Only with the *GRE*® revised General Test

NO LONGER PROPERTY OF SEATTLE PUBLIC LIBRARY

D0517712

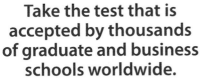

Take the test that is accepted by thousands of graduate and business schools worldwide.

You can use *GRE*® scores to apply to master's, MBA, specialized master's in business and Ph.D. programs around the world. So you can take the test now, even if you are still deciding what to do.

Use the test-taker friendly design to do your best.

You can preview questions, skip and go back to more challenging questions, and even change your answers, all within a section. The test-taker friendly design helps you feel good on test day.

Send only your best scores.

GRE tests all provide the *ScoreSelect*® option, which means you can take a GRE test once now, or again in the future, and only send the GRE test scores from whichever test date(s) you want schools to see. Best of all, you always have 5 years to decide how to use any of your scores.

TakeTheGRE.com

For graduate school. For business school. For your future.

Copyright © 2016 by Educational Testing Service. All rights reserved. ETS, the ETS logo, GRE and SCORESELECT are registered trademarks of Educational Testing Service (ETS) in the United States and other countries. MEASURING THE POWER OF LEARNING is a trademark of ETS. 33558

 **GRE**®

Measuring the Power of Learning.™

& WORLD REPORT
U.S.News

2017 EDITION

Best
GRAD
SCHOOLS

Dartmouth College
ELLEN WEBBER FOR USN&WR

HOW TO ORDER: Additional copies of U.S.News & World Report's **Best Graduate Schools 2017** guidebook
are available for·purchase at usnews.com/gradguide or by calling (800) 836-6397.
To order custom reprints, please call (877) 652-5295 or email usnews@wrightsmedia.com.
For permission to republish articles, data or other content from this book, email permissions@usnews.com.

Copyright © 2016 by U.S.News & World Report L.P., 1050 Thomas Jefferson Street N.W., Washington, D.C. 20007-3837.
Published in three editions: hardcover, ISBN 978-1-931469-81-4; softcover, 978-1-931469-82-1; e-book, ISBN 978-1-931469-83-8.
All rights reserved. Published by U.S.News & World Report L.P., Washington, D.C. The Best Graduate Schools 2017 guidebook is printed primarily on recycled paper.

Prestigious

The University of Tampa's prestigious **AACSB-accredited** graduate business programs are recognized for their academic rigor, superior faculty and alumni outcomes. Hundreds of companies **recruit on campus** annually, including Citigroup, The Nielsen Company, Coca-Cola, Verizon and Raymond James Financial Services. Within six months of graduation, 94 percent of alumni report **achieving their goals**, including a new job or a promotion. UT is proud to be:

- Named by The Princeton Review as one of the 296 best business schools in the world
- Listed in *U.S. News & World Report* among the nation's best part-time MBA programs
- Named the nation's #7 best value business school by *Business Insider*

We offer **full-time, part-time and executive options** in our MBA and M.S. programs. When you're ready to invest in yourself, invest in the best: a degree from the Sykes College of Business at The University of Tampa.

Take the next step!
Visit www.ut.edu/graduate
or call (813) 258-7409.

THE UNIVERSITY OF TAMPA
SYKES COLLEGE OF BUSINESS

AACSB ACCREDITED

MBA (eight concentrations) | Executive MBA

M.S. in Accounting | M.S. in Finance | M.S. in Marketing | Nonprofit Management Certificate

CONTENTS

RACHELLE HACMAC FOR USN&WR

80

CONTINUED ON PAGE 6

Prep smart, go far.
Enjoy the ride.

- Score improvement guaranteed: **+5 points for GRE, +50 points for GMAT**
- Unbeatable price in test prep
- Study anywhere, anytime on desktop or mobile
- Learn more at **www.magoosh.com/bestgrad**

GRE®
GMAT®
LSAT®
Praxis®
TOEFL®
SAT®
ACT®

GMAT® is a registered trademark of the Graduate Management Admission Council (GMAC). This website is not endorsed or approved by GMAC. GRE®, TOEFL®, and Praxis® are registered trademarks of Educational Testing Service (ETS). This website is not endorsed or approved by ETS. SAT® is a registered trademark of the College Board, which was not involved in the production of, and does not endorse this product. LSAT® is a registered trademark of the Law School Admission Council, Inc. This website is not endorsed or approved by the LSAC. ACT® is a registered trademark of ACT, inc. This website is not endorsed or approved by ACT, inc.

CONTENTS

THE RANKINGS

34

BRETT ZIEGLER FOR USN&WR

Invigorate your mind.

Academically rigorous.
Amazingly affordable.
Truly global.

- More than 100 graduate programs

- An accessible, award-winning faculty dedicated to scholarship and research

- One of the top 5 colleges in the U.S. for giving students the "Best Bang for the Buck" (*Washington Monthly*)

Apply now for Fall 2016. Learn more at
qc.cuny.edu/exploregrad

QUEENS COLLEGE   CU NY

@ USNEWS.COM / EDUCATION

Prospective graduate students researching their options will find the **U.S. News** website (home of the **Best Graduate Schools** and **Best Colleges** rankings) full of tips on everything from choosing a school to landing the most generous scholarships. Here's a sampling:

MBA Admissions Blog
usnews.com/mbaadmissions

Get admissions advice from blogger Stacy Blackman, a business school specialist with degrees from Wharton and Kellogg and co-author of "The MBA Application Roadmap: The Essential Guide to Getting into a Top Business School." Learn how to master those application essays, prepare for your interviews, and find the money for business school.

Online Education
usnews.com/online

Want to get that MBA without spending time in the classroom? See our rankings of the best online degree programs in business, education, engineering, computer information technology, criminal justice and nursing. And read time-management and funding tips from students who have completed online degree programs.

Law Admissions Blog
usnews.com/lawadmissions

Get the lowdown on admissions from bloggers at Stratus Prep, a global test preparation and admissions counseling firm based in New York City. Learn how to do your best on the LSAT, determine the value of a dual J.D./MBA degree, and examine potential career paths.

Medical School Admissions Blog
usnews.com/medadmissions

Wade through the medical school admissions process with tips from experts and students in the field. Learn how to choose the right undergrad major for med school, avoid MCAT prep mistakes, decide between an M.D. and a D.O. degree, and submit a winning application.

Morse Code Blog
usnews.com/morsecode

Get an insider's view of the rankings from Chief Data Strategist Bob Morse, the mastermind behind them. Morse explains the methods we use to rank graduate programs and keeps you up to date on all the commentary and controversy.

Paying for Graduate School
usnews.com/payforgrad

Find tips and tools for financing your education, including guidance on scholarships, grants and loans. Read about your borrowing options, including loan forgiveness and repayment assistance programs for people who work in public service, nonprofits or underserved areas.

U.S. News Graduate School Compass
usnews.com/gradcompass

Gain access to the U.S. News Graduate School Compass, a wealth of searchable data with tools and an expanded directory of programs. (Subscribe at usnews.com/compassdiscount to get a 25 percent discount.) Are you curious about how much you could make coming out of law school? Or which medical residency programs are the most popular? Check the Graduate School Compass.

BEST GRADUATE SCHOOLS
2017 EDITION

Executive Committee Chairman and Editor-in-Chief Mortimer B. Zuckerman
Editor and Chief Content Officer Brian Kelly
Executive Editor Margaret Mannix
Managing Editor Anne McGrath
Chief Data Strategist Robert J. Morse
Senior Data Analyst Eric Brooks
Data Collection Manager Matthew Mason
Art Director Rebecca Pajak
Director of Photography Avijit Gupta
Photography Editor Brett Ziegler
News Editor Elizabeth Whitehead
Contributors Lindsay Cates, Elizabeth Gardner, Christopher J. Gearon, Beth Howard, Margaret Loftus, Linda Marsa, Michael Morella, Courtney Rubin, Arlene Weintraub
Research Manager Myke Freeman
Directory Janie S. Price

USNEWS.COM/EDUCATION
Senior Vice President Chris DiCosmo
Vice President and General Manager Michael Nolan
Managing Editor Anita Narayan
Senior Editor Allison Gualtieri
Reporters/Writers Jordan Friedman, Kelly Mae Ross, Delece Smith-Barrow
Web Producers Briana Boyington, Alexandra Pannoni
Product Manager Erica Ryan

ACADEMIC INSIGHTS
General Manager Evan Jones
Account Manager Cale Gosnell
Sales Manager Megan Trudeau
Product Marketing Specialist Taylor Suggs

INFORMATION SERVICES
Vice President, Data and Information Strategy Stephanie Salmon
Data Analysts Kenneth Hines, Alexis Krivian, Anjelica Pitts
Data Collection Jessica Benenson, Geneva Dampare, Kelsey Page-Campbell

TECHNOLOGY
Vice President Yingjie Shu
Director of Web Technology Patrick Peak
Director of Engineering Matt Kupferman
Senior Systems Manager Cathy Cacho
Software Team Lead David Jessup, Bethany Morin
Primary Developers William Garcia, Josh Brown, Jose Velazquez, Jon Lewis, Robert Miller, Alan Weinstein
Digital Production Michael A. Brooks, Manager; Michael Fingerhuth

President and Chief Executive Officer William D. Holiber

ADVERTISING
Publisher and Chief Advertising Officer Kerry Dyer
National Advertising Director Ed Hannigan
Director of Sales Strategy and Planning Alexandra Kalaf
Managing Editor, BrandFuse Jada Graves
Director, Integrated Media Solutions Peter Bowes
Health Care Manager Colin Hamilton
Finance Manager Heather Levine
Senior Account Executives Steve Hiel, Michelle Rosen, Brian Roy, Shannon Tkach
Account Executives Taylor Kiefer, Ivy Zenati
Account Executive, Integrated Media Solutions Dustin Hill
Senior Manager, Programmatic and Revenue Platforms Joe Hayden
Programmatic and Data Analyst Liam Kristinnsson
Managers, Sales Strategy Tina Lopez, Riki Smolen
Sales Planners Gary DeNardis, Michael Machado, Spencer Vastoler
Senior Manager, Client Services Rachel Wulfow
Account Managers Rachel Halasz, Katie Harper, Dana Jelen
Senior Manager Advertising Operations Cory Nesser
Advertising Operations Manager Samit Khatri
Director of Advertising Services Phyllis Panza
Business Operations Karolee Jarnecki
Executive Assistant to the President Judy David
Executive Assistant to the Publisher Anny Lasso
Sales Administration Coordinator Carmen Caraballo

Vice President, Specialty Marketing Mark W. White
Director of Specialty Marketing Abbe Weintraub

Chief Operating Officer Karen S. Chevalier
Chief Product Officer Chad Smolinski
Chief Financial Officer Neil Maheshwari
Senior Vice President, Strategic Development and General Counsel Peter M. Dwoskin
Senior Vice President, Human Resources Jeff Zomper
Senior Vice President Planning Thomas H. Peck

Additional copies of the **2017** edition of **U.S.News & World Report's Best Graduate Schools** guidebook are available for purchase at (800) 836-6397 or online at **usnews.com/gradguide**. To order custom reprints, please call (877) 652-5295 or email **usnews@wrightsmedia.com**. For all other permissions, email **permissions@usnews.com**.

Printed primarily on recycled paper

We know NURSING.

Take your career to the next level at Wayne State University. When you become a College of Nursing graduate student, you'll grow as a leader, scholar and practitioner. Wayne State M.S.N. and D.N.P. students apply evidence in practice to improve the health of individuals, families and communities in a range of health care settings. Ph.D. students advance nursing knowledge and build the science on which practice is based.

Located in the heart of Detroit and surrounded by world-class health care institutions, Wayne State University's College of Nursing is committed to diversity and excellence.

Join us to make a lasting impact on urban health.

nursing.wayne.edu

Master of Science in Nursing
- Clinical specialties:
  - Neonatal Nurse Practitioner
  - Nurse-Midwife
  - Pediatric Nurse Practitioner-Acute Care
  - Pediatric Nurse Practitioner-Primary Care
  - Psychiatric-Mental Health Nurse Practitioner
- M.S.N. in Advanced Public Health Nursing

Doctor of Nursing Practice
Pathways:
- B.S.N. to D.N.P.
- M.S.N. to D.N.P. *(APRN certified)*
- M.S.N. to D.N.P. *(need certification)*

Clinical specialties:
- Adult-Gerontology Acute Care Nurse Practitioner
- Adult-Gerontology Primary Care Nurse Practitioner
- Family Nurse Practitioner
- Nurse-Midwife
- Neonatal Nurse Practitioner
- Pediatric Nurse Practitioner-Acute Care
- Pediatric Nurse Practitioner-Primary Care
- Psychiatric-Mental Health Nurse Practitioner

Doctor of Philosophy in Nursing
Pathways:
- M.S.N. to Ph.D.
- B.S.N. to Ph.D.

Graduate Certificates
- Nursing Education
- Clinical specialties:
  - Adult-Gerontology Acute Care Nurse Practitioner
  - Nurse-Midwife
  - Pediatric Nurse Practitioner-Acute Care
  - Pediatric Nurse Practitioner-Primary Care

SHOULD *You* GO TO Grad School?

Depending on your discipline and the cost of a degree, the answer will vary

By **LINDA MARSA**

Kristofferson Culmer (right) guides Josh Ehrich on a class project.

>>> **Since Kristofferson Culmer** had no plans to teach, he hadn't considered pursuing a Ph.D. in computer science. But that quickly changed once he started a master's program at the University of Missouri and realized that a doctorate is now a good way for job candidates outside the ivory tower to demonstrate the inventiveness and ability to solve complex technical problems that employers prize. "It opens doors that wouldn't be there with just a master's degree," says Culmer, who intends to work in industry. His decision should pay off. The tech business pays a premium for people

in computer science, with median salaries of about $108,000 in a field projected to grow by 11 percent in the decade ending in 2024.

Still, based on the struggles of people he knows or has heard about in other fields or who are aiming for academia, Culmer, 38, has turned frugality into an art form. Even though his tuition is covered and an assistantship pays him $12,000 a year, "it's not enough to live on," he says. He supplements his income with summer jobs and has learned to live with less to avoid the perils many graduates face when freighted down by debt. "They're having trouble finding academic jobs, so they take anything," says Culmer, "and they're looking at loan repayments of tens of thousands of dollars."

The type of return-on-investment calculations Culmer made, which take into account the prospects for finding work and career satisfaction as well as the financial picture, are a key exercise for anyone pondering grad school. While advanced degrees are pro forma in such arenas as medicine, law and academia, grad school may not mean an instant salary bump or career advancement in other fields. On average, people with a bachelor's and at least three years in the workforce out-earn those freshly out of grad school, according to a report released last year by Georgetown University's Center on Education and the Workforce. Experts believe hiring managers often place a higher premium on experience than academic credentials.

"Employers are risk averse about hiring people

straight out of school, because the soft skills needed in the workplace – the professionalism, the ability to communicate and work as part of a team – aren't taught in academia," says Andrew R. Hanson, a senior analyst at the center. Moreover, the average graduate student now finishes up owing $57,600 (including undergrad loans), and that figure can easily hit $100,000 or more. "More than half the people who get a master's degree leave with debt," says Jason Delisle, director of the Federal Education Budget Project at the think tank New America. And many prospective grad students neglect to figure in lost wages and retirement savings.

The good news is that in many fields, at least, people with the extra degree generally do catch up eventually. Median annual earnings in 2014 were $99,000 for people with a doctoral or professional degree versus $69,000 for those with a bachelor's, according to the Bureau of Labor Statistics, a difference that, taking pro-

jected raises into account, can add a very tidy sum to a paycheck over a lifetime. And people with advanced degrees enjoy lower rates of unemployment – 2.8 percent for those with a master's in 2014, compared to 3.5 percent for people with a bachelor's.

What's more, while nearly 6 million high school-level jobs were wiped out in the last recession, those that require a master's or doctoral degree are experiencing high growth, according to the BLS, with anticipated increases of 18 percent and 16 percent respectively this decade. (The BLS reports projected job growth across occupations as well as educational requirements in its Occupational Outlook Handbook at www.bls.gov/ooh.)

"We're becoming more of a graduate school economy," says Hanson. "Because our infrastructure is now so complex, these positions require a lot of cognitive ability." Employers, he notes, are thus looking for highly educated candidates.

That includes people with Ph.D.s, who face a shortage of tenure-track positions and are increasingly stepping out of the ivory tower. Only about half of people with doctorates now work in higher education, according to the Council of Graduate Schools. Stanford University, which tracks doctoral alumni, has found that nearly half have parlayed their intellectual depth and critical thinking skills into jobs in business, government or nonprofits, including at places like Intel, Microsoft, Goldman Sachs and the International Monetary Fund.

"In all parts of industry, there is a market for Ph.D.s," says Suzanne Ortega, president of the Council of Graduate Schools. "They not only have specialized knowledge, but have the ability to engage in high levels of research across a range of sectors, to ask good research questions, to develop original and innovative ideas, and to work independently."

Keep in mind as you weigh your options that despite the rosy-sounding averages, employment and salary prospects vary considerably by discipline. It should come as no surprise that "what you study has a huge impact on your earnings," says Hanson. An earlier Georgetown study found that chemists, materials scientists and financial professionals get about a $1 million lifetime paycheck boost with a grad degree, for example. Computer software engineers make nearly $300,000 extra with a master's over a lifetime, while teachers make $400,000 extra with a master's. People with an extra diploma and some experience in engineering and business can command starting salaries in the very high five-figure range. But the added degree has

Grad school may not mean an instant PAY BUMP.

#RadyMade
Scientist > Entrepreneur

"As a scientist turned entrepreneur, my Rady MBA provided me the business acumen and opportunities to catapult my entrepreneurial journey. Today, I have built a female-focused business accelerator and angel network/fund that has helped launch 56 startups, facilitated 82 women-owned small businesses to think big and created over 50 new jobs."

Silvia Mah, Ph.D., MBA '10
CEO, Hera Labs & Founding Partner, Hera Fund

— I am RadyMade —

NEVER STOP STARTING UP

Rady | UC San Diego
School of Management

To see more stories:
rady.ucsd.edu/radymade

MBA | MFIN | MSBA | Ph.D. | ExecEd

a negligible impact on lifetime earnings for writers, editors and even computer programmers. Here are some other factors to consider as you plot your path:

1. The purpose of getting that extra degree. "Ask yourself: Where do you want to go careerwise?" advises Hanson. "What will you be able to do with a graduate degree that you can't do now?" Grad school shouldn't be automatically assumed to be a résumé enhancer, and the cost is too great to use it as a way to mark time until the job picture improves. Make sure an extra degree is required or desirable in your chosen field; if it isn't, you could be seen as overqualified.

In many instances, it will be a boon. A 2014 survey of 19 major employers found that their human resources administrators do look more favorably upon both job applicants and internal candidates for promotion who have that added diploma. They use it as a sorting mechanism that signals discipline and drive, although the preferred candidates also had the requisite experience. If your ultimate goal is a leadership or adminis-

BRUSHING UP YOUR SKILLS WITH A CERTIFICATE

These quickly earned credentials are now hot at the graduate level

Mandi Martini of Cincinnati considered getting her MBA. Instead, the medical devices sales rep for Ethicon, a subsidiary of Johnson & Johnson, enrolled last fall in a 12-credit graduate certificate program in business foundations at the University of Cincinnati's Carl H. Lindner College of Business. Even though she'd earned a bachelor's in marketing from UC in 2009, "If you don't use it, you lose it," says Martini, 30. She views the extra helpings of accounting, finance and marketing as a key step in her pursuit of "more cross-functional roles" at Johnson & Johnson, including in sales training and marketing.

Martini's path is increasingly well-traveled. In the 2013-14 school year, U.S. graduate schools awarded some 36,000 certificates, nearly 5 percent more than a year earlier, according to the Council of Graduate Schools. The credentials, long associated with blue-collar jobs, are rapidly becoming popular at the graduate level as a way for professionals who already have secured a bachelor's degree to quickly develop specific skills and advance or switch careers. Typically, all or some of the credits earned in graduate certificate programs can be applied to a master's degree.

The 65 certificates UC offers today, for example, represent "triple the number the graduate school offered five years ago," says Margaret Hanson, associate university dean of the grad school. They range widely across disciplines: Asian studies, corporate taxation, data science, and film and media studies, for example.

A bridge. The certificate route can be appealing to adults who want to return to school but are not ready to commit to the time and expense of a master's program. "There is a certain level

> **'This is a way to advance or SWITCH careers.**

of anxiety when you're going back to school," says Martini, who wanted "an easier bridge" but may eventually also decide on an MBA. Martini's certificate cost her about $10,500, about one-third of the cost of a full-blown MBA at UC. The programs are taught online, in class or as hybrid programs, like the one Martini is finishing this spring. More than half of East Carolina University's 60 graduate certificates can be completed entirely online, for example.

Whether sought as a freestanding award, a prelude to a full-fledged graduate degree, or in conjunction with a master's or doctoral program, certificates typically involve a package of four to six classes that can be taken over a couple semesters. An engineer who needs to enhance his or her bona fides in noise control engineering, for example, could get a certificate from Purdue University by taking master's level courses in engineering acoustics and mechanical vibrations plus two related electives.

Or consider Beverly Bragg, 43, of Nashville, Indiana, who is working on her doctorate of nursing practice at Purdue and has added a certificate in gerontology. "I want to be a primary provider seeing patients and have an independent clinic in a rural setting," she says. About 60 percent of certificates awarded in the 2013-14 academic year were in education, health sciences and business, according to CGS.

For Joseph Biggio Jr., director of maternal-fetal medicine at the University of Alabama–Birmingham's medical school, a certificate in health care quality and safety from the university provided the know-how he felt he needed to respond to the growing emphasis on improving care and measuring outcomes. The certificate helped him gain his department's position of vice-chair for quality and research. UAB offers 24 certificates in subjects ranging from social media to sustainable engineering to mentoring and leadership. Indeed, says Jeffrey Engler, associate dean for academic affairs at the graduate school, the programs are "a growth industry." –*Christopher J. Gearon*

EXPLORE YOUR PASSION.

DEVELOP YOUR EXPERTISE IN OVER

180 GRADUATE AND PROFESSIONAL PROGRAMS.

17 TOP 100 GRADUATE PROGRAMS (U.S. NEWS & WORLD REPORT)

Aerospace Engineering, Audiology, Ceramics, Chemical Engineering, Civil Engineering, Clinical Psychology, Fine Arts, Industrial Engineering, Law, MBA, Mechanical Engineering, Nursing, Pharmacy, Physical Therapy, Psychology, Rehabilitation Counseling and Rural Medicine

AT WEST VIRGINIA UNIVERSITY, WE HAVE

1,800 GRADUATE ASSISTANTS

WHO STUDY, LEARN AND TEACH AT ONE OF THE HIGHEST TIER RESEARCH ACTIVITY UNIVERSITIES IN THE U.S.

West Virginia University®
graduate.wvu.edu | MOUNTAINEERS GO FIRST.

Aimee Liu hosts alumni of the Goddard writing program and prospective students.

trative post, says Ortega, "an advanced degree may be required."

2. Your various program options. There's been a groundswell of innovation lately as programs try to do a better job of prepping students for the real world. So it pays to look around carefully. Many programs, in fields from business to law to education, are adding a big dose of training in technology and big data, for instance. And "professional" master's degree programs have been spreading that combine academics with job-specific training and the hands-on experience needed in the workplace.

"Industry and academia are coming together at long last to find ways of preparing this great talent pool," says Elizabeth Watkins, dean of the graduate division at the University of California–San Francisco. There's more of a focus, too, on building networks with classmates and mentors that can later be tapped when prospecting for jobs.

At Michigan State University, for instance, a formal program provides mentoring, workshops and overall guidance to doctoral candidates on cultivating skills that are transferable to the business world as well as academia. "This is a growing trend and a high priority for graduate schools nationally," says Judith Stoddart, interim dean of the MSU Graduate School. To find out whether a particular school offers these hybrid programs, check their websites. "How visible are their professional development programs? What kind of investments have they made? Find out where their graduates are. This will tell you a lot about the culture of the institution," says Stoddart.

For midlife professionals at a career crossroads, the costs of attending grad school full time can be prohibitive. But here again, there are alternatives. For Aimee Liu, a Los Angeles writer who enjoyed teaching adults at UCLA Extension but wanted a permanent gig on a regular faculty, the answer was a "low residency" master of fine arts program at Bennington College in Vermont. The program, pursued mostly independently, required only a 10-day residency on campus per semester for four semesters. The total cost was about $24,000, much less than for a traditional program, and she wouldn't have to uproot her family.

"I did a hard-nosed calculation of what this will mean for

FROM LEFT: JENNIFER EMERLING FOR USN&WR; YULIA TRENIKHINA

my career and the cost benefit," says Liu. Her gamble paid off after graduation in the form of a position teaching remotely and occasionally on-site in a low residency MFA program at Goddard College, which has campuses in Vermont and Washington. "The degree was basically paid for within the year," says Liu.

3. The true cost of attendance. The tab for tuition and fees for two-year master's programs at most public universities now runs $20,000 a year or more and at private universities the bill can be more than double. And that does not include living costs, which can easily add another $2,000 a month. Even with an assistantship, which normally includes a full or partial tuition waiver and a stipend in exchange for teaching classes or doing research (story, Page 21), your living costs can saddle you with debt. Ask yourself if the future earnings boost will more than make up for the lost income and lost retirement savings while you are in school.

4. Getting the best loan terms. The government's Stafford and Grad PLUS loan programs offer the best deals. Interest rates for the former are about 5.84 percent while the latter clocks in at around 6.84 percent. You aren't disqualified because of a spotty credit history, payments are deferred until you're out of school, and you may be eligible for income-based repayment programs that cap monthly payments. But annual borrowing limits are $20,500 and aggregate caps are $138,500 (medical students can borrow up to $224,000), including any lingering undergraduate debts.

Another advantage: If public service is your goal, any remaining debt is forgiven after 10 years of full-time employment. "The definition of public service is very broad," says Mark Kantrowitz, publisher and vice president of strategy for Cappex.com, a resource for planning and paying for higher education. It includes "public librarians, social workers, teachers, prosecutors or working for any 501(c)(3) charitable organization."

Private loans through banks are normally a last resort because interest rates are usually higher and may be variable instead of fixed, your credit record can't have blemishes, and you may need a cosigner in order to qualify. Often, private loans won't be forgiven in the event of disability or death (which means the borrower's estate could be on the hook for student loans). Federal loans are discharged in the event of death or total and permanent disability.

5. A reasonable debt load. Research your probable first-year earnings (tip: check Glassdoor.com). Disparities within professions can be huge. For example, the most recent data from NALP, the association of law placement professionals, show that the largest law firms commonly pay first-year associates $160,000 while the median for beginning public defenders is just $50,400. The rule of thumb from financial advisors is that loans stop being affordable when monthly payments eat up more than 10 percent of income; total debt at graduation, they say, should be less than your starting salary.

"Don't borrow more than you can repay in 10 years," says Kantrowitz. "Assume every dollar of debt will cost you $2 by the time you pay it back."

While the financial realities are clearly a key measure in your decision-making, they shouldn't be your only yardstick. Satisfaction counts, too. The desire for more of that is what motivated Andrew Solomon to go back to school. Solomon, 35, worked for an alternative investment firm after graduating from Columbia University but realized when the financial crisis hit in 2008 that what he wanted more than that earning potential was to be in a field where he could have more of a social impact.

Believing that an advanced degree would help him hone his skills for a leadership role in the nonprofit world, he enrolled in a three-year program sponsored jointly by Harvard's Kennedy School and the Wharton School at the University of Pennsylvania that awards a dual master's in public administration and an MBA. Partial scholarships from both of the schools, along with a year off to work between the first and second years of his studies, defrayed Solomon's educational costs, and the two degrees positioned him for his current job as chief financial officer and chief operating officer of a network of charter schools in Boston.

"My education gave me the skills I needed to help our teachers, families and students," he says. "This was an investment in my future." ∎

WHY I PICKED...

Cornell University
ITHACA, N.Y.

SAM POSEN, '15
Associate scientist

❯❯ Students in Cornell's world-class physics Ph.D. program perform research using state-of-the-art resources including a particle accelerator X-ray source and a nanofabrication facility. Working closely with top researchers, they get advanced, hands-on experimental experience and develop theories for complex physical phenomena.

I found Cornell's research community refreshingly collaborative – interdisciplinary cooperation is encouraged and assisted. For example, in my research, I investigated superconducting materials for particle accelerator cavities. When my experiments showed performance-limiting nanometer-scale defects, I consulted with a professor, a world expert in condensed matter theory, to better understand the physical mechanism involved. Cornell also sent me to international conferences, where I built my knowledge and network. This excellent training prepared me well to join Fermi National Accelerator Laboratory outside Chicago, where I perform R&D on particle accelerators. ∎

Exploring a Fellowship

A host of programs fund graduate school, research or a job • By LINDSAY CATES

>>> **Grad school always appealed** to Jacob Calvert, but it wasn't until late in his junior year at the University of Illinois in Urbana-Champaign that the bioengineering major zeroed in on a subject area that really spoke to him: complex systems mathematics. After discovering a center focused on that field at the University of Bristol in the United Kingdom, he strategically sought out several fellowship programs that could pay his way. With the help of an adviser, Calvert applied for and earned a Marshall Scholarship, which funds up to 40 American students each year who are pursuing graduate degrees in the U.K. Calvert's scholarship covers the $30,000 tuition toward

a math master's degree and gives him an additional $20,000 for expenses. Thanks to the fellowship, "I really got to choose my own experience," says Calvert, who will complete his degree this year.

Many fellowships can be thought of as scholarships that cover tuition for one to three years of graduate study and sometimes include extra funding for living expenses or attending academic conferences. Other awards are given for teaching, research or short-term jobs. Besides the generous funding, it's often the specialized opportunities and a chance to build both a network and a résumé that lead recent college grads and young professionals to pursue fellowships. In-

Molly Rockett's fellowships support a job at FairVote.

BRETT ZIEGLER FOR USN&WR

Graduate School
Costs Covered

Cover up to 100% of school-certified costs with zero fees.
Get a cash reward for good grades.

DiscoverStudentLoans.com   1-800-STUDENT (788-3368)

DISCOVER | STUDENT LOANS

Discover Student Loans are made by Discover Bank | © 2016 Discover Bank, Member FDIC
Aggregate loan limits apply. Reward redemption period is limited.
Visit DiscoverStudentLoans.com/Reward for reward and redemption terms and conditions.

deed, becoming part of a cohort of highly qualified peers and having access to personalized professional development can be just as valuable as the monetary benefits, says Kyle Mox, vice president of the National Association of Fellowship Advisors.

Hundreds of programs exist in the U.S. and abroad, and fellowships attract tens of thousands of applicants every year. Many are highly selective. The Fulbright Program, for instance, receives more than 10,000 U.S. student applications each year, and fewer than 20 percent earn the State Department-funded award. (Fulbright also has research fellowships for faculty and other scholars.) The Rhodes and the Mitchell scholarships accept between 3 and 5 percent of those who apply from the U.S.

Some fellowships are based at particular schools, while others are targeted at people in certain disciplines. Fulbright winners represent a broad spectrum of disciplines and schools. The Rhodes is exclusive to the University of Oxford in the U.K.; the Mitchell is for American students enrolling in a graduate program in Ireland or Northern Ireland. The Truman is for those interested in public service. Plus, "there's just a whole alphabet soup" of offerings in the sciences, notes Suzanne Mc-Cray, vice president for enrollment management and director of the Office of Nationally Competitive Awards at the University of Arkansas. Aspiring scientists might consider the National Defense Science and Engineering Graduate Fellowship (180 awarded annually in fields of interest to the Department of Defense) or the Hertz Foundation Graduate Fellowship (12 to 15 awarded per year to people pursuing a Ph.D. in science, math or engineering), among many others.

A number of opportunities are earmarked for students from underrepresented minority groups. The National Academies of Sciences, Engineering, and Medicine administer a fellowship on behalf of the Ford Foundation, for example, that invests in about 120 doctoral students in a variety of disciplines each year with a goal of diversifying teaching faculty. The Paul and Daisy Soros Fellowships for New Americans program annually supports 30 naturalized U.S. citizens, other immigrants and children of immigrants for two years of study in any field.

Often, a fellowship offers a way for people who have already

completed graduate study to take advantage of research opportunities. "I couldn't finance my own research projects overseas without funding," says Fulbright fellow Kate Witt, 30, who finished a master's in intercultural communication at the University of Maryland–Baltimore County in 2013. This year, she began a Fulbright Scholar fellowship in Paraguay studying sociolinguistics, and she eventually

hopes to earn a Ph.D. in the field. "If you have an idea, find a program that will fund it," she advises.

To help students sort through their options, many universities have dedicated fellowship advisers and detailed databases of offerings. Schools like Cornell (gradschool.cornell.edu/fellowships) and UCLA (grad.ucla.edu/funding) offer publicly searchable collections of fellowships. Mox suggests working with your school's advisers to find programs whose goals align with your interests. It's important to start thinking about applying junior year – or even earlier. Applications for many competitive programs are due early in the fall. They often require a personal statement, letters of recommendation and extensive interviews. Depending on the program, you typically will either apply to a fellowship organization or be nominated by your undergraduate institution.

Selection committees want applicants to make clear how a fellowship is critical to their career path, rather than framing it as a study-abroad experience, for example. "It's not a gap year," McCray says. "It's a supplemental experience that really is going to enable you to do what it is you want to do." Other desirable attributes generally include top-notch academic performance and leadership skills.

"What we're looking for is people who apply their intellectual skills, their people skills, and their grit and determination to an issue that they care about," says Rob Garris, director of admissions for the Schwarzman Scholars program, which is backed by a range of individuals, corporations and private foundations and will enroll its inaugural class of 111 this year. Participants study at Tsinghua University in Beijing in a fully funded one-year master's program specializing in international studies, public policy or business and economics.

In addition to helping the award winners make real progress toward their educational goals, applying for a fellowship can even sometimes benefit those who are not selected. Mitchell applicants, for instance, can choose to have their submissions shared with companies that help sponsor the program, such as Morgan Stanley or CRH, an international building materials firm. "Our entire applicant pool is highly impressive, and that's of interest to companies," says Trina Vargo, founder and president of the US-Ireland Alliance, which administers the Mitchell.

For Molly Rockett, the biggest perk has been getting to know and learn from others who are also interested in politics and public service. A 2015 University of Connecticut political science grad, Rockett, 22, earned several fellowships that support a year of work in the communications department at FairVote, a nonpartisan voting rights organization in Washington, D.C. She plans to attend law school and focus on voting rights litigation or run for office. "You have this really exciting and unique chance right after you graduate to do something really different," she says. "Grad school is not going anywhere." ∎

> ‘Make clear how a program is **critical** to your CAREER path.

How to Raise the Money

Smart ways to cover your tuition and repay all those loans • By **MICHAEL MORELLA**

>>> **As an undergrad at Florida** International University in Miami, her hometown, Lucia Lopez volunteered in poor communities and saw firsthand the health care challenges many people face. When she finished her master's in physician assistant studies at Wake Forest University in 2013, Lopez, 27, found a job as a PA at a Wake Forest Baptist Medical Center clinic in Winston-Salem, North Carolina, where she serves mostly high-need patients, many of them uninsured. Now, she says, "I just can't see myself practicing anywhere outside of an underserved population."

Lopez's passion is rewarding in more ways than one: It has paid off in a $50,000 grant from the National Health Service Corps, a federal program that offers loan repayment assistance to health professionals who agree to work in low-income communities for at least two years. Lopez's award will wipe out nearly half of the $120,000 loan debt she accumulated in grad school. For the rest, she pays a "very reasonable" $485 each month thanks to another federal program that ties her monthly obligation to her $86,000 income.

Devising that kind of multipronged payment strategy is the key to keeping graduate school affordable, whether you plan to be a doctor or lawyer or are destined for a teaching career. Prospective students should keep costs, job and salary potential, and their repayment options top of mind from the beginning of the application process, rather than as "the last piece of the puzzle," says David Sheridan, director of financial aid at Columbia University's School of International and Public Affairs.

A Council of Graduate Schools website, GradSense.org, features a budget calculator and other resources that can help you do the research. A science teacher-to-be, for example, can see that graduates of education master's degree programs come out with a median debt load of $33,250 and command a median salary of about $62,000. If those loans carry a typical 5.84 percent interest rate, it would cost just over $365 a month to pay back the balance over the standard 10 years.

Nationwide, about 70 percent of grad students receive financial aid in the form of grants, teaching or research assistantships, and loans. Here are several potential ways to get your share:

Find a sponsor. Fifty-two percent of companies offer tuition assistance for job-related courses, according to the Society for Human Resource Management. More typical in fields like business and education, employer-sponsored funding helps about 15 percent of grad students pay for school, and up to $5,250 annually of such aid qualifies as a tax-free benefit. Most university employees have access to discounted coursework, too.

Seek out scholarships. At the graduate level, scholarships tend to be awarded based on a student's credentials or course of study rather than financial need. Such grants are more common for Ph.D. students, many of whom are able to tap into research funding. Awards can come from a wide range of government agencies, foundations and other sources (story, Page 18). In 2015, the National Science Foundation, for instance, awarded $138,000 each to 2,000 individuals to pursue grad degrees across a range of scientific disciplines as part of its Graduate Research Fellowship program. The U.S. Department of Labor (careerinfonet.org/scholarshipsearch) and FastWeb (fastweb.com) offer lists of scholarships that can be searched based on academic interests, location and other factors. Applying early could give students an edge in the competition for institutional money; schools with rolling admissions deadlines could see their funding dry up by late spring.

Work for the school. Teaching or research assistantships are often awarded to Ph.D. students, many of whom will go on to become faculty members or researchers. Awards typically include tuition plus a stipend for other expenses and entail 20 or so hours of work a week. At many institutions, assistantships are viewed "not first and foremost as employment but as part of their training," says W. Jeffrey Hughes, associate dean of the graduate school of arts and sciences at Boston University.

Obtaining an assistantship can be competitive, so students should "make sure that they are marketing skill sets" that they would bring to the table, says Carol Shanklin, dean of the graduate school at Kansas State University. For instance, an aspiring Shakespeare scholar who has taught high school English might have the edge for a coveted TA position over an applicant with equal academic creds who is arriving straight out of college.

Borrow carefully — and have a payback plan. Nearly half of all grad students take out loans, particularly in professional fields like law and medicine, where average debt levels exceed $100,000. Currently, grad students can borrow up to $20,500 per year in federal loans at a 5.84 percent interest rate. That rate is fixed for the life of the loan, but the interest figure for new loans is adjusted each summer based on the 10-year U.S. Treasury note. For those who need to borrow more, federal PLUS loans are available up to the cost of attendance at 6.84 percent interest.

Federal loans feature a range of flexible repayment options that allow borrowers to adjust monthly payments based on their salary or have their loan balances forgiven after a certain period of consistent payments. Lopez, for example, is taking advantage of the Pay As You Earn plan, which caps her monthly loan bill at approximately 10 percent of her discretionary income. Teachers who work in qualifying low-income schools for five consecutive years can have up to $17,500 in direct loans forgiven, while those who work in certain government or public-interest jobs can have their loans fully expunged after 10 years of payments.

Like the National Health Service Corps, a number of government agencies, states and graduate schools, especially in medicine and law, also offer loan forgiveness or repayment assistance programs for public servants.

Federal loans offer a range of flexible REPAYMENT options.

Private loans tend to carry variable interest rates and have fewer repayment safeguards. "There's far less risk with a federal loan than a private lender," says Tracy Kitchel, assistant vice provost for graduate and postdoctoral affairs at the University of Missouri. The rate on loans at several private lenders, for instance, can swing by about 5 percentage points depending on market conditions.

Dustin Rynders sought out a variety of state, federal and legal sector funding sources to keep his burden manageable. After graduating from the University of Houston Law Center in 2006 with some $100,000 in debt, Rynders, 36, took a job as an attorney at a state agency in Houston representing children with disabilities in education matters. Under a standard 10-year loan repayment plan, he owed about $1,100 a month from his $38,000 starting salary.

That might have been "a pretty insurmountable barrier" to a public service career, he says, if not for a fellowship from Equal Justice Works – a nonprofit that sponsors dozens of public interest lawyers nationwide – that covered most of his payments for two years. Next, Rynders turned to the Texas Access to Justice Foundation for additional aid. The foundation gives about 120 public-interest lawyers in the state as much as $400 a month toward their loans for up to 10 years, and Rynders is among them. ■

Shop the U.S. News Store

U.S. News
Grad Compass

· See complete U.S. News rankings

· Expanded data on 1,900 programs

· Compare schools side by side

· Financial aid information

· See entering LSAT, MCAT, GMAT and GRE scores

visit **usnews.com/store**

U.S. News publications also available on Kindle and iPad

About the Rankings

Objective measures are important, as are the opinions of experts

By ROBERT J. MORSE

Each year, U.S. News ranks professional school programs in business, education, engineering, law, nursing and medicine. The rankings in these six areas are based on two types of data: expert opinions about program excellence and statistical indicators that measure the quality of a school's faculty, research and students. The data come from statistical surveys sent to administrators at more than 1,900 graduate programs and from reputation surveys sent to more than 18,400 academics and professionals in the disciplines. The surveys were conducted during the fall of 2015 and in early 2016. In each field, we also present rankings of programs in various specialty areas based on reputation data alone.

As you research course offerings and weigh schools' intangible attributes, the data in these pages can help you compare concrete factors such as faculty-student ratio and placement success upon graduation. It's important that you use the rankings to supplement, not substitute for, careful thought and your own research. In each of the six major disciplines, the ranking tables show approximately the top half of the schools that were eligible to be ranked; longer lists and more complete data can be found at usnews.com/grad. Detailed information about the various methodologies can be found on the website, too; summaries appear with each ranking in these pages. (Note that the formula used to rank nursing master's programs has been revised and improved this year.)

Beyond the six disciplines ranked annually, we also periodically rank programs in the sciences, social sciences, humanities, the health arena and many other areas based solely on the ratings of academic experts. This year, new rankings of graduate programs based on peer assessment only are published for public affairs, fine arts and nine health fields: audiology, clinical psychology, nurse anesthesia, nurse midwifery, occupational therapy, pharmacy, physical therapy, social work and speech-language pathology. The rankings of other health programs, as well as those of Ph.D. programs in the sciences and social sciences and humanities, are based on earlier surveys and are republished.

> **Use the rankings to supplement YOUR OWN research.**

Full rankings in all categories, plus a new ranking of Doctor of Nursing Practice programs and rankings based on earlier surveys of programs in library and information studies, are available at usnews.com/grad. It's a good idea to check the site every now and then, as U.S. News occasionally adds content when additional data we think useful becomes available – whether on job placement, GPA, test scores or other factors – or new information changes the data.

To gather the peer assessment data, we asked deans, program directors and senior faculty to judge the academic quality of programs in their field on a scale of 1 (marginal) to 5 (outstanding). In business, education, engineering, law and medicine, we also surveyed professionals who hire new graduates and have used their three most recent years' responses to calculate the results.

Statistical indicators fall into two categories: inputs, or measures of the qualities that students and faculty bring to the educational experience; and outputs, measures of graduates' achievements linked to their degrees. As inputs, for example, we use admission test scores. Output measures for business include starting salaries and grads' ability to find jobs; in law, we look at employment rates at graduation and 10 months later, and at bar exam pass rates.

Scoring system. To arrive at a school's rank, we examined the data for individual indicators and standardized the value of each indicator about its mean. The weight applied to each indicator reflects our judgment about its relative importance, as determined in consultation with experts in each field. Final scores were rescaled so that the highest-scoring school was assigned 100; the other schools' scores were recalculated as a percentage of that top score. The scores were then rounded to the nearest whole number. Schools with a score of 100 accumulated the highest composite score. A school's rank reflects the number of schools that sit above it; if three schools are tied at 1, the next school will be ranked 4, not 2. Tied schools are listed alphabetically. ∎

KENDRICK BRINSON FOR USN&WR

A view of the quad
at Emory University

Explore the U.S. News
Community College Directory

Search among nearly 950 schools across the U.S.

U.S.News & WORLD REPORT

Visit: **usnews.com/education/community-colleges**

BUSINESS

THE **U.S. NEWS** RANKINGS

At the Stanford Graduate School of Business
BRETT ZIEGLER FOR USN&WR

B-SCHOOL
GOES
GL⊕BAL

>>> **During Lonzyo Holcomb's** two years at the University of Michigan's Ross School of Business, he spent one week in Brazil and another in Ecuador working with a services development team for General Motors. He then made a two-week trip to China, where Cheung Kong Graduate School of Business in Beijing served as a base as he attended lectures and visited companies to learn about one of the world's largest emerging markets. "I needed to shore up my core finance skills in valuation and assessing emerging markets at a high level. I definitely accomplished that goal," says Holcomb, 27. He credits the global experience for his early job offer from Citigroup, where he will work as an investment banker after earning his MBA.

Michigan is one of the multitude of business schools that have focused on broadening students' horizons over the last couple of years. The depth of international experiences available varies widely. Some schools simply add a quick spring break foreign tour to a semester-long course; others, like New York University and Duke, have opened satellite campuses in fast-growing economies where they provide business courses to native students as well as to visiting Americans. Many are partnering with foreign B-schools to provide "action-based" learning that allows students to complete real projects for

multinational companies. Some experiences come with language training and company internships.

All told, nearly half of the 100 or so action projects Michigan MBA students complete each year include international experience, says M.S. Krishnan, associate dean for global initiatives. Holcomb and his classmates assessed a premium service offered by GM in Brazil and the viability of rolling it out elsewhere in South America. Another team in India analyzed mobile-payment opportunities for a large bank there. "Because

> ## MBA programs are adding a wide range of ways to gain experience in international markets
> *By* **ARLENE WEINTRAUB**

One of Lonzyo Holcomb's global experiences entailed two weeks in China.

CLOCKWISE FROM TOP LEFT: GETTY IMAGES (2); JONATHAN ERDTSIECK

Shanghai is a draw for students interested in learning about emerging markets.

of technology, boundaries across all industries are breaking down," Krishnan says. "The contextual and cultural immersion in important markets becomes an advantage for students when they go into the job market."

Many of the experiences are focused on providing the knowledge large companies are looking for as they expand into emerging markets. NYU's Stern School of Business has created a series of market-specific DBi ("Doing Business in") courses, for example, by partnering with business schools in 25 countries that provide course materials used for the semester and host students for one- or two-week trips. NYU also has set up its own (mostly undergraduate) campuses in Abu Dhabi and Shanghai that offer degrees to locals and are a base for traveling graduate business students. Those taking the DBi course about China begin visiting the Shanghai campus this spring.

It is certainly possible to teach students about emerging markets without leaving the U.S., says Tom Pugel, vice dean for MBA programs at NYU. But immersing them in these countries – even for a short time – offers potential employers a clear sign of more nuanced understanding of "the issues that can arise in conducting business across borders and across cultures." Among the companies that have been hiring Stern graduates with international experience: McKinsey, Apple and Samsung.

The list of countries that open their doors to U.S.-based MBA programs has grown so diverse that students can choose from a wide range of ultraspecialized pursuits, from entrepreneurship in Israel to fashion in London to telecom in India. NYU has sent students to Panama to learn the ins and outs of operating a major canal. Yale students can go to Spain to consider the European debt crisis or to the Philippines to study ecotourism. Or they can try their hand at "social entrepreneurship," assisting nonprofits and social-services startups in countries like India and Ghana. In the summer of 2015, five Massachusetts Institute of Technology MBA students worked in Malaysia with an Asian regional airline to redesign its scheduling system.

"They did data analytics using a number of different software tools," says Charles Fine, dean of the new Asia School of Business, launched last year as a partnership between MIT and Malaysia's central bank. "They proposed a new approach to scheduling that would generate over $100 million in profit." The airline is now implementing the students' recommendations, he says. The Asia School of Business offers MBAs to students from around the world as well as expanded opportunities for MIT students to work on projects for companies there.

Even students who are working full time and earning their MBAs at night are now offered travel abroad. Gabriella Pearlman, a physician and student in the University of Pennsylvania's Wharton executive MBA program in San Francisco, took a one-week trip to Cuba, for example, as part of a project with other students to develop a business plan for starting a medical school in the country. "I wanted a program that would give me an opportunity to go somewhere and use my health care background," says Pearlman, who plans to transition into hospital administration. Other industry-focused trips Wharton has offered include consulting for Taiwan's pharmaceutical companies, assisting Israeli tech entrepreneurs, and determining a strategy for building cancer research centers in sub-Saharan Africa.

Most schools are offering these opportunities not just to MBA students but also to those earning other business master's degrees. "You can't learn how business is done in other cultures without experiencing it," says Austin Taylor, who received a master's in management studies from the Duke University Fuqua School of Business in May 2015 after spending four months of his 10-month program in China working with appliance-maker Bosch to assess the market for high-end auto parts.

The China program, which started on Duke's North Carolina campus with courses in business basics, helped Taylor land a job as a corporate finance analyst with General Motors in Detroit after he graduated. And he expects it could someday lead to a job outside of the U.S. "Having that experi-

AN ESSAY OF FEWER WORDS

Top B-schools want applicants to be succinct or even send a video

French philosopher Blaise Pascal famously noted that he didn't have time to pen a short letter, so he wrote a long one instead. The fact that writing effectively but concisely is a rare skill is one reason applicants to some top B-schools are facing fewer and shorter essays. "We prioritize communicating in a clear, concise, compelling way, and shortening or having fewer essays really forces applicants to reflect on what they want to share," says Kate Smith, assistant dean of admissions and financial aid at Northwestern's Kellogg School of Management, which reduced its essay count in 2014 from three to two and asked for shorter responses. "Being asked to write less is actually more challenging."

Harvard now requires just one essay, down from seven a decade ago. The Class of 2018 applicants are asked how they would introduce themselves to their section mates when they arrive on campus. The University of Pennsylvania's Wharton School, which asked for four essays five years ago, wants just one of 500 words from Class of 2018 hopefuls. One of Columbia University's four writing assignments asks applicants to describe their immediate post-MBA goal in just 50 charac-

ters, or a little over a third of a single tweet. That figure has been gradually whittled down from 200 characters four years ago.

"Shortening is definitely the big trend of the past four to five years," said Matt Symonds, co-author of "The MBA Admissions Edge" and co-director of Fortuna Admissions, a business school admissions consulting firm. Symonds attributes the change also to

> ‘**Writing less is actually MORE challenging.**

the fact that admissions committees have been taxed lately by a sharp rise in applications to near-record levels. The trend is confined to elite schools at the moment, he says, though he expects others to follow suit.

Business schools are also experimenting with different formats for the essay. The University of Chicago Booth School of Business asked applicants for entry this fall to pick one of 16 school-related photos to use as a jumping-off point to discuss "why the Booth community is the right fit for you" and told them to "feel free" to submit a slide presenta-

tion or "any format that you feel best captures your response." The University of Toronto's Rotman School of Management introduced a video essay in 2012, using it to replace two written essays. Yale's School of Management and Northwestern's Kellogg have since added a video essay. All three use a platform that poses the question and offers limited time to respond, so the focus in on the applicant's answer rather than his or her production ability.

No right answer. One reason admissions staffers like the video approach is that it's tougher for applicants to be coached. "Unfortunately, with the proliferation of online message boards and admissions consultants who try to convince applicants that there is a 'right' answer to these questions, [written essay] submissions often sound very similar," wrote Niki da Silva, Rotman's director of recruitment and admissions, in a blog post debuting the video format.

Moreover, the ability to present yourself well during a videoconference is a crucial business skill, says Smith. She recalls that while she was considering introducing the video essay, one convincing factor was a conversation she'd had with a Kellogg student who mentioned that her first round of interviews at Nike had included a video component.

How to prepare? You don't want to look overpracticed, Symonds cautions; the goal is to gauge your presentation skills, thoughtfulness and "apparent spontaneity." Speak about your goals and your history concisely, he advises, and if you lose your train of thought, "take a breath, compose yourself, and bounce back." –*Courtney Rubin*

State of Confidence

It's time. All of the reasons you think you can't are reasons you should.
Gain the confidence to do more and be more. Challenge yourself to keep
learning with Colorado's top-ranked MBA program. You're ready.

Colorado State University

COLLEGE OF BUSINESS

CSUonlineMBA.com
The Online Professional MBA

WHY I PICKED...

University of North Carolina

CHAPEL HILL

LAUREN CRUZ, '15
Marketing associate

» UNC Kenan-Flagler embraces diversity, collaboration and teamwork and offers excellent educational and experiential opportunities. In assessing MBA programs, I looked for these strengths as I didn't have a traditional undergrad business education. After college, I founded and operated a personal training studio and became enthralled with running my own enterprise. I felt Kenan-Flagler's program would build my leadership skills while surrounding me with the passionate and open-minded students and faculty I sought.

My classwork was flanked by great opportunities: a Leadership Immersion course, study abroad in Barcelona, and a business trip to Africa. The 10-week leadership course began with a week in the woods through Outward Bound, included team-based "Apprentice"-like challenges, and ended with executing a charity basketball tournament. UNC's strong career center helped me land a marketing role with Ethicon, a Johnson & Johnson medical device company. ■

ence positions me well to be a candidate for overseas jobs," he says.

Duke has also established a campus outside of Shanghai, a joint venture with Wuhan University. In addition, partnering with more than 40 business schools in other countries has allowed the school to offer short-term study opportunities in markets from Brazil to South Africa.

Like Taylor, many business students are looking for much more than a week or two stay. Wharton's two-year joint MBA/master's program with Penn's Joseph H. Lauder Institute of Management and International Studies now provides for two months of study in one of more than 20 locations and includes language instruction.

The Lauder component is designed to enhance understanding of cultural differences. Alumni have landed jobs with

nese or Arabic get three years to complete the program to ensure they master the language.

Among the large companies recently hosting Moore interns are BMW in Germany, Nissan in Japan, and a Brazilian TV channel. In France, Michelin has asked its Moore interns to develop an Internet-based training program focused on supply chain management.

Meanwhile, some students are opting to earn their entire MBA abroad. Surveys by the Graduate Management Admission Council report that 3.2 percent of U.S. students now say they prefer to get their business degrees in Europe. European business schools report that the proportion of their applications coming in from U.S. students is running about 5 percent. Popular choices include the Insead Business School in

Students want more than a one- or two-week STAY.

organizations ranging from the International Finance Corporation to major pharmaceutical and tech giants.

Those choosing the Africa specialty, new in 2016, start in the summer, learning French and traveling for two months throughout the western region of the continent to work with companies and meet local officials. "Africa is a very interesting economy to observe," says Mauro Guillen, director of the Lauder Institute. "They have natural resources, but they also have a growing population. If you look at the 20 economies that are growing the fastest, 10 are in sub-Saharan Africa. It will be a very important part of the global economy."

At the University of South Carolina Darla Moore School of Business, students who enroll in the two-year International MBA program get a full eight months on the ground in their chosen country. While abroad, they complete intensive language study and internships and work with business anthropologists who help them analyze and understand cultural variables.

Students who study Chinese, Japa-

France, the University of Oxford Said Business School in London, and the Frankfurt School of Finance and Management in Germany.

One of those adventurers is Scott Gabrielson of Minneapolis, who decided to enroll in Said after looking around for a program that would allow him to earn an MBA in one year instead of two. Gabrielson, 28, had been working for an investment bank but knew he wanted to start a clothing label, and he saw Oxford as the best one-year MBA program located conveniently in the center of a world fashion capital.

"Oxford is really entrepreneurial – 35 percent of the graduates start companies," says Gabrielson. After he graduated in 2015, he launched Oliver Cabell, a fashion label based in Minneapolis that plans to market high-end clothing and accessories at discount prices. The Oxford program "helped me really understand digital marketing, supply chain logistics, and reputation management," he says. And it got him to London, home to "many of the best designers in the world." ■

CRUZ PORTRAIT DESIGN

THE JOB MARKET

A Close Eye on the Pipeline

By **COURTNEY RUBIN**

》》 When Nest Labs wants to increase profitability, it's up to Tejash Patel to help figure out how. Has the engineering department at the maker of smart thermostats, security cameras and other devices for the home put in features that don't address customer needs? Should the global supply manager negotiate better prices on certain parts? To find answers, Patel, a business operations systems manager in Nest's supply chain arm, analyzes data and meets frequently with the operations, engineering and marketing departments. "You can really have an impact on how the company operates," says Patel, 34. "You're not just sitting behind your computer not ever talking to anyone."

It's a rare kid who dreams of working in supply chain management, a field where responsibilities typically divide into four parts: Plan, source, make and deliver the product. Patel certainly didn't. He grew up intrigued by the computers his father, an engineer, brought home, and he studied computer science at the University of Illinois–Urbana-Champaign. But demand for MBAs to fill these functions has been growing along with the geographical reach and complexity of supply and distribution channels, say B-school placement professionals. Companies focus on finding cost savings in their supply chain to avoid raising prices, says Dean Vera, director of the MBA Office of Career Management and assistant dean at Rutgers Business School–Newark and New Brunswick. Consulting firms also are looking for supply chain experts.

Patel didn't know much about the

Tejash Patel
University of Chicago Booth
School of Business, 2015

field until he entered it. After college, he worked for several years in software development and as an information technology consultant. Eventually, tired of "clients in random cities with small problems," he headed to the University of Chicago Booth School of Business, thinking that perhaps he would target Silicon Valley.

Best of both worlds. A summer internship at Nest in Palo Alto, where a major project involved analyzing data and developing insights that would help upper management make strategic decisions, led to his current job after graduation in 2015. He's glad that it offers the best of both worlds. There's a technical component; one responsibility is to supervise software developers creating the tools used to analyze data. And, he says, you can "touch different areas of the business that you don't often get to in other roles." ∎

...More Hot Jobs

MARKET RESEARCHER

To help them beat the competition, companies need people who can analyze numbers and point to the next profitable niche. Expert projections put job growth in this field at 19 percent over the next 10 years or much faster than average. Market research analysts at the upper end of the pay scale can command a salary nearing $120,000.

TECHNOLOGY PRODUCT MANAGER

New tech products constantly are debuting, and that spurs demand for tech-savvy brand managers. Unlike a product manager for a leading toothpaste, say, who can be effective at the job without ever having formulated toothpaste, technology brand managers are expected to be very familiar with a product's inner workings. Among 2015 MBA grads of the Massachusetts Institute of Technology, the mean salary for this type of job was $124,927, with a $25,265 signing bonus.

LEADER-IN-TRAINING

Leadership development programs that rotate employees through company departments were among the first budget items cut during the financial downturn. Now they are being reinstated by employers in need of new managers to take over the business. Much of the action is in the manufacturing sector, experts say, where the workforce is older. A Northwestern B-school report puts the average base salary around $120,000.

COURTESY OF TEJASH PATEL

Schools of Business

THE TOP MBA PROGRAMS

Rank School	Overall score	Peer assessment score (5.0=highest)	Recruiter assessment score (5.0=highest)	'15 full-time average undergrad GPA	'15 full-time average GMAT score	'15 full-time acceptance rate	'15 average starting salary and bonus	'15 graduates employed at graduation	Employed 3 months after graduation	'15 out-of-state tuition and fees	'15 total full-time enrollment
1. Harvard University (MA)	100	4.8	4.6	3.66	725	10.7%	$149,784	81.0%	91.1%	$72,312	1,872
2. Stanford University (CA)	98	4.8	4.5	3.75	733	6.1%	$145,173	71.7%	86.2%	$64,050	824
2. University of Chicago (Booth) (IL)	98	4.7	4.5	3.59	726	24.4%	$143,475	86.5%	95.0%	$65,069	1,180
4. University of Pennsylvania (Wharton)	97	4.7	4.5	3.60	732	19.8%	$146,761	80.8%	93.6%	$70,870	1,715
5. Massachusetts Institute of Technology (Sloan)	96	4.7	4.5	3.54	716	14.6%	$146,201	86.1%	92.4%	$65,750	806
5. Northwestern University (Kellogg) (IL)	96	4.6	4.5	3.60	724	20.6%	$140,107	86.3%	93.8%	$65,284	1,272
7. University of California–Berkeley (Haas)	94	4.6	4.3	3.66	715	13.0%	$143,485	72.0%	93.8%	$55,968	502
8. Dartmouth College (Tuck) (NH)	90	4.3	4.2	3.52	717	22.6%	$148,025	83.3%	95.1%	$67,394	563
8. Yale University (CT)	90	4.3	4.3	3.60	721	20.7%	$139,310	76.6%	92.2%	$63,380	668
10. Columbia University (NY)	89	4.4	4.1	3.50	715	18.0%	$146,436	76.7%	92.5%	$68,724	1,287
11. University of Virginia (Darden)	87	4.1	4.0	3.53	706	27.8%	$146,136	88.9%	95.3%	$61,150	656
12. Duke University (Fuqua) (NC)	86	4.3	4.1	3.40	696	23.1%	$143,382	85.4%	94.4%	$63,036	894
12. University of Michigan–Ann Arbor (Ross)	86	4.4	4.1	3.36	708	28.3%	$143,195	86.3%	92.1%	$61,918	836
14. Cornell University (Johnson) (NY)	80	4.1	4.1	3.35	697	32.4%	$144,813	79.5%	88.2%	$62,100	535
15. University of California–Los Angeles (Anderson)	79	4.1	3.9	3.48	713	19.8%	$132,827	72.3%	87.1%	$57,844	725
16. U. of North Carolina–Chapel Hill (Kenan-Flagler)	76	3.9	3.7	3.41	701	33.8%	$129,016	81.7%	94.3%	$57,839	558
16. University of Texas–Austin (McCombs)	76	3.9	4.1	3.40	694	29.7%	$133,647	74.1%	87.0%	$49,532	543
18. Carnegie Mellon University (Tepper) (PA)	75	4.0	3.8	3.33	690	30.6%	$135,548	82.1%	89.5%	$60,746	417
19. Emory University (Goizueta) (GA)	73	3.7	3.8	3.35	678	30.1%	$132,779	78.5%	94.4%	$50,140	345
20. New York University (Stern)	72	4.2	4.0	3.51	720	20.0%	$137,534	78.8%	89.0%	$66,192	799
21. Washington University in St. Louis (Olin) (MO)	71	3.6	3.6	3.40	695	30.1%	$112,957	79.6%	97.1%	$54,225	280
22. Georgetown University (McDonough) (DC)	69	3.6	3.8	3.36	692	43.3%	$130,659	72.7%	85.9%	$56,962	519
22. Indiana University (Kelley School)	69	3.8	3.6	3.36	668	29.2%	$123,855	77.0%	89.1%	$46,561	372
22. Vanderbilt University (Owen) (TN)	69	3.5	3.6	3.36	690	42.1%	$126,959	80.9%	91.9%	$50,380	346
25. Rice University (Jones) (TX)	66	3.4	3.5	3.30	676	27.2%	$129,954	82.3%	90.6%	$54,493	225
25. University of Notre Dame (Mendoza) (IN)	66	3.5	3.5	3.31	682	40.5%	$125,227	76.4%	92.7%	$49,180	302
27. Ohio State University (Fisher)	65	3.5	3.4	3.46	664	34.1%	$110,358	72.3%	95.7%	$50,611	220

PETER HOFFMAN FOR USN&WR

University of Chicago, tied at No. 2

The Kelley Effect

As lived by Greg Mattes, MBA'14

GREG MATTES
1 Success Story
growing with every moment

HARSHA KALAPALA
1 of 400 Peer Mentors
fellow students giving him feedback and collaborating

DON KURATKO
1 of 45 Professors
amplify his education through personal attention

MANDY SU
1 of 10,000 Future Clients
whose business he will develop and enrich

RAY LUTHER
1 of 30 Inspiring Alumni
whose achievements showed him the power of a Kelley education

The pivotal moments in Greg's life mean a lot more than most. Each one starts a chain reaction of new paths, connections and opportunity. Greg has an MBA from Kelley, so his moments go much farther. The skills, confidence and network Greg gained from Kelley gave him the momentum to bring his startup, Analog Computing Solutions, to market.

See more of Greg's story, and start building your momentum
gokelley.iu.edu/mbaBGG

KELLEY
SCHOOL OF BUSINESS
GO FROM MOMENT TO MOMENTUM

THE TOP MBA PROGRAMS continued

Rank	School	Overall score	Peer assessment score (5.0=highest)	Recruiter assessment score (5.0=highest)	'15 full-time average undergrad GPA	'15 full-time average GMAT score	'15 full-time acceptance rate	'15 average starting salary and bonus	'15 graduates employed at graduation	Employed 3 months after graduation	'15 out-of-state tuition and fees	'15 total full-time enrollment
27.	University of Minnesota–Twin Cities (Carlson)	65	3.5	3.4	3.41	680	39.1%	$120,000	75.3%	89.2%	$51,085	195
27.	University of Washington (Foster)	65	3.4	3.2	3.35	688	25.6%	$118,405	80.1%	95.6%	$45,450	234
27.	University of Wisconsin–Madison	65	3.6	3.4	3.38	669	20.0%	$114,815	76.8%	89.5%	$30,435	197
31.	Brigham Young University (Marriott) (UT)	64	3.0	3.5	3.54	674	48.1%	$120,853	84.3%	91.8%	$11,970	320
31.	Texas A&M University–College Station (Mays)	64	3.3	3.5	3.50	654	23.5%	$110,625	75.0%	93.8%	$40,416	123
31.	University of Southern California (Marshall)	64	3.8	3.6	3.31	679	28.9%	$120,207	60.8%	80.7%	$60,287	438
34.	Georgia Institute of Technology (Scheller)	63	3.2	3.6	3.18	678	25.2%	$118,233	83.9%	96.4%	$41,676	123
35.	Arizona State University (Carey)	62	3.4	3.4	3.37	672	31.4%	$113,243	71.2%	90.9%	$42,780	150
35.	Michigan State University (Broad)	62	3.3	3.4	3.34	664	30.7%	$117,326	85.9%	90.6%	$44,895	154
37.	University of Florida (Hough)	61	3.3	2.7	3.46	681	15.8%	$109,171	85.1%	95.7%	$31,130	109
37.	University of Texas–Dallas	61	2.9	4.2	3.47	678	21.9%	$86,285	58.1%	93.0%	$30,935	123
39.	University of Illinois–Urbana-Champaign	60	3.4	3.3	3.38	654	32.1%	$99,495	80.9%	94.1%	$39,420	160
39.	University of Rochester (Simon) (NY)	60	3.2	3.0	3.40	667	32.8%	$112,512	77.7%	95.7%	$47,053	209
41.	Boston University (Questrom) (MA)	57	3.1	3.0	3.33	682	35.7%	$109,358	76.3%	93.0%	$48,182	281
41.	Pennsylvania State U.–University Park (Smeal)	57	3.2	3.5	3.37	636	17.1%	$114,035	71.2%	86.4%	$39,210	146
41.	Temple University (Fox) (PA)	57	2.9	3.5	3.59	632	40.3%	$83,800	76.9%	97.4%	$43,744	90
41.	University of Maryland–College Park (Smith)	57	3.4	3.4	3.35	658	30.8%	$108,031	63.5%	82.4%	$54,409	190
45.	University of California–Davis	56	3.2	3.2	3.26	683	17.8%	$112,202	51.4%	94.3%	$52,508	87
45.	University of Iowa (Tippie)	56	3.1	3.0	3.27	670	40.7%	$102,619	79.2%	97.9%	$41,870	119
47.	Purdue University–West Lafayette (Krannert) (IN)	55	3.4	3.4	3.38	635	26.0%	$103,386	66.2%	80.9%	$42,184	150
48.	Southern Methodist University (Cox) (TX)	54	3.1	3.2	3.40	656	35.9%	$111,355	66.7%	82.4%	$51,395	206
48.	University of California–Irvine (Merage)	54	3.1	3.4	3.36	656	25.2%	$94,765	60.9%	89.1%	$48,608	195
50.	Boston College (Carroll) (MA)	53	3.2	3.2	3.26	664	38.3%	$102,206	71.3%	87.5%	$45,630	182
51.	George Washington University (DC)	52	3.1	3.3	3.24	642	42.7%	$107,628	61.6%	93.2%	$1,610*	180
52.	North Carolina State University (Jenkins)	51	2.6	3.3	3.57	639	38.4%	$85,968	77.8%	91.7%	$69,122†	83
53.	Rutgers, The State U. of N.J.–Newark & New Brunswick	50	2.8	3.0	3.33	642	42.5%	$99,772	72.9%	98.3%	$49,383	146
53.	University of Alabama (Manderson)	50	2.7	3.4	3.59	679	58.3%	$70,340	62.1%	84.5%	$28,780	192
55.	University of Georgia (Terry)	49	3.2	3.1	3.43	643	30.9%	$90,978	68.6%	80.0%	$33,768	98
55.	University of Pittsburgh (Katz) (PA)	49	3.2	3.3	3.27	607	22.2%	$94,404	69.6%	87.5%	$65,256†	152
57.	Baylor University (Hankamer) (TX)	48	2.7	3.0	3.32	634	36.1%	$83,411	87.0%	95.7%	$40,598	96
57.	Northeastern University (MA)	48	2.8	3.3	3.29	644	22.5%	$84,047	64.3%	95.2%	$1,476*	166
59.	University of Missouri (Trulaske)	47	2.7	3.2	3.50	648	40.7%	$63,045	65.5%	90.9%	$937*	135
60.	Babson College (Olin) (MA)	46	3.2	3.3	3.20	628	55.9%	$85,959	52.8%	85.9%	$101,566†	348
60.	University of Arizona (Eller)	46	3.3	2.9	3.30	654	38.8%	$86,009	46.2%	84.6%	$46,384	81
62.	Louisiana State University–Baton Rouge (Ourso)	45	2.7	2.8	3.35	626	41.6%	$67,100	90.5%	97.6%	$64,144†	96
63.	Texas Christian University (Neeley)	44	2.7	3.1	3.26	642	54.5%	$92,981	70.5%	88.6%	$48,850	88
63.	University of Arkansas–Fayetteville (Walton)	44	3.0	2.5	3.58	630	64.4%	$67,214	71.9%	87.5%	$44,499	88
63.	University of Cincinnati (Lindner) (OH)	44	2.6	3.0	3.59	651	53.2%	$64,538	52.9%	88.2%	$40,677†	115
63.	University of Oklahoma (Price)	44	2.8	2.8	3.38	628	55.0%	$86,835	69.0%	89.7%	$32,848	82
63.	University of Tennessee–Knoxville	44	2.8	3.4	3.42	616	50.5%	$84,571	63.4%	77.5%	$43,774	144

SPECIALTIES

PROGRAMS RANKED BEST BY BUSINESS SCHOOL DEANS AND MBA PROGRAM DIRECTORS

ACCOUNTING

1. **University of Texas–Austin** (McCombs)
2. **University of Chicago** (Booth) (IL)
2. **University of Pennsylvania** (Wharton)
4. **University of Illinois–Urbana-Champaign**
5. **U. of Michigan–Ann Arbor** (Ross)
6. **Stanford University** (CA)
7. **Brigham Young University** (Marriott) (UT)
8. **New York University** (Stern)
9. **University of Southern California** (Marshall)
10. **University of North Carolina–Chapel Hill** (Kenan-Flagler)
11. **Indiana University** (Kelley School)
12. **Columbia University** (NY)
13. **Ohio State University** (Fisher)
13. **University of Notre Dame** (Mendoza) (IN)
15. **Fairfield University** (Dolan) (CT)
16. **Boston College** (Carroll) (MA)
16. **Gonzaga University** (WA)
16. **Loyola Marymount University** (CA)
16. **Seattle University** (Albers) (WA)

ENTREPRENEURSHIP

1. **Babson College** (Olin) (MA)
1. **Stanford University** (CA)
3. **Harvard University** (MA)
3. **Massachusetts Institute of Technology** (Sloan)
5. **University of California–Berkeley** (Haas)
6. **University of Texas–Austin** (McCombs)
7. **University of Pennsylvania** (Wharton)
8. **Indiana University** (Kelley School)
9. **U. of Michigan–Ann Arbor** (Ross)
10. **Loyola Marymount University** (CA)
10. **University of Southern California** (Marshall)
12. **University of Arizona** (Eller)

EXECUTIVE MBA

1. **University of Pennsylvania** (Wharton)
2. **University of Chicago** (Booth) (IL)

*Tuition is reported on a per-credit-hour basis. †Total program tuition
Sources: U.S. News and the schools. Assessment data collected by Ipsos Public Affairs.

RECRUITED BY MORE THAN 500 TOP COMPANIES.

INSPIRED BY WORLD-RENOWNED RESEARCH.

ENHANCED BY A LIFELONG PROFESSIONAL COMMUNITY.

Our globally recognized faculty and forward-thinking curriculum provide an outstanding business education and a distinct hiring advantage. We offer exceptional return on investment and the sure path for advancing your career. Let's begin.

go.wisc.edu/UWBusiness

WISCONSIN
SCHOOL OF BUSINESS
UNIVERSITY OF WISCONSIN–MADISON

TOGETHER FORWARD®

© 2016 Board of Regents of the University of Wisconsin System

SPECIALTIES continued

3. **Northwestern U.** (Kellogg) (IL)
4. **Columbia University** (NY)
5. **New York University** (Stern)
6. **Duke University** (Fuqua) (NC)
6. **U. of Michigan–Ann Arbor** (Ross)
8. **University of California–Berkeley** (Haas)
9. **University of California–Los Angeles** (Anderson)
10. **University of North Carolina–Chapel Hill** (Kenan-Flagler)
11. **Massachusetts Institute of Technology** (Sloan)
12. **Seattle University** (Albers) (WA)
12. **St. Joseph's University** (Haub) (PA)

FINANCE
1. **University of Pennsylvania** (Wharton)
2. **University of Chicago** (Booth) (IL)
3. **New York University** (Stern)
4. **Stanford University** (CA)
5. **Columbia University** (NY)
6. **Massachusetts Institute of Technology** (Sloan)
7. **University of California–Berkeley** (Haas)
8. **Harvard University** (MA)
9. **U. of Michigan–Ann Arbor** (Ross)
10. **Northwestern U.** (Kellogg) (IL)
11. **University of California–Los Angeles** (Anderson)
12. **Boston College** (Carroll) (MA)
13. **St. Joseph's University** (Haub) (PA)
14. **Fairfield University** (Dolan) (CT)
15. **Creighton University** (NE)
15. **Duke University** (Fuqua) (NC)
15. **University of Texas–Austin** (McCombs)

INFORMATION SYSTEMS
1. **Massachusetts Institute of Technology** (Sloan)
2. **Carnegie Mellon University** (Tepper) (PA)
3. **University of Texas–Austin** (McCombs)
4. **University of Minnesota–Twin Cities** (Carlson)
5. **University of Arizona** (Eller)
6. **New York University** (Stern)
7. **Stanford University** (CA)
7. **University of Maryland–College Park** (Smith)
9. **University of Pennsylvania** (Wharton)
10. **Arizona State University** (Carey)
11. **Georgia Institute of Technology** (Scheller)

INTERNATIONAL
1. **University of South Carolina** (Moore)
2. **Harvard University** (MA)
3. **Thunderbird School of Global Management** (AZ)
3. **University of California–Berkeley** (Haas)
5. **Columbia University** (NY)
5. **University of Pennsylvania** (Wharton)
7. **U. of Michigan–Ann Arbor** (Ross)
8. **Stanford University** (CA)
9. **New York University** (Stern)
10. **Duke University** (Fuqua) (NC)
11. **University of Southern California** (Marshall)

MANAGEMENT
1. **Harvard University** (MA)

2. **Stanford University** (CA)
3. **University of Pennsylvania** (Wharton)
4. **Northwestern U.** (Kellogg) (IL)
5. **U. of Michigan–Ann Arbor** (Ross)
6. **University of Virginia** (Darden)
7. **University of California–Berkeley** (Haas)
8. **Dartmouth College** (Tuck) (NH)
8. **University of Chicago** (Booth) (IL)
10. **Columbia University** (NY)
10. **Duke University** (Fuqua) (NC)
12. **University of Texas–Austin** (McCombs)

MARKETING
1. **Northwestern U.** (Kellogg) (IL)
2. **University of Pennsylvania** (Wharton)
3. **Harvard University** (MA)
4. **Stanford University** (CA)
5. **Columbia University** (NY)
6. **Duke University** (Fuqua) (NC)
6. **U. of Michigan–Ann Arbor** (Ross)
8. **University of Chicago** (Booth) (IL)
9. **University of California–Berkeley** (Haas)
10. **New York University** (Stern)
11. **University of California–Los Angeles** (Anderson)
11. **University of Texas–Austin** (McCombs)
13. **Loyola Marymount University** (CA)
13. **St. Joseph's University** (Haub) (PA)

NONPROFIT
1. **Yale University** (CT)
2. **Harvard University** (MA)
2. **Stanford University** (CA)

4. **University of California–Berkeley** (Haas)
5. **Northwestern U.** (Kellogg) (IL)
6. **Duke University** (Fuqua) (NC)

PRODUCTION/OPERATIONS
1. **Massachusetts Institute of Technology** (Sloan)
2. **University of Pennsylvania** (Wharton)
3. **Carnegie Mellon University** (Tepper) (PA)
4. **U. of Michigan–Ann Arbor** (Ross)
5. **Stanford University** (CA)
6. **Purdue University–West Lafayette** (Krannert) (IN)
7. **Northwestern U.** (Kellogg) (IL)
8. **Columbia University** (NY)
9. **Harvard University** (MA)
10. **Ohio State University** (Fisher)
11. **Michigan State University** (Broad)

SUPPLY CHAIN/LOGISTICS
1. **Massachusetts Institute of Technology** (Sloan)
2. **Michigan State University** (Broad)
3. **Pennsylvania State University–University Park** (Smeal)
4. **Arizona State University** (Carey)
5. **U. of Michigan–Ann Arbor** (Ross)
6. **Stanford University** (CA)
7. **Ohio State University** (Fisher)
8. **University of Tennessee–Knoxville**
9. **Carnegie Mellon University** (Tepper) (PA)
10. **University of Pennsylvania** (Wharton)
11. **Rutgers, The State U. of New Jersey–Newark and New Brunswick**

METHODOLOGY

The 470 master's programs in business administration accredited by the Association to Advance Collegiate Schools of Business were surveyed; 379 responded, with 129 MBA programs providing the data needed to calculate rankings based on a weighted average of eight indicators:

Quality assessment: Two surveys were conducted in fall 2015. Business school deans and directors of accredited MBA programs were asked to rate the overall academic quality of the MBA programs at each school on a scale from marginal (1) to outstanding (5); 41 percent responded. The average score is

weighted by .25 in the ranking model. Corporate recruiters and company contacts who hired MBA grads, whose names were supplied by previously ranked MBA programs, also were asked to rate the programs. The last three years' recruiter responses were averaged and are weighted by .15 in the model.

Placement success (weighted by .35): Based on average starting salary and bonus (40 percent of this measure) and employment rates for full-time 2015 graduates at graduation (20 percent) and three months later (40 percent). Calculations for MBA placement rates exclude

those not seeking jobs and those for whom the school has no information. To be included in the full-time MBA rankings, a program needed 20 or more of its 2015 full-time graduates to be seeking employment. Salary is based on the number of graduates reporting data. Signing bonus is weighted by the proportion of graduates reporting salaries who received a bonus since not everyone with a base salary received a signing bonus.

Student selectivity (.25): The strength of full-time students entering in the fall of 2015 was measured by the average GMAT and GRE scores (65 percent),

average undergraduate GPA (30 percent), and the proportion of applicants accepted by the school (5 percent).

Overall rank: Data were standardized about their means, and standardized scores were weighted, totaled and rescaled so that the top school received 100; others received their percentage of the top score.

Specialty rankings: Based solely on ratings by educators at peer schools. B-school deans and MBA program heads were asked to nominate up to 10 programs for excellence. Those receiving the most nominations are listed.

BRETT ZIEGLER FOR USN&WR

The Wharton School,
No. 4

Best Part-Time MBA Programs

Part-time business programs play a vital role for working people who can't go to school full time because of family or financial reasons. The U.S. News part-time MBA ranking is based on five factors: average peer assessment score (50 percent of the overall score); average GMAT score and GRE scores of part-time MBA students entering in the fall of 2015 (15 percent); average undergraduate GPA (5 percent); work experience (15 percent); and the percentage of the fall 2015 MBA enrollment that is part time (15 percent). The average peer assessment score is calculated from a fall 2015 survey that asked business school deans and MBA program directors at each of the nation's 344 part-time MBA programs to rate the other part-time programs on a 5-point scale, from marginal (1) to outstanding (5); 44 percent responded. For the purpose of calculating this year's rankings, the two most recent years of peer assessment survey results were averaged. To be eligible for the part-time ranking, a program needed to be accredited by the Association to Advance Collegiate Schools of Business and have at least 20 students enrolled part time in the fall of 2015; 296 programs met those criteria.

THE TOP PART-TIME PROGRAMS

Rank School	Overall score	Peer assessment score (5.0=highest)	'15 part-time average GMAT score	'15 part-time acceptance rate	'15 total part-time enrollment
1. University of California–Berkeley (Haas)	100	4.5	694	43.6%	799
2. University of Chicago (Booth) (IL)	98	4.7	676	N/A	1,329
3. Northwestern University (Kellogg) (IL)	93	4.6	669	N/A	688
4. University of California–Los Angeles (Anderson)	89	4.2	676	64.8%	971
5. University of Michigan–Ann Arbor (Ross)	85	4.3	655	72.7%	463
6. Indiana University (Kelley School)	84	3.9	670	51.2%	305
7. University of Texas–Austin (McCombs)	78	4.0	630	70.0%	436
8. Carnegie Mellon University (Tepper) (PA)	77	4.1	643	70.0%	164
8. Ohio State University (Fisher)	77	3.7	621	69.3%	332
10. New York University (Stern)	76	4.3	669	59.4%	1,540
11. University of Minnesota–Twin Cities (Carlson)	75	3.7	603	82.2%	1,047
12. Georgetown University (McDonough) (DC)	73	3.7	666	61.9%	391
13. Emory University (Goizueta) (GA)	72	3.8	639	70.0%	250
13. University of Washington (Foster)	72	3.6	638	71.6%	356
15. University of Southern California (Marshall)	71	3.9	614	53.0%	513
16. Temple University (Fox) (PA)	70	3.1	597	60.3%	638
16. University of Massachusetts–Amherst (Isenberg)	70	3.1	570	87.2%	1,248
16. Virginia Tech (Pamplin)	70	3.1	634	88.9%	145
19. University of Maryland–College Park (Smith)	69	3.5	579	87.8%	646
19. Wake Forest University (NC)	69	3.3	587	84.0%	305
19. Washington University in St. Louis (Olin) (MO)	69	3.8	585	90.0%	350
22. University of Wisconsin–Madison	68	3.7	598	81.0%	163
23. Georgia Institute of Technology (Scheller)	67	3.4	615	79.5%	369
24. Rice University (Jones) (TX)	66	3.5	629	69.1%	292
24. University of South Carolina (Moore)	66	3.1	619	87.6%	462
26. University of Texas–Dallas	65	3.0	634	41.5%	803
27. Georgia State University (Robinson)	64	3.0	621	53.6%	452
28. Miami University (Farmer) (OH)	63	2.8	593	70.7%	107
28. University of Florida (Hough)	63	3.3	584	63.5%	392
30. Texas A&M University–College Station (Mays)	62	3.4	609	80.9%	98
30. University of California–Davis	62	3.3	584	67.0%	424
30. University of Iowa (Tippie)	62	3.2	568	88.4%	743
30. Washington State University	62	2.6	571	44.3%	556
34. North Carolina State University (Jenkins)	61	2.7	664	75.8%	227
34. University of Georgia (Terry)	61	3.3	561	84.5%	288
36. University of California–Irvine (Merage)	60	3.4	579	82.1%	333
37. Boston College (Carroll) (MA)	59	3.4	593	90.1%	363
37. Santa Clara University (Leavey) (CA)	59	2.9	624	72.2%	490
39. Arizona State University (Carey)	58	3.4	584	75.4%	234
39. Babson College (Olin) (MA)	58	3.3	570	92.7%	263
39. Boston University (Questrom) (MA)	58	3.3	577	94.7%	671
39. Villanova University (PA)	58	2.8	610	78.1%	138

More @ usnews.com/grad

Rank School	Overall score	Peer assessment score (5.0=highest)	'15 part-time average GMAT score	'15 part-time acceptance rate	'15 total part-time enrollment
43. Clemson University (SC)	57	2.9	606	88.5%	281
43. Loyola University Chicago (Quinlan) (IL)	57	2.9	566	45.6%	557
43. Purdue University–West Lafayette (Krannert) (IN)	57	3.4	592	83.8%	57
43. Rutgers, The State U. of N.J.–Newark & New Brunswick	57	2.9	587	75.9%	987
43. University of Houston (Bauer) (TX)	57	2.9	610	58.2%	359
48. Lehigh University (PA)	56	2.6	613	73.5%	154
48. Pepperdine University (Graziadio) (CA)	56	3.1	551	91.8%	922
48. University of Arizona (Eller)	56	3.3	505	93.6%	204
51. Case Western Reserve University (Weatherhead) (OH)	55	3.3	562	85.9%	104
51. Colorado State University	55	2.7	531	98.6%	889
51. Southern Methodist University (Cox) (TX)	55	3.2	590	74.8%	243
51. University of Delaware (Lerner)	55	2.6	610	87.3%	209
55. Fordham University (Gabelli) (NY)	54	2.9	611	85.7%	366
55. George Washington University (DC)	54	3.2	553	70.4%	286
55. James Madison University (VA)	54	2.6	568	93.1%	35
55. Loyola Marymount University (CA)	54	3.0	586	57.8%	177
59. Kennesaw State University (Coles) (GA)	53	2.5	595	29.0%	165
59. Seattle University (Albers) (WA)	53	2.7	580	87.9%	591
59. University of Colorado–Boulder (Leeds)	53	3.2	578	96.3%	101
59. University of Connecticut	53	2.8	574	94.2%	813
59. University of Nebraska–Lincoln	53	2.9	622	64.3%	70
59. University of North Carolina–Charlotte (Belk)	53	2.7	604	63.8%	271
59. University of Richmond (Robins) (VA)	53	2.7	606	82.0%	78
66. CUNY Bernard M. Baruch College (Zicklin) (NY)	52	2.9	603	60.2%	613
66. College of William and Mary (Mason) (VA)	52	3.1	584	97.8%	178
66. Florida State University	52	2.9	577	63.5%	65
66. University of Oklahoma (Price)	52	2.9	601	74.3%	147
66. University of Pittsburgh (Katz) (PA)	52	3.2	559	89.2%	424
66. University of Rochester (Simon) (NY)	52	3.3	585	92.5%	185
72. St. Louis University (Cook) (MO)	51	2.9	539	88.1%	225
72. University of Kansas	51	3.0	562	97.3%	166
74. Bentley University (MA)	50	2.8	583	91.0%	223
74. DePaul University (Kellstadt) (IL)	50	2.9	558	79.4%	776
74. Elon University (Love) (NC)	50	2.5	562	83.8%	122
74. George Mason University (VA)	50	2.7	570	57.3%	192
78. Gonzaga University (WA)	49	2.7	570	67.2%	220
78. University of California–San Diego (Rady)	49	3.1	582	81.0%	98
78. University of Illinois–Chicago (Liautaud)	49	2.7	581	57.9%	278
78. University of Utah (Eccles)	49	2.9	550	69.0%	313
82. Butler University (IN)	48	2.5	578	45.5%	208
82. University of Cincinnati (Lindner) (OH)	48	2.7	639	78.4%	148
82. University of Kentucky (Gatton)	48	2.8	609	92.3%	125
82. University of Massachusetts–Lowell	48	2.2	559	85.0%	586
82. University of Texas–Arlington	48	2.6	518	65.8%	494
87. Northeastern University (MA)	47	2.8	543	88.4%	362
87. Xavier University (Williams) (OH)	47	2.6	568	80.6%	362
89. Loyola University Maryland (Sellinger)	46	2.7	525	52.6%	295
89. Rutgers, The State University of New Jersey–Camden	46	2.7	560	63.4%	187
89. University of Alabama–Birmingham	46	2.6	552	70.4%	247
89. University of Colorado–Denver	46	2.7	580	70.4%	533
93. St. Joseph's University (Haub) (PA)	45	2.5	535	59.1%	1,227
93. Texas Christian University (Neeley)	45	2.8	550	84.9%	177
93. University of Louisville (KY)	45	2.7	550	73.0%	160
93. University of Nebraska–Omaha	45	2.5	572	69.8%	250
97. Hofstra University (Zarb) (NY)	44	2.5	561	77.5%	804
97. University of New Mexico (Anderson)	44	2.6	503	N/A	146

THE TOP PART-TIME PROGRAMS continued

Rank School	Overall score	Peer assessment score (5.0=highest)	'15 part-time average GMAT score	'15 part-time acceptance rate	'15 total part-time enrollment
97. University of Portland (Pamplin) (OR)	44	2.5	523	86.9%	89
97. University of San Diego (CA)	44	2.7	609	87.2%	89
97. University of Wisconsin–Milwaukee (Lubar)	44	2.7	547	69.2%	430
102. American University (Kogod) (DC)	43	2.7	580	88.0%	80
102. Creighton University (NE)	43	2.7	518	45.2%	142
102. Marquette University (WI)	43	2.8	549	71.4%	236
102. Seton Hall University (Stillman) (NJ)	43	2.5	559	69.2%	185
102. University of Hawaii–Manoa (Shidler)	43	2.5	594	88.2%	94
102. University of Nevada–Las Vegas	43	2.3	585	55.1%	154
102. University of South Florida	43	2.4	572	38.5%	230
102. University of Wisconsin–Eau Claire	43	2.4	529	91.7%	207
102. Virginia Commonwealth University	43	2.6	550	62.9%	163
111. SUNY–Oswego (NY)	42	1.9	560	86.5%	156
111. University of Colorado–Colorado Springs	42	2.4	514	70.9%	206
111. University of Michigan–Dearborn	42	2.3	586	66.1%	119
114. Bradley University (Foster) (IL)	41	2.3	567	84.6%	49
114. University of Michigan–Flint	41	2.2	548	54.1%	154
114. University of New Hampshire (Paul)	41	2.4	537	100.0%	126
114. University of Northern Iowa	41	2.1	545	54.8%	67
114. University of St. Thomas (MN)	41	2.5	525	100.0%	626
119. Drexel University (LeBow) (PA)	40	2.6	483	99.1%	247
119. Louisiana State University–Baton Rouge (Ourso)	40	2.7	599	84.1%	62
119. Old Dominion University (VA)	40	2.4	558	55.2%	106
119. Portland State University (OR)	40	2.4	607	59.8%	38
119. University of Central Florida	40	2.4	N/A	65.7%	360
124. Fairfield University (Dolan) (CT)	39	2.5	523	52.4%	57
124. Northern Illinois University	39	2.3	485	92.4%	589
124. University of Denver (Daniels) (CO)	39	2.7	569	91.4%	122
124. University of North Carolina–Greensboro (Bryan)	39	2.4	570	86.5%	90
124. University of North Carolina–Wilmington (Cameron)	39	2.1	564	72.1%	44
124. University of Washington–Bothell	39	2.2	540	66.4%	101
130. Boise State University (ID)	38	2.3	540	79.5%	67
130. Duquesne University (Donahue) (PA)	38	2.4	548	95.8%	235
130. John Carroll University (Boler) (OH)	38	2.4	540	98.0%	89
130. Ohio University	38	2.4	N/A	82.7%	106
130. Oklahoma State University (Spears)	38	2.7	554	86.2%	103
130. University of Texas–San Antonio	38	2.3	571	40.0%	156
136. Florida International University	37	2.3	N/A	47.0%	557
136. Pennsylvania State U., The Behrend College (Black)	37	2.3	549	76.5%	124
136. San Diego State University (CA)	37	2.7	583	36.2%	271
136. University at Buffalo–SUNY (NY)	37	2.6	576	94.9%	200
136. University of Washington–Tacoma Milgard	37	2.1	470	91.7%	56
141. Bowling Green State University (OH)	36	2.3	547	88.6%	86
141. Clark University (MA)	36	2.3	560	100.0%	95
141. University of Akron (OH)	36	2.0	567	60.6%	490
141. University of Missouri–Kansas City (Bloch)	36	2.5	588	47.4%	143
141. University of Scranton (PA)	36	2.4	531	28.8%	141
141. Valparaiso University (IN)	36	2.2	534	100.0%	64
141. Wichita State University (Barton) (KS)	36	2.3	533	51.1%	205
148. California State University–Northridge (Nazarian)	35	2.2	583	24.9%	138
148. Texas State University (McCoy)	35	2.2	520	46.5%	271
148. University of Alabama–Huntsville	35	2.3	533	92.9%	126

Note: The data listed for acceptance rate and enrollment are for informational purposes only and are not used in the computation of the part-time MBA program rankings. N/A=Data were not provided by the school. Sources: U.S. News and the schools. Assessment data collected by Ipsos Public Affairs.

ENGINEERING

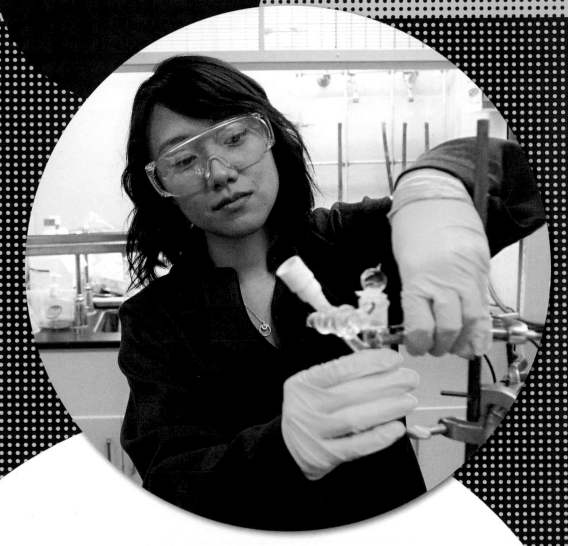

THE U.S. NEWS RANKINGS

In a research lab, University of Southern California
TROY HARVEY FOR USN&WR

A **WARMER** WELCOME

Wanted: Women and members of other underrepresented groups

By **MICHAEL MORELLA**

⟩⟩⟩ **Rice University** Ph.D. student Sydney Gibson spends her days in the lab, working with tissue and natural biomaterials like collagen and elastin to model vascular processes in lung cancer. The fast-growing field of bioengineering attracted Gibson, 26, because "you experience cutting-edge technology" while also having a direct – even lifesaving – impact on patients. Rice stood out among her grad school possibilities. As an African-American woman, Gibson was impressed by its efforts to draw women and students of color into a still mostly white male domain through social activities, mentoring opportunities and professional development programs. Women now earn more than 30 percent of engineering grad degrees there, compared to the national average of about 23 percent. And "students actively practice diversity and inclusion," she says.

Rice is one of the many engineering schools that are ramping up programs to recruit, retain and advance women and other underrepresented students in the face of stubbornly discouraging demographics. Women comprise only 15 percent of the engineering workforce, and black, Hispanic and American Indian workers account for just about 1 in 10. Intel, whose percentages of black and

TROY HARVEY FOR USN&WR

Hispanic employees are in the single digits and whose male employees outnumber women 3 to 1, announced a $300 million initiative last year to radically change those figures by 2020. It will be tough: Just 24 percent of engineering master's students and 22 percent of doctoral candidates are women, according to the American Society for Engineering Education. African-Americans, American Indians, and Hispanics together make up roughly one-third of the country's population but only about 13 percent of engineering graduate students. Given what employers say is a critical need to train more scientists and engineers, expanding the pipeline is not simply "a feel-good initiative," says Gabriel Montaño, who works in the Center for Integrated Nanotechnologies at Los Alamos National Laboratory in New Mexico and is president of the Society for Advancement of Chicanos/Hispanics and Native Americans in Science.

Last year, some 150 engineering deans pledged to craft detailed plans to boost recruitment and retention of underrepresented students and faculty. "This can't be solved overnight. But I think if there is a commitment at the university level, it can be changed," says Yannis C. Yortsos, dean of the Viterbi School of Engineering at the University of Southern California.

For starters, educators have realized that there's a benefit in moving away from the traditional sink-or-swim mentality and instead finding ways to better engage and support all students. That has meant fewer lectures and more emphasis on bringing engineering principles to life through real-world problem-solving and community service. At the University of Michigan, for example, teams that might include business, art and other students as well as engineers tackle actual problems for university or industry partners. One group is working with General Motors to boost transmission efficiency. Another is partnering with Procter & Gamble to craft a robotic arm that should improve the shipping process. Rice students have worked with Queen Elizabeth Central Hospital in Malawi to develop low-cost blood pressure monitors and CPAP systems for infants with respiratory problems.

Cornell biomedical engineering Ph.D. candidates can spend a summer of "clinical immersion" in New York City at the university's medical school or affiliated New York-Presbyterian Hospital. They are paired with physician mentors in fields like cardiology and oncology to observe surgery and other treatments and use engineering principles to solve clinical challenges. "I was lucky to see many orthopedic medical procedures," says fourth-year Ph.D. student Ashley Torres, 25, who shadowed an orthopedic trauma surgeon and has taken that perspective back to her research on understanding and preventing stress fractures. She also contributed to a published paper on walking speed in elderly trauma patients.

An opportunity to tackle real work with a public service component "goes a long way" in keeping students, particularly women, committed to the pro-

Some participants in the USC Women in Science and Engineering Program

WHY I PICKED...

Purdue University

WEST LAFAYETTE, INDIANA

JOSEPH LUKENS, '15
Research scientist

>> For graduate school, I looked for programs with excellent research opportunities and supportive advisers. Purdue turned out to be a great match. As an electrical engineer, I studied how optics and lasers can improve communications. The engineering department is huge, but once you specialize you work with very small groups of faculty and students and can build strong relationships.

I had a great adviser who gave me engineering problems to tackle and some general guidance, then allowed me to move ahead on my own. He also helped me get funding for research, including studying how lasers can hide data in a kind of temporal invisibility cloak, a real plus for cybersecurity. I also took courses outside my specialty, like one in estimation theory, so helpful to me now in my current job as a research scientist working on optics and communications at Oak Ridge National Laboratory. ∎

gram, says Karen Horting, executive director and CEO of the Society of Women Engineers. Some of the evidence is at the undergraduate level: About 70 percent of the students who participate in Purdue University's Engineering Projects in Community Service program report that it increased their motivation to continue studying engineering. Roughly two-fifths are women. Their efforts have included developing a mobile app to track nutrition and collaborating with the city of West Lafayette, Indiana, to prevent erosion in a park. Disciplines like environmental and biomedical engineering, where projects might involve pressing societal issues like climate change or cancer treatment, enroll much more balanced numbers of women and men at the graduate level than other fields do.

A number of schools are also embracing entrepreneurship as a way to foster teamwork and make theory meaningful and concrete. Harvard, Northwestern and New York University, among others, have established innovation centers where future engineers and business students, say, can collaborate on carrying ideas from concept to market. And many programs have introduced classes on intellectual property and finance. Kay Igwe, who recently completed her electrical engineering master's at Columbia, took a class in which small groups of students from a range of disciplines developed ideas, crafted business plans, and created prototypes. Igwe, 28, helped build an app that alerts students when they are in the same area as a peer taking the same class, so they might study together. She later worked with other engineering and public health students on a project to decontaminate electrical equipment used in treating patients with the Ebola virus.

Beyond experiential learning, many schools are courting women and students of color with scholarships and fellowships. More than 100 universities are members of the National GEM Consortium, for example, which awards approximately 125 fellowships to those pursuing grad degrees in science and engineering. The fellowships provide full tuition plus a stipend, and include internships at one of about three dozen sponsoring employers such as Intel,

Corning, Northrop Grumman and several national labs. Gibson's GEM fellowship to Rice supported a summer position at Draper Laboratory in Cambridge, Massachusetts, where she worked on tissue engineering.

At Cornell, Torres, who is Mexican-American, is receiving tuition funding and an annual stipend from a university fellowship that also assigns her a faculty mentor and provides workshops on such topics as securing research funding and networking. "I really don't think I would be here if it wasn't for the support," she says. Cornell has more than doubled its graduate enrollment of women and underrepresented minorities in the last 10 years.

Because work at the graduate level is so research-intensive and individual, finding a community and a mentor or two on campus can make a big difference in a student's satisfaction level, says Adrienne Minerick, associate dean for research and innovation in the College of Engineering at Michigan Technological University and chair of ASEE's diversity committee. A number of institutions, including Cornell, UCLA and the University of Virginia, have established full-fledged diversity centers as vehicles. USC's Center for Engineering Diversity acts as a central hub for programming

FROM LEFT: ANGELA M. LUKENS; BRANDON THIBODEAUX – MJR FOR USN&WR

Rice Ph.D. student Sydney Gibson (center) works with postdoc Jade Li in their lab.

geared toward underrepresented minority students; along with student groups like the Minority Engineering Graduate Association, the center coordinates everything from social activities around Los Angeles to workshops in leadership. USC also has a universitywide Women in Science and Engineering initiative, established in 2000, that offers funding, networking opportunities, and other programming for female students and faculty. Just since 2013, the female grad student engineering population has risen from 26 to 29 percent.

Georgia Tech's center, in addition to offering mentoring and enrichment programs, puts on a summer engineering institute for underrepresented high school students that relies on grad students as chaperones and mentors. Often, this type of engagement reaffirms the older students' interest in engineering and is thus "mutually beneficial," says Dean Gary May. Georgia Tech's longstanding relationship with two historically black colleges in Atlanta, Morehouse and Spelman, has created something of a pipeline for African-American students interested in a graduate degree in engineering.

Purdue's Women in Engineering Program offers similar opportunities for 700 female

graduate students. They can apply for funding to attend academic and professional conferences and are invited to exclusive networking events with alumnae; last fall, grads from 3M, NASA, General Electric and other companies visited campus. A student-led mentoring program connects grad students with peers who counsel them on academic, professional and personal questions. The peer mentoring has been shown to significantly improve retention and self-confidence, says Beth Holloway, director of Women in Engineering and assistant dean for undergraduate education in Purdue's College of Engineering. "We can come together and make everybody successful," says Catherine Berdanier, 28, who will graduate in May with a Ph.D. in engineering education and has both been mentored and served as a mentor.

Each year, the University of Michigan hosts NextProf, a workshop for underrepresented grad students and postdocs from across the country interested in academic careers. Guest experts discuss topics like securing a tenure-track position,

negotiating a job offer and building a research program. "An entire roadmap was played out," says Mauro Rodriguez, 27, a mechanical engineering Ph.D. candidate at Michigan who attended the program in 2014. The son of Mexican immigrants and the first in his family to attend college, Rodriguez decided on an academic career as a way to combine his interests in teaching, research and service.

Universities are also putting a premium on recruiting more women and minority faculty members, so valuable as role models. Women represent only 15.2 percent of tenure-track faculty members in engineering, with African-American and Hispanic professors accounting for just 2.5 and 3.9 percent, respectively. Doctoral students considering a career in academia should focus a job search on schools where faculty members mentor junior faculty and where women and minority professors are offered training on promotion and tenure, for example, advises Sonya T. Smith, who teaches mechanical engineering at Howard University in Washington, D.C., and has led a program there on diversifying STEM faculty. The idea is to find "a climate conducive to your being successful," she says.

In addition to exploring university supports, applicants should look into what additional resources are available on campus. Organizations like SWE, the National Society of Black Engineers and the Society of Hispanic Professional Engineers are active at hundreds of campuses, hosting social events, meet-and-greets with faculty and employers, and national conferences that draw thousands of students, faculty and recruiters from industry. "It's a really nice ecosystem," says Ritu Raman, 24, a mechanical engineering Ph.D. candidate at the University of Illinois–Urbana-Champaign who helped establish a graduate chapter of SWE there four years ago. Today, the group has about 400 members.

Rodriguez has met several of his own mentors through the Society of Hispanic Professional Engineers, and he pays his good fortune forward by working on projects with middle and high school students in Detroit through Michigan's Center for Engineering Diversity and Outreach. "I care a lot," he says, "about the entire pipeline." ■

THE JOB MARKET

SPOTLIGHT ON: BIOMEDICAL ENGINEERING

From Lab to Bedside

By **CHRISTOPHER J. GEARON**

》 As a senior in high school, Melanie McWade knew she wanted to become one of the lucky people who apply engineering science to medicine, repairing the body's worn parts and coming up with new medical devices and drugs. "Brains controlling prosthetic limbs? As an 18-year-old, I wanted to be part of that," she says.

So she completed an accelerated bachelor's/master's program in biomedical engineering in four years at Vanderbilt University, followed by a fellowship at the Bionics Institute in Melbourne, Australia. There she worked on retinal implants that restore vision to people with macular degeneration and on cochlear implant stimulation strategies for hearing loss. She then entered Vandy's doctoral program.

A scouting role. Hoping to get even closer to translating science into results at the bedside, McWade, 26, sought out a fellowship last summer at Allied Minds, a Boston venture capital firm that looks to commercialize promising research. She worked alongside the investment team, scouting for possibilities and gaining experience with investment analysis. After finishing her degree this spring, she'll take a position as vice president of emerging therapies at Rosellini Scientific, bringing biomedical technology to market by directing studies and helping to gain funding and Food and Drug Administration approval. "I get to be on the cusp of research and also turn the research into a real commercial product," she says.

The field is young: Of the country's 90-plus accredited programs at all

Melanie McWade
Vanderbilt University School
of Engineering, 2016

degree levels, 68 have earned that status just since 2000. "There was a concern at one time that industry didn't know what biomedical engineering brought to the table," notes Rich Hart, chair of Ohio State University's department and president of the Biomedical Engineering Society. Today, the future is bright; government projections put job growth at 23 percent – more than three times the average for all jobs – during the decade ending in 2024.

Graduates follow a number of different paths, says Hart. They work in hospitals, at medical device-makers, pharmaceutical and other life sciences companies, and at government agencies from the FDA to NASA, as well as pursue research and teaching positions in academia. In 2014, the median salary for biomedical engineers was $87,000. ∎

... More Hot Jobs

ENVIRONMENTAL ENGINEER

Using soil science, biology and chemistry, these pros develop solutions to environmental problems. Work ranges from preparing investigation reports to designing water reclamation and air pollution control systems to advising corporations on contaminated site cleanup. Job growth through 2024 will likely run 12 percent. The median salary is now about $83,000, but pay can exceed $125,000.

PETROLEUM ENGINEER

Despite the recent drop in oil prices and a growing push for clean energy, the job outlook for petroleum engineers appears strong for the foreseeable future. Oil prices will be a factor, however: It will take higher prices to prompt companies to drill in deeper waters and less hospitable places and to try new extraction methods. Also, many petroleum engineers are expected to retire over the next decade. Median salary was approximately $130,000 in 2014.

CIVIL ENGINEER

These experts are needed to deal with the country's aging infrastructure – the bridge rebuilds, road repairs, levee and dam upgrades, and the execution of new projects such as water systems and waste treatment plants. They also will facilitate the economy's move toward alternative energy and already play a big role in the rebuilding after natural disasters. Median pay in 2014 was about $82,000.

COURTESY OF MELANIE MCWADE

Schools of Engineering

THE TOP SCHOOLS

Rank School	Overall score	Peer assessment score (5.0=highest)	Recruiter assessment score (5.0=highest)	'15 average quantitative GRE score[1]	'15 accept-ance rate	'15 Ph.D students/ faculty	'15 faculty membership in National Academy of Engineering	'15 engineering school research expenditures (in millions)	'15 research expenditures per faculty member (in thousands)	Ph.D.s granted 2014-2015	'15 total graduate engineering enrollment
1. Massachusetts Institute of Technology	100	4.9	4.7	167	13.6%	5.6	13.6%	$465.5	$1,238.0	348	3,123
2. Stanford University (CA)	87	4.9	4.6	167	15.4%	7.2	18.5%	$200.4	$831.7	279	3,601
3. University of California–Berkeley	81	4.7	4.6	166	15.7%	5.4	15.7%	$207.0	$821.6	218	1,973
4. California Institute of Technology	75	4.6	4.6	168	9.6%	5.2	16.5%	$110.9	$1,192.3	75	545
5. Carnegie Mellon University (PA)	73	4.3	4.3	165	22.5%	4.5	10.9%	$202.5	$800.3	217	3,648
6. University of Michigan–Ann Arbor	72	4.4	4.1	166	27.6%	4.3	4.2%	$265.6	$742.0	257	3,364
7. Georgia Institute of Technology	71	4.6	4.4	164	30.2%	4.4	3.4%	$195.5	$365.4	411	7,504
7. University of Illinois–Urbana-Champaign	71	4.5	4.3	165	25.3%	4.0	3.5%	$222.1	$537.9	304	3,421
9. Purdue University–West Lafayette (IN)	70	4.2	4.2	164	22.8%	4.8	4.7%	$230.7	$642.6	311	3,542
10. University of Texas–Austin (Cockrell)	68	4.2	4.1	165	16.5%	5.2	7.6%	$199.4	$664.6	240	2,373
11. Texas A&M University–College Station (Look)	67	3.8	3.8	163	20.8%	3.6	3.5%	$309.2	$820.1	221	3,480
12. Cornell University (NY)	66	4.3	4.1	166	27.6%	4.3	12.0%	$136.3	$671.4	165	2,001
12. University of Southern California (Viterbi)	66	3.6	3.8	163	21.8%	5.2	10.3%	$188.8	$1,048.8	157	5,195
14. Columbia University (Fu Foundation) (NY)	64	3.7	3.8	166	24.4%	5.0	13.2%	$144.6	$957.6	135	3,212
14. University of California–Los Angeles (Samueli)	64	3.7	3.9	165	27.6%	5.7	19.5%	$104.6	$683.7	159	2,064
14. University of Wisconsin–Madison	64	4.0	3.9	163	8.9%	4.4	3.9%	$194.7	$905.7	165	1,939
17. University of California–San Diego (Jacobs)	63	3.6	4.0	166	25.6%	5.2	11.3%	$162.4	$832.7	163	2,244
18. Princeton University (NJ)	62	4.1	4.1	167	11.7%	4.1	16.2%	$90.7	$677.0	93	568
19. Northwestern University (McCormick) (IL)	56	3.9	3.9	166	23.5%	4.8	4.3%	$109.9	$587.8	137	1,980
19. University of Pennsylvania	56	3.6	3.8	166	21.0%	3.8	9.5%	$103.4	$884.1	78	1,577
21. Johns Hopkins University (Whiting) (MD)	55	3.9	4.0	165	29.3%	4.5	2.5%	$112.9	$723.8	112	3,472
21. Virginia Tech	55	3.8	3.9	163	31.1%	3.3	2.0%	$175.4	$531.6	193	2,257
23. University of California–Santa Barbara	54	3.5	3.7	164	15.5%	3.8	11.8%	$102.9	$714.5	89	743
24. Harvard University (MA)	53	3.6	4.0	166	11.0%	4.7	12.5%	$47.7	$644.6	64	448
24. University of Maryland–College Park (Clark)	53	3.6	3.7	164	32.5%	4.0	4.3%	$152.9	$599.7	152	2,318
24. University of Washington	53	3.7	3.8	164	19.3%	3.6	4.7%	$141.8	$576.4	131	2,333
27. North Carolina State University	51	3.3	3.5	164	16.1%	3.2	4.2%	$175.7	$532.3	181	3,362
27. Pennsylvania State University–University Park	51	3.7	3.8	164	24.0%	3.3	1.8%	$101.1	$331.5	228	1,840
27. University of Minnesota–Twin Cities	51	3.6	3.8	169	23.3%	3.8	4.2%	$110.3	$477.6	152	1,901
30. Duke University (Pratt) (NC)	50	3.6	3.7	164	24.5%	4.2	3.1%	$96.9	$775.0	74	1,067
31. Ohio State University	49	3.5	3.5	165	17.5%	3.9	2.4%	$120.4	$470.4	169	1,883
31. Rice University (Brown) (TX)	49	3.6	3.8	165	22.6%	5.4	6.8%	$61.0	$530.7	77	903
33. University of California–Davis	47	3.4	3.8	163	19.8%	4.1	5.6%	$80.8	$459.1	110	1,131
33. University of Colorado–Boulder	47	3.4	3.4	162	31.0%	4.7	4.9%	$93.4	$591.2	112	1,803
35. Boston University (MA)	46	3.0	3.4	164	24.0%	3.9	6.7%	$99.1	$832.6	59	1,002
36. Vanderbilt University (TN)	45	3.3	3.6	163	17.1%	4.2	2.2%	$69.3	$778.7	63	503
37. University of California–Irvine (Samueli)	44	3.2	3.6	164	16.7%	4.1	3.7%	$79.0	$434.1	127	1,470
38. Yale University (CT)	43	3.3	3.8	168	16.4%	3.3	6.8%	$32.4	$599.4	35	282
39. Rensselaer Polytechnic Institute (NY)	42	3.4	3.8	163	26.8%	3.4	2.1%	$59.7	$403.4	103	681
39. University of Virginia	42	3.2	3.6	164	24.9%	3.3	3.6%	$66.8	$506.4	81	681
41. University of Rochester (NY)	41	2.7	3.3	164	37.6%	3.6	4.5%	$89.3	$970.5	46	602
42. Northeastern University (MA)	40	2.9	3.5	161	37.5%	3.9	2.6%	$69.5	$466.6	65	3,574
43. Arizona State University (Fulton)	39	3.2	3.3	162	44.2%	3.1	1.8%	$92.7	$349.9	124	3,610
43. University of Florida	39	3.3	3.4	163	41.5%	3.0	0.4%	$65.7	$239.8	193	2,797
43. University of Pittsburgh (Swanson) (PA)	39	3.0	3.3	163	33.0%	3.3	0.7%	$87.5	$620.8	77	1,064
46. Case Western Reserve University (OH)	38	3.2	3.5	165	34.1%	3.2	2.7%	$41.3	$362.0	64	671
46. New York University	38	2.6	3.3	164	33.9%	3.5	10.8%	$26.7	$405.2	32	2,496
48. Iowa State University	37	3.2	3.3	162	21.3%	2.6	1.2%	$88.1	$361.3	81	1,363
48. Michigan State University	37	3.1	3.4	163	10.4%	3.1	2.2%	$49.0	$273.8	104	807
48. University of Notre Dame (IN)	37	3.1	3.5	163	20.1%	3.9	2.4%	$42.4	$334.0	61	511
51. Lehigh University (Rossin) (PA)	36	3.0	3.5	165	26.0%	5.0	3.4%	$20.7	$183.0	61	828
51. University of Delaware	36	2.8	3.4	163	37.7%	4.5	4.6%	$45.9	$355.6	72	881
51. University of Utah	36	2.8	3.2	163	35.9%	2.7	3.4%	$80.4	$444.3	100	1,219
51. Washington University in St. Louis (MO)	36	3.2	3.6	164	51.1%	4.0	1.1%	$20.9	$237.7	62	1,187

[1]GRE scores displayed are for master's and Ph.D. students and are only for those GRE exams taken during or after August 2011 using the new 130-170 score scale.
N/A=Data were not provided by the school. Sources: U.S. News and the schools. Assessment data collected by Ipsos Public Affairs.

▶ More @ usnews.com/grad

THE TOP SCHOOLS continued

Rank School	Overall score	Peer assessment score (5.0=highest)	Recruiter assessment score (5.0=highest)	'15 average quantitative GRE score[1]	'15 acceptance rate	'15 Ph.D. students/ faculty	'15 faculty membership in National Academy of Engineering	'15 engineering school research expenditures (in millions)	'15 research expenditures per faculty member (in thousands)	Ph.D.s granted 2014-2015	'15 total graduate engineering enrollment
55. Colorado School of Mines	35	2.9	3.6	159	38.3%	2.8	1.6%	$51.4	$270.3	124	1,261
55. University of Arizona	35	3.0	3.2	162	41.1%	2.6	4.8%	$62.0	$373.6	102	1,098
57. Dartmouth College (Thayer) (NH)	34	2.9	3.6	165	26.2%	2.5	3.6%	$24.3	$476.2	14	304
57. Rutgers, The State Univ. of N.J.–New Brunswick	34	2.9	3.3	164	19.9%	2.1	3.1%	$59.5	$323.2	88	1,355
57. University of Massachusetts–Amherst	34	2.8	3.4	162	24.5%	3.4	1.2%	$50.3	$312.2	79	864
60. University of Illinois–Chicago	33	2.8	3.3	160	26.8%	4.1	1.9%	$26.0	$268.5	65	1,539
61. University at Buffalo–SUNY (NY)	32	2.7	3.0	162	30.8%	3.2	1.2%	$58.6	$361.8	78	1,749
62. Auburn University (Ginn) (AL)	31	2.9	3.2	160	45.5%	2.0	N/A	$58.3	$416.6	73	850
62. Stony Brook University–SUNY (NY)	31	2.7	3.1	165	32.0%	3.8	2.4%	$30.1	$194.3	90	1,534
62. University of Tennessee–Knoxville	31	2.7	3.1	160	31.3%	3.3	2.2%	$64.1	$348.5	85	1,008
65. Brown University (RI)	30	3.2	3.6	144	27.2%	2.6	5.0%	$23.8	$316.7	34	429
65. Clemson University (SC)	30	2.9	3.2	162	31.7%	2.6	0.5%	$34.5	$160.4	105	1,457
65. Drexel University (PA)	30	2.8	3.4	160	33.0%	2.7	2.1%	$29.6	$184.7	92	1,225
65. Tufts University (MA)	30	2.8	3.3	161	39.8%	2.7	3.7%	$20.7	$262.6	25	618
65. University of Dayton (OH)	30	2.1	2.7	156	15.5%	3.1	N/A	$89.8	$1,448.0	18	729
65. University of Iowa	30	2.7	3.1	160	16.9%	2.2	1.1%	$46.3	$520.7	40	364
71. Colorado State University	29	2.6	3.1	161	49.0%	1.1	0.9%	$61.9	$600.6	48	817
71. University of California–Riverside (Bourns)	29	2.2	2.8	162	25.3%	4.8	1.9%	$48.3	$508.1	102	747
73. Illinois Institute of Technology (Armour)	28	2.6	3.1	160	50.7%	3.1	3.1%	$18.5	$189.1	44	1,840
73. University of Connecticut	28	2.6	2.9	163	26.0%	3.3	1.4%	$42.3	$308.6	72	892
73. University of Houston (Cullen) (TX)	28	2.4	3.0	162	31.0%	3.5	4.1%	$30.1	$210.6	74	1,499
73. University of Texas–Dallas (Jonsson)	28	2.4	3.1	161	32.8%	1.8	3.2%	$47.0	$315.3	64	2,552
77. Oregon State University	27	2.6	3.2	161	25.2%	2.6	0.6%	$38.5	$242.1	58	1,150
77. Stevens Institute of Technology (Schaefer) (NJ)	27	2.4	3.2	161	59.0%	2.4	1.2%	$28.3	$358.8	43	2,073
77. Syracuse University (NY)	27	2.5	3.2	163	34.4%	3.0	2.7%	$11.5	$168.7	31	1,147
80. University of North Carolina–Chapel Hill	26	2.8	3.4	159	36.7%	1.8	N/A	$6.6	$214.1	11	112
80. Washington State University	26	2.6	3.1	161	24.4%	2.8	0.7%	$28.1	$216.3	61	732
82. Michigan Technological University	25	2.6	3.1	162	31.4%	1.9	N/A	$28.3	$197.7	49	1,060
82. University of Central Florida	25	2.3	3.0	159	38.3%	4.2	0.8%	$36.0	$285.9	77	1,325
82. University of Cincinnati (OH)	25	2.5	3.0	161	16.5%	2.6	N/A	$23.4	$203.4	55	808
82. University of New Mexico	25	2.4	2.8	157	45.9%	4.4	1.0%	$29.8	$304.2	64	853
82. University of Texas–Arlington	25	2.3	2.8	156	48.3%	3.0	1.5%	$41.2	$311.7	74	3,320
87. Rochester Institute of Technology (Gleason) (NY)	24	2.7	3.5	159	39.1%	0.7	N/A	$29.0	$246.1	17	1,160
87. University of Alabama–Huntsville	24	2.3	2.9	157	72.3%	1.6	N/A	$58.1	$806.6	24	740
87. University of California–Santa Cruz (Baskin)	24	2.2	2.9	163	32.6%	2.9	N/A	$33.3	$416.6	35	453
87. Worcester Polytechnic Institute (MA)	24	2.5	3.3	163	47.8%	1.6	0.9%	$25.0	$215.7	35	1,124
91. University of Missouri	23	2.5	2.9	162	25.7%	1.9	N/A	$22.6	$199.8	43	644
92. George Washington University (DC)	22	2.4	3.1	162	43.3%	1.5	N/A	$11.1	$132.3	62	1,590
92. Missouri University of Science & Technology	22	2.6	3.3	157	54.5%	2.1	0.6%	$26.5	$149.0	75	1,174
92. New Jersey Institute of Technology	22	2.4	2.9	157	86.1%	1.4	N/A	$47.6	$340.3	48	2,271
92. Texas Tech University (Whitacre)	22	2.3	2.8	159	25.8%	2.7	3.1%	$18.4	$138.6	60	892
92. University of Kentucky	22	2.4	2.8	161	51.7%	1.8	0.7%	$41.1	$275.7	55	489
92. University of Nebraska–Lincoln	22	2.5	2.9	160	35.6%	1.8	N/A	$31.2	$177.1	52	627

SPECIALTIES
PROGRAMS RANKED BEST BY ENGINEERING SCHOOL DEPARTMENT HEADS

Rank School	Average assessment score (5.0=highest)
AEROSPACE/AERONAUTICAL/ASTRONAUTICAL	
1. Massachusetts Institute of Technology	4.7
2. Georgia Institute of Technology	4.6
2. Stanford University (CA)	4.6
4. California Institute of Technology	4.4
4. University of Michigan–Ann Arbor	4.4
6. Purdue University–West Lafayette (IN)	4.3
7. University of Texas–Austin (Cockrell)	4.0
8. University of Colorado–Boulder	3.9
8. University of Illinois–Urbana-Champaign	3.9
10. Texas A&M University–College Station (Look)	3.8
10. University of Maryland–College Park (Clark)	3.8

Rank School	Average assessment score (5.0=highest)
BIOLOGICAL/AGRICULTURAL	
1. Purdue University–West Lafayette (IN)	4.9
2. Iowa State University	4.6
3. Texas A&M University–College Station (Look)	4.4
3. University of Florida	4.4
3. University of Illinois–Urbana-Champaign	4.4
6. Cornell University (NY)	4.3
7. University of California–Davis	4.1
8. University of Nebraska–Lincoln	3.9
8. Virginia Tech	3.9
10. North Carolina State University	3.8

Rank School	Average assessment score (5.0=highest)
BIOMEDICAL/BIOENGINEERING	
1. Johns Hopkins University (Whiting) (MD)	4.6
2. Georgia Institute of Technology	4.5
2. Massachusetts Institute of Technology	4.5
4. University of California–San Diego (Jacobs)	4.4
5. Stanford University (CA)	4.3
6. Duke University (Pratt) (NC)	4.2
6. University of California–Berkeley	4.2
8. University of Pennsylvania	4.0
9. Boston University (MA)	3.9
9. Northwestern University (McCormick) (IL)	3.9
9. Rice University (Brown) (TX)	3.9

Photo Credit: Patrick Mansell

GO BEYOND

...the expected and ordinary. Take a long look at what really shapes your graduate school experience—the people, the research, the labs, the partnerships. We are certain you will find what you are looking for at the Penn State College of Engineering.

If you are ready to take that step towards your successful future, the Penn State College of Engineering is ready for you.

www.engr.psu.edu/gobeyond

Degree options in 13 academic areas

New professional 1-year Master's programs

Expansive labs and research facilities

Relaxing and affordable location

© 2016 The Pennsylvania State University. All Rights Reserved. Penn State is an equal opportunity, affirmative action employer, and is committed to providing employment opportunities to all qualified applicants without regard to race, color, religion, age, sex, sexual orientation, gender identity, national origin, disability or protected veteran status. U.Ed. ENG 16-159

Penn State
College of Engineering

SPECIALTIES continued

Rank School	Average assessment score (5.0=highest)
9. University of Michigan–Ann Arbor	3.9
9. University of Washington	3.9
CHEMICAL	
1. Massachusetts Institute of Technology	4.9
2. California Institute of Technology	4.7
2. University of California–Berkeley	4.7
2. University of Minnesota–Twin Cities	4.7
5. Stanford University (CA)	4.6
6. University of Wisconsin–Madison	4.5
7. University of Texas–Austin (Cockrell)	4.4
8. Georgia Institute of Technology	4.3
9. Princeton University (NJ)	4.2
9. University of California–Santa Barbara	4.2
9. University of Delaware	4.2
CIVIL	
1. University of California–Berkeley	4.7
2. University of Illinois–Urbana-Champaign	4.6
2. University of Texas–Austin (Cockrell)	4.6
4. Georgia Institute of Technology	4.5
4. Stanford University (CA)	4.5
6. Purdue University–West Lafayette (IN)	4.3
7. Massachusetts Institute of Technology	4.2
8. University of Michigan–Ann Arbor	4.1
8. Virginia Tech	4.1
10. Cornell University (NY)	4.0
COMPUTER	
1. Massachusetts Institute of Technology	4.9
2. Carnegie Mellon University (PA)	4.8
2. Stanford University (CA)	4.8
2. University of California–Berkeley	4.8
5. University of Illinois–Urbana-Champaign	4.6
6. Georgia Institute of Technology	4.3
7. University of Michigan–Ann Arbor	4.2
7. University of Washington	4.2
9. California Institute of Technology	4.1
9. Purdue University–West Lafayette (IN)	4.1
ELECTRICAL/ELECTRONIC/COMMUNICATIONS	
1. Massachusetts Institute of Technology	4.9

Rank School	Average assessment score (5.0=highest)
1. Stanford University (CA)	4.9
1. University of California–Berkeley	4.9
4. California Institute of Technology	4.6
4. University of Illinois–Urbana-Champaign	4.6
6. Georgia Institute of Technology	4.4
6. University of Michigan–Ann Arbor	4.4
8. Carnegie Mellon University (PA)	4.2
8. Cornell University (NY)	4.2
8. Purdue University–West Lafayette (IN)	4.2
8. University of Texas–Austin (Cockrell)	4.2
ENVIRONMENTAL/ENVIRONMENTAL HEALTH	
1. University of California–Berkeley	4.8
2. Stanford University (CA)	4.5
3. University of Illinois–Urbana-Champaign	4.4
4. University of Texas–Austin (Cockrell)	4.2
5. Georgia Institute of Technology	4.1
5. University of Michigan–Ann Arbor	4.1
7. Carnegie Mellon University (PA)	3.9
7. Virginia Tech	3.9
9. Johns Hopkins University (Whiting) (MD)	3.8
9. Massachusetts Institute of Technology	3.8
9. Yale University (CT)	3.8
INDUSTRIAL/MANUFACTURING/SYSTEMS	
1. Georgia Institute of Technology	4.7
2. University of California–Berkeley	4.5
2. University of Michigan–Ann Arbor	4.5
4. Northwestern University (McCormick) (IL)	4.4
4. Stanford University (CA)	4.4
6. Massachusetts Institute of Technology	4.1
7. Cornell University (NY)	4.0
7. University of Wisconsin–Madison	4.0
9. Purdue University–West Lafayette (IN)	3.9
9. Virginia Tech	3.9
MATERIALS	
1. Massachusetts Institute of Technology	4.7
2. Northwestern University (McCormick) (IL)	4.5
2. University of California–Santa Barbara	4.5
4. Stanford University (CA)	4.4
4. University of Illinois–Urbana-Champaign	4.4

Rank School	Average assessment score (5.0=highest)
6. University of California–Berkeley	4.3
7. California Institute of Technology	4.2
8. Georgia Institute of Technology	4.1
9. Cornell University (NY)	4.0
9. University of Michigan–Ann Arbor	4.0
MECHANICAL	
1. Massachusetts Institute of Technology	4.8
1. Stanford University (CA)	4.8
3. University of California–Berkeley	4.7
4. California Institute of Technology	4.6
4. University of Michigan–Ann Arbor	4.6
6. Georgia Institute of Technology	4.4
6. University of Illinois–Urbana-Champaign	4.4
8. Carnegie Mellon University (PA)	4.1
8. Cornell University (NY)	4.1
8. Purdue University–West Lafayette (IN)	4.1
NUCLEAR	
1. University of Michigan–Ann Arbor	4.8
2. Massachusetts Institute of Technology	4.5
3. Texas A&M University–College Station (Look)	4.2
4. University of Wisconsin–Madison	4.1
5. University of California–Berkeley	3.9
6. North Carolina State University	3.8
7. University of Tennessee–Knoxville	3.7
8. Georgia Institute of Technology	3.6
9. University of Illinois–Urbana-Champaign	3.5
10. Pennsylvania State University–University Park	3.4
10. Purdue University–West Lafayette (IN)	3.4
PETROLEUM ENGINEERING	
1. University of Texas–Austin (Cockrell)	4.7
2. Stanford University (CA)	4.3
2. Texas A&M University–College Station (Look)	4.3
4. University of Tulsa (OK)	3.9
5. Colorado School of Mines	3.7
5. Pennsylvania State University–University Park	3.7
7. University of Oklahoma	3.5
8. University of Southern California (Viterbi)	3.3
9. Texas Tech University (Whitacre)	2.6
9. University of Wyoming	2.6

METHODOLOGY

Programs at the 215 engineering schools that grant doctoral degrees were surveyed; 194 responded and were eligible to be ranked based on a weighted average of 10 indicators described below.

Quality assessment: Two surveys were conducted in the fall of 2015. In one, engineering school deans and deans of graduate studies at engineering schools were asked to rate program quality from marginal (1) to outstanding (5); 33 percent responded. The two most recent years' peer results were averaged and the resulting score is weighted by .25 in the overall score. Corporate recruiters and company contacts (names were supplied by the schools) who hire engineers from previously ranked engineering schools were also asked to rate programs. The three most recent years' results were averaged and are weighted by .15.

Student selectivity (.10): The strength of master's and Ph.D. students entering in fall 2015 was measured by their mean GRE quantitative score (67.5 percent of this measure) and acceptance rate (32.5 percent). Scores for the new and old GRE were converted to a common scale; new scores are displayed.

Faculty resources (.25): This score is based on the 2015 ratio of full-time doctoral students to full-time faculty (30 percent) and full-time master's students to full-time faculty (15 percent); the proportion of full-time faculty who were members of the National Academy of Engineering in 2015 (30 percent); and the number of engineering doctoral degrees granted in the past school year (25 percent).

Research activity (.25): Based on total externally funded engineering research expenditures (60 percent) and research dollars per full-time tenured and tenure-track faculty member (40 percent). Expenditures refer to separately funded research, public and private, averaged over fiscal years 2014 and 2015.

Overall rank: Data were standardized about their means, and standardized scores were weighted, totaled and rescaled so the top-scoring school received 100; others received their percentage of the top score.

Specialty rankings: Rankings are based solely on assessments by department heads in the specialty, who rated other schools on a 5-point scale. The top-rated schools appear here. Names of department heads surveyed are from the American Society for Engineering Education.

LAW

THE U.S. NEWS RANKINGS

At Northwestern's Pritzker School of Law
PETER HOFFMAN FOR USN&WR

Breaking
WITH
Tradition

Many law schools are overhauling their programs to build in extensive hands-on practice. Here's a look at five pioneers

By **MARGARET LOFTUS**

>>> **Law school continues** to be more of a buyer's market than in years past, as many programs invent new ways to reel in applicants who've been wary of the poor job outlook and steep tuitions. The legal education community is still trying to regain its footing after the Great Recession forced firms to radically tighten their belts, shutting out many new grads and sending applications into a spiral. First-year enrollment in 2014 was down by 30 percent at private law schools and 18 percent at public schools from 2009. Meanwhile, tuition climbed 46 percent at the privates and 132 percent at the publics between 1999 and 2014. In 2015, an American Bar Association task force urged law schools to get creative about improving curricula and holding the line on costs. (It wouldn't be necessary for the ABA to impose any "tough love," the task force noted, "because the market is already doing it – in some instances brutally.") On the bright side, hiring seems to be inching up slightly. And fewer graduates should mean less competition for those spots.

Among the more unconventional curricular experiments law schools will keep an eye on are several new programs. The Mitchell Hamline School of Law – a merger of Minnesota's William Mitchell College of Law and Hamline University School of Law – will offer a first-of-its-kind, hybrid on-campus/online curriculum. Students will take online courses for 12 or 13 weeks a semester and visit the campus 10 times during the four-year program to participate in skills workshops. The UNT Dallas College of Law is teaching skills like research, writing and deposition-taking in courses on legal theory like Contracts and Civil Procedure, and lectures are videotaped so students can review them at will. The school vows to close the "justice gap" by attracting nontraditional students (the average age is above 30). Tuition is comparatively affordable: $14,500 for state residents, compared to the national average of $23,214 for public law schools.

Meanwhile, more established schools continue to recast their programs by condensing coursework, addressing tuition, and adding intensive on-the-job training, perhaps the biggest trend of all. "I see more and more law schools going in this direction," says Judith Lipton, associate dean for experiential education at Case Western Reserve School of Law. "Students will demand it." Here's a look at what's happening at a few of the pioneers:

Elon University School of Law
Greensboro, North Carolina

Before committing to a career in law, Caitlin Mitchell tested the waters by working as a paralegal for a firm in Roanoke, Virginia. When the time came, she knew she wanted a law school that would teach her not only legal theory but also how to act like an attorney. She was surprised to find that many schools operate as if new J.D.s graduate and then "serve as an apprentice for years." But firms no longer have the resources (or the patience) to train apprentices.

▶ **More on law schools** @ usnews.com/lawschools

So Mitchell, 25, jumped at the chance to enter Elon last year as it unveiled a completely overhauled curriculum emphasizing practice. The new program focuses heavily on individualized mentorship by working attorneys and faculty members and extensive experiential coursework, and it has been condensed into two and a half years. Meanwhile, the school reduced tuition by 12 percent to a flat $100,000 for the whole package.

In the first year, "lab" components of foundational courses connect theory to practice. In a criminal law lab, for instance, students might observe a plea agreement negotiation in court before doing their own simulated plea deal. Second-year students spend one trimester in a full-time "residency" in a legal setting – such as the North Carolina Business Court conveniently located on campus – while taking a related class. These experiences culminate in a third-year "bridge-to-practice" course tailored to a student's intended career path. Family law students, for example, might participate in an extended simulation of a divorce case.

Throughout it all, each student depends for guidance on his or her personal "student success team," which includes a faculty adviser, an attorney mentor, an executive coach from the school's leadership program, and a professional development adviser. Mitchell had barely started her first trimester when her mentor, an Elon alum who works at a local firm, brought her to a court hearing. The judge's line of questioning was relevant to what she was then covering in class. That realization, she says, "was really energizing."

Case Western Reserve University School of Law
Cleveland

At Case Western, which also has overhauled its curriculum to make experiential learning central to all three years of coursework, new students right off the bat find themselves work-

Elon students are introduced to business court by Judge James L. Gale and Julia Ebert (second from right), legal counsel at Volvo Group North America and their attorney mentor.

ALEX BOERNER FOR USN&WR

Sultana Kelantan and Benjamin Schuppel chose Pepperdine's two-year option.

ing with real clients of the Cleveland Legal Aid Society. While they can't offer advice, the students do the initial interviews, present the problem to volunteer attorneys, and sit in on problem-solving sessions. Lipton is one of the faculty who meet with students to discuss their experiences. "It becomes a wonderful conversation about what it means to be a lawyer," she says.

Other first-year experiences include a residency program that puts selected 1Ls to work assisting 3L interns in the school's in-house legal clinics, which aid clients who can't afford counsel in criminal cases, civil litigation, health issues and other areas of law. They research and draft memos and

pleadings and participate in team strategy sessions. "I was taking civil procedure class, and [the clinic work] really helped because I could see it in action," says Kory Wiita, 23, who helped pilot the litigation residency last year and is now in his second year at Case. "It was a good incubator."

Simulations keep students focused on "real lawyering" as well, says Lipton. Wiita, for example, found it helpful to role-play taking a deposition in his Legal Writing 3 class from a "client" suing a department store for a false imprisonment claim after a shoplifting allegation. Meanwhile, many 2Ls and all 3Ls work full time for a semester (or half time for both semesters) in an externship. For most, that

ARE LAW SCHOOLS DOING THEIR JOB?

Bar exam scores dropped again last year. The mean score on the multiple-choice section of the July 2015 exam was 139.9, down 1.6 points from the previous summer's score – which itself represented a low not seen since 1988. Several states saw their pass rates slip significantly. In New York, for instance, 61 percent of those who sat for the July test passed, down from 65 percent in July 2014; California's rate slipped 2 percentage points to

just under 47 percent. (A national pass rate for July 2015 was to be announced after press time; in 2014, the U.S. rate for the July test was 67 percent.)

The National Conference of Bar Examiners, which is responsible for the standardized portion of the bar exam, blames the slump on a lowering of standards for admission to law school that has resulted from the drop in applications (54,130 people applied to law school in 2015, down from

BOBBY CURTIS FOR USN&WR

means working in the clinics. Others go abroad to work in the International Criminal Court or find spots in law firms or nonprofits to get experience in areas not practiced in the clinics, such as environmental or labor law.

University of Denver Sturm College of Law

Denver

L ast year, Tyler McAnelly, 27, logged 40 to 60 hours a week working in the Arapahoe County public defender's office, handling cases from DUIs to child abuse. "I carried around 50 cases," he says. "They treated me pretty much the way they treated every attorney." Only McAnelly hasn't graduated from law school yet; he was participating in Denver Law's "semester in practice" program, in which third-year students hold down a real job and attend a seminar every week to discuss their experiences.

In the school's new curriculum, one-third of the load consists of hands-on practice-based opportunities. In the first-year Lawyering Process course, a legal research, writing and analysis class, students might partner with a nonprofit to help it decide whether to pursue public interest litigation, for example. Similarly, potentially dry classes such as Contracts and Corporations have been recast as simulations. Professor Roberto Corrada uses the novel "Jurassic Park" to inspire students in his administrative law class, for instance; they work in teams to draft and present legislation to Congress establishing regulations for a dinosaur theme park, which may include guidance on handling dinosaur DNA and fence electrification. And five in-house clinics offer hands-on practice.

McAnelly is convinced his background will prove valuable in the job search. "I don't think a class exists that gets into the misdemeanor stuff I learned every day," he says. "I feel like I'll be properly prepared to handle a full caseload."

University of Kansas School of Law

Lawrence, Kansas

F rom the moment she first tagged along with her father to a courtroom as a little girl, Ashley Akers, 25, was hooked. "I figured out you could just go to the courthouse and look at the docket and go to any trial you wanted.

87,900 in 2010). Others question whether schools are doing enough to prepare students for the bar. The schools contend that the curriculum does indeed cover much of the material and note that students never have had the bandwidth to fit in the whole range of electives beyond the foundational courses. Whatever the explanation, experts say, a test prep course may be a wise investment. –M.L.

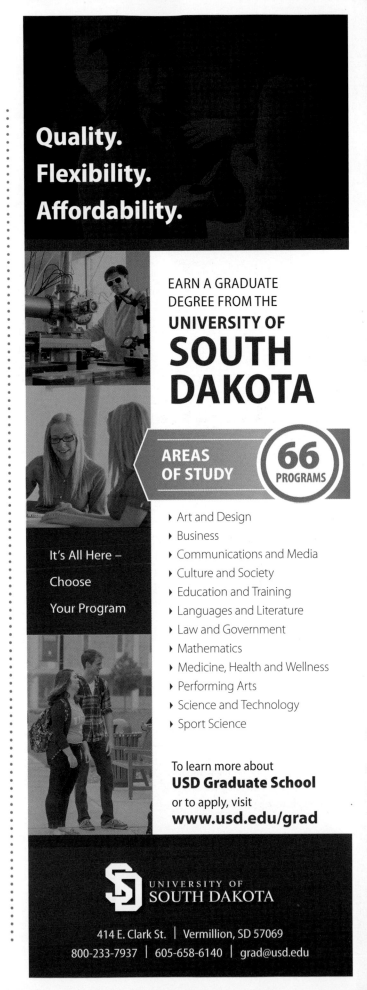

Quality.
Flexibility.
Affordability.

EARN A GRADUATE DEGREE FROM THE

UNIVERSITY OF
SOUTH DAKOTA

AREAS OF STUDY **66 PROGRAMS**

It's All Here – Choose Your Program

▸ Art and Design
▸ Business
▸ Communications and Media
▸ Culture and Society
▸ Education and Training
▸ Languages and Literature
▸ Law and Government
▸ Mathematics
▸ Medicine, Health and Wellness
▸ Performing Arts
▸ Science and Technology
▸ Sport Science

To learn more about **USD Graduate School** or to apply, visit **www.usd.edu/grad**

UNIVERSITY OF SOUTH DAKOTA

414 E. Clark St. | Vermillion, SD 57069
800-233-7937 | 605-658-6140 | grad@usd.edu

WHY I PICKED...

University of Texas

AUSTIN

MEGAN SHEFFIELD, '13
Public interest attorney

» When looking at law schools, I came across a video of the UT immigration clinic's work to end the detention of families with children. I was inspired by the group's advocacy and knew it was something I wanted to do.

At UT, professors make themselves available, and people in general are very kind and helpful. It's not the stereotypical cutthroat law school environment you hear about. The school's strong pro bono program offers opportunities from working on expunging juvenile records to domestic violence cases. It also gives students hands-on experience assisting clients. In addition, each January, UT takes students to the Rio Grande Valley to help people with needs ranging from wills to asylum applications.

I now work with the nonprofit Equal Justice Center and feel well-prepared by UT not just in the law, but also in serving the center's low-income clients and engaging other pro bono attorneys to aid our important work. ■

I've seen multiple murder trials. I decided around fourth grade that I wanted to be a lawyer." Today the Casper, Wyoming, native is a third-year student at the University of Kansas School of Law, getting ready for the courtroom herself through an intense, immersive skills workshop on using expert witnesses, one of a series that forms the core of the school's experiential offerings. (Another feature of the program that appealed to her: At $20,000 per year for in-staters and $34,000 for out-of-state students, "the tuition is so reasonable," she says. "That was the clincher.")

The skills workshops are modeled on those that some of the largest law firms still use to train new associates. The school partners with local firms to teach the skills, using a combination of lectures and simulations over the course of four 10-hour days. Each workshop focuses only on one skill, such as taking depositions, qualifying expert witnesses at trial, and selecting a jury through voir dire. While legal doctrines take time to absorb, such practice-related skills are mastered most effectively "in these short bursts," says KU law professor Lumen Mulligan.

In her crash course, Akers first got a primer on cross-examination strategies by local attorneys and then was thrown into a simulated trial about a wrongful death case for which she had to cross-examine multiple expert witnesses. Local attorneys played the roles of judge and opposing counsel and later weighed in with feedback.

"The experience was so cool," she says. "It undoubtedly prepared me for cross-examinations in the future." That future is taking shape. After a yearlong clerkship for the 9th U.S. Circuit Court of Appeals that begins this summer, Akers will become an associate in products liability defense for one of the university's partnering law firms.

Pepperdine University School of Law
Malibu, California

Students in Pepperdine's accelerated J.D. program get their experiential learning at a somewhat reduced cost by packing three years of law school into two. But it isn't easy, says Benjamin Schuppel, 30, a 2016 grad who is a captain in the U.S. Army and spent eight years on active duty, including a stint in Iraq. There certainly is no time to waste. He once had a 20-page paper for the summer semester due on the first day of the fall term.

Like Schuppel, though, most students who choose accelerated programs like Pepperdine's have already been out in the professional world and are willing to double down to get back to it sooner. Tuition typically runs the same as for the traditional track, but saving a year of living expenses and lost income is a big selling point.

The streamlined approach has been lauded as a way to cut down on student debt by President Barack Obama. It had a setback last fall when the Northwestern University Pritzker School of Law, one of the movement's pioneers, ended its program after failing to reach its goal of 30 students per class. And Gonzaga University School of Law is no longer accepting applications for its accelerated program. Nonetheless, others, such as those at Brooklyn Law School and the University of Dayton School of Law, are still going strong. Drexel University's law school launched a two-year program in 2014.

Pepperdine's accelerated students start off with a 12-credit summer semester, then join traditional 1Ls in the fall and spring semesters. They get a good dose of experiential learning about dispute resolution, in particular, through simulations in courses on mediation and negotiation offered by the school's Straus Institute for Dispute Resolution (and, as a bonus, they graduate with a certificate in the field). They also do an externship while taking six classroom credits the next summer, and then wrap up the program by taking the traditional 2L coursework.

It's certainly a heavy load, says Schuppel, who nevertheless has found ways to build in the occasional break to lounge on the beach, learn how to surf, and otherwise make the most of Pepperdine's enviable location overlooking the Pacific Ocean. That, he notes, is not a feature you often find at the competition. ■

COURTESY OF CAROL SHEFFIELD

THE JOB MARKET

Keeping It In-House

By **CHRISTOPHER J. GEARON**

>> When Justin Grad went to the University of Iowa's law school, he wanted to land a job at a prestigious firm and get on the lucrative partnership track. Upon graduating in 2009, he did go on to practice corporate law at Latham & Watkins' Orange County, California, office. Grad was involved in mergers and acquisitions and capital market work and was "running my own deals." He loved his job, but 80-hour-plus weeks were not conducive to spending time with his family.

So in 2014 Grad shifted gears into a position as corporate counsel at Amazon in Seattle, where he could indulge his interest in technology and aim for a better work-life balance. He's found the right mix at Amazon, where he is providing legal, compliance and development-related support for Kindle products and associated services. Grad feels he is staying challenged and likes the small team-based practice approach he's found at the company.

Business-minded counsel. For many young attorneys, the in-house choice has become an increasingly common route. "Corporate legal departments are expanding their teams to bring more work in-house and reduce spending on outside counsel," notes the Robert Half Legal "2016 Salary Guide for the Legal Field." Companies want people "who can handle a wide range of business-related legal matters, including expansion into new products and markets, executive compensation, and labor and employment disputes."

Amar Sarwal, vice president and chief legal strategist at the Association

Justin Grad
University of Iowa
College of Law, 2009

of Corporate Counsel, has advice for law school students thinking about in-house careers: Take some business courses. Companies want attorneys who are not afraid of math, "are business-minded and who can manage teams," he says.

Three-quarters of in-house lawyers in the U.S. earn a base salary between $100,000 and $299,000; half of these earn less than $200,000, according to the association's "2015 ACC Global Census." While many attorneys who make the jump from a law firm to a company can expect a pay cut as a trade-off for enjoying the better hours, Grad says he lucked out with his job change; Amazon's offer was on the generous side. For many in-house attorneys, part of the compensation package comes in the form of company stock. Over time, Grad says, "One can win big or lose big." ∎

... More Hot Jobs

HEALTH CARE ATTORNEY

Robert Half Legal, one of the nation's largest legal staffing companies, forecasts that lawyers with health care expertise will find their skills in high demand by government agencies, medical providers and law firms involved with issues tied to medical research, Medicare fraud and health care implementation. Government projections put job growth for health care attorneys at 23 percent through 2024.

DATA PRIVACY ATTORNEY

Cyberattacks and privacy breaches are increasingly top of mind for companies, governments and other entities and so are changes in state and federal regulatory law that are being made to address these challenges. Charles Volkert, executive director of Robert Half Legal, notes that attorneys entering this in-demand practice area are receiving increases of 5 to 7 percent over the average base salaries seen by their peers.

REGULATED SUBSTANCES SPECIALIST

ArcView Market Research reports that U.S. legal cannabis market sales grew from $4.6 billion to $5.4 billion in 2015, driving expansion of law firms' regulated substances practices and even stand-alone cannabis specialties. So far, mostly regional or smaller firms have ventured into advising clients ranging from growers and dispensers to security firms. But big law is also eyeing the potential.

COURTESY OF JUSTIN GRAD

Schools of Law

THE TOP SCHOOLS

Rank School	Overall score	Peer assessment score (5.0=highest)	Assessment score by lawyers/ judges (5.0=highest)	'15 undergrad GPA 25th-75th percentile	'15 LSAT score 25th-75th percentile	'15 acceptance rate	'15 student/ faculty ratio	'14 grads employed at graduation[†]	Employed 10 months after graduation[†]	School's bar passage rate in jurisdiction	Jurisdiction's overall bar passage rate
1. Yale University (CT)	100	4.8	4.7	3.86-3.98	171-176	10%	7.8	84.8%	86.1%	96.4%/NY	73%
2. Harvard University (MA)	97	4.8	4.8	3.75-3.96	170-175	18%	10.9	92.7%	94.4%	97.3%/NY	73%
2. Stanford University (CA)	97	4.8	4.8	3.78-3.97	169-173	11%	7.3	90.9%	93.0%	86.8%/CA	60%
4. Columbia University (NY)	94	4.6	4.6	3.59-3.81	168-173	21%	6.1	93.6%	95.7%	92.4%/NY	73%
4. University of Chicago (IL)	94	4.6	4.7	3.69-3.97	166-172	22%	8.6	94.8%	96.2%	97.3%/IL	85%
6. New York University	91	4.5	4.5	3.61-3.87	166-171	33%	8.4	96.5%	96.7%	95.7%/NY	73%
7. University of Pennsylvania	89	4.4	4.4	3.52-3.95	163-170	19%	10.1	98.2%	97.8%	99.3%/NY	73%
8. University of California–Berkeley	86	4.5	4.5	3.66-3.9	162-168	21%	13.0	88.5%	95.5%	87.9%/CA	60%
8. University of Michigan–Ann Arbor	86	4.4	4.5	3.54-3.87	164-169	28%	10.7	88.5%	93.3%	92.9%/NY	73%
8. University of Virginia	86	4.3	4.5	3.59-3.94	163-170	20%	9.7	98.3%	96.6%	98.0%/NY	73%
11. Duke University (NC)	84	4.2	4.4	3.56-3.84	166-170	23%	9.1	86.5%	93.0%	94.3%/NY	73%
12. Northwestern University (Pritzker) (IL)	83	4.2	4.4	3.56-3.85	163-169	23%	6.5	79.0%	90.0%	92.4%/IL	85%
13. Cornell University (NY)	82	4.2	4.3	3.62-3.82	164-168	31%	8.5	94.2%	96.3%	91.6%/NY	73%
14. Georgetown University (DC)	77	4.1	4.3	3.47-3.85	161-168	28%	10.9	81.8%	87.2%	90.5%/NY	73%
15. University of Texas–Austin	76	4.0	4.2	3.48-3.86	162-169	22%	9.8	68.9%	86.9%	88.0%/TX	77%
16. Vanderbilt University (TN)	75	3.9	4.1	3.5-3.83	161-168	38%	10.9	82.5%	87.1%	93.2%/TN	72%
17. University of California–Los Angeles	74	3.9	4.1	3.51-3.86	162-169	30%	11.4	58.9%	87.5%	81.4%/CA	60%
18. Washington University in St. Louis (MO)	73	3.5	3.9	3.18-3.8	161-168	28%	9.6	67.1%	91.1%	93.0%/MO	87%
19. University of Southern California (Gould)	71	3.4	3.8	3.49-3.86	161-167	30%	10.2	77.4%	85.7%	86.4%/CA	60%
20. Boston University (MA)	68	3.4	3.5	3.41-3.75	160-164	38%	10.6	57.7%	80.5%	95.4%/MA	81%
20. University of Iowa	68	3.3	3.6	3.44-3.79	156-162	43%	8.7	67.6%	86.9%	90.8%/IA	84%
22. Emory University (GA)	67	3.5	3.8	3.45-3.88	156-166	32%	11.4	62.3%	89.9%	88.4%/GA	80%
22. University of Minnesota	67	3.5	3.7	3.48-3.9	158-166	44%	9.3	69.9%	81.5%	89.9%/MN	84%
22. University of Notre Dame (IN)	67	3.4	3.9	3.46-3.79	161-165	35%	10.1	62.6%	85.5%	93.9%/IL	85%
25. Arizona State University (O'Connor)	64	3.1	3.2	3.39-3.8	158-163	43%	9.8	65.2%	88.4%	89.5%/AZ	74%
25. George Washington University (DC)	64	3.3	3.7	3.38-3.8	158-166	40%	15.9	81.2%	89.2%	92.2%/NY	73%
25. Indiana University–Bloomington (Maurer)	64	3.3	3.7	3.31-3.88	155-162	53%	8.3	48.0%	82.4%	94.0%/IN	79%
28. University of Alabama	63	3.2	3.2	3.29-3.93	156-164	37%	9.5	49.7%	85.4%	94.8%/AL	79%
28. University of California–Irvine	63	3.2	3.5	3.38-3.7	161-165	27%	7.3	46.2%	84.9%	77.9%/CA	60%
30. Boston College (MA)	61	3.2	3.7	3.39-3.65	158-163	45%	10.3	57.1%	83.9%	90.9%/MA	81%
30. Ohio State University (Moritz)	61	3.3	3.5	3.44-3.81	156-161	50%	10.1	46.7%	89.0%	92.6%/OH	81%
30. University of California–Davis	61	3.3	3.6	3.27-3.68	159-165	31%	10.1	54.4%	82.2%	86.0%/CA	60%
33. Col. of William and Mary (Marshall-Wythe) (VA)	60	3.2	3.6	3.4-3.86	158-164	36%	12.0	65.1%	82.3%	85.0%/VA	72%
33. University of Georgia	60	3.2	3.4	3.36-3.83	156-164	33%	12.2	47.7%	77.9%	92.8%/GA	80%
33. University of Washington	60	3.2	3.5	3.41-3.78	159-166	27%	7.6	46.5%	74.5%	84.3%/WA	80%
33. University of Wisconsin–Madison	60	3.4	3.6	3.27-3.76	155-162	49%	8.2	45.8%	79.7%	100.0%/WI	81%
37. Fordham University (NY)	59	3.1	3.5	3.35-3.69	160-165	35%	11.0	54.9%	74.3%	85.8%/NY	73%
38. Brigham Young University (Clark) (UT)	58	2.8	3.2	3.45-3.86	156-164	40%	12.3	56.5%	88.4%	84.9%/UT	87%
38. University of North Carolina–Chapel Hill	58	3.4	3.9	3.31-3.68	160-164	45%	11.1	47.3%	77.0%	88.2%/NC	69%
40. University of Arizona (Rogers)	57	3.1	3.3	3.22-3.68	155-162	33%	8.8	36.1%	81.9%	88.2%/AZ	74%
40. University of Colorado–Boulder	57	3.1	3.3	3.28-3.77	157-163	46%	9.9	50.3%	78.8%	82.4%/CO	78%
40. University of Illinois–Urbana-Champaign	57	3.1	3.5	3.26-3.68	158-163	46%	11.0	61.1%	82.2%	84.9%/IL	85%

For top schools and second tier: [†]Represents the percentage of all graduates who had a full-time job lasting at least a year for which bar passage was required or a J.D. degree was an advantage. These employment rates are part of the data on placement success used to determine a school's ranking. N/A=Data were not provided by the school. [1]Law school declined to fill out the U.S. News statistical survey. Numbers appearing with an * are from the fall 2015 entering class or school year and 2014 graduating class as reported to the American Bar Association. [2]William Mitchell College of Law and Hamline University School of Law have merged to become Mitchell Hamline School of Law. Belmont University in Tennessee, Concordia University in Idaho, Lincoln Memorial University in Tennessee, the University of La Verne in California, and the University of Massachusetts–Dartmouth are unranked because, as of January 2016, they were only provisionally approved by the American Bar Association. Also unranked are Inter-American University in Puerto Rico, University of Puerto Rico, and Pontifical Catholic University of Puerto Rico. The state bar examination pass rates for first-time test-takers in summer 2014 and winter 2014 were provided by the National Conference of Bar Examiners. Sources: U.S. News and the schools. Assessment data collected by Ipsos Public Affairs.

UNIVERSITY of **HOUSTON** | LAW CENTER

THE POWER OF LEGAL EDUCATION

The University of Houston Law Center is a dynamic, top tier school, empowering our students through legal education.

- Ranked in the Top 10 by U.S. News & World Report for Intellectual Property and Health Law programs

- Recognized for diversity by preLaw and The National Jurist magazines

- Ranked 31st by The National Law Journal among 'Go to' law schools for graduates hired by the top 250 law firms

- Named a 'Best Value' school by The National Jurist

- Offers JD/MBA, JD/MA, JD/MSW, JD/MPH, JD/MD, and JD/Ph.D.

- Offers joint JD program with University of Calgary law school in International Energy Law allowing students to earn both Canadian and American law degrees in 4 years

- Hands-on clinical programs in precedent-setting cases in state and federal courts, including the U.S. Supreme Court

- Named one of the best schools for big and small law firms by The National Jurist

APPLY NOW: LAW.UH.EDU/ADMISSIONS

The University of Houston is a Carnegie-designated Tier One public research university and an EO/AA institution.

THE TOP SCHOOLS continued

Rank School	Overall score	Peer assessment score (5.0=highest)	Assessment score by lawyers/ judges (5.0=highest)	'15 undergrad GPA 25th-75th percentile	'15 LSAT score 25th-75th percentile	'15 acceptance rate	'15 student/ faculty ratio	'14 grads employed at graduation†	Employed 10 months after graduation†	School's bar passage rate in jurisdiction	Jurisdiction's overall bar passage rate
40. Wake Forest University (NC)	57	3.0	3.5	3.37-3.73	157-162	56%	10.9	37.4%	83.4%	78.0%/NC	69%
40. Washington and Lee University (VA)	57	3.0	3.7	3.08-3.58	158-162	49%	8.9	45.7%	74.8%	89.2%/VA	72%
45. George Mason University (VA)	54	2.7	3.1	3.15-3.68	156-162	35%	10.6	56.0%	79.9%	72.4%/VA	72%
45. Southern Methodist University (Dedman) (TX)	54	2.6	3.3	3.27-3.75	156-163	47%	13.9	55.1%	82.7%	84.1%/TX	77%
45. University of Utah (Quinney)	54	2.8	3.2	3.36-3.76	154-160	47%	6.8	39.8%	78.0%	91.3%/UT	87%
48. University of Florida (Levin)	52	3.1	3.4	3.28-3.68	155-160	62%	12.0	42.7%	76.1%	89.0%/FL	72%
48. University of Maryland (Carey)	52	3.0	3.2	3.25-3.63	154-160	54%	10.3	50.0%	77.4%	78.0%/MD	76%
50. Florida State University	51	2.9	3.0	3.26-3.68	156-161	44%	11.0	36.2%	77.2%	82.2%/FL	72%
50. Temple University (Beasley) (PA)	51	2.6	3.1	3.29-3.69	155-162	43%	9.0	46.8%	71.4%	84.1%/PA	81%
50. Tulane University (LA)	51	3.0	3.4	3.15-3.59	155-161	60%	12.7	42.0%	76.1%	80.2%/LA	69%
50. University of California (Hastings)	51	3.1	3.7	3.28-3.64	155-161	42%	13.9	30.1%	58.0%	68.4%/CA	60%
50. University of Houston (TX)	51	2.6	2.9	3.29-3.71	155-161	38%	9.7	56.3%	83.6%	86.0%/TX	77%
55. Baylor University (TX)	50	2.4	3.4	3.28-3.72	158-162	29%	12.9	36.8%	73.5%	90.8%/TX	77%
55. University of Richmond (VA)	50	2.4	3.0	3.23-3.66	155-161	42%	8.9	31.5%	81.9%	86.2%/VA	72%
57. Case Western Reserve University (OH)	48	2.6	3.2	3.12-3.66	156-162	42%	8.1	33.3%	66.1%	78.0%/OH	81%
57. Georgia State University	48	2.6	2.9	3.12-3.6	155-160	28%	8.9	45.2%	79.7%	91.6%/GA	80%
57. University of Nebraska–Lincoln	48	2.5	3.0	3.4-3.85	152-158	62%	11.5	52.1%	87.2%	90.4%/NE	77%
60. University of Cincinnati (OH)	47	2.4	3.1	3.23-3.78	152-157	58%	8.6	47.2%	82.4%	86.3%/OH	81%
60. University of Kentucky	47	2.6	3.1	3.17-3.69	152-158	60%	11.0	63.7%	88.7%	89.8%/KY	81%
60. University of Miami (FL)	47	2.7	3.1	3.15-3.6	154-160	54%	11.6	40.4%	79.4%	81.1%/FL	72%
60. University of New Mexico	47	2.3	2.8	3.21-3.73	150-157	42%	8.9	60.4%	86.5%	88.1%/NM	88%
60. University of Oklahoma	47	2.4	3.2	3.33-3.8	154-159	49%	13.6	47.6%	79.0%	90.7%/OK	84%
65. Loyola Marymount University (CA)	46	2.6	3.1	3.28-3.65	156-161	45%	12.8	36.6%	71.0%	81.7%/CA	60%
65. Pepperdine University (CA)	46	2.6	3.2	3.24-3.71	154-161	49%	11.8	34.3%	59.6%	78.9%/CA	60%
65. Seton Hall University (NJ)	46	2.3	2.9	3.12-3.68	153-159	49%	10.4	61.8%	83.5%	83.0%/NJ	76%
65. University of Connecticut	46	2.7	2.9	3.12-3.62	153-158	51%	7.9	42.2%	69.0%	89.7%/CT	86%
65. University of Kansas	46	2.7	3.3	3.16-3.66	152-159	66%	10.8	37.0%	79.8%	83.0%/KS	86%
65. University of Missouri	46	2.6	3.1	3.08-3.72	154-159	59%	10.7	43.0%	80.7%	92.2%/MO	87%
65. University of Tennessee–Knoxville	46	2.7	2.9	3.31-3.8	153-161	37%	9.4	27.8%	66.9%	83.7%/TN	72%
72. Loyola University Chicago (IL)	45	2.5	3.2	3.07-3.55	155-160	54%	10.3	32.1%	71.8%	83.5%/IL	85%
72. University of Denver (Sturm) (CO)	45	2.7	3.1	3.14-3.61	154-158	45%	9.3	36.1%	65.3%	83.5%/CO	78%
74. St. John's University (NY)	44	2.1	2.9	3.26-3.73	154-159	41%	12.8	35.8%	73.9%	85.3%/NY	73%
74. University of San Diego (CA)	44	2.6	3.0	3.19-3.63	156-161	40%	11.0	38.4%	58.6%	73.3%/CA	60%
74. Villanova University (PA)	44	2.3	3.2	3.27-3.74	152-158	49%	13.2	48.2%	77.7%	94.6%/PA	81%
74. Yeshiva University (Cardozo) (NY)	44	2.7	2.9	3.15-3.62	156-161	56%	12.5	36.7%	67.3%	85.5%/NY	73%
78. American University (Washington) (DC)	43	2.7	3.2	2.96-3.48	152-158	59%	11.0	57.8%	70.2%	73.7%/NY	73%
78. University of Nevada–Las Vegas	43	2.4	2.6	2.98-3.58	155-161	32%	9.1	40.3%	71.2%	68.9%/NV	68%
78. University of Oregon	43	2.7	3.2	2.97-3.55	154-159	49%	10.3	31.5%	59.8%	83.8%/OR	73%
78. University of Pittsburgh (PA)	43	2.6	3.2	3.03-3.63	153-159	37%	9.5	33.5%	71.5%	90.4%/PA	81%
82. Louisiana State U.–Baton Rouge (Hebert)	42	2.2	3.0	3.12-3.7	153-158	59%	18.4	40.4%	82.0%	84.4%/LA	69%
82. Northeastern University (MA)	42	2.4	2.9	3.3-3.75	152-162	35%	12.6	18.1%	61.1%	80.4%/MA	81%
82. St. Louis University (MO)	42	2.3	3.0	3.17-3.66	152-158	66%	10.8	44.9%	78.3%	84.1%/MO	87%
82. University of New Hampshire School of Law	42	1.9	2.8	3.18-3.65	153-159	53%	8.3	38.9%	73.0%	93.2%/NH	86%
86. Illinois Institute of Technology (Chicago-Kent)	41	2.5	2.7	3.09-3.58	152-158	62%	10.2	32.1%	67.6%	88.5%/IL	85%
86. Pennsylvania State University (Dickinson)	41	2.1	2.9	3.15-3.72	158-161	39%	8.3	44.9%	72.2%	82.5%/PA	81%
86. Pennsylvania State University–University Park	41	2.1	2.7	3.15-3.73	152-159	43%	9.1	44.9%	72.2%	87.5%/PA	81%
86. Syracuse University (NY)	41	2.3	3.0	3.07-3.51	151-156	55%	9.5	42.7%	72.0%	86.2%/NY	73%
86. University of Arkansas–Fayetteville	41	2.3	2.8	3.06-3.65	151-158	67%	11.6	30.2%	79.1%	73.2%/AR	76%
86. University of Tulsa (OK)	41	2.0	2.6	2.98-3.57	151-156	37%	9.4	41.8%	84.7%	90.4%/OK	84%
92. Lewis & Clark College (Northwestern) (OR)	40	2.4	3.1	3.08-3.59	154-161	59%	10.3	29.9%	64.1%	80.6%/OR	73%
92. Rutgers, The State University of New Jersey	40	2.4	3.0	2.96-3.54	153-158	49%	12.6	53.3%	71.1%	80.1%/NJ	76%
92. University of Hawaii–Manoa (Richardson)	40	2.5	2.7	2.91-3.6	151-158	37%	7.3	48.6%	72.4%	68.5%/HI	74%
92. University of Louisville (Brandeis) (KY)	40	2.2	2.8	3.12-3.7	151-157	68%	10.7	41.1%	81.3%	82.7%/KY	81%

JEREMY M. LANGE FOR USN&WR

Duke University,
No. 11

LAW

THE TOP SCHOOLS continued

Rank School	Overall score	Peer assessment score (5.0=highest)	Assessment score by lawyers/judges (5.0=highest)	'15 undergrad GPA 25th-75th percentile	'15 LSAT score 25th-75th percentile	'15 acceptance rate	'15 student/faculty ratio	'14 grads employed at graduation†	Employed 10 months after graduation†	School's bar passage rate in jurisdiction	Jurisdiction's overall bar passage rate
92. University of South Carolina	40	2.4	2.9	3-3.56	152-157	59%	13.3	38.1%	74.8%	78.8%/SC	73%
97. Brooklyn Law School (NY)	39	2.4	2.8	3.11-3.59	152-158	52%	16.2	38.2%	63.9%	84.8%/NY	73%
97. Wayne State University (MI)	39	2.0	2.6	3.05-3.61	154-159	52%	10.3	22.5%	62.1%	82.8%/MI	73%
97. West Virginia University	39	2.2	2.7	3.11-3.69	151-157	53%	8.1	41.9%	79.1%	75.8%/WV	82%
100. Indiana University–Indianapolis (McKinney)	38	2.4	3.1	3.03-3.55	148-156	70%	15.6	39.4%	76.0%	79.1%/IN	79%
100. Michigan State University	38	2.3	2.9	3.19-3.72	150-157	46%	14.1	16.0%	66.2%	84.4%/MI	73%
100. SUNY Buffalo Law School (NY)	38	2.2	2.7	3.21-3.66	150-157	52%	16.7	41.4%	70.7%	76.4%/NY	73%
103. The Catholic University of America (DC)	37	2.1	2.9	2.93-3.45	150-156	55%	9.7	40.2%	70.9%	69.7%/MD	76%
103. Florida International University	37	1.6	1.9	3.14-3.76	151-158	29%	12.7	N/A	78.6%	79.4%/FL	72%
103. Stetson University (FL)	37	2.1	2.7	3-3.59	152-156	51%	12.4	27.4%	74.9%	79.9%/FL	72%
106. Cleveland State U. (Cleveland-Marshall) (OH)	35	1.8	2.5	3.13-3.68	150-155	47%	8.7	33.8%	68.2%	78.7%/OH	81%
106. Creighton University (NE)	35	1.9	2.9	2.91-3.56	149-154	79%	11.7	40.6%	76.7%	69.7%/NE	77%
106. Howard University (DC)	35	2.3	2.8	3-3.55	148-153	43%	11.4	47.8%	66.4%	81.3%/NY	73%
106. University of Mississippi	35	2.2	2.7	3.04-3.65	151-157	48%	12.5	26.3%	68.2%	83.8%/MS	87%
106. Washburn University (KS)	35	1.9	2.8	2.86-3.52	149-155	59%	9.2	50.0%	79.5%	81.7%/KS	86%
111. DePaul University (IL)	34	2.2	2.9	3.07-3.49	149-154	67%	12.3	30.1%	69.2%	86.9%/IL	85%
111. Drake University (IA)	34	1.9	2.9	3-3.56	148-154	75%	10.0	35.4%	77.7%	84.0%/IA	84%
111. Drexel University (Kline) (PA)	34	2.0	2.6	3-3.57	153-158	54%	10.3	32.6%	70.2%	85.8%/PA	81%
111. Duquesne University (PA)	34	1.8	2.7	3.07-3.64	150-155	64%	11.4	28.2%	73.5%	90.3%/PA	81%
111. Hofstra University (Deane) (NY)	34	2.2	2.7	2.99-3.6	147-155	60%	13.6	36.3%	71.9%	73.7%/NY	73%
111. New York Law School	34	1.9	2.6	2.88-3.48	149-154	55%	13.7	33.7%	64.3%	69.0%/NY	73%
111. Seattle University (WA)	34	2.3	2.9	2.99-3.49	151-157	58%	11.5	N/A	58.3%	75.3%/WA	80%
111. Texas A&M University	34	2.1	2.4	3.13-3.56	154-158	20%	11.1	22.8%	63.8%	76.6%/TX	77%
111. University of Baltimore (MD)	34	2.0	2.6	2.97-3.51	149-155	52%	11.7	41.4%	73.2%	79.6%/MD	76%
111. University of Idaho	34	2.1	2.7	2.94-3.44	147-155	66%	9.9	N/A	75.6%	65.8%/ID	73%
111. University of Maine	34	2.2	2.7	3.07-3.65	149-157	69%	10.7	32.6%	70.5%	75.9%/ME	76%
111. University of St. Thomas (MN)	34	1.9	2.5	3.21-3.65	149-157	64%	12.0	21.7%	76.9%	79.4%/MN	84%
123. Marquette University (WI)	33	2.3	3.0	2.89-3.42	150-155	77%	17.0	36.0%	67.8%	99.5%/WI	81%
123. Mercer University (George) (GA)	33	2.0	2.6	3.06-3.48	150-154	50%	12.5	39.9%	74.1%	80.2%/GA	80%
123. Texas Tech University	33	1.9	2.9	3.07-3.6	151-156	54%	13.5	31.9%	71.8%	79.2%/TX	77%
123. University of Missouri–Kansas City	33	2.2	2.6	3.03-3.57	150-155	57%	11.0	33.6%	72.7%	89.3%/MO	87%
123. University of Montana	33	2.0	2.5	3.06-3.63	149-156	65%	13.3	47.5%	75.0%	71.4%/MT	70%
123. University of Wyoming	33	2.1	2.7	3.1-3.55	149-155	78%	9.1	38.0%	62.0%	81.6%/WY	78%
129. Albany Law School (NY)	32	1.9	2.5	2.98-3.54	149-154	62%	11.6	41.7%	72.5%	74.5%/NY	73%
129. Santa Clara University (CA)	32	2.4	3.1	3.06-3.41	153-157	61%	10.1	23.4%	47.9%	60.7%/CA	60%
131. CUNY (NY)	31	2.1	2.5	3.09-3.59	150-156	45%	7.4	N/A	50.3%	77.4%/NY	73%
132. Gonzaga University (WA)	30	2.0	2.9	2.98-3.49	151-156	66%	14.8	21.0%	67.3%	75.7%/WA	80%
132. Quinnipiac University (CT)	30	1.9	2.3	3.09-3.55	149-155	63%	10.6	23.0%	58.4%	88.1%/CT	86%
132. Vermont Law School	30	2.1	2.8	2.82-3.52	146-156	71%	18.3	24.6%	63.1%	79.2%/NY	73%
132. Willamette University (Collins) (OR)	30	2.0	2.7	2.8-3.44	150-157	100%	11.1	36.1%	73.8%	65.6%/OR	73%
136. Chapman University (Fowler) (CA)	29	1.8	2.2	3.08-3.47	152-158	47%	10.3	26.8%	55.1%	74.8%/CA	60%
136. Pace University (NY)	29	1.9	2.3	2.88-3.48	147-153	63%	11.4	N/A	68.7%	70.1%/NY	73%
136. University of Akron (OH)	29	1.8	2.4	2.88-3.56	147-154	65%	13.1	31.0%	72.2%	83.6%/OH	81%
136. University of Arkansas–Little Rock (Bowen)	29	2.2	2.7	2.99-3.53	146-155	71%	15.5	20.8%	72.0%	74.8%/AR	76%
140. Hamline University[2] (MN)	28	1.6	2.4	3-3.52	149-156	62%	13.9	29.2%	74.4%	75.2%/MN	84%
140. Loyola University New Orleans (LA)	28	2.0	3.0	2.87-3.52	147-154	76%	10.3	21.1%	60.1%	69.2%/LA	69%
140. William Mitchell College of Law[2] (MN)	28	1.7	2.6	2.92-3.52	148-156	57%	22.2	25.0%	71.5%	80.9%/MN	84%
143. University of South Dakota	27	1.8	2.3	3.01-3.67	144-151	66%	11.1	44.4%	79.0%	75.4%/SD	75%
144. Campbell University (NC)	25	1.5	2.3	2.94-3.48	150-156	62%	14.3	13.6%	72.1%	85.7%/NC	69%
144. Northern Illinois University	25	1.6	2.2	2.77-3.34	145-150	65%	9.9	N/A	73.7%	84.9%/IL	85%
144. Oklahoma City University	25	1.6	2.1	2.79-3.53	146-151	72%	14.3	N/A	87.0%	78.3%/OK	84%
144. University of North Dakota	25	1.9	2.6	2.9-3.45	145-152	68%	11.9	N/A	64.5%	56.0%/ND	65%
144. University of the Pacific (McGeorge) (CA)	25	1.8	2.5	2.9-3.42	148-154	72%	13.6	26.7%	59.4%	63.4%/CA	60%
144. University of Toledo (OH)	25	1.8	2.2	2.94-3.53	147-154	68%	10.6	33.3%	58.5%	83.1%/OH	81%

Other Schools to Consider

The country's other law schools can be considered broadly similar in quality. To be included in the ranking, a law school had to be accredited and fully approved by the American Bar Association, and it had to draw most of its students from the United States.

Remember, as you weigh your options, that you should look not only at a law school's position in the ranking, but also at its many other key characteristics, both tangible and intangible – location, the cost of spending three years there, faculty expertise and the breadth of the course offerings, to name a few – and certainly your prospects of being offered a job upon graduation. More information on all of the law schools is available in the directory at the back of the book, as well as at usnews.com/lawschools.

SECOND TIER (Schools are not ranked, but listed alphabetically.)

School	Peer assessment score (5.0=highest)	Assessment score by lawyers/ judges (5.0=highest)	'15 undergrad GPA 25th-75th percentile	'15 LSAT score 25th-75th percentile	'15 acceptance rate	'15 student/ faculty ratio	'14 grads employed at graduation[1]	Employed 10 months after graduation[1]	School's bar passage rate in jurisdiction	Jurisdiction's overall bar passage rate
Appalachian School of Law[1] (VA)	1.2	1.5	2.78-3.41*	142-150*	40%*	N/A	N/A	42.1%*	33.3%/VA*	72%
Arizona Summit Law School[1]	1.2	1.4	2.54-3.34*	140-148*	73%*	N/A	N/A	60.1%*	54.7%/AZ*	74%
Atlanta's John Marshall Law School[1] (GA)	1.4	1.7	2.7-3.26*	145-150*	57%*	N/A	N/A	66.3%*	62.3%/GA*	80%
Ave Maria School of Law (FL)	1.1	1.7	2.71-3.39	142-153	57%	13.9	9.1%	45.5%	54.4%/FL	72%
Barry University (FL)	1.1	1.4	2.64-3.29	144-150	61%	N/A	N/A	56.9%*	62.2%/FL	72%
California Western School of Law	1.5	2.0	2.87-3.41	147-153	70%	12.3	N/A	56.6%	71.4%/CA	60%
Capital University (OH)	1.5	2.0	2.81-3.45	144-152	76%	12.1	17.5%	46.3%	84.7%/OH	81%
Charleston School of Law (SC)	1.2	1.9	2.59-3.21	143-149	79%	17.5	N/A	62.7%	69.2%/SC	73%
Charlotte School of Law[1] (NC)	1.1	1.6	2.51-3.17*	140-145*	65%*	N/A	N/A	51.3%*	57.0%/NC*	69%
Elon University (NC)	1.6	2.3	2.8-3.42	145-150	47%	10.5	20.2%	52.9%	66.7%/NC	69%
Faulkner University[1] (Jones) (AL)	1.3	1.5	2.68-3.44*	142-149*	70%*	N/A	N/A	68.7%*	69.0%/AL*	79%
Florida A&M University[1]	1.4	1.6	2.72-3.26*	144-149*	55%*	N/A	N/A	43.1%*	73.2%/FL*	72%
Florida Coastal School of Law	1.1	1.5	2.54-3.3	141-148	71%	19.3	N/A	45.2%	60.8%/FL	72%
Golden Gate University (CA)	1.6	2.0	2.72-3.28	145-151	66%	11.0	N/A	31.7%	45.1%/CA	60%
The John Marshall Law School (IL)	1.7	2.6	2.75-3.36	145-151	73%	17.3	37.0%	69.7%	84.5%/IL	85%
Liberty University (VA)	1.2	1.5	2.98-3.76	150-157	50%	8.0	23.7%	56.6%	52.8%/VA	72%
Mississippi College	1.6	1.8	2.73-3.33	142-150	85%	12.9	22.3%	61.7%	45.8%/MS	87%
New England Law Boston (MA)	1.4	2.1	2.78-3.47	144-151	80%	N/A	N/A	59.9%	74.2%/MA	81%
North Carolina Central University	1.5	2.1	2.97-3.41	142-149	56%	12.5	N/A	46.5%	74.3%/NC	69%
Northern Kentucky University (Chase)	1.6	2.0	2.9-3.41	144-152	82%	12.3	N/A	68.6%	79.4%/OH	81%
Nova Southeastern University (Broad) (FL)	1.6	1.9	2.79-3.33	146-151	54%	13.7	22.9%	67.1%	70.4%/FL	72%
Ohio Northern University (Pettit)	1.5	2.2	3-3.5	144-152	50%	11.1	N/A	58.5%	75.6%/OH	81%
Regent University (VA)	1.3	1.7	3-3.55	149-154	55%	11.7	22.1%	63.1%	75.0%/VA	72%
Roger Williams University (RI)	1.6	2.2	2.83-3.48	145-152	80%	14.1	N/A	54.9%	80.2%/MA	81%
Samford University (Cumberland) (AL)	1.7	2.5	2.98-3.53	148-153	65%	16.3	23.5%	63.2%	84.3%/AL	79%
Southern Illinois University–Carbondale	1.7	2.4	2.66-3.32	145-152	79%	13.5	22.9%	70.5%	85.5%/IL	85%
Southern University Law Center (LA)	1.4	2.0	2.53-3.16	141-147	69%	15.0	N/A	57.6%	55.8%/LA	69%
South Texas College of Law	1.6	2.3	2.78-3.34	147-153	63%	20.1	N/A	72.8%	83.6%/TX	77%
Southwestern Law School (CA)	1.8	2.2	2.91-3.39	149-154	59%	12.9	27.5%	55.9%	56.1%/CA	60%
St. Mary's University (TX)	1.6	2.3	2.57-3.37	149-154	66%	14.8	N/A	69.4%	69.7%/TX	77%
St. Thomas University[1] (FL)	1.3	1.7	2.71-3.3*	145-151*	59%*	N/A	N/A	50.9%*	67.4%/FL*	72%
Suffolk University (MA)	1.8	2.6	3.02-3.48	145-154	70%	15.9	27.6%	63.1%	75.8%/MA	81%
Texas Southern University[1] (Marshall)	1.4	1.8	2.8-3.44*	141-146*	55%*	N/A	N/A	46.0%*	63.3%/TX*	77%
Thomas Jefferson School of Law (CA)	1.2	1.8	2.49-3.12	141-149	83%	15.9	11.9%	41.0%	44.7%/CA	60%
Touro College (Fuchsberg) (NY)	1.5	1.8	2.77-3.31	145-149	61%	N/A	N/A	64.3%	65.3%/NY	73%
University of Dayton (OH)	1.7	2.6	2.84-3.43	144-151	58%	14.2	27.9%	72.9%	66.2%/OH	81%
University of Detroit Mercy (MI)	1.5	1.9	2.85-3.34	147-155	61%	13.2	N/A	46.4%	67.2%/MI	73%
University of Memphis (Humphreys) (TN)	1.9	2.2	2.89-3.41	149-156	60%	12.2	22.1%	61.8%	71.9%/TN	72%
University of San Francisco (CA)	2.0	2.9	2.85-3.38	149-154	61%	12.5	22.8%	46.7%	62.1%/CA	60%
University of the District of Columbia (Clarke)	1.4	1.5	2.65-3.32	145-151	30%	11.5	N/A	44.7%	52.2%/MD	76%
Valparaiso University (IN)	1.7	2.7	2.63-3.27	142-148	66%	11.6	N/A	58.7%	60.9%/IN	79%
Western Michigan U. Thomas M. Cooley Law Sch.	1.1	1.7	2.51-3.19	138-147	88%	N/A	N/A	44.1%	61.5%/MI	73%
Western New England University[1] (MA)	1.4	1.8	2.84-3.45*	143-152*	69%*	N/A	N/A	55.1%*	73.3%/MA*	81%
Western State Col. of Law at Argosy U. (CA)	1.1	1.6	2.78-3.3	146-151	63%	20.4	N/A	44.7%	62.7%/CA	60%
Whittier College (CA)	1.3	2.1	2.59-3.24	146-151	63%	11.8	N/A	43.8%	45.9%/CA	60%
Widener University (Commonwealth) (PA)	1.6	2.0	2.82-3.39	145-151	67%	9.3	20.4%	67.3%	81.1%/PA	81%
Widener University (DE)	1.7	2.1	2.74-3.44	147-151	64%	8.7	25.4%	54.7%	70.4%/PA	81%

Note: Key to footnotes, Page 60.

NEIL BLAKE FOR USN&WR

University of Michigan, tied at No. 8

SPECIALTIES
PROGRAMS RANKED BEST BY FACULTY WHO TEACH IN THE FIELD

CLINICAL TRAINING
1. Georgetown University (DC)
2. American University (Washington) (DC)
3. CUNY (NY)
3. New York University
5. Washington University in St. Louis (MO)
6. Yale University (CT)
7. University of Maryland (Carey)

8. Northwestern University (Pritzker) (IL)
8. Stanford University (CA)
10. University of the District of Columbia (Clarke)
11. University of New Mexico
12. University of Michigan–Ann Arbor
13. University of California–Irvine
14. Seattle University (WA)
14. University of Denver (Sturm) (CO)
16. University of California–Berkeley

17. Suffolk University (MA)
17. University of California (Hastings)
19. University of Tennessee–Knoxville
20. Harvard University (MA)

DISPUTE RESOLUTION
1. Ohio State University (Moritz)
2. Pepperdine University (CA)
3. University of Missouri
4. Harvard University (MA)
5. Hamline University[2] (MN)
6. Yeshiva University (Cardozo) (NY)

7. Marquette University (WI)
7. University of Oregon
9. University of Nevada–Las Vegas
10. Northwestern University (Pritzker) (IL)

ENVIRONMENTAL LAW
1. Vermont Law School
2. Lewis & Clark College (Northwestern) (OR)
3. Pace University (NY)
4. University of California–Berkeley

Note: Key to footnotes, Page 60.

5. **Georgetown University** (DC)
5. **University of California–Los Angeles**
7. **University of Utah** (Quinney)
8. **George Washington University** (DC)
8. **University of Colorado–Boulder**
10. **Tulane University** (LA)
11. **Duke University** (NC)
11. **New York University**

HEALTH LAW
1. **St. Louis University** (MO)
2. **Boston University** (MA)
2. **University of Houston** (TX)
4. **University of Maryland** (Carey)
5. **Georgetown University** (DC)
6. **Georgia State University**
7. **Harvard University** (MA)
8. **Loyola University Chicago** (IL)
9. **Case Western Reserve University** (OH)
9. **Seton Hall University** (NJ)
11. **Indiana University–Indianapolis** (McKinney)
12. **Hamline University**[2] (MN)
12. **University of Pittsburgh** (PA)

INTELLECTUAL PROPERTY LAW
1. **University of California–Berkeley**
2. **Stanford University** (CA)

3. **New York University**
4. **George Washington University** (DC)
5. **University of New Hampshire School of Law**
6. **Santa Clara University** (CA)
7. **Yeshiva University** (Cardozo) (NY)
8. **University of Houston** (TX)
9. **American University** (Washington) (DC)
10. **Boston University** (MA)
11. **Duke University** (NC)
12. **University of Washington**
13. **Illinois Institute of Technology** (Chicago-Kent)
14. **Columbia University** (NY)
14. **Texas A&M University**
14. **University of Pennsylvania**

INTERNATIONAL LAW
1. **New York University**
2. **Columbia University** (NY)
3. **Harvard University** (MA)
4. **Georgetown University** (DC)
5. **American University** (Washington) (DC)
6. **University of Michigan–Ann Arbor**
6. **Yale University** (CT)
8. **George Washington University** (DC)
9. **Duke University** (NC)
10. **University of California–Berkeley**

11. **Case Western Reserve University** (OH)
12. **Temple University** (Beasley) (PA)
12. **University of Virginia**
14. **Stanford University** (CA)
15. **Cornell University** (NY)
15. **Northwestern University** (Pritzker) (IL)
15. **University of Pennsylvania**

LEGAL WRITING
1. **Seattle University** (WA)
2. **University of Nevada–Las Vegas**
3. **Stetson University** (FL)
4. **University of Oregon**
5. **The John Marshall Law School** (IL)
6. **Suffolk University** (MA)
7. **Arizona State University** (O'Connor)
7. **University of Denver** (Sturm) (CO)
9. **Mercer University** (George) (GA)
10. **Temple University** (Beasley) (PA)
11. **Georgetown University** (DC)
11. **Marquette University** (WI)
13. **Ohio State University** (Moritz)
13. **Washburn University** (KS)

TAX LAW
1. **New York University**
2. **Georgetown University** (DC)
3. **University of Florida** (Levin)

4. **Northwestern University** (Pritzker) (IL)
5. **Loyola Marymount University** (CA)
6. **University of Virginia**
7. **Harvard University** (MA)
8. **Boston University** (MA)
9. **Columbia University** (NY)
9. **University of California–Los Angeles**
9. **University of Michigan–Ann Arbor**
12. **University of Miami** (FL)
12. **University of San Diego** (CA)
12. **University of Southern California** (Gould)

TRIAL ADVOCACY
1. **Stetson University** (FL)
2. **Temple University** (Beasley) (PA)
3. **Illinois Institute of Technology** (Chicago-Kent)
4. **Baylor University** (TX)
5. **Georgetown University** (DC)
6. **South Texas College of Law**
6. **University of Denver** (Sturm) (CO)
8. **American University** (Washington) (DC)
8. **Loyola Marymount University** (CA)
10. **Loyola University Chicago** (IL)
10. **Northwestern University** (Pritzker) (IL)

METHODOLOGY

Our annual rankings of 196 accredited law schools are based on a weighted average of 12 factors, described below. With rare exception, a law school official at each school – in many cases the dean – verified the data submitted on the U.S. News statistical survey.

Quality assessment: Quality was measured by two surveys conducted in the fall of 2015. The dean and three faculty members at each school were asked to rate schools from marginal (1) to outstanding (5); 67 percent voted. Their average rating is weighted by .25 in the overall ranking. Lawyers, recruiters and judges whose names were provided by the law schools also rated schools. Their three most recent years of responses were averaged and weighted by .15.

Selectivity (weighted at .25): This measure combines the following fall 2015 data for all full-time and part-time entering J.D. students: median LSAT scores

(50 percent of this indicator), median undergrad GPA (40 percent), and the acceptance rate (10 percent).

Placement success (.20): Success is determined by calculating employment rates for 2014 grads at graduation (20 percent) and 10 months after (70 percent) as well as their bar passage rate (10 percent). For ranking purposes only, the placement measure was calculated by assigning various weights to the number of grads employed in up to 43 different types and durations of jobs as defined by the American Bar Association. Full weight was given for graduates who had a full-time job not funded by their school lasting at least a year for which bar passage was required or a J.D. degree was an advantage; less weight went to full-time long-term jobs that were professional or nonprofessional and did not require bar passage, to pursuit of an additional advanced

degree, and to positions whose start dates were deferred. The least weight was applied to jobs categorized as part-time and short-term. (Employment rates published in the tables reflect all full-time jobs lasting at least a year for which bar passage was required or a J.D. degree was an advantage). For the second year, U.S. News discounted the value of jobs that were funded by the law school or university even if they were full-time, at least yearlong, and required bar passage or were jobs for which a J.D. was a benefit. Other types of school-funded jobs were discounted more. The bar passage indicator is the ratio of a school's pass rate in the cited jurisdiction to the overall state rate for first-time test-takers in summer and winter 2014. The jurisdiction is the state where the largest number of 2014 grads first took the test.

Faculty resources (.15): Resources are based on average fiscal year 2014 and 2015

expenditures per student for instruction, library and supporting services (65 percent) and on all other items, including financial aid (10 percent). Also: 2015 student/teacher ratio (20 percent) and total number of volumes and titles in the library (5 percent).

Overall rank: Scores on each indicator were standardized about their means. Then scores were weighted, totaled and rescaled so that the top school received 100, and other schools received a percentage of the top score.

Specialty rankings: Results are based solely on votes by faculty who were surveyed in the fall of 2015 and asked to identify up to 15 top schools in the particular field. Names of those surveyed were supplied by the law schools. Those with the most votes were ranked. Half of schools receiving a statistically significant number of votes appear.

Best Part-Time J.D. Programs

The American Bar Association's latest data reveal that in the fall of 2015, some 15,292 law students, or about 13.4 percent of the 113,394 total number, were enrolled part time. For many working adults, part-time study is the only way to afford a law degree and still meet other commitments. Fewer than half of the country's law schools offer these programs, which generally require four years to complete. Below, U.S. News presents the top half of accredited law schools offering a part-time pathway. The ranking is based on four factors as described in the methodology below: reputation among deans and faculty at peer schools, LSAT scores and undergraduate GPAs of students entering in the fall of 2015, and the breadth of each school's part-time program.

THE TOP PART-TIME PROGRAMS

Rank School	Overall score	Peer assessment score (5.0=highest)	'15 part-time LSAT score 25th-75th percentile	'15 part-time acceptance rate	'15 part-time enrollment
1. Georgetown University (DC)	100	4.1	160-167	5.1%	241
2. Fordham University (NY)	79	3.4	157-163	25.8%	195
3. George Washington University (DC)	78	3.4	152-165	21.6%	237
4. George Mason University (VA)	70	2.8	157-162	21.1%	155
5. University of Maryland (Carey)	66	3.0	152-159	27.9%	130
6. Temple University (Beasley) (PA)	62	2.7	155-162	37.6%	150
6. University of Connecticut	62	2.8	152-158	37.1%	105
6. University of Denver (Sturm) (CO)	62	2.9	154-160	48.4%	116
6. University of Houston (TX)	62	2.7	154-162	16.0%	126
10. Southern Methodist University (Dedman) (TX)	59	2.6	152-162	12.3%	180
11. American University (Washington) (DC)	58	2.8	152-157	55.4%	236
11. Loyola Marymount University (CA)	58	2.5	155-159	30.3%	182
11. Loyola University Chicago (IL)	58	2.5	153-162	40.9%	72
14. Georgia State University	57	2.5	154-159	23.8%	178
14. Lewis & Clark College (Northwestern) (OR)	57	2.5	152-160	50.0%	174
16. Santa Clara University (CA)	56	2.4	153-161	51.9%	147
17. University of San Diego (CA)	54	2.6	153-160	34.3%	103
18. Illinois Institute of Technology (Chicago-Kent)	53	2.6	152-159	44.2%	112
18. University of Nevada–Las Vegas	53	2.5	154-161	24.2%	103
20. Brooklyn Law School (NY)	52	2.5	153-159	35.6%	247
21. Rutgers, The State University of New Jersey	51	2.6	151-155	32.0%	250
22. St. John's University (NY)	50	2.2	149-160	32.7%	116
23. Indiana University–Indianapolis (McKinney)	49	2.4	146-154	79.2%	297
23. Seattle University (WA)	49	2.5	151-157	52.8%	151
25. DePaul University (IL)	48	2.3	149-154	49.5%	125
25. St. Louis University (MO)	48	2.4	148-157	57.5%	77
27. The Catholic University of America (DC)	46	2.2	152-158	50.7%	137
28. Stetson University (FL)	45	2.2	150-154	37.6%	164
28. Texas A&M University	45	2.1	153-157	18.5%	185
28. University of Hawaii–Manoa (Richardson)	45	2.4	151-158	40.8%	73
28. William Mitchell College of Law[1] (MN)	45	2.0	148-156	45.2%	363
32. Wayne State University (MI)	43	2.0	155-160	27.9%	51
32. Yeshiva University (Cardozo) (NY)	43	2.6	152-156	49.5%	75
34. Seton Hall University (NJ)	42	2.3	147-156	35.3%	172
35. Quinnipiac University (CT)	41	1.9	149-155	55.7%	59
36. University of Baltimore (MD)	40	2.1	147-153	35.9%	283
36. University of San Francisco (CA)	40	2.0	150-153	49.4%	97
38. Cleveland State U. (Cleveland-Marshall) (OH)	38	1.9	150-155	48.0%	97
38. New York Law School	38	1.9	148-154	41.8%	315
38. Suffolk University (MA)	38	1.9	146-156	60.5%	393
38. University of the Pacific (McGeorge) (CA)	38	1.9	147-154	62.0%	121

METHODOLOGY

The ranking of 79 part-time law programs is based on a weighted average of four measures of quality. For a school's program to be eligible for the part-time ranking, it had to have reported at least 20 part-time students enrolled in the fall of 2015 and supplied data on fall 2015 applications and acceptances to its part-time program.

Quality assessment (weighted by .50): In the fall of 2015, deans and three faculty members at each school were asked to rate programs from marginal (1) to outstanding (5); 59 percent responded, and scores for each school were averaged.

Selectivity (weighted by .275): For part-time students entering in 2015, this measure combines median LSAT scores (81.8 percent of this indicator) and undergraduate GPAs (18.2 percent).

Part-time focus (weighted by .225): An index was created from data reported by the schools about their 2015 part-time J.D. programs. Factors used in the creation of this index include the size of part-time first-year sections; the size of part-time first-year small sections; and the number of positions filled by part-time students in seminars, simulation courses, field placements, law journals, interschool skills competitions and independent study. Schools received credit for reporting data and additional credit for surpassing a threshold value in the various factors used.

Overall rank: Schools' scores on each indicator were standardized, weighted, totaled and rescaled so that the top school received 100, and other schools received a percentage of the top score.

[1]William Mitchell College of Law and Hamline University School of Law have merged to become Mitchell Hamline School of Law. The data listed for acceptance rate and enrollment are for informational purposes only and are not used in the computation of the part-time J.D. program ranking. Only part-time J.D. programs ranked in the top half appear. Sources: U.S. News and the schools. Assessment data collected by Ipsos Public Affairs.

EDUCATION

THE U.S. NEWS RANKINGS

At Johns Hopkins University
BRETT ZIEGLER FOR USN&WR

7
Great PATHS BEYOND *Teaching*

From counseling to health instruction and game design, there are many entries to education

By **CHRISTOPHER J. GEARON**

>>> **Interested in education** but not in entering (or staying in) the classroom? With K-12 improvements a national priority and educational processes at all levels being transformed by new learning insights and technological advances, the field can now be accessed by many doors. Columbia University's Teachers College, one of the most comprehensive graduate schools of education in the nation, now boasts 100-plus advanced degrees and areas of study, nearly two-thirds of which lead to nonclassroom careers. A grad degree in education can take you into foundations, state agencies, corporations, media outlets, startups and even health care. Here are seven possible avenues to explore:

1. TECHNOLOGY AND NEW MEDIA. Technology and mobile devices have teachers flipping their classrooms, colleges rolling out online degrees, and workers in all sorts of fields earning digital badges by mastering new skills. School systems and universities are hiring experts to rethink curriculum design and re-equip classrooms for tomorrow's learning. Still, "a lot of the work is located beyond the school walls," notes Lalitha Vasudevan, associate professor and program coordinator for the Communication, Media, and Learning Technologies Design Program at Teachers College. Grads are tak-

ing their master's and doctoral degrees in instructional technology and media into jobs with community organizations, museums, after-school programs, design companies and industry. They are people like Carla Fisher, director of production innovation for kids and families at Netflix, who earned her Ed.D. in 2012 and now oversees a team that "makes sure our members 12 and under are getting the best viewing experience." Other schools offering programs in educational technology include Harvard University, George Washington University and Ball State University.

One cutting-edge path into educational tech is New York University's pioneering M.S. program in games for learning. The 36-credit program combines cognitive science and education theory with the technical aspects of game design and doesn't require any prior programming experience. "We put a strong focus on how learning works," says Jan Plass, who directs and teaches in the program and notes that inquiries about entering it "have at least doubled" in each of its three years. Teachers College plans to roll out a similar degree. Investments in learning technology companies are "astonishing," according to Ambient Insights, a market research firm. Some $3.7 billion was invested in such firms worldwide in the first nine months of 2015, up from $2.4 billion for all of 2014.

NYU grads' work includes a game teaching special needs stu-

More on education schools @ usnews.com/educationschools

dents to navigate urban environments in a 3-D virtual world, a multimedia app to connect grandparents and grandchildren, and a game teaching the economics and operations of a startup aimed at low-income youth.

2. SPEECH-LANGUAGE PATHOLOGY. Ask Tim Asfazadour what his toughest hiring challenge is and the chief human resources officer for the San Diego Unified School District immediately says, "No. 1: speech-language pathologists!" To attract these professionals, the district has boosted first-year pay to that of a teacher with 10 years' experience. The demand for speech pathologists — who work in both education and health care aiding children or adults with speaking problems such as stuttering and struggles resulting from stroke, brain injury or Alzheimer's, for instance – will rise by 21 percent through 2024, according to the U.S. Bureau of Labor Statistics, nearly twice the growth rate for all jobs.

"There is no way to get bored in this career," says Natalie Hall, who in 2014 earned an M.S. in communicative disorders from California State University–Northridge and is working in two San Diego elementary schools helping at-risk students gain the communication skills they need to access the full curricu-

NYU students try out an educational game by Geoffrey Suthers (standing).

lum. "No single day is the same." Florida State University and the universities of Pittsburgh, Oregon and Washington are among those offering similar programs.

3. EDUCATION LEADERSHIP. Top-notch management is particularly needed now in education to navigate the changing terrain. As part of a Carnegie Foundation for the Advancement of Teaching-supported initiative, the Carnegie Project on the Education Doctorate, 80-plus ed schools are redesigning all aspects of the professional practice Ed.D. degree to better prepare the next generation of K-12 and college leaders. To that end, highly ranked Johns Hopkins School of Education in 2013 introduced an online doctoral program emphasizing the ability to systematically analyze problems and implement empirically supported interventions to improve outcomes.

About half of the program's students come from the K-12 arena; others include an NCAA official seeking ways to improve the success and completion rates of African-American student-athletes, an administrator trying to raise the teaching acumen of

WHY I PICKED...

Michigan State University
EAST LANSING

LATEEFAH ID-DEEN, '15
Assistant professor

» After getting my master's and teaching high school math for nearly six years, I decided to earn my Ph.D. and become a math education professor. The MSU College of Education appealed to me because of its outstanding faculty, international research opportunities, and curricular emphasis on diversity. The school encourages students of color to apply with its Advance to Adventure program, which paid for my campus visit. I met with professors and was impressed by their availability.

MSU promotes research on teaching practices through field experiences. For example, I observed schooling systems in China and assessed whether STEM programs raised student confidence in Iowa. For my dissertation, I examined how teacher turnover affected student-teacher relationships in an urban school. Now that I'm at the University of Louisville, I feel MSU gave me a great foundation to prepare future math teachers and to improve instruction for students of color. ■

adjunct community college faculty, and a person working to improve school access in war-torn parts of Africa. "Everybody in the program is bringing some problem of practice they are working on," says Rich Rosen, a retired engineer in the program who ran Battelle's education and philanthropy group and helped businesses and educational organizations build partnerships. Harvard, Stanford and Vanderbilt all offer such leadership degrees, along with the rest of the Carnegie group.

4. SCHOOL PSYCHOLOGY. Traditionally, school psychologists assessed and diagnosed struggling students. Today, their role is much expanded, as school districts are asked to support all students' behavioral, social and emotional health as well as their academics. "There are shortages of school psychologists all over the country," says Angela Whalen, a clinical associate professor in the field at the University of Oregon.

"I don't know of any other field where you can have such an impact," says Billie Jo Rodriguez, who earned an Oregon Ph.D. in school psychology and now works for Springfield Public Schools in the state. Besides working with students and families, she helps set districtwide social and emotional learning policies, evaluates student performance and coaches teachers. Beyond K-12 schools, opportunities can be found at universities, in independent practice, and at state agencies. Other notable programs include those at Lehigh University, the University of Minnesota, Stanford University and the University of Maryland.

5. ADULT LEARNING. To ensure that their employees' skills are up to par, corporations spent about the same amount on corporate training in 2014 – more than $70 billion – as the U.S. government spends annually on postsecondary education.

That's where programs like Michigan State University's master of arts in higher, adult and lifelong education come in. Unlike younger learners, a class of adults has "a reservoir of experiences they are drawing on," notes William Arnold, an MSU assistant professor in educational administration. "And they tend to be much more focused in terms of their needs." The MSU program and others like it – at Texas A&M, East Carolina University and

Indiana University, for example – prepare students to teach adult learners in a variety of settings.

6. HEALTH EDUCATION. At the current rate, 1 in 3 adult Americans will have diabetes by 2050, according to the American Diabetes Association. And that's just one of the chronic diseases that explain why the need for health educators is booming. The Bureau of Labor Statistics projects that the job market for these pros will expand by 13 percent between 2014 and 2024.

Most grad degrees in health education, including those at the University of Cincinnati and Boston University, take a general approach, teaching strategies to promote wellness in individuals and communities. Working as a nurse in Montgomery, Alabama, at Medical Outreach Ministries, Chris Anderson realized that she wanted "to know everything there was to know" about helping her uninsured, low-income patients avoid the ravages of diabetes. So she chose to instead pursue a highly specialized online master of science in diabetes education and management from Teachers College and finished last May. The degree was just what she has needed, she says, to build an education program right for her population.

7. POLICY/RESEARCH. Too often, researchers and the people in the trenches operate in different worlds, says Chad Nash, director of college success initiatives at the Denver Scholarship Foundation, which provides access to higher education for minority, first-generation and low-income students. "Being able to speak both languages is key in leadership positions." Nash, who manages partnerships with 33 Colorado colleges and universities and oversees the foundation's research and evaluation department, landed his position after earning his doctorate in the University of Colorado–Boulder's Educational Foundations, Policy and Practice program.

The coursework, which covers policy analysis, curriculum theory, and the study of education historically and culturally, is designed to lead to careers in academia and at think tanks and research centers. The University of California–Los Angeles and the universities of Michigan and Wisconsin–Madison offer such programs, too. ■

CAMERON GAMES VISUALS

THE JOB MARKET

Training Future Scientists

By **CHRISTOPHER J. GEARON**

>> As a kid, Blake Nathan wanted to fly planes and learn everything there was to know about aircraft. So he pursued a bachelor's degree in aeronautical and industrial technology at Tennessee State University. But the year before graduating in 2012, while holding part-time jobs as a caregiver at a daycare center and as a middle school math tutor, Nathan discovered another passion. And a lightbulb went off. "Teaching was more satisfying than wanting to fly a plane," he says.

So after graduation, Nathan applied and was accepted into the four-year Woodrow Wilson Teaching Fellowship program, which provides entry to an established master's track at a school of education, in Nathan's case at Indiana University–Purdue University Indianapolis. The fellowship helps make students who have been educated in science, technology, engineering or math ready for the classroom.

Acute needs. Nathan got a $30,000 stipend the first year while he juggled a full course load – including pedagogy, theory, classroom management and courses in his engineering concentration – and student-taught at an Indianapolis high school. That led to a post teaching technology to middle schoolers, where Nathan is now a full-time, certified teacher. (After Year One, students must teach three years in a high-needs school as part of the program.)

"There are acute needs to find effective teachers" of STEM subjects, notes Arthur Levine, president of the Woodrow Wilson National Fellowship

Blake Nathan
Indiana University–Purdue
University Indianapolis, 2016

Foundation, and these include adding women and people of color, who are significantly underrepresented, to the ranks. Ten of the top 14 fastest-growing industries require know-how in STEM, according to 100Kin10, a network supporting the national effort to get more STEM teachers into schools.

Now, in the final year of his program, Nathan has his middle school students hard at work building rockets, assembling an LED circuit, and making stop-motion animation films. "We do a lot of cool hands-on projects," he explains.

Nathan earns "over $40,000" and says he loves what he does. He has also started a nonprofit, Educate ME, to mentor African-American males in high school and beyond who want to pursue careers in education and teaching. ∎

... More Hot Jobs

POSTSECONDARY TEACHER

The demand for teachers in public and private colleges and universities, professional schools, community colleges, and career and vocational schools will grow by 13 percent for the decade ending in 2024, estimates the Bureau of Labor Statistics. While a Ph.D. is most often required at the university level, a master's degree may suffice for positions at community colleges and other schools. The median annual wage for postsecondary teachers in 2014 was $70,790.

ADMINISTRATOR

A master's or doctorate in education policy has become a sought-after pathway for postsecondary administrators, says Thomas Rock, vice provost for enrollment services at Teachers College, the nation's oldest graduate school of education at Columbia University. Positions range from registrars to admissions officers to academic deans; such openings are expected to grow by 9 percent through 2024. More than 40 percent of advertised salaries for these positions are for $65,000 plus.

SPECIAL EDUCATION TEACHER

While the BLS says tight budgets may moderate hiring of special ed teachers to 6 percent growth overall by 2024, job prospects are "good" and are aided by the number of teachers who leave the occupation each year. At the preschool level, the growth rate should run 9 percent. Some states require a master's degree in special education to become fully certified. The median 2014 annual wage was $55,980.

COURTESY OF BLAKE NATHAN

Schools of Education

THE TOP SCHOOLS

Rank School	Overall score	Peer assessment score (5.0=highest)	Administrators/ experts assessment score (5.0=highest)	'15 mean GRE scores (verbal/ quantitative)[1]	'15 doctoral acceptance rate	'15 doctoral students/ faculty[2]	Doctorals granted/ faculty 2014-15	'15 funded research (in millions)	'15 funded research/faculty member (in thousands)	'15 total graduate education enrollment
1. Stanford University (CA)	100	4.7	4.9	164/162	4.7%	3.0	0.8	$30.0	$625.1	373
2. Harvard University (MA)	97	4.3	4.6	165/161	4.9%	4.2	1.0	$32.6	$776.8	891
2. Johns Hopkins University (MD)	97	4.0	4.1	163/161	19.5%	1.2	0.2	$45.8	$694.6	2,161
4. University of Wisconsin–Madison	95	4.3	4.5	155/152	31.3%	4.1	0.9	$59.7	$510.0	1,030
5. Vanderbilt University (Peabody) (TN)	94	4.4	4.6	164/159	5.2%	2.5	0.6	$36.2	$430.5	908
6. University of Pennsylvania	93	4.0	4.4	161/159	4.5%	1.6	0.3	$43.5	$621.1	1,140
7. Teachers College, Columbia University (NY)	91	4.3	4.4	159/156	14.6%	4.6	1.3	$58.0	$394.5	4,920
8. Northwestern University (IL)	89	3.9	4.2	163/158	7.5%	1.9	0.3	$24.4	$763.3	318
8. University of Washington	89	3.8	4.3	156/152	29.7%	4.2	1.8	$45.8	$881.6	938
10. University of Texas–Austin	88	4.0	4.2	155/152	28.4%	4.0	1.1	$55.1	$509.8	1,025
11. University of California–Los Angeles	84	4.0	4.3	156/158	27.7%	8.7	2.2	$37.1	$883.4	686
12. University of Michigan–Ann Arbor	83	4.3	4.6	159/155	15.8%	4.4	1.0	$19.4	$388.3	524
12. University of Oregon	83	3.5	3.9	158/153	19.3%	4.4	1.0	$35.9	$919.7	592
14. Arizona State University	82	3.7	3.8	158/153	21.1%	1.6	0.8	$56.3	$625.6	2,627
15. Michigan State University	79	4.2	4.4	156/153	33.8%	5.1	1.0	$29.6	$262.4	1,862
15. New York University (Steinhardt)	79	3.9	4.2	159/154	8.6%	5.3	0.9	$37.1	$340.1	3,117
15. University of Kansas	79	3.7	4.1	155/155	44.2%	4.7	0.9	$40.5	$518.7	1,209
18. Ohio State University	78	3.9	4.1	154/152	44.2%	3.3	0.4	$48.6	$376.4	989
18. University of California–Berkeley	78	4.2	4.6	158/154	8.8%	8.8	1.0	$13.2	$487.7	343
20. University of Minnesota–Twin Cities	77	3.8	4.0	157/152	36.1%	4.3	1.1	$44.4	$366.5	1,861
21. University of Southern California (Rossier)	76	3.9	4.1	161/157	15.6%	15.5	8.8	$20.1	$1,004.9	1,866
21. University of Virginia (Curry)	76	4.0	4.3	159/156	17.3%	2.6	0.7	$21.9	$296.0	937
23. Boston College (Lynch) (MA)	72	3.7	4.1	161/155	13.9%	2.1	0.7	$15.3	$273.7	793
23. University of Illinois–Urbana-Champaign	72	4.0	4.2	160/155	18.0%	4.2	0.9	$11.8	$147.2	792
25. University of California–Irvine	68	3.4	3.7	160/159	15.9%	2.9	0.4	$9.6	$415.6	274
26. University of Connecticut (Neag)	67	3.7	4.0	157/154	25.8%	1.8	0.4	$15.1	$228.5	720
26. University of Maryland–College Park	67	3.9	4.1	160/156	21.3%	4.2	0.8	$9.9	$110.2	992
28. Indiana University–Bloomington	66	3.9	3.9	154/150	44.7%	3.2	0.7	$18.5	$201.6	925
28. University of Colorado–Boulder	66	3.7	3.7	160/153	13.9%	2.4	0.6	$8.5	$273.4	345
30. University of Florida	65	3.6	3.9	153/155	48.8%	3.9	1.1	$20.8	$335.1	1,088
30. University of Pittsburgh (PA)	65	3.6	3.9	161/153	45.7%	4.0	0.8	$25.0	$472.3	943
30. Utah State University	65	2.9	3.0	156/152	28.4%	1.1	0.2	$50.6	$372.2	956
33. Virginia Commonwealth University	64	3.1	3.5	156/151	55.0%	2.2	0.6	$19.3	$428.0	818
34. University of Georgia	63	3.8	4.2	153/153	38.5%	3.2	0.7	$14.7	$89.8	1,636
35. University of Delaware	62	3.3	3.4	157/157	44.8%	2.0	0.8	$14.3	$398.3	294
35. University of North Carolina–Chapel Hill	62	3.8	4.2	158/154	26.0%	5.0	0.8	$5.7	$143.2	436
37. Florida State University	61	3.5	3.7	154/151	40.0%	4.1	0.8	$17.3	$228.2	1,048
37. Pennsylvania State University–University Park	61	3.8	4.2	154/152	35.8%	3.7	0.8	$7.7	$70.1	1,297
39. Texas A&M University–College Station	60	3.6	3.8	152/152	56.3%	3.8	1.0	$21.9	$209.0	1,568
39. University of Nebraska–Lincoln	60	3.5	3.5	154/151	29.2%	2.8	1.0	$16.3	$201.8	954
41. University of Illinois–Chicago	59	3.5	3.6	155/152	51.2%	3.7	0.5	$12.1	$302.0	676
42. Purdue University–West Lafayette (IN)	58	3.5	3.7	154/153	44.8%	1.7	0.5	$9.6	$133.7	604
42. University of Iowa	58	3.5	3.9	153/153	45.3%	5.4	0.8	$9.7	$151.8	716
42. University of Massachusetts–Amherst	58	3.5	3.8	155/152	43.9%	3.8	0.5	$7.4	$126.7	604
45. Boston University (MA)	57	3.4	3.8	156/152	25.0%	2.9	0.6	$3.2	$110.3	507
45. Fordham University (NY)	57	3.1	3.5	165/160	39.3%	5.4	1.5	$8.0	$258.9	958
45. George Washington University (DC)	57	3.4	3.9	157/151	50.2%	4.4	1.4	$8.9	$170.9	1,422
45. University of Missouri	57	3.4	3.7	153/149	33.1%	4.7	0.9	$16.7	$185.6	1,501
49. Lehigh University (PA)	56	3.0	3.3	158/157	18.9%	3.0	0.7	$7.1	$253.6	463
49. University of California–Santa Barbara (Gevirtz)	56	3.4	3.5	157/153	17.7%	5.0	0.7	$4.0	$91.7	328

Rank	School	Overall score	Peer assessment score (5.0=highest)	Administrators/experts assessment score (5.0=highest)	'15 mean GRE scores (verbal/quantitative)[1]	'15 doctoral acceptance rate	'15 doctoral students/faculty[2]	Doctorals granted/faculty 2014-15	'15 funded research (in millions)	'15 funded research/faculty member (in thousands)	'15 total graduate education enrollment
51.	George Mason University (VA)	55	3.3	3.6	152/147	41.8%	2.4	0.5	$15.3	$218.6	2,216
51.	North Carolina State University–Raleigh	55	3.3	3.2	155/151	27.8%	3.0	0.9	$13.6	$186.4	1,187
51.	University of California–Davis	55	3.5	3.8	150/144	30.4%	4.4	0.9	$7.8	$277.8	416
51.	University of Utah	55	3.2	3.3	160/158	35.7%	3.1	0.4	$6.7	$122.7	627
55.	College of William and Mary (VA)	54	3.3	3.8	159/152	58.3%	2.3	1.0	$5.2	$148.5	387
55.	Syracuse University (NY)	54	3.4	3.8	152/149	40.9%	2.9	0.2	$6.3	$109.7	621
55.	Temple University (PA)	54	3.1	3.4	155/150	18.9%	4.6	0.9	$11.4	$247.1	885
55.	University of Arizona	54	3.7	3.8	151/149	57.7%	4.2	0.7	$6.9	$114.7	770
59.	Georgia State University	53	3.1	3.2	155/151	29.4%	2.4	0.6	$17.1	$155.4	1,347
59.	Tufts University (MA)	53	3.3	3.6	162/163	21.1%	1.8	N/A	$0.5	N/A	147
59.	University of Kentucky	53	3.3	3.4	153/152	48.9%	3.1	0.4	$13.1	$148.9	783
62.	Loyola Marymount University (CA)	52	2.9	3.5	156/149	26.9%	2.1	0.4	$6.4	$219.9	1,321
62.	Rutgers, The State Univ. of N.J.–New Brunswick	52	3.4	3.7	158/152	49.1%	2.5	0.8	$9.0	$192.3	1,023
62.	University of California–Riverside	52	3.2	3.4	158/154	20.7%	4.8	0.7	$1.3	$69.0	246
62.	University of Tennessee–Knoxville	52	3.3	3.6	154/152	60.0%	1.6	0.4	$8.7	$83.5	686
66.	University at Albany–SUNY (NY)	51	3.2	3.5	153/151	37.8%	2.6	0.5	$6.3	$107.4	862
66.	University of Hawaii–Manoa	51	3.0	2.9	155/148	61.7%	1.0	0.3	$19.9	$167.1	873
66.	University of Vermont	51	3.1	3.5	155/149	67.7%	1.0	0.3	$7.7	$186.9	268
69.	San Diego State University (CA)	50	3.2	3.3	149/144	73.3%	1.0	0.5	$16.9	$241.5	1,174
69.	University of Miami (FL)	50	3.1	3.4	154/149	26.7%	3.5	0.8	$3.5	$110.1	389
71.	Boise State University (ID)	49	2.8	3.0	155/150	32.0%	1.0	0.3	$9.5	$201.8	1,245
71.	University at Buffalo–SUNY (NY)	49	3.1	3.5	152/151	50.5%	5.1	0.9	$3.2	$67.6	1,023
71.	University of Massachusetts–Boston	49	2.9	3.0	160/153	38.8%	1.5	0.3	$4.3	$90.7	1,000
74.	Auburn University (AL)	48	3.4	3.5	150/147	37.8%	2.9	0.7	$4.7	$52.9	996
74.	Clemson University (Moore) (SC)	48	3.1	3.4	154/147	45.8%	1.6	0.3	$6.0	$93.2	611
74.	University of California–San Diego	48	3.3	3.4	155/147	57.1%	3.8	0.8	$1.1	$87.0	152
74.	University of Wisconsin–Milwaukee	48	3.2	3.4	154/149	31.5%	1.9	0.3	$1.9	$28.0	671
78.	Baylor University (TX)	47	3.2	3.3	156/152	46.2%	1.4	0.3	$0.3	$10.8	177
78.	Brigham Young University–Provo (McKay) (UT)	47	3.1	3.4	155/149	31.3%	0.6	0.4	$1.8	$22.8	326

An ed class at No. 4 University of Wisconsin–Madison

DARREN HAUCK FOR USN&WR

THE TOP SCHOOLS continued

Rank	School	Overall score	Peer assessment score (5.0=highest)	Administrators/ experts assessment score (5.0=highest)	'15 mean GRE scores (verbal/ quantitative)[1]	'15 doctoral acceptance rate	'15 doctoral students/ faculty[2]	Doctorals granted/ faculty 2014-15	'15 funded research (in millions)	'15 funded research/faculty member (in thousands)	'15 total graduate education enrollment
78.	Iowa State University	47	3.1	3.7	152/147	40.3%	1.6	0.3	$3.3	$56.8	405
78.	University of California–Santa Cruz	47	2.7	2.8	158/157	31.4%	2.0	0.2	$1.5	$99.5	106
78.	University of Louisville (KY)	47	3.0	3.5	153/148	35.5%	1.8	0.4	$4.3	$63.6	1,085
78.	University of North Carolina–Greensboro	47	3.1	3.4	154/148	38.0%	2.7	0.6	$4.3	$63.8	935
78.	University of Oklahoma (Rainbolt)	47	3.1	3.5	152/148	41.6%	3.3	0.5	$7.9	$122.2	776
78.	University of South Carolina	47	3.2	3.5	154/150	37.0%	2.5	0.7	$2.5	$32.3	1,269
78.	University of South Florida	47	3.0	3.0	152/147	61.6%	3.2	0.6	$20.0	$194.1	1,240
78.	Virginia Tech	47	3.1	3.8	153/147	48.4%	4.0	1.3	$5.2	$110.6	685
78.	Washington University in St. Louis (MO)	47	3.2	3.6	154/152	16.7%	1.3	N/A	$0.0	$0.0	32
89.	Kansas State University	46	3.0	3.3	152/147	70.7%	2.2	0.6	$10.2	$238.1	947
89.	University of North Carolina–Charlotte	46	3.1	3.5	151/145	54.4%	1.3	0.4	$6.9	$67.8	1,362
91.	University of Arkansas–Fayetteville	45	2.9	3.1	150/146	82.5%	1.8	0.5	$16.3	$194.6	1,077
91.	University of Central Florida	45	3.0	2.9	154/150	39.2%	3.5	1.1	$5.9	$85.3	1,844
93.	Ball State University (IN)	44	3.1	3.3	151/147	32.7%	1.6	0.5	$2.0	$23.3	2,805
93.	Montclair State University (NJ)	44	2.8	3.1	157/149	50.0%	0.7	0.1	$4.1	$35.6	2,048
93.	University of Cincinnati (OH)	44	3.0	3.2	154/152	23.1%	1.6	0.3	$5.6	$71.7	1,591
93.	University of Maine	44	2.9	3.0	N/A	10.0%	0.9	0.2	$3.3	$137.5	341
93.	University of Mississippi	44	2.9	3.2	151/145	64.0%	1.6	0.4	$9.2	$190.9	601
93.	University of San Diego (CA)	44	2.8	3.0	155/151	45.3%	1.8	0.3	$2.5	$75.9	711
99.	Louisiana State University–Baton Rouge	43	3.0	3.5	151/145	59.1%	2.1	0.7	$4.5	$84.0	469
99.	Loyola University Chicago (IL)	43	3.1	3.1	154/147	27.0%	5.7	1.0	$2.0	$51.9	666
99.	Mills College (CA)	43	2.6	3.2	N/A	55.8%	2.3	1.0	$2.8	$284.6	214
99.	Ohio University	43	3.0	3.5	148/147	39.8%	1.6	0.6	$1.8	$27.4	838
99.	Southern Illinois University–Carbondale	43	2.8	3.1	140/145	96.8%	2.4	0.5	$19.9	$279.7	971
99.	Towson University (MD)	43	2.7	3.1	157/149	42.4%	0.6	0.1	$2.6	$22.8	1,381
99.	University of Colorado–Denver	43	3.2	3.0	N/A	69.5%	3.6	0.3	$4.7	$119.4	1,365
99.	West Virginia University	43	2.9	3.0	154/148	34.5%	2.0	0.1	$3.3	$54.1	965
107.	Howard University (DC)	42	3.0	3.3	150/145	50.0%	5.3	1.1	$3.1	$100.3	216
107.	Kent State University (OH)	42	2.9	3.3	149/145	38.6%	3.1	0.6	$6.3	$56.7	1,679
107.	Miami University (OH)	42	3.1	3.6	N/A	64.6%	0.6	0.3	$1.7	$20.1	725
107.	Old Dominion University (Darden) (VA)	42	2.8	2.9	153/149	50.8%	1.4	0.7	$11.9	$129.2	1,528
107.	Texas Tech University	42	2.9	3.2	152/147	50.2%	4.6	1.0	$7.1	$106.1	1,308
107.	University of Alabama	42	3.1	3.3	150/146	60.5%	3.3	1.2	$4.5	$54.0	999
107.	University of Dayton (OH)	42	2.5	3.2	154/146	24.1%	1.0	0.1	$4.1	$77.1	874
107.	University of Houston (TX)	42	2.9	3.1	153/148	27.5%	4.4	1.4	$4.4	$86.3	738
115.	Illinois State University	41	2.8	2.8	152/149	74.4%	0.8	0.4	$8.9	$65.6	829
115.	Marquette University (WI)	41	3.0	2.8	N/A	16.7%	0.8	N/A	$0.1	$7.2	139
115.	Mississippi State University	41	2.8	2.8	147/147	72.5%	1.4	0.4	$4.3	$45.0	725
115.	St. John's University (NY)	41	2.9	3.3	151/147	81.4%	2.1	1.0	$4.1	$86.6	1,425
115.	University of Alabama–Birmingham	41	2.9	3.0	154/149	78.6%	0.8	0.3	$5.0	$125.6	768
120.	Bowling Green State University (OH)	40	2.8	3.4	N/A	43.9%	0.7	0.1	$1.4	$17.1	852
120.	Colorado State University	40	2.9	3.3	154/148	24.0%	5.6	2.1	$0.3	$15.6	702
120.	Oklahoma State University	40	2.8	3.2	N/A	51.2%	3.9	0.5	$5.0	$59.1	854
120.	University of North Texas	40	2.7	2.9	151/149	45.0%	2.8	0.8	$6.8	$97.3	1,281
120.	University of Texas–Arlington	40	2.7	2.8	156/147	41.4%	1.3	0.7	$2.7	$89.9	1,801
120.	Wayne State University (MI)	40	2.8	2.9	149/149	6.5%	3.4	0.7	$4.5	$84.2	1,494
126.	Drexel University (PA)	39	2.6	2.9	156/152	55.3%	5.3	2.2	$2.5	$139.1	942
126.	Pennsylvania State University–Harrisburg	39	2.6	3.3	158/148	100.0%	2.0	0.2	$1.9	$209.0	297
126.	Texas Christian University	39	2.8	3.2	N/A	73.7%	3.4	0.3	$2.8	$115.8	195
126.	University of Nevada–Reno	39	2.6	2.6	150/146	71.4%	1.4	0.3	$8.5	$188.6	512
126.	University of Wyoming	39	2.8	3.0	153/147	44.4%	2.1	0.5	$1.3	$24.5	576
126.	Western Michigan University	39	2.8	3.2	146/143	36.8%	1.7	0.3	$2.4	$25.2	1,363

[1]GRE scores are for doctoral students only, and all those displayed are for exams taken during or after August 2011 using the new 130-170 score scale.
[2]Student/faculty ratio is for all full-time equivalent doctoral students and full-time faculty.
N/A=Data were not provided by the school. Sources: U.S. News and the schools. Assessment data collected by Ipsos Public Affairs.

SPECIALTIES
PROGRAMS RANKED BEST BY EDUCATION SCHOOL DEANS

ADMINISTRATION/SUPERVISION
1. Vanderbilt University (Peabody) (TN)
2. University of Wisconsin–Madison
3. University of Texas–Austin
4. Harvard University (MA)
5. Stanford University (CA)
6. Teachers College, Columbia University (NY)
7. Michigan State University
8. University of Virginia (Curry)
9. Pennsylvania State University–University Park
9. University of Washington
11. Ohio State University

COUNSELING/PERSONNEL SERVICES
1. U. of Maryland–College Park
2. University of North Carolina–Greensboro
3. University of Georgia
4. University of Missouri
5. Pennsylvania State University–University Park
6. University of Florida
6. University of Wisconsin–Madison

CURRICULUM/INSTRUCTION
1. University of Wisconsin–Madison
2. Stanford University (CA)
2. Teachers College, Columbia University (NY)
4. Michigan State University
5. University of Michigan–Ann Arbor
6. Vanderbilt University (Peabody) (TN)
7. University of Texas–Austin
8. University of Georgia
9. Ohio State University
10. Indiana University–Bloomington
10. U. of Illinois–Urbana-Champaign

EDUCATION POLICY
1. Stanford University (CA)

2. Harvard University (MA)
3. University of Wisconsin–Madison
4. Vanderbilt University (Peabody) (TN)
5. Teachers College, Columbia University (NY)
6. University of Michigan–Ann Arbor
7. University of California–Berkeley
8. University of Pennsylvania
9. University of California–Los Angeles
10. University of Colorado–Boulder

EDUCATIONAL PSYCHOLOGY
1. University of Wisconsin–Madison
2. University of Michigan–Ann Arbor
3. Stanford University (CA)
4. U. of Maryland–College Park
5. Michigan State University
6. University of Texas–Austin
7. U. of Illinois–Urbana-Champaign
8. Vanderbilt University (Peabody) (TN)
9. University of California–Berkeley
10. University of Minnesota–Twin Cities

ELEMENTARY EDUCATION
1. Michigan State University
2. Teachers College, Columbia University (NY)
3. University of Michigan–Ann Arbor
4. University of Wisconsin–Madison
5. Vanderbilt University (Peabody) (TN)
6. University of Georgia
7. University of Washington
8. Stanford University (CA)
9. Indiana University–Bloomington
10. University of Virginia (Curry)

HIGHER EDUCATION ADMINISTRATION
1. University of Michigan–Ann Arbor
2. Michigan State University

3. University of California–Los Angeles
4. University of Pennsylvania
4. University of Southern California (Rossier)
6. University of Georgia
7. Pennsylvania State University–University Park
8. Vanderbilt University (Peabody) (TN)
9. Indiana University–Bloomington

SECONDARY EDUCATION
1. Michigan State University
2. University of Michigan–Ann Arbor
3. University of Wisconsin–Madison
4. University of Georgia
5. Stanford University (CA)
6. Teachers College, Columbia University (NY)
7. University of Virginia (Curry)
8. University of Washington
9. Vanderbilt University (Peabody) (TN)
10. Indiana University–Bloomington

SPECIAL EDUCATION
1. University of Kansas
2. Vanderbilt University (Peabody) (TN)
3. University of Oregon
4. University of Texas–Austin
5. University of Florida
5. University of Virginia (Curry)
7. University of Washington
8. University of Minnesota–Twin Cities
9. University of Wisconsin–Madison
10. U. of Illinois–Urbana-Champaign
11. Ohio State University

VOCATIONAL/TECHNICAL
1. Ohio State University
1. Pennsylvania State University–University Park

METHODOLOGY

Graduate programs at 376 schools granting education doctoral degrees were surveyed; 255 responded and provided data needed to calculate rankings based on 10 measures:

Quality assessment: Two surveys were conducted in the fall of 2015. Education school deans and deans of graduate studies were asked to rate program quality from marginal (1) to outstanding (5); 34 percent responded. The resulting score is weighted by .25. Education schools provided names of superintendents, people who hire graduates, and education experts familiar with them, who were also asked to rate programs. The three most recent years' results were averaged and weighted by .15.

Student selectivity (weighted by .18): Combines mean verbal and quantitative GRE scores of doctoral students entering in fall 2015 and the acceptance rate of doctoral applicants for the 2015-2016 academic year (each accounts for one-third of the measure). Where scores are not available for doctoral students, mean GRE scores for all entering students may be substituted. Scores for the new and old GRE were converted to a common scale; new scores are displayed.

Faculty resources (.12): Resources include the 2015 ratio of full-time-equivalent doctoral students to full-time faculty (37.5 percent); average percentage of full-time faculty holding awards or editorships at selected education journals in 2014 and 2015 (20.8 percent); and ratio of doctoral degrees granted to full-time faculty in the 2014-2015 school year (41.7 percent).

Research activity (.30): This measure uses average total education school research expenditures (50 percent) and average expenditures per full-time faculty member (50 percent). Expenditures refer to separately funded research, public and private, averaged over fiscal years 2014 and 2015.

Overall rank: Data were standardized about their means, and standardized scores were weighted, totaled and rescaled so that the top school received 100; other schools received their percentage of the top score.

Specialty rankings: These ratings are based solely on nominations by deans and deans of graduate studies, who were asked to choose up to 10 programs for excellence in each specialty. The top ones are listed.

Find the right school for you with the

U.S. News Graduate School

Compass

Buy today and save 25%!
www.usnews.com/compassdiscount

Compass is our exclusive online tool that gives you unlimited access to the most comprehensive graduate school directory anywhere. You'll find in-depth profiles on more than 1,900 programs, average LSAT, GMAT, MCAT, and GRE scores, financial aid availability, and more!

Plus, essential information on major disciplines, including:

BUSINESS
Average starting salary and bonus of MBA graduates

LAW
Median private and public sector starting salaries

NURSING
Acceptance rates for masters and doctoral programs

MEDICAL
Most popular residency programs

ENGINEERING
Research spending per faculty member

Andrey Popov/Getty Images

CHAPTER 5

HEALTH&MEDICINE

A UC–San Francisco
nursing student

DAVID BUTOW – REDUX FOR USN&WR

THE U.S. NEWS RANKINGS

A BIG DOSE *of* PUBLIC HEALTH

Future doctors are learning lifestyle medicine and how to take care of whole populations

By **BETH HOWARD**

>>> **As part of her dual degree** program in medicine and public health at the University of Wisconsin, fourth-year student Nayeli Spahr, 32, devotes much of her time to the Sixteenth Street Community Health Centers. Here, deep in the underserved south side of Milwaukee, Spahr runs two-hour group well-child visits for 12 immigrant families with babies. The group approach has "eased the time pressure of a 15-minute doctor visit," says Spahr, and encourages the parents to open up about their challenges and share solutions. "You can address things like social support through medical visits," she says, "if you think a little outside the box."

Medical schools are increasingly doing just that themselves as they scramble to prep students like Spahr to take charge of a health system centered on preventive medicine and population health, or care that's tailored to provide the best outcomes for a population of patients given their environment and culture. Across the country, schools are injecting principles of population medicine into their curriculums, putting even first-year students out in the community to tackle real health problems, and teaching future doctors about nutrition and exercise. Public health topics like epidemiology, biostatistics, and the effects of factors like poverty, race and education on well-being are also popping up in the coursework.

The reason for the push: As a reformed health system increasingly rewards better care and preventive care rather than number of procedures, medicine will be less about treating episodes of acute illness and more about managing chronic diseases. To date, medical education hasn't kept up with calls for change. It's been "building a Pinto for a market that wants a Tesla," says David Nash, founding dean of the Thomas Jefferson College of Population Health in Philadelphia.

But now all kinds of new ideas are being embraced. "Schools are clamoring for this," says Eric Kasowski, a branch chief at the Centers for Disease Control and Prevention who oversees an initiative in which the agency collaborates with schools of medicine, nursing, physical therapy and other allied health professions to improve public health.

While some schools have simply expanded the curriculum, others have created a certificate program or public health track students can opt to take along with the traditional courses. A number have added dual MD/master's of public health programs. Students at Jefferson's Sidney Kimmel Medical College can follow a population health track that earns them credits toward an MPH at the School of Popu-

▶ **More on medical schools** @ usnews.com/medschools

Miami medical student Sandy Jiang gets active with Fit2Play participants.

lation Health. At the University of Arizona College of Medicine–Phoenix, public health is entwined into all four years of coursework. The University of New Mexico School of Medicine requires its medical students to graduate with a certificate in public health. At Tufts University School of Medicine in Massachusetts, the combined MD/MPH pathway allows students to complete both degrees in four years. Such programs are expected not only to produce doctors well-suited to the medicine of the future but also leaders in public health, policy and research.

At the University of Wisconsin School of Medicine and Public Health, "we emphasize that we're not just treating disease but preventing it," says Robert Golden, the school's dean. "From the start, we want students thinking not only about patients and families but populations."

In Wisconsin's popular public health case studies, first- and second-year students examine a scenario from multiple perspectives, such as that of a drunk driver who is severely injured. What is the cost to the health system? How do drunk driving and seatbelt laws affect the epidemiology of such accidents? Third- and fourth-year students do most of their clinical rotations in underserved rural or urban areas, where they might also stage disaster drills or provide health education to diabetic children, say. Students can pursue a public health pathway or dual degrees; those who decide to get the MPH typically take a detour between the second and third

years of medical school to complete it.

The University of Pittsburgh School of Medicine, which offers a public health concentration, is another pioneer. The first week of school, new students can expect to visit a community in need and then explore factors that affect health, from unemployment to poor air quality. The ultimate aim: to bring awareness of public health realities to the bedside. "For that moment that you are in the room with a patient, the rest of the world is ignored," says John Mahoney, associate dean for medical education. "But when you step outside, you need to be thinking, 'Wow, that's the fourth antibiotic I've given out in the last hour. Am I contributing to antibiotic resistance in my community?'"

Second year brings another powerful learning experience, the poverty simulation. In a large room with areas designated for utility companies, businesses, homes, schools, a jail, a pawn shop, social services agencies and health facilities, faculty and other volunteers play business owners, civil servants,

Healthful cooking is on West Virginia University medical school's course menu.

police, teachers, doctors and the odd thief or drug dealer. Students act the part of members of needy families struggling to get kids to school or daycare and show up at jobs, pay the bills, and get services in the face of various obstacles. Think: The line to pay your gas bill was so long that you are late getting to work, and you lose your job. Or a thief steals your mortgage money, and you have no way to replace it.

The hope is that students who can put themselves in their future patient's shoes – the guy who "has to get up at 5:30 to take a two-hour bus ride to get dialysis" – will have more empathy, says Jason Morrow, professor of ethics and medical humanities at the University of Texas Health Science Center School of Medicine in San Antonio, which stages the same simulation.

Brown University in Rhode Island has devised another way to help students walk the walk. Through a new dual degree program, Primary Care–Population Medicine, first-year students act as patient navigators, each guiding a person to needed care over time. "Medical students typically see one episode of care, like surgery or a doctor visit," says Paul George, director of the program. "This way, they are able to see the full spectrum of care from the first contact." The challenges faced by first-year student Elise Presser's assigned patient, who uses a wheelchair and has had to struggle with public transportation to get around, have become very apparent as she has spent time accompanying him to his doctor's appointments, she says. The integrated

Brown program can be completed in four years.

At the same time, schools are paying greater attention to the role of lifestyle choices in disease prevention. Little wonder: The World Health Organization predicts that two-thirds of disease globally will be the result of poor lifestyle habits by 2020. Yet research has shown that fewer than half of primary care doctors in the U.S. routinely offer guidance on weight control, nutrition or exercise.

While it's still true that fewer than a third of medical schools are meeting the minimum number of hours of nutrition education recommended by the National Academy of Sciences, changes are afoot. At Boston University School of Medicine, students are matched with interning dietitians at the university's Sargent College of Health and Rehabilitation Sciences for a monthlong collaboration. The interning

THE SECOND TIME AROUND

By 2025, the country will be short up to 90,000 physicians, according to the Association of American Medical Colleges. One solution: buffing up the skills of retired and otherwise inactive doctors and drawing them back into the fold. A growing number of medical institutions aim to do just that.

The Reentry Program at Cedars-Sinai Medical Center in Los Angeles, for example, lets doctors who have been away from practice while they raise a family, pursue research, or try out retirement seek to re-earn their staff privileges. The on-site training takes from one to three months and is tailored to the doctor's needs and specialty. Drexel's Physician Refresher/Re-entry program requires six to 12 weeks on the Philadelphia campus. The KSTAR (Knowledge, Skills, Training, Assessment and Research) Program at the Texas A&M Health Science Center consists of a three-month miniresidency

FROM LEFT: JOEY STEVENSON; JOEL E. ANDERSON

dietitian analyzes the medical student's diet and provides tips for improving it, the two shop for groceries together, the med student practices mock nutrition intake interviews, and they work together on a nutrition-related case study. "It's a win-win," says Joan Salge Blake, a clinical associate professor at Sargent and the dietetic internship director. Reports third-year student Sean Burns, 26, a recent convert to vegetarianism: "My intern really opened up my eyes to what I didn't know."

In a state whose rates of obesity and

physical inactivity are among the highest nationwide, students at West Virginia University School of Medicine learn about exercise science and nutrition intensively their third year; training includes hands-on experience preparing healthy meals. And last year in New Orleans, Tulane University's medical school christened a gleaming new teaching kitchen near a community clinic in what used to be one of the city's "food deserts," or places where access to fresh foods is severely limited. Besides the kitchen, where the students learn "culinary medicine" and members of the community can take cooking classes, the complex houses a new Whole Foods Market and a job-training organization that equips local residents to work in the food service industry.

Lifestyle medicine is incorporated into courses, rotations and scholarly concentrations at the new University of South Carolina School of Medicine Greenville, with experts in exercise and

in partnership with the University of Texas Medical Branch in Galveston. And the two-year-old Physician Retraining & Reentry program created by doctors at the University of California–San Diego School of Medicine equips specialists of all backgrounds to re-enter the workforce in primary care. Completed mostly online, the self-paced program is open to physicians nationwide and has revived the careers of more than 40 doctors since 2013. –B.H.

nutrition co-teaching with physicians. Students practice what they'll be preaching; they can often be spotted on group bike rides and runs. Third-year students have a required project and an optional clerkship in lifestyle medicine.

The Greenville Health System, where students get their bedside training, has embraced the focus. Electronic health records now prompt physicians to ask about lifestyle habits and give out "exercise prescriptions" to be filled through a collaboration with the local YMCA, where patients can get low-cost personalized fitness training. "It's classroom to community," says Jennifer L. Trilk, a clinical assistant professor of physiology and exercise science at the school. Nutrition and physical activity concepts are also woven into the curriculum at the University of Colorado School of Medicine and Anschutz Medical Campus in Aurora and the Feinberg School of Medicine at Northwestern University.

As part of her studies at the University of Miami Miller School of Medicine, Sandy Jiang, 24, has created a wellness curriculum for at-risk youth that will be launched next year. "It's been great practice for me to take what I'm learning and put it in lay terms so kids can learn why it's better to eat right," says Jiang, a second-year student working toward dual degrees in medicine and public health.

That program is an offshoot of a larger effort to train future doctors to help stem the tide of obesity and diabetes by intervening before problems develop. Teaming up with the Miami-Dade Department of County Parks, Recreation and Open Spaces, the juvenile services department and Florida International University, medical faculty and students have served some 1,600 children in Fit-2Play, a program in local parks that uses physical activity and interactive learning to promote healthy lifestyles. Based on evidence that kids in the program significantly reduced their body mass index and blood pressure, pediatricians are now offering "park prescriptions."

"The goal is to prevent childhood obesity and break the chain," says Sarah Messiah, the University of Miami research associate professor of pediatrics who created the program. "We're showing students how to make that happen." ∎

WHY I PICKED...

University of Missouri

COLUMBIA

SARAH KIRCHHOFF, '15
Family doctor

❯❯ I knew in high school I wanted to be a doctor. I attended Southeast Missouri State University for undergrad because they partnered with Mizzou for the Bryant Scholars program, a preadmission track to medical school geared toward students who want to practice primary care in rural areas. I was interested in family medicine and continued in the rural track at Mizzou, where I was able to get hands-on experience at practices around Missouri.

Mizzou also emphasizes a patient-based learning curriculum that mimics real-life medicine. Students work in small groups to analyze an actual patient case and learn about the diagnosis and management of an array of health issues.

Another great Mizzou practice: You get a fourth-year student and a faculty adviser to help you navigate school and the future, which is so helpful. My adviser happens to be the clinic director at the rural practice where I now work. ∎

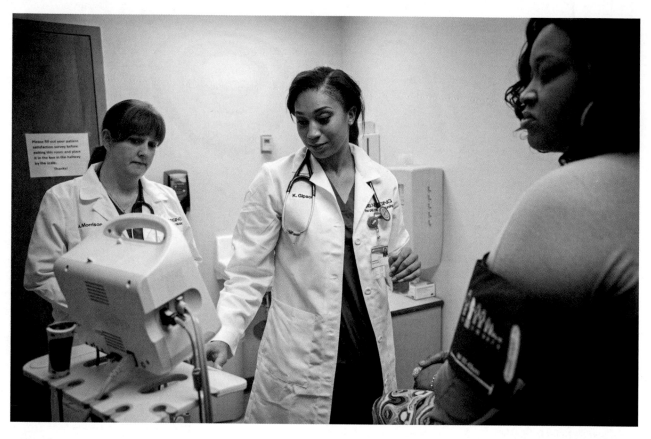

Moving to a Sizzling Field

The many ways liberal arts grads can enter the health arena • *By* **LINDA MARSA**

>>> **John Derksen majored** in political science. But interning at the National Institutes of Health and working for a nonprofit coordinating patient care for immigrants altered his path. The 26-year-old Orrville, Ohio, native is now in a three-year master's program in health care administration at the University of Alabama–Birmingham. "I had no science background whatsoever, but getting this degree looked like a great opportunity," says Derksen, who will wrap up his studies with a yearlong fellowship at a hospital chain in Louisiana, where he will be partnered with a top executive. He believes the extra diploma will give him a leg up in a field with great potential.

Derksen's right about that. Job openings for health care managers are anticipated to swell by 17 percent in the decade ending in 2024, according to government projections. That's much faster than the average for all occupations. All told, the health care field is expected to account for about 1 in 4 new jobs over that period. The Affordable Care Act has given millions of Americans better access to the system even as chronic disease and an aging population translate to more people needing more care.

As Derksen has discovered, the opportunities are hardly limited to people with undergraduate science or allied health degrees. A wide range of health care arenas will be adding new positions that liberal arts majors can qualify for after getting an advanced degree. They range from social work and mental health counseling to public health, regulatory compliance and policy analysis. "A lot of health systems have huge marketing divisions and are looking for people who can write and communicate, which are tasks humanities grads can handle," says Richard Oliver, immediate past president of the Association of Schools of Allied Health Professions and former dean of the school of health professions at the University of Missouri in Columbia. "Health or strate-

Nursing students in UAB's accelerated master's program see a patient in the heart failure clinic.

KEVIN D. LILES FOR USN&WR

New jobs,
New industries.

See which jobs are in-demand in
the following industries:

Business

Construction

Creative & Media

Education

Engineering

Health Care

Health Care Support

Maintenance & Repair

Sales & Marketing

Science

Social Services

STEM

Technology

Visit **usnews.com/careers**

for rankings and analysis of the greatest occupations of this decade.

WHY I PICKED...

University of California

SAN FRANCISCO

GINA INTINARELLI, '13
Health care executive

» **Many senior administrators in health care lack clinical experience, and now more than ever leaders with this background, especially nurses, need to be at the table when policy is made. That's why I applied to UCSF's School of Nursing, which has a well-designed interdisciplinary health policy program. Already an experienced critical care nurse, I learned institutional and policy theory, health care economics and comparative analysis of international health care systems.**

All UCSF students must complete a policy residency; I did mine at the World Health Organization in Geneva, studying global efforts to curb tobacco use. UCSF gave me the skills to perform population health analysis, to implement large programs and to design and use technology to move more patient care into the home, all of which prepared me to be successful in my new role as the executive director for population health and accountable care at UCSF Health. ■

gic communications are also hot areas."

Besides hospital and other clinical practice settings, work can be found in academia, think tanks, governmental agencies and large health care corporations. And people who either have had or are game to take some science prerequisites can opt for "entry-level" master's programs to become a registered nurse or speech therapist, for instance.

At Alabama, students in the health care administration master's program "run the gamut from English, economics and business to engineering backgrounds," says program director Amy Yarbrough Landry, who is also an associate professor of health services administration. (There is a second "low-residency" track for professionals with at least five years of health care experience that entails mostly online coursework and one week on campus each semester.) Graduates work in middle to upper management in a broad range of organizations, including hospitals, physician group practices, insurance companies and consulting firms.

For Kaylan Agnew, 26, the shift has been

from a college major in sociocultural anthropology to a career in global health. Stints during college volunteering in Kenya with botanists studying medicinal plants, doing research at a Palestinian refugee clinic, and working on a water project in Sierra Leone "made me realize how much anthropology and culture play a role in health," says Agnew. Last fall, she started the master's program in global health at the University of California–San Francisco. It's a degree that "will give me a lot of latitude," she thinks. For example, public health pros are needed in hospitals, community clinics, government agencies and nonprofits; median salaries are often in the $60,000 range.

Agnew's one-year program, similar to ones offered at Duke, Notre Dame and other universities, includes nine weeks of fieldwork in a public health project in the U.S. or abroad, and prepares graduates for careers in academia, research, organizational leadership and program management. (The school also launched a Ph.D. track this year.) While applicants are best served by having a solid math

background and a statistics course as well as some health-related science such as nutrition or anatomy, "these can be done in a summer or a semester," says Madhavi Dandu, director of the program. "We have students with all kinds of undergraduate degrees, like anthropology and sociology. We've even had geographers and journalists."

A good way to find out about programs open to liberal arts majors is to search for schools of health sciences or health professions and look at admission requirements for programs of interest. And "contact the program's director," advises Edelma Huntley, dean in residence at the Council of Graduate Schools. "They can tell you if you qualify, or if you need to take some prerequisite classes, and they can give you a realistic assessment of your chances for success if you matriculate." Most occupations have national organizations – the American Occupational Therapy Association and the American Nurses Association, for example – that can provide information on the best places to get an advanced degree.

They can also refer people interested in a career such as nursing or speech-language pathology to fast-track programs for liberal arts grads motivated to take some science prerequisites. Within the next five years, the country will need an additional half million RNs and advanced practice nurses (such as nurse practitioners and nurse anesthetists) along with several hundred thousand to replace retiring nurses. While a bachelor's in nursing is normally needed to enter a master's program, there are now more than 60 master's programs – UAB offers one – for people with an undergrad degree in another field who want to earn both their nursing license and an advanced degree.

Typically these are three-year programs in which the first year is packed with the science needed to prepare for the licensing exam and the last two cover both academics and extensive clinical training. Nursing has created the greatest number of accelerated programs, says Oliver, "because of the magnitude of the demand."

The take-home message? There are many entryways to health care open even to people who struggled with high-school chemistry. ■

COURTESY OF RONALD PALMA

THE JOB MARKET

SPOTLIGHT ON: RURAL MEDICINE

Life as a Country Doctor

By **COURTNEY RUBIN**

>> When she was a child living on a ranch in Montana and attending elementary school in a one-room schoolhouse with four other children, a career as a physician didn't occur to KayCee Gardner. She'd never needed one. For a long time, says Gardner, 31, "I didn't even know doctors existed." (She recalls, however, that she always "enjoyed doctoring our cows.")

Gardner's plan as she went off to Montana State University was to become an engineer. But she soon got the feeling that the work would lack the humanitarian rewards she craved. Searching for a better fit, she shadowed an X-ray technician and later a doctor on a Northern Cheyenne reservation. Both experiences impressed upon her that it must be possible to prevent a good many health conditions by giving people better access to physicians.

According to the National Rural Health Association, just 10 percent of doctors practice in the wide swath of America where nearly a quarter of the population lives. The shortage of rural doctors has only grown more acute as the Affordable Care Act has expanded the ranks of people with insurance.

Fast start. Gardner decided on medical school at the University of Washington and participated in a new track that would lead her to primary care in a rural and underserved area. She was assigned a mentor and sent to work in a small town before school even started. The first week, she delivered a baby.

Gardner graduated in 2012, did her residency at Montana Family Medicine in Billings, and is all set to begin practicing in Miles City (popula-

KayCee Gardner
University of Washington School of Medicine, 2012

tion 8,000) this fall after she wraps up a rural medicine fellowship with a focus on high-risk obstetrics. That should help equip her for the huge range of tasks she expects to face – everything from putting tubes in tracheas to treating trauma patients and performing cesarean sections.

Primary care doctors are paid less than specialists, and rural doctors sit on the lower end of the primary care spectrum. (A survey of 35,000 doctors by the physician network Doximity puts state averages for primary care physicians at $191,500 to $330,000.) Gardner has no complaints: "I'm still going to be in the top 1 percent of income compared to people I'll be living with," she notes. To draw grads to rural medicine, many states and agencies help with loan repayment. If Gardner commits for 10 years in the state, Montana will repay her loans. ∎

... More Hot Jobs

PHYSICIAN ASSISTANT

With the expanding demand for health care services, the need for physician assistants is projected to rise by 30 percent in the next 10 years, according to government data – growth that is "much faster" than the overall average. The job, which involves diagnosing and treating patients and can include writing prescriptions, typically requires a master's degree and a license. The median pay is just under $96,000.

ONCOLOGIST

Cancer continues to be a formidable foe, and since oncologists "tend to follow their patients for years and years," says Colleen Christmas, associate professor of medicine at Johns Hopkins, "they have a reduced ability to take in new patients." Rapid discoveries in genomics and immunology, for example, make the field a dynamic one. According to the physician network Doximity, oncologists' pay averages $353,000.

GERIATRICIAN

There are currently some 7,400 geriatricians in the country, or one for every 2,526 Americans age 75 or older, according to the American Geriatrics Society. But thanks to the aging population and a "plateauing" of the number of these specialists, that ratio is expected to sink to one for every 4,484 people in 2030. After they finish medical school and residency, geriatricians typically spend at least one additional year studying conditions specific to aging.

COURTESY OF MULTICARE

Schools of Medicine

THE TOP SCHOOLS - RESEARCH

Rank School	Overall score	Peer assessment score (5.0=highest)	Assessment score, residency directors (5.0=highest)	'15 median undergrad GPA	'15 median MCAT score	'15 acceptance rate	'15 NIH research grants (in millions)	'15 NIH research grants per faculty member (in thousands)	'15 faculty/ student ratio	'15 out-of-state tuition and fees	'15 total medical school enrollment
1. Harvard University (MA)	100	4.8	4.7	3.92	36	3.7%	$1,419.6	$150.3	13.3	$57,485	710
2. Stanford University (CA)	88	4.7	4.6	3.85	35	2.6%	$375.3	$397.6	2.0	$53,445	482
3. Johns Hopkins University (MD)	83	4.8	4.7	3.90	36	6.3%	$521.6	$188.9	5.8	$53,804	472
3. University of California–San Francisco	83	4.8	4.7	3.75	34	3.8%	$531.1	$234.0	3.5	$49,589	647
3. University of Pennsylvania (Perelman)	83	4.5	4.6	3.87	38	5.4%	$514.2	$177.6	4.7	$56,784	616
6. Washington University in St. Louis (MO)	79	4.6	4.5	3.88	38	8.9%	$352.3	$190.3	3.8	$58,460	484
7. Columbia University (NY)	77	4.4	4.5	3.82	36	4.0%	$399.5	$208.8	2.9	$61,485	670
8. Duke University (NC)	76	4.4	4.5	3.80	36	3.6%	$326.3	$229.8	3.1	$57,329	453
8. University of Washington	76	4.4	4.3	3.73	31	3.6%	$605.2	$222.0	2.8	$64,399	959
8. Yale University (CT)	76	4.4	4.2	3.87	36	6.5%	$344.3	$234.9	3.7	$56,645	396
11. New York University	74	3.7	3.8	3.87	36	5.5%	$324.3	$311.5	1.7	$54,030	615
11. University of Chicago (Pritzker) (IL)	74	4.1	4.1	3.87	37	4.9%	$233.7	$260.2	2.5	$54,784	363
11. University of Michigan–Ann Arbor	74	4.4	4.4	3.78	35	6.8%	$385.4	$210.9	2.6	$51,182	710
14. University of California–Los Angeles (Geffen)	73	4.1	4.3	3.82	35	3.1%	$472.9	$185.3	3.4	$48,647	748
15. Vanderbilt University (TN)	72	4.2	4.3	3.88	37	4.4%	$344.3	$131.6	6.5	$50,932	402
16. University of Pittsburgh (PA)	71	4.0	4.1	3.81	36	7.3%	$399.6	$194.2	3.5	$52,306	583
17. Northwestern University (Feinberg) (IL)	68	4.0	4.2	3.88	36	7.8%	$290.1	$147.0	3.1	$58,210	639
18. Cornell University (Weill) (NY)	67	4.1	4.3	3.84	36	5.0%	$280.3	$110.5	6.0	$54,650	423
18. University of California–San Diego	67	3.9	3.8	3.77	34	3.4%	$315.6	$228.2	2.7	$49,232	521
20. Baylor College of Medicine (TX)	65	3.7	4.1	3.86	35	4.1%	$290.2	$143.1	2.7	$31,663	742
21. Icahn School of Medicine at Mount Sinai (NY)	64	3.6	3.7	3.82	35	9.0%	$319.1	$181.3	3.2	$53,608	556
22. University of North Carolina–Chapel Hill	63	4.0	3.8	3.73	32	3.8%	$278.7	$182.3	1.8	$50,651	829
23. Emory University (GA)	61	3.9	4.1	3.70	34	5.8%	$251.9	$131.6	3.4	$50,860	562
24. Mayo Medical School (MN)	59	3.8	4.0	3.80	34	1.8%	$240.3	$72.0	16.0	$49,900	208
25. Case Western Reserve University (OH)	58	3.5	3.7	3.73	35	9.7%	$296.5	$111.2	3.0	$59,303	883
25. University of Wisconsin–Madison	58	3.7	3.7	3.80	32	5.7%	$198.6	$162.7	1.7	$37,155	727
25. U. of Texas Southwestern Medical Center	58	4.0	3.9	3.83	34	8.4%	$189.9	$84.5	2.4	$32,443	955
28. University of Virginia	56	3.6	3.9	3.86	34	10.4%	$115.8	$112.0	1.6	$58,160	629
29. Boston University (MA)	54	3.3	3.5	3.74	35	4.1%	$177.1	$107.0	2.4	$56,304	702
29. University of Rochester (NY)	54	3.5	3.7	3.79	34	4.8%	$139.6	$91.5	3.5	$52,799	435
31. Oregon Health and Science University	53	3.6	3.8	3.68	31	3.9%	$230.4	$103.3	4.0	$57,856	556
31. University of Southern California (Keck)	53	3.4	3.7	3.72	35	4.9%	$144.6	$87.9	2.2	$59,388	743
33. Ohio State University	52	3.4	3.5	3.77	34	6.5%	$182.7	$97.4	2.5	$36,361	756
33. University of Iowa (Carver)	52	3.7	3.6	3.76	32	8.0%	$103.5	$103.3	1.7	$52,319	600
35. Brown University (Alpert) (RI)	51	3.4	3.7	3.69	33	2.8%	$86.4	$118.1	1.4	$57,783	526
35. University of Alabama–Birmingham	51	3.6	3.5	3.80	30	7.1%	$165.3	$119.4	1.8	$64,514	780
35. University of Colorado	51	3.7	3.6	3.71	33	4.4%	$188.6	$54.9	5.2	$63,270	664
35. University of Minnesota	51	3.5	3.6	3.79	32	6.0%	$150.3	$74.0	2.1	$53,397	975
39. Yeshiva University (Einstein) (NY)	50	3.3	3.4	3.83	33	4.5%	$148.7	$77.8	2.5	$54,512	773
40. Dartmouth College (Geisel) (NH)	49	3.5	3.7	3.64	32	4.7%	$85.5	$103.5	2.2	$60,012	369
40. University of Cincinnati (OH)	49	3.1	3.2	3.73	33	7.6%	$191.2	$106.9	2.6	$50,438	692
40. University of Florida	49	3.2	3.3	3.87	33	5.3%	$104.6	$77.3	2.5	$49,385	551
40. University of Maryland	49	3.2	3.3	3.76	32	6.5%	$153.5*	$121.9*	1.9	$61,253	651
44. University of California–Irvine	48	3.0	3.2	3.70	33	3.7%	$115.6	$164.9	1.6	$49,979	437
44. University of Miami (Miller) (FL)	48	3.1	3.4	3.77	33	4.5%	$113.7	$80.9	1.7	$42,626	809
46. University of Utah	47	3.3	3.5	3.71	30	5.9%	$133.9	$80.9	4.1	$67,374	406
47. Georgetown University (DC)	46	3.3	3.7	3.60	31	2.8%	$147.7	$68.6	2.7	$56,648	793
47. Indiana University–Indianapolis	46	3.4	3.6	3.80	30	9.4%	$111.5*	$54.4*	1.5	$56,230	1,404
47. Tufts University (MA)	46	3.3	3.6	3.67	33	5.7%	$70.4	$45.6	1.9	$59,080	819

► More @ usnews.com/grad

TRUE MEDICINE

TRUE. SGU is the #1 provider of doctors into first-year US residencies for the past 5 years combined, including over 830 US residencies in 2015.*

TRUE. SGU has a network of over 13,000 graduate physicians who have impacted health care worldwide.

TRUE. SGU's US and Canadian students achieved a 97% first-time pass rate on the USMLE I in 2014, surpassing students from US and Canadian schools 5 years in a row.

FIND YOUR TRUE CALLING

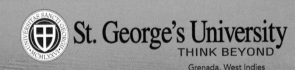

St. George's University
THINK BEYOND

Grenada, West Indies

sgu.edu/md | 800.899.6337

*According to published information as of April 2015

THE TOP SCHOOLS - RESEARCH continued

Rank School	Overall score	Peer assessment score (5.0=highest)	Assessment score, residency directors (5.0=highest)	'15 median undergrad GPA	'15 median MCAT score	'15 acceptance rate	'15 NIH research grants (in millions)	'15 NIH research grants per faculty member (in thousands)	'15 faculty/ student ratio	'15 out-of-state tuition and fees	'15 total medical school enrollment
47. University of California–Davis	46	3.2	3.3	3.58	29	2.8%	$127.2	$173.8	1.7	$53,467	433
47. University of Illinois	46	3.1	3.2	3.69	32	12.8%	$113.7	$121.9	0.7	$76,716	1,317
52. University of Massachusetts–Worcester	44	3.1	3.0	3.70	32	16.9%	$140.5*	$104.7*	2.6	N/A	515
52. Wake Forest University (NC)	44	3.2	3.5	3.58	31	2.9%	$87.1	$75.3	2.5	$51,800	467
54. Temple University (Katz) (PA)	43	2.8	2.9	3.69	31	4.3%	$92.6	$158.2	0.7	$54,339	867
55. Medical College of Wisconsin	42	3.2	3.3	3.75	30	8.3%	$94.5	$59.3	1.9	$50,935	845
56. Stony Brook University–SUNY (NY)	41	2.9	2.9	3.70	32	7.2%	$67.6	$89.2	1.5	$66,411	516
56. Thomas Jefferson University (Kimmel) (PA)	41	3.0	3.3	3.70	32	4.2%	$70.8	$23.8	2.8	$54,161	1,056
56. University of Vermont	41	2.9	3.1	3.65	31	4.1%	$66.6	$104.2	1.4	$60,776	464
56. Univ. of Texas Health Science Center–Houston	41	3.0	3.2	3.79	32	13.6%	$51.0*	$40.0*	1.3	$31,192	982

THE TOP SCHOOLS - PRIMARY CARE

Rank School	Overall score	Peer assessment score (5.0=highest)	Assessment score, residency directors (5.0=highest)	Selectivity rank	'15 median undergrad GPA	'15 median MCAT score	'15 acceptance rate	% '13-'15 graduates entering primary care	'15 faculty/ student ratio	'15 out-of-state tuition and fees	'15 total medical school enrollment
1. University of Washington	100	4.2	4.5	53	3.73	31	3.6%	56.3%	2.8	$64,399	959
2. University of North Carolina–Chapel Hill	98	3.7	4.1	40	3.73	32	3.8%	65.0%	1.8	$50,651	829
3. University of California–San Francisco	82	3.8	4.5	30	3.75	34	3.8%	42.7%	3.5	$49,589	647
4. University of Michigan–Ann Arbor	80	3.6	4.3	18	3.78	35	6.8%	44.5%	2.6	$51,182	710
5. University of Nebraska Medical Center	79	3.1	3.3	53	3.75	31	9.1%	64.0%	1.4	$74,365	503
6. Oregon Health and Science University	78	3.8	4.1	62	3.68	31	3.9%	45.6%	4.0	$57,856	556
6. University of California–Los Angeles (Geffen)	78	3.3	4.1	16	3.82	35	3.1%	47.2%	3.4	$48,647	748
8. Duke University (NC)	75	3.2	4.2	12	3.80	36	3.6%	44.6%	3.1	$57,329	453
9. Baylor College of Medicine (TX)	74	3.0	4.1	12	3.86	35	4.1%	48.3%	2.7	$31,663	742
9. University of Minnesota	74	3.4	3.7	35	3.79	32	6.0%	49.4%	2.1	$53,397	975
11. University of Colorado	73	3.7	3.9	35	3.71	33	4.4%	41.4%	5.2	$63,270	664
11. University of Pennsylvania (Perelman)	73	3.3	4.4	1	3.87	38	5.4%	37.0%	4.7	$56,784	616
11. University of Pittsburgh (PA)	73	3.5	4.1	12	3.81	36	7.3%	39.0%	3.5	$52,306	583
14. University of Wisconsin–Madison	71	3.6	3.9	34	3.80	32	5.7%	41.5%	1.7	$37,155	727
15. Michigan State U. (College of Osteopathic Medicine)	70	2.2	3.1	92	3.65	29	8.2%	80.0%	0.2	$88,788	1,242
16. University of Massachusetts–Worcester	69	3.2	3.4	62	3.70	32	16.9%	51.5%	2.6	N/A	515
17. Harvard University (MA)	68	3.0	4.4	5	3.92	36	3.7%	38.0%	13.3	$57,485	710
17. Johns Hopkins University (MD)	68	3.1	4.5	6	3.90	36	6.3%	36.0%	5.8	$53,804	472
17. Northwestern University (Feinberg) (IL)	68	3.1	4.2	7	3.88	36	7.8%	39.4%	3.1	$58,210	639
20. University of Chicago (Pritzker) (IL)	67	3.0	4.0	3	3.87	37	4.9%	40.7%	2.5	$54,784	363
21. University of Alabama–Birmingham	66	3.3	3.9	53	3.80	30	7.1%	43.7%	1.8	$64,514	780
21. University of California–San Diego	66	3.3	3.8	27	3.77	34	3.4%	39.9%	2.7	$49,232	521
21. U. of Texas Southwestern Medical Center	66	3.1	3.8	20	3.83	34	8.4%	43.5%	2.4	$32,443	955
21. Washington University in St. Louis (MO)	66	3.1	4.2	1	3.88	38	8.9%	35.0%	3.8	$58,460	484
25. Icahn School of Medicine at Mount Sinai (NY)	64	2.6	3.6	17	3.82	35	9.0%	49.3%	3.2	$53,608	556
25. University of Iowa (Carver)	64	3.5	3.8	40	3.76	32	8.0%	38.0%	1.7	$52,319	600
25. University of Virginia	64	3.2	3.9	18	3.86	34	10.4%	38.4%	1.6	$58,160	629
25. Vanderbilt University (TN)	64	3.1	4.1	3	3.88	37	4.4%	34.9%	6.5	$50,932	402
29. Cornell University (Weill) (NY)	63	2.8	4.0	10	3.84	36	5.0%	41.0%	6.0	$54,650	423
29. Emory University (GA)	63	3.1	3.9	33	3.70	34	5.8%	40.7%	3.4	$50,860	562
29. Ohio State University	63	3.0	3.7	30	3.77	34	6.5%	43.7%	2.5	$36,361	756
32. Brown University (Alpert) (RI)	62	3.1	3.8	38	3.69	33	2.8%	42.0%	1.4	$57,783	526
32. East Carolina University (Brody) (NC)	62	2.9	3.0	91	3.69	29	12.7%	56.0%	1.3	N/A	311
32. Mayo Medical School (MN)	62	3.0	4.1	20	3.80	34	1.8%	38.0%	16.0	$49,900	208
32. New York University	62	2.9	3.6	7	3.87	36	5.5%	41.0%	1.7	$54,030	615
32. Yeshiva University (Einstein) (NY)	62	2.9	3.4	27	3.83	33	4.5%	46.0%	2.5	$54,512	773

N/A=Data were not provided by the school. *The medical school's National Institutes of Health grants do not include any grants to affiliated hospitals.
Sources: U.S. News and the schools. Peer assessment data collected by Ipsos Public Affairs.

DISCOVER ONE OF THE MOST GENEROUS SCHOLARSHIP PROGRAMS.

The U.S. Army's Health Professions Scholarship Program (HPSP) offers qualified medical, dental, veterinary, optometry, clinical psychology and specialty nursing students full tuition for a graduate-level degree at the school of your choice:

- You'll receive a monthly stipend, as well as payment for books, equipment and academic fees.

- Medical and dental students may qualify for a sign-on bonus.

- As you serve, you'll enjoy the potential to train, perform research and grow as a leader.

To learn more, call 800-431-6691 or visit healthcare.goarmy.com/at60

U.S.ARMY

©2016. Paid for by the United States Army. All rights reserved.

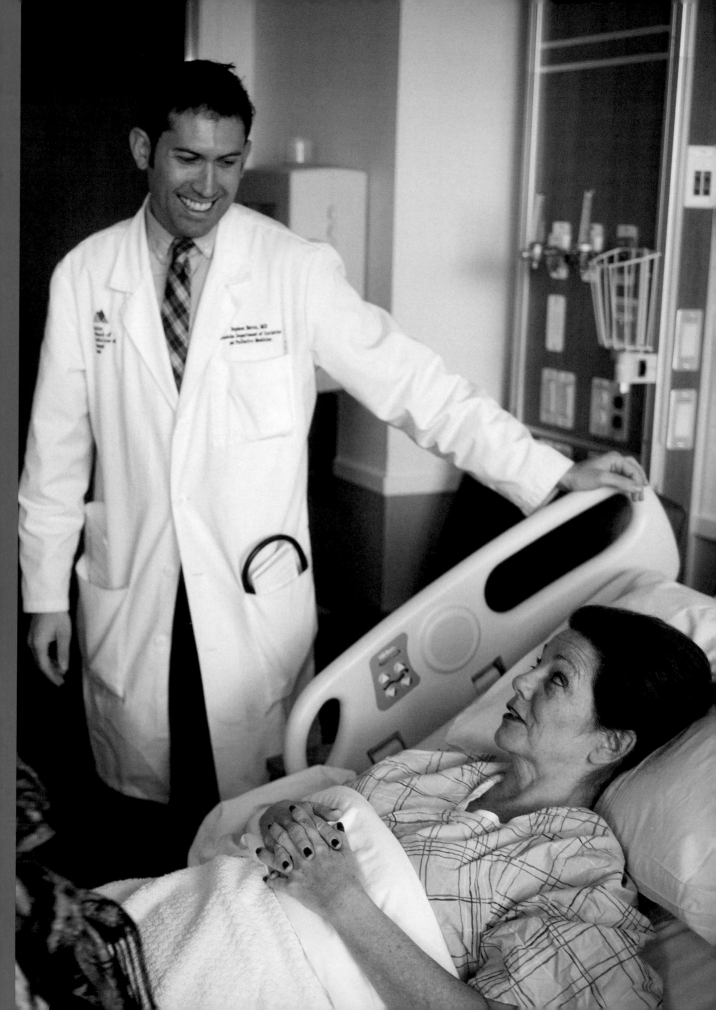

THE TOP SCHOOLS - PRIMARY CARE continued

Rank	School	Overall score	Peer assessment score (5.0=highest)	Assessment score, residency directors (5.0=highest)	Selectivity rank	'15 median undergrad GPA	'15 median MCAT score	'15 acceptance rate	% '13-'15 graduates entering primary care	'15 faculty/ student ratio	'15 out-of-state tuition and fees	'15 total medical school enrollment
37.	Stanford University (CA)	61	3.0	4.5	12	3.85	35	2.6%	33.0%	2.0	$53,445	482
37.	University of California–Davis	61	3.3	3.6	96	3.58	29	2.8%	44.7%	1.7	$53,467	433
37.	Yale University (CT)	61	3.0	4.0	7	3.87	36	6.5%	35.0%	3.7	$56,645	396
40.	Boston University (MA)	60	2.9	3.6	20	3.74	35	4.1%	42.6%	2.4	$56,304	702
40.	University of Arkansas for Medical Sciences	60	3.0	3.1	96	3.67	29	21.1%	52.3%	1.9	$55,606	684
40.	University of Kansas Medical Center	60	3.1	3.5	76	3.78	29	7.4%	46.0%	1.1	$60,431	838
40.	University of Rochester (NY)	60	3.3	3.7	24	3.79	34	4.8%	35.6%	3.5	$52,799	435
40.	Virginia Commonwealth University	60	2.9	3.3	84	3.60	31	4.3%	50.1%	1.8	$49,193	833
45.	Dartmouth College (Geisel) (NH)	59	3.1	3.7	58	3.64	32	4.7%	41.6%	2.2	$60,012	369
45.	Tufts University (MA)	59	2.8	3.6	45	3.67	33	5.7%	45.6%	1.9	$59,080	819
45.	University of New Mexico	59	3.4	3.1	94	3.68	28	8.4%	45.6%	2.2	$49,109	422
48.	St. Louis University (MO)	58	2.6	3.4	24	3.87	33	6.4%	47.6%	0.9	$51,130	731
48.	University of Vermont	58	3.2	3.5	71	3.65	31	4.1%	42.0%	1.4	$60,776	464
50.	Columbia University (NY)	57	3.0	4.2	11	3.82	36	4.0%	30.4%	2.9	$61,485	670
50.	Indiana University–Indianapolis	57	3.4	3.7	58	3.80	30	9.4%	35.0%	1.5	$56,230	1,404
50.	University of Connecticut	57	2.7	3.4	50	3.70	32	7.1%	48.0%	2.6	$65,630	392
50.	University of North Texas Health Science Center	57	2.2	2.9	96	3.70	28	13.9%	65.7%	0.5	$34,710	919
54.	Medical College of Wisconsin	56	3.1	3.6	67	3.75	30	8.3%	40.3%	1.9	$50,935	845
54.	Thomas Jefferson University (Kimmel) (PA)	56	2.8	3.5	47	3.70	32	4.2%	44.4%	2.8	$54,161	1,056
54.	University of Missouri	56	3.1	3.3	58	3.79	30	8.9%	42.7%	1.5	$57,613	397
54.	University of Southern California (Keck)	56	3.0	3.7	24	3.72	35	4.9%	36.3%	2.2	$59,388	743
54.	University of Utah	56	3.2	3.8	76	3.71	30	5.9%	37.3%	4.1	$67,374	406

SPECIALTIES

MEDICAL SCHOOL DEANS AND SENIOR FACULTY SELECT THE BEST PROGRAMS

DRUG/ALCOHOL ABUSE
1. Harvard University (MA)
2. University of California–San Francisco
3. Columbia University (NY)
3. Yale University (CT)
5. Johns Hopkins University (MD)
6. University of California–Los Angeles (Geffen)

FAMILY MEDICINE
1. University of Washington
2. Oregon Health and Science University
2. University of North Carolina–Chapel Hill
4. University of California–San Francisco
5. University of Colorado
5. University of Wisconsin–Madison
7. University of Missouri
8. University of Michigan–Ann Arbor

GERIATRICS
1. Johns Hopkins University (MD)
2. Harvard University (MA)
3. Icahn School of Medicine at Mount Sinai (NY)
4. University of Michigan–Ann Arbor
5. University of California–Los Angeles (Geffen)
6. University of California–San Francisco
7. Duke University (NC)

INTERNAL MEDICINE
1. Harvard University (MA)
2. Johns Hopkins University (MD)
3. University of California–San Francisco
4. University of Pennsylvania (Perelman)
5. Duke University (NC)
6. University of Michigan–Ann Arbor
7. University of Washington

8. Washington University in St. Louis (MO)
9. Columbia University (NY)
10. Stanford University (CA)
10. Vanderbilt University (IN)

PEDIATRICS
1. University of Pennsylvania (Perelman)
2. Harvard University (MA)
3. University of Cincinnati (OH)
4. University of Colorado
5. University of Washington
6. Johns Hopkins University (MD)
7. Baylor College of Medicine (TX)
7. University of California–San Francisco
9. University of Pittsburgh (PA)
9. Washington University in St. Louis (MO)

RURAL MEDICINE
1. University of Washington
2. University of New Mexico
2. University of North Carolina–Chapel Hill
4. Oregon Health and Science University
5. University of Minnesota
6. University of Colorado
6. University of North Dakota

WOMEN'S HEALTH
1. Harvard University (MA)
2. University of California–San Francisco
3. University of Pennsylvania (Perelman)
4. Johns Hopkins University (MD)
5. University of Pittsburgh (PA)
6. Columbia University (NY)
6. University of Michigan–Ann Arbor

Palliative care at the Icahn School of Medicine is taught via simulated talks with "patients."

MATT SLABY – LUCEO FOR USN&WR

METHODOLOGY

The 140 medical schools fully accredited in 2015 by the Liaison Committee on Medical Education and the 30 schools of osteopathic medicine fully accredited in 2015 by the American Osteopathic Association were surveyed for the rankings of research- and primary care-oriented medical schools; 116 schools provided the data needed to calculate the two rankings. The research model is based on a weighted average of eight indicators; the primary care model is based on seven indicators. Most are the same for both. The research model factors in NIH research activity; the primary care model uses proportion of graduates entering primary care.

Quality assessment: Three assessment surveys were conducted in the fall of 2015. In a peer survey, medical and osteopathic school deans, deans of academic affairs, and heads of internal medicine or the directors of admissions were asked to rate program quality on a scale of marginal (1) to outstanding (5). Respondents were asked to rate research and primary care programs separately. The response rate was 31 percent. Average peer assessment score in the research model is weighted by .20; average score in the primary care model, by .25. In two separate surveys, residency program directors were asked to rate programs using the same 5-point scale. One survey dealt with research and was sent to a sample of residency program directors designated by the medical schools as being involved in research. The other survey was sent to residency directors designated by the medical schools as being involved in clinical practice. Residency directors' ratings for the three most recent years were averaged and weighted .20 for research and .15 for primary care. Schools supplied U.S. News names of residency program directors who were sent either of the surveys.

Research activity (weighted by .30 in the research model only): Research was measured as the total dollar amount of National Institutes of Health research grants awarded to the medical school and its affiliated hospitals (50 percent of this measure) and the average amount of those grants per full-time medical school science or clinical faculty member (50 percent); for the rankings, both factors were averaged for fiscal years 2014 and 2015. An asterisk indicates schools that reported only NIH research grants going to their medical school in 2015. The NIH figures published are for fiscal year 2015 only.

Primary care rate (.30 in primary care model only): The percentage of medical or osteopathic school graduates entering primary care residencies in the fields of family practice, pediatrics and internal medicine was averaged over the 2013, 2014 and 2015 graduating classes.

Student selectivity (.20 in research model, .15 in primary care model): Based on three measures describing the class entering in fall 2015: median Medical College Admission Test total score (65 percent of this measure), median undergraduate GPA (30 percent), and the acceptance rate (5 percent).

Faculty resources (.10 in research model, .15 in primary care model): Faculty resources were measured as the ratio of full-time science and clinical faculty to medical or osteopathic students in 2014.

Overall rank: Indicators were standardized about their means, and standardized scores were weighted, totaled and rescaled so that the top school received 100; other schools received their percentage of the top school's score.

Specialty rankings: Based solely on ratings by medical school deans and senior faculty at peer schools, who identified up to 10 schools offering the best programs in each specialty. The top half of programs (by number of nominations) appear.

Advance your practice:

Our learning environment transforms lives

U-M's global network means lifelong connections

Our DNP, PhD and Master's grads are sought after by the best health systems

NURSING

Join us at University of Michigan:
Learning at the edge of discovery.

nursing.umich.edu/gograd • 734.763.5985

MS in **Management**
Information Systems

Ranked #18
2016 Best Online Programs

A·ACSB
ACCREDITED

- Available online or on-campus
- 100% placement record
- Graduate Certificate in Business Process Management
- Graduate Certificate in IT Project Management
- Graduate Certificate in Business Intelligence

Combining a high level of competency in information technology with the fundamental principles of management to produce today's sought-after technology and business leaders.

Visit us: **mis.uis.edu**   Contact us: MIS@uis.edu

UNIVERSITY OF
ILLINOIS
SPRINGFIELD

LEADERSHIP lived

Schools of Nursing

THE TOP SCHOOLS - MASTER'S

Rank School	Overall score	Peer assessment score (5.0=highest)	'15 master's acceptance rate	'15 mean full-time undergrad GPA (master's)	'15 master's student/ faculty ratio	'15 percent of faculty in active nursing practice	'15 master's degrees awarded	'15 NIH and all other research grants (in thousands)	'15 NIH and all other teaching and practice grants (in thousands)	'15 out-of-state tuition and fees	'15 master's program enrollment full-/part-time
1. Johns Hopkins University (MD)	100	4.5	57.2%	3.46	3.6	68.4%	96	$31,942.8	$4,376.5	$37,191	188/222
2. University of Pennsylvania	97	4.6	48.2%	3.58	1.9	53.6%	294	$12,376.5	$4,871.2	$42,026	208/353
3. University of California–San Francisco	91	4.4	32.9%	3.53	3.8	22.4%	157	$16,042.6	$5,159.0	$39,048	400/N/A
4. Duke University (NC)	90	4.3	48.6%	3.65	2.0	63.6%	207	$6,111.0	$2,052.0	$1,568*	94/380
4. University of Washington	90	4.3	83.7%	3.54	0.2	100.0%	28	$14,702.6	$2,660.8	$32,011	12/49
6. New York University	89	4.1	69.2%	3.50	3.4	47.1%	198	$9,090.1	$4,015.0	$40,174	48/552
7. University of Michigan–Ann Arbor	88	4.2	67.1%	3.64	4.9	62.9%	96	$8,296.1	$858.3	$43,342	151/176
8. Case Western Reserve University (OH)	87	4.1	71.2%	3.52	2.0	100.0%	122	$4,786.9	$3,664.4	$1,891*	147/140
8. Columbia University (NY)	87	4.2	37.3%	3.80	4.6	93.1%	208	$3,720.3	$1,325.6	$1,408*	317/161
8. Emory University (GA)	87	4.1	80.7%	3.46	2.1	62.8%	83	$14,478.3	$3,822.3	$1,750*	201/27
8. University of Maryland–Baltimore	87	4.2	55.8%	3.34	1.7	93.1%	358	$2,341.2	$6,006.0	$1,251*	235/326
12. University of California–Los Angeles	85	3.9	65.1%	3.55	11.3	35.7%	170	$4,929.7	$2,227.0	$34,983	316/N/A
13. University of Pittsburgh (PA)	83	4.2	33.5%	3.66	1.4	50.8%	73	$4,288.6	$2,274.9	$44,571	120/58
13. Vanderbilt University (TN)	83	4.1	52.5%	3.47	3.3	55.8%	398	$3,048.5	$2,481.5	$1,219*	408/203
15. University of Alabama–Birmingham	82	4.0	57.1%	3.56	5.0	37.5%	488	$1,709.7	$4,006.3	$493*	255/1,101
16. Rush University (IL)	81	4.1	41.4%	3.56	3.3	49.7%	229	$1,779.7	$3,624.8	$947*	276/61
17. University of Texas–Austin	79	3.9	56.8%	3.45	3.2	96.4%	75	$3,526.7	$1,314.4	$22,655	205/41
18. University of Virginia	77	4.0	43.3%	3.57	2.0	65.7%	111	$1,205.6	$1,440.3	$26,888	108/157
19. Rutgers University–Newark (NJ)	76	3.5	62.0%	N/A	0.8	96.8%	237	$2,591.9	$40,391.0	$1,124*	30/286
19. Yale University (CT)	76	4.1	29.1%	3.61	2.2	78.7%	87	$2,960.8	$651.3	$39,779	253/12
21. Ohio State University	75	4.1	57.7%	3.49	4.2	26.8%	162	$3,147.5	$1,732.8	$1,940*	445/182
21. U. of North Carolina–Chapel Hill	75	4.1	28.6%	3.70	1.6	14.3%	91	$3,087.2	$1,651.9	$33,291	138/80
23. Indiana Univ.-Purdue Univ.–Indianapolis	74	3.8	80.4%	3.61	0.9	62.9%	110	$3,808.5	$2,355.7	$1,435*	19/277
23. University of Colorado	74	3.8	48.5%	3.20	3.4	88.8%	151	$556.2	$5,332.8	$1,020*	314/95
23. University of Illinois–Chicago	74	4.1	64.4%	3.45	2.5	26.5%	191	$3,994.9	$1,058.6	$35,452	298/190
23. University of Iowa	74	4.1	80.0%	N/A	0.1	33.7%	5	$3,252.9	$829.9	$32,085	N/A/14
23. U. of Texas Health Sci. Ctr.–Houston	74	3.7	57.5%	3.49	2.6	90.2%	114	$1,477.8	$2,580.4	$946*	179/244
28. Georgetown University (DC)	73	3.6	42.3%	3.50	4.7	75.2%	406	$3,561.9	$311.8	$1,863*	273/613
28. University of Cincinnati (OH)	73	3.6	55.6%	3.47	4.4	77.3%	666	$1,175.7	$2,122.2	$26,917	225/1,252
30. Arizona State University	72	3.7	90.5%	3.57	0.2	84.0%	12	$6,567.4	$1,343.8	$22,516	16/12
30. Oregon Health and Science University	72	4.1	34.0%	3.53	1.1	N/A	40	$2,576.8	$2,160.9	$740*	153/37
30. University of Arizona	72	3.8	31.2%	3.35	6.8	11.8%	148	$1,474.2	$1,058.2	$800*	158/302
33. Boston College (MA)	71	3.8	72.3%	3.53	3.4	66.1%	98	$737.9	$525.0	$1,248*	171/63
34. George Washington University (DC)	70	3.7	58.9%	3.46	3.4	69.6%	97	$498.4	$1,615.9	$1,030*	39/364
34. Medical University of South Carolina	70	3.5	17.8%	3.60	0.4	69.4%	17	$6,631.8	$1,106.1	$32,419	15/11
34. University of San Diego (CA)	70	3.5	26.2%	3.45	3.6	58.2%	113	$1,519.7	$2,654.1	$1,390*	144/49
34. University of Utah	70	3.7	85.7%	3.45	0.4	64.7%	20	$7,386.6	$444.9	$35,891	27/18
38. University of Rochester (NY)	67	3.7	70.6%	3.21	0.8	75.0%	52	$2,969.1	$587.2	$24,740	2/200
39. University of Missouri–Kansas City	66	3.3	81.8%	3.59	1.0	63.5%	116	$765.4	$6,511.4	$400*	9/105
40. Loyola University Chicago (IL)	65	3.6	73.9%	3.47	1.9	65.1%	78	$677.9	$1,728.6	$1,060*	138/206
40. Penn. State University–University Park	65	3.6	46.3%	3.91	3.4	41.7%	53	$363.1	$674.5	$29,943	64/88
40. University of Miami (FL)	65	3.4	53.2%	3.33	1.5	81.6%	112	$1,935.0	$997.8	$41,790	34/135
40. University of South Florida	65	3.5	41.6%	N/A	4.3	40.8%	333	$2,037.2	$1,138.8	$772*	83/636
40. University of Tennessee–Knoxville	65	3.4	53.9%	3.60	2.0	100.0%	57	$252.3	$3,027.1	$1,660*	98/26
40. Washington State University	65	3.5	68.8%	3.77	0.2	88.4%	26	$3,530.1	$1,418.1	$33,248	5/34
46. Florida Atlantic University (Lynn)	64	3.1	51.8%	N/A	2.7	87.3%	153	$2,907.6	$1,147.1	$928*	8/381
46. University of Nebraska Medical Center	64	3.8	65.7%	3.50	1.5	11.0%	78	$2,055.3	$788.1	$933*	117/155
48. Frontier Nursing University (KY)	63	3.4	49.0%	3.60	13.1	100.0%	433	N/A	$1,013.0	$535*	915/499

N/A=Data were not provided by the school. *Tuition is reported on a per-credit-hour basis. Sources: U.S. News and the schools. Peer assessment data collected by Ipsos Public Affairs.

UC–San Francisco, No. 3

DAVID BUTOW –REDUX FOR USN&WR

Rank School	Overall score	Peer assessment score (5.0=highest)	'15 master's acceptance rate	'15 mean full-time undergrad GPA (master's)	'15 master's student/faculty ratio	'15 percent of faculty in active nursing practice	'15 master's degrees awarded	'15 NIH and all other research grants (in thousands)	'15 NIH and all other teaching and practice grants (in thousands)	'15 out-of-state tuition and fees	'15 master's program enrollment full-/part-time
48. University of Kansas	63	3.7	97.9%	3.44	0.6	29.5%	71	$1,530.6	$340.7	$615*	5/90
48. University of Massachusetts–Amherst	63	3.4	82.6%	3.48	0.3	69.6%	18	$1,544.2	$1,531.0	$750*	1/34
48. University of Missouri	63	3.6	81.3%	N/A	0.3	16.1%	29	$5,004.9	$1,170.8	$422*	1/39
52. California State University–Los Angeles	62	3.2	43.1%	3.60	8.1	91.3%	40	N/A	$9,000.0	$16,830	188/5
52. Uniformed Svces U. of the Hlth. Sci. (MD)	62	3.6	N/A	N/A	0.0	90.9%	7	$1,495.8	$100.0	N/A	1/N/A
52. University of Alabama	62	3.5	49.4%	3.33	1.3	76.6%	55	$300.7	$1,384.5	$360*	56/72
52. University of Connecticut	62	3.5	54.2%	3.43	0.9	69.4%	49	$642.2	$1,189.0	$36,082	34/77
52. University of Massachusetts–Boston	62	3.5	75.5%	3.40	1.1	59.4%	50	$2,418.8	$727.0	$32,967	49/93
52. University of Massachusetts–Worcester	62	3.4	66.7%	3.10	4.1	100.0%	43	$542.1	$479.5	$750*	90/12
58. Baylor University (TX)	61	3.5	70.0%	3.49	1.0	70.0%	19	$537.1	$227.1	$1,515*	15/5
58. Florida International University	61	3.0	33.8%	3.39	3.2	79.3%	174	$3,995.1	$1,819.2	$1,133*	200/61
58. Marquette University (WI)	61	3.5	57.1%	3.45	2.9	64.1%	84	$815.3	$926.7	$1,050*	119/182
58. Michigan State University	61	3.5	39.6%	3.71	1.6	41.9%	61	$3,036.5	$371.2	$1,320*	71/105
58. Purdue University–West Lafayette (IN)	61	3.4	97.2%	3.46	1.3	38.6%	20	$1,420.8	$2,217.6	$29,598	49/4
58. Texas Woman's University	61	3.5	69.1%	N/A	2.4	N/A	242	$363.7	$4,149.0	$688*	31/819
58. University of California–Davis	61	3.5	56.7%	3.54	2.7	N/A	29	$1,853.7	$347.6	$39,392	65/N/A
58. Univ. of South Carolina	61	3.4	81.5%	3.55	2.2	77.2%	31	$1,849.3	$588.4	$1,304*	101/119
58. Villanova University (PA)	61	3.7	85.8%	3.57	2.6	97.1%	64	$133.1	$732.5	$837*	142/108
58. Virginia Commonwealth University	61	3.7	53.8%	3.50	1.8	20.2%	99	$969.3	$500.0	$28,536	75/147
68. CUNY–Hunter College (NY)	59	3.4	47.2%	3.55	2.8	81.8%	53	$318.0	$373.0	$20,179	3/492
68. Northeastern University (MA)	59	3.4	42.0%	3.48	3.1	8.3%	92	$3,053.8	$1,477.7	$1,335*	225/106
70. South Dakota State University	58	3.0	40.8%	3.65	4.8	66.7%	12	$623.9	$1,321.6	$582*	8/62
70. St. John Fisher College (NY)	58	3.0	50.0%	3.40	2.3	100.0%	25	$1,012.2	$670.5	$860*	7/129
70. Thomas Jefferson University (PA)	58	3.3	54.7%	3.40	3.7	100.0%	182	N/A	$975.6	$1,075*	46/384
70. U. of Texas Medical Branch–Galveston	58	3.3	27.3%	N/A	4.0	19.7%	169	$1,568.8	$1,562.8	$675*	110/381
70. Wayne State University (MI)	58	3.4	18.3%	N/A	1.3	41.2%	108	$100.7	$3,534.3	$1,463*	50/91
75. Texas Tech U. Health Sciences Center	57	3.3	33.8%	N/A	1.4	18.2%	152	$4,488.2	$1,663.5	$6,590	7/498
75. University at Buffalo–SUNY (NY)	57	3.3	62.5%	N/A	0.1	57.9%	7	$342.7	$787.9	$24,505	N/A/8
75. University of Texas–Arlington	57	3.0	57.0%	3.60	12.3	81.1%	291	$1,415.9	$498.5	$17,865	72/1,842
78. The Catholic University of America (DC)	56	3.5	65.8%	3.30	1.7	N/A	12	N/A	$1,200.0	$41,800	27/94
78. Mercer University (GA)	56	3.1	70.5%	3.52	2.1	33.3%	N/A	$1,100.0	$800.0	$29,784	62/26
78. St. Louis University (MO)	56	3.4	69.0%	3.60	3.3	100.0%	124	N/A	$316.2	$1,050*	210/127
78. University of Colorado–Colorado Springs	56	3.4	55.7%	N/A	4.8	38.9%	39	$1,067.9	N/A	$20,668	11/151
78. University of Wisconsin–Milwaukee	56	3.6	84.0%	3.32	1.2	24.3%	16	$1,015.3	$497.9	$25,855	103/4
78. U. of Oklahoma Health Sciences Center	56	3.6	46.1%	3.19	1.2	27.3%	88	$319.8	$4,823.7	$835*	52/149
84. George Mason University (VA)	55	3.2	48.1%	3.55	0.9	80.2%	48	N/A	$1,557.8	$1,260*	18/98
85. Duquesne University (PA)	54	3.3	81.9%	3.47	1.8	59.3%	39	$417.0	$382.4	$1,218*	91/87
85. Samford University (AL)	54	3.3	72.3%	3.20	6.0	71.7%	116	$39.5	$2,796.0	$785*	276/N/A
85. University of Detroit Mercy (MI)	54	3.4	25.0%	N/A	2.5	58.7%	61	$522.0	$450.0	$925*	72/132
83. Auburn University (AL)	53	3.2	56.6%	3.54	2.7	100.0%	32	N/A	N/A	$28,022	13/107
88. East Carolina University (NC)	53	3.1	67.5%	3.17	1.6	30.6%	181	$994.6	$3,696.3	$960*	59/308
88. SUNY Downstate Medical Center (NY)	53	3.1	23.4%	3.50	14.9	100.0%	62	$571.7	N/A	$22,344	126/84
88. University of Louisville (KY)	53	3.3	69.8%	3.34	1.7	46.0%	50	$1,626.8	$336.0	$24,470	90/22
88. University of Michigan–Flint	53	3.3	N/A	N/A	0.4	81.3%	16	$100.0	$3,006.9	$14,751	12/1
88. U. of Texas Health Sci. Ctr.–San Antonio	53	3.6	36.9%	3.40	1.4	28.5%	109	$25.0	$1,763.0	$23,489	109/87
88. Xavier University (OH)	53	3.1	85.6%	3.56	2.3	75.7%	70	$392.0	$1,461.2	N/A	61/166
95. Augusta University (GA)	52	3.2	37.1%	3.45	5.2	63.8%	162	$270.2	$358.7	$1,198*	311/16
95. Stony Brook University–SUNY (NY)	52	3.1	57.8%	N/A	7.2	35.9%	152	$135.0	$2,038.4	$23,761	10/788
95. University of Alabama–Huntsville	52	3.4	90.0%	3.33	2.6	20.7%	80	$456.4	$456.4	$1,500*	73/174
98. West Virginia University	50	3.0	83.1%	3.49	3.6	57.7%	44	$742.2	N/A	$23,256	53/67
99. Brigham Young University (UT)	49	3.3	31.9%	3.73	0.7	73.6%	14	N/A	N/A	$764*	30/N/A
99. Seattle University (WA)	49	3.3	21.2%	N/A	3.0	97.1%	57	N/A	N/A	$690*	190/N/A
99. University of Missouri–St. Louis	49	3.3	55.1%	3.64	1.1	51.7%	55	$54.2	$747.0	$1,049*	2/200
99. University of North Carolina–Greensboro	49	3.1	84.4%	N/A	1.7	72.6%	N/A	N/A	$1,761.2	$16,484	89/50
99. University of Portland (OR)	49	3.5	100.0%	3.65	0.6	50.0%	4	$5.0	N/A	$685*	8/N/A

THE TOP SCHOOLS - MASTER'S continued

Rank	School	Overall score	Peer assessment score (5.0=highest)	'15 master's acceptance rate	'15 mean full-time undergrad GPA (master's)	'15 master's student/ faculty ratio	'15 percent of faculty in active nursing practice	'15 master's degrees awarded	'15 NIH and all other research grants (in thousands)	'15 NIH and all other teaching and practice grants (in thousands)	'15 out-of-state tuition and fees	'15 master's program enrollment full-/part-time
104.	Pace University (NY)	48	3.3	66.3%	N/A	1.9	80.2%	131	$130.4	$88.1	$1,150*	2/366
104.	University of Hawaii–Manoa	48	3.0	76.9%	3.29	1.7	38.7%	56	$314.7	$2,731.5	$1,770*	105/57
104.	University of Massachusetts–Lowell	48	3.2	56.3%	3.55	1.1	88.0%	35	$83.2	N/A	$18,587	22/48
104.	University of Southern Indiana	48	3.0	76.4%	3.60	5.2	73.0%	108	N/A	$627.3	$438*	104/323
104.	University of Vermont	48	3.0	100.0%	3.90	1.8	86.7%	25	N/A	$281.6	$1,544*	40/8
109.	Loyola University New Orleans (LA)	47	3.2	88.6%	3.17	15.4	100.0%	139	N/A	$22.3	$818*	271/79
109.	Montana State University	47	3.1	100.0%	N/A	0.1	N/A	10	$830.2	$1,007.2	$892*	N/A/17
109.	Texas Christian University	47	3.3	80.0%	3.27	1.0	75.0%	33	$10.8	$628.0	$1,415*	55/14
109.	University of Central Florida	47	3.2	60.9%	3.42	1.4	38.4%	90	$2,052.1	$41.0	$1,194*	31/180
113.	East Tennessee State University	46	3.1	76.9%	3.61	2.2	100.0%	58	N/A	N/A	$1,292*	58/270
114.	Binghamton University–SUNY (NY)	45	3.0	84.5%	3.55	1.7	47.5%	61	$367.0	$500.0	$24,061	61/64
114.	Fairfield University (CT)	45	3.2	56.6%	N/A	0.7	5.1%	12	N/A	$492.0	$850*	N/A/101
114.	Mississippi University for Women	45	2.9	38.9%	3.45	4.6	100.0%	38	N/A	N/A	$16,142	33/2
114.	University of North Carolina–Charlotte	45	3.2	21.1%	3.38	3.7	23.7%	112	$522.0	$335.0	$19,703	133/77
118.	Indiana State University	44	3.0	74.7%	N/A	2.0	93.1%	58	N/A	N/A	$485*	N/A/241
118.	Shenandoah University (VA)	44	2.6	78.8%	3.04	1.1	97.2%	32	N/A	$1,325.1	$830	24/35
118.	University of Saint Francis (IN)	44	2.7	90.5%	3.72	4.8	100.0%	33	N/A	$350.0	$870*	45/58
121.	Robert Morris University (PA)	43	2.9	71.4%	N/A	0.5	89.2%	10	N/A	$325.0	N/A	N/A/69
121.	University of Indianapolis (IN)	43	3.3	87.2%	N/A	1.5	17.9%	77	N/A	N/A	N/A	N/A/277
121.	University of Tennessee–Chattanooga	43	3.1	24.4%	N/A	2.6	96.3%	41	N/A	N/A	$1,589*	65/N/A
124.	Hawaii Pacific University	42	2.8	74.4%	3.43	4.6	91.7%	20	N/A	N/A	$1,275*	36/20
124.	Monmouth University (NJ)	42	2.5	98.8%	3.28	5.9	83.3%	68	$148.0	N/A	$1,047*	14/240
124.	Notre Dame of Maryland University	42	2.9	95.7%	N/A	2.0	75.0%	40	N/A	N/A	$626*	19/90
124.	University of St. Francis (IL)	42	2.7	41.8%	3.37	13.9	78.3%	99	N/A	$581.7	N/A	70/303
128.	Alverno College (WI)	41	'3.1	94.5%	3.39	11.3	50.0%	33	N/A	N/A	N/A	102/100
128.	Creighton University (NE)	41	3.4	100.0%	N/A	1.1	50.0%	54	$234.2	$25.0	$800*	42/63
128.	Georgia Southern University	41	3.0	N/A	N/A	0.6	52.5%	19	$8.5	$1,588.8	$1,105*	18/N/A
128.	St. Xavier University (IL)	41	3.0	52.8%	3.23	6.1	44.1%	92	N/A	$686.9	$690*	145/134
128.	University of Massachusetts–Dartmouth	41	3.3	100.0%	3.32	0.2	N/A	4	N/A	N/A	$20,727	N/A/27

SPECIALTIES

ADMINISTRATION
1. Johns Hopkins University (MD)
1. University of Pennsylvania
3. University of Iowa
4. U. of North Carolina–Chapel Hill
5. University of Maryland–Baltimore
6. University of Alabama–Birmingham
6. University of Michigan–Ann Arbor

CLINICAL NURSE LEADER
1. University of Maryland–Baltimore
2. University of Virginia
3. Rush University (IL)
4. University of Pittsburgh (PA)

INFORMATICS
1. University of Maryland–Baltimore
2. University of Minnesota–Twin Cities
3. Duke University (NC)
4. Vanderbilt University (TN)
5. Columbia University (NY)

6. New York University
6. University of Colorado

NURSE PRACTITIONER
ADULT / GERONTOLOGY, ACUTE CARE
1. University of Pennsylvania
2. Johns Hopkins University (MD)
3. Vanderbilt University (TN)
4. Rush University (IL)
5. University of Pittsburgh (PA)
6. Columbia University (NY)
6. Duke University (NC)

NURSE PRACTITIONER
ADULT / GERONTOLOGY, PRIMARY CARE
1. University of Pennsylvania
2. Johns Hopkins University (MD)
2. New York University
4. Rush University (IL)
5. University of Washington
6. University of California–San Francisco

6. Vanderbilt University (TN)
8. University of Maryland–Baltimore

NURSE PRACTITIONER
FAMILY
1. University of Washington
2. Duke University (NC)
2. University of Pennsylvania
4. Johns Hopkins University (MD)
5. University of California–San Francisco
5. Vanderbilt University (TN)
7. University of Illinois–Chicago
8. University of Maryland–Baltimore
9. Rush University (IL)
10. Columbia University (NY)
10. Emory University (GA)
10. University of North Carolina–Chapel Hill

NURSE PRACTITIONER
PEDIATRIC, PRIMARY CARE
1. University of Pennsylvania

2. Johns Hopkins University (MD)
3. University of California–San Francisco
4. Vanderbilt University (TN)
5. Duke University (NC)
5. Rush University (IL)
5. Yale University (CT)
8. University of Colorado

NURSE PRACTITIONER
PSYCHIATRIC / MENTAL HEALTH, ACROSS THE LIFESPAN
1. University of Pennsylvania
2. Rush University (IL)
3. Vanderbilt University (TN)
4. University of California–San Francisco
5. University of Washington
6. Yale University (CT)
7. New York University
7. University of Virginia

The University of
Texas–Austin, No. 17

METHODOLOGY

Programs at the 519 nursing schools with master's or doctoral programs accredited in late summer 2015 by either the Commission on Collegiate Nursing Education or the Accreditation Commission for Education in Nursing were surveyed; 259 responded and were eligible to be included in the rankings of master's programs based on a weighted average of 14 indicators described below.

Quality assessment: One survey was conducted in the fall of 2015. Nursing school deans and deans of graduate studies at nursing schools were asked to rate the quality of master's programs from marginal (1) to outstanding (5); 32 percent responded. The resulting peer assessment score is weighted by .40 in the overall score.

Student selectivity and master's program size (weighted by .1125): The strength of full-time and part-time nursing students entering master's programs in the fall of 2015 was measured by their mean undergraduate grade point average (.05 percent of this measure), and the acceptance rate of master's students in fall 2015 (.0125). Size was measured by the percent of the fall 2015 total full-time and part-time graduate nursing program's enrollment that was in the master's program (.0125); and by the number of master's degrees awarded for the 2015 graduating class (.0375).

Faculty resources (.2375): This score is based on the 2015 ratio of full-time equivalent master's students to full-time equivalent faculty (.05), the proportion of 2015 full-time faculty with doctoral degrees (.05); the proportion of total full- and part-time faculty who were members or fellows in the fall of 2015 of a list of 19 organizations provided by the American Association of

Colleges of Nursing including: the National Academy of Medicine, the National Institutes of Health, the American Academy of Nursing, and the American Association of Nurse Practitioners (.0375); the proportion of 2015 total full- and part-time faculty in active nursing practice (.075); and the number of 2015 master's degrees in nursing awarded per full-time equivalent faculty member in the past school year (.025).

Research activity (.25): Based on total dollar amount of National Institutes of Health and other federal and nonfederal research grants to the nursing school (.075); average NIH and other federal and nonfederal research grants per full-time equivalent nursing faculty member (.05); total dollar amount of NIH and other non-NIH nursing educational and practice initiative grants to the nursing school (.075); and average NIH

and other non-NIH nursing educational and practice initiative grants per full-time equivalent nursing faculty member (.05). NIH and other federal and nonfederal research grants and all educational and practice initiative grants awarded to the nursing school are for fiscal year 2015.

Overall rank: Data were standardized about their means, and standardized scores were weighted, totaled and rescaled so the top-scoring school received 100; others received their percentage of the top score.

Specialty rankings: These rankings are based solely on assessments by nursing school deans and deans of graduate studies who identified up to 10 schools offering the best programs in each specialty area. The top half of ranked programs (based on the number of nominations received) appear.

BRETT ZIEGLER FOR USN&WR

Health Disciplines

SCHOOLS RANKED BEST BY PROGRAM DIRECTORS AND FACULTY

AUDIOLOGY

DOCTORATE Ranked in 2016

Rank	School	Average assessment score (5.0=highest)
1.	Vanderbilt University (TN)	4.6
2.	University of Iowa	4.3
3.	Washington University in St. Louis (MO)	4.1
4.	University of North Carolina–Chapel Hill	4.0
4.	University of Texas–Dallas	4.0
4.	University of Washington	4.0
7.	Northwestern University (IL)	3.7
7.	University of Pittsburgh (PA)	3.7
9.	Arizona State University	3.6
9.	Ohio State University	3.6
9.	Rush University Medical Center (IL)	3.6
9.	University of Arizona	3.6
13.	Indiana University–Bloomington	3.5
13.	Purdue University–West Lafayette (IN)	3.5
13.	University of Minnesota–Twin Cities	3.5
13.	University of Texas–Austin	3.5
17.	James Madison University (VA)	3.4
17.	University at Buffalo–SUNY (NY)	3.4
17.	University of Colorado–Boulder	3.4
17.	University of Maryland–College Park	3.4
17.	University of Memphis (TN)	3.4
17.	University of South Florida	3.4
17.	University of Wisconsin AuD Consortium	3.4

CLINICAL PSYCHOLOGY

DOCTORATE Ranked in 2016

Rank	School	Average assessment score (5.0=highest)
1.	University of California–Los Angeles	4.7
2.	University of California–Berkeley	4.5
2.	University of North Carolina–Chapel Hill	4.5
4.	Stony Brook University–SUNY (NY)	4.4
4.	University of Minnesota–Twin Cities	4.4
4.	University of Wisconsin–Madison	4.4
4.	Yale University (CT)	4.4
8.	University of Texas–Austin	4.3
8.	University of Virginia	4.3
8.	University of Washington	4.3
11.	Duke University (NC)	4.2
11.	Emory University (GA)	4.2
11.	Univ. of Illinois–Urbana-Champaign	4.2
11.	University of Pennsylvania	4.2
11.	University of Pittsburgh (PA)	4.2
16.	Harvard University (MA)	4.1
16.	Indiana University–Bloomington	4.1

Rank	School	Average assessment score (5.0=highest)
16.	Northwestern University (IL)	4.1
16.	University of Colorado–Boulder	4.1
16.	University of Michigan–Ann Arbor	4.1
16.	University of Southern California	4.1
16.	U. of Kansas (Clin. Child Psych. Prog.)	4.1
16.	Vanderbilt University (TN)	4.1
16.	Washington University in St. Louis	4.1
25.	Penn. State University–University Park	4.0
25.	San Diego State Univ. - U. of Calif.–SD (CA)	4.0
25.	Temple University (PA)	4.0
25.	University of Iowa	4.0
25.	University of Miami (FL)	4.0
25.	University of Oregon	4.0
31.	Boston University (MA)	3.9
31.	University of Arizona	3.9
31.	University of Florida	3.9
31.	University of Kansas	3.9
31.	University of Maryland–College Park	3.9

HEALTH CARE MANAGEMENT

MASTER'S Ranked in 2015

Rank	School	Average assessment score (5.0=highest)
1.	University of Michigan–Ann Arbor	4.4
2.	University of Alabama–Birmingham	4.3
3.	University of Minnesota–Twin Cities	4.2
3.	Virginia Commonwealth University	4.2
5.	Rush University (IL)	4.0
5.	University of North Carolina–Chapel Hill	4.0
7.	Johns Hopkins University (MD)	3.6
7.	St. Louis University	3.6
7.	U.S. Army-Baylor University (TX)	3.6
10.	Northwestern University (Kellogg) (IL)	3.5
10.	Ohio State University	3.5
10.	Trinity University (TX)	3.5
10.	University of Iowa	3.5
10.	University of Washington	3.5
15.	Cornell University (Sloan) (NY)	3.4
15.	University of California–Los Angeles	3.4
17.	George Washington University (DC)	3.3
18.	Baylor University (TX)	3.2
18.	Boston University	3.2
18.	Medical University of South Carolina	3.2
18.	New York University	3.2
18.	U. of Col.–Denver/Network for Hlthcare Mgmt.	3.2
23.	Columbia University (NY)	3.1
23.	Georgetown University (DC)	3.1

Rank	School	Average assessment score (5.0=highest)
23.	Tulane University (LA)	3.1
23.	University of Colorado–Denver	3.1
23.	University of Southern California	3.1

NURSE ANESTHESIA

MASTER'S/DOCTORATE Ranked in 2016

Rank	School	Average assessment score (5.0=highest)
1.	Virginia Commonwealth University	4.0
2.	Baylor College of Medicine (TX)	3.8
3.	Duke University (NC)	3.7
4.	Kaiser Perm. Sch. of Anesth.-Cal. St. U.–Fullerton	3.6
4.	Rush University (IL)	3.6
4.	Uniformed Svces U. of the Hlth. Sci. (MD)	3.6
4.	University of Pittsburgh (PA)	3.6
8.	U. of Texas Health Science Ctr.–Houston	3.5
8.	U.S. Army Grad Prog., Anesth. Nursing (TX)	3.5
10.	Georgetown University (DC)	3.4
10.	Mayo School of Health Sciences (MN)	3.4
10.	University at Buffalo–SUNY (NY)	3.4
10.	University of Detroit Mercy (MI)	3.4
10.	University of Iowa	3.4
10.	University of Maryland–Baltimore	3.4
10.	University of Southern California	3.4
10.	Wake Forest Baptist Hlth.-WF Sch. of Med. (NC)	3.4
18.	Goldfarb Sch. of Nursing, Barnes-Jewish	3.3
18.	Oakland University–Beaumont (MI)	3.3
18.	Sacred Heart Medical Ctr. - Gonzaga U (WA)	3.3
18.	Samuel Merritt University (CA)	3.3

Note: All schools have either a master's or a doctoral program.

NURSE MIDWIFERY

MASTER'S/DOCTORATE Ranked in 2016

Rank	School	Average assessment score (5.0=highest)
1.	UC–San Francisco/S.F. General Hospital	4.2
1.	University of Michigan–Ann Arbor	4.2
1.	Vanderbilt University (TN)	4.2
4.	Oregon Health and Science University	4.0
4.	University of Minnesota–Twin Cities	4.0
4.	Yale University (CT)	4.0
7.	University of New Mexico	3.9
7.	University of Pennsylvania	3.9
9.	University of Utah	3.8
10.	Baylor University (TX)	3.7
10.	University of Illinois–Chicago	3.7

Note: All schools have either a master's or a doctoral program; some have both.

More @ usnews.com/grad

OCCUPATIONAL THERAPY

MASTER'S/DOCTORATE Ranked in 2016

Rank School	Average assessment score (5.0=highest)
1. Boston University (Sargent) (MA)	4.6
1. Washington University in St. Louis	4.6
3. University of Southern California	4.5
4. University of Illinois–Chicago	4.3
4. University of Pittsburgh (PA)	4.3
6. Colorado State University	4.1
6. Thomas Jefferson University (PA)	4.1
6. Tufts U.–Boston Sch. of Occup. Therapy (MA)	4.1
9. University of Kansas Medical Center	4.0
9. University of North Carolina–Chapel Hill	4.0
11. Columbia University (NY)	3.9
12. New York University	3.8
12. Ohio State University	3.8
14. University of Washington	3.7
14. University of Wisconsin–Madison	3.7
14. U. of Texas Medical Branch–Galveston	3.7
17. Medical University of South Carolina	3.6
17. Texas Woman's University	3.6
17. University of Florida	3.6
17. University of Wisconsin–Milwaukee	3.6
17. Virginia Commonwealth University	3.6

Note: All schools listed have master's programs; some may not have doctoral programs.

PHARMACY

PHARM.D. Ranked in 2016

Rank School	Average assessment score (5.0=highest)
1. University of North Carolina–Chapel Hill	4.7
2. University of Minnesota	4.5
3. University of California–San Francisco	4.4
3. University of Michigan–Ann Arbor	4.4
3. University of Texas–Austin	4.4
6. Ohio State University	4.2
6. University of Illinois–Chicago	4.2
6. University of Kentucky	4.2
9. Purdue University (IN)	4.1
9. University of Florida	4.1
9. University of Maryland–Baltimore	4.1
9. University of Pittsburgh (PA)	4.1
9. University of Southern California	4.1
9. University of Washington	4.1
9. University of Wisconsin–Madison	4.1
16. University of Arizona	4.0
17. University of Iowa	3.9
17. University of Utah	3.9
17. U. of Tennessee Health Science Center	3.9
17. Virginia Commonwealth University	3.9
21. University of Kansas	3.8
22. University at Buffalo–SUNY (NY)	3.7
22. University of Colorado–Denver	3.7

PHYSICAL THERAPY

MASTER'S/DOCTORATE Ranked in 2016

Rank School	Average assessment score (5.0=highest)
1. University of Delaware	4.3
1. University of Pittsburgh (PA)	4.3
1. University of Southern California	4.3
1. Washington University in St. Louis	4.3
5. Emory University (GA)	4.1
6. Northwestern University (IL)	4.0
6. University of Iowa	4.0
8. MGH Inst. of Health Professions (MA)	3.8
8. U.S. Army-Baylor University (TX)	3.8
10. Duke University (NC)	3.7
10. Ohio State University	3.7
10. University of Florida	3.7
10. University of Miami (FL)	3.7
14. Boston University (MA)	3.6
15. Creighton University (NE)	3.5
15. Marquette University (WI)	3.5
15. University of Colorado–Denver	3.5
15. University of Illinois–Chicago	3.5
15. University of North Carolina–Chapel Hill	3.5
20. Arcadia University (PA)	3.4
20. Mayo Sch. of Hlth. Related Sciences (MN)	3.4
20. University of Alabama–Birmingham	3.4
20. University of Kansas Medical Center	3.4
20. University of Minnesota–Twin Cities	3.4
20. University of Utah	3.4
20. Univ. of Calif.–San Francisco - SF State U.	3.4
20. Virginia Commonwealth University	3.4

Note: All schools have a doctoral program and may have a master's.

PHYSICIAN ASSISTANT

MASTER'S Ranked in 2015

Rank School	Average assessment score (5.0=highest)
1. Duke University (NC)	4.4
2. University of Iowa	4.3
3. Emory University (GA)	4.1
3. George Washington University (DC)	4.1
5. Oregon Health and Sciences University	4.0
5. Quinnipiac University (CT)	4.0
5. University of Colorado–Denver	4.0
5. University of Utah	4.0
9. University of Nebraska Medical Center	3.9
9. Wake Forest University (NC)	3.9
11. Interservice Physician Asst. Prog. (TX)	3.8
11. University of Washington	3.8
13. Baylor College of Medicine (TX)	3.7
13. Drexel University (PA)	3.7
15. U. of Texas Southwest. Med. Ctr.–Dallas	3.6
16. Rutgers Biomedical and Health Sci. (NJ)	3.5
16. Shenandoah University (VA)	3.5
16. Stony Brook University–SUNY	3.5

Rank School	Average assessment score (5.0=highest)
16. University of Alabama–Birmingham	3.5
20. Midwestern University (IL)	3.4
20. Midwestern University (AZ)	3.4
20. Northeastern University (MA)	3.4
20. Rosalind Franklin U. of Med. and Sci. (IL)	3.4
20. University of Southern California (Keck)	3.4
20. Yale University (CT)	3.4

PUBLIC HEALTH

MASTER'S/DOCTORATE Ranked in 2015

Rank School	Average assessment score (5.0=highest)
1. Johns Hopkins University (MD)	4.8
2. Harvard University (MA)	4.7
2. University of North Carolina–Chapel Hill	4.7
4. University of Michigan–Ann Arbor	4.5
5. Columbia University (NY)	4.4
6. University of Washington	4.2
7. Emory University (GA)	4.1
8. University of Minnesota–Twin Cities	4.0
9. University of California–Berkeley	3.9
10. Boston University	3.6
10. University of California–Los Angeles	3.6
12. Tulane University (LA)	3.5
13. University of Pittsburgh	3.4
14. George Washington University (DC)	3.2
14. Yale University (CT)	3.2
16. University of South Florida	3.1
17. University of Illinois–Chicago	3.0
17. University of Iowa	3.0
19. Ohio State University	2.9
19. University of Alabama–Birmingham	2.9
21. U. of Texas–Houston Health Sciences Ctr.	2.8
22. University of Maryland–College Park	2.7
23. St. Louis University	2.6
23. University of South Carolina	2.6

Note: All schools listed have master's programs; some may not have doctoral programs.

REHABILITATION COUNSELING

MASTER'S/DOCTORATE Ranked in 2015

Rank School	Average assessment score (5.0=highest)
1. Michigan State University	4.5
1. University of Wisconsin–Madison	4.5
3. University of Iowa	4.2
4. Southern Illinois University–Carbondale	4.0
4. Virginia Commonwealth University	4.0
6. George Washington University (DC)	3.8
6. Penn. State University–University Park	3.8
6. University of Arizona	3.8
6. University of Kentucky	3.8
10. San Diego State University	3.7

REHABILITATION COUNSELING Continued

Rank	School	Average assessment score (5.0=highest)
10.	University of Wisconsin–Stout	3.7
10.	Utah State University	3.7
13.	Illinois Institute of Technology	3.5
13.	University of Arkansas–Fayetteville	3.5
15.	University of Northern Colorado	3.4
15.	University of North Texas	3.4
15.	University of Texas–Pan American	3.4
18.	East Carolina University (NC)	3.3
18.	Portland State University (OR)	3.3
18.	University of Pittsburgh	3.3
21.	University at Buffalo–SUNY	3.2
21.	University of Memphis	3.2
21.	University of North Carolina–Chapel Hill	3.2

Note: All schools listed have master's programs; some may not have doctoral programs.

SOCIAL WORK

MASTER'S Ranked in 2016

Rank	School	Average assessment score (5.0=highest)
1.	University of Michigan–Ann Arbor	4.5
2.	Washington University in St. Louis	4.4
3.	University of California–Berkeley	4.3
3.	University of Chicago (IL)	4.3
3.	University of Washington	4.3
6.	Columbia University (NY)	4.2
7.	University of North Carolina–Chapel Hill	4.1
7.	University of Texas–Austin	4.1
9.	Case Western Reserve University (OH)	4.0
10.	Boston College (MA)	3.9
10.	University of Pittsburgh (PA)	3.9
12.	Boston University (MA)	3.8
12.	University of California–Los Angeles	3.8
12.	University of Pennsylvania	3.8
12.	University of Southern California	3.8

Rank	School	Average assessment score (5.0=highest)
12.	University of Wisconsin–Madison	3.8
17.	New York University	3.7
17.	Ohio State University	3.7
17.	University of Denver (CO)	3.7
17.	Univ. of Illinois–Urbana-Champaign	3.7
17.	University of Maryland–Baltimore	3.7
22.	Fordham University (NY)	3.6
22.	Rutgers University–New Brunswick (NJ)	3.6
22.	Smith College (MA)	3.6
22.	University of Kansas	3.6
22.	Virginia Commonwealth University	3.6

SPEECH–LANGUAGE PATHOLOGY

MASTER'S Ranked in 2016

Rank	School	Average assessment score (5.0=highest)
1.	University of Iowa	4.5
1.	Vanderbilt University (TN)	4.5
3.	University of Washington	4.4
3.	University of Wisconsin–Madison	4.4
5.	Northwestern University (IL)	4.3
5.	Purdue University–West Lafayette (IN)	4.3
7.	MGH Institute of Health Professions (MA)	4.1
7.	University of Arizona	4.1
7.	University of Kansas	4.1
7.	University of Pittsburgh (PA)	4.1
7.	University of Texas–Austin	4.1
12.	Boston University (MA)	4.0
12.	Indiana University	4.0
12.	University of North Carolina–Chapel Hill	4.0
12.	University of Texas–Dallas	4.0
16.	University of Minnesota–Twin Cities	3.9
17.	Arizona State University	3.8
17.	Ohio State University	3.8
17.	Univ. of Illinois–Urbana-Champaign	3.8
20.	Emerson College (MA)	3.7

Rank	School	Average assessment score (5.0=highest)
20.	Penn. State University–University Park	3.7
20.	University of Maryland–College Park	3.7
20.	University of Nebraska–Lincoln	3.7
24.	Rush University Medical Center (IL)	3.6
24.	San Diego State University (CA)	3.6
24.	University of Colorado–Boulder	3.6
24.	University of Memphis (TN)	3.6
28.	Florida State University	3.5
28.	University of Florida	3.5
30.	Northeastern University (MA)	3.4
30.	Syracuse University (NY)	3.4
30.	Teachers College, Columbia Univ. (NY)	3.4
30.	Temple University (PA)	3.4
30.	University at Buffalo–SUNY (NY)	3.4
30.	University of Connecticut	3.4
30.	University of North Carolina–Greensboro	3.4
30.	University of South Carolina	3.4
30.	University of Utah	3.4

VETERINARY MEDICINE

DOCTOR OF VETERINARY MEDICINE
Ranked in 2015

Rank	School	Average assessment score (5.0=highest)
1.	University of California–Davis	4.5
2.	Cornell University (NY)	4.1
3.	Colorado State University	3.9
3.	North Carolina State University	3.9
5.	Ohio State University	3.7
5.	University of Wisconsin–Madison	3.7
7.	Texas A&M University–College Station	3.6
7.	University of Pennsylvania	3.6
9.	University of Minnesota–Twin Cities	3.4
10.	Tufts University (MA)	3.3
10.	University of Georgia	3.3
12.	Michigan State University	3.2
13.	Iowa State University	3.1

METHODOLOGY

The health rankings are based solely on the results of peer assessment surveys sent to deans, other administrators, and/or faculty at accredited degree programs or schools in each discipline. Respondents rated the academic quality of programs on a 5-point scale: outstanding (5 points), strong (4), good (3), adequate (2), or marginal (1). They were instructed to select "don't know" if they did not have enough knowledge to rate a program.

Only fully accredited programs in good standing during the survey period are ranked. Those with the highest average scores appear.

In the fall of 2015, surveys were conducted for the 2016 rankings of doctor of pharmacy programs accredited by the Accreditation Council for Pharmacy Education (response rate: 40 percent); doctoral programs in clinical psychology accredited by the American Psychological Association (21 percent); graduate programs in occupational therapy accredited by the American Occupational Therapy Association (42 percent); audiology programs and speech-language pathology programs accredited by the American Speech-Language-Hearing Association (58 percent and 33 percent, respectively); physical therapy programs accredited by the Commission on Accreditation in Physical Therapy Education (39 percent); master of social work programs accredited by the Commission on Accreditation of the Council on Social Work Education (51 percent); graduate programs in nurse midwifery accredited by the Accreditation Commission for Midwifery Education (62 percent); and graduate programs in nurse anesthesia accredited by the Council on Accreditation of Nurse Anesthesia Educational Programs (54 percent).

In the fall of 2014, surveys were conducted for 2015 rankings of schools of public health accredited by the Council on Education for Public Health (response rate: 59 percent); health care management programs accredited by the Commission on Accreditation of Healthcare Management Education (57 percent); physician assistant programs accredited by the Accreditation Review Commission on Education for the Physician Assistant (50 percent); rehabilitation counselor education programs accredited by the Commission on Standards and Accreditation: Council on Rehabilitation Education (38 percent); and veterinary schools accredited by the American Veterinary Medical Association (49 percent).

Surveys for both sets of rankings were conducted by research firm Ipsos Public Affairs.

MAKE A DIFFERENCE

The Colorado State Doctor of Veterinary Medicine Program offers exceptional veterinary teaching, based on world-class research and compassionate clinical care – all in colorful Colorado. Our veterinary school consistently ranks in the top three in the nation, according to *U.S. News & World Report*.

www.cvmbs.colostate.edu
dvmadmissions@colostate.edu
970.491.7051

Colorado State University
COLLEGE OF VETERINARY MEDICINE
AND BIOMEDICAL SCIENCES

ACADEMIC INSIGHTS
YOUR SCHOOL BY THE NUMBERS

Designed for schools, U.S. News Academic Insights provides instant access to a rich historical archive of undergraduate and graduate school rankings data.

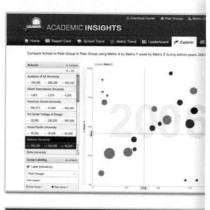

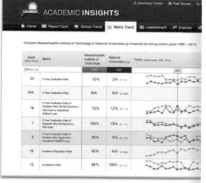

Advanced Visualizations
Take complex data and turn it into six easily understandable and exportable views.

Download Center
Export large data sets from the new Download Center to create custom reports.

Dedicated Account Management
Have access to full analyst support for training, troubleshooting and advanced reporting.

Peer-Group Analysis
Flexibility to create your own peer groups to compare your institution on more than 5 M + data points.

Historical Trending
Find out how institutions have performed over time based on more than 350 metrics.

To request a demo visit **AI.USNEWS.COM**   or call **202.955.2121**

The *REST* *of the* RANKINGS

At California Institute of Technology

DAVID BUTOW – REDUX FOR USN&WR

THE U.S. NEWS RANKINGS

Choosing the Arts

Is an advanced degree a wise investment for artists? Here are some trade-offs they should consider

By **ELIZABETH GARDNER**

>>> **The decision to get a** master's degree in an artistic field can be a fraught one. If you're good, after all, you should be able to make it without one, right? And you're already looking at a high probability of living in relative poverty (at least compared with MBAs and techies), so why make matters worse with thousands in debt? The occasional superstar notwithstanding, government data puts median annual earnings at around $44,000 for "fine artists" – including painters, sculptors and illustrators – and at about $30,000 for photographers. Choreographers earn $44,250, producers and directors about $69,000. Uncle Sam doesn't even bother trying to estimate earnings for actors and dancers, and doesn't break out "novelist" or "poet" among writing occupations. Architects ($74,520) and graphic designers ($46,000) may enjoy more job opportunities and better earning power, but a steep investment in a graduate degree can still be a tough call.

"It's a big responsibility to put young people out in the world following this track, and it weighs on you as a professor," says Mary Ellen Strom, who teaches courses in video and directs the MFA program at the School of the Museum of Fine Arts in Boston, where tuition runs $42,000. While several members of the class of 2015 landed tenure-track teaching positions at major universities, would-be professors should know that most academic openings are for adjuncts, instructors, and other part-time or temporary teachers. Some students develop their own studios and exhibit in galleries and museums; others have started creative agencies, curated exhibitions, or worked as studio assistants to established artists.

"It's always a debate whether to get a degree or just go and do it," agrees Patti Phillips, dean of graduate studies at Rhode Island School of Design in Providence, where tuition tops $45,000 per year.

Despite the less-than-terrific earnings potential, graduate programs in artistic fields are enjoying relatively healthy growth. More than 17,000 master's degrees in the visual and performing arts were awarded in 2012 (the most recent data available), for example, according to the National Center for Education Statistics – 2.5 times more than were earned in 1970. Arts master's haven't enjoyed the meteoric growth of health care (up 16 times), business (seven times) or psychology (five times), but they're surpassing other labors of love like English literature or library science (both virtually flat). RISD's 18 art and design grad programs, which run the gamut from sculpture to jewelry and metalsmithing to landscape architecture, are having a banner year, with a record 470 enrolled last fall.

There's no doubt that such aptitudes can translate into interesting and perhaps even lucrative careers as long as you're willing to create in diverse and unexpected places: anywhere from Fortune 500 companies to Etsy. Do-it-yourself career

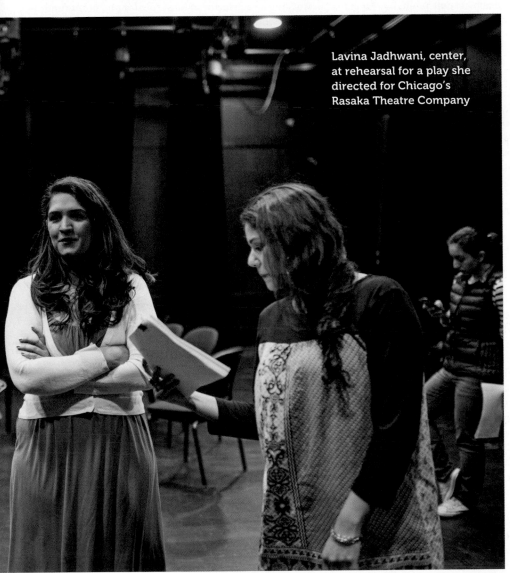

Lavina Jadhwani, center, at rehearsal for a play she directed for Chicago's Rasaka Theatre Company

paths – a staple of artists for millennia – have received a huge boost from the Internet. A 2015 New York Times Magazine cover story was enthusiastic about the opportunities to monetize artistic output via the multitude of outlets that didn't exist as recently as 10 years ago: e-books, YouTube channels and streaming services, for instance.

"The MFA is the new MBA," was author Daniel Pink's perhaps hyperbolic catchphrase in his 2005 bestseller "A Whole New Mind." He posited that highly trained right-brain think-

ers ought to flourish in the evolving creative economy, where computers handle many analytical left-brain tasks and businesses are hungry for new ideas and approaches.

But there are impassioned voices advising against going into massive debt to earn a fine arts degree. In 2014, a small group of artist activists calling themselves "BFAMFAPhD" looked at whether arts studies at the undergraduate level are worth the money, using primarily census data. Their bottom line, in a report displayed on the group's website (bfamfaphd.com) called "Artists Report Back," is no, if your only metric is whether you will make a living at your art.

The analysis revealed that there are some 2 million holders of undergrad degrees in a wide range of studio and performing arts in the country and about 1.2 million people who identify as working artists. But the overlap between the two groups is only 200,000, suggesting that lack of formal training doesn't keep people from following their muse and having training is no guarantee of a career as an artist.

So how do believers justify the decision to go to graduate school? College-level teaching positions in the fine and performing arts, and even those in some high schools, require an MFA. And while entry-level jobs in architecture and graphic design usually require no more than a bachelor's degree in those disciplines, a master's can help employees move up in the profession.

But unlike fields such as social work, where a master's is a hard-and-fast entry credential, advanced study in the arts is often more about the process than achieving a practical outcome. Students can immerse themselves in their art in a way often not possible in day-to-day life and widen their horizons by being part of a community of artists, notes RISD's Phillips. And perhaps they can even propel themselves from good to great.

"I've learned more per month here than I did in the whole five years I lived and worked in Brooklyn," says Ryan Leitner, 29, a professional photographer who's pursuing his master's in studio arts at Boston's SMFA and will complete his degree this year. "The agency world was stifling," he says. "I wanted a place to conceptualize my work." The school awarded him a merit scholarship that covers part of the cost, and he works as a retoucher at a commercial photography studio. He has applied for several artist-in-residence positions sponsored by arts organizations that would allow him to continue concentrating on his studio work after he graduates, but if one of those doesn't pan out, he'll rely on his retouching job and also try to sell his work. "I would like to teach at some point, but I feel I need more art industry experience," he says.

Grad programs can also be appealing for the intense collaborations with fellow students, faculty and visiting artists that are possible or required, and professional contacts that may pay off in a big way later. "I had a lot of new doors open to me," says Lavina Jadhwani, 32, one of only two candidates admitted to the directing program at the Theatre School at DePaul University for the class that graduated in June 2015.

Jadhwani worked last fall as assistant director for a production of "Never the Sinner" by screenwriter and playwright John Logan (whose credits include "Skyfall" and "Spectre") at the Victory Gardens Theater in Chicago, home to DePaul and some 200 theaters. She met Gary Griffin, the play's director, when he took part in a DePaul seminar and was teamed up with him as part of the theater community's initiative aimed at bringing artists of varied backgrounds together. Students often look upon the three-year DePaul program as a way to "pivot from their local community scene to the national level," says Assistant Dean Jason Beck.

And an advanced degree can certainly be the ticket to a redirected career path. Lea Hershkowitz, 26, who's due to graduate from RISD this year with a master's in interior architecture, sought the technical skills and credentials necessary to switch careers after majoring in psychology and photography and working as a creative marketing producer at Juicy Couture. She says the cutting-edge digital design skills she's gained at RISD have caused associates at architecture firms she has worked with on projects to ask her to teach them the technologies.

Hershkowitz also has been able to pursue her

interest in designing health-promoting environments by taking a course focused on intensive care units conducted in collaboration with New York University's Langone Medical Center. Her work developing a method of improving air quality by introducing plant microbes into the ventilation system has attracted the attention of several potential employers who build health care facilities. She already has two job offers in hand and is expecting to get at least one more.

Arts programs vary widely in their ability to help students with expenses. Some offer a full ride, but most can't afford to be so generous. DePaul typically offers half-tuition scholarships; Jadhwani footed the rest of the bill out of savings from several years working as a director in local theater and grant funding she found from the state of Illinois. Hershkowitz has supported her studies with a scholarship from RISD, multiple grants from other sources, several assistantships that involve both research and teaching, a work-study job, and a part-time consulting gig, though she says she still has incurred significant debt. The average merit award for the 46 students entering Boston's SMFA last fall was $14,500.

Caroline Woolard, one of the artists behind BFAMFAPhD who earned her BFA in 2007 at (then) tuition-free Cooper Union in New York City and lectures at the School of Visual Arts and The New School in the city, points out that there are several lists online of fully funded or low-cost MFA programs. One can be found on the "about" page at bfamfaphd.com.

Studying the arts is often more about PROCESS than an outcome.

Because of the money and time commitment and the uncertainty of the payback, it's essential to be clear-eyed about what you hope to gain by pursuing an advanced degree, whether it's to develop your studio work, land a specific job, or change direction. "The worst reason to do an MFA is because you don't know what else to do," cautions Jeannene Przyblyski, provost at California Institute of the Arts in Valencia. She advises researching programs thoroughly, including opportunities to study with particular people whose work you admire. The institute recruits many of its graduate faculty from working professionals in nearby Los Angeles. Professors not only mentor their students through the postgraduate employment search, but also they sometimes hire them onto current projects or refer them to colleagues while they're still in school. "Art is not theoretical here. It's a set of working practices in the world," Przyblyski says.

Check out studios, performance spaces and equipment resources as well. While Jadhwani didn't pick DePaul for its facilities, the new building that opened in her second year there is "quite astonishing," she says, with two state-of-the-art theaters, 10 acting labs that can also host performances, and over 7,000 square feet of scenery-building space. Working in such an environment was part of the reason, she says, that the program turned out to be even more rewarding than she'd hoped. ∎

The Fine Arts

MASTER'S PROGRAMS RANKED BEST BY DEANS AND DEPARTMENT CHAIRS

THE TOP SCHOOLS Ranked in 2016

Rank	School	Average assessment score (5.0=highest)
1.	Yale University (CT)	4.6
2.	University of California–Los Angeles	4.4
2.	Virginia Commonwealth University	4.4
4.	Rhode Island School of Design	4.3
4.	School of the Art Inst. of Chicago (IL)	4.3
6.	Carnegie Mellon University (PA)	4.2
6.	Columbia University (NY)	4.2
6.	Cranbrook Academy of Art (MI)	4.2
9.	Alfred U.–N.Y. State College of Ceramics	4.1
9.	California Institute of the Arts	4.1
9.	Maryland Institute College of Art	4.1
12.	Washington University in St. Louis	4.0
13.	Bard College (NY)	3.9
13.	University of California–San Diego	3.9
15.	California College of the Arts	3.8
15.	Pratt Institute (NY)	3.8
15.	Stanford University (CA)	3.8
15.	Temple University (PA)	3.8
15.	University of Wisconsin–Madison	3.8
20.	Arizona State University	3.7
20.	Art Center College of Design (CA)	3.7
20.	CUNY–Hunter College (NY)	3.7
20.	Rutgers, The State U. of N.J.–New Brunswick	3.7
20.	School of Visual Arts (NY)	3.7
20.	University of Michigan	3.7
20.	University of Washington	3.7
27.	Cornell University (NY)	3.6
27.	New School–Parsons Sch. of Design (NY)	3.6
27.	Purchase College–SUNY (NY)	3.6
27.	University of California–Berkeley	3.6
27.	University of California–Davis	3.6
27.	University of Texas–Austin	3.6
33.	Indiana University–Bloomington	3.5
33.	Ohio State University	3.5
33.	Ohio University	3.5
33.	Otis College of Art and Design (CA)	3.5
33.	Rensselaer Polytechnic Institute (NY)	3.5
33.	Rochester Institute of Technology (NY)	3.5
33.	San Francisco Art Institute (CA)	3.5
33.	Syracuse University (NY)	3.5
33.	University of California–Irvine	3.5
33.	University of Chicago (IL)	3.5
33.	University of Illinois–Chicago	3.5
33.	University of Illinois–Urbana-Champaign	3.5
33.	University of Iowa	3.5
33.	University of Pennsylvania	3.5
33.	University of Tennessee–Knoxville	3.5
48.	College for Creative Studies (MI)	3.4
48.	Massachusetts College of Art	3.4
48.	Minneapolis Coll. of Art and Design (MN)	3.4
48.	New York University	3.4
48.	Northwestern University (IL)	3.4
48.	University of Georgia	3.4
48.	University of New Mexico	3.4
55.	California State University–Los Angeles	3.3
55.	University of Arizona	3.3
55.	University of Cincinnati (OH)	3.3
55.	University of Minnesota–Twin Cities	3.3

FINE ARTS SPECIALTIES

CERAMICS
1 Alfred University–New York State College of Ceramics
2 Cranbrook Academy of Art (MI)
3 Ohio University
4 Ohio State University
5 Rhode Island School of Design
5 University of Colorado–Boulder

FIBER ARTS
1 Cranbrook Academy of Art (MI)
1 School of the Art Institute of Chicago (IL)

GLASS
1 Rhode Island School of Design
2 Temple University (PA)

GRAPHIC DESIGN
1 Rhode Island School of Design
2 Yale University (CT)
3 Maryland Institute College of Art
4 Cranbrook Academy of Art (MI)

METALS/JEWELRY
1 Cranbrook Academy of Art (MI)
1 Rhode Island School of Design

PAINTING/DRAWING
1 Yale University (CT)
2 Rhode Island School of Design
2 School of the Art Institute of Chicago (IL)
4 Maryland Institute College of Art
5 Columbia University (NY)

PHOTOGRAPHY
1 Yale University (CT)
2 School of the Art Institute of Chicago (IL)
3 University of California–Los Angeles
4 Rochester Institute of Technology (NY)
5 School of Visual Arts (NY)
5 University of New Mexico

PRINTMAKING
1 University of Wisconsin–Madison
2 University of Tennessee–Knoxville
3 Rhode Island School of Design
4 School of the Art Institute of Chicago (IL)

5 Arizona State University
5 University of Iowa

SCULPTURE
1 Virginia Commonwealth University
2 Yale University (CT)
3 Maryland Institute College of Art
4 School of the Art Institute of Chicago (IL)
5 Rhode Island School of Design
5 University of California–Los Angeles

TIME-BASED/NEW MEDIA
1 Carnegie Mellon University (PA)
2 University of California–Los Angeles
3 University of California–San Diego

METHODOLOGY

The Master of Fine Arts rankings are based solely on the results of a peer assessment survey conducted in the fall of 2015. Art school deans or department chairs at 229 MFA programs in art and design were surveyed; one survey was sent to each school. Respondents were asked to rate the academic quality of programs on a scale of 1 (marginal) to 5 (outstanding). Scores for each school were totaled and divided by the number of respondents who rated that school and sorted in descending order. The response rate was 29 percent. The lists of schools and individuals surveyed and specialty concentrations spotlighted were developed in cooperation with the Department of Art and Visual Technology at the College of Visual and Performing Arts at George Mason University in Virginia. Institutions listed in the specialty rankings received the most nominations from respondents at peer institutions for excellence in the specialty. Assessment surveys were conducted by Ipsos Public Affairs.

University of
Wisconsin–Madison,
tied at No. 13

Public Affairs

ACADEMICS AT PEER INSTITUTIONS WEIGH IN ON PROGRAM EXCELLENCE

THE TOP SCHOOLS Ranked in 2016

Rank	School	Average assessment score (5.0=highest)
1.	Indiana University–Bloomington	4.4
1.	Syracuse University (Maxwell) (NY)	4.4
3.	Harvard University (Kennedy) (MA)	4.2
4.	Princeton University (Wilson) (NJ)	4.1
4.	University of Georgia	4.1
4.	University of Southern California (Price)	4.1
4.	University of Washington (Evans)	4.1
8.	Univ. of California–Berkeley (Goldman)	4.0
8.	University of Michigan–Ann Arbor (Ford)	4.0
8.	U. of Minnesota–Twin Cities (Humphrey)	4.0
11.	New York University (Wagner)	3.9
11.	University of Texas–Austin (LBJ)	3.9
13.	Arizona State University	3.8
13.	Carnegie Mellon University (Heinz) (PA)	3.8
13.	Duke University (Sanford) (NC)	3.8
13.	George Washington U. (Trachtenberg) (DC)	3.8
13.	University of Chicago (Harris) (IL)	3.8
13.	U. of Wisconsin–Madison (La Follette)	3.8
19.	American University (DC)	3.7
19.	Columbia University (SIPA) (NY)	3.7
19.	Florida State University (Askew)	3.7
19.	Univ. at Albany–SUNY (Rockefeller) (NY)	3.7
19.	Univ. of California–Los Angeles (Luskin)	3.7
19.	University of Kansas	3.7
25.	Georgetown University (McCourt) (DC)	3.6
25.	Georgia State University (Young)	3.6
25.	Ohio State University (Glenn)	3.6
25.	University of Kentucky (Martin)	3.6
25.	University of Nebraska–Omaha	3.6
25.	University of North Carolina–Chapel Hill	3.6
31.	Texas A&M U.–College Station (Bush)	3.5
31.	University of Maryland–College Park	3.5
33.	University of Missouri (Truman)	3.4
34.	Johns Hopkins University (DC)	3.3
34.	Rutgers, The State U. of N.J.–Newark	3.3
34.	Stanford University (CA)	3.3
34.	University of Arizona	3.3
34.	University of Colorado–Denver	3.3
34.	University of Pittsburgh (PA)	3.3
34.	Virginia Tech	3.3
41.	Cornell University (NY)	3.2
41.	George Mason University (VA)	3.2
41.	Indiana Univ.-Purdue Univ.–Indianapolis	3.2
41.	University of Virginia (Batten)	3.2
45.	Brandeis University (Heller) (MA)	3.1
45.	Cleveland State University (Levin) (OH)	3.1
45.	CUNY–Baruch College (NY)	3.1
45.	Georgia Institute of Technology	3.1
45.	North Carolina State University	3.1
45.	Northern Illinois University	3.1
45.	Portland State University (Hatfield) (OR)	3.1
45.	University of Connecticut	3.1
45.	University of Delaware	3.1
45.	University of Illinois–Chicago	3.1
45.	University of Pennsylvania (Fels)	3.1

PUBLIC AFFAIRS SPECIALTIES

CITY MANAGEMENT
1 University of Kansas
2 New York University (Wagner)
3 University of Southern California (Price)
4 Arizona State University

ENVIRONMENTAL POLICY & MANAGEMENT
1 Indiana University–Bloomington
2 University of Washington (Evans)
3 Duke University (Sanford) (NC)
3 University of California–Berkeley (Goldman)

HEALTH POLICY & MANAGEMENT
1 Harvard University (Kennedy) (MA)
2 New York University (Wagner)
3 Duke University (Sanford) (NC)
3 University of Southern California (Price)

INFORMATION & TECHNOLOGY MANAGEMENT
1 Carnegie Mellon Univ. (Heinz) (PA)
2 Georgia Institute of Technology
3 Syracuse University (Maxwell) (NY)
3 University at Albany–SUNY (Rockefeller) (NY)

NONPROFIT MANAGEMENT
1 Indiana University–Bloomington
2 University of Minnesota–Twin Cities (Humphrey)
3 Syracuse University (Maxwell) (NY)
4 Indiana University-Purdue University–Indianapolis

PUBLIC FINANCE & BUDGETING
1 Indiana University–Bloomington
2 University of Georgia
3 Syracuse University (Maxwell) (NY)
4 University of Kentucky (Martin)

PUBLIC MANAGEMENT/ADMIN.
1 Syracuse University (Maxwell) (NY)
2 University of Georgia
3 Indiana University–Bloomington
4 University of Southern California (Price)
5 American University (DC)

PUBLIC POLICY ANALYSIS
1 University of California–Berkeley (Goldman)
2 Harvard University (Kennedy) (MA)
3 University of Michigan–Ann Arbor (Ford)
4 Duke University (Sanford) (NC)

SOCIAL POLICY
1 University of Michigan–Ann Arbor (Ford)
2 Harvard University (Kennedy) (MA)
2 University of Wisconsin–Madison (La Follette)
4 University of California–Berkeley (Goldman)

METHODOLOGY

Rankings are based solely on results of a peer assessment survey conducted in the fall of 2015. Deans, directors and department chairs representing 272 master's programs in public affairs and administration were surveyed; two surveys were sent to each school. Respondents were asked to rate the academic quality of master's programs on a scale of 1 (marginal) to 5 (outstanding). Scores for each school were totaled and divided by the number of respondents who rated that school and sorted in descending order. The response rate was 43 percent. The lists of schools and individuals surveyed were provided by NASPAA (Network of Schools of Public Policy, Affairs and Administration) and the Association for Public Policy Analysis and Management. For the specialty rankings, deans and other academics at public affairs schools were asked to nominate up to 10 programs for excellence in each specialty. Those with the most nominations appear. Assessment survey data were collected by Ipsos Public Affairs.

Social Sciences & Humanities

PH.D. PROGRAMS RANKED BEST BY DEPARTMENT CHAIRS AND SENIOR FACULTY

ECONOMICS Ranked in 2013

Rank	School	Average assessment score (5.0=highest)
1.	Harvard University (MA)	5.0
1.	Massachusetts Institute of Technology	5.0
1.	Princeton University (NJ)	5.0
1.	University of Chicago	5.0
5.	Stanford University (CA)	4.9
5.	University of California–Berkeley	4.9
7.	Northwestern University (IL)	4.8
7.	Yale University (CT)	4.8
9.	University of Pennsylvania	4.5
10.	Columbia University (NY)	4.4
11.	New York University	4.3
11.	University of Minnesota–Twin Cities	4.3
13.	University of Michigan–Ann Arbor	4.2
13.	University of Wisconsin–Madison	4.2
15.	California Institute of Technology	4.1
15.	University of California–Los Angeles	4.1
15.	University of California–San Diego	4.1
18.	Cornell University (NY)	3.9

Rank	School	Average assessment score (5.0=highest)
19.	Brown University (RI)	3.8
19.	Carnegie Mellon University (Tepper) (PA)	3.8
19.	Duke University (NC)	3.8
22.	University of Maryland–College Park	3.7
22.	University of Rochester (NY)	3.7
24.	Boston University	3.6
24.	Johns Hopkins University (MD)	3.6
26.	University of Texas–Austin	3.5
27.	Ohio State University	3.4
27.	Penn. State University–University Park	3.4
27.	Washington University in St. Louis	3.4
30.	Michigan State University	3.3
30.	University of Virginia	3.3
32.	Boston College	3.2
32.	University of California–Davis	3.2
32.	University of Illinois–Urbana-Champaign	3.2
32.	University of North Carolina–Chapel Hill	3.2
36.	Arizona State University	3.1

Rank	School	Average assessment score (5.0=highest)
36.	University of Arizona	3.1
36.	University of Pittsburgh	3.1
36.	Vanderbilt University (TN)	3.1
40.	University of Iowa (Tippie)	3.0
40.	University of Washington	3.0
42.	Indiana University–Bloomington	2.9
42.	Purdue–West Lafayette (Krannert) (IN)	2.9
42.	Texas A&M University–College Station	2.9
42.	University of California–Santa Barbara	2.9
46.	Georgetown University (DC)	2.8
46.	University of California–Irvine	2.8
48.	North Carolina State University–Raleigh	2.7
48.	Rice University (TX)	2.7
48.	Rutgers, the State U. of N. J.–New Bruns.	2.7
48.	University of Florida	2.7
48.	University of Southern California	2.7

ECONOMICS SPECIALTIES

DEVELOPMENT ECONOMICS
1. Harvard University (MA)
2. Massachusetts Institute of Tech.
3. Princeton University (NJ)
3. Yale University (CT)
5. University of California–Berkeley

ECONOMETRICS
1. Massachusetts Institute of Tech.
1. Yale University (CT)
3. Princeton University (NJ)
4. University of California–San Diego
5. Harvard University (MA)
6. Northwestern University (IL)
6. University of California–Berkeley

INDUSTRIAL ORGANIZATION
1. Stanford University (CA)
2. Harvard University (MA)
2. Northwestern University (IL)
4. Yale University (CT)
5. University of Chicago
6. Massachusetts Institute of Tech.
6. University of California–Berkeley

INTERNATIONAL ECONOMICS
1. Harvard University (MA)
2. Princeton University (NJ)
3. Columbia University (NY)
4. University of California–Berkeley
5. Massachusetts Institute of Tech.

LABOR ECONOMICS
1. Harvard University (MA)
1. Princeton University (NJ)
3. Massachusetts Institute of Tech.
4. University of California–Berkeley
5. University of Chicago

MACROECONOMICS
1. Harvard University (MA)
2. Massachusetts Institute of Tech.
3. Princeton University (NJ)
4. New York University
5. University of Minnesota–Twin Cities
6. University of Chicago
6. University of Pennsylvania

MICROECONOMICS
1. Stanford University (CA)
2. Massachusetts Institute of Tech.
3. Harvard University (MA)
4. Yale University (CT)
5. Northwestern University (IL)
5. Princeton University (NJ)
7. University of Chicago

PUBLIC FINANCE
1. University of California–Berkeley
2. Harvard University (MA)
2. Massachusetts Institute of Tech.
4. Stanford University (CA)
5. University of Michigan–Ann Arbor

ENGLISH Ranked in 2013

Rank	School	Average assessment score (5.0=highest)
1.	University of California–Berkeley	4.9
2.	Harvard University (MA)	4.8
2.	Stanford University (CA)	4.8
4.	Columbia University (NY)	4.7
4.	Princeton University (NJ)	4.7
4.	University of Pennsylvania	4.7
4.	Yale University (CT)	4.7
8.	Cornell University (NY)	4.6
8.	University of Chicago	4.6
10.	Duke University (NC)	4.4
10.	University of California–Los Angeles	4.4
10.	University of Virginia	4.4

Rank	School	Average assessment score (5.0=highest)
13.	Johns Hopkins University (MD)	4.3
13.	University of Michigan–Ann Arbor	4.3
15.	Brown University (RI)	4.2
15.	University of North Carolina–Chapel Hill	4.2
17.	Rutgers, the State U. of N. J.–New Bruns.	4.1
17.	University of Texas–Austin	4.1
17.	University of Wisconsin–Madison	4.1
20.	New York University	4.0
20.	Northwestern University (IL)	4.0
22.	CUNY Grad School and University Ctr.	3.9
22.	Indiana University–Bloomington	3.9
22.	University of California–Irvine	3.9

Rank	School	Average assessment score (5.0=highest)
22.	University of Illinois–Urbana-Champaign	3.9
26.	Emory University (GA)	3.7
26.	Ohio State University	3.7
26.	Penn. State University–University Park	3.7
26.	University of California–Davis	3.7
26.	University of California–Santa Barbara	3.7
26.	Vanderbilt University (TN)	3.7
32.	University of Iowa	3.6
32.	University of Maryland–College Park	3.6
32.	University of Washington	3.6
32.	Washington University in St. Louis	3.6
36.	Rice University (TX)	3.5

More @ usnews.com/grad

Rank	School	Average assessment score (5.0=highest)
36.	University of Minnesota–Twin Cities	3.5
36.	University of Southern California	3.5
39.	Carnegie Mellon University (PA)	3.4
39.	University of California–San Diego	3.4
39.	University of California–Santa Cruz	3.4

Rank	School	Average assessment score (5.0=highest)
39.	University of Notre Dame (IN)	3.4
39.	University of Pittsburgh	3.4
44.	Boston University	3.3
44.	Brandeis University (MA)	3.3

Rank	School	Average assessment score (5.0=highest)
44.	Claremont Graduate University (CA)	3.3
44.	University at Buffalo–SUNY	3.3
44.	University of California–Riverside	3.3
44.	University of Illinois–Chicago	3.3

ENGLISH SPECIALTIES

AFRICAN-AMERICAN LITERATURE
1. Harvard University (MA)
2. Yale University (CT)
3. Princeton University (NJ)
4. Duke University (NC)
4. University of California–Berkeley
4. Vanderbilt University (TN)

AMERICAN LITERATURE BEFORE 1865
1. University of California–Berkeley
2. Harvard University (MA)
2. University of Pennsylvania
2. Yale University (CT)
5. University of Virginia

AMERICAN LITERATURE AFTER 1865
1. University of California–Berkeley
2. University of Chicago
3. Stanford University (CA)
4. Columbia University (NY)
4. Harvard University (MA)
4. University of Pennsylvania
4. University of Virginia
4. Yale University (CT)

18TH THROUGH 20TH CENTURY BRITISH LITERATURE
1. University of California–Berkeley
2. Harvard University (MA)
2. University of Pennsylvania

2. University of Virginia
5. Stanford University (CA)
6. Columbia University (NY)
6. University of California–Los Angeles
6. Yale University (CT)

GENDER AND LITERATURE
1. University of California–Berkeley
2. Duke University (NC)
3. University of Michigan–Ann Arbor
4. Princeton University (NJ)
4. Stanford University (CA)

LITERARY CRITICISM AND THEORY
1. Duke University (NC)

2. University of California–Berkeley
3. Cornell University (NY)
3. University of California–Irvine
5. Stanford University (CA)
6. Johns Hopkins University (MD)

MEDIEVAL/RENAISSANCE LITERATURE
1. Harvard University (MA)
2. University of California–Berkeley
3. University of Pennsylvania
3. Yale University (CT)
5. Stanford University (CA)
6. University of Notre Dame (IN)

HISTORY Ranked in 2013

Rank	School	Average assessment score (5.0=highest)
1.	Princeton University (NJ)	4.8
1.	University of California–Berkeley	4.8
1.	Yale University (CT)	4.8
4.	Harvard University (MA)	4.7
4.	Stanford University (CA)	4.7
4.	University of Chicago	4.7
7.	Columbia University (NY)	4.6
7.	University of Michigan–Ann Arbor	4.6
9.	University of California–Los Angeles	4.5
9.	University of Pennsylvania	4.5
11.	Cornell University (NY)	4.4
11.	Johns Hopkins University (MD)	4.4

Rank	School	Average assessment score (5.0=highest)
11.	University of North Carolina–Chapel Hill	4.4
14.	Duke University (NC)	4.3
14.	Northwestern University (IL)	4.3
14.	University of Wisconsin–Madison	4.3
17.	University of Texas–Austin	4.2
18.	Brown University (RI)	4.1
18.	New York University	4.1
20.	Rutgers, the State U. of N. J.–New Bruns.	4.0
20.	University of Illinois–Urbana-Champaign	4.0
20.	University of Virginia (Corcoran)	4.0
23.	Indiana University–Bloomington	3.9
24.	Ohio State University	3.8

Rank	School	Average assessment score (5.0=highest)
24.	University of Minnesota–Twin Cities	3.8
24.	Vanderbilt University (TN)	3.8
27.	Emory University (GA)	3.7
27.	Massachusetts Institute of Technology	3.7
27.	University of California–Davis	3.7
30.	CUNY Grad School and University Ctr.	3.6
30.	Georgetown University (DC)	3.6
30.	Rice University (TX)	3.6
30.	University of California–San Diego	3.6
30.	University of Washington	3.6
30.	Washington University in St. Louis	3.6

HISTORY SPECIALTIES

AFRICAN HISTORY
1. University of Wisconsin–Madison
2. University of Michigan–Ann Arbor
3. Michigan State University
4. Northwestern University (IL)
4. University of California–Los Angeles

AFRICAN-AMERICAN HISTORY
1. Yale University (CT)
2. Duke University (NC)
3. University of Michigan–Ann Arbor
4. Harvard University (MA)
5. Columbia University (NY)
6. Princeton University (NJ)
6. Univ. of North Carolina–Chapel Hill

ASIAN HISTORY
1. Harvard University (MA)
1. University of California–Berkeley
3. Yale University (CT)

4. Princeton University (NJ)
4. Stanford University (CA)
4. University of California–Los Angeles

CULTURAL HISTORY
1. University of California–Berkeley
2. University of Michigan–Ann Arbor
3. Yale University (CT)
4. Princeton University (NJ)
5. Columbia University (NY)

EUROPEAN HISTORY
1. University of California–Berkeley
1. Yale University (CT)
3. Harvard University (MA)
3. University of Michigan–Ann Arbor
5. University of Chicago
6. Columbia University (NY)
7. Princeton University (NJ)

LATIN AMERICAN HISTORY
1. University of Texas–Austin
2. Yale University (CT)
3. University of Wisconsin–Madison
4. Duke University (NC)
5. University of California–Los Angeles
6. University of Chicago
6. University of Michigan–Ann Arbor

MODERN U.S. HISTORY
1. Yale University (CT)
2. Harvard University (MA)
2. University of California–Berkeley
4. Columbia University (NY)
4. Princeton University (NJ)
6. University of Michigan–Ann Arbor
6. University of Wisconsin–Madison
8. University of Pennsylvania

U.S. COLONIAL HISTORY
1. Harvard University (MA)
2. University of Pennsylvania
3. Col. of William and Mary (Tyler) (VA)
4. Yale University (CT)
5. University of Virginia (Corcoran)
6. Johns Hopkins University (MD)
7. University of Michigan–Ann Arbor

WOMEN'S HISTORY
1. Rutgers, the State U. of New Jersey–New Brunswick
2. University of Wisconsin–Madison
3. University of Michigan–Ann Arbor
4. University of Pennsylvania
4. Yale University (CT)
6. New York University
7. Univ. of California–Santa Barbara
7. University of Minnesota–Twin Cities

POLITICAL SCIENCE Ranked in 2013

Rank	School	Average assessment score (5.0=highest)
1.	Harvard University (MA)	4.9
2.	Princeton University (NJ)	4.8
2.	Stanford University (CA)	4.8
4.	University of Michigan–Ann Arbor	4.7
4.	Yale University (CT)	4.7
6.	University of California–Berkeley	4.6
7.	Columbia University (NY)	4.4
8.	Massachusetts Institute of Technology	4.3
8.	University of California–San Diego	4.3
10.	Duke University (NC)	4.2
10.	University of California–Los Angeles	4.2
12.	University of Chicago	4.1
13.	University of North Carolina–Chapel Hill	4.0
13.	Washington University in St. Louis	4.0
15.	New York University	3.9

Rank	School	Average assessment score (5.0=highest)
15.	Ohio State University	3.9
15.	University of Rochester (NY)	3.9
15.	University of Wisconsin–Madison	3.9
19.	Cornell University (NY)	3.8
19.	University of Minnesota–Twin Cities	3.8
21.	Northwestern University (IL)	3.6
21.	University of Texas–Austin	3.6
23.	University of California–Davis	3.5
23.	University of Illinois–Urbana-Champaign	3.5
25.	Emory University (GA)	3.4
25.	Indiana University–Bloomington	3.4
25.	Texas A&M University–College Station	3.4
28.	Penn. State University–University Park	3.3
28.	University of Maryland–College Park	3.3
28.	University of Pennsylvania	3.3

Rank	School	Average assessment score (5.0=highest)
28.	University of Washington	3.3
32.	Michigan State University	3.2
32.	Rice University (TX)	3.2
32.	Stony Brook University–SUNY	3.2
32.	University of Iowa	3.2
36.	George Washington University (DC)	3.1
36.	University of Notre Dame (IN)	3.1
36.	University of Virginia	3.1
36.	Vanderbilt University (TN)	3.1
40.	Florida State University	3.0
40.	Georgetown University (DC)	3.0
40.	Johns Hopkins University (MD)	3.0
40.	University of California–Irvine	3.0
40.	University of Pittsburgh	3.0

POLITICAL SCIENCE SPECIALTIES

AMERICAN POLITICS
1. Harvard University (MA)
2. Stanford University (CA)
3. University of Michigan–Ann Arbor
4. Princeton University (NJ)
5. University of California–Berkeley
6. Yale University (CT)
7. Duke University (NC)
8. University of California–Los Angeles
9. Columbia University (NY)

COMPARATIVE POLITICS
1. Harvard University (MA)
2. Stanford University (CA)
3. Princeton University (NJ)
3. University of California–Berkeley
5. Columbia University (NY)
6. Yale University (CT)
7. University of Michigan–Ann Arbor
8. University of California–Los Angeles
9. Duke University (NC)

INTERNATIONAL POLITICS
1. Harvard University (MA)
2. Stanford University (CA)
3. Princeton University (NJ)
4. Columbia University (NY)
5. University of California–San Diego
6. University of Michigan–Ann Arbor
7. New York University
8. Ohio State University
8. Yale University (CT)

POLITICAL METHODOLOGY
1. Harvard University (MA)
2. Stanford University (CA)
3. New York University
3. University of Michigan–Ann Arbor
5. Washington University in St. Louis
6. Princeton University (NJ)
7. University of Rochester (NY)
8. University of California–Berkeley

POLITICAL THEORY
1. Princeton University (NJ)
2. Harvard University (MA)
3. University of Chicago
4. Yale University (CT)
5. Johns Hopkins University (MD)
6. University of California–Berkeley
7. Duke University (NC)
8. Northwestern University (IL)

PSYCHOLOGY Ranked in 2013

Rank	School	Average assessment score (5.0=highest)
1.	Stanford University (CA)	4.8
2.	University of California–Berkeley	4.7
2.	University of California–Los Angeles	4.7
4.	Harvard University (MA)	4.6
4.	University of Michigan–Ann Arbor	4.6
4.	Yale University (CT)	4.6
7.	Princeton University (NJ)	4.5
7.	University of Illinois–Urbana-Champaign	4.5
9.	Massachusetts Institute of Technology	4.4
9.	University of Minnesota–Twin Cities	4.4
9.	University of Wisconsin–Madison	4.4
12.	University of North Carolina–Chapel Hill	4.3
12.	University of Pennsylvania	4.3
14.	Columbia University (NY)	4.2
14.	Cornell University (NY)	4.2
14.	Northwestern University (IL)	4.2
14.	University of California–San Diego	4.2
14.	University of Texas–Austin	4.2
14.	University of Washington	4.2
14.	Washington University in St. Louis	4.2
21.	Carnegie Mellon University (PA)	4.1
21.	Duke University (NC)	4.1
21.	Ohio State University	4.1
21.	University of California–Davis	4.1
21.	University of Chicago	4.1
26.	Brown University (RI)	4.0

Rank	School	Average assessment score (5.0=highest)
26.	Indiana University–Bloomington	4.0
26.	Johns Hopkins University (MD)	4.0
26.	University of Virginia	4.0
30.	New York University	3.9
30.	Penn. State University–University Park	3.9
30.	University of California–Irvine	3.9
30.	University of Colorado–Boulder	3.9
30.	University of Iowa	3.9
30.	University of Oregon	3.9
30.	University of Pittsburgh	3.9
30.	Vanderbilt University (TN)	3.9
38.	Arizona State University	3.8
38.	Emory University (GA)	3.8
40.	University of Arizona	3.7
40.	University of California–Santa Barbara	3.7
40.	University of Florida	3.7
40.	University of Kansas	3.7
40.	University of Maryland–College Park	3.7
40.	University of Southern California	3.7
46.	Boston University	3.6
46.	Dartmouth College (NH)	3.6
46.	Michigan State University	3.6
46.	Purdue University–West Lafayette (IN)	3.6
46.	Stony Brook University–SUNY	3.6
46.	University of Massachusetts–Amherst	3.6
52.	Oregon Health and Science University	3.5

Rank	School	Average assessment score (5.0=highest)
52.	San Diego State - U. of Calif.–San Diego	3.5
52.	Temple University (PA)	3.5
52.	University of Connecticut	3.5
52.	University of Georgia	3.5
52.	University of Miami (FL)	3.5
52.	University of Missouri	3.5
52.	University of Rochester (NY)	3.5
60.	Florida State University	3.4
60.	Rutgers, the State U. of N. J.–New Bruns.	3.4
60.	University of Illinois–Chicago	3.4
63.	Georgia Institute of Technology	3.3
63.	Teachers College, Columbia Univ. (NY)	3.3
63.	University at Buffalo–SUNY	3.3
63.	University of California–Riverside	3.3
67.	Binghamton University–SUNY	3.2
67.	Boston College	3.2
67.	Brandeis University (MA)	3.2
67.	Rice University (TX)	3.2
67.	Rutgers, the State U. of N. J.–Newark	3.2
67.	Texas A&M University–College Station	3.2
67.	Tufts University (MA)	3.2
67.	University of Delaware	3.2
67.	University of Notre Dame (IN)	3.2
67.	University of Utah	3.2
67.	Virginia Tech	3.2

PSYCHOLOGY SPECIALTIES

BEHAVIORAL NEUROSCIENCE
1. University of California–San Diego
2. Massachusetts Institute of Tech.
3. University of Michigan–Ann Arbor
4. Harvard University (MA)
4. University of California–Los Angeles
6. Duke University (NC)
7. Johns Hopkins University (MD)
7. University of California–Berkeley

COGNITIVE PSYCHOLOGY
1. Stanford University (CA)

2. Harvard University (MA)
3. University of California–San Diego
3. Univ. of Illinois–Urbana-Champaign
5. Carnegie Mellon University (PA)
5. University of Michigan–Ann Arbor
5. Yale University (CT)

DEVELOPMENTAL PSYCHOLOGY
1. University of Minnesota–Twin Cities
2. University of Michigan–Ann Arbor
3. Stanford University (CA)
4. Harvard University (MA)

5. Pennsylvania State University–University Park
5. University of California–Berkeley
5. University of California–Los Angeles
5. Univ. of North Carolina–Chapel Hill
5. University of Virginia
5. University of Wisconsin–Madison

INDUSTRIAL AND ORGANIZATIONAL PSYCHOLOGY
1. Michigan State University
1. University of Minnesota–Twin Cities

SOCIAL PSYCHOLOGY
1. Ohio State University
1. University of Michigan–Ann Arbor
3. Harvard University (MA)
3. Princeton University (NJ)
3. Stanford University (CA)
3. University of California–Los Angeles
3. Yale University (CT)

SOCIOLOGY Ranked in 2013

Rank	School	Average assessment score (5.0=highest)
1.	Princeton University (NJ)	4.7
1.	University of California–Berkeley	4.7
1.	University of Wisconsin–Madison	4.7
4.	Stanford University (CA)	4.6
4.	University of Michigan–Ann Arbor	4.6
6.	Harvard University (MA)	4.5
6.	University of Chicago	4.5
6.	University of North Carolina–Chapel Hill	4.5
9.	University of California–Los Angeles	4.4
10.	Northwestern University (IL)	4.3
10.	University of Pennsylvania	4.3
12.	Columbia University (NY)	4.2
12.	Indiana University–Bloomington	4.2
14.	Duke University (NC)	4.1
14.	University of Texas–Austin	4.1
16.	New York University	4.0
17.	Cornell University (NY)	3.9
17.	Ohio State University	3.9
17.	Penn. State University–University Park	3.9
20.	University of Arizona	3.8
20.	University of Minnesota–Twin Cities	3.8
20.	University of Washington	3.8
20.	Yale University (CT)	3.8
24.	University of Maryland–College Park	3.7
25.	Brown University (RI)	3.6
25.	University of California–Irvine	3.6
27.	Johns Hopkins University (MD)	3.5
28.	CUNY Grad School and University Ctr.	3.4
28.	Rutgers, the State U. of N. J.–New Bruns.	3.4
28.	University at Albany–SUNY	3.4
31.	University of California–Davis	3.3
31.	University of California–Santa Barbara	3.3
31.	University of Massachusetts–Amherst	3.3
31.	Vanderbilt University (TN)	3.3
35.	Emory University (GA)	3.2
35.	University of California–San Diego	3.2
35.	University of Iowa	3.2
35.	University of Virginia	3.2
39.	Florida State University	3.1
39.	University of Illinois–Chicago	3.1
39.	University of Southern California	3.1

SOCIOLOGY SPECIALTIES

ECONOMIC SOCIOLOGY
1. Stanford University (CA)
2. Princeton University (NJ)
2. University of California–Berkeley
2. University of Wisconsin–Madison
5. Harvard University (MA)

HISTORICAL SOCIOLOGY
1. Harvard University (MA)
1. University of California–Berkeley

SEX AND GENDER
1. Univ. of California–Santa Barbara
2. University of California–Berkeley
2. University of Wisconsin–Madison
4. Stanford University (CA)

SOCIAL PSYCHOLOGY
1. Stanford University (CA)
2. Indiana University–Bloomington
3. University of Iowa

SOCIAL STRATIFICATION
1. University of Wisconsin–Madison
2. Stanford University (CA)
3. University of California–Los Angeles
3. University of Michigan–Ann Arbor
5. University of California–Berkeley

SOCIOLOGY OF CULTURE
1. Princeton University (NJ)
2. University of California–Berkeley
3. Northwestern University (IL)

SOCIOLOGY OF POPULATION
1. University of Michigan–Ann Arbor
2. University of Wisconsin–Madison
3. Univ. of North Carolina–Chapel Hill
4. University of Pennsylvania
4. University of Texas–Austin
6. Pennsylvania State University–University Park
7. Princeton University (NJ)
7. University of California–Los Angeles

METHODOLOGY

Rankings of doctoral programs in the social sciences and humanities are based solely on the results of peer assessment surveys sent to academics in each discipline. Each school offering a doctoral program was sent two surveys. The questionnaires asked respondents to rate the academic quality of the program at each institution on a 5-point scale: outstanding (5), strong (4), good (3), adequate (2), or marginal (1). Individuals who were unfamiliar with a particular

school's programs were asked to select "don't know." Scores for each school were determined by computing a trimmed mean (eliminating the two highest and two lowest responses) of the ratings of all respondents who rated that school for the last two surveys; average scores were then sorted in descending order.

Surveys were conducted in the fall of 2012 by Ipsos Public Affairs. Questionnaires were sent to department heads and directors of graduate studies (or, alternatively, a senior faculty

member who teaches graduate students) at schools that had granted a total of five or more doctorates in each discipline during the five-year period from 2005 through 2009, as indicated by the 2010 Survey of Earned Doctorates. The surveys asked about Ph.D. programs in economics (response rate: 25 percent), English (21 percent), history (19 percent), political science (30 percent), psychology (16 percent), and sociology (31 percent). Survey results from fall 2008 and fall 2012 were aver-

aged to compute the scores.

In psychology, a school was listed once on the survey even if it grants a doctoral degree in psychology in multiple departments. Programs in clinical psychology are ranked separately in the health professions section. Specialty rankings are based solely on nominations by department heads and directors of graduate studies at peer schools from the list of schools surveyed. They named up to 10 programs in each area. Those with the most votes appear.

The Sciences
PH.D. PROGRAMS RANKED BEST BY DEANS AND DEPARTMENT CHAIRS

BIOLOGICAL SCIENCES Ranked in 2014

Listed schools may have multiple programs.

Rank	School	Average assessment score (5.0=highest)
1.	Harvard University (MA)	4.9
1.	Massachusetts Institute of Technology	4.9
1.	Stanford University (CA)	4.9
4.	University of California–Berkeley	4.8
5.	California Institute of Technology	4.7
5.	Johns Hopkins University (MD)	4.7
7.	University of California–San Francisco	4.6
7.	Yale University (CT)	4.6
9.	Princeton University (NJ)	4.5
9.	Scripps Research Institute (CA)	4.5
11.	Cornell University (NY)	4.4
11.	Duke University (NC)	4.4
11.	Washington University in St. Louis	4.4
14.	Columbia University (NY)	4.3
14.	Rockefeller University (NY)	4.3
14.	University of California–San Diego	4.3
14.	University of Chicago	4.3
18.	University of Wisconsin–Madison	4.2
19.	University of California–Davis	4.1
19.	University of California–Los Angeles	4.1
19.	University of Michigan–Ann Arbor	4.1
19.	University of Pennsylvania	4.1
19.	University of Washington	4.1
19.	U. of Texas Southwest. Med. Ctr.–Dallas	4.1
25.	Baylor College of Medicine (TX)	4.0
26.	Cornell University (Weill) (NY)	3.9
26.	Northwestern University (IL)	3.9
26.	University of North Carolina–Chapel Hill	3.9
26.	Vanderbilt University (TN)	3.9
30.	Emory University (GA)	3.8
30.	University of Colorado–Boulder	3.8
30.	University of Illinois–Urbana-Champaign	3.8
30.	University of Texas–Austin	3.8
34.	Brown University (RI)	3.7
34.	Indiana University–Bloomington	3.7
34.	University of California–Irvine	3.7
34.	University of Minnesota–Twin Cities	3.7
38.	Case Western Reserve University (OH)	3.6
38.	Dartmouth College (NH)	3.6
38.	Mayo Medical School (MN)	3.6
38.	University of Arizona	3.6
42.	Carnegie Mellon University (PA)	3.5
42.	Icahn Sch. of Medicine at Mt. Sinai (NY)	3.5
42.	Ohio State University	3.5
42.	Penn. State University–University Park	3.5
42.	Rice University (TX)	3.5
42.	University of Alabama–Birmingham	3.5
42.	University of Georgia	3.5
42.	University of Pittsburgh	3.5
50.	Michigan State University	3.4
50.	University of California–Santa Barbara	3.4
50.	University of Virginia	3.4
50.	U. of Mass. Medical Center–Worcester	3.4
50.	Yeshiva University (Einstein) (NY)	3.4
55.	Arizona State University	3.3
55.	Brandeis University (MA)	3.3
55.	Georgia Institute of Technology	3.3
55.	Purdue University–West Lafayette (IN)	3.3
55.	Stony Brook University–SUNY	3.3
55.	University of California–Santa Cruz	3.3
55.	University of Florida	3.3
55.	University of Iowa	3.3
55.	University of Maryland–College Park	3.3
55.	University of Massachusetts–Amherst	3.3
55.	University of Oregon	3.3
55.	University of Southern California	3.3
55.	University of Utah	3.3
68.	New York University	3.2
68.	Oregon Health and Science University	3.2
68.	Rutgers, the State U. of N.J.–New Bruns.	3.2
68.	Tufts University (MA)	3.2
68.	University of California–Riverside	3.2
68.	University of Kansas	3.2
68.	University of Rochester (NY)	3.2
75.	Colorado State University	3.1
75.	Iowa State University	3.1
75.	North Carolina State University	3.1
75.	Oregon State University	3.1
75.	Texas A&M University–College Station	3.1
75.	University of Colorado–Denver	3.1
75.	University of Connecticut	3.1
75.	University of Illinois–Chicago	3.1
75.	U. of Texas Health Sci. Ctr.–Houston	3.1

BIOLOGICAL SCIENCES SPECIALTIES

BIOCHEMISTRY/BIOPHYSICS/STRUCTURAL BIOLOGY
1. Harvard University (MA)
1. Stanford University (CA)
3. California Institute of Technology
3. Yale University (CT)

CELL BIOLOGY
1. Yale University (CT)
2. Stanford University (CA)
3. Harvard University (MA)
3. Johns Hopkins University (MD)

ECOLOGY/EVOLUTIONARY BIOLOGY
1. University of California–Berkeley
2. Cornell University (NY)
3. University of California–Davis
4. Stanford University (CA)
4. University of Chicago

GENETICS/GENOMICS/BIOINFORMATICS
1. Harvard University (MA)
1. Stanford University (CA)
3. University of California–Berkeley
3. University of Washington

IMMUNOLOGY/INFECTIOUS DISEASE
1. Johns Hopkins University (MD)
2. University of California–San Francisco
3. Harvard University (MA)

MICROBIOLOGY
1. Harvard University (MA)
2. Stanford University (CA)

MOLECULAR BIOLOGY
1. Harvard University (MA)

1. University of California–Berkeley
3. Johns Hopkins University (MD)
4. Massachusetts Institute of Technology
4. Stanford University (CA)

NEUROSCIENCE/NEUROBIOLOGY
1. Stanford University (CA)
2. University of California–San Diego
3. California Institute of Technology
3. Johns Hopkins University (MD)

▶ More @ usnews.com/grad

CHEMISTRY Ranked in 2014

Rank	School	Average assessment score (5.0=highest)
1.	California Institute of Technology	5.0
1.	Massachusetts Institute of Technology	5.0
1.	University of California–Berkeley	5.0
4.	Harvard University (MA)	4.9
4.	Stanford University (CA)	4.9
6.	University of Illinois–Urbana-Champaign	4.7
7.	Northwestern University (IL)	4.6
7.	Scripps Research Institute (CA)	4.6
9.	University of Wisconsin–Madison	4.5
10.	Columbia University (NY)	4.4
10.	Cornell University (NY)	4.4
12.	University of Chicago	4.3
12.	University of Texas–Austin	4.3
12.	Yale University (CT)	4.3
15.	Princeton University (NJ)	4.2
15.	University of California–Los Angeles	4.2
15.	University of Michigan–Ann Arbor	4.2
15.	University of North Carolina–Chapel Hill	4.2
19.	Texas A&M University–College Station	4.0
19.	University of Pennsylvania	4.0
21.	Penn. State University–University Park	3.9
21.	Purdue University–West Lafayette (IN)	3.9
21.	University of California–San Diego	3.9
24.	Georgia Institute of Technology	3.8
24.	Indiana University–Bloomington	3.8
24.	Johns Hopkins University (MD)	3.8
24.	University of California–Irvine	3.8
24.	University of Colorado–Boulder	3.8
24.	University of Minnesota–Twin Cities	3.8
24.	University of Washington	3.8
31.	Ohio State University	3.7
31.	University of California–San Francisco	3.7
33.	Rice University (TX)	3.6
33.	University of California–Santa Barbara	3.6
35.	Emory University (GA)	3.5
35.	University of California–Davis	3.5
35.	University of Florida	3.5
35.	University of Pittsburgh	3.5
35.	University of Utah	3.5
35.	Washington University in St. Louis	3.5
41.	Duke University (NC)	3.4
41.	University of Arizona	3.4
41.	University of Maryland–College Park	3.4
41.	U. of Texas Southwest. Med. Ct.–Dallas	3.4
45.	Carnegie Mellon University (PA)	3.3
45.	Iowa State University	3.3
45.	Michigan State University	3.3
45.	Vanderbilt University (TN)	3.3
49.	Boston College	3.2
49.	Colorado State University	3.2
49.	Florida State University	3.2
49.	Rockefeller University (NY)	3.2
49.	University of Rochester (NY)	3.2
49.	University of Southern California	3.2
49.	University of Virginia	3.2
56.	North Carolina State University	3.1
56.	Stony Brook University–SUNY	3.1
56.	University of Georgia	3.1
56.	University of Massachusetts–Amherst	3.1
60.	Arizona State University	3.0
60.	Boston University	3.0
60.	Brown University (RI)	3.0
60.	New York University	3.0
60.	Rutgers, the State U. of N.J.–New Bruns.	3.0
60.	University of California–Riverside	3.0
60.	University of Delaware	3.0
60.	University of Iowa	3.0
60.	University of Notre Dame (IN)	3.0
60.	University of Oregon	3.0
60.	Virginia Tech	3.0

CHEMISTRY SPECIALTIES

ANALYTICAL
1. Purdue Univ.–West Lafayette (IN)
2. University of North Carolina–Chapel Hill
3. University of Illinois–Urbana-Champaign
4. University of Texas–Austin
5. Indiana University–Bloomington
6. University of Wisconsin–Madison

BIOCHEMISTRY
1. University of California–Berkeley
2. Scripps Research Institute (CA)
2. University of Wisconsin–Madison
4. Harvard University (MA)
5. University of California–San Francisco
6. Stanford University (CA)
7. Mass. Institute of Technology

INORGANIC
1. Mass. Institute of Technology
2. California Institute of Technology
3. University of California–Berkeley
4. Northwestern University (IL)
5. Texas A&M University–College Station
6. University of Wisconsin–Madison

ORGANIC
1. Harvard University (MA)
2. California Institute of Technology
3. University of California–Berkeley
4. Mass. Institute of Technology
5. Stanford University (CA)
6. Scripps Research Institute (CA)
7. Princeton University (NJ)
8. University of Wisconsin–Madison

PHYSICAL
1. University of California–Berkeley
2. California Institute of Technology
3. Mass. Institute of Technology
4. Stanford University (CA)
5. Northwestern University (IL)
6. University of Chicago

THEORETICAL
1. University of California–Berkeley
2. California Institute of Technology
3. Harvard University (MA)
3. University of Chicago
5. Columbia University (NY)
5. Yale University (CT)
7. Mass. Institute of Technology
7. Stanford University (CA)

GETTY IMAGES

COMPUTER SCIENCE Ranked in 2014

Rank School	Average assessment score (5.0=highest)
1. Carnegie Mellon University (PA)	5.0
1. Massachusetts Institute of Technology	5.0
1. Stanford University (CA)	5.0
1. University of California–Berkeley	5.0
5. University of Illinois–Urbana-Champaign	4.6
6. Cornell University (NY)	4.5
6. University of Washington	4.5
8. Princeton University (NJ)	4.4
9. Georgia Institute of Technology	4.3
9. University of Texas–Austin	4.3
11. California Institute of Technology	4.2
11. University of Wisconsin–Madison	4.2
13. University of California–Los Angeles	4.1
13. University of Michigan–Ann Arbor	4.1
15. Columbia University (NY)	4.0
15. University of California–San Diego	4.0
15. University of Maryland–College Park	4.0

Rank School	Average assessment score (5.0=highest)
18. Harvard University (MA)	3.9
19. University of Pennsylvania	3.8
20. Brown University (RI)	3.7
20. Purdue University–West Lafayette (IN)	3.7
20. Rice University (TX)	3.7
20. University of Southern California	3.7
20. Yale University (CT)	3.7
25. Duke University (NC)	3.6
25. University of Massachusetts–Amherst	3.6
25. University of North Carolina–Chapel Hill	3.6
28. Johns Hopkins University (MD)	3.5
29. New York University	3.4
29. Penn. State University–University Park	3.4
29. University of California–Irvine	3.4
29. University of Minnesota–Twin Cities	3.4
29. University of Virginia	3.4
34. Northwestern University (IL)	3.3

Rank School	Average assessment score (5.0=highest)
34. Ohio State University	3.3
34. Rutgers, the State U. of N.J.–New Bruns.	3.3
34. University of California–Davis	3.3
34. University of California–Santa Barbara	3.3
34. University of Chicago	3.3
40. Dartmouth College (NH)	3.1
40. Stony Brook University–SUNY	3.1
40. Texas A&M University–College Station	3.1
40. University of Arizona	3.1
40. University of Colorado–Boulder	3.1
40. University of Utah	3.1
40. Virginia Tech	3.1
40. Washington University in St. Louis	3.1
48. Arizona State University	3.0
48. Boston University	3.0
48. North Carolina State University	3.0
48. University of Florida	3.0

COMPUTER SCIENCE SPECIALTIES

ARTIFICIAL INTELLIGENCE
1. Stanford University (CA)
2. Carnegie Mellon University (PA)
3. Mass. Institute of Technology
4. University of California–Berkeley
5. University of Washington
6. Georgia Institute of Technology
7. University of Illinois–Urbana-Champaign
7. University of Texas–Austin
9. Cornell University (NY)
9. University of California–Los Angeles

PROGRAMMING LANGUAGE
1. Carnegie Mellon University (PA)
2. University of California–Berkeley
3. Stanford University (CA)
4. Mass. Institute of Technology
5. Princeton University (NJ)
6. Cornell University (NY)
7. University of Pennsylvania
8. University of Texas–Austin
9. University of Illinois–Urbana-Champaign
10. University of Wisconsin–Madison

SYSTEMS
1. University of California–Berkeley
2. Mass. Institute of Technology
3. Stanford University (CA)
4. Carnegie Mellon University (PA)
5. University of Washington
6. Georgia Institute of Technology
7. University of Illinois–Urbana-Champaign
8. University of Texas–Austin
8. University of Wisconsin–Madison
10. University of Michigan–Ann Arbor

THEORY
1. University of California–Berkeley
2. Mass. Institute of Technology
3. Stanford University (CA)
4. Princeton University (NJ)
5. Carnegie Mellon University (PA)
6. Cornell University (NY)
7. Harvard University (MA)
8. Georgia Institute of Technology
9. University of Washington

EARTH SCIENCES Ranked in 2014

Rank School	Average assessment score (5.0=highest)
1. California Institute of Technology	4.9
2. Massachusetts Institute of Technology	4.8
3. Stanford University (CA)	4.6
3. University of California–Berkeley	4.6
5. Columbia University (NY)	4.5
6. Penn. State University–University Park	4.4
7. University of Arizona	4.3
8. Harvard University (MA)	4.2
8. University of Michigan–Ann Arbor	4.2
8. University of Texas–Austin	4.2
11. Princeton University (NJ)	4.1
11. University of Washington	4.1
13. University of California–Los Angeles	4.0
13. University of Wisconsin–Madison	4.0

Rank School	Average assessment score (5.0=highest)
13. Yale University (CT)	4.0
16. Brown University (RI)	3.9
16. Cornell University (NY)	3.9
16. University of California–San Diego	3.9
16. University of California–Santa Cruz	3.9
20. Arizona State University	3.8
20. University of California–Davis	3.8
20. University of Chicago	3.8
23. University of California–Santa Barbara	3.7
23. University of Colorado–Boulder	3.7
25. Colorado School of Mines	3.6
25. Rice University (TX)	3.6
25. University of Minnesota–Twin Cities	3.6
25. University of Southern California	3.6

Rank School	Average assessment score (5.0=highest)
25. Washington University in St. Louis	3.6
30. Johns Hopkins University (MD)	3.5
30. Virginia Tech	3.5
32. Texas A&M University–College Station	3.4
32. University of Maryland–College Park	3.4
34. Northwestern University (IL)	3.3
34. Ohio State University	3.3
34. Oregon State University	3.3
34. Stony Brook University–SUNY	3.3
34. University of California–Irvine	3.3
34. University of Hawaii–Manoa	3.3
34. University of Illinois–Urbana-Champaign	3.3
34. University of Oregon	3.3

EARTH SCIENCES SPECIALTIES

ENVIRONMENTAL SCIENCES
1. Stanford University (CA)
2. Pennsylvania State University–University Park
3. Columbia University (NY)
3. University of California–Berkeley
5. University of Michigan–Ann Arbor
5. University of Wisconsin–Madison

GEOCHEMISTRY
1. California Institute of Technology
2. Pennsylvania State University–University Park

GEOLOGY
1. Pennsylvania State University–University Park

2. University of Michigan–Ann Arbor
3. Stanford University (CA)
3. University of Arizona
5. California Institute of Technology
5. University of Texas–Austin

GEOPHYSICS AND SEISMOLOGY
1. University of California–Berkeley

2. California Institute of Technology
3. Stanford University (CA)
4. Massachusetts Institute of Technology

PALEONTOLOGY
1. University of Chicago
2. University of California–Berkeley

MATHEMATICS Ranked in 2014

Rank	School	Average assessment score (5.0=highest)
1.	Massachusetts Institute of Technology	5.0
1.	Princeton University (NJ)	5.0
3.	Harvard University (MA)	4.9
3.	University of California–Berkeley	4.9
5.	Stanford University (CA)	4.8
5.	University of Chicago	4.8
7.	California Institute of Technology	4.6
7.	University of California–Los Angeles	4.6
9.	Columbia University (NY)	4.5
9.	New York University	4.5
9.	University of Michigan–Ann Arbor	4.5
9.	Yale University (CT)	4.5
13.	Cornell University (NY)	4.3
14.	Brown University (RI)	4.2
14.	University of Texas–Austin	4.2
14.	University of Wisconsin–Madison	4.2
17.	Duke University (NC)	4.0
17.	Northwestern University (IL)	4.0
17.	University of Illinois–Urbana-Champaign	4.0
17.	University of Maryland–College Park	4.0
17.	University of Minnesota–Twin Cities	4.0
17.	University of Pennsylvania	4.0
23.	Rutgers, the State U. of N.J.–New Bruns.	3.9
23.	University of California–San Diego	3.9
25.	Johns Hopkins University (MD)	3.8
25.	Stony Brook University–SUNY	3.8
25.	University of Washington	3.8
28.	Georgia Institute of Technology	3.7
28.	Ohio State University	3.7
28.	Penn. State University–University Park	3.7
28.	Purdue University–West Lafayette (IN)	3.7
28.	Rice University (TX)	3.7
28.	University of North Carolina–Chapel Hill	3.7
34.	Carnegie Mellon University (PA)	3.6
34.	Indiana University–Bloomington	3.6
34.	University of California–Davis	3.6
34.	University of Illinois–Chicago	3.6
34.	University of Utah	3.6
39.	CUNY Grad School and University Ctr.	3.5
39.	Washington University in St. Louis	3.5
41.	Brandeis University (MA)	3.4
41.	Texas A&M University–College Station	3.4
41.	University of Arizona	3.4
41.	University of California–Irvine	3.4
41.	University of Notre Dame (IN)	3.4
46.	Boston University	3.3
46.	Michigan State University	3.3
46.	University of California–Santa Barbara	3.3
46.	University of Colorado–Boulder	3.3
46.	University of Southern California	3.3
46.	Vanderbilt University (TN)	3.3
52.	Dartmouth College (NH)	3.2
52.	North Carolina State University	3.2
52.	University of Georgia	3.2
52.	University of Virginia	3.2
56.	Rensselaer Polytechnic Institute (NY)	3.1
56.	University of Florida	3.1
56.	University of Iowa	3.1
56.	University of Oregon	3.1

MATHEMATICS SPECIALTIES

ALGEBRA/NUMBER THEORY/ALGEBRAIC GEOMETRY
1. Harvard University (MA)
2. Princeton University (NJ)
3. University of California–Berkeley
4. University of Chicago
5. Mass. Institute of Technology
5. University of California–Los Angeles

ANALYSIS
1. University of California–Los Angeles
2. University of California–Berkeley
3. Princeton University (NJ)
4. University of Chicago
5. Mass. Institute of Technology

6. New York University
6. Stanford University (CA)
8. University of Texas–Austin

APPLIED MATH
1. New York University
2. University of California–Los Angeles
3. California Institute of Technology
4. Mass. Institute of Technology
5. Brown University (RI)
5. University of Minnesota–Twin Cities
7. Princeton University (NJ)

DISCRETE MATHEMATICS AND COMBINATIONS
1. Mass. Institute of Technology

2. Princeton University (NJ)
3. University of California–San Diego
4. Georgia Institute of Technology
5. University of Michigan–Ann Arbor
6. University of California–Berkeley
6. University of California–Los Angeles

GEOMETRY
1. Harvard University (MA)
2. Mass. Institute of Technology
2. Stanford University (CA)
3. Stony Brook University–SUNY
4. University of California–Berkeley
6. Princeton University (NJ)

LOGIC
1. University of California–Berkeley
2. University of California–Los Angeles
3. University of Notre Dame (IN)
4. University of Illinois–Urbana-Champaign
4. University of Wisconsin–Madison

TOPOLOGY
1. University of California–Berkeley
2. Stanford University (CA)
3. Princeton University (NJ)
4. Harvard University (MA)
4. Mass. Institute of Technology
6. University of Chicago

PHYSICS Ranked in 2014

Rank	School	Average assessment score (5.0=highest)
1.	Massachusetts Institute of Technology	5.0
2.	California Institute of Technology	4.9
2.	Harvard University (MA)	4.9
2.	Princeton University (NJ)	4.9
2.	Stanford University (CA)	4.9
2.	University of California–Berkeley	4.9
7.	Cornell University (NY)	4.7
7.	University of Chicago	4.7
9.	University of Illinois–Urbana-Champaign	4.6
10.	University of California–Santa Barbara	4.5
11.	Columbia University (NY)	4.3
11.	University of Michigan–Ann Arbor	4.3
11.	Yale University (CT)	4.3
14.	University of Maryland–College Park	4.2
14.	University of Texas–Austin	4.2
16.	University of California–San Diego	4.1
16.	University of Pennsylvania	4.1
18.	Johns Hopkins University (MD)	4.0
18.	University of California–Los Angeles	4.0
18.	University of Colorado–Boulder	4.0
18.	University of Wisconsin–Madison	4.0
22.	University of Washington	3.9
23.	Ohio State University	3.8
23.	Penn. State University–University Park	3.8
23.	Stony Brook University–SUNY	3.8
26.	Northwestern University (IL)	3.7
26.	Rice University (TX)	3.7
26.	University of Minnesota–Twin Cities	3.7
29.	Brown University (RI)	3.6
29.	Duke University (NC)	3.6
29.	Georgia Institute of Technology	3.6
29.	Michigan State University	3.6
29.	Rutgers, the State U. of N.J.–New Bruns.	3.6
29.	University of California–Davis	3.6
29.	University of California–Irvine	3.6
36.	Carnegie Mellon University (PA)	3.5
36.	New York University	3.5
36.	University of Florida	3.5
39.	Boston University	3.4
39.	Indiana University–Bloomington	3.4
39.	University of Arizona	3.4
39.	University of California–Santa Cruz	3.4
39.	University of North Carolina–Chapel Hill	3.4
44.	Florida State University	3.3
44.	Purdue University–West Lafayette (IN)	3.3
44.	Texas A&M University–College Station	3.3
44.	University of Rochester (NY)	3.3
44.	University of Virginia	3.3
44.	Washington University in St. Louis	3.3
50.	Arizona State University	3.2
50.	Iowa State University	3.2
50.	University of Massachusetts–Amherst	3.2
50.	University of Pittsburgh	3.2

PHYSICS SPECIALTIES

ATOMIC/MOLECULAR/OPTICAL
1. University of Colorado–Boulder
2. Massachusetts Institute of Technology
3. Harvard University (MA)
4. Stanford University (CA)
5. University of California–Berkeley
6. University of Maryland–College Park
6. University of Rochester (NY)
8. California Institute of Technology

CONDENSED MATTER
1. University of Illinois–Urbana-Champaign
2. Stanford University (CA)
3. Massachusetts Institute of Technology
3. University of California–Berkeley
5. University of California–Santa Barbara
6. Cornell University (NY)
7. Harvard University (MA)
8. Princeton University (NJ)
9. California Institute of Technology

COSMOLOGY/RELATIVITY/GRAVITY
1. Princeton University (NJ)
2. California Institute of Technology
3. University of Chicago
4. Harvard University (MA)
5. Stanford University (CA)
5. University of California–Berkeley
7. Massachusetts Institute of Technology
8. University of California–Santa Barbara

ELEMENTARY PARTICLES/FIELDS/STRING THEORY
1. Princeton University (NJ)
2. Harvard University (MA)
3. Stanford University (CA)
4. University of California–Berkeley
5. Massachusetts Institute of Technology
6. California Institute of Technology
7. University of California–Santa Barbara

NUCLEAR
1. Michigan State University
2. University of Washington
3. Massachusetts Institute of Technology
4. Stony Brook University–SUNY
5. Indiana University–Bloomington
6. California Institute of Technology
6. Duke University (NC)
6. University of California–Berkeley
6. Yale University (CT)

PLASMA
1. Princeton University (NJ)
2. University of California–Los Angeles
3. Massachusetts Institute of Technology
3. University of Maryland–College Park
3. University of Texas–Austin
3. University of Wisconsin–Madison

QUANTUM
1. California Institute of Technology
2. Stanford University (CA)
3. Harvard University (MA)
3. Massachusetts Institute of Technology
5. Princeton University (NJ)

STATISTICS Ranked in 2014

Rank	School	Average assessment score (5.0=highest)
1.	Stanford University (CA)	4.9
2.	University of California–Berkeley	4.7
3.	Harvard University (MA)*	4.6
3.	University of Washington*	4.6
5.	Johns Hopkins University (MD)*	4.4
5.	University of Chicago	4.4
7.	Harvard University (MA)	4.3
7.	University of Washington	4.3
9.	Carnegie Mellon University (PA)	4.2
10.	Duke University (NC)	4.1

Rank	School	Average assessment score (5.0=highest)
10.	University of Pennsylvania	4.1
12.	University of Michigan–Ann Arbor*	4.0
12.	University of North Carolina–Chapel Hill*	4.0
12.	University of Wisconsin–Madison	4.0
15.	North Carolina State University	3.9
15.	Texas A&M University–College Station	3.9
15.	University of California–Berkeley*	3.9
15.	University of Michigan–Ann Arbor	3.9
19.	Iowa State University	3.8
20.	Columbia University (NY)	3.7

Rank	School	Average assessment score (5.0=highest)
20.	Pennsylvania State University	3.7
20.	University of Minnesota–Twin Cities	3.7
20.	University of North Carolina–Chapel Hill	3.7
24.	Cornell University (NY)	3.6
24.	Purdue University–West Lafayette (IN)	3.6
24.	University of Minnesota–Twin Cities*	3.6
27.	Ohio State University	3.5
27.	University of California–Davis	3.5
27.	University of Pennsylvania (Perelman)*	3.5

*Denotes a department of biostatistics

METHODOLOGY

Rankings of doctoral programs in the sciences are based on the results of surveys sent to academics in the biological sciences, chemistry, computer science, earth sciences, mathematics, physics and statistics during the fall of 2013. The individuals rated the quality of the program at each institution from marginal (1) to outstanding (5). Individuals who were unfamiliar with a particular school's programs were asked to select "don't know." The schools with the highest average scores were sorted in descending order and appear here. Results from fall 2009 and fall 2013 were averaged to compute the scores; programs had to be rated by at least 10 respondents to be ranked. Surveys were conducted by Ipsos Public Affairs. The universe surveyed in the biological sciences, chemistry, computer science, earth sciences, mathematics and physics consisted of schools that awarded at least five doctoral degrees in 2006 through 2010, according to the National Science Foundation report "Science and Engineering Doctorate Awards." The American Statistical Association provided U.S. News with eligible programs for statistics. In the biological sciences, programs may be offered in a university's medical school or college of arts and sciences. In statistics, programs may be offered through a biostatistics or statistics department. Questionnaires were sent to the department heads and directors of graduate studies at each program in each discipline. Response rates were: for biological sciences, 9 percent; chemistry, 18 percent; computer science, 35 percent; earth sciences, 17 percent; mathematics, 24 percent; physics, 29 percent; and statistics, 39 percent.

Specialty rankings are based solely on nominations by department heads and directors of graduate studies at peer schools. These respondents ranked up to 10 programs in each area. Those with the most votes appear here.

Best Online Programs

For our rankings of online graduate degree programs in business, computer information technology, criminal justice, education, engineering and nursing, U.S. News started by surveying nearly 1,000 master's programs at regionally accredited colleges that deliver all required classes predominantly online. Programs were ranked based on their success at promoting student engagement, the training and credentials of their faculty, the selectivity of their admissions processes, the services and technologies available to distance learners, and the opinions of deans and other academics at peer distance-education programs in their disciplines. Although the methodologies used in each discipline rely on varying criteria, individual ranking factors common to all include retention and graduation rates, student indebtedness at graduation, the average undergraduate GPAs of new entrants, proportion of faculty members with terminal degrees, proportion of full-time faculty who are tenured or tenure-track, and whether the program offers support services like mentoring and academic advising so they are accessible to students remotely. The top programs in each of the six disciplines are listed below. To find more detail on the methodologies and to see the complete rankings, visit usnews.com/online.

BUSINESS (MBA PROGRAMS)

Rank. School	Overall score	Average peer assessment score (5.0=highest)	'15 total enrollment	'15-'16 total program cost[1]	Entrance test required	'15 average undergrad GPA	'15 acceptance rate	'15 full-time faculty with terminal degree	'15 tenured or tenure-track faculty[2]	'15 retention rate	'15 three-year graduation rate
1. Temple University (Fox) (PA)	100	3.4	240	$59,760	GMAT or GRE	3.3	66%	100%	78%	100%	94%
2. Indiana University–Bloomington (Kelley)	99	4.2	737	N/A	GMAT or GRE	3.3	76%	83%	83%	99%	64%
3. U. of N. Carolina–Chapel Hill (Kenan-Flagler)	97	4.2	782	$99,660	GMAT or GRE	3.3	49%	87%	67%	96%	100%
4. University of Florida (Hough)	92	3.8	424	$53,440	GMAT or GRE	3.3	61%	95%	67%	96%	92%
5. Arizona State University (Carey)	91	3.8	409	N/A	GMAT or GRE	3.3	65%	93%	53%	98%	89%
6. Carnegie Mellon University (Tepper) (PA)	88	4.1	62	$120,000	GMAT or GRE	3.3	72%	91%	87%	100%	N/A
7. Pennsylvania State University–World Campus	86	3.2	282	N/A	GMAT or GRE	3.4	79%	100%	91%	90%	83%
8. Lehigh University (PA)	83	3.2	188	N/A	GMAT or GRE	3.2	85%	86%	64%	89%	41%
9. University of Texas–Dallas	82	3.3	272	$75,701	GMAT or GRE	3.4	50%	67%	41%	82%	46%
10. Arkansas State University–Jonesboro	80	2.1	118	$19,140	GMAT or GRE	3.7	85%	100%	100%	94%	92%
10. Auburn University (Harbert) (AL)	80	3.3	224	$29,255	GMAT or GRE	3.3	55%	96%	92%	94%	48%
12. Ball State University (Miller) (IN)	78	2.7	254	$17,370	GMAT or GRE	3.4	80%	100%	100%	93%	65%
12. Univ. of Massachusetts–Amherst (Isenberg)	78	3.3	1,259	$32,175	GMAT or GRE	3.3	88%	94%	71%	96%	56%
12. University of Wisconsin MBA Consortium	78	2.8	240	N/A	GMAT or GRE	3.2	92%	87%	87%	95%	78%
15. North Carolina State University (Jenkins)	76	2.9	224	N/A	GMAT or GRE	3.2	89%	92%	92%	100%	100%
15. Pepperdine University (Graziadio) (CA)	76	3.5	99	$84,240	GMAT or GRE	3.1	76%	80%	50%	94%	N/A
15. University of Nebraska–Lincoln	76	3.3	365	$25,488	GMAT or GRE	3.3	82%	94%	106%	87%	35%
15. University of North Texas	76	2.7	157	$24,948	GMAT	3.5	39%	100%	87%	93%	71%
15. U. of South Florida–St. Petersburg (Tiedemann)	76	2.3	288	$32,664	GMAT or GRE	3.4	40%	100%	85%	95%	89%
20. Cleveland State University (Ahuja) (OH)	75	2.4	38	$37,500	GMAT or GRE	3.4	34%	100%	100%	88%	N/A
20. SUNY–Oswego (NY)	75	2.6	140	$36,576	GMAT	3.3	93%	91%	91%	87%	79%
22. Georgia College & State University (Bunting)	74	2.6	61	$22,170	GMAT or GRE	3.1	91%	100%	100%	91%	100%
22. Mississippi State University	74	3.0	250	$12,323	GMAT or GRE	3.3	67%	100%	100%	85%	51%
22. University of Mississippi	74	3.0	135	N/A	GMAT or GRE	3.2	42%	92%	67%	80%	N/A
22. University of Tennessee–Martin	74	2.4	67	N/A	GMAT	3.2	53%	100%	100%	82%	100%
22. Washington State University	74	3.0	702	N/A	GMAT	3.5	46%	88%	81%	75%	N/A
27. University of Wisconsin–Whitewater	73	2.8	312	$22,608	GMAT or GRE	3.3	96%	100%	100%	97%	78%
28. Georgia Southern University	72	2.6	102	N/A	GMAT or GRE	3.1	60%	100%	100%	96%	96%
28. James Madison University (VA)	72	3.0	38	$37,800	GMAT or GRE	3.1	96%	100%	100%	N/A	N/A
28. Kennesaw State University (Coles) (GA)	72	2.8	115	N/A	GMAT or GRE	3.1	65%	100%	100%	94%	81%
31. Rochester Institute of Tech. (Saunders) (NY)	70	3.2	24	N/A	None	3.2	92%	83%	75%	100%	69%
31. University of Nevada–Reno	70	2.5	30	$24,000	GMAT or GRE	3.1	94%	100%	100%	N/A	100%
31. University of North Dakota	70	2.7	80	$13,686	GMAT or GRE	3.3	74%	88%	75%	88%	58%
34. George Mason University (VA)	69	3.2	65	N/A	GMAT or GRE	3.1	43%	100%	75%	74%	70%
34. Southern Illinois University–Carbondale	69	2.8	96	$35,868	GMAT or GRE	3.3	60%	91%	91%	88%	81%
36. Central Michigan University	68	2.6	189	N/A	GMAT	3.2	47%	88%	81%	89%	37%
36. Clarkson University (NY)	68	2.5	52	$61,194	GMAT or GRE	3.4	77%	87%	67%	93%	60%
36. Northeastern University (MA)	68	3.2	1,016	$73,800	None	3.2	89%	95%	79%	81%	59%
36. West Texas A&M University	68	2.2	500	$14,810	None	3.6	72%	97%	89%	82%	80%
36. West Virginia University	68	2.7	108	$42,144	GMAT or GRE	3.1	88%	96%	91%	91%	84%
41. Oklahoma State University (Spears)	67	3.1	412	$33,012	GMAT	3.2	94%	100%	100%	N/A	57%
41. University of Arizona (Eller)	67	3.5	121	$27,000	GMAT	3.3	75%	83%	87%	97%	N/A

▶ More @ usnews.com/grad

N/A=Data were not provided by the school; programs that received insufficient numbers of ratings do not have their peer-assessment scores published. [1]Tuition is reported for part-time, out-of-state students. [2]Percentage reported of full-time faculty.

BUSINESS (MBA PROGRAMS) continued

Rank	School	Overall score	Average peer assessment score (5.0=highest)	'15 total enrollment	'15-'16 total program cost[1]	Entrance test required	'15 average undergrad GPA	'15 acceptance rate	'15 full-time faculty with terminal degree	'15 tenured or tenure-track faculty[2]	'15 retention rate	'15 three-year graduation rate
41.	University of Colorado–Colorado Springs	67	2.8	117	N/A	GMAT or GRE	3.0	90%	86%	86%	67%	50%
44.	Creighton University (NE)	66	2.7	29	$33,000	GMAT or GRE	3.4	45%	100%	71%	100%	N/A
44.	Florida State University	66	3.1	173	N/A	GMAT or GRE	N/A	63%	100%	100%	N/A	78%
44.	George Washington University (DC)	66	3.3	394	N/A	GMAT or GRE	3.2	69%	100%	82%	85%	71%
44.	Syracuse University (Whitman) (NY)	66	3.3	445	$74,952	N/A	3.1	71%	77%	59%	96%	47%
44.	University of Michigan–Dearborn	66	2.9	107	N/A	GMAT or GRE	3.3	43%	100%	100%	71%	17%
44.	University of Utah (Eccles)	66	3.1	72	N/A	GMAT or GRE	3.4	64%	100%	56%	90%	N/A
50.	Colorado State University	65	3.2	1,174	N/A	GMAT or GRE	3.1	57%	100%	96%	83%	N/A
50.	Quinnipiac University (CT)	65	2.5	314	$41,170	GMAT or GRE	3.2	86%	97%	91%	79%	44%
52.	Marist College (NY)	63	2.4	239	$22,500	GMAT or GRE	3.4	37%	83%	75%	75%	52%
52.	University of Cincinnati (OH)	63	2.9	53	$35,303	GMAT or GRE	3.4	65%	82%	73%	83%	N/A
52.	University of South Dakota	63	2.4	207	$14,223	GMAT	3.2	84%	100%	93%	86%	57%
55.	Hofstra University (Zarb) (NY)	62	2.7	44	N/A	GMAT or GRE	N/A	70%	100%	94%	91%	78%
55.	University of West Georgia	62	2.5	111	N/A	GMAT or GRE	3.1	88%	100%	100%	94%	75%
55.	West Chester University of Pennsylvania	62	N/A	143	$14,370	GMAT or GRE	3.3	75%	100%	100%	93%	68%
58.	Old Dominion University (VA)	61	2.6	20	$20,040	GMAT or GRE	3.3	71%	100%	93%	N/A	N/A
59.	St. Joseph's University (Haub) (PA)	60	2.6	337	N/A	GMAT or GRE	3.2	72%	91%	100%	79%	44%
60.	Florida International University	59	2.5	744	$42,000	None	3.3	62%	93%	63%	N/A	N/A
60.	University of Louisiana–Monroe	59	2.3	102	$16,683	GMAT or GRE	3.0	95%	83%	83%	71%	43%
62.	Baldwin Wallace University (OH)	58	1.7	49	N/A	GMAT	3.5	100%	90%	80%	100%	100%
62.	Columbus State University (Turner) (GA)	58	2.3	22	N/A	GMAT or GRE	2.9	100%	100%	100%	100%	N/A
62.	Portland State University (OR)	58	2.7	113	N/A	GMAT or GRE	3.3	62%	75%	N/A	97%	76%
62.	Univ. of Massachusetts–Dartmouth (Charlton)	58	2.9	27	N/A	GMAT	3.5	86%	100%	100%	N/A	N/A
66.	Robert Morris University (PA)	57	1.9	57	N/A	GMAT	3.3	36%	100%	100%	100%	71%
66.	Sam Houston State University (TX)	57	2.1	350	$20,034	GMAT	3.4	80%	100%	94%	73%	55%
66.	University of Tennessee–Chattanooga	57	2.7	110	$28,128	GMAT or GRE	3.4	40%	92%	92%	N/A	N/A
69.	Baylor University (Hankamer) (TX)	56	3.3	103	$49,296	None	3.0	77%	92%	69%	N/A	N/A
69.	University of Massachusetts–Lowell	56	2.6	321	$18,900	None	3.4	N/A	88%	83%	N/A	N/A
69.	Valdosta State University (Langdale) (GA)	56	2.4	49	$22,170	GMAT or GRE	N/A	N/A	90%	100%	93%	77%

COMPUTER INFORMATION TECHNOLOGY

Rank	School	Overall score	Average peer assessment score (5.0=highest)	'15 total enrollment	'15-'16 total program cost[1]	Entrance test required	'15 average undergrad GPA	'15 acceptance rate	'15 full-time faculty with terminal degree	'15 tenured or tenure-track faculty[2]	'15 retention rate	'15 three-year graduation rate
1.	University of Southern California	100	4.0	105	N/A	GRE	3.4	56%	100%	50%	91%	88%
2.	Virginia Tech	88	3.7	369	$29,700	None	3.3	91%	100%	88%	90%	78%
3.	Boston University (MA)	75	3.7	879	$32,800	None	3.2	74%	100%	N/A	86%	58%
4.	Pennsylvania State University–World Campus	74	3.2	286	N/A	GRE	3.4	86%	100%	59%	79%	64%
5.	Johns Hopkins University (Whiting) (MD)	67	3.6	767	N/A	None	3.5	33%	N/A	N/A	83%	41%
6.	Sam Houston State University (TX)	66	2.7	50	$20,034	GRE	3.4	62%	83%	83%	78%	21%
7.	North Carolina State University	64	3.7	54	$31,837	GRE	3.5	62%	100%	93%	100%	17%
8.	Drexel University (PA)	63	3.4	179	$52,065	GRE	3.5	79%	100%	69%	89%	34%
8.	Missouri University of Science & Technology	63	2.7	61	N/A	GRE	3.3	94%	88%	83%	78%	N/A
10.	Stevens Institute of Technology (Schaefer) (NJ)	62	N/A	91	N/A	GRE	N/A	57%	83%	50%	85%	N/A
11.	Florida Institute of Technology	60	N/A	498	N/A	None	3.1	44%	100%	N/A	74%	54%
11.	Syracuse University (NY)	60	3.4	78	$49,968	None	3.3	81%	83%	70%	95%	52%
11.	Texas Tech University (Whitacre)	60	3.1	33	$19,800	GRE	3.8	48%	100%	100%	100%	N/A
14.	Pace University (NY)	56	2.4	105	N/A	None	3.3	84%	100%	100%	71%	35%
14.	University of South Florida	56	2.4	13	N/A	None	3.5	52%	100%	80%	N/A	53%

CRIMINAL JUSTICE

Rank	School	Overall score	Average peer assessment score (5.0=highest)	'15 total enrollment	'15-'16 total program cost[1]	Entrance test required	'15 average undergrad GPA	'15 acceptance rate	'15 full-time faculty with terminal degree	'15 tenured or tenure-track faculty[2]	'15 retention rate	'15 three-year graduation rate
1.	Boston University (MA)	100	2.8	498	$32,800	None	3.3	70%	100%	N/A	89%	66%
2.	Arizona State University	98	3.6	565	$16,236	None	3.3	73%	64%	73%	90%	73%
3.	Sam Houston State University (TX)	97	3.4	241	$20,034	None	3.3	92%	100%	81%	78%	63%

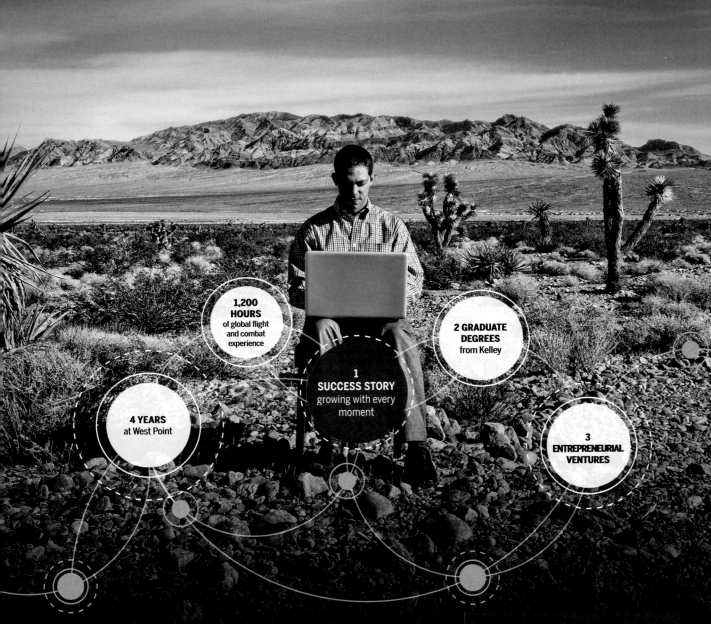

1,200 HOURS
of global flight and combat experience

2 GRADUATE DEGREES
from Kelley

1 SUCCESS STORY
growing with every moment

4 YEARS
at West Point

3 ENTREPRENEURIAL VENTURES

The pivotal moments in Tony's life mean a lot more than most. Each one starts a chain reaction of new paths, connections and opportunities. Tony earned his MBA and MS from Kelley online, so his moments go much farther.

Start building your momentum
gokelley.iu.edu/BestOnlineMBA

KELLEY
SCHOOL OF BUSINESS
GO FROM MOMENT TO MOMENTUM

CRIMINAL JUSTICE continued

Rank	School	Overall score	Average peer assessment score (5.0=highest)	'15 total enrollment	'15-'16 total program cost[1]	Entrance test required	'15 average undergrad GPA	'15 acceptance rate	'15 full-time faculty with terminal degree	'15 tenured or tenure-track faculty[2]	'15 retention rate	'15 three-year graduation rate
4.	University of California–Irvine	96	3.8	118	N/A	None	3.3	75%	93%	100%	93%	79%
5.	Florida State University	90	3.8	82	N/A	GRE	3.3	89%	100%	90%	91%	63%
6.	Columbia College (MO)	87	N/A	233	N/A	None	2.8	87%	100%	100%	87%	61%
6.	Pace University (NY)	87	N/A	18	$34,560	None	3.1	70%	100%	90%	82%	26%
8.	Indiana University of Pennsylvania	85	3.3	19	N/A	None	3.4	68%	100%	100%	N/A	95%
9.	University of Louisville (KY)	84	3.0	89	N/A	N/A	3.4	82%	100%	100%	N/A	N/A
10.	Bowling Green State University (OH)	82	2.7	17	$15,660	None	3.1	86%	100%	100%	N/A	100%
10.	Faulkner University (AL)	82	N/A	71	$14,400	None	3.1	54%	100%	100%	85%	59%
12.	University of Colorado–Denver	79	2.4	N/A	$21,996	GMAT or GRE	N/A	N/A	100%	100%	70%	N/A
12.	Western Kentucky University	79	N/A	20	$21,516	GRE	3.0	N/A	100%	100%	100%	N/A
14.	University of Cincinnati (OH)	78	4.2	820	$21,120	None	3.1	81%	100%	100%	81%	69%
14.	University of New Haven (CT)	78	2.3	76	N/A	None	N/A	N/A	100%	100%	70%	N/A
16.	Michigan State University	76	3.7	152	N/A	N/A	3.4	79%	100%	100%	N/A	84%
17.	University of the Cumberlands (KY)	74	N/A	50	N/A	None	3.2	87%	67%	33%	N/A	N/A
18.	Colorado State University–Global Campus	71	N/A	111	$18,000	None	3.0	98%	N/A	N/A	79%	N/A
18.	University of Nebraska–Omaha	71	N/A	N/A	$19,260	None	N/A	N/A	100%	100%	56%	N/A
18.	University of North Texas	71	N/A	68	N/A	None	3.4	67%	100%	100%	N/A	N/A

EDUCATION

Rank	School	Overall score	Average peer assessment score (5.0=highest)	'15 total enrollment	'15-'16 total program cost[1]	Entrance test required	'15 average undergrad GPA	'15 acceptance rate	'15 full-time faculty with terminal degree	'15 tenured or tenure-track faculty[2]	'15 retention rate	'15 three-year graduation rate
1.	University of Florida	100	3.5	206	$24,840	GRE	3.4	63%	96%	64%	100%	85%
1.	University of Houston (TX)	100	2.9	108	N/A	GRE	3.3	75%	100%	65%	96%	93%
3.	Florida State University	94	3.4	125	N/A	GRE	3.5	46%	83%	83%	88%	62%
3.	University of Georgia	94	3.6	89	$22,277	GRE	3.4	84%	100%	87%	97%	N/A
5.	Northern Illinois University	88	3.1	166	N/A	GRE	3.2	100%	100%	77%	97%	85%
6.	Pennsylvania State University–World Campus	87	3.8	347	N/A	GRE	3.5	78%	100%	54%	84%	49%
7.	Auburn University (AL)	86	3.3	165	$17,220	GRE	3.3	66%	98%	88%	90%	78%
7.	University of Illinois–Urbana-Champaign	86	3.5	236	$11,008	None	3.5	90%	100%	100%	90%	89%
9.	George Washington University (DC)	85	3.5	153	N/A	GRE	3.4	88%	100%	64%	94%	72%
9.	University of Massachusetts–Lowell	85	3.2	250	$14,100	None	3.4	90%	100%	86%	93%	72%
11.	Ball State University (IN)	84	3.3	2,410	$17,370	None	3.2	92%	94%	74%	84%	58%
11.	Michigan State University	84	3.7	822	$23,025	None	3.5	78%	93%	72%	91%	74%
11.	St. John's University (NY)	84	3.0	37	N/A	None	3.2	90%	100%	93%	90%	N/A
14.	East Carolina University (NC)	83	2.9	366	N/A	None	3.3	98%	100%	95%	93%	74%
14.	University at Albany–SUNY	83	N/A	278	$59,572	None	N/A	79%	100%	94%	97%	84%
14.	University of Nebraska–Lincoln	83	3.4	109	$21,924	None	N/A	50%	100%	88%	86%	52%
17.	Central Michigan University	82	2.7	463	N/A	None	3.3	88%	97%	90%	80%	65%
17.	North Carolina Central University	82	N/A	32	$53,123	None	3.3	89%	100%	100%	100%	93%
17.	University of Iowa	82	3.3	24	$19,944	GRE	3.3	80%	100%	33%	93%	100%
17.	Utah State University	82	3.0	91	$15,383	None	3.5	85%	63%	63%	77%	84%
17.	Wright State University (OH)	82	2.5	96	$18,240	None	3.5	100%	100%	100%	95%	N/A
22.	Graceland University (IA)	81	N/A	129	$13,500	None	3.5	98%	100%	100%	95%	82%
22.	Indiana University–Bloomington	81	3.7	206	$18,000	GRE	3.4	86%	100%	100%	81%	58%
22.	University of South Carolina	81	3.1	381	$22,500	GRE	3.3	83%	100%	90%	N/A	73%
25.	New York Institute of Technology	80	2.4	225	N/A	None	3.4	71%	90%	100%	90%	76%
25.	University of Dayton (OH)	80	2.3	455	$18,090	N/A	3.3	64%	86%	68%	75%	69%
25.	University of Mississippi	80	3.0	57	N/A	None	3.4	55%	100%	100%	100%	79%
25.	University of Nebraska–Kearney	80	2.6	841	$14,580	None	3.4	97%	85%	80%	95%	40%
25.	William Carey University (MS)	80	N/A	235	$9,900	None	3.3	86%	100%	100%	97%	100%
30.	Emporia State University (KS)	79	2.7	1,223	$12,276	None	3.3	49%	95%	88%	84%	70%
30.	Sam Houston State University (TX)	79	2.5	856	$20,034	GRE	3.3	95%	100%	84%	79%	59%
30.	University of Cincinnati (OH)	79	2.9	906	$19,650	None	3.4	75%	95%	84%	85%	73%
30.	University of Texas–Arlington	79	2.5	2,033	N/A	GRE	3.4	64%	100%	75%	93%	79%
34.	Arizona State University	78	3.6	2,190	$16,650	None	3.4	91%	96%	65%	93%	77%
34.	California State University–Fullerton	78	3.1	377	N/A	None	3.3	79%	100%	79%	90%	72%

OUR ALUMNI *Never Begin* SENTENCES *With*

"If I only knew someone who worked in ______________."

Tap into the power of more than 225,000 alumni throughout the world from anywhere, any time.

Join the George Washington community and work the network. Select online programs include:

- Online Healthcare MBA
- Master's in Strategic Public Relations Online
- Master's in Political Management Online
- Master's in Paralegal Studies Online

Connect now.

Visit **mygraduateprogram.com**

The George Washington University does not unlawfully discriminate in its admissions programs against any person based on that person's race, color, religion, sex, national origin, age, disability, veteran status, sexual orientation, or gender identity or expression.

THE GEORGE WASHINGTON UNIVERSITY

WASHINGTON, DC

EDUCATION continued

Rank	School	Overall score	Average peer assessment score (5.0=highest)	'15 total enrollment	'15-'16 total program cost[1]	Entrance test required	'15 average undergrad GPA	'15 acceptance rate	'15 full-time faculty with terminal degree	'15 tenured or tenure-track faculty[2]	'15 retention rate	'15 three-year graduation rate
36.	Angelo State University (TX)	77	N/A	573	N/A	None	3.2	96%	56%	56%	97%	100%
36.	Creighton University (NE)	77	2.6	116	N/A	None	N/A	80%	100%	100%	95%	N/A
36.	Georgia State University	77	3.1	128	N/A	GRE	3.3	100%	100%	76%	86%	65%
36.	University of Colorado–Denver	77	3.2	407	N/A	None	3.3	N/A	100%	100%	73%	58%
36.	University of South Florida	77	3.2	N/A	N/A	None	3.3	72%	100%	83%	72%	60%
41.	Purdue University–West Lafayette (IN)	75	3.5	259	N/A	GRE	3.4	73%	91%	64%	91%	56%
41.	Stony Brook University–SUNY	75	3.3	308	N/A	GRE	3.4	88%	100%	100%	81%	61%
41.	University at Buffalo–SUNY	75	3.3	89	$33,300	None	3.4	97%	100%	55%	83%	N/A
44.	Texas A&M University–College Station	74	3.4	551	N/A	None	3.4	73%	100%	51%	N/A	75%
44.	Western Kentucky University	74	2.7	333	N/A	GRE	3.0	N/A	97%	92%	76%	41%
46.	Regent University (VA)	73	1.8	831	$15,525	None	3.6	75%	100%	78%	87%	48%
46.	University of North Florida	73	2.6	95	N/A	GRE	3.2	52%	88%	76%	N/A	80%
48.	Brenau University (GA)	72	1.8	116	$22,356	None	3.3	44%	100%	N/A	85%	71%
48.	College of St. Scholastica (MN)	72	N/A	76	N/A	None	3.5	91%	83%	83%	92%	59%
48.	Fort Hays State University (KS)	72	2.6	1,156	$9,108	None	3.4	91%	92%	83%	90%	22%
48.	Old Dominion University (Darden) (VA)	72	2.8	540	$30,218	GRE	N/A	N/A	82%	73%	81%	89%
48.	University of Colorado–Colorado Springs	72	N/A	93	N/A	None	N/A	N/A	89%	100%	82%	44%
53.	Armstrong State University (GA)	71	N/A	80	$12,000	None	3.3	88%	86%	79%	80%	86%
53.	Augustana University (SD)	71	2.2	221	N/A	None	3.5	100%	100%	88%	99%	93%
53.	Boise State University (ID)	71	3.2	633	$12,518	None	3.5	58%	100%	93%	88%	66%
53.	Drexel University (PA)	71	2.8	915	N/A	None	3.3	88%	98%	39%	85%	57%
53.	Kansas State University	71	3.0	462	N/A	None	3.4	95%	100%	93%	76%	89%
53.	University of Alaska–Anchorage	71	N/A	298	N/A	None	3.2	45%	81%	56%	93%	59%
53.	University of Arkansas–Fayetteville	71	3.0	268	$13,200	GRE	3.4	67%	100%	71%	77%	37%
53.	University of North Carolina–Pembroke	71	2.6	35	N/A	None	3.2	100%	100%	100%	100%	N/A
53.	University of North Carolina–Wilmington	71	2.8	289	$26,565	GRE	N/A	N/A	100%	100%	N/A	80%
62.	Concordia University (IL)	70	1.8	1,798	$13,350	None	N/A	73%	75%	51%	84%	78%
62.	Ohio University	70	2.9	868	$21,240	None	3.4	85%	100%	67%	71%	55%
62.	Pittsburg State University (KS)	70	2.6	396	N/A	None	3.3	N/A	91%	77%	82%	62%
62.	University of San Diego (CA)	70	3.3	133	$21,300	None	3.2	95%	100%	100%	96%	N/A

ENGINEERING

Rank	School	Overall score	Average peer assessment score (5.0=highest)	'15 total enrollment	'15-'16 total program cost[1]	Entrance test required	'15 average undergrad GPA	'15 acceptance rate	'15 full-time faculty with terminal degree	'15 tenured or tenure-track faculty[2]	'15 retention rate	'15 three-year graduation rate
1.	University of California–Los Angeles (Samueli)	100	3.5	329	$34,650	GRE	3.5	43%	100%	100%	87%	77%
2.	University of Southern California (Viterbi)	97	4.0	828	N/A	GRE	3.4	48%	100%	63%	92%	83%
3.	Columbia University (Fu Foundation) (NY)	93	3.7	296	N/A	GRE	3.7	92%	100%	78%	95%	92%
4.	Pennsylvania State University–World Campus	86	3.5	740	N/A	None	3.3	92%	98%	76%	92%	79%
5.	Purdue University–West Lafayette (IN)	84	3.9	770	$34,890	None	3.5	65%	100%	93%	88%	53%
6.	University of Wisconsin–Madison	78	3.8	222	$48,000	None	3.3	64%	78%	71%	93%	55%
7.	Mississippi State University (Bagley)	76	2.6	175	N/A	GRE	3.2	71%	100%	98%	98%	100%
8.	Cornell University (NY)	75	3.8	103	N/A	GRE	N/A	83%	92%	62%	N/A	85%
9.	Missouri University of Science & Technology	73	2.6	998	N/A	GRE	3.3	88%	96%	71%	82%	67%
9.	Virginia Tech	73	3.6	34	N/A	GRE	3.5	16%	100%	100%	94%	N/A
11.	Johns Hopkins University (Whiting) (MD)	71	3.3	2,226	N/A	None	3.4	49%	100%	33%	89%	41%
12.	Arizona State University (Fulton)	70	3.3	345	N/A	None	3.3	59%	98%	89%	78%	31%
12.	New York University	70	2.9	134	N/A	None	3.5	51%	57%	25%	76%	60%
12.	North Carolina State University	70	3.4	659	$26,100	GRE	3.4	69%	100%	98%	N/A	31%
12.	University of Nebraska–Lincoln	70	2.2	46	$27,000	None	N/A	77%	100%	100%	82%	73%
16.	California State University–Fullerton	69	2.4	189	N/A	None	3.3	72%	100%	100%	82%	84%
16.	Texas Tech University (Whitacre)	69	2.4	128	N/A	GRE	3.2	38%	100%	100%	87%	56%
16.	University of Maryland–College Park (Clark)	69	3.6	427	$31,980	None	3.3	54%	100%	100%	71%	42%
19.	University of North Carolina–Charlotte (Lee)	67	2.5	77	$24,720	GRE	3.3	46%	100%	86%	100%	79%
20.	University of South Florida	66	2.3	144	N/A	GRE	3.4	67%	100%	75%	92%	76%
21.	University of Illinois–Chicago	65	2.7	113	$29,880	None	N/A	29%	100%	100%	N/A	N/A
22.	Kansas State University	64	2.6	188	$23,190	None	3.3	82%	100%	91%	80%	74%

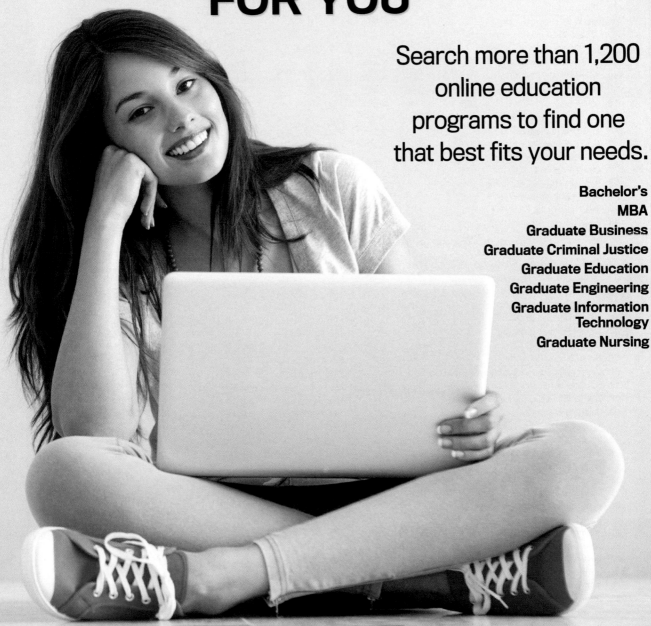

FIND THE BEST ONLINE PROGRAM FOR YOU

Search more than 1,200 online education programs to find one that best fits your needs.

Bachelor's
MBA
Graduate Business
Graduate Criminal Justice
Graduate Education
Graduate Engineering
Graduate Information Technology
Graduate Nursing

U.S.News & WORLD REPORT

Start your search today: **usnews.com/education/online-education**

ENGINEERING continued

Rank	School	Overall score	Average peer assessment score (5.0=highest)	'15 total enrollment	'15-'16 total program cost[1]	Entrance test required	'15 average undergrad GPA	'15 acceptance rate	'15 full-time faculty with terminal degree	'15 tenured or tenure-track faculty[2]	'15 retention rate	'15 three-year graduation rate
22.	University of Virginia	64	2.9	58	N/A	GRE	3.2	76%	100%	88%	73%	N/A
24.	Drexel University (PA)	63	2.9	402	N/A	None	3.1	74%	100%	35%	90%	38%
25.	Calif. Polytechnic State Univ.–San Luis Obispo	62	2.3	51	N/A	None	3.2	97%	100%	80%	76%	78%
25.	Ohio State University	62	3.1	44	N/A	None	3.3	95%	93%	71%	92%	N/A
27.	Auburn University (AL)	61	3.1	102	N/A	GRE	3.1	73%	100%	98%	90%	26%
27.	Villanova University (PA)	61	2.3	400	$36,500	None	3.5	72%	92%	92%	91%	73%
29.	Ohio University (Russ)	60	2.3	231	$21,250	None	3.2	94%	96%	92%	79%	59%
29.	Rutgers, the State Univ. of N.J.–New Brunswick	60	2.7	N/A	N/A	GRE	3.1	38%	100%	100%	75%	N/A
29.	University of Colorado–Colorado Springs	60	2.1	68	N/A	None	3.1	88%	100%	50%	79%	44%

NURSING

Rank	School	Overall score	Average peer assessment score (5.0=highest)	'15 total enrollment	'15-'16 total program cost[1]	Entrance test required	'15 average undergrad GPA	'15 acceptance rate	'15 full-time faculty with terminal degree	'15 tenured or tenure-track faculty[2]	'15 retention rate	'15 three-year graduation rate
1.	University of South Carolina	100	3.3	118	N/A	None	3.4	72%	87%	67%	97%	79%
2.	Medical University of South Carolina	98	3.6	238	$59,100	None	3.7	42%	92%	100%	100%	100%
3.	St. Xavier University (IL)	96	3.3	234	N/A	None	3.5	91%	90%	100%	98%	99%
4.	Ohio State University	94	3.7	111	$50,065	None	3.5	45%	68%	27%	100%	86%
5.	Duke University (NC)	93	4.0	547	$65,856	GRE	3.5	48%	98%	48%	98%	89%
6.	Johns Hopkins University (MD)	92	4.1	53	N/A	None	3.6	37%	100%	42%	93%	45%
7.	University of Texas–Tyler	91	3.3	334	$16,280	None	3.2	64%	100%	96%	100%	86%
8.	Georgia College & State University	90	3.0	120	N/A	GRE	3.4	96%	91%	100%	100%	87%
8.	University of Cincinnati (OH)	90	3.5	1,306	$30,785	None	3.5	51%	79%	79%	90%	77%
10.	Stony Brook University–SUNY (NY)	89	3.3	563	$11,881	None	3.4	61%	86%	14%	95%	85%
11.	Oregon Health and Science University	88	3.7	52	$38,054	None	3.5	92%	92%	33%	89%	84%
11.	Rush University (IL)	88	3.9	558	N/A	GRE	3.3	75%	80%	49%	88%	68%
13.	George Washington University (DC)	87	3.5	529	$49,400	None	3.4	64%	92%	75%	94%	78%
13.	Samford University (AL)	87	2.9	276	N/A	None	3.5	65%	95%	85%	93%	87%
13.	University of Colorado–Colorado Springs	87	3.5	222	N/A	None	3.5	63%	78%	44%	86%	27%
13.	University of Nevada–Las Vegas	87	3.4	73	$33,350	None	3.6	52%	56%	36%	97%	65%
17.	University of Alabama–Birmingham	86	N/A	1,930	$52,246	GRE	3.4	69%	84%	24%	97%	71%
18.	Duquesne University (PA)	85	3.6	171	N/A	None	3.5	81%	86%	82%	98%	39%
18.	Eastern Kentucky University	85	3.0	341	$23,790	None	3.6	68%	89%	89%	N/A	N/A
20.	Graceland University (MO)	84	2.8	523	N/A	None	3.6	83%	64%	73%	94%	83%
20.	Texas Christian University	84	3.2	103	$56,600	GRE	3.4	96%	100%	58%	N/A	97%
20.	University of Texas Medical Branch–Galveston	84	3.3	544	$33,056	None	3.3	33%	75%	29%	96%	82%
23.	Ball State University (IN)	83	3.1	476	$27,213	None	3.6	55%	90%	N/A	92%	61%
23.	East Carolina University (NC)	83	3.3	435	N/A	GRE	3.3	40%	62%	38%	91%	N/A
23.	University of Arizona	83	3.3	365	$30,000	None	3.4	64%	56%	41%	88%	N/A
23.	University of Missouri–Kansas City	83	3.5	219	$17,200	None	3.6	88%	89%	11%	89%	75%
23.	University of Pittsburgh (PA)	83	3.6	105	$28,296	GRE	3.7	80%	100%	26%	70%	52%
28.	Clarion U. of Pennsylvania/Edinboro U. of Penn.	82	2.6	108	$25,110	None	3.5	82%	100%	100%	N/A	47%
28.	Frontier Nursing University (KY)	82	3.5	1,757	$34,240	None	3.6	54%	82%	N/A	N/A	82%
28.	Georgetown University (DC)	82	3.6	1,062	$81,972	None	3.5	33%	97%	N/A	61%	88%
31.	Augusta University (GA)	81	3.0	151	$52,072	GRE	3.5	50%	83%	33%	N/A	100%
31.	Michigan State University	81	3.5	40	$34,874	None	3.5	91%	77%	46%	100%	59%
31.	Old Dominion University (VA)	81	3.2	118	N/A	GRE	3.3	30%	100%	55%	86%	77%
31.	University of Kansas	81	3.8	104	N/A	None	3.5	90%	94%	54%	75%	20%
31.	University of West Georgia	81	2.9	87	$22,212	None	3.3	90%	100%	100%	88%	73%
36.	Texas A&M University–Corpus Christi	80	3.2	449	N/A	None	3.4	41%	89%	100%	80%	69%
36.	Texas Tech University Health Sciences Center	80	3.5	735	N/A	None	3.6	39%	91%	39%	N/A	82%
36.	Vanderbilt University (TN)	80	3.8	10	$23,770	GRE	3.3	67%	100%	N/A	N/A	81%
39.	Angelo State University (TX)	79	3.1	87	N/A	None	3.4	40%	77%	46%	95%	89%
39.	Clarkson College (NE)	79	3.1	508	$25,145	None	3.5	45%	100%	N/A	90%	74%
39.	Jacksonville University (FL)	79	2.8	486	$20,100	None	3.9	89%	100%	46%	95%	93%

DIRECTORY OF GRADUATE SCHOOLS

Schools are listed alphabetically by state within each discipline; data are accurate as of late February 2016. A key to the terminology used in the directory can be found at the beginning of each area of study.

BUSINESS

The business directory lists all 470 U.S. schools offering master's programs in business accredited by AACSB International–the Association to Advance Collegiate Schools of Business, as of August 2015. Most offer the MBA degree; a few offer the master of business. Three hundred and seventy-nine schools responded to the U.S. News survey conducted in the fall of 2015 and early 2016. Schools that did not respond to the survey have abbreviated entries.

KEY TO THE TERMINOLOGY

1. A school whose name is footnoted with the numeral 1 did not return the U.S. News statistical survey; limited data appear in its entry.
N/A. Not available from the school or not applicable.
Email. The address of the admissions office. If instead of an email address a website is given in this field, the website will automatically present an email screen programmed to reach the admissions office.
Application deadline. For fall 2017 enrollment. "Rolling" means there is no application deadline; the school acts on applications as they are received. "Varies" means deadlines vary according to department or whether applicants are U.S. citizens or foreign nationals.
Tuition. For the 2015-16 academic year or for the cost of the total graduate business degree program, if specified. Includes required annual student fees.
Credit hour. The cost per credit hour for the 2015-16 academic year.
Room/board/expenses. For the 2015-16 academic year.
College-funded aid and international student aid. "Yes" means the school provides its own financial aid to students.
Average indebtedness. Computed for 2015 graduates who incurred business school debt.
Enrollment. Full-time and part-time program totals are for fall 2015.
Minorities. For fall 2015, percentage of students who are black or African-American, Asian, American Indian or Alaska Native, Native Hawaiian or other Pacific Islander, Hispanic/Latino, or two or more races. The minority percentage was reported by each school.
Acceptance rate. Percentage of applicants to the full-time program who were accepted for fall 2015.
Average Graduate Management Admission Test (GMAT) score. Calculated

separately for full-time and part-time students who entered in fall 2015.
Average undergraduate grade point average (1.0 to 4.0). For full-time program applicants who entered in fall 2015.
Average age of entrants. Calculated for full-time students who entered in fall 2015.
Average months of work experience. Calculated only for full-time program students who entered in fall 2015. Refers to post-baccalaureate work experience only.
TOEFL requirement. "Yes" means that students from non-English-speaking countries must submit scores for the Test of English as a Foreign Language.
Minimum TOEFL score. The lowest score on the paper TOEFL accepted for admission. (The computer-administered TOEFL is graded on a different scale.)
Most popular departments. Based on highest student demand in the 2015-16 academic year.
Mean starting base salary for 2015 graduates. Calculated only for graduates who were full-time students, had accepted full-time job offers, and reported salary data. Excludes employer-sponsored students, signing bonuses of any kind and other forms of guaranteed compensation, such as stock options.
Employment locations. For the 2015 graduating class. Calculated only for full-time students who had accepted job offers. Abbreviations: **Intl.**, international; **N.E.**, Northeast (Conn., Maine, Mass., N.H., N.J., N.Y., R.I., Vt.); **M.A.**, Middle Atlantic (Del., D.C., Md., Pa., Va., W.Va.); **S.**, South (Ala., Ark., Fla., Ga., Ky., La., Miss., N.C., S.C., Tenn.); **M.W.**, Midwest (Ill., Ind., Iowa, Kan., Mich., Minn., Mo., Neb., N.D., Ohio, S.D., Wis.); **S.W.**, Southwest (Ariz., Colo., N.M., Okla., Texas); **W.**, West (Alaska, Calif., Hawaii, Idaho, Mont., Nev., Ore., Utah, Wash., Wyo.).

ALABAMA

Auburn University (Harbert)
415 W. Magnolia, Suite 503
Auburn, AL 36849-5240
www.business.auburn.edu/mba
Public
Admissions: (334) 844-4060
Email: mbadmis@auburn.edu
Financial aid: (334) 844-4367
Application deadline: 02/01
In-state tuition: total program: $24,227 (full time); part time: N/A
Out-of-state tuition: total program: $50,633 (full time)
Room/board/expenses: $19,776
College-funded aid: Yes
International student aid: Yes
Average student indebtedness at graduation: $34,408
Full-time enrollment: 72
men: 60%; women: 40%;
minorities: 6%; international: 21%
Part-time enrollment: N/A
men: N/A; women: N/A; minorities: N/A; international: N/A
Acceptance rate (full time): 47%
Average GMAT (full time): 578
Average GPA (full time): 3.28
Average age of entrants to full-time program: 25
Average months of prior work experience (full time): 56
TOEFL requirement: Yes
Minimum TOEFL score: 550
Most popular departments: finance, human resources management, management information systems, supply chain management, statistics and operations research
Mean starting base salary for 2015 full-time graduates: $54,111
Employment location for 2015 class: Intl. N/A; N.E. N/A; M.A. N/A; S. 100%; M.W. N/A; S.W. N/A; W. N/A

Auburn University-Montgomery
7300 East Drive
Montgomery, AL 36117
www.aum.edu
Public
Admissions: (334) 244-3623
Email: awarren3@aum.edu
Financial aid: (334) 244-3571
Application deadline: 08/01
In-state tuition: full time: $359/credit hour; part time: $359/credit hour
Out-of-state tuition: full time: $807/credit hour
Room/board/expenses: N/A
College-funded aid: Yes
International student aid: Yes
Full-time enrollment: 58
men: 47%; women: 53%;
minorities: 12%; international: 41%
Part-time enrollment: 45
men: 53%; women: 47%;
minorities: 16%; international: 16%
Acceptance rate (full time): 86%
Average GMAT (full time): 489
TOEFL requirement: Yes
Minimum TOEFL score: 500

Jacksonville State University[1]
700 Pelham Road N
Jacksonville, AL 36265
www.jsu.edu/ccba/
Public
Admissions: (256) 782-5268
Email: info@jsu.edu
Financial aid: N/A
Tuition: N/A
Room/board/expenses: N/A
Enrollment: N/A

Samford University (Brock)
800 Lakeshore Drive
Birmingham, AL 35229
www.samford.edu/business/
Private
Admissions: (205) 726-2040
Email: gradbusi@samford.edu
Financial aid: (205) 726-2905
Application deadline: rolling
Tuition: full time: N/A; part time: $766/credit hour
Room/board/expenses: N/A
College-funded aid: Yes
International student aid: No
Full-time enrollment: N/A
men: N/A; women: N/A; minorities: N/A; international: N/A
Part-time enrollment: 97
men: 56%; women: 44%;
minorities: 15%; international: 6%
Average GMAT (part time): 533
TOEFL requirement: Yes
Minimum TOEFL score: N/A

University of Alabama-Birmingham
1720 2nd Avenue South
Birmingham, AL 35294-4460
www.uab.edu/mba
Public
Admissions: (205) 934-8817
Email: cmanning@uab.edu
Financial aid: (205) 934-8223
Application deadline: 07/01
In-state tuition: full time: N/A; part time: $457/credit hour
Out-of-state tuition: full time: N/A
Room/board/expenses: N/A
College-funded aid: Yes
International student aid: No
Full-time enrollment: N/A
men: N/A; women: N/A; minorities: N/A; international: N/A
Part-time enrollment: 247
men: 58%; women: 42%;
minorities: 18%; international: 12%
Average GMAT (part time): 552
TOEFL requirement: Yes
Minimum TOEFL score: 550
Most popular departments: finance, health care administration, marketing, management information systems

University of Alabama-Huntsville
BAB 202
Huntsville, AL 35899
cba.uah.edu/
Public
Admissions: (256) 824-6681
Email: gradbiz@uah.edu
Financial aid: (256) 824-6241

Application deadline: 06/01
In-state tuition: full time: $9,548;
part time: $675/credit hour
Out-of-state tuition: full time:
$21,402
Room/board/expenses: $11,000
College-funded aid: Yes
International student aid: Yes
Average student indebtedness at
graduation: $15,480
Full-time enrollment: 69
men: 57%; women: 43%;
minorities: 14%; international: 17%
Part-time enrollment: 126
men: 58%; women: 42%;
minorities: 16%; international: 1%
Acceptance rate (full time): 92%
Average GMAT (full time): 500
Average GMAT (part time): 533
Average GPA (full time): 3.13
Average age of entrants to full-time
program: 29
Average months of prior work
experience (full time): 100
TOEFL requirement: Yes
Minimum TOEFL score: 550
Most popular departments:
accounting, general management,
manufacturing and technology
management, supply chain
management, technology

University of Alabama (Manderson)

Box 870223
Tuscaloosa, AL 35487
www.cba.ua.edu/~mba
Public
Admissions: (888) 863-2622
Email: mba@cba.ua.edu
Financial aid: (205) 348-6517
Application deadline: 04/15
In-state tuition: full time: $13,000;
part time: N/A
Out-of-state tuition: full time:
$28,780
Room/board/expenses: N/A
College-funded aid: Yes
International student aid: Yes
Full-time enrollment: 192
men: 71%; women: 29%;
minorities: 9%; international: 8%
Part-time enrollment: N/A
men: N/A; women: N/A; minorities:
N/A; international: N/A
Acceptance rate (full time): 58%
Average GMAT (full time): 679
Average GPA (full time): 3.59
Average age of entrants to full-time
program: 22
Average months of prior work
experience (full time): 40
TOEFL requirement: Yes
Minimum TOEFL score: 550
Most popular departments:
consulting, management
information systems, operations
management, supply chain
management, statistics and
operations research
Mean starting base salary for 2015
full-time graduates: $66,755
Employment location for 2015 class:
Intl. 0%; N.E. 4%; M.A. 2%; S.
80%; M.W. 8%; S.W. 2%; W. 4%

University of Montevallo

Morgan Hall 201, Station 6540
Montevallo, AL 35115
www.montevallo.edu/grad/
Public
Admissions: (205) 665-6350
Email: graduate@montevallo.edu
Financial aid: (205) 665-6050
Application deadline: 07/01

In-state tuition: full time: $391/
credit hour; part time: $391/
credit hour
Out-of-state tuition: full time: $803/
credit hour
Room/board/expenses: N/A
College-funded aid: Yes
International student aid: N/A
men: N/A; women: N/A; minorities:
N/A; international: N/A
Part-time enrollment: 36
men: 61%; women: 39%;
minorities: 50%; international: 11%
TOEFL requirement: Yes
Minimum TOEFL score: 525

University of South Alabama (Mitchell)[1]

307 N. University Boulevard
Mobile, AL 36688
mcob.usouthal.edu
Public
Admissions: (251) 460-6418
Financial aid: N/A
Tuition: N/A
Room/board/expenses: N/A
Enrollment: N/A

ALASKA

University of Alaska-Anchorage[1]

3211 Providence Drive
Anchorage, AK 99508
www.uaa.alaska.edu/cbpp/
Public
Admissions: (907) 786-1480
Email:
admissions@uaa.alaska.edu
Financial aid: N/A
Tuition: N/A
Room/board/expenses: N/A
Enrollment: N/A

University of Alaska-Fairbanks

PO Box 756080
Fairbanks, AK 99775-6080
www.uaf.edu/index.html
Public
Admissions: (800) 478-1823
Email: admissions@uaf.edu
Financial aid: (888) 474-7256
Application deadline: 06/01
In-state tuition: full time: $491/
credit hour; part time: $491/
credit hour
Out-of-state tuition: full time: $932/
credit hour
Room/board/expenses: $12,430
College-funded aid: Yes
International student aid: Yes
Average student indebtedness at
graduation: $15,006
Full-time enrollment: 19
men: 37%; women: 63%;
minorities: 5%; international: 5%
Part-time enrollment: 44
men: 55%; women: 45%;
minorities: 18%; international: 2%
Acceptance rate (full time): 61%
Average GMAT (part time): 430
Average age of entrants to full-time
program: 25
TOEFL requirement: Yes
Minimum TOEFL score: N/A
Most popular departments: finance,
general management

Arizona State University (Carey)

PO Box 874906
Tempe, AZ 85287-4906
wpcarey.asu.edu/
mba-programs
Public
Admissions: (480) 965-3332
Email: wpcareymasters@asu.edu
Financial aid: (480) 965-6890
Application deadline: 06/30
In-state tuition: full time: $26,304;
part time: $26,554
Out-of-state tuition: full time:
$42,780
Room/board/expenses: $19,044
College-funded aid: Yes
International student aid: Yes
Average student indebtedness at
graduation: $45,662
Full-time enrollment: 150
men: 71%; women: 29%;
minorities: 17%; international: 28%
Part-time enrollment: 234
men: 73%; women: 27%;
minorities: 22%; international: 9%
Acceptance rate (full time): 31%
Average GMAT (full time): 672
Average GMAT (part time): 584
Average GPA (full time): 3.37
Average age of entrants to full-time
program: 28
Average months of prior work
experience (full time): 59
TOEFL requirement: Yes
Minimum TOEFL score: 550
Most popular departments:
finance, marketing, management
information systems, supply chain
management, other
Mean starting base salary for 2015
full-time graduates: $98,945
Employment location for 2015 class:
Intl. 2%; N.E. 5%; M.A. 0%; S. 7%;
M.W. 7%; S.W. 42%; W. 38%

Northern Arizona University (Franke)

PO Box 15066
Flagstaff, AZ 86011-5066
www.franke.nau.edu/gradu-
ateprograms
Public
Admissions: (928) 523-7342
Email: fcb-gradprog@nau.edu
Financial aid: (928) 523-4951
Application deadline: rolling
In-state tuition: total program:
$17,977 (full time); part time: N/A
Out-of-state tuition: total program:
$29,617 (full time)
Room/board/expenses: N/A
College-funded aid: Yes
International student aid: Yes
Full-time enrollment: 36
men: 58%; women: 42%;
minorities: 14%; international: 6%
Part-time enrollment: N/A
men: N/A; women: N/A; minorities:
N/A; international: N/A
Acceptance rate (full time): 96%
Average GMAT (full time): 559
Average GPA (full time): 3.53
Average age of entrants to full-time
program: 25
Average months of prior work
experience (full time): 24
TOEFL requirement: Yes
Minimum TOEFL score: 550
Mean starting base salary for 2015
full-time graduates: $55,151

Thunderbird School of Global Management

1 Global Place
Glendale, AZ 85306-6000
www.thunderbird.edu
Public
Admissions: (602) 978-7100
Email:
admissions@thunderbird.edu
Financial aid: (602) 978-7130
Application deadline: 05/10
In-state tuition: total program:
$70,000 (full time); part time: N/A
Out-of-state tuition: total program:
$70,000 (full time)
Room/board/expenses: $5,265
College-funded aid: Yes
International student aid: Yes
Average student indebtedness at
graduation: $81,852
Full-time enrollment: 141
men: 77%; women: 23%;
minorities: 6%; international: 61%
Part-time enrollment: N/A
men: N/A; women: N/A; minorities:
N/A; international: N/A
Acceptance rate (full time): 71%
Average GMAT (full time): 570
Average GPA (full time): 3.20
Average age of entrants to full-time
program: 30
Average months of prior work
experience (full time): 74
TOEFL requirement: Yes
Minimum TOEFL score: 600
Most popular departments:
accounting, finance, general
management, international
business, marketing
Mean starting base salary for 2015
full-time graduates: $74,784
Employment location for 2015 class:
Intl. 23%; N.E. 6%; M.A. 2%; S.
4%; M.W. 17%; S.W. 32%; W. 16%

University of Arizona (Eller)

McClelland Hall, Room 417
Tucson, AZ 85721-0108
ellermba.arizona.edu
Public
Admissions: (520) 621-6227
Email: mba_admissions@
eller.arizona.edu
Financial aid: (520) 621-1858
Application deadline: 05/01
In-state tuition: full time: $23,562;
part time: $25,500
Out-of-state tuition: full time:
$41,884
Room/board/expenses: $13,200
College-funded aid: Yes
International student aid: Yes
Average student indebtedness at
graduation: $32,649
Full-time enrollment: 81
men: 68%; women: 32%;
minorities: 15%; international: 41%
Part-time enrollment: 204
men: 61%; women: 39%;
minorities: 34%; international: 4%
Acceptance rate (full time): 39%
Average GMAT (full time): 654
Average GMAT (part time): 505
Average GPA (full time): 3.30
Average age of entrants to full-time
program: 26
Average months of prior work
experience (full time): 39
TOEFL requirement: Yes
Minimum TOEFL score: 600
Most popular departments:
entrepreneurship, finance, health
care administration, marketing,
management information systems
Mean starting base salary for 2015
full-time graduates: $78,009

Employment location for 2015 class:
Intl. 9%; N.E. 5%; M.A. 5%; S. 5%;
M.W. 18%; S.W. 50%; W. 9%

Arkansas State University-Jonesboro

PO Box 970
State University, AR 72467
www2.astate.edu/business/
Public
Admissions: (870) 972-3029
Email: gradsch@astate.edu
Financial aid: (870) 972-2310
Application deadline: 06/01
In-state tuition: full time: $372/
credit hour; part time: $372/
credit hour
Out-of-state tuition: full time: $626/
credit hour
Room/board/expenses: $15,176
College-funded aid: Yes
International student aid: Yes
Average student indebtedness at
graduation: $42,000
Full-time enrollment: 138
men: 52%; women: 48%;
minorities: 4%; international: 81%
Part-time enrollment: 124
men: 56%; women: 44%;
minorities: 17%; international: 6%
Acceptance rate (full time): 73%
Average GMAT (full time): 546
Average GMAT (part time): 538
Average GPA (full time): 3.38
Average age of entrants to full-time
program: 26
Average months of prior work
experience (full time): 18
TOEFL requirement: Yes
Minimum TOEFL score: 550
Most popular departments: finance,
health care administration,
international business, non-
profit management, supply chain
management
Mean starting base salary for 2015
full-time graduates: $63,000
Employment location for 2015 class:
Intl. 30%; N.E. 4%; M.A. 11%; S.
30%; M.W. 11%; S.W. 11%; W. 4%

Arkansas Tech University[1]

1605 North Coliseum Drive
Russellville, AR 72801
www.atu.edu/business/
Public
Admissions: (479) 968-0398
Email: gradcollege@atu.edu
Financial aid: N/A
Tuition: N/A
Room/board/expenses: N/A
Enrollment: N/A

Henderson State University[1]

1100 Henderson Street
Box 7801
Arkadelphia, AR 71999-0001
www.hsu.edu/schoolofbusiness
Public
Admissions: N/A
Email: grad@hsu.edu
Financial aid: N/A
Tuition: N/A
Room/board/expenses: N/A
Enrollment: N/A

Southern Arkansas University[1]

100 E. University
Magnolia, AR 71753
web.saumag.edu/graduate/
programs/mba/
Public
Admissions: N/A
Financial aid: N/A
Tuition: N/A
Room/board/expenses: N/A
Enrollment: N/A

University of Arkansas-Fayetteville (Walton)

310 Williard J. Walker Hall
Fayetteville, AR 72701
gsb.uark.edu
Public
Admissions: (479) 575-2851
Email: gsb@walton.uark.edu
Financial aid: (479) 575-2711
Application deadline: rolling
In-state tuition: full time: $18,004;
part time: N/A
Out-of-state tuition: full time:
$44,438
Room/board/expenses: $20,518
College-funded aid: Yes
International student aid: Yes
Full-time enrollment: 88
men: 61%; women: 39%;
minorities: 14%; international:
30%
Part-time enrollment: N/A
men: N/A; women: N/A; minorities:
N/A; international: N/A
Acceptance rate (full time): 64%
Average GMAT (full time): 630
Average GPA (full time): 3.58
**Average age of entrants to full-time
program:** 25
**Average months of prior work
experience (full time):** 24
TOEFL requirement: Yes
Minimum TOEFL score: 550
Most popular departments:
entrepreneurship, finance,
marketing, non-profit
management, supply chain
management
**Mean starting base salary for 2015
full-time graduates:** $65,406
Employment location for 2015 class:
Intl. 11%; N.E. 0%; M.A. 4%; S.
67%; M.W. 4%; S.W. 15%; W. 0%

University of Arkansas-Little Rock

2801 S. University Avenue
Little Rock, AR 72204
ualr.edu/cob
Public
Admissions: (501) 569-3356
Email: mbaadvising@ualr.edu
Financial aid: (501) 569-3035
Application deadline: 07/15
In-state tuition: full time: N/A; part
time: N/A
Out-of-state tuition: full time: N/A
Room/board/expenses: N/A
College-funded aid: Yes
International student aid: Yes
Full-time enrollment: 25
men: 52%; women: 48%;
minorities: 16%; international:
28%
Part-time enrollment: 139
men: 58%; women: 42%;
minorities: 25%; international: 6%
Average GMAT (part time): 521
**Average age of entrants to full-time
program:** 34
TOEFL requirement: Yes
Minimum TOEFL score: 550

University of Central Arkansas

201 Donaghey
Conway, AR 72035
www.uca.edu/mba
Public
Admissions: (501) 450-5316
Email: mrubach@uca.edu
Financial aid: (501) 450-3140
Application deadline: 07/15
In-state tuition: full time: $243/
credit hour; part time: $243/
credit hour
Out-of-state tuition: full time: $486/
credit hour
Room/board/expenses: $17,007
College-funded aid: Yes
International student aid: No
**Average student indebtedness at
graduation:** $5,853
Full-time enrollment: 37
men: 59%; women: 41%;
minorities: 16%; international: 41%
Part-time enrollment: 42
men: 60%; women: 40%;
minorities: 10%; international: 12%
Acceptance rate (full time): 100%
Average GMAT (full time): 500
**Average age of entrants to full-time
program:** 25
TOEFL requirement: Yes
Minimum TOEFL score: 550
Most popular departments: finance,
health care administration,
international business

CALIFORNIA

California Polytechnic State University-San Luis Obispo (Orfalea)

1 Grand Avenue
San Luis Obispo, CA 93407
www.cob.calpoly.edu/
gradprograms/
Public
Admissions: (805) 756-2311
Email: admissions@calpoly.edu
Financial aid: (805) 756-2927
Application deadline: 04/01
In-state tuition: full time: $24,384;
part time: N/A
Out-of-state tuition: full time:
$36,288
Room/board/expenses: $15,765
College-funded aid: Yes
International student aid: Yes
**Average student indebtedness at
graduation:** $18,100
Full-time enrollment: 35
men: 63%; women: 37%;
minorities: 0%; international: 9%
Part-time enrollment: N/A
men: N/A; women: N/A; minorities:
N/A; international: N/A
Acceptance rate (full time): 61%
Average GMAT (full time): 595
Average GPA (full time): 3.15
**Average months of prior work
experience (full time):** 52
TOEFL requirement: Yes
Minimum TOEFL score: 550
Most popular departments:
general management, industrial
management, other

California State Polytechnic University-Pomona

3801 W. Temple Avenue
Pomona, CA 91768
www.csupomona.edu/~mba
Public
Admissions: (909) 869-3210
Email:
admissions@csupomona.edu
Financial aid: (909) 869-3700
Application deadline: 06/01
In-state tuition: full time: $12,298;
part time: $7,438
Out-of-state tuition: full time:
$18,250
Room/board/expenses: N/A
College-funded aid: Yes
International student aid: Yes
Full-time enrollment: 39
men: 33%; women: 67%;
minorities: 15%; international:
28%
Part-time enrollment: 37
men: 46%; women: 54%;
minorities: 19%; international: 11%
Acceptance rate (full time): 27%
Average GMAT (full time): 490
Average GPA (full time): 3.05
**Average months of prior work
experience (full time):** 24
TOEFL requirement: Yes
Minimum TOEFL score: 580

California State University-Bakersfield[1]

9001 Stockdale Highway
Bakersfield, CA 93311-1099
www.csub.edu/BPA
Public
Admissions: (661) 664-3036
Email: admissions@csub.edu
Financial aid: N/A
Tuition: N/A
Room/board/expenses: N/A
Enrollment: N/A

California State University-Chico

Tehama Hall 301
Chico, CA 95929-0001
www.csuchico.edu/MBA
Public
Admissions: (530) 898-6880
Email:
graduatestudies@csuchico.edu
Financial aid: (530) 898-6451
Application deadline: 03/21
In-state tuition: total program:
$16,500 (full time); $16,500 (part
time)
Out-of-state tuition: total program:
$27,500 (full time)
Room/board/expenses: $15,000
College-funded aid: Yes
International student aid: Yes
Full-time enrollment: 63
men: 59%; women: 41%;
minorities: N/A; international: 37%
Part-time enrollment: N/A
men: N/A; women: N/A; minorities:
N/A; international: N/A
Acceptance rate (full time): 65%
Average GMAT (full time): 560
Average GPA (full time): 3.20
**Average age of entrants to full-time
program:** 26
**Average months of prior work
experience (full time):** 36
TOEFL requirement: Yes
Minimum TOEFL score: 550

California State University-East Bay

25800 Carlos Bee Boulevard
Hayward, CA 94542
www.csueastbay.edu
Public
Admissions: (510) 885-2784
Email:
admissions@csueastbay.edu
Financial aid: (510) 885-2784
Application deadline: rolling

In-state tuition: total program:
$21,256 (full time); $31,696 (part
time)
Out-of-state tuition: total program:
$37,128 (full time)
Room/board/expenses: $15,000
College-funded aid: Yes
International student aid: No
**Average student indebtedness at
graduation:** $4,445
Full-time enrollment: 22
men: 45%; women: 55%;
minorities: 0%; international: 68%
Part-time enrollment: 277
men: 51%; women: 49%;
minorities: 71%; international: 21%
Acceptance rate (full time): 67%
Average GMAT (part time): 540
Average GPA (full time): 3.07
**Average age of entrants to full-time
program:** 24
TOEFL requirement: Yes
Minimum TOEFL score: 550
Most popular departments: finance,
human resources management,
international business, marketing,
supply chain management

California State University-Fresno (Craig)[1]

5245 N. Backer Avenue
Fresno, CA 93740-8001
www.craig.csufresno.edu/mba
Public
Admissions: (559) 278-2107
Email: mbainfo@csufresno.edu
Financial aid: N/A
Tuition: N/A
Room/board/expenses: N/A
Enrollment: N/A

California State University-Fullerton (Mihaylo)

PO Box 6848
Fullerton, CA 92834-6848
business.fullerton.edu
Public
Admissions: (657) 278-4035
Email: mba@fullerton.edu
Financial aid: (657) 278-3125
Application deadline: 04/01
In-state tuition: full time: $12,279;
part time: $6,399
Out-of-state tuition: full time:
$18,975
Room/board/expenses: $19,274
College-funded aid: Yes
International student aid: Yes
Full-time enrollment: 33
men: 55%; women: 45%;
minorities: 33%; international:
67%
Part-time enrollment: 302
men: 67%; women: 33%;
minorities: 70%; international:
30%
Acceptance rate (full time): 47%
Average GMAT (full time): 554
Average GMAT (part time): 558
Average GPA (full time): 3.22
**Average age of entrants to full-time
program:** 28
**Average months of prior work
experience (full time):** 59
TOEFL requirement: Yes
Minimum TOEFL score: N/A
Most popular departments: finance,
general management, marketing,
statistics and operations
research

California State University-Long Beach[1]

1250 Bellflower Boulevard
Long Beach, CA 90840-8501
www.csulb.edu/colleges/cba/mba
Public
Admissions: (562) 985-8627
Email: mba@csulb.edu
Financial aid: (562) 985-4141
Tuition: N/A
Room/board/expenses: N/A
Enrollment: N/A

California State University-Los Angeles[1]

5151 State University Drive
Los Angeles, CA 90032-8120
www.calstatela.edu/business/
graddprog
Public
Admissions: (323) 343-2800
Email: ehsieh@calstatela.edu
Financial aid: (323) 343-6260
Tuition: N/A
Room/board/expenses: N/A
Enrollment: N/A

California State University-Northridge (Nazarian)

18111 Nordhoff Street
Northridge, CA 91330-8380
www.csun.edu/mba/
Public
Admissions: (818) 677-2467
Email: MBA@csun.edu
Financial aid: (818) 677-4085
Application deadline: 05/01
In-state tuition: full time: $12,382;
part time: $8,026
Out-of-state tuition: full time:
$19,078
Room/board/expenses: $17,870
College-funded aid: Yes
International student aid: Yes
Full-time enrollment: N/A
men: N/A; women: N/A; minorities:
N/A; international: N/A
Part-time enrollment: 138
men: 62%; women: 38%;
minorities: 25%; international: 7%
Average GMAT (part time): 583
TOEFL requirement: Yes
Minimum TOEFL score: 550
Most popular departments:
finance, general management,
human resources management,
marketing, operations
management

California State University-Sacramento[1]

6000 J Street
Sacramento, CA 95819-6088
www.csus.edu/cbagrad
Public
Admissions: (916) 278-6772
Email: cbagrad@csus.edu
Financial aid: (916) 278-6554
Tuition: N/A
Room/board/expenses: N/A
Enrollment: N/A

California State University-San Bernardino

5500 University Parkway
San Bernardino, CA 92407
www.cpba.csusb.edu/
mba_program/welcome
Public
Admissions: (909) 537-5703
Email: mba@csusb.edu
Financial aid: (909) 537-5227
Application deadline: 07/05
In-state tuition: full time: $7,860;
part time: $5,031
Out-of-state tuition: full time:
$7,860
Room/board/expenses: $20,518
College-funded aid: Yes
International student aid: Yes
**Average student indebtedness at
graduation:** $39,076
Full-time enrollment: 178
men: 66%; women: 34%;
minorities: 37%; international:
38%
Part-time enrollment: 29
men: 41%; women: 59%;
minorities: 48%; international:
31%
Acceptance rate (full time): 53%
Average GMAT (full time): 526
Average GPA (full time): 3.25
**Average age of entrants to full-time
program:** 31
**Average months of prior work
experience (full time):** 104
TOEFL requirement: Yes
Minimum TOEFL score: 550
Most popular departments:
accounting, entrepreneurship,
finance, general management,
marketing

California State University-Stanislaus[1]

1 University Circle
Turlock, CA 95382
www.csustan.edu/cba
Public
Admissions: (209) 667-3288
Email:
graduate_school@csustan.edu
Financial aid: N/A
Tuition: N/A
Room/board/expenses: N/A
Enrollment: N/A

Chapman University (Argyros)

1 University Drive
Orange, CA 92866
www.chapman.edu/argyros
Private
Admissions: (714) 997-6596
Email: mba@chapman.edu
Financial aid: (714) 997-6741
Application deadline: 06/01
Tuition: full time: $1,470/credit
hour; part time: $1,470/credit hour
Room/board/expenses: $20,100
College-funded aid: Yes
International student aid: Yes
**Average student indebtedness at
graduation:** $100,518
Full-time enrollment: 69
men: 57%; women: 43%;
minorities: 20%; international:
32%
Part-time enrollment: 132
men: 43%; women: 57%;
minorities: 27%; international:
27%
Acceptance rate (full time): 59%
Average GMAT (full time): 627
Average GMAT (part time): 520
Average GPA (full time): 3.34

**Average age of entrants to full-time
program:** 25
**Average months of prior work
experience (full time):** 27
TOEFL requirement: Yes
Minimum TOEFL score: N/A
**Mean starting base salary for 2015
full-time graduates:** $55,947
Employment location for 2015 class:
Intl. N/A; N.E. N/A; M.A. N/A; S.
N/A; M.W. N/A; S.W. N/A; W. 100%

Claremont Graduate University (Drucker)

1021 N. Dartmouth Avenue
Claremont, CA 91711-6184
www.drucker.cgu.edu
Private
Admissions: (800) 944-4312
Email: drucker@cgu.edu
Financial aid: (909) 621-8337
Application deadline: 02/01
Tuition: full time: $1,793/credit
hour; part time: $1,793/credit hour
Room/board/expenses: $23,000
College-funded aid: Yes
International student aid: Yes
**Average student indebtedness at
graduation:** $93,004
Full-time enrollment: 82
men: 66%; women: 34%;
minorities: 21%; international:
48%
Part-time enrollment: 31
men: 45%; women: 55%;
minorities: 61%; international: 13%
TOEFL requirement: Yes
Minimum TOEFL score: N/A
Most popular departments: arts
administration, entrepreneurship,
general management, marketing,
other

Loyola Marymount University

1 LMU Drive, MS 8387
Los Angeles, CA 90045-2659
mba.lmu.edu
Private
Admissions: (310) 338-2848
Email: Mba.office@lmu.edu
Financial aid: (310) 338-2753
Application deadline: 06/01
Tuition: full time: N/A; total
program: $86,500 (part time)
Room/board/expenses: N/A
College-funded aid: Yes
International student aid: Yes
Full-time enrollment: N/A
men: N/A; women: N/A; minorities:
N/A; international: N/A
Part-time enrollment: 177
men: 56%; women: 44%;
minorities: 37%; international:
19%
Average GMAT (part time): 586
TOEFL requirement: Yes
Minimum TOEFL score: 600
Most popular departments:
entrepreneurship, finance,
general management,
international business, marketing

Monterey Institute of International Studies (Fisher)[1]

460 Pierce Street
Monterey, CA 93940
www.miis.edu/academics/pro-
grams/mba
Private
Admissions: (831) 647-4123
Email: admit@miis.edu
Financial aid: N/A

Tuition: N/A
Room/board/expenses: N/A
Enrollment: N/A

Naval Postgraduate School[1]

555 Dyer Road
Monterey, CA 93943
www.nps.edu/academics/
schools/GSBPP/
Public
Admissions: N/A
Financial aid: N/A
Tuition: N/A
Room/board/expenses: N/A
Enrollment: N/A

Pepperdine University (Graziadio)

24255 Pacific Coast Highway
Malibu, CA 90263-4100
www.bschool.pepperdine.edu
Private
Admissions: (310) 568-5530
Email: gsbmadm@pepperdine.edu
Financial aid: (310) 568-5530
Application deadline: 05/01
Tuition: full time: $46,480; part
time: $1,620/credit hour
Room/board/expenses: $14,800
College-funded aid: Yes
International student aid: Yes
**Average student indebtedness at
graduation:** $103,721
Full-time enrollment: 160
men: 63%; women: 38%;
minorities: 18%; international:
44%
Part-time enrollment: 922
men: 60%; women: 40%;
minorities: 46%; international:
13%
Acceptance rate (full time): 45%
Average GMAT (full time): 631
Average GMAT (part time): 551
Average GPA (full time): 3.23
**Average age of entrants to full-time
program:** 28
**Average months of prior work
experience (full time):** 50
TOEFL requirement: Yes
Minimum TOEFL score: 550
Most popular departments: finance,
general management, leadership,
marketing, management
information systems
**Mean starting base salary for 2015
full-time graduates:** $75,821
Employment location for 2015 class:
Intl. 3%; N.E. 3%; M.A. 3%; S. 5%;
M.W. 8%; S.W. 5%; W. 75%

San Diego State University

5500 Campanile Drive
San Diego, CA 92182-8228
www.sdsu.edu/business
Public
Admissions: (619) 594-6336
Email: admissions@sdsu.edu
Financial aid: (619) 594-6323
Application deadline: 03/01
In-state tuition: full time: $14,338;
part time: $11,506
Out-of-state tuition: full time:
$23,266
Room/board/expenses: $15,875
College-funded aid: Yes
International student aid: Yes
**Average student indebtedness at
graduation:** $17,376
Full-time enrollment: 319
men: 48%; women: 52%;
minorities: 13%; international:
58%

Part-time enrollment: 271
men: 53%; women: 47%;
minorities: 25%; international:
16%
Acceptance rate (full time): 36%
Average GMAT (full time): 603
Average GMAT (part time): 583
Average GPA (full time): 3.37
**Average age of entrants to full-time
program:** 27
**Average months of prior work
experience (full time):** 36
TOEFL requirement: Yes
Minimum TOEFL score: N/A
**Mean starting base salary for 2015
full-time graduates:** $54,848
Employment location for 2015 class:
Intl. 3%; N.E. N/A; M.A. N/A; S.
N/A; M.W. N/A; S.W. N/A; W. 97%

San Francisco State University

835 Market Street, Suite 600
San Francisco, CA 94103
mba.sfsu.edu
Public
Admissions: (415) 817-4300
Email: mba@sfsu.edu
Financial aid: (415) 338-1581
Application deadline: 05/15
In-state tuition: full time: $16,238;
part time: $10,358
Out-of-state tuition: full time:
$25,166
Room/board/expenses: $30,000
College-funded aid: Yes
International student aid: No
Full-time enrollment: 105
men: 57%; women: 43%;
minorities: 32%; international:
41%
Part-time enrollment: 82
men: 54%; women: 46%;
minorities: 52%; international: 7%
Acceptance rate (full time): 30%
Average GMAT (full time): 566
Average GMAT (part time): 544
Average GPA (full time): 3.30
**Average age of entrants to full-time
program:** 27
**Average months of prior work
experience (full time):** 47
TOEFL requirement: Yes
Minimum TOEFL score: 590
Most popular departments:
accounting, finance, leadership,
marketing, statistics and
operations research

San Jose State University (Lucas)

1 Washington Square
San Jose, CA 95192-0162
www.sjsu.edu/lucasgsb
Public
Admissions: (408) 924-3420
Email: lucas-school@sjsu.edu
Financial aid: (408) 283-7500
Application deadline: 05/01
In-state tuition: total program:
$30,340 (full time); $35,700 (part
time)
Out-of-state tuition: total program:
$45,964 (full time)
Room/board/expenses: N/A
College-funded aid: Yes
International student aid: No
Full-time enrollment: 106
men: 47%; women: 53%;
minorities: N/A; international: N/A
Part-time enrollment: 45
men: 69%; women: 31%;
minorities: N/A; international: N/A
Acceptance rate (full time): 52%
Average GMAT (full time): 560
Average GMAT (part time): 527
Average GPA (full time): 3.28

**Average age of entrants to full-time
program:** 26
TOEFL requirement: Yes
Minimum TOEFL score: N/A

Santa Clara University (Leavey)

Lucas Hall
Santa Clara, CA 95053
www.scu.edu/business
Private
Admissions: (408) 554-4539
Email: gradbusiness@scu.edu
Financial aid: (408) 554-4505
Application deadline: rolling
Tuition: full time: N/A; part time:
$983/credit hour
Room/board/expenses: N/A
College-funded aid: Yes
International student aid: Yes
Full-time enrollment: N/A
men: N/A; women: N/A; minorities:
N/A; international: N/A
Part-time enrollment: 490
men: 58%; women: 42%;
minorities: 35%; international:
30%
Average GMAT (part time): 624
TOEFL requirement: Yes
Minimum TOEFL score: N/A
Most popular departments:
entrepreneurship, finance,
leadership, marketing, other

Sonoma State University

1801 E. Cotati Avenue
Rohnert Park, CA 94928
www.sonoma.edu/admissions
Public
Admissions: (707) 664-2252
Email:
rosanna.kelley@sonoma.edu
Financial aid: (707) 664-2389
Application deadline: 03/31
In-state tuition: total program:
$21,523 (full time); $22,597 (part
time)
Out-of-state tuition: total program:
$30,451 (full time)
Room/board/expenses: $18,850
College-funded aid: Yes
International student aid: Yes
Full-time enrollment: N/A
men: N/A; women: N/A; minorities:
N/A; international: N/A
Part-time enrollment: 59
men: 49%; women: 51%;
minorities: 24%; international: 8%
TOEFL requirement: Yes
Minimum TOEFL score: N/A

Stanford University

655 Knight Way
Stanford, CA 94305-7298
www.gsb.stanford.edu/mba
Private
Admissions: (650) 723-2766
Email: mba.admissions@
gsb.stanford.edu
Financial aid: (650) 723-3282
Application deadline: N/A
Tuition: full time: $64,050; part
time: N/A
Room/board/expenses: $39,369
College-funded aid: Yes
International student aid: Yes
**Average student indebtedness at
graduation:** $83,762
Full-time enrollment: 824
men: 60%; women: 40%;
minorities: 20%; international:
31%
Part-time enrollment: N/A
men: N/A; women: N/A; minorities:
N/A; international: N/A

Acceptance rate (full time): 6%
Average GMAT (full time): 733
Average GPA (full time): 3.75
Average months of prior work experience (full time): 49
TOEFL requirement: Yes
Minimum TOEFL score: 600
Most popular departments: entrepreneurship, finance, general management, leadership, organizational behavior
Mean starting base salary for 2015 full-time graduates: $133,406
Employment location for 2015 class: Intl. 7%; N.E. 17%; M.A. 2%; S. 1%; M.W. 1%; S.W. 4%; W. 68%

St. Mary's College of California

1928 Saint Mary's Road
Moraga, CA 94556
www.smcmba.com
Private
Admissions: (925) 631-4888
Email: smcmba@stmarys-ca.edu
Financial aid: N/A
Application deadline: rolling
Tuition: full time: N/A; part time: $3,000/credit hour
Room/board/expenses: N/A
College-funded aid: Yes
International student aid: Yes
Full-time enrollment: N/A
men: N/A; women: N/A; minorities: N/A; international: N/A
Part-time enrollment: 150
men: 69%; women: 31%; minorities: 30%; international: 2%
Average GMAT (part time): 527
TOEFL requirement: Yes
Minimum TOEFL score: N/A

University of California-Berkeley (Haas)

545 Student Services Building
Berkeley, CA 94720-1900
mba.haas.berkeley.edu
Public
Admissions: (510) 642-1405
Email: mbaadm@haas.berkeley.edu
Financial aid: (510) 643-0183
Application deadline: N/A
In-state tuition: full time: $53,907; part time: $3,047/credit hour
Out-of-state tuition: full time: $55,968
Room/board/expenses: $25,486
College-funded aid: Yes
International student aid: Yes
Average student indebtedness at graduation: $79,453
Full-time enrollment: 502
men: 57%; women: 43%; minorities: 23%; international: 40%
Part-time enrollment: 799
men: 73%; women: 27%; minorities: 43%; international: 22%
Acceptance rate (full time): 13%
Average GMAT (full time): 715
Average GMAT (part time): 694
Average GPA (full time): 3.66
Average age of entrants to full-time program: 28
Average months of prior work experience (full time): 62
TOEFL requirement: Yes
Minimum TOEFL score: 570
Most popular departments: entrepreneurship, finance, leadership, marketing, technology
Mean starting base salary for 2015 full-time graduates: $123,403

Employment location for 2015 class: Intl. 11%; N.E. 7%; M.A. 1%; S. 1%; M.W. 1%; S.W. 1%; W. 78%

University of California-Davis

1 Shields Avenue
Davis, CA 95616-8609
gsm.ucdavis.edu
Public
Admissions: (530) 752-7658
Email: admissions@gsm.ucdavis.edu
Financial aid: (530) 752-7658
Application deadline: 11/02
In-state tuition: full time: $38,277; total program: $85,104 (part time)
Out-of-state tuition: full time: $52,508
Room/board/expenses: $22,518
College-funded aid: Yes
International student aid: Yes
Average student indebtedness at graduation: $70,273
Full-time enrollment: 87
men: 74%; women: 26%; minorities: 18%; international: 36%
Part-time enrollment: 424
men: 61%; women: 39%; minorities: 39%; international: 6%
Acceptance rate (full time): 18%
Average GMAT (full time): 683
Average GMAT (part time): 584
Average GPA (full time): 3.26
Average age of entrants to full-time program: 29
Average months of prior work experience (full time): 71
TOEFL requirement: Yes
Minimum TOEFL score: 600
Most popular departments: entrepreneurship, finance, marketing, technology, other
Mean starting base salary for 2015 full-time graduates: $101,877
Employment location for 2015 class: Intl. N/A; N.E. N/A; M.A. N/A; S. 3%; M.W. N/A; S.W. N/A; W. 97%

University of California-Irvine (Merage)

5300 SB1, 4293 Pereira Drive
Irvine, CA 92697-3125
www.merage.uci.edu
Public
Admissions: (949) 824-4622
Email: mba@merage.uci.edu
Financial aid: (949) 824-7967
Application deadline: 04/01
In-state tuition: full time: $40,533; total program: $98,703 (part time)
Out-of-state tuition: full time: $48,608
Room/board/expenses: $28,766
College-funded aid: Yes
International student aid: Yes
Average student indebtedness at graduation: $57,243
Full-time enrollment: 195
men: 72%; women: 28%; minorities: 23%; international: 49%
Part-time enrollment: 333
men: 63%; women: 37%; minorities: 56%; international: 2%
Acceptance rate (full time): 25%
Average GMAT (full time): 656
Average GMAT (part time): 579
Average GPA (full time): 3.36
Average age of entrants to full-time program: 29
Average months of prior work experience (full time): 70
TOEFL requirement: Yes
Minimum TOEFL score: 600

Most popular departments: finance, marketing, organizational behavior, statistics and operations research, other
Mean starting base salary for 2015 full-time graduates: $88,765
Employment location for 2015 class: Intl. 9%; N.E. 0%; M.A. 0%; S. 2%; M.W. 2%; S.W. 0%; W. 88%

University of California-Los Angeles (Anderson)

110 Westwood Plaza
Box 951481
Los Angeles, CA 90095-1481
www.anderson.ucla.edu
Public
Admissions: (310) 825-6944
Email: mba.admissions@anderson.ucla.edu
Financial aid: (310) 825-2746
Application deadline: 04/12
In-state tuition: full time: $53,717; part time: $43,175
Out-of-state tuition: full time: $57,844
Room/board/expenses: $27,647
College-funded aid: Yes
International student aid: Yes
Average student indebtedness at graduation: $88,654
Full-time enrollment: 725
men: 69%; women: 31%; minorities: 26%; international: 29%
Part-time enrollment: 971
men: 70%; women: 30%; minorities: 44%; international: 10%
Acceptance rate (full time): 20%
Average GMAT (full time): 713
Average GMAT (part time): 676
Average GPA (full time): 3.48
Average age of entrants to full-time program: 28
Average months of prior work experience (full time): 59
TOEFL requirement: Yes
Minimum TOEFL score: 560
Most popular departments: accounting, consulting, finance, marketing, technology
Mean starting base salary for 2015 full-time graduates: $114,392
Employment location for 2015 class: Intl. 4%; N.E. 7%; M.A. 1%; S. 0%; M.W. 3%; S.W. 3%; W. 83%

University of California-Riverside (Anderson)

900 University Avenue
Riverside, CA 92521-0203
www.agsm.ucr.edu/mba/
Public
Admissions: (951) 827-6200
Email: mba@ucr.edu
Financial aid: (951) 827-3878
Application deadline: 09/01
In-state tuition: full time: $40,656; part time: $1,313/credit hour
Out-of-state tuition: full time: $52,902
Room/board/expenses: $15,045
College-funded aid: Yes
International student aid: Yes
Average student indebtedness at graduation: $81,116
Full-time enrollment: 117
men: 54%; women: 46%; minorities: 15%; international: 73%
Part-time enrollment: 69
men: 57%; women: 43%; minorities: 14%; international: 75%
Acceptance rate (full time): 62%

Average GMAT (full time): 587
Average GMAT (part time): 488
Average GPA (full time): 3.17
Average age of entrants to full-time program: 25
Average months of prior work experience (full time): 34
TOEFL requirement: Yes
Minimum TOEFL score: 550
Mean starting base salary for 2015 full-time graduates: $71,382
Employment location for 2015 class: Intl. 23%; N.E. 2%; M.A. 0%; S. 0%; M.W. 0%; S.W. 0%; W. 74%

University of California-San Diego (Rady)

9500 Gilman Drive #0553
San Diego, CA 92093-0553
www.rady.ucsd.edu/mba/
Public
Admissions: (858) 534-0864
Email: mbaadmissions@ucsd.edu
Financial aid: N/A
Application deadline: 06/01
In-state tuition: full time: $50,365; part time: $1,152/credit hour
Out-of-state tuition: full time: $54,865
Room/board/expenses: $21,742
College-funded aid: Yes
International student aid: Yes
Full-time enrollment: 124
men: 70%; women: 30%; minorities: 11%; international: 64%
Part-time enrollment: 98
men: 71%; women: 29%; minorities: 32%; international: 1%
Acceptance rate (full time): 42%
Average GMAT (full time): 657
Average GMAT (part time): 582
Average GPA (full time): 3.33
Average age of entrants to full-time program: 31
Average months of prior work experience (full time): 79
TOEFL requirement: Yes
Minimum TOEFL score: 550
Most popular departments: entrepreneurship, finance, general management, marketing, technology
Mean starting base salary for 2015 full-time graduates: $80,265
Employment location for 2015 class: Intl. 9%; N.E. 0%; M.A. 0%; S. 0%; M.W. 0%; S.W. 0%; W. 91%

University of San Diego

5998 Alcala Park
San Diego, CA 92110-2492
www.sandiego.edu/mba
Private
Admissions: (619) 260-4860
Email: mba@sandiego.edu
Financial aid: (619) 260-4514
Application deadline: 05/01
Tuition: full time: $1,380/credit hour; part time: $1,380/credit hour
Room/board/expenses: $17,891
College-funded aid: Yes
International student aid: Yes
Average student indebtedness at graduation: $50,054
Full-time enrollment: 80
men: 55%; women: 45%; minorities: 13%; international: 64%
Part-time enrollment: 89
men: 62%; women: 38%; minorities: 15%; international: 15%
Acceptance rate (full time): 55%
Average GMAT (full time): 621
Average GMAT (part time): 609
Average GPA (full time): 3.40

Average age of entrants to full-time program: 28
Average months of prior work experience (full time): 59
TOEFL requirement: Yes
Minimum TOEFL score: 580
Most popular departments: entrepreneurship, finance, general management, marketing, supply chain management
Mean starting base salary for 2015 full-time graduates: $74,706
Employment location for 2015 class: Intl. 9%; N.E. N/A; M.A. N/A; S. N/A; M.W. 5%; S.W. N/A; W. 86%

University of San Francisco

101 Howard Street, Suite 500
San Francisco, CA 94105-1080
www.usfca.edu/management/graduate/
Private
Admissions: (415) 422-2221
Email: management@usfca.edu
Financial aid: (415) 422-2020
Application deadline: 06/15
Tuition: full time: $1,330/credit hour; part time: N/A
Room/board/expenses: N/A
College-funded aid: Yes
International student aid: Yes
Average student indebtedness at graduation: $82,470
Full-time enrollment: 122
men: 60%; women: 40%; minorities: 30%; international: 43%
Part-time enrollment: 67
men: 45%; women: 55%; minorities: 48%; international: 1%
Acceptance rate (full time): 59%
Average GMAT (full time): 559
Average GMAT (part time): 543
Average GPA (full time): 3.10
Average age of entrants to full-time program: 28
Average months of prior work experience (full time): 40
TOEFL requirement: Yes
Minimum TOEFL score: 580
Mean starting base salary for 2015 full-time graduates: $70,357
Employment location for 2015 class: Intl. 18%; N.E. 6%; M.A. N/A; S. N/A; M.W. N/A; S.W. N/A; W. 76%

University of Southern California (Marshall)

University Park
Los Angeles, CA 90089-1421
www.marshall.usc.edu
Private
Admissions: (213) 740-7846
Email: marshallmba@marshall.usc.edu
Financial aid: (213) 740-1111
Application deadline: 04/15
Tuition: full time: $53,865; part time: $1,710/credit hour
Room/board/expenses: $21,943
College-funded aid: Yes
International student aid: Yes
Full-time enrollment: 438
men: 70%; women: 30%; minorities: 30%; international: 27%
Part-time enrollment: 513
men: 68%; women: 32%; minorities: 47%; international: 2%
Acceptance rate (full time): 29%
Average GMAT (full time): 679
Average GMAT (part time): 614
Average GPA (full time): 3.31
Average age of entrants to full-time program: 27
Average months of prior work experience (full time): 59

TOEFL requirement: Yes
Minimum TOEFL score: 600
Mean starting base salary for 2015 full-time graduates: $105,171
Employment location for 2015 class: Intl. 6%; N.E. 8%; M.A. 0%; S. 2%; M.W. 3%; S.W. 4%; W. 77%

University of the Pacific (Eberhardt)

3601 Pacific Avenue
Stockton, CA 95211
www.pacific.edu/mba
Private
Admissions: (209) 946-2629
Email: mba@pacific.edu
Financial aid: (209) 946-2421
Application deadline: 03/01
Tuition: total program: $65,040 (full time); part time: $1,325/credit hour
Room/board/expenses: $25,416
College-funded aid: Yes
International student aid: Yes
Full-time enrollment: 17
men: 53%; women: 47%; minorities: 53%; international: 18%
Part-time enrollment: 13
men: 46%; women: 54%; minorities: 46%; international: 0%
Acceptance rate (full time): 77%
Average GMAT (full time): 552
Average GMAT (part time): 510
Average GPA (full time): 3.41
Average age of entrants to full-time program: 23
Average months of prior work experience (full time): 11
TOEFL requirement: Yes
Minimum TOEFL score: 550
Mean starting base salary for 2015 full-time graduates: $59,517
Employment location for 2015 class: Intl. N/A; N.E. N/A; M.A. N/A; S. N/A; M.W. N/A; S.W. N/A; W. 100%

Woodbury University[1]

7500 N. Glenoaks Boulevard
Burbank, CA 91504
woodbury.edu/
Private
Admissions: (818) 252-5221
Email: business@woodbury.edu
Financial aid: N/A
Tuition: N/A
Room/board/expenses: N/A
Enrollment: N/A

COLORADO

Colorado State University

110 Rockwell Hall West
Fort Collins, CO 80523-1270
www.csumba.com
Public
Admissions: (970) 491-3704
Email: gradadmissions@business.colostate.edu
Financial aid: (970) 491-6321
Application deadline: 06/01
In-state tuition: full time: $693/credit hour; part time: $918/credit hour
Out-of-state tuition: full time: $1,447/credit hour
Room/board/expenses: $13,500
College-funded aid: No
International student aid: No
Average student indebtedness at graduation: $32,556
Full-time enrollment: 103
men: 50%; women: 50%; minorities: 10%; international: 39%

Part-time enrollment: 889
men: 67%; women: 33%; minorities: 22%; international: 1%
Acceptance rate (full time): 70%
Average GMAT (full time): 545
Average GMAT (part time): 531
Average GPA (full time): 3.38
Average age of entrants to full-time program: 25
Average months of prior work experience (full time): 46
TOEFL requirement: Yes
Minimum TOEFL score: N/A
Most popular departments: general management, marketing, management information systems, operations management, technology

Colorado State University-Pueblo[1]

2200 Bonforte Boulevard
Pueblo, CO 81001
hsb.colostate-pueblo.edu
Public
Admissions: (719) 549-2461
Email: mba@colostate-pueblo.edu
Financial aid: N/A
Tuition: N/A
Room/board/expenses: N/A
Enrollment: N/A

University of Colorado-Boulder (Leeds)

995 Regent Drive 419 UCB
Boulder, CO 80309
leeds.colorado.edu/mba
Public
Admissions: (303) 492-8397
Email: leedsmba@Colorado.edu
Financial aid: (303) 492-8223
Application deadline: 04/01
In-state tuition: full time: $19,385; total program: $49,000 (part time)
Out-of-state tuition: full time: $34,343
Room/board/expenses: $18,453
College-funded aid: Yes
International student aid: Yes
Average student indebtedness at graduation: $56,255
Full-time enrollment: 157
men: 69%; women: 31%; minorities: 6%; international: 18%
Part-time enrollment: 101
men: 63%; women: 37%; minorities: 13%; international: 6%
Acceptance rate (full time): 75%
Average GMAT (full time): 616
Average GMAT (part time): 578
Average GPA (full time): 3.33
Average age of entrants to full-time program: 29
Average months of prior work experience (full time): 60
TOEFL requirement: Yes
Minimum TOEFL score: N/A
Most popular departments: entrepreneurship, finance, general management, real estate, other
Mean starting base salary for 2015 full-time graduates: $75,095
Employment location for 2015 class: Intl. 0%; N.E. 2%; M.A. 2%; S. 0%; M.W. 5%; S.W. 84%; W. 7%

University of Colorado-Colorado Springs

1420 Austin Bluffs Parkway
Colorado Springs, CO 80918
www.uccs.edu/mba
Public
Admissions: (719) 255-3122

Email: mbacred@uccs.edu
Financial aid: (719) 255-3460
Application deadline: 06/01
In-state tuition: full time: $11,734; part time: $4,406
Out-of-state tuition: full time: $20,644
Room/board/expenses: $15,120
College-funded aid: Yes
International student aid: Yes
Full-time enrollment: N/A
men: N/A; women: N/A; minorities: N/A; international: N/A
Part-time enrollment: 206
men: 62%; women: 38%; minorities: 16%; international: 5%
Average GMAT (part time): 514
TOEFL requirement: Yes
Minimum TOEFL score: 550
Most popular departments: accounting, finance, general management, marketing, other

University of Colorado-Denver

Campus Box 165
PO Box 173364
Denver, CO 80217-3364
www.ucdenver.edu/business/
Public
Admissions: (303) 315-8200
Email: bschool.admissions@ucdenver.edu
Financial aid: (303) 315-1850
Application deadline: 04/15
In-state tuition: full time: $41,570; part time: $506/credit hour
Out-of-state tuition: full time: $41,570
Room/board/expenses: $15,489
College-funded aid: Yes
International student aid: Yes
Full-time enrollment: 23
men: 52%; women: 48%; minorities: 4%; international: 17%
Part-time enrollment: 533
men: 61%; women: 39%; minorities: 11%; international: 4%
Acceptance rate (full time): 70%
Average GMAT (full time): 601
Average GMAT (part time): 580
Average GPA (full time): 3.16
Average age of entrants to full-time program: 29
Average months of prior work experience (full time): 31
TOEFL requirement: Yes
Minimum TOEFL score: 560

University of Denver (Daniels)

2101 S. University Boulevard
Denver, CO 80208
www.daniels.du.edu/
Private
Admissions: (303) 871-3416
Email: daniels@du.edu
Financial aid: (303) 871-3416
Application deadline: 05/15
Tuition: full time: $85,000; total program: $89,952 (part time)
Room/board/expenses: $16,000
College-funded aid: Yes
International student aid: Yes
Full-time enrollment: 101
men: 63%; women: 37%; minorities: 12%; international: 21%
Part-time enrollment: 122
men: 61%; women: 39%; minorities: 18%; international: 1%
Acceptance rate (full time): 68%
Average GMAT (full time): 588
Average GMAT (part time): 569
Average GPA (full time): 3.19
Average age of entrants to full-time program: 29
Average months of prior work experience (full time): 73

TOEFL requirement: Yes
Minimum TOEFL score: 587
Most popular departments: entrepreneurship, finance, general management, marketing, real estate
Mean starting base salary for 2015 full-time graduates: $61,401
Employment location for 2015 class: Intl. 3%; N.E. 6%; M.A. 0%; S. 3%; M.W. 12%; S.W. 64%; W. 12%

University of Northern Colorado (Monfort)[1]

800 17th Street
Greeley, CO 80639
mcb.unco.edu/MBA/information.cfm
Public
Admissions: N/A
Financial aid: N/A
Tuition: N/A
Room/board/expenses: N/A
Enrollment: N/A

Central Connecticut State University[1]

1615 Stanley Street
New Britain, CT 06050
www.ccsu.edu/
Public
Admissions: (860) 832-2350
Financial aid: N/A
Tuition: N/A
Room/board/expenses: N/A
Enrollment: N/A

Fairfield University (Dolan)

1073 N. Benson Road
Fairfield, CT 06824
www.fairfield.edu/dsb/graduateprograms/mba/
Private
Admissions: (203) 254-4000
Email: dsbgrad@fairfield.edu
Financial aid: (203) 254-4125
Application deadline: 08/01
Tuition: full time: N/A; part time: $840/credit hour
Room/board/expenses: N/A
College-funded aid: Yes
International student aid: No
Full-time enrollment: N/A
men: N/A; women: N/A; minorities: N/A; international: N/A
Part-time enrollment: 57
men: 56%; women: 44%; minorities: 16%; international: 14%
Average GMAT (part time): 523
TOEFL requirement: Yes
Minimum TOEFL score: 550
Most popular departments: accounting, finance, general management, marketing, tax

Quinnipiac University[1]

275 Mount Carmel Avenue
Hamden, CT 06518
www.quinnipiac.edu/
Private
Admissions: (800) 462-1944
Email: graduate@quinnipiac.edu
Financial aid: (203) 582-8384
Tuition: N/A
Room/board/expenses: N/A
Enrollment: N/A

Sacred Heart University (Welch)

5151 Park Avenue
Fairfield, CT 06825
www.sacredheart.edu/johnfwelchcob.cfm
Private
Admissions: (203) 365-7619
Email: gradstudies@sacredheart.edu
Financial aid: (203) 371-7980
Application deadline: rolling
Tuition: full time: N/A; part time: $850/credit hour
Room/board/expenses: N/A
College-funded aid: Yes
International student aid: Yes
Full-time enrollment: 27
men: 48%; women: 52%; minorities: 26%; international: 11%
Part-time enrollment: 107
men: 55%; women: 45%; minorities: 32%; international: 3%
Average GMAT (part time): 501
TOEFL requirement: Yes
Minimum TOEFL score: 570

University of Connecticut

2100 Hillside Road, Unit 1041
Storrs, CT 06269-1041
www.business.uconn.edu
Public
Admissions: (860) 486-2872
Email: uconnmba@business.uconn.edu
Financial aid: (860) 486-2819
Application deadline: 06/01
In-state tuition: full time: $13,852; part time: $825/credit hour
Out-of-state tuition: full time: $34,638
Room/board/expenses: $25,750
College-funded aid: Yes
International student aid: Yes
Average student indebtedness at graduation: $58,767
Full-time enrollment: 96
men: 66%; women: 34%; minorities: 9%; international: 55%
Part-time enrollment: 813
men: 68%; women: 32%; minorities: 17%; international: 1%
Acceptance rate (full time): 42%
Average GMAT (full time): 625
Average GMAT (part time): 574
Average GPA (full time): 3.43
Average age of entrants to full-time program: 29
Average months of prior work experience (full time): 73
TOEFL requirement: Yes
Minimum TOEFL score: 575
Most popular departments: finance, general management, marketing, portfolio management, other
Mean starting base salary for 2015 full-time graduates: $89,232
Employment location for 2015 class: Intl. N/A; N.E. 68%; M.A. N/A; S. 5%; M.W. 16%; S.W. 5%; W. 5%

University of Hartford (Barney)[1]

200 Bloomfield Avenue
West Hartford, CT 06117
www.hartford.edu/barney
Private
Admissions: N/A
Financial aid: N/A
Tuition: N/A
Room/board/expenses: N/A
Enrollment: N/A

University of New Haven[1]

300 Boston Post Rd
West Haven, CT 06516
Private
Admissions: N/A
Financial aid: N/A
Tuition: N/A
Room/board/expenses: N/A
Enrollment: N/A

Yale University

165 Whitney Avenue
New Haven, CT 06511-3729
som.yale.edu
Private
Admissions: (203) 432-5635
Email: mba.admissions@yale.edu
Financial aid: (203) 432-5875
Application deadline: 04/21
Tuition: full time: $63,380; part time: N/A
Room/board/expenses: $25,100
College-funded aid: Yes
International student aid: Yes
Full-time enrollment: 668
men: 61%; women: 39%;
minorities: 24%; international: 39%
Part-time enrollment: N/A
men: N/A; women: N/A; minorities: N/A; international: N/A
Acceptance rate (full time): 21%
Average GMAT (full time): 721
Average GPA (full time): 3.60
Average age of entrants to full-time program: 28
Average months of prior work experience (full time): 57
TOEFL requirement: No
Minimum TOEFL score: N/A
Mean starting base salary for 2015 full-time graduates: $119,066
Employment location for 2015 class: Intl. 14%; N.E. 51%; M.A. 4%; S. 3%; M.W. 5%; S.W. 3%; W. 20%

DELAWARE

Delaware State University[1]

1200 DuPont Highway
Dover, DE 19901
www.desu.edu/business-administration-mba-program
Public
Admissions: (302) 857-6978
Email: dkim@desu.edu
Financial aid: (302) 857-6250
Tuition: N/A
Room/board/expenses: N/A
Enrollment: N/A

University of Delaware (Lerner)

103 Alfred Lerner Hall
Newark, DE 19716
www.mba.udel.edu
Public
Admissions: (302) 831-2221
Email: mbaprogram@udel.edu
Financial aid: (302) 831-8761
Application deadline: rolling
In-state tuition: full time: $14,292; part time: $750/credit hour
Out-of-state tuition: full time: $24,792
Room/board/expenses: $13,058
College-funded aid: Yes
International student aid: Yes
Full-time enrollment: 120
men: 61%; women: 39%;
minorities: 71%; international: 54%

Part-time enrollment: 209
men: 59%; women: 41%;
minorities: 40%; international: 6%
Acceptance rate (full time): 45%
Average GMAT (full time): 610
Average GMAT (part time): 610
Average GPA (full time): 3.20
Average age of entrants to full-time program: 28
Average months of prior work experience (full time): 42
TOEFL requirement: Yes
Minimum TOEFL score: 600
Most popular departments:
entrepreneurship, finance, international business, marketing, technology
Mean starting base salary for 2015 full-time graduates: $92,813
Employment location for 2015 class: Intl. N/A; N.E. 25%; M.A. 75%; S. N/A; M.W. N/A; S.W. N/A; W. N/A

DISTRICT OF COLUMBIA

American University (Kogod)

4400 Massachusetts Avenue NW
Washington, DC 20016
www.kogod.american.edu
Private
Admissions: (202) 885-1913
Email: kogodgrad@american.edu
Financial aid: (202) 885-1907
Application deadline: rolling
Tuition: full time: $1,526/credit hour; total program: $90,712 (part time)
Room/board/expenses: $21,933
College-funded aid: Yes
International student aid: Yes
Average student indebtedness at graduation: $12,598
Full-time enrollment: 69
men: 51%; women: 49%;
minorities: 41%; international: 20%
Part-time enrollment: 80
men: 51%; women: 49%;
minorities: 30%; international: 9%
Acceptance rate (full time): 72%
Average GMAT (full time): 530
Average GMAT (part time): 580
Average GPA (full time): 3.00
Average age of entrants to full-time program: 27
Average months of prior work experience (full time): 41
TOEFL requirement: Yes
Minimum TOEFL score: N/A
Most popular departments:
consulting, finance, international business, marketing, management information systems
Mean starting base salary for 2015 full-time graduates: $78,556
Employment location for 2015 class: Intl. 5%; N.E. 5%; M.A. 86%; S. N/A; M.W. 5%; S.W. N/A; W. N/A

Georgetown University (McDonough)

Rafik B. Hariri Building
37th and O Streets NW
Washington, DC 20057
msb.georgetown.edu
Private
Admissions: (202) 687-4200
Email: georgetownmba@georgetown.edu
Financial aid: (202) 687-4547
Application deadline: N/A
Tuition: full time: $56,962; part time: $1,715/credit hour
Room/board/expenses: $25,558
College-funded aid: Yes

International student aid: Yes
Full-time enrollment: 519
men: 68%; women: 32%;
minorities: 17%; international: 38%
Part-time enrollment: 391
men: 66%; women: 34%;
minorities: 20%; international: 7%
Acceptance rate (full time): 43%
Average GMAT (full time): 692
Average GMAT (part time): 666
Average GPA (full time): 3.36
Average age of entrants to full-time program: 28
Average months of prior work experience (full time): 60
TOEFL requirement: Yes
Minimum TOEFL score: 600
Most popular departments:
consulting, finance, general management, international business, marketing
Mean starting base salary for 2015 full-time graduates: $108,789
Employment location for 2015 class: Intl. 7%; N.E. 42%; M.A. 32%; S. 5%; M.W. 5%; S.W. 3%; W. 7%

George Washington University

2201 G Street NW
Washington, DC 20052
business.gwu.edu/grad/mba/
Private
Admissions: (202) 994-1212
Email: gwmba@gwu.edu
Financial aid: (202) 994-6822
Application deadline: 05/26
Tuition: full time: $1,610/credit hour; part time: $1,610/credit hour
Room/board/expenses: $24,000
College-funded aid: Yes
International student aid: Yes
Average student indebtedness at graduation: $79,456
Full-time enrollment: 180
men: 59%; women: 41%;
minorities: 16%; international: 53%
Part-time enrollment: 286
men: 59%; women: 41%;
minorities: 33%; international: 8%
Acceptance rate (full time): 43%
Average GMAT (full time): 642
Average GMAT (part time): 553
Average GPA (full time): 3.24
Average age of entrants to full-time program: 30
Average months of prior work experience (full time): 60
TOEFL requirement: Yes
Minimum TOEFL score: 600
Most popular departments:
consulting, finance, international business, management information systems, public policy
Mean starting base salary for 2015 full-time graduates: $98,055
Employment location for 2015 class: Intl. 6%; N.E. 16%; M.A. 51%; S. 3%; M.W. 10%; S.W. 3%; W. 10%

Howard University

2600 Sixth Street NW
Suite 236
Washington, DC 20059
www.bschool.howard.edu
Private
Admissions: (202) 806-1725
Email: MBA_bschool@howard.edu
Financial aid: (202) 806-2820
Application deadline: 04/01
Tuition: full time: $33,166; part time: $1,840/credit hour
Room/board/expenses: $26,518
College-funded aid: Yes
International student aid: Yes

FLORIDA

Barry University

11300 N.E. Second Avenue
Miami Shores, FL 33161-6695
www.barry.edu/mba
Private
Admissions: (305) 899-3146
Email: dfletcher@mail.barry.edu
Financial aid: (305) 899-3673
Application deadline: rolling
Tuition: full time: $990/credit hour; part time: $990/credit hour
Room/board/expenses: N/A
College-funded aid: Yes
International student aid: Yes
Full-time enrollment: N/A
men: N/A; women: N/A; minorities: N/A; international: N/A
Part-time enrollment: 76
men: 47%; women: 53%;
minorities: 49%; international: 36%
Average GMAT (part time): 485
TOEFL requirement: Yes
Minimum TOEFL score: 550

Florida Atlantic University

777 Glades Road
Boca Raton, FL 33431
www.business.fau.edu
Public
Admissions: (561) 297-3624
Email: graduatecollege@fau.edu
Financial aid: (561) 297-3530
Application deadline: rolling
In-state tuition: full time: $304/credit hour; part time: $304/credit hour
Out-of-state tuition: full time: $928/credit hour
Room/board/expenses: $17,424
College-funded aid: Yes
International student aid: Yes
Full-time enrollment: N/A
men: N/A; women: N/A; minorities: N/A; international: N/A
Part-time enrollment: 144
men: 54%; women: 46%;
minorities: 29%; international: 15%
Average GMAT (part time): 530
TOEFL requirement: Yes
Minimum TOEFL score: 600
Most popular departments:
accounting, general management, health care administration, international business, tax

Average student indebtedness at graduation: $47,661
Full-time enrollment: 58
men: 45%; women: 55%;
minorities: 84%; international: 16%
Part-time enrollment: 24
men: 29%; women: 71%;
minorities: 100%; international: 0%
Acceptance rate (full time): 47%
Average GMAT (full time): 494
Average GPA (full time): 3.28
Average age of entrants to full-time program: 27
Average months of prior work experience (full time): 50
TOEFL requirement: Yes
Minimum TOEFL score: 550
Most popular departments:
finance, general management, international business, marketing, supply chain management
Mean starting base salary for 2015 full-time graduates: $95,824
Employment location for 2015 class: Intl. 0%; N.E. 9%; M.A. 36%; S. 5%; M.W. 27%; S.W. 23%; W. 0%

Florida Gulf Coast University (Lutgert)

10501 FGCU Boulevard S
Fort Myers, FL 33965-6565
www.fgcu.edu/cob/
Public
Admissions: (239) 590-7988
Email: graduate@fgcu.edu
Financial aid: (239) 590-7920
Application deadline: 06/01
In-state tuition: full time: $373/credit hour; part time: $373/credit hour
Out-of-state tuition: full time: $1,301/credit hour
Room/board/expenses: $11,259
College-funded aid: Yes
International student aid: Yes
Average student indebtedness at graduation: $25,466
Full-time enrollment: 31
men: 58%; women: 42%;
minorities: 10%; international: 13%
Part-time enrollment: 89
men: 54%; women: 46%;
minorities: 2%; international: 1%
Average GMAT (full time): 510
Average GMAT (part time): 540
Average GPA (full time): 3.41
Average age of entrants to full-time program: 28
TOEFL requirement: Yes
Minimum TOEFL score: 550

Florida International University

1050 S.W. 112 Avenue
CBC 300
Miami, FL 33199-0001
business.fiu.edu
Public
Admissions: (305) 348-7398
Email: chapman@fiu.edu
Financial aid: (305) 348-7272
Application deadline: 07/01
In-state tuition: total program: $35,000 (full time); $48,000 (part time)
Out-of-state tuition: total program: $40,000 (full time)
Room/board/expenses: $18,000
College-funded aid: Yes
International student aid: Yes
Full-time enrollment: 52
men: 56%; women: 44%;
minorities: 48%; international: 37%
Part-time enrollment: 557
men: 42%; women: 58%;
minorities: 72%; international: 15%
Acceptance rate (full time): 33%
Average GMAT (full time): 590
Average GPA (full time): 3.42
Average age of entrants to full-time program: 25
Average months of prior work experience (full time): 37
TOEFL requirement: Yes
Minimum TOEFL score: 550
Most popular departments: finance, general management, health care administration, international business, management information systems
Mean starting base salary for 2015 full-time graduates: $34,750
Employment location for 2015 class: Intl. 0%; N.E. 0%; M.A. 0%; S. 100%; M.W. 0%; S.W. 0%; W. 0%

Florida Southern College

111 Lake Hollingsworth Drive
Lakeland, FL 33801
www.flsouthern.edu/
Private
Admissions: N/A
Financial aid: N/A
Application deadline: 07/01
Tuition: total program: $32,180 (full time); part time: N/A
Room/board/expenses: N/A
College-funded aid: Yes
International student aid: Yes
Full-time enrollment: 86
men: 56%; women: 44%; minorities: 26%; international: 15%
Part-time enrollment: N/A
men: N/A; women: N/A; minorities: N/A; international: N/A
Acceptance rate (full time): 58%
Average GMAT (full time): 552
Average GPA (full time): 3.28
Average age of entrants to full-time program: 29
Average months of prior work experience (full time): 66
TOEFL requirement: Yes
Minimum TOEFL score: N/A
Most popular departments: accounting, general management, health care administration, supply chain management

Florida State University

Graduate Programs, 233 Rovetta Building
Tallahassee, FL 32306-1110
business.fsu.edu/academics/graduate-programs/masters-degrees
Public
Admissions: (850) 644-1147
Email: gradprograms@business.fsu.edu
Financial aid: (850) 644-5716
Application deadline: 06/01
In-state tuition: full time: $480/credit hour; part time: $480/credit hour
Out-of-state tuition: full time: $1,110/credit hour
Room/board/expenses: $52,500
College-funded aid: Yes
International student aid: Yes
Average student indebtedness at graduation: $24,501
Full-time enrollment: 31
men: 74%; women: 26%; minorities: 10%; international: 3%
Part-time enrollment: 65
men: 65%; women: 35%; minorities: 20%; international: N/A
Acceptance rate (full time): 58%
Average GMAT (full time): 573
Average GMAT (part time): 577
Average GPA (full time): 3.22
Average age of entrants to full-time program: 24
Average months of prior work experience (full time): 29
TOEFL requirement: Yes
Minimum TOEFL score: 600
Most popular departments: accounting, finance, general management, insurance, marketing
Mean starting base salary for 2015 full-time graduates: $58,346
Employment location for 2015 class: Intl. N/A; N.E. N/A; M.A. N/A; S. 100%; M.W. N/A; S.W. N/A; W. N/A

Jacksonville University

2800 University Blvd N
Jacksonville, FL 32211
www.ju.edu
Private
Admissions: (904) 256-7000
Email: mba@ju.edu
Financial aid: (904) 256-7956
Application deadline: 08/01
Tuition: full time: $720/credit hour; part time: $720/credit hour
Room/board/expenses: $13,000
College-funded aid: Yes
International student aid: Yes
Average student indebtedness at graduation: $23,719
Full-time enrollment: 63
men: 48%; women: 52%; minorities: 21%; international: 37%
Part-time enrollment: 153
men: 59%; women: 41%; minorities: 22%; international: 6%
Acceptance rate (full time): 75%
Average GMAT (full time): 403
Average GMAT (part time): 455
Average GPA (full time): 3.33
Average age of entrants to full-time program: 25
Average months of prior work experience (full time): 72
TOEFL requirement: Yes
Minimum TOEFL score: 500
Most popular departments: accounting, finance, general management, leadership, marketing
Mean starting base salary for 2015 full-time graduates: $36,359
Employment location for 2015 class: Intl. 0%; N.E. 20%; M.A. 0%; S. 80%; M.W. 0%; S.W. 0%; W. 0%

Rollins College (Crummer)[1]

1000 Holt Avenue
Winter Park, FL 32789-4499
www.rollins.edu/business/
Private
Admissions: N/A
Financial aid: N/A
Tuition: N/A
Room/board/expenses: N/A
Enrollment: N/A

Stetson University

421 N. Woodland Boulevard
Unit 8398
DeLand, FL 32723
www.stetson.edu/graduate
Private
Admissions: (386) 822-7100
Email: gradadmissions@stetson.edu
Financial aid: (800) 688-7120
Application deadline: rolling
Tuition: full time: $943/credit hour; part time: $943/credit hour
Room/board/expenses: N/A
College-funded aid: Yes
International student aid: Yes
Average student indebtedness at graduation: $26,447
Full-time enrollment: 71
men: 69%; women: 31%; minorities: 24%; international: 10%
Part-time enrollment: 57
men: 44%; women: 56%; minorities: 26%; international: 2%
Acceptance rate (full time): 69%
Average GMAT (full time): 503
Average GPA (full time): 3.24
Average age of entrants to full-time program: 28
TOEFL requirement: Yes
Minimum TOEFL score: N/A
Mean starting base salary for 2015 full-time graduates: $46,571

University of Central Florida

PO Box 161400
Orlando, FL 32816-1400
www.ucf.edu
Public
Admissions: (407) 235-3917
Email: cbagrad@ucf.edu
Financial aid: (407) 823-2827
Application deadline: 07/15
In-state tuition: full time: N/A; part time: $5,550
Out-of-state tuition: full time: N/A
Room/board/expenses: N/A
College-funded aid: Yes
International student aid: Yes
Average student indebtedness at graduation: $27,212
Full-time enrollment: 63
men: N/A; women: N/A; minorities: N/A; international: N/A
Part-time enrollment: 360
men: 54%; women: 46%; minorities: 35%; international: 1%
Average GPA (full time): N/A
TOEFL requirement: Yes
Minimum TOEFL score: 577
Most popular departments: accounting, entrepreneurship, general management, human resources management, technology

University of Florida (Hough)

Hough Hall 310
Gainesville, FL 32611-7152
www.floridamba.ufl.edu
Public
Admissions: (352) 392-7992
Email: floridamba@warrington.ufl.edu
Financial aid: (352) 392-1275
Application deadline: 03/15
In-state tuition: full time: $12,737; part time: $24,166
Out-of-state tuition: full time: $30,130
Room/board/expenses: $16,630
College-funded aid: Yes
International student aid: Yes
Average student indebtedness at graduation: $30,549
Full-time enrollment: 109
men: 66%; women: 34%; minorities: 18%; international: 13%
Part-time enrollment: 392
men: 73%; women: 27%; minorities: 26%; international: 11%
Acceptance rate (full time): 16%
Average GMAT (full time): 681
Average GMAT (part time): 584
Average GPA (full time): 3.46
Average age of entrants to full-time program: 25
Average months of prior work experience (full time): 39
TOEFL requirement: Yes
Minimum TOEFL score: 550
Most popular departments: consulting, finance, marketing, real estate, supply chain management
Mean starting base salary for 2015 full-time graduates: $99,241
Employment location for 2015 class: Intl. 0%; N.E. 7%; M.A. 4%; S. 47%; M.W. 4%; S.W. 36%; W. 2%

University of Miami

PO Box 248027
Coral Gables, FL 33124-6520
www.bus.miami.edu/grad
Private
Admissions: (305) 284-2510
Email: mba@miami.edu
Financial aid: (305) 284-5212

University of North Florida (Coggin)

1 UNF Drive
Jacksonville, FL 32224-2645
www.unf.edu/coggin
Public
Admissions: (904) 620-1360
Email: l.reigger@unf.edu
Financial aid: (904) 620-5555
Application deadline: 08/01
In-state tuition: full time: $11,848; part time: $494/credit hour
Out-of-state tuition: full time: $25,066
Room/board/expenses: $20,131
College-funded aid: Yes
International student aid: Yes
Average student indebtedness at graduation: $31,307
Full-time enrollment: 78
men: 54%; women: 46%; minorities: 26%; international: 12%
Part-time enrollment: 171
men: 59%; women: 41%; minorities: 15%; international: 1%
Average GMAT (part time): 528
TOEFL requirement: Yes
Minimum TOEFL score: 550
Most popular departments: accounting, e-commerce, finance, general management, supply chain management

University of South Florida

4202 Fowler Avenue BSN 3404
Tampa, FL 33620
www.mba.usf.edu
Public
Admissions: (813) 974-3335
Email: bsn-mba@usf.edu
Financial aid: (813) 974-4700
Application deadline: 01/07
In-state tuition: full time: $467/credit hour; part time: $467/credit hour
Out-of-state tuition: full time: $913/credit hour
Room/board/expenses: $26,000
College-funded aid: Yes
International student aid: Yes
Average student indebtedness at graduation: $27,667

Application deadline: 05/15
Tuition: full time: $1,850/credit hour; part time: N/A
Room/board/expenses: $21,704
College-funded aid: Yes
International student aid: Yes
Average student indebtedness at graduation: $62,877
Full-time enrollment: 164
men: 63%; women: 37%; minorities: 38%; international: 30%
Part-time enrollment: N/A
men: N/A; women: N/A; minorities: N/A; international: N/A
Acceptance rate (full time): 23%
Average GMAT (full time): 643
Average GPA (full time): 3.26
Average age of entrants to full-time program: 27
Average months of prior work experience (full time): 48
TOEFL requirement: Yes
Minimum TOEFL score: 587
Most popular departments: finance, general management, marketing, statistics and operations research, other
Mean starting base salary for 2015 full-time graduates: $77,967
Employment location for 2015 class: Intl. 6%; N.E. 10%; M.A. 0%; S. 80%; M.W. 0%; S.W. 2%; W. 2%

Full-time enrollment: 50
men: 60%; women: 40%; minorities: 20%; international: 6%
Part-time enrollment: 230
men: 63%; women: 37%; minorities: 23%; international: 21%
Acceptance rate (full time): 100%
Average GMAT (full time): 525
Average GMAT (part time): 572
Average GPA (full time): 3.49
Average age of entrants to full-time program: 23
Average months of prior work experience (full time): 21
TOEFL requirement: N/A
Minimum TOEFL score: N/A
Most popular departments: entrepreneurship, finance, leadership, marketing, management information systems
Mean starting base salary for 2015 full-time graduates: $45,000
Employment location for 2015 class: Intl. 4%; N.E. 7%; M.A. 7%; S. 59%; M.W. 0%; S.W. 22%; W. 0%

University of South Florida-Sarasota-Manatee

8350 N. Tamiami Trail
Sarasota, FL 34243
usfsm.edu/college-of-business
Public
Admissions: N/A
Financial aid: N/A
Application deadline: 07/01
In-state tuition: full time: $380/credit hour; part time: $380/credit hour
Out-of-state tuition: full time: $826/credit hour
Room/board/expenses: N/A
College-funded aid: Yes
International student aid: Yes
Average student indebtedness at graduation: $36,690
Full-time enrollment: N/A
men: N/A; women: N/A; minorities: N/A; international: N/A
Part-time enrollment: 69
men: 46%; women: 54%; minorities: 29%; international: 0%
Average GMAT (part time): 573
TOEFL requirement: Yes
Minimum TOEFL score: 550

University of South Florida-St. Petersburg

140 7th Ave S, BAY III
St. Petersburg, FL 33701
www.usfsp.edu/mba
Public
Admissions: (727) 873-4622
Email: mba@usfsp.edu
Financial aid: (727) 873-4128
Application deadline: 11/01
In-state tuition: full time: $462/credit hour; part time: $462/credit hour
Out-of-state tuition: full time: $907/credit hour
Room/board/expenses: N/A
College-funded aid: Yes
International student aid: Yes
Average student indebtedness at graduation: $25,714
Full-time enrollment: N/A
men: N/A; women: N/A; minorities: N/A; international: N/A
Part-time enrollment: 288
men: 52%; women: 48%; minorities: 24%; international: 2%
Average GMAT (part time): 540
TOEFL requirement: Yes
Minimum TOEFL score: 550

Most popular departments: accounting, finance, marketing, management information systems
Mean starting base salary for 2015 full-time graduates: $68,000

University of Tampa (Sykes)
401 W. Kennedy Boulevard
Tampa, FL 33606-1490
grad.ut.edu
Private
Admissions: (813) 257-3642
Email: utgrad@ut.edu
Financial aid: (813) 253-6219
Application deadline: rolling
Tuition: full time: $573/credit hour; part time: $573/credit hour
Room/board/expenses: $13,330
College-funded aid: Yes
International student aid: Yes
Average student indebtedness at graduation: $39,080
Full-time enrollment: 271
men: 66%; women: 34%; minorities: 5%; international: 50%
Part-time enrollment: 92
men: 51%; women: 49%; minorities: 9%; international: 2%
Acceptance rate (full time): 29%
Average GMAT (full time): 550
Average GMAT (part time): 560
Average GPA (full time): 3.40
Average age of entrants to full-time program: 26
Average months of prior work experience (full time): 54
TOEFL requirement: Yes
Minimum TOEFL score: 577
Mean starting base salary for 2015 full-time graduates: $56,719
Employment location for 2015 class: Intl. 11%; N.E. 9%; M.A. 2%; S. 72%; M.W. 0%; S.W. 2%; W. 4%

University of West Florida[1]
11000 University Parkway
Pensacola, FL 32514
uwf.edu
Public
Admissions: (850) 474-2230
Email: mba@uwf.edu
Financial aid: N/A
Tuition: N/A
Room/board/expenses: N/A
Enrollment: N/A

GEORGIA

Augusta University[1]
1120 15th Street
Augusta, GA 30912
www.gru.edu/hull/grad/mba.php
Public
Admissions: (706) 737-1418
Email: hull@gru.edu
Financial aid: N/A
Tuition: N/A
Room/board/expenses: N/A
Enrollment: N/A

Berry College (Campbell)
PO Box 495024
Mount Berry, GA 30149-5024
www.berry.edu/academics/campbell/
Private
Admissions: (706) 236-2215
Email: admissions@berry.edu
Financial aid: (706) 236-1714
Application deadline: 07/21
Tuition: full time: $576/credit hour; part time: $576/credit hour

Room/board/expenses: N/A
College-funded aid: Yes
International student aid: Yes
Full-time enrollment: N/A
men: N/A; women: N/A; minorities: N/A; international: N/A
Part-time enrollment: 23
men: 30%; women: 70%; minorities: N/A; international: N/A
TOEFL requirement: Yes
Minimum TOEFL score: N/A

Clark Atlanta University
223 James P. Brawley Drive SW
Atlanta, GA 30314
www.cau.edu
Private
Admissions: (404) 880-8443
Email: pkamos@cau.edu
Financial aid: (404) 880-6265
Application deadline: rolling
Tuition: full time: $861/credit hour; part time: $861/credit hour
Room/board/expenses: $16,278
College-funded aid: Yes
International student aid: No
Full-time enrollment: 84
men: 45%; women: 55%; minorities: 55%; international: 23%
Part-time enrollment: 4
men: 50%; women: 50%; minorities: 75%; international: 0%
Acceptance rate (full time): 24%
Average GMAT (full time): 323
Average GPA (full time): 3.13
Average age of entrants to full-time program: 26
TOEFL requirement: Yes
Minimum TOEFL score: N/A
Most popular departments: accounting, marketing
Mean starting base salary for 2015 full-time graduates: $81,862
Employment location for 2015 class: Intl. N/A; N.E. 13%; M.A. N/A; S. 25%; M.W. N/A; S.W. 13%; W. 50%

Clayton State University
2000 Clayton State Boulevard
Morrow, GA 30260-0285
www.clayton.edu/mba
Public
Admissions: (678) 466-4113
Email: graduate@clayton.edu
Financial aid: N/A
Application deadline: 07/15
In-state tuition: full time: $335/credit hour; part time: $335/credit hour
Out-of-state tuition: full time: $1,335/credit hour
Room/board/expenses: N/A
College-funded aid: Yes
Average student indebtedness at graduation: $17,000
Full-time enrollment: 15
men: N/A; women: N/A; minorities: N/A; international: N/A
Part-time enrollment: 136
men: N/A; women: N/A; minorities: N/A; international: N/A
TOEFL requirement: Yes
Minimum TOEFL score: N/A
Most popular departments: accounting, human resources management, international business, supply chain management, other

Columbus State University (Turner)
4225 University Avenue
Columbus, GA 31907
cobcs.columbusstate.edu
Public
Admissions: (706) 507-8800
Email: lovell_susan@columbusstate.edu
Financial aid: N/A
Application deadline: 06/30
In-state tuition: full time: $250/credit hour; part time: $250/credit hour
Out-of-state tuition: full time: $1,000/credit hour
Room/board/expenses: N/A
College-funded aid: Yes
International student aid: Yes
Full-time enrollment: 12
men: 58%; women: 42%; minorities: 25%; international: 33%
Part-time enrollment: 21
men: 57%; women: 43%; minorities: 24%; international: 0%
Average GMAT (full time): 600
Average GMAT (part time): 570
Average GPA (full time): 3.37
TOEFL requirement: Yes
Minimum TOEFL score: 550

Emory University (Goizueta)
1300 Clifton Road NE
Atlanta, GA 30322
www.goizueta.emory.edu
Private
Admissions: (404) 727-6311
Email: mbaadmissions@emory.edu
Financial aid: (404) 727-6039
Application deadline: 03/11
Tuition: full time: $50,140; total program: $73,600 (part time)
Room/board/expenses: $23,864
College-funded aid: Yes
International student aid: Yes
Average student indebtedness at graduation: $77,343
Full-time enrollment: 345
men: 69%; women: 31%; minorities: 19%; international: 39%
Part-time enrollment: 250
men: 72%; women: 28%; minorities: 28%; international: 9%
Acceptance rate (full time): 30%
Average GMAT (full time): 678
Average GMAT (part time): 639
Average GPA (full time): 3.35
Average age of entrants to full-time program: 29
Average months of prior work experience (full time): 68
TOEFL requirement: Yes
Minimum TOEFL score: N/A
Most popular departments: consulting, finance, general management, marketing, operations management
Mean starting base salary for 2015 full-time graduates: $113,295
Employment location for 2015 class: Intl. 3%; N.E. 20%; M.A. 1%; S. 58%; M.W. 1%; S.W. 8%; W. 9%

Georgia College & State University (Bunting)
Campus Box 019
Milledgeville, GA 31061
mba.gcsu.edu
Public
Admissions: (478) 445-6283
Email: grad-admit@gcsu.edu
Financial aid: (478) 445-5149

Application deadline: 07/01
In-state tuition: full time: $288/credit hour; part time: $288/credit hour
Out-of-state tuition: full time: $1,027/credit hour
Room/board/expenses: $15,531
College-funded aid: Yes
International student aid: Yes
Average student indebtedness at graduation: $25,939
Full-time enrollment: 8
men: 50%; women: 50%; minorities: 25%; international: 25%
Part-time enrollment: 169
men: 63%; women: 37%; minorities: 28%; international: 7%
Average GMAT (part time): 520
TOEFL requirement: Yes
Minimum TOEFL score: 550

Georgia Institute of Technology (Scheller)
800 W. Peachtree Street NW
Atlanta, GA 30332-0520
scheller.gatech.edu
Public
Admissions: (404) 894-8722
Email: mba@scheller.gatech.edu
Financial aid: (404) 894-4160
Application deadline: 05/15
In-state tuition: full time: $31,088; part time: $1,107/credit hour
Out-of-state tuition: full time: $41,676
Room/board/expenses: $16,194
College-funded aid: Yes
International student aid: Yes
Average student indebtedness at graduation: $47,727
Full-time enrollment: 123
men: 80%; women: 20%; minorities: 15%; international: 28%
Part-time enrollment: 369
men: 73%; women: 27%; minorities: 28%; international: 7%
Acceptance rate (full time): 25%
Average GMAT (full time): 678
Average GMAT (part time): 615
Average GPA (full time): 3.18
Average age of entrants to full-time program: 28
Average months of prior work experience (full time): 70
TOEFL requirement: Yes
Minimum TOEFL score: 600
Most popular departments: consulting, entrepreneurship, operations management, supply chain management, technology
Mean starting base salary for 2015 full-time graduates: $103,454
Employment location for 2015 class: Intl. N/A; N.E. 9%; M.A. N/A; S. 69%; M.W. 9%; S.W. 2%; W. 11%

Georgia Southern University
PO Box 8002
Statesboro, GA 30460-8050
coba.georgiasouthern.edu/mba
Public
Admissions: (912) 478-2357
Email: mba@georgiasouthern.edu
Financial aid: (912) 478-5413
Application deadline: 07/31
In-state tuition: full time: $11,916; part time: $410/credit hour
Out-of-state tuition: full time: $31,804
Room/board/expenses: $16,656
College-funded aid: Yes
International student aid: Yes
Full-time enrollment: N/A
men: N/A; women: N/A; minorities: N/A; international: N/A

Part-time enrollment: 93
men: 61%; women: 39%; minorities: 25%; international: 9%
Average GMAT (part time): 491
TOEFL requirement: Yes
Minimum TOEFL score: 550

Georgia Southwestern State University[1]
800 Georgia Southwestern State University Drive
Americus, GA 31709
gsw.edu/
Public
Admissions: N/A
Financial aid: N/A
Tuition: N/A
Room/board/expenses: N/A
Enrollment: N/A

Georgia State University (Robinson)
PO Box 3989
Atlanta, GA 30302-3989
robinson.gsu.edu/
Public
Admissions: (404) 413-7167
Email: rcbgradadmissions@gsu.edu
Financial aid: (404) 413-2400
Application deadline: 05/01
In-state tuition: full time: N/A; part time: $483/credit hour
Out-of-state tuition: full time: N/A
Room/board/expenses: N/A
College-funded aid: Yes
International student aid: Yes
Full-time enrollment: 31
men: 42%; women: 58%; minorities: 58%; international: 10%
Part-time enrollment: 452
men: 53%; women: 47%; minorities: 38%; international: 8%
Acceptance rate (full time): 84%
Average GMAT (part time): 621
Average age of entrants to full-time program: 29
Average months of prior work experience (full time): 57
TOEFL requirement: Yes
Minimum TOEFL score: 610
Most popular departments: finance, general management, health care administration, marketing, statistics and operations research

Kennesaw State University (Coles)
MD 3306
Kennesaw, GA 30144-5591
www.kennesaw.edu/graduate/admissions
Public
Admissions: (470) 578-4377
Email: ksugrad@kennesaw.edu
Financial aid: (470) 578-6525
Application deadline: 07/01
In-state tuition: full time: N/A; part time: $339/credit hour
Out-of-state tuition: full time: N/A
Room/board/expenses: N/A
College-funded aid: Yes
International student aid: Yes
Full-time enrollment: N/A
men: N/A; women: N/A; minorities: N/A; international: N/A
Part-time enrollment: 165
men: 56%; women: 44%; minorities: 32%; international: 4%
Average GMAT (part time): 595
TOEFL requirement: Yes
Minimum TOEFL score: N/A

Mercer University-Atlanta (Stetson)

3001 Mercer University Drive
Atlanta, GA 30341-4155
business.mercer.edu
Private
Admissions: (678) 547-6300
Email: business.admissions@
mercer.edu
Financial aid: (678) 547-6444
Application deadline: 06/15
Tuition: full time: $706/credit hour;
part time: $706/credit hour
Room/board/expenses: N/A
College-funded aid: No
International student aid: No
**Average student indebtedness at
graduation:** $24,271
Full-time enrollment: 25
men: 56%; women: 44%;
minorities: 68%; international:
20%
Part-time enrollment: 363
men: 48%; women: 52%;
minorities: 50%; international:
14%
Acceptance rate (full time): 77%
Average GMAT (full time): 510
Average GMAT (part time): 537
Average GPA (full time): 3.13
**Average age of entrants to full-time
program:** 27
**Average months of prior work
experience (full time):** 73
TOEFL requirement: Yes
Minimum TOEFL score: 550
Most popular departments:
accounting, economics, finance,
health care administration,
marketing
**Mean starting base salary for 2015
full-time graduates:** $49,583
Employment location for 2015 class:
Intl. N/A; N.E. N/A; M.A. N/A; S.
92%; M.W. 8%; S.W. N/A; W. N/A

Savannah State University

PO Box 20359
Savannah, GA 31404
www.savannahstate.edu/coba/
programs-mba.shtml
Public
Admissions: (912) 358-3406
Email: mba@savannahstate.edu
Financial aid: (912) 358-4162
Application deadline: rolling
In-state tuition: full time: N/A; total
program: $10,275 (part time)
Out-of-state tuition: full time: N/A
Room/board/expenses: N/A
College-funded aid: Yes
Full-time enrollment: N/A
men: N/A; women: N/A; minorities:
N/A; international: N/A
Part-time enrollment: 37
men: 27%; women: 73%;
minorities: N/A; international: N/A
TOEFL requirement: Yes
Minimum TOEFL score: N/A

University of Georgia (Terry)

335 Brooks Hall
Athens, GA 30602-6251
terry.uga.edu/mba
Public
Admissions: (706) 542-5671
Email: ugamba@uga.edu
Financial aid: (706) 542-6147
Application deadline: 03/09
In-state tuition: full time: $15,450;
total program: $56,400 (part time)
Out-of-state tuition: full time:
$33,768
Room/board/expenses: $22,796
College-funded aid: Yes

International student aid: Yes
**Average student indebtedness at
graduation:** $37,565
Full-time enrollment: 98
men: 72%; women: 28%;
minorities: 14%; international:
38%
Part-time enrollment: 288
men: 59%; women: 41%;
minorities: 37%; international: 2%
Acceptance rate (full time): 31%
Average GMAT (full time): 643
Average GMAT (part time): 561
Average GPA (full time): 3.43
**Average age of entrants to full-time
program:** 28
**Average months of prior work
experience (full time):** 51
TOEFL requirement: Yes
Minimum TOEFL score: N/A
Most popular departments: finance,
human resources management,
marketing, operations
management, statistics and
operations research
**Mean starting base salary for 2015
full-time graduates:** $84,364
Employment location for 2015 class:
Intl. 4%; N.E. 7%; M.A. 4%; S.
75%; M.W. 4%; S.W. 7%; W. 0%

University of North Georgia

82 College Circle
Dahlonega, GA 30597
ung.edu/master-business-
administration/
Public
Admissions: (470) 239-3030
Email: mba@ung.edu
Financial aid: (706) 864-1412
Application deadline: 07/01
In-state tuition: full time: N/A; part
time: $520/credit hour
Out-of-state tuition: full time: N/A
Room/board/expenses: N/A
College-funded aid: Yes
International student aid: No
Full-time enrollment: N/A
men: N/A; women: N/A; minorities:
N/A; international: N/A
Part-time enrollment: 24
men: 58%; women: 42%;
minorities: 17%; international: 0%
Average GMAT (part time): 468
TOEFL requirement: Yes
Minimum TOEFL score: 550

University of West Georgia (Richards)

1601 Maple Street
Carrollton, GA 30118-3000
www.westga.edu/business
Public
Admissions: (678) 839-5355
Email: hudombon@westga.edu
Financial aid: (678) 839-6421
Application deadline: 07/15
In-state tuition: full time: $9,292;
part time: $306/credit hour
Out-of-state tuition: full time:
$26,976
Room/board/expenses: $11,948
College-funded aid: Yes
International student aid: Yes
Full-time enrollment: N/A
men: N/A; women: N/A; minorities:
N/A; international: N/A
Part-time enrollment: 95
men: 51%; women: 49%;
minorities: 38%; international: 8%
Average GMAT (part time): 476
TOEFL requirement: Yes
Minimum TOEFL score: 550
Most popular departments:
accounting, economics, finance,
general management

Valdosta State University (Langdale)[1]

1500 N. Patterson Street
Valdosta, GA 31698
www.valdosta.edu/lcoba/grad/
Public
Admissions: (229) 245-3822
Email: mschnake@valdosta.edu
Financial aid: (229) 333-5935
Tuition: N/A
Room/board/expenses: N/A
Enrollment: N/A

HAWAII

University of Hawaii-Manoa (Shidler)

2404 Maile Way, Business
Administration C-204
Honolulu, HI 96822
www.shidler.hawaii.edu
Public
Admissions: (808) 956-8266
Email: mba@hawaii.edu
Financial aid: (808) 956-7251
Application deadline: rolling
In-state tuition: full time: $21,032;
part time: $843/credit hour
Out-of-state tuition: full time:
$36,704
Room/board/expenses: $20,000
College-funded aid: Yes
International student aid: Yes
Full-time enrollment: 59
men: 59%; women: 41%;
minorities: 69%; international:
14%
Part-time enrollment: 94
men: 54%; women: 46%;
minorities: 83%; international: 0%
Acceptance rate (full time): 90%
Average GMAT (full time): 587
Average GMAT (part time): 594
Average GPA (full time): 3.35
**Average age of entrants to full-time
program:** 29
**Average months of prior work
experience (full time):** 63
TOEFL requirement: Yes
Minimum TOEFL score: N/A
Most popular departments:
accounting, entrepreneurship,
finance, health care
administration, international
business

IDAHO

Boise State University

1910 University Drive,
MBEB4101
Boise, ID 83725-1600
cobe.boisestate.edu/graduate
Public
Admissions: (208) 426-3116
Email: graduatebusiness@
boisestate.edu
Financial aid: (208) 426-1664
Application deadline: rolling
In-state tuition: full time: $8,166;
part time: $358/credit hour
Out-of-state tuition: full time: N/A
Room/board/expenses: N/A
College-funded aid: Yes
International student aid: Yes
**Average student indebtedness at
graduation:** $34,330
Full-time enrollment: 71
men: 54%; women: 46%;
minorities: 8%; international: 11%
Part-time enrollment: 67
men: 67%; women: 33%;
minorities: 9%; international: 1%
Acceptance rate (full time): 61%
Average GMAT (full time): 574
Average GMAT (part time): 540
Average GPA (full time): 3.56

**Average age of entrants to full-time
program:** 27
**Average months of prior work
experience (full time):** 24
TOEFL requirement: Yes
Minimum TOEFL score: 587
**Mean starting base salary for 2015
full-time graduates:** $55,437
Employment location for 2015 class:
Intl. N/A; N.E. 7%; M.A. N/A; S. N/A;
M.W. 7%; S.W. N/A; W. 87%

Idaho State University[1]

921 S. 8th Ave Stop 8020
Pocatello, ID 83209
www.isu.edu/cob/mba.shtml
Public
Admissions: (208) 282-2966
Email: mba@isu.edu
Financial aid: N/A
Tuition: N/A
Room/board/expenses: N/A
Enrollment: N/A

University of Idaho[1]

PO Box 443161
Moscow, ID 83844-3161
www.uidaho.edu
Public
Admissions: (800) 885-4001
Email: graduateadmissions@
uidaho.edu
Financial aid: N/A
Tuition: N/A
Room/board/expenses: N/A
Enrollment: N/A

ILLINOIS

Bradley University (Foster)

1501 W. Bradley Avenue
Peoria, IL 61625
www.bradley.edu/mba
Private
Admissions: (309) 677-3714
Email: mba@bradley.edu
Financial aid: (309) 677-3089
Application deadline: 08/01
Tuition: full time: N/A; part time:
$830/credit hour
Room/board/expenses: N/A
College-funded aid: Yes
International student aid: Yes
Full-time enrollment: N/A
men: N/A; women: N/A; minorities:
N/A; international: N/A
Part-time enrollment: 49
men: 55%; women: 45%;
minorities: 10%; international: 16%
Average GMAT (part time): 567
TOEFL requirement: Yes
Minimum TOEFL score: N/A
Most popular departments: finance,
general management, marketing

DePaul University (Kellstadt)

1 E. Jackson Boulevard
Chicago, IL 60604-2287
www.kellstadt.depaul.edu/
Private
Admissions: (312) 362-8810
Email: kgsb@depaul.edu
Financial aid: (312) 362-8091
Application deadline: 08/01
Tuition: full time: $1,000/credit
hour; part time: $1,000/credit
hour
Room/board/expenses: $15,000
College-funded aid: Yes
International student aid: Yes
**Average student indebtedness at
graduation:** $64,759

Full-time enrollment: 46
men: 52%; women: 48%;
minorities: 17%; international: 22%
Part-time enrollment: 776
men: 64%; women: 36%;
minorities: 21%; international: 5%
Acceptance rate (full time): 34%
Average GMAT (full time): 626
Average GMAT (part time): 558
Average GPA (full time): 3.40
**Average age of entrants to full-time
program:** 28
**Average months of prior work
experience (full time):** 43
TOEFL requirement: Yes
Minimum TOEFL score: 550
**Mean starting base salary for 2015
full-time graduates:** $73,258
Employment location for 2015 class:
Intl. N/A; N.E. N/A; M.A. N/A; S.
N/A; M.W. 100%; S.W. N/A; W. N/A

Dominican University (Brennan)

7900 West Division Street
River Forest, IL 60305
business.dom.edu/
Private
Admissions: N/A
Financial aid: N/A
Application deadline: rolling
Tuition: full time: N/A; part time:
$932/credit hour
Room/board/expenses: N/A
College-funded aid: Yes
International student aid: Yes
Full-time enrollment: N/A
men: N/A; women: N/A; minorities:
N/A; international: N/A
Part-time enrollment: 165
men: 36%; women: 64%;
minorities: 24%; international: 7%
Average GMAT (part time): 450
TOEFL requirement: Yes
Minimum TOEFL score: N/A
Most popular departments: finance,
general management, health
care administration, international
business, marketing

Eastern Illinois University (Lumpkin)

600 Lincoln Avenue
Charleston, IL 61920-3099
www.eiu.edu/mba
Public
Admissions: (217) 581-3028
Email: mba@eiu.edu
Financial aid: N/A
Application deadline: 01/06
In-state tuition: full time: $285/
credit hour; part time: $285/
credit hour
Out-of-state tuition: full time: $684/
credit hour
Room/board/expenses: $10,546
College-funded aid: Yes
International student aid: Yes
Full-time enrollment: 47
men: 49%; women: 51%;
minorities: 11%; international: 32%
Part-time enrollment: 43
men: 51%; women: 49%;
minorities: 5%; international: 2%
Acceptance rate (full time): 85%
Average GMAT (full time): 458
Average GMAT (part time): 522
Average GPA (full time): 3.36
TOEFL requirement: Yes
Minimum TOEFL score: 550
Most popular departments:
accounting, general management,
other

Illinois Institute of Technology (Stuart)[1]

10 W. 35th Street
Chicago, IL 60616
www.stuart.iit.edu
Private
Admissions: (312) 567-3020
Email: admission@stuart.iit.edu
Financial aid: (312) 567-7219
Tuition: N/A
Room/board/expenses: N/A
Enrollment: N/A

Illinois State University

MBA Program
Campus Box 5570
Normal, IL 61790-5570
business.illinoisstate.edu/mba/
Public
Admissions: (309) 438-8388
Email: admissions@ilstu.edu
Financial aid: (309) 438-2231
Application deadline: 07/01
In-state tuition: full time: $374/
credit hour; part time: $374/
credit hour
Out-of-state tuition: full time: $777/
credit hour
Room/board/expenses: $15,161
College-funded aid: Yes
International student aid: Yes
Full-time enrollment: N/A
men: N/A; women: N/A; minorities:
N/A; international: N/A
Part-time enrollment: 114
men: 54%; women: 46%;
minorities: 11%; international: 17%
Average GMAT (part time): 535
TOEFL requirement: Yes
Minimum TOEFL score: 600
Most popular departments: finance,
human resources management,
insurance, leadership, marketing

Loyola University Chicago (Quinlan)

820 N. Michigan Avenue
Chicago, IL 60611
www.luc.edu/quinlan/mba/
index.shtml
Private
Admissions: (312) 915-8908
Email: quinlangrad@luc.edu
Financial aid: (773) 508-7704
Application deadline: 07/15
Tuition: full time: $1,460/credit
hour; part time: $1,460/credit
hour
Room/board/expenses: $22,023
College-funded aid: Yes
International student aid: Yes
Full-time enrollment: N/A
men: N/A; women: N/A; minorities:
N/A; international: N/A
Part-time enrollment: 557
men: 45%; women: 55%;
minorities: 16%; international:
34%
Average GMAT (part time): 566
TOEFL requirement: Yes
Minimum TOEFL score: 577
Most popular departments:
accounting, finance, human
resources management,
marketing, supply chain
management

Northern Illinois University

Office of MBA Programs,
Barsema Hall 203
De Kalb, IL 60115-2897
www.cob.niu.edu/mbaprograms
Public
Admissions: (866) 648-6221
Email: mba@niu.edu
Financial aid: (815) 753-1395
Application deadline: 07/15
In-state tuition: total program:
$50,000 (full time); part time:
$894/credit hour
Out-of-state tuition: total program:
$61,000 (full time)
Room/board/expenses: $10,000
College-funded aid: Yes
International student aid: Yes
Full-time enrollment: 30
men: 57%; women: 43%;
minorities: 13%; international:
43%
Part-time enrollment: 589
men: 68%; women: 32%;
minorities: 28%; international:
12%
Acceptance rate (full time): 78%
Average GMAT (full time): 475
Average GMAT (part time): 485
Average GPA (full time): 3.06
**Average age of entrants to full-time
program:** 25
**Average months of prior work
experience (full time):** 90
TOEFL requirement: Yes
Minimum TOEFL score: N/A
Most popular departments: finance,
international business, leadership,
marketing, management
information systems

Northwestern University (Kellogg)

2001 Sheridan Road
Evanston, IL 60208-2001
www.kellogg.northwestern.edu
Private
Admissions: (847) 491-3308
Email: mbaadmissions@
kellogg.northwestern.edu
Financial aid: (847) 491-3308
Application deadline: 04/06
Tuition: full time: $65,284; part
time: $6,208/credit hour
Room/board/expenses: $21,108
College-funded aid: Yes
International student aid: Yes
Full-time enrollment: 1,272
men: 61%; women: 39%;
minorities: 24%; international:
35%
Part-time enrollment: 688
men: 73%; women: 27%;
minorities: 19%; international: 9%
Acceptance rate (full time): 21%
Average GMAT (full time): 724
Average GMAT (part time): 669
Average GPA (full time): 3.60
**Average age of entrants to full-time
program:** 28
**Average months of prior work
experience (full time):** 60
TOEFL requirement: Yes
Minimum TOEFL score: N/A
Most popular departments:
entrepreneurship, finance,
general management, marketing,
organizational behavior
**Mean starting base salary for 2015
full-time graduates:** $121,516
Employment location for 2015 class:
Intl. 12%; N.E. 20%; M.A. 3%; S.
3%; M.W. 33%; S.W. 6%; W. 22%

Purdue University-Calumet[1]

2200 169th Street
Hammond, IN 46323
Public
Admissions: N/A
Financial aid: N/A
Tuition: N/A
Room/board/expenses: N/A
Enrollment: N/A

Southern Illinois University-Carbondale

133 Rehn Hall
Carbondale, IL 62901-4625
mba.business.siu.edu
Public
Admissions: (618) 453-3030
Email: cobgp@business.siu.edu
Financial aid: (618) 453-4334
Application deadline: 07/31
In-state tuition: full time: $480/
credit hour; part time: $480/
credit hour
Out-of-state tuition: full time:
$1,044/credit hour
Room/board/expenses: N/A
College-funded aid: Yes
International student aid: Yes
Full-time enrollment: 72
men: 56%; women: 44%;
minorities: 21%; international: 31%
Part-time enrollment: N/A
men: N/A; women: N/A; minorities:
N/A; international: N/A
Acceptance rate (full time): 49%
Average GMAT (full time): 560
Average GPA (full time): 3.53
**Average age of entrants to full-time
program:** 27
**Average months of prior work
experience (full time):** 74
TOEFL requirement: Yes
Minimum TOEFL score: 550
Most popular departments: finance,
general management, marketing

Southern Illinois University-Edwardsville

Box 1051
Edwardsville, IL 62026-1051
www.siue.edu/business
Public
Admissions: (618) 650-3840
Email: mba@siue.edu
Financial aid: (618) 650-3880
Application deadline: rolling
In-state tuition: full time: $293/
credit hour; part time: $293/
credit hour
Out-of-state tuition: full time: $733/
credit hour
Room/board/expenses: $24,000
College-funded aid: Yes
International student aid: Yes
Full-time enrollment: N/A
men: N/A; women: N/A; minorities:
N/A; international: N/A
Part-time enrollment: 133
men: 59%; women: 41%;
minorities: 10%; international: 4%
Average GMAT (part time): 505
TOEFL requirement: Yes
Minimum TOEFL score: N/A

St. Xavier University

3700 West 103rd Street
Chicago, IL 60655
www.sxu.edu/academics/
colleges_schools/gsm/
Private
Admissions: (773) 298-3053
Email: graduateadmission@
sxu.edu

Financial aid: N/A
Application deadline: N/A
Tuition: full time: $915/credit hour;
part time: N/A
Room/board/expenses: N/A
College-funded aid: Yes
International student aid: Yes
**Average student indebtedness at
graduation:** $8,366
Full-time enrollment: 256
men: 48%; women: 52%;
minorities: 41%; international: 2%
Part-time enrollment: 90
men: 50%; women: 50%;
minorities: 42%; international: 0%
Acceptance rate (full time): 90%
Average GPA (full time): 3.21
**Average age of entrants to full-time
program:** 33
TOEFL requirement: Yes
Minimum TOEFL score: 550
Most popular departments: general
management, human resources
management, marketing, other

University of Chicago (Booth)

5807 S. Woodlawn Avenue
Chicago, IL 60637
ChicagoBooth.edu
Private
Admissions: (773) 702-7369
Email:
admissions@ChicagoBooth.edu
Financial aid: (773) 702-7369
Application deadline: 04/04
Tuition: full time: $65,069; part
time: $6,338/credit hour
Room/board/expenses: $25,870
College-funded aid: Yes
International student aid: Yes
Full-time enrollment: 1,180
men: 61%; women: 39%;
minorities: 23%; international:
35%
Part-time enrollment: 1,329
men: 75%; women: 25%;
minorities: 26%; international:
16%
Acceptance rate (full time): 24%
Average GMAT (full time): 726
Average GMAT (part time): 676
Average GPA (full time): 3.59
**Average age of entrants to full-time
program:** 27
**Average months of prior work
experience (full time):** 55
TOEFL requirement: Yes
Minimum TOEFL score: 600
Most popular departments:
economics, entrepreneurship,
finance, organizational behavior,
other
**Mean starting base salary for 2015
full-time graduates:** $123,561
Employment location for 2015 class:
Intl. 17%; N.E. 23%; M.A. 2%; S.
2%; M.W. 31%; S.W. 5%; W. 19%

University of Illinois-Chicago (Liautaud)

601 South Morgan Street
University Hall, 11th Floor
Chicago, IL 60607
www.mba.uic.edu/
Public
Admissions: (312) 996-4573
Email: mba@uic.edu
Financial aid: (312) 996-3126
Application deadline: 06/15
In-state tuition: full time: $24,912;
part time: $18,020
Out-of-state tuition: full time:
$37,152
Room/board/expenses: N/A
College-funded aid: Yes
International student aid: Yes
Full-time enrollment: N/A

men: N/A; women: N/A; minorities:
N/A; international: N/A
Part-time enrollment: 278
men: 63%; women: 37%;
minorities: 25%; international:
12%
Average GMAT (part time): 581
TOEFL requirement: Yes
Minimum TOEFL score: 550
Most popular departments:
entrepreneurship, finance,
general management, marketing,
management information systems

University of Illinois-Springfield

1 University Plaza
MS UHB 4000
Springfield , IL 62703
www.uis.edu/admissions
Public
Admissions: (888) 977-4847
Email: admissions@uis.edu
Financial aid: (217) 206-6724
Application deadline: rolling
In-state tuition: full time: $329/
credit hour; part time: $329/
credit hour
Out-of-state tuition: full time: $675/
credit hour
Room/board/expenses: N/A
College-funded aid: Yes
International student aid: Yes
Full-time enrollment: N/A
men: N/A; women: N/A; minorities:
N/A; international: N/A
Part-time enrollment: 117
men: 64%; women: 36%;
minorities: 12%; international: 15%
Average GMAT (part time): 445
TOEFL requirement: Yes
Minimum TOEFL score: 550

University of Illinois-Urbana-Champaign

515 E. Gregory Drive
3019 BIF, MC 520
Champaign, IL 61820
www.mba.illinois.edu
Public
Admissions: (217) 244-7602
Email: mba@illinois.edu
Financial aid: (217) 333-0100
Application deadline: 02/03
In-state tuition: full time: $27,830;
part time: $23,070
Out-of-state tuition: full time:
$39,420
Room/board/expenses: $21,658
College-funded aid: Yes
International student aid: Yes
**Average student indebtedness at
graduation:** $53,820
Full-time enrollment: 160
men: 73%; women: 27%;
minorities: 24%; international:
41%
Part-time enrollment: N/A
men: N/A; women: N/A; minorities:
N/A; international: N/A
Acceptance rate (full time): 32%
Average GMAT (full time): 654
Average GPA (full time): 3.38
**Average age of entrants to full-time
program:** 28
**Average months of prior work
experience (full time):** 49
TOEFL requirement: Yes
Minimum TOEFL score: 610
Most popular departments:
consulting, finance, general
management, marketing,
technology
**Mean starting base salary for 2015
full-time graduates:** $91,195

Employment location for 2015 class: Intl. 22%; N.E. 8%; M.A. N/A; S. 8%; M.W. 50%; S.W. N/A; W. 13%

Western Illinois University
1 University Circle
Macomb, IL 61455
www.wiu.edu/cbt
Public
Admissions: (309) 298-2442
Email: wj-polley@wiu.edu
Financial aid: (309) 298-2446
Application deadline: rolling
In-state tuition: full time: $324/credit hour; part time: $324/credit hour
Out-of-state tuition: full time: $485/credit hour
Room/board/expenses: N/A
College-funded aid: Yes
International student aid: Yes
Full-time enrollment: 53
men: 53%; women: 47%; minorities: 4%; international: 19%
Part-time enrollment: 31
men: 61%; women: 39%; minorities: 6%; international: 6%
Acceptance rate (full time): 81%
Average GMAT (full time): 500
Average GMAT (part time): 443
Average GPA (full time): 3.20
Average months of prior work experience (full time): 118
TOEFL requirement: Yes
Minimum TOEFL score: 550
Most popular departments: accounting, economics, finance, general management, supply chain management

INDIANA

Ball State University (Miller)
Whitinger Building,147
Muncie, IN 47306
www.bsu.edu/mba/
Public
Admissions: (765) 285-1931
Email: mba@bsu.edu
Financial aid: (765) 285-5600
Application deadline: rolling
In-state tuition: total program: $18,633 (full time); $18,633 (part time)
Out-of-state tuition: total program: $38,823 (full time)
Room/board/expenses: $10,015
College-funded aid: Yes
International student aid: Yes
Average student indebtedness at graduation: $32,666
Full-time enrollment: 39
men: 56%; women: 44%; minorities: 10%; international: 26%
Part-time enrollment: 15
men: 60%; women: 40%; minorities: 0%; international: 0%
Acceptance rate (full time): 100%
Average GMAT (full time): 519
Average GPA (full time): 3.35
Average age of entrants to full-time program: 25
Average months of prior work experience (full time): 24
TOEFL requirement: Yes
Minimum TOEFL score: 550
Most popular departments: entrepreneurship, finance, general management, operations management, other
Mean starting base salary for 2015 full-time graduates: $102,000
Employment location for 2015 class: Intl. N/A; N.E. 20%; M.A. N/A; S. N/A; M.W. 80%; S.W. N/A; W. N/A

Butler University
4600 Sunset Avenue
Indianapolis, IN 46208-3485
www.butlermba.com
Private
Admissions: (317) 940-9842
Email: mba@butler.edu
Financial aid: (317) 940-8200
Application deadline: 08/01
Tuition: full time: N/A; part time: $760/credit hour
Room/board/expenses: N/A
College-funded aid: No
International student aid: No
Full-time enrollment: N/A
men: N/A; women: N/A; minorities: N/A; international: N/A
Part-time enrollment: 208
men: 70%; women: 30%; minorities: 4%; international: 3%
Average GMAT (part time): 578
TOEFL requirement: Yes
Minimum TOEFL score: 550

Indiana State University
MBA Program, 30 N 7th Street
Terre Haute, IN 47809
www.indstate.edumba/
Public
Admissions: (812) 237-2002
Email: ISU-MBA@mail.indstate.edu
Financial aid: (812) 237-2215
Application deadline: rolling
In-state tuition: full time: $388/credit hour; part time: $388/credit hour
Out-of-state tuition: full time: $762/credit hour
Room/board/expenses: N/A
College-funded aid: Yes
International student aid: Yes
Full-time enrollment: 27
men: 81%; women: 19%; minorities: 11%; international: 33%
Part-time enrollment: 59
men: 53%; women: 47%; minorities: 15%; international: 2%
Acceptance rate (full time): 65%
Average GMAT (full time): 528
Average GPA (full time): 3.24
Average age of entrants to full-time program: 31
Average months of prior work experience (full time): 156
TOEFL requirement: Yes
Minimum TOEFL score: 550
Most popular departments: accounting, finance, marketing, operations management, supply chain management
Employment location for 2015 class: Intl. 50%; N.E. 0%; M.A. 0%; S. 0%; M.W. 50%; S.W. 0%; W. 0%

Indiana University (Kelley School)
1275 E. 10th Street, Suite 2010
Bloomington, IN 47405-1703
kelley.iu.edu/mba
Public
Admissions: (812) 855-8006
Email: iumba@indiana.edu
Financial aid: (812) 855-8006
Application deadline: 04/15
In-state tuition: full time: $27,601; part time: $750/credit hour
Out-of-state tuition: full time: $46,561
Room/board/expenses: $18,540
College-funded aid: Yes
International student aid: Yes
Average student indebtedness at graduation: $64,438

Full-time enrollment: 372
men: 70%; women: 30%; minorities: 19%; international: 34%
Part-time enrollment: 305
men: 79%; women: 21%; minorities: 12%; international: 38%
Acceptance rate (full time): 29%
Average GMAT (full time): 668
Average GMAT (part time): 670
Average GPA (full time): 3.36
Average age of entrants to full-time program: 28
Average months of prior work experience (full time): 61
TOEFL requirement: Yes
Minimum TOEFL score: 600
Most popular departments: finance, general management, marketing, supply chain management, other
Mean starting base salary for 2015 full-time graduates: $107,006
Employment location for 2015 class: Intl. 5%; N.E. 7%; M.A. 5%; S. 4%; M.W. 55%; S.W. 11%; W. 13%

Indiana University-Kokomo[1]
2300 S. Washington Street
Kokomo, IN 46904-9003
www.iuk.edu/index.php
Public
Admissions: (765) 455-9275
Financial aid: N/A
Tuition: N/A
Room/board/expenses: N/A
Enrollment: N/A

Indiana University Northwest
3400 Broadway
Gary, IN 46408-1197
www.indiana.edu/~bulletin/iun/grad/busec.html#pro
Public
Admissions: (219) 980-6635
Email: iunbiz@iun.edu
Financial aid: (219) 980-6778
Application deadline: 08/01
In-state tuition: full time: N/A; part time: N/A
Out-of-state tuition: full time: N/A
Room/board/expenses: N/A
College-funded aid: Yes
International student aid: No
Full-time enrollment: N/A
men: N/A; women: N/A; minorities: N/A; international: N/A
Part-time enrollment: 55
men: N/A; women: N/A; minorities: N/A; international: N/A
TOEFL requirement: Yes
Minimum TOEFL score: 550

Indiana University-Purdue University-Fort Wayne (Doermer)
2101 E. Coliseum Boulevard
Fort Wayne, IN 46805-1499
www.ipfw.edu/mba
Public
Admissions: (260) 481-6498
Email: mba@ipfw.edu
Financial aid: (260) 481-6820
Application deadline: 05/15
In-state tuition: full time: $733/credit hour; part time: $420/credit hour
Out-of-state tuition: full time: $1,152/credit hour
Room/board/expenses: N/A
College-funded aid: Yes
International student aid: Yes

Full-time enrollment: 25
men: 72%; women: 28%; minorities: 44%; international: 4%
Part-time enrollment: 29
men: 66%; women: 34%; minorities: 17%; international: 14%
Acceptance rate (full time): 84%
Average GMAT (part time): 544
Average age of entrants to full-time program: 35
Average months of prior work experience (full time): 60
TOEFL requirement: Yes
Minimum TOEFL score: 550
Employment location for 2015 class: Intl. N/A; N.E. N/A; M.A. N/A; S. N/A; M.W. 100%; S.W. N/A; W. N/A

Indiana University-South Bend[1]
1700 Mishawaka Avenue
PO Box 7111
South Bend, IN 46634-7111
www.iusb.edu/buse
Public
Admissions: (574) 520-4497
Email: graduate@iusb.edu
Financial aid: N/A
Tuition: N/A
Room/board/expenses: N/A
Enrollment: N/A

Indiana University-Southeast
4201 Grant Line Road
New Albany, IN 47150
www.ius.edu/graduatebusiness
Public
Admissions: (812) 941-2364
Email: iusmba@ius.edu
Financial aid: (812) 941-2246
Application deadline: 07/20
In-state tuition: full time: N/A; part time: $391
Out-of-state tuition: full time: N/A
Room/board/expenses: N/A
College-funded aid: Yes
International student aid: Yes
Full-time enrollment: N/A
men: N/A; women: N/A; minorities: N/A; international: N/A
Part-time enrollment: 199
men: 61%; women: 39%; minorities: 13%; international: 2%
Average GMAT (part time): 525
TOEFL requirement: Yes
Minimum TOEFL score: 550

Purdue University-West Lafayette (Krannert)
100 S. Grant Street
Rawls Hall, Room 2020
West Lafayette, IN 47907-2076
www.krannert.purdue.edu/programs/masters
Public
Admissions: (765) 494-0773
Email: krannertmasters@purdue.edu
Financial aid: (765) 494-0998
Application deadline: 05/01
In-state tuition: full time: $22,418; part time: $24,870
Out-of-state tuition: full time: $42,184
Room/board/expenses: $13,030
College-funded aid: Yes
International student aid: Yes
Average student indebtedness at graduation: $45,807
Full-time enrollment: 150
men: 74%; women: 26%; minorities: 16%; international: 46%

Part-time enrollment: 57
men: 72%; women: 28%; minorities: 14%; international: 7%
Acceptance rate (full time): 26%
Average GMAT (full time): 635
Average GMAT (part time): 592
Average GPA (full time): 3.38
Average age of entrants to full-time program: 26
Average months of prior work experience (full time): 50
TOEFL requirement: Yes
Minimum TOEFL score: 600
Most popular departments: finance, human resources management, marketing, operations management, supply chain management
Mean starting base salary for 2015 full-time graduates: $92,546
Employment location for 2015 class: Intl. 9%; N.E. 16%; M.A. 2%; S. 9%; M.W. 42%; S.W. 9%; W. 13%

University of Notre Dame (Mendoza)
204 Mendoza College of Business
Notre Dame, IN 46556
mendoza.nd.edu/programs/mba-programs/two-year-mba/
Private
Admissions: (574) 631-8488
Email: mba.business@nd.edu
Financial aid: (574) 631-6436
Application deadline: rolling
Tuition: full time: $49,180; part time: N/A
Room/board/expenses: $19,950
College-funded aid: Yes
International student aid: Yes
Average student indebtedness at graduation: $69,632
Full-time enrollment: 302
men: 72%; women: 28%; minorities: 13%; international: 27%
Part-time enrollment: N/A
men: N/A; women: N/A; minorities: N/A; international: N/A
Acceptance rate (full time): 40%
Average GMAT (full time): 682
Average GPA (full time): 3.31
Average age of entrants to full-time program: 27
Average months of prior work experience (full time): 60
TOEFL requirement: Yes
Minimum TOEFL score: 600
Most popular departments: consulting, finance, leadership, marketing, other
Mean starting base salary for 2015 full-time graduates: $108,219
Employment location for 2015 class: Intl. 4%; N.E. 23%; M.A. 4%; S. 7%; M.W. 33%; S.W. 11%; W. 19%

University of Southern Indiana
8600 University Boulevard
Evansville, IN 47712
www.usi.edu/graduatestudies
Public
Admissions: (812) 465-7015
Email: graduate.studeis@usi.edu
Financial aid: (812) 464-1767
Application deadline: rolling
In-state tuition: full time: $338/credit hour; part time: $338/credit hour
Out-of-state tuition: full time: $666/credit hour
Room/board/expenses: $9,316
College-funded aid: Yes
International student aid: Yes
Average student indebtedness at graduation: $22,598

Full-time enrollment: 8
men: 63%; women: 38%;
minorities: 0%; international: 38%
Part-time enrollment: 99
men: 62%; women: 38%;
minorities: 6%; international: 3%
Acceptance rate (full time): 100%
Average GMAT (part time): 547
Average GPA (full time): 3.31
Average age of entrants to full-time program: 22
TOEFL requirement: Yes
Minimum TOEFL score: N/A

Valparaiso University

Urschel Hall, 1909 Chapel Drive
Valparaiso, IN 46383
www.valpo.edu/mba/
Private
Admissions: (219) 465-7952
Email: mba@valpo.edu
Financial aid: (219) 464-5015
Application deadline: 06/30
Tuition: full time: $833/credit hour; part time: $833/credit hour
Room/board/expenses: $19,998
College-funded aid: No
International student aid: No
Average student indebtedness at graduation: $45,926
Full-time enrollment: 7
men: 43%; women: 57%;
minorities: 0%; international: 57%
Part-time enrollment: 64
men: 58%; women: 42%;
minorities: 9%; international: 2%
Acceptance rate (full time): 42%
Average GMAT (full time): 463
Average GMAT (part time): 534
Average GPA (full time): 3.51
Average age of entrants to full-time program: 25
Average months of prior work experience (full time): 46
TOEFL requirement: Yes
Minimum TOEFL score: 575
Most popular departments:
finance, general management, manufacturing and technology management, marketing, statistics and operations research
Mean starting base salary for 2015 full-time graduates: $45,250
Employment location for 2015 class: Intl. 0%; N.E. 0%; M.A. 0%; S. 0%; M.W. 100%; S.W. 0%; W. 0%

IOWA

Iowa State University

1360 Gerdin Business Building
Ames, IA 50011-1350
www.business.iastate.edu
Public
Admissions: (515) 294-8118
Email: busgrad@iastate.edu
Financial aid: (515) 294-2223
Application deadline: 06/01
In-state tuition: full time: $10,952; part time: $549/credit hour
Out-of-state tuition: full time: $23,890
Room/board/expenses: N/A
College-funded aid: Yes
International student aid: Yes
Full-time enrollment: 82
men: 61%; women: 39%;
minorities: 6%; international: 32%
Part-time enrollment: 60
men: 72%; women: 28%;
minorities: 10%; international: 2%
Acceptance rate (full time): 55%
Average GMAT (full time): 613
Average GPA (full time): 3.48
Average age of entrants to full-time program: 24
TOEFL requirement: Yes
Minimum TOEFL score: 600

Most popular departments:
accounting, finance, marketing, supply chain management, technology
Mean starting base salary for 2015 full-time graduates: $65,360
Employment location for 2015 class: Intl. N/A; N.E. N/A; M.A. N/A; S. 10%; M.W. 86%; S.W. 5%; W. N/A

University of Iowa (Tippie)

108 John Pappajohn Business Building, Suite W160
Iowa City, IA 52242-1000
tippie.uiowa.edu/mba
Public
Admissions: (319) 335-1039
Email: tippiemba@uiowa.edu
Financial aid: (319) 335-1039
Application deadline: 07/30
In-state tuition: full time: $19,936; part time: $665/credit hour
Out-of-state tuition: full time: $36,580
Room/board/expenses: $17,085
College-funded aid: Yes
International student aid: Yes
Average student indebtedness at graduation: $46,523
Full-time enrollment: 119
men: 73%; women: 27%;
minorities: 10%; international: 34%
Part-time enrollment: 743
men: 67%; women: 33%;
minorities: 12%; international: 6%
Acceptance rate (full time): 41%
Average GMAT (full time): 670
Average GMAT (part time): 568
Average GPA (full time): 3.27
Average age of entrants to full-time program: 27
Average months of prior work experience (full time): 43
TOEFL requirement: Yes
Minimum TOEFL score: 600
Most popular departments:
finance, marketing, operations management, portfolio management, supply chain management
Mean starting base salary for 2015 full-time graduates: $94,088
Employment location for 2015 class: Intl. 4%; N.E. 4%; M.A. 9%; S. 13%; M.W. 51%; S.W. 4%; W. 15%

University of Northern Iowa

Curris Business Building 325
Cedar Falls, IA 50614-0123
www.cba.uni.edu/mba/
Public
Admissions: (319) 273-6243
Email: mba@uni.edu
Financial aid: (319) 273-2700
Application deadline: 05/30
In-state tuition: full time: $10,803; part time: $536/credit hour
Out-of-state tuition: full time: $20,973
Room/board/expenses: $11,680
College-funded aid: Yes
International student aid: No
Full-time enrollment: N/A
men: N/A; women: N/A; minorities: N/A; international: N/A
Part-time enrollment: 67
men: 67%; women: 33%;
minorities: 7%; international: 58%
Average GMAT (part time): 545
TOEFL requirement: Yes
Minimum TOEFL score: 550
Most popular departments: general management

KANSAS

Emporia State University[1]

1 Kellogg Circle, ESU Box 4039
Emporia, KS 66801-5087
emporia.edu/business/programs/mba
Public
Admissions: (800) 950-4723
Email: gradinfo@emporia.edu
Financial aid: (620) 341-5457
Tuition: N/A
Room/board/expenses: N/A
Enrollment: N/A

Kansas State University

112 Calvin Hall
Manhattan, KS 66506-0501
www.cba.ksu.edu/cba/
Public
Admissions: (785) 532-7190
Email: gradbusiness@ksu.edu
Financial aid: (785) 532-6420
Application deadline: 02/01
In-state tuition: full time: $12,212; part time: $380/credit hour
Out-of-state tuition: full time: $25,135
Room/board/expenses: $22,000
College-funded aid: Yes
International student aid: Yes
Full-time enrollment: 40
men: 65%; women: 35%;
minorities: 25%; international: 33%
Part-time enrollment: 4
men: N/A; women: N/A; minorities: N/A; international: N/A
Acceptance rate (full time): 71%
Average GMAT (full time): 525
Average GMAT (part time): 584
Average GPA (full time): 3.22
Average age of entrants to full-time program: 25
Average months of prior work experience (full time): 46
TOEFL requirement: Yes
Minimum TOEFL score: 550
Most popular departments:
finance, general management, management information systems, supply chain management

Pittsburg State University (Kelce)

1701 S. Broadway
Pittsburg, KS 66762
www.pittstate.edu/kelce/graduate.html
Public
Admissions: (620) 235-4218
Email: grad@pittstate.edu
Financial aid: (620) 235-4240
Application deadline: 07/15
In-state tuition: full time: $8,632; part time: $305/credit hour
Out-of-state tuition: full time: $18,392
Room/board/expenses: $6,734
College-funded aid: Yes
International student aid: Yes
Average student indebtedness at graduation: $19,500
Full-time enrollment: 39
men: 51%; women: 49%;
minorities: N/A; international: N/A
Part-time enrollment: 20
men: 50%; women: 50%;
minorities: N/A; international: N/A
Acceptance rate (full time): 94%
Average GMAT (full time): 460
Average GMAT (part time): 400

Average age of entrants to full-time program: 25
TOEFL requirement: Yes
Minimum TOEFL score: 550

University of Kansas

1300 Sunnyside Avenue
Lawrence, KS 66045-7585
www.mba.ku.edu
Public
Admissions: (785) 864-7556
Email: bschoolmba@ku.edu
Financial aid: (785) 864-7596
Application deadline: 06/01
In-state tuition: full time: $376/credit hour; part time: $442/credit hour
Out-of-state tuition: full time: $880/credit hour
Room/board/expenses: $14,000
College-funded aid: Yes
International student aid: Yes
Full-time enrollment: 54
men: 81%; women: 19%;
minorities: 17%; international: 24%
Part-time enrollment: 166
men: 70%; women: 30%;
minorities: 11%; international: 7%
Acceptance rate (full time): 54%
Average GMAT (full time): 604
Average GMAT (part time): 562
Average GPA (full time): 3.21
Average age of entrants to full-time program: 28
Average months of prior work experience (full time): 46
TOEFL requirement: Yes
Minimum TOEFL score: N/A
Most popular departments:
finance, general management, international business, marketing, supply chain management
Mean starting base salary for 2015 full-time graduates: $60,067
Employment location for 2015 class: Intl. 5%; N.E. 0%; M.A. 0%; S. 5%; M.W. 75%; S.W. 5%; W. 10%

Washburn University[1]

1700 S.W. College Avenue
Topeka, KS 66621
www.washburn.edu/business
Public
Admissions: N/A
Financial aid: N/A
Tuition: N/A
Room/board/expenses: N/A
Enrollment: N/A

Wichita State University (Barton)

1845 N. Fairmount, Box 48
Wichita, KS 67260-0048
www.wichita.edu/mba
Public
Admissions: (316) 978-3230
Email: grad.business@wichita.edu
Financial aid: N/A
Application deadline: 07/01
In-state tuition: full time: N/A; total program: $12,525 (part time)
Out-of-state tuition: full time: N/A
Room/board/expenses: N/A
College-funded aid: Yes
International student aid: Yes
Full-time enrollment: N/A
men: N/A; women: N/A; minorities: N/A; international: N/A
Part-time enrollment: 205
men: 69%; women: 31%;
minorities: 19%; international: 19%
Average GMAT (part time): 533
TOEFL requirement: Yes
Minimum TOEFL score: 570

Average age of entrants to full-time program: 25
TOEFL requirement: Yes
Minimum TOEFL score: 550

University of Kansas

Most popular departments:
economics, finance, health care administration, management information systems, other

KENTUCKY

Bellarmine University (Rubel)

2001 Newburg Road
Louisville, KY 40205-0671
www.bellarmine.edu/business/
Private
Admissions: N/A
Email: gradadmissions@bellarmine.edu
Financial aid: (502) 452-8124
Application deadline: rolling
Tuition: total program: $34,850 (full time); part time: $750/credit hour
Room/board/expenses: N/A
College-funded aid: Yes
International student aid: Yes
Full-time enrollment: 46
men: 57%; women: 43%;
minorities: 13%; international: 0%
Part-time enrollment: 43
men: 40%; women: 60%;
minorities: 7%; international: 0%
Average GMAT (full time): 450
Average GMAT (part time): 469
Average GPA (full time): 3.14
Average age of entrants to full-time program: 27
TOEFL requirement: Yes
Minimum TOEFL score: N/A

Eastern Kentucky University[1]

521 Lancaster Avenue
Richmond, KY 40475
cbt.eku.edu/
Public
Admissions: (859) 622-1742
Email: graduateschool@eku.edu
Financial aid: N/A
Tuition: N/A
Room/board/expenses: N/A
Enrollment: N/A

Morehead State University[1]

Combs Building 214
Morehead, KY 40351
www.moreheadstate.edu/mba
Public
Admissions: (606) 783-2000
Email: admissions@moreheadstate.edu
Financial aid: N/A
Tuition: N/A
Room/board/expenses: N/A
Enrollment: N/A

Murray State University (Bauernfeind)[1]

109 Business Building
Murray, KY 42071
murraystate.edu/business.aspx
Public
Admissions: (270) 809-3779
Email: Msu.graduateadmissions@murraystate.edu
Financial aid: (270) 809-2546
Tuition: N/A
Room/board/expenses: N/A
Enrollment: N/A

Northern Kentucky University

Suite 401, BEP Center
Highland Heights, KY 41099
cob.nku.edu/
graduatedegrees.html
Public
Admissions: (859) 572-6336
Email: mbusiness@nku.edu
Financial aid: N/A
Application deadline: 12/31
In-state tuition: full time: N/A; part time: $602/credit hour
Out-of-state tuition: full time: N/A
Room/board/expenses: N/A
College-funded aid: Yes
Full-time enrollment: N/A
men: N/A; women: N/A; minorities: N/A; international: N/A
Part-time enrollment: 56
men: 57%; women: 43%; minorities: 11%; international: 0%
Average GMAT (part time): 585
TOEFL requirement: Yes
Minimum TOEFL score: 550

University of Kentucky (Gatton)

145 Gatton College of Business and Economics
Lexington, KY 40506-0034
gatton.uky.edu
Public
Admissions: (859) 257-1306
Email: ukmba@uky.edu
Financial aid: (859) 257-1306
Application deadline: 05/11
In-state tuition: full time: $23,410; part time: $718/credit hour
Out-of-state tuition: full time: $37,946
Room/board/expenses: $13,500
College-funded aid: Yes
International student aid: Yes
Full-time enrollment: 49
men: 67%; women: 33%; minorities: 8%; international: 6%
Part-time enrollment: 125
men: 62%; women: 38%; minorities: 12%; international: 2%
Acceptance rate (full time): 73%
Average GMAT (full time): 636
Average GMAT (part time): 609
Average GPA (full time): 3.47
Average age of entrants to full-time program: 24
Average months of prior work experience (full time): 9
TOEFL requirement: Yes
Minimum TOEFL score: 550
Most popular departments: finance, general management, marketing, supply chain management, other
Mean starting base salary for 2015 full-time graduates: $58,119
Employment location for 2015 class: Intl. 0%; N.E. 8%; M.A. 3%; S. 67%; M.W. 14%; S.W. 6%; W. 3%

University of Louisville

Belknap Campus
Louisville, KY 40292
business.louisville.edu/uoflmba
Public
Admissions: (502) 852-7257
Email: mba@louisville.edu
Financial aid: (502) 852-5511
Application deadline: 07/01
In-state tuition: total program: $32,196 (full time); $32,196 (part time)
Out-of-state tuition: total program: $32,196 (full time)
Room/board/expenses: $13,000
College-funded aid: Yes
International student aid: Yes

Average student indebtedness at graduation: $31,272
Full-time enrollment: 50
men: 66%; women: 34%; minorities: 16%; international: 8%
Part-time enrollment: 160
men: 74%; women: 26%; minorities: 9%; international: 6%
Acceptance rate (full time): 41%
Average GMAT (full time): 625
Average GMAT (part time): 550
Average GPA (full time): 3.40
Average age of entrants to full-time program: 25
Average months of prior work experience (full time): 32
TOEFL requirement: Yes
Minimum TOEFL score: 550
Most popular departments: entrepreneurship, finance, health care administration, marketing, statistics and operations research
Mean starting base salary for 2015 full-time graduates: $57,272
Employment location for 2015 class: Intl. 0%; N.E. 0%; M.A. 0%; S. 88%; M.W. 9%; S.W. 0%; W. 3%

Western Kentucky University (Ford)

434 A. Grise Hall
Bowling Green, KY 42101-1056
www.wku.edu/mba/
Public
Admissions: (270) 745-2446
Email: mba@wku.edu
Financial aid: (270) 745-2755
Application deadline: 03/15
In-state tuition: full time: $543/credit hour; part time: $5,285
Out-of-state tuition: full time: $763/credit hour
Room/board/expenses: $0
College-funded aid: Yes
International student aid: No
Average student indebtedness at graduation: $17,695
Full-time enrollment: 36
men: 67%; women: 33%; minorities: 6%; international: 31%
Part-time enrollment: 80
men: 60%; women: 40%; minorities: 6%; international: 13%
Acceptance rate (full time): 53%
Average GMAT (full time): 512
Average GMAT (part time): 516
Average GPA (full time): 3.26
Average age of entrants to full-time program: 28
TOEFL requirement: Yes
Minimum TOEFL score: 550
Most popular departments: accounting, economics, health care administration, other

LOUISIANA

Louisiana State University- Baton Rouge (Ourso)

4000 Business Education Complex
Baton Rouge, LA 70803
mba.lsu.edu
Public
Admissions: (225) 578-8867
Email: busmba@lsu.edu
Financial aid: (225) 578-3103
Application deadline: 05/15
In-state tuition: total program: $32,620 (full time); $52,322 (part time)
Out-of-state tuition: total program: $68,436 (full time)
Room/board/expenses: $20,000
College-funded aid: Yes

International student aid: Yes
Average student indebtedness at graduation: $22,499
Full-time enrollment: 96
men: 47%; women: 53%; minorities: 18%; international: 18%
Part-time enrollment: 62
men: 68%; women: 32%; minorities: 18%; international: 0%
Acceptance rate (full time): 42%
Average GMAT (full time): 626
Average GMAT (part time): 599
Average GPA (full time): 3.35
Average age of entrants to full-time program: 24
Average months of prior work experience (full time): 32
TOEFL requirement: Yes
Minimum TOEFL score: 550
Mean starting base salary for 2015 full-time graduates: $62,957
Employment location for 2015 class: Intl. 0%; N.E. 5%; M.A. 2%; S. 51%; M.W. 0%; S.W. 39%; W. 2%

Louisiana State University-Shreveport

1 University Place
Shreveport, LA 71115
www.lsus.edu/ba/mba
Public
Admissions: (318) 797-5213
Email: bill.bigler@lsus.edu
Financial aid: (318) 797-5363
Application deadline: rolling
In-state tuition: full time: $331/credit hour; part time: $331/credit hour
Out-of-state tuition: full time: $331/credit hour
Room/board/expenses: N/A
College-funded aid: Yes
International student aid: Yes
Full-time enrollment: 245
men: 40%; women: 60%; minorities: N/A; international: N/A
Part-time enrollment: 859
men: 44%; women: 56%; minorities: N/A; international: N/A
TOEFL requirement: Yes
Minimum TOEFL score: N/A
Most popular departments: accounting, finance, general management

Louisiana Tech University

PO Box 10318
Ruston, LA 71272
www.latech.edu/graduate_school
Public
Admissions: (318) 257-2924
Email: gschool@latech.edu
Financial aid: (318) 257-2641
Application deadline: 08/01
In-state tuition: full time: $7,080; part time: $5,793
Out-of-state tuition: full time: $16,383
Room/board/expenses: $9,912
College-funded aid: Yes
International student aid: Yes
Average student indebtedness at graduation: $17,461
Full-time enrollment: 104
men: 60%; women: 40%; minorities: 8%; international: 19%
Part-time enrollment: 32
men: 53%; women: 47%; minorities: 0%; international: 0%
Acceptance rate (full time): 91%
TOEFL requirement: Yes
Minimum TOEFL score: 550
Most popular departments: accounting, finance, general management, management information systems

Loyola University New Orleans (Butt)

6363 St. Charles Avenue
Campus Box 15
New Orleans, LA 70118
www.business.loyno.edu
Private
Admissions: (504) 864-7953
Email: mba@loyno.edu
Financial aid: (504) 865-3231
Application deadline: 06/30
Tuition: full time: $1,005/credit hour; part time: $1,005/credit hour
Room/board/expenses: N/A
College-funded aid: Yes
International student aid: Yes
Full-time enrollment: 29
men: 48%; women: 52%; minorities: 34%; international: 14%
Part-time enrollment: 50
men: 42%; women: 58%; minorities: 24%; international: 2%
Acceptance rate (full time): 74%
Average GMAT (full time): 450
Average GMAT (part time): 547
Average age of entrants to full-time program: 25
TOEFL requirement: Yes
Minimum TOEFL score: 580
Most popular departments: entrepreneurship, leadership, marketing, supply chain management, statistics and operations research
Employment location for 2015 class: Intl. N/A; N.E. 4%; M.A. N/A; S. 88%; M.W. 4%; S.W. 2%; W. 2%

McNeese State University[1]

PO Box 91660
Lake Charles, LA 70609
www.mcneese.edu/colleges/bus
Public
Admissions: (337) 475-5576
Email: mba@mcneese.edu
Financial aid: (337) 475-5065
Tuition: N/A
Room/board/expenses: N/A
Enrollment: N/A

Nicholls State University[1]

PO Box 2015
Thibodaux, LA 70310
www.nicholls.edu/business/
Public
Admissions: (985) 448-4507
Email: becky.leblanc-durocher@nicholls.edu
Financial aid: (985) 448-4048
Tuition: N/A
Room/board/expenses: N/A
Enrollment: N/A

Southeastern Louisiana University

SLU 10735
Hammond, LA 70402
www.selu.edu/acad_research/programs/grad_bus
Public
Admissions: (985) 549-5637
Email: admissions@selu.edu
Financial aid: (985) 549-2244
Application deadline: 07/15
In-state tuition: full time: $7,844; part time: $436/credit hour
Out-of-state tuition: full time: $20,321
Room/board/expenses: $12,802
College-funded aid: Yes

International student aid: No
Average student indebtedness at graduation: $19,654
Full-time enrollment: 56
men: 48%; women: 52%; minorities: 16%; international: 13%
Part-time enrollment: N/A
men: N/A; women: N/A; minorities: N/A; international: N/A
Acceptance rate (full time): 100%
Average GMAT (full time): 485
Average age of entrants to full-time program: 25
TOEFL requirement: Yes
Minimum TOEFL score: 500
Most popular departments: general management

Southern University and A&M College[1]

PO Box 9723
Baton Rouge, LA 70813
www.subr.edu/index.cfm/page/121
Public
Admissions: (225) 771-5390
Email: gradschool@subr.edu
Financial aid: N/A
Tuition: N/A
Room/board/expenses: N/A
Enrollment: N/A

Tulane University (Freeman)

7 McAlictor Drive
New Orleans, LA 70118-5669
freeman.tulane.edu
Private
Admissions: (504) 865-5410
Email: freeman.admissions@tulane.edu
Financial aid: (504) 865-5410
Application deadline: 06/01
Tuition: full time: $53,530; part time: $1,600/credit hour
Room/board/expenses: $19,140
College-funded aid: Yes
International student aid: Yes
Full-time enrollment: 85
men: 73%; women: 27%; minorities: 9%; international: 27%
Part-time enrollment: N/A
men: N/A; women: N/A; minorities: N/A; international: N/A
Acceptance rate (full time): 78%
Average GMAT (full time): 664
Average GPA (full time): 3.25
Average age of entrants to full-time program: 28
Average months of prior work experience (full time): 43
TOEFL requirement: Yes
Minimum TOEFL score: N/A
Most popular departments: entrepreneurship, finance, general management, international business, other
Mean starting base salary for 2015 full-time graduates: $82,000
Employment location for 2015 class: Intl. 4%; N.E. 4%; M.A. 9%; S. 61%; M.W. 9%; S.W. 13%; W. 0%

University of Louisiana-Lafayette (Moody)

USL Box 44568
Lafayette, LA 70504-4568
gradschool.louisiana.edu/
Public
Admissions: (337) 482-6965
Email: gradschool@louisiana.edu
Financial aid: (337) 482-6506
Application deadline: 06/30
In-state tuition: full time: $8,890; part time: $5,920

Out-of-state tuition: full time: $22,905
Room/board/expenses: $10,300
College-funded aid: Yes
International student aid: Yes
Full-time enrollment: N/A
men: N/A; women: N/A; minorities: N/A; international: N/A
Part-time enrollment: 179
men: 47%; women: 53%; minorities: 18%; international: 8%
Average GMAT (part time): 480
TOEFL requirement: Yes
Minimum TOEFL score: N/A
Most popular departments: accounting, finance, health care administration, international business, marketing

University of Louisiana-Monroe[1]
700 University Avenue
Monroe, LA 71209
www.ulm.edu/cbss/
Public
Admissions: N/A
Financial aid: N/A
Tuition: N/A
Room/board/expenses: N/A
Enrollment: N/A

University of New Orleans[1]
2000 Lakeshore Drive
New Orleans, LA 70148
www.uno.edu/admissions/
contact.aspx
Public
Admissions: (504) 280-6595
Email: pec@uno.edu
Financial aid: (504) 280-6603
Tuition: N/A
Room/board/expenses: N/A
Enrollment: N/A

MAINE

University of Maine[1]
Donald P. Corbett Business Building
Orono, ME 04469-5723
www.umaine.edu/business/mba
Public
Admissions: (207) 581-1971
Email: mba@maine.edu
Financial aid: (207) 581-1324
Tuition: N/A
Room/board/expenses: N/A
Enrollment: N/A

University of Southern Maine
PO Box 9300
Portland, ME 04104
www.usm.maine.edu/sb
Public
Admissions: (207) 780-4184
Email: mba@usm.maine.edu
Financial aid: (207) 780-5250
Application deadline: rolling
In-state tuition: full time: $380/credit hour; part time: $380/credit hour
Out-of-state tuition: full time: $1,026/credit hour
Room/board/expenses: $21,250
College-funded aid: Yes
International student aid: Yes
Full-time enrollment: N/A
men: N/A; women: N/A; minorities: N/A; international: N/A
Part-time enrollment: 67
men: 57%; women: 43%;
minorities: 3%; international: N/A

Average GMAT (part time): 485
TOEFL requirement: Yes
Minimum TOEFL score: 550

MARYLAND

Frostburg State University[1]
125 Guild Center
101 Braddock Road
Frostburg, MD 21532-2303
www.frostburg.edu/colleges/cob/mba
Public
Admissions: (301) 687-7053
Email: gradservices@frostburg.edu
Financial aid: (301) 687-4301
Tuition: N/A
Room/board/expenses: N/A
Enrollment: N/A

Loyola University Maryland (Sellinger)
4501 N. Charles Street
Baltimore, MD 21210-2699
www.loyola.edu/sellinger/
Private
Admissions: (410) 617-5020
Email: graduate@loyola.edu
Financial aid: (410) 617-2576
Application deadline: 08/20
Tuition: total program: $63,500 (full time); part time: $925/credit hour
Room/board/expenses: N/A
College-funded aid: Yes
International student aid: Yes
Average student indebtedness at graduation: $69,100
Full-time enrollment: 8
men: 50%; women: 50%; minorities: 25%; international: 0%
Part-time enrollment: 295
men: 60%; women: 40%; minorities: 13%; international: 1%
Acceptance rate (full time): 71%
Average GMAT (full time): 544
Average GMAT (part time): 525
Average GPA (full time): 3.17
Average age of entrants to full-time program: 25
Average months of prior work experience (full time): 11
TOEFL requirement: Yes
Minimum TOEFL score: 550
Employment location for 2015 class: Intl. N/A; N.E. 77%; M.A. 23%; S. N/A; M.W. N/A; S.W. N/A; W. N/A

Morgan State University (Graves)[1]
1700 E. Cold Spring Lane
Baltimore, MD 21251
www.morgan.edu/sbm
Public
Admissions: (443) 885-3185
Financial aid: N/A
Tuition: N/A
Room/board/expenses: N/A
Enrollment: N/A

Salisbury University (Perdue)
1101 Camden Avenue
Salisbury, MD 21801-6860
www.salisbury.edu/Schools/perdue/welcome.html
Public
Admissions: (410) 543-6161
Email: admissions@salisbury.edu
Financial aid: N/A
Application deadline: 03/01

In-state tuition: full time: $370/credit hour; part time: $370/credit hour
Out-of-state tuition: full time: $659/credit hour
Room/board/expenses: N/A
College-funded aid: Yes
International student aid: Yes
Full-time enrollment: 34
men: 47%; women: 53%; minorities: 9%; international: 6%
Part-time enrollment: 18
men: 67%; women: 33%; minorities: 11%; international: 17%
Acceptance rate (full time): 73%
Average age of entrants to full-time program: 26
TOEFL requirement: Yes
Minimum TOEFL score: 550
Mean starting base salary for 2015 full-time graduates: $37,500
Employment location for 2015 class: Intl. N/A; N.E. N/A; M.A. 100%; S. N/A; M.W. N/A; S.W. N/A; W. N/A

University of Baltimore (Merrick)
1420 N. Charles Street
Baltimore, MD 21201
www.ubalt.edu/gradadmission
Public
Admissions: (410) 837-6565
Email: gradadmissions@ubalt.edu
Financial aid: (410) 837-4763
Application deadline: 08/17
In-state tuition: full time: $800/credit hour; part time: $800/credit hour
Out-of-state tuition: full time: $1,116/credit hour
Room/board/expenses: N/A
College-funded aid: Yes
International student aid: Yes
Full-time enrollment: N/A
men: N/A; women: N/A; minorities: N/A; international: N/A
Part-time enrollment: 469
men: 49%; women: 51%; minorities: 31%; international: 9%
Average GMAT (part time): 522
TOEFL requirement: Yes
Minimum TOEFL score: 550
Most popular departments: finance, general management, health care administration, leadership, marketing

University of Maryland-College Park (Smith)
2308 Van Munching Hall
College Park, MD 20742
www.rhsmith.umd.edu
Public
Admissions: (301) 405-0202
Email: mba_info@rhsmith.umd.edu
Financial aid: (301) 314-8297
Application deadline: 03/01
In-state tuition: full time: $45,499; part time: $1,610/credit hour
Out-of-state tuition: full time: $54,409
Room/board/expenses: N/A
College-funded aid: Yes
International student aid: Yes
Full-time enrollment: 190
men: 64%; women: 36%; minorities: 18%; international: 39%
Part-time enrollment: 646
men: 63%; women: 37%; minorities: 31%; international: 8%
Acceptance rate (full time): 31%
Average GMAT (full time): 658
Average GMAT (part time): 579
Average GPA (full time): 3.35
Average age of entrants to full-time program: 28

Average months of prior work experience (full time): 63
TOEFL requirement: Yes
Minimum TOEFL score: 600
Most popular departments: consulting, entrepreneurship, finance, general management, marketing
Mean starting base salary for 2015 full-time graduates: $90,479
Employment location for 2015 class: Intl. 0%; N.E. 22%; M.A. 56%; S. 1%; M.W. 10%; S.W. 4%; W. 6%

MASSACHUSETTS

Babson College (Olin)
231 Forest Street
Babson Park, MA 02457-0310
www.babson.edu/graduate
Private
Admissions: (781) 239-4317
Email: gradadmissions@babson.edu
Financial aid: (781) 239-4219
Application deadline: rolling
Tuition: total program: $101,566 (full time); part time: $1,604/credit hour
Room/board/expenses: $52,858
College-funded aid: Yes
International student aid: Yes
Average student indebtedness at graduation: $74,294
Full-time enrollment: 348
men: 69%; women: 31%; minorities: 10%; international: 62%
Part-time enrollment: 263
men: 66%; women: 34%; minorities: 11%; international: 11%
Acceptance rate (full time): 56%
Average GMAT (full time): 628
Average GMAT (part time): 570
Average GPA (full time): 3.20
Average age of entrants to full-time program: 28
Average months of prior work experience (full time): 60
TOEFL requirement: Yes
Minimum TOEFL score: N/A
Most popular departments: entrepreneurship, finance, marketing, other
Mean starting base salary for 2015 full-time graduates: $81,715
Employment location for 2015 class: Intl. 36%; N.E. 53%; M.A. 1%; S. 6%; M.W. 1%; S.W. 1%; W. 3%

Bentley University
175 Forest Street
Waltham, MA 02452-4705
www.bentley.edu/graduate/admission-financial-aid
Private
Admissions: (781) 891-2108
Email: bentleygraduateadmissions@bentley.edu
Financial aid: (781) 891-3441
Application deadline: 03/15
Tuition: full time: $37,865; part time: $1,355/credit hour
Room/board/expenses: $19,430
College-funded aid: Yes
International student aid: Yes
Average student indebtedness at graduation: $36,844
Full-time enrollment: 142
men: 61%; women: 39%; minorities: 9%; international: 61%
Part-time enrollment: 223
men: 58%; women: 42%; minorities: 17%; international: 4%
Acceptance rate (full time): 75%
Average GMAT (part time): 583
TOEFL requirement: Yes

Minimum TOEFL score: 600
Most popular departments: accounting, finance, marketing, management information systems, statistics and operations research

Boston College (Carroll)
140 Commonwealth Avenue
Fulton Hall 320
Chestnut Hill, MA 02467
www.bc.edu/mba
Private
Admissions: (617) 552-3920
Email: bcmba@bc.edu
Financial aid: (800) 294-0294
Application deadline: 04/15
Tuition: full time: $45,630; part time: $1,550/credit hour
Room/board/expenses: $19,560
College-funded aid: Yes
International student aid: Yes
Average student indebtedness at graduation: $63,080
Full-time enrollment: 182
men: 64%; women: 36%; minorities: 12%; international: 32%
Part-time enrollment: 363
men: 62%; women: 38%; minorities: 36%; international: 3%
Acceptance rate (full time): 38%
Average GMAT (full time): 664
Average GMAT (part time): 593
Average GPA (full time): 3.26
Average age of entrants to full-time program: 28
Average months of prior work experience (full time): 53
TOEFL requirement: Yes
Minimum TOEFL score: 600
Most popular departments: accounting, finance, general management, marketing, statistics and operations research
Mean starting base salary for 2015 full-time graduates: $93,522
Employment location for 2015 class: Intl. 3%; N.E. 83%; M.A. 0%; S. 6%; M.W. 3%; S.W. 0%; W. 6%

Boston University (Questrom)
595 Commonwealth Avenue
Boston, MA 02215-1704
www.bu.edu/questrom
Private
Admissions: (617) 353-2670
Email: mba@bu.edu
Financial aid: (617) 353-2670
Application deadline: rolling
Tuition: full time: $48,182; part time: $1,482/credit hour
Room/board/expenses: $18,364
College-funded aid: Yes
International student aid: Yes
Average student indebtedness at graduation: $67,582
Full-time enrollment: 281
men: 61%; women: 39%; minorities: 17%; international: 37%
Part-time enrollment: 671
men: 59%; women: 41%; minorities: 19%; international: 10%
Acceptance rate (full time): 36%
Average GMAT (full time): 682
Average GMAT (part time): 577
Average GPA (full time): 3.33
Average age of entrants to full-time program: 28
Average months of prior work experience (full time): 57
TOEFL requirement: Yes
Minimum TOEFL score: 600

Most popular departments: finance, health care administration, marketing, non-profit management, other
Mean starting base salary for 2015 full-time graduates: $100,010
Employment location for 2015 class: Intl. 3%; N.E. 77%; M.A. 7%; S. 0%; M.W. 3%; S.W. 1%; W. 10%

Brandeis University[1]
415 South Street
Waltham, MA 02454-9110
www.brandeis.edu/global
Private
Admissions: (781) 736-4829
Email: admissions@
lemberg.brandeis.edu
Financial aid: N/A
Tuition: N/A
Room/board/expenses: N/A
Enrollment: N/A

Clark University
950 Main Street
Worcester, MA 01610
www.clarku.edu/gsom
Private
Admissions: (508) 793-7373
Email:
gradadmissions@clarku.edu
Financial aid: (508) 793-7373
Application deadline: rolling
Tuition: full time: $1,025/credit hour; part time: $1,025/credit hour
Room/board/expenses: $12,000
College-funded aid: Yes
International student aid: Yes
Full-time enrollment: 99
men: 47%; women: 53%;
minorities: N/A; international: 45%
Part-time enrollment: 95
men: 55%; women: 45%;
minorities: N/A; international: 1%
Acceptance rate (full time): 47%
Average GMAT (full time): 533
Average GMAT (part time): 560
Average GPA (full time): 3.24
Average age of entrants to full-time program: 26
Average months of prior work experience (full time): 36
TOEFL requirement: Yes
Minimum TOEFL score: N/A
Mean starting base salary for 2015 full-time graduates: $55,940
Employment location for 2015 class: Intl. N/A; N.E. 85%; M.A. N/A; S. N/A; M.W. 15%; S.W. N/A; W. N/A

Harvard University
Soldiers Field
Boston, MA 02163
www.hbs.edu
Private
Admissions: (617) 495-6128
Email: admissions@hbs.edu
Financial aid: (617) 495-6640
Application deadline: 04/04
Tuition: full time: $72,312; part time: N/A
Room/board/expenses: $26,088
College-funded aid: Yes
International student aid: Yes
Average student indebtedness at graduation: $79,667
Full-time enrollment: 1,872
men: 59%; women: 41%;
minorities: 26%; international: 35%
Part-time enrollment: N/A
men: N/A; women: N/A; minorities: N/A; international: N/A
Acceptance rate (full time): 11%
Average GMAT (full time): 725
Average GPA (full time): 3.66

Average age of entrants to full-time program: 27
Average months of prior work experience (full time): 51
TOEFL requirement: Yes
Minimum TOEFL score: N/A
Mean starting base salary for 2015 full-time graduates: $131,646
Employment location for 2015 class: Intl. 15%; N.E. 41%; M.A. 5%; S. 3%; M.W. 5%; S.W. 6%; W. 26%

Massachusetts Institute of Technology (Sloan)
238 Main Street, E48-500
Cambridge, MA 02142
mitsloan.mit.edu/mba
Private
Admissions: (617) 258-5434
Email: mbaadmissions@
sloan.mit.edu
Financial aid: (617) 253-4971
Application deadline: 04/11
Tuition: full time: $65,750; part time: N/A
Room/board/expenses: $32,996
College-funded aid: Yes
International student aid: Yes
Average student indebtedness at graduation: $107,172
Full-time enrollment: 806
men: 60%; women: 40%;
minorities: 20%; international: 42%
Part-time enrollment: N/A
men: N/A; women: N/A; minorities: N/A; international: N/A
Acceptance rate (full time): 15%
Average GMAT (full time): 716
Average GPA (full time): 3.54
Average age of entrants to full-time program: 28
Average months of prior work experience (full time): 58
TOEFL requirement: No
Minimum TOEFL score: N/A
Most popular departments: entrepreneurship, finance, international business, manufacturing and technology management, operations management
Mean starting base salary for 2015 full-time graduates: $126,316
Employment location for 2015 class: Intl. 11%; N.E. 37%; M.A. 4%; S. 3%; M.W. 4%; S.W. 7%; W. 34%

Northeastern University
360 Huntington Avenue
350 Dodge Hall
Boston, MA 02115
www.mba.northeastern.edu
Private
Admissions: (617) 373-5992
Email: gradbusiness@neu.edu
Financial aid: (617) 373-5899
Application deadline: 04/15
Tuition: full time: $1,476/credit hour; part time: $1,476/credit hour
Room/board/expenses: $25,350
College-funded aid: Yes
International student aid: Yes
Full-time enrollment: 166
men: 69%; women: 31%;
minorities: 12%; international: 39%
Part-time enrollment: 362
men: 59%; women: 41%;
minorities: 18%; international: 3%
Acceptance rate (full time): 23%
Average GMAT (full time): 644
Average GMAT (part time): 543
Average GPA (full time): 3.29

Average age of entrants to full-time program: 26
Average months of prior work experience (full time): 33
TOEFL requirement: Yes
Minimum TOEFL score: 600
Most popular departments: entrepreneurship, finance, international business, marketing, supply chain management
Mean starting base salary for 2015 full-time graduates: $81,797
Employment location for 2015 class: Intl. 5%; N.E. 88%; M.A. 3%; S. 3%; M.W. 0%; S.W. 0%; W. 3%

Simmons College[1]
300 The Fenway
Boston, MA 02115
www.simmons.edu/som
Private
Admissions: N/A
Financial aid: N/A
Tuition: N/A
Room/board/expenses: N/A
Enrollment: N/A

Suffolk University (Sawyer)
8 Ashburton Place
Boston, MA 02108
www.suffolk.edu/business
Private
Admissions: (617) 573-8302
Email:
grad.admission@suffolk.edu
Financial aid: (617) 573-8470
Application deadline: 03/03
Tuition: full time: $40,172; part time: $1,337/credit hour
Room/board/expenses: $20,400
College-funded aid: Yes
International student aid: Yes
Average student indebtedness at graduation: $59,435
Full-time enrollment: 116
men: 50%; women: 50%;
minorities: 21%; international: 32%
Part-time enrollment: 288
men: 48%; women: 52%;
minorities: 22%; international: 1%
Acceptance rate (full time): 54%
Average GMAT (full time): 511
Average GMAT (part time): 453
Average GPA (full time): 3.21
Average age of entrants to full-time program: 27
Average months of prior work experience (full time): 44
TOEFL requirement: Yes
Minimum TOEFL score: 550
Most popular departments: accounting, finance, marketing, tax
Mean starting base salary for 2015 full-time graduates: $71,691
Employment location for 2015 class: Intl. 19%; N.E. 81%; M.A. N/A; S. N/A; M.W. N/A; S.W. N/A; W. N/A

University of Massachusetts-Amherst (Isenberg)
121 Presidents Drive
Amherst, MA 01003
www.isenberg.umass.edu/mba
Public
Admissions: (413) 545-5608
Email: mba@isenberg.umass.edu
Financial aid: (413) 577-0555
Application deadline: 12/01
In-state tuition: full time: $2,640; part time: $825/credit hour
Out-of-state tuition: full time: $9,938

Room/board/expenses: $13,904
College-funded aid: Yes
International student aid: Yes
Average student indebtedness at graduation: $26,482
Full-time enrollment: 46
men: 65%; women: 35%;
minorities: 22%; international: 22%
Part-time enrollment: 1,248
men: 71%; women: 29%;
minorities: 21%; international: 6%
Acceptance rate (full time): 34%
Average GMAT (full time): 639
Average GMAT (part time): 570
Average GPA (full time): 3.36
Average age of entrants to full-time program: 28
Average months of prior work experience (full time): 51
TOEFL requirement: Yes
Minimum TOEFL score: 600
Most popular departments: entrepreneurship, finance, health care administration, marketing, sports business
Mean starting base salary for 2015 full-time graduates: $75,088
Employment location for 2015 class: Intl. 0%; N.E. 88%; M.A. 6%; S. 0%; M.W. 0%; S.W. 0%; W. 6%

University of Massachusetts-Boston
100 Morrissey Boulevard
Boston, MA 02125-3393
www.umb.edu/cmgrad
Public
Admissions: (617) 287-7720
Email: gradcm@umb.edu
Financial aid: (617) 287-6300
Application deadline: 06/01
In-state tuition: full time: $672/credit hour; part time: $672/credit hour
Out-of-state tuition: full time: $1,297/credit hour
Room/board/expenses: $16,000
College-funded aid: Yes
International student aid: Yes
Full-time enrollment: 222
men: 49%; women: 51%;
minorities: 13%; international: 61%
Part-time enrollment: 238
men: 58%; women: 42%;
minorities: 25%; international: 7%
Acceptance rate (full time): 69%
Average GMAT (full time): 520
Average GMAT (part time): 491
Average GPA (full time): 3.29
Average age of entrants to full-time program: 26
Average months of prior work experience (full time): 48
TOEFL requirement: Yes
Minimum TOEFL score: 600
Mean starting base salary for 2015 full-time graduates: $63,575
Employment location for 2015 class: Intl. 30%; N.E. 50%; M.A. 10%; S. 10%; M.W. N/A; S.W. N/A; W. N/A

University of Massachusetts-Dartmouth
285 Old Westport Road
North Dartmouth, MA 02747
www.umassd.edu/charlton/
Public
Admissions: (508) 999-8604
Email: graduate@umassd.edu
Financial aid: (508) 999-8643
Application deadline: 07/01
In-state tuition: full time: $14,699; part time: $86/credit hour

---

Out-of-state tuition: full time: $20,727
Room/board/expenses: $14,476
College-funded aid: Yes
International student aid: Yes
Full-time enrollment: 243
men: 51%; women: 49%;
minorities: 10%; international: 49%
Part-time enrollment: 70
men: 46%; women: 54%;
minorities: 16%; international: 0%
Acceptance rate (full time): 84%
Average GMAT (full time): 484
Average GMAT (part time): 481
Average GPA (full time): 3.22
Average age of entrants to full-time program: 30
TOEFL requirement: Yes
Minimum TOEFL score: 500
Most popular departments: accounting, finance, general management, leadership, supply chain management
Employment location for 2015 class: Intl. N/A; N.E. 100%; M.A. N/A; S. N/A; M.W. N/A; S.W. N/A; W. N/A

University of Massachusetts-Lowell
1 University Avenue
Lowell, MA 01854
www.uml.edu/grad
Public
Admissions: (978) 934-2390
Email: graduate_admissions@
uml.edu
Financial aid: (978) 934-4220
Application deadline: rolling
In-state tuition: full time: $1,637; part time: $91/credit hour
Out-of-state tuition: full time: $6,425
Room/board/expenses: $18,200
College-funded aid: Yes
International student aid: Yes
Average student indebtedness at graduation: $23,741
Full-time enrollment: 78
men: 54%; women: 46%;
minorities: 22%; international: 54%
Part-time enrollment: 586
men: 69%; women: 31%;
minorities: 19%; international: 4%
Acceptance rate (full time): 84%
Average GMAT (full time): 580
Average GMAT (part time): 559
Average GPA (full time): 3.41
Average age of entrants to full-time program: 28
Average months of prior work experience (full time): 48
TOEFL requirement: Yes
Minimum TOEFL score: 600
Most popular departments: accounting, finance, general management, marketing, management information systems

Western New England University
1215 Wilbraham Road
Springfield, MA 01119-2684
www1.wne.edu/business/
Private
Admissions: (800) 325-1122
Email: study@wne.edu
Financial aid: (413) 796-2080
Application deadline: rolling
Tuition: full time: N/A; part time: $784/credit hour
Room/board/expenses: N/A
College-funded aid: No
International student aid: No
Full-time enrollment: N/A
men: N/A; women: N/A; minorities: N/A; international: N/A

Part-time enrollment: 115
men: 61%; women: 39%;
minorities: 10%; international: 4%
Average GMAT (part time): 500
TOEFL requirement: Yes
Minimum TOEFL score: N/A
Most popular departments:
accounting, general management,
leadership

Worcester Polytechnic Institute[1]

100 Institute Road
Worcester, MA 01609
business.wpi.edu
Private
Admissions: (508) 831-4665
Email: business@wpi.edu
Financial aid: (508) 831-5469
Tuition: N/A
Room/board/expenses: N/A
Enrollment: N/A

MICHIGAN

Central Michigan University[1]

252 ABSC - Grawn Hall
Mount Pleasant, MI 48859
www.cmich.edu/colleges/cba/
Pages/default.aspx
Public
Admissions: (989) 774-4723
Email: grad@cmich.edu
Financial aid: N/A
Tuition: N/A
Room/board/expenses: N/A
Enrollment: N/A

Eastern Michigan University

404 Gary M. Owen Building
Ypsilanti, MI 48197
www.cob.emich.edu
Public
Admissions: (734) 487-4444
Email: cob.graduate@emich.edu
Financial aid: (734) 487-0455
Application deadline: 05/15
In-state tuition: full time: $709/
credit hour; part time: $709/
credit hour
Out-of-state tuition: full time:
$1,212/credit hour
Room/board/expenses: $10,433
College-funded aid: Yes
International student aid: Yes
**Average student indebtedness at
graduation:** $35,951
Full-time enrollment: 238
men: 47%; women: 53%;
minorities: 30%; international:
34%
Part-time enrollment: 512
men: 40%; women: 60%;
minorities: 33%; international: 5%
Average GMAT (part time): 507
TOEFL requirement: Yes
Minimum TOEFL score: 550
Most popular departments:
accounting, finance, general
management, management
information systems, supply chain
management

Grand Valley State University (Seidman)[1]

50 Front Ave. SW
Grand Rapids, MI 49504-6424
www.gvsu.edu
Public
Admissions: (616) 331-7400
Email: go2gvmba@gvsu.edu
Financial aid: (616) 331-3234

Tuition: N/A
Room/board/expenses: N/A
Enrollment: N/A

Michigan State University (Broad)

Eppley Center, 645 N. Shaw
Lane, Rm 211
East Lansing, MI 48824-1121
www.mba.msu.edu
Public
Admissions: (517) 355-7604
Email: mba@msu.edu
Financial aid: (517) 355-7604
Application deadline: N/A
In-state tuition: full time: $28,313;
part time: N/A
Out-of-state tuition: full time:
$44,895
Room/board/expenses: $20,030
College-funded aid: Yes
International student aid: Yes
**Average student indebtedness at
graduation:** $55,539
Full-time enrollment: 154
men: 68%; women: 32%;
minorities: 14%; international:
40%
Part-time enrollment: N/A
men: N/A; women: N/A; minorities:
N/A; international: N/A
Acceptance rate (full time): 31%
Average GMAT (full time): 664
Average GPA (full time): 3.34
**Average age of entrants to full-time
program:** 27
**Average months of prior work
experience (full time):** 49
TOEFL requirement: Yes
Minimum TOEFL score: N/A
Most popular departments:
finance, general management,
human resources management,
marketing, supply chain
management
**Mean starting base salary for 2015
full-time graduates:** $101,430
Employment location for 2015 class:
Intl. 4%; N.E. 16%; M.A. 2%; S.
4%; M.W. 51%; S.W. 9%; W. 16%

Michigan Technological University

1400 Townsend Drive
Houghton, MI 49931-1295
www.mtu.edu/business/graduate/
techmba/
Public
Admissions: (906) 487-3055
Email: mba@mtu.edu
Financial aid: (906) 487-3055
Application deadline: 07/01
In-state tuition: full time: $862/
credit hour; part time: $862/
credit hour
Out-of-state tuition: full time: $862/
credit hour
Room/board/expenses: $13,707
College-funded aid: Yes
International student aid: Yes
Full-time enrollment: 26
men: 62%; women: 38%;
minorities: 8%; international: 23%
Part-time enrollment: N/A
men: N/A; women: N/A; minorities:
N/A; international: N/A
Acceptance rate (full time): 24%
Average GPA (full time): 3.19
**Average age of entrants to full-time
program:** 28
**Average months of prior work
experience (full time):** 103
TOEFL requirement: Yes
Minimum TOEFL score: 590

Most popular departments:
entrepreneurship, manufacturing
and technology management,
technology

Northern Michigan University[1]

1401 Presque Isle Avenue
Marquette, MI 49855
www.nmu.edu/graduatestudies
Public
Admissions: (906) 227-2300
Email: gradapp@nmu.edu
Financial aid: (906) 227-2327
Tuition: N/A
Room/board/expenses: N/A
Enrollment: N/A

Oakland University

238 Elliott Hall
Rochester, MI 48309-4493
www.oakland.edu/business/grad
Public
Admissions: (248) 370-3287
Email: gbp@lists.oakland.edu
Financial aid: (248) 370-2550
Application deadline: 07/15
In-state tuition: full time: N/A; part
time: $655/credit hour
Out-of-state tuition: full time: N/A
Room/board/expenses: N/A
College-funded aid: Yes
International student aid: Yes
Full-time enrollment: N/A
men: N/A; women: N/A; minorities:
N/A; international: N/A
Part-time enrollment: 301
men: 68%; women: 32%;
minorities: 14%; international: 9%
Average GMAT (part time): 454
TOEFL requirement: Yes
Minimum TOEFL score: 550
Most popular departments: finance,
human resources management,
international business, marketing,
management information systems

Saginaw Valley State University

7400 Bay Road
University Center, MI 48710
www.svsu.edu/cbm/
Public
Admissions: (989) 964-4064
Email: cbmdean@svsu.edu
Financial aid: (989) 964-4103
Application deadline: rolling
In-state tuition: full time: $514/
credit hour; part time: $514/
credit hour
Out-of-state tuition: full time: $980/
credit hour
Room/board/expenses: N/A
College-funded aid: Yes
International student aid: Yes
**Average student indebtedness at
graduation:** $29,551
Full-time enrollment: N/A
men: N/A; women: N/A; minorities:
N/A; international: N/A
Part-time enrollment: 97
men: 64%; women: 36%;
minorities: 7%; international: 52%
TOEFL requirement: Yes
Minimum TOEFL score: 550

University of Detroit Mercy

4001 W. McNichols Road
Detroit, MI 48221-3038
business.udmercy.edu
Private
Admissions: (800) 635-5020
Email: admissions@udmercy.edu
Financial aid: N/A

Application deadline: rolling
Tuition: full time: $1,489/credit
hour; part time: $1,489/credit hour
Room/board/expenses: N/A
College-funded aid: Yes
International student aid: Yes
**Average student indebtedness at
graduation:** $33,684
Full-time enrollment: 32
men: 56%; women: 44%;
minorities: 38%; international:
25%
Part-time enrollment: 70
men: 47%; women: 53%;
minorities: 53%; international: 3%
Acceptance rate (full time): 81%
Average GPA (full time): 3.39
**Average age of entrants to full-time
program:** 25
TOEFL requirement: No
Minimum TOEFL score: N/A

University of Michigan-Ann Arbor (Ross)

701 Tappan Street
Ann Arbor, MI 48109-1234
michiganross.umich.edu/
Public
Admissions: (734) 763-5796
Email: rossadmissions@umich.
edu
Financial aid: (734) 764-5139
Application deadline: 03/21
In-state tuition: full time: $56,918;
part time: $1,867/credit hour
Out-of-state tuition: full time:
$61,918
Room/board/expenses: $20,654
College-funded aid: Yes
International student aid: Yes
**Average student indebtedness at
graduation:** $100,611
Full-time enrollment: 836
men: 68%; women: 32%;
minorities: 25%; international:
33%
Part-time enrollment: 463
men: 81%; women: 19%;
minorities: 19%; international:
20%
Acceptance rate (full time): 28%
Average GMAT (full time): 708
Average GMAT (part time): 655
Average GPA (full time): 3.36
**Average age of entrants to full-time
program:** 27
**Average months of prior work
experience (full time):** 64
TOEFL requirement: Yes
Minimum TOEFL score: N/A
Most popular departments:
consulting, finance, marketing,
operations management,
technology
**Mean starting base salary for 2015
full-time graduates:** $118,274
Employment location for 2015 class:
Intl. 6%; N.E. 20%; M.A. 1%; S.
5%; M.W. 38%; S.W. 7%; W. 23%

University of Michigan-Dearborn

19000 Hubbard Drive
Dearborn, MI 48126-2638
umdearborn.edu/cob
Public
Admissions: (313) 593-5460
Email: umd-gradbusiness@
umich.edu
Financial aid: (313) 593-5300
Application deadline: rolling
In-state tuition: full time: N/A; part
time: $633/credit hour
Out-of-state tuition: full time: N/A
Room/board/expenses: N/A
College-funded aid: Yes
International student aid: Yes

Full-time enrollment: N/A
men: N/A; women: N/A; minorities:
N/A; international: N/A
Part-time enrollment: 119
men: 65%; women: 35%;
minorities: 10%; international: 8%
Average GMAT (part time): 586
TOEFL requirement: Yes
Minimum TOEFL score: 560
Most popular departments:
finance, international business,
marketing, management
information systems, supply chain
management

University of Michigan-Flint

303 E. Kearsley Street
Flint, MI 48502-1950
mba.umflint.edu
Public
Admissions: (810) 762-3171
Email: graduate@umflint.edu.
Financial aid: (810) 762-3444
Application deadline: 08/01
In-state tuition: full time: $11,970;
part time: $641/credit hour
Out-of-state tuition: full time:
$14,751
Room/board/expenses: $10,866
College-funded aid: Yes
International student aid: No
Full-time enrollment: N/A
men: N/A; women: N/A; minorities:
N/A; international: N/A
Part-time enrollment: 154
men: 62%; women: 38%;
minorities: 21%; international: 14%
Average GMAT (part time): 548
TOEFL requirement: Yes
Minimum TOEFL score: 500
Most popular departments:
accounting, finance, health care
administration, international
business, marketing

Wayne State University

5201 Cass Avenue
Prentis Building
Detroit, MI 48202
www.ilitchbusiness.wayne.edu
Public
Admissions: (313) 577-4511
Email: gradbusiness@wayne.edu
Financial aid: (313) 577-2100
Application deadline: 07/01
In-state tuition: full time: $685/
credit hour; part time: $685/
credit hour
Out-of-state tuition: full time:
$1,371/credit hour
Room/board/expenses: $16,431
College-funded aid: Yes
International student aid: Yes
Full-time enrollment: N/A
men: N/A; women: N/A; minorities:
N/A; international: N/A
Part-time enrollment: 743
men: 59%; women: 41%;
minorities: 29%; international: 6%
Average GMAT (part time): 489
TOEFL requirement: Yes
Minimum TOEFL score: 550
Most popular departments:
finance, general management,
marketing, management
information systems, supply chain
management

Western Michigan University (Haworth)

1903 W. Michigan Avenue
Kalamazoo, MI 49008-5480
www.wmich.edu/mba
Public
Admissions: (269) 387-5133
Email: mba-advising@wmich.edu
Financial aid: (269) 387-6000
Application deadline: 07/15
In-state tuition: full time: N/A; part time: $530/credit hour
Out-of-state tuition: full time: N/A
Room/board/expenses: N/A
College-funded aid: Yes
International student aid: No
Full-time enrollment: N/A
men: N/A; women: N/A; minorities: N/A; international: N/A
Part-time enrollment: 352
men: 67%; women: 33%; minorities: 10%; international: 14%
Average GMAT (part time): 532
TOEFL requirement: Yes
Minimum TOEFL score: 550
Most popular departments: finance, general management, marketing, management information systems, other

MINNESOTA

Minnesota State University-Mankato

120 Morris Hall
Mankato, MN 56001
grad.mnsu.edu
Public
Admissions: (507) 389-2321
Financial aid: (507) 389-1419
Application deadline: 06/01
In-state tuition: full time: N/A; part time: $566/credit hour
Out-of-state tuition: full time: N/A
Room/board/expenses: N/A
College-funded aid: Yes
International student aid: Yes
Full-time enrollment: N/A
men: N/A; women: N/A; minorities: N/A; international: N/A
Part-time enrollment: 53
men: 74%; women: 26%; minorities: 19%; international: 17%
Average GMAT (part time): 532
TOEFL requirement: Yes
Minimum TOEFL score: 500
Most popular departments: leadership

Minnesota State University-Moorhead

1104 7th Ave South
Moorhead, MN 56563
www.mnstate.edu/
Public
Admissions: (218) 477-2134
Email: graduate@mnstate.edu
Financial aid: N/A
Application deadline: 06/15
In-state tuition: full time: $375/credit hour; part time: $375/credit hour
Out-of-state tuition: full time: $750/credit hour
Room/board/expenses: N/A
College-funded aid: Yes
International student aid: No
Full-time enrollment: N/A
men: N/A; women: N/A; minorities: N/A; international: N/A
Part-time enrollment: 34
men: 44%; women: 56%; minorities: 21%; international: 0%
TOEFL requirement: No
Minimum TOEFL score: N/A

St. Cloud State University (Herberger)[1]

720 Fourth Avenue S
St. Cloud, MN 56301-4498
www.stcloudstate.edu/mba
Public
Admissions: (320) 308-3212
Email: mba@stcloudstate.edu
Financial aid: N/A
Tuition: N/A
Room/board/expenses: N/A
Enrollment: N/A

University of Minnesota-Duluth (Labovitz)

1318 Kirby Drive
Duluth, MN 55812-2496
lsbe.d.umn.edu/mba/mba.php
Public
Admissions: (218) 726-8839
Email: grad@d.umn.edu
Financial aid: (218) 726-8000
Application deadline: 07/15
In-state tuition: full time: N/A; part time: $900/credit hour
Out-of-state tuition: full time: N/A
Room/board/expenses: N/A
College-funded aid: Yes
International student aid: No
Full-time enrollment: N/A
men: N/A; women: N/A; minorities: N/A; international: N/A
Part-time enrollment: 4
men: 75%; women: 25%; minorities: 50%; international: 25%
Average GMAT (part time): 553
TOEFL requirement: Yes
Minimum TOEFL score: 550

University of Minnesota-Twin Cities (Carlson)

321 19th Avenue S
Office 4-300
Minneapolis, MN 55455
www.carlsonschool.umn.edu/mba
Public
Admissions: (612) 625-5555
Email: mba@umn.edu
Financial aid: (612) 624-1111
Application deadline: 04/01
In-state tuition: full time: $40,725; part time: $1,302/credit hour
Out-of-state tuition: full time: $51,085
Room/board/expenses: $17,000
College-funded aid: Yes
International student aid: Yes
Average student indebtedness at graduation: $54,723
Full-time enrollment: 195
men: 73%; women: 27%; minorities: 14%; international: 23%
Part-time enrollment: 1,047
men: 68%; women: 32%; minorities: 9%; international: 5%
Acceptance rate (full time): 39%
Average GMAT (full time): 680
Average GMAT (part time): 603
Average GPA (full time): 3.41
Average age of entrants to full-time program: 29
Average months of prior work experience (full time): 54
TOEFL requirement: Yes

Minimum TOEFL score: 580
Most popular departments: finance, general management, health care administration, marketing, supply chain management
Mean starting base salary for 2015 full-time graduates: $106,435
Employment location for 2015 class: Intl. 2%; N.E. 4%; M.A. 4%; S. 1%; M.W. 76%; S.W. 6%; W. 7%

University of St. Thomas

1000 LaSalle Avenue SCH200
Minneapolis, MN 55403
www.stthomas.edu/business
Private
Admissions: (651) 962-8800
Email: ustmba@stthomas.edu
Financial aid: (651) 962-6550
Application deadline: 08/01
Tuition: full time: $33,640; part time: $1,044/credit hour
Room/board/expenses: $16,520
College-funded aid: Yes
International student aid: Yes
Average student indebtedness at graduation: $47,876
Full-time enrollment: 73
men: 56%; women: 44%; minorities: 55%; international: 16%
Part-time enrollment: 626
men: 56%; women: 44%; minorities: 17%; international: 1%
Acceptance rate (full time): 78%
Average GMAT (full time): 546
Average GMAT (part time): 525
Average GPA (full time): 3.20
Average age of entrants to full-time program: 28
Average months of prior work experience (full time): 53
TOEFL requirement: Yes
Minimum TOEFL score: 550
Most popular departments: accounting, entrepreneurship, finance, general management, marketing

MISSISSIPPI

Jackson State University[1]

1400 J.R. Lynch Street
Jackson, MS 39217
www.jsums.edu/business
Public
Admissions: N/A
Financial aid: N/A
Tuition: N/A
Room/board/expenses: N/A
Enrollment: N/A

Millsaps College (Else)[1]

1701 N. State Street
Jackson, MS 39210
millsaps.edu/esom
Private
Admissions: N/A
Financial aid: N/A
Tuition: N/A
Room/board/expenses: N/A
Enrollment: N/A

Mississippi State University

PO Box 5288
Mississippi State, MS 39762
www.business.msstate.edu/gsb
Public
Admissions: (662) 325-1891
Email: gsb@business.msstate.edu
Financial aid: (662) 325-2450
Application deadline: 03/01

In-state tuition: total program: $10,107 (full time); part time: N/A
Out-of-state tuition: total program: $26,960 (full time)
Room/board/expenses: $16,356
College-funded aid: Yes
International student aid: Yes
Full-time enrollment: 24
men: 63%; women: 38%; minorities: 8%; international: 8%
Part-time enrollment: N/A
men: N/A; women: N/A; minorities: N/A; international: N/A
Acceptance rate (full time): 50%
Average GMAT (full time): 554
Average GPA (full time): 3.48
Average age of entrants to full-time program: 23
TOEFL requirement: Yes
Minimum TOEFL score: 575
Most popular departments: accounting, marketing, management information systems, other
Mean starting base salary for 2015 full-time graduates: $65,500
Employment location for 2015 class: Intl. 10%; N.E. 10%; M.A. 20%; S. 60%; M.W. 0%; S.W. 0%; W. 0%

University of Mississippi

253 Holman Hall
University, MS 38677
www.olemissbusiness.com/mba
Public
Admissions: (662) 915-5483
Email: ajones@bus.olemiss.edu
Financial aid: (800) 891-4596
Application deadline: 07/01
In-state tuition: total program: $17,975 (full time); part time: $595/credit hour
Out-of-state tuition: total program: $40,694 (full time)
Room/board/expenses: $20,398
College-funded aid: Yes
International student aid: Yes
Average student indebtedness at graduation: $24,923
Full-time enrollment: 49
men: 71%; women: 29%; minorities: 16%; international: 10%
Part-time enrollment: N/A
men: N/A; women: N/A; minorities: N/A; international: N/A
Acceptance rate (full time): 33%
Average GMAT (full time): 604
Average GPA (full time): 3.31
Average age of entrants to full-time program: 25
TOEFL requirement: Yes
Minimum TOEFL score: 600
Mean starting base salary for 2015 full-time graduates: $51,929
Employment location for 2015 class: Intl. 0%; N.E. 0%; M.A. 2%; S. 70%; M.W. 9%; S.W. 15%; W. 4%

University of Southern Mississippi

118 College Drive, #5096
Hattiesburg, MS 39406-5096
www.usm.edu/gulfcoast/college-business/mba-ap
Public
Admissions: (601) 266-5137
Email: gc-business@usm.edu
Financial aid: (601) 266-4774
Application deadline: 04/01
In-state tuition: full time: $402/credit hour; part time: $402/credit hour
Out-of-state tuition: full time: $895/credit hour
Room/board/expenses: N/A
College-funded aid: Yes

International student aid: Yes
Full-time enrollment: 24
men: 67%; women: 33%; minorities: 0%; international: 29%
Part-time enrollment: 46
men: 48%; women: 52%; minorities: 13%; international: 11%
Acceptance rate (full time): 77%
Average GMAT (full time): 468
Average GMAT (part time): 472
Average GPA (full time): 3.49
Average age of entrants to full-time program: 24
Average months of prior work experience (full time): 31
TOEFL requirement: Yes
Minimum TOEFL score: N/A
Most popular departments: accounting, health care administration, international business, marketing, sports business

MISSOURI

Drury University[1]

900 North Benton Avenue
Springfield, MO 65802
www.drury.edu/mba/
Private
Admissions: (417) 873-6948
Email: grad@drury.edu
Financial aid: (417) 873-7312
Tuition: N/A
Room/board/expenses: N/A
Enrollment: N/A

Missouri State University

901 S. National Avenue
Glass Hall 400
Springfield, MO 65897
www.mba.missouristate.edu
Public
Admissions: (417) 836-5331
Email: graduatecollege@missouristate.edu
Financial aid: (417) 836-5262
Application deadline: rolling
In-state tuition: full time: $287/credit hour; part time: $287/credit hour
Out-of-state tuition: full time: $543/credit hour
Room/board/expenses: $8,130
College-funded aid: Yes
International student aid: Yes
Full-time enrollment: 356
men: 55%; women: 45%; minorities: 10%; international: 29%
Part-time enrollment: N/A
men: N/A; women: N/A; minorities: N/A; international: N/A
Acceptance rate (full time): 78%
Average GMAT (full time): 542
Average GPA (full time): 3.10
Average age of entrants to full-time program: 26
TOEFL requirement: Yes
Minimum TOEFL score: 550

Missouri University of Science & Technology

1870 Miner Circle
Rolla, MO
bit.mst.edu/
Public
Admissions: (573) 341-4165
Email: admissions@mst.edu
Financial aid: N/A
Application deadline: rolling
In-state tuition: full time: $387/credit hour; part time: $387/credit hour
Out-of-state tuition: full time: $1,074/credit hour

Room/board/expenses: N/A
College-funded aid: Yes
International student aid: Yes
Average student indebtedness at graduation: $10,141
Full-time enrollment: 65
men: 58%; women: 42%;
minorities: 6%; international: 77%
Part-time enrollment: 52
men: 69%; women: 31%;
minorities: 15%; international: 31%
Acceptance rate (full time): 85%
Average GMAT (full time): 555
Average GPA (full time): 3.33
Average age of entrants to full-time program: 25
Average months of prior work experience (full time): 25
TOEFL requirement: Yes
Minimum TOEFL score: 570
Most popular departments: general management, leadership, management information systems, statistics and operations research, technology
Mean starting base salary for 2015 full-time graduates: $74,500
Employment location for 2015 class: Intl. 0%; N.E. 22%; M.A. 11%; S. 0%; M.W. 22%; S.W. 33%; W. 11%

Rockhurst University (Helzberg)

1100 Rockhurst Road
Kansas City, MO 64110
www.rockhurst.edu/helzberg
Private
Admissions: (816) 501-4632
Email: mba@rockhurst.edu
Financial aid: (816) 501-4831
Application deadline: rolling
Tuition: full time: N/A; part time: $640/credit hour
Room/board/expenses: N/A
College-funded aid: Yes
International student aid: Yes
Full-time enrollment: N/A
men: N/A; women: N/A; minorities: N/A; international: N/A
Part-time enrollment: 310
men: 66%; women: 34%;
minorities: 15%; international: 2%
Average GMAT (part time): 513
TOEFL requirement: Yes
Minimum TOEFL score: 550
Most popular departments: accounting, finance, general management, health care administration, statistics and operations research

Southeast Missouri State University (Harrison)

1 University Plaza, MS 5890
Cape Girardeau, MO 63701
www.semo.edu/mba
Public
Admissions: (573) 651-2590
Email: mba@semo.edu
Financial aid: (573) 651-2039
Application deadline: 08/01
In-state tuition: full time: $261/credit hour; part time: $261/credit hour
Out-of-state tuition: full time: $487/credit hour
Room/board/expenses: $11,374
College-funded aid: Yes
International student aid: Yes
Full-time enrollment: 66
men: 41%; women: 59%;
minorities: 6%; international: 67%
Part-time enrollment: 123
men: 68%; women: 32%;
minorities: 12%; international: 13%
Acceptance rate (full time): 95%
Average GMAT (full time): 495

Average GMAT (part time): 549
Average GPA (full time): 3.48
Average age of entrants to full-time program: 25
TOEFL requirement: Yes
Minimum TOEFL score: 550

St. Louis University (Cook)

3674 Lindell Boulevard
St. Louis, MO 63108
www.slu.edu/gradbiz.xml
Private
Admissions: (314) 977-2125
Email: gradbiz@slu.edu
Financial aid: (314) 977-2350
Application deadline: 08/01
Tuition: full time: $55,886; part time: $995/credit hour
Room/board/expenses: $18,940
College-funded aid: Yes
International student aid: Yes
Average student indebtedness at graduation: $48,206
Full-time enrollment: 29
men: 66%; women: 34%;
minorities: 14%; international: 24%
Part-time enrollment: 225
men: 64%; women: 36%;
minorities: 15%; international: 7%
Acceptance rate (full time): 62%
Average GMAT (full time): 567
Average GMAT (part time): 539
Average GPA (full time): 3.26
Average age of entrants to full-time program: 26
Average months of prior work experience (full time): 35
TOEFL requirement: Yes
Minimum TOEFL score: 570
Most popular departments: finance, general management, international business, marketing, supply chain management
Mean starting base salary for 2015 full-time graduates: $63,623
Employment location for 2015 class: Intl. N/A; N.E. N/A; M.A. N/A; S. N/A; M.W. 100%; S.W. N/A; W. N/A

Truman State University[1]

100 E. Normal
Kirksville, MO 63501
gradstudies.truman.edu
Public
Admissions: (660) 785-4109
Email: gradinfo@truman.edu
Financial aid: (660) 785-4130
Tuition: N/A
Room/board/expenses: N/A
Enrollment: N/A

University of Central Missouri (Harmon)

Ward Edwards 1600
Warrensburg, MO 64093
www.ucmo.edu/mba
Public
Admissions: (660) 543-8617
Email: mba@ucmo.edu
Financial aid: (800) 729-2678
Application deadline: 07/14
In-state tuition: full time: $278/credit hour; part time: $278/credit hour
Out-of-state tuition: full time: $557/credit hour
Room/board/expenses: N/A
College-funded aid: Yes
International student aid: Yes
Full-time enrollment: 113
men: N/A; women: N/A; minorities: N/A; international: N/A

Part-time enrollment: N/A
men: N/A; women: N/A; minorities: N/A; international: N/A
TOEFL requirement: Yes
Minimum TOEFL score: 550
Most popular departments: finance, general management, marketing

University of Missouri-Kansas City (Bloch)

5100 Rockhill Road
Kansas City, MO 64110
www.bloch.umkc.edu/graduate-program/mba
Public
Admissions: (816) 235-5254
Email: bloch@umkc.edu
Financial aid: (816) 235-1154
Application deadline: 06/15
In-state tuition: full time: $345/credit hour; part time: $345/credit hour
Out-of-state tuition: full time: $891/credit hour
Room/board/expenses: $18,998
College-funded aid: Yes
International student aid: Yes
Full-time enrollment: 71
men: 56%; women: 44%;
minorities: 41%; international: 27%
Part-time enrollment: 143
men: 65%; women: 35%;
minorities: 10%; international: 6%
Average GMAT (part time): 588
TOEFL requirement: Yes
Minimum TOEFL score: 550

University of Missouri-St. Louis[1]

1 University Boulevard
St. Louis, MO 63121
mba.umsl.edu
Public
Admissions: N/A
Financial aid: N/A
Tuition: N/A
Room/board/expenses: N/A
Enrollment: N/A

University of Missouri (Trulaske)

213 Cornell Hall
Columbia, MO 65211
mba.missouri.edu
Public
Admissions: (573) 882-2750
Email: mba@missouri.edu
Financial aid: (573) 882-2750
Application deadline: 07/31
In-state tuition: full time: $350/credit hour; part time: $350/credit hour
Out-of-state tuition: full time: $937/credit hour
Room/board/expenses: $14,391
College-funded aid: Yes
International student aid: Yes
Average student indebtedness at graduation: $22,616
Full-time enrollment: 135
men: 67%; women: 33%;
minorities: 4%; international: 31%
Part-time enrollment: N/A
men: N/A; women: N/A; minorities: N/A; international: N/A
Acceptance rate (full time): 41%
Average GMAT (full time): 648
Average GPA (full time): 3.50
Average age of entrants to full-time program: 24
Average months of prior work experience (full time): 21
TOEFL requirement: Yes
Minimum TOEFL score: 550

Most popular departments: entrepreneurship, finance, general management, marketing, statistics and operations research
Mean starting base salary for 2015 full-time graduates: $61,972
Employment location for 2015 class: Intl. 2%; N.E. 10%; M.A. 6%; S. 4%; M.W. 62%; S.W. 12%; W. 4%

Washington University in St. Louis (Olin)

1 Brookings Drive
Campus Box 1133
St. Louis, MO 63130-4899
www.olin.wustl.edu/academicprograms/MBA/Pages/default.aspx
Private
Admissions: (314) 935-7301
Email: mba@wustl.edu
Financial aid: (314) 935-7301
Application deadline: 04/01
Tuition: full time: $54,225; part time: $1,560/credit hour
Room/board/expenses: $25,746
College-funded aid: Yes
International student aid: Yes
Average student indebtedness at graduation: $62,053
Full-time enrollment: 280
men: 66%; women: 34%;
minorities: 21%; international: 37%
Part-time enrollment: 350
men: 71%; women: 29%;
minorities: 21%; international: 4%
Acceptance rate (full time): 30%
Average GMAT (full time): 695
Average GMAT (part time): 585
Average GPA (full time): 3.40
Average age of entrants to full-time program: 28
Average months of prior work experience (full time): 52
TOEFL requirement: Yes
Minimum TOEFL score: N/A
Most popular departments: consulting, entrepreneurship, finance, marketing, supply chain management
Mean starting base salary for 2015 full-time graduates: $99,383
Employment location for 2015 class: Intl. 4%; N.E. 7%; M.A. 8%; S. 10%; M.W. 57%; S.W. 10%; W. 4%

MONTANA

University of Montana[1]

32 Campus Drive
Missoula, MT 59812-6808
www.business.umt.edu/
Public
Admissions: N/A
Email: mba@business.umt.edu
Financial aid: N/A
Tuition: N/A
Room/board/expenses: N/A
Enrollment: N/A

NEBRASKA

Creighton University

2500 California Plaza
Omaha, NE 68178-0130
business.creighton.edu
Private
Admissions: (402) 280-2841
Email: busgradadmit@creighton.edu
Financial aid: (402) 280-2731
Application deadline: rolling
Tuition: full time: N/A; part time: $800/credit hour
Room/board/expenses: N/A
College-funded aid: Yes
International student aid: Yes

Full-time enrollment: N/A
men: N/A; women: N/A; minorities: N/A; international: N/A
Part-time enrollment: 142
men: 71%; women: 29%;
minorities: 8%; international: 3%
Average GMAT (part time): 518
TOEFL requirement: Yes
Minimum TOEFL score: 550
Most popular departments: accounting, finance, leadership, management information systems, portfolio management

University of Nebraska-Kearney[1]

905 West 25th Street
Kearney, NE 68849
www.unk.edu
Public
Admissions: (800) 717-7881
Email: gradstudies@unk.edu
Financial aid: N/A
Tuition: N/A
Room/board/expenses: N/A
Enrollment: N/A

University of Nebraska-Lincoln

P.O. Box 880405
Lincoln, NE 68588-0405
www.mba.unl.edu
Public
Admissions: (402) 472-2338
Email: cbagrad@unl.edu
Financial aid: (402) 472-2030
Application deadline: 07/01
In-state tuition: full time: N/A; part time: $359/credit hour
Out-of-state tuition: full time: N/A
Room/board/expenses: N/A
College-funded aid: Yes
International student aid: Yes
Full-time enrollment: N/A
men: N/A; women: N/A; minorities: N/A; international: N/A
Part-time enrollment: 70
men: 63%; women: 37%;
minorities: 3%; international: 39%
Average GMAT (part time): 622
TOEFL requirement: Yes
Minimum TOEFL score: 550
Most popular departments: finance, international business, marketing, supply chain management, statistics and operations research

University of Nebraska-Omaha

6708 Pine St
Omaha, NE 68182-0048
mba.unomaha.edu
Public
Admissions: (402) 554-2303
Email: mba@unomaha.edu
Financial aid: (402) 554-2327
Application deadline: 07/01
In-state tuition: full time: N/A; part time: $325/credit hour
Out-of-state tuition: full time: N/A
Room/board/expenses: N/A
College-funded aid: Yes
International student aid: Yes
Full-time enrollment: N/A
men: N/A; women: N/A; minorities: N/A; international: N/A
Part-time enrollment: 250
men: 62%; women: 38%;
minorities: 9%; international: 8%
Average GMAT (part time): 572
TOEFL requirement: Yes
Minimum TOEFL score: 550

Most popular departments: finance, health care administration, human resources management, international business, other

NEVADA

University of Nevada-Las Vegas
4505 Maryland Parkway
PO Box 456031
Las Vegas, NV 89154-6031
business.unlv.edu
Public
Admissions: (702) 895-3655
Email: lbsmba@unlv.edu
Financial aid: (702) 895-3682
Application deadline: 07/15
In-state tuition: full time: $364/credit hour; part time: $364/credit hour
Out-of-state tuition: full time: $22,646
Room/board/expenses: N/A
College-funded aid: Yes
International student aid: Yes
Full-time enrollment: N/A
men: N/A; women: N/A; minorities: N/A; international: N/A
Part-time enrollment: 154
men: 66%; women: 34%; minorities: 32%; international: 9%
Average GMAT (part time): 585
TOEFL requirement: Yes
Minimum TOEFL score: 550

University of Nevada-Reno
1664 N. Virginia Street
Reno, NV 89557
www.coba.unr.edu
Public
Admissions: (775) 784-4912
Email: vkrentz@unr.edu
Financial aid: (775) 784-4666
Application deadline: 03/15
In-state tuition: full time: N/A; part time: $365/credit hour
Out-of-state tuition: full time: N/A
Room/board/expenses: N/A
College-funded aid: Yes
International student aid: Yes
Full-time enrollment: N/A
men: N/A; women: N/A; minorities: N/A; international: N/A
Part-time enrollment: 205
men: 68%; women: 32%; minorities: 19%; international: 6%
Average GMAT (part time): 524
TOEFL requirement: Yes
Minimum TOEFL score: 550
Most popular departments: entrepreneurship, finance, general management, marketing

NEW HAMPSHIRE

Dartmouth College (Tuck)
100 Tuck Hall
Hanover, NH 03755-9000
www.tuck.dartmouth.edu
Private
Admissions: (603) 646-3162
Email: tuck.admissions@tuck.dartmouth.edu
Financial aid: (603) 646-0640
Application deadline: 04/04
Tuition: full time: $67,394; part time: N/A
Room/board/expenses: $28,560
College-funded aid: Yes
International student aid: Yes
Full-time enrollment: 563
men: 63%; women: 37%; minorities: 17%; international: 33%

Part-time enrollment: N/A
men: N/A; women: N/A; minorities: N/A; international: N/A
Acceptance rate (full time): 23%
Average GMAT (full time): 717
Average GPA (full time): 3.52
Average age of entrants to full-time program: 28
Average months of prior work experience (full time): 52
TOEFL requirement: Yes
Minimum TOEFL score: N/A
Mean starting base salary for 2015 full-time graduates: $123,900
Employment location for 2015 class: Intl. 8%; N.E. 51%; M.A. 3%; S. 5%; M.W. 8%; S.W. 5%; W. 21%

University of New Hampshire (Paul)
10 Garrison Avenue
Durham, NH 03824
www.mba.unh.edu
Public
Admissions: (603) 862-1367
Email: info.mba@unh.edu
Financial aid: (603) 862-3600
Application deadline: 06/01
In-state tuition: total program: $29,953 (full time); part time: $800/credit hour
Out-of-state tuition: total program: $43,953 (full time)
Room/board/expenses: $14,000
College-funded aid: Yes
International student aid: Yes
Average student indebtedness at graduation: $35,708
Full-time enrollment: 29
men: 59%; women: 41%; minorities: 10%; international: 24%
Part-time enrollment: 126
men: 62%; women: 38%; minorities: 5%; international: 6%
Acceptance rate (full time): 85%
Average GMAT (full time): 567
Average GMAT (part time): 537
Average GPA (full time): 3.44
Average age of entrants to full-time program: 27
Average months of prior work experience (full time): 48
TOEFL requirement: Yes
Minimum TOEFL score: 550
Most popular departments: entrepreneurship, finance, general management, marketing
Mean starting base salary for 2015 full-time graduates: $65,786
Employment location for 2015 class: Intl. 0%; N.E. 100%; M.A. 0%; S. 0%; M.W. 0%; S.W. 0%; W. 0%

NEW JERSEY

Fairleigh Dickinson University (Silberman)
1000 River Road
Teaneck, NJ 07666
www.fduinfo.com/depts/sctab.php
Private
Admissions: (201) 692-2554
Email: grad@fdu.edu
Financial aid: N/A
Application deadline: 08/22
Tuition: full time: $1,220/credit hour; part time: $1,220/credit hour
Room/board/expenses: N/A
College-funded aid: Yes
International student aid: Yes
Full-time enrollment: 262
men: N/A; women: N/A; minorities: N/A; international: N/A

Part-time enrollment: 219
men: N/A; women: N/A; minorities: N/A; international: N/A
Acceptance rate (full time): 58%
Average GMAT (full time): 478
TOEFL requirement: Yes
Minimum TOEFL score: 550
Most popular departments: accounting, finance, marketing, organizational behavior, other

Monmouth University
400 Cedar Avenue
West Long Branch, NJ 07764
www.monmouth.edu
Private
Admissions: (732) 571-3452
Email: gradadm@monmouth.edu
Financial aid: (732) 571-3463
Application deadline: 07/15
Tuition: full time: $1,047/credit hour; part time: $1,047/credit hour
Room/board/expenses: $44,674
College-funded aid: Yes
International student aid: Yes
Average student indebtedness at graduation: $16,800
Full-time enrollment: 15
men: 40%; women: 60%; minorities: 0%; international: 0%
Part-time enrollment: 167
men: 53%; women: 47%; minorities: 13%; international: 2%
Acceptance rate (full time): 83%
Average GMAT (full time): 474
Average GPA (full time): 3.67
Average age of entrants to full-time program: 22
TOEFL requirement: Yes
Minimum TOEFL score: 550

Montclair State University (Feliciano)
Feliciano School of Business
1 Normal Avenue
Montclair, NJ 07043
www.montclair.edu/mba
Public
Admissions: (973) 655-5147
Email: graduate.school@montclair.edu
Financial aid: (973) 655-4461
Application deadline: rolling
In-state tuition: full time: $671/credit hour; part time: $671/credit hour
Out-of-state tuition: full time: $671/credit hour
Room/board/expenses: $19,491
College-funded aid: Yes
International student aid: Yes
Average student indebtedness at graduation: $45,281
Full-time enrollment: N/A
men: N/A; women: N/A; minorities: N/A; international: N/A
Part-time enrollment: 348
men: 53%; women: 47%; minorities: 42%; international: 11%
TOEFL requirement: Yes
Minimum TOEFL score: 550

New Jersey Institute of Technology
University Heights
Newark, NJ 07102
management.njit.edu/
Public
Admissions: (973) 596-3300
Email: admissions@njit.edu
Financial aid: (973) 596-3479
Application deadline: rolling
In-state tuition: full time: $21,152; part time: $1,006/credit hour
Out-of-state tuition: full time: $29,992
Room/board/expenses: $19,500

College-funded aid: Yes
International student aid: Yes
Average student indebtedness at graduation: $33,078
Full-time enrollment: 80
men: 68%; women: 33%; minorities: 28%; international: 64%
Part-time enrollment: 63
men: 73%; women: 27%; minorities: 63%; international: 5%
Acceptance rate (full time): 91%
Average GMAT (full time): 548
Average GPA (full time): 3.09
Average age of entrants to full-time program: 26
TOEFL requirement: Yes
Minimum TOEFL score: 550
Mean starting base salary for 2015 full-time graduates: $81,250
Employment location for 2015 class: Intl. N/A; N.E. 94%; M.A. N/A; S. N/A; M.W. N/A; S.W. N/A; W. 6%

Ramapo College of New Jersey
505 Ramapo Valley Road
Mahwah, NJ 07430
www.ramapo.edu/admissions/
Public
Admissions: (201) 684-7300
Email: admissions@ramapo.edu
Financial aid: (201) 684-7549
Application deadline: 05/01
In-state tuition: full time: N/A; part time: $836/credit hour
Out-of-state tuition: full time: N/A
Room/board/expenses: N/A
College-funded aid: Yes
International student aid: Yes
Full-time enrollment: N/A
men: N/A; women: N/A; minorities: N/A; international: N/A
Part-time enrollment: 62
men: 55%; women: 45%; minorities: 31%; international: 3%
TOEFL requirement: Yes
Minimum TOEFL score: 550

Rider University
2083 Lawrenceville Road
Lawrenceville, NJ 08648-3099
www.rider.edu/mba
Private
Admissions: (609) 896-5036
Email: gradadm@rider.edu
Financial aid: (609) 896-5360
Application deadline: rolling
Tuition: full time: N/A; part time: $980/credit hour
Room/board/expenses: N/A
College-funded aid: Yes
International student aid: Yes
Full-time enrollment: N/A
men: N/A; women: N/A; minorities: N/A; international: N/A
Part-time enrollment: 136
men: 49%; women: 51%; minorities: 18%; international: 8%
Average GMAT (part time): 480
TOEFL requirement: Yes
Minimum TOEFL score: 550
Most popular departments: accounting, finance, international business, management information systems, statistics and operations research

Rowan University (Rohrer)
201 Mullica Hill Road
Glassboro, NJ 08028
www.rowancgce.com
Public
Admissions: (856) 256-5435
Email: cgceadmissions@rowan.edu

Financial aid: (856) 256-5186
Application deadline: rolling
In-state tuition: full time: $714/credit hour; part time: $714/credit hour
Out-of-state tuition: full time: $714/credit hour
Room/board/expenses: $16,904
College-funded aid: Yes
International student aid: No
Average student indebtedness at graduation: $9,152
Full-time enrollment: 35
men: 71%; women: 29%; minorities: 23%; international: 6%
Part-time enrollment: 98
men: 61%; women: 39%; minorities: 11%; international: 1%
Average GMAT (full time): 466
Average GPA (full time): 3.73
TOEFL requirement: Yes
Minimum TOEFL score: 550
Most popular departments: accounting, finance, general management, marketing, management information systems

Rutgers, The State University of New Jersey-Camden
227 Penn Street
Camden, NJ 08102
camden-sbc.rutgers.edu
Public
Admissions: (856) 225-6104
Email: camden@camuga.rutgers.edu
Financial aid: (856) 225-6039
Application deadline: rolling
In-state tuition: full time: $940/credit hour; part time: $940/credit hour
Out-of-state tuition: full time: $1,593/credit hour
Room/board/expenses: N/A
College-funded aid: Yes
International student aid: Yes
Full-time enrollment: N/A
men: N/A; women: N/A; minorities: N/A; international: N/A
Part-time enrollment: 187
men: 66%; women: 34%; minorities: 36%; international: 3%
Average GMAT (part time): 560
TOEFL requirement: Yes
Minimum TOEFL score: N/A

Rutgers, The State University of New Jersey-Newark and New Brunswick
1 Washington Park
Newark, NJ 07102-3122
www.business.rutgers.edu
Public
Admissions: (973) 353-1234
Email: admit@business.rutgers.edu
Financial aid: (973) 353-5151
Application deadline: 05/01
In-state tuition: full time: $30,681; part time: $1,059/credit hour
Out-of-state tuition: full time: $49,383
Room/board/expenses: $30,000
College-funded aid: Yes
International student aid: No
Average student indebtedness at graduation: $44,000
Full-time enrollment: 146
men: 54%; women: 46%; minorities: 26%; international: 40%
Part-time enrollment: 987
men: 64%; women: 36%; minorities: 45%; international: 2%
Acceptance rate (full time): 43%

Average GMAT (full time): 642
Average GMAT (part time): 587
Average GPA (full time): 3.33
Average age of entrants to full-time program: 27
Average months of prior work experience (full time): 56
TOEFL requirement: Yes
Minimum TOEFL score: 600
Most popular departments: entrepreneurship, finance, general management, marketing, supply chain management
Mean starting base salary for 2015 full-time graduates: $91,588
Employment location for 2015 class: Intl. 0%; N.E. 72%; M.A. 7%; S. 0%; M.W. 4%; S.W. 11%; W. 7%

Seton Hall University (Stillman)

400 S. Orange Avenue
South Orange, NJ 07079
www.shu.edu/academics/business/
Private
Admissions: (973) 761-9262
Email: mba@shu.edu
Financial aid: (973) 761-9350
Application deadline: 05/31
Tuition: full time: N/A; part time: $1,222/credit hour
Room/board/expenses: $17,600
College-funded aid: Yes
International student aid: Yes
Full-time enrollment: N/A
men: N/A; women: N/A; minorities: N/A; international: N/A
Part-time enrollment: 185
men: 67%; women: 33%; minorities: 37%; international: 15%
Average GMAT (part time): 559
TOEFL requirement: Yes
Minimum TOEFL score: 607

Stevens Institute of Technology

1 Castle Point Terrace
Hoboken, NJ 07030
Private
Admissions: N/A
Financial aid: N/A
Application deadline: 06/01
Tuition: full time: $33,350; part time: $1,450/credit hour
Room/board/expenses: $15,750
College-funded aid: Yes
International student aid: Yes
Full-time enrollment: 426
men: 61%; women: 39%; minorities: 4%; international: 93%
Part-time enrollment: 376
men: 31%; women: 69%; minorities: 50%; international: 3%
Acceptance rate (full time): 58%
Average GMAT (full time): 642
Average GMAT (part time): 554
Average GPA (full time): 3.22
Average age of entrants to full-time program: 24
Average months of prior work experience (full time): 20
TOEFL requirement: Yes
Minimum TOEFL score: 537
Most popular departments: finance, general management, management information systems, statistics and operations research, other
Mean starting base salary for 2015 full-time graduates: $72,800
Employment location for 2015 class: Intl. 8%; N.E. 84%; M.A. 2%; S. 2%; M.W. N/A; S.W. N/A; W. 4%

William Paterson University (Cotsakos)

1600 Valley Road
Wayne, NJ 07470
www.wpunj.edu/ccob/programs/mbaprogram.dot
Public
Admissions: (973) 720-2237
Email: graduate@wpunj.edu
Financial aid: (973) 720-3945
Application deadline: rolling
In-state tuition: full time: $577/credit hour; part time: $577/credit hour
Out-of-state tuition: full time: $951/credit hour
Room/board/expenses: $14,770
College-funded aid: Yes
International student aid: Yes
Average student indebtedness at graduation: $30,115
Full-time enrollment: 46
men: 52%; women: 48%; minorities: 35%; international: 20%
Part-time enrollment: 112
men: 52%; women: 48%; minorities: 38%; international: 2%
Acceptance rate (full time): 100%
Average GMAT (full time): 506
Average GMAT (part time): 477
Average GPA (full time): 3.35
Average age of entrants to full-time program: 28
TOEFL requirement: Yes
Minimum TOEFL score: 550

NEW MEXICO

New Mexico State University

P.O. Box 30001, MSC 3GSP
Las Cruces, NM 88003
business.nmsu.edu/mba
Public
Admissions: (505) 646-8003
Email: mba@nmsu.edu
Financial aid: (505) 646-4105
Application deadline: 07/15
In-state tuition: full time: $4,941; part time: $227/credit hour
Out-of-state tuition: full time: $15,107
Room/board/expenses: $13,050
College-funded aid: Yes
International student aid: Yes
Full-time enrollment: N/A
men: N/A; women: N/A; minorities: N/A; international: N/A
Part-time enrollment: 158
men: 50%; women: 50%; minorities: 42%; international: 10%
Average GMAT (part time): 465
TOEFL requirement: Yes
Minimum TOEFL score: 550
Most popular departments: finance, general management, management information systems, other

University of New Mexico (Anderson)

MSC05 3090
1 University of New Mexico
Albuquerque, NM 87131-0001
www.mgt.unm.edu
Public
Admissions: (505) 277-3290
Email: andersonadvising@unm.edu
Financial aid: (505) 277-8900
Application deadline: 04/01
In-state tuition: full time: $438/credit hour; part time: $438/credit hour

Out-of-state tuition: full time: $1,049/credit hour
Room/board/expenses: N/A
College-funded aid: Yes
International student aid: Yes
Average student indebtedness at graduation: $27,454
Full-time enrollment: 161
men: 56%; women: 44%; minorities: 48%; international: 15%
Part-time enrollment: 146
men: 58%; women: 42%; minorities: 50%; international: 3%
Average GMAT (full time): 582
Average GMAT (part time): 503
Average GPA (full time): 3.63
Average age of entrants to full-time program: 26
TOEFL requirement: Yes
Minimum TOEFL score: 550
Most popular departments: accounting, finance, marketing, organizational behavior, technology
Mean starting base salary for 2015 full-time graduates: $45,743

NEW YORK

Adelphi University

1 South Avenue
Garden City, NY 11530
www.adelphi.edu
Private
Admissions: (516) 877-3050
Email: admissions@adelphi.edu
Financial aid: (516) 877-3080
Application deadline: rolling
Tuition: full time: N/A; part time: $1,110/credit hour
Room/board/expenses: N/A
College-funded aid: Yes
International student aid: Yes
Full-time enrollment: N/A
men: N/A; women: N/A; minorities: N/A; international: N/A
Part-time enrollment: 305
men: 52%; women: 48%; minorities: 25%; international: 32%
Average GMAT (part time): 492
TOEFL requirement: Yes
Minimum TOEFL score: N/A
Most popular departments: accounting, finance, health care administration, marketing

Alfred University

Saxon Drive
Alfred, NY 14802
business.alfred.edu/mba.html
Private
Admissions: (800) 541-9229
Email: gradinquiry@alfred.edu
Financial aid: (607) 871-2159
Application deadline: 08/01
Tuition: full time: $38,990; part time: $810/credit hour
Room/board/expenses: $15,260
College-funded aid: Yes
International student aid: Yes
Full-time enrollment: 26
men: 62%; women: 38%; minorities: 27%; international: 0%
Part-time enrollment: 14
men: 64%; women: 36%; minorities: 14%; international: 7%
Acceptance rate (full time): 97%
Average GPA (full time): 3.33
Average age of entrants to full-time program: 22
TOEFL requirement: Yes
Minimum TOEFL score: 550
Most popular departments: accounting, general management
Mean starting base salary for 2015 full-time graduates: $43,482

Binghamton University-SUNY

PO Box 6000
Binghamton, NY 13902-6000
www.binghamton.edu/som/graduate/index.html
Public
Admissions: (607) 777-2012
Email: awheeler@binghamton.edu
Financial aid: (607) 777-2470
Application deadline: 03/01
In-state tuition: full time: $16,511; part time: $600/credit hour
Out-of-state tuition: full time: $26,491
Room/board/expenses: $19,122
College-funded aid: Yes
International student aid: Yes
Average student indebtedness at graduation: $26,694
Full-time enrollment: 78
men: 63%; women: 37%; minorities: 15%; international: 33%
Part-time enrollment: 2
men: 50%; women: 50%; minorities: 0%; international: 50%
Acceptance rate (full time): 63%
Average GMAT (full time): 621
Average GPA (full time): 3.50
Average age of entrants to full-time program: 23
Average months of prior work experience (full time): 20
TOEFL requirement: Yes
Minimum TOEFL score: 590
Mean starting base salary for 2015 full-time graduates: $62,136
Employment location for 2015 class: Intl. 5%; N.E. 95%; M.A. 0%; S. 0%; M.W. 0%; S.W. 0%; W. 0%

Canisius College (Wehle)

2001 Main Street
Buffalo, NY 14208
www.canisius.edu/business/graduate_programs.asp
Public
Admissions: (800) 950-2505
Email: gradubus@canisius.edu
Financial aid: (716) 888-2300
Application deadline: rolling
In-state tuition: total program: $38,709 (full time); part time: $780/credit hour
Out-of-state tuition: total program: $38,709 (full time)
Room/board/expenses: $15,266
College-funded aid: Yes
International student aid: Yes
Average student indebtedness at graduation: $36,979
Full-time enrollment: 25
men: 52%; women: 48%; minorities: 16%; international: 12%
Part-time enrollment: 250
men: 60%; women: 40%; minorities: 0%; international: 4%
Acceptance rate (full time): 63%
Average GMAT (full time): 518
Average GMAT (part time): 430
Average GPA (full time): 3.39
Average age of entrants to full-time program: 25
TOEFL requirement: Yes
Minimum TOEFL score: 550
Most popular departments: accounting, general management
Mean starting base salary for 2015 full-time graduates: $45,466
Employment location for 2015 class: Intl. N/A; N.E. 100%; M.A. N/A; S. N/A; M.W. N/A; S.W. N/A; W. N/A

Clarkson University

Snell Hall 322E, Box 5770
Potsdam, NY 13699-5770
www.clarkson.edu/business/graduate
Private
Admissions: (315) 268-6613
Email: busgrad@clarkson.edu
Financial aid: (315) 268-7699
Application deadline: rolling
Tuition: full time: $55,956; part time: $1,457/credit hour
Room/board/expenses: $14,734
College-funded aid: Yes
International student aid: Yes
Average student indebtedness at graduation: $36,014
Full-time enrollment: 62
men: 56%; women: 44%; minorities: 3%; international: 34%
Part-time enrollment: N/A
men: N/A; women: N/A; minorities: N/A; international: N/A
Acceptance rate (full time): 73%
Average GMAT (full time): 565
Average GPA (full time): 3.26
Average age of entrants to full-time program: 27
Average months of prior work experience (full time): 73
TOEFL requirement: Yes
Minimum TOEFL score: 550
Most popular departments: accounting, entrepreneurship, general management, supply chain management, other
Mean starting base salary for 2015 full-time graduates: $61,188
Employment location for 2015 class: Intl. 6%; N.E. 50%; M.A. 0%; S. 6%; M.W. 13%; S.W. 13%; W. 13%

College at Brockport-SUNY[1]

119 Hartwell Hall
Brockport, NY 14420
www.brockport.edu/business
Public
Admissions: N/A
Financial aid: N/A
Tuition: N/A
Room/board/expenses: N/A
Enrollment: N/A

Columbia University

3022 Broadway, 216 Uris Hall
New York, NY 10027
www.gsb.columbia.edu
Private
Admissions: (212) 854-1961
Email: apply@gsb.columbia.edu
Financial aid: (212) 854-4057
Application deadline: 04/12
Tuition: full time: $68,724; part time: N/A
Room/board/expenses: $26,442
College-funded aid: Yes
International student aid: Yes
Full-time enrollment: 1,287
men: 63%; women: 37%; minorities: 24%; international: 34%
Part-time enrollment: N/A
men: N/A; women: N/A; minorities: N/A; international: N/A
Acceptance rate (full time): 18%
Average GMAT (full time): 715
Average GPA (full time): 3.50
Average age of entrants to full-time program: 28
Average months of prior work experience (full time): 60
TOEFL requirement: Yes
Minimum TOEFL score: N/A

Most popular departments: entrepreneurship, finance, general management, leadership, marketing
Mean starting base salary for 2015 full-time graduates: $127,637

Cornell University (Johnson)

Sage Hall, Cornell University
Ithaca, NY 14853-6201
www.johnson.cornell.edu
Private
Admissions: (607) 255-0600
Email: mba@cornell.edu
Financial aid: (607) 255-6116
Application deadline: 03/17
Tuition: full time: $62,100; part time: N/A
Room/board/expenses: $22,860
College-funded aid: Yes
International student aid: Yes
Average student indebtedness at graduation: $115,048
Full-time enrollment: 535
men: 73%; women: 27%; minorities: 27%; international: 33%
Part-time enrollment: N/A
men: N/A; women: N/A; minorities: N/A; international: N/A
Acceptance rate (full time): 32%
Average GMAT (full time): 697
Average GPA (full time): 3.35
Average age of entrants to full-time program: 28
Average months of prior work experience (full time): 58
TOEFL requirement: Yes
Minimum TOEFL score: 600
Most popular departments: consulting, finance, leadership, marketing, technology
Mean starting base salary for 2015 full-time graduates: $119,051
Employment location for 2015 class: Intl. 10%; N.E. 48%; M.A. 4%; S. 3%; M.W. 10%; S.W. 5%; W. 21%

CUNY Bernard M. Baruch College (Zicklin)

1 Bernard Baruch Way
New York, NY 10010
zicklin.baruch.cuny.edu
Public
Admissions: (646) 312-1300
Email: zicklingradadmissions@baruch.cuny.edu
Financial aid: (646) 312-1370
Application deadline: 04/15
In-state tuition: full time: $19,618; part time: $665/credit hour
Out-of-state tuition: full time: $35,318
Room/board/expenses: $21,000
College-funded aid: Yes
International student aid: Yes
Full-time enrollment: 99
men: 69%; women: 31%; minorities: 28%; international: 37%
Part-time enrollment: 613
men: 59%; women: 41%; minorities: 32%; international: 5%
Acceptance rate (full time): 29%
Average GMAT (full time): 615
Average GMAT (part time): 603
Average GPA (full time): 3.29
Average age of entrants to full-time program: 28
Average months of prior work experience (full time): 52
TOEFL requirement: Yes
Minimum TOEFL score: N/A

Most popular departments: accounting, finance, general management, marketing, management information systems
Mean starting base salary for 2015 full-time graduates: $70,771
Employment location for 2015 class: Intl. 3%; N.E. 92%; M.A. N/A; S. N/A; M.W. 3%; S.W. 3%; W. N/A

Fordham University (Gabelli)

113 W. 60th Street, Room 624
New York, NY 10023
www.fordham.edu/gabelli
Private
Admissions: (212) 636-6200
Email: admissionsgb@fordham.edu
Financial aid: (212) 636-6700
Application deadline: 06/01
Tuition: full time: $1,352/credit hour; part time: $1,352/credit hour
Room/board/expenses: $29,945
College-funded aid: Yes
International student aid: Yes
Average student indebtedness at graduation: $69,293
Full-time enrollment: 107
men: 56%; women: 44%; minorities: 12%; international: 49%
Part-time enrollment: 366
men: 61%; women: 39%; minorities: 15%; international: 16%
Acceptance rate (full time): 58%
Average GMAT (full time): 605
Average GMAT (part time): 611
Average GPA (full time): 3.16
Average age of entrants to full-time program: 28
Average months of prior work experience (full time): 63
TOEFL requirement: Yes
Minimum TOEFL score: N/A
Most popular departments: accounting, finance, general management, marketing, other
Mean starting base salary for 2015 full-time graduates: $84,357
Employment location for 2015 class: Intl. N/A; N.E. 89%; M.A. N/A; S. 5%; M.W. N/A; S.W. N/A; W. 5%

Hofstra University (Zarb)

300 Weller Hall
Hempstead, NY 11549
www.hofstra.edu/graduate
Private
Admissions: (516) 463-4723
Email: graduateadmission@hofstra.edu
Financial aid: (516) 463-8000
Application deadline: rolling
Tuition: full time: $1,218/credit hour; part time: $1,218/credit hour
Room/board/expenses: $22,305
College-funded aid: Yes
International student aid: Yes
Full-time enrollment: 71
men: 55%; women: 45%; minorities: 10%; international: 75%
Part-time enrollment: 804
men: 49%; women: 51%; minorities: 14%; international: 54%
Acceptance rate (full time): 44%
Average GMAT (full time): 577
Average GMAT (part time): 561
Average GPA (full time): 3.17
Average age of entrants to full-time program: 26
Average months of prior work experience (full time): 42
TOEFL requirement: Yes
Minimum TOEFL score: 550

Most popular departments: accounting, finance, general management, health care administration, marketing
Mean starting base salary for 2015 full-time graduates: $55,571
Employment location for 2015 class: Intl. 7%; N.E. 93%; M.A. 0%; S. 0%; M.W. 0%; S.W. 0%; W. 0%

Iona College (Hagan)

715 North Avenue
New Rochelle, NY 10801
www.iona.edu/hagan
Private
Admissions: (800) 231-4662
Email: aletang@iona.edu
Financial aid: (914) 633-2497
Application deadline: rolling
Tuition: full time: N/A; part time: $1,023/credit hour
Room/board/expenses: N/A
College-funded aid: Yes
International student aid: Yes
Full-time enrollment: N/A
men: N/A; women: N/A; minorities: N/A; international: N/A
Part-time enrollment: 332
men: 55%; women: 45%; minorities: 22%; international: 25%
Average GMAT (part time): 350
TOEFL requirement: Yes
Minimum TOEFL score: N/A
Most popular departments: accounting, finance, general management, health care administration, marketing

Ithaca College

953 Danby Road
Ithaca, NY 14850-7000
www.ithaca.edu/gradadmission
Private
Admissions: (607) 274-3124
Email: admission@ithaca.edu
Financial aid: (607) 274-3131
Application deadline: 05/15
Tuition: full time: $902/credit hour; part time: $902/credit hour
Room/board/expenses: N/A
College-funded aid: Yes
International student aid: Yes
Full-time enrollment: 31
men: 58%; women: 42%; minorities: 6%; international: 6%
Part-time enrollment: 5
men: 60%; women: 40%; minorities: 0%; international: 0%
Acceptance rate (full time): 77%
Average GMAT (full time): 434
Average GPA (full time): 3.43
Average age of entrants to full-time program: 23
TOEFL requirement: Yes
Minimum TOEFL score: 550

Le Moyne College

1419 Salt Springs Road
Syracuse, NY 13214-1301
www.lemoyne.edu/madden
Private
Admissions: (315) 445-5444
Email: business@lemoyne.edu
Financial aid: (315) 445-4400
Application deadline: 07/01
Tuition: full time: $778/credit hour; part time: $778/credit hour
Room/board/expenses: N/A
College-funded aid: Yes
International student aid: Yes
Average student indebtedness at graduation: $15,230
Full-time enrollment: 43
men: 67%; women: 33%; minorities: 14%; international: 2%

Part-time enrollment: 82
men: 61%; women: 39%; minorities: 7%; international: 1%
Acceptance rate (full time): 100%
Average GMAT (part time): 456
Average GPA (full time): 3.08
Average age of entrants to full-time program: 25
TOEFL requirement: Yes
Minimum TOEFL score: 550

LIU Post[1]

720 Northern Boulevard
Brookville, NY 11548-1300
www.liu.edu/postmba
Private
Admissions: (516) 299-2900
Email: enroll@cwpost.liu.edu
Financial aid: (516) 299-2338
Tuition: N/A
Room/board/expenses: N/A
Enrollment: N/A

Manhattan College[1]

4513 Manhattan College Parkway
Riverdale, NY 10471
Private
Admissions: N/A
Financial aid: N/A
Tuition: N/A
Room/board/expenses: N/A
Enrollment: N/A

Marist College

127 Dyson Center
Poughkeepsie, NY 12601
www.marist.edu/mba
Private
Admissions: (845) 575-3800
Email: graduate@marist.edu
Financial aid: (845) 575-3230
Application deadline: rolling
Tuition: full time: N/A; part time: $750/credit hour
Room/board/expenses: N/A
College-funded aid: Yes
International student aid: No
Full-time enrollment: N/A
men: N/A; women: N/A; minorities: N/A; international: N/A
Part-time enrollment: 173
men: 60%; women: 40%; minorities: 20%; international: 0%
Average GMAT (part time): 537
TOEFL requirement: Yes
Minimum TOEFL score: 550
Most popular departments: finance, general management, health care administration, international business, leadership

New York Institute of Technology[1]

1855 Broadway
New York, NY 10023
Private
Admissions: N/A
Financial aid: N/A
Tuition: N/A
Room/board/expenses: N/A
Enrollment: N/A

New York University (Stern)

44 W. Fourth Street
New York, NY 10012-1126
www.stern.nyu.edu
Private
Admissions: (212) 998-0600
Email: sternmba@stern.nyu.edu
Financial aid: (212) 998-0790

Application deadline: 03/15
Tuition: full time: $66,192; part time: $2,010/credit hour
Room/board/expenses: $36,300
College-funded aid: Yes
International student aid: Yes
Average student indebtedness at graduation: $107,458
Full-time enrollment: 799
men: 64%; women: 36%; minorities: 25%; international: 27%
Part-time enrollment: 1,540
men: 65%; women: 35%; minorities: 27%; international: 12%
Acceptance rate (full time): 20%
Average GMAT (full time): 720
Average GMAT (part time): 669
Average GPA (full time): 3.51
Average age of entrants to full-time program: 28
Average months of prior work experience (full time): 56
TOEFL requirement: Yes
Minimum TOEFL score: N/A
Most popular departments: entrepreneurship, finance, general management, marketing, other
Mean starting base salary for 2015 full-time graduates: $114,863
Employment location for 2015 class: Intl. 7%; N.E. 74%; M.A. 3%; S. 1%; M.W. 1%; S.W. 1%; W. 12%

Niagara University

PO Box 1909
Niagara University, NY 14109
mba.niagara.edu
Private
Admissions: (716) 286-8051
Email: mbadirector@niagara.edu
Financial aid: (716) 286-8686
Application deadline: rolling
Tuition: full time: $835/credit hour; part time: $835/credit hour
Room/board/expenses: $14,170
College-funded aid: Yes
International student aid: Yes
Full-time enrollment: 183
men: 57%; women: 43%; minorities: 7%; international: 43%
Part-time enrollment: 67
men: 40%; women: 60%; minorities: 16%; international: 6%
Average age of entrants to full-time program: 25
TOEFL requirement: Yes
Minimum TOEFL score: N/A
Most popular departments: accounting, finance, general management, marketing, operations management

Pace University (Lubin)

1 Pace Plaza
New York, NY 10038
www.pace.edu/lubin/
Private
Admissions: (212) 346-1531
Email: graduateadmission@pace.edu
Financial aid: (914) 773-3751
Application deadline: rolling
Tuition: full time: $1,170/credit hour; part time: $1,170/credit hour
Room/board/expenses: $20,682
College-funded aid: Yes
International student aid: Yes
Average student indebtedness at graduation: $41,991
Full-time enrollment: 261
men: 54%; women: 46%; minorities: 21%; international: 51%

Part-time enrollment: 153
men: 50%; women: 50%;
minorities: 29%; international:
25%
Acceptance rate (full time): 59%
Average GMAT (full time): 536
Average GMAT (part time): 525
Average GPA (full time): 3.31
**Average age of entrants to full-time
program:** 25
TOEFL requirement: Yes
Minimum TOEFL score: 577
Most popular departments:
accounting, finance, general
management, human resources
management, marketing
**Mean starting base salary for 2015
full-time graduates:** $61,365
Employment location for 2015 class:
Intl. N/A; N.E. 96%; M.A. N/A; S.
N/A; M.W. 2%; S.W. 1%; W. 1%

Rensselaer Polytechnic Institute (Lally)

110 Eighth Street
Pittsburgh Building 5202
Troy, NY 12180-3590
lallyschool.rpi.edu
Private
Admissions: (518) 276-6565
Email: lallymba@rpi.edu
Financial aid: (518) 276-6565
Application deadline: 04/15
Tuition: full time: $50,439; part
time: $1,600/credit hour
Room/board/expenses: $17,634
College-funded aid: Yes
International student aid: Yes
Full-time enrollment: 21
men: 62%; women: 38%;
minorities: 19%; international:
33%
Part-time enrollment: 28
men: 68%; women: 32%;
minorities: 18%; international: N/A
Acceptance rate (full time): 56%
Average GMAT (full time): 608
Average GPA (full time): 3.42
**Average age of entrants to full-time
program:** 25
**Average months of prior work
experience (full time):** 29
TOEFL requirement: Yes
Minimum TOEFL score: 577
Most popular departments:
entrepreneurship, finance,
marketing, supply chain
management, technology
**Mean starting base salary for 2015
full-time graduates:** $70,167
Employment location for 2015 class:
Intl. 25%; N.E. 58%; M.A. 17%; S.
N/A; M.W. N/A; S.W. N/A; W. N/A

Rochester Institute of Technology (Saunders)

105 Lomb Memorial Drive
Rochester, NY 14623-5608
saunders.rit.edu
Private
Admissions: (585) 475-7284
Email: gradinfo@rit.edu
Financial aid: (585) 475-2186
Application deadline: rolling
Tuition: full time: $40,426; part
time: $1,673/credit hour
Room/board/expenses: $13,944
College-funded aid: Yes
International student aid: Yes
Full-time enrollment: 130
men: 54%; women: 46%;
minorities: 6%; international: 61%
Part-time enrollment: 61
men: 59%; women: 41%;
minorities: 5%; international: 15%

Acceptance rate (full time): 48%
Average GMAT (full time): 536
Average GMAT (part time): 563
Average GPA (full time): 3.42
**Average age of entrants to full-time
program:** 25
**Average months of prior work
experience (full time):** 25
TOEFL requirement: Yes
Minimum TOEFL score: N/A
Most popular departments: finance,
general management, leadership,
marketing, technology
**Mean starting base salary for 2015
full-time graduates:** $58,315

Siena College[1]

515 Loudon Road
Loudonville, NY 12211-1462
https://www.siena.edu/
Private
Admissions: N/A
Financial aid: N/A
Tuition: N/A
Room/board/expenses: N/A
Enrollment: N/A

St. Bonaventure University

3261 West State Road
St. Bonaventure, NY 14778
www.sbu.edu/admission-aid/
graduate-admissions
Private
Admissions: (716) 375-2021
Email: gradsch@sbu.edu
Financial aid: (716) 375-2528
Application deadline: 10/08
Tuition: full time: $711/credit hour;
part time: $711/credit hour
Room/board/expenses: $25,458
College-funded aid: Yes
International student aid: Yes
**Average student indebtedness at
graduation:** $16,197
Full-time enrollment: 49
men: 51%; women: 49%;
minorities: 18%; international: 2%
Part-time enrollment: 33
men: 42%; women: 58%;
minorities: 9%; international: 0%
Average GMAT (full time): 469
Average GPA (full time): 3.41
**Average age of entrants to full-time
program:** 25
TOEFL requirement: Yes
Minimum TOEFL score: 550

St. John Fisher College

3690 East Avenue
Rochester, NY 14618
www.sjfc.edu/academics/
business/about/index.dot
Private
Admissions: (585) 385-8161
Email: grad@sjfc.edu
Financial aid: (585) 385-8042
Application deadline: rolling
Tuition: full time: $990/credit hour;
part time: $990/credit hour
Room/board/expenses: N/A
College-funded aid: Yes
International student aid: Yes
Full-time enrollment: 66
men: 56%; women: 44%;
minorities: 6%; international: 5%
Part-time enrollment: 89
men: 55%; women: 45%;
minorities: 19%; international: 0%
Acceptance rate (full time): 77%
Average GMAT (full time): 470
Average GMAT (part time): 490
Average GPA (full time): 3.50
**Average age of entrants to full-time
program:** 22
TOEFL requirement: Yes
Minimum TOEFL score: 575

St. John's University (Tobin)

8000 Utopia Parkway
Queens, NY 11439
www.stjohns.edu/tobin
Private
Admissions: (718) 990-1345
Email: tobingradnyc@stjohns.edu
Financial aid: (718) 990-2000
Application deadline: 05/01
Tuition: full time: $1,155/credit
hour; part time: $1,155/credit hour
Room/board/expenses: $22,608
College-funded aid: Yes
International student aid: Yes
**Average student indebtedness at
graduation:** $37,473
Full-time enrollment: 377
men: 50%; women: 50%;
minorities: 20%; international:
49%
Part-time enrollment: 204
men: 59%; women: 41%;
minorities: 35%; international:
20%
Acceptance rate (full time): 74%
Average GMAT (full time): 537
Average GMAT (part time): 533
Average GPA (full time): 3.62
**Average age of entrants to full-time
program:** 23
**Average months of prior work
experience (full time):** 20
TOEFL requirement: Yes
Minimum TOEFL score: 550
Most popular departments:
accounting, finance, general
management, international
business, marketing
**Mean starting base salary for 2015
full-time graduates:** $43,000
Employment location for 2015 class:
Intl. 7%; N.E. 89%; M.A. 2%; S.
2%; M.W. 1%; S.W. N/A; W. N/A

SUNY-Geneseo[1]

1 College Circle
Geneseo, NY 14454
www.geneseo.edu/business
Public
Admissions: N/A
Financial aid: N/A
Tuition: N/A
Room/board/expenses: N/A
Enrollment: N/A

SUNY-New Paltz

1 Hawk Drive
New Paltz, NY
www.newpaltz.edu/graduate
Public
Admissions: (845) 257-3947
Email: gradschool@newpaltz.edu
Financial aid: N/A
Application deadline: rolling
In-state tuition: full time: $15,677;
part time: $600/credit hour
Out-of-state tuition: full time:
$25,657
Room/board/expenses: N/A
College-funded aid: Yes
International student aid: No
Full-time enrollment: 45
men: 56%; women: 44%;
minorities: 31%; international: 18%
Part-time enrollment: 43
men: 44%; women: 56%;
minorities: 35%; international: 9%
Acceptance rate (full time): 93%
Average GMAT (full time): 478
Average GPA (full time): 3.42
**Average age of entrants to full-time
program:** 24
TOEFL requirement: Yes
Minimum TOEFL score: N/A

Most popular departments:
accounting, general management

SUNY-Oswego

138 Rich Hall
Oswego, NY 13126
www.oswego.edu/academics/
colleges_and_departments/
business/index.html
Public
Admissions: (315) 312-3152
Email: gradstudies@oswego.edu
Financial aid: (315) 312-2248
Application deadline: rolling
In-state tuition: full time: $14,410;
part time: $600/credit hour
Out-of-state tuition: full time:
$24,390
Room/board/expenses: $16,922
College-funded aid: Yes
International student aid: Yes
**Average student indebtedness at
graduation:** $11,023
Full-time enrollment: 83
men: 67%; women: 33%;
minorities: 25%; international: 4%
Part-time enrollment: 156
men: 69%; women: 31%;
minorities: 16%; international: 0%
Acceptance rate (full time): 80%
Average GMAT (full time): 504
Average GMAT (part time): 560
Average GPA (full time): 3.35
**Average age of entrants to full-time
program:** 24
**Average months of prior work
experience (full time):** 94
TOEFL requirement: Yes
Minimum TOEFL score: 560
Most popular departments:
accounting, general management,
health care administration,
marketing, tax

SUNY Polytechnic Institute

100 Seymour Road
Utica, NY 13502
www.sunypoly.edu/graduate/
mbatm/
Public
Admissions: (315) 792-7347
Email: gradcenter@sunyit.edu
Financial aid: (315) 792-7210
Application deadline: 07/15
In-state tuition: full time: $15,699;
part time: $600/credit hour
Out-of-state tuition: full time:
$25,679
Room/board/expenses: $15,770
College-funded aid: Yes
International student aid: Yes
Full-time enrollment: 23
men: 61%; women: 39%;
minorities: 43%; international: 0%
Part-time enrollment: 101
men: 58%; women: 42%;
minorities: 17%; international: 0%
Acceptance rate (full time): 55%
Average GMAT (full time): 512
Average GMAT (part time): 509
**Average age of entrants to full-time
program:** 27
TOEFL requirement: Yes
Minimum TOEFL score: 550
Most popular departments:
accounting, finance, human
resources management,
marketing, other

Syracuse University (Whitman)

721 University Avenue
Suite 315
Syracuse, NY 13244-2450
whitman.syr.edu/mba/fulltime
Private
Admissions: (315) 443-9214
Email: busgrad@syr.edu
Financial aid: (315) 443-3727
Application deadline: 04/19
Tuition: full time: $42,814; part
time: $1,388/credit hour
Room/board/expenses: $20,630
College-funded aid: Yes
International student aid: Yes
**Average student indebtedness at
graduation:** $34,592
Full-time enrollment: 81
men: 70%; women: 30%;
minorities: 7%; international: 65%
Part-time enrollment: N/A
men: N/A; women: N/A; minorities:
N/A; international: N/A
Acceptance rate (full time): 65%
Average GMAT (full time): 631
Average GPA (full time): 3.53
**Average age of entrants to full-time
program:** 25
**Average months of prior work
experience (full time):** 35
TOEFL requirement: Yes
Minimum TOEFL score: 600
Most popular departments:
entrepreneurship, finance,
general management, marketing,
supply chain management
**Mean starting base salary for 2015
full-time graduates:** $73,536
Employment location for 2015 class:
Intl. 16%; N.E. 53%; M.A. 11%; S.
5%; M.W. 5%; S.W. 5%; W. 5%

Union Graduate College[1]

80 Nott Terrace
Schenectady, NY 12308-3107
www.uniongraduatecollege.edu/
management
Private
Admissions: (518) 631-9831
Financial aid: N/A
Tuition: N/A
Room/board/expenses: N/A
Enrollment: N/A

University at Albany-SUNY

1400 Washington Avenue
Massry Center for Business
Albany, NY 12222
graduatebusiness.albany.edu
Public
Admissions: (518) 442-4961
Email: busweb@uamail.albany.edu
Financial aid: (518) 442-5757
Application deadline: 05/01
In-state tuition: full time: $16,017;
part time: $600/credit hour
Out-of-state tuition: full time:
$25,997
Room/board/expenses: $12,422
College-funded aid: Yes
International student aid: No
Full-time enrollment: 83
men: 61%; women: 39%;
minorities: 13%; international: 19%
Part-time enrollment: 212
men: 35%; women: 65%;
minorities: 19%; international: 5%
Acceptance rate (full time): 37%
Average GMAT (full time): 563
Average GMAT (part time): 533
Average GPA (full time): 3.50
**Average months of prior work
experience (full time):** 90
TOEFL requirement: Yes

Minimum TOEFL score: 600
Most popular departments: finance, human resources management, marketing, management information systems, other
Mean starting base salary for 2015 full-time graduates: $68,000
Employment location for 2015 class: Intl. 3%; N.E. 90%; M.A. 7%; S. 0%; M.W. 0%; S.W. 0%; W. 0%

University at Buffalo-SUNY

203 Alfiero Center
Buffalo, NY 14260-4010
mgt.buffalo.edu/mba
Public
Admissions: (716) 645-3204
Email: som-apps@buffalo.edu
Financial aid: (716) 645-8232
Application deadline: 05/15
In-state tuition: full time: $18,674; part time: $760/credit hour
Out-of-state tuition: full time: $28,654
Room/board/expenses: $21,000
College-funded aid: Yes
International student aid: Yes
Average student indebtedness at graduation: $29,881
Full-time enrollment: 236
men: 67%; women: 33%;
minorities: 3%; international: 32%
Part-time enrollment: 200
men: 64%; women: 37%;
minorities: 10%; international: 4%
Acceptance rate (full time): 58%
Average GMAT (full time): 611
Average GMAT (part time): 576
Average GPA (full time): 3.36
Average age of entrants to full-time program: 26
Average months of prior work experience (full time): 31
TOEFL requirement: Yes
Minimum TOEFL score: 570
Most popular departments: consulting, finance, health care administration, marketing, other
Mean starting base salary for 2015 full-time graduates: $60,168
Employment location for 2015 class: Intl. 7%; N.E. 80%; M.A. 2%; S. 4%; M.W. 2%; S.W. 2%; W. 2%

University of Rochester (Simon)

Schlegel Hall
Rochester, NY 14627
www.simon.rochester.edu
Private
Admissions: (585) 275-3533
Email: admissions@simon.rochester.edu
Financial aid: (585) 275-3533
Application deadline: 05/15
Tuition: full time: $47,053; part time: $1,745/credit hour
Room/board/expenses: $17,765
College-funded aid: Yes
International student aid: Yes
Average student indebtedness at graduation: $55,548
Full-time enrollment: 209
men: 65%; women: 35%;
minorities: 22%; international: 54%
Part-time enrollment: 185
men: 29%; women: 71%;
minorities: 15%; international: 3%
Acceptance rate (full time): 33%
Average GMAT (full time): 667
Average GMAT (part time): 542
Average GPA (full time): 3.40
Average age of entrants to full-time program: 28
Average months of prior work experience (full time): 66

TOEFL requirement: Yes
Minimum TOEFL score: N/A
Most popular departments: accounting, finance, marketing, operations management, other
Mean starting base salary for 2015 full-time graduates: $98,206
Employment location for 2015 class: Intl. 6%; N.E. 50%; M.A. 4%; S. 12%; M.W. 12%; S.W. 4%; W. 11%

Yeshiva University (Syms)[1]

500 West 185th Street
New York, NY 10033
www.yu.edu/syms/
Private
Admissions: N/A
Financial aid: N/A
Tuition: N/A
Room/board/expenses: N/A
Enrollment: N/A

NORTH CAROLINA

Appalachian State University (Walker)

Box 32037
Boone, NC 28608-2037
www.business.appstate.edu/grad/mba.asp
Public
Admissions: (828) 262-2130
Email: mba@appstate.edu
Financial aid: (828) 262-2190
Application deadline: 07/01
In-state tuition: total program: $17,700 (full time); $15,263 (part time)
Out-of-state tuition: total program: $33,200 (full time)
Room/board/expenses: N/A
College-funded aid: Yes
International student aid: Yes
Full-time enrollment: 79
men: N/A; women: N/A; minorities: N/A; international: N/A
Part-time enrollment: 31
men: N/A; women: N/A; minorities: N/A; international: N/A
Acceptance rate (full time): 84%
Average GMAT (full time): 493
Average GMAT (part time): 542
Average GPA (full time): 3.50
Average age of entrants to full-time program: 24
Average months of prior work experience (full time): 54
TOEFL requirement: Yes
Minimum TOEFL score: N/A
Mean starting base salary for 2015 full-time graduates: $57,118
Employment location for 2015 class: Intl. 0%; N.E. 0%; M.A. 0%; S. 95%; M.W. 0%; S.W. 0%; W. 5%

Duke University (Fuqua)

100 Fuqua Drive Box 90120
Durham, NC 27708-0120
www.fuqua.duke.edu
Private
Admissions: (919) 660-7705
Email: admissions-info@fuqua.duke.edu
Financial aid: (919) 660-7687
Application deadline: 03/22
Tuition: full time: $63,036; part time: N/A
Room/board/expenses: $21,224
College-funded aid: Yes
International student aid: Yes
Average student indebtedness at graduation: $114,498

Full-time enrollment: 894
men: 65%; women: 35%;
minorities: 19%; international: 38%
Part-time enrollment: N/A
men: N/A; women: N/A; minorities: N/A; international: N/A
Acceptance rate (full time): 23%
Average GMAT (full time): 696
Average GPA (full time): 3.40
Average age of entrants to full-time program: 29
Average months of prior work experience (full time): 64
TOEFL requirement: No
Minimum TOEFL score: N/A
Most popular departments: consulting, finance, health care administration, marketing, statistics and operations research
Mean starting base salary for 2015 full-time graduates: $119,056
Employment location for 2015 class: Intl. 13%; N.E. 27%; M.A. 8%; S. 13%; M.W. 15%; S.W. 7%; W. 17%

East Carolina University

3203 Bate Building
Greenville, NC 27858-4353
www.business.ecu.edu/grad/
Public
Admissions: (252) 328-6970
Email: gradbus@ecu.edu
Financial aid: (252) 328-6610
Application deadline: 06/01
In-state tuition: full time: $371/credit hour; part time: $342/credit hour
Out-of-state tuition: full time: $1,071/credit hour
Room/board/expenses: N/A
College-funded aid: Yes
International student aid: Yes
Full-time enrollment: 146
men: 58%; women: 42%;
minorities: 29%; international: 5%
Part-time enrollment: 560
men: 58%; women: 43%;
minorities: 26%; international: 2%
Acceptance rate (full time): 78%
Average GMAT (full time): 498
Average GMAT (part time): 534
Average GPA (full time): 3.32
Average age of entrants to full-time program: 27
TOEFL requirement: Yes
Minimum TOEFL score: 550
Most popular departments: finance, health care administration, marketing, management information systems, sports business

Elon University (Love)

100 Campus Drive
Elon, NC 27244-2010
elon.edu/mba
Private
Admissions: (336) 278-7600
Email: gradadm@elon.edu
Financial aid: (336) 278-7600
Application deadline: rolling
Tuition: full time: N/A; part time: $852/credit hour
Room/board/expenses: N/A
College-funded aid: No
International student aid: No
Full-time enrollment: N/A
men: N/A; women: N/A; minorities: N/A; international: N/A
Part-time enrollment: 122
men: 65%; women: 35%;
minorities: 22%; international: 4%
Average GMAT (part time): 562
TOEFL requirement: Yes
Minimum TOEFL score: 550

Most popular departments: entrepreneurship, general management, human resources management, leadership, marketing

Fayetteville State University

1200 Murchison Road
Newbold Station
Fayetteville, NC 28301-1033
mba.uncfsu.edu/
Public
Admissions: (910) 672-1197
Email: mbaprogram@uncfsu.edu
Financial aid: (910) 672-1325
Application deadline: 06/30
In-state tuition: full time: $3,280; part time: $205/credit hour
Out-of-state tuition: full time: $14,129
Room/board/expenses: N/A
College-funded aid: Yes
International student aid: No
Full-time enrollment: N/A
men: N/A; women: N/A; minorities: N/A; international: N/A
Part-time enrollment: 106
men: 54%; women: 46%;
minorities: 41%; international: 3%
Average GMAT (part time): 471
TOEFL requirement: Yes
Minimum TOEFL score: 550
Most popular departments: entrepreneurship, finance, general management, health care administration, operations management

Meredith College

3800 Hillsborough Street
Raleigh, NC 27607
www.meredith.edu/mba
Private
Admissions: (919) 760-8212
Email: mba@meredith.edu
Financial aid: (919) 760-8565
Application deadline: 06/01
Tuition: full time: $12,585; part time: $7,659
Room/board/expenses: $12,890
College-funded aid: Yes
International student aid: Yes
Average student indebtedness at graduation: $27,581
Full-time enrollment: 49
men: 20%; women: 80%;
minorities: 29%; international: 6%
Part-time enrollment: 18
men: 17%; women: 83%;
minorities: 39%; international: 6%
Acceptance rate (full time): 86%
Average GMAT (full time): 415
Average GPA (full time): 3.02
Average age of entrants to full-time program: 40
Average months of prior work experience (full time): 144
TOEFL requirement: Yes
Minimum TOEFL score: 550
Most popular departments: general management, human resources management
Mean starting base salary for 2015 full-time graduates: $91,483
Employment location for 2015 class: Intl. 0%; N.E. 0%; M.A. 0%; S. 100%; M.W. 0%; S.W. 0%; W. 0%

North Carolina A&T State University

1601 E. Market Street
Greensboro, NC 27411
www.ncat.edu/~business/
Public
Admissions: (336) 334-7920
Email: jjtaylor@ncat.edu

Financial aid: (336) 334-7973
Application deadline: 05/01
In-state tuition: full time: $7,947; part time: $297/credit hour
Out-of-state tuition: full time: $20,352
Room/board/expenses: $11,500
College-funded aid: Yes
International student aid: Yes
Average student indebtedness at graduation: $45,000
Full-time enrollment: 45
men: 56%; women: 44%;
minorities: 62%; international: 31%
Part-time enrollment: 11
men: 27%; women: 73%;
minorities: 82%; international: 9%
Acceptance rate (full time): 78%
Average GMAT (full time): 487
Average GPA (full time): 3.34
Average age of entrants to full-time program: 27
Average months of prior work experience (full time): 45
TOEFL requirement: Yes
Minimum TOEFL score: 550

North Carolina Central University[1]

1801 Fayetteville Street
Durham, NC 27707
www.nccu.edu/academics/business/index.cfm
Public
Admissions: (919) 530-6405
Email: mba@nccu.edu
Financial aid: N/A
Tuition: N/A
Room/board/expenses: N/A
Enrollment: N/A

North Carolina State University (Jenkins)

2130 Nelson Hall
Campus Box 8114
Raleigh, NC 27695-8114
www.mba.ncsu.edu
Public
Admissions: (919) 515-5584
Email: mba@ncsu.edu
Financial aid: (919) 515-2866
Application deadline: 03/01
In-state tuition: total program: $44,698 (full time); part time: $979/credit hour
Out-of-state tuition: total program: $73,866 (full time)
Room/board/expenses: $27,504
College-funded aid: Yes
International student aid: Yes
Average student indebtedness at graduation: $36,759
Full-time enrollment: 83
men: 60%; women: 40%;
minorities: 12%; international: 28%
Part-time enrollment: 227
men: 61%; women: 39%;
minorities: 32%; international: 4%
Acceptance rate (full time): 38%
Average GMAT (full time): 639
Average GMAT (part time): 664
Average GPA (full time): 3.57
Average age of entrants to full-time program: 28
Average months of prior work experience (full time): 45
TOEFL requirement: Yes
Minimum TOEFL score: 650
Most popular departments: entrepreneurship, manufacturing and technology management, marketing, operations management, supply chain management

Mean starting base salary for 2015 full-time graduates: $82,389
Employment location for 2015 class: Intl. 0%; N.E. 3%; M.A. 6%; S. 70%; M.W. 9%; S.W. 9%; W. 3%

Queens University of Charlotte (McColl)[1]

1900 Selwyn Avenue
Charlotte, NC 28274
mccoll.queens.edu/
Private
Admissions: (704) 337-2224
Email: MBA@Queens.edu
Financial aid: (704) 337-2225
Tuition: N/A
Room/board/expenses: N/A
Enrollment: N/A

University of North Carolina-Chapel Hill (Kenan-Flagler)

CB 3490, McColl Building
Chapel Hill, NC 27599-3490
www.kenan-flagler.unc.edu
Public
Admissions: (919) 962-3236
Email: mba_info@unc.edu
Financial aid: (919) 962-9096
Application deadline: N/A
In-state tuition: full time: $40,441; part time: N/A
Out-of-state tuition: full time: $57,839
Room/board/expenses: $23,520
College-funded aid: Yes
International student aid: Yes
Average student indebtedness at graduation: $93,898
Full-time enrollment: 558
men: 72%; women: 28%; minorities: 15%; international: 33%
Part-time enrollment: N/A
men: N/A; women: N/A; minorities: N/A; international: N/A
Acceptance rate (full time): 34%
Average GMAT (full time): 701
Average GPA (full time): 3.41
Average age of entrants to full-time program: 28
Average months of prior work experience (full time): 61
TOEFL requirement: Yes
Minimum TOEFL score: N/A
Most popular departments: consulting, entrepreneurship, finance, marketing, real estate
Mean starting base salary for 2015 full-time graduates: $108,627
Employment location for 2015 class: Intl. 2%; N.E. 23%; M.A. 10%; S. 40%; M.W. 6%; S.W. 4%; W. 16%

University of North Carolina-Charlotte (Belk)

9201 University City Boulevard
Charlotte, NC 28223
www.mba.uncc.edu
Public
Admissions: (704) 687-7566
Email: mba@uncc.edu
Financial aid: (704) 687-2461
Application deadline: rolling
In-state tuition: full time: $13,032; part time: $9,377
Out-of-state tuition: full time: $25,703
Room/board/expenses: N/A
College-funded aid: Yes
International student aid: Yes

Full-time enrollment: N/A
men: N/A; women: N/A; minorities: N/A; international: N/A
Part-time enrollment: 271
men: 66%; women: 34%; minorities: 21%; international: 18%
Average GMAT (part time): 604
TOEFL requirement: Yes
Minimum TOEFL score: N/A

University of North Carolina-Greensboro (Bryan)

PO Box 26170
Greensboro, NC 27402-6170
mba.uncg.edu
Public
Admissions: (336) 334-5390
Email: mba@uncg.edu
Financial aid: (336) 334-5702
Application deadline: 07/01
In-state tuition: full time: $9,673; part time: $809/credit hour
Out-of-state tuition: full time: $23,122
Room/board/expenses: $11,767
College-funded aid: Yes
International student aid: Yes
Full-time enrollment: 55
men: 51%; women: 49%; minorities: 22%; international: 27%
Part-time enrollment: 90
men: 73%; women: 27%; minorities: 20%; international: 4%
Acceptance rate (full time): 74%
Average GMAT (full time): 605
Average GMAT (part time): 570
Average GPA (full time): 3.30
Average age of entrants to full-time program: 25
Average months of prior work experience (full time): 22
TOEFL requirement: Yes
Minimum TOEFL score: 550
Most popular departments: finance, general management, marketing, management information systems, supply chain management
Mean starting base salary for 2015 full-time graduates: $59,500
Employment location for 2015 class: Intl. N/A; N.E. N/A; M.A. N/A; S. 100%; M.W. N/A; S.W. N/A; W. N/A

University of North Carolina-Pembroke

PO Box 1510
One University Drive
Pembroke, NC 28372
www.uncp.edu/grad
Public
Admissions: (910) 521-6271
Email: grad@uncp.edu
Financial aid: (910) 521-6255
Application deadline: 08/15
In-state tuition: full time: $5,637; part time: $3,900
Out-of-state tuition: full time: $15,429
Room/board/expenses: $12,015
College-funded aid: Yes
Average student indebtedness at graduation: $19,790
Full-time enrollment: 14
men: 14%; women: 86%; minorities: 57%; international: 14%
Part-time enrollment: 53
men: 38%; women: 62%; minorities: 43%; international: 4%
Acceptance rate (full time): 100%
Average GMAT (full time): 428
Average GMAT (part time): 430
Average GPA (full time): 3.34

Average age of entrants to full-time program: 29
TOEFL requirement: No
Minimum TOEFL score: N/A

University of North Carolina-Wilmington (Cameron)

601 S. College Road
Wilmington, NC 28403-5680
www.csb.uncw.edu/gradprograms
Public
Admissions: (910) 962-3903
Email: barnhillk@uncw.edu
Financial aid: (910) 962-3177
Application deadline: 06/01
In-state tuition: total program: $18,850 (full time); $8,745 (part time)
Out-of-state tuition: total program: $18,850 (full time)
Room/board/expenses: $16,844
College-funded aid: Yes
International student aid: Yes
Average student indebtedness at graduation: $24,247
Full-time enrollment: N/A
men: N/A; women: N/A; minorities: N/A; international: N/A
Part-time enrollment: 44
men: 82%; women: 18%; minorities: 5%; international: 7%
Acceptance rate (full time): 100%
Average GMAT (part time): 564
Average GPA (full time): 3.18
Average age of entrants to full-time program: 25
Average months of prior work experience (full time): 27
TOEFL requirement: Yes
Minimum TOEFL score: 550
Most popular departments: consulting, finance, general management, marketing

Wake Forest University

PO Box 7659
Winston-Salem, NC 27109
www.business.wfu.edu
Private
Admissions: (336) 758-5422
Email: busadmissions@wfu.edu
Financial aid: (336) 758-4424
Application deadline: rolling
Tuition: full time: N/A; part time: $37,476
Room/board/expenses: N/A
College-funded aid: Yes
International student aid: Yes
Full-time enrollment: N/A
men: N/A; women: N/A; minorities: N/A; international: N/A
Part-time enrollment: 305
men: 71%; women: 29%; minorities: 25%; international: 3%
Average GMAT (part time): 587
TOEFL requirement: Yes
Minimum TOEFL score: N/A

Western Carolina University

Forsyth Building
Cullowhee, NC 28723
grad.wcu.edu
Public
Admissions: (828) 227-3174
Email: gradsch@email.wcu.edu
Financial aid: (828) 227-7290
Application deadline: 07/15
In-state tuition: full time: $4,847; part time: $4,207
Out-of-state tuition: full time: $10,500
Room/board/expenses: N/A

College-funded aid: Yes
International student aid: No
Full-time enrollment: 43
men: 58%; women: 42%; minorities: 21%; international: 7%
Part-time enrollment: 186
men: 57%; women: 43%; minorities: 25%; international: 2%
Average GMAT (full time): 473
Average GMAT (part time): 517
Average GPA (full time): 3.36
Average age of entrants to full-time program: 28
TOEFL requirement: Yes
Minimum TOEFL score: 550

Winston-Salem State University[1]

RJR Center, Suite 109
Winston-Salem, NC 27110
www.wssu.edu/
Public
Admissions: (336) 750-3045
Email: graduate@wssu.edu
Financial aid: N/A
Tuition: N/A
Room/board/expenses: N/A
Enrollment: N/A

NORTH DAKOTA

North Dakota State University[1]

NDSU Department 2400
PO Box 6050
Fargo, ND 58108-6050
www.ndsu.edu/
Public
Admissions: N/A
Financial aid: N/A
Tuition: N/A
Room/board/expenses: N/A
Enrollment: N/A

University of North Dakota[1]

293 Centennial Drive
Stop 8098
Grand Forks, ND 58202
business.und.edu/
Public
Admissions: N/A
Financial aid: N/A
Tuition: N/A
Room/board/expenses: N/A
Enrollment: N/A

OHIO

Bowling Green State University

371 Business Administration Building
Bowling Green, OH 43403
www.bgsumba.com
Public
Admissions: (800) 247-8622
Email: mba@bgsu.edu
Financial aid: (419) 372-2651
Application deadline: 03/01
In-state tuition: total program: $17,997 (full time); $18,009 (part time)
Out-of-state tuition: total program: $28,959 (full time)
Room/board/expenses: N/A
College-funded aid: Yes
International student aid: Yes
Full-time enrollment: 34
men: 53%; women: 47%; minorities: 3%; international: 41%
Part-time enrollment: 86
men: 73%; women: 27%; minorities: 16%; international: 1%

Acceptance rate (full time): 40%
Average GMAT (full time): 505
Average GMAT (part time): 547
Average GPA (full time): 3.30
Average age of entrants to full-time program: 25
Average months of prior work experience (full time): 24
TOEFL requirement: Yes
Minimum TOEFL score: 550
Most popular departments: accounting, finance, supply chain management
Mean starting base salary for 2015 full-time graduates: $54,166
Employment location for 2015 class: Intl. N/A; N.E. N/A; M.A. 17%; S. N/A; M.W. 83%; S.W. N/A; W. N/A

Case Western Reserve University (Weatherhead)

Peter B. Lewis Building, 10900 Euclid Avenue
Cleveland, OH 44106-7235
www.weatherhead.case.edu
Private
Admissions: (216) 368-6702
Email: wsomadmissions@case.edu
Financial aid: (216) 368-8907
Application deadline: 05/29
Tuition: full time: $37,700; part time: $30,120
Room/board/expenses: $21,880
College-funded aid: Yes
International student aid: Yes
Average student indebtedness at graduation: $65,393
Full-time enrollment: 122
men: 60%; women: 40%; minorities: 13%; international: 45%
Part-time enrollment: 104
men: 59%; women: 41%; minorities: 16%; international: 9%
Acceptance rate (full time): 60%
Average GMAT (full time): 642
Average GMAT (part time): 562
Average GPA (full time): 3.23
Average age of entrants to full-time program: 27
Average months of prior work experience (full time): 50
TOEFL requirement: Yes
Minimum TOEFL score: 600
Mean starting base salary for 2015 full-time graduates: $79,641
Employment location for 2015 class: Intl. 9%; N.E. 9%; M.A. 3%; S. 0%; M.W. 70%; S.W. 3%; W. 6%

Cleveland State University (Ahuja)

1860 E. 18th Street, BU420
Cleveland, OH 44115
www.csuohio.edu/business/mba
Public
Admissions: (216) 687-5599
Email: cbacsu@csuohio.edu
Financial aid: (216) 687-3764
Application deadline: 08/18
In-state tuition: full time: $569/credit hour; part time: $569/credit hour
Out-of-state tuition: full time: $1,074/credit hour
Room/board/expenses: $15,818
College-funded aid: Yes
International student aid: Yes
Average student indebtedness at graduation: $41,152
Full-time enrollment: 282
men: 53%; women: 47%; minorities: 17%; international: 40%

Part-time enrollment: 505
men: 53%; women: 47%;
minorities: 23%; international: 7%
Acceptance rate (full time): 63%
Average GMAT (full time): 490
Average GMAT (part time): 490
Average GPA (full time): 3.23
Average age of entrants to full-time
program: 27
Average months of prior work
experience (full time): 36
TOEFL requirement: Yes
Minimum TOEFL score: 550
Most popular departments:
accounting, finance, health care
administration, marketing, supply
chain management
Mean starting base salary for 2015
full-time graduates: $50,000
Employment location for 2015 class:
Intl. N/A; N.E. 100%; M.A. N/A; S.
N/A; M.W. N/A; S.W. N/A; W. N/A

John Carroll University (Boler)

1 John Carroll Boulevard
University Heights, OH 44118
www.jcu.edu/mba
Private
Admissions: (216) 397-1970
Email: gradbusiness@jcu.edu
Financial aid: (216) 397-4248
Application deadline: 07/15
Tuition: full time: N/A; part time:
$855/credit hour
Room/board/expenses: N/A
College-funded aid: Yes
International student aid: Yes
Full-time enrollment: N/A
men: N/A; women: N/A; minorities:
N/A; international: N/A
Part-time enrollment: 89
men: 62%; women: 38%;
minorities: 9%; international: 10%
Average GMAT (part time): 540
TOEFL requirement: Yes
Minimum TOEFL score: 550
Most popular departments:
accounting, finance, human
resources management,
marketing

Kent State University

PO Box 5190
Kent, OH 44242-0001
www.kent.edu/business/grad
Public
Admissions: (330) 672-2282
Email: gradbus@kent.edu
Financial aid: (330) 672-2972
Application deadline: 04/01
In-state tuition: full time: $12,064;
part time: $495/credit hour
Out-of-state tuition: full time:
$19,580
Room/board/expenses: $11,250
College-funded aid: Yes
International student aid: Yes
Full-time enrollment: 61
men: 67%; women: 33%;
minorities: 5%; international: 44%
Part-time enrollment: 61
men: 61%; women: 39%;
minorities: 5%; international: 0%
Acceptance rate (full time): 61%
Average GMAT (full time): 568
Average GMAT (part time): 543
Average GPA (full time): 3.27
Average age of entrants to full-time
program: 24
Average months of prior work
experience (full time): 16
TOEFL requirement: Yes
Minimum TOEFL score: 550
Most popular departments:
finance, general management,
human resources management,
international business, marketing

Miami University (Farmer)

800 E. High Street
Oxford, OH 45056
mba.muohio.edu
Public
Admissions: (513) 895-8876
Email: miamimba@muohio.edu
Financial aid: (513) 529-8710
Application deadline: rolling
In-state tuition: full time: N/A; total
program: $34,200 (part time)
Out-of-state tuition: full time: N/A
Room/board/expenses: N/A
College-funded aid: No
International student aid: No
Full-time enrollment: N/A
men: N/A; women: N/A; minorities:
N/A; international: N/A
Part-time enrollment: 107
men: 66%; women: 34%;
minorities: 17%; international: 1%
Average GMAT (part time): 593
TOEFL requirement: Yes
Minimum TOEFL score: 550

Ohio State University (Fisher)

100 Gerlach Hall
2108 Neil Avenue
Columbus, OH 43210-1144
fisher.osu.edu/master
Public
Admissions: (614) 292-8511
Email: mba@fisher.osu.edu
Financial aid: (614) 292-8511
Application deadline: 04/15
In-state tuition: full time: $31,139;
part time: $1,574/credit hour
Out-of-state tuition: full time:
$50,611
Room/board/expenses: $17,772
College-funded aid: Yes
International student aid: Yes
Average student indebtedness at
graduation: $56,154
Full-time enrollment: 220
men: 71%; women: 29%;
minorities: 15%; international:
34%
Part-time enrollment: 332
men: 69%; women: 31%;
minorities: 16%; international: 12%
Acceptance rate (full time): 34%
Average GMAT (full time): 664
Average GMAT (part time): 621
Average GPA (full time): 3.46
Average age of entrants to full-time
program: 27
Average months of prior work
experience (full time): 51
TOEFL requirement: Yes
Minimum TOEFL score: 600
Most popular departments:
consulting, finance, marketing,
operations management, supply
chain management
Mean starting base salary for 2015
full-time graduates: $98,388
Employment location for 2015 class:
Intl. 1%; N.E. 11%; M.A. 5%; S. 5%;
M.W. 68%; S.W. 3%; W. 7%

Ohio University

409 Copeland Hall
Athens, OH 45701
www.business.ohio.edu
Public
Admissions: (740) 593-2053
Email: vvalentv@ohio.edu
Financial aid: (740) 593-4141

Application deadline: 03/01
In-state tuition: total program:
$20,770 (full time); $40,723 (part
time)
Out-of-state tuition: total program:
$32,758 (full time)
Room/board/expenses: $15,700
College-funded aid: Yes
International student aid: Yes
Average student indebtedness at
graduation: $16,551
Full-time enrollment: 19
men: 58%; women: 42%;
minorities: 11%; international: 11%
Part-time enrollment: 106
men: 63%; women: 37%;
minorities: 9%; international: 4%
Acceptance rate (full time): 52%
Average GMAT (full time): 510
Average GPA (full time): 3.50
Average age of entrants to full-time
program: 23
TOEFL requirement: Yes
Minimum TOEFL score: N/A

University of Akron

CBA 412
Akron, OH 44325-4805
mba.uakron.edu
Public
Admissions: (330) 972-7043
Email: gradcba@uakron.edu
Financial aid: (330) 972-7032
Application deadline: 07/15
In-state tuition: full time: N/A; part
time: $461/credit hour
Out-of-state tuition: full time: N/A
Room/board/expenses: N/A
College-funded aid: Yes
International student aid: Yes
Full-time enrollment: N/A
men: N/A; women: N/A; minorities:
N/A; international: N/A
Part-time enrollment: 490
men: 59%; women: 41%;
minorities: 8%; international: 34%
Average GMAT (part time): 567
TOEFL requirement: Yes
Minimum TOEFL score: 550
Most popular departments:
accounting, finance, general
management, management
information systems, tax

University of Cincinnati (Lindner)

606 Lindner Hall
Cincinnati, OH 45221-0020
www.business.uc.edu/mba
Public
Admissions: (513) 556-7024
Email: graduate@uc.edu
Financial aid: (513) 556-6982
Application deadline: rolling
In-state tuition: total program:
$31,437 (full time); part time:
$890/credit hour
Out-of-state tuition: total program:
$43,194 (full time)
Room/board/expenses: $25,000
College-funded aid: Yes
International student aid: Yes
Average student indebtedness at
graduation: $30,862
Full-time enrollment: 115
men: 60%; women: 40%;
minorities: 15%; international:
25%
Part-time enrollment: 148
men: 65%; women: 35%;
minorities: 14%; international: 9%
Acceptance rate (full time): 53%
Average GMAT (full time): 651
Average GMAT (part time): 639
Average GPA (full time): 3.59
Average age of entrants to full-time
program: 25

Average months of prior work
experience (full time): 43
TOEFL requirement: Yes
Minimum TOEFL score: 600
Mean starting base salary for 2015
full-time graduates: $62,646
Employment location for 2015 class:
Intl. 4%; N.E. 9%; M.A. 2%; S. 11%;
M.W. 62%; S.W. 4%; W. 7%

University of Dayton

300 College Park Avenue
Dayton, OH 45469-2234
business.udayton.edu/mba
Private
Admissions: (937) 229-3733
Email: mba@udayton.edu
Financial aid: (937) 229-4311
Application deadline: rolling
Tuition: full time: $951/credit hour;
part time: $951/credit hour
Room/board/expenses: N/A
College-funded aid: Yes
International student aid: Yes
Full-time enrollment: 92
men: 62%; women: 38%;
minorities: 1%; international: 24%
Part-time enrollment: 82
men: 57%; women: 43%;
minorities: 1%; international: 5%
Acceptance rate (full time): 18%
Average GMAT (full time): 557
Average GMAT (part time): 557
Average GPA (full time): 3.30
Average age of entrants to full-time
program: 25
TOEFL requirement: Yes
Minimum TOEFL score: 550

University of Toledo[1]

Stranahan Hall North
Room 3130
Toledo, OH 43606-3390
utoledo.edu/business/
gradprograms/
Public
Admissions: (419) 530-2087
Email: COBIadvising@utoledo.edu
Financial aid: (419) 530-5800
Tuition: N/A
Room/board/expenses: N/A
Enrollment: N/A

Wright State University (Soin)[1]

3640 Colonel Glenn Highway
Dayton, OH 45435-0001
www.wright.edu/business
Public
Admissions: (937) 775-2437
Email: mba@wright.edu
Financial aid: N/A
Tuition: N/A
Room/board/expenses: N/A
Enrollment: N/A

Xavier University (Williams)

1002 Francis Xavier Way
Cincinnati, OH 45207-1221
www.xavier.edu/MBA
Private
Admissions: (513) 745-3525
Email: xumba@xu.edu
Financial aid: (513) 745-3142
Application deadline: 08/01
Tuition: full time: $799/credit hour;
part time: $799/credit hour
Room/board/expenses: $15,200
College-funded aid: Yes
International student aid: Yes
Average student indebtedness at
graduation: $29,519

Full-time enrollment: 105
men: 63%; women: 37%;
minorities: 47%; international:
27%
Part-time enrollment: 362
men: 65%; women: 35%;
minorities: 17%; international: 1%
Acceptance rate (full time): 79%
Average GMAT (full time): 548
Average GMAT (part time): 568
Average GPA (full time): 3.20
Average age of entrants to full-time
program: 25
Average months of prior work
experience (full time): 36
TOEFL requirement: Yes
Minimum TOEFL score: 550
Most popular departments:
finance, general management,
international business, marketing,
other

Youngstown State University (Williamson)

1 University Plaza
Youngstown, OH 44555
web.ysu.edu/mba
Public
Admissions: N/A
Email: graduateschool@ysu.edu
Financial aid: N/A
Application deadline: 07/14
In-state tuition: full time: $470/
credit hour; part time: $470/
credit hour
Out-of-state tuition: full time: $720/
credit hour
Room/board/expenses: N/A
College-funded aid: Yes
Full-time enrollment: N/A
men: N/A; women: N/A; minorities:
N/A; international: N/A
Part-time enrollment: 175
men: N/A; women: N/A; minorities:
N/A; international: N/A
TOEFL requirement: Yes
Minimum TOEFL score: 550

OKLAHOMA

Oklahoma City University

2501 N Blackwelder
Oklahoma City, OK 73106
www.okcu.edu/mba/
Private
Admissions: (405) 208-5351
Email: gadmissions@okcu.edu
Financial aid: (405) 208-5211
Application deadline: rolling
Tuition: full time: $590/credit hour;
part time: $590/credit hour
Room/board/expenses: N/A
College-funded aid: Yes
International student aid: Yes
Average student indebtedness at
graduation: $14,500
Full-time enrollment: 61
men: 67%; women: 33%;
minorities: 18%; international:
26%
Part-time enrollment: 47
men: 62%; women: 38%;
minorities: 30%; international: 4%
Average GMAT (full time): 480
Average age of entrants to full-time
program: 28
TOEFL requirement: Yes
Minimum TOEFL score: N/A

Oklahoma State University (Spears)

102 Gundersen
Stillwater, OK 74078-4022
spears.okstate.edu/
Public
Admissions: (405) 744-2951
Email: spearsmasters@
okstate.edu
Financial aid: (405) 744-6604
Application deadline: 04/15
In-state tuition: full time: $196/
credit hour; part time: $196/
credit hour
Out-of-state tuition: full time: $786/
credit hour
Room/board/expenses: $14,620
College-funded aid: Yes
International student aid: No
Full-time enrollment: 70
men: 64%; women: 36%;
minorities: 19%; international:
34%
Part-time enrollment: 103
men: 78%; women: 22%;
minorities: 12%; international: 0%
Acceptance rate (full time): 83%
Average GMAT (full time): 560
Average GMAT (part time): 554
Average GPA (full time): 3.24
Average age of entrants to full-time
program: 25
Average months of prior work
experience (full time): 57
TOEFL requirement: Yes
Minimum TOEFL score: 575
Most popular departments:
entrepreneurship, finance,
general management, non-profit
management, other
Mean starting base salary for 2015
full-time graduates: $56,933
Employment location for 2015 class:
Intl. 4%; N.E. 4%; M.A. N/A; S. N/A;
M.W. 11%; S.W. 78%; W. 4%

Southeastern Oklahoma State University

1405 N. Fourth Avenue
PMB 4205
Durant, OK 74701-0609
www.se.edu/bus/
Public
Admissions: N/A
Email: kluke@se.edu
Financial aid: (580) 745-2186
Application deadline: rolling
In-state tuition: full time: $212/
credit hour; part time: $212/
credit hour
Out-of-state tuition: full time: $532/
credit hour
Room/board/expenses: $1,755
College-funded aid: Yes
International student aid: Yes
Full-time enrollment: 16
men: 44%; women: 56%;
minorities: 50%; international: 0%
Part-time enrollment: 50
men: 48%; women: 52%;
minorities: 56%; international: 6%
Average age of entrants to full-time
program: 23
TOEFL requirement: Yes
Minimum TOEFL score: N/A

University of Oklahoma (Price)

Adams Hall, 307 West Brooks
Norman, OK 73019-4004
ou.edu/mba
Public
Admissions: (405) 325-5623
Email: rebecca_watts@ou.edu
Financial aid: (405) 325-4521

Application deadline: 05/15
In-state tuition: full time: $15,903;
part time: $12,962
Out-of-state tuition: full time:
$32,848
Room/board/expenses: $14,000
College-funded aid: Yes
International student aid: Yes
Full-time enrollment: 82
men: 74%; women: 26%;
minorities: 11%; international: 29%
Part-time enrollment: 147
men: 80%; women: 20%;
minorities: 14%; international: 1%
Acceptance rate (full time): 55%
Average GMAT (full time): 628
Average GMAT (part time): 601
Average GPA (full time): 3.38
Average age of entrants to full-time
program: 26
Average months of prior work
experience (full time): 33
TOEFL requirement: Yes
Minimum TOEFL score: 600
Most popular departments:
entrepreneurship, finance,
management information
systems, other
Mean starting base salary for 2015
full-time graduates: $82,335
Employment location for 2015 class:
Intl. 5%; N.E. N/A; M.A. 5%; S. N/A;
M.W. N/A; S.W. 90%; W. N/A

University of Tulsa (Collins)

800 S. Tucker Drive
Tulsa, OK 74104-9700
www.utulsa.edu/graduate/
business
Private
Admissions: (918) 631-2242
Email: graduate-business@
utulsa.edu
Financial aid: (918) 631-2526
Application deadline: 07/01
Tuition: full time: $1,176/credit
hour; part time: $1,176/credit hour
Room/board/expenses: $15,932
College-funded aid: Yes
International student aid: Yes
Average student indebtedness at
graduation: $32,736
Full-time enrollment: 42
men: 57%; women: 43%;
minorities: 10%; international:
26%
Part-time enrollment: 41
men: 66%; women: 34%;
minorities: 22%; international: 2%
Acceptance rate (full time): 64%
Average GMAT (full time): 596
Average GMAT (part time): 553
Average GPA (full time): 3.50
Average age of entrants to full-time
program: 25
Average months of prior work
experience (full time): 20
TOEFL requirement: Yes
Minimum TOEFL score: 575
Most popular departments:
accounting, finance, general
management, marketing, other
Mean starting base salary for 2015
full-time graduates: $55,500
Employment location for 2015 class:
Intl. 0%; N.E. 7%; M.A. 0%; S. 7%;
M.W. 0%; S.W. 73%; W. 13%

OREGON

Oregon State University

Bexell Hall 200
Corvallis, OR 97331
business.oregonstate.edu/mba/
Public
Admissions: (541) 737-5510
Email:
osumba@bus.oregonstate.edu
Financial aid: (541) 737-2241
Application deadline: 08/14
In-state tuition: full time: $20,985;
part time: $699/credit hour
Out-of-state tuition: full time:
$33,621
Room/board/expenses: $15,237
College-funded aid: Yes
International student aid: Yes
Average student indebtedness at
graduation: $31,633
Full-time enrollment: 137
men: 59%; women: 41%;
minorities: 2%; international: 86%
Part-time enrollment: 36
men: 39%; women: 61%;
minorities: 14%; international: 17%
Acceptance rate (full time): 63%
Average GMAT (full time): 569
Average GPA (full time): 3.15
Average age of entrants to full-time
program: 26
Average months of prior work
experience (full time): 47
TOEFL requirement: Yes
Minimum TOEFL score: 575
Most popular departments:
accounting, finance, leadership,
supply chain management, other
Mean starting base salary for 2015
full-time graduates: $57,840
Employment location for 2015 class:
Intl. N/A; N.E. 20%; M.A. N/A; S.
N/A; M.W. N/A; S.W. N/A; W. 80%

Portland State University

PO Box 751
Portland, OR 97207-0751
www.mba.pdx.edu
Public
Admissions: (503) 725-3714
Email: gradinfo@sba.pdx.edu
Financial aid: (503) 725-5442
Application deadline: 05/02
In-state tuition: full time: $591/
credit hour; part time: $591/
credit hour
Out-of-state tuition: full time: $716/
credit hour
Room/board/expenses: $20,000
College-funded aid: Yes
International student aid: Yes
Full-time enrollment: 31
men: 45%; women: 55%;
minorities: 13%; international:
42%
Part-time enrollment: 38
men: 55%; women: 45%;
minorities: 16%; international: 5%
Acceptance rate (full time): 42%
Average GMAT (full time): 622
Average GMAT (part time): 607
Average GPA (full time): 3.31
Average age of entrants to full-time
program: 32
Average months of prior work
experience (full time): 79
TOEFL requirement: Yes
Minimum TOEFL score: 550
Most popular departments:
entrepreneurship, finance,
general management, marketing,
supply chain management
Mean starting base salary for 2015
full-time graduates: $69,568

Employment location for 2015 class:
Intl. 0%; N.E. 0%; M.A. 0%; S. 5%;
M.W. 14%; S.W. 0%; W. 82%

University of Oregon (Lundquist)

1208 University of Oregon
Eugene, OR 97403-1208
business.uoregon.edu/mba
Public
Admissions: (541) 346-3306
Email: mbainfo@uoregon.edu
Financial aid: (541) 346-3221
Application deadline: rolling
In-state tuition: full time: $29,774;
part time: N/A
Out-of-state tuition: full time:
$39,944
Room/board/expenses: $14,568
College-funded aid: Yes
International student aid: Yes
Average student indebtedness at
graduation: $37,794
Full-time enrollment: 97
men: 67%; women: 33%;
minorities: 16%; international: 21%
Part-time enrollment: N/A
men: N/A; women: N/A; minorities:
N/A; international: N/A
Acceptance rate (full time): 44%
Average GMAT (full time): 621
Average GPA (full time): 3.37
Average age of entrants to full-time
program: 26
Average months of prior work
experience (full time): 44
TOEFL requirement: Yes
Minimum TOEFL score: 600
Most popular departments:
accounting, entrepreneurship,
finance, sports business, other
Mean starting base salary for 2015
full-time graduates: $63,300
Employment location for 2015 class:
Intl. 0%; N.E. 21%; M.A. 0%; S.
7%; M.W. 0%; S.W. 0%; W. 71%

University of Portland (Pamplin)

5000 N. Willamette Boulevard
Portland, OR 97203-5798
business.up.edu
Private
Admissions: (503) 943-7225
Email: mba-up@up.edu
Financial aid: (503) 943-7311
Application deadline: 07/15
Tuition: full time: $1,170/credit
hour; part time: $1,170/credit hour
Room/board/expenses: $10,000
College-funded aid: Yes
International student aid: Yes
Full-time enrollment: 53
men: 60%; women: 40%;
minorities: 13%; international:
42%
Part-time enrollment: 89
men: 66%; women: 34%;
minorities: 9%; international: 12%
Acceptance rate (full time): 84%
Average GMAT (full time): 549
Average GMAT (part time): 523
Average GPA (full time): 3.29
Average age of entrants to full-time
program: 29
Average months of prior work
experience (full time): 72
TOEFL requirement: Yes
Minimum TOEFL score: 570

Willamette University (Atkinson)

900 State Street
Salem, OR 97301-3922
www.willamette.edu/mba
Private
Admissions: (503) 370-6167
Email: mba-admission@
willamette.edu
Financial aid: (503) 370-6273
Application deadline: 05/01
Tuition: full time: $37,780; total
program: $66,600 (part time)
Room/board/expenses: $13,000
College-funded aid: Yes
International student aid: Yes
Average student indebtedness at
graduation: $68,590
Full-time enrollment: 189
men: 55%; women: 45%;
minorities: 14%; international:
43%
Part-time enrollment: 116
men: 50%; women: 50%;
minorities: 17%; international: 0%
Acceptance rate (full time): 70%
Average GMAT (full time): 561
Average GMAT (part time): 528
Average GPA (full time): 3.30
Average age of entrants to full-time
program: 24
Average months of prior work
experience (full time): 19
TOEFL requirement: Yes
Minimum TOEFL score: 580
Most popular departments:
accounting, entrepreneurship,
finance, marketing, organizational
behavior
Mean starting base salary for 2015
full-time graduates: $63,917
Employment location for 2015 class:
Intl. 17%; N.E. 7%; M.A. 0%; S. 0%;
M.W. 0%; S.W. 2%; W. 73%

PENNSYLVANIA

Bloomsburg University of Pennsylvania

Sutliff Hall, Room 212
400 Second Street
Bloomsburg, PA 17815-1301
cob.bloomu.edu/
Public
Admissions: (570) 389-4394
Financial aid: (570) 389-4297
Application deadline: 06/01
In-state tuition: full time: N/A; part
time: $470/credit hour
Out-of-state tuition: full time: N/A
Room/board/expenses: N/A
College-funded aid: Yes
International student aid: Yes
Full-time enrollment: N/A
men: N/A; women: N/A; minorities:
N/A; international: N/A
Part-time enrollment: 33
men: 52%; women: 48%;
minorities: 6%; international: 9%
Average GMAT (part time): 490
TOEFL requirement: Yes
Minimum TOEFL score: 590

Carnegie Mellon University (Tepper)

5000 Forbes Avenue
Pittsburgh, PA 15213
www.tepper.cmu.edu
Private
Admissions: (412) 268-2272
Email: mba-admissions@
andrew.cmu.edu
Financial aid: (412) 268-7581
Application deadline: 03/13
Tuition: full time: $60,000; part
time: $1,875/credit hour
Room/board/expenses: $21,152

College-funded aid: Yes
International student aid: Yes
Average student indebtedness at
graduation: $93,267
Full-time enrollment: 417
men: 74%; women: 26%;
minorities: 26%; international:
34%
Part-time enrollment: 164
men: 80%; women: 20%;
minorities: 18%; international: 9%
Acceptance rate (full time): 31%
Average GMAT (full time): 690
Average GMAT (part time): 643
Average GPA (full time): 3.33
Average age of entrants to full-time
program: 28
Average months of prior work
experience (full time): 63
TOEFL requirement: Yes
Minimum TOEFL score: 600
Most popular departments:
entrepreneurship, finance,
management information
systems, organizational behavior,
other
Mean starting base salary for 2015
full-time graduates: $115,253
Employment location for 2015 class:
Intl. 5%; N.E. 24%; M.A. 11%; S.
6%; M.W. 14%; S.W. 5%; W. 36%

Clarion University of Pennsylvania

840 Wood Street
Clarion, PA 16214
www.clarion.edu/admissions/
graduate
Public
Admissions: (814) 393-2337
Email: gradstudies@clarion.edu
Financial aid: (800) 672-7171
Application deadline: 07/15
In-state tuition: full time: $470/
credit hour; part time: $470/
credit hour
Out-of-state tuition: full time: $705/
credit hour
Room/board/expenses: N/A
College-funded aid: Yes
International student aid: Yes
Average student indebtedness at
graduation: $27,343
Full-time enrollment: 19
men: 42%; women: 58%;
minorities: 5%; international: 11%
Part-time enrollment: 80
men: 53%; women: 48%;
minorities: 13%; international: 1%
Acceptance rate (full time): 100%
Average GMAT (full time): 470
Average GMAT (part time): 483
Average GPA (full time): 3.44
Average age of entrants to full-time
program: 24
Average months of prior work
experience (full time): 1.3
TOEFL requirement: Yes
Minimum TOEFL score: 550
Most popular departments:
accounting, economics, finance,
general management

Drexel University (LeBow)

3141 Chestnut Street
Philadelphia, PA 19104
www.lebow.drexel.edu/
Private
Admissions: (215) 895-6804
Email: mba@drexel.edu
Financial aid: N/A
Application deadline: 09/01
Tuition: total program: $65,400
(full time); part time: $1,106/
credit hour
Room/board/expenses: N/A
College-funded aid: Yes

International student aid: Yes
Average student indebtedness at
graduation: $53,899
Full-time enrollment: 57
men: 60%; women: 40%;
minorities: 12%; international: 47%
Part-time enrollment: 247
men: 57%; women: 43%;
minorities: 18%; international: 11%
Acceptance rate (full time): 46%
Average GMAT (full time): 546
Average GMAT (part time): 483
Average GPA (full time): 3.28
Average age of entrants to full-time
program: 28
Average months of prior work
experience (full time): 49
TOEFL requirement: Yes
Minimum TOEFL score: 577
Most popular departments:
entrepreneurship, finance, health
care administration, marketing,
other
Mean starting base salary for 2015
full-time graduates: $78,071
Employment location for 2015 class:
Intl. 0%; N.E. 12%; M.A. 71%; S.
0%; M.W. 0%; S.W. 0%; W. 18%

Duquesne University (Donahue)

704 Rockwell Hall
Pittsburgh, PA 15282
www.duq.edu/business/grad
Private
Admissions: (412) 396-6276
Email: grad-bus@duq.edu
Financial aid: (412) 396-6607
Application deadline: 07/01
Tuition: total program: $52,824
(full time); part time: $1,189/
credit hour
Room/board/expenses: $15,018
College-funded aid: Yes
International student aid: Yes
Average student indebtedness at
graduation: $43,800
Full-time enrollment: 14
men: 29%; women: 71%;
minorities: 21%; international: 21%
Part-time enrollment: 235
men: 63%; women: 37%;
minorities: 4%; international: 14%
Acceptance rate (full time): 87%
Average GMAT (full time): 540
Average GMAT (part time): 548
Average GPA (full time): 3.41
Average age of entrants to full-time
program: 26
Average months of prior work
experience (full time): 41
TOEFL requirement: Yes
Minimum TOEFL score: 577
Most popular departments: finance,
general management, marketing,
supply chain management, other
Employment location for 2015 class:
Intl. 13%; N.E. 0%; M.A. 63%; S.
13%; M.W. 0%; S.W. 0%; W. 13%

Indiana University of Pennsylvania (Eberly)

664 Pratt Drive, Room 402
Indiana, PA 15705
www.eberly.iup.edu/mba
Public
Admissions: (724) 357-2522
Email: iup-mba@iup.edu
Financial aid: (724) 357-2218
Application deadline: rolling
In-state tuition: full time: $11,687;
part time: $495/credit hour
Out-of-state tuition: full time:
$16,139
Room/board/expenses: $14,980
College-funded aid: Yes
International student aid: Yes

Average student indebtedness at
graduation: $38,678
Full-time enrollment: 234
men: 68%; women: 32%;
minorities: 1%; international: 91%
Part-time enrollment: 11
men: 64%; women: 36%;
minorities: 0%; international: 36%
Acceptance rate (full time): 77%
Average GMAT (full time): 489
Average GMAT (part time): 560
Average age of entrants to full-time
program: 23
TOEFL requirement: Yes
Minimum TOEFL score: 540

King's College (McGowan)[1]

133 N. River Street
Wilkes-Barre, PA 18711
www.kings.edu/academics/
colleges_and_programs/business
Private
Admissions: (570) 208-5991
Email: gradprograms@kings.edu
Financial aid: N/A
Tuition: N/A
Room/board/expenses: N/A
Enrollment: N/A

Kutztown University of Pennsylvania

PO Box 730
Kutztown, PA 19530
www.kutztown.edu/admissions/
graduate-admissions.htm
Public
Admissions: (610) 683-4200
Email: graduate@kutztown.edu
Financial aid: (610) 683-4077
Application deadline: 08/01
In-state tuition: full time: $470/
credit hour; part time: $470/
credit hour
Out-of-state tuition: full time: $705/
credit hour
Room/board/expenses: N/A
College-funded aid: Yes
International student aid: Yes
Full-time enrollment: 20
men: 65%; women: 35%;
minorities: 15%; international: 5%
Part-time enrollment: 14
men: 50%; women: 50%;
minorities: 7%; international: 0%
Acceptance rate (full time): 76%
Average GMAT (full time): 482
Average GMAT (part time): 493
Average GPA (full time): 3.32
Average age of entrants to full-time
program: 25
Average months of prior work
experience (full time): 24
TOEFL requirement: Yes
Minimum TOEFL score: 550
Most popular departments:
marketing, operations
management

La Salle University

1900 W. Olney Avenue
Philadelphia, PA 19141
www.lasalle.edu/mba
Private
Admissions: (215) 951-1057
Email: mba@lasalle.edu
Financial aid: (215) 951-1070
Application deadline: rolling
Tuition: full time: $22,920; part
time: $940/credit hour
Room/board/expenses: N/A
College-funded aid: Yes
International student aid: Yes
Average student indebtedness at
graduation: $25,273

Full-time enrollment: 61
men: 57%; women: 43%;
minorities: 33%; international:
25%
Part-time enrollment: 280
men: 49%; women: 51%;
minorities: 27%; international: 0%
Acceptance rate (full time): 70%
Average GMAT (full time): 450
Average GMAT (part time): 496
Average GPA (full time): 3.35
Average age of entrants to full-time
program: 24
Average months of prior work
experience (full time): 60
TOEFL requirement: Yes
Minimum TOEFL score: 573
Most popular departments:
accounting, finance, general
management, marketing, other
Mean starting base salary for 2015
full-time graduates: $53,625
Employment location for 2015 class:
Intl. 2%; N.E. 5%; M.A. 91%; S.
2%; M.W. 0%; S.W. 0%; W. 0%

Lehigh University

621 Taylor Street
Bethlehem, PA 18015
www.lehigh.edu/mba
Private
Admissions: (610) 758-3418
Email: mba.admissions@
lehigh.edu
Financial aid: (610) 758-4450
Application deadline: 08/01
Tuition: full time: $1,050/credit
hour; part time: $1,050/credit
hour
Room/board/expenses: $17,000
College-funded aid: Yes
International student aid: Yes
Average student indebtedness at
graduation: $17,325
Full-time enrollment: 24
men: 58%; women: 42%;
minorities: 17%; international:
46%
Part-time enrollment: 154
men: 75%; women: 25%;
minorities: 17%; international: 5%
Acceptance rate (full time): 57%
Average GMAT (full time): 601
Average GMAT (part time): 613
Average GPA (full time): 3.00
Average age of entrants to full-time
program: 31
Average months of prior work
experience (full time): 71
TOEFL requirement: Yes
Minimum TOEFL score: 600
Most popular departments:
entrepreneurship, finance, supply
chain management, other
Employment location for 2015 class:
Intl. 17%; N.E. 50%; M.A. 17%; S.
0%; M.W. 0%; S.W. 0%; W. 17%

Pennsylvania State University-Erie, The Behrend College (Black)

5101 Jordan Road
Erie, PA 16563
www.pennstatebehrend.psu.edu
Public
Admissions: (814) 898-7255
Email: behrend.admissions@
psu.edu
Financial aid: (814) 898-6162
Application deadline: rolling
In-state tuition: full time: N/A; part
time: $821/credit hour
Out-of-state tuition: full time: N/A
Room/board/expenses: $22,422
College-funded aid: Yes
International student aid: Yes

Full-time enrollment: N/A
men: N/A; women: N/A; minorities:
N/A; international: N/A
Part-time enrollment: 124
men: 73%; women: 27%;
minorities: 3%; international: 1%
Average GMAT (part time): 549
TOEFL requirement: Yes
Minimum TOEFL score: 550

Pennsylvania State University-Great Valley[1]

30 E. Swedesford Road
Malvern, PA 19355
www.sgps.psu.edu
Public
Admissions: (610) 648-3242
Email: gvadmiss@psu.edu
Financial aid: N/A
Tuition: N/A
Room/board/expenses: N/A
Enrollment: N/A

Pennsylvania State University-Harrisburg

777 W. Harrisburg Pike
Middletown, PA 17057-4898
php.scripts.psu.edu/dept/lit/cl/
sba/Graduate.php
Public
Admissions: (717) 948-6250
Email: mbahbg@psu.edu
Financial aid: (717) 948-6307
Application deadline: 07/18
In-state tuition: full time: N/A; part
time: $821/credit hour
Out-of-state tuition: full time: N/A
Room/board/expenses: N/A
College-funded aid: Yes
International student aid: Yes
Full-time enrollment: N/A
men: N/A; women: N/A; minorities:
N/A; international: N/A
Part-time enrollment: 128
men: 66%; women: 34%;
minorities: 13%; international: 9%
Average GMAT (part time): 534
TOEFL requirement: Yes
Minimum TOEFL score: 550

Pennsylvania State University-University Park (Smeal)

220 Business Building
University Park, PA 16802
www.smeal.psu.edu/mba
Public
Admissions: (814) 863-0474
Email: smealmba@psu.edu
Financial aid: (814) 865-6301
Application deadline: 04/01
In-state tuition: full time: $24,850;
part time: N/A
Out-of-state tuition: full time:
$39,210
Room/board/expenses: $21,750
College-funded aid: Yes
International student aid: Yes
Average student indebtedness at
graduation: $36,234
Full-time enrollment: 146
men: 75%; women: 25%;
minorities: 16%; international:
40%
Part-time enrollment: N/A
men: N/A; women: N/A; minorities:
N/A; international: N/A
Acceptance rate (full time): 17%
Average GMAT (full time): 636
Average GPA (full time): 3.37
Average age of entrants to full-time
program: 28

Average months of prior work experience (full time): 61
TOEFL requirement: Yes
Minimum TOEFL score: N/A
Most popular departments: entrepreneurship, finance, leadership, marketing, supply chain management
Mean starting base salary for 2015 full-time graduates: $101,072
Employment location for 2015 class: Intl. 4%; N.E. 18%; M.A. 28%; S. 4%; M.W. 18%; S.W. 21%; W. 9%

Robert Morris University

6001 University Boulevard
Moon Township, PA 15108-1189
mba.rmu.edu/
Private
Admissions: (800) 762-0097
Email: enrollmentoffice@rmu.edu
Financial aid: (412) 397-6250
Application deadline: rolling
Tuition: full time: N/A; part time: $875/credit hour
Room/board/expenses: N/A
College-funded aid: Yes
International student aid: Yes
Full-time enrollment: N/A
men: N/A; women: N/A; minorities: N/A; international: N/A
Part-time enrollment: 196
men: 58%; women: 42%;
minorities: 6%; international: 3%
Average GMAT (part time): 500
TOEFL requirement: Yes
Minimum TOEFL score: 550
Most popular departments: general management, human resources management, tax

Shippensburg University of Pennsylvania (Grove)

1871 Old Main Drive
Shippensburg, PA 17257
www.ship.edu/mba
Public
Admissions: (717) 477-1231
Email: admiss@ship.edu
Financial aid: (717) 477-1131
Application deadline: rolling
In-state tuition: full time: $470/credit hour; part time: $470/credit hour
Out-of-state tuition: full time: $705/credit hour
Room/board/expenses: N/A
College-funded aid: Yes
International student aid: Yes
Full-time enrollment: 55
men: 75%; women: 25%;
minorities: 5%; international: 38%
Part-time enrollment: 280
men: 61%; women: 39%;
minorities: 10%; international: 2%
Acceptance rate (full time): 58%
Average GMAT (full time): 483
Average GMAT (part time): 539
Average GPA (full time): 3.29
Average age of entrants to full-time program: 28
Average months of prior work experience (full time): 56
TOEFL requirement: Yes
Minimum TOEFL score: 500

St. Joseph's University (Haub)

5600 City Avenue
Philadelphia, PA 19131
www.sju.edu/haubmba
Private
Admissions: (610) 660-1690
Email: sjumba@sju.edu

Financial aid: (610) 660-2000
Application deadline: 07/15
Tuition: full time: $974/credit hour; part time: $974/credit hour
Room/board/expenses: N/A
College-funded aid: Yes
International student aid: Yes
Full-time enrollment: N/A
men: N/A; women: N/A; minorities: N/A; international: N/A
Part-time enrollment: 1,227
men: 59%; women: 41%;
minorities: 17%; international: 24%
Average GMAT (part time): 535
TOEFL requirement: Yes
Minimum TOEFL score: 550
Most popular departments: finance, general management, human resources management, marketing, management information systems

Temple University (Fox)

Alter Hall
1801 Liacouras Walk
Suite A701
Philadelphia, PA 19122-6083
sbm.temple.edu/
Public
Admissions: (215) 204-7678
Email: foxinfo@temple.edu
Financial aid: (215) 204-7678
Application deadline: 12/10
In-state tuition: full time: $30,375; part time: $1,125/credit hour
Out-of-state tuition: full time: $42,579
Room/board/expenses: $19,096
College-funded aid: Yes
International student aid: Yes
Average student indebtedness at graduation: $31,615
Full-time enrollment: 90
men: 48%; women: 52%;
minorities: N/A; international: 16%
Part-time enrollment: 638
men: 61%; women: 39%;
minorities: N/A; international: 11%
Acceptance rate (full time): 40%
Average GMAT (full time): 632
Average GMAT (part time): 597
Average GPA (full time): 3.59
Average age of entrants to full-time program: 28
Average months of prior work experience (full time): 51
TOEFL requirement: Yes
Minimum TOEFL score: 600
Most popular departments: finance, general management, health care administration, marketing, management information systems
Mean starting base salary for 2015 full-time graduates: $75,473
Employment location for 2015 class: Intl. 5%; N.E. 11%; M.A. 71%; S. 3%; M.W. 3%; S.W. 0%; W. 8%

University of Pennsylvania (Wharton)

420 Jon M. Huntsman Hall
3730 Walnut Street
Philadelphia, PA 19104
www.wharton.edu
Private
Admissions: (215) 898-6183
Email: mbaadmiss@wharton.upenn.edu
Financial aid: (215) 898-8728
Application deadline: N/A
Tuition: full time: $70,870; part time: N/A
Room/board/expenses: $29,584
College-funded aid: Yes
International student aid: Yes

Full-time enrollment: 1,715
men: 58%; women: 42%;
minorities: 30%; international: 34%
Part-time enrollment: N/A
men: N/A; women: N/A; minorities: N/A; international: N/A
Acceptance rate (full time): 20%
Average GMAT (full time): 732
Average GPA (full time): 3.60
Average age of entrants to full-time program: 28
Average months of prior work experience (full time): 60
TOEFL requirement: Yes
Minimum TOEFL score: N/A
Most popular departments: entrepreneurship, finance, general management, health care administration, other
Mean starting base salary for 2015 full-time graduates: $127,280
Employment location for 2015 class: Intl. 16%; N.E. 42%; M.A. 9%; S. 3%; M.W. 5%; S.W. 4%; W. 22%

University of Pittsburgh (Katz)

372 Mervis Hall
Pittsburgh, PA 15260
www.business.pitt.edu/katz
Public
Admissions: (412) 648-1700
Email: mba@katz.pitt.edu
Financial aid: (412) 648-1700
Application deadline: 04/01
In-state tuition: total program: $57,596 (full time); part time: $1,218/credit hour
Out-of-state tuition: total program: $72,856 (full time)
Room/board/expenses: $36,040
College-funded aid: Yes
International student aid: Yes
Full-time enrollment: 152
men: 67%; women: 33%;
minorities: 19%; international: 36%
Part-time enrollment: 424
men: 66%; women: 34%;
minorities: 13%; international: 2%
Acceptance rate (full time): 22%
Average GMAT (full time): 607
Average GMAT (part time): 559
Average GPA (full time): 3.27
Average age of entrants to full-time program: 28
Average months of prior work experience (full time): 54
TOEFL requirement: Yes
Minimum TOEFL score: N/A
Most popular departments: finance, marketing, management information systems, operations management, supply chain management
Mean starting base salary for 2015 full-time graduates: $88,027
Employment location for 2015 class: Intl. 0%; N.E. 12%; M.A. 51%; S. 2%; M.W. 22%; S.W. 0%; W. 12%

University of Scranton

800 Linden Street
Scranton, PA 18510-4632
www.scranton.edu
Private
Admissions: (570) 941-7540
Email: robackj2@scranton.edu
Financial aid: (570) 941-7700
Application deadline: rolling
Tuition: full time: $965/credit hour; part time: $965/credit hour
Room/board/expenses: N/A
College-funded aid: Yes
International student aid: Yes

Full-time enrollment: N/A
men: N/A; women: N/A; minorities: N/A; international: N/A
Part-time enrollment: 141
men: 75%; women: 25%;
minorities: 1%; international: 43%
Average GMAT (part time): 531
TOEFL requirement: Yes
Minimum TOEFL score: 550
Most popular departments: accounting, finance, general management, management information systems, operations management

Villanova University

Bartley Hall
800 Lancaster Avenue
Villanova, PA 19085
mba.villanova.edu
Private
Admissions: (610) 519-4336
Email: claire.vanna@villanova.edu
Financial aid: (610) 519-4010
Application deadline: 06/30
Tuition: full time: N/A; part time: $1,060/credit hour
Room/board/expenses: N/A
College-funded aid: Yes
International student aid: Yes
Full-time enrollment: N/A
men: N/A; women: N/A; minorities: N/A; international: N/A
Part-time enrollment: 138
men: 61%; women: 39%;
minorities: 17%; international: 3%
Average GMAT (part time): 610
TOEFL requirement: Yes
Minimum TOEFL score: 550

West Chester University of Pennsylvania

1160 McDermott Drive
West Chester, PA 19383
www.wcupa.edu/mba
Public
Admissions: (610) 436-2943
Email: gradstudy@wcupa.edu
Financial aid: (610) 436-2627
Application deadline: rolling
In-state tuition: full time: N/A; part time: $470/credit hour
Out-of-state tuition: full time: N/A
Room/board/expenses: N/A
College-funded aid: Yes
International student aid: Yes
Full-time enrollment: N/A
men: N/A; women: N/A; minorities: N/A; international: N/A
Part-time enrollment: 111
men: 66%; women: 34%;
minorities: 16%; international: 0%
Average GMAT (part time): 526
TOEFL requirement: Yes
Minimum TOEFL score: 550
Most popular departments: entrepreneurship, general management

Widener University

1 University Place
Chester, PA 19013
www.widener.edu/sba
Private
Admissions: (610) 499-4305
Email: sbagradv@mail.widener.edu
Financial aid: (610) 499-4174
Application deadline: rolling
Tuition: full time: $984/credit hour; part time: $984/credit hour
Room/board/expenses: N/A
College-funded aid: Yes
International student aid: Yes

Full-time enrollment: 48
men: 67%; women: 33%;
minorities: 15%; international: 48%
Part-time enrollment: 80
men: 53%; women: 48%;
minorities: 23%; international: 6%
TOEFL requirement: Yes
Minimum TOEFL score: N/A

RHODE ISLAND

Bryant University

1150 Douglas Pike
Smithfield, RI 02917
www.bryant.edu/
Private
Admissions: (401) 232-6230
Email: gradprog@bryant.edu
Financial aid: (401) 232-6020
Application deadline: 04/15
Tuition: full time: $1,118/credit hour; part time: $1,118/credit hour
Room/board/expenses: $17,400
College-funded aid: Yes
International student aid: Yes
Average student indebtedness at graduation: $34,935
Full-time enrollment: 35
men: 63%; women: 37%;
minorities: 11%; international: 26%
Part-time enrollment: 52
men: 69%; women: 31%;
minorities: 13%; international: 2%
Acceptance rate (full time): 65%
Average GMAT (full time): 481
Average GMAT (part time): 474
Average GPA (full time): 3.39
Average age of entrants to full-time program: 23
TOEFL requirement: Yes
Minimum TOEFL score: N/A
Most popular departments: finance, general management, international business, supply chain management, other
Mean starting base salary for 2015 full-time graduates: $54,000
Employment location for 2015 class: Intl. 7%; N.E. 93%; M.A. N/A; S. N/A; M.W. N/A; S.W. N/A; W. N/A

Providence College

One Cunningham Square
Providence, RI 02918
providence.edu/mba
Private
Admissions: (401) 865-2294
Email: mba@providence.edu
Financial aid: (401) 865-2286
Application deadline: 07/01
Tuition: full time: $10,800; part time: $7,200
Room/board/expenses: $11,600
College-funded aid: Yes
International student aid: No
Full-time enrollment: N/A
men: N/A; women: N/A; minorities: N/A; international: N/A
Part-time enrollment: 134
men: 57%; women: 43%;
minorities: 6%; international: 3%
Average GMAT (part time): 524
TOEFL requirement: Yes
Minimum TOEFL score: 577
Most popular departments: accounting, finance, general management, international business, marketing

University of Rhode Island[1]

7 Lippitt Road
Kingston, RI 02881
web.uri.edu/business/
Public
Admissions: (401) 874-2842
Email: gradadm@etal.uri.edu
Financial aid: N/A
Tuition: N/A
Room/board/expenses: N/A
Enrollment: N/A

SOUTH CAROLINA

The Citadel

171 Moultrie Street
Charleston, SC 29409
www.citadel.edu/csba/
Public
Admissions: (843) 953-5089
Email: cgc@citadel.edu
Financial aid: (843) 953-5187
Application deadline: rolling
In-state tuition: full time: $551/
credit hour; part time: $551/
credit hour
Out-of-state tuition: full time: $927/
credit hour
Room/board/expenses: $22,804
College-funded aid: Yes
International student aid: Yes
**Average student indebtedness at
graduation:** $26,104
Full-time enrollment: 24
men: 83%; women: 17%;
minorities: 17%; international: 0%
Part-time enrollment: 179
men: 60%; women: 40%;
minorities: 10%; international: 1%
Average GMAT (full time): 485
Average GMAT (part time): 485
Average GPA (full time): 3.25
**Average age of entrants to full-time
program:** 24
TOEFL requirement: No
Minimum TOEFL score: N/A

Clemson University

55 East Camperdown Way
Greenville, SC 29601
www.clemson.edu/cbbs/
departments/mba
Public
Admissions: (864) 656-8173
Email: mba@clemson.edu
Financial aid: (864) 656-2280
Application deadline: 07/15
In-state tuition: full time: $18,666;
part time: $663/credit hour
Out-of-state tuition: full time:
$30,672
Room/board/expenses: $13,500
College-funded aid: Yes
International student aid: Yes
Full-time enrollment: 136
men: 67%; women: 33%;
minorities: 33%; international:
22%
Part-time enrollment: 281
men: 68%; women: 32%;
minorities: 21%; international: 3%
Acceptance rate (full time): 65%
Average GMAT (full time): 579
Average GMAT (part time): 606
Average GPA (full time): 3.32
**Average age of entrants to full-time
program:** 27
**Average months of prior work
experience (full time):** 51
TOEFL requirement: Yes
Minimum TOEFL score: N/A

Coastal Carolina University

PO Box 261954
Conway, SC 29528-6054
www.coastal.edu/admissions
Public
Admissions: (843) 349-2026
Email: admissions@coastal.edu
Financial aid: (843) 349-2313
Application deadline: 06/15
In-state tuition: full time: $16,410;
part time: $533/credit hour
Out-of-state tuition: full time:
$29,520
Room/board/expenses: $5,030
College-funded aid: Yes
International student aid: Yes
**Average student indebtedness at
graduation:** $23,063
Full-time enrollment: 56
men: 66%; women: 34%;
minorities: 18%; international: 18%
Part-time enrollment: 34
men: 59%; women: 41%;
minorities: 21%; international: 0%
Acceptance rate (full time): 84%
Average GMAT (full time): 505
Average GPA (full time): 3.38
**Average age of entrants to full-time
program:** 25
TOEFL requirement: Yes
Minimum TOEFL score: 550
Employment location for 2015 class:
Intl. 3%; N.E. 5%; M.A. 5%; S.
87%; M.W. N/A; S.W. N/A; W. N/A

College of Charleston

66 George St.
Charleston, SC 29424
www.mbacharleston.com/
Public
Admissions: (843) 953-8112
Email: mba@cofc.edu
Financial aid: (843) 953-5540
Application deadline: 05/01
In-state tuition: total program:
$25,650 (full time); part time:
$500/credit hour
Out-of-state tuition: total program:
$25,650 (full time)
Room/board/expenses: $15,534
College-funded aid: Yes
International student aid: Yes
**Average student indebtedness at
graduation:** $21,547
Full-time enrollment: 50
men: 54%; women: 46%;
minorities: 12%; international: 4%
Part-time enrollment: N/A
men: N/A; women: N/A; minorities:
N/A; international: N/A
Acceptance rate (full time): 62%
Average GMAT (full time): 555
Average GPA (full time): 3.26
**Average age of entrants to full-time
program:** 25
**Average months of prior work
experience (full time):** 39
TOEFL requirement: Yes
Minimum TOEFL score: N/A
**Mean starting base salary for 2015
full-time graduates:** $52,634
Employment location for 2015 class:
Intl. 0%; N.E. 0%; M.A. 11%; S.
67%; M.W. 11%; S.W. 6%; W. 6%

Francis Marion University

Box 100547
Florence, SC 29501
www.fmarion.edu/academics/
mba
Public
Admissions: (843) 661-1281
Email: graduate@fmarion.edu
Financial aid: N/A
Application deadline: rolling

In-state tuition: total program: N/A
(full time); $16,602 (part time)
Out-of-state tuition: full time: N/A
Room/board/expenses: N/A
College-funded aid: No
Full-time enrollment: N/A
men: N/A; women: N/A; minorities:
N/A; international: N/A
Part-time enrollment: 43
men: N/A; women: N/A; minorities:
N/A; international: N/A
Average GMAT (part time): 425
TOEFL requirement: Yes
Minimum TOEFL score: N/A

South Carolina State University

300 College Street NE
Orangeburg, SC 29117
www.scsu.edu/
schoolofgraduatestudies.aspx
Public
Admissions: (803) 536-7133
Email: graduateschool@scsu.edu
Financial aid: (803) 536-7067
Application deadline: rolling
In-state tuition: full time: $10,088;
part time: $560/credit hour
Out-of-state tuition: full time:
$19,856
Room/board/expenses: N/A
College-funded aid: Yes
International student aid: Yes
Full-time enrollment: 22
men: 41%; women: 59%;
minorities: 95%; international: 5%
Part-time enrollment: 4
men: 75%; women: 25%;
minorities: 100%; international:
0%
Acceptance rate (full time): 100%
**Average age of entrants to full-time
program:** 24
TOEFL requirement: Yes
Minimum TOEFL score: 550

University of South Carolina (Moore)

1014 Greene Street
Columbia, SC 29208
moore.sc.edu/
Public
Admissions: (803) 777-4346
Email: gradinfo@moore.sc.edu
Financial aid: (803) 777-8134
Application deadline: rolling
In-state tuition: total program:
$44,422 (full time); part time:
$690/credit hour
Out-of-state tuition: total program:
$72,860 (full time)
Room/board/expenses: $17,961
College-funded aid: Yes
International student aid: Yes
**Average student indebtedness at
graduation:** $36,537
Full-time enrollment: 73
men: 75%; women: 25%;
minorities: 14%; international: 18%
Part-time enrollment: 462
men: 74%; women: 26%;
minorities: 18%; international: 2%
Acceptance rate (full time): 53%
Average GMAT (full time): 669
Average GMAT (part time): 619
Average GPA (full time): 3.23
**Average age of entrants to full-time
program:** 28
**Average months of prior work
experience (full time):** 53
TOEFL requirement: Yes
Minimum TOEFL score: 600
**Mean starting base salary for 2015
full-time graduates:** $85,708

Employment location for 2015 class:
Intl. 0%; N.E. 12%; M.A. 4%; S.
38%; M.W. 12%; S.W. 8%; W. 27%

Winthrop University

Thurmond Building
Rock Hill, SC 29733
www.winthrop.edu/cba
Public
Admissions: (803) 323-2204
Email: gradschool@winthrop.edu
Financial aid: N/A
Application deadline: 07/15
In-state tuition: full time: N/A; part
time: N/A
Out-of-state tuition: full time: N/A
Room/board/expenses: N/A
Full-time enrollment: N/A
men: N/A; women: N/A; minorities:
N/A; international: N/A
Part-time enrollment: 171
men: 44%; women: 56%;
minorities: N/A; international: N/A
Minimum TOEFL score: N/A

SOUTH DAKOTA

Black Hills State University

1200 University Street
Spearfish, SD 57799
www.bhsu.edu/
Public
Admissions: (800) 255-2478
Email: BHSUGraduateStudies@
bhsu.edu
Financial aid: N/A
Application deadline: rolling
In-state tuition: full time: N/A; part
time: N/A
Out-of-state tuition: full time: N/A
Room/board/expenses: N/A
College-funded aid: Yes
International student aid: Yes
Full-time enrollment: N/A
men: N/A; women: N/A; minorities:
N/A; international: N/A
Part-time enrollment: 17
men: 47%; women: 53%;
minorities: N/A; international: 12%
TOEFL requirement: Yes
Minimum TOEFL score: 500

University of South Dakota

414 E. Clark Street
Vermillion, SD 57069
www.usd.edu/mba
Public
Admissions: (605) 677-5232
Email: mba@usd.edu
Financial aid: (605) 677-5446
Application deadline: 06/01
In-state tuition: full time: $219/
credit hour; part time: $431/
credit hour
Out-of-state tuition: full time: $464/
credit hour
Room/board/expenses: N/A
College-funded aid: Yes
International student aid: Yes
**Average student indebtedness at
graduation:** $20,632
Full-time enrollment: 25
men: 68%; women: 32%;
minorities: 8%; international: 4%
Part-time enrollment: 261
men: 71%; women: 29%;
minorities: 6%; international: 8%
Acceptance rate (full time): 93%
Average GMAT (full time): 522
Average GMAT (part time): 552
Average GPA (full time): 3.37
**Average age of entrants to full-time
program:** 23

**Average months of prior work
experience (full time):** 8
TOEFL requirement: Yes
Minimum TOEFL score: 550
Most popular departments:
general management, health care
administration, other
Employment location for 2015 class:
Intl. N/A; N.E. N/A; M.A. N/A; S.
N/A; M.W. 88%; S.W. 13%; W. N/A

TENNESSEE

Belmont University (Massey)

1900 Belmont Boulevard
Nashville, TN 37212
www.belmont.edu/business/
graduatebusiness
Private
Admissions: (615) 460-6480
Email: masseyadmissions@
belmont.edu
Financial aid: (615) 460-6403
Application deadline: 06/01
Tuition: total program: $52,330
(full time); $52,330 (part time)
Room/board/expenses: N/A
College-funded aid: Yes
International student aid: Yes
Full-time enrollment: 24
men: 54%; women: 46%;
minorities: 21%; international: 4%
Part-time enrollment: 119
men: 58%; women: 42%;
minorities: 13%; international: 5%
Acceptance rate (full time): 92%
Average GMAT (full time): 526
Average GMAT (part time): 525
Average GPA (full time): 3.51
**Average age of entrants to full-time
program:** 23
TOEFL requirement: Yes
Minimum TOEFL score: 550
Most popular departments:
entrepreneurship, finance,
general management, health care
administration, marketing
**Mean starting base salary for 2015
full-time graduates:** $45,572
Employment location for 2015 class:
Intl. N/A; N.E. N/A; M.A. N/A; S.
92%; M.W. 8%; S.W. N/A; W. N/A

East Tennessee State University[1]

PO Box 70699
Johnson City, TN 37614
www.etsu.edu/cbat
Public
Admissions: (423) 439-5314
Email: business@etsu.edu
Financial aid: N/A
Tuition: N/A
Room/board/expenses: N/A
Enrollment: N/A

Middle Tennessee State University[1]

PO Box 290
Murfreesboro, TN 37132
www.mtsu.edu
Public
Admissions: (615) 898-2840
Email: graduate@mtsu.edu
Financial aid: N/A
Tuition: N/A
Room/board/expenses: N/A
Enrollment: N/A

Tennessee State University[1]

330 N. 10th Avenue
Nashville, TN 37203
www.tnstate.edu/business
Public
Admissions: (615) 963-5145
Email: cobinfo@tnstate.edu
Financial aid: N/A
Tuition: N/A
Room/board/expenses: N/A
Enrollment: N/A

Tennessee Technological University

Box 5023
Cookeville, TN 38505
www.tntech.edu/mba
Public
Admissions: (931) 372-3600
Email: mbastudies@tntech.edu
Financial aid: (931) 372-3073
Application deadline: 07/01
In-state tuition: full time: $447/
credit hour; part time: $447/
credit hour
Out-of-state tuition: full time: $706/
credit hour
Room/board/expenses: $25,600
College-funded aid: Yes
International student aid: Yes
**Average student indebtedness at
graduation:** $9,294
Full-time enrollment: 47
men: 62%; women: 38%;
minorities: 13%; international: 11%
Part-time enrollment: 165
men: 63%; women: 37%;
minorities: 4%; international: 2%
Acceptance rate (full time): 54%
Average GMAT (full time): 516
Average GMAT (part time): 536
Average GPA (full time): 3.38
**Average age of entrants to full-time
program:** 24
TOEFL requirement: Yes
Minimum TOEFL score: 550
Most popular departments:
accounting, general management,
human resources management,
marketing, management
information systems

Union University[1]

1050 Union University Drive
Jackson, TN 38305
www.uu.edu/
Private
Admissions: N/A
Financial aid: N/A
Tuition: N/A
Room/board/expenses: N/A
Enrollment: N/A

University of Memphis (Fogelman)

3675 Central Avenue
Memphis, TN 38152
fcbe.memphis.edu/
Public
Admissions: (901) 678-3721
Email: krishnan@memphis.edu
Financial aid: (901) 678-4825
Application deadline: rolling
In-state tuition: full time: $479/
credit hour; part time: $479/
credit hour
Out-of-state tuition: full time: $967/
credit hour
Room/board/expenses: N/A
College-funded aid: Yes
International student aid: Yes
**Average student indebtedness at
graduation:** $33,248

Full-time enrollment: 54
men: 48%; women: 52%;
minorities: 9%; international: 39%
Part-time enrollment: 127
men: 69%; women: 31%;
minorities: 33%; international: 5%
Acceptance rate (full time): 58%
Average GMAT (full time): 544
Average GMAT (part time): 543
Average GPA (full time): 3.38
**Average age of entrants to full-time
program:** 28
**Average months of prior work
experience (full time):** 15
TOEFL requirement: Yes
Minimum TOEFL score: 550

University of Tennessee-Chattanooga

615 McCallie Avenue
Chattanooga, TN 37403
www.utc.edu/Academic/
Business/
Public
Admissions: (423) 425-4666
Email: bonny-clark@utc.edu
Financial aid: (423) 425-4677
Application deadline: rolling
In-state tuition: full time: N/A; part
time: $441/credit hour
Out-of-state tuition: full time: N/A
Room/board/expenses: N/A
College-funded aid: Yes
International student aid: No
Full-time enrollment: N/A
men: N/A; women: N/A; minorities:
N/A; international: N/A
Part-time enrollment: 276
men: 58%; women: 42%;
minorities: 17%; international: 2%
Average GMAT (part time): 484
TOEFL requirement: Yes
Minimum TOEFL score: 550
Most popular departments:
accounting, finance, general
management, human resources
management, marketing

University of Tennessee-Knoxville

504 Haslam Business Building
Knoxville, TN 37996-4150
mba.utk.edu
Public
Admissions: (865) 974-5033
Email: mba@utk.edu
Financial aid: (865) 974-3131
Application deadline: 02/01
In-state tuition: full time: $24,356;
part time: N/A
Out-of-state tuition: full time:
$42,774
Room/board/expenses: $16,000
College-funded aid: Yes
International student aid: Yes
**Average student indebtedness at
graduation:** $38,294
Full-time enrollment: 144
men: 80%; women: 20%;
minorities: 8%; international: 22%
Part-time enrollment: N/A
men: N/A; women: N/A; minorities:
N/A; international: N/A
Acceptance rate (full time): 50%
Average GMAT (full time): 616
Average GPA (full time): 3.42
**Average age of entrants to full-time
program:** 27
**Average months of prior work
experience (full time):** 51
TOEFL requirement: Yes
Minimum TOEFL score: 600
**Mean starting base salary for 2015
full-time graduates:** $79,407

Employment location for 2015 class:
Intl. N/A; N.E. 4%; M.A. 2%; S.
67%; M.W. 16%; S.W. 9%; W. 2%

University of Tennessee-Martin

103 Business Administration
Building
Martin, TN 38238
www.utm.edu/departments/
cbga/mba
Public
Admissions: (731) 881-7012
Email: jcunningham@utm.edu
Financial aid: (731) 881-7040
Application deadline: rolling
In-state tuition: full time: $538/
credit hour; part time: $538/
credit hour
Out-of-state tuition: full time:
$1,313/credit hour
Room/board/expenses: N/A
College-funded aid: Yes
International student aid: Yes
Full-time enrollment: 13
men: 54%; women: 46%;
minorities: 8%; international: 31%
Part-time enrollment: 14
men: 79%; women: 21%;
minorities: 7%; international: 0%
Acceptance rate (full time): 68%
Average GMAT (full time): 440
Average GMAT (part time): 470
Average GPA (full time): 3.19
**Average age of entrants to full-time
program:** 25
**Average months of prior work
experience (full time):** 14
TOEFL requirement: Yes
Minimum TOEFL score: 525
Most popular departments: other

Vanderbilt University (Owen)

401 21st Avenue S
Nashville, TN 37203
www.owen.vanderbilt.edu
Private
Admissions: (615) 322-6469
Email: mba@owen.vanderbilt.edu
Financial aid: (615) 322-3591
Application deadline: 05/03
Tuition: full time: $50,380; part
time: N/A
Room/board/expenses: $24,910
College-funded aid: Yes
International student aid: Yes
**Average student indebtedness at
graduation:** $76,448
Full-time enrollment: 346
men: 72%; women: 28%;
minorities: 11%; international: 18%
Part-time enrollment: N/A
men: N/A; women: N/A; minorities:
N/A; international: N/A
Acceptance rate (full time): 42%
Average GMAT (full time): 690
Average GPA (full time): 3.36
**Average age of entrants to full-time
program:** 28
**Average months of prior work
experience (full time):** 64
TOEFL requirement: Yes
Minimum TOEFL score: N/A
Most popular departments: finance,
health care administration,
marketing, operations
management, organizational
behavior
**Mean starting base salary for 2015
full-time graduates:** $108,255
Employment location for 2015 class:
Intl. 2%; N.E. 13%; M.A. 2%; S.
49%; M.W. 10%; S.W. 9%; W. 15%

Abilene Christian University[1]

ACU Box 29300
Abilene, TX 79699-9300
www.acu.edu/academics/coba/
index.html
Private
Admissions: (800) 460-6228
Email: info@admissions.acu.edu
Financial aid: N/A
Tuition: N/A
Room/board/expenses: N/A
Enrollment: N/A

Baylor University (Hankamer)

1 Bear Place #98013
Waco, TX 76798-8013
www.baylor.edu/mba
Private
Admissions: (254) 710-3718
Email: mba_info@baylor.edu
Financial aid: (254) 710-2611
Application deadline: 06/15
Tuition: full time: $40,598; part
time: N/A
Room/board/expenses: $19,900
College-funded aid: Yes
International student aid: Yes
**Average student indebtedness at
graduation:** $19,300
Full-time enrollment: 96
men: 68%; women: 32%;
minorities: 17%; international: 11%
Part-time enrollment: N/A
men: N/A; women: N/A; minorities:
N/A; international: N/A
Acceptance rate (full time): 36%
Average GMAT (full time): 634
Average GPA (full time): 3.32
**Average age of entrants to full-time
program:** 26
**Average months of prior work
experience (full time):** 33
TOEFL requirement: Yes
Minimum TOEFL score: 600
**Mean starting base salary for 2015
full-time graduates:** $77,900
Employment location for 2015 class:
Intl. N/A; N.E. N/A; M.A. N/A; S.
5%; M.W. N/A; S.W. 90%; W. 5%

Lamar University

4400 Martin Luther King
Parkway
Beaumont, TX 77710
mba.lamar.edu
Public
Admissions: (409) 880-8888
Email: gradmissions@lamar.edu
Financial aid: (409) 880-8450
Application deadline: 07/01
In-state tuition: full time: $13,365;
part time: $10,395
Out-of-state tuition: full time:
$23,895
Room/board/expenses: N/A
College-funded aid: Yes
International student aid: Yes
**Average student indebtedness at
graduation:** $18,999
Full-time enrollment: 152
men: 49%; women: 51%;
minorities: 26%; international:
30%
Part-time enrollment: N/A
men: N/A; women: N/A; minorities:
N/A; international: N/A
Acceptance rate (full time): 54%
Average GMAT (full time): 465
Average GPA (full time): 3.29
**Average age of entrants to full-time
program:** 35
TOEFL requirement: Yes
Minimum TOEFL score: 550

Employment location for 2015 class:
Intl. 7%; N.E. N/A; M.A. N/A; S. N/A;
M.W. N/A; S.W. 93%; W. N/A

Midwestern State University[1]

3410 Taft Boulevard
Wichita Falls, TX 76308
www.mwsu.edu
Public
Admissions: N/A
Financial aid: N/A
Tuition: N/A
Room/board/expenses: N/A
Enrollment: N/A

Prairie View A&M University

PO Box 519; MS 2300
Prairie View, TX 77446
pvamu.edu/business
Public
Admissions: (936) 261-9215
Email: mba@pvamu.edu
Financial aid: N/A
Application deadline: rolling
In-state tuition: full time: $261/
credit hour; part time: $261/
credit hour
Out-of-state tuition: full time: $680/
credit hour
Room/board/expenses: $13,801
College-funded aid: Yes
International student aid: Yes
Full-time enrollment: 79
men: 44%; women: 56%;
minorities: 80%; international:
14%
Part-time enrollment: 170
men: 43%; women: 57%;
minorities: 95%; international: 1%
Acceptance rate (full time): 73%
Average GPA (full time): 3.00
**Average age of entrants to full-time
program:** 29
TOEFL requirement: Yes
Minimum TOEFL score: 500
Most popular departments:
accounting, finance, general
management, international
business, management
information systems

Rice University (Jones)

PO Box 2932
Houston, TX 77252-2932
business.rice.edu
Private
Admissions: (713) 348-4918
Email: ricemba@rice.edu
Financial aid: (713) 348-4958
Application deadline: rolling
Tuition: full time: $54,493; part
time: $98,593
Room/board/expenses: $24,490
College-funded aid: Yes
International student aid: Yes
**Average student indebtedness at
graduation:** $55,156
Full-time enrollment: 225
men: 66%; women: 34%;
minorities: 39%; international:
28%
Part-time enrollment: 292
men: 78%; women: 22%;
minorities: 20%; international:
10%
Acceptance rate (full time): 27%
Average GMAT (full time): 690
Average GMAT (part time): 629
Average GPA (full time): 3.30
**Average age of entrants to full-time
program:** 28
**Average months of prior work
experience (full time):** 63
TOEFL requirement: Yes
Minimum TOEFL score: N/A

Most popular departments: consulting, entrepreneurship, finance, general management, other
Mean starting base salary for 2015 full-time graduates: $111,433
Employment location for 2015 class: Intl. 1%; N.E. 6%; M.A. 0%; S. 6%; M.W. 0%; S.W. 80%; W. 7%

Sam Houston State University

PO Box 2056
Huntsville, TX 77341
coba.shsu.edu/
Public
Admissions: (936) 294-1246
Email: busgrad@shsu.edu
Financial aid: (936) 294-1724
Application deadline: 08/01
In-state tuition: full time: $286/credit hour; part time: $286/credit hour
Out-of-state tuition: full time: $676/credit hour
Room/board/expenses: $11,344
College-funded aid: Yes
International student aid: Yes
Average student indebtedness at graduation: $22,941
Full-time enrollment: 81
men: 43%; women: 57%; minorities: 31%; international: 14%
Part-time enrollment: 224
men: 61%; women: 39%; minorities: 33%; international: 1%
Acceptance rate (full time): 71%
Average GMAT (full time): 496
Average GMAT (part time): 525
Average GPA (full time): 3.55
Average age of entrants to full-time program: 79
Average months of prior work experience (full time): 79
TOEFL requirement: Yes
Minimum TOEFL score: 550
Most popular departments: economics, finance, general management

Southern Methodist University (Cox)

PO Box 750333
Dallas, TX 75275-0333
www.coxmba.com
Private
Admissions: (214) 768-1214
Email: mbainfo@cox.smu.edu
Financial aid: (214) 768-2371
Application deadline: 05/02
Tuition: full time: $51,395; part time: $46,316
Room/board/expenses: $19,664
College-funded aid: Yes
International student aid: Yes
Full-time enrollment: 206
men: 67%; women: 33%; minorities: 10%; international: 28%
Part-time enrollment: 243
men: 72%; women: 28%; minorities: 26%; international: 5%
Acceptance rate (full time): 36%
Average GMAT (full time): 656
Average GMAT (part time): 590
Average GPA (full time): 3.40
Average age of entrants to full-time program: 28
Average months of prior work experience (full time): 54
TOEFL requirement: Yes
Minimum TOEFL score: 600
Most popular departments: entrepreneurship, finance, marketing, real estate, other
Mean starting base salary for 2015 full-time graduates: $100,304

Employment location for 2015 class: Intl. 1%; N.E. 2%; M.A. 1%; S. 34%; M.W. 2%; S.W. 48%; W. 11%

Stephen F. Austin State University[1]

PO Box 13004, SFA Station
Nacogdoches, TX 75962-3004
www.sfasu.edu/cob/
Public
Admissions: (936) 468-2807
Email: gschool@titan.sfasu.edu
Financial aid: N/A
Tuition: N/A
Room/board/expenses: N/A
Enrollment: N/A

St. Mary's University (Greehey)

1 Camino Santa Maria
San Antonio, TX 78228-8607
www.stmarytx.edu/mba
Private
Admissions: (210) 436-3708
Email: ebroughton@stmarytx.edu
Financial aid: (210) 436-3141
Application deadline: rolling
Tuition: full time: $830/credit hour; part time: $830/credit hour
Room/board/expenses: $19,774
College-funded aid: Yes
International student aid: Yes
Full-time enrollment: 50
men: 70%; women: 30%; minorities: 30%; international: 10%
Part-time enrollment: 3
men: 67%; women: 33%; minorities: 33%; international: 0%
Acceptance rate (full time): 57%
Average GMAT (full time): 543
Average GPA (full time): 3.08
Average age of entrants to full-time program: 28
TOEFL requirement: Yes
Minimum TOEFL score: N/A

Texas A&M International University

5201 University Boulevard
Western Hemispheric Trade Center, Suite 203
Laredo, TX 78041-1900
www.tamiu.edu
Public
Admissions: (956) 326-3020
Email: GraduateSchool@tamiu.edu
Financial aid: (956) 326-2225
Application deadline: 04/30
In-state tuition: full time: $77/credit hour; part time: $77/credit hour
Out-of-state tuition: full time: $467/credit hour
Room/board/expenses: $12,162
College-funded aid: Yes
International student aid: Yes
Average student indebtedness at graduation: $15,835
Full-time enrollment: 110
men: 68%; women: 32%; minorities: 32%; international: 68%
Part-time enrollment: 170
men: 59%; women: 41%; minorities: 75%; international: 23%
Acceptance rate (full time): 99%
Average GMAT (full time): 398
Average GMAT (part time): 310
Average GPA (full time): 3.20
Average age of entrants to full-time program: 25
Average months of prior work experience (full time): 36
TOEFL requirement: Yes

Minimum TOEFL score: 550
Most popular departments: accounting, finance, general management, international business, management information systems

Texas A&M University-College Station (Mays)

4117 TAMU
390 Wehner Building
College Station, TX 77843-4117
ftmba.tamu.edu
Public
Admissions: (979) 845-4714
Email: ftmba@tamu.edu
Financial aid: (979) 845-3236
Application deadline: 04/15
In-state tuition: full time: $27,100; part time: $59,000
Out-of-state tuition: full time: $40,416
Room/board/expenses: $19,944
College-funded aid: Yes
International student aid: Yes
Average student indebtedness at graduation: $42,833
Full-time enrollment: 123
men: 73%; women: 27%; minorities: 15%; international: 39%
Part-time enrollment: 98
men: 73%; women: 27%; minorities: 20%; international: 7%
Acceptance rate (full time): 24%
Average GMAT (full time): 654
Average GMAT (part time): 609
Average GPA (full time): 3.50
Average age of entrants to full-time program: 28
Average months of prior work experience (full time): 64
TOEFL requirement: Yes
Minimum TOEFL score: 600
Mean starting base salary for 2015 full-time graduates: $100,675
Employment location for 2015 class: Intl. 2%; N.E. 4%; M.A. N/A; S. 2%; M.W. N/A; S.W. 82%; W. 9%

Texas A&M University-Commerce[1]

PO Box 3011
Commerce, TX 75429-3011
www.tamuc.edu
Public
Admissions: N/A
Financial aid: N/A
Tuition: N/A
Room/board/expenses: N/A
Enrollment: N/A

Texas A&M University-Corpus Christi

6300 Ocean Drive
Corpus Christi, TX 78412-5807
www.cob.tamucc.edu/prstudents/graduate.html
Public
Admissions: (361) 825-2177
Email: maria.martinez@tamucc.edu
Financial aid: (361) 825-2338
Application deadline: 07/15
In-state tuition: full time: $208/credit hour; part time: $213/credit hour
Out-of-state tuition: full time: $598/credit hour
Room/board/expenses: N/A
College-funded aid: Yes
International student aid: Yes

Full-time enrollment: N/A
men: N/A; women: N/A; minorities: N/A; international: N/A
Part-time enrollment: 471
men: N/A; women: N/A; minorities: N/A; international: N/A
TOEFL requirement: Yes
Minimum TOEFL score: 550
Most popular departments: finance, health care administration, international business

Texas Christian University (Neeley)

PO Box 298540
Fort Worth, TX 76129
www.mba.tcu.edu
Private
Admissions: (817) 257-7531
Email: mbainfo@tcu.edu
Financial aid: (817) 257-7531
Application deadline: 11/01
Tuition: full time: $48,850; part time: $31,870
Room/board/expenses: $13,000
College-funded aid: Yes
International student aid: Yes
Average student indebtedness at graduation: $48,048
Full-time enrollment: 88
men: 75%; women: 25%; minorities: 13%; international: 22%
Part-time enrollment: 177
men: 72%; women: 28%; minorities: 14%; international: 2%
Acceptance rate (full time): 54%
Average GMAT (full time): 642
Average GMAT (part time): 550
Average GPA (full time): 3.26
Average age of entrants to full-time program: 28
Average months of prior work experience (full time): 57
TOEFL requirement: Yes
Minimum TOEFL score: N/A
Mean starting base salary for 2015 full-time graduates: $89,579
Employment location for 2015 class: Intl. 0%; N.E. 3%; M.A. 3%; S. 3%; M.W. 3%; S.W. 88%; W. 3%

Texas Southern University (Jones)

3100 Cleburne Avenue
Houston, TX 77004
www.tsu.edu/academics/colleges_schools/Jesse_H_Jones_School_of_Business/
Public
Admissions: (713) 313-7590
Email: haidern@tsu.edu
Financial aid: (713) 313-7480
Application deadline: 07/15
In-state tuition: full time: $7,391; part time: $5,174
Out-of-state tuition: full time: $13,511
Room/board/expenses: N/A
College-funded aid: Yes
International student aid: Yes
Full-time enrollment: 222
men: 52%; women: 48%; minorities: 68%; international: 7%
Part-time enrollment: N/A
men: N/A; women: N/A; minorities: N/A; international: N/A
Acceptance rate (full time): 61%
Average GMAT (full time): 346
Average GPA (full time): 3.01
Average age of entrants to full-time program: 29
Average months of prior work experience (full time): 85
TOEFL requirement: Yes
Minimum TOEFL score: 550

Most popular departments: accounting, general management, health care administration, management information systems, other

Texas State University (McCoy)

601 University Drive
San Marcos, TX 78666-4616
www.txstate.edu
Public
Admissions: (512) 245-3591
Email: gradcollege@txstate.edu
Financial aid: (512) 245-2315
Application deadline: 06/01
In-state tuition: total program: $16,649 (full time); $16,649 (part time)
Out-of-state tuition: total program: $33,027 (full time)
Room/board/expenses: N/A
College-funded aid: Yes
International student aid: Yes
Full-time enrollment: 17
men: 47%; women: 53%; minorities: 47%; international: 12%
Part-time enrollment: 271
men: 59%; women: 41%; minorities: 35%; international: 7%
Acceptance rate (full time): 52%
Average GMAT (full time): 539
Average GMAT (part time): 520
Average GPA (full time): 3.33
Average age of entrants to full-time program: 26
Average months of prior work experience (full time): 55
TOEFL requirement: Yes
Minimum TOEFL score: N/A
Most popular departments: general management, health care administration, human resources management, international business, manufacturing and technology management

Texas Tech University (Rawls)

PO Box 42101
Lubbock, TX 79409-2101
texastechmba.com
Public
Admissions: (806) 742-3184
Email: rawls.mba@ttu.edu
Financial aid: (806) 742-0454
Application deadline: 07/01
In-state tuition: full time: $269/credit hour; part time: $269/credit hour
Out-of-state tuition: full time: $625/credit hour
Room/board/expenses: N/A
College-funded aid: Yes
International student aid: Yes
Full-time enrollment: 193
men: 68%; women: 32%; minorities: 41%; international: 6%
Part-time enrollment: N/A
men: N/A; women: N/A; minorities: N/A; international: N/A
Acceptance rate (full time): 69%
Average GMAT (full time): 583
Average GPA (full time): 3.44
Average age of entrants to full-time program: 25
TOEFL requirement: Yes
Minimum TOEFL score: 550
Most popular departments: general management, health care administration, other
Mean starting base salary for 2015 full-time graduates: $59,855
Employment location for 2015 class: Intl. N/A; N.E. N/A; M.A. N/A; S. 7%; M.W. N/A; S.W. 93%; W. N/A

Texas Wesleyan University

1201 Wesleyan Street
Fort Worth, TX 76105
https://txwes.edu/
Private
Admissions: (817) 531-4930
Email: graduate@txwes.edu
Financial aid: N/A
Application deadline: rolling
Tuition: full time: $742/credit hour;
part time: $742/credit hour
Room/board/expenses: $8,651
College-funded aid: No
Full-time enrollment: N/A
men: N/A; women: N/A; minorities:
N/A; international: N/A
Part-time enrollment: 44
men: 59%; women: 41%;
minorities: 75%; international:
70%
Average GMAT (part time): 446
TOEFL requirement: Yes
Minimum TOEFL score: 550
Most popular departments: general
management

University of Dallas

1845 East Northgate Drive
Irving, TX 75062
www.udallas.edu/cob/
Private
Admissions: N/A
Email: admiss@udallas.edu
Financial aid: N/A
Application deadline: rolling
Tuition: full time: N/A; part time:
$1,250/credit hour
Room/board/expenses: N/A
College-funded aid: Yes
International student aid: Yes
**Average student indebtedness at
graduation:** $45,845
Full-time enrollment: N/A
men: N/A; women: N/A; minorities:
N/A; international: N/A
Part-time enrollment: 735
men: 64%; women: 36%;
minorities: 43%; international:
28%
Average GMAT (part time): 473
TOEFL requirement: Yes
Minimum TOEFL score: N/A
Most popular departments:
accounting, finance, general
management, management
information systems, technology

University of Houston (Bauer)

334 Melcher Hall, Suite 330
Houston, TX 77204-6021
www.bauer.uh.edu/graduate
Public
Admissions: (713) 743-4638
Email: houstonmba@uh.edu
Financial aid: (713) 743-2062
Application deadline: 06/01
In-state tuition: full time: $23,604;
part time: $14,544
Out-of-state tuition: full time:
$38,304
Room/board/expenses: $17,860
College-funded aid: Yes
International student aid: Yes
Full-time enrollment: 82
men: 67%; women: 33%;
minorities: 23%; international:
38%
Part-time enrollment: 359
men: 72%; women: 28%;
minorities: 32%; international:
22%
Acceptance rate (full time): 35%
Average GMAT (full time): 605
Average GMAT (part time): 610
Average GPA (full time): 3.29

**Average age of entrants to full-time
program:** 27
**Average months of prior work
experience (full time):** 52
TOEFL requirement: Yes
Minimum TOEFL score: 603
**Mean starting base salary for 2015
full-time graduates:** $64,852
Employment location for 2015 class:
Intl. 4%; N.E. 0%; M.A. 4%; S. 0%;
M.W. 0%; S.W. 92%; W. 0%

University of Houston-Clear Lake

2700 Bay Area Boulevard
Box 71
Houston, TX 77058
www.uhcl.edu/admissions
Public
Admissions: (281) 283-2500
Email: admissions@uhcl.edu
Financial aid: (281) 283-2480
Application deadline: 08/01
In-state tuition: full time: N/A; part
time: $416/credit hour
Out-of-state tuition: full time: N/A
Room/board/expenses: N/A
College-funded aid: Yes
International student aid: Yes
Full-time enrollment: N/A
men: N/A; women: N/A; minorities:
N/A; international: N/A
Part-time enrollment: 248
men: 57%; women: 43%;
minorities: 33%; international:
13%
Average GMAT (part time): 507
TOEFL requirement: Yes
Minimum TOEFL score: 550
Most popular departments: finance,
human resources management,
international business,
manufacturing and technology
management, other

University of Houston-Downtown

One Main St.
Houston, TX 77002
www.uhd.edu/admissions/Pages/
admissions-index.aspx
Public
Admissions: (713) 221-8093
Email: gradadmission@uhd.edu
Financial aid: (713) 221-8041
Application deadline: 08/15
In-state tuition: full time: N/A; part
time: $428/credit hour
Out-of-state tuition: full time: N/A
Room/board/expenses: $18,602
College-funded aid: Yes
International student aid: Yes
Full-time enrollment: N/A
men: N/A; women: N/A; minorities:
N/A; international: N/A
Part-time enrollment: 765
men: 47%; women: 53%;
minorities: 76%; international: 4%
Average GMAT (part time): 423
TOEFL requirement: Yes
Minimum TOEFL score: 550
Most popular departments:
finance, general management,
human resources management,
leadership, supply chain
management

University of Houston-Victoria

University West Room 214,
3007 N. Ben Wilson
Victoria, TX 77901
www.uhv.edu/bus/default.asp
Public
Admissions: (361) 570-4110
Email: admissions@uhv.edu

Financial aid: (361) 570-4131
Application deadline: rolling
In-state tuition: full time: $310/
credit hour; part time: $310/
credit hour
Out-of-state tuition: full time: $700/
credit hour
Room/board/expenses: $8,000
College-funded aid: Yes
International student aid: No
**Average student indebtedness at
graduation:** $59,513
Full-time enrollment: 170
men: 45%; women: 55%;
minorities: 37%; international: 12%
Part-time enrollment: 453
men: 55%; women: 45%;
minorities: 38%; international: 8%
Acceptance rate (full time): 51%
Average GMAT (full time): 514
Average GMAT (part time): 459
**Average age of entrants to full-time
program:** 30
TOEFL requirement: Yes
Minimum TOEFL score: 550
Most popular departments:
accounting, entrepreneurship,
finance, general management,
international business

University of North Texas

1155 Union Circle #311160
Denton, TX 76203-5017
www.cob.unt.edu
Public
Admissions: (940) 369-8977
Email: mbacob@unt.edu
Financial aid: (940) 565-2302
Application deadline: 06/15
In-state tuition: full time: $303/
credit hour; part time: $303/
credit hour
Out-of-state tuition: full time: $693/
credit hour
Room/board/expenses: $14,865
College-funded aid: Yes
International student aid: Yes
**Average student indebtedness at
graduation:** $33,408
Full-time enrollment: 198
men: 61%; women: 39%;
minorities: 24%; international:
31%
Part-time enrollment: 316
men: 63%; women: 37%;
minorities: 23%; international: 9%
Acceptance rate (full time): 40%
Average GMAT (full time): 520
Average GMAT (part time): 522
Average GPA (full time): 3.30
**Average age of entrants to full-time
program:** 25
TOEFL requirement: Yes
Minimum TOEFL score: 550
Most popular departments:
accounting, finance, general
management, marketing,
organizational behavior

University of St. Thomas-Houston

3800 Montrose Blvd.
Houston, TX 77006
www.stthom.edu/bschool
Private
Admissions: (713) 525-2100
Email: cameron@stthom.edu
Financial aid: (713) 525-2170
Application deadline: 07/15
Tuition: full time: $1,119/credit
hour; part time: $1,119/credit hour
Room/board/expenses: N/A
College-funded aid: Yes
International student aid: Yes

Full-time enrollment: 224
men: 47%; women: 53%;
minorities: 44%; international:
27%
Part-time enrollment: N/A
men: N/A; women: N/A; minorities:
N/A; international: N/A
Acceptance rate (full time): 91%
Average GMAT (full time): 385
Average GPA (full time): 3.26
**Average age of entrants to full-time
program:** 30
TOEFL requirement: Yes
Minimum TOEFL score: N/A
Most popular departments:
finance, general management,
international business, marketing,
management information systems

University of Texas-Arlington

UTA Box 19377
Arlington, TX 76019-0376
wweb.uta.edu/business/gradbiz
Public
Admissions: (817) 272-3004
Financial aid: (817) 272-3561
Application deadline: rolling
In-state tuition: full time: $8,710;
part time: $6,210
Out-of-state tuition: full time:
$17,690
Room/board/expenses: $14,812
College-funded aid: Yes
International student aid: Yes
Full-time enrollment: N/A
men: N/A; women: N/A; minorities:
N/A; international: N/A
Part-time enrollment: 494
men: 56%; women: 44%;
minorities: 28%; international:
40%
Average GMAT (part time): 518
TOEFL requirement: Yes
Minimum TOEFL score: 550
Most popular departments:
accounting, general management,
health care administration,
human resources management,
management information systems

University of Texas-Austin (McCombs)

MBA Program
2110 Speedway, Stop B6004
Austin, TX 78712-1750
www.mccombs.utexas.edu/mba/
full-time
Public
Admissions: (512) 471-7698
Email: TexasMBA@
mccombs.utexas.edu
Financial aid: (512) 471-7698
Application deadline: 03/28
In-state tuition: full time: $33,298;
total program: $104,000 (part
time)
Out-of-state tuition: full time:
$48,832
Room/board/expenses: $19,394
College-funded aid: Yes
International student aid: Yes
**Average student indebtedness at
graduation:** $62,525
Full-time enrollment: 543
men: 68%; women: 32%;
minorities: 21%; international:
26%
Part-time enrollment: 436
men: 75%; women: 25%;
minorities: 35%; international: 9%
Acceptance rate (full time): 30%
Average GMAT (full time): 694
Average GMAT (part time): 630
Average GPA (full time): 3.40
**Average age of entrants to full-time
program:** 28

**Average months of prior work
experience (full time):** 67
TOEFL requirement: Yes
Minimum TOEFL score: 620
Most popular departments:
consulting, entrepreneurship,
finance, marketing, management
information systems
**Mean starting base salary for 2015
full-time graduates:** $113,787
Employment location for 2015 class:
Intl. 3%; N.E. 9%; M.A. 1%; S. 4%;
M.W. 6%; S.W. 64%; W. 13%

University of Texas-Dallas

800 W. Campbell Road SM 40
Richardson, TX 75080-3021
jindal.utdallas.edu/mba
Public
Admissions: (972) 883-6191
Email: mba@utdallas.edu
Financial aid: (972) 883-2941
Application deadline: 07/01
In-state tuition: full time: $15,242;
part time: $12,714
Out-of-state tuition: full time:
$30,855
Room/board/expenses: $15,000
College-funded aid: Yes
International student aid: Yes
Full-time enrollment: 123
men: 66%; women: 34%;
minorities: 20%; international:
43%
Part-time enrollment: 803
men: 64%; women: 36%;
minorities: 32%; international:
27%
Acceptance rate (full time): 22%
Average GMAT (full time): 678
Average GMAT (part time): 634
Average GPA (full time): 3.47
**Average age of entrants to full-time
program:** 29
**Average months of prior work
experience (full time):** 68
TOEFL requirement: Yes
Minimum TOEFL score: 550
Most popular departments:
accounting, finance,
manufacturing and technology
management, supply chain
management, statistics and
operations research
**Mean starting base salary for 2015
full-time graduates:** $82,551
Employment location for 2015 class:
Intl. 0%; N.E. 5%; M.A. 0%; S. 3%;
M.W. 0%; S.W. 90%; W. 3%

University of Texas-El Paso

500 W. University Avenue
El Paso, TX 79968
mba.utep.edu
Public
Admissions: (915) 747-7726
Email: mba@utep.edu
Financial aid: (915) 747-5204
Application deadline: rolling
In-state tuition: full time: $248/
credit hour; part time: N/A
Out-of-state tuition: full time: $645/
credit hour
Room/board/expenses: N/A
College-funded aid: Yes
International student aid: Yes
**Average student indebtedness at
graduation:** $32,659
Full-time enrollment: 179
men: 56%; women: 44%;
minorities: 69%; international:
17%
Part-time enrollment: 2
men: 100%; women: N/A;
minorities: 100%; international:
N/A

Acceptance rate (full time): 83%
Average GMAT (full time): 476
Average GPA (full time): 3.26
Average age of entrants to full-time program: 28
Average months of prior work experience (full time): 73
TOEFL requirement: Yes
Minimum TOEFL score: N/A
Most popular departments: finance, general management, human resources management, international business, marketing
Mean starting base salary for 2015 full-time graduates: $82,750
Employment location for 2015 class: Intl. N/A; N.E. N/A; M.A. 25%; S. 0%; M.W. 0%; S.W. 75%; W. N/A

University of Texas of the Permian Basin

4901 E. University
Odessa, TX 79762
www.utpb.edu/
Public
Admissions: N/A
Financial aid: N/A
Application deadline: 07/15
In-state tuition: full time: $168/credit hour; part time: $168/credit hour
Out-of-state tuition: full time: $203/credit hour
Room/board/expenses: $11,721
College-funded aid: Yes
International student aid: Yes
Full-time enrollment: 22
men: 55%; women: 45%;
minorities: 45%; international: 5%
Part-time enrollment: 64
men: 50%; women: 50%;
minorities: 61%; international: 0%
Average GMAT (full time): 460
Average GMAT (part time): 460
Average age of entrants to full-time program: 25
TOEFL requirement: Yes
Minimum TOEFL score: 550

University of Texas-Rio Grande Valley

1201 W University Dr
Edinburg, TX 78539
Public
Admissions: N/A
Financial aid: N/A
Application deadline: 07/01
In-state tuition: full time: $6,498; part time: $405/credit hour
Out-of-state tuition: full time: $13,518
Room/board/expenses: $10,814
College-funded aid: Yes
International student aid: Yes
Full-time enrollment: 94
men: 56%; women: 44%;
minorities: 54%; international: 33%
Part-time enrollment: 261
men: 56%; women: 44%;
minorities: 74%; international: 6%
TOEFL requirement: Yes
Minimum TOEFL score: 550
Most popular departments: accounting, finance, general management, marketing, management information systems

University of Texas-San Antonio

1 UTSA Circle
San Antonio, TX 78249
www.graduateschool.utsa.edu
Public
Admissions: (210) 458-4331

Email: graduateadmissions@utsa.edu
Financial aid: (210) 458-8000
Application deadline: 07/01
In-state tuition: full time: $310/credit hour; part time: $310/credit hour
Out-of-state tuition: full time: $1,107/credit hour
Room/board/expenses: $15,054
College-funded aid: Yes
International student aid: Yes
Full-time enrollment: 80
men: 60%; women: 40%;
minorities: 29%; international: 16%
Part-time enrollment: 156
men: 77%; women: 23%;
minorities: 35%; international: 1%
Acceptance rate (full time): 39%
Average GMAT (full time): 600
Average GMAT (part time): 571
Average GPA (full time): 3.10
Average age of entrants to full-time program: 29
Average months of prior work experience (full time): 79
TOEFL requirement: Yes
Minimum TOEFL score: 550
Most popular departments: finance, health care administration, marketing, statistics and operations research, other
Mean starting base salary for 2015 full-time graduates: $54,000
Employment location for 2015 class: Intl. 18%; N.E. 9%; M.A. N/A; S. N/A; M.W. N/A; S.W. 73%; W. N/A

University of Texas-Tyler[1]

3900 University Boulevard
Tyler, TX 75799
www.uttyler.edu/cbt/
Public
Admissions: (903) 566-7360
Email: cbtinfo@uttyler.edu
Financial aid: N/A
Tuition: N/A
Room/board/expenses: N/A
Enrollment: N/A

West Texas A&M University

WTAMU Box 60768
Canyon, TX 79016
www.wtamu.edu/academics/online-mba.aspx
Public
Admissions: (806) 651-2501
Email: lmills@wtamu.edu
Financial aid: (806) 651-2055
Application deadline: rolling
In-state tuition: total program: $13,200 (full time); $13,700 (part time)
Out-of-state tuition: total program: $15,200 (full time)
Room/board/expenses: $15,000
College-funded aid: Yes
International student aid: Yes
Average student indebtedness at graduation: $13,000
Full-time enrollment: 305
men: 54%; women: 46%;
minorities: 20%; international: 34%
Part-time enrollment: 645
men: 55%; women: 45%;
minorities: 48%; international: 0%
Acceptance rate (full time): 72%
Average GMAT (full time): 540
Average GMAT (part time): 530
Average GPA (full time): 3.52
Average age of entrants to full-time program: 25
Average months of prior work experience (full time): 18

TOEFL requirement: Yes
Minimum TOEFL score: 525
Most popular departments: accounting, finance, health care administration, marketing, management information systems
Mean starting base salary for 2015 full-time graduates: $60,000
Employment location for 2015 class: Intl. 14%; N.E. 3%; M.A. 3%; S. 5%; M.W. 11%; S.W. 52%; W. 11%

UTAH

Brigham Young University (Marriott)

W-437 TNRB
Provo, UT 84602
mba.byu.edu
Private
Admissions: (801) 422-3500
Email: mba@byu.edu
Financial aid: (801) 422-5195
Application deadline: 05/01
Tuition: full time: $11,970; part time: N/A
Room/board/expenses: $20,280
College-funded aid: Yes
International student aid: Yes
Average student indebtedness at graduation: $22,521
Full-time enrollment: 320
men: 81%; women: 19%;
minorities: 7%; international: 19%
Part-time enrollment: N/A
men: N/A; women: N/A; minorities: N/A; international: N/A
Acceptance rate (full time): 48%
Average GMAT (full time): 674
Average GPA (full time): 3.54
Average age of entrants to full-time program: 29
Average months of prior work experience (full time): 46
TOEFL requirement: Yes
Minimum TOEFL score: 590
Most popular departments: entrepreneurship, finance, human resources management, marketing, supply chain management
Mean starting base salary for 2015 full-time graduates: $102,793
Employment location for 2015 class: Intl. 0%; N.E. 10%; M.A. 5%; S. 5%; M.W. 20%; S.W. 16%; W. 44%

Southern Utah University

351 W. University Boulevard
Cedar City, UT 84720
www.suu.edu/business
Public
Admissions: (435) 586-5462
Financial aid: (435) 586-7735
Application deadline: 03/01
In-state tuition: total program: $13,206 (full time); part time: $393/credit hour
Out-of-state tuition: total program: $37,222 (full time)
Room/board/expenses: $9,900
College-funded aid: Yes
International student aid: No
Average student indebtedness at graduation: $17,520
Full-time enrollment: 42
men: 74%; women: 26%;
minorities: 17%; international: 7%
Part-time enrollment: 15
men: 60%; women: 40%;
minorities: N/A; international: N/A
Acceptance rate (full time): 97%
Average GMAT (full time): 475
Average GMAT (part time): 510
Average GPA (full time): 3.30
Average age of entrants to full-time program: 33

TOEFL requirement: Yes
Minimum TOEFL score: 525

University of Utah (Eccles)

1655 E. Campus Center Drive
Room 1113
Salt Lake City, UT 84112-9301
www.business.utah.edu
Public
Admissions: (801) 585-6291
Email: christine.harris@eccles.utah.edu
Financial aid: (801) 585-6291
Application deadline: 05/01
In-state tuition: total program: $51,850 (full time); $58,450 (part time)
Out-of-state tuition: total program: $96,850 (full time)
Room/board/expenses: $17,263
College-funded aid: Yes
International student aid: Yes
Average student indebtedness at graduation: $19,846
Full-time enrollment: 134
men: 78%; women: 22%;
minorities: 10%; international: 5%
Part-time enrollment: 313
men: 77%; women: 23%;
minorities: 8%; international: 0%
Acceptance rate (full time): 64%
Average GMAT (full time): 621
Average GMAT (part time): 550
Average GPA (full time): 3.44
Average age of entrants to full-time program: 27
Average months of prior work experience (full time): 35
TOEFL requirement: Yes
Minimum TOEFL score: N/A
Most popular departments: entrepreneurship, general management, health care administration, marketing, management information systems
Mean starting base salary for 2015 full-time graduates: $77,733
Employment location for 2015 class: Intl. 0%; N.E. 6%; M.A. 0%; S. 0%; M.W. 9%; S.W. 9%; W. 76%

Utah State University (Huntsman)[1]

3500 Old Main Hill
Logan, UT 84322-3500
www.huntsman.usu.edu/mba/
Public
Admissions: (435) 797-3624
Email: HuntsmanMBA@usu.edu
Financial aid: N/A
Tuition: N/A
Room/board/expenses: N/A
Enrollment: N/A

Utah Valley University

800 W. University Parkway
Orem, UT 84058
www.uvu.edu/woodbury
Public
Admissions: (801) 863-8367
Financial aid: N/A
Application deadline: 04/01
In-state tuition: total program: $22,330 (full time); $22,850 (part time)
Out-of-state tuition: total program: $45,050 (full time)
Room/board/expenses: N/A
College-funded aid: Yes
International student aid: Yes
Full-time enrollment: 37
men: 76%; women: 24%;
minorities: 22%; international: 14%

Part-time enrollment: 96
men: 81%; women: 19%;
minorities: 7%; international: 1%
Acceptance rate (full time): 85%
Average age of entrants to full-time program: 26
TOEFL requirement: Yes
Minimum TOEFL score: N/A

Weber State University (Goddard)

2750 N. University Park
Boulevard - MC102
Layton, UT 84041-9099
weber.edu/mba
Public
Admissions: (801) 395-3528
Email: mba@weber.edu
Financial aid: (801) 626-7569
Application deadline: N/A
In-state tuition: full time: N/A; part time: $656/credit hour
Out-of-state tuition: full time: N/A
Room/board/expenses: N/A
College-funded aid: Yes
International student aid: Yes
Full-time enrollment: N/A
men: N/A; women: N/A; minorities: N/A; international: N/A
Part-time enrollment: 149
men: 74%; women: 26%;
minorities: N/A; international: 3%
Average GMAT (part time): 563
TOEFL requirement: Yes
Minimum TOEFL score: N/A

VERMONT

University of Vermont

55 Colchester Avenue
Burlington, VT 05405
www.uvm.edu/business
Public
Admissions: (802) 656-0794
Email: mba@uvm.edu
Financial aid: N/A
Application deadline: 03/15
In-state tuition: total program: $29,850 (full time); part time: N/A
Out-of-state tuition: total program: $71,804 (full time)
Room/board/expenses: $16,055
College-funded aid: Yes
International student aid: Yes
Average student indebtedness at graduation: $45,051
Full-time enrollment: 16
men: 44%; women: 56%;
minorities: 19%; international: 0%
Part-time enrollment: N/A
men: N/A; women: N/A; minorities: N/A; international: N/A
Acceptance rate (full time): 87%
Average GMAT (full time): 544
Average GPA (full time): 3.20
Average age of entrants to full-time program: 28
Average months of prior work experience (full time): 68
TOEFL requirement: Yes
Minimum TOEFL score: 550
Most popular departments: entrepreneurship, other
Mean starting base salary for 2015 full-time graduates: $45,542
Employment location for 2015 class: Intl. 38%; N.E. 54%; M.A. N/A; S. N/A; M.W. N/A; S.W. N/A; W. 8%

VIRGINIA

College of William and Mary (Mason)
PO Box 8795
Williamsburg, VA 23187-8795
mason.wm.edu
Public
Admissions: (757) 221-2900
Email: admissions@mason.wm.edu
Financial aid: (757) 221-2944
Application deadline: 07/15
In-state tuition: full time: $31,226;
part time: $750/credit hour
Out-of-state tuition: full time:
$41,682
Room/board/expenses: $17,130
College-funded aid: Yes
International student aid: Yes
Average student indebtedness at graduation: $72,197
Full-time enrollment: 198
men: 69%; women: 31%;
minorities: 23%; international:
41%
Part-time enrollment: 178
men: 62%; women: 38%;
minorities: 27%; international: 1%
Acceptance rate (full time): 60%
Average GMAT (full time): 608
Average GMAT (part time): 584
Average GPA (full time): 3.20
Average age of entrants to full-time program: 28
Average months of prior work experience (full time): 56
TOEFL requirement: Yes
Minimum TOEFL score: N/A
Most popular departments:
entrepreneurship, finance,
general management, operations
management, real estate
Mean starting base salary for 2015 full-time graduates: $80,742
Employment location for 2015 class:
Intl. 16%; N.E. 11%; M.A. 47%; S.
5%; M.W. 8%; S.W. 5%; W. 8%

George Mason University
4400 University Drive
Fairfax, VA 22030
business.gmu.edu
Public
Admissions: (703) 993-2136
Email: mba@gmu.edu
Financial aid: (703) 993-2353
Application deadline: 06/01
In-state tuition: full time: $916/
credit hour; part time: $889/
credit hour
Out-of-state tuition: full time:
$1,663/credit hour
Room/board/expenses: N/A
College-funded aid: Yes
International student aid: Yes
Full-time enrollment: 38
men: 45%; women: 55%;
minorities: 29%; international:
26%
Part-time enrollment: 192
men: 61%; women: 39%;
minorities: 29%; international: 4%
Acceptance rate (full time): 51%
Average GMAT (part time): 570
Average GPA (full time): 3.39
Average age of entrants to full-time program: 24
Average months of prior work experience (full time): 6
TOEFL requirement: Yes
Minimum TOEFL score: N/A

James Madison University
Showker Hall
Harrisonburg, VA 22807
www.jmu.edu/cob/mba
Public
Admissions: (540) 568-3236
Email: busingme@jmu.edu
Financial aid: (540) 568-3139
Application deadline: 07/01
In-state tuition: full time: N/A; part
time: $500/credit hour
Out-of-state tuition: full time: N/A
Room/board/expenses: N/A
College-funded aid: Yes
International student aid: Yes
Full-time enrollment: N/A
men: N/A; women: N/A; minorities:
N/A; international: N/A
Part-time enrollment: 35
men: 63%; women: 37%;
minorities: 11%; international: 3%
Average GMAT (part time): 568
TOEFL requirement: Yes
Minimum TOEFL score: 570
Most popular departments:
e-commerce, entrepreneurship,
finance, marketing, technology

Longwood University[1]
201 High Street
Farmville, VA 23909
www.longwood.edu/business/
Public
Admissions: (877) 267-7883
Email: graduate@longwood.edu
Financial aid: N/A
Tuition: N/A
Room/board/expenses: N/A
Enrollment: N/A

Old Dominion University
1026 Constant Hall
Norfolk, VA 23529
odu.edu/mba
Public
Admissions: (757) 683-3585
Email: mbainfo@odu.edu
Financial aid: (757) 683-3683
Application deadline: 06/01
In-state tuition: full time: $464/
credit hour; part time: $464/
credit hour
Out-of-state tuition: full time:
$1,160/credit hour
Room/board/expenses: $18,500
College-funded aid: Yes
International student aid: Yes
Full-time enrollment: 22
men: 41%; women: 59%;
minorities: 27%; international: 18%
Part-time enrollment: 106
men: 57%; women: 43%;
minorities: 25%; international: 4%
Average GMAT (part time): 558
TOEFL requirement: Yes
Minimum TOEFL score: 550
Most popular departments:
entrepreneurship, general
management, health care
administration, public
administration, other

Radford University
PO Box 6956
Radford, VA 24142
www.radford.edu
Public
Admissions: (540) 831-6296
Email: gradcoll@radford.edu
Financial aid: (540) 831-5408
Application deadline: rolling
In-state tuition: full time: $318/
credit hour; part time: $318/
credit hour

Out-of-state tuition: full time: $683/
credit hour
Room/board/expenses: $19,861
College-funded aid: Yes
International student aid: Yes
Average student indebtedness at graduation: $29,050
Full-time enrollment: 13
men: 77%; women: 23%;
minorities: 38%; international:
46%
Part-time enrollment: 33
men: 67%; women: 33%;
minorities: 0%; international: 6%
Acceptance rate (full time): 38%
Average GMAT (full time): 560
Average GMAT (part time): 425
Average GPA (full time): 2.79
Average age of entrants to full-time program: 25
Average months of prior work experience (full time): 48
TOEFL requirement: Yes
Minimum TOEFL score: 550
Employment location for 2015 class:
Intl. N/A; N.E. 67%; M.A. N/A; S.
N/A; M.W. 33%; S.W. N/A; W. N/A

Shenandoah University (Byrd)
Halpin Harrison, Room 103
Winchester, VA 22601
www.su.edu/
Private
Admissions: (540) 665-4581
Email: admit@su.edu
Financial aid: (540) 665-4621
Application deadline: 11/01
Tuition: full time: $15,560; part
time: $830/credit hour
Room/board/expenses: $14,420
College-funded aid: Yes
International student aid: Yes
Average student indebtedness at graduation: $104,900
Full-time enrollment: 55
men: 55%; women: 45%;
minorities: 36%; international:
27%
Part-time enrollment: 43
men: 40%; women: 60%;
minorities: 35%; international: 5%
Acceptance rate (full time): 40%
Average GPA (full time): 3.42
Average age of entrants to full-time program: 28
TOEFL requirement: Yes
Minimum TOEFL score: 550

University of Richmond (Robins)
1 Gateway Road
Richmond, VA 23173
robins.richmond.edu/mba/
Private
Admissions: (804) 289-8553
Email: mba@richmond.edu
Financial aid: (804) 289-8438
Application deadline: rolling
Tuition: full time: N/A; part time:
$1,380/credit hour
Room/board/expenses: N/A
College-funded aid: Yes
International student aid: Yes
Full-time enrollment: N/A
men: N/A; women: N/A; minorities:
N/A; international: N/A
Part-time enrollment: 78
men: 59%; women: 41%;
minorities: 12%; international: 6%
Average GMAT (part time): 606
TOEFL requirement: Yes
Minimum TOEFL score: 600

University of Virginia (Darden)
PO Box 6550
Charlottesville, VA 22906-6550
www.darden.virginia.edu
Public
Admissions: (434) 924-7281
Email: darden@virginia.edu
Financial aid: (434) 924-7739
Application deadline: 04/08
In-state tuition: full time: $58,832;
part time: N/A
Out-of-state tuition: full time:
$61,150
Room/board/expenses: $26,287
College-funded aid: Yes
International student aid: Yes
Average student indebtedness at graduation: $100,083
Full-time enrollment: 656
men: 66%; women: 34%;
minorities: 16%; international:
32%
Part-time enrollment: N/A
men: N/A; women: N/A; minorities:
N/A; international: N/A
Acceptance rate (full time): 28%
Average GMAT (full time): 706
Average GPA (full time): 3.53
Average age of entrants to full-time program: 27
Average months of prior work experience (full time): 58
TOEFL requirement: No
Minimum TOEFL score: N/A
Most popular departments:
consulting, entrepreneurship,
finance, general management,
marketing
Mean starting base salary for 2015 full-time graduates: $119,819
Employment location for 2015 class:
Intl. 6%; N.E. 33%; M.A. 20%; S.
11%; M.W. 9%; S.W. 9%; W. 12%

Virginia Commonwealth University
301 W. Main Street
Richmond, VA 23284-4000
www.business.vcu.edu/graduate
Public
Admissions: (804) 828-4622
Email: gsib@vcu.edu
Financial aid: (804) 828-6669
Application deadline: rolling
In-state tuition: full time: $13,549;
part time: $590/credit hour
Out-of-state tuition: full time:
$24,772
Room/board/expenses: $19,700
College-funded aid: Yes
International student aid: Yes
Full-time enrollment: N/A
men: N/A; women: N/A; minorities:
N/A; international: N/A
Part-time enrollment: 163
men: 68%; women: 32%;
minorities: 16%; international: 7%
Average GMAT (part time): 550
TOEFL requirement: Yes
Minimum TOEFL score: 600
Most popular departments:
entrepreneurship, finance,
general management,
international business, statistics
and operations research

Virginia Tech (Pamplin)
1044 Pamplin Hall (0209)
Blacksburg, VA 24061
www.mba.vt.edu
Public
Admissions: (703) 538-8410
Email: mba@vt.edu
Financial aid: (540) 231-5179

Application deadline: 08/01
In-state tuition: full time: N/A; part
time: $745/credit hour
Out-of-state tuition: full time: N/A
Room/board/expenses: N/A
College-funded aid: Yes
International student aid: Yes
Full-time enrollment: N/A
men: N/A; women: N/A; minorities:
N/A; international: N/A
Part-time enrollment: 145
men: 66%; women: 34%;
minorities: 28%; international: 5%
Average GMAT (part time): 634
TOEFL requirement: Yes
Minimum TOEFL score: 550

WASHINGTON

Eastern Washington University[1]
668 N. Riverpoint Boulevard
Suite A
Spokane, WA 99202-1677
www.ewu.edu/mba
Public
Admissions: (509) 828-1248
Email: mbaprogram@ewu.edu
Financial aid: N/A
Tuition: N/A
Room/board/expenses: N/A
Enrollment: N/A

Gonzaga University
502 E. Boone Avenue
Spokane, WA 99258-0009
www.gonzaga.edu/mba
Private
Admissions: (509) 313-4622
Email: chatman@gonzaga.edu
Financial aid: (509) 313-6581
Application deadline: 05/30
Tuition: full time: $935/credit hour;
part time: $935/credit hour
Room/board/expenses: $15,325
College-funded aid: Yes
International student aid: Yes
Full-time enrollment: N/A
men: N/A; women: N/A; minorities:
N/A; international: N/A
Part-time enrollment: 220
men: 63%; women: 37%;
minorities: 21%; international: 6%
Average GMAT (part time): 570
TOEFL requirement: Yes
Minimum TOEFL score: 570
Most popular departments:
accounting, entrepreneurship,
finance, health care
administration, tax

Pacific Lutheran University
Morken Center for Learning
and Technology, Room 176
Tacoma, WA 98447
www.plu.edu/mba
Private
Admissions: (253) 535-7330
Email: plumba@plu.edu
Financial aid: (253) 535-7134
Application deadline: rolling
Tuition: full time: N/A; total
program: $41,760 (part time)
Room/board/expenses: $13,888
College-funded aid: Yes
International student aid: Yes
Full-time enrollment: 30
men: 60%; women: 40%;
minorities: 27%; international: 13%
Part-time enrollment: 25
men: 68%; women: 32%;
minorities: 24%; international: N/A
Acceptance rate (full time): 94%
Average GMAT (full time): 528
Average GPA (full time): 3.27

Average age of entrants to full-time program: 33
TOEFL requirement: Yes
Minimum TOEFL score: 570
Most popular departments: entrepreneurship, general management, health care administration, technology

Seattle Pacific University
3307 Third Avenue W, Suite 201
Seattle, WA 98119-1950
www.spu.edu/sbe
Private
Admissions: (206) 281-2753
Email: drj@spu.edu
Financial aid: (206) 281-2469
Application deadline: 08/01
Tuition: full time: N/A; part time: $798/credit hour
Room/board/expenses: N/A
College-funded aid: No
International student aid: No
Full-time enrollment: N/A
men: N/A; women: N/A; minorities: N/A; international: N/A
Part-time enrollment: 49
men: 53%; women: 47%; minorities: 45%; international: 16%
TOEFL requirement: Yes
Minimum TOEFL score: N/A
Most popular departments: finance, general management, human resources management, management information systems, other

Seattle University (Albers)
901 12th Avenue
PO Box 222000
Seattle, WA 98122-1090
www.seattleu.edu/albers/gradoverview/
Private
Admissions: (206) 296-5708
Email: millardj@seattleu.edu
Financial aid: (206) 220-8020
Application deadline: 08/20
Tuition: full time: N/A; part time: $815/credit hour
Room/board/expenses: N/A
College-funded aid: Yes
International student aid: Yes
Full-time enrollment: N/A
men: N/A; women: N/A; minorities: N/A; international: N/A
Part-time enrollment: 591
men: 50%; women: 50%; minorities: 24%; international: 23%
Average GMAT (part time): 580
TOEFL requirement: Yes
Minimum TOEFL score: 580
Most popular departments: accounting, finance, marketing, statistics and operations research, other

University of Washington-Bothell
18115 Campus Way NW
Box 358533
Bothell, WA 98011
www.uwb.edu/mba/mbaadmissions
Public
Admissions: (425) 352-5394
Email: vtolbert@uwb.edu
Financial aid:
Application deadline: 04/15
In-state tuition: full time: N/A; part time: $23,202
Out-of-state tuition: full time: N/A

Room/board/expenses: N/A
College-funded aid: Yes
International student aid: Yes
Full-time enrollment: N/A
men: N/A; women: N/A; minorities: N/A; international: N/A
Part-time enrollment: 101
men: 62%; women: 38%; minorities: 36%; international: 10%
Average GMAT (part time): 540
TOEFL requirement: Yes
Minimum TOEFL score: 580
Most popular departments: consulting, entrepreneurship, human resources management, leadership, technology

University of Washington (Foster)
PO Box 353200
Seattle, WA 98195-3200
foster.washington.edu/mba/
Public
Admissions: (206) 543-4661
Email: mba@uw.edu
Financial aid: (206) 543-4661
Application deadline: 03/15
In-state tuition: full time: $31,200; part time: $23,811
Out-of-state tuition: full time: $45,450
Room/board/expenses: $29,211
College-funded aid: Yes
International student aid: Yes
Average student indebtedness at graduation: $35,104
Full-time enrollment: 234
men: 68%; women: 32%; minorities: 10%; international: 33%
Part-time enrollment: 356
men: 67%; women: 33%; minorities: 29%; international: 7%
Acceptance rate (full time): 26%
Average GMAT (full time): 688
Average GMAT (part time): 638
Average GPA (full time): 3.35
Average age of entrants to full-time program: 29
Average months of prior work experience (full time): 70
TOEFL requirement: Yes
Minimum TOEFL score: 600
Most popular departments: consulting, entrepreneurship, finance, international business, marketing
Mean starting base salary for 2015 full-time graduates: $104,884
Employment location for 2015 class: Intl. 4%; N.E. 4%; M.A. 0%; S. 0%; M.W. 1%; S.W. 5%; W. 87%

University of Washington-Tacoma (Milgard)
1900 Commerce Street
Box 358420
Tacoma, WA 98402
www.tacoma.uw.edu/mba_apply
Public
Admissions: (253) 692-5630
Email: uwtmba@uw.edu
Financial aid: (253) 692-4374
Application deadline: 06/01
In-state tuition: full time: N/A; part time: $28,616
Out-of-state tuition: full time: N/A
Room/board/expenses: N/A
College-funded aid: Yes
International student aid: Yes
Full-time enrollment: N/A
men: N/A; women: N/A; minorities: N/A; international: N/A

Part-time enrollment: 56
men: 64%; women: 36%; minorities: 30%; international: 0%
Average GMAT (part time): 470
TOEFL requirement: Yes
Minimum TOEFL score: 580

Washington State University
PO Box 644744
Pullman, WA 99164-4744
https://business.wsu.edu/graduate-programs/
Public
Admissions: (509) 335-7617
Email: mba@wsu.edu
Financial aid: (509) 335-9711
Application deadline: 03/31
In-state tuition: total program: $21,000 (full time); part time: $890/credit hour
Out-of-state tuition: total program: $40,000 (full time)
Room/board/expenses: $16,032
College-funded aid: Yes
International student aid: Yes
Average student indebtedness at graduation: $28,495
Full-time enrollment: 35
men: 77%; women: 23%; minorities: 14%; international: 6%
Part-time enrollment: 556
men: 67%; women: 33%; minorities: 24%; international: 5%
Acceptance rate (full time): 48%
Average GMAT (full time): 559
Average GMAT (part time): 571
Average GPA (full time): 3.43
Average age of entrants to full-time program: 25
Average months of prior work experience (full time): 57
TOEFL requirement: Yes
Minimum TOEFL score: 580
Most popular departments: finance, general management, hotel administration, international business, marketing

Western Washington University[1]
516 High Street, MS 9072
Bellingham, WA 98225-9072
www.cbe.wwu.edu/mba/
Public
Admissions: (360) 650-3898
Email: mba@wwu.edu
Financial aid: N/A
Tuition: N/A
Room/board/expenses: N/A
Enrollment: N/A

WEST VIRGINIA

Marshall University (Lewis)
1 John Marshall Drive
Huntington, WV 25755-2020
www.marshall.edu/lcob/
Public
Admissions: (800) 642-9842
Email: johnson73@marshall.edu
Financial aid: (800) 438-5390
Application deadline: rolling
In-state tuition: full time: $7,668; part time: $427/credit hour
Out-of-state tuition: full time: $18,058
Room/board/expenses: N/A
College-funded aid: Yes
International student aid: Yes
Full-time enrollment: 153
men: 70%; women: 30%; minorities: 10%; international: 45%

Part-time enrollment: 37
men: 54%; women: 46%; minorities: 8%; international: 8%
Acceptance rate (full time): 82%
Average GPA (full time): 3.12
Average age of entrants to full-time program: 26
TOEFL requirement: Yes
Minimum TOEFL score: N/A
Most popular departments: finance, general management, health care administration, human resources management, marketing

West Virginia University
PO Box 6027
Morgantown, WV 26506
www.be.wvu.edu
Public
Admissions: (304) 293-7937
Email: mba@wvu.edu
Financial aid: (304) 293-5242
Application deadline: 03/01
In-state tuition: total program: $26,424 (full time); part time: N/A
Out-of-state tuition: total program: $60,588 (full time)
Room/board/expenses: $15,712
College-funded aid: Yes
International student aid: Yes
Average student indebtedness at graduation: $35,319
Full-time enrollment: 45
men: 78%; women: 22%; minorities: 27%; international: 24%
Part-time enrollment: N/A
men: N/A; women: N/A; minorities: N/A; international: N/A
Acceptance rate (full time): 65%
Average GMAT (full time): 618
Average GPA (full time): 3.30
Average age of entrants to full-time program: 25
Average months of prior work experience (full time): 21
TOEFL requirement: Yes
Minimum TOEFL score: 580
Most popular departments: finance, human resources management
Mean starting base salary for 2015 full-time graduates: $62,000
Employment location for 2015 class: Intl. 4%; N.E. 43%; M.A. 26%; S. 9%; M.W. 17%; S.W. N/A; W. N/A

WISCONSIN

Marquette University
PO Box 1881
Milwaukee, WI 53201-1881
www.marquette.edu/gsm
Private
Admissions: (414) 288-7145
Email: mba@Marquette.edu
Financial aid: (414) 288-7137
Application deadline: rolling
Tuition: full time: $1,050/credit hour; part time: $1,050/credit hour
Room/board/expenses: $17,518
College-funded aid: Yes
International student aid: Yes
Full-time enrollment: 155
men: 37%; women: 63%; minorities: 6%; international: 46%
Part-time enrollment: 236
men: 72%; women: 28%; minorities: 6%; international: 2%
Acceptance rate (full time): 59%
Average GMAT (full time): 591
Average GMAT (part time): 549
Average GPA (full time): 3.47
Average age of entrants to full-time program: 23
Average months of prior work experience (full time): 16
TOEFL requirement: Yes

Minimum TOEFL score: N/A
Most popular departments: accounting, finance, human resources management, international business

University of Wisconsin-Eau Claire
Schneider Hall 215
Eau Claire, WI 54702-4004
www.uwec.edu/academics/college-business/
Public
Admissions: (715) 836-5415
Email: uwecmba@uwec.edu
Financial aid: (715) 836-3373
Application deadline: 09/04
In-state tuition: full time: $525/credit hour; part time: $525/credit hour
Out-of-state tuition: full time: $1,034/credit hour
Room/board/expenses: $9,374
College-funded aid: Yes
International student aid: Yes
Average student indebtedness at graduation: $28,299
Full-time enrollment: 29
men: 79%; women: 21%; minorities: 7%; international: 3%
Part-time enrollment: 207
men: 54%; women: 46%; minorities: 9%; international: 1%
Acceptance rate (full time): 92%
Average GMAT (full time): 553
Average GMAT (part time): 529
Average GPA (full time): 3.12
Average age of entrants to full-time program: 35
TOEFL requirement: Yes
Minimum TOEFL score: 550
Most popular departments: accounting, general management, health care administration, marketing, management information systems

University of Wisconsin-La Crosse
1725 State Street
La Crosse, WI 54601
www.uwlax.edu
Public
Admissions: (608) 785-8939
Email: admissions@uwlax.edu
Financial aid: (608) 785-8604
Application deadline: 06/15
In-state tuition: total program: $12,000 (full time); part time: $530/credit hour
Out-of-state tuition: total program: $24,268 (full time)
Room/board/expenses: N/A
College-funded aid: Yes
International student aid: Yes
Full-time enrollment: 38
men: 66%; women: 34%; minorities: 0%; international: 24%
Part-time enrollment: N/A
men: N/A; women: N/A; minorities: N/A; international: N/A
Acceptance rate (full time): 96%
Average GMAT (full time): 573
Average GPA (full time): 3.38
Average age of entrants to full-time program: 29
Average months of prior work experience (full time): 76
TOEFL requirement: Yes
Minimum TOEFL score: 550
Most popular departments: finance, general management, health care administration, marketing

University of Wisconsin-Madison

975 University Avenue
Suite 2450
Madison, WI 53706-1323
www.bus.wisc.edu/mba
Public
Admissions: (608) 262-4000
Email: mba@bus.wisc.edu
Financial aid: (608) 262-4000
Application deadline: 04/11
In-state tuition: full time: $15,618; part time: $18,508
Out-of-state tuition: full time: $30,435
Room/board/expenses: $16,895
College-funded aid: Yes
International student aid: Yes
Average student indebtedness at graduation: $15,481
Full-time enrollment: 197
men: 64%; women: 36%;
minorities: 16%; international: 23%
Part-time enrollment: 163
men: 68%; women: 32%;
minorities: 10%; international: 6%
Acceptance rate (full time): 20%
Average GMAT (full time): 669
Average GMAT (part time): 598
Average GPA (full time): 3.38
Average age of entrants to full-time program: 29
Average months of prior work experience (full time): 66
TOEFL requirement: Yes
Minimum TOEFL score: N/A
Most popular departments: finance, general management, marketing, operations management, real estate
Mean starting base salary for 2015 full-time graduates: $100,653
Employment location for 2015 class: Intl. 1%; N.E. 7%; M.A. 6%; S. 5%; M.W. 59%; S.W. 10%; W. 12%

University of Wisconsin-Milwaukee (Lubar)

PO Box 742
Milwaukee, WI 53201-9863
lubar.uwm.edu/programs
Public
Admissions: (414) 229-5403
Email: mba-ms@uwm.edu

Financial aid: (414) 229-4541
Application deadline: rolling
In-state tuition: full time: $17,018; part time: $13,842
Out-of-state tuition: full time: $33,378
Room/board/expenses: $14,100
College-funded aid: Yes
International student aid: Yes
Full-time enrollment: 17
men: 41%; women: 59%;
minorities: 24%; international: 0%
Part-time enrollment: 430
men: 67%; women: 33%;
minorities: 9%; international: 19%
Acceptance rate (full time): 91%
Average GMAT (part time): 547
Average GPA (full time): 3.16
Average age of entrants to full-time program: 24
Average months of prior work experience (full time): 35
TOEFL requirement: Yes
Minimum TOEFL score: 550

University of Wisconsin-Oshkosh

800 Algoma Boulevard
Oshkosh, WI 54901
www.uwosh.edu/coba/
Public
Admissions: (800) 633-1430
Email: mba@uwosh.edu
Financial aid: (920) 424-3377
Application deadline: rolling
In-state tuition: full time: N/A; part time: N/A
Out-of-state tuition: full time: N/A
Room/board/expenses: N/A
College-funded aid: Yes
International student aid: Yes
Full-time enrollment: 12
men: 75%; women: 25%;
minorities: 17%; international: 17%
Part-time enrollment: 387
men: 59%; women: 41%;
minorities: 9%; international: 1%
TOEFL requirement: Yes
Minimum TOEFL score: 550

University of Wisconsin-Parkside

PO Box 2000
Kenosha, WI 53141-2000
uwp.edu/learn/programs/mbamasters.cfm
Public
Admissions: (262) 595-2355
Email: admissions@uwp.edu
Financial aid: (262) 595-2574
Application deadline: rolling
In-state tuition: full time: $495/credit hour; part time: $495/credit hour
Out-of-state tuition: full time: $1,018/credit hour
Room/board/expenses: $9,000
College-funded aid: Yes
International student aid: Yes
Full-time enrollment: 16
men: 44%; women: 56%;
minorities: 19%; international: 56%
Part-time enrollment: 69
men: 61%; women: 39%;
minorities: 26%; international: 3%
Acceptance rate (full time): 100%
Average GMAT (full time): 452
Average GMAT (part time): 479
Average GPA (full time): 3.27
Average age of entrants to full-time program: 32
Average months of prior work experience (full time): 20
TOEFL requirement: Yes
Minimum TOEFL score: 550

University of Wisconsin-River Falls

410 S. Third Street
River Falls, WI 54022-5001
www.uwrf.edu/mba
Public
Admissions: (715) 425-3335
Email: mbacbe@uwrf.edu
Financial aid: (715) 425-4111
Application deadline: rolling
In-state tuition: full time: $692/credit hour; part time: $692/credit hour
Out-of-state tuition: full time: $692/credit hour
Room/board/expenses: N/A
College-funded aid: Yes
International student aid: Yes

Average student indebtedness at graduation: $51,694
Full-time enrollment: 30
men: 60%; women: 40%;
minorities: 10%; international: 17%
Part-time enrollment: 74
men: 42%; women: 58%;
minorities: 8%; international: 0%
Acceptance rate (full time): 100%
Average GMAT (full time): 277
Average GMAT (part time): 438
Average age of entrants to full-time program: 32
Average months of prior work experience (full time): 8
TOEFL requirement: Yes
Minimum TOEFL score: 550

University of Wisconsin-Whitewater

800 W. Main Street
Whitewater, WI 53190
www.uww.edu/gradstudies/admission
Public
Admissions: (262) 472-1945
Email: gradbus@uww.edu
Financial aid: (262) 472-1130
Application deadline: 07/15
In-state tuition: full time: $9,118; part time: $507/credit hour
Out-of-state tuition: full time: $18,274
Room/board/expenses: $6,800
College-funded aid: Yes
International student aid: Yes
Average student indebtedness at graduation: $8,000
Full-time enrollment: 88
men: 56%; women: 44%;
minorities: 19%; international: 17%
Part-time enrollment: 434
men: 59%; women: 41%;
minorities: 14%; international: 2%
Acceptance rate (full time): 98%
Average GMAT (full time): 461
Average GMAT (part time): 498
Average GPA (full time): 3.30
Average age of entrants to full-time program: 30
Average months of prior work experience (full time): 50
TOEFL requirement: Yes
Minimum TOEFL score: 550

Most popular departments: finance, general management, marketing, management information systems, supply chain management
Employment location for 2015 class: Intl. N/A; N.E. N/A; M.A. N/A; S. N/A; M.W. 100%; S.W. N/A; W. N/A

WYOMING

University of Wyoming

PO Box 3275
Laramie, WY 82071-3275
www.uwyo.edu/business/
Public
Admissions: N/A
Financial aid: N/A
Application deadline: 06/30
In-state tuition: full time: $595/credit hour; part time: $630/credit hour
Out-of-state tuition: full time: $906/credit hour
Room/board/expenses: $4,240
College-funded aid: Yes
International student aid: Yes
Full-time enrollment: 35
men: 77%; women: 23%;
minorities: 3%; international: 6%
Part-time enrollment: 68
men: 54%; women: 46%;
minorities: 10%; international: 3%
Acceptance rate (full time): 40%
Average GMAT (full time): 560
Average GMAT (part time): 583
Average GPA (full time): 3.35
Average age of entrants to full-time program: 26
Average months of prior work experience (full time): 25
TOEFL requirement: Yes
Minimum TOEFL score: N/A
Most popular departments: entrepreneurship, finance, marketing, supply chain management
Employment location for 2015 class: Intl. 5%; N.E. N/A; M.A. N/A; S. N/A; M.W. 29%; S.W. 24%; W. 43%

EDUCATION

Here you'll find information on 374 schools nation-wide that offer doctoral programs in education. Two hundred fifty-five responded to the U.S. News survey, which was conducted in the fall of 2015 and early 2016. They provided information on matters of interest to applicants such as entrance requirements, enrollment, costs, location and specialties. Schools that did not respond to the survey have abbreviated entries.

KEY TO THE TERMINOLOGY

1. A school whose name has been footnoted with the numeral 1 did not return the U.S. News statistical survey; limited data appear in its entry.
N/A. Not available from the school or not applicable.
Admissions. The admissions office phone number.
Email. The address of the admissions office. If instead of an email address a website is listed, the website will automatically present an email screen programmed to reach the admissions office.
Financial aid. The financial aid office phone number.
Application deadline. For fall 2017 enrollment. "Rolling" means there is no deadline; the school acts on applications as they are received. "Varies" means deadlines vary according to department or whether applicants are U.S. citizens or foreign nationals.
Tuition. For the 2015-16 academic year. Includes fees.
Credit hour. The cost per credit hour for the 2015-16 academic year.
Room/board/expenses. For the 2015-16 academic year.
Enrollment. Full-time and part-time graduate-level enrollment at the education school for fall 2015.
Minorities. Full-time and part-time graduate-level minority enrollment percentage for fall 2015. It is the share of students who are black or African-American, Asian, American Indian or Alaska Native, Native Hawaiian or other Pacific Islander, Hispanic/Latino, or two or more races. The minority percentage was reported by each school.
Acceptance rate. Percentage of applicants who were accepted among those who applied for fall 2015 for both master's and doctoral programs.

Entrance test required. GRE means that scores on the Graduate Record Examination are required by some or all departments. GRE scores displayed are for both the master's and Ph.D. students and are only for those GRE exams taken by the fall 2015 entering students during or after August 2011 using the new GRE 130-170 score scale. MAT means that the Miller Analogies Test is required by some or all departments. GRE or MAT means that some or all departments require either the GRE or MAT.
Average GRE scores. Average verbal and quantitative scores for students who entered in fall 2015. Averages are based on the number of students who provided the school with scores. That number may be less than the total number of students who entered in fall 2015. (The GRE scores published in the ranking table refer to the scores of a school's entering doctoral students and may not be the same as the average GRE scores for the overall entering class printed in the directory.)
Total research assistantships. For the 2015-16 academic year.
Students reporting specialty. The percentage of graduate students, both full and part time, reporting a program specialization in fall 2015. If a school's figure is less than 50 percent, then its directory entry does not include this information or an enumeration of student specialties.
Student specialties. Proportion of students in the specialty-reporting population (not necessarily the entire student body) who are enrolled in a particular specialty. Numbers may not add up to 100 percent because of rounding or students enrolled in multiple specialties. The largest specialty areas in graduate education are listed.

ALABAMA

Alabama State University[1]
915 S. Jackson Street
Montgomery, AL 36101
www.alasu.edu/Education/
Public
Admissions: (334) 229-4275
Financial aid: (334) 229-4324
Tuition: N/A
Room/board/expenses: N/A
Enrollment: N/A

Auburn University
3084 Haley Center
Auburn, AL 36849-5218
www.auburn.edu/
Public
Admissions: (334) 844-4700
Email: gradadm@auburn.edu
Financial aid: (334) 844-4634
Application deadline: rolling
In-state tuition: full time: $10,418; part time: $489/credit hour
Out-of-state tuition: full time: $28,022
Room/board/expenses: $19,370
Full-time enrollment: 465
doctoral students: 38%;
master's students: 60%;
education specialists: 2%; men: 33%; women: 67%; minorities: 26%; international: 6%
Part-time enrollment: 523
doctoral students: 49%;
master's students: 42%;
education specialists: 9%; men: 33%; women: 67%; minorities: 26%; international: 1%
Acceptance rate (master's): 71%
Acceptance rate (doctoral): 38%
Entrance test required: GRE
Avg. GRE (of all entering students with scores): quantitative: 147; verbal: 149
Research assistantships: 14
Students reporting specialty: 100%
Students specializing in: admin.: 11%; instructional media design: 1%; educational psych: 7%; elementary: 3%; higher education admin.: 9%; secondary: 11%; special: 9%; counseling: 9%; technical (vocational): 6%; other: 34%

Samford University (Beeson)
800 Lakeshore Drive
Birmingham, AL 35229
samford.edu/education
Private
Admissions: (205) 726-2451
Email: lsennis@samford.edu
Financial aid: (205) 726-2905
Application deadline: 07/15
Tuition: full time: $766/credit hour; part time: $766/credit hour
Room/board/expenses: $1,100
Full-time enrollment: 197
doctoral students: 29%;
master's students: 58%;
education specialists: 12%; men: 25%; women: 75%; minorities: 19%; international: 1%

Part-time enrollment: 98
doctoral students: 63%;
master's students: 37%;
education specialists: 0%; men: 30%; women: 70%; minorities: 24%; international: N/A
Acceptance rate (master's): 85%
Acceptance rate (doctoral): 70%
Entrance test required: GRE
Avg. GRE (of all entering students with scores): quantitative: 146; verbal: 148
Research assistantships: 0
Students reporting specialty: 100%
Students specializing in: admin.: 68%; elementary: 2%; secondary: 14%; special: 9%; other: 7%

University of Alabama
Box 870231
Tuscaloosa, AL 35487-0231
graduate.ua.edu
Public
Admissions: (205) 348-5921
Email: gradschool@ua.edu
Financial aid: (205) 348-7949
Application deadline: rolling
In-state tuition: full time: $10,170; part time: N/A
Out-of-state tuition: full time: $25,950
Room/board/expenses: $12,796
Full-time enrollment: 374
doctoral students: 51%;
master's students: 46%;
education specialists: 3%; men: 32%; women: 68%; minorities: 26%; international: 7%
Part-time enrollment: 563
doctoral students: 52%;
master's students: 35%;
education specialists: 13%; men: 29%; women: 71%; minorities: 22%; international: 2%
Acceptance rate (master's): 61%
Acceptance rate (doctoral): 61%
Entrance test required: GRE
Avg. GRE (of all entering students with scores): quantitative: 146; verbal: 149
Research assistantships: 51
Students reporting specialty: 100%
Students specializing in: admin.: 30%; evaluation/research/statistics: 2%; educational psych: 9%; elementary: 4%; higher education admin.: 14%; secondary: 13%; special: 6%; counseling: 3%; other: 22%

University of Alabama-Birmingham
1530 Third Avenue S, EB 217
Birmingham, AL 35294-1250
www.uab.edu/graduate
Public
Admissions: (205) 934-8227
Email: gradschool@uab.edu
Financial aid: (205) 934-8223
Application deadline: 07/01
In-state tuition: full time: $7,340; part time: $383/credit hour
Out-of-state tuition: full time: $16,628
Room/board/expenses: $14,409

Full-time enrollment: 164
doctoral students: 9%; master's
students: 88%; education
specialists: 3%; men: 26%;
women: 74%; minorities: 23%;
international: 7%
Part-time enrollment: 553
doctoral students: 12%;
master's students: 74%;
education specialists: 14%; men:
23%; women: 77%; minorities:
27%; international: 0%
Acceptance rate (master's): 93%
Acceptance rate (doctoral): 79%
Entrance test required: GRE
Avg. GRE (of all entering students
with scores): quantitative: 147;
verbal: 152
Research assistantships: 3
Students reporting specialty: 100%
Students specializing in: admin.:
20%; evaluation/research/
statistics: 3%; elementary: 3%;
secondary: 14%; special: 8%;
counseling: 11%; other: 42%

University of South Alabama[1]
UCOM 3600
Mobile, AL 36688
www.southalabama.edu/
Public
Admissions: N/A
Financial aid: N/A
Tuition: N/A
Room/board/expenses: N/A
Enrollment: N/A

ARIZONA

Arizona State University
PO Box 37100, MC 1252
Phoenix, AZ 85069-7100
www.asu.edu/graduate
Public
Admissions: (480) 965-6113
Email: gograd@asu.edu
Financial aid: (855) 278-5080
Application deadline: rolling
In-state tuition: full time: $11,304;
part time: $758/credit hour
Out-of-state tuition: full time:
$27,780
Room/board/expenses: $19,044
Full-time enrollment: 745
doctoral students: 15%;
master's students: 85%;
education specialists: N/A; men:
31%; women: 69%; minorities:
32%; international: 4%
Part-time enrollment: 1,761
doctoral students: 7%; master's
students: 93%; education
specialists: N/A; men: 17%;
women: 83%; minorities: 31%;
international: 3%
Acceptance rate (master's): 88%
Acceptance rate (doctoral): 21%
Entrance test required: GRE
Avg. GRE (of all entering students
with scores): quantitative: 153;
verbal: 158
Research assistantships: 47
Students reporting specialty: 100%
Students specializing in:
curriculum/instr.: 55%; admin.:
11%; policy: 0%; evaluation/
research/statistics: 0%;
instructional media design:
2%; educational psych:
0%; elementary: 5%; higher
education admin.: 5%;
secondary: 6%; special: 4%;
other: 9%

Grand Canyon University[1]
3300 W. Camelback Road
Phoenix, AZ 85017
www.gcu.edu
Private
Admissions: N/A
Financial aid: N/A
Tuition: N/A
Room/board/expenses: N/A
Enrollment: N/A

Northcentral University
8667 E. Hartford Drive, Suite 100
Scottsdale, AZ 85255
www.ncu.edu
Private
Admissions: (866) 776-0331
Email: admissions@ncu.edu
Financial aid: (866) 776-0331
Application deadline: N/A
Tuition: full time: $16,821; part
time: $935/credit hour
Room/board/expenses: N/A
Full-time enrollment: 2,240
doctoral students: 88%;
master's students: 9%;
education specialists: 2%; men:
29%; women: 71%; minorities:
59%; international: 3%
Part-time enrollment: 1,687
doctoral students: 57%;
master's students: 35%;
education specialists: 8%; men:
27%; women: 73%; minorities:
62%; international: 2%
Acceptance rate (master's): 52%
Acceptance rate (doctoral): 56%
Entrance test required: N/A
Avg. GRE (of all entering students
with scores): quantitative: N/A;
verbal: N/A
Students reporting specialty: 100%
Students specializing in:
curriculum/instr.: 17%; admin.:
23%; policy: 0%; educational
tech.: 11%; elementary: 8%;
higher education admin.: 9%;
special: 10%; other: 23%

Northern Arizona University
PO Box 5774
Flagstaff, AZ 86011-5774
nau.edu/GradCol/Welcome/
Public
Admissions: (928) 523-4348
Email: Graduate@nau.edu
Financial aid: (928) 523-4951
Application deadline: rolling
In-state tuition: full time: $9,606;
part time: $431/credit hour
Out-of-state tuition: full time:
$21,246
Room/board/expenses: $15,202
Full-time enrollment: 570
doctoral students: 11%; master's
students: 84%; education
specialists: 5%; men: 27%;
women: 73%; minorities: 32%;
international: 2%
Part-time enrollment: 966
doctoral students: 15%;
master's students: 83%;
education specialists: 2%; men:
30%; women: 70%; minorities:
36%; international: N/A
Acceptance rate (master's): 85%
Acceptance rate (doctoral): 80%
Entrance test required: GRE
Avg. GRE (of all entering students
with scores): quantitative: 148;
verbal: 153
Research assistantships: 3

Students reporting specialty: 100%
Students specializing in:
curriculum/instr.: 3%; admin.:
44%; educational psych:
2%; educational tech.: 5%;
elementary: 7%; secondary:
0%; special: 3%; counseling:
20%; technical (vocational): 0%;
other: 16%

Prescott College
220 Grove Ave.
Prescott, AZ 86301
www.prescott.edu/learn/
index.html
Private
Admissions: N/A
Financial aid: N/A
Application deadline: rolling
Tuition: full time: $796/credit
hour; part time: N/A
Room/board/expenses: $2,696
Full-time enrollment: 3
doctoral students: N/A; master's
students: 100%; education
specialists: N/A; men: 33%;
women: 67%; minorities: 33%;
international: N/A
Part-time enrollment: 11
doctoral students: N/A; master's
students: 100%; education
specialists: N/A; men: 36%;
women: 64%; minorities: 45%;
international: N/A
Acceptance rate (master's): 70%
Acceptance rate (doctoral): N/A
Entrance test required: N/A
Avg. GRE (of all entering students
with scores): quantitative: N/A;
verbal: N/A
Research assistantships: 0
Students reporting specialty: 15%
Students specializing in: N/A

University of Arizona
Box 210069
1430 E. Second Street
Tucson, AZ 85721-0069
grad.arizona.edu/admissions
Public
Admissions: (520) 626-8851
Email: gradadmissions@
grad.arizona.edu
Financial aid: (520) 621-5200
Application deadline: rolling
In-state tuition: full time: $13,034;
part time: $789/credit hour
Out-of-state tuition: full time:
$31,434
Room/board/expenses: $17,150
Full-time enrollment: 462
doctoral students: 44%;
master's students: 53%;
education specialists: 3%; men:
30%; women: 70%; minorities:
41%; international: 6%
Part-time enrollment: 305
doctoral students: 36%;
master's students: 56%;
education specialists: 8%; men:
24%; women: 76%; minorities:
34%; international: 2%
Acceptance rate (master's): 69%
Acceptance rate (doctoral): 58%
Entrance test required: GRE
Avg. GRE (of all entering students
with scores): quantitative: 149;
verbal: 151
Research assistantships: 28
Students reporting specialty: 88%
Students specializing in:
curriculum/instr.: 11%; admin.:
15%; policy: 0%; evaluation/
research/statistics: 2%;
educational psych: 7%;
elementary: 2%; higher
education admin.: 14%; junior

high: 2%; secondary: 7%; social/
philosophical foundations: 7%;
special: 17%; counseling: 6%;
other: 11%

University of Phoenix[1]
1625 W. Fountainhead Pkwy
Tempe, AZ 85282-2371
Private
Admissions: N/A
Financial aid: N/A
Tuition: N/A
Room/board/expenses: N/A
Enrollment: N/A

ARKANSAS

Arkansas State University-Jonesboro
PO Box 10
State University, AR 72467
www.astate.edu/college/
graduate-school/
Public
Admissions: N/A
Financial aid: N/A
Application deadline: N/A
In-state tuition: full time: $254/
credit hour; part time: $254/
credit hour
Out-of-state tuition: full time:
$508/credit hour
Room/board/expenses: $14,053
Full-time enrollment: 135
doctoral students: 3%; master's
students: 61%; education
specialists: 36%; men: 34%;
women: 66%; minorities: 23%;
international: 4%
Part-time enrollment: 2,266
doctoral students: 3%; master's
students: 75%; education
specialists: 22%; men: 29%;
women: 71%; minorities: 17%;
international: N/A
Acceptance rate (master's): 76%
Acceptance rate (doctoral): 100%
Entrance test required: GRE
Avg. GRE (of all entering students
with scores): quantitative: N/A;
verbal: N/A
Students reporting specialty: 92%
Students specializing in:
curriculum/instr.: 23%; admin.:
51%; elementary: 0%; special:
21%; counseling: 5%

Harding University
Box 12234
Searcy, AR 72149
www.harding.edu/education/
grad.html/
Private
Admissions: (501) 279-4315
Email:
gradstudiesedu@harding.edu
Financial aid: (501) 279-4081
Application deadline: N/A
Tuition: full time: $439/credit
hour; part time: $439/credit
hour
Room/board/expenses: N/A
Full-time enrollment: 83
doctoral students: 0%; master's
students: 99%; education
specialists: 1%; men: 19%;
women: 81%; minorities: 20%;
international: 8%
Part-time enrollment: 325
doctoral students: 10%;
master's students: 87%;
education specialists: 3%; men:
29%; women: 71%; minorities:
23%; international: 0%
Acceptance rate (master's): 100%
Acceptance rate (doctoral): 100%

Entrance test required: GRE
Avg. GRE (of all entering students
with scores): quantitative: N/A;
verbal: N/A
Research assistantships: 0
Students reporting specialty: 82%
Students specializing in:
curriculum/instr.: 2%; admin.:
25%; instructional media design:
1%; elementary: 3%; junior
high: 10%; secondary: 22%;
counseling: 26%; technical
(vocational): 11%

University of Arkansas-Fayetteville
324 Graduate Education Building
Fayetteville, AR 72701
coehp.uark.edu
Public
Admissions: (479) 575-6247
Email: gradinfo@uark.edu
Financial aid: (479) 575-3276
Application deadline: rolling
In-state tuition: full time: $399/
credit hour; part time: $399/
credit hour
Out-of-state tuition: full time:
$987/credit hour
Room/board/expenses: $15,726
Full-time enrollment: 485
doctoral students: 21%;
master's students: 79%;
education specialists: 0%; men:
29%; women: 71%; minorities:
25%; international: 8%
Part-time enrollment: 471
doctoral students: 37%;
master's students: 59%;
education specialists: 4%; men:
34%; women: 66%; minorities:
21%; international: 2%
Acceptance rate (master's): 92%
Acceptance rate (doctoral): 82%
Entrance test required: GRE
Avg. GRE (of all entering students
with scores): quantitative: 146;
verbal: 150
Research assistantships: 55
Students reporting specialty: 92%
Students specializing in:
curriculum/instr.: 7%; admin.:
7%; policy: 2%; evaluation/
research/statistics: 2%;
educational psych: 0%;
educational tech.: 4%;
elementary: 8%; higher
education admin.: 9%;
secondary: 5%; special: 2%;
counseling: 10%; technical
(vocational): 6%; other: 54%

University of Arkansas-Little Rock[1]
2801 S. University Avenue
Little Rock, AR 72204
ualr.edu/www/
Public
Admissions: N/A
Financial aid: N/A
Tuition: N/A
Room/board/expenses: N/A
Enrollment: N/A

CALIFORNIA

Alliant International University
1 Beach Street
San Francisco, CA 94133-1221
www.alliant.edu/
Private
Admissions: (866) 825-5426
Email: admissions@alliant.edu
Financial aid: (858) 635-4559
Application deadline: rolling

Tuition: full time: $630/credit hour; part time: $630/credit hour
Room/board/expenses: $26,160
Full-time enrollment: 135
doctoral students: 13%; master's students: 87%; education specialists: N/A; men: 28%; women: 72%; minorities: 44%; international: 13%
Part-time enrollment: 180
doctoral students: 38%; master's students: 62%; education specialists: N/A; men: 34%; women: 66%; minorities: 52%; international: 3%
Acceptance rate (master's): N/A
Acceptance rate (doctoral): N/A
Entrance test required: N/A
Avg. GRE (of all entering students with scores): quantitative: N/A; verbal: N/A
Students reporting specialty: 100%
Students specializing in: curriculum/instr.: 13%; admin.: 12%; educational psych: 31%; elementary: 1%; higher education admin.: 1%; secondary: 4%; special: 3%; counseling: 4%; other: 31%

Azusa Pacific University
PO Box 7000
Azusa, CA 91702
www.apu.edu
Private
Admissions: N/A
Financial aid: N/A
Application deadline: N/A
Tuition: full time: N/A; part time: N/A
Room/board/expenses: N/A
Full-time enrollment: 538
doctoral students: 3%; master's students: 85%; education specialists: 12%; men: 20%; women: 80%; minorities: 43%; international: 1%
Part-time enrollment: 433
doctoral students: 14%; master's students: 82%; education specialists: 4%; men: 32%; women: 68%; minorities: 44%; international: N/A
Acceptance rate (master's): 91%
Acceptance rate (doctoral): 73%
Entrance test required: GRE
Avg. GRE (of all entering students with scores): quantitative: N/A; verbal: N/A
Students reporting specialty: 100%
Students specializing in: admin.: 13%; educational psych: 7%; educational tech.: 2%; elementary: 16%; secondary: 14%; special: 29%; counseling: 13%; other: 5%

California Lutheran University[1]
60 West Olsen Road
Thousand Oaks, CA 91360
www.callutheran.edu/
Private
Admissions: N/A
Financial aid: N/A
Tuition: N/A
Room/board/expenses: N/A
Enrollment: N/A

California State University-East Bay
25800 Carlos Bee Boulevard
Hayward, CA 94542
www.csueastbay.edu
Public
Admissions: N/A
Financial aid: N/A
Application deadline: 07/15
In-state tuition: full time: $7,830; part time: N/A
Out-of-state tuition: full time: $248/credit hour
Room/board/expenses: $15,084
Full-time enrollment: 270
doctoral students: 0%; master's students: 100%; education specialists: 0%; men: 26%; women: 74%; minorities: 61%; international: 2%
Part-time enrollment: 142
doctoral students: 39%; master's students: 61%; education specialists: 0%; men: 36%; women: 64%; minorities: 25%; international: 2%
Acceptance rate (master's): 58%
Acceptance rate (doctoral): N/A
Entrance test required: GRE
Avg. GRE (of all entering students with scores): quantitative: N/A; verbal: N/A
Students reporting specialty: 88%
Students specializing in: admin.: 26%; special: 4%; counseling: 16%; other: 54%

California State University-Fresno[1]
5150 N. Maple
Fresno, CA 93740
www.fresnostate.edu
Public
Admissions: N/A
Financial aid: N/A
Tuition: N/A
Room/board/expenses: N/A
Enrollment: N/A

California State University-Fullerton[1]
800 N. State College Boulevard
Fullerton, CA 92831-3599
ed.fullerton.edu/
Public
Admissions: N/A
Financial aid: N/A
Tuition: N/A
Room/board/expenses: N/A
Enrollment: N/A

California State University-Long Beach[1]
1250 Bellflower Boulevard
Long Beach, CA 90840
www.ced.csulb.edu
Public
Admissions: (562) 985-4547
Email: nmcgloth@csulb.edu
Financial aid: (562) 985-8403
Tuition: N/A
Room/board/expenses: N/A
Enrollment: N/A

California State University-Los Angeles[1]
5151 State University Drive
Los Angeles, CA 90032
www.calstatela.edu/academic/ccoe/
Public
Admissions: N/A
Financial aid: N/A

Tuition: N/A
Room/board/expenses: N/A
Enrollment: N/A

California State University-Northridge
18111 Nordhoff Street
Northridge, CA 91330-8265
www.csun.edu/
Public
Admissions: N/A
Financial aid: N/A
Application deadline: N/A
In-state tuition: full time: $8,927; part time: N/A
Out-of-state tuition: full time: $372/credit hour
Room/board/expenses: $14,594
Full-time enrollment: 345
doctoral students: 0%; master's students: 100%; education specialists: N/A; men: 16%; women: 84%; minorities: N/A; international: N/A
Part-time enrollment: 542
doctoral students: 11%; master's students: 89%; education specialists: N/A; men: 22%; women: 78%; minorities: N/A; international: N/A
Acceptance rate (master's): N/A
Acceptance rate (doctoral): N/A
Entrance test required: N/A
Avg. GRE (of all entering students with scores): quantitative: N/A; verbal: N/A
Students reporting specialty: 0%
Students specializing in: N/A

California State University-Sacramento[1]
6000 J Street
Sacramento, CA 95819-2694
www.csus.edu/
Public
Admissions: N/A
Financial aid: N/A
Tuition: N/A
Room/board/expenses: N/A
Enrollment: N/A

California State University-San Bernardino[1]
5500 University Parkway
San Bernardino, CA 92407
www.csusb.edu/
Public
Admissions: N/A
Financial aid: N/A
Tuition: N/A
Room/board/expenses: N/A
Enrollment: N/A

California State University-Stanislaus[1]
801 W. Monte Vista Avenue
Turlock, CA 95382
www.csustan.edu/
Public
Admissions: N/A
Financial aid: N/A
Tuition: N/A
Room/board/expenses: N/A
Enrollment: N/A

Chapman University
1 University Drive
Orange, CA 92866
www.chapman.edu/ces
Private
Admissions: (888) 282-7759
Email: admit@chapman.edu
Financial aid: (714) 997-6741

Application deadline: rolling
Tuition: full time: $840/credit hour; part time: $840/credit hour
Room/board/expenses: $1,560
Full-time enrollment: 173
doctoral students: 8%; master's students: 67%; education specialists: 25%; men: 19%; women: 81%; minorities: 42%; international: 3%
Part-time enrollment: 178
doctoral students: 34%; master's students: 61%; education specialists: 5%; men: 29%; women: 71%; minorities: 35%; international: 1%
Acceptance rate (master's): 70%
Acceptance rate (doctoral): 74%
Entrance test required: GRE
Avg. GRE (of all entering students with scores): quantitative: 147; verbal: 149
Research assistantships: 23
Students reporting specialty: 100%
Students specializing in: curriculum/instr.: 7%; educational psych: 17%; elementary: 17%; higher education admin.: 6%; secondary: 15%; special: 20%; counseling: 5%; other: 12%

Claremont Graduate University
150 E. 10th Street
Claremont, CA 91711
www.cgu.edu/pages/267.asp
Private
Admissions: (909) 621-8263
Email: admiss@cgu.edu
Financial aid: (909) 621-8337
Application deadline: N/A
Tuition: full time: $43,632; part time: $1,793/credit hour
Room/board/expenses: $26,000
Full-time enrollment: 78
doctoral students: 74%; master's students: 26%; education specialists: N/A; men: 26%; women: 74%; minorities: 69%; international: 6%
Part-time enrollment: 290
doctoral students: 82%; master's students: 18%; education specialists: N/A; men: 29%; women: 71%; minorities: 52%; international: 3%
Acceptance rate (master's): 94%
Acceptance rate (doctoral): 83%
Entrance test required: GRE
Avg. GRE (of all entering students with scores): quantitative: 146; verbal: 150
Research assistantships: 13
Students reporting specialty: 100%
Students specializing in: curriculum/instr.: 0%; admin.: 15%; policy: 6%; elementary: 6%; higher education admin.: 11%; secondary: 10%; special: 8%; other: 46%

Fielding Graduate University[1]
2020 De La Vina St.
Santa Barbara, CA 93105
www.fielding.edu/programs/education/default.aspx
Private
Admissions: (800) 340-1099
Email: admission@fielding.edu
Financial aid: (805) 898-4009
Tuition: N/A
Room/board/expenses: N/A
Enrollment: N/A

La Sierra University[1]
4700 Pierce Street
Riverside, CA 92515
lasierra.edu
Private
Admissions: N/A
Financial aid: N/A
Tuition: N/A
Room/board/expenses: N/A
Enrollment: N/A

Loyola Marymount University
1 LMU Drive
Los Angeles, CA 90045
soe.lmu.edu
Private
Admissions: (310) 338-7845
Email: soeinfo@lmu.edu
Financial aid: (310) 338-2753
Application deadline: 06/15
Tuition: full time: $1,123/credit hour; part time: $1,123/credit hour
Room/board/expenses: $23,106
Full-time enrollment: 787
doctoral students: 8%; master's students: 86%; education specialists: 6%; men: 26%; women: 74%; minorities: 61%; international: 5%
Part-time enrollment: 167
doctoral students: 0%; master's students: 100%; education specialists: 0%; men: 25%; women: 75%; minorities: 59%; international: 3%
Acceptance rate (master's): 30%
Acceptance rate (doctoral): 27%
Entrance test required: GRE
Avg. GRE (of all entering students with scores): quantitative: 148; verbal: 152
Research assistantships: 17
Students reporting specialty: 100%
Students specializing in: admin.: 11%; educational psych: 4%; elementary: 22%; higher education admin.: 1%; secondary: 24%; special: 13%; counseling: 14%; other: 16%

Mills College
5000 MacArthur Boulevard
Oakland, CA 94613
www.mills.edu/
Private
Admissions: (510) 430-3309
Email: grad-studies@mills.edu
Financial aid: (510) 430-2000
Application deadline: 12/15
Tuition: full time: $32,738; part time: $7,905/credit hour
Room/board/expenses: $16,904
Full-time enrollment: 147
doctoral students: 13%; master's students: 87%; education specialists: N/A; men: 12%; women: 88%; minorities: 45%; international: 5%
Part-time enrollment: 67
doctoral students: 30%; master's students: 70%; education specialists: N/A; men: 22%; women: 78%; minorities: 42%; international: 5%
Acceptance rate (master's): 81%
Acceptance rate (doctoral): 56%
Entrance test required: N/A
Avg. GRE (of all entering students with scores): quantitative: N/A; verbal: N/A
Research assistantships: 21
Students reporting specialty: 100%

Students specializing in: admin.: 41%; elementary: 21%; secondary: 40%; special: 5%; other: 32%

Pepperdine University
6100 Center Drive, Fifth Floor
Los Angeles, CA 90045-4301
gsep.pepperdine.edu/
Private
Admissions: (310) 568-5744
Email: barbara.moore@pepperdine.edu
Financial aid: (310) 568-2304
Application deadline: rolling
Tuition: full time: $1,145/credit hour; part time: $1,145/credit hour
Room/board/expenses: $10,200
Full-time enrollment: 345
doctoral students: 50%; master's students: 50%; education specialists: N/A; men: 27%; women: 73%; minorities: 42%; international: 9%
Part-time enrollment: 316
doctoral students: 97%; master's students: 3%; education specialists: N/A; men: 36%; women: 64%; minorities: 40%; international: 6%
Acceptance rate (master's): 59%
Acceptance rate (doctoral): 75%
Entrance test required: GRE
Avg. GRE (of all entering students with scores): quantitative: 143; verbal: 148
Research assistantships: 27
Students reporting specialty: 97%
Students specializing in: admin.: 63%; evaluation/research/statistics: 2%; instructional media design: 16%; educational tech.: 16%; elementary: 14%; junior high: 14%; secondary: 14%; social/philosophical foundations: 13%; other: 7%

San Diego State University
5500 Campanile Drive
San Diego, CA 92182
edweb.sdsu.edu/
Public
Admissions: (619) 594-6336
Email: barata@mail.sdsu.edu
Financial aid: (619) 594-6323
Application deadline: 03/01
In-state tuition: full time: $8,242; part time: $5,410
Out-of-state tuition: full time: $372/credit hour
Room/board/expenses: $15,902
Full-time enrollment: 420
doctoral students: 10%; master's students: 81%; education specialists: 10%; men: 25%; women: 75%; minorities: 60%; international: 6%
Part-time enrollment: 278
doctoral students: 27%; master's students: 73%; education specialists: 0%; men: 26%; women: 74%; minorities: 53%; international: 6%
Acceptance rate (master's): 61%
Acceptance rate (doctoral): 73%
Entrance test required: GRE
Avg. GRE (of all entering students with scores): quantitative: 145; verbal: 149
Research assistantships: 19
Students reporting specialty: 100%

Students specializing in: curriculum/instr.: 5%; admin.: 9%; policy: 2%; instructional media design: 0%; elementary: 19%; higher education admin.: 9%; secondary: 15%; special: 11%; counseling: 23%; other: 7%

San Francisco State University[1]
1600 Holloway Avenue
San Francisco, CA 94132
www.sfsu.edu/
Public
Admissions: N/A
Financial aid: N/A
Tuition: N/A
Room/board/expenses: N/A
Enrollment: N/A

Stanford University
485 Lasuen Mall
Stanford, CA 94305-3096
ed.stanford.edu
Private
Admissions: (650) 723-4794
Email: info@gse.stanford.edu
Financial aid: (650) 723-4794
Application deadline: N/A
Tuition: full time: $46,320; part time: N/A
Room/board/expenses: $23,730
Full-time enrollment: 373
doctoral students: 43%; master's students: 57%; education specialists: N/A; men: 33%; women: 67%; minorities: 36%; international: 16%
Part-time enrollment: N/A
doctoral students: N/A; master's students: N/A; education specialists: N/A; men: N/A; women: N/A; minorities: N/A; international: N/A
Acceptance rate (master's): 24%
Acceptance rate (doctoral): 5%
Entrance test required: GRE
Avg. GRE (of all entering students with scores): quantitative: 160; verbal: 162
Research assistantships: 521
Students reporting specialty: 100%
Students specializing in: curriculum/instr.: 11%; policy: 16%; evaluation/research/statistics: 10%; instructional media design: 7%; educational psych: 7%; educational tech.: 8%; elementary: 6%; higher education admin.: 1%; secondary: 19%; social/philosophical foundations: 7%; other: 9%

St. Mary's College of California[1]
1928 St. Mary's Road
Moraga, CA 94556
www.stmarys-ca.edu
Private
Admissions: N/A
Financial aid: N/A
Tuition: N/A
Room/board/expenses: N/A
Enrollment: N/A

Trident University International[1]
5757 Plaza Dr #100
Cypress, CA 90630
Private
Admissions: N/A
Financial aid: N/A
Tuition: N/A

Room/board/expenses: N/A
Enrollment: N/A

University of California-Berkeley
1600 Tolman Hall, MC #1670
Berkeley, CA 94720-1670
gse.berkeley.edu
Public
Admissions: (510) 642-0841
Email: gse_info@berkeley.edu
Financial aid: (510) 643-1720
Application deadline: 12/01
In-state tuition: full time: $17,356; part time: N/A
Out-of-state tuition: full time: $26,322/credit hour
Room/board/expenses: $25,120
Full-time enrollment: 343
doctoral students: 67%; master's students: 33%; education specialists: N/A; men: 31%; women: 69%; minorities: 38%; international: 13%
Part-time enrollment: N/A
doctoral students: N/A; master's students: N/A; education specialists: N/A; men: N/A; women: N/A; minorities: N/A; international: N/A
Acceptance rate (master's): 33%
Acceptance rate (doctoral): 9%
Entrance test required: GRE
Avg. GRE (of all entering students with scores): quantitative: 154; verbal: 158
Research assistantships: 93
Students reporting specialty: 100%
Students specializing in: admin.: 19%; policy: 7%; evaluation/research/statistics: 6%; educational psych: 15%; elementary: 5%; secondary: 13%; social/philosophical foundations: 9%; special: 6%; other: 20%

University of California-Davis
School of Education
1 Shields Avenue
Davis, CA 95616
education.ucdavis.edu
Public
Admissions: (530) 752-5887
Email: eduadvising@ucdavis.edu
Financial aid: (530) 752-2396
Application deadline: N/A
In-state tuition: full time: $26,330; part time: $20,719
Out-of-state tuition: full time: $41,432
Room/board/expenses: $21,919
Full-time enrollment: 118
doctoral students: 98%; master's students: 2%; education specialists: N/A; men: 35%; women: 65%; minorities: 49%; international: 3%
Part-time enrollment: 171
doctoral students: 13%; master's students: 87%; education specialists: N/A; men: 23%; women: 77%; minorities: 42%; international: 1%
Acceptance rate (master's): 50%
Acceptance rate (doctoral): 30%
Entrance test required: GRE
Avg. GRE (of all entering students with scores): quantitative: 149; verbal: 157
Research assistantships: 100

Room/board/expenses: N/A
Enrollment: N/A

University of California-Irvine
3200 Education
Irvine, CA 92697-5500
education.uci.edu
Public
Admissions: (949) 824-7465
Email: gseinfo@uci.edu
Financial aid: (949) 824-5337
Application deadline: rolling
In-state tuition: full time: $16,494; part time: $10,884
Out-of-state tuition: full time: $31,596
Room/board/expenses: $18,877
Full-time enrollment: 178
doctoral students: 40%; master's students: 60%; education specialists: N/A; men: 24%; women: 76%; minorities: 51%; international: 6%
Part-time enrollment: N/A
doctoral students: N/A; master's students: N/A; education specialists: N/A; men: N/A; women: N/A; minorities: N/A; international: N/A
Acceptance rate (master's): 81%
Acceptance rate (doctoral): 16%
Entrance test required: GRE
Avg. GRE (of all entering students with scores): quantitative: 151; verbal: 154
Research assistantships: 30
Students reporting specialty: 100%
Students specializing in: other: 100%

University of California-Los Angeles
1009 Moore Hall, MB 951521
Los Angeles, CA 90095-1521
www.gseis.ucla.edu
Public
Admissions: (310) 825-8326
Email: info@gseis.ucla.edu
Financial aid: (310) 206-0400
Application deadline: 12/01
In-state tuition: full time: $15,830; part time: N/A
Out-of-state tuition: full time: $30,932
Room/board/expenses: $20,588
Full-time enrollment: 686
doctoral students: 53%; master's students: 47%; education specialists: N/A; men: 28%; women: 72%; minorities: 60%; international: 6%
Part-time enrollment: N/A
doctoral students: N/A; master's students: N/A; education specialists: N/A; men: N/A; women: N/A; minorities: N/A; international: N/A
Acceptance rate (master's): 46%
Acceptance rate (doctoral): 28%
Entrance test required: GRE
Avg. GRE (of all entering students with scores): quantitative: 152; verbal: 154
Research assistantships: 176
Students reporting specialty: 100%
Students specializing in: curriculum/instr.: 2%; admin.: 15%; policy: 17%; evaluation/research/statistics: 6%; instructional media design: 1%; educational psych: 7%; elementary: 11%; higher education admin.: 14%; secondary: 22%; social/philosophical foundations: 13%; special: 3%; counseling: 2%

University of California-Irvine

University of California-Riverside
1207 Sproul Hall
Riverside, CA 92521
www.education.ucr.edu
Public
Admissions: (951) 827-6362
Email: edgrad@ucr.edu
Financial aid: (951) 827-3878
Application deadline: N/A
In-state tuition: full time: $16,665; part time: N/A
Out-of-state tuition: full time: $31,767
Room/board/expenses: $16,550
Full-time enrollment: 213
doctoral students: 40%; master's students: 60%; education specialists: N/A; men: 24%; women: 76%; minorities: 61%; international: 7%
Part-time enrollment: N/A
doctoral students: N/A; master's students: N/A; education specialists: N/A; men: N/A; women: N/A; minorities: N/A; international: N/A
Acceptance rate (master's): 70%
Acceptance rate (doctoral): 21%
Entrance test required: GRE
Avg. GRE (of all entering students with scores): quantitative: 152; verbal: 156
Research assistantships: 20
Students reporting specialty: 28%
Students specializing in: N/A

University of California-San Diego
9500 Gilman Drive
La Jolla, CA 92093
eds.ucsd.edu
Public
Admissions: (858) 534-2958
Email: gvanluit@ucsd.edu
Financial aid: (858) 534-3800
Application deadline: rolling
In-state tuition: full time: $16,435; part time: $10,825
Out-of-state tuition: full time: $31,537
Room/board/expenses: $18,455
Full-time enrollment: 152
doctoral students: 35%; master's students: 59%; education specialists: 6%; men: 31%; women: 69%; minorities: 48%; international: N/A
Part-time enrollment: N/A
doctoral students: N/A; master's students: N/A; education specialists: N/A; men: N/A; women: N/A; minorities: N/A; international: N/A
Acceptance rate (master's): 88%
Acceptance rate (doctoral): 57%
Entrance test required: GRE
Avg. GRE (of all entering students with scores): quantitative: 148; verbal: 153
Research assistantships: 6
Students reporting specialty: 100%
Students specializing in: curriculum/instr.: 38%; admin.: 25%; elementary: 34%; higher education admin.: 9%; junior high: 31%; secondary: 31%; special: 6%

University of California-Santa Barbara (Gevirtz)

Education Building
Santa Barbara, CA 93106-9490
www.education.ucsb.edu
Public
Admissions: (805) 893-2137
Email: sao@education.ucsb.edu
Financial aid: (805) 893-2432
Application deadline: N/A
In-state tuition: full time: $15,966; part time: N/A
Out-of-state tuition: full time: $31,068
Room/board/expenses: $20,224
Full-time enrollment: 328
doctoral students: 67%; master's students: 30%; education specialists: 2%; men: 23%; women: 77%; minorities: 44%; international: 9%
Part-time enrollment: N/A
doctoral students: N/A; master's students: N/A; education specialists: N/A; men: N/A; women: N/A; minorities: N/A; international: N/A
Acceptance rate (master's): 67%
Acceptance rate (doctoral): 18%
Entrance test required: GRE
Avg. GRE (of all entering students with scores): quantitative: 152; verbal: 156
Research assistantships: 30
Students reporting specialty: 100%
Students specializing in: curriculum/instr.: 8%; admin.: 0%; policy: 5%; evaluation/research/statistics: 1%; elementary: 10%; secondary: 13%; social/philosophical foundations: 7%; special: 7%; counseling: 24%; other: 24%

University of California-Santa Cruz

1156 High Street
Santa Cruz, CA 95064
www.graddiv.ucsc.edu/
Public
Admissions: (831) 459-5905
Email: gradadm@ucsc.edu
Financial aid: (831) 459-2963
Application deadline: N/A
In-state tuition: full time: $17,250; part time: $11,640
Out-of-state tuition: full time: $32,352
Room/board/expenses: $22,764
Full-time enrollment: 104
doctoral students: 22%; master's students: 78%; education specialists: N/A; men: 29%; women: 71%; minorities: 35%; international: 2%
Part-time enrollment: 2
doctoral students: 100%; master's students: 0%; education specialists: N/A; men: N/A; women: 100%; minorities: N/A; international: N/A
Acceptance rate (master's): 84%
Acceptance rate (doctoral): 31%
Entrance test required: GRE
Avg. GRE (of all entering students with scores): quantitative: 156; verbal: 157
Research assistantships: 7
Students reporting specialty: 100%
Students specializing in: evaluation/research/statistics: 100%

University of La Verne

1950 Third Street
La Verne, CA 91750
www.laverne.edu/academics/education/
Private
Admissions: (877) 468-6858
Email: gradadmt@ulv.edu
Financial aid: (800) 649-0160
Application deadline: rolling
Tuition: full time: $695/credit hour; part time: $695/credit hour
Room/board/expenses: N/A
Full-time enrollment: 420
doctoral students: 34%; master's students: 63%; education specialists: 3%; men: 19%; women: 81%; minorities: 48%; international: 1%
Part-time enrollment: 461
doctoral students: 12%; master's students: 78%; education specialists: 10%; men: 19%; women: 81%; minorities: 55%; international: 0%
Acceptance rate (master's): 63%
Acceptance rate (doctoral): 57%
Entrance test required: N/A
Avg. GRE (of all entering students with scores): quantitative: N/A; verbal: N/A
Research assistantships: 0
Students reporting specialty: 100%
Students specializing in: admin.: 21%; elementary: 11%; secondary: 8%; special: 9%; counseling: 21%; other: 30%

University of Redlands

PO Box 3080
Redlands, CA 92373
www.redlands.edu
Private
Admissions: (909) 748-8064
Email: education@redlands.edu
Financial aid: (909) 748-8047
Application deadline: rolling
Tuition: full time: $685/credit hour; part time: $685/credit hour
Room/board/expenses: N/A
Full-time enrollment: 532
doctoral students: 5%; master's students: 92%; education specialists: 4%; men: 29%; women: 71%; minorities: 50%; international: N/A
Part-time enrollment: 45
doctoral students: 44%; master's students: 22%; education specialists: 33%; men: 22%; women: 78%; minorities: 60%; international: N/A
Acceptance rate (master's): N/A
Acceptance rate (doctoral): N/A
Entrance test required: N/A
Avg. GRE (of all entering students with scores): quantitative: N/A; verbal: N/A
Students reporting specialty: 0%
Students specializing in: N/A

University of San Diego

5998 Alcala Park
San Diego, CA 92110-2492
www.sandiego.edu/soles/
Private
Admissions: (619) 260-4524
Email: grads@sandiego.edu
Financial aid: (619) 260-2700
Application deadline: 07/01
Tuition: full time: $1,370/credit hour; part time: $1,370/credit hour

Room/board/expenses: $17,891
Full-time enrollment: 328
doctoral students: 14%; master's students: 86%; education specialists: N/A; men: 21%; women: 79%; minorities: 41%; international: 7%
Part-time enrollment: 338
doctoral students: 9%; master's students: 91%; education specialists: N/A; men: 20%; women: 80%; minorities: 39%; international: 1%
Acceptance rate (master's): 60%
Acceptance rate (doctoral): 45%
Entrance test required: GRE
Avg. GRE (of all entering students with scores): quantitative: 150; verbal: 154
Research assistantships: 17
Students reporting specialty: 100%
Students specializing in: curriculum/instr.: 21%; admin.: 20%; instructional media design: 3%; elementary: 6%; higher education admin.: 17%; secondary: 15%; special: 5%; counseling: 6%; other: 19%

University of San Francisco

2130 Fulton Street
San Francisco, CA 94117-1080
www.usfca.edu
Private
Admissions: (415) 422-6563
Email: graduate@usfca.edu
Financial aid: (415) 422-6303
Application deadline: N/A
Tuition: full time: $1,110/credit hour; part time: $1,110/credit hour
Room/board/expenses: $21,220
Full-time enrollment: 827
doctoral students: 13%; master's students: 87%; education specialists: N/A; men: 25%; women: 75%; minorities: 8%; international: 47%
Part-time enrollment: 245
doctoral students: 38%; master's students: 62%; education specialists: N/A; men: 23%; women: 77%; minorities: 4%; international: 44%
Acceptance rate (master's): 75%
Acceptance rate (doctoral): 84%
Entrance test required: GRE
Avg. GRE (of all entering students with scores): quantitative: N/A; verbal: N/A
Research assistantships: 36
Students reporting specialty: 100%
Students specializing in: curriculum/instr.: 4%; admin.: 3%; evaluation/research/statistics: 6%; instructional media design: 1%; educational tech.: 2%; elementary: 13%; higher education admin.: 4%; secondary: 9%; special: 3%; counseling: 1%; other: 54%

University of Southern California (Rossier)

3470 Trousdale Parkway
Waite Phillips Hall
Los Angeles, CA 90089-0031
rossier.usc.edu
Private
Admissions: (213) 740-0224
Email: rsoeadm@rossier.usc.edu
Financial aid: (213) 740-1111
Application deadline: 12/01

Tuition: full time: $1,666/credit hour; part time: $1,666/credit hour
Room/board/expenses: $19,136
Full-time enrollment: 628
doctoral students: 8%; master's students: 92%; education specialists: N/A; men: 26%; women: 74%; minorities: 50%; international: 12%
Part-time enrollment: 1,225
doctoral students: 67%; master's students: 33%; education specialists: N/A; men: 33%; women: 67%; minorities: 56%; international: 6%
Acceptance rate (master's): 68%
Acceptance rate (doctoral): 16%
Entrance test required: GRE
Avg. GRE (of all entering students with scores): quantitative: 151; verbal: 152
Research assistantships: 39
Students reporting specialty: 100%
Students specializing in: admin.: 45%; policy: 3%; instructional media design: 1%; elementary: 11%; higher education admin.: 6%; secondary: 15%; special: 1%; counseling: 3%; other: 16%

University of the Pacific[1]

3601 Pacific Avenue
Stockton, CA 95211
www.pacific.edu
Private
Admissions: N/A
Financial aid: N/A
Tuition: N/A
Room/board/expenses: N/A
Enrollment: N/A

COLORADO

Colorado State University

1588 Campus Delivery
Fort Collins, CO 80523-1588
www.colostate.edu/
Public
Admissions: (970) 491-6909
Email: gschool@grad.colostate.edu
Financial aid: (970) 491-6321
Application deadline: rolling
In-state tuition: full time: $519/credit hour; part time: $519/credit hour
Out-of-state tuition: full time: $1,273/credit hour
Room/board/expenses: $14,736
Full-time enrollment: 386
doctoral students: 22%; master's students: 78%; education specialists: N/A; men: 30%; women: 70%; minorities: 25%; international: 2%
Part-time enrollment: 238
doctoral students: 47%; master's students: 53%; education specialists: N/A; men: 34%; women: 66%; minorities: 19%; international: 0%
Acceptance rate (master's): 47%
Acceptance rate (doctoral): 24%
Entrance test required: GRE
Avg. GRE (of all entering students with scores): quantitative: 148; verbal: 154
Research assistantships: 2
Students reporting specialty: 89%

Students specializing in: admin.: 2%; higher education admin.: 34%; secondary: 9%; counseling: 7%; other: 48%

Jones International University[1]

9697 East Mineral Avenue
Centennial, CO 80112
www.jiu.edu/academics/education
Private
Admissions: N/A
Financial aid: N/A
Tuition: N/A
Room/board/expenses: N/A
Enrollment: N/A

University of Colorado-Boulder

Campus Box 249
Boulder, CO 80309-0249
www.colorado.edu/education
Public
Admissions: (303) 492-6555
Email: edadvise@colorado.edu
Financial aid: (303) 492-5091
Application deadline: 12/15
In-state tuition: full time: $12,320; part time: $585/credit hour
Out-of-state tuition: full time: $29,618
Room/board/expenses: $19,024
Full-time enrollment: 154
doctoral students: 50%; master's students: 50%; education specialists: N/A; men: 33%; women: 67%; minorities: 32%; international: 2%
Part-time enrollment: 191
doctoral students: 2%; master's students: 98%; education specialists: N/A; men: 17%; women: 83%; minorities: 27%; international: 1%
Acceptance rate (master's): 66%
Acceptance rate (doctoral): 14%
Entrance test required: GRE
Avg. GRE (of all entering students with scores): quantitative: 153; verbal: 160
Research assistantships: 112
Students reporting specialty: 100%
Students specializing in: curriculum/instr.: 30%; evaluation/research/statistics: 2%; educational psych.: 7%; secondary: 7%; social/philosophical foundations: 61%; other: 68%

University of Colorado-Colorado Springs

PO Box 7150
Colorado Springs, CO 80933
www.uccs.edu/~coe/
Public
Admissions: (719) 255-4996
Email: education@uccs.edu
Financial aid: (719) 255-3460
Application deadline: rolling
In-state tuition: full time: $11,068; part time: $4,185
Out-of-state tuition: full time: $19,330
Room/board/expenses: $17,100
Full-time enrollment: 162
doctoral students: 7%; master's students: 93%; education specialists: N/A; men: 34%; women: 66%; minorities: 17%; international: 5%

Part-time enrollment: 240
doctoral students: 19%;
master's students: 81%;
education specialists: N/A; men:
30%; women: 70%; minorities:
22%; international: 3%
Acceptance rate (master's): 84%
Acceptance rate (doctoral): 78%
Entrance test required: GRE
**Avg. GRE (of all entering students
with scores):** quantitative: 146;
verbal: 151
Research assistantships: 1
Students reporting specialty: 100%
Students specializing in:
curriculum/instr.: 25%; admin.:
23%; evaluation/research/
statistics: 13%; special: 10%;
counseling: 29%

University of
Colorado-Denver
PO Box 173364, Campus Box 106
Denver, CO 80217-3364
www.ucdenver.edu/education
Public
Admissions: (303) 315-6300
Email: education@ucdenver.edu
Financial aid: (303) 315-1850
Application deadline: rolling
In-state tuition: full time: $356/
credit hour; part time: $356/
credit hour
Out-of-state tuition: full time:
$1,207/credit hour
Room/board/expenses: $21,345
Full-time enrollment: 947
doctoral students: 14%;
master's students: 79%;
education specialists: 7%; men:
20%; women: 80%; minorities:
18%; international: 2%
Part-time enrollment: 406
doctoral students: 3%; master's
students: 92%; education
specialists: 4%; men: 19%;
women: 81%; minorities: 16%;
international: N/A
Acceptance rate (master's): 71%
Acceptance rate (doctoral): 69%
Entrance test required: GRE
**Avg. GRE (of all entering students
with scores):** quantitative: N/A;
verbal: N/A
Research assistantships: 39
Students reporting specialty: 100%
Students specializing in:
curriculum/instr.: 7%; admin.:
16%; policy: 0%; evaluation/
research/statistics: 0%;
instructional media design:
2%; educational psych:
16%; educational tech.: 8%;
elementary: 16%; secondary:
12%; special: 10%; counseling:
11%; other: 25%

University of
Denver (Morgridge)
Ruffatto Hall
1999 East Evans Avenue
Denver, CO 80208
www.du.edu/education/
Private
Admissions: (303) 871-2509
Email: edinfo@du.edu
Financial aid: (303) 871-2509
Application deadline: rolling
Tuition: full time: $1,199/credit
hour; part time: $1,199/credit
hour
Room/board/expenses: N/A

Full-time enrollment: 598
doctoral students: 24%;
master's students: 66%;
education specialists: 10%; men:
25%; women: 75%; minorities:
23%; international: 6%
Part-time enrollment: 219
doctoral students: 62%;
master's students: 38%;
education specialists: 0%; men:
24%; women: 76%; minorities:
24%; international: 1%
Acceptance rate (master's): 75%
Acceptance rate (doctoral): 37%
Entrance test required: GRE
**Avg. GRE (of all entering students
with scores):** quantitative: 150;
verbal: 152
Research assistantships: 23
Students reporting specialty: 100%
Students specializing in:
curriculum/instr.: 23%; admin.:
19%; evaluation/research/
statistics: 6%; higher education
admin.: 12%; special: 2%; other:
37%

University of
Northern Colorado[1]
McKee 125
Greeley, CO 80639
www.unco.edu/grad/index.html
Public
Admissions: (970) 351-2831
Email: gradsch@unco.edu
Financial aid: (970) 351-2502
Tuition: N/A
Room/board/expenses: N/A
Enrollment: N/A

CONNECTICUT

Central Connecticut
State University
1615 Stanley Street
New Britain, CT 06050
www.ccsu.edu/grad/
Public
Admissions: (860) 832-2350
Email: graduateadmissions@
mail.ccsu.edu
Financial aid: (860) 832-2200
Application deadline: 06/01
In-state tuition: full time: $10,454;
part time: $577/credit hour
Out-of-state tuition: full time:
$21,506
Room/board/expenses: $14,361
Full-time enrollment: 192
doctoral students: 1%; master's
students: 99%; education
specialists: N/A; men: 21%;
women: 79%; minorities: 19%;
international: 5%
Part-time enrollment: 648
doctoral students: 8%; master's
students: 92%; education
specialists: N/A; men: 26%;
women: 74%; minorities: 15%;
international: 5%
Acceptance rate (master's): 66%
Acceptance rate (doctoral): 51%
Entrance test required: GRE
**Avg. GRE (of all entering students
with scores):** quantitative: N/A;
verbal: N/A
Students reporting specialty: 100%
Students specializing in: admin.:
14%; instructional media design:
4%; elementary: 1%; social/
philosophical foundations: 2%;
special: 12%; counseling: 23%;
technical (vocational): 5%;
other: 40%

Southern Connecticut
State University
501 Crescent Street
New Haven, CT 06515
www.southernct.edu/
Public
Admissions: (203) 392-5240
Email: GradInfo@southernCT.edu
Financial aid: (203) 392-5222
Application deadline: rolling
In-state tuition: full time: N/A; part
time: N/A
Out-of-state tuition: full time: N/A
Room/board/expenses: N/A
Full-time enrollment: 211
doctoral students: 3%; master's
students: 82%; education
specialists: 15%; men: 18%;
women: 82%; minorities: 13%;
international: 2%
Part-time enrollment: 511
doctoral students: 12%;
master's students: 51%;
education specialists: 37%; men:
23%; women: 77%; minorities:
12%; international: 0%
Acceptance rate (master's): 24%
Acceptance rate (doctoral): 29%
Entrance test required: GRE
**Avg. GRE (of all entering students
with scores):** quantitative: N/A;
verbal: N/A
Students reporting specialty: 0%
Students specializing in: N/A

University of
Bridgeport
126 Park Avenue
Bridgeport, CT 06604
www.bridgeport.edu/
Private
Admissions: (203) 576-4552
Email: admit@bridgeport.edu
Financial aid: (203) 576-4568
Application deadline: rolling
Tuition: full time: $690/credit
hour; part time: $690/credit
hour
Room/board/expenses: $16,090
Full-time enrollment: 204
doctoral students: 9%; master's
students: 85%; education
specialists: 6%; men: 30%;
women: 70%; minorities: 24%;
international: 1%
Part-time enrollment: 290
doctoral students: 5%; master's
students: 59%; education
specialists: 36%; men: 32%;
women: 68%; minorities: 28%;
international: 0%
Acceptance rate (master's): 43%
Acceptance rate (doctoral): 53%
Entrance test required: GRE
**Avg. GRE (of all entering students
with scores):** quantitative: N/A;
verbal: N/A
Students reporting specialty: 100%
Students specializing in: admin.:
27%; elementary: 34%;
secondary: 20%; counseling:
18%

University of
Connecticut (Neag)
249 Glenbrook Road
Storrs, CT 06269-2064
www.grad.uconn.edu
Public
Admissions: (860) 486-3617
Email: gradschool@uconn.edu
Financial aid: (860) 486-2819
Application deadline: rolling
In-state tuition: full time: $15,174;
part time: $724/credit hour

Out-of-state tuition: full time:
$35,640
Room/board/expenses: $18,933
Full-time enrollment: 417
doctoral students: 23%;
master's students: 77%;
education specialists: N/A; men:
27%; women: 73%; minorities:
18%; international: 6%
Part-time enrollment: 140
doctoral students: 56%;
master's students: 44%;
education specialists: N/A; men:
31%; women: 69%; minorities:
21%; international: 6%
Acceptance rate (master's): 42%
Acceptance rate (doctoral): 26%
Entrance test required: GRE
**Avg. GRE (of all entering students
with scores):** quantitative: 153;
verbal: 156
Research assistantships: 98
Students reporting specialty: 100%
Students specializing in:
curriculum/instr.: 7%; admin.:
18%; policy: 1%; evaluation/
research/statistics: 4%;
instructional media design:
3%; educational psych:
6%; educational tech.: 2%;
elementary: 7%; higher
education admin.: 6%;
secondary: 18%; special: 15%;
counseling: 7%; other: 8%

University of Hartford
200 Bloomfield Avenue
West Hartford, CT 06117
www.hartford.edu/enhp
Private
Admissions: (860) 768-4371
Email: gradstudy@hartford.edu
Financial aid: (860) 768-4296
Application deadline: rolling
Tuition: full time: $11,778; part
time: $540/credit hour
Room/board/expenses: N/A
Full-time enrollment: 102
doctoral students: 50%;
master's students: 50%;
education specialists: N/A; men:
28%; women: 72%; minorities:
20%; international: 5%
Part-time enrollment: 86
doctoral students: 34%;
master's students: 66%;
education specialists: N/A; men:
19%; women: 81%; minorities:
14%; international: 1%
Acceptance rate (master's): 63%
Acceptance rate (doctoral): 59%
Entrance test required: GRE
**Avg. GRE (of all entering students
with scores):** quantitative: 144;
verbal: 150
Research assistantships: 10
Students reporting specialty: 100%
Students specializing in: admin.:
17%; elementary: 16%; higher
education admin.: 39%; special:
5%; other: 22%

Western Connecticut
State University[1]
181 White Street
Danbury, CT 06810
www.wcsu.edu
Public
Admissions: N/A
Financial aid: N/A
Tuition: N/A
Room/board/expenses: N/A
Enrollment: N/A

DELAWARE

Delaware State
University[1]
1200 N. DuPont Highway
Dover, DE 19901
www.desu.edu
Public
Admissions: N/A
Financial aid: N/A
Tuition: N/A
Room/board/expenses: N/A
Enrollment: N/A

University of Delaware
113 Willard Hall Education Building
Newark, DE 19716
www.education.udel.edu
Public
Admissions: (302) 831-2129
Email: marym@udel.edu
Financial aid: (302) 831-2129
Application deadline: rolling
In-state tuition: full time: $625/
credit hour; part time: $625/
credit hour
Out-of-state tuition: full time:
$1,674/credit hour
Room/board/expenses: $14,424
Full-time enrollment: 93
doctoral students: 41%;
master's students: 49%;
education specialists: 10%; men:
25%; women: 75%; minorities:
14%; international: 29%
Part-time enrollment: 201
doctoral students: 53%;
master's students: 42%;
education specialists: 5%; men:
30%; women: 70%; minorities:
15%; international: 3%
Acceptance rate (master's): 63%
Acceptance rate (doctoral): 45%
Entrance test required: GRE
**Avg. GRE (of all entering students
with scores):** quantitative: 155;
verbal: 155
Research assistantships: 23
Students reporting specialty: 69%
Students specializing in: admin.:
67%; educational psych: 12%;
educational tech.: 9%; special:
17%; other: 16%

Wilmington University[1]
320 DuPont Highway
Wilmington, DE 19720
www.wilmu.edu
Private
Admissions: N/A
Financial aid: N/A
Tuition: N/A
Room/board/expenses: N/A
Enrollment: N/A

DISTRICT OF COLUMBIA

American University[1]
4400 Massachusetts Avenue NW
Washington, DC 20016-8030
www.american.edu/cas/seth/
Private
Admissions: N/A
Financial aid: N/A
Tuition: N/A
Room/board/expenses: N/A
Enrollment: N/A

The Catholic
University of America
Cardinal Station
Washington, DC 20064
admissions.cua.edu/graduate/
Private
Admissions: (800) 673-2772
Email: cua-admissions@cua.edu

Financial aid: (202) 319-5307
Application deadline: rolling
Tuition: full time: $41,800; part time: $1,650/credit hour
Room/board/expenses: $18,812
Full-time enrollment: 4
doctoral students: N/A; master's students: 100%; education specialists: N/A; men: 25%; women: 75%; minorities: N/A; international: 25%
Part-time enrollment: 36
doctoral students: 42%; master's students: 42%; education specialists: 17%; men: 25%; women: 75%; minorities: 11%; international: N/A
Acceptance rate (master's): 63%
Acceptance rate (doctoral): 25%
Entrance test required: GRE
Avg. GRE (of all entering students with scores): quantitative: 143; verbal: 147
Research assistantships: 0
Students reporting specialty: 100%
Students specializing in: secondary: 13%; special: 20%; other: 68%

Gallaudet University

800 Florida Avenue NE
Washington, DC 20002-3695
gradschool.gallaudet.edu
Private
Admissions: (202) 651-5717
Email: graduate.school@gallaudet.edu
Financial aid: (202) 651-5290
Application deadline: rolling
Tuition: full time: $15,604; part time: $1,448
Room/board/expenses: $19,884
Full-time enrollment: 58
doctoral students: 5%; master's students: 74%; education specialists: 21%; men: 16%; women: 84%; minorities: 43%; international: 10%
Part-time enrollment: 30
doctoral students: 47%; master's students: 33%; education specialists: 20%; men: 17%; women: 83%; minorities: 30%; international: 3%
Acceptance rate (master's): 63%
Acceptance rate (doctoral): 0%
Entrance test required: GRE
Avg. GRE (of all entering students with scores): quantitative: N/A; verbal: N/A
Research assistantships: 0
Students reporting specialty: 90%
Students specializing in: special: 54%; counseling: 26%; technical (vocational): 3%; other: 27%

George Washington University

2134 G Street NW
Washington, DC 20052
gsehd.gwu.edu
Private
Admissions: (202) 994-9283
Email: gsehdadm@gwu.edu
Financial aid: (202) 994-6822
Application deadline: rolling
Tuition: full time: $1,530/credit hour; part time: $1,530/credit hour
Room/board/expenses: $24,000
Full-time enrollment: 408
doctoral students: 23%; master's students: 76%; education specialists: 0%; men: 21%; women: 79%; minorities: 31%; international: 16%

Part-time enrollment: 816
doctoral students: 51%; master's students: 44%; education specialists: 5%; men: 29%; women: 71%; minorities: 35%; international: 3%
Acceptance rate (master's): 74%
Acceptance rate (doctoral): 50%
Entrance test required: GRE
Avg. GRE (of all entering students with scores): quantitative: 150; verbal: 154
Research assistantships: 16
Students reporting specialty: 98%
Students specializing in: curriculum/instr.: 5%; admin.: 20%; evaluation/research/statistics: 0%; instructional media design: 2%; educational tech.: 4%; elementary: 2%; higher education admin.: 9%; secondary: 2%; special: 15%; counseling: 31%; other: 11%

Howard University

2441 Fourth Street NW
Washington, DC 20059
www.howard.edu/schooleducation
Private
Admissions: (202) 806-7523
Email: hugsadmission@howard.edu
Financial aid: (202) 806-2820
Application deadline: rolling
Tuition: full time: $31,778; part time: $1,700/credit hour
Room/board/expenses: $25,587
Full-time enrollment: 183
doctoral students: 83%; master's students: 17%; education specialists: N/A; men: 25%; women: 75%; minorities: 91%; international: 21%
Part-time enrollment: 33
doctoral students: 18%; master's students: 82%; education specialists: N/A; men: 27%; women: 73%; minorities: 79%; international: 21%
Acceptance rate (master's): 61%
Acceptance rate (doctoral): 50%
Entrance test required: GRE
Avg. GRE (of all entering students with scores): quantitative: 145; verbal: 150
Research assistantships: 4
Students reporting specialty: 100%
Students specializing in: curriculum/instr.: 1%; admin.: 33%; educational psych: 7%; elementary: 2%; secondary: 1%; special: 1%; counseling: 21%; other: 33%

FLORIDA

Barry University (Dominican)[1]

11300 N.E. Second Avenue
Miami Shores, FL 33161-6695
www.barry.edu/
Private
Admissions: N/A
Financial aid: N/A
Tuition: N/A
Room/board/expenses: N/A
Enrollment: N/A

Florida A&M University

Gore Education Center
Tallahassee, FL 32307
www.famu.edu/education/
Public
Admissions: (850) 599-3315

Email: adm@famu.edu
Financial aid: (850) 599-3730
Application deadline: 05/01
In-state tuition: full time: $406/credit hour; part time: $406/credit hour
Out-of-state tuition: full time: $1,022/credit hour
Room/board/expenses: $15,524
Full-time enrollment: 67
doctoral students: 45%; master's students: 55%; education specialists: N/A; men: 30%; women: 70%; minorities: 96%; international: N/A
Part-time enrollment: 53
doctoral students: 62%; master's students: 38%; education specialists: N/A; men: 36%; women: 64%; minorities: 98%; international: N/A
Acceptance rate (master's): 57%
Acceptance rate (doctoral): 56%
Entrance test required: GRE
Avg. GRE (of all entering students with scores): quantitative: 141; verbal: 145
Research assistantships: 0
Students reporting specialty: 88%
Students specializing in: curriculum/instr.: 8%; admin.: 68%; counseling: 24%

Florida Atlantic University

777 Glades Road
PO Box 3091
Boca Raton, FL 33431-0991
www.coe.fau.edu/menu.htm
Public
Admissions: (561) 297-3624
Email: gradadm@fau.edu
Financial aid: (561) 297-3131
Application deadline: rolling
In-state tuition: full time: $370/credit hour; part time: $370/credit hour
Out-of-state tuition: full time: $1,024/credit hour
Room/board/expenses: $17,424
Full-time enrollment: 350
doctoral students: 19%; master's students: 78%; education specialists: 3%; men: 26%; women: 74%; minorities: 33%; international: 5%
Part-time enrollment: 496
doctoral students: 39%; master's students: 55%; education specialists: 5%; men: 26%; women: 74%; minorities: 28%; international: 1%
Acceptance rate (master's): 37%
Acceptance rate (doctoral): 47%
Entrance test required: GRE
Avg. GRE (of all entering students with scores): quantitative: 147; verbal: 149
Research assistantships: 45
Students reporting specialty: 95%
Students specializing in: curriculum/instr.: 19%; admin.: 20%; elementary: 3%; higher education admin.: 17%; social/philosophical foundations: 2%; special: 6%; counseling: 14%; other: 19%

Florida Gulf Coast University

10501 FGCU Boulevard S
Fort Myers, FL 33965
coe.fgcu.edu/
Public
Admissions: N/A
Email: graduate@fgcu.edu
Financial aid: N/A

Application deadline: rolling
In-state tuition: full time: $8,961; part time: N/A
Out-of-state tuition: full time: $30,157
Room/board/expenses: $11,220
Full-time enrollment: 22
doctoral students: 23%; master's students: 77%; education specialists: N/A; men: 14%; women: 86%; minorities: 18%; international: 5%
Part-time enrollment: 183
doctoral students: 26%; master's students: 74%; education specialists: N/A; men: 32%; women: 68%; minorities: 19%; international: 1%
Acceptance rate (master's): 87%
Acceptance rate (doctoral): 17%
Entrance test required: GRE
Avg. GRE (of all entering students with scores): quantitative: 145; verbal: 151
Students reporting specialty: 91%
Students specializing in: curriculum/instr.: 27%; admin.: 30%; special: 5%; counseling: 3%; other: 35%

Florida Institute of Technology

150 W. University Boulevard
Melbourne, FL 32901
www.fit.edu
Private
Admissions: (800) 944-4348
Email: grad-admissions@fit.edu
Financial aid: (321) 674-8070
Application deadline: rolling
Tuition: full time: $1,205/credit hour; part time: $1,205/credit hour
Room/board/expenses: $17,700
Full-time enrollment: 40
doctoral students: 50%; master's students: 48%; education specialists: 3%; men: 50%; women: 50%; minorities: 20%; international: 50%
Part-time enrollment: 17
doctoral students: 65%; master's students: 35%; education specialists: N/A; men: 24%; women: 76%; minorities: 29%; international: 24%
Acceptance rate (master's): 43%
Acceptance rate (doctoral): 73%
Entrance test required: N/A
Avg. GRE (of all entering students with scores): quantitative: N/A; verbal: N/A
Research assistantships: 0
Students reporting specialty: 89%
Students specializing in: secondary: 4%; other: 91%

Florida International University

11200 S.W. Eighth Street
Miami, FL 33199
education.fiu.edu
Public
Admissions: (305) 348-7442
Email: gradadm@fiu.edu
Financial aid: (305) 348-7272
Application deadline: rolling
In-state tuition: full time: $11,334; part time: $456/credit hour
Out-of-state tuition: full time: $24,438
Room/board/expenses: $25,620

Full-time enrollment: 409
doctoral students: 10%; master's students: 85%; education specialists: 5%; men: 24%; women: 76%; minorities: 71%; international: 9%
Part-time enrollment: 582
doctoral students: 21%; master's students: 75%; education specialists: 5%; men: 22%; women: 78%; minorities: 83%; international: 9%
Acceptance rate (master's): 57%
Acceptance rate (doctoral): 44%
Entrance test required: GRE
Avg. GRE (of all entering students with scores): quantitative: 145; verbal: 148
Research assistantships: 7
Students reporting specialty: 99%
Students specializing in: curriculum/instr.: 18%; admin.: 8%; higher education admin.: 13%; special: 9%; counseling: 15%; other: 38%

Florida State University

Suite 1100 Stone Building
1114 W. Call Street
Tallahassee, FL 32306-4450
www.education.fsu.edu
Public
Admissions: (850) 644-6200
Email: admissions@fsu.edu
Financial aid: (850) 644-0539
Application deadline: rolling
In-state tuition: full time: $404/credit hour; part time: $404/credit hour
Out-of-state tuition: full time: $1,035/credit hour
Room/board/expenses: $16,478
Full-time enrollment: 663
doctoral students: 38%; master's students: 51%; education specialists: 11%; men: 35%; women: 65%; minorities: 19%; international: 27%
Part-time enrollment: 351
doctoral students: 40%; master's students: 47%; education specialists: 13%; men: 35%; women: 65%; minorities: 26%; international: 8%
Acceptance rate (master's): 66%
Acceptance rate (doctoral): 40%
Entrance test required: GRE
Avg. GRE (of all entering students with scores): quantitative: 150; verbal: 152
Research assistantships: 113
Students reporting specialty: 100%
Students specializing in: curriculum/instr.: 14%; admin.: 9%; policy: 4%; evaluation/research/statistics: 5%; instructional media design: 14%; educational psych: 8%; elementary: 3%; higher education admin.: 10%; secondary: 3%; social/philosophical foundations: 3%; special: 5%; counseling: 13%; other: 14%

Keiser University

1500 NW 49th St
Fort Lauderdale, FL 33309
Private
Admissions: N/A
Financial aid: N/A
Application deadline: N/A
Tuition: full time: $22,104; part time: N/A
Room/board/expenses: N/A

Full-time enrollment: 63
doctoral students: 8%; master's students: 92%; education specialists: N/A; men: N/A; women: N/A; minorities: 89%; international: N/A
Part-time enrollment: 273
doctoral students: 92%; master's students: 4%; education specialists: 5%; men: N/A; women: N/A; minorities: 95%; international: N/A
Acceptance rate (master's): N/A
Acceptance rate (doctoral): N/A
Entrance test required: N/A
Avg. GRE (of all entering students with scores): quantitative: N/A; verbal: N/A
Students reporting specialty: 0%
Students specializing in: N/A

Lynn University
3601 North Military Trail
Boca Raton, FL 33431
www.lynn.edu
Private
Admissions: (561) 237-7834
Email: admission@lynn.edu
Financial aid: (561) 237-7816
Application deadline: 08/14
Tuition: full time: $710/credit hour; part time: $710/credit hour
Room/board/expenses: N/A
Full-time enrollment: 48
doctoral students: 21%; master's students: 79%; education specialists: N/A; men: 40%; women: 60%; minorities: 33%; international: 13%
Part-time enrollment: 51
doctoral students: 96%; master's students: 4%; education specialists: N/A; men: 29%; women: 71%; minorities: 22%; international: 6%
Acceptance rate (master's): 77%
Acceptance rate (doctoral): 75%
Entrance test required: N/A
Avg. GRE (of all entering students with scores): quantitative: N/A; verbal: N/A
Students reporting specialty: 99%
Students specializing in: admin.: 80%; elementary: 1%; special: 19%

Nova Southeastern University (Fischler)
3301 College Avenue
Fort Lauderdale, FL 33314
www.schoolofed.nova.edu
Private
Admissions: (954) 262-8500
Financial aid: (954) 262-3380
Application deadline: rolling
Tuition: full time: $895/credit hour; part time: $895/credit hour
Room/board/expenses: $11,820
Full-time enrollment: N/A
doctoral students: N/A; master's students: N/A; education specialists: N/A; men: N/A; women: N/A; minorities: N/A; international: N/A
Part-time enrollment: N/A
doctoral students: N/A; master's students: N/A; education specialists: N/A; men: N/A; women: N/A; minorities: N/A; international: N/A
Acceptance rate (master's): 74%
Acceptance rate (doctoral): 100%
Entrance test required: GRE
Avg. GRE (of all entering students with scores): quantitative: N/A; verbal: N/A

Students reporting specialty: 19%
Students specializing in: N/A

University of Central Florida
4000 Central Florida Boulevard
Orlando, FL 32816-1250
www.graduate.ucf.edu
Public
Admissions: (407) 823-0549
Email: graduate@mail.ucf.edu
Financial aid: (407) 823-2827
Application deadline: 01/15
In-state tuition: full time: $288/credit hour; part time: $288/credit hour
Out-of-state tuition: full time: $1,073/credit hour
Room/board/expenses: $15,853
Full-time enrollment: 724
doctoral students: 30%; master's students: 63%; education specialists: 7%; men: 25%; women: 75%; minorities: 29%; international: 5%
Part-time enrollment: 877
doctoral students: 11%; master's students: 88%; education specialists: 1%; men: 22%; women: 78%; minorities: 31%; international: N/A
Acceptance rate (master's): 58%
Acceptance rate (doctoral): 39%
Entrance test required: GRE
Avg. GRE (of all entering students with scores): quantitative: 149; verbal: 152
Research assistantships: 13
Students reporting specialty: 100%
Students specializing in: curriculum/instr.: 7%; admin.: 21%; instructional media design: 5%; educational psych: 3%; educational tech.: 2%; elementary: 4%; higher education admin.: 6%; junior high: 2%; secondary: 3%; special: 10%; counseling: 4%; technical (vocational): 2%; other: 33%

University of Florida
140 Norman Hall
PO Box 117040
Gainesville, FL 32611-7040
education.ufl.edu/
Public
Admissions: (352) 273-4116
Email: tla@coe.ufl.edu
Financial aid: (352) 392-1275
Application deadline: rolling
In-state tuition: full time: $449/credit hour; part time: $449/credit hour
Out-of-state tuition: full time: $1,253/credit hour
Room/board/expenses: $16,630
Full-time enrollment: 549
doctoral students: 32%; master's students: 50%; education specialists: 19%; men: 18%; women: 82%; minorities: 22%; international: 17%
Part-time enrollment: 473
doctoral students: 54%; master's students: 37%; education specialists: 8%; men: 24%; women: 76%; minorities: 27%; international: 4%
Acceptance rate (master's): 58%
Acceptance rate (doctoral): 49%
Entrance test required: GRE
Avg. GRE (of all entering students with scores): quantitative: 152; verbal: 152
Research assistantships: 83
Students reporting specialty: 100%

Students specializing in:
curriculum/instr.: 32%; admin.: 11%; evaluation/research/statistics: 2%; elementary: 8%; higher education admin.: 6%; special: 8%; counseling: 10%; other: 23%

University of Miami
PO Box 248212
Coral Gables, FL 33124
www.education.miami.edu
Private
Admissions: (305) 284-2167
Email: soegradadmissions@miami.edu
Financial aid: (305) 284-5212
Application deadline: rolling
Tuition: full time: $1,850/credit hour; part time: $1,850/credit hour
Room/board/expenses: $20,978
Full-time enrollment: 244
doctoral students: 45%; master's students: 55%; education specialists: 0%; men: 33%; women: 67%; minorities: 46%; international: 14%
Part-time enrollment: 144
doctoral students: 0%; master's students: 100%; education specialists: 0%; men: 56%; women: 44%; minorities: 37%; international: N/A
Acceptance rate (master's): 68%
Acceptance rate (doctoral): 27%
Entrance test required: GRE
Avg. GRE (of all entering students with scores): quantitative: 148; verbal: 149
Research assistantships: 32
Students reporting specialty: 100%
Students specializing in: admin.: 5%; evaluation/research/statistics: 3%; higher education admin.: 17%; other: 76%

University of North Florida
1 UNF Drive
Jacksonville, FL 32224-2676
www.unf.edu/graduatestudies
Public
Admissions: (904) 620-1360
Email: graduatestudies@unf.edu
Financial aid: (904) 620-5555
Application deadline: rolling
In-state tuition: full time: $494/credit hour; part time: $494/credit hour
Out-of-state tuition: full time: $1,044/credit hour
Room/board/expenses: $14,678
Full-time enrollment: 118
doctoral students: 4%; master's students: 96%; education specialists: N/A; men: 17%; women: 83%; minorities: 35%; international: 10%
Part-time enrollment: 358
doctoral students: 24%; master's students: 76%; education specialists: N/A; men: 26%; women: 74%; minorities: 30%; international: 2%
Acceptance rate (master's): 64%
Acceptance rate (doctoral): 62%
Entrance test required: GRE
Avg. GRE (of all entering students with scores): quantitative: 144; verbal: 148
Research assistantships: 12
Students reporting specialty: 88%
Students specializing in: admin.: 56%; elementary: 7%; secondary: 6%; special: 14%; counseling: 10%; other: 7%

University of South Florida
4202 E. Fowler Avenue, EDU 105
Tampa, FL 33620
www.grad.usf.edu
Public
Admissions: (813) 974-8800
Email: admissions@grad.usf.edu
Financial aid: (813) 974-4700
Application deadline: rolling
In-state tuition: full time: $431/credit hour; part time: $431/credit hour
Out-of-state tuition: full time: $877/credit hour
Room/board/expenses: $15,650
Full-time enrollment: 467
doctoral students: 39%; master's students: 59%; education specialists: 2%; men: 31%; women: 69%; minorities: 29%; international: 17%
Part-time enrollment: 773
doctoral students: 43%; master's students: 54%; education specialists: 3%; men: 28%; women: 72%; minorities: 26%; international: 4%
Acceptance rate (master's): 46%
Acceptance rate (doctoral): 62%
Entrance test required: GRE
Avg. GRE (of all entering students with scores): quantitative: 147; verbal: 150
Research assistantships: 28
Students reporting specialty: 100%
Students specializing in: admin.: 10%; evaluation/research/statistics: 3%; educational psych: 5%; educational tech.: 6%; elementary: 5%; higher education admin.: 7%; junior high: 1%; secondary: 12%; special: 8%; counseling: 8%; technical (vocational): 4%; other: 32%

University of West Florida[1]
11000 University Parkway
Pensacola, FL 32514-5750
uwf.edu
Public
Admissions: N/A
Financial aid: N/A
Tuition: N/A
Room/board/expenses: N/A
Enrollment: N/A

GEORGIA

Clark Atlanta University
223 James P. Brawley Drive SW
Atlanta, GA 30314
www.cau.edu/
Private
Admissions: (404) 880-6605
Email: cauadmissions@cau.edu
Financial aid: (404) 880-8992
Application deadline: rolling
Tuition: full time: $861/credit hour; part time: $861/credit hour
Room/board/expenses: $15,757
Full-time enrollment: 92
doctoral students: 35%; master's students: 65%; education specialists: 0%; men: 29%; women: 71%; minorities: 87%; international: 14%
Part-time enrollment: 71
doctoral students: 55%; master's students: 42%; education specialists: 3%; men: 31%; women: 69%; minorities: 86%; international: 3%

Acceptance rate (master's): 40%
Acceptance rate (doctoral): 41%
Entrance test required: GRE
Avg. GRE (of all entering students with scores): quantitative: N/A; verbal: N/A
Students reporting specialty: 100%
Students specializing in: admin.: 60%; secondary: 1%; special: 2%; counseling: 21%; other: 15%

Columbus State University
4225 University Ave.
Columbus, GA 31907
www.columbusstate.edu
Public
Admissions: (706) 507-8800
Financial aid: (706) 507-8800
Application deadline: 06/30
In-state tuition: full time: $201/credit hour; part time: $201/credit hour
Out-of-state tuition: full time: $801/credit hour
Room/board/expenses: N/A
Full-time enrollment: 275
doctoral students: 4%; master's students: 46%; education specialists: 50%; men: 29%; women: 71%; minorities: 45%; international: N/A
Part-time enrollment: 496
doctoral students: 20%; master's students: 48%; education specialists: 33%; men: 24%; women: 76%; minorities: 45%; international: 1%
Acceptance rate (master's): 63%
Acceptance rate (doctoral): 58%
Entrance test required: GRE
Avg. GRE (of all entering students with scores): quantitative: 145; verbal: 151
Students reporting specialty: 100%
Students specializing in: admin.: 36%; junior high: 2%; secondary: 8%; special: 11%; counseling: 10%; other: 33%

Georgia Southern University
U.S. Highway 301 S
P.O. Box 8033
Statesboro, GA 30460
coe.georgiasouthern.edu/ger/
Public
Admissions: (912) 478-5648
Email: GradAdmissions@georgiasouthern.edu
Financial aid: (912) 478-5413
Application deadline: rolling
In-state tuition: full time: $302/credit hour; part time: $302/credit hour
Out-of-state tuition: full time: $1,130/credit hour
Room/board/expenses: $16,656
Full-time enrollment: 317
doctoral students: 8%; master's students: 77%; education specialists: 15%; men: 23%; women: 77%; minorities: 30%; international: 1%
Part-time enrollment: 904
doctoral students: 27%; master's students: 60%; education specialists: 13%; men: 20%; women: 80%; minorities: 33%; international: 0%
Acceptance rate (master's): 82%
Acceptance rate (doctoral): 50%
Entrance test required: GRE
Avg. GRE (of all entering students with scores): quantitative: 146; verbal: 150

Research assistantships: 2
Students reporting specialty: 100%
Students specializing in:
curriculum/instr.: 12%; admin.:
26%; instructional media design:
12%; higher education admin.:
12%; junior high: 2%; secondary:
6%; counseling: 6%; other: 36%

Georgia State University
PO Box 3980
Atlanta, GA 30302-3980
education.gsu.edu/admissions/
graduate-admissions/
Public
Admissions: (404) 413-8000
Email: educadmissions@gsu.edu
Financial aid: (404) 413-2400
Application deadline: rolling
In-state tuition: full time: $382/
credit hour; part time: $382/
credit hour
Out-of-state tuition: full time:
$1,243/credit hour
Room/board/expenses: $14,690
Full-time enrollment: 745
doctoral students: 28%;
master's students: 65%;
education specialists: 7%; men:
25%; women: 75%; minorities:
47%; international: 5%
Part-time enrollment: 435
doctoral students: 43%;
master's students: 50%;
education specialists: 6%; men:
27%; women: 73%; minorities:
45%; international: 0%
Acceptance rate (master's): 47%
Acceptance rate (doctoral): 29%
Entrance test required: GRE
**Avg. GRE (of all entering students
with scores):** quantitative: 148;
verbal: 152
Research assistantships: 467
Students reporting specialty: 77%
Students specializing in:
curriculum/instr.: 2%; admin.:
7%; policy: 6%; evaluation/
research/statistics: 1%;
educational psych: 5%;
educational tech.: 5%;
elementary: 15%; junior high:
3%; secondary: 27%; social/
philosophical foundations: 1%;
special: 9%; counseling: 6%;
other: 13%

Kennesaw State University[1]
1000 Chastain Road
Campus Box 0123
Kennesaw, GA 30144
www.kennesaw.edu
Public
Admissions: N/A
Financial aid: N/A
Tuition: N/A
Room/board/expenses: N/A
Enrollment: N/A

Mercer University[1]
1400 Coleman Avenue
Macon, GA 31207
www.mercer.edu/
Private
Admissions: N/A
Financial aid: N/A
Tuition: N/A
Room/board/expenses: N/A
Enrollment: N/A

Piedmont College[1]
165 Central Avenue
PO Box 10
Demorest, GA 30535
www.piedmont.edu
Private
Admissions: N/A
Financial aid: N/A
Tuition: N/A
Room/board/expenses: N/A
Enrollment: N/A

University of Georgia
G-3 Aderhold Hall
Athens, GA 30602-7101
www.coe.uga.edu/
Public
Admissions: (706) 542-1739
Email: gradadm@uga.edu
Financial aid: (706) 542-6147
Application deadline: 07/01
In-state tuition: full time: $10,750;
part time: $354/credit hour
Out-of-state tuition: full time:
$26,348
Room/board/expenses: $12,526
Full-time enrollment: 945
doctoral students: 45%;
master's students: 54%;
education specialists: 1%; men:
30%; women: 70%; minorities:
20%; international: 20%
Part-time enrollment: 619
doctoral students: 42%;
master's students: 44%;
education specialists: 14%; men:
28%; women: 72%; minorities:
46%; international: 24%
Acceptance rate (master's): 55%
Acceptance rate (doctoral): 39%
Entrance test required: GRE
**Avg. GRE (of all entering students
with scores):** quantitative: 151;
verbal: 152
Research assistantships: 117
Students reporting specialty: 100%
Students specializing in: admin.:
2%; policy: 2%; evaluation/
research/statistics: 2%;
instructional media design:
2%; educational psych:
8%; educational tech.: 6%;
elementary: 5%; higher
education admin.: 3%; junior
high: 2%; secondary: 21%;
social/philosophical foundations:
0%; special: 4%; counseling:
18%; technical (vocational): 3%;
other: 23%

University of West Georgia
1601 Maple Street
Carrollton, GA 30118
www.westga.edu/ogia
Public
Admissions: (678) 839-1394
Email: graduate@westga.edu
Financial aid: (678) 839-6421
Application deadline: rolling
In-state tuition: full time: $7,278;
part time: $222/credit hour
Out-of-state tuition: full time:
$22,620
Room/board/expenses: $11,948
Full-time enrollment: 352
doctoral students: 2%; master's
students: 85%; education
specialists: 13%; men: 20%;
women: 80%; minorities: 36%;
international: 1%
Part-time enrollment: 909
doctoral students: 11%; master's
students: 54%; education
specialists: 35%; men: 19%;
women: 81%; minorities: 36%;
international: 1%

IDAHO

Boise State University
1910 University Drive
Boise, ID 83725-1700
www.boisestate.edu/
Public
Admissions: (208) 426-3903
Email: gradcoll@boisestate.edu

Acceptance rate (master's): 73%
Acceptance rate (doctoral): 100%
Entrance test required: GRE
**Avg. GRE (of all entering students
with scores):** quantitative: 145;
verbal: 148
Research assistantships: 0
Students reporting specialty: 100%
Students specializing in: admin.:
4%; instructional media
design: 24%; elementary: 9%;
secondary: 1%; special: 7%;
counseling: 17%; other: 38%

Valdosta State University[1]
1500 N. Patterson Street
Valdosta, GA 31698
www.valdosta.edu/
Public
Admissions: (229) 333-5694
Email: rlwaters@valdosta.edu
Financial aid: (229) 333-5935
Tuition: N/A
Room/board/expenses: N/A
Enrollment: N/A

HAWAII

University of Hawaii-Manoa
1776 University Avenue
Everly Hall 128
Honolulu, HI 96822
manoa.hawaii.edu/graduate/
Public
Admissions: (808) 956-8544
Email: graduate.education@
hawaii.edu
Financial aid: (808) 956-7251
Application deadline: rolling
In-state tuition: full time: $637/
credit hour; part time: $637/
credit hour
Out-of-state tuition: full time:
$1,532/credit hour
Room/board/expenses: $17,560
Full-time enrollment: 226
doctoral students: 16%;
master's students: 84%;
education specialists: N/A; men:
29%; women: 71%; minorities:
60%; international: 8%
Part-time enrollment: 551
doctoral students: 39%;
master's students: 61%;
education specialists: N/A; men:
30%; women: 70%; minorities:
73%; international: 2%
Acceptance rate (master's): 66%
Acceptance rate (doctoral): 62%
Entrance test required: GRE
**Avg. GRE (of all entering students
with scores):** quantitative: 147;
verbal: 152
Research assistantships: 26
Students reporting specialty: 67%
Students specializing in:
curriculum/instr.: 28%; admin.:
6%; policy: 0%; educational
psych: 10%; educational
tech.: 23%; elementary: 8%;
higher education admin.:
8%; secondary: 12%; social/
philosophical foundations: 11%;
special: 19%

Idaho

Boise State University

Financial aid: (800) 824-7017
Application deadline: 03/01
In-state tuition: full time: $8,166;
part time: $358/credit hour
Out-of-state tuition: full time:
$22,216
Room/board/expenses: $13,572
Full-time enrollment: 107
doctoral students: 20%;
master's students: 79%;
education specialists: 1%; men:
18%; women: 82%; minorities:
14%; international: 10%
Part-time enrollment: 662
doctoral students: 12%;
master's students: 84%;
education specialists: 4%; men:
38%; women: 62%; minorities:
10%; international: 3%
Acceptance rate (master's): 58%
Acceptance rate (doctoral): 32%
Entrance test required: GRE
**Avg. GRE (of all entering students
with scores):** quantitative: 150;
verbal: 155
Research assistantships: 25
Students reporting specialty: 9%
Students specializing in: N/A

Idaho State University[1]
921 S. Eighth Avenue
Pocatello, ID 83209-8059
ed.isu.edu/
Public
Admissions: N/A
Financial aid: N/A
Tuition: N/A
Room/board/expenses: N/A
Enrollment: N/A

Northwest Nazarene University[1]
623 Holly Street
Nampa, ID 83686
www.nnu.edu
Private
Admissions: (208) 467-8341
Email: empoe@nnu.edu
Financial aid: (208) 467-8424
Tuition: N/A
Room/board/expenses: N/A
Enrollment: N/A

University of Idaho
PO Box 443080
Moscow, ID 83844-3080
www.uidaho.edu/ed
Public
Admissions: (208) 885-4001
Email: graduateadmissions@
uidaho.edu
Financial aid: N/A
Application deadline: 02/01
In-state tuition: full time: $8,222;
part time: $7,312
Out-of-state tuition: full time:
$22,226
Room/board/expenses: $15,142
Full-time enrollment: N/A
doctoral students: N/A; master's
students: N/A; education
specialists: N/A; men: N/A;
women: N/A; minorities: N/A;
international: N/A
Part-time enrollment: N/A
doctoral students: N/A; master's
students: N/A; education
specialists: N/A; men: N/A;
women: N/A; minorities: N/A;
international: N/A
Acceptance rate (master's): N/A
Acceptance rate (doctoral): N/A
Entrance test required: GRE
**Avg. GRE (of all entering students
with scores):** quantitative: N/A;
verbal: N/A

Students reporting specialty: 54%
Students specializing in:
curriculum/instr.: 45%; admin.:
55%

ILLINOIS

Argosy University[1]
225 N. Michigan Avenue
Chicago, IL 60601
www.argosy.edu/colleges/
education/default.aspx
Private
Admissions: N/A
Financial aid: N/A
Tuition: N/A
Room/board/expenses: N/A
Enrollment: N/A

Aurora University[1]
347 S. Gladstone Avenue
Aurora, IL 60506-4892
www.aurora.edu
Private
Admissions: N/A
Financial aid: N/A
Tuition: N/A
Room/board/expenses: N/A
Enrollment: N/A

Benedictine University[1]
5700 College Road
Lisle, IL 60532
www.ben.edu
Private
Admissions: N/A
Financial aid: N/A
Tuition: N/A
Room/board/expenses: N/A
Enrollment: N/A

Chicago State University
9501 S. King Drive, ED 320
Chicago, IL 60628
www.csu.edu/
Public
Admissions: N/A
Financial aid: N/A
Application deadline: 03/15
In-state tuition: full time: $8,320;
part time: $5,330
Out-of-state tuition: full time:
$13,252
Room/board/expenses: $14,423
Full-time enrollment: 59
doctoral students: 0%; master's
students: 100%; education
specialists: N/A; men: 29%;
women: 71%; minorities: 95%;
international: 2%
Part-time enrollment: 205
doctoral students: 29%;
master's students: 71%;
education specialists: N/A; men:
32%; women: 68%; minorities:
90%; international: 2%
Acceptance rate (master's): N/A
Acceptance rate (doctoral): N/A
Entrance test required: N/A
**Avg. GRE (of all entering students
with scores):** quantitative: N/A;
verbal: N/A
Research assistantships: 0
Students reporting specialty: 100%
Students specializing in:
curriculum/instr.: 3%; admin.:
36%; elementary: 4%;
secondary: 2%; special: 17%;
technical (vocational): 1%; other:
37%

Concordia University[1]

7400 Augusta Street
River Forest, IL 60305-1499
www.cuchicago.edu
Private
Admissions: N/A
Financial aid: N/A
Tuition: N/A
Room/board/expenses: N/A
Enrollment: N/A

DePaul University

1 E. Jackson Boulevard
Chicago, IL 60604-2287
education.depaul.edu
Private
Admissions: (773) 325-4405
Email: edgradadmissions@
depaul.edu
Financial aid: (312) 362-8610
Application deadline: rolling
Tuition: full time: $610/credit
hour; part time: $610/credit hour
Room/board/expenses: $13,951
Full-time enrollment: 637
doctoral students: 9%; master's
students: 91%; education
specialists: N/A; men: 23%;
women: 77%; minorities: 18%;
international: 3%
Part-time enrollment: 299
doctoral students: 24%;
master's students: 76%;
education specialists: N/A; men:
23%; women: 77%; minorities:
31%; international: 5%
Acceptance rate (master's): 78%
Acceptance rate (doctoral): 64%
Entrance test required: GRE
**Avg. GRE (of all entering students
with scores):** quantitative: N/A;
verbal: N/A
Research assistantships: 11
Students reporting specialty: 86%
Students specializing in:
curriculum/instr.: 8%; admin.:
16%; elementary: 11%; junior
high: 0%; secondary: 20%;
social/philosophical foundations:
3%; special: 10%; counseling:
26%; other: 6%

Governors State University

1 University Parkway
University Park, IL 60466
www.govst.edu
Public
Admissions: (708) 534-4490
Email: gsunow@govst.edu
Financial aid: (708) 534-4590
Application deadline: rolling
In-state tuition: full time: $7,368;
part time: $307/credit hour
Out-of-state tuition: full time:
$14,736
Room/board/expenses: $15,338
Full-time enrollment: 94
doctoral students: N/A; master's
students: 100%; education
specialists: N/A; men: 15%;
women: 85%; minorities: 91%;
international: 2%
Part-time enrollment: 329
doctoral students: N/A; master's
students: 100%; education
specialists: N/A; men: 18%;
women: 82%; minorities: 48%;
international: 0%
Acceptance rate (master's): 49%
Acceptance rate (doctoral): N/A
Entrance test required: GRE
**Avg. GRE (of all entering students
with scores):** quantitative: 143;
verbal: 148
Students reporting specialty: 21%
Students specializing in: N/A

Illinois State University

Campus Box 5300
Normal, IL 61790-5300
www.illinoisstate.edu
Public
Admissions: (309) 438-2181
Email:
admissions@illinoisstate.edu
Financial aid: (309) 438-2231
Application deadline: rolling
In-state tuition: full time: $374/
credit hour; part time: $374/
credit hour
Out-of-state tuition: full time: $777/
credit hour
Room/board/expenses: $11,983
Full-time enrollment: 214
doctoral students: 20%;
master's students: 73%;
education specialists: 7%; men:
17%; women: 83%; minorities:
22%; international: 4%
Part-time enrollment: 584
doctoral students: 36%;
master's students: 58%;
education specialists: 6%; men:
27%; women: 73%; minorities:
12%; international: 0%
Acceptance rate (master's): 40%
Acceptance rate (doctoral): 74%
Entrance test required: GRE
**Avg. GRE (of all entering students
with scores):** quantitative: 149;
verbal: 151
Research assistantships: 101
Students reporting specialty: 100%
Students specializing in:
curriculum/instr.: 16%; admin.:
21%; educational psych: 5%;
educational tech.: 2%; special:
9%; counseling: 6%; other: 41%

Lewis University[1]

One University Parkway
Romeoville, IL 60446
www.lewisu.edu/
Private
Admissions: N/A
Financial aid: N/A
Tuition: N/A
Room/board/expenses: N/A
Enrollment: N/A

Loyola University Chicago

820 N. Michigan Avenue
Chicago, IL 60611
www.luc.edu/education/
Private
Admissions: (312) 915-6722
Email: schleduc@luc.edu
Financial aid: (773) 508-7704
Application deadline: N/A
Tuition: full time: $930/credit
hour; part time: $930/credit
hour
Room/board/expenses: $25,675
Full-time enrollment: 437
doctoral students: 38%;
master's students: 47%;
education specialists: 15%; men:
22%; women: 78%; minorities:
34%; international: 5%
Part-time enrollment: 195
doctoral students: 38%;
master's students: 61%;
education specialists: 1%; men:
24%; women: 76%; minorities:
40%; international: 1%
Acceptance rate (master's): 70%
Acceptance rate (doctoral): 27%
Entrance test required: GRE
**Avg. GRE (of all entering students
with scores):** quantitative: 148;
verbal: 152

Research assistantships: 87
Students reporting specialty: 100%
Students specializing in:
curriculum/instr.: 10%;
admin.: 16%; policy: 4%;
evaluation/research/
statistics: 3%; educational
psych: 4%; elementary: 4%;
higher education admin.:
21%; secondary: 2%; social/
philosophical foundations: 5%;
special: 2%; counseling: 16%;
other: 14%

National-Louis University[1]

122 S. Michigan Avenue
Chicago, IL 60603
www.nl.edu
Private
Admissions: N/A
Financial aid: N/A
Tuition: N/A
Room/board/expenses: N/A
Enrollment: N/A

Northern Illinois University[1]

321 Graham Hall
DeKalb, IL 60115
www.niu.edu
Public
Admissions: N/A
Financial aid: N/A
Tuition: N/A
Room/board/expenses: N/A
Enrollment: N/A

Northwestern University

2120 Campus Drive
Evanston, IL 60208
www.sesp.northwestern.edu
Private
Admissions: (847) 467-2789
Email: sesp@northwestern.edu
Financial aid: (847) 467-2789
Application deadline: rolling
Tuition: full time: $49,024; part
time: $5,766/credit hour
Room/board/expenses: N/A
Full-time enrollment: 149
doctoral students: 42%;
master's students: 58%;
education specialists: N/A; men:
24%; women: 76%; minorities:
16%; international: 10%
Part-time enrollment: 134
doctoral students: N/A; master's
students: 100%; education
specialists: N/A; men: 29%;
women: 71%; minorities: 8%;
international: 1%
Acceptance rate (master's): 65%
Acceptance rate (doctoral): 8%
Entrance test required: GRE
**Avg. GRE (of all entering students
with scores):** quantitative: 157;
verbal: 161
Research assistantships: 30
Students reporting specialty: 100%
Students specializing in:
elementary: 4%; higher
education admin.: 19%;
secondary: 14%; other: 63%

Roosevelt University

430 S. Michigan Avenue
Chicago, IL 60605
www.roosevelt.edu
Private
Admissions: (877) 277-5978
Email:
admissions@roosevelt.edu
Financial aid: (866) 421-0935

Application deadline: rolling
Tuition: full time: $17,325; part
time: $811/credit hour
Room/board/expenses: $800
Full-time enrollment: 90
doctoral students: 0%; master's
students: 100%; education
specialists: N/A; men: 22%;
women: 78%; minorities: 34%;
international: N/A
Part-time enrollment: 190
doctoral students: 13%;
master's students: 87%;
education specialists: 0%; men:
23%; women: 77%; minorities:
42%; international: N/A
Acceptance rate (master's): 64%
Acceptance rate (doctoral): N/A
Entrance test required: N/A
**Avg. GRE (of all entering students
with scores):** quantitative: N/A;
verbal: N/A
Research assistantships: 0
Students reporting specialty: 91%
Students specializing in:
curriculum/instr.: 17%; admin.:
18%; elementary: 15%;
secondary: 10%; special: 4%;
counseling: 16%; other: 20%

Southern Illinois University-Carbondale

Wham Building 115
Carbondale, IL 62901-4624
web.coehs.siu.edu/Public/
Public
Admissions: (618) 536-7791
Email: gradschl@siu.edu
Financial aid: (618) 453-4334
Application deadline: rolling
In-state tuition: full time: $1,326/
credit hour; part time: $1,326/
credit hour
Out-of-state tuition: full time:
$1,952/credit hour
Room/board/expenses: $17,421
Full-time enrollment: 528
doctoral students: 18%;
master's students: 82%;
education specialists: N/A; men:
28%; women: 72%; minorities:
28%; international: 17%
Part-time enrollment: 443
doctoral students: 38%;
master's students: 62%;
education specialists: N/A; men:
33%; women: 67%; minorities:
26%; international: 7%
Acceptance rate (master's): 87%
Acceptance rate (doctoral): 97%
Entrance test required: GRE
**Avg. GRE (of all entering students
with scores):** quantitative: 145;
verbal: 142
Research assistantships: 115
Students reporting specialty: 100%
Students specializing in:
curriculum/instr.: 16%; admin.:
7%; elementary: 1%; secondary:
4%; social/philosophical
foundations: 1%; special: 1%;
counseling: 3%; technical
(vocational): 1%; other: 69%

Southern Illinois University-Edwardsville

Campus Box 1049
Edwardsville, IL 62026
www.siue.edu/education/
Public
Admissions: N/A
Financial aid: N/A
Application deadline: rolling
In-state tuition: full time: $6,997;
part time: $5,237

Out-of-state tuition: full time:
$14,915
Room/board/expenses: $13,473
Full-time enrollment: 43
doctoral students: 0%; master's
students: 93%; education
specialists: 7%; men: 19%;
women: 81%; minorities: 16%;
international: 16%
Part-time enrollment: 301
doctoral students: 6%; master's
students: 78%; education
specialists: 16%; men: 28%;
women: 72%; minorities: 23%;
international: 0%
Acceptance rate (master's): 69%
Acceptance rate (doctoral): 100%
Entrance test required: GRE
**Avg. GRE (of all entering students
with scores):** quantitative: 150;
verbal: 153
Research assistantships: 12
Students reporting specialty: 94%
Students specializing in:
curriculum/instr.: 22%; admin.:
29%; educational tech.:
15%; secondary: 8%; social/
philosophical foundations: 6%;
counseling: 12%; other: 8%

University of Illinois-Chicago

1040 W. Harrison Street
Chicago, IL 60607-7133
www.education.uic.edu
Public
Admissions: (312) 996-4532
Email: aelami2@uic.edu
Financial aid: (312) 996-3126
Application deadline: rolling
In-state tuition: full time: $14,560;
part time: $10,734
Out-of-state tuition: full time:
$26,800
Room/board/expenses: $17,958
Full-time enrollment: 146
doctoral students: 51%;
master's students: 49%;
education specialists: N/A; men:
25%; women: 75%; minorities:
38%; international: 10%
Part-time enrollment: 500
doctoral students: 48%;
master's students: 52%;
education specialists: N/A; men:
27%; women: 73%; minorities:
41%; international: 3%
Acceptance rate (master's): 73%
Acceptance rate (doctoral): 51%
Entrance test required: GRE
**Avg. GRE (of all entering students
with scores):** quantitative: 153;
verbal: 155
Research assistantships: 87
Students reporting specialty: 100%
Students specializing in:
curriculum/instr.: 11%; admin.:
15%; policy: 2%; evaluation/
research/statistics: 11%;
educational psych: 13%;
elementary: 2%; secondary: 5%;
social/philosophical foundations:
4%; special: 16%; other: 21%

University of Illinois-Urbana-Champaign

1310 S. Sixth Street
Champaign, IL 61820
education.illinois.edu
Public
Admissions: (217) 333-2800
Email: saao@education.illinois.
edu
Financial aid: (217) 333-2800
Application deadline: 04/01

In-state tuition: full time: $15,818; part time: $11,798
Out-of-state tuition: full time: $29,816
Room/board/expenses: $17,900
Full-time enrollment: 372
doctoral students: 75%; master's students: 25%; education specialists: N/A; men: 32%; women: 68%; minorities: 40%; international: 20%
Part-time enrollment: 409
doctoral students: 27%; master's students: 73%; education specialists: N/A; men: 30%; women: 70%; minorities: 25%; international: 6%
Acceptance rate (master's): 63%
Acceptance rate (doctoral): 18%
Entrance test required: GRE
Avg. GRE (of all entering students with scores): quantitative: N/A; verbal: N/A
Research assistantships: 126
Students reporting specialty: 100%
Students specializing in: curriculum/instr.: 19%; admin.: 9%; policy: 27%; evaluation/research/statistics: 2%; educational psych: 8%; educational tech.: 2%; elementary: 2%; higher education admin.: 7%; junior high: 5%; secondary: 3%; social/philosophical foundations: 24%; special: 8%; counseling: 2%; other: 26%

Western Illinois University[1]

1 University Circle
Macomb, IL 61455
www.wiu.edu
Public
Admissions: N/A
Financial aid: N/A
Tuition: N/A
Room/board/expenses: N/A
Enrollment: N/A

INDIANA

Ball State University

2000 W. University Avenue
Muncie, IN 47306
www.bsu.edu/gradschool/
Public
Admissions: (765) 285-1297
Email: gradschool@bsu.edu
Financial aid: (765) 285-5600
Application deadline: rolling
In-state tuition: full time: $386/credit hour; part time: $386/credit hour
Out-of-state tuition: full time: $1,059/credit hour
Room/board/expenses: $13,922
Full-time enrollment: 623
doctoral students: 13%; master's students: 84%; education specialists: 3%; men: 20%; women: 80%; minorities: 13%; international: 5%
Part-time enrollment: 1,996
doctoral students: 8%; master's students: 92%; education specialists: 1%; men: 20%; women: 80%; minorities: 13%; international: 2%
Acceptance rate (master's): 73%
Acceptance rate (doctoral): 33%
Entrance test required: GRE
Avg. GRE (of all entering students with scores): quantitative: 148; verbal: 151
Research assistantships: 70

Students reporting specialty: 100%
Students specializing in: curriculum/instr.: 2%; admin.: 19%; instructional media design: 0%; educational psych: 3%; elementary: 5%; junior high: 0%; secondary: 1%; special: 73%; counseling: 2%; technical (vocational): 0%; other: 24%

Indiana State University

401 N. Seventh Street
Terre Haute, IN 47809
www.coe.indstate.edu/
Public
Admissions: (800) 444-4723
Email: grdstudy@indstate.edu
Financial aid: (800) 841-4744
Application deadline: rolling
In-state tuition: full time: $388/credit hour; part time: $388/credit hour
Out-of-state tuition: full time: $762/credit hour
Room/board/expenses: $13,156
Full-time enrollment: 303
doctoral students: 45%; master's students: 52%; education specialists: 3%; men: 30%; women: 70%; minorities: 15%; international: 13%
Part-time enrollment: 334
doctoral students: 63%; master's students: 27%; education specialists: 10%; men: 37%; women: 63%; minorities: 14%; international: 4%
Acceptance rate (master's): 24%
Acceptance rate (doctoral): 31%
Entrance test required: GRE
Avg. GRE (of all entering students with scores): quantitative: N/A; verbal: N/A
Research assistantships: 2
Students reporting specialty: 100%
Students specializing in: curriculum/instr.: 16%; admin.: 32%; instructional media design: 0%; educational psych: 2%; elementary: 2%; higher education admin.: 13%; special: 9%; counseling: 16%; other: 10%

Indiana University-Bloomington

201 N. Rose Avenue
Bloomington, IN 47405-1006
education.indiana.edu/
Public
Admissions: (812) 856-8504
Email: educate@indiana.edu
Financial aid: (812) 855-3278
Application deadline: 01/01
In-state tuition: full time: $416/credit hour; part time: $416/credit hour
Out-of-state tuition: full time: $1,222/credit hour
Room/board/expenses: $20,016
Full-time enrollment: 421
doctoral students: 50%; master's students: 47%; education specialists: 3%; men: 31%; women: 69%; minorities: 20%; international: 28%
Part-time enrollment: 460
doctoral students: 50%; master's students: 45%; education specialists: 5%; men: 32%; women: 68%; minorities: 16%; international: 18%
Acceptance rate (master's): 50%
Acceptance rate (doctoral): 45%
Entrance test required: GRE

Avg. GRE (of all entering students with scores): quantitative: 151; verbal: 153
Research assistantships: 106
Students reporting specialty: 100%
Students specializing in: curriculum/instr.: 10%; admin.: 14%; policy: 5%; evaluation/research/statistics: 2%; instructional media design: 13%; educational psych: 11%; elementary: 2%; higher education admin.: 8%; secondary: 1%; social/philosophical foundations: 5%; special: 4%; counseling: 16%; other: 8%

Oakland City University[1]

143 N. Lucretia Street
Oakland City, IN 47660
www.oak.edu
Private
Admissions: N/A
Financial aid: N/A
Tuition: N/A
Room/board/expenses: N/A
Enrollment: N/A

Purdue University-West Lafayette

100 N. University Street
West Lafayette, IN 47907-2098
www.education.purdue.edu/
Public
Admissions: (765) 494-2345
Email: education-gradoffice@purdue.edu
Financial aid: (765) 494-5050
Application deadline: rolling
In-state tuition: full time: $10,002; part time: $348/credit hour
Out-of-state tuition: full time: $28,804
Room/board/expenses: $12,820
Full-time enrollment: 129
doctoral students: 74%; master's students: 26%; education specialists: 0%; men: 30%; women: 70%; minorities: 17%; international: 38%
Part-time enrollment: 437
doctoral students: 24%; master's students: 75%; education specialists: 1%; men: 31%; women: 69%; minorities: 16%; international: 8%
Acceptance rate (master's): 80%
Acceptance rate (doctoral): 45%
Entrance test required: GRE
Avg. GRE (of all entering students with scores): quantitative: 152; verbal: 153
Research assistantships: 58
Students reporting specialty: 100%
Students specializing in: curriculum/instr.: 18%; admin.: 8%; educational psych: 9%; educational tech.: 36%; higher education admin.: 0%; special: 19%; counseling: 7%; technical (vocational): 2%

IOWA

Drake University

3206 University Avenue
Des Moines, IA 50311-4505
www.drake.edu/soe/
Private
Admissions: (515) 271-2552
Email: soegradadmission@drake.edu
Financial aid: (515) 271-3048
Application deadline: rolling

Tuition: full time: $34,050; part time: $665/credit hour
Room/board/expenses: $10,742
Full-time enrollment: 86
doctoral students: N/A; master's students: 98%; education specialists: 2%; men: 28%; women: 72%; minorities: 5%; international: 3%
Part-time enrollment: 440
doctoral students: 14%; master's students: 79%; education specialists: 7%; men: 25%; women: 75%; minorities: 4%; international: 1%
Acceptance rate (master's): 80%
Acceptance rate (doctoral): 100%
Entrance test required: GRE
Avg. GRE (of all entering students with scores): quantitative: 151; verbal: 154
Research assistantships: 1
Students reporting specialty: 100%
Students specializing in: curriculum/instr.: 19%; admin.: 16%; elementary: 8%; higher education admin.: 12%; junior high: 1%; secondary: 9%; special: 1%; counseling: 11%; other: 24%

Iowa State University

E262 Lagomarcino Hall
Ames, IA 50011
www.grad-college.iastate.edu/
Public
Admissions: (515) 294-5836
Email: admissions@iastate.edu
Financial aid: (515) 294-2223
Application deadline: rolling
In-state tuition: full time: $9,172; part time: $452/credit hour
Out-of-state tuition: full time: $22,096
Room/board/expenses: $12,303
Full-time enrollment: 155
doctoral students: 26%; master's students: 74%; education specialists: N/A; men: 33%; women: 67%; minorities: 18%; international: 12%
Part-time enrollment: 222
doctoral students: 41%; master's students: 59%; education specialists: N/A; men: 31%; women: 69%; minorities: 11%; international: 5%
Acceptance rate (master's): 61%
Acceptance rate (doctoral): 40%
Entrance test required: GRE
Avg. GRE (of all entering students with scores): quantitative: 150; verbal: 152
Research assistantships: 31
Students reporting specialty: 100%
Students specializing in: curriculum/instr.: 9%; admin.: 9%; evaluation/research/statistics: 1%; educational psych: 0%; educational tech.: 10%; higher education admin.: 51%; junior high: 4%; secondary: 4%; social/philosophical foundations: 1%; special: 3%; other: 15%

University of Iowa

Lindquist Center
Iowa City, IA 52242
www.education.uiowa.edu
Public
Admissions: (319) 335-5359
Email: edu-educationservices@uiowa.edu
Financial aid: (319) 335-1450
Application deadline: rolling

In-state tuition: full time: $11,223; part time: $544/credit hour
Out-of-state tuition: full time: $28,133
Room/board/expenses: $16,250
Full-time enrollment: 432
doctoral students: 66%; master's students: 34%; education specialists: 0%; men: 31%; women: 69%; minorities: 16%; international: 21%
Part-time enrollment: 213
doctoral students: 57%; master's students: 38%; education specialists: 5%; men: 46%; women: 54%; minorities: 11%; international: 10%
Acceptance rate (master's): 58%
Acceptance rate (doctoral): 45%
Entrance test required: GRE
Avg. GRE (of all entering students with scores): quantitative: 151; verbal: 152
Research assistantships: 198
Students reporting specialty: 100%
Students specializing in: admin.: 9%; evaluation/research/statistics: 10%; educational psych: 4%; elementary: 1%; higher education admin.: 11%; secondary: 21%; social/philosophical foundations: 5%; special: 12%; counseling: 6%; other: 24%

University of Northern Iowa

205 Schindler Center
Cedar Falls, IA 50614-0610
www.uni.edu/coe
Public
Admissions: (319) 273-2623
Email: registrar@uni.edu
Financial aid: (800) 772-2736
Application deadline: rolling
In-state tuition: full time: $9,219; part time: $448/credit hour
Out-of-state tuition: full time: $19,389
Room/board/expenses: $11,320
Full-time enrollment: 141
doctoral students: 15%; master's students: 80%; education specialists: 5%; men: 30%; women: 70%; minorities: 9%; international: 16%
Part-time enrollment: 385
doctoral students: 17%; master's students: 80%; education specialists: 3%; men: 27%; women: 73%; minorities: 7%; international: 5%
Acceptance rate (master's): 66%
Acceptance rate (doctoral): 55%
Entrance test required: GRE
Avg. GRE (of all entering students with scores): quantitative: 146; verbal: 150
Research assistantships: 15
Students reporting specialty: 76%
Students specializing in: curriculum/instr.: 6%; admin.: 6%; educational psych: 2%; educational tech.: 10%; elementary: 4%; secondary: 9%; social/philosophical foundations: 1%; special: 5%; counseling: 7%; other: 50%

KANSAS

Baker University
PO Box 65
Baldwin City, KS 66006
www.bakeru.edu/
soe-prospective-students2
Private
Admissions: (913) 491-4432
Email: education@bakeru.edu
Financial aid: N/A
Application deadline: rolling
Tuition: full time: $375/credit
hour; part time: $375/credit hour
Room/board/expenses: N/A
Full-time enrollment: 434
doctoral students: 32%;
master's students: 68%;
education specialists: N/A; men:
28%; women: 72%; minorities:
13%; international: N/A
Part-time enrollment: 82
doctoral students: 100%;
master's students: N/A;
education specialists: N/A; men:
44%; women: 56%; minorities:
27%; international: N/A
Acceptance rate (master's): N/A
Acceptance rate (doctoral): 75%
Entrance test required: N/A
**Avg. GRE (of all entering students
with scores):** quantitative: N/A;
verbal: N/A
Students reporting specialty: 15%
Students specializing in: N/A

Kansas State University
006 Bluemont Hall
Manhattan, KS 66506
www.ksu.edu/
Public
Admissions: (785) 532-5765
Email: coegrads@ksu.edu
Financial aid: (785) 532-6420
Application deadline: rolling
In-state tuition: full time: $478/
credit hour; part time: $478/
credit hour
Out-of-state tuition: full time:
$957/credit hour
Room/board/expenses: $11,604
Full-time enrollment: 192
doctoral students: 25%;
master's students: 75%;
education specialists: N/A; men:
38%; women: 63%; minorities:
19%; international: 19%
Part-time enrollment: 609
doctoral students: 24%;
master's students: 76%;
education specialists: N/A; men:
31%; women: 69%; minorities:
17%; international: 1%
Acceptance rate (master's): 97%
Acceptance rate (doctoral): 71%
Entrance test required: GRE
**Avg. GRE (of all entering students
with scores):** quantitative: 147;
verbal: 151
Research assistantships: 16
Students reporting specialty: 84%
Students specializing in:
curriculum/instr.: 22%; admin.:
15%; special: 3%; counseling:
17%; other: 43%

Southwestern College[1]
100 College Street
Winfield, KS 67156-2499
www.sckans.edu/
Private
Admissions: N/A
Financial aid: N/A
Tuition: N/A
Room/board/expenses: N/A
Enrollment: N/A

University of Kansas
217 Joseph R. Pearson Hall
Lawrence, KS 66045
www.soe.ku.edu
Public
Admissions: (785) 864-4510
Email: khuggett@ku.edu
Financial aid: (785) 864-4700
Application deadline: N/A
In-state tuition: full time: $378/
credit hour; part time: $378/
credit hour
Out-of-state tuition: full time:
$881/credit hour
Room/board/expenses: N/A
Full-time enrollment: 536
doctoral students: 63%;
master's students: 35%;
education specialists: 2%; men:
36%; women: 64%; minorities:
16%; international: 21%
Part-time enrollment: 580
doctoral students: 14%;
master's students: 86%;
education specialists: 0%; men:
20%; women: 80%; minorities:
14%; international: 1%
Acceptance rate (master's): 79%
Acceptance rate (doctoral): 44%
Entrance test required: GRE
**Avg. GRE (of all entering students
with scores):** quantitative: 153;
verbal: 154
Research assistantships: 80
Students reporting specialty: 100%
Students specializing in:
curriculum/instr.: 25%; admin.:
11%; policy: 1%; evaluation/
research/statistics: 3%;
educational psych: 2%;
educational tech.: 4%;
higher education admin.:
10%; secondary: 1%; social/
philosophical foundations: 2%;
special: 29%; counseling: 6%;
other: 6%

Wichita State University[1]
1845 N. Fairmount
Wichita, KS 67260-0131
www.wichita.edu
Public
Admissions: N/A
Financial aid: N/A
Tuition: N/A
Room/board/expenses: N/A
Enrollment: N/A

KENTUCKY

Eastern Kentucky University[1]
521 Lancaster Avenue
Richmond, KY 40475
www.eku.edu
Public
Admissions: N/A
Financial aid: N/A
Tuition: N/A
Room/board/expenses: N/A
Enrollment: N/A

Morehead State University
Ginger Hall 100
Morehead, KY 40351
www.moreheadstate.edu/
education/
Public
Admissions: N/A
Financial aid: N/A
Application deadline: rolling
In-state tuition: full time: $10,422;
part time: $579/credit hour

Out-of-state tuition: full time:
$10,422
Room/board/expenses: $11,485
Full-time enrollment: 52
doctoral students: 8%; master's
students: 88%; education
specialists: 4%; men: 25%;
women: 75%; minorities: 10%;
international: 4%
Part-time enrollment: 495
doctoral students: 13%;
master's students: 74%;
education specialists: 13%; men:
31%; women: 69%; minorities:
4%; international: N/A
Acceptance rate (master's): N/A
Acceptance rate (doctoral): N/A
Entrance test required: GRE
**Avg. GRE (of all entering students
with scores):** quantitative: N/A;
verbal: N/A
Students reporting specialty: 100%
Students specializing in:
curriculum/instr.: 9%; admin.:
17%; instructional media design:
9%; educational tech.: 9%;
elementary: 3%; junior high: 0%;
secondary: 12%; special: 2%;
counseling: 17%; other: 23%

Northern Kentucky University[1]
Nunn Drive
Highland Heights, KY 41099
www.nku.edu
Public
Admissions: N/A
Financial aid: N/A
Tuition: N/A
Room/board/expenses: N/A
Enrollment: N/A

Spalding University[1]
851 S. Fourth Street
Louisville, KY 40203
spalding.edu/
Private
Admissions: N/A
Financial aid: N/A
Tuition: N/A
Room/board/expenses: N/A
Enrollment: N/A

University of Kentucky
103 Dickey Hall
Lexington, KY 40506-0033
www.gradschool.uky.edu/
Public
Admissions: (859) 257-4905
Email: Brian.Jackson@uky.edu
Financial aid: (859) 257-3172
Application deadline: rolling
In-state tuition: full time: $12,901;
part time: $617/credit hour
Out-of-state tuition: full time:
$27,403
Room/board/expenses: $16,032
Full-time enrollment: 489
doctoral students: 47%;
master's students: 49%;
education specialists: 4%; men:
34%; women: 66%; minorities:
20%; international: 7%
Part-time enrollment: 268
doctoral students: 56%;
master's students: 41%;
education specialists: 3%; men:
38%; women: 62%; minorities:
12%; international: N/A
Acceptance rate (master's): 77%
Acceptance rate (doctoral): 49%
Entrance test required: GRE
**Avg. GRE (of all entering students
with scores):** quantitative: 149;
verbal: 151

Research assistantships: 40
Students reporting specialty: 60%
Students specializing in:
curriculum/instr.: 2%; admin.:
28%; policy: 9%; evaluation/
research/statistics: 16%;
instructional media design:
1%; educational psych:
6%; educational tech.: 1%;
elementary: 0%; higher
education admin.: 5%;
secondary: 10%; social/
philosophical foundations: 2%;
special: 11%; other: 16%

University of Louisville
Cardinal Boulevard
and First Street
Louisville, KY 40292
www.louisville.edu/education
Public
Admissions: (502) 852-3101
Email: gradadm@louisville.edu
Financial aid: (502) 852-5511
Application deadline: rolling
In-state tuition: full time: $11,860;
part time: $649/credit hour
Out-of-state tuition: full time:
$24,470
Room/board/expenses: $14,506
Full-time enrollment: 359
doctoral students: 25%;
master's students: 75%;
education specialists: 0%; men:
34%; women: 66%; minorities:
22%; international: 4%
Part-time enrollment: 633
doctoral students: 18%;
master's students: 76%;
education specialists: 6%; men:
37%; women: 63%; minorities:
24%; international: 1%
Acceptance rate (master's): 66%
Acceptance rate (doctoral): 35%
Entrance test required: GRE
**Avg. GRE (of all entering students
with scores):** quantitative: 147;
verbal: 151
Research assistantships: 38
Students reporting specialty: 100%
Students specializing in:
curriculum/instr.: 4%; admin.:
13%; elementary: 3%; higher
education admin.: 9%; special:
5%; counseling: 19%; other: 48%

University of the Cumberlands
7792 College Station Drive
Williamsburg, KY 40769
www.ucumberlands.edu
Private
Admissions: (606) 539-4530
Email:
gradadm@ucumberlands.edu
Financial aid: (606) 539-4239
Application deadline: rolling
Tuition: full time: $315/credit
hour; part time: $315/credit hour
Room/board/expenses: $400
Full-time enrollment: 2,568
doctoral students: 4%; master's
students: 88%; education
specialists: 8%; men: 79%;
women: 21%; minorities: 15%;
international: 0%
Part-time enrollment: 486
doctoral students: 13%;
master's students: 62%;
education specialists: 25%;
men: 51%; women: 49%;
minorities: 25%; international:
N/A
Acceptance rate (master's): 78%
Acceptance rate (doctoral): 22%
Entrance test required: GRE

**Avg. GRE (of all entering students
with scores):** quantitative: N/A;
verbal: 149
Research assistantships: 2
Students reporting specialty: 100%
Students specializing in: admin.:
13%; evaluation/research/
statistics: 5%; elementary: 31%;
junior high: 6%; secondary: 13%;
special: 17%; counseling: 16%

Western Kentucky University
1906 College Heights Boulevard
Bowling Green, KY 42101
www.wku.edu/cebs
Public
Admissions: (270) 745-2446
Email:
graduate.studies@wku.edu
Financial aid: (270) 745-2755
Application deadline: rolling
In-state tuition: full time: $362/
credit hour; part time: $395/
credit hour
Out-of-state tuition: full time:
$763/credit hour
Room/board/expenses: $11,749
Full-time enrollment: 163
doctoral students: 3%; master's
students: 88%; education
specialists: 9%; men: 11%;
women: 89%; minorities: 5%;
international: 4%
Part-time enrollment: 425
doctoral students: 7%; master's
students: 90%; education
specialists: 3%; men: 16%;
women: 84%; minorities: 11%;
international: N/A
Acceptance rate (master's): 43%
Acceptance rate (doctoral): 100%
Entrance test required: GRE
**Avg. GRE (of all entering students
with scores):** quantitative: 147;
verbal: 152
Research assistantships: 21
Students reporting specialty: 100%
Students specializing in: admin.:
9%; elementary: 14%; junior
high: 3%; secondary: 7%;
special: 8%; other: 59%

LOUISIANA

Grambling State University
GSU Box 4305
Grambling, LA 71245
www.gram.edu/
Public
Admissions: N/A
Financial aid: N/A
Application deadline: 07/01
In-state tuition: full time: $6,822;
part time: $284/credit hour
Out-of-state tuition: full time:
$12,447
Room/board/expenses: $18,045
Full-time enrollment: 19
doctoral students: 21%;
master's students: 79%;
education specialists: N/A; men:
16%; women: 84%; minorities:
84%; international: 16%
Part-time enrollment: 107
doctoral students: 62%;
master's students: 38%;
education specialists: N/A; men:
23%; women: 77%; minorities:
82%; international: 1%
Acceptance rate (master's): 32%
Acceptance rate (doctoral): 43%
Entrance test required: N/A
**Avg. GRE (of all entering students
with scores):** quantitative: N/A;
verbal: N/A

Students reporting specialty: 100%
Students specializing in:
curriculum/instr.: 6%;
admin.: 7%; elementary: 14%;
secondary: 2%; special: 3%;
other: 68%

Louisiana State University-Baton Rouge

223 Peabody Hall
Baton Rouge, LA 70803
www.lsu.edu/coe
Public
Admissions: (225) 578-1641
Email: graddeanoffice@lsu.edu
Financial aid: (225) 578-3103
Application deadline: rolling
In-state tuition: full time: $10,602;
part time: $6,022
Out-of-state tuition: full time:
$27,822
Room/board/expenses: $14,856
Full-time enrollment: 230
doctoral students: 30%;
master's students: 70%;
education specialists: 0%; men:
21%; women: 79%; minorities:
29%; international: 4%
Part-time enrollment: 239
doctoral students: 32%;
master's students: 63%;
education specialists: 5%; men:
18%; women: 82%; minorities:
33%; international: N/A
Acceptance rate (master's): 78%
Acceptance rate (doctoral): 59%
Entrance test required: GRE
**Avg. GRE (of all entering students
with scores):** quantitative: 147;
verbal: 151
Research assistantships: 31
Students reporting specialty: 100%
Students specializing in:
curriculum/instr.: 16%; admin.:
28%; educational psych:
5%; elementary: 4%; higher
education admin.: 19%;
secondary: 3%; special: 3%;
counseling: 6%; other: 17%

Louisiana Tech University

PO Box 3163
Ruston, LA 71272-0001
www.latech.edu/education/
Public
Admissions: (318) 257-2924
Email: gschool@latech.edu
Financial aid: (318) 257-2641
Application deadline: 08/01
In-state tuition: full time: $7,080;
part time: $5,793
Out-of-state tuition: full time:
$16,383
Room/board/expenses: $11,460
Full-time enrollment: 284
doctoral students: 26%;
master's students: 74%;
education specialists: N/A; men:
30%; women: 70%; minorities:
11%; international: 4%
Part-time enrollment: 168
doctoral students: 34%;
master's students: 66%;
education specialists: N/A; men:
26%; women: 74%; minorities:
23%; international: 1%
Acceptance rate (master's): 68%
Acceptance rate (doctoral): 60%
Entrance test required: GRE
**Avg. GRE (of all entering students
with scores):** quantitative: 146;
verbal: 149
Research assistantships: 20

Students reporting specialty: 48%
Students specializing in: N/A

Southeastern Louisiana University

SLU 10671
Hammond, LA 70402
www.southeastern.edu/
Public
Admissions: N/A
Email: admissions@selu.edu
Financial aid: (985) 549-2244
Application deadline: 07/15
In-state tuition: full time: $7,844;
part time: $436/credit hour
Out-of-state tuition: full time:
$20,321
Room/board/expenses: $12,292
Full-time enrollment: 11
doctoral students: 9%; master's
students: 91%; education
specialists: N/A; men: N/A;
women: 100%; minorities: 18%;
international: N/A
Part-time enrollment: 233
doctoral students: 32%;
master's students: 68%;
education specialists: N/A; men:
17%; women: 83%; minorities:
34%; international: 0%
Acceptance rate (master's): 76%
Acceptance rate (doctoral): 92%
Entrance test required: GRE
**Avg. GRE (of all entering students
with scores):** quantitative: 143;
verbal: 147
Students reporting specialty: 100%
Students specializing in:
curriculum/instr.: 8%; admin.:
50%; elementary: 3%; special:
11%; other: 29%

Southern University and A&M College[1]

JC Clark Adminstration Building
4th Floor
Baton Rouge, LA 70813
www.subr.edu/
Public
Admissions: N/A
Financial aid: N/A
Tuition: N/A
Room/board/expenses: N/A
Enrollment: N/A

University of Louisiana-Lafayette

PO Drawer 44872
Lafayette, LA 70504-4872
www.louisiana.edu
Public
Admissions: N/A
Financial aid: N/A
Application deadline: rolling
In-state tuition: full time: $8,014;
part time: $445/credit hour
Out-of-state tuition: full time:
$21,741
Room/board/expenses: $14,192
Full-time enrollment: 97
doctoral students: 9%; master's
students: 91%; education
specialists: N/A; men: 24%;
women: 76%; minorities: 29%;
international: N/A
Part-time enrollment: 212
doctoral students: 46%;
master's students: 54%;
education specialists: N/A; men:
24%; women: 76%; minorities:
30%; international: N/A
Acceptance rate (master's): 57%
Acceptance rate (doctoral): 56%
Entrance test required: GRE

**Avg. GRE (of all entering students
with scores):** quantitative: 145;
verbal: 149
Research assistantships: 0
Students reporting specialty: 100%
Students specializing in:
curriculum/instr.: 7%; admin.:
44%; elementary: 4%; higher
education admin.: 4%;
secondary: 3%; special: 4%;
counseling: 24%; other: 10%

University of Louisiana-Monroe

Walker Hall 2-37
Monroe, LA 71209-0001
www.ulm.edu
Public
Admissions: (318) 342-1036
Email: admissions@ulm.edu
Financial aid: (318) 342-5320
Application deadline: 07/01
In-state tuition: full time: $8,005;
part time: $6,183
Out-of-state tuition: full time:
$20,105
Room/board/expenses: $12,209
Full-time enrollment: 50
doctoral students: 12%;
master's students: 88%;
education specialists: N/A; men:
18%; women: 82%; minorities:
30%; international: 2%
Part-time enrollment: 115
doctoral students: 0%; master's
students: 100%; education
specialists: N/A; men: 13%;
women: 87%; minorities: 30%;
international: 1%
Acceptance rate (master's): 79%
Acceptance rate (doctoral): 72%
Entrance test required: GRE
**Avg. GRE (of all entering students
with scores):** quantitative: N/A;
verbal: N/A
Research assistantships: 7
Students reporting specialty: 92%
Students specializing in:
curriculum/instr.: 42%; admin.:
15%; educational tech.: 8%;
elementary: 23%; secondary:
12%; special: 13%

University of New Orleans[1]

2000 Lakeshore Drive
New Orleans, LA 70148
coehd.uno.edu/
Public
Admissions: N/A
Financial aid: N/A
Tuition: N/A
Room/board/expenses: N/A
Enrollment: N/A

MAINE

University of Maine

Shibles Hall
Orono, ME 04469-5766
www.umaine.edu/edhd/
Public
Admissions: (207) 581-3219
Email: graduate@maine.edu
Financial aid: (207) 581-1324
Application deadline: rolling
In-state tuition: full time: $418/
credit hour; part time: $418/
credit hour
Out-of-state tuition: full time:
$1,330/credit hour
Room/board/expenses: $16,102
Full-time enrollment: 116
doctoral students: 6%; master's
students: 88%; education
specialists: 6%; men: 29%;

women: 71%; minorities: 14%;
international: 3%
Part-time enrollment: 208
doctoral students: 20%;
master's students: 64%;
education specialists: 16%; men:
22%; women: 78%; minorities:
3%; international: 1%
Acceptance rate (master's): 48%
Acceptance rate (doctoral): 10%
Entrance test required: GRE
**Avg. GRE (of all entering students
with scores):** quantitative: 148;
verbal: 152
Students reporting specialty: 100%
Students specializing in:
curriculum/instr.: 13%; admin.:
16%; educational tech.: 6%;
higher education admin.: 9%;
secondary: 1%; special: 16%;
counseling: 9%; other: 32%

MARYLAND

Bowie State University

14000 Jericho Park Road
Bowie, MD 20715-9465
www.bowiestate.edu/academics-
research/the-graduate-school/
Public
Admissions: (301) 860-3415
Email: gradadmissions@
bowiestate.edu
Financial aid: (301) 860-3540
Application deadline: N/A
In-state tuition: full time: $391/
credit hour; part time: $391/
credit hour
Out-of-state tuition: full time:
$681/credit hour
Room/board/expenses: $12,084
Full-time enrollment: 87
doctoral students: 2%; master's
students: 98%; education
specialists: N/A; men: 29%;
women: 71%; minorities: 34%;
international: 9%
Part-time enrollment: 82
doctoral students: 33%;
master's students: 67%;
education specialists: N/A; men:
34%; women: 66%; minorities:
85%; international: 10%
Acceptance rate (master's): 67%
Acceptance rate (doctoral): 100%
Entrance test required: GRE
**Avg. GRE (of all entering students
with scores):** quantitative: N/A;
verbal: N/A
Students reporting specialty: 0%
Students specializing in: N/A

Johns Hopkins University

2800 N. Charles Street
Baltimore, MD 21218
education.jhu.edu/admission/
Private
Admissions: (877) 548-7631
Email: soe.info@jhu.edu
Financial aid: (410) 516-9808
Application deadline: 04/01
Tuition: full time: $1,000/credit
hour; part time: $740/credit hour
Room/board/expenses: N/A
Full-time enrollment: 320
doctoral students: 6%; master's
students: 94%; education
specialists: N/A; men: 21%;
women: 79%; minorities: 42%;
international: 5%
Part-time enrollment: 1,675
doctoral students: 12%;
master's students: 88%;
education specialists: N/A; men:
25%; women: 75%; minorities:
39%; international: 3%

Acceptance rate (master's): 69%
Acceptance rate (doctoral): 19%
Entrance test required: GRE
**Avg. GRE (of all entering students
with scores):** quantitative: 151;
verbal: 154
Students reporting specialty: 100%
Students specializing in:
curriculum/instr.: 3%; admin.:
8%; evaluation/research/
statistics: 1%; educational
tech.: 3%; elementary: 18%;
secondary: 28%; special: 7%;
counseling: 12%; other: 34%

Morgan State University[1]

1700 E. Cold Spring Lane
Baltimore, MD 21251
www.morgan.edu/
Public
Admissions: N/A
Financial aid: N/A
Tuition: N/A
Room/board/expenses: N/A
Enrollment: N/A

Notre Dame of Maryland University[1]

4701 North Charles Street
Baltimore, MD 21210
www.ndm.edu
Private
Admissions: (410) 532-5317
Email: gradadm@ndm.edu
Financial aid: (410) 532-5369
Tuition: N/A
Room/board/expenses: N/A
Enrollment: N/A

Towson University

8000 York Road
Towson, MD 21252
grad.towson.edu
Public
Admissions: (410) 704-2501
Email: grads@towson.edu
Financial aid: (410) 704-4236
Application deadline: rolling
In-state tuition: full time: $372/
credit hour; part time: $372/
credit hour
Out-of-state tuition: full time:
$770/credit hour
Room/board/expenses: $16,106
Full-time enrollment: 290
doctoral students: 20%;
master's students: 80%;
education specialists: N/A; men:
16%; women: 84%; minorities:
14%; international: 3%
Part-time enrollment: 917
doctoral students: 3%; master's
students: 97%; education
specialists: N/A; men: 15%;
women: 85%; minorities: 13%;
international: 0%
Acceptance rate (master's): 49%
Acceptance rate (doctoral): 42%
Entrance test required: GRE
**Avg. GRE (of all entering students
with scores):** quantitative: 149;
verbal: 153
Research assistantships: 2
Students reporting specialty: 100%
Students specializing in: admin.:
18%; instructional media
design: 12%; educational psych:
3%; educational tech.: 2%;
elementary: 3%; secondary: 5%;
special: 14%; other: 43%

University of Maryland–College Park

3119 Benjamin Building
College Park, MD 20742-1121
www.education.umd.edu/
GraduatePrograms
Public
Admissions: (301) 405-5609
Email: pdowdcll@umd.edu
Financial aid: (301) 314-9000
Application deadline: rolling
In-state tuition: full time: $632/
credit hour; part time: $632/
credit hour
Out-of-state tuition: full time:
$1,363/credit hour
Room/board/expenses: $14,591
Full-time enrollment: 603
doctoral students: 57%;
master's students: 43%;
education specialists: 0%; men:
23%; women: 77%; minorities:
33%; international: 12%
Part-time enrollment: 346
doctoral students: 11%; master's
students: 89%; education
specialists: 0%; men: 17%;
women: 83%; minorities: 34%;
international: 1%
Acceptance rate (master's): 62%
Acceptance rate (doctoral): 21%
Entrance test required: GRE
Avg. GRE (of all entering students
with scores): quantitative: 154;
verbal: 157
Research assistantships: 47
Students reporting specialty: 99%
Students specializing in: admin.:
7%; policy: 6%; evaluation/
research/statistics: 5%;
educational psych: 8%;
educational tech.: 0%;
elementary: 4%; higher
education admin.: 4%; junior
high: 2%; secondary: 40%;
social/philosophical foundations:
1%; special: 9%; counseling: 14%

University of Maryland–Eastern Shore[1]

1 Backbone Road
Princess Anne, MD 21853
www.umes.edu
Public
Admissions: N/A
Financial aid: N/A
Tuition: N/A
Room/board/expenses: N/A
Enrollment: N/A

MASSACHUSETTS

American International College

1000 State Street
Springfield, MA 01109
www.aic.edu
Private
Admissions: (413) 205-3703
Email: kerry.barnes@aic.edu
Financial aid: (413) 205-3280
Application deadline: rolling
Tuition: full time: $439/credit
hour; part time: $439/credit
hour
Room/board/expenses: $14,100
Full-time enrollment: 1,186
doctoral students: 5%; master's
students: 95%; education
specialists: N/A; men: 20%;
women: 80%; minorities: 9%;
international: N/A

Part-time enrollment: 103
doctoral students: 7%; master's
students: 93%; education
specialists: N/A; men: 36%;
women: 64%; minorities: 12%;
international: N/A
Acceptance rate (master's): 92%
Acceptance rate (doctoral): 81%
Entrance test required: N/A
Avg. GRE (of all entering students
with scores): quantitative: N/A;
verbal: N/A
Research assistantships: 0
Students reporting specialty: 98%
Students specializing in: admin.:
16%; elementary: 11%; junior
high: 8%; secondary: 10%;
special: 27%; counseling: 3%;
other: 26%

Boston College (Lynch)

Campion Hall
Chestnut Hill, MA 02467-3813
www.bc.edu/schools/lsoe/
gradadmission
Private
Admissions: (617) 552-4214
Email: gsoe@bc.edu
Financial aid: (617) 552-3300
Application deadline: 12/31
Tuition: full time: $1,310/credit
hour; part time: $1,310/credit
hour
Room/board/expenses: $22,443
Full-time enrollment: 361
doctoral students: 16%;
master's students: 84%;
education specialists: N/A; men:
20%; women: 80%; minorities:
22%; international: 20%
Part-time enrollment: 432
doctoral students: 40%;
master's students: 60%;
education specialists: N/A; men:
27%; women: 73%; minorities:
19%; international: 5%
Acceptance rate (master's): 93%
Acceptance rate (doctoral): 14%
Entrance test required: GRE
Avg. GRE (of all entering students
with scores): quantitative: 152;
verbal: 155
Research assistantships: 414
Students reporting specialty: 100%
Students specializing in:
curriculum/instr.: 19%; admin.:
10%; evaluation/research/
statistics: 7%; educational
psych: 5%; elementary: 3%;
higher education admin.: 15%;
secondary: 7%; special: 9%;
counseling: 25%; other: 1%

Boston University

2 Silber Way
Boston, MA 02215
www.bu.edu/sed
Private
Admissions: (617) 353-4237
Email: sedgrad@bu.edu
Financial aid: (617) 353-4238
Application deadline: rolling
Tuition: full time: $48,102; part
time: $741/credit hour
Room/board/expenses: $18,086
Full-time enrollment: 204
doctoral students: 26%;
master's students: 74%;
education specialists: 0%; men:
25%; women: 75%; minorities:
19%; international: 23%
Part-time enrollment: 303
doctoral students: 18%;
master's students: 78%;

education specialists: 4%; men:
29%; women: 71%; minorities:
25%; international: 3%
Acceptance rate (master's): 66%
Acceptance rate (doctoral): 25%
Entrance test required: GRE
Avg. GRE (of all entering students
with scores): quantitative: 153;
verbal: 155
Research assistantships: 16
Students reporting specialty: 100%
Students specializing in:
curriculum/instr.: 32%; admin.:
14%; elementary: 1%; higher
education admin.: 14%;
secondary: 11%; special: 6%;
counseling: 18%; other: 17%

Cambridge College[1]

1000 Massachusetts Avenue
Cambridge, MA 02138
www.cambridgecollege.edu/
Private
Admissions: N/A
Financial aid: N/A
Tuition: N/A
Room/board/expenses: N/A
Enrollment: N/A

Harvard University

Appian Way
Cambridge, MA 02138
www.gse.harvard.edu
Private
Admissions: (617) 495-3414
Email:
gseadmissions@harvard.edu
Financial aid: (617) 495-3416
Application deadline: 12/01
Tuition: full time: $46,712; part
time: $25,072
Room/board/expenses: $24,032
Full-time enrollment: 817
doctoral students: 23%;
master's students: 77%;
education specialists: N/A; men:
28%; women: 72%; minorities:
30%; international: 19%
Part-time enrollment: 74
doctoral students: 4%; master's
students: 96%; education
specialists: N/A; men: 30%;
women: 70%; minorities: 23%;
international: 1%
Acceptance rate (master's): 54%
Acceptance rate (doctoral): 5%
Entrance test required: GRE
Avg. GRE (of all entering students
with scores): quantitative: 156;
verbal: 160
Research assistantships: 91
Students reporting specialty: 100%
Students specializing in:
curriculum/instr.: 4%; admin.:
19%; policy: 25%; evaluation/
research/statistics: 4%;
educational tech.: 4%;
higher education admin.: 7%;
secondary: 4%; counseling: 5%;
other: 38%

Lesley University[1]

29 Everett Street
Cambridge, MA 02138-2790
www.lesley.edu/soe.html
Private
Admissions: N/A
Financial aid: N/A
Tuition: N/A
Room/board/expenses: N/A
Enrollment: N/A

Northeastern University[1]

360 Huntington Avenue
50 Nightingale Hall
Boston, MA 02115
www.northeastern.edu/
Private
Admissions: N/A
Financial aid: N/A
Tuition: N/A
Room/board/expenses: N/A
Enrollment: N/A

Tufts University

Paige Hall
12 Upper Campus Road
Medford, MA 02155
www.tufts.edu/
Private
Admissions: N/A
Financial aid: N/A
Application deadline: 01/02
Tuition: full time: $41,958; part
time: $4,840/credit hour
Room/board/expenses: $10,952
Full-time enrollment: 100
doctoral students: 9%; master's
students: 91%; education
specialists: 0%; men: 14%;
women: 86%; minorities: 16%;
international: 7%
Part-time enrollment: 34
doctoral students: 18%;
master's students: 79%;
education specialists: 3%; men:
21%; women: 79%; minorities:
29%; international: 3%
Acceptance rate (master's): 77%
Acceptance rate (doctoral): 21%
Entrance test required: GRE
Avg. GRE (of all entering students
with scores): quantitative: 155;
verbal: 156
Research assistantships: 12
Students reporting specialty: 100%
Students specializing in: policy:
7%; evaluation/research/
statistics: 7%; educational
psych: 29%; elementary: 5%;
junior high: 29%; secondary:
29%; social/philosophical
foundations: 7%; other: 25%

University of Massachusetts–Amherst

Furcolo Hall
813 N. Pleasant Street
Amherst, MA 01003-9308
www.umass.edu/education
Public
Admissions: (413) 545-0722
Email:
gradadm@grad.umass.edu
Financial aid: (413) 545-0801
Application deadline: 01/02
In-state tuition: full time: $110/
credit hour; part time: $110/
credit hour
Out-of-state tuition: full time:
$414/credit hour
Room/board/expenses: $13,700
Full-time enrollment: 379
doctoral students: 50%;
master's students: 38%;
education specialists: 12%; men:
28%; women: 72%; minorities:
18%; international: 26%
Part-time enrollment: 223
doctoral students: 61%;
master's students: 33%;
education specialists: 6%; men:
33%; women: 67%; minorities:
20%; international: 5%
Acceptance rate (master's): 49%

Acceptance rate (doctoral): 44%
Entrance test required: GRE
Avg. GRE (of all entering students
with scores): quantitative: 152;
verbal: 155
Research assistantships: 153
Students reporting specialty: 100%
Students specializing in:
curriculum/instr.: 24%; admin.:
6%; policy: 7%; evaluation/
research/statistics: 4%;
educational psych: 7%;
educational tech.: 4%;
elementary: 4%; higher
education admin.: 13%; junior
high: 2%; secondary: 9%; social/
philosophical foundations: 5%;
special: 5%; counseling: 12%;
other: 4%

University of Massachusetts–Boston

100 Morrissey Boulevard
Boston, MA 02125-3393
www.umb.edu/academics/
graduate?nossl
Public
Admissions: (617) 287-6400
Email: bos.gadm@umb.edu
Financial aid: (617) 287-6300
Application deadline: N/A
In-state tuition: full time: $16,115;
part time: $108/credit hour
Out-of-state tuition: full time:
$23,283
Room/board/expenses: $14,850
Full-time enrollment: 388
doctoral students: 10%;
master's students: 86%;
education specialists: 4%; men:
20%; women: 80%; minorities:
12%; international: 6%
Part-time enrollment: 466
doctoral students: 22%;
master's students: 65%;
education specialists: 12%; men:
29%; women: 71%; minorities:
30%; international: 2%
Acceptance rate (master's): 77%
Acceptance rate (doctoral): 39%
Entrance test required: GRE
Avg. GRE (of all entering students
with scores): quantitative: 148;
verbal: 153
Research assistantships: 67
Students reporting specialty: 100%
Students specializing in: admin.:
9%; evaluation/research/
statistics: 3%; educational
psych: 7%; elementary: 34%;
special: 10%; counseling: 7%;
other: 31%

University of Massachusetts–Lowell

510 O'Leary Library
61 Wilder Street
Lowell, MA 01854
www.uml.edu
Public
Admissions: (978) 934-2373
Email: Graduate_Admissions@
uml.edu
Financial aid: (978) 934-2000
Application deadline: 08/01
In-state tuition: full time: $701/
credit hour; part time: $701/
credit hour
Out-of-state tuition: full time:
$1,295/credit hour
Room/board/expenses: $1,150
Full-time enrollment: 33
doctoral students: 6%; master's
students: 94%; education
specialists: 0%; men: 39%;

women: 61%; minorities: 15%;
international: 3%
Part-time enrollment: 351
doctoral students: 26%;
master's students: 60%;
education specialists: 14%; men:
26%; women: 74%; minorities:
9%; international: 0%
Acceptance rate (master's): 90%
Acceptance rate (doctoral): 91%
Entrance test required: GRE
**Avg. GRE (of all entering students
with scores):** quantitative: 146;
verbal: 152
Research assistantships: 1
Students reporting specialty: 72%
Students specializing in:
curriculum/instr.: 35%;
admin.: 16%; elementary: 5%;
higher education admin.: 11%;
secondary: 15%; special: 1%;
other: 18%

MICHIGAN

Andrews University
8975 US-31
Berrien Springs, MI 49104-0103
www.andrews.edu/
Private
Admissions: (800) 253-2874
Email: enroll@andrews.edu
Financial aid: (269) 471-3334
Application deadline: 07/15
Tuition: full time: $1,188/credit
hour; part time: $1,188/credit
hour
Room/board/expenses: $16,035
Full-time enrollment: 143
doctoral students: 74%;
master's students: 20%;
education specialists: 6%; men:
32%; women: 68%; minorities:
45%; International: 33%
Part-time enrollment: 87
doctoral students: 55%;
master's students: 37%;
education specialists: 8%; men:
47%; women: 53%; minorities:
32%; international: 23%
Acceptance rate (master's): 92%
Acceptance rate (doctoral): 97%
Entrance test required: GRE
**Avg. GRE (of all entering students
with scores):** quantitative: N/A;
verbal: N/A
Research assistantships: 4
Students reporting specialty: 100%
Students specializing in:
curriculum/instr.: 10%;
admin.: 9%; educational
psych: 10%; elementary: 0%;
higher education admin.: 7%;
secondary: 2%; special: 2%;
counseling: 32%; other: 27%

Central Michigan University[1]
105 Warriner
Mount Pleasant, MI 48859
www.cmich.edu/
Public
Admissions: N/A
Financial aid: N/A
Tuition: N/A
Room/board/expenses: N/A
Enrollment: N/A

Eastern Michigan University
310 Porter Building
Ypsilanti, MI 48197
www.emich.edu/coe/
Public
Admissions: (734) 487-3400

Email: graduate.admissions@
emich.edu
Financial aid: (734) 487-0455
Application deadline: rolling
In-state tuition: full time: $597/
credit hour; part time: $597/
credit hour
Out-of-state tuition: full time:
$1,100/credit hour
Room/board/expenses: $13,154
Full-time enrollment: 192
doctoral students: 0%; master's
students: 100%; education
specialists: 0%; men: 16%;
women: 84%; minorities: 13%;
international: 4%
Part-time enrollment: 779
doctoral students: 18%;
master's students: 74%;
education specialists: 7%; men:
25%; women: 75%; minorities:
20%; international: 2%
Acceptance rate (master's): 54%
Acceptance rate (doctoral): 43%
Entrance test required: GRE
**Avg. GRE (of all entering students
with scores):** quantitative: 147;
verbal: 152
Research assistantships: 3
Students reporting specialty: 100%
Students specializing in: admin.:
27%; evaluation/research/
statistics: 0%; instructional
media design: 4%; educational
psych: 4%; elementary: 2%;
higher education admin.:
10%; secondary: 4%; social/
philosophical foundations: 1%;
special: 23%; counseling: 5%;
other: 18%

Ferris State University
1349 Cramer Circle
Bishop 421
Big Rapids, MI 49307
www.ferris.edu/education/
education/
Public
Admissions: N/A
Financial aid: N/A
Application deadline: rolling
In-state tuition: full time: $527/
credit hour; part time: $527/
credit hour
Out-of-state tuition: full time:
$790/credit hour
Room/board/expenses: $500
Full-time enrollment: N/A
doctoral students: N/A; master's
students: N/A; education
specialists: N/A; men: N/A;
women: N/A; minorities: N/A;
international: N/A
Part-time enrollment: 83
doctoral students: N/A; master's
students: 100%; education
specialists: N/A; men: 37%;
women: 63%; minorities: N/A;
international: N/A
Acceptance rate (master's): 60%
Acceptance rate (doctoral): N/A
Entrance test required: N/A
**Avg. GRE (of all entering students
with scores):** quantitative: N/A;
verbal: N/A
Research assistantships: 0
Students reporting specialty: 77%
Students specializing in:
curriculum/instr.: 43%; admin.:
29%; higher education admin.:
11%; special: 17%

Michigan State University
620 Farm Lane, Room 501
East Lansing, MI 48824-1034
www.educ.msu.edu
Public
Admissions: (517) 355-8332
Email: admis@msu.edu
Financial aid: (517) 353-5940
Application deadline: rolling
In-state tuition: full time: $705/
credit hour; part time: $705/
credit hour
Out-of-state tuition: full time:
$1,353/credit hour
Room/board/expenses: $11,807
Full-time enrollment: 967
doctoral students: 56%;
master's students: 43%;
education specialists: 1%; men:
33%; women: 67%; minorities:
20%; international: 17%
Part-time enrollment: 363
doctoral students: 12%;
master's students: 88%;
education specialists: 0%; men:
24%; women: 76%; minorities:
10%; international: 3%
Acceptance rate (master's): 37%
Acceptance rate (doctoral): 34%
Entrance test required: GRE
**Avg. GRE (of all entering students
with scores):** quantitative: 140;
verbal: 143
Research assistantships: 203
Students reporting specialty: 72%
Students specializing in:
curriculum/instr.: 28%;
admin.: 8%; policy: 4%;
evaluation/research/
statistics: 2%; educational
psych: 2%; educational
tech.: 10%; elementary: 4%;
higher education admin.:
15%; secondary: 2%; social/
philosophical foundations: 2%;
special: 8%; counseling: 6%;
other: 9%

Oakland University
415 Pawley Hall
Rochester, MI 48309-4494
www.oakland.edu/grad
Public
Admissions: (248) 370-3167
Email: gradmail@oakland.edu
Financial aid: (248) 370-2550
Application deadline: rolling
In-state tuition: full time: $15,720;
part time: $655/credit hour
Out-of-state tuition: full time:
$24,648
Room/board/expenses: $11,886
Full-time enrollment: 325
doctoral students: 12%;
master's students: 88%;
education specialists: 0%; men:
20%; women: 80%; minorities:
18%; international: 8%
Part-time enrollment: 691
doctoral students: 14%;
master's students: 69%;
education specialists: 18%; men:
19%; women: 81%; minorities:
16%; international: 0%
Acceptance rate (master's): 53%
Acceptance rate (doctoral): 20%
Entrance test required: N/A
**Avg. GRE (of all entering students
with scores):** quantitative: N/A;
verbal: N/A
Students reporting specialty: 97%

Students specializing in:
curriculum/instr.: 1%; admin.:
18%; elementary: 7%; higher
education admin.: 1%;
secondary: 6%; special: 12%;
counseling: 23%; other: 31%

University of Michigan-Ann Arbor
610 E. University Street
Ann Arbor, MI 48109-1259
www.soe.umich.edu/
Public
Admissions: (734) 615-1528
Email: ed.grad.admit@umich.edu
Financial aid: (734) 615-1528
Application deadline: N/A
In-state tuition: full time: $21,368;
part time: $1,495/credit hour
Out-of-state tuition: full time:
$42,858
Room/board/expenses: $20,130
Full-time enrollment: 363
doctoral students: 60%;
master's students: 40%;
education specialists: N/A; men:
34%; women: 66%; minorities:
32%; international: 13%
Part-time enrollment: 56
doctoral students: 21%;
master's students: 79%;
education specialists: N/A; men:
29%; women: 71%; minorities:
14%; international: 14%
Acceptance rate (master's): 77%
Acceptance rate (doctoral): 16%
Entrance test required: GRE
**Avg. GRE (of all entering students
with scores):** quantitative: 154;
verbal: 157
Research assistantships: 136
Students reporting specialty: 81%
Students specializing in:
curriculum/instr.: 24%; admin.:
5%; policy: 6%; educational
psych: 8%; educational
tech.: 2%; elementary: 5%;
higher education admin.:
25%; secondary: 11%; social/
philosophical foundations: 8%;
other: 5%

University of Michigan-Dearborn[1]
19000 Hubbard Drive
Dearborn, MI 48126
www.soe.umd.umich.edu/
Public
Admissions: (313) 593-5006
Email: Joanno@umd.umich.edu
Financial aid: (313) 593-5300
Tuition: N/A
Room/board/expenses: N/A
Enrollment: N/A

Wayne State University
5425 Gullen Mall
Detroit, MI 48202-3489
www.coe.wayne.edu/
Public
Admissions: (313) 577-1605
Email:
gradadmissions@wayne.edu
Financial aid: (313) 577-2100
Application deadline: rolling
In-state tuition: full time: $590/
credit hour; part time: $590/
credit hour
Out-of-state tuition: full time:
$1,278/credit hour
Room/board/expenses: $16,431

Full-time enrollment: 513
doctoral students: 25%;
master's students: 71%;
education specialists: 4%; men:
24%; women: 76%; minorities:
31%; international: 10%
Part-time enrollment: 904
doctoral students: 12%;
master's students: 77%;
education specialists: 11%; men:
26%; women: 74%; minorities:
42%; international: 2%
Acceptance rate (master's): 44%
Acceptance rate (doctoral): 6%
Entrance test required: GRE
**Avg. GRE (of all entering students
with scores):** quantitative: 148;
verbal: 150
Research assistantships: 14
Students reporting specialty: 100%
Students specializing in:
curriculum/instr.: 5%; admin.:
13%; policy: 2%; evaluation/
research/statistics: 2%;
instructional media design:
9%; educational psych: 5%;
elementary: 4%; secondary:
6%; special: 6%; counseling:
15%; technical (vocational): 1%;
other: 33%

Western Michigan University
1903 W. Michigan Avenue
Kalamazoo, MI 49008-5229
www.wmich.edu/education/
Public
Admissions: (269) 387-2000
Email: ask-wmu@wmich.edu
Financial aid: (269) 387-6000
Application deadline: rolling
In-state tuition: full time: $530/
credit hour; part time: $530/
credit hour
Out-of-state tuition: full time:
$1,123/credit hour
Room/board/expenses: $13,751
Full-time enrollment: 683
doctoral students: 16%;
master's students: 84%;
education specialists: 0%; men:
28%; women: 72%; minorities:
23%; international: 14%
Part-time enrollment: 676
doctoral students: 27%;
master's students: 72%;
education specialists: 0%; men:
32%; women: 68%; minorities:
20%; international: 6%
Acceptance rate (master's): 75%
Acceptance rate (doctoral): 37%
Entrance test required: GRE
**Avg. GRE (of all entering students
with scores):** quantitative: 145;
verbal: 147
Research assistantships: 72
Students reporting specialty: 100%
Students specializing in:
admin.: 17%; evaluation/
research/statistics: 4%;
instructional media design:
4%; higher education admin.:
5%; secondary: 0%; social/
philosophical foundations: 1%;
special: 5%; counseling: 14%;
technical (vocational): 2%;
other: 51%

MINNESOTA

Bethel University[1]
3900 Bethel Drive
St. Paul, MN 55112-6999
gs.bethel.edu
Private
Admissions: N/A
Financial aid: N/A
Tuition: N/A
Room/board/expenses: N/A
Enrollment: N/A

Capella University[1]
225 South 6th Street
Minneapolis, MN 55402
www.capella.edu
Private
Admissions: N/A
Financial aid: N/A
Tuition: N/A
Room/board/expenses: N/A
Enrollment: N/A

Hamline University
1536 Hewitt Avenue
St. Paul, MN 55104-1284
www.hamline.edu
Private
Admissions: (651) 523-2900
Email: gradprog@hamline.edu
Financial aid: N/A
Application deadline: rolling
Tuition: full time: $437/credit hour; part time: $437/credit hour
Room/board/expenses: $11,512
Full-time enrollment: 269
doctoral students: 1%; master's students: 99%; education specialists: N/A; men: 29%; women: 71%; minorities: 11%; international: 3%
Part-time enrollment: 541
doctoral students: 9%; master's students: 91%; education specialists: N/A; men: 24%; women: 76%; minorities: 10%; international: 1%
Acceptance rate (master's): 72%
Acceptance rate (doctoral): 48%
Entrance test required: N/A
Avg. GRE (of all entering students with scores): quantitative: N/A; verbal: N/A
Research assistantships: 0
Students reporting specialty: 100%
Students specializing in: admin.: 9%; elementary: 24%; secondary: 22%; social/philosophical foundations: 13%; other: 32%

Minnesota State University-Mankato[1]
118 Armstrong Hall
Mankato, MN 56001
www.mnsu.edu
Public
Admissions: N/A
Financial aid: N/A
Tuition: N/A
Room/board/expenses: N/A
Enrollment: N/A

St. Cloud State University[1]
720 S. Fourth Avenue
St. Cloud, MN 56301
www.stcloudstate.edu
Public
Admissions: N/A
Financial aid: N/A
Tuition: N/A
Room/board/expenses: N/A
Enrollment: N/A

St. Mary's University of Minnesota
700 Terrace Heights
Winona, MN 55987-1700
www.smumn.edu
Private
Admissions: N/A
Financial aid: N/A
Application deadline: rolling
Tuition: full time: N/A; part time: N/A
Room/board/expenses: N/A
Full-time enrollment: 952
doctoral students: 7%; master's students: 93%; education specialists: 0%; men: 29%; women: 71%; minorities: 8%; international: 1%
Part-time enrollment: 493
doctoral students: 27%; master's students: 71%; education specialists: 3%; men: 33%; women: 67%; minorities: 10%; international: 2%
Acceptance rate (master's): N/A
Acceptance rate (doctoral): N/A
Entrance test required: N/A
Avg. GRE (of all entering students with scores): quantitative: N/A; verbal: N/A
Students reporting specialty: 100%
Students specializing in: instructional media design: 3%; higher education admin.: 27%; other: 70%

University of Minnesota-Duluth
1207 Ordean Court
Duluth, MN 55812
www.d.umn.edu/grad/graduate-programs.php
Public
Admissions: (218) 726-7523
Email: grad@d.umn.edu
Financial aid: N/A
Application deadline: 04/15
In-state tuition: full time: $644/credit hour; part time: $644/credit hour
Out-of-state tuition: full time: $1,020/credit hour
Room/board/expenses: $10,778
Full-time enrollment: 38
doctoral students: 8%; master's students: 92%; education specialists: N/A; men: 42%; women: 58%; minorities: 11%; international: 5%
Part-time enrollment: 72
doctoral students: 32%; master's students: 68%; education specialists: N/A; men: 32%; women: 68%; minorities: 28%; international: 3%
Acceptance rate (master's): 93%
Acceptance rate (doctoral): 0%
Entrance test required: GRE
Avg. GRE (of all entering students with scores): quantitative: N/A; verbal: N/A
Research assistantships: 2
Students reporting specialty: 80%
Students specializing in: special: 1%; other: 99%

University of Minnesota-Twin Cities
104 Burton Hall, 178 Pillsbury Drive SE
Minneapolis, MN 55455
www.cehd.umn.edu
Public
Admissions: (612) 625-3339
Email: cehdinfo@umn.edu
Financial aid: (612) 624-1111

Application deadline: rolling
In-state tuition: full time: $16,973; part time: $1,320/credit hour
Out-of-state tuition: full time: $25,637
Room/board/expenses: $14,466
Full-time enrollment: 904
doctoral students: 48%; master's students: 52%; education specialists: 0%; men: 31%; women: 69%; minorities: 16%; international: 15%
Part-time enrollment: 466
doctoral students: 57%; master's students: 43%; education specialists: 0%; men: 32%; women: 68%; minorities: 18%; international: 8%
Acceptance rate (master's): 61%
Acceptance rate (doctoral): 36%
Entrance test required: GRE
Avg. GRE (of all entering students with scores): quantitative: 152; verbal: 157
Research assistantships: 179
Students reporting specialty: 100%
Students specializing in: curriculum/instr.: 12%; admin.: 4%; evaluation/research/statistics: 2%; educational psych: 5%; educational tech.: 3%; elementary: 7%; higher education admin.: 7%; secondary: 17%; social/philosophical foundations: 5%; special: 7%; counseling: 5%; other: 26%

University of St. Thomas
1000 LaSalle Avenue
Minneapolis, MN 55403
www.stthomas.edu/education
Private
Admissions: (651) 962-4550
Email: education@stthomas.edu
Financial aid: (651) 962-6550
Application deadline: rolling
Tuition: full time: $825/credit hour; part time: $825/credit hour
Room/board/expenses: $1,350
Full-time enrollment: 394
doctoral students: 8%; master's students: 84%; education specialists: 8%; men: 34%; women: 66%; minorities: 19%; international: 10%
Part-time enrollment: 421
doctoral students: 21%; master's students: 66%; education specialists: 13%; men: 32%; women: 68%; minorities: 16%; international: 3%
Acceptance rate (master's): 96%
Acceptance rate (doctoral): N/A
Entrance test required: N/A
Avg. GRE (of all entering students with scores): quantitative: N/A; verbal: N/A
Research assistantships: 2
Students reporting specialty: 81%
Students specializing in: curriculum/instr.: 5%; admin.: 30%; elementary: 4%; higher education admin.: 6%; junior high: 0%; secondary: 6%; special: 45%; other: 10%

Walden University[1]
155 Fifth Avenue, S
Minneapolis, MN 55401
www.waldenu.edu/acad-prog/index.html
Private
Admissions: N/A
Financial aid: N/A

Tuition: N/A
Room/board/expenses: N/A
Enrollment: N/A

MISSISSIPPI

Delta State University
1003 W. Sunflower Road
Cleveland, MS 38733
www.deltastate.edu/pages/251.asp
Public
Admissions: (662) 846-4875
Email: grad-info@deltastate.edu
Financial aid: (662) 846-4670
Application deadline: rolling
In-state tuition: full time: $6,112; part time: $334/credit hour
Out-of-state tuition: full time: $6,112
Room/board/expenses: $12,205
Full-time enrollment: 81
doctoral students: 2%; master's students: 79%; education specialists: 19%; men: 12%; women: 88%; minorities: 68%; international: 1%
Part-time enrollment: 332
doctoral students: 26%; master's students: 42%; education specialists: 33%; men: 18%; women: 82%; minorities: 53%; international: 1%
Acceptance rate (master's): 81%
Acceptance rate (doctoral): 96%
Entrance test required: GRE
Avg. GRE (of all entering students with scores): quantitative: N/A; verbal: N/A
Students reporting specialty: 100%
Students specializing in: admin.: 31%; elementary: 21%; higher education admin.: 5%; secondary: 4%; special: 4%; counseling: 20%; other: 14%

Jackson State University[1]
1400 John R. Lynch Street
Administration Tower
Jackson, MS 39217
www.jsums.edu/
Public
Admissions: N/A
Financial aid: N/A
Tuition: N/A
Room/board/expenses: N/A
Enrollment: N/A

Mississippi College[1]
P.O. Box 4026
Clinton, MS 39058
www.mc.edu/
Private
Admissions: N/A
Financial aid: N/A
Tuition: N/A
Room/board/expenses: N/A
Enrollment: N/A

Mississippi State University
PO Box 9710
Mississippi State, MS 39762
www.educ.msstate.edu/
Public
Admissions: (662) 325-2224
Email: grad@grad.msstate.edu
Financial aid: (662) 325-2450
Application deadline: rolling
In-state tuition: full time: $7,502; part time: $411/credit hour
Out-of-state tuition: full time: $20,142

Room/board/expenses: $18,190
Full-time enrollment: 272
doctoral students: 24%; master's students: 71%; education specialists: 5%; men: 36%; women: 64%; minorities: 25%; international: 5%
Part-time enrollment: 453
doctoral students: 44%; master's students: 50%; education specialists: 6%; men: 29%; women: 71%; minorities: 40%; international: 0%
Acceptance rate (master's): 76%
Acceptance rate (doctoral): 72%
Entrance test required: GRE
Avg. GRE (of all entering students with scores): quantitative: 145; verbal: 147
Research assistantships: 14
Students reporting specialty: 100%
Students specializing in: curriculum/instr.: 5%; admin.: 25%; educational psych: 5%; elementary: 2%; junior high: 9%; secondary: 11%; special: 3%; counseling: 18%; technical (vocational): 0%; other: 22%

University of Mississippi
222 Guyton Hall
University, MS 38677
education.olemiss.edu
Public
Admissions: (662) 915-7226
Email: admissions@olemiss.edu
Financial aid: (662) 915-5788
Application deadline: 03/01
In-state tuition: full time: $408/credit hour; part time: $408/credit hour
Out-of-state tuition: full time: $1,143/credit hour
Room/board/expenses: $21,200
Full-time enrollment: 200
doctoral students: 16%; master's students: 79%; education specialists: 6%; men: 24%; women: 76%; minorities: 24%; international: 2%
Part-time enrollment: 401
doctoral students: 34%; master's students: 50%; education specialists: 16%; men: 31%; women: 69%; minorities: 39%; international: 0%
Acceptance rate (master's): 35%
Acceptance rate (doctoral): 64%
Entrance test required: GRE
Avg. GRE (of all entering students with scores): quantitative: 145; verbal: 151
Research assistantships: 15
Students reporting specialty: 96%
Students specializing in: curriculum/instr.: 35%; admin.: 22%; higher education admin.: 28%; counseling: 16%

University of Southern Mississippi[1]
118 College Drive
Box 5023
Hattiesburg, MS 39406
www.usm.edu
Public
Admissions: N/A
Financial aid: N/A
Tuition: N/A
Room/board/expenses: N/A
Enrollment: N/A

William Carey University
498 Tuscan Avenue
Hattiesburg, MS 39401-5499
www.wmcarey.edu/
Private
Admissions: (601) 318-6774
Email: robbie.stewart@
wmcarey.edu
Financial aid: (601) 318-6153
Application deadline: 08/18
Tuition: full time: $330/credit
hour; part time: $330/credit
hour
Room/board/expenses: $4,020
Full-time enrollment: 391
doctoral students: 6%; master's
students: 76%; education
specialists: 18%; men: 19%;
women: 81%; minorities: 19%;
international: 0%
Part-time enrollment: 356
doctoral students: 2%; master's
students: 82%; education
specialists: 15%; men: 20%;
women: 80%; minorities: 20%;
international: 1%
Acceptance rate (master's): 82%
Acceptance rate (doctoral): 24%
Entrance test required: GRE
**Avg. GRE (of all entering students
with scores):** quantitative: N/A;
verbal: N/A
Research assistantships: 1
Students reporting specialty: 100%
Students specializing in:
curriculum/instr.: 17%; admin.:
29%; elementary: 31%;
higher education admin.: 3%;
secondary: 10%; special: 6%;
counseling: 3%

MISSOURI

Lindenwood University
209 S. Kings Highway
St. Charles, MO 63301
www.lindenwood.edu
Private
Admissions: (636) 949-4933
Email: eveningadmissions@
lindenwood.edu
Financial aid: (636) 949-4923
Application deadline: rolling
Tuition: full time: $16,022; part
time: $453/credit hour
Room/board/expenses: $12,614
Full-time enrollment: 300
doctoral students: 3%; master's
students: 94%; education
specialists: 4%; men: 27%;
women: 73%; minorities: 17%;
international: 1%
Part-time enrollment: 1,335
doctoral students: 25%;
master's students: 62%;
education specialists: 12%; men:
26%; women: 74%; minorities:
23%; international: 1%
Acceptance rate (master's): 72%
Acceptance rate (doctoral): 91%
Entrance test required: GRE
**Avg. GRE (of all entering students
with scores):** quantitative: N/A;
verbal: N/A
Research assistantships: 0
Students reporting specialty: 100%
Students specializing in: admin.:
42%; evaluation/research/
statistics: 0%; educational
tech.: 4%; elementary: 8%;
higher education admin.: 0%;
junior high: 1%; secondary: 2%;
special: 5%; counseling: 15%;
other: 22%

Maryville University of St. Louis
650 Maryville University Drive
St. Louis, MO 63141
maryville.edu
Private
Admissions: (314) 529-9350
Email: admissions@maryville.edu
Financial aid: (314) 529-9361
Application deadline: 08/15
Tuition: full time: $26,458; part
time: $766/credit hour
Room/board/expenses: $15,100
Full-time enrollment: 16
doctoral students: 0%; master's
students: 100%; education
specialists: N/A; men: 19%;
women: 81%; minorities: 6%;
international: 13%
Part-time enrollment: 250
doctoral students: 73%;
master's students: 27%;
education specialists: N/A; men:
30%; women: 70%; minorities:
22%; international: 1%
Acceptance rate (master's): N/A
Acceptance rate (doctoral): N/A
Entrance test required: N/A
**Avg. GRE (of all entering students
with scores):** quantitative: N/A;
verbal: N/A
Research assistantships: 0
Students reporting specialty: 100%
Students specializing in:
curriculum/instr.: 7%; admin.:
72%; elementary: 1%; higher
education admin.: 15%; junior
high: 0%; special: 1%; other: 4%

Missouri Baptist University[1]
1 College Park Drive
St. Louis, MO 63141
www.mobap.edu/academics/
graduate-education-division/
Private
Admissions: N/A
Financial aid: N/A
Tuition: N/A
Room/board/expenses: N/A
Enrollment: N/A

St. Louis University
3500 Lindell Boulevard
St. Louis, MO 63103-3412
www.slu.edu/x7039.xml
Private
Admissions: (314) 977-2500
Email: mwikete@slu.edu
Financial aid: (314) 977-2350
Application deadline: rolling
Tuition: full time: $1,050/credit
hour; part time: $1,050/credit
hour
Room/board/expenses: $18,940
Full-time enrollment: 188
doctoral students: 85%;
master's students: 14%;
education specialists: 2%; men:
37%; women: 63%; minorities:
20%; international: 15%
Part-time enrollment: 49
doctoral students: 63%;
master's students: 31%;
education specialists: 6%; men:
35%; women: 65%; minorities:
18%; international: 6%
Acceptance rate (master's): 67%
Acceptance rate (doctoral): 68%
Entrance test required: GRE
**Avg. GRE (of all entering students
with scores):** quantitative: N/A;
verbal: N/A
Research assistantships: 24
Students reporting specialty: 38%
Students specializing in: N/A

University of Central Missouri
Lovinger 2190
Warrensburg, MO 64093
www.ucmo.edu/graduate
Public
Admissions: N/A
Financial aid: N/A
Application deadline: rolling
In-state tuition: full time: $278/
credit hour; part time: $278/
credit hour
Out-of-state tuition: full time:
$557/credit hour
Room/board/expenses: N/A
Full-time enrollment: 126
doctoral students: 0%; master's
students: 97%; education
specialists: 3%; men: 25%;
women: 75%; minorities: 13%;
international: 3%
Part-time enrollment: 720
doctoral students: 2%; master's
students: 77%; education
specialists: 21%; men: 21%;
women: 79%; minorities: 7%;
international: 0%
Acceptance rate (master's): N/A
Acceptance rate (doctoral): N/A
Entrance test required: GRE
**Avg. GRE (of all entering students
with scores):** quantitative: N/A;
verbal: N/A
Students reporting specialty: 100%
Students specializing in:
curriculum/instr.: 13%; admin.:
18%; instructional media
design: 11%; educational
tech.: 0%; elementary: 6%;
higher education admin.: 8%;
secondary: 3%; special: 4%;
counseling: 1%; other: 36%

University of Missouri
118 Hill Hall
Columbia, MO 65211
gradadmin@missouri.edu
Public
Admissions: (573) 882-6311
Email: chvalkb@missouri.edu
Financial aid: (573) 882-7506
Application deadline: rolling
In-state tuition: full time: $350/
credit hour; part time: $350/
credit hour
Out-of-state tuition: full time:
$937/credit hour
Room/board/expenses: $17,048
Full-time enrollment: 621
doctoral students: 44%;
master's students: 53%;
education specialists: 3%; men:
32%; women: 68%; minorities:
14%; international: 9%
Part-time enrollment: 880
doctoral students: 27%;
master's students: 61%;
education specialists: 12%; men:
36%; women: 64%; minorities:
9%; international: 3%
Acceptance rate (master's): 50%
Acceptance rate (doctoral): 33%
Entrance test required: GRE
**Avg. GRE (of all entering students
with scores):** quantitative: 148;
verbal: 153
Research assistantships: 122
Students reporting specialty: 100%
Students specializing in:
curriculum/instr.: 23%; admin.:
26%; evaluation/research/
statistics: 0%; instructional
media design: 13%; educational
psych.: 2%; educational tech.:
6%; special: 4%; counseling:
25%; technical (vocational): 1%

University of Missouri-Kansas City
5100 Rockhill Road
Kansas City, MO 64110-2499
www.umkc.edu/
Public
Admissions: (816) 235-1111
Email: admit@umkc.edu
Financial aid: (816) 235-1154
Application deadline: 06/15
In-state tuition: full time: $345/
credit hour; part time: $345/
credit hour
Out-of-state tuition: full time:
$891/credit hour
Room/board/expenses: $14,081
Full-time enrollment: 186
doctoral students: 18%;
master's students: 76%;
education specialists: 5%; men:
27%; women: 73%; minorities:
26%; international: 11%
Part-time enrollment: 379
doctoral students: 13%;
master's students: 73%;
education specialists: 13%; men:
26%; women: 74%; minorities:
21%; international: 2%
Acceptance rate (master's): 65%
Acceptance rate (doctoral): 21%
Entrance test required: GRE
**Avg. GRE (of all entering students
with scores):** quantitative: 148;
verbal: 154
Research assistantships: 14
Students reporting specialty: 100%
Students specializing in:
curriculum/instr.: 35%; admin.:
20%; educational psych.: 7%;
elementary: 0%; secondary: 0%;
social/philosophical foundations:
0%; special: 3%; counseling:
18%; technical (vocational): 4%;
other: 13%

University of Missouri-St. Louis
1 University Boulevard
St. Louis, MO 63121
coe.umsl.edu
Public
Admissions: (314) 516-5458
Email: gradadm@umsl.edu
Financial aid: (314) 516-5508
Application deadline: rolling
In-state tuition: full time: $436/
credit hour; part time: $436/
credit hour
Out-of-state tuition: full time:
$1,049/credit hour
Room/board/expenses: $18,440
Full-time enrollment: 172
doctoral students: 17%;
master's students: 70%;
education specialists: 12%; men:
24%; women: 76%; minorities:
7%; international: 8%
Part-time enrollment: 1,039
doctoral students: 22%;
master's students: 76%;
education specialists: 2%; men:
26%; women: 74%; minorities:
28%; international: 1%
Acceptance rate (master's): 88%
Acceptance rate (doctoral): 72%
Entrance test required: GRE
**Avg. GRE (of all entering students
with scores):** quantitative: 149;
verbal: 152
Research assistantships: 26
Students reporting specialty: 100%
Students specializing in: admin.:
11%; evaluation/research/
statistics: 0%; elementary: 16%;
secondary: 20%; special: 7%;
counseling: 17%; other: 30%

Washington University in St. Louis
1 Brookings Drive
Box 1183
St. Louis, MO 63130-4899
education.wustl.edu
Private
Admissions: (314) 935-6791
Email: nkolk@artsci.wustl.edu
Financial aid: (314) 935-6880
Application deadline: N/A
Tuition: full time: $49,132; part
time: $1,971/credit hour
Room/board/expenses: N/A
Full-time enrollment: 28
doctoral students: 43%;
master's students: 57%;
education specialists: N/A; men:
29%; women: 71%; minorities:
21%; international: 18%
Part-time enrollment: 2
doctoral students: 0%; master's
students: 100%; education
specialists: N/A; men: 100%;
women: N/A; minorities: 50%;
international: N/A
Acceptance rate (master's): 49%
Acceptance rate (doctoral): 17%
Entrance test required: GRE
**Avg. GRE (of all entering students
with scores):** quantitative: 151;
verbal: 156
Research assistantships: 1
Students reporting specialty: 100%
Students specializing in: policy:
38%; elementary: 25%;
secondary: 38%

William Woods University
One University Ave
Fulton, MO 65251
www.williamwoods.edu/
academics/graduate/
education_graduate/index.html
Private
Admissions: N/A
Financial aid: N/A
Application deadline: rolling
Tuition: full time: $325/credit
hour; part time: $325/credit
hour
Room/board/expenses: $2,450
Full-time enrollment: 34
doctoral students: 0%; master's
students: 65%; education
specialists: N/A; men: 29%;
women: 71%; minorities: 6%;
international: N/A
Part-time enrollment: 902
doctoral students: 14%;
master's students: 59%;
education specialists: 27%; men:
39%; women: 61%; minorities:
3%; international: 1%
Acceptance rate (master's): 100%
Acceptance rate (doctoral): 100%
Entrance test required: N/A
**Avg. GRE (of all entering students
with scores):** quantitative: N/A;
verbal: N/A
Research assistantships: 15
Students reporting specialty: 100%
Students specializing in:
curriculum/instr.: 14%; admin.:
77%; instructional media design:
8%; other: 2%

MONTANA

Montana State University
215 Reid Hall
Bozeman, MT 59717
www.montana.edu/wwweduc/
Public
Admissions: (406) 994-4145
Email: gradstudy@montana.edu
Financial aid: (406) 994-2845
Application deadline: 04/01
In-state tuition: full time: $5,200;
part time: $267/credit hour
Out-of-state tuition: full time:
$15,500
Room/board/expenses: $9,600
Full-time enrollment: 24
doctoral students: 29%;
master's students: 71%;
education specialists: 0%; men:
21%; women: 79%; minorities:
4%; international: 4%
Part-time enrollment: 246
doctoral students: 29%;
master's students: 70%;
education specialists: 0%; men:
37%; women: 63%; minorities:
5%; international: 4%
Acceptance rate (master's): 88%
Acceptance rate (doctoral): 81%
Entrance test required: GRE
**Avg. GRE (of all entering students
with scores):** quantitative: 153;
verbal: 153
Research assistantships: 5
Students reporting specialty: 98%
Students specializing in:
curriculum/instr.: 62%; admin.:
21%; higher education admin.:
15%; counseling: 2%

University of Montana
PJWEC Room 321
Missoula, MT 59812
www.coehs.umt.edu
Public
Admissions: (406) 243-2572
Email:
grad.school@umontana.edu
Financial aid: (406) 243-5373
Application deadline: rolling
In-state tuition: full time: $6,959;
part time: $215/credit hour
Out-of-state tuition: full time:
$20,396
Room/board/expenses: $13,696
Full-time enrollment: N/A
doctoral students: N/A; master's
students: N/A; education
specialists: N/A; men: N/A;
women: N/A; minorities: N/A;
international: N/A
Part-time enrollment: N/A
doctoral students: N/A; master's
students: N/A; education
specialists: N/A; men: N/A;
women: N/A; minorities: N/A;
international: N/A
Acceptance rate (master's): 40%
Acceptance rate (doctoral): 76%
Entrance test required: GRE
**Avg. GRE (of all entering students
with scores):** quantitative: 157;
verbal: 152
Research assistantships: 5
Students reporting specialty: 91%
Students specializing in:
curriculum/instr.: 39%; admin.:
21%; counseling: 21%; other:
19%

NEBRASKA

College of St. Mary
7000 Mercy Road
Omaha, NE 68106
www.csm.edu
Private
Admissions: (800) 926-5534
Financial aid: N/A
Application deadline: rolling
Tuition: full time: $615/credit
hour; part time: $615/credit hour
Room/board/expenses: $15,730
Full-time enrollment: 80
doctoral students: 1%; master's
students: 99%; education
specialists: N/A; men: 14%;
women: 86%; minorities: 16%;
international: N/A
Part-time enrollment: 66
doctoral students: 64%;
master's students: 36%;
education specialists: N/A; men:
6%; women: 94%; minorities:
9%; international: N/A
Acceptance rate (master's): 68%
Acceptance rate (doctoral): 50%
Entrance test required: N/A
**Avg. GRE (of all entering students
with scores):** quantitative: N/A;
verbal: N/A
Research assistantships: 0
Students reporting specialty: 100%
Students specializing in:
curriculum/instr.: 11%;
admin.: 8%; elementary: 18%;
secondary: 30%; special: 12%;
other: 22%

University of Nebraska-Lincoln
233 Mabel Lee Hall
Lincoln, NE 68588-0234
cehs.unl.edu
Public
Admissions: (402) 472-2878
Email: graduate@unl.edu
Financial aid: (402) 472-2030
Application deadline: rolling
In-state tuition: full time: $290/
credit hour; part time: $290/
credit hour
Out-of-state tuition: full time:
$830/credit hour
Room/board/expenses: $11,810
Full-time enrollment: 306
doctoral students: 39%;
master's students: 59%;
education specialists: 2%; men:
22%; women: 78%; minorities:
15%; international: 13%
Part-time enrollment: 579
doctoral students: 53%;
master's students: 46%;
education specialists: 2%; men:
30%; women: 70%; minorities:
15%; international: 5%
Acceptance rate (master's): 69%
Acceptance rate (doctoral): 29%
Entrance test required: GRE
**Avg. GRE (of all entering students
with scores):** quantitative: 150;
verbal: 153
Research assistantships: 118
Students reporting specialty: 100%
Students specializing in:
curriculum/instr.: 24%; admin.:
19%; evaluation/research/
statistics: 3%; educational
psych: 1%; educational tech.:
2%; elementary: 1%; higher
education admin.: 19%;
secondary: 2%; special: 9%;
counseling: 7%; other: 12%

University of Nebraska-Omaha[1]
6001 Dodge Street
Omaha, NE 68182
www.unomaha.edu
Public
Admissions: (402) 554-2936
Email: graduate@unomaha.edu
Financial aid: (402) 554-3408
Tuition: N/A
Room/board/expenses: N/A
Enrollment: N/A

NEVADA

University of Nevada-Las Vegas
4505 Maryland Parkway
Box 453001
Las Vegas, NV 89154-3001
www.unlv.edu/gradcollege/
futurestudents
Public
Admissions: (702) 895-3320
Email:
GradAdmissions@unlv.edu
Financial aid: (702) 895-3424
Application deadline: 06/01
In-state tuition: full time: $6,800;
part time: $264/credit hour
Out-of-state tuition: full time:
$20,710
Room/board/expenses: $20,572
Full-time enrollment: 556
doctoral students: 10%;
master's students: 86%;
education specialists: 3%; men:
27%; women: 73%; minorities:
45%; international: 2%
Part-time enrollment: 522
doctoral students: 26%;
master's students: 72%;
education specialists: 2%; men:
30%; women: 70%; minorities:
39%; international: 3%
Acceptance rate (master's): 82%
Acceptance rate (doctoral): 72%
Entrance test required: GRE
**Avg. GRE (of all entering students
with scores):** quantitative: 148;
verbal: 151
Research assistantships: 59
Students reporting specialty: 94%
Students specializing in:
curriculum/instr.: 49%;
educational psych: 9%; special:
26%; counseling: 8%; other: 8%

University of Nevada-Reno
MS278
Reno, NV 89557-0278
www.unr.edu/grad
Public
Admissions: (775) 784-6869
Email: gradadmissions@unr.edu
Financial aid: (775) 784-4666
Application deadline: rolling
In-state tuition: full time: $264/
credit hour; part time: $264/
credit hour
Out-of-state tuition: full time:
$15,313
Room/board/expenses: $19,248
Full-time enrollment: 187
doctoral students: 17%;
master's students: 83%;
education specialists: N/A; men:
28%; women: 72%; minorities:
28%; international: 5%
Part-time enrollment: 304
doctoral students: 23%;
master's students: 77%;
education specialists: N/A; men:
26%; women: 74%; minorities:
20%; international: 3%

Acceptance rate (master's): 79%
Acceptance rate (doctoral): 71%
Entrance test required: GRE
**Avg. GRE (of all entering students
with scores):** quantitative: 146;
verbal: 153
Research assistantships: 14
Students reporting specialty: 88%
Students specializing in: admin.:
6%; educational psych:
0%; educational tech.: 1%;
elementary: 15%; higher
education admin.: 16%;
secondary: 16%; special: 12%;
counseling: 6%; other: 29%

NEW HAMPSHIRE

New England College[1]
98 Bridge Street
Henniker, NH 03242
Private
Admissions: N/A
Financial aid: N/A
Tuition: N/A
Room/board/expenses: N/A
Enrollment: N/A

Plymouth State University[1]
17 High Street MSC 11
Plymouth, NH 03264
www.plymouth.edu/???
Public
Admissions: N/A
Financial aid: N/A
Tuition: N/A
Room/board/expenses: N/A
Enrollment: N/A

Rivier University[1]
420 Main Street
Nashua, NH 03060
www.rivier.edu/
Private
Admissions: N/A
Financial aid: N/A
Tuition: N/A
Room/board/expenses: N/A
Enrollment: N/A

University of New Hampshire[1]
Morrill Hall
Durham, NH 03824-3595
www.unh.edu/education/
Public
Admissions: (603) 862-2381
Financial aid: (603) 862-3600
Tuition: N/A
Room/board/expenses: N/A
Enrollment: N/A

NEW JERSEY

College of St. Elizabeth
2 Convent Road
Morristown, NJ 07960-6989
www.cse.edu
Private
Admissions: (800) 210-7900
Email: apply@cse.edu
Financial aid: (973) 290-4432
Application deadline: rolling
Tuition: full time: $23,462; part
time: $1,001/credit hour
Room/board/expenses: N/A
Full-time enrollment: 18
doctoral students: 22%;
master's students: 78%;
education specialists: N/A; men:
11%; women: 89%; minorities:
39%; international: 6%

Part-time enrollment: 107
doctoral students: 43%;
master's students: 57%;
education specialists: N/A; men:
30%; women: 70%; minorities:
25%; international: N/A
Acceptance rate (master's): 76%
Acceptance rate (doctoral): 88%
Entrance test required: N/A
**Avg. GRE (of all entering students
with scores):** quantitative: N/A;
verbal: N/A
Students reporting specialty: 76%
Students specializing in: admin.:
70%; other: 30%

Kean University[1]
1000 Morris Avenue
Union, NJ 07083
www.kean.edu/
Public
Admissions: N/A
Financial aid: N/A
Tuition: N/A
Room/board/expenses: N/A
Enrollment: N/A

Montclair State University
1 Normal Avenue
Upper Montclair, NJ 07043
cehs.montclair.edu/
Public
Admissions: (973) 655-5147
Email: Graduate.School@
montclair.edu
Financial aid: (973) 655-4461
Application deadline: rolling
In-state tuition: full time: $564/
credit hour; part time: $564/
credit hour
Out-of-state tuition: full time:
$854/credit hour
Room/board/expenses: N/A
Full-time enrollment: 677
doctoral students: 8%; master's
students: 92%; education
specialists: N/A; men: 24%;
women: 76%; minorities: 32%;
international: 4%
Part-time enrollment: 1,077
doctoral students: 6%; master's
students: 94%; education
specialists: N/A; men: 24%;
women: 76%; minorities: 31%;
international: 0%
Acceptance rate (master's): 69%
Acceptance rate (doctoral): 50%
Entrance test required: GRE
**Avg. GRE (of all entering students
with scores):** quantitative: 147;
verbal: 149
Research assistantships: 84
Students reporting specialty: 100%
Students specializing in: admin.:
20%; evaluation/research/
statistics: 0%; special: 7%;
counseling: 18%; other: 55%

Rowan University
201 Mullica Hill Road
Glassboro, NJ 08028
www.rowan.edu/
Public
Admissions: (856) 256-4050
Email: gradoffice@rowan.edu
Financial aid: (856) 256-4250
Application deadline: rolling
In-state tuition: full time: $661/
credit hour; part time: $661/
credit hour
Out-of-state tuition: full time:
$661/credit hour
Room/board/expenses: N/A

Full-time enrollment: 166
doctoral students: 1%; master's
students: 89%; education
specialists: 10%; men: 20%;
women: 80%; minorities: 16%;
international: N/A
Part-time enrollment: 591
doctoral students: 38%;
master's students: 57%;
education specialists: 5%; men:
26%; women: 74%; minorities:
17%; international: N/A
Acceptance rate (master's): 42%
Acceptance rate (doctoral): 41%
Entrance test required: GRE
Avg. GRE (of all entering students
with scores): quantitative: 145;
verbal: 147
Research assistantships: 8
Students reporting specialty: 66%
Students specializing in:
curriculum/instr.: 0%; admin.:
59%; educational psych: 13%;
special: 15%; counseling: 13%

Rutgers, The State University of New Jersey-New Brunswick

10 Seminary Place
New Brunswick, NJ 08901-1183
www.gse.rutgers.edu
Public
Admissions: (732) 932-7711
Email: gradadm@rci.rutgers.edu
Financial aid: (848) 932-2622
Application deadline: 02/01
In-state tuition: full time: $18,032;
part time: $678/credit hour
Out-of-state tuition: full time:
$29,408
Room/board/expenses: $18,160
Full-time enrollment: 341
doctoral students: 12%;
master's students: 88%;
education specialists: N/A; men:
23%; women: 77%; minorities:
28%; international: 6%
Part-time enrollment: 405
doctoral students: 55%;
master's students: 45%;
education specialists: N/A; men:
29%; women: 71%; minorities:
26%; international: 3%
Acceptance rate (master's): 64%
Acceptance rate (doctoral): 49%
Entrance test required: GRE
Avg. GRE (of all entering students
with scores): quantitative: 150;
verbal: 153
Research assistantships: 0
Students reporting specialty: 100%
Students specializing in: admin.:
11%; policy: 1%; evaluation/
research/statistics: 3%;
instructional media design:
3%; educational psych:
4%; educational tech.: 1%;
elementary: 9%; higher
education admin.: 5%; junior
high: 2%; secondary: 22%;
social/philosophical foundations:
5%; special: 24%; counseling:
4%; other: 14%

Seton Hall University[1]

400 S. Orange Avenue
South Orange, NJ 07079
www.shu.edu/academics/
education/
Private
Admissions: N/A
Financial aid: N/A
Tuition: N/A
Room/board/expenses: N/A
Enrollment: N/A

St. Peter's University[1]

2641 Kennedy Boulevard
Jersey City, NJ 07306
www.spc.edu
Private
Admissions: (201) 915-9220
Email: gradadmit@spc.edu
Financial aid: (201) 915-4929
Tuition: N/A
Room/board/expenses: N/A
Enrollment: N/A

NEW MEXICO

New Mexico State University

PO Box 30001, MSC 3AC
Las Cruces, NM 88003-8001
education.nmsu.edu
Public
Admissions: (575) 646-3121
Email: admissions@nmsu.edu
Financial aid: (505) 646-4105
Application deadline: N/A
In-state tuition: full time: $4,941;
part time: $227/credit hour
Out-of-state tuition: full time:
$15,107
Room/board/expenses: $13,050
Full-time enrollment: 287
doctoral students: 26%;
master's students: 69%;
education specialists: 5%; men:
25%; women: 75%; minorities:
53%; international: 11%
Part-time enrollment: 463
doctoral students: 32%;
master's students: 67%;
education specialists: 2%; men:
24%; women: 76%; minorities:
58%; international: 2%
Acceptance rate (master's): 53%
Acceptance rate (doctoral): 26%
Entrance test required: GRE
Avg. GRE (of all entering students
with scores): quantitative: 145;
verbal: 150
Research assistantships: 33
Students reporting specialty: 96%
Students specializing in:
curriculum/instr.: 43%; admin.:
16%; educational psych: 2%;
elementary: 1%; secondary: 1%;
special: 19%; counseling: 9%;
other: 11%

University of New Mexico

MSC05 3040
Albuquerque, NM 87131-0001
www.unm.edu
Public
Admissions: (505) 277-2447
Financial aid: (505) 277-8900
Application deadline: rolling
In-state tuition: full time: $5,821;
part time: $312/credit hour
Out-of-state tuition: full time:
$16,696
Room/board/expenses: $15,684
Full-time enrollment: 345
doctoral students: 30%;
master's students: 66%;
education specialists: 4%; men:
36%; women: 64%; minorities:
39%; international: 17%
Part-time enrollment: 567
doctoral students: 35%;
master's students: 63%;
education specialists: 2%; men:
26%; women: 74%; minorities:
51%; international: 4%
Acceptance rate (master's): 64%
Acceptance rate (doctoral): 40%
Entrance test required: GRE

Avg. GRE (of all entering students
with scores): quantitative: 147;
verbal: 149
Research assistantships: 44
Students reporting specialty: 100%
Students specializing in:
curriculum/instr.: 2%; admin.:
11%; educational psych: 3%;
elementary: 9%; secondary: 8%;
social/philosophical foundations:
18%; special: 15%; counseling:
10%; other: 24%

NEW YORK

Binghamton University-SUNY

PO Box 6000
Binghamton, NY 13902-6000
gse.binghamton.edu
Public
Admissions: N/A
Financial aid: N/A
Application deadline: rolling
In-state tuition: full time: $453/
credit hour; part time: $453/
credit hour
Out-of-state tuition: full time:
$925/credit hour
Room/board/expenses: N/A
Full-time enrollment: 111
doctoral students: 7%; master's
students: 93%; education
specialists: N/A; men: 32%;
women: 68%; minorities: 14%;
international: 4%
Part-time enrollment: 101
doctoral students: 41%;
master's students: 59%;
education specialists: N/A; men:
18%; women: 82%; minorities:
8%; international: 2%
Acceptance rate (master's): N/A
Acceptance rate (doctoral): N/A
Entrance test required: GRE
Avg. GRE (of all entering students
with scores): quantitative: N/A;
verbal: N/A
Students reporting specialty: 0%
Students specializing in: N/A

Cornell University[1]

Kennedy Hall
Ithaca, NY 14853
www.cornell.edu
Private
Admissions: N/A
Financial aid: N/A
Tuition: N/A
Room/board/expenses: N/A
Enrollment: N/A

CUNY-Graduate Center[1]

365 Fifth Avenue
New York, NY 10016
www.gc.cuny.edu
Public
Admissions: (212) 817-7470
Email: admissions@gc.cuny.edu
Financial aid: (212) 817-7460
Tuition: N/A
Room/board/expenses: N/A
Enrollment: N/A

Dowling College[1]

Idle Hour Blvd.
Oakdale Long Island, NY 11769
www.dowling.edu/
school-education/index.shtm
Private
Admissions: (631) 244-3303
Financial aid: (631) 244-3220
Tuition: N/A
Room/board/expenses: N/A
Enrollment: N/A

D'Youville College[1]

1 D'Youville Square
320 Porter Avenue
Buffalo, NY 14201-1084
www.dyc.edu/academics/
education/index.asp
Private
Admissions: (716) 829-7676
Email: graduateadmissions@
dyc.edu
Financial aid: (716) 829-7500
Tuition: N/A
Room/board/expenses: N/A
Enrollment: N/A

Fordham University

113 W. 60th Street
New York, NY 10023
www.fordham.edu/gse
Private
Admissions: (212) 636-6401
Email: gse_admiss@fordham.edu
Financial aid: (212) 636-7611
Application deadline: rolling
Tuition: full time: $1,302/credit
hour; part time: $1,302/credit
hour
Room/board/expenses: $24,146
Full-time enrollment: 251
doctoral students: 25%;
master's students: 65%;
education specialists: 10%; men:
20%; women: 80%; minorities:
46%; international: 13%
Part-time enrollment: 701
doctoral students: 40%;
master's students: 56%;
education specialists: 4%; men:
24%; women: 76%; minorities:
32%; international: 2%
Acceptance rate (master's): 76%
Acceptance rate (doctoral): 39%
Entrance test required: GRE
Avg. GRE (of all entering students
with scores): quantitative: 160;
verbal: 165
Research assistantships: 55
Students reporting specialty: 100%
Students specializing in:
curriculum/instr.: 0%; admin.:
23%; educational psych: 1%;
elementary: 16%; secondary:
16%; special: 5%; counseling:
29%; other: 10%

Hofstra University

Hagedorn Hall
Hempstead, NY 11549
www.hofstra.edu/graduate
Private
Admissions: (516) 463-4723
Email: graduateadmission@
hofstra.edu
Financial aid: (516) 463-6680
Application deadline: rolling
Tuition: full time: $1,192/credit
hour; part time: $1,192/credit
hour
Room/board/expenses: $22,305
Full-time enrollment: 272
doctoral students: 14%;
master's students: 86%;
education specialists: N/A; men:
23%; women: 77%; minorities:
19%; international: 8%
Part-time enrollment: 343
doctoral students: 39%;
master's students: 61%;
education specialists: N/A; men:
29%; women: 71%; minorities:
27%; international: 1%
Acceptance rate (master's): 89%
Acceptance rate (doctoral): 66%
Entrance test required: GRE
Avg. GRE (of all entering students
with scores): quantitative: 149;
verbal: 152

Research assistantships: 19
Students reporting specialty: 96%
Students specializing in:
curriculum/instr.: 0%; admin.:
11%; instructional media design:
1%; elementary: 4%; higher
education admin.: 5%; junior
high: 0%; secondary: 2%; social/
philosophical foundations: 0%;
special: 20%; other: 60%

LIU Post

720 Northern Boulevard
Brookville, NY 11548
www.liu.edu/post/Academics/
schools/CEIS
Private
Admissions: N/A
Financial aid: N/A
Application deadline: rolling
Tuition: full time: $1,155/credit
hour; part time: $1,155/credit
hour
Room/board/expenses: N/A
Full-time enrollment: 439
doctoral students: 0%; master's
students: 100%; education
specialists: N/A; men: 15%;
women: 85%; minorities: 4%;
international: 1%
Part-time enrollment: 767
doctoral students: 13%;
master's students: 87%;
education specialists: N/A; men:
22%; women: 78%; minorities:
8%; international: 0%
Acceptance rate (master's): 73%
Acceptance rate (doctoral): 65%
Entrance test required: N/A
Avg. GRE (of all entering students
with scores): quantitative: N/A;
verbal: N/A
Students reporting specialty: 29%
Students specializing in: N/A

Manhattanville College[1]

2900 Purchase Street
Purchase, NY 10577
www.mville.edu/
Private
Admissions: (914) 323-3208
Email: polia@mville.edu
Financial aid: (914) 323-5376
Tuition: N/A
Room/board/expenses: N/A
Enrollment: N/A

New York University (Steinhardt)

82 Washington Square E
Fourth Floor
New York, NY 10003
www.steinhardt.nyu.edu/
Private
Admissions: (212) 998-5030
Email: steinhardt.
gradadmission@nyu.edu
Financial aid: (212) 998-4444
Application deadline: rolling
Tuition: full time: $39,304; part
time: $1,538/credit hour
Room/board/expenses: $33,954
Full-time enrollment: 2,052
doctoral students: 17%;
master's students: 83%;
education specialists: N/A; men:
23%; women: 77%; minorities:
25%; international: 28%
Part-time enrollment: 1,065
doctoral students: 14%;
master's students: 86%;
education specialists: N/A; men:
23%; women: 77%; minorities:
29%; international: 16%

Acceptance rate (master's): 51%
Acceptance rate (doctoral): 9%
Entrance test required: GRE
Avg. GRE (of all entering students with scores): quantitative: 155; verbal: 156
Research assistantships: 37
Students reporting specialty: 100%
Students specializing in: curriculum/instr.: 10%; admin.: 3%; policy: 4%; evaluation/research/statistics: 1%; instructional media design: 3%; educational tech.: 1%; elementary: 1%; higher education admin.: 4%; social/philosophical foundations: 1%; special: 2%; counseling: 6%; other: 65%

The Sage Colleges[1]
65 1st Street
Troy, NY 12180
www.sage.edu/academics/education/
Private
Admissions: N/A
Financial aid: N/A
Tuition: N/A
Room/board/expenses: N/A
Enrollment: N/A

St. John's University
8000 Utopia Parkway
Queens, NY 11439
www.stjohns.edu/academics/graduate/education
Private
Admissions: (718) 990-2304
Email: graded@stjohns.edu
Financial aid: (718) 990-2000
Application deadline: 08/17
Tuition: full time: $1,145/credit hour; part time: $1,145/credit hour
Room/board/expenses: $1,668
Full-time enrollment: 283
doctoral students: 5%; master's students: 92%; education specialists: 4%; men: 16%; women: 84%; minorities: 39%; international: 13%
Part-time enrollment: 1,121
doctoral students: 21%; master's students: 59%; education specialists: 19%; men: 28%; women: 72%; minorities: 40%; international: 2%
Acceptance rate (master's): 89%
Acceptance rate (doctoral): 81%
Entrance test required: GRE
Avg. GRE (of all entering students with scores): quantitative: N/A; verbal: N/A
Research assistantships: 0
Students reporting specialty: 100%
Students specializing in: curriculum/instr.: 8%; admin.: 23%; elementary: 3%; secondary: 5%; special: 18%; counseling: 3%; other: 40%

Syracuse University
230 Huntington Hall
Syracuse, NY 13244-2340
soe.syr.edu
Private
Admissions: (315) 443-2505
Email: gradrcrt@gwmail.syr.edu
Financial aid: (315) 443-1513
Application deadline: rolling
Tuition: full time: $1,388/credit hour; part time: $1,388/credit hour
Room/board/expenses: $17,350

Full-time enrollment: 357
doctoral students: 35%; master's students: 65%; education specialists: N/A; men: 28%; women: 72%; minorities: 25%; international: 19%
Part-time enrollment: 189
doctoral students: 46%; master's students: 54%; education specialists: N/A; men: 35%; women: 65%; minorities: 15%; international: 2%
Acceptance rate (master's): 66%
Acceptance rate (doctoral): 41%
Entrance test required: GRE
Avg. GRE (of all entering students with scores): quantitative: 149; verbal: 152
Research assistantships: 20
Students reporting specialty: 100%
Students specializing in: curriculum/instr.: 11%; admin.: 14%; instructional media design: 11%; educational tech.: 1%; elementary: 5%; higher education admin.: 16%; secondary: 10%; social/philosophical foundations: 13%; special: 10%; counseling: 7%; other: 12%

Teachers College, Columbia University
525 W. 120th Street
New York, NY 10027
www.tc.columbia.edu/
Private
Admissions: (212) 678-3710
Email: tcinfo@tc.columbia.edu
Financial aid: (212) 678-3714
Application deadline: rolling
Tuition: full time: $1,454/credit hour; part time: $1,454/credit hour
Room/board/expenses: $27,032
Full-time enrollment: 1,713
doctoral students: 22%; master's students: 78%; education specialists: N/A; men: 23%; women: 77%; minorities: 30%; international: 29%
Part-time enrollment: 3,207
doctoral students: 30%; master's students: 70%; education specialists: N/A; men: 24%; women: 76%; minorities: 35%; international: 15%
Acceptance rate (master's): 60%
Acceptance rate (doctoral): 15%
Entrance test required: GRE
Avg. GRE (of all entering students with scores): quantitative: 156; verbal: 157
Research assistantships: 110
Students reporting specialty: 95%
Students specializing in: curriculum/instr.: 11%; admin.: 6%; policy: 2%; evaluation/research/statistics: 2%; instructional media design: 2%; educational psych.: 6%; educational tech.: 1%; elementary: 9%; higher education admin.: 5%; secondary: 13%; social/philosophical foundations: 10%; special: 4%; counseling: 19%; other: 12%

University at Albany-SUNY
1400 Washington Avenue, ED 212
Albany, NY 12222
www.albany.edu/education
Public
Admissions: (518) 442-3980
Email: graduate@uamail.albany.edu

Financial aid: (518) 442-5757
Application deadline: rolling
In-state tuition: full time: $12,477; part time: $453/credit hour
Out-of-state tuition: full time: $23,817
Room/board/expenses: $13,100
Full-time enrollment: 371
doctoral students: 25%; master's students: 70%; education specialists: 5%; men: 23%; women: 77%; minorities: 16%; international: 10%
Part-time enrollment: 491
doctoral students: 37%; master's students: 56%; education specialists: 6%; men: 22%; women: 78%; minorities: 11%; international: 6%
Acceptance rate (master's): 76%
Acceptance rate (doctoral): 38%
Entrance test required: GRE
Avg. GRE (of all entering students with scores): quantitative: N/A; verbal: N/A
Research assistantships: 75
Students reporting specialty: 100%
Students specializing in: curriculum/instr.: 13%; admin.: 6%; policy: 3%; evaluation/research/statistics: 2%; instructional media design: 4%; educational psych.: 6%; educational tech.: 7%; elementary: 6%; higher education admin.: 6%; secondary: 5%; special: 9%; counseling: 5%; other: 30%

University at Buffalo-SUNY
367 Baldy Hall
Buffalo, NY 14260-1000
www.gse.buffalo.edu
Public
Admissions: (716) 645-2110
Email: gseinfo@buffalo.edu
Financial aid: (716) 645-8232
Application deadline: rolling
In-state tuition: full time: $13,165; part time: $453/credit hour
Out-of-state tuition: full time: $24,505
Room/board/expenses: $17,223
Full-time enrollment: 453
doctoral students: 36%; master's students: 64%; education specialists: N/A; men: 25%; women: 75%; minorities: 25%; international: 19%
Part-time enrollment: 443
doctoral students: 44%; master's students: 56%; education specialists: N/A; men: 29%; women: 71%; minorities: 15%; international: 4%
Acceptance rate (master's): 72%
Acceptance rate (doctoral): 51%
Entrance test required: GRE
Avg. GRE (of all entering students with scores): quantitative: 151; verbal: 151
Research assistantships: 80
Students reporting specialty: 99%
Students specializing in: curriculum/instr.: 17%; admin.: 7%; policy: 0%; educational psych.: 3%; educational tech.: 1%; elementary: 8%; higher education admin.: 11%; secondary: 7%; social/philosophical foundations: 3%; special: 1%; counseling: 10%; other: 33%

University of Rochester (Warner)[1]
2-147 Dewey Hall
Rochester, NY 14627
www.rochester.edu/warner/
Private
Admissions: N/A
Financial aid: N/A
Tuition: N/A
Room/board/expenses: N/A
Enrollment: N/A

Yeshiva University (Azrieli)[1]
245 Lexington Avenue
New York, NY 10016
www.yu.edu/azrieli/
Private
Admissions: N/A
Financial aid: N/A
Tuition: N/A
Room/board/expenses: N/A
Enrollment: N/A

NORTH CAROLINA

Appalachian State University
College of Education Building
Boone, NC 28608-2068
graduate.appstate.edu
Public
Admissions: (828) 262-2130
Email: ParsonDO@appstate.edu
Financial aid: (828) 262-2190
Application deadline: rolling
In-state tuition: full time: $7,267; part time: $247/credit hour
Out-of-state tuition: full time: $19,809
Room/board/expenses: N/A
Full-time enrollment: 318
doctoral students: 5%; master's students: 95%; education specialists: 0%; men: 16%; women: 84%; minorities: 9%; international: 1%
Part-time enrollment: 492
doctoral students: 15%; master's students: 73%; education specialists: 13%; men: 21%; women: 79%; minorities: 10%; international: 0%
Acceptance rate (master's): 47%
Acceptance rate (doctoral): 68%
Entrance test required: GRE
Avg. GRE (of all entering students with scores): quantitative: 148; verbal: 152
Research assistantships: 42
Students reporting specialty: 100%
Students specializing in: curriculum/instr.: 3%; admin.: 26%; instructional media design: 10%; educational psych: 3%; elementary: 0%; higher education admin.: 12%; junior high: 0%; secondary: 4%; special: 1%; counseling: 13%; other: 28%

East Carolina University
E. Fifth Street
Greenville, NC 27858
www.ecu.edu/gradschool/
Public
Admissions: (252) 328-6012
Email: gradschool@ecu.edu
Financial aid: (252) 737-6610
Application deadline: N/A
In-state tuition: full time: $6,857; part time: $5,748

Out-of-state tuition: full time: $19,459
Room/board/expenses: $15,308
Full-time enrollment: 191
doctoral students: 26%; master's students: 74%; education specialists: 1%; men: 27%; women: 73%; minorities: 31%; international: 1%
Part-time enrollment: 701
doctoral students: 9%; master's students: 89%; education specialists: 2%; men: 19%; women: 81%; minorities: 22%; international: 0%
Acceptance rate (master's): 90%
Acceptance rate (doctoral): 50%
Entrance test required: GRE
Avg. GRE (of all entering students with scores): quantitative: 147; verbal: 152
Research assistantships: 44
Students reporting specialty: 62%
Students specializing in: admin.: 55%; instructional media design: 22%; elementary: 2%; junior high: 2%; special: 8%; counseling: 10%; technical (vocational): 1%

Fayetteville State University[1]
1200 Murchison Road
Fayetteville, NC 28301
www.uncfsu.edu/???
Public
Admissions: N/A
Financial aid: N/A
Tuition: N/A
Room/board/expenses: N/A
Enrollment: N/A

Gardner-Webb University
110 S. Main Street
Boiling Springs, NC 28017
www.gardner-webb.edu
Private
Admissions: (800) 492-4723
Email: gradschool@gardner-webb.edu
Financial aid: (704) 406-3271
Application deadline: rolling
Tuition: full time: $410/credit hour; part time: $410/credit hour
Room/board/expenses: $12,223
Full-time enrollment: 19
doctoral students: 89%; master's students: 11%; education specialists: 0%; men: 26%; women: 74%; minorities: 32%; international: N/A
Part-time enrollment: 803
doctoral students: 40%; master's students: 56%; education specialists: 5%; men: 23%; women: 77%; minorities: 38%; international: 0%
Acceptance rate (master's): 56%
Acceptance rate (doctoral): 41%
Entrance test required: GRE
Avg. GRE (of all entering students with scores): quantitative: N/A; verbal: N/A
Students reporting specialty: 100%
Students specializing in: curriculum/instr.: 38%; admin.: 57%; counseling: 2%; other: 4%

North Carolina State University-Raleigh

Campus Box 7801
Raleigh, NC 27695-7801
ced.ncsu.edu/
Public
Admissions: (919) 515-2872
Email: graduate_admissions@ncsu.edu
Financial aid: (919) 515-3325
Application deadline: N/A
In-state tuition: full time: $11,922; part time: $6,416
Out-of-state tuition: full time: $26,022
Room/board/expenses: $18,133
Full-time enrollment: 379
doctoral students: 32%; master's students: 68%; education specialists: N/A; men: 26%; women: 74%; minorities: 25%; international: 8%
Part-time enrollment: 610
doctoral students: 51%; master's students: 49%; education specialists: N/A; men: 26%; women: 74%; minorities: 27%; international: 1%
Acceptance rate (master's): 46%
Acceptance rate (doctoral): 28%
Entrance test required: GRE
Avg. GRE (of all entering students with scores): quantitative: 150; verbal: 153
Research assistantships: 38
Students reporting specialty: 80%
Students specializing in: curriculum/instr.: 12%; admin.: 28%; policy: 12%; evaluation/research/statistics: 12%; instructional media design: 3%; educational psych: 2%; elementary: 3%; higher education admin.: 5%; junior high: 1%; secondary: 7%; special: 1%; counseling: 12%; technical (vocational): 2%

University of North Carolina-Chapel Hill

CB#3500
101 Peabody Hall
Chapel Hill, NC 27599-3500
soe.unc.edu
Public
Admissions: (919) 966-1346
Email: ed@unc.edu
Financial aid: (919) 966-1346
Application deadline: rolling
In-state tuition: full time: $11,074; part time: $8,788
Out-of-state tuition: full time: $28,285
Room/board/expenses: $23,740
Full-time enrollment: 319
doctoral students: 60%; master's students: 40%; education specialists: N/A; men: 24%; women: 76%; minorities: 32%; international: 13%
Part-time enrollment: 102
doctoral students: 26%; master's students: 74%; education specialists: N/A; men: 16%; women: 84%; minorities: 40%; international: 8%
Acceptance rate (master's): 59%
Acceptance rate (doctoral): 26%
Entrance test required: GRE
Avg. GRE (of all entering students with scores): quantitative: N/A; verbal: N/A
Research assistantships: 30
Students reporting specialty: 100%

Students specializing in: curriculum/instr.: 8%; admin.: 23%; policy: 3%; evaluation/research/statistics: 3%; educational psych: 12%; elementary: 2%; junior high: 1%; secondary: 2%; social/philosophical foundations: 9%; special: 4%; counseling: 6%; other: 26%

University of North Carolina-Charlotte

9201 University City Boulevard
Charlotte, NC 28223
education.uncc.edu/
Public
Admissions: (704) 687-3366
Email: gradadm@uncc.edu
Financial aid: (704) 687-5547
Application deadline: N/A
In-state tuition: full time: $7,032; part time: $6,000
Out-of-state tuition: full time: $19,703
Room/board/expenses: $13,376
Full-time enrollment: 205
doctoral students: 35%; master's students: 65%; education specialists: N/A; men: 15%; women: 85%; minorities: 28%; international: 4%
Part-time enrollment: 556
doctoral students: 25%; master's students: 75%; education specialists: N/A; men: 22%; women: 78%; minorities: 27%; international: 1%
Acceptance rate (master's): 80%
Acceptance rate (doctoral): 54%
Entrance test required: GRE
Avg. GRE (of all entering students with scores): quantitative: 147; verbal: 151
Research assistantships: 36
Students reporting specialty: 98%
Students specializing in: curriculum/instr.: 5%; admin.: 12%; instructional media design: 3%; elementary: 2%; special: 9%; counseling: 14%; other: 57%

University of North Carolina-Greensboro

School of Education Building
P.O. Box 26170
Greensboro, NC 27402-6170
www.uncg.edu/grs
Public
Admissions: (336) 334-5596
Email: inquiries@uncg.edu
Financial aid: (336) 334-5702
Application deadline: rolling
In-state tuition: full time: $7,477; part time: $5,041
Out-of-state tuition: full time: $20,926
Room/board/expenses: $11,048
Full-time enrollment: 645
doctoral students: 23%; master's students: 70%; education specialists: 7%; men: 21%; women: 79%; minorities: 28%; international: 3%
Part-time enrollment: 194
doctoral students: 53%; master's students: 45%; education specialists: 2%; men: 25%; women: 75%; minorities: 21%; international: 3%
Acceptance rate (master's): 52%
Acceptance rate (doctoral): 38%
Entrance test required: GRE

Avg. GRE (of all entering students with scores): quantitative: 147; verbal: 153
Research assistantships: 17
Students reporting specialty: 100%
Students specializing in: curriculum/instr.: 20%; admin.: 14%; evaluation/research/statistics: 6%; educational psych: 0%; elementary: 3%; higher education admin.: 9%; junior high: 2%; secondary: 3%; special: 9%; counseling: 12%; other: 29%

University of North Carolina-Wilmington

601 S. College Road
Wilmington, NC 28403
uncw.edu/gradschool/
Public
Admissions: N/A
Financial aid: N/A
Application deadline: 05/15
In-state tuition: full time: $7,252; part time: N/A
Out-of-state tuition: full time: $19,241
Room/board/expenses: $2,499
Full-time enrollment: N/A
doctoral students: N/A; master's students: N/A; education specialists: N/A; men: N/A; women: N/A; minorities: N/A; international: N/A
Part-time enrollment: N/A
doctoral students: N/A; master's students: N/A; education specialists: N/A; men: N/A; women: N/A; minorities: N/A; international: N/A
Acceptance rate (master's): 76%
Acceptance rate (doctoral): 0%
Entrance test required: GRE
Avg. GRE (of all entering students with scores): quantitative: N/A; verbal: N/A
Research assistantships: 0
Students reporting specialty: 47%
Students specializing in: N/A

Western Carolina University

Killian Building, Room 204
Cullowhee, NC 28723
www.wcu.edu/
Public
Admissions: (828) 227-7398
Email: grad@wcu.edu
Financial aid: (828) 227-7290
Application deadline: rolling
In-state tuition: full time: $13,363; part time: $630/credit hour
Out-of-state tuition: full time: $23,770
Room/board/expenses: $12,941
Full-time enrollment: 121
doctoral students: 0%; master's students: 87%; education specialists: 13%; men: 9%; women: 91%; minorities: 12%; international: 2%
Part-time enrollment: 186
doctoral students: 14%; master's students: 85%; education specialists: 1%; men: 26%; women: 74%; minorities: 11%; international: N/A
Acceptance rate (master's): 90%
Acceptance rate (doctoral): 42%
Entrance test required: GRE
Avg. GRE (of all entering students with scores): quantitative: 144; verbal: 148

Research assistantships: 16
Students reporting specialty: 100%
Students specializing in: admin.: 25%; junior high: 0%; counseling: 6%; other: 69%

Wingate University[1]

220 North Camden Road
Wingate, NC 28174
www.wingate.edu/matthews/grad-ed
Private
Admissions: N/A
Financial aid: N/A
Tuition: N/A
Room/board/expenses: N/A
Enrollment: N/A

NORTH DAKOTA

North Dakota State University

Box 6050
Department 2600
Fargo, ND 58108-6050
www.ndsu.edu/gradschool/
Public
Admissions: (701) 231-7033
Email: ndsu.grad.school@ndsu.edu
Financial aid: (701) 231-6200
Application deadline: rolling
In-state tuition: full time: $345/credit hour; part time: $345/credit hour
Out-of-state tuition: full time: $345/credit hour
Room/board/expenses: N/A
Full-time enrollment: 32
doctoral students: 31%; master's students: 69%; education specialists: 0%; men: 19%; women: 81%; minorities: 9%; international: N/A
Part-time enrollment: 218
doctoral students: 39%; master's students: 57%; education specialists: 4%; men: 27%; women: 73%; minorities: 7%; international: 2%
Acceptance rate (master's): 69%
Acceptance rate (doctoral): 47%
Entrance test required: N/A
Avg. GRE (of all entering students with scores): quantitative: N/A; verbal: N/A
Research assistantships: 5
Students reporting specialty: 100%
Students specializing in: curriculum/instr.: 22%; admin.: 24%; evaluation/research/statistics: 14%; higher education admin.: 8%; secondary: 8%; counseling: 7%; other: 16%

University of North Dakota[1]

Box 7189
Grand Forks, ND 58202-7189
und.edu/
Public
Admissions: N/A
Financial aid: N/A
Tuition: N/A
Room/board/expenses: N/A
Enrollment: N/A

OHIO

Ashland University (Schar)[1]

401 College Avenue
Ashland, OH 44805
www.ashland.edu
Private
Admissions: N/A
Financial aid: N/A
Tuition: N/A
Room/board/expenses: N/A
Enrollment: N/A

Bowling Green State University

444 Education Building
Bowling Green, OH 43403
www.bgsu.edu/colleges/edhd/
Public
Admissions: (419) 372-BGSU
Email: prospct@bgsu.edu
Financial aid: (419) 372-2651
Application deadline: rolling
In-state tuition: full time: $12,560; part time: $424/credit hour
Out-of-state tuition: full time: $20,096
Room/board/expenses: $14,487
Full-time enrollment: 352
doctoral students: 11%; master's students: 89%; education specialists: 0%; men: 29%; women: 71%; minorities: 11%; international: 10%
Part-time enrollment: 422
doctoral students: 17%; master's students: 79%; education specialists: 3%; men: 23%; women: 77%; minorities: 10%; international: 3%
Acceptance rate (master's): 55%
Acceptance rate (doctoral): 44%
Entrance test required: GRE
Avg. GRE (of all entering students with scores): quantitative: N/A; verbal: N/A
Research assistantships: 46
Students reporting specialty: 100%
Students specializing in: curriculum/instr.: 7%; admin.: 12%; instructional media design: 0%; educational tech.: 5%; higher education admin.: 5%; special: 13%; counseling: 13%; other: 55%

Cleveland State University

2121 Euclid Avenue, JH 210
Cleveland, OH 44115
www.csuohio.edu/cehs/
Public
Admissions: (216) 687-5599
Email: graduate.admissions@csuohio.edu
Financial aid: (216) 687-5411
Application deadline: rolling
In-state tuition: full time: $13,876; part time: $531/credit hour
Out-of-state tuition: full time: $26,031
Room/board/expenses: $15,000
Full-time enrollment: 1,120
doctoral students: 10%; master's students: 90%; education specialists: N/A; men: 22%; women: 78%; minorities: 31%; international: 9%
Part-time enrollment: N/A
doctoral students: N/A; master's students: N/A; education specialists: N/A; men: N/A; women: N/A; minorities: N/A; international: N/A

Acceptance rate (master's): 83%
Acceptance rate (doctoral): 40%
Entrance test required: GRE
Avg. GRE (of all entering students with scores): quantitative: 146; verbal: 151
Research assistantships: 37
Students reporting specialty: 100%
Students specializing in: curriculum/instr.: 35%; admin.: 15%; policy: 2%; evaluation/research/ statistics: 0%; educational tech.: 3%; elementary: 5%; higher education admin.: 1%; secondary: 3%; special: 18%; counseling: 5%; other: 48%

Kent State University

PO Box 5190
Kent, OH 44242-0001
www.ehhs.kent.edu
Public
Admissions: (330) 672-2576
Email: ogs@kent.edu
Financial aid: (330) 672-2972
Application deadline: rolling
In-state tuition: full time: $8,910; part time: $495/credit hour
Out-of-state tuition: full time: $15,066
Room/board/expenses: $16,950
Full-time enrollment: 880
doctoral students: 36%; master's students: 60%; education specialists: 4%; men: 26%; women: 74%; minorities: 11%; international: 10%
Part-time enrollment: 483
doctoral students: 18%; master's students: 79%; education specialists: 3%; men: 24%; women: 76%; minorities: 13%; international: 3%
Acceptance rate (master's): 49%
Acceptance rate (doctoral): 39%
Entrance test required: GRE
Avg. GRE (of all entering students with scores): quantitative: 148; verbal: 150
Research assistantships: 70
Students reporting specialty: 100%
Students specializing in: curriculum/instr.: 6%; admin.: 3%; evaluation/research/ statistics: 3%; instructional media design: 4%; educational psych: 3%; higher education admin.: 10%; junior high: 0%; secondary: 1%; social/ philosophical foundations: 3%; special: 6%; counseling: 15%; technical (vocational): 2%; other: 45%

Miami University

207 McGuffey Hall
Oxford, OH 45056
www.miami.muohio.edu/ graduate-studies/index.html
Public
Admissions: (513) 529-3734
Email: gradschool@muohio.edu
Financial aid: (513) 529-8734
Application deadline: rolling
In-state tuition: full time: $6,937; part time: $537/credit hour
Out-of-state tuition: full time: $15,004
Room/board/expenses: $1,250
Full-time enrollment: 213
doctoral students: 15%; master's students: 77%; education specialists: 8%; men: 24%; women: 76%; minorities: 17%; international: 10%

Part-time enrollment: 432
doctoral students: 13%; master's students: 87%; education specialists: 0%; men: 22%; women: 78%; minorities: 13%; international: 0%
Acceptance rate (master's): 96%
Acceptance rate (doctoral): 65%
Entrance test required: GRE
Avg. GRE (of all entering students with scores): quantitative: N/A; verbal: N/A
Research assistantships: 7
Students reporting specialty: 50%
Students specializing in: curriculum/instr.: 1%; admin.: 40%; instructional media design: 2%; educational psych.: 5%; higher education admin.: 16%; secondary: 4%; special: 24%; counseling: 8%; other: 0%

Ohio State University

1945 N. High Street
Columbus, OH 43210-1172
ehe.osu.edu/
Public
Admissions: (614) 292-9444
Email: domestic.grad@osu.edu
Financial aid: (614) 292-0300
Application deadline: 12/01
In-state tuition: full time: $12,803; part time: $723/credit hour
Out-of-state tuition: full time: $32,275
Room/board/expenses: $21,380
Full-time enrollment: 655
doctoral students: 58%; master's students: 40%; education specialists: 2%; men: 27%; women: 73%; minorities: 21%; international: 26%
Part-time enrollment: 205
doctoral students: 24%; master's students: 71%; education specialists: 5%; men: 30%; women: 70%; minorities: 17%; international: 6%
Acceptance rate (master's): 51%
Acceptance rate (doctoral): 44%
Entrance test required: GRE
Avg. GRE (of all entering students with scores): quantitative: 152; verbal: 154
Research assistantships: 66
Students reporting specialty: 87%
Students specializing in: curriculum/instr.: 24%; admin.: 9%; policy: 2%; evaluation/ research/statistics: 2%; educational psych: 2%; educational tech.: 3%; elementary: 12%; higher education admin.: 9%; junior high: 2%; secondary: 6%; social/ philosophical foundations: 3%; special: 5%; counseling: 12%; technical (vocational): 7%; other: 2%

Ohio University

133 McCracken Hall
Athens, OH 45701-2979
www.ohio.edu/education/
Public
Admissions: (740) 593-2800
Email: graduate@ohio.edu
Financial aid: (740) 593-4141
Application deadline: rolling
In-state tuition: full time: $10,536; part time: $583/credit hour
Out-of-state tuition: full time: $19,500
Room/board/expenses: $16,016

Full-time enrollment: 295
doctoral students: 22%; master's students: 78%; education specialists: N/A; men: 38%; women: 62%; minorities: 11%; international: 22%
Part-time enrollment: 543
doctoral students: 25%; master's students: 75%; education specialists: N/A; men: 54%; women: 46%; minorities: 18%; international: 6%
Acceptance rate (master's): 52%
Acceptance rate (doctoral): 40%
Entrance test required: GRE
Avg. GRE (of all entering students with scores): quantitative: 147; verbal: 148
Research assistantships: 25
Students reporting specialty: 100%
Students specializing in: curriculum/instr.: 15%; admin.: 11%; evaluation/research/ statistics: 2%; instructional media design: 8%; higher education admin.: 15%; secondary: 2%; counseling: 12%; other: 37%

University of Akron

302 Buchtel Common
Akron, OH 44325-4201
www.uakron.edu/admissions/ graduate
Public
Admissions: (330) 972-7663
Email: gradschool@uakron.edu
Financial aid: (330) 972-5858
Application deadline: rolling
In-state tuition: full time: $430/ credit hour; part time: $430/ credit hour
Out-of-state tuition: full time: $735/credit hour
Room/board/expenses: $14,068
Full-time enrollment: 117
doctoral students: 7%; master's students: 93%; education specialists: N/A; men: 40%; women: 60%; minorities: 10%; international: 18%
Part-time enrollment: 248
doctoral students: 15%; master's students: 85%; education specialists: N/A; men: 25%; women: 75%; minorities: 20%; international: 2%
Acceptance rate (master's): 85%
Acceptance rate (doctoral): N/A
Entrance test required: GRE
Avg. GRE (of all entering students with scores): quantitative: 146; verbal: 149
Research assistantships: 2
Students reporting specialty: 100%
Students specializing in: admin.: 8%; evaluation/research/ statistics: 7%; instructional media design: 16%; elementary: 4%; higher education admin.: 11%; junior high: 1%; secondary: 10%; social/philosophical foundations: 0%; special: 14%; technical (vocational): 2%; other: 28%

University of Cincinnati

PO Box 210002
Cincinnati, OH 45221-0002
www.cech.uc.edu
Public
Admissions: (513) 556-1427
Email: kendalce@ucmail.uc.edu
Financial aid: (513) 556-4170
Application deadline: rolling

In-state tuition: full time: $12,790; part time: $640/credit hour
Out-of-state tuition: full time: $24,532
Room/board/expenses: $16,296
Full-time enrollment: 256
doctoral students: 38%; master's students: 54%; education specialists: 7%; men: 23%; women: 77%; minorities: 19%; international: 10%
Part-time enrollment: 840
doctoral students: 9%; master's students: 91%; education specialists: 1%; men: 18%; women: 82%; minorities: 20%; international: 2%
Acceptance rate (master's): 57%
Acceptance rate (doctoral): 23%
Entrance test required: GRE
Avg. GRE (of all entering students with scores): quantitative: 151; verbal: 152
Research assistantships: 48
Students reporting specialty: 92%
Students specializing in: curriculum/instr.: 16%; admin.: 3%; evaluation/research/ statistics: 1%; educational psych: 40%; secondary: 0%; social/philosophical foundations: 6%; special: 9%; counseling: 1%; other: 43%

University of Dayton

300 College Park/Fitz Hall
Dayton, OH 45469-2969
www.udayton.edu/education
Private
Admissions: (937) 229-4411
Email: gradadmission@udayton.edu
Financial aid: (800) 229-4338
Application deadline: rolling
Tuition: full time: $603/credit hour; part time: $603/credit hour
Room/board/expenses: N/A
Full-time enrollment: 378
doctoral students: 14%; master's students: 83%; education specialists: 3%; men: 28%; women: 72%; minorities: 12%; international: 15%
Part-time enrollment: 254
doctoral students: 0%; master's students: 95%; education specialists: 5%; men: 24%; women: 76%; minorities: 12%; international: 9%
Acceptance rate (master's): 32%
Acceptance rate (doctoral): 24%
Entrance test required: GRE
Avg. GRE (of all entering students with scores): quantitative: 147; verbal: 153
Research assistantships: 19
Students reporting specialty: 100%
Students specializing in: admin.: 39%; instructional media design: 2%; educational psych: 4%; educational tech.: 2%; elementary: 8%; higher education admin.: 3%; junior high: 1%; secondary: 1%; special: 6%; counseling: 12%; other: 28%

University of Toledo

2801 W. Bancroft Street
Toledo, OH 43606
www.utoledo.edu/education/ index.html
Public
Admissions: N/A
Financial aid: N/A
Application deadline: rolling

In-state tuition: full time: $548/ credit hour; part time: $548/ credit hour
Out-of-state tuition: full time: $978/credit hour
Room/board/expenses: $10,310
Full-time enrollment: 209
doctoral students: 27%; master's students: 69%; education specialists: 4%; men: 30%; women: 70%; minorities: 20%; international: 17%
Part-time enrollment: 375
doctoral students: 43%; master's students: 43%; education specialists: 13%; men: 27%; women: 73%; minorities: 19%; international: 2%
Acceptance rate (master's): 75%
Acceptance rate (doctoral): 91%
Entrance test required: GRE
Avg. GRE (of all entering students with scores): quantitative: N/A; verbal: N/A
Research assistantships: 37
Students reporting specialty: 100%
Students specializing in: curriculum/instr.: 17%; admin.: 4%; evaluation/research/ statistics: 1%; instructional media design: 2%; educational psych: 1%; higher education admin.: 18%; secondary: 5%; social/philosophical foundations: 9%; special: 12%; other: 32%

Youngstown State University[1]

1 University Plaza
Youngstown, OH 44555
bcoe.ysu.edu/bcoe
Public
Admissions: N/A
Financial aid: N/A
Tuition: N/A
Room/board/expenses: N/A
Enrollment: N/A

OKLAHOMA

Oklahoma State University

325 Willard Hall
Stillwater, OK 74078-4033
www.okstate.edu/education/
Public
Admissions: (405) 744-6368
Email: grad-i@okstate.edu
Financial aid: (405) 744-6604
Application deadline: rolling
In-state tuition: full time: $196/ credit hour; part time: $196/ credit hour
Out-of-state tuition: full time: $786/credit hour
Room/board/expenses: $12,420
Full-time enrollment: 628
doctoral students: 41%; master's students: 57%; education specialists: 2%; men: 36%; women: 64%; minorities: 33%; international: 5%
Part-time enrollment: 226
doctoral students: 72%; master's students: 27%; education specialists: 1%; men: 35%; women: 65%; minorities: 22%; international: 3%
Acceptance rate (master's): 76%
Acceptance rate (doctoral): 51%
Entrance test required: GRE
Avg. GRE (of all entering students with scores): quantitative: 145; verbal: 150
Research assistantships: 73
Students reporting specialty: 100%

Students specializing in: curriculum/instr.: 6%; admin.: 10%; policy: 5%; evaluation/research/statistics: 2%; instructional media design: 1%; educational psych: 14%; educational tech.: 3%; elementary: 4%; higher education admin.: 1%; junior high: 4%; secondary: 4%; social/philosophical foundations: 2%; special: 5%; counseling: 3%; technical (vocational): 5%; other: 31%

Oral Roberts University[1]

7777 S. Lewis Avenue
Tulsa, OK 74171
www.oru.edu/
Private
Admissions: (918) 495-6553
Email: gradedu@oru.edu
Financial aid: (918) 495-6602
Tuition: N/A
Room/board/expenses: N/A
Enrollment: N/A

University of Oklahoma (Rainbolt)

820 Van Vleet Oval, No. 100
Norman, OK 73019-2041
www.ou.edu/education
Public
Admissions: (405) 325-2252
Email: admrec@ou.edu
Financial aid: (405) 325-4521
Application deadline: rolling
In-state tuition: full time: $8,611; part time: $191/credit hour
Out-of-state tuition: full time: $21,792
Room/board/expenses: $17,315
Full-time enrollment: 535
doctoral students: 28%; master's students: 72%; education specialists: N/A; men: 33%; women: 67%; minorities: 25%; international: 5%
Part-time enrollment: 232
doctoral students: 60%; master's students: 40%; education specialists: N/A; men: 25%; women: 75%; minorities: 25%; international: 3%
Acceptance rate (master's): 83%
Acceptance rate (doctoral): 42%
Entrance test required: GRE
Avg. GRE (of all entering students with scores): quantitative: 148; verbal: 152
Research assistantships: 125
Students reporting specialty: 100%
Students specializing in: curriculum/instr.: 23%; admin.: 25%; evaluation/research/statistics: 5%; higher education admin.: 26%; social/philosophical foundations: 4%; special: 8%; counseling: 7%; other: 1%

OREGON

George Fox University[1]

414 N. Meridian Street
Newberg, OR 97132
www.georgefox.edu
Private
Admissions: N/A
Financial aid: N/A
Tuition: N/A
Room/board/expenses: N/A
Enrollment: N/A

Lewis & Clark College

0615 S.W. Palatine Hill Road
Portland, OR 97219-7899
graduate.lclark.edu
Private
Admissions: (503) 768-6200
Email: gseadmit@lclark.edu
Financial aid: (503) 768-7090
Application deadline: rolling
Tuition: full time: N/A; part time: N/A
Room/board/expenses: $24,075
Full-time enrollment: 179
doctoral students: 0%; master's students: 82%; education specialists: 18%; men: 21%; women: 79%; minorities: 16%; international: 2%
Part-time enrollment: 83
doctoral students: N/A; master's students: 40%; education specialists: 35%; men: 27%; women: 73%; minorities: 22%; international: N/A
Acceptance rate (master's): 82%
Acceptance rate (doctoral): 100%
Entrance test required: GRE
Avg. GRE (of all entering students with scores): quantitative: N/A; verbal: N/A
Research assistantships: 0
Students reporting specialty: 100%
Students specializing in: curriculum/instr.: 2%; admin.: 42%; educational psych: 13%; elementary: 8%; higher education admin.: 6%; secondary: 14%; special: 1%; counseling: 13%; other: 2%

Oregon State University

104 Furman Hall
Corvallis, OR 97331-3502
oregonstate.edu/education/
Public
Admissions: (541) 737-4411
Email: osuadmit@oregonstate.edu
Financial aid: (541) 737-2241
Application deadline: 06/01
In-state tuition: full time: $13,722; part time: $450/credit hour
Out-of-state tuition: full time: $22,524
Room/board/expenses: $16,125
Full-time enrollment: 185
doctoral students: 23%; master's students: 77%; education specialists: N/A; men: 32%; women: 68%; minorities: 18%; international: 2%
Part-time enrollment: 235
doctoral students: 43%; master's students: 57%; education specialists: N/A; men: 26%; women: 74%; minorities: 24%; international: 0%
Acceptance rate (master's): 61%
Acceptance rate (doctoral): 41%
Entrance test required: N/A
Avg. GRE (of all entering students with scores): quantitative: N/A; verbal: N/A
Research assistantships: 5
Students reporting specialty: 100%
Students specializing in: admin.: 8%; elementary: 6%; secondary: 23%; counseling: 38%; other: 25%

Portland State University

PO Box 751
Portland, OR 97207-0751
www.ed.pdx.edu/admissions.shtml
Public
Admissions: (503) 725-3511
Email: adm@pdx.edu
Financial aid: (503) 725-3461
Application deadline: rolling
In-state tuition: full time: $10,896; part time: $356/credit hour
Out-of-state tuition: full time: $16,296
Room/board/expenses: $15,681
Full-time enrollment: 480
doctoral students: 2%; master's students: 98%; education specialists: N/A; men: 26%; women: 74%; minorities: 26%; international: 3%
Part-time enrollment: 542
doctoral students: 12%; master's students: 88%; education specialists: N/A; men: 24%; women: 76%; minorities: 21%; international: 3%
Acceptance rate (master's): 74%
Acceptance rate (doctoral): 100%
Entrance test required: N/A
Avg. GRE (of all entering students with scores): quantitative: N/A; verbal: N/A
Research assistantships: 6
Students reporting specialty: 100%
Students specializing in: curriculum/instr.: 15%; admin.: 32%; instructional media design: 0%; elementary: 15%; higher education admin.: 1%; secondary: 12%; special: 12%; counseling: 14%

University of Oregon

1215 University of Oregon
Eugene, OR 97403-1215
education.uoregon.edu/
Public
Admissions: (541) 346-5134
Email: gradsch@uoregon.edu
Financial aid: (541) 346-3221
Application deadline: rolling
In-state tuition: full time: $17,816; part time: $539/credit hour
Out-of-state tuition: full time: $24,536
Room/board/expenses: $14,568
Full-time enrollment: 428
doctoral students: 41%; master's students: 59%; education specialists: N/A; men: 24%; women: 76%; minorities: 23%; international: 6%
Part-time enrollment: 51
doctoral students: 18%; master's students: 82%; education specialists: N/A; men: 35%; women: 65%; minorities: 18%; international: 18%
Acceptance rate (master's): 50%
Acceptance rate (doctoral): 19%
Entrance test required: GRE
Avg. GRE (of all entering students with scores): quantitative: 151; verbal: 154
Students reporting specialty: 100%
Students specializing in: admin.: 29%; evaluation/research/statistics: 4%; special: 15%; other: 52%

Arcadia University[1]

450 S. Easton Road
Glenside, PA 19038-3295
www.arcadia.edu/
Private
Admissions: (877) 272-2342
Email: admiss@arcadia.edu
Financial aid: (215) 572-2980
Tuition: N/A
Room/board/expenses: N/A
Enrollment: N/A

Drexel University

3141 Chestnut Street
Philadelphia, PA 19104
goodwin.drexel.edu/soe
Private
Admissions: (215) 895-2400
Email: admissions@drexel.edu
Financial aid: (215) 895-1627
Application deadline: rolling
Tuition: full time: $1,157/credit hour; part time: $1,157/credit hour
Room/board/expenses: N/A
Full-time enrollment: 32
doctoral students: 25%; master's students: 75%; education specialists: N/A; men: 19%; women: 81%; minorities: 19%; international: 9%
Part-time enrollment: 804
doctoral students: 35%; master's students: 65%; education specialists: N/A; men: 27%; women: 73%; minorities: 25%; international: 2%
Acceptance rate (master's): 87%
Acceptance rate (doctoral): 55%
Entrance test required: GRE
Avg. GRE (of all entering students with scores): quantitative: N/A; verbal: N/A
Research assistantships: 11
Students reporting specialty: 100%
Students specializing in: curriculum/instr.: 3%; admin.: 33%; policy: 0%; evaluation/research/statistics: 30%; instructional media design: 4%; educational tech.: 4%; elementary: 12%; higher education admin.: 11%; secondary: 12%; social/philosophical foundations: 6%; special: 9%; counseling: 3%; other: 6%

Duquesne University

600 Forbes Avenue
Pittsburgh, PA 15282
www.duq.edu/education/
Private
Admissions: (412) 396-6093
Email: edinfo@duq.edu
Financial aid: (412) 396-6607
Application deadline: 08/25
Tuition: full time: $1,189/credit hour; part time: $1,189/credit hour
Room/board/expenses: $15,018
Full-time enrollment: 484
doctoral students: 45%; master's students: 55%; education specialists: N/A; men: 28%; women: 72%; minorities: 13%; international: 8%
Part-time enrollment: 65
doctoral students: 8%; master's students: 92%; education specialists: N/A; men: 18%; women: 82%; minorities: 14%; international: 18%
Acceptance rate (master's): 48%

Acceptance rate (doctoral): 49%
Entrance test required: GRE
Avg. GRE (of all entering students with scores): quantitative: 149; verbal: 150
Research assistantships: 39
Students reporting specialty: 100%
Students specializing in: curriculum/instr.: 0%; admin.: 6%; evaluation/research/statistics: 0%; educational psych: 17%; educational tech.: 12%; elementary: 6%; junior high: 1%; secondary: 6%; social/philosophical foundations: 6%; special: 3%; counseling: 33%; other: 11%

East Stroudsburg University of Pennsylvania

200 Prospect Street
East Stroudsburg, PA 18301-2999
www.esu.edu
Public
Admissions: (570) 422-3536
Email: grad@po-box.esu.edu
Financial aid: (570) 422-2800
Application deadline: 08/11
In-state tuition: full time: $470/credit hour; part time: $470/credit hour
Out-of-state tuition: full time: $705/credit hour
Room/board/expenses: $12,928
Full-time enrollment: 46
doctoral students: N/A; master's students: 87%; education specialists: 13%; men: 39%; women: 61%; minorities: 15%; international: 4%
Part-time enrollment: 117
doctoral students: N/A; master's students: 99%; education specialists: 1%; men: 21%; women: 79%; minorities: 6%; international: N/A
Acceptance rate (master's): 79%
Acceptance rate (doctoral): N/A
Entrance test required: GRE
Avg. GRE (of all entering students with scores): quantitative: N/A; verbal: N/A
Students reporting specialty: 100%
Students specializing in: admin.: 1%; educational tech.: 13%; elementary: 5%; secondary: 32%; special: 21%; other: 28%

Immaculata University[1]

1145 King Road
Immaculata, PA 19345
www.immaculata.edu
Private
Admissions: N/A
Financial aid: N/A
Tuition: N/A
Room/board/expenses: N/A
Enrollment: N/A

Indiana University of Pennsylvania

104 Stouffer Hall
Indiana, PA 15705-1083
www.iup.edu/graduate
Public
Admissions: (724) 357-2222
Email: graduate-admissions@iup.edu
Financial aid: (724) 357-2218
Application deadline: rolling
In-state tuition: full time: $11,175; part time: $470/credit hour
Out-of-state tuition: full time: $15,405

Room/board/expenses: $14,535
Full-time enrollment: 249
doctoral students: 4%; master's students: 94%; education specialists: 2%; men: 23%; women: 77%; minorities: 11%; international: 3%
Part-time enrollment: 398
doctoral students: 51%; master's students: 46%; education specialists: 3%; men: 27%; women: 73%; minorities: 11%; international: 3%
Acceptance rate (master's): 45%
Acceptance rate (doctoral): 65%
Entrance test required: GRE
Avg. GRE (of all entering students with scores): quantitative: 147; verbal: 150
Students reporting specialty: 100%
Students specializing in: admin.: 14%; educational psych: 3%; elementary: 14%; special: 5%; counseling: 16%; other: 48%

Lehigh University
111 Research Drive
Bethlehem, PA 18015
coe.lehigh.edu/
Private
Admissions: (610) 758-3231
Email: ineduc@lehigh.edu
Financial aid: (610) 758-3181
Application deadline: rolling
Tuition: full time: $565/credit hour; part time: $565/credit hour
Room/board/expenses: $19,820
Full-time enrollment: 148
doctoral students: 43%; master's students: 52%; education specialists: 5%; men: 14%; women: 86%; minorities: 10%; international: 22%
Part-time enrollment: 274
doctoral students: 28%; master's students: 69%; education specialists: 3%; men: 28%; women: 72%; minorities: 8%; international: 6%
Acceptance rate (master's): 57%
Acceptance rate (doctoral): 19%
Entrance test required: GRE
Avg. GRE (of all entering students with scores): quantitative: 155; verbal: 156
Research assistantships: 38
Students reporting specialty: 100%
Students specializing in: admin.: 25%; instructional media design: 10%; educational psych: 14%; elementary: 3%; secondary: 3%; special: 10%; counseling: 13%; other: 21%

Neumann University[1]
1 Neumann Drive
Aston, PA 19014
www.neumann.edu
Private
Admissions: N/A
Financial aid: N/A
Tuition: N/A
Room/board/expenses: N/A
Enrollment: N/A

Pennsylvania State University-Harrisburg
777 W. Harrisburg Pike
Middletown, PA 17057
hbg.psu.edu/admissions/index.php
Public
Admissions: (717) 948-6250
Email: hbgadmit@psu.edu
Financial aid: (717) 948-6307

Application deadline: rolling
In-state tuition: full time: $20,280; part time: $805/credit hour
Out-of-state tuition: full time: $26,488
Room/board/expenses: $19,316
Full-time enrollment: 10
doctoral students: 20%; master's students: 80%; education specialists: N/A; men: N/A; women: 100%; minorities: 20%; international: 20%
Part-time enrollment: 209
doctoral students: 18%; master's students: 82%; education specialists: N/A; men: 15%; women: 85%; minorities: 11%; international: N/A
Acceptance rate (master's): 99%
Acceptance rate (doctoral): 100%
Entrance test required: GRE
Avg. GRE (of all entering students with scores): quantitative: 150; verbal: 158
Research assistantships: 0
Students reporting specialty: 62%
Students specializing in: curriculum/instr.: 58%; secondary: 9%; special: 3%; other: 30%

Pennsylvania State University-University Park
274 Chambers Building
University Park, PA 16802-3206
ed.psu.edu/graduate
Public
Admissions: (814) 865-1795
Email: gswww@psu.edu
Financial aid: (814) 865-2514
Application deadline: rolling
In-state tuition: full time: $20,270; part time: $805/credit hour
Out-of-state tuition: full time: $34,084
Room/board/expenses: $18,486
Full-time enrollment: 593
doctoral students: 62%; master's students: 38%; education specialists: N/A; men: 31%; women: 69%; minorities: 18%; international: 28%
Part-time enrollment: 623
doctoral students: 32%; master's students: 68%; education specialists: N/A; men: 29%; women: 71%; minorities: 14%; international: 6%
Acceptance rate (master's): 49%
Acceptance rate (doctoral): 36%
Entrance test required: GRE
Avg. GRE (of all entering students with scores): quantitative: 151; verbal: 154
Research assistantships: 79
Students reporting specialty: 100%
Students specializing in: curriculum/instr.: 15%; admin.: 18%; policy: 4%; evaluation/research/statistics: 26%; instructional media design: 9%; educational psych: 3%; educational tech.: 4%; elementary: 0%; higher education admin.: 13%; secondary: 0%; social/philosophical foundations: 5%; special: 8%; counseling: 11%; technical (vocational): 8%; other: 17%

Robert Morris University
6001 University Boulevard
Moon Township, PA 15108-1189
www.rmu.edu
Private
Admissions: (412) 397-5200
Email: graduateadmissions@rmu.edu
Financial aid: (412) 397-6260
Application deadline: rolling
Tuition: full time: N/A; part time: $815/credit hour
Room/board/expenses: N/A
Full-time enrollment: N/A
doctoral students: N/A; master's students: N/A; education specialists: N/A; men: N/A; women: N/A; minorities: N/A; international: N/A
Part-time enrollment: 147
doctoral students: 43%; master's students: 57%; education specialists: N/A; men: 34%; women: 66%; minorities: 9%; international: 1%
Acceptance rate (master's): 39%
Acceptance rate (doctoral): 42%
Entrance test required: N/A
Avg. GRE (of all entering students with scores): quantitative: N/A; verbal: N/A
Research assistantships: 3
Students reporting specialty: 93%
Students specializing in: curriculum/instr.: 25%; admin.: 53%; instructional media design: 1%; educational tech.: 1%; elementary: 4%; higher education admin.: 11%; special: 6%

St. Joseph's University[1]
5600 City Avenue
Philadelphia, PA 19131
www.sju.edu
Private
Admissions: N/A
Financial aid: N/A
Tuition: N/A
Room/board/expenses: N/A
Enrollment: N/A

Temple University
OSS RA238
Philadelphia, PA 19122
www.temple.edu/
Public
Admissions: (215) 204-8011
Email: educate@temple.edu
Financial aid: (215) 204-1492
Application deadline: rolling
In-state tuition: full time: $853/credit hour; part time: $853/credit hour
Out-of-state tuition: full time: $1,169/credit hour
Room/board/expenses: $16,450
Full-time enrollment: 381
doctoral students: 45%; master's students: 49%; education specialists: 6%; men: 27%; women: 73%; minorities: 24%; international: 9%
Part-time enrollment: 309
doctoral students: 26%; master's students: 74%; education specialists: 0%; men: 36%; women: 64%; minorities: 28%; international: 2%
Acceptance rate (master's): 49%
Acceptance rate (doctoral): 19%
Entrance test required: GRE

Avg. GRE (of all entering students with scores): quantitative: 148; verbal: 152
Research assistantships: 14
Students reporting specialty: 100%
Students specializing in: curriculum/instr.: 10%; admin.: 10%; instructional media design: 1%; educational psych: 7%; elementary: 1%; higher education admin.: 10%; junior high: 1%; secondary: 5%; social/philosophical foundations: 7%; special: 9%; counseling: 13%; technical (vocational): 8%; other: 19%

University of Pennsylvania
3700 Walnut Street
Philadelphia, PA 19104-6216
www.gse.upenn.edu
Private
Admissions: (215) 898-6455
Email: admissions@gse.upenn.edu
Financial aid: (215) 898-6455
Application deadline: rolling
Tuition: full time: $50,050; part time: $1,480/credit hour
Room/board/expenses: $27,310
Full-time enrollment: 882
doctoral students: 12%; master's students: 88%; education specialists: N/A; men: 23%; women: 77%; minorities: 30%; international: 30%
Part-time enrollment: 188
doctoral students: 2%; master's students: 98%; education specialists: N/A; men: 28%; women: 72%; minorities: 31%; international: 15%
Acceptance rate (master's): 73%
Acceptance rate (doctoral): 5%
Entrance test required: GRE
Avg. GRE (of all entering students with scores): quantitative: 156; verbal: 156
Research assistantships: 97
Students reporting specialty: 100%
Students specializing in: curriculum/instr.: 33%; admin.: 4%; policy: 7%; evaluation/research/statistics: 4%; educational psych: 4%; educational tech.: 2%; elementary: 3%; higher education admin.: 10%; junior high: 4%; secondary: 11%; social/philosophical foundations: 4%; special: 3%; counseling: 11%

University of Pittsburgh
5601 Wesley W. Posvar Hall
Pittsburgh, PA 15260
www.education.pitt.edu
Public
Admissions: (412) 648-2230
Email: soeinfo@pitt.edu
Financial aid: (412) 648-2230
Application deadline: rolling
In-state tuition: full time: $22,060; part time: $858/credit hour
Out-of-state tuition: full time: $35,744
Room/board/expenses: $17,458
Full-time enrollment: 482
doctoral students: 33%; master's students: 67%; education specialists: N/A; men: 24%; women: 76%; minorities: 14%; international: 21%

Part-time enrollment: 367
doctoral students: 53%; master's students: 47%; education specialists: N/A; men: 29%; women: 71%; minorities: 15%; international: 1%
Acceptance rate (master's): 85%
Acceptance rate (doctoral): 46%
Entrance test required: GRE
Avg. GRE (of all entering students with scores): quantitative: 156; verbal: 153
Research assistantships: 24
Students reporting specialty: 87%
Students specializing in: curriculum/instr.: 1%; admin.: 7%; policy: 2%; evaluation/research/statistics: 4%; educational psych: 9%; elementary: 6%; higher education admin.: 16%; secondary: 24%; social/philosophical foundations: 11%; special: 15%; other: 11%

Widener University[1]
1 University Place
Chester, PA 19013-5792
www.widener.edu
Private
Admissions: N/A
Financial aid: N/A
Tuition: N/A
Room/board/expenses: N/A
Enrollment: N/A

Wilkes University[1]
84 W. South Street
Wilkes-Barre, PA 18766
www.wilkes.edu
Private
Admissions: N/A
Financial aid: N/A
Room/board/expenses: N/A
Enrollment: N/A

RHODE ISLAND

Johnson & Wales University
8 Abbott Park Place
Providence, RI 02903-3703
www.jwu.edu
Private
Admissions: N/A
Financial aid: N/A
Application deadline: rolling
Tuition: full time: $422/credit hour; part time: $422/credit hour
Room/board/expenses: N/A
Full-time enrollment: 73
doctoral students: 89%; master's students: 11%; education specialists: N/A; men: 30%; women: 70%; minorities: N/A; international: N/A
Part-time enrollment: N/A
doctoral students: N/A; master's students: N/A; education specialists: N/A; men: N/A; women: N/A; minorities: N/A; international: N/A
Acceptance rate (master's): 30%
Acceptance rate (doctoral): 53%
Entrance test required: N/A
Avg. GRE (of all entering students with scores): quantitative: N/A; verbal: N/A
Students reporting specialty: 89%
Students specializing in: admin.: 54%; higher education admin.: 46%

University of Rhode Island–Rhode Island College (Feinstein)[1]
600 Mount Pleasant Avenue
Providence, RI 02908
www.uri.edu/prov
Public
Admissions: N/A
Financial aid: N/A
Tuition: N/A
Room/board/expenses: N/A
Enrollment: N/A

SOUTH CAROLINA

Clemson University (Moore)
102 Tillman Hall
Clemson, SC 29634-0702
www.grad.clemson.edu
Public
Admissions: (864) 656-3195
Email: grdapp@clemson.edu
Financial aid: (864) 656-2280
Application deadline: rolling
In-state tuition: full time: $4,468; part time: $448/credit hour
Out-of-state tuition: full time: $8,511
Room/board/expenses: $0
Full-time enrollment: 255 doctoral students: 24%; master's students: 75%; education specialists: 1%; men: 29%; women: 71%; minorities: 21%; international: 4%
Part-time enrollment: 356 doctoral students: 27%; master's students: 61%; education specialists: 12%; men: 32%; women: 68%; minorities: 21%; international: 0%
Acceptance rate (master's): 52%
Acceptance rate (doctoral): 46%
Entrance test required: GRE
Avg. GRE (of all entering students with scores): quantitative: 148; verbal: 151
Research assistantships: 6
Students reporting specialty: 100%
Students specializing in: curriculum/instr.: 6%; admin.: 30%; evaluation/research/statistics: 1%; junior high: 5%; secondary: 3%; special: 3%; counseling: 26%; other: 26%

Columbia International University[1]
7435 Monticello Road
Columbia, SC 29203
www.ciu.edu/
Private
Admissions: N/A
Financial aid: N/A
Tuition: N/A
Room/board/expenses: N/A
Enrollment: N/A

South Carolina State University
PO Box 7298
300 College Street NE
Orangeburg, SC 29117
www.scsu.edu/schoolofgraduatestudies.aspx
Public
Admissions: (803) 536-7133
Email: graduateschool@scsu.edu
Financial aid: (803) 536-7067
Application deadline: N/A

In-state tuition: full time: $10,088; part time: $560/credit hour
Out-of-state tuition: full time: $19,856
Room/board/expenses: N/A
Full-time enrollment: 80 doctoral students: 4%; master's students: 86%; education specialists: 10%; men: 29%; women: 71%; minorities: 98%; international: N/A
Part-time enrollment: 135 doctoral students: 39%; master's students: 44%; education specialists: 17%; men: 30%; women: 70%; minorities: 96%; international: N/A
Acceptance rate (master's): 98%
Acceptance rate (doctoral): 100%
Entrance test required: GRE
Avg. GRE (of all entering students with scores): quantitative: N/A; verbal: N/A
Students reporting specialty: 100%
Students specializing in: admin.: 40%; elementary: 11%; secondary: 8%; counseling: 31%; other: 9%

University of South Carolina
Wardlaw Building
Columbia, SC 29208
www.ed.sc.edu
Public
Admissions: (803) 777-4243
Email: gradapp@mailbox.sc.edu
Financial aid: (803) 777-8134
Application deadline: rolling
In-state tuition: full time: $12,784; part time: $516/credit hour
Out-of-state tuition: full time: $26,932
Room/board/expenses: $16,300
Full-time enrollment: 464 doctoral students: 14%; master's students: 79%; education specialists: 7%; men: 34%; women: 66%; minorities: 18%; international: 2%
Part-time enrollment: 783 doctoral students: 51%; master's students: 45%; education specialists: 4%; men: 26%; women: 74%; minorities: 21%; international: 2%
Acceptance rate (master's): 66%
Acceptance rate (doctoral): 37%
Entrance test required: GRE
Avg. GRE (of all entering students with scores): quantitative: 150; verbal: 152
Research assistantships: 33
Students reporting specialty: 99%
Students specializing in: curriculum/instr.: 17%; admin.: 30%; evaluation/research/statistics: 0%; educational psych: 9%; educational tech.: 1%; elementary: 2%; higher education admin.: 2%; secondary: 7%; social/philosophical foundations: 1%; special: 3%; counseling: 8%; other: 19%

SOUTH DAKOTA

University of South Dakota
414 E. Clark Street
Vermillion, SD 57069
www.usd.edu/grad
Public
Admissions: (605) 677-6240
Email: grad@usd.edu
Financial aid: (605) 677-5446

Application deadline: rolling
In-state tuition: full time: $219/credit hour; part time: $219/credit hour
Out-of-state tuition: full time: $464/credit hour
Room/board/expenses: $11,526
Full-time enrollment: 170 doctoral students: 18%; master's students: 69%; education specialists: 14%; men: 32%; women: 68%; minorities: 5%; international: 4%
Part-time enrollment: 325 doctoral students: 37%; master's students: 43%; education specialists: 19%; men: 34%; women: 66%; minorities: 10%; international: 1%
Acceptance rate (master's): 80%
Acceptance rate (doctoral): 81%
Entrance test required: GRE
Avg. GRE (of all entering students with scores): quantitative: 148; verbal: 149
Research assistantships: 8
Students reporting specialty: 100%
Students specializing in: curriculum/instr.: 7%; admin.: 35%; instructional media design: 2%; educational psych: 11%; elementary: 2%; higher education admin.: 16%; secondary: 2%; special: 4%; counseling: 14%; other: 6%

TENNESSEE

East Tennessee State University (Clemmer)
PO Box 70720
Johnson City, TN 37614-0720
www.etsu.edu/coe/
Public
Admissions: (423) 439-4221
Email: gradsch@etsu.edu
Financial aid: (423) 439-4300
Application deadline: rolling
In-state tuition: full time: $9,171; part time: $434/credit hour
Out-of-state tuition: full time: $23,085
Room/board/expenses: $15,542
Full-time enrollment: 288 doctoral students: 16%; master's students: 84%; education specialists: 0%; men: 39%; women: 61%; minorities: 9%; international: 7%
Part-time enrollment: 342 doctoral students: 56%; master's students: 43%; education specialists: 1%; men: 29%; women: 71%; minorities: 13%; international: 1%
Acceptance rate (master's): N/A
Acceptance rate (doctoral): N/A
Entrance test required: GRE
Avg. GRE (of all entering students with scores): quantitative: 146; verbal: 147
Students reporting specialty: 100%
Students specializing in: admin.: 37%; instructional media design: 9%; elementary: 2%; secondary: 2%; special: 2%; counseling: 12%; other: 37%

Lincoln Memorial University[1]
6965 Cumberland Gap Parkway
Harrogate, TN 37752
www.lmunet.edu/
Private
Admissions: N/A
Financial aid: N/A
Tuition: N/A

Room/board/expenses: N/A
Enrollment: N/A

Lipscomb University[1]
3901 Granny White Pike
Nashville, TN 37204-3951
www.lipscomb.edu/
Private
Admissions: (615) 279-6067
Email: junior.high@lipscomb.edu
Financial aid: (615) 269-1791
Tuition: N/A
Room/board/expenses: N/A
Enrollment: N/A

Middle Tennessee State University
1301 E. Main Street
CAB Room 205
Murfreesboro, TN 37132
www.mtsu.edu/education/index.php
Public
Admissions: N/A
Financial aid: N/A
Application deadline: rolling
In-state tuition: full time: $432/credit hour; part time: $432/credit hour
Out-of-state tuition: full time: $1,197/credit hour
Room/board/expenses: $17,192
Full-time enrollment: 129 doctoral students: 3%; master's students: 95%; education specialists: 2%; men: 22%; women: 78%; minorities: 16%; international: 22%
Part-time enrollment: 324 doctoral students: 19%; master's students: 69%; education specialists: 11%; men: 19%; women: 81%; minorities: 16%; international: 3%
Acceptance rate (master's): 51%
Acceptance rate (doctoral): 86%
Entrance test required: GRE
Avg. GRE (of all entering students with scores): quantitative: N/A; verbal: N/A
Students reporting specialty: 100%
Students specializing in: curriculum/instr.: 36%; admin.: 30%; evaluation/research/statistics: 7%; special: 3%; counseling: 13%; other: 11%

Tennessee State University[1]
3500 John A. Merritt Boulevard
Nashville, TN 37209-1561
www.tnstate.edu
Public
Admissions: N/A
Financial aid: N/A
Tuition: N/A
Room/board/expenses: N/A
Enrollment: N/A

Tennessee Technological University
Box 5012
Cookeville, TN 38505-0001
www.tntech.edu/
Public
Admissions: (931) 372-3233
Email: gradstudies@tntech.edu
Financial aid: (931) 372-3073
Application deadline: 07/01
In-state tuition: full time: $15,667; part time: $511/credit hour
Out-of-state tuition: full time: $36,847

Room/board/expenses: $16,400
Full-time enrollment: 145 doctoral students: 10%; master's students: 81%; education specialists: 9%; men: 32%; women: 68%; minorities: 12%; international: 4%
Part-time enrollment: 249 doctoral students: 10%; master's students: 66%; education specialists: 23%; men: 29%; women: 71%; minorities: 10%; international: 1%
Acceptance rate (master's): 67%
Acceptance rate (doctoral): 80%
Entrance test required: GRE
Avg. GRE (of all entering students with scores): quantitative: N/A; verbal: N/A
Research assistantships: 11
Students reporting specialty: 99%
Students specializing in: curriculum/instr.: 17%; admin.: 11%; evaluation/research/statistics: 10%; educational psych: 3%; educational tech.: 4%; elementary: 4%; secondary: 14%; special: 5%; counseling: 16%; other: 15%

Trevecca Nazarene University[1]
333 Murfreesboro Road
Nashville, TN 37210
www.trevecca.edu/academics/schools-colleges/education/
Private
Admissions: N/A
Financial aid: N/A
Tuition: N/A
Room/board/expenses: N/A
Enrollment: N/A

Union University
1050 Union University Drive
Jackson, TN 38305
www.uu.edu/
Private
Admissions: (731) 661-5928
Email: crbrown@uu.edu
Financial aid: (731) 661-5015
Application deadline: rolling
Tuition: full time: $485/credit hour; part time: $485/credit hour
Room/board/expenses: N/A
Full-time enrollment: N/A doctoral students: N/A; master's students: N/A; education specialists: N/A; men: N/A; women: N/A; minorities: N/A; international: N/A
Part-time enrollment: N/A doctoral students: N/A; master's students: N/A; education specialists: N/A; men: N/A; women: N/A; minorities: N/A; international: N/A
Acceptance rate (master's): N/A
Acceptance rate (doctoral): N/A
Entrance test required: GRE
Avg. GRE (of all entering students with scores): quantitative: N/A; verbal: N/A
Research assistantships: 1
Students reporting specialty: 100%
Students specializing in: admin.: 17%; higher education admin.: 6%; other: 77%

University of Memphis[1]
215 Ball Hall
Memphis, TN 38152-6015
www.memphis.edu/admissions.htm
Public
Admissions: (901) 678-2911
Email: admissions@memphis.edu
Financial aid: (901) 678-4825
Tuition: N/A
Room/board/expenses: N/A
Enrollment: N/A

University of Tennessee-Chattanooga
615 McCallie Avenue
Chattanooga, TN 37403
www.utc.edu/graduate-school
Public
Admissions: (423) 425-4478
Financial aid: (423) 425-4677
Application deadline: rolling
In-state tuition: full time: $9,670;
part time: $441/credit hour
Out-of-state tuition: full time:
$25,788
Room/board/expenses: $17,400
Full-time enrollment: 81
doctoral students: N/A; master's
students: 62%; education
specialists: 38%; men: 26%;
women: 74%; minorities: 15%;
international: 1%
Part-time enrollment: 76
doctoral students: N/A; master's
students: 88%; education
specialists: 12%; men: 21%;
women: 79%; minorities: 24%;
international: N/A
Acceptance rate (master's): 92%
Acceptance rate (doctoral): N/A
Entrance test required: GRE
**Avg. GRE (of all entering students
with scores):** quantitative: 145;
verbal: 147
Research assistantships: 31
Students reporting specialty: 100%
Students specializing in:
admin.: 17%; elementary: 7%;
secondary: 34%; special: 5%;
counseling: 14%; other: 24%

University of Tennessee-Knoxville
335 Claxton Complex
Knoxville, TN 37996-3400
cehhs.utk.edu
Public
Admissions: (865) 974-3251
Email: nfox@utk.edu
Financial aid: (865) 974-3131
Application deadline: rolling
In-state tuition: full time: $12,166;
part time: $591/credit hour
Out-of-state tuition: full time:
$30,356
Room/board/expenses: $19,250
Full-time enrollment: 345
doctoral students: 34%;
master's students: 64%;
education specialists: 2%; men:
20%; women: 80%; minorities:
13%; international: 3%
Part-time enrollment: 266
doctoral students: 58%; master's
students: 38%;
education specialists: 4%; men:
26%; women: 74%; minorities:
13%; international: 2%
Acceptance rate (master's): 77%
Acceptance rate (doctoral): 60%
Entrance test required: GRE
**Avg. GRE (of all entering students
with scores):** quantitative: 150;
verbal: 154

Research assistantships: 88
Students reporting specialty: 100%
Students specializing in: admin.:
4%; policy: 3%; evaluation/
research/statistics: 1%;
educational psych: 8%;
educational tech.: 4%;
elementary: 10%; higher
education admin.: 5%; junior
high: 1%; secondary: 12%;
social/philosophical foundations:
0%; special: 6%; counseling:
9%; other: 37%

Vanderbilt University (Peabody)
PO Box 227
Nashville, TN 37203-9418
peabody.vanderbilt.edu
Private
Admissions: (615) 322-8410
Email: peabody.admissions@
vanderbilt.edu
Financial aid: (615) 322-8410
Application deadline: rolling
Tuition: full time: $1,818/credit
hour; part time: $1,818/credit
hour
Room/board/expenses: $19,845
Full-time enrollment: 704
doctoral students: 26%;
master's students: 74%;
education specialists: N/A; men:
20%; women: 80%; minorities:
16%; international: 13%
Part-time enrollment: 186
doctoral students: 37%;
master's students: 63%;
education specialists: N/A; men:
35%; women: 65%; minorities:
19%; international: N/A
Acceptance rate (master's): 66%
Acceptance rate (doctoral): 5%
Entrance test required: GRE
**Avg. GRE (of all entering students
with scores):** quantitative: 155;
verbal: 158
Research assistantships: 207
Students reporting specialty: 100%
Students specializing in:
curriculum/instr.: 12%; admin.:
6%; policy: 14%; evaluation/
research/statistics: 13%;
elementary: 3%; higher
education admin.: 10%;
secondary: 5%; special: 15%;
counseling: 10%; other: 12%

TEXAS

Baylor University
1 Bear Place, #97304
Waco, TX 76798-7304
www.baylor.edu/SOE/
Private
Admissions: (254) 710-3584
Email:
graduate_school@baylor.edu
Financial aid: (254) 710-2611
Application deadline: 02/01
Tuition: full time: $1,515/credit
hour; part time: $1,515/credit
hour
Room/board/expenses: $12,414
Full-time enrollment: 133
doctoral students: 26%;
master's students: 56%;
education specialists: 17%; men:
26%; women: 74%; minorities:
26%; international: 5%
Part-time enrollment: 44
doctoral students: 36%;
master's students: 64%;
education specialists: 0%; men:
34%; women: 66%; minorities:
32%; international: 2%

Acceptance rate (master's): 60%
Acceptance rate (doctoral): 46%
Entrance test required: GRE
**Avg. GRE (of all entering students
with scores):** quantitative: 151;
verbal: 154
Research assistantships: 45
Students reporting specialty: 100%
Students specializing in:
curriculum/instr.: 21%; admin.:
19%; educational psych: 41%;
other: 19%

Dallas Baptist University (Bush)[1]
3000 Mountain Creek Parkway
Dallas, TX 75211-9299
www.dbu.edu/
Private
Admissions: N/A
Financial aid: N/A
Tuition: N/A
Room/board/expenses: N/A
Enrollment: N/A

Lamar University
PO Box 10034
Lamar University Station
Beaumont, TX 77710
dept.lamar.edu/education/
Public
Admissions: (409) 880-8356
Email: gradmissions@hal.lamar.
edu
Financial aid: (409) 880-8450
Application deadline: rolling
In-state tuition: full time: $6,733;
part time: $330/credit hour
Out-of-state tuition: full time:
$11,803
Room/board/expenses: $14,070
Full-time enrollment: 44
doctoral students: 59%;
master's students: 41%;
education specialists: N/A; men:
32%; women: 68%; minorities:
36%; international: 9%
Part-time enrollment: 3,282
doctoral students: 7%; master's
students: 93%; education
specialists: N/A; men: 21%;
women: 79%; minorities: 39%;
international: 0%
Acceptance rate (master's): 82%
Acceptance rate (doctoral): 69%
Entrance test required: GRE
**Avg. GRE (of all entering students
with scores):** quantitative: N/A;
verbal: N/A
Students reporting specialty: 100%
Students specializing in:
curriculum/instr.: 5%; admin.:
34%; educational tech.: 5%;
technical (vocational): 4%;
other: 53%

Prairie View A&M University[1]
PO Box 3089
Office of Admissions and Records
Prarie View, TX 77446-0188
www.pvamu.edu/
Public
Admissions: N/A
Financial aid: N/A
Tuition: N/A
Room/board/expenses: N/A
Enrollment: N/A

Sam Houston State University
PO Box 2119
Huntsville, TX 77341
www.shsu.edu/~grs_www
Public
Admissions: (936) 294-1971
Email: graduate@shsu.edu
Financial aid: (936) 294-1724
Application deadline: 08/01
In-state tuition: full time: $286/
credit hour; part time: $286/
credit hour
Out-of-state tuition: full time:
$676/credit hour
Room/board/expenses: $11,366
Full-time enrollment: 145
doctoral students: 5%; master's
students: 80%; education
specialists: 15%; men: 17%;
women: 83%; minorities: 23%;
international: 1%
Part-time enrollment: 1,039
doctoral students: 20%;
master's students: 80%;
education specialists: 0%; men:
18%; women: 82%; minorities:
23%; international: 3%
Acceptance rate (master's): 91%
Acceptance rate (doctoral): 60%
Entrance test required: GRE
**Avg. GRE (of all entering students
with scores):** quantitative: 141;
verbal: 148
Research assistantships: 16
Students reporting specialty: 100%
Students specializing in:
curriculum/instr.: 14%; admin.:
9%; evaluation/research/
statistics: 0%; educational
psych: 2%; educational tech.:
5%; higher education admin.:
5%; special: 7%; counseling:
17%; other: 42%

Southern Methodist University[1]
PO Box 750181
Dallas, TX 75275-0181
www.smu.edu/???
Private
Admissions: N/A
Financial aid: N/A
Tuition: N/A
Room/board/expenses: N/A
Enrollment: N/A

Stephen F. Austin State University
PO Box 13024
SFA Station
Nacogdoches, TX 75962
www.sfasu.edu/graduate
Public
Admissions: (936) 468-2807
Email: gschool@sfasu.edu
Financial aid: (936) 468-2403
Application deadline: rolling
In-state tuition: full time: $266/
credit hour; part time: $266/
credit hour
Out-of-state tuition: full time:
$656/credit hour
Room/board/expenses: $11,614
Full-time enrollment: 230
doctoral students: 15%;
master's students: 85%;
education specialists: N/A; men:
26%; women: 74%; minorities:
31%; international: 3%
Part-time enrollment: 760
doctoral students: 4%; master's
students: 96%; education
specialists: N/A; men: 19%;
women: 81%; minorities: 31%;
international: 1%

Acceptance rate (master's): N/A
Acceptance rate (doctoral): N/A
Entrance test required: GRE
**Avg. GRE (of all entering students
with scores):** quantitative: N/A;
verbal: N/A
Research assistantships: 24
Students reporting specialty: 100%
Students specializing in: admin.:
34%; elementary: 7%;
secondary: 5%; special: 17%;
counseling: 1%; other: 36%

Tarleton State University
Box T-0350
Stephenville, TX 76402
www.tarleton.edu
Public
Admissions: N/A
Financial aid: N/A
Application deadline: 06/15
In-state tuition: full time: $204/
credit hour; part time: $204/
credit hour
Out-of-state tuition: full time:
$594/credit hour
Room/board/expenses: N/A
Full-time enrollment: 141
doctoral students: 55%;
master's students: 45%;
education specialists: N/A; men:
30%; women: 70%; minorities:
36%; international: 1%
Part-time enrollment: 478
doctoral students: 9%; master's
students: 91%; education
specialists: N/A; men: 26%;
women: 74%; minorities: 25%;
international: 4%
Acceptance rate (master's): 89%
Acceptance rate (doctoral): 56%
Entrance test required: GRE
**Avg. GRE (of all entering students
with scores):** quantitative: N/A;
verbal: N/A
Research assistantships: 6
Students reporting specialty: 80%
Students specializing in:
curriculum/instr.: 26%; admin.:
20%; educational psych: 32%;
counseling: 6%; other: 16%

Texas A&M University-College Station
4222 TAMUS
College Station, TX 77843-4222
www.cehd.tamu.edu/
Public
Admissions: (979) 845-1071
Email: admissions@tamu.edu
Financial aid: (979) 845-3236
Application deadline: N/A
In-state tuition: full time: $241/
credit hour; part time: $241/
credit hour
Out-of-state tuition: full time:
$638/credit hour
Room/board/expenses: $15,358
Full-time enrollment: 681
doctoral students: 45%;
master's students: 55%;
education specialists: N/A; men:
30%; women: 70%; minorities:
29%; international: 24%
Part-time enrollment: 877
doctoral students: 35%;
master's students: 65%;
education specialists: N/A; men:
29%; women: 71%; minorities:
36%; international: 1%
Acceptance rate (master's): 74%
Acceptance rate (doctoral): 56%
Entrance test required: GRE

Avg. GRE (of all entering students with scores): quantitative: 151; verbal: 152
Research assistantships: 77
Students reporting specialty: 99%
Students specializing in: curriculum/instr.: 28%; admin.: 16%; educational psych: 12%; educational tech.: 2%; special: 4%; counseling: 3%; other: 35%

Texas A&M University-Commerce[1]

PO Box 3011
Commerce, TX 75429-3011
www.tamuc.edu/
Public
Admissions: N/A
Financial aid: N/A
Tuition: N/A
Room/board/expenses: N/A
Enrollment: N/A

Texas A&M University-Corpus Christi[1]

6300 Ocean Drive
Corpus Christi, TX 78412
gradschool.tamucc.edu
Public
Admissions: (361) 825-2177
Email: gradweb@tamucc.edu
Financial aid: (361) 825-2332
Tuition: N/A
Room/board/expenses: N/A
Enrollment: N/A

Texas A&M University-Kingsville

700 University Boulevard
Kingsville, TX 78363
www.tamuk.edu/grad
Public
Admissions: (361) 593-2808
Email: gradschool@tamuk.edu
Financial aid: (361) 593-2174
Application deadline: 07/15
In-state tuition: full time: $5,248; part time: $684/credit hour
Out-of-state tuition: full time: $12,269
Room/board/expenses: $13,968
Full-time enrollment: 140
doctoral students: 20%; master's students: 80%; education specialists: N/A; men: 25%; women: 75%; minorities: 80%; international: 7%
Part-time enrollment: 262
doctoral students: 37%; master's students: 63%; education specialists: N/A; men: 29%; women: 71%; minorities: 72%; international: 8%
Acceptance rate (master's): 94%
Acceptance rate (doctoral): 67%
Entrance test required: GRE
Avg. GRE (of all entering students with scores): quantitative: 143; verbal: 143
Students reporting specialty: 100%
Students specializing in: admin.: 29%; instructional media design: 5%; special: 4%; counseling: 28%; other: 34%

Texas Christian University

3000 Bellaire Drive N
Fort Worth, TX 76129
www.coe.tcu.edu
Private
Admissions: (817) 257-7661

Financial aid: (817) 257-7872
Application deadline: N/A
Tuition: full time: $1,415/credit hour; part time: $1,415/credit hour
Room/board/expenses: $17,380
Full-time enrollment: 165
doctoral students: 43%; master's students: 57%; education specialists: N/A; men: 20%; women: 80%; minorities: 34%; international: 4%
Part-time enrollment: 30
doctoral students: 67%; master's students: 33%; education specialists: N/A; men: 27%; women: 73%; minorities: 40%; international: N/A
Acceptance rate (master's): 86%
Acceptance rate (doctoral): 74%
Entrance test required: GRE
Avg. GRE (of all entering students with scores): quantitative: N/A; verbal: N/A
Research assistantships: 8
Students reporting specialty: 100%
Students specializing in: curriculum/instr.: 14%; admin.: 50%; elementary: 1%; higher education admin.: 17%; special: 3%; counseling: 23%; other: 9%

Texas Southern University[1]

3100 Cleburne Street
Houston, TX 77004
www.tsu.edu/academics/colleges__schools/The_Graduate_School/admissions.php
Public
Admissions: (713) 313-7435
Email: graduateadmissions@tsu.edu
Financial aid: (713) 313-7071
Tuition: N/A
Room/board/expenses: N/A
Enrollment: N/A

Texas State University

601 University Drive
San Marcos, TX 78666
www.txstate.edu
Public
Admissions: (512) 245-2581
Email: gradcollege@txstate.edu
Financial aid: (512) 245-2315
Application deadline: rolling
In-state tuition: full time: $7,089; part time: $301/credit hour
Out-of-state tuition: full time: $14,109
Room/board/expenses: $11,720
Full-time enrollment: 523
doctoral students: 12%; master's students: 79%; education specialists: 9%; men: 27%; women: 73%; minorities: 38%; international: 4%
Part-time enrollment: 612
doctoral students: 18%; master's students: 79%; education specialists: 3%; men: 25%; women: 75%; minorities: 40%; international: 1%
Acceptance rate (master's): 67%
Acceptance rate (doctoral): 55%
Entrance test required: GRE
Avg. GRE (of all entering students with scores): quantitative: 147; verbal: 149
Research assistantships: 46
Students reporting specialty: 100%
Students specializing in: admin.: 26%; instructional media design: 2%; educational psych: 22%; elementary: 15%; higher educa-

tion admin.: 3%; secondary: 7%; special: 4%; other: 22%

Texas Tech University

Box 41071
Lubbock, TX 79409-1071
www.educ.ttu.edu/
Public
Admissions: (806) 742-2787
Email: gradschool@ttu.edu
Financial aid: (806) 742-3681
Application deadline: rolling
In-state tuition: full time: $270/credit hour; part time: $270/credit hour
Out-of-state tuition: full time: $660/credit hour
Room/board/expenses: $14,705
Full-time enrollment: 338
doctoral students: 43%; master's students: 57%; education specialists: N/A; men: 23%; women: 77%; minorities: 30%; international: 17%
Part-time enrollment: 772
doctoral students: 52%; master's students: 48%; education specialists: N/A; men: 26%; women: 74%; minorities: 32%; international: 4%
Acceptance rate (master's): 60%
Acceptance rate (doctoral): 50%
Entrance test required: GRE
Avg. GRE (of all entering students with scores): quantitative: 146; verbal: 150
Research assistantships: 80
Students reporting specialty: 100%
Students specializing in: curriculum/instr.: 20%; admin.: 6%; evaluation/research/statistics: 13%; instructional media design: 5%; educational psych: 4%; special: 25%; counseling: 12%; other: 16%

Texas Wesleyan University

1201 Wesleyan
Fort Worth, TX 76105
www.txwes.edu/
Private
Admissions: N/A
Financial aid: (817) 531-4420
Application deadline: rolling
Tuition: full time: $510/credit hour; part time: $510/credit hour
Room/board/expenses: $12,551
Full-time enrollment: 34
doctoral students: 6%; master's students: 94%; education specialists: N/A; men: 26%; women: 74%; minorities: 44%; international: 9%
Part-time enrollment: 189
doctoral students: 33%; master's students: 67%; education specialists: N/A; men: 11%; women: 89%; minorities: 54%; international: 3%
Acceptance rate (master's): 86%
Acceptance rate (doctoral): 86%
Entrance test required: GRE
Avg. GRE (of all entering students with scores): quantitative: N/A; verbal: N/A
Students reporting specialty: 99%
Students specializing in: curriculum/instr.: 9%; admin.: 17%; counseling: 61%; technical (vocational): 7%; other: 6%

Texas Woman's University[1]

PO Box 425769
Denton, TX 76204-5769
www.twu.edu/
Public
Admissions: N/A
Financial aid: N/A
Tuition: N/A
Room/board/expenses: N/A
Enrollment: N/A

University of Houston

3657 Cullen Boulevard, Room 214
Houston, TX 77204-5023
www.coe.uh.edu/
Public
Admissions: (713) 743-4997
Email: coegrad@uh.edu
Financial aid: (713) 743-1010
Application deadline: rolling
In-state tuition: full time: $8,406; part time: $414/credit hour
Out-of-state tuition: full time: $17,226
Room/board/expenses: $16,238
Full-time enrollment: 373
doctoral students: 47%; master's students: 53%; education specialists: N/A; men: 23%; women: 77%; minorities: 40%; international: 11%
Part-time enrollment: 307
doctoral students: 60%; master's students: 40%; education specialists: N/A; men: 29%; women: 71%; minorities: 50%; international: 2%
Acceptance rate (master's): 66%
Acceptance rate (doctoral): 28%
Entrance test required: GRE
Avg. GRE (of all entering students with scores): quantitative: 148; verbal: 152
Research assistantships: 48
Students reporting specialty: 92%
Students specializing in: curriculum/instr.: 30%; admin.: 34%; educational psych: 9%; higher education admin.: 7%; special: 2%; counseling: 11%; other: 8%

University of Houston-Clear Lake[1]

2700 Bay Area Boulevard
Houston, TX 77058
www.uhcl.edu
Public
Admissions: N/A
Financial aid: N/A
Tuition: N/A
Room/board/expenses: N/A
Enrollment: N/A

University of Mary Hardin-Baylor[1]

UMHB Box 8017
900 College Street
Belton, TX 76513
www.umhb.edu/
Private
Admissions: N/A
Financial aid: N/A
Tuition: N/A
Room/board/expenses: N/A
Enrollment: N/A

University of North Texas

1155 Union Circle, #311337
Denton, TX 76203-1337
tsgs.unt.edu/overview
Public
Admissions: (940) 565-2383
Email: gradsch@unt.edu
Financial aid: (940) 565-2302
Application deadline: rolling
In-state tuition: full time: $303/credit hour; part time: $303/credit hour
Out-of-state tuition: full time: $664/credit hour
Room/board/expenses: $11,766
Full-time enrollment: 351
doctoral students: 26%; master's students: 74%; education specialists: N/A; men: 28%; women: 72%; minorities: 33%; international: 11%
Part-time enrollment: 854
doctoral students: 34%; master's students: 66%; education specialists: N/A; men: 26%; women: 74%; minorities: 33%; international: 3%
Acceptance rate (master's): 33%
Acceptance rate (doctoral): 45%
Entrance test required: GRE
Avg. GRE (of all entering students with scores): quantitative: 148; verbal: 151
Research assistantships: 28
Students reporting specialty: 82%
Students specializing in: curriculum/instr.: 8%; admin.: 33%; evaluation/research/statistics: 3%; educational psych: 6%; elementary: 1%; higher education admin.: 12%; secondary: 0%; special: 12%; counseling: 24%

University of Texas-Arlington

701 S. Nedderman Drive
Arlington, TX 76019
www.uta.edu
Public
Admissions: N/A
Financial aid: N/A
Application deadline: rolling
In-state tuition: full time: $8,197; part time: $6,230
Out-of-state tuition: full time: $15,951
Room/board/expenses: $13,812
Full-time enrollment: 72
doctoral students: 24%; master's students: 76%; education specialists: N/A; men: 21%; women: 79%; minorities: 43%; international: 11%
Part-time enrollment: 1,704
doctoral students: 4%; master's students: 96%; education specialists: N/A; men: 21%; women: 79%; minorities: 45%; international: 1%
Acceptance rate (master's): 67%
Acceptance rate (doctoral): 41%
Entrance test required: GRE
Avg. GRE (of all entering students with scores): quantitative: 148; verbal: 152
Research assistantships: 6
Students reporting specialty: 100%
Students specializing in: curriculum/instr.: 57%; admin.: 39%; educational psych: 1%; elementary: 2%; junior high: 0%; secondary: 1%

University of Texas-Austin

1 University Station, D5000
Sanchez Building, Room 210
Austin, TX 78712
www.edb.utexas.edu/education/
Public
Admissions: (512) 475-7398
Email:
adgrd@utxdp.dp.utexas.edu
Financial aid: (512) 475-6282
Application deadline: rolling
In-state tuition: full time: $8,402;
part time: $8,066
Out-of-state tuition: full time:
$16,338
Room/board/expenses: $16,465
Full-time enrollment: 752
doctoral students: 52%;
master's students: 48%;
education specialists: N/A; men:
30%; women: 70%; minorities:
33%; international: 13%
Part-time enrollment: 269
doctoral students: 51%;
master's students: 49%;
education specialists: N/A; men:
32%; women: 68%; minorities:
34%; international: 2%
Acceptance rate (master's): 60%
Acceptance rate (doctoral): 28%
Entrance test required: GRE
**Avg. GRE (of all entering students
with scores):** quantitative: 151;
verbal: 156
Research assistantships: 290
Students reporting specialty: 94%
Students specializing in:
curriculum/instr.: 29%; admin.:
8%; policy: 5%; evaluation/
research/statistics: 3%;
educational psych: 16%;
educational tech.: 4%; higher
education admin.: 11%; special:
12%; counseling: 4%; other: 11%

University of Texas-El Paso[1]

500 W. University Avenue
El Paso, TX 79968
www.utep.edu/
Public
Admissions: N/A
Financial aid: N/A
Tuition: N/A
Room/board/expenses: N/A
Enrollment: N/A

University of Texas-Rio Grande Valley[1]

Marialice Shary Shivers
Building, 1.158
Edinburg, TX 78539-2999
Public
Admissions: N/A
Financial aid: N/A
Tuition: N/A
Room/board/expenses: N/A
Enrollment: N/A

University of Texas-San Antonio

1 UTSA Circle
San Antonio, TX 78249-0617
www.graduateschool.utsa.edu
Public
Admissions: (210) 458-4331
Email:
graduatestudies@usta.edu
Financial aid: (210) 458-8000
Application deadline: rolling
In-state tuition: full time: $260/
credit hour; part time: $260/
credit hour

Out-of-state tuition: full time:
$1,057/credit hour
Room/board/expenses: $15,054
Full-time enrollment: 488
doctoral students: 11%; master's
students: 89%; education
specialists: N/A; men: 24%;
women: 76%; minorities: 56%;
international: 3%
Part-time enrollment: 936
doctoral students: 17%;
master's students: 83%;
education specialists: N/A; men:
24%; women: 76%; minorities:
62%; international: 1%
Acceptance rate (master's): 92%
Acceptance rate (doctoral): 50%
Entrance test required: GRE
**Avg. GRE (of all entering students
with scores):** quantitative: 145;
verbal: 151
Research assistantships: 60
Students reporting specialty: 100%
Students specializing in:
curriculum/instr.: 7%; admin.:
22%; policy: 20%; educational
tech.: 3%; elementary: 3%;
higher education admin.: 5%;
special: 5%; counseling: 10%;
other: 47%

University of the Incarnate Word

4301 Broadway
San Antonio, TX 78209
www.uiw.edu
Private
Admissions: (210) 829-6005
Email: admis@uiwtx.edu
Financial aid: (210) 829-6008
Application deadline: rolling
Tuition: full time: $850/credit
hour; part time: $850/credit
hour
Room/board/expenses: N/A
Full-time enrollment: 31
doctoral students: 35%;
master's students: 65%;
education specialists: N/A; men:
26%; women: 74%; minorities:
39%; international: 52%
Part-time enrollment: 209
doctoral students: 70%;
master's students: 30%;
education specialists: N/A; men:
33%; women: 67%; minorities:
60%; international: 11%
Acceptance rate (master's): 64%
Acceptance rate (doctoral): 70%
Entrance test required: N/A
**Avg. GRE (of all entering students
with scores):** quantitative: N/A;
verbal: N/A
Research assistantships: 20
Students reporting specialty: 100%
Students specializing in:
elementary: 6%; secondary: 2%;
other: 92%

UTAH

Brigham Young University-Provo (McKay)

301 MCKB
Provo, UT 84602
www.byu.edu/gradstudies
Private
Admissions: (801) 422-4091
Email: admissions@byu.edu
Financial aid: (801) 422-4104
Application deadline: 02/01
Tuition: full time: $6,500; part
time: $382/credit hour
Room/board/expenses: $15,712

Full-time enrollment: 237
doctoral students: 45%;
master's students: 43%;
education specialists: 13%; men:
41%; women: 59%; minorities:
11%; international: 3%
Part-time enrollment: 84
doctoral students: 26%;
master's students: 67%;
education specialists: 7%; men:
35%; women: 65%; minorities:
5%; international: 4%
Acceptance rate (master's): 40%
Acceptance rate (doctoral): 31%
Entrance test required: GRE
**Avg. GRE (of all entering students
with scores):** quantitative: 151;
verbal: 150
Research assistantships: 97
Students reporting specialty: 68%
Students specializing in: admin.:
17%; policy: 16%; evaluation/
research/statistics: 9%;
instructional media design: 33%;
higher education admin.: 17%;
special: 2%; counseling: 15%

University of Utah

1721 E. Campus Center Drive
Salt Lake City, UT 84112-9251
admissions.utah.edu
Public
Admissions: (801) 581-7281
Email: admissions@utah.edu
Financial aid: (801) 581-6211
Application deadline: 04/01
In-state tuition: full time: $6,720;
part time: $320/credit hour
Out-of-state tuition: full time:
$21,294
Room/board/expenses: $15,362
Full-time enrollment: 394
doctoral students: 34%;
master's students: 66%;
education specialists: N/A; men:
27%; women: 73%; minorities:
21%; international: 4%
Part-time enrollment: 206
doctoral students: 51%;
master's students: 49%;
education specialists: N/A; men:
33%; women: 67%; minorities:
15%; international: 0%
Acceptance rate (master's): 63%
Acceptance rate (doctoral): 36%
Entrance test required: GRE
**Avg. GRE (of all entering students
with scores):** quantitative: 153;
verbal: 156
Research assistantships: 9
Students reporting specialty: 61%
Students specializing in: admin.:
21%; policy: 9%; instructional
media design: 11%; educational
psych: 54%; elementary: 3%;
higher education admin.: 23%;
secondary: 8%; special: 15%;
counseling: 10%; other: 26%

Utah State University

2800 Old Main Hill
Logan, UT 84322-2800
www.rgs.usu.edu/graduateschool
Public
Admissions: (435) 797-1189
Email: graduateschool@usu.edu
Financial aid: (435) 797-0173
Application deadline: rolling
In-state tuition: full time: $6,092;
part time: $5,598
Out-of-state tuition: full time:
$18,951
Room/board/expenses: $11,514
Full-time enrollment: 300
doctoral students: 32%;
master's students: 61%;
education specialists: 7%; men:

30%; women: 70%; minorities:
11%; international: 3%
Part-time enrollment: 568
doctoral students: 26%;
master's students: 74%;
education specialists: 0%; men:
35%; women: 65%; minorities:
5%; international: 3%
Acceptance rate (master's): 46%
Acceptance rate (doctoral): 28%
Entrance test required: GRE
**Avg. GRE (of all entering students
with scores):** quantitative: 165;
verbal: 166
Research assistantships: 98
Students reporting specialty: 62%
Students specializing in:
curriculum/instr.: 14%; admin.:
9%; instructional media design:
26%; elementary: 7%; junior
high: 1%; secondary: 8%;
special: 10%; counseling: 25%

VERMONT

University of Vermont

309 Waterman Building
Burlington, VT 05405-0160
www.uvm.edu/~gradcoll
Public
Admissions: (802) 656-2699
Email: graduate.admissions@
uvm.edu
Financial aid: (802) 656-3156
Application deadline: 02/01
In-state tuition: full time: $12,862;
part time: $611/credit hour
Out-of-state tuition: full time:
$29,656
Room/board/expenses: $15,548
Full-time enrollment: 113
doctoral students: 15%;
master's students: 45%;
education specialists: 40%;
men: 41%; women: 59%;
minorities: 14%; international:
6%
Part-time enrollment: 153
doctoral students: 35%;
master's students: 22%;
education specialists: 43%;
men: 34%; women: 66%;
minorities: 7%; international: 3%
Acceptance rate (master's): 53%
Acceptance rate (doctoral): 68%
Entrance test required: GRE
**Avg. GRE (of all entering students
with scores):** quantitative: 149;
verbal: 153
Research assistantships: 2
Students reporting specialty: 85%
Students specializing in:
curriculum/instr.: 13%; admin.:
40%; higher education admin.:
15%; special: 16%; other: 16%

VIRGINIA

College of William and Mary

PO Box 8795
Williamsburg, VA 23187-8795
education.wm.edu/
Public
Admissions: (757) 221-2317
Email: GradEd@wm.edu
Financial aid: (757) 221-2317
Application deadline: 01/15
In-state tuition: full time: $13,657;
part time: $6,098
Out-of-state tuition: full time:
$29,400
Room/board/expenses: $19,300
Full-time enrollment: 206
doctoral students: 21%;
master's students: 75%;
education specialists: 3%; men:

20%; women: 80%; minorities:
17%; international: 6%
Part-time enrollment: 181
doctoral students: 73%;
master's students: 23%;
education specialists: 4%; men:
25%; women: 75%; minorities:
25%; international: N/A
Acceptance rate (master's): 63%
Acceptance rate (doctoral): 58%
Entrance test required: GRE
**Avg. GRE (of all entering students
with scores):** quantitative: 153;
verbal: 157
Students reporting specialty: 100%
Students specializing in:
curriculum/instr.: 24%; admin.:
52%; counseling: 20%; other:
4%

George Mason University

4400 University Drive, MSN 2F1
Fairfax, VA 22030-4444
cehd.gmu.edu
Public
Admissions: (703) 993-2892
Email: cehdgrad@gmu.edu
Financial aid: (703) 993-2349
Application deadline: rolling
In-state tuition: full time: $340/
credit hour; part time: $340/
credit hour
Out-of-state tuition: full time:
$572/credit hour
Room/board/expenses: $23,648
Full-time enrollment: 310
doctoral students: 28%;
master's students: 72%;
education specialists: N/A; men:
18%; women: 82%; minorities:
26%; international: 13%
Part-time enrollment: 1,906
doctoral students: 14%;
master's students: 86%;
education specialists: N/A; men:
20%; women: 80%; minorities:
25%; international: 1%
Acceptance rate (master's): 81%
Acceptance rate (doctoral): 42%
Entrance test required: GRE
**Avg. GRE (of all entering students
with scores):** quantitative: 149;
verbal: 153
Research assistantships: 94
Students reporting specialty: 84%
Students specializing in:
curriculum/instr.: 51%; admin.:
16%; educational psych: 2%;
special: 28%; counseling: 4%

Hampton University[1]

Graduate College
Hampton, VA 23668
www.hamptonu.edu/
GraduateCollege/home.html
Private
Admissions: (757) 727-5454
Email: hugrad@hamptonu.edu
Financial aid: (757) 727-5332
Tuition: N/A
Room/board/expenses: N/A
Enrollment: N/A

Liberty University

1971 University Boulevard
Lynchburg, VA 24502
www.liberty.edu/academics/
graduate
Private
Admissions: (800) 424-9596
Email: gradadmissions@liberty.
edu
Financial aid: (434) 582-2270
Application deadline: rolling

Tuition: full time: $540/credit hour; part time: $590/credit hour
Room/board/expenses: N/A
Full-time enrollment: 1,879
doctoral students: 17%; master's students: 56%; education specialists: 27% men: 25%; women: 75%; minorities: 21%; international: 0%
Part-time enrollment: 4,230
doctoral students: 19%; master's students: 73%; education specialists: 8%; men: 24%; women: 76%; minorities: 25%; international: 0%
Acceptance rate (master's): 49%
Acceptance rate (doctoral): 15%
Entrance test required: GRE
Avg. GRE (of all entering students with scores): quantitative: N/A; verbal: N/A
Students reporting specialty: 100%
Students specializing in: curriculum/instr.: 9%; admin.: 39%; instructional media design: 6%; elementary: 11%; junior high: 1%; secondary: 6%; special: 9%; counseling: 17%; other: 3%

Old Dominion University (Darden)

Education Building, Room 218
Norfolk, VA 23529
education.odu.edu
Public
Admissions: (757) 683-3685
Email: admit@odu.edu
Financial aid: (757) 683-3683
Application deadline: rolling
In-state tuition: full time: $464/credit hour; part time: $464/credit hour
Out-of-state tuition: full time: $1,160/credit hour
Room/board/expenses: $13,869
Full-time enrollment: 515
doctoral students: 12%; master's students: 85%; education specialists: 3%; men: 20%; women: 80%; minorities: 25%; international: 3%
Part-time enrollment: 755
doctoral students: 31%; master's students: 59%; education specialists: 10%; men: 26%; women: 74%; minorities: 27%; international: 1%
Acceptance rate (master's): 57%
Acceptance rate (doctoral): 51%
Entrance test required: GRE
Avg. GRE (of all entering students with scores): quantitative: 147; verbal: 151
Research assistantships: 19
Students reporting specialty: 84%
Students specializing in: admin.: 27%; instructional media design: 0%; educational tech.: 4%; elementary: 17%; higher education admin.: 3%; secondary: 8%; special: 7%; counseling: 15%; other: 19%

Regent University

1000 Regent University Drive
Virginia Beach, VA 23464
www.regent.edu/acad/schedu
Private
Admissions: (888) 713-1595
Email: education@regent.edu
Financial aid: (757) 352-4125
Application deadline: rolling
Tuition: full time: $575/credit hour; part time: $575/credit hour

Room/board/expenses: $15,705
Full-time enrollment: 71
doctoral students: 0%; master's students: 97%; education specialists: 3%; men: 18%; women: 82%; minorities: 38%; international: 3%
Part-time enrollment: 867
doctoral students: 23%; master's students: 68%; education specialists: 9%; men: 21%; women: 79%; minorities: 37%; international: 2%
Acceptance rate (master's): 57%
Acceptance rate (doctoral): 32%
Entrance test required: GRE
Avg. GRE (of all entering students with scores): quantitative: 145; verbal: 152
Research assistantships: 0
Students reporting specialty: 100%
Students specializing in: curriculum/instr.: 6%; admin.: 19%; educational psych.: 1%; educational tech.: 1%; elementary: 0%; higher education admin.: 3%; special: 17%; other: 52%

Shenandoah University

1460 University Drive
Winchester, VA 22601
www.su.edu
Private
Admissions: (540) 665-4581
Email: admit@su.edu
Financial aid: (540) 665-4621
Application deadline: rolling
Tuition: full time: $9,770; part time: $500/credit hour
Room/board/expenses: $15,420
Full-time enrollment: 16
doctoral students: 25%; master's students: 75%; education specialists: N/A; men: 25%; women: 75%; minorities: 19%; international: 6%
Part-time enrollment: 233
doctoral students: 37%; master's students: 63%; education specialists: N/A; men: 33%; women: 67%; minorities: 13%; international: 1%
Acceptance rate (master's): 96%
Acceptance rate (doctoral): 79%
Entrance test required: N/A
Avg. GRE (of all entering students with scores): quantitative: N/A; verbal: N/A
Research assistantships: 0
Students reporting specialty: 79%
Students specializing in: admin.: 31%; elementary: 2%; junior high: 0%; secondary: 1%; special: 1%; other: 76%

University of Virginia (Curry)

405 Emmet Street S
Charlottesville, VA 22903-2495
curry.virginia.edu
Public
Admissions: (434) 924-0742
Email: curry-admissions@virginia.edu
Financial aid: (434) 982-6000
Application deadline: N/A
In-state tuition: full time: $17,452; part time: $802/credit hour
Out-of-state tuition: full time: $26,884
Room/board/expenses: $20,933
Full-time enrollment: 563
doctoral students: 27%; master's students: 73%; education specialists: 0%; men:

24%; women: 76%; minorities: 18%; international: 5%
Part-time enrollment: 302
doctoral students: 28%; master's students: 58%; education specialists: 14%; men: 29%; women: 71%; minorities: 13%; international: 1%
Acceptance rate (master's): 55%
Acceptance rate (doctoral): 17%
Entrance test required: GRE
Avg. GRE (of all entering students with scores): quantitative: 153; verbal: 156
Research assistantships: 91
Students reporting specialty: 97%
Students specializing in: curriculum/instr.: 23%; admin.: 13%; policy: 1%; evaluation/research/statistics: 1%; educational psych.: 3%; educational tech.: 2%; elementary: 9%; higher education admin.: 9%; secondary: 6%; social/philosophical foundations: 6%; special: 6%; counseling: 8%; other: 16%

Virginia Commonwealth University

1015 W. Main Street
PO Box 842020
Richmond, VA 23284-2020
www.soe.vcu.edu
Public
Admissions: (804) 828-3382
Email: htclark@vcu.edu
Financial aid: (804) 828-6181
Application deadline: 02/01
In-state tuition: full time: $13,107; part time: $571/credit hour
Out-of-state tuition: full time: $23,655
Room/board/expenses: $15,557
Full-time enrollment: 353
doctoral students: 13%; master's students: 86%; education specialists: 0%; men: 24%; women: 76%; minorities: 27%; international: 3%
Part-time enrollment: 295
doctoral students: 47%; master's students: 47%; education specialists: 6%; men: 22%; women: 78%; minorities: 23%; international: 2%
Acceptance rate (master's): 70%
Acceptance rate (doctoral): 55%
Entrance test required: GRE
Avg. GRE (of all entering students with scores): quantitative: 148; verbal: 151
Research assistantships: 17
Students reporting specialty: 84%
Students specializing in: curriculum/instr.: 4%; admin.: 15%; evaluation/research/statistics: 2%; instructional media design: 1%; educational psych.: 2%; educational tech.: 0%; elementary: 21%; secondary: 8%; special: 13%; counseling: 14%; other: 20%

Virginia State University[1]

1 Hayden Street
Petersburg, VA 23806
www.vsu.edu/
Public
Admissions: (804) 524-5985
Email: gradadmiss@vsu.edu
Financial aid: N/A
Tuition: N/A

Room/board/expenses: N/A
Enrollment: N/A

Virginia Tech

226 War Memorial Hall, 0313
Blacksburg, VA 24061
www.graduateschool.vt.edu/
Public
Admissions: (540) 231-8636
Email: gradappl@vt.edu
Financial aid: (540) 231-4558
Application deadline: rolling
In-state tuition: full time: $14,116; part time: $674/credit hour
Out-of-state tuition: full time: $26,377
Room/board/expenses: $14,284
Full-time enrollment: 318
doctoral students: 42%; master's students: 56%; education specialists: 2%; men: 31%; women: 69%; minorities: 19%; international: 12%
Part-time enrollment: 367
doctoral students: 49%; master's students: 42%; education specialists: 9%; men: 36%; women: 64%; minorities: 18%; international: 3%
Acceptance rate (master's): 64%
Acceptance rate (doctoral): 48%
Entrance test required: GRE
Avg. GRE (of all entering students with scores): quantitative: 148; verbal: 151
Research assistantships: 9
Students reporting specialty: 100%
Students specializing in: curriculum/instr.: 52%; admin.: 34%; evaluation/research/statistics: 3%; counseling: 8%; other: 4%

Seattle Pacific University[1]

3307 Third Avenue W
Seattle, WA 98119-1997
www.spu.edu
Private
Admissions: N/A
Financial aid: N/A
Tuition: N/A
Room/board/expenses: N/A
Enrollment: N/A

Seattle University[1]

901 12th Avenue
Seattle, WA 98122
www.seattleu.edu/education
Private
Admissions: (206) 296-2000
Email: grad-admissions@seattleu.edu
Financial aid: (206) 296-2000
Tuition: N/A
Room/board/expenses: N/A
Enrollment: N/A

University of Washington

PO Box 353600
206 Miller
Seattle, WA 98195-3600
education.uw.edu/home
Public
Admissions: (206) 543-7834
Email: edinfo@u.washington.edu
Financial aid: (206) 543-7834
Application deadline: N/A
In-state tuition: full time: $17,607; part time: $737/credit hour
Out-of-state tuition: full time: $30,813

Room/board/expenses: $19,392
Full-time enrollment: 626
doctoral students: 31%; master's students: 63%; education specialists: 6%; men: 23%; women: 77%; minorities: 32%; international: 9%
Part-time enrollment: 177
doctoral students: 35%; master's students: 65%; education specialists: 0%; men: 27%; women: 73%; minorities: 28%; international: 6%
Acceptance rate (master's): 65%
Acceptance rate (doctoral): 30%
Entrance test required: GRE
Avg. GRE (of all entering students with scores): quantitative: 151; verbal: 154
Research assistantships: 76
Students reporting specialty: 88%
Students specializing in: curriculum/instr.: 22%; admin.: 26%; policy: 24%; evaluation/research/statistics: 2%; educational psych: 15%; elementary: 11%; higher education admin.: 5%; secondary: 8%; social/philosophical foundations: 8%; special: 19%; counseling: 7%

Washington State University[1]

PO Box 642114
Pullman, WA 99164-2114
www.wsu.edu/
Public
Admissions: N/A
Financial aid: N/A
Tuition: N/A
Room/board/expenses: N/A
Enrollment: N/A

Marshall University[1]

100 Angus E. Peyton Drive
South Charleston, WV 25303
www.marshall.edu/gsepd/
Public
Admissions: N/A
Financial aid: N/A
Tuition: N/A
Room/board/expenses: N/A
Enrollment: N/A

West Virginia University

802 Allen Hall
PO Box 6122
Morgantown, WV 26506-6122
www.wvu.edu
Public
Admissions: (304) 293-2124
Email: graded@mail.wvu.edu
Financial aid: (304) 293-5242
Application deadline: rolling
In-state tuition: full time: $9,126; part time: $406/credit hour
Out-of-state tuition: full time: $22,950
Room/board/expenses: $12,600
Full-time enrollment: 465
doctoral students: 16%; master's students: 84%; education specialists: N/A; men: 19%; women: 81%; minorities: 10%; international: 2%
Part-time enrollment: 429
doctoral students: 22%; master's students: 78%; education specialists: N/A; men: 19%; women: 81%; minorities: 5%; international: 2%

Acceptance rate (master's): 47%
Acceptance rate (doctoral): 35%
Entrance test required: GRE
Avg. GRE (of all entering students with scores): quantitative: 148; verbal: 151
Research assistantships: 29
Students reporting specialty: 87%
Students specializing in: admin.: 3%; instructional media design: 5%; educational psych: 2%; higher education admin.: 1%; special: 29%; counseling: 6%; other: 55%

WISCONSIN

Cardinal Stritch University
6801 N. Yates Road
Milwaukee, WI 53217
www.stritch.edu/
Private
Admissions: N/A
Financial aid: N/A
Application deadline: rolling
Tuition: full time: $11,880; part time: $740/credit hour
Room/board/expenses: N/A
Full-time enrollment: 142
doctoral students: 4%; master's students: 96%; education specialists: N/A; men: 27%; women: 73%; minorities: 20%; international: 1%
Part-time enrollment: 361
doctoral students: 40%; master's students: 60%; education specialists: N/A; men: 39%; women: 61%; minorities: 23%; international: 3%
Acceptance rate (master's): 99%
Acceptance rate (doctoral): 100%
Entrance test required: GRE
Avg. GRE (of all entering students with scores): quantitative: N/A; verbal: N/A
Research assistantships: 0
Students reporting specialty: 98%
Students specializing in: admin.: 50%; instructional media design: 1%; elementary: 14%; secondary: 5%; special: 13%; other: 16%

Edgewood College
1000 Edgewood College Drive
Madison, WI 53711
www.edgewood.edu
Private
Admissions: (608) 663-3297
Email: gps@edgewood.edu
Financial aid: (608) 663-4300
Application deadline: rolling
Tuition: full time: $867/credit hour; part time: $867/credit hour
Room/board/expenses: N/A
Full-time enrollment: 156
doctoral students: 69%; master's students: 31%; education specialists: N/A; men: 35%; women: 65%; minorities: 12%; international: 9%
Part-time enrollment: 175
doctoral students: 20%; master's students: 80%; education specialists: N/A; men: 22%; women: 78%; minorities: 18%; international: 6%
Acceptance rate (master's): N/A
Acceptance rate (doctoral): N/A
Entrance test required: N/A
Avg. GRE (of all entering students with scores): quantitative: N/A; verbal: N/A
Students reporting specialty: 0%
Students specializing in: N/A

Marquette University
Schroeder Complex Box 1881
Milwaukee, WI 53201
www.grad.marquette.edu
Private
Admissions: (414) 288-7137
Email: mugs@marquette.edu
Financial aid: (414) 288-5325
Application deadline: rolling
Tuition: full time: $785/credit hour; part time: $785/credit hour
Room/board/expenses: $17,206
Full-time enrollment: 43
doctoral students: 5%; master's students: 95%; education specialists: N/A; men: 12%; women: 88%; minorities: N/A; international: 9%
Part-time enrollment: 73
doctoral students: 30%; master's students: 70%; education specialists: N/A; men: 30%; women: 70%; minorities: N/A; international: 12%
Acceptance rate (master's): 87%
Acceptance rate (doctoral): 17%
Entrance test required: GRE
Avg. GRE (of all entering students with scores): quantitative: 151; verbal: 153
Research assistantships: 5
Students reporting specialty: 95%
Students specializing in: curriculum/instr.: 1%; admin.: 17%; elementary: 18%; higher education admin.: 20%; junior high: 30%; secondary: 25%; social/philosophical foundations: 27%; counseling: 7%

University of Wisconsin-Madison
1000 Bascom Mall, Suite 377
Madison, WI 53706-1326
www.education.wisc.edu
Public
Admissions: (608) 262-2433
Email: gradamiss@grad.wisc.edu
Financial aid: (608) 262-2087
Application deadline: rolling
In-state tuition: full time: $11,870; part time: $786/credit hour
Out-of-state tuition: full time: $25,197
Room/board/expenses: $14,291
Full-time enrollment: 726
doctoral students: 61%; master's students: 39%; education specialists: N/A; men: 31%; women: 69%; minorities: 24%; international: 20%
Part-time enrollment: 292
doctoral students: 47%; master's students: 53%; education specialists: N/A; men: 35%; women: 65%; minorities: 19%; international: 7%
Acceptance rate (master's): 28%
Acceptance rate (doctoral): 31%
Entrance test required: GRE
Avg. GRE (of all entering students with scores): quantitative: 154; verbal: 156

Research assistantships: 17
Students reporting specialty: 99%
Students specializing in: curriculum/instr.: 26%; admin.: 25%; policy: 8%; educational psych: 12%; secondary: 4%; special: 3%; counseling: 6%; other: 16%

University of Wisconsin-Milwaukee
PO Box 413
Milwaukee, WI 53201
www.graduateschool.uwm.edu
Public
Admissions: (414) 229-4495
Email: gradschool@uwm.edu
Financial aid: (414) 229-4541
Application deadline: rolling
In-state tuition: full time: $13,063; part time: $1,196/credit hour
Out-of-state tuition: full time: $26,100
Room/board/expenses: $12,830
Full-time enrollment: 261
doctoral students: 36%; master's students: 61%; education specialists: 3%; men: 26%; women: 74%; minorities: 30%; international: 5%
Part-time enrollment: 377
doctoral students: 16%; master's students: 81%; education specialists: 3%; men: 27%; women: 73%; minorities: 26%; international: 2%
Acceptance rate (master's): 60%
Acceptance rate (doctoral): 32%
Entrance test required: GRE
Avg. GRE (of all entering students with scores): quantitative: 149; verbal: 153
Research assistantships: 18
Students reporting specialty: 100%
Students specializing in: curriculum/instr.: 13%; admin.: 41%; educational psych: 31%; social/philosophical foundations: 8%; special: 5%; other: 3%

WYOMING

University of Wyoming
Department 3374
1000 E. University Avenue
Laramie, WY 82071
www.uwyo.edu/education/
Public
Admissions: (307) 766-5160
Email: admissions@uwyo.edu
Financial aid: N/A
Application deadline: N/A
In-state tuition: full time: $232/credit hour; part time: $232/credit hour
Out-of-state tuition: full time: $693/credit hour
Room/board/expenses: $16,782
Full-time enrollment: 148
doctoral students: 42%; master's students: 58%; education specialists: N/A; men: 32%; women: 68%; minorities: 7%; international: 9%
Part-time enrollment: 358
doctoral students: 42%; master's students: 58%; education specialists: N/A; men: 37%; women: 63%; minorities: 11%; international: 2%
Acceptance rate (master's): 83%
Acceptance rate (doctoral): 44%
Entrance test required: GRE
Avg. GRE (of all entering students with scores): quantitative: 148; verbal: 154
Research assistantships: 15
Students reporting specialty: 100%
Students specializing in: curriculum/instr.: 3%; admin.: 5%; special: 1%; counseling: 11%; other: 81%

ENGINEERING

The engineering directory lists the country's 215 schools offering doctoral programs. One hundred ninety-five schools responded to the U.S. News survey conducted in the fall of 2015 and early 2016. Information about entrance requirements, enrollment and costs is reported. Institutions that did not respond to the survey have abbreviated entries.

KEY TO THE TERMINOLOGY

1. A school footnoted with the numeral 1 did not return the U.S. News statistical survey; limited data appear in its entry.

N.A. Not available from the school or not applicable.

Admissions. The admissions office phone number.

Email. The address of the admissions office. If instead of an email address a website is listed, the website will automatically present an email screen programmed to reach the admissions office.

Financial aid. The financial aid office phone number.

Application deadline. For fall 2017 enrollment. "Rolling" means there is no deadline; the school acts on applications as they are received. "Varies" means deadlines vary according to department or whether applicants are U.S. citizens or foreign nationals.

Tuition. For the 2015-16 academic year. Includes fees.

Credit hour. The cost per credit hour for the 2015-16 academic year.

Room/board/expenses. For the 2015-16 academic year.

Enrollment. Full and part time for fall 2015. The total is the combination of master's and doctoral students if the school offers both degrees. Where available, the breakdown for men, women, minorities and international students is provided. Percentages for men and women may not add up to 100 because of rounding.

Minorities. For fall 2015, the percentage of students who are black or African-American, Asian, American Indian or Alaska Native, Native Hawaiian or other Pacific Islander, Hispanic/Latino, or two or more races. The minority percentage was reported by each school.

Acceptance rate. Percentage of applicants who were accepted for fall 2015, including both master's and doctoral degree programs.

GRE requirement. "Yes" means Graduate Record Examination scores are required by some or all departments.

Average GRE scores. Combined for both master's and doctoral degree students who entered in fall 2015. GRE scores displayed are for fall 2015 entering master's and Ph.D. students and are only for those GRE exams taken during or after August 2011 using the new 130-170 score scale.

TOEFL requirement. "Yes" means that students from non-English-speaking countries must submit scores for the Test of English as a Foreign Language.

Minimum TOEFL score. The score listed is the minimum acceptable score for the paper TOEFL. (The computer-administered TOEFL is graded on a different scale.)

Total fellowships, teaching assistantships and research assistantships. The number of student appointments for the 2015-16 academic year. Students may hold multiple appointments and would therefore be counted more than once.

Student specialties. Proportion of master's and doctoral students, both full and part time, in the specialty-reporting population (not necessarily the entire student body) who were enrolled in a particular specialty in fall 2015. Specialty fields listed are aerospace/aeronautical/astronautical; biological/agricultural; architectural engineering; bioengineering/biomedical; chemical; civil; computer engineering; computer science; electrical/electronic/communications; engineering management; engineering science and physics; environmental/environmental health; industrial/manufacturing/systems; materials; mechanical; mining; nuclear; petroleum; and other. Numbers may not add up to 100 percent from rounding or because students are enrolled in multiple specialties.

ALABAMA

Auburn University (Ginn)
1301 Shelby Center
Auburn, AL 36849-5330
www.grad.auburn.edu
Public
Admissions: (334) 844-4700
Email: gradadm@auburn.edu
Financial aid: (334) 844-4367
Application deadline: rolling
In-state tuition: full time: $10,418; part time: $489/credit hour
Out-of-state tuition: full time: $28,022
Room/board/expenses: $19,370
Full-time enrollment: 552
men: 77%; women: 23%; minorities: 2%; international: 81%
Part-time enrollment: 298
men: 82%; women: 18%; minorities: 15%; international: 17%
Acceptance rate: 46%
GRE requirement: Yes
Avg. GRE: quantitative: 160
TOEFL requirement: Yes
Minimum TOEFL score: 550
Fellowships: 113
Teaching assistantships: 199
Research assistantships: 321
Students reporting specialty: 100%
Students specializing in:
aerospace: 6%; agriculture: 3%; chemical: 9%; civil: 14%; computer science: 14%; electrical: 17%; industrial: 17%; materials: 4%; mechanical: 14%; other: 1%

Tuskegee University[1]
202 Engineering Building
Tuskegee, AL 36088-1920
www.tuskegee.edu
Private
Admissions: (334) 727-8500
Email: adm@tuskegee.edu
Financial aid: N/A
Tuition: N/A
Room/board/expenses: N/A
Enrollment: N/A

University of Alabama
Box 870200
Tuscaloosa, AL 35487-0200
www.coeweb.eng.ua.edu/
Public
Admissions: (205) 348-5921
Email: gradschool@ua.edu
Financial aid: (205) 348-2976
Application deadline: rolling
In-state tuition: full time: $10,170; part time: N/A
Out-of-state tuition: full time: $25,950
Room/board/expenses: $12,796
Full-time enrollment: 282
men: 80%; women: 20%; minorities: 6%; international: 53%
Part-time enrollment: 77
men: 91%; women: 9%; minorities: 12%; international: 18%
Acceptance rate: 31%
GRE requirement: Yes
Avg. GRE: quantitative: 161
TOEFL requirement: Yes
Minimum TOEFL score: 550
Fellowships: 0
Teaching assistantships: 77
Research assistantships: 119
Students reporting specialty: 100%
Students specializing in:
aerospace: 19%; chemical: 7%; civil: 18%; computer science: 12%; electrical: 16%; materials: 10%; mechanical: 19%; other: 1%

University of Alabama-Birmingham
1720 2nd Avenue S, HOEN 100
Birmingham, AL 35294-4440
www.uab.edu/engineering
Public
Admissions: (205) 934-8232
Email: gradschool@uab.edu
Financial aid: (205) 934-8132
Application deadline: 03/01
In-state tuition: full time: $7,786; part time: $383/credit hour
Out-of-state tuition: full time: $17,074
Room/board/expenses: $11,460
Full-time enrollment: 134
men: 83%; women: 17%; minorities: 19%; international: 49%
Part-time enrollment: 352
men: 81%; women: 19%; minorities: 34%; international: 6%
Acceptance rate: 86%
GRE requirement: Yes
Avg. GRE: quantitative: 156
TOEFL requirement: Yes
Minimum TOEFL score: 550
Fellowships: 32
Teaching assistantships: 1
Research assistantships: 54
Students reporting specialty: 100%
Students specializing in:
biomedical: 7%; civil: 8%; computer: 4%; electrical: 5%; management: 57%; materials: 6%; mechanical: 3%; other: 10%

University of Alabama-Huntsville
301 Sparkman Drive, EB 102
Huntsville, AL 35899
www.uah.edu
Public
Admissions: (256) 824-6198
Email: berkowd@uah.edu
Financial aid: (256) 824-6241
Application deadline: rolling
In-state tuition: full time: $9,548; part time: $547/credit hour
Out-of-state tuition: full time: $21,402
Room/board/expenses: $12,429
Full-time enrollment: 315
men: 73%; women: 27%; minorities: 10%; international: 62%
Part-time enrollment: 425
men: 81%; women: 19%; minorities: 13%; international: 4%
Acceptance rate: 72%
GRE requirement: Yes
Avg. GRE: quantitative: 157
TOEFL requirement: Yes
Minimum TOEFL score: 550
Fellowships: 0
Teaching assistantships: 93
Research assistantships: 88
Students reporting specialty: 100%
Students specializing in:
aerospace: 9%; biomedical: 4%; chemical: 1%; civil: 3%; computer: 7%; computer science: 18%; electrical: 18%; management: 4%; industrial: 10%; materials: 1%; mechanical: 14%; other: 10%

ALASKA

University of Alaska-Fairbanks
PO Box 755960
Fairbanks, AK 99775-5960
www.uaf.edu/cem
Public
Admissions: (800) 478-1823
Email: admissions@uaf.edu
Financial aid: (888) 474-7256
Application deadline: 06/01

In-state tuition: full time: $423/
credit hour; part time: $423/
credit hour
Out-of-state tuition: full time: $864/
credit hour
Room/board/expenses: $12,534
Full-time enrollment: 70
men: 79%; women: 21%;
minorities: 9%; international: 46%
Part-time enrollment: 52
men: 81%; women: 19%;
minorities: 17%; international: 19%
Acceptance rate: 36%
GRE requirement: Yes
Avg. GRE: quantitative: 159
TOEFL requirement: N/A
Minimum TOEFL score: N/A
Teaching assistantships: 36
Research assistantships: 29
Students reporting specialty: 100%
Students specializing in: civil:
10%; computer science: 2%;
electrical: 16%; management: 3%;
environmental: 6%; mechanical:
6%; mining: 4%; petroleum: 25%;
other: 29%

ARIZONA

Arizona State University (Fulton)

Box 879309
Tempe, AZ 85287-9309
engineering.asu.edu
Public
Admissions: (480) 965-6113
Email: gograd@asu.edu
Financial aid: (480) 965-3355
Application deadline: rolling
In-state tuition: full time: $12,103;
part time: $1,022/credit hour
Out-of-state tuition: full time:
$28,579
Room/board/expenses: $19,044
Full-time enrollment: 2,789
men: 77%; women: 23%;
minorities: 6%; international: 81%
Part-time enrollment: 821
men: 78%; women: 22%;
minorities: 22%; international:
36%
Acceptance rate: 44%
GRE requirement: Yes
Avg. GRE: quantitative: 162
TOEFL requirement: Yes
Minimum TOEFL score: 550
Fellowships: 284
Teaching assistantships: 286
Research assistantships: 641
Students reporting specialty: 100%
Students specializing in:
aerospace: 2%; biomedical: 5%;
chemical: 3%; civil: 6%; computer:
7%; computer science: 25%;
electrical: 23%; environmental:
2%; industrial: 6%; materials: 4%;
mechanical: 11%; other: 7%

University of Arizona

Civil Engineering Building
Room 100
Tucson, AZ 85721-0072
grad.arizona.edu
Public
Admissions: (520) 621-3471
Email: gradadmission@grad.
arizona.edu
Financial aid: (520) 621-1858
Application deadline: rolling
In-state tuition: full time: $12,062;
part time: $789/credit hour
Out-of-state tuition: full time:
$30,384
Room/board/expenses: $17,150
Full-time enrollment: 801
men: 78%; women: 22%;
minorities: 13%; international:
56%
Part-time enrollment: 297
men: 84%; women: 16%;
minorities: 28%; international:
14%
Acceptance rate: 41%
GRE requirement: Yes
Avg. GRE: quantitative: 162
TOEFL requirement: Yes
Minimum TOEFL score: 550
Fellowships: 120
Teaching assistantships: 82

Research assistantships: 195
Students reporting specialty: 100%
Students specializing in:
aerospace: 3%; agriculture:
2%; biomedical: 3%; chemical:
4%; civil: 4%; computer:
25%; computer science: 6%;
electrical: 25%; management: 3%;
environmental: 3%; industrial: 6%;
materials: 4%; mechanical: 4%;
mining: 3%; other: 30%

ARKANSAS

University of Arkansas-Fayetteville

Bell Engineering Center
Room 4183
Fayetteville, AR 72701
www.engr.uark.edu
Public
Admissions: (479) 575-4401
Email: gradinfo@uark.edu
Financial aid: (479) 575-3806
Application deadline: 08/01
In-state tuition: full time: $400/
credit hour; part time: $400/
credit hour
Out-of-state tuition: full time: $988/
credit hour
Room/board/expenses: $12,538
Full-time enrollment: 337
men: 77%; women: 23%;
minorities: 10%; international: 61%
Part-time enrollment: 161
men: 87%; women: 13%;
minorities: 14%; international:
22%
Acceptance rate: 34%
GRE requirement: Yes
Avg. GRE: quantitative: 158
TOEFL requirement: Yes
Minimum TOEFL score: 555
Fellowships: 41
Teaching assistantships: 57
Research assistantships: 184
Students reporting specialty: 100%
Students specializing in:
agriculture: 5%; biomedical:
5%; chemical: 8%; civil: 11%;
computer: 6%; computer science:
8%; electrical: 24%; industrial:
10%; mechanical: 7%; other: 16%

University of Arkansas-Little Rock[1]

2801 S University Avenue
Little Rock, AR 72204
ualr.edu/eit/
Public
Admissions: (501) 569-3127
Email: admissions@ualr.edu
Financial aid: N/A
Tuition: N/A
Room/board/expenses: N/A
Enrollment: N/A

CALIFORNIA

California Institute of Technology

1200 E. California Boulevard
Pasadena, CA 91125-4400
www.gradoffice.caltech.edu
Private
Admissions: (626) 395-6346
Email: gradofc@its.caltech.edu
Financial aid: (626) 395-6346
Application deadline: 12/15
Tuition: full time: $45,264; part
time: N/A
Room/board/expenses: $30,171
Full-time enrollment: 545
men: 77%; women: 23%;
minorities: 6%; international: 54%
Part-time enrollment: N/A
men: N/A; women: N/A; minorities:
N/A; international: N/A
Acceptance rate: 10%
GRE requirement: Yes
Avg. GRE: quantitative: 168
TOEFL requirement: Yes
Minimum TOEFL score: N/A
Fellowships: 227
Teaching assistantships: 95
Research assistantships: 353

Students reporting specialty: 100%
Students specializing in:
aerospace: 13%; biomedical:
2%; chemical: 10%; civil: 3%;
computer science: 8%; electrical:
26%; science and physics: 11%;
environmental: 5%; materials:
12%; mechanical: 10%

California State University-Long Beach

1250 Bellflower Boulevard
Long Beach, CA 90840-8306
www.csulb.edu/colleges/coe/
Public
Admissions: (562) 985-5121
Email: coe-gr@csulb.edu
Financial aid: N/A
Application deadline: 04/01
In-state tuition: full time: $7,718;
part time: $4,886
Out-of-state tuition: full time:
$14,414
Room/board/expenses: $17,500
Full-time enrollment: 347
men: 79%; women: 21%;
minorities: 89%; international:
85%
Part-time enrollment: 325
men: 84%; women: 16%;
minorities: 72%; international:
47%
Acceptance rate: 27%
GRE requirement: Yes
Avg. GRE: quantitative: 157
TOEFL requirement: Yes
Minimum TOEFL score: 550
Fellowships: 12
Teaching assistantships: 18
Research assistantships: 20
Students reporting specialty: 97%
Students specializing in:
aerospace: 5%; civil: 10%;
computer: 2%; computer science:
27%; electrical: 41%; industrial:
3%; mechanical: 11%

Naval Postgraduate School[1]

1 University Circle
Monterey, CA 93943-5001
www.nps.edu/Academics/
Schools/GSEAS/
Public
Admissions: (831) 656-3093
Email: grad-ed@nps.edu
Financial aid: N/A
Tuition: N/A
Room/board/expenses: N/A
Enrollment: N/A

Northwestern Polytechnic University[1]

47671 Westinghouse Drive
Fremont, CA 94539
www.npu.edu
Private
Admissions: (510) 592-9688
Email: admission@npu.edu
Financial aid: N/A
Tuition: N/A
Room/board/expenses: N/A
Enrollment: N/A

San Diego State University

5500 Campanile Drive
San Diego, CA 92182
engineering.sdsu.edu
Public
Admissions: (619) 594-6061
Email: admissions@sdsu.edu
Financial aid: (619) 594-6323
Application deadline: N/A
In-state tuition: full time: $8,242;
part time: $5,410
Out-of-state tuition: full time: $372/
credit hour
Room/board/expenses: $18,434

Full-time enrollment: 236
men: 69%; women: 31%;
minorities: 18%; international:
69%
Part-time enrollment: 244
men: 73%; women: 27%;
minorities: 38%; international:
45%
Acceptance rate: 43%
GRE requirement: Yes
Avg. GRE: quantitative: 155
TOEFL requirement: N/A
Minimum TOEFL score: N/A
Teaching assistantships: 24
Students reporting specialty: 85%
Students specializing in:
aerospace: 13%; biomedical:
7%; civil: 16%; computer: 1%;
electrical: 29%; science and
physics: 6%; environmental: 5%;
industrial: 3%; mechanical: 21%

Santa Clara University

500 El Camino Real
Santa Clara, CA 95053-0583
www.scu.edu/engineering/
graduate
Private
Admissions: (408) 554-4313
Email: gradengineer@scu.edu
Financial aid: (408) 554-4505
Application deadline: rolling
Tuition: full time: $892/credit hour;
part time: $892/credit hour
Room/board/expenses: N/A
Full-time enrollment: 543
men: 57%; women: 43%;
minorities: 87%; international:
79%
Part-time enrollment: 345
men: 71%; women: 29%;
minorities: 67%; international:
27%
Acceptance rate: 37%
GRE requirement: Yes
Avg. GRE: quantitative: 161
TOEFL requirement: Yes
Minimum TOEFL score: 550
Teaching assistantships: 39
Research assistantships: 12
Students reporting specialty: 100%
Students specializing in:
biomedical: 4%; civil: 2%;
computer: 56%; electrical: 14%;
management: 11%; environmental:
1%; mechanical: 10%; other: 1%

Stanford University

Huang Engineering Center
Stanford, CA 94305-4121
gradadmissions.stanford.edu
Private
Admissions: (866) 732-7472
Email:
gradadmissions@stanford.edu
Financial aid: (650) 723-3058
Application deadline: rolling
Tuition: full time: $49,383; part
time: N/A
Room/board/expenses: $28,410
Full-time enrollment: 3,300
men: 71%; women: 29%;
minorities: 24%; international:
45%
Part-time enrollment: 301
men: 75%; women: 25%;
minorities: 36%; international:
24%
Acceptance rate: 15%
GRE requirement: Yes
Avg. GRE: quantitative: 167
TOEFL requirement: Yes
Minimum TOEFL score: 575
Fellowships: 1,203
Teaching assistantships: 558
Research assistantships: 1,117
Students reporting specialty: 100%
Students specializing in:
aerospace: 6%; biomedical:
4%; civil: 13%;
computer science: 15%; electrical:
21%; management: 8%; materials:
6%; mechanical: 14%; petroleum:
1%; other: 7%

University of California-Berkeley

320 McLaughlin Hall, #1700
Berkeley, CA 94720-1700
www.grad.berkeley.edu/
Public
Admissions: (510) 642-7405
Email: gradadm@berkeley.edu
Financial aid: (510) 642-6442
Application deadline: 02/10
In-state tuition: full time: $17,270;
part time: N/A
Out-of-state tuition: full time:
$32,372
Room/board/expenses: $22,100
Full-time enrollment: 1,877
men: 71%; women: 29%;
minorities: 21%; international:
43%
Part-time enrollment: 96
men: 55%; women: 45%;
minorities: 33%; international:
20%
Acceptance rate: 16%
GRE requirement: Yes
Avg. GRE: quantitative: 166
TOEFL requirement: Yes
Minimum TOEFL score: 570
Fellowships: 777
Teaching assistantships: 367
Research assistantships: 781
Students reporting specialty: 100%
Students specializing in:
biomedical: 11%; chemical:
7%; civil: 18%; computer: 11%;
electrical: 18%; industrial: 7%;
materials: 5%; mechanical: 18%;
nuclear: 3%; other: 2%

University of California-Davis

1042 Kemper Hall
1 Shields Avenue
Davis, CA 95616-5294
engineering.ucdavis.edu
Public
Admissions: (530) 752-1473
Email: gradadmit@ucdavis.edu
Financial aid: (530) 752-8864
Application deadline: N/A
In-state tuition: full time: $13,164;
part time: $7,554
Out-of-state tuition: full time:
$28,266
Room/board/expenses: $21,919
Full-time enrollment: 1,097
men: 73%; women: 27%;
minorities: 21%; international:
42%
Part-time enrollment: 34
men: 74%; women: 26%;
minorities: 21%; international: 12%
Acceptance rate: 20%
GRE requirement: Yes
Avg. GRE: quantitative: 163
TOEFL requirement: Yes
Minimum TOEFL score: 550
Fellowships: 280
Teaching assistantships: 226
Research assistantships: 393
Students reporting specialty: 98%
Students specializing in:
aerospace: 14%; agriculture:
4%; biomedical: 9%; chemical:
6%; civil: 19%; computer: 20%;
computer science: 19%; electrical:
20%; science and physics: 1%;
environmental: 19%; materials:
6%; mechanical: 14%; other: 4%

University of California-Irvine (Samueli)

305 EH 5200
Irvine, CA 92697-2700
www.eng.uci.edu
Public
Admissions: (949) 824-4334
Email: gradengr@uci.edu
Financial aid: (949) 824-4889
Application deadline: rolling
In-state tuition: full time: $16,493;
part time: $10,883
Out-of-state tuition: full time:
$31,595
Room/board/expenses: $18,877

Full-time enrollment: 1,352
men: 70%; women: 30%; minorities: 14%; international: 67%
Part-time enrollment: 118
men: 74%; women: 26%; minorities: 27%; international: 42%
Acceptance rate: 17%
GRE requirement: Yes
Avg. GRE: quantitative: 164
TOEFL requirement: Yes
Minimum TOEFL score: N/A
Students reporting specialty: 100%
Students specializing in: aerospace: 3%; biomedical: 8%; chemical: 6%; civil: 8%; computer: 9%; computer science: 28%; electrical: 15%; management: 1%; environmental: 3%; industrial: 2%; materials: 5%; mechanical: 7%; other: 4%

University of California-Los Angeles (Samueli)

6426 Boelter Hall
Box 951601
Los Angeles, CA 90095-1601
www.engineer.ucla.edu
Public
Admissions: (310) 825-2514
Email: gradadm@seas.ucla.edu
Financial aid: (310) 206-0400
Application deadline: 12/01
In-state tuition: full time: $12,630; part time: N/A
Out-of-state tuition: full time: $27,732
Room/board/expenses: $19,974
Full-time enrollment: 2,064
men: 77%; women: 23%; minorities: 24%; international: 55%
Part-time enrollment: N/A
men: N/A; women: N/A; minorities: N/A; international: N/A
Acceptance rate: 28%
GRE requirement: Yes
Avg. GRE: quantitative: 165
TOEFL requirement: Yes
Minimum TOEFL score: 560
Fellowships: 617
Teaching assistantships: 664
Research assistantships: 1,502
Students reporting specialty: 100%
Students specializing in: aerospace: 3%; biomedical: 8%; chemical: 5%; civil: 9%; computer science: 16%; electrical: 26%; materials: 7%; mechanical: 12%; other: 15%

University of California-Merced

5200 North Lake Road
Merced, CA 95343
engineering.ucmerced.edu/
Public
Admissions: (202) 228-4400
Email: engineering@ucmerced.edu
Financial aid: (209) 228-4405
Application deadline: 01/15
In-state tuition: full time: $12,829; part time: $7,219
Out-of-state tuition: full time: $27,931
Room/board/expenses: $17,519
Full-time enrollment: 143
men: 72%; women: 28%; minorities: 20%; international: 53%
Part-time enrollment: N/A
men: N/A; women: N/A; minorities: N/A; international: N/A
Acceptance rate: 42%
GRE requirement: Yes
Avg. GRE: quantitative: 160
TOEFL requirement: Yes
Minimum TOEFL score: 550
Fellowships: 2
Teaching assistantships: 54
Research assistantships: 33
Students reporting specialty: 100%
Students specializing in: biomedical: 15%; electrical: 29%; environmental: 31%; mechanical: 24%

University of California-Riverside (Bourns)

University Office Building
Riverside, CA 92521-0208
www.graddiv.ucr.edu
Public
Admissions: (951) 827-3313
Email: grdadmis@ucr.edu
Financial aid: (951) 827-3387
Application deadline: 01/05
In-state tuition: full time: $11,220; part time: $5,610
Out-of-state tuition: full time: $26,322
Room/board/expenses: $20,100
Full-time enrollment: 747
men: 75%; women: 25%; minorities: 76%; international: 61%
Part-time enrollment: N/A
men: N/A; women: N/A; minorities: N/A; international: N/A
Acceptance rate: 25%
GRE requirement: Yes
Avg. GRE: quantitative: 162
TOEFL requirement: Yes
Minimum TOEFL score: 550
Fellowships: 173
Teaching assistantships: 232
Research assistantships: 288
Students reporting specialty: 100%
Students specializing in: biomedical: 13%; chemical: 13%; computer: 5%; computer science: 24%; electrical: 21%; materials: 11%; mechanical: 10%; other: 3%

University of California-San Diego (Jacobs)

9500 Gilman Drive
La Jolla, CA 92093-0403
www.jacobsschool.ucsd.edu
Public
Admissions: (858) 534-3555
Email: gradadmissions@ucsd.edu
Financial aid: (858) 534-4480
Application deadline: N/A
In-state tuition: full time: $13,021; part time: $7,411
Out-of-state tuition: full time: $28,123
Room/board/expenses: $21,869
Full-time enrollment: 2,119
men: 77%; women: 23%; minorities: 19%; international: 60%
Part-time enrollment: 125
men: 80%; women: 20%; minorities: 43%; international: 18%
Acceptance rate: 26%
GRE requirement: Yes
Avg. GRE: quantitative: 166
TOEFL requirement: Yes
Minimum TOEFL score: 550
Fellowships: 420
Teaching assistantships: 580
Research assistantships: 970
Students reporting specialty: 100%
Students specializing in: aerospace: 1%; biomedical: 11%; chemical: 2%; civil: 9%; computer: 7%; computer science: 22%; electrical: 23%; science and physics: 2%; materials: 8%; mechanical: 11%; other: 4%

University of California-Santa Barbara

Harold Frank Hall, 1038
Santa Barbara, CA 93106-5130
www.graddiv.ucsb.edu
Public
Admissions: (805) 893-2277
Email: gradadmissions@graddiv.ucsb.edu
Financial aid: (805) 893-2432
Application deadline: N/A
In-state tuition: full time: $13,194; part time: N/A
Out-of-state tuition: full time: $29,250
Room/board/expenses: $16,851
Full-time enrollment: 743
men: 78%; women: 22%; minorities: 13%; international: 47%
Part-time enrollment: N/A
men: N/A; women: N/A; minorities: N/A; international: N/A
Acceptance rate: 15%
GRE requirement: Yes
Avg. GRE: quantitative: 164
TOEFL requirement: Yes
Minimum TOEFL score: 550
Fellowships: 194
Teaching assistantships: 145
Research assistantships: 363
Students reporting specialty: 100%
Students specializing in: chemical: 11%; computer science: 22%; electrical: 37%; management: 3%; materials: 17%; mechanical: 10%

University of California-Santa Cruz (Baskin)

1156 High Street
Santa Cruz, CA 95064
ga.soe.ucsc.edu/
Public
Admissions: (831) 459-5905
Email: soegradadm@soe.ucsc.edu
Financial aid: (831) 459-2963
Application deadline: N/A
In-state tuition: full time: $17,250; part time: $11,640
Out-of-state tuition: full time: $32,352
Room/board/expenses: $22,764
Full-time enrollment: 409
men: 76%; women: 24%; minorities: 14%; international: 50%
Part-time enrollment: 44
men: 84%; women: 16%; minorities: 34%; international: 23%
Acceptance rate: 33%
GRE requirement: Yes
Avg. GRE: quantitative: 163
TOEFL requirement: Yes
Minimum TOEFL score: 570
Fellowships: 124
Teaching assistantships: 329
Research assistantships: 308
Students reporting specialty: 100%
Students specializing in: biomedical: 9%; computer: 25%; computer science: 31%; electrical: 19%; other: 16%

University of Southern California (Viterbi)

University Park
Olin Hall 200
Los Angeles, CA 90089-1450
viterbi.usc.edu
Private
Admissions: (213) 740-4530
Email: viterbi.gradadmission@usc.edu
Financial aid: (213) 740-0119
Application deadline: 01/15
Tuition: full time: $29,275; part time: $1,774/credit hour
Room/board/expenses: $21,724
Full-time enrollment: 3,530
men: 71%; women: 29%; minorities: 8%; international: 85%
Part-time enrollment: 1,665
men: 71%; women: 29%; minorities: 19%; international: 58%
Acceptance rate: 22%
GRE requirement: Yes
Avg. GRE: quantitative: 163
TOEFL requirement: Yes
Minimum TOEFL score: N/A
Fellowships: 353
Teaching assistantships: 684
Research assistantships: 1,024
Students reporting specialty: 100%
Students specializing in: aerospace: 5%; biomedical: 4%; chemical: 3%; civil: 5%; computer: 2%; computer science: 38%; electrical: 23%; management: 2%; environmental: 1%; industrial: 5%; materials: 3%; mechanical: 6%; petroleum: 4%; other: 0%

COLORADO

Colorado School of Mines

1500 Illinois Street
Golden, CO 80401-1887
gradschool.mines.edu
Public
Admissions: (303) 273-3247
Email: grad-app@mines.edu
Financial aid: (303) 273-3207
Application deadline: 06/01
In-state tuition: full time: $17,353; part time: $846/credit hour
Out-of-state tuition: full time: $34,828
Room/board/expenses: $19,800
Full-time enrollment: 1,104
men: 71%; women: 29%; minorities: 11%; international: 34%
Part-time enrollment: 157
men: 74%; women: 26%; minorities: 19%; international: 9%
Acceptance rate: 38%
GRE requirement: Yes
Avg. GRE: quantitative: 159
TOEFL requirement: Yes
Minimum TOEFL score: 550
Fellowships: 74
Teaching assistantships: 177
Research assistantships: 508
Students reporting specialty: 100%
Students specializing in: chemical: 10%; civil: 10%; electrical: 7%; science and physics: 6%; materials: 10%; mechanical: 11%; mining: 4%; petroleum: 8%; other: 34%

Colorado State University

Campus Delivery 1301
Fort Collins, CO 80523-1301
graduateschool.colostate.edu
Public
Admissions: (970) 491-6817
Email: gradschool@colostate.edu
Financial aid: (970) 491-6321
Application deadline: 04/01
In-state tuition: full time: $11,328; part time: $629/credit hour
Out-of-state tuition: full time: $24,896
Room/board/expenses: $15,336
Full-time enrollment: 408
men: 75%; women: 25%; minorities: 5%; international: 57%
Part-time enrollment: 409
men: 76%; women: 24%; minorities: 6%; international: 47%
Acceptance rate: 49%
GRE requirement: Yes
Avg. GRE: quantitative: 161
TOEFL requirement: Yes
Minimum TOEFL score: 550
Fellowships: 53
Teaching assistantships: 54
Research assistantships: 235
Students reporting specialty: 100%
Students specializing in: biomedical: 5%; chemical: 4%; civil: 29%; electrical: 35%; management: 0%; industrial: 1%; mechanical: 15%; other: 10%

University of Colorado-Boulder

422 UCB
Boulder, CO 80309-0422
www.colorado.edu/engineering
Public
Admissions: (303) 492-5071
Financial aid: (303) 492-5091
Application deadline: N/A
In-state tuition: full time: $15,470; part time: $10,910
Out-of-state tuition: full time: $32,120
Room/board/expenses: $25,712
Full-time enrollment: 1,580
men: 74%; women: 26%; minorities: 10%; international: 42%
Part-time enrollment: 223
men: 81%; women: 19%; minorities: 17%; international: 15%
Acceptance rate: 31%
GRE requirement: Yes
Avg. GRE: quantitative: 162
TOEFL requirement: Yes
Minimum TOEFL score: N/A
Fellowships: 74
Teaching assistantships: 146
Research assistantships: 477
Students reporting specialty: 100%
Students specializing in: aerospace: 14%; architectural: 2%; chemical: 6%; civil: 12%; computer science: 16%; electrical: 17%; management: 9%; environmental: 0%; materials: 2%; mechanical: 10%; other: 12%

University of Colorado-Colorado Springs

1420 Austin Bluffs Parkway
Colorado Springs, CO 80918
www.uccs.edu
Public
Admissions: (719) 255-3383
Email: admrec@uccs.edu
Financial aid: (719) 255-3460
Application deadline: 06/01
In-state tuition: full time: $11,734; part time: $4,407
Out-of-state tuition: full time: $20,644
Room/board/expenses: $17,100
Full-time enrollment: 32
men: 69%; women: 31%; minorities: 9%; international: 166%
Part-time enrollment: 276
men: 80%; women: 20%; minorities: 16%; international: 19%
Acceptance rate: 67%
GRE requirement: Yes
Avg. GRE: quantitative: 154
TOEFL requirement: Yes
Minimum TOEFL score: N/A
Research assistantships: 5
Students reporting specialty: 100%
Students specializing in: computer science: 21%; electrical: 17%; management: 56%; mechanical: 6%

University of Colorado-Denver[1]

PO Box 173364
Campus Box 104
Denver, CO 80217-3364
www.ucdenver.edu/
Public
Admissions: (303) 556-2704
Email: admissions@ucdenver.edu
Financial aid: (303) 556-2886
Tuition: N/A
Room/board/expenses: N/A
Enrollment: N/A

University of Denver

2135 E. Wesley Avenue
Denver, CO 80208
www.du.edu/secs/
Private
Admissions: (303) 871-2831
Email: grad-info@du.edu
Financial aid: (303) 871-4020
Application deadline: 02/01
Tuition: full time: $29,022; part time: $1,199/credit hour
Room/board/expenses: $15,255
Full-time enrollment: 161
men: 78%; women: 22%; minorities: 6%; international: 69%
Part-time enrollment: 52
men: 79%; women: 21%; minorities: 17%; international: 4%
Acceptance rate: 64%
GRE requirement: Yes
Avg. GRE: quantitative: 159
TOEFL requirement: Yes
Minimum TOEFL score: 550
Fellowships: 0
Teaching assistantships: 35
Research assistantships: 29
Students reporting specialty: 100%

Students specializing in: biomedical: 4%; computer: 10%; computer science: 20%; electrical: 24%; materials: 5%; mechanical: 12%; other: 25%

CONNECTICUT

University of Bridgeport
221 University Avenue
Bridgeport, CT 06604
www.bridgeport.edu/sed
Private
Admissions: (203) 576-4552
Email: admit@bridgeport.edu
Financial aid: (203) 576-4568
Application deadline: rolling
Tuition: full time: $790/credit hour; part time: $790/credit hour
Room/board/expenses: $16,090
Full-time enrollment: 788
men: 76%; women: 24%; minorities: 3%; international: 97%
Part-time enrollment: 224
men: 83%; women: 17%; minorities: 12%; international: 77%
Acceptance rate: 57%
GRE requirement: No
Avg. GRE: quantitative: N/A
TOEFL requirement: Yes
Minimum TOEFL score: 550
Teaching assistantships: 34
Research assistantships: 44
Students reporting specialty: 100%
Students specializing in: biomedical: 8%; computer: 9%; computer science: 34%; electrical: 25%; management: 11%; mechanical: 13%

University of Connecticut
261 Glenbrook Road
Unit 3237
Storrs, CT 06269-3237
www.uconn.edu
Public
Admissions: (860) 486-0974
Email: gradadmissions@uconn.edu
Financial aid: (860) 486-2819
Application deadline: rolling
In-state tuition: full time: $14,724; part time: $724/credit hour
Out-of-state tuition: full time: $35,640
Room/board/expenses: $21,629
Full-time enrollment: 639
men: 70%; women: 30%; minorities: 10%; international: 63%
Part-time enrollment: 253
men: 79%; women: 21%; minorities: 19%; international: 14%
Acceptance rate: 26%
GRE requirement: Yes
Avg. GRE: quantitative: 163
TOEFL requirement: Yes
Minimum TOEFL score: N/A
Fellowships: 221
Teaching assistantships: 70
Research assistantships: 306
Students reporting specialty: 100%
Students specializing in: biomedical: 14%; chemical: 6%; civil: 9%; computer: 16%; computer science: 16%; electrical: 17%; environmental: 4%; materials: 11%; mechanical: 21%; other: 3%

Yale University
226 Dunham Lab
10 Hillhouse Avenue
New Haven, CT 06520
www.seas.yale.edu
Private
Admissions: (203) 432-2771
Email: graduate.admissions@yale.edu
Financial aid: (203) 432-2739
Application deadline: 01/02
Tuition: full time: $38,700; part time: $4,838/credit hour
Room/board/expenses: $28,274

Full-time enrollment: 281
men: 68%; women: 32%; minorities: 11%; international: 59%
Part-time enrollment: 1
men: 100%; women: 0%; minorities: 0%; international: 0%
Acceptance rate: 16%
GRE requirement: Yes
Avg. GRE: quantitative: 168
TOEFL requirement: Yes
Minimum TOEFL score: 600
Fellowships: 90
Teaching assistantships: 124
Research assistantships: 144
Students reporting specialty: 100%
Students specializing in: biomedical: 26%; chemical: 22%; computer science: 21%; electrical: 16%; mechanical: 14%; other: 1%

DELAWARE

University of Delaware
102 DuPont Hall
Newark, DE 19716-3101
www.engr.udel.edu
Public
Admissions: (302) 831-2129
Email: gradadmission@udel.edu
Financial aid: (302) 831-8189
Application deadline: rolling
In-state tuition: full time: $1,674/credit hour; part time: $1,674/credit hour
Out-of-state tuition: full time: $1,674/credit hour
Room/board/expenses: $15,388
Full-time enrollment: 813
men: 73%; women: 27%; minorities: 10%; international: 59%
Part-time enrollment: 68
men: 82%; women: 18%; minorities: 18%; international: 19%
Acceptance rate: 38%
GRE requirement: Yes
Avg. GRE: quantitative: 163
TOEFL requirement: Yes
Minimum TOEFL score: 570
Fellowships: 36
Teaching assistantships: 58
Research assistantships: 386
Students reporting specialty: 100%
Students specializing in: biomedical: 6%; chemical: 17%; civil: 14%; computer: 25%; computer science: 14%; electrical: 25%; environmental: 16%; materials: 8%; mechanical: 10%; other: 4%

DISTRICT OF COLUMBIA

The Catholic University of America
620 Michigan Avenue NE
Washington, DC 20064
admissions.cua.edu/graduate/
Private
Admissions: (800) 673-2772
Email: cua-admissions@cua.edu
Financial aid: (202) 319-5307
Application deadline: 07/15
Tuition: full time: $42,320; part time: $1,650/credit hour
Room/board/expenses: $18,812
Full-time enrollment: 80
men: 79%; women: 21%; minorities: 10%; international: 84%
Part-time enrollment: 106
men: 75%; women: 25%; minorities: 25%; international: 43%
Acceptance rate: 69%
GRE requirement: No
Avg. GRE: quantitative: N/A
TOEFL requirement: Yes
Minimum TOEFL score: 580
Fellowships: 4
Teaching assistantships: 8
Research assistantships: 4
Students reporting specialty: 100%
Students specializing in: biomedical: 14%; civil: 19%; computer science: 14%; electrical: 16%; management: 20%; materials: 6%; mechanical: 11%

George Washington University
Science and Engineering Hall
800 22nd Street NW
Washington, DC 20052
www.seas.gwu.edu/
Private
Admissions: (202) 994-8675
Email: engineering@gwu.edu
Financial aid: (202) 994-6822
Application deadline: 01/15
Tuition: full time: $1,585/credit hour; part time: $1,585/credit hour
Room/board/expenses: $24,000
Full-time enrollment: 614
men: 72%; women: 28%; minorities: 8%; international: 82%
Part-time enrollment: 976
men: 74%; women: 26%; minorities: 30%; international: 15%
Acceptance rate: 43%
GRE requirement: Yes
Avg. GRE: quantitative: 162
TOEFL requirement: Yes
Minimum TOEFL score: 550
Fellowships: 112
Teaching assistantships: 86
Research assistantships: 99
Students reporting specialty: 100%
Students specializing in: biomedical: 2%; civil: 2%; computer: 0%; computer science: 25%; electrical: 13%; management: 48%; mechanical: 9%

Howard University
2300 Sixth Street, NW
Washington, DC 20059
www.gs.howard.edu
Private
Admissions: (202) 806-4676
Email: HUGS@howard.edu
Financial aid: (202) 806-2864
Application deadline: 01/15
Tuition: full time: $33,211; part time: $1,700/credit hour
Room/board/expenses: $25,587
Full-time enrollment: 53
men: 68%; women: 32%; minorities: 43%; international: 55%
Part-time enrollment: 16
men: 69%; women: 31%; minorities: 63%; international: 25%
Acceptance rate: 78%
GRE requirement: Yes
Avg. GRE: quantitative: N/A
TOEFL requirement: Yes
Minimum TOEFL score: 550
Fellowships: 10
Teaching assistantships: 4
Research assistantships: 12
Students reporting specialty: 100%
Students specializing in: chemical: 9%; civil: 20%; computer science: 20%; electrical: 41%; mechanical: 10%

FLORIDA

Embry-Riddle Aeronautical University
600 S. Clyde Morris Boulevard
Daytona Beach, FL 32114
daytonabeach.erau.edu/
admissions/index.html
Private
Admissions: (800) 388-3728
Email: graduate.admissions@erau.edu
Financial aid: (855) 661-7968
Application deadline: rolling
Tuition: full time: $1,331/credit hour; part time: $1,331/credit hour
Room/board/expenses: $16,240
Full-time enrollment: 275
men: 80%; women: 20%; minorities: 9%; international: 64%
Part-time enrollment: 68
men: 76%; women: 24%; minorities: 21%; international: 26%

Acceptance rate: 42%
GRE requirement: Yes
Avg. GRE: quantitative: 156
TOEFL requirement: Yes
Minimum TOEFL score: 550
Fellowships: 41
Teaching assistantships: 38
Research assistantships: 5
Students reporting specialty: 100%
Students specializing in: aerospace: 45%; computer science: 3%; electrical: 9%; science and physics: 10%; mechanical: 18%; other: 17%

Florida A&M University-Florida State University
2525 Pottsdamer Street
Tallahassee, FL 32310
www.eng.fsu.edu
Public
Admissions: (850) 410-6423
Email: perry@eng.fsu.edu
Financial aid: (850) 410-6423
Application deadline: 03/01
In-state tuition: full time: $404/credit hour; part time: $404/credit hour
Out-of-state tuition: full time: $1,005/credit hour
Room/board/expenses: $16,478
Full-time enrollment: 331
men: 78%; women: 22%; minorities: 75%; international: 56%
Part-time enrollment: N/A
men: N/A; women: N/A; minorities: N/A; international: N/A
Acceptance rate: 43%
GRE requirement: Yes
Avg. GRE: quantitative: 159
TOEFL requirement: Yes
Minimum TOEFL score: 550
Fellowships: 22
Teaching assistantships: 94
Research assistantships: 125
Students reporting specialty: 100%
Students specializing in: biomedical: 3%; chemical: 9%; civil: 15%; electrical: 28%; industrial: 21%; mechanical: 24%

Florida Atlantic University
777 Glades Road
Boca Raton, FL 33431-0991
www.eng.fau.edu
Public
Admissions: (561) 297-3642
Email: graduatecollege@fau.edu
Financial aid: (561) 297-3530
Application deadline: rolling
In-state tuition: full time: $370/credit hour; part time: $370/credit hour
Out-of-state tuition: full time: $1,025/credit hour
Room/board/expenses: $15,450
Full-time enrollment: 144
men: 73%; women: 27%; minorities: 15%; international: 45%
Part-time enrollment: 153
men: 78%; women: 22%; minorities: 40%; international: 14%
Acceptance rate: 46%
GRE requirement: Yes
Avg. GRE: quantitative: 157
TOEFL requirement: Yes
Minimum TOEFL score: 550
Fellowships: 3
Teaching assistantships: 45
Research assistantships: 51
Students reporting specialty: 99%
Students specializing in: biomedical: 5%; civil: 10%; computer: 12%; computer science: 25%; electrical: 15%; mechanical: 16%; other: 17%

Florida Institute of Technology
150 W. University Boulevard
Melbourne, FL 32901-6975
www.fit.edu
Private
Admissions: (800) 944-4348
Email: grad-admissions@fit.edu
Financial aid: (321) 674-8070
Application deadline: rolling
Tuition: full time: $1,205/credit hour; part time: $1,205/credit hour
Room/board/expenses: $17,700
Full-time enrollment: 729
men: 76%; women: 24%; minorities: 3%; international: 84%
Part-time enrollment: 314
men: 84%; women: 16%; minorities: 16%; international: 46%
Acceptance rate: 42%
GRE requirement: Yes
Avg. GRE: quantitative: 148
TOEFL requirement: Yes
Minimum TOEFL score: 550
Fellowships: 0
Teaching assistantships: 71
Research assistantships: 72
Students reporting specialty: 100%
Students specializing in: aerospace: 6%; biomedical: 3%; chemical: 1%; civil: 4%; computer: 1%; computer science: 34%; electrical: 20%; management: 5%; environmental: 2%; mechanical: 9%; other: 15%

Florida International University
10555 W. Flagler Street
Miami, FL 33174
www.eng.fiu.edu/
Public
Admissions: (305) 348-7442
Email: gradadm@fiu.edu
Financial aid: (305) 348-7272
Application deadline: 02/15
In-state tuition: full time: $11,334; part time: $456/credit hour
Out-of-state tuition: full time: $24,438
Room/board/expenses: $25,620
Full-time enrollment: 608
men: 72%; women: 28%; minorities: 27%; international: 68%
Part-time enrollment: 278
men: 77%; women: 23%; minorities: 63%; international: 23%
Acceptance rate: 41%
GRE requirement: Yes
Avg. GRE: quantitative: 157
TOEFL requirement: Yes
Minimum TOEFL score: 550
Fellowships: 39
Teaching assistantships: 117
Research assistantships: 122
Students reporting specialty: 99%
Students specializing in: biomedical: 4%; civil: 11%; computer: 6%; computer science: 22%; electrical: 16%; management: 16%; environmental: 1%; materials: 4%; mechanical: 6%; other: 12%

University of Central Florida
4000 Central Florida Boulevard
Orlando, FL 32816-2993
www.cecs.ucf.edu/future-students/admissions-graduate-students/
Public
Admissions: (407) 823-2455
Email: gradengr@ucf.edu
Financial aid: (407) 823-2827
Application deadline: 07/15
In-state tuition: full time: $370/credit hour; part time: $370/credit hour
Out-of-state tuition: full time: $1,194/credit hour
Room/board/expenses: $15,853

Full-time enrollment: 897
men: 79%; women: 21%;
minorities: 13%; international: 66%
Part-time enrollment: 428
men: 79%; women: 21%;
minorities: 36%; international: 0%
Acceptance rate: 38%
GRE requirement: Yes
Avg. GRE: quantitative: 159
TOEFL requirement: Yes
Minimum TOEFL score: 550
Fellowships: 42
Teaching assistantships: 182
Research assistantships: 251
Students reporting specialty: 100%
Students specializing in: aerospace: 3%; civil: 11%; computer: 7%; computer science: 18%; electrical: 17%; management: 5%; environmental: 3%; industrial: 11%; materials: 4%; mechanical: 11%; other: 9%

University of Florida

300 Weil Hall
Gainesville, FL 32611-6550
www.eng.ufl.edu
Public
Admissions: (352) 392-0943
Email: admissions@eng.ufl.edu
Financial aid: (352) 392-0943
Application deadline: 06/01
In-state tuition: full time: $12,737; part time: $531/credit hour
Out-of-state tuition: full time: $30,130
Room/board/expenses: $16,630
Full-time enrollment: 2,230
men: 76%; women: 24%;
minorities: 9%; international: 71%
Part-time enrollment: 567
men: 75%; women: 25%;
minorities: 18%; international: 31%
Acceptance rate: 41%
GRE requirement: Yes
Avg. GRE: quantitative: 163
TOEFL requirement: Yes
Minimum TOEFL score: 550
Fellowships: 170
Teaching assistantships: 150
Research assistantships: 667
Students reporting specialty: 100%
Students specializing in: aerospace: 4%; agriculture: 2%; biomedical: 6%; chemical: 6%; civil: 7%; computer: 7%; computer science: 12%; electrical: 21%; environmental: 5%; industrial: 6%; materials: 8%; mechanical: 13%; nuclear: 2%

University of Miami

1251 Memorial Drive
Coral Gables, FL 33146
www.miami.edu/engineering
Private
Admissions: (305) 284-2942
Email: gradadm.eng@miami.edu
Financial aid: (305) 284-5212
Application deadline: 12/01
Tuition: full time: $1,850/credit hour; part time: $1,850/credit hour
Room/board/expenses: $20,978
Full-time enrollment: 233
men: 73%; women: 27%;
minorities: 24%; international: 56%
Part-time enrollment: 20
men: 85%; women: 15%;
minorities: 55%; international: 30%
Acceptance rate: 50%
GRE requirement: Yes
Avg. GRE: quantitative: 159
TOEFL requirement: Yes
Minimum TOEFL score: 550
Fellowships: 8
Teaching assistantships: 33
Research assistantships: 65
Students reporting specialty: 100%
Students specializing in: architectural: 2%; biomedical: 25%; civil: 10%; computer science: 6%; electrical: 17%; industrial: 26%; mechanical: 15%; other: 0%

University of South Florida

4202 E. Fowler Avenue, ENB118
Tampa, FL 33620
www.usf.edu/admissions/
Public
Admissions: (813) 974-3350
Email: admissions@grad.usf.edu
Financial aid: (813) 974-4700
Application deadline: 02/15
In-state tuition: full time: $10,502; part time: $467/credit hour
Out-of-state tuition: full time: $21,200
Room/board/expenses: $15,850
Full-time enrollment: 891
men: 77%; women: 23%;
minorities: 9%; international: 73%
Part-time enrollment: 150
men: 81%; women: 19%;
minorities: 41%; international: 0%
Acceptance rate: 49%
GRE requirement: Yes
Avg. GRE: quantitative: 157
TOEFL requirement: Yes
Minimum TOEFL score: 550
Fellowships: 73
Teaching assistantships: 227
Research assistantships: 196
Students reporting specialty: 100%
Students specializing in: biomedical: 5%; chemical: 4%; civil: 13%; computer: 9%; computer science: 15%; electrical: 32%; management: 11%; science and physics: 2%; environmental: 3%; industrial: 4%; materials: 1%; mechanical: 9%

GEORGIA

Georgia Institute of Technology

225 North Avenue
Atlanta, GA 30332-0360
www.gradadmiss.gatech.edu/
Public
Admissions: (404) 894-1610
Email: gradstudies@gatech.edu
Financial aid: (404) 894-4160
Application deadline: rolling
In-state tuition: full time: $15,644; part time: $561/credit hour
Out-of-state tuition: full time: $30,064
Room/board/expenses: $16,194
Full-time enrollment: 3,889
men: 77%; women: 23%;
minorities: 15%; international: 58%
Part-time enrollment: 3,615
men: 85%; women: 15%;
minorities: 27%; international: 24%
Acceptance rate: 30%
GRE requirement: Yes
Avg. GRE: quantitative: 164
TOEFL requirement: Yes
Minimum TOEFL score: 550
Fellowships: 861
Teaching assistantships: 487
Research assistantships: 1,911
Students reporting specialty: 99%
Students specializing in: aerospace: 7%; biomedical: 3%; chemical: 3%; civil: 4%; computer science: 49%; electrical: 16%; science and physics: 0%; environmental: 1%; industrial: 5%; materials: 2%; mechanical: 10%; nuclear: 1%; other: 1%

University of Georgia[1]

Paul D. Coverdell Center
Athens, GA 30602
grad.uga.edu
Public
Admissions: (706) 542-1739
Email: gradadm@uga.edu
Financial aid: (706) 542-6147
Tuition: N/A
Room/board/expenses: N/A
Enrollment: N/A

HAWAII

University of Hawaii-Manoa[1]

2540 Dole Street
Holmes Hall 240
Honolulu, HI 96822
www.eng.hawaii.edu/current-students/graduate-students
Public
Admissions: (808) 956-8544
Email: gradadm@hawaii.edu
Financial aid: (808) 956-7251
Tuition: N/A
Room/board/expenses: N/A
Enrollment: N/A

IDAHO

Boise State University

1910 University Drive
Boise, ID 83725
graduatecollege.boisestate.edu
Public
Admissions: (208) 426-3903
Email: gradcollege@boisestate.edu
Financial aid: (208) 426-1664
Application deadline: rolling
In-state tuition: full time: $8,166; part time: $358/credit hour
Out-of-state tuition: full time: $22,216
Room/board/expenses: $13,572
Full-time enrollment: 116
men: 73%; women: 27%;
minorities: 7%; international: 53%
Part-time enrollment: 56
men: 84%; women: 16%;
minorities: 14%; international: 39%
Acceptance rate: 48%
GRE requirement: Yes
Avg. GRE: quantitative: 159
TOEFL requirement: Yes
Minimum TOEFL score: 550
Fellowships: 2
Teaching assistantships: 8
Research assistantships: 48
Students reporting specialty: 100%
Students specializing in: civil: 7%; computer: 1%; computer science: 32%; electrical: 29%; materials: 26%; mechanical: 5%

Idaho State University[1]

921 S. Eighth Street, MS 8060
Pocatello, ID 83209-8060
www.isu.edu/cse
Public
Admissions: (208) 282-2150
Email: graddean@isu.edu
Financial aid: N/A
Tuition: N/A
Room/board/expenses: N/A
Enrollment: N/A

University of Idaho[1]

PO Box 441011
Moscow, ID 83844-1011
www.engr.uidaho.edu/
Public
Admissions: (208) 885-4001
Email: gadms@uidaho.edu
Financial aid: N/A
Tuition: N/A
Room/board/expenses: N/A
Enrollment: N/A

ILLINOIS

Illinois Institute of Technology (Armour)

10 West 33rd Street, Perlstein Hall, Suite 224
Chicago, IL 60616
www.iit.edu/engineering
Private
Admissions: (312) 567-3020
Email: gradstu@iit.edu
Financial aid: (312) 567-7219
Application deadline: 01/01
Tuition: full time: $1,313/credit hour; part time: $1,313/credit hour
Room/board/expenses: $17,706
Full-time enrollment: 1,511
men: 78%; women: 22%;
minorities: 2%; international: 93%
Part-time enrollment: 329
men: 78%; women: 22%;
minorities: 11%; international: 61%
Acceptance rate: 51%
GRE requirement: Yes
Avg. GRE: quantitative: 160
TOEFL requirement: Yes
Minimum TOEFL score: 550
Fellowships: 25
Teaching assistantships: 92
Research assistantships: 240
Students reporting specialty: 100%
Students specializing in: aerospace: 9%; agriculture: 0%; architectural: 1%; biomedical: 3%; chemical: 6%; civil: 8%; computer: 7%; computer science: 40%; electrical: 24%; environmental: 2%; industrial: 0%; materials: 2%; mechanical: 9%

Northwestern University (McCormick)

2145 Sheridan Road
Evanston, IL 60208
www.tgs.northwestern.edu/
Private
Admissions: (847) 491-5279
Email: gradapp@northwestern.edu
Financial aid: (847) 491-8495
Application deadline: N/A
Tuition: full time: $48,954; part time: $5,766/credit hour
Room/board/expenses: $22,590
Full-time enrollment: 1,674
men: 69%; women: 31%;
minorities: 15%; international: 54%
Part-time enrollment: 306
men: 67%; women: 33%;
minorities: 17%; international: 49%
Acceptance rate: 23%
GRE requirement: Yes
Avg. GRE: quantitative: 166
TOEFL requirement: Yes
Minimum TOEFL score: 550
Fellowships: 210
Teaching assistantships: 85
Research assistantships: 550
Students reporting specialty: 70%
Students specializing in: biomedical: 10%; chemical: 9%; civil: 9%; computer: 4%; computer science: 14%; electrical: 11%; management: 6%; science and physics: 4%; industrial: 4%; materials: 18%; mechanical: 11%

Southern Illinois University-Carbondale

900 S. Normal Avenue
Mailcode 4716
Carbondale, IL 62901-6603
gradschool.siuc.edu/
Public
Admissions: (618) 536-7791
Email: gradschl@siu.edu
Financial aid: (618) 453-4334
Application deadline: rolling
In-state tuition: full time: $418/credit hour; part time: $418/credit hour
Out-of-state tuition: full time: $1,044/credit hour
Room/board/expenses: $17,421
Full-time enrollment: 223
men: 78%; women: 22%;
minorities: 4%; international: 88%
Part-time enrollment: 116
men: 85%; women: 15%;
minorities: 5%; international: 67%
Acceptance rate: 55%
GRE requirement: Yes
Avg. GRE: quantitative: 160
TOEFL requirement: Yes
Minimum TOEFL score: 550
Fellowships: 10
Teaching assistantships: 128
Research assistantships: 52
Students reporting specialty: 85%
Students specializing in: biomedical: 2%; civil: 15%; computer: 63%; electrical: 63%; environmental: 15%; mechanical: 17%; mining: 3%

University of Illinois-Chicago

851 S. Morgan Street
Chicago, IL 60607-7043
www.uic.edu/
Public
Admissions: (312) 996-5133
Email: uicgrad@uic.edu
Financial aid: (312) 996-3126
Application deadline: 05/15
In-state tuition: full time: $18,300; part time: $13,228
Out-of-state tuition: full time: $30,540
Room/board/expenses: $17,958
Full-time enrollment: 1,324
men: 73%; women: 27%;
minorities: 7%; international: 81%
Part-time enrollment: 215
men: 81%; women: 19%;
minorities: 36%; international: 34%
Acceptance rate: 27%
GRE requirement: Yes
Avg. GRE: quantitative: 160
TOEFL requirement: Yes
Minimum TOEFL score: 550
Fellowships: 29
Teaching assistantships: 245
Research assistantships: 186
Students reporting specialty: 100%
Students specializing in: biomedical: 10%; chemical: 4%; civil: 8%; computer science: 22%; electrical: 25%; mechanical: 30%

University of Illinois-Urbana-Champaign

1308 W. Green
Urbana, IL 61801
engineering.illinois.edu
Public
Admissions: (217) 333-0035
Email: engineering@illinois.edu
Financial aid: (217) 333-0100
Application deadline: rolling
In-state tuition: full time: $23,401; part time: N/A
Out-of-state tuition: full time: $35,384
Room/board/expenses: $17,900
Full-time enrollment: 3,195
men: 78%; women: 22%;
minorities: 11%; international: 65%
Part-time enrollment: 226
men: 82%; women: 18%;
minorities: 14%; international: 35%
Acceptance rate: 25%
GRE requirement: Yes
Avg. GRE: quantitative: 165
TOEFL requirement: Yes
Minimum TOEFL score: N/A
Fellowships: 299
Teaching assistantships: 845
Research assistantships: 1,762
Students reporting specialty: 100%
Students specializing in: aerospace: 5%; agriculture: 2%; biomedical: 3%; chemical: 3%; civil: 18%; computer: 15%; computer science: 18%; electrical: 15%; science and physics: 8%; environmental: 3%; industrial: 6%; materials: 6%; mechanical: 12%; nuclear: 3%

INDIANA

Indiana University-Purdue University-Indianapolis

799 W. Michigan Street, ET 219
Indianapolis, IN 46202-5160
engr.iupui.edu
Public
Admissions: (317) 278-4960
Email: gradengr@iupui.edu
Financial aid: N/A
Application deadline: 06/01

In-state tuition: full time: $374/credit hour; part time: $374/credit hour
Out-of-state tuition: full time: $1,069/credit hour
Room/board/expenses: $2,650
Full-time enrollment: 278
men: 78%; women: 22%; minorities: 3%; international: 86%
Part-time enrollment: 56
men: 91%; women: 9%; minorities: 23%; international: 9%
Acceptance rate: 54%
GRE requirement: Yes
Avg. GRE: quantitative: 160
TOEFL requirement: Yes
Minimum TOEFL score: 550
Fellowships: 5
Teaching assistantships: 21
Research assistantships: 69
Students reporting specialty: 100%
Students specializing in:
biomedical: 8%; computer: 18%; electrical: 28%; mechanical: 46%

Purdue University-West Lafayette
701 W. Stadium Avenue
Suite 3000 ARMS
West Lafayette, IN 47907-2045
engineering.purdue.edu
Public
Admissions: (765) 494-2598
Email: gradinfo@purdue.edu
Financial aid: (765) 494-2598
Application deadline: rolling
In-state tuition: full time: $11,124; part time: $329/credit hour
Out-of-state tuition: full time: $29,926
Room/board/expenses: $13,190
Full-time enrollment: 2,787
men: 78%; women: 22%; minorities: 8%; international: 70%
Part-time enrollment: 755
men: 81%; women: 19%; minorities: 15%; international: 22%
Acceptance rate: 23%
GRE requirement: Yes
Avg. GRE: quantitative: 164
TOEFL requirement: Yes
Minimum TOEFL score: 550
Fellowships: 355
Teaching assistantships: 564
Research assistantships: 1,350
Students reporting specialty: 99%
Students specializing in:
aerospace: 13%; agriculture: 3%; biomedical: 3%; chemical: 4%; civil: 11%; computer: 5%; computer science: 8%; electrical: 16%; environmental: 1%; industrial: 6%; materials: 3%; mechanical: 15%; nuclear: 1%; other: 13%

University of Notre Dame
257 Fitzpatrick Hall of Engineering
Notre Dame, IN 46556
www.nd.edu
Private
Admissions: (574) 631-7706
Email: gradad@nd.edu
Financial aid: (574) 631-7706
Application deadline: rolling
Tuition: full time: $47,765; part time: $2,628/credit hour
Room/board/expenses: $19,910
Full-time enrollment: 508
men: 76%; women: 24%; minorities: 10%; international: 50%
Part-time enrollment: 3
men: 67%; women: 33%; minorities: 67%; international: 0%
Acceptance rate: 20%
GRE requirement: Yes
Avg. GRE: quantitative: 163
TOEFL requirement: Yes
Minimum TOEFL score: N/A
Fellowships: 43
Teaching assistantships: 44
Research assistantships: 372
Students reporting specialty: 100%
Students specializing in:
biomedical: 5%; chemical: 15%;

civil: 17%; computer science: 23%; electrical: 21%; mechanical: 19%; other: 0%

IOWA

Iowa State University
4565 Memorial Union
Ames, IA 50011-1130
www.engineering.iastate.edu/
Public
Admissions: (800) 262-3810
Email: grad_admissions@iastate.edu
Financial aid: (515) 294-2223
Application deadline: rolling
In-state tuition: full time: $10,676; part time: $1,825
Out-of-state tuition: full time: $23,554
Room/board/expenses: $13,745
Full-time enrollment: 1,363
men: 76%; women: 24%; minorities: 8%; international: 57%
Part-time enrollment: N/A
men: N/A; women: N/A; minorities: N/A; international: N/A
Acceptance rate: 21%
GRE requirement: Yes
Avg. GRE: quantitative: 162
TOEFL requirement: Yes
Minimum TOEFL score: 550
Fellowships: 46
Teaching assistantships: 216
Research assistantships: 614
Students reporting specialty: 100%
Students specializing in:
aerospace: 7%; agriculture: 5%; chemical: 5%; civil: 15%; computer: 13%; electrical: 15%; industrial: 14%; materials: 6%; mechanical: 19%; other: 1%

University of Iowa
3100 Seamans Center
Iowa City, IA 52242-1527
www.uiowa.edu/admissions/graduate/index.html
Public
Admissions: (319) 335-1525
Email: admissions@uiowa.edu
Financial aid: (319) 335-1450
Application deadline: rolling
In-state tuition: full time: $10,094; part time: N/A
Out-of-state tuition: full time: $27,272
Room/board/expenses: $15,740
Full-time enrollment: 330
men: 79%; women: 21%; minorities: 8%; international: 58%
Part-time enrollment: 34
men: 71%; women: 29%; minorities: 9%; international: 15%
Acceptance rate: 17%
GRE requirement: Yes
Avg. GRE: quantitative: 160
TOEFL requirement: Yes
Minimum TOEFL score: N/A
Fellowships: 14
Teaching assistantships: 79
Research assistantships: 200
Students reporting specialty: 100%
Students specializing in:
biomedical: 17%; chemical: 8%; civil: 15%; computer science: 22%; electrical: 18%; industrial: 5%; mechanical: 15%

KANSAS

Kansas State University
1046 Rathbone Hall
Manhattan, KS 66506-5201
www.engg.ksu.edu/
Public
Admissions: (785) 532-6191
Email: grad@ksu.edu
Financial aid: (785) 532-6420
Application deadline: rolling
In-state tuition: full time: $381/credit hour; part time: $381/credit hour
Out-of-state tuition: full time: $859/credit hour
Room/board/expenses: $9,380

Full-time enrollment: 266
men: 73%; women: 27%; minorities: 6%; international: 63%
Part-time enrollment: 200
men: 81%; women: 20%; minorities: 15%; international: 13%
Acceptance rate: 50%
GRE requirement: Yes
Avg. GRE: quantitative: 159
TOEFL requirement: Yes
Minimum TOEFL score: 550
Fellowships: 13
Teaching assistantships: 102
Research assistantships: 135
Students reporting specialty: 100%
Students specializing in:
agriculture: 8%; architectural: 3%; chemical: 7%; civil: 18%; computer science: 17%; electrical: 17%; industrial: 17%; mechanical: 10%; nuclear: 4%

University of Kansas
1 Eaton Hall
1520 W. 15th Street
Lawrence, KS 66045-7621
www.engr.ku.edu
Public
Admissions: (785) 864-3881
Email: kuengrgrad@ku.edu
Financial aid: (785) 864-5491
Application deadline: 12/15
In-state tuition: full time: $376/credit hour; part time: $376/credit hour
Out-of-state tuition: full time: $880/credit hour
Room/board/expenses: $12,850
Full-time enrollment: 421
men: 73%; women: 27%; minorities: 6%; international: 66%
Part-time enrollment: 266
men: 74%; women: 26%; minorities: 15%; international: 22%
Acceptance rate: 41%
GRE requirement: Yes
Avg. GRE: quantitative: 160
TOEFL requirement: Yes
Minimum TOEFL score: N/A
Fellowships: 109
Teaching assistantships: 112
Research assistantships: 150
Students reporting specialty: 100%
Students specializing in:
aerospace: 7%; architectural: 1%; biomedical: 7%; chemical: 5%; civil: 18%; computer: 2%; computer science: 13%; electrical: 12%; management: 17%; environmental: 2%; mechanical: 8%; petroleum: 2%; other: 6%

Wichita State University
1845 N. Fairmount
Wichita, KS 67260-0044
www.wichita.edu/engineering
Public
Admissions: (316) 978-3095
Email: jordan.oleson@wichita.edu
Financial aid: (316) 978-3430
Application deadline: rolling
In-state tuition: full time: $274/credit hour; part time: $274/credit hour
Out-of-state tuition: full time: $672/credit hour
Room/board/expenses: $13,342
Full-time enrollment: 460
men: 80%; women: 20%; minorities: 4%; international: 90%
Part-time enrollment: 319
men: 79%; women: 21%; minorities: 19%; international: 55%
Acceptance rate: 50%
GRE requirement: Yes
Avg. GRE: quantitative: 155
TOEFL requirement: Yes
Minimum TOEFL score: 550
Fellowships: 21
Teaching assistantships: 63
Research assistantships: 169
Students reporting specialty: 92%
Students specializing in:
aerospace: 18%; computer: 12%;

computer science: 11%; electrical: 20%; management: 6%; industrial: 23%; mechanical: 15%

KENTUCKY

University of Kentucky
351 Ralph G. Anderson Building
Lexington, KY 40506-0503
www.engr.uky.edu
Public
Admissions: (859) 257-4905
Email: grad.admit@uky.edu
Financial aid: (859) 257-3172
Application deadline: 07/14
In-state tuition: full time: $11,652; part time: $617/credit hour
Out-of-state tuition: full time: $26,154
Room/board/expenses: $11,151
Full-time enrollment: 430
men: 79%; women: 21%; minorities: 5%; international: 60%
Part-time enrollment: 59
men: 88%; women: 12%; minorities: 22%; international: 19%
Acceptance rate: 52%
GRE requirement: Yes
Avg. GRE: quantitative: 161
TOEFL requirement: Yes
Minimum TOEFL score: 550
Fellowships: 24
Teaching assistantships: 101
Research assistantships: 170
Students reporting specialty: 100%
Students specializing in:
agriculture: 5%; biomedical: 7%; chemical: 9%; civil: 13%; computer science: 19%; electrical: 13%; industrial: 2%; materials: 7%; mechanical: 18%; mining: 6%

University of Louisville (Speed)
2301 S. Third Street
Louisville, KY 40292
louisville.edu/speed/
Public
Admissions: (502) 852-3101
Email: gradadm@louisville.edu
Financial aid: (502) 852-5511
Application deadline: rolling
In-state tuition: full time: $11,860; part time: $649/credit hour
Out-of-state tuition: full time: $24,470
Room/board/expenses: $14,330
Full-time enrollment: 332
men: 75%; women: 25%; minorities: 6%; international: 48%
Part-time enrollment: 306
men: 84%; women: 16%; minorities: 17%; international: 19%
Acceptance rate: 58%
GRE requirement: Yes
Avg. GRE: quantitative: 160
TOEFL requirement: Yes
Minimum TOEFL score: 550
Fellowships: 35
Teaching assistantships: 48
Research assistantships: 49
Students reporting specialty: 100%
Students specializing in:
biomedical: 5%; chemical: 6%; civil: 7%; computer: 10%; computer science: 9%; electrical: 10%; management: 21%; industrial: 14%; mechanical: 18%

LOUISIANA

Louisiana State University-Baton Rouge
3304 Patrick F. Taylor Building
Baton Rouge, LA 70803
www.eng.lsu.edu
Public
Admissions: (225) 578-1641
Email: graddeanoffice@lsu.edu
Financial aid: (225) 578-3103
Application deadline: rolling
In-state tuition: full time: $10,602; part time: $6,022

Out-of-state tuition: full time: $27,822
Room/board/expenses: $14,856
Full-time enrollment: 531
men: 75%; women: 25%; minorities: 7%; international: 72%
Part-time enrollment: 111
men: 81%; women: 19%; minorities: 21%; international: 22%
Acceptance rate: 35%
GRE requirement: Yes
Avg. GRE: quantitative: 159
TOEFL requirement: Yes
Minimum TOEFL score: 550
Fellowships: 17
Teaching assistantships: 109
Research assistantships: 221
Students reporting specialty: 100%
Students specializing in:
agriculture: 2%; chemical: 9%; civil: 15%; computer science: 11%; electrical: 17%; science and physics: 11%; industrial: 2%; mechanical: 12%; petroleum: 11%; other: 11%

Louisiana Tech University
PO Box 10348
Ruston, LA 71272
www.latech.edu/tech/engr
Public
Admissions: (318) 257-2924
Email: gschool@latech.edu
Financial aid: (318) 257-2641
Application deadline: rolling
In-state tuition: full time: $7,080; part time: $5,793
Out-of-state tuition: full time: $16,383
Room/board/expenses: $11,460
Full-time enrollment: 251
men: 75%; women: 25%; minorities: 7%; international: 61%
Part-time enrollment: 91
men: 79%; women: 21%; minorities: 14%; international: 27%
Acceptance rate: 38%
GRE requirement: Yes
Avg. GRE: quantitative: 157
TOEFL requirement: Yes
Minimum TOEFL score: 550
Fellowships: 15
Teaching assistantships: 73
Research assistantships: 63
Students reporting specialty: 53%
Students specializing in:
biomedical: 18%; chemical: 4%; civil: 4%; computer science: 13%; electrical: 13%; management: 40%; industrial: 2%; mechanical: 8%

Tulane University
201 Lindy Boggs Building
New Orleans, LA 70118
tulane.edu/sse/academics/graduate/index.cfm
Private
Admissions: (504) 865-5764
Email: segrad@tulane.edu
Financial aid: (504) 865-5764
Application deadline: rolling
Tuition: full time: $49,638; part time: $2,692/credit hour
Room/board/expenses: $18,300
Full-time enrollment: 95
men: 65%; women: 35%; minorities: 13%; international: 42%
Part-time enrollment: N/A
men: N/A; women: N/A; minorities: N/A; international: N/A
Acceptance rate: 30%
GRE requirement: Yes
Avg. GRE: quantitative: 160
TOEFL requirement: Yes
Minimum TOEFL score: N/A
Fellowships: 15
Teaching assistantships: 22
Research assistantships: 34
Students reporting specialty: 82%
Students specializing in:
biomedical: 67%; chemical: 51%; computer science: 1%; science and physics: 3%

University of Louisiana-Lafayette

PO Box 42251
Lafayette, LA 70504
engineering.louisiana.edu/
Public
Admissions: (337) 482-6467
Email: gradschool@louisiana.edu
Financial aid: (337) 482-6506
Application deadline: rolling
In-state tuition: full time: $8,014; part time: $445/credit hour
Out-of-state tuition: full time: $21,741
Room/board/expenses: $14,192
Full-time enrollment: 264
men: 79%; women: 21%; minorities: 6%; international: 75%
Part-time enrollment: 62
men: 85%; women: 15%; minorities: 13%; international: 45%
Acceptance rate: 34%
GRE requirement: Yes
Avg. GRE: quantitative: 157
TOEFL requirement: Yes
Minimum TOEFL score: N/A
Students reporting specialty: 100%
Students specializing in: chemical: 7%; civil: 6%; computer: 17%; computer science: 34%; industrial: 5%; mechanical: 7%; petroleum: 23%

University of New Orleans

2000 Lakeshore Drive
New Orleans, LA 70148
www.uno.edu
Public
Admissions: (504) 280-6595
Email: pec@uno.edu
Financial aid: (504) 280-6603
Application deadline: rolling
In-state tuition: full time: $7,938; part time: $5,202
Out-of-state tuition: full time: $21,377
Room/board/expenses: $14,069
Full-time enrollment: 93
men: 78%; women: 22%; minorities: 2%; international: 61%
Part-time enrollment: 84
men: 85%; women: 15%; minorities: 7%; international: 19%
Acceptance rate: 40%
GRE requirement: Yes
Avg. GRE: quantitative: 156
TOEFL requirement: Yes
Minimum TOEFL score: 550
Students reporting specialty: 100%
Students specializing in: civil: 15%; computer science: 11%; electrical: 14%; mechanical: 10%; other: 50%

MAINE

University of Maine

Advanced Manufacturing Center
Orono, ME 04469
www.engineering.umaine.edu/
Public
Admissions: (207) 581-3291
Email: graduate@maine.edu
Financial aid: (207) 581-1324
Application deadline: rolling
In-state tuition: full time: $418/credit hour; part time: $418/credit hour
Out-of-state tuition: full time: $1,330/credit hour
Room/board/expenses: $16,102
Full-time enrollment: 153
men: 78%; women: 22%; minorities: 7%; international: 44%
Part-time enrollment: 34
men: 88%; women: 12%; minorities: 6%; international: 15%
Acceptance rate: 60%
GRE requirement: Yes
Avg. GRE: quantitative: 156
TOEFL requirement: Yes
Minimum TOEFL score: N/A
Fellowships: 6
Teaching assistantships: 23
Research assistantships: 36
Students reporting specialty: 100%
Students specializing in: biomedical: 4%; chemical: 8%; civil: 24%; computer: 4%; computer science: 11%; electrical: 12%; science and physics: 1%; mechanical: 15%; other: 22%

MARYLAND

Johns Hopkins University (Whiting)

3400 N. Charles Street
Baltimore, MD 21218
engineering.jhu.edu
Private
Admissions: (410) 516-8174
Email: graduateadmissions@jhu.edu
Financial aid: (410) 516-8028
Application deadline: N/A
Tuition: full time: $49,210; part time: $1,624/credit hour
Room/board/expenses: $17,766
Full-time enrollment: 1,206
men: 70%; women: 30%; minorities: 14%; international: 57%
Part-time enrollment: 2,266
men: 77%; women: 23%; minorities: 23%; international: 5%
Acceptance rate: 29%
GRE requirement: Yes
Avg. GRE: quantitative: 165
TOEFL requirement: Yes
Minimum TOEFL score: 600
Fellowships: 175
Teaching assistantships: 81
Research assistantships: 521
Students reporting specialty: 100%
Students specializing in: aerospace: 1%; biomedical: 6%; chemical: 3%; civil: 2%; computer science: 19%; electrical: 13%; management: 2%; science and physics: 1%; environmental: 6%; materials: 3%; mechanical: 6%; other: 38%

Morgan State University (Mitchell)

1700 E. Coldspring Lane
Baltimore, MD 21251
www.morgan.edu/Prospective_Grad_Students.html
Public
Admissions: (443) 885-3185
Email: mark.garrison@morgan.edu
Financial aid: (443) 885-3170
Application deadline: rolling
In-state tuition: full time: $382/credit hour; part time: $382/credit hour
Out-of-state tuition: full time: $580/credit hour
Room/board/expenses: $15,646
Full-time enrollment: 94
men: 71%; women: 29%; minorities: 49%; international: 38%
Part-time enrollment: 40
men: 73%; women: 28%; minorities: 78%; international: 10%
Acceptance rate: 86%
GRE requirement: Yes
Avg. GRE: quantitative: 152
TOEFL requirement: Yes
Minimum TOEFL score: N/A
Teaching assistantships: 2
Research assistantships: 2
Students reporting specialty: 0%
Students specializing in: N/A

University of Maryland-Baltimore County

1000 Hilltop Circle
Baltimore, MD 21250
www.umbc.edu/gradschool/
Public
Admissions: (410) 455-2537
Email: umbcgrad@umbc.edu
Financial aid: (410) 455-2387
Application deadline: N/A
In-state tuition: full time: $585/credit hour; part time: $585/credit hour
Out-of-state tuition: full time: $968/credit hour
Room/board/expenses: $19,434
Full-time enrollment: 325
men: 72%; women: 28%; minorities: 16%; international: 58%
Part-time enrollment: 314
men: 81%; women: 19%; minorities: 34%; international: 6%
Acceptance rate: 43%
GRE requirement: Yes
Avg. GRE: quantitative: 166
TOEFL requirement: Yes
Minimum TOEFL score: 550
Fellowships: 0
Teaching assistantships: 91
Research assistantships: 103
Students reporting specialty: 100%
Students specializing in: chemical: 4%; computer: 6%; computer science: 25%; electrical: 9%; management: 12%; environmental: 3%; mechanical: 12%; other: 30%

University of Maryland-College Park (Clark)

3110 Jeong H. Kim Engineering Building
College Park, MD 20742-2831
www.eng.umd.edu
Public
Admissions: (301) 405-0376
Email: gradschool@umd.edu
Financial aid: (301) 314-9000
Application deadline: N/A
In-state tuition: full time: $15,682; part time: $632/credit hour
Out-of-state tuition: full time: $30,302
Room/board/expenses: $18,294
Full-time enrollment: 1,750
men: 77%; women: 23%; minorities: 12%; international: 64%
Part-time enrollment: 568
men: 84%; women: 16%; minorities: 33%; international: 11%
Acceptance rate: 32%
GRE requirement: Yes
Avg. GRE: quantitative: 164
TOEFL requirement: Yes
Minimum TOEFL score: 574
Fellowships: 154
Teaching assistantships: 308
Research assistantships: 775
Students reporting specialty: 92%
Students specializing in: aerospace: 8%; biomedical: 4%; chemical: 3%; civil: 14%; computer science: 11%; electrical: 23%; materials: 4%; mechanical: 15%; other: 20%

MASSACHUSETTS

Boston University

44 Cummington Street
Boston, MA 02215
www.bu.edu/eng
Private
Admissions: (617) 353-9760
Email: enggrad@bu.edu
Financial aid: (617) 353-9760
Application deadline: 12/15
Tuition: full time: $48,122; part time: $1,482/credit hour
Room/board/expenses: $20,440
Full-time enrollment: 854
men: 71%; women: 29%; minorities: 13%; international: 56%
Part-time enrollment: 148
men: 77%; women: 23%; minorities: 13%; international: 45%
Acceptance rate: 24%
GRE requirement: Yes
Avg. GRE: quantitative: 164
TOEFL requirement: Yes
Minimum TOEFL score: 550
Fellowships: 103
Teaching assistantships: 100
Research assistantships: 375
Students reporting specialty: 100%
Students specializing in: biomedical: 24%; computer: 12%; computer science: 10%; electrical: 21%; industrial: 0%; materials: 6%; mechanical: 15%; other: 12%

Harvard University

29 Oxford Street
Room 217A, Pierce Hall
Cambridge, MA 02138
www.gsas.harvard.edu
Private
Admissions: (617) 495-5315
Email: admiss@fas.harvard.edu
Financial aid: (617) 495-5396
Application deadline: 12/15
Tuition: full time: $45,264; part time: N/A
Room/board/expenses: $27,350
Full-time enrollment: 434
men: 74%; women: 26%; minorities: 16%; international: 49%
Part-time enrollment: 14
men: 93%; women: 7%; minorities: 21%; international: 71%
Acceptance rate: 11%
GRE requirement: Yes
Avg. GRE: quantitative: 166
TOEFL requirement: Yes
Minimum TOEFL score: N/A
Fellowships: 104
Teaching assistantships: 126
Research assistantships: 279
Students reporting specialty: 100%
Students specializing in: computer: 13%; computer science: 16%; science and physics: 35%; other: 36%

Massachusetts Institute of Technology

77 Massachusetts Avenue
Room 1-206
Cambridge, MA 02139-4307
web.mit.edu/admissions/graduate/
Private
Admissions: (617) 253-3400
Email: mitgrad@mit.edu
Financial aid: (617) 253-4971
Application deadline: N/A
Tuition: full time: $46,704; part time: N/A
Room/board/expenses: $31,422
Full-time enrollment: 3,106
men: 72%; women: 28%; minorities: 21%; international: 43%
Part-time enrollment: 17
men: 65%; women: 35%; minorities: 53%; international: 12%
Acceptance rate: 14%
GRE requirement: Yes
Avg. GRE: quantitative: 167
Minimum TOEFL score: N/A
Fellowships: 620
Teaching assistantships: 299
Research assistantships: 1,624
Students reporting specialty: 100%
Students specializing in: aerospace: 7%; biomedical: 8%; chemical: 7%; civil: 4%; computer science: 15%; electrical: 12%; management: 10%; environmental: 2%; materials: 6%; mechanical: 18%; nuclear: 3%; petroleum: 0%; other: 7%

Northeastern University

130 Snell Engineering Center
Boston, MA 02115-5000
www.coe.neu.edu/gse
Private
Admissions: (617) 373-2711
Email: grad-eng@coe.neu.edu
Financial aid: (617) 373-3190
Application deadline: 01/15
Tuition: full time: $1,422/credit hour; part time: $1,422/credit hour
Room/board/expenses: $18,900
Full-time enrollment: 3,359
men: 69%; women: 31%; minorities: 3%; international: 88%
Part-time enrollment: 215
men: 80%; women: 20%; minorities: 17%; international: 9%
Acceptance rate: 37%
GRE requirement: Yes
Avg. GRE: quantitative: 161
TOEFL requirement: Yes
Minimum TOEFL score: 550
Fellowships: 80
Teaching assistantships: 105
Research assistantships: 388
Students reporting specialty: 100%
Students specializing in: biomedical: 1%; chemical: 2%; civil: 5%; computer: 2%; computer science: 20%; electrical: 12%; management: 9%; industrial: 12%; mechanical: 8%; other: 29%

Tufts University

Anderson Hall
Medford, MA 02155
asegrad.tufts.edu/
Private
Admissions: (617) 627-3395
Email: gradadmissions@tufts.edu
Financial aid: (617) 627-2000
Application deadline: N/A
Tuition: full time: $30,878; part time: $4,876/credit hour
Room/board/expenses: $22,350
Full-time enrollment: 549
men: 64%; women: 36%; minorities: 15%; international: 33%
Part-time enrollment: 69
men: 72%; women: 28%; minorities: 22%; international: 6%
Acceptance rate: 40%
GRE requirement: Yes
Avg. GRE: quantitative: 161
TOEFL requirement: Yes
Minimum TOEFL score: N/A
Fellowships: 18
Teaching assistantships: 70
Research assistantships: 172
Students reporting specialty: 100%
Students specializing in: biomedical: 14%; chemical: 8%; civil: 5%; computer science: 12%; electrical: 12%; management: 30%; environmental: 7%; mechanical: 9%; other: 2%

University of Massachusetts-Amherst

Room 125, Marston Hall
Amherst, MA 01003
www.umass.edu/gradschool
Public
Admissions: (413) 545-0722
Email: gradadm@grad.umass.edu
Financial aid: (413) 577-0555
Application deadline: 02/01
In-state tuition: full time: $15,329; part time: $110/credit hour
Out-of-state tuition: full time: $22,626
Room/board/expenses: $14,503
Full-time enrollment: 864
men: 69%; women: 31%; minorities: 8%; international: 63%
Part-time enrollment: N/A
men: N/A; women: N/A; minorities: N/A; international: N/A
Acceptance rate: 24%
GRE requirement: Yes
Avg. GRE: quantitative: 162
TOEFL requirement: Yes
Minimum TOEFL score: 550
Fellowships: 127
Teaching assistantships: 69
Research assistantships: 473
Students reporting specialty: 100%
Students specializing in: chemical: 7%; civil: 13%; computer science: 26%; electrical: 28%; management: 1%; industrial: 2%; materials: 12%; mechanical: 11%

University of Massachusetts-Dartmouth

285 Old Westport Road
North Dartmouth, MA 02747-2300
www.umassd.edu/graduate
Public
Admissions: (508) 999-8604
Email: graduate@umassd.edu
Financial aid: (508) 999-8632
Application deadline: 02/15
In-state tuition: full time: $14,699; part time: $86/credit hour
Out-of-state tuition: full time: $20,727
Room/board/expenses: $14,476
Full-time enrollment: 173
men: 71%; women: 29%; minorities: 4%; international: 80%
Part-time enrollment: 118
men: 82%; women: 18%; minorities: 8%; international: 58%
Acceptance rate: 75%
GRE requirement: Yes
Avg. GRE: quantitative: 154
TOEFL requirement: Yes
Minimum TOEFL score: 550
Fellowships: 11
Teaching assistantships: 35
Research assistantships: 29
Students reporting specialty: 100%
Students specializing in: biomedical: 9%; civil: 3%; computer: 9%; computer science: 42%; electrical: 19%; science and physics: 9%; mechanical: 8%; other: 2%

University of Massachusetts-Lowell (Francis)

1 University Avenue
Lowell, MA 01854
www.uml.edu/grad
Public
Admissions: (978) 934-2390
Email: graduate_school@uml.edu
Financial aid: (978) 934-4226
Application deadline: rolling
In-state tuition: full time: $13,799; part time: $766/credit hour
Out-of-state tuition: full time: $24,478
Room/board/expenses: $13,170
Full-time enrollment: 520
men: 74%; women: 26%; minorities: 7%; international: 70%
Part-time enrollment: 429
men: 81%; women: 19%; minorities: 22%; international: 16%
Acceptance rate: 62%
GRE requirement: Yes
Avg. GRE: quantitative: 158
TOEFL requirement: Yes
Minimum TOEFL score: 550
Fellowships: 12
Teaching assistantships: 127
Research assistantships: 173
Students reporting specialty: 100%
Students specializing in: biomedical: 13%; chemical: 4%; civil: 9%; computer: 10%; computer science: 19%; electrical: 18%; materials: 11%; mechanical: 15%; nuclear: 1%

Worcester Polytechnic Institute

100 Institute Road
Worcester, MA 01609-2280
grad.wpi.edu/
Private
Admissions: (508) 831-5301
Email: grad@wpi.edu
Financial aid: (508) 831-5469
Application deadline: rolling
Tuition: full time: $24,648; part time: $1,366/credit hour
Room/board/expenses: $23,373
Full-time enrollment: 463
men: 76%; women: 24%; minorities: 6%; international: 64%
Part-time enrollment: 661
men: 81%; women: 19%; minorities: 19%; international: 21%
Acceptance rate: 48%
GRE requirement: Yes
Avg. GRE: quantitative: 163
TOEFL requirement: Yes
Minimum TOEFL score: 563
Fellowships: 22
Teaching assistantships: 90
Research assistantships: 131
Students reporting specialty: 100%
Students specializing in: aerospace: 2%; biomedical: 4%; chemical: 3%; civil: 4%; computer science: 10%; electrical: 22%; environmental: 2%; industrial: 3%; materials: 8%; mechanical: 12%; other: 31%

MICHIGAN

Lawrence Technological University

21000 W. Ten Mile Road
Southfield, MI 48075
www.ltu.edu
Private
Admissions: (248) 204-3160
Email: admissions@ltu.edu
Financial aid: (248) 204-2126
Application deadline: rolling
Tuition: full time: $14,850; part time: $8,550
Room/board/expenses: $15,070
Full-time enrollment: 54
men: 81%; women: 19%; minorities: 2%; international: 83%
Part-time enrollment: 668
men: 87%; women: 13%; minorities: 2%; international: 79%
Acceptance rate: 42%
GRE requirement: No
Avg. GRE: quantitative: N/A
TOEFL requirement: Yes
Minimum TOEFL score: 550
Fellowships: 0
Teaching assistantships: 0
Research assistantships: 3
Students reporting specialty: 94%
Students specializing in: architectural: 2%; biomedical: 0%; civil: 10%; electrical: 22%; management: 9%; industrial: 10%; mechanical: 33%; other: 20%

Michigan State University

428 S.Shaw Lane
3410 Engineering Building
East Lansing, MI 48824
www.egr.msu.edu
Public
Admissions: (517) 355-8332
Email: egrgrad@egr.msu.edu
Financial aid: (517) 353-5940
Application deadline: 12/31
In-state tuition: full time: $747/credit hour; part time: $747/credit hour
Out-of-state tuition: full time: $1,401/credit hour
Room/board/expenses: $13,802
Full-time enrollment: 807
men: 78%; women: 22%; minorities: 7%; international: 64%
Part-time enrollment: N/A
men: N/A; women: N/A; minorities: N/A; international: N/A
Acceptance rate: 10%
GRE requirement: Yes
Avg. GRE: quantitative: 163
TOEFL requirement: Yes
Minimum TOEFL score: 550
Fellowships: 82
Teaching assistantships: 182
Research assistantships: 464
Students reporting specialty: 100%
Students specializing in: agriculture: 5%; chemical: 8%; civil: 12%; computer science: 18%; electrical: 27%; environmental: 7%; materials: 6%; mechanical: 17%

Michigan Technological University

1400 Townsend Drive
Houghton, MI 49931-1295
www.mtu.edu/gradschool/
Public
Admissions: (906) 487-2327
Email: gradadms@mtu.edu
Financial aid: (906) 487-2622
Application deadline: rolling
In-state tuition: full time: $17,655; part time: $862/credit hour
Out-of-state tuition: full time: $17,655
Room/board/expenses: $13,707
Full-time enrollment: 827
men: 78%; women: 22%; minorities: 3%; international: 79%
Part-time enrollment: 233
men: 82%; women: 18%; minorities: 8%; international: 46%
Acceptance rate: 31%
GRE requirement: Yes
Avg. GRE: quantitative: 162
TOEFL requirement: Yes
Minimum TOEFL score: 550
Fellowships: 49
Teaching assistantships: 95
Research assistantships: 138
Students reporting specialty: 100%
Students specializing in: biomedical: 4%; chemical: 4%; civil: 7%; computer: 2%; computer science: 4%; electrical: 24%; environmental: 10%; materials: 4%; mechanical: 35%; mining: 0%; other: 6%

Oakland University

2200 Squirrel Road
Rochester, MI 48309
oakland.edu/secs/
Public
Admissions: (248) 370-2700
Email: gradinfo@oakland.edu
Financial aid: (248) 370-2550
Application deadline: 07/15
In-state tuition: full time: $655/credit hour; part time: $655/credit hour
Out-of-state tuition: full time: $1,027/credit hour
Room/board/expenses: $11,658
Full-time enrollment: 262
men: 70%; women: 30%; minorities: 6%; international: 63%
Part-time enrollment: 367
men: 85%; women: 15%; minorities: 13%; international: 17%
Acceptance rate: 31%
GRE requirement: Yes
Avg. GRE: quantitative: N/A
TOEFL requirement: Yes
Minimum TOEFL score: 550
Teaching assistantships: 36
Research assistantships: 41
Students reporting specialty: 100%
Students specializing in: computer: 6%; computer science: 17%; electrical: 26%; management: 12%; industrial: 9%; mechanical: 31%

University of Detroit Mercy

4001 W. McNichols
Detroit, MI 48221-3038
www.udmercy.edu
Private
Admissions: (313) 993-1592
Email: admissions@udmercy.edu
Financial aid: N/A
Application deadline: rolling
Tuition: full time: $1,516/credit hour; part time: $1,516/credit hour
Room/board/expenses: N/A
Full-time enrollment: 111
men: 79%; women: 21%; minorities: 5%; international: 85%
Part-time enrollment: 70
men: 83%; women: 17%; minorities: 20%; international: 34%
Acceptance rate: 70%
GRE requirement: No
Avg. GRE: quantitative: N/A
TOEFL requirement: No
Minimum TOEFL score: N/A
Students reporting specialty: 89%
Students specializing in: civil: 11%; computer: 14%; computer science: 7%; electrical: 3%; management: 8%; environmental: 20%; mechanical: 17%; other: 20%

University of Michigan-Ann Arbor

Robert H. Lurie Engineering Center
Ann Arbor, MI 48109-2102
www.engin.umich.edu/college/academics/grad
Public
Admissions: (734) 647-7077
Email: coe-grad-ed@umich.edu
Financial aid: (734) 647-7077
Application deadline: rolling
In-state tuition: full time: $23,693; part time: $1,266/credit hour
Out-of-state tuition: full time: $44,405
Room/board/expenses: $20,130
Full-time enrollment: 3,005
men: 76%; women: 24%; minorities: 13%; international: 57%
Part-time enrollment: 359
men: 82%; women: 18%; minorities: 10%; international: 35%
Acceptance rate: 28%
GRE requirement: Yes
Avg. GRE: quantitative: 166
TOEFL requirement: Yes
Minimum TOEFL score: N/A
Teaching assistantships: 290
Research assistantships: 979
Students reporting specialty: 100%
Students specializing in: aerospace: 6%; biomedical: 6%; chemical: 5%; civil: 4%; computer science: 10%; electrical: 20%; environmental: 2%; industrial: 6%; materials: 5%; mechanical: 14%; nuclear: 4%; other: 22%

University of Michigan-Dearborn

4901 Evergreen Road
Dearborn, MI 48128
www.engin.umd.umich.edu/
Public
Admissions: (313) 593-1494
Email: umdgrad@umd.umich.edu
Financial aid: (517) 353-5940
Application deadline: 08/01
In-state tuition: full time: $730/credit hour; part time: $730/credit hour
Out-of-state tuition: full time: $1,230/credit hour
Room/board/expenses: $10,908
Full-time enrollment: 342
men: 77%; women: 23%; minorities: 4%; international: 94%
Part-time enrollment: 714
men: 81%; women: 19%; minorities: 19%; international: 28%
Acceptance rate: 53%
GRE requirement: Yes
Avg. GRE: quantitative: 156
TOEFL requirement: Yes
Minimum TOEFL score: 560
Teaching assistantships: 11
Research assistantships: 32
Students reporting specialty: 100%
Students specializing in: computer: 3%; computer science: 7%; electrical: 14%; management: 9%; science and physics: 13%; industrial: 8%; mechanical: 24%; other: 22%

Wayne State University

5050 Anthony Wayne Drive
Detroit, MI 48202
engineering.wayne.edu
Public
Admissions: (313) 577-2170
Email: gradadmissions@wayne.edu
Financial aid: (313) 577-2100
Application deadline: 06/01
In-state tuition: full time: $685/credit hour; part time: $685/credit hour
Out-of-state tuition: full time: $1,371/credit hour
Room/board/expenses: $16,431
Full-time enrollment: 1,055
men: 82%; women: 18%; minorities: 7%; international: 83%
Part-time enrollment: 379
men: 78%; women: 22%; minorities: 24%; international: 31%
Acceptance rate: 43%
GRE requirement: Yes
Avg. GRE: quantitative: 155
TOEFL requirement: Yes
Minimum TOEFL score: 550
Fellowships: 21
Teaching assistantships: 102
Research assistantships: 78
Students reporting specialty: 100%
Students specializing in: biomedical: 7%; chemical: 2%; civil: 6%; computer: 3%; computer science: 13%; electrical: 13%; management: 5%; industrial: 23%; materials: 2%; mechanical: 22%; other: 3%

Western Michigan University

1903 W. Michigan Avenue
Kalamazoo, MI 49008-5314
www.wmich.edu/engineer/
Public
Admissions: (269) 387-2000
Email: ask-wmu@wmich.edu
Financial aid: (269) 387-6000
Application deadline: rolling
In-state tuition: full time: $530/credit hour; part time: $530/credit hour
Out-of-state tuition: full time: $1,123/credit hour
Room/board/expenses: $13,751
Full-time enrollment: 499
men: 82%; women: 18%; minorities: 3%; international: 87%
Part-time enrollment: 140
men: 87%; women: 13%; minorities: 6%; international: 49%
Acceptance rate: 50%
GRE requirement: Yes
Avg. GRE: quantitative: 152
TOEFL requirement: Yes
Minimum TOEFL score: 550
Teaching assistantships: 62
Research assistantships: 35
Students reporting specialty: 100%
Students specializing in: aerospace: 1%; chemical: 2%; civil: 11%; computer: 3%; computer science: 15%; electrical: 23%; management: 8%; industrial: 17%; mechanical: 14%; other: 6%

MINNESOTA

Mayo Graduate School[1]

200 First Street SW
Rochester, MN 55905
www.mayo.edu/mgs/
Private
Admissions: N/A
Financial aid: N/A
Tuition: N/A
Room/board/expenses: N/A
Enrollment: N/A

University of Minnesota-Twin Cities

117 Pleasant Street SE
Minneapolis, MN 55455
www.cse.umn.edu
Public
Admissions: (612) 625-3014
Email: gsquest@umn.edu
Financial aid: (612) 624-1111
Application deadline: 12/15
In-state tuition: full time: $17,572; part time: $1,320/credit hour

More @ usnews.com/grad

Out-of-state tuition: full time: $26,236
Room/board/expenses: $15,466
Full-time enrollment: 1,563
men: 77%; women: 23%; minorities: 8%; international: 60%
Part-time enrollment: 338
men: 80%; women: 20%; minorities: 13%; international: 28%
Acceptance rate: 23%
GRE requirement: Yes
Avg. GRE: quantitative: 169
TOEFL requirement: Yes
Minimum TOEFL score: 550
Fellowships: 230
Teaching assistantships: 319
Research assistantships: 660
Students reporting specialty: 100%
Students specializing in: aerospace: 5%; biomedical: 9%; chemical: 7%; civil: 7%; computer science: 19%; electrical: 23%; management: 2%; industrial: 3%; materials: 5%; mechanical: 15%; other: 7%

MISSISSIPPI

Jackson State University

1400 John R. Lynch Street
Jackson, MS 39217
www.jsums.edu/
Public
Admissions: N/A
Email: graduate@jsums.edu
Financial aid: N/A
Application deadline: rolling
In-state tuition: full time: $6,866; part time: $381/credit hour
Out-of-state tuition: full time: $16,841
Room/board/expenses: $10,526
Full-time enrollment: 62
men: 77%; women: 23%; minorities: 82%; international: 55%
Part-time enrollment: 33
men: 70%; women: 30%; minorities: 61%; international: 15%
Acceptance rate: 33%
GRE requirement: Yes
Avg. GRE: quantitative: N/A
TOEFL requirement: Yes
Minimum TOEFL score: N/A
Students reporting specialty: 100%
Students specializing in: computer: 68%; computer science: 32%

Mississippi State University (Bagley)

PO Box 9544
Mississippi State, MS 39762
www.bagley.msstate.edu/
Public
Admissions: (662) 325-7400
Email: gradapps@grad.msstate.edu
Financial aid: (662) 325-2450
Application deadline: 07/01
In-state tuition: full time: $7,392; part time: $411/credit hour
Out-of-state tuition: full time: $20,032
Room/board/expenses: $18,190
Full-time enrollment: 357
men: 77%; women: 23%; minorities: 9%; international: 53%
Part-time enrollment: 269
men: 83%; women: 17%; minorities: 28%; international: 7%
Acceptance rate: 42%
GRE requirement: Yes
Avg. GRE: quantitative: 163
TOEFL requirement: Yes
Minimum TOEFL score: 477
Fellowships: 53
Teaching assistantships: 77
Research assistantships: 196
Students reporting specialty: 95%
Students specializing in: aerospace: 10%; agriculture: 0%; biomedical: 4%; chemical: 3%; civil: 16%; computer science: 11%; electrical: 16%; industrial: 16%; mechanical: 18%; other: 6%

University of Mississippi

Brevard Hall, Room 227
University, MS 38677-1848
www.engineering.olemiss.edu/
Public
Admissions: (662) 915-7474
Email: gschool@olemiss.edu
Financial aid: (800) 891-4596
Application deadline: 04/01
In-state tuition: full time: $7,344; part time: $408/credit hour
Out-of-state tuition: full time: $20,574
Room/board/expenses: $17,698
Full-time enrollment: 132
men: 77%; women: 23%; minorities: 10%; international: 51%
Part-time enrollment: 22
men: 86%; women: 14%; minorities: 9%; international: 18%
Acceptance rate: 26%
GRE requirement: Yes
Avg. GRE: quantitative: 156
TOEFL requirement: Yes
Minimum TOEFL score: N/A
Fellowships: 15
Teaching assistantships: 81
Research assistantships: 15
Students reporting specialty: 100%
Students specializing in: chemical: 5%; civil: 19%; computer science: 34%; electrical: 12%; mechanical: 12%; other: 17%

University of Southern Mississippi[1]

118 College Drive, #5050
Hattiesburg, MS 39406
www.usm.edu/graduate-school
Public
Admissions: (601) 266-4369
Financial aid: N/A
Tuition: N/A
Room/board/expenses: N/A
Enrollment: N/A

MISSOURI

Missouri University of Science & Technology

500 W. 16th Street, 110 ERL
Rolla, MO 65409-0840
www.mst.edu
Public
Admissions: (800) 522-0938
Email: admissions@mst.edu
Financial aid: (800) 522-0938
Application deadline: 07/01
In-state tuition: full time: $10,537; part time: $387/credit hour
Out-of-state tuition: full time: $27,015
Room/board/expenses: $14,076
Full-time enrollment: 800
men: 82%; women: 19%; minorities: 4%; international: 72%
Part-time enrollment: 374
men: 80%; women: 20%; minorities: 11%; international: 32%
Acceptance rate: 55%
GRE requirement: Yes
Avg. GRE: quantitative: 157
TOEFL requirement: Yes
Minimum TOEFL score: N/A
Fellowships: 19
Teaching assistantships: 90
Research assistantships: 335
Students reporting specialty: 100%
Students specializing in: aerospace: 3%; chemical: 5%; civil: 8%; computer: 4%; computer science: 7%; electrical: 18%; management: 9%; environmental: 1%; industrial: 2%; materials: 2%; mechanical: 11%; mining: 3%; nuclear: 4%; petroleum: 7%; other: 16%

St. Louis University (Parks)

3450 Lindell Boulevard
St. Louis, MO 63103
parks.slu.edu/grad
Private
Admissions: (314) 977-8306
Email: parksgraduateprograms@slu.edu
Financial aid: (314) 977-2350
Application deadline: 06/30
Tuition: full time: $1,050/credit hour; part time: $1,050/credit hour
Room/board/expenses: $18,940
Full-time enrollment: 81
men: 72%; women: 28%; minorities: 20%; international: 37%
Part-time enrollment: 18
men: 94%; women: 6%; minorities: 17%; international: 6%
Acceptance rate: 68%
GRE requirement: Yes
Avg. GRE: quantitative: N/A
TOEFL requirement: Yes
Minimum TOEFL score: 550
Fellowships: 7
Teaching assistantships: 0
Research assistantships: 18
Students reporting specialty: 79%
Students specializing in: aerospace: 37%; biomedical: 24%; civil: 31%; computer: 5%; electrical: 5%; mechanical: 37%; other: 3%

University of Missouri

W1025 Thomas and Nell Lafferre Hall
Columbia, MO 65211
www.missouri.edu/
Public
Admissions: (573) 882-7786
Email: gradadmin@missouri.edu
Financial aid: (573) 882-2751
Application deadline: rolling
In-state tuition: full time: $8,423; part time: $464/credit hour
Out-of-state tuition: full time: $17,493
Room/board/expenses: $17,048
Full-time enrollment: 361
men: 78%; women: 22%; minorities: 4%; international: 76%
Part-time enrollment: 283
men: 79%; women: 21%; minorities: 3%; international: 78%
Acceptance rate: 26%
GRE requirement: Yes
Avg. GRE: quantitative: 162
TOEFL requirement: Yes
Minimum TOEFL score: N/A
Fellowships: 34
Teaching assistantships: 98
Research assistantships: 196
Students reporting specialty: 100%
Students specializing in: biomedical: 8%; chemical: 5%; civil: 12%; computer: 3%; computer science: 20%; electrical: 21%; industrial: 5%; mechanical: 18%; nuclear: 5%; other: 2%

University of Missouri-Kansas City

534 R. H. Flarsheim Hall, 5100 Rockhill Road
Kansas City, MO 64110-2499
www.umkc.edu/sce
Public
Admissions: (816) 235-1111
Email: graduate@umkc.edu
Financial aid: (816) 235-1154
Application deadline: rolling
In-state tuition: full time: $345/credit hour; part time: $345/credit hour
Out-of-state tuition: full time: $891/credit hour
Room/board/expenses: $14,081
Full-time enrollment: 555
men: 72%; women: 28%; minorities: 2%; international: 96%
Part-time enrollment: 247
men: 77%; women: 23%; minorities: 4%; international: 72%
Acceptance rate: 41%
GRE requirement: Yes
Avg. GRE: quantitative: N/A
TOEFL requirement: Yes
Minimum TOEFL score: 550
Teaching assistantships: 20
Research assistantships: 28
Students reporting specialty: 0%
Students specializing in: N/A

Washington University in St. Louis

1 Brookings Drive
Campus Box 1100
St. Louis, MO 63130
www.engineering.wustl.edu/
Private
Admissions: (314) 935-7974
Email: gradengineering@seas.wustl.edu
Financial aid: (314) 935-5900
Application deadline: 01/15
Tuition: full time: $47,640; part time: $1,971/credit hour
Room/board/expenses: $22,200
Full-time enrollment: 826
men: 74%; women: 26%; minorities: 8%; international: 67%
Part-time enrollment: 361
men: 78%; women: 22%; minorities: 23%; international: 8%
Acceptance rate: 51%
GRE requirement: Yes
Avg. GRE: quantitative: 164
TOEFL requirement: Yes
Minimum TOEFL score: 550
Fellowships: 46
Teaching assistantships: 0
Research assistantships: 312
Students reporting specialty: 100%
Students specializing in: aerospace: 4%; biomedical: 11%; computer: 3%; computer science: 14%; electrical: 19%; management: 1%; environmental: 11%; industrial: 2%; materials: 1%; mechanical: 13%; other: 22%

MONTANA

Montana State University

212 Roberts Hall
PO Box 173820
Bozeman, MT 59717-3820
www.montana.edu/wwwdg
Public
Admissions: (406) 994-4145
Email: gradstudy@montana.edu
Financial aid: (406) 994-2845
Application deadline: rolling
In-state tuition: full time: $7,920; part time: $267/credit hour
Out-of-state tuition: full time: $17,020
Room/board/expenses: $12,950
Full-time enrollment: 98
men: 74%; women: 26%; minorities: 7%; international: 37%
Part-time enrollment: 109
men: 76%; women: 24%; minorities: 1%; international: 24%
Acceptance rate: 39%
GRE requirement: Yes
Avg. GRE: quantitative: 157
TOEFL requirement: Yes
Minimum TOEFL score: 580
Teaching assistantships: 66
Research assistantships: 73
Students reporting specialty: 100%
Students specializing in: biomedical: 0%; chemical: 11%; civil: 18%; computer science: 24%; electrical: 15%; environmental: 5%; industrial: 8%; mechanical: 17%; other: 1%

NEBRASKA

University of Nebraska-Lincoln

114 Othmer Hall
Lincoln, NE 68588-0642
www.engineering.unl.edu/graduate-programs
Public
Admissions: (402) 472-2875
Email: graduate@unl.edu
Financial aid: (402) 472-2030
Application deadline: rolling
In-state tuition: full time: $401/credit hour; part time: $401/credit hour
Out-of-state tuition: full time: $1,071/credit hour
Room/board/expenses: $13,320
Full-time enrollment: 531
men: 79%; women: 21%; minorities: 4%; international: 66%
Part-time enrollment: 96
men: 82%; women: 18%; minorities: 10%; international: 19%
Acceptance rate: 36%
GRE requirement: Yes
Avg. GRE: quantitative: 160
TOEFL requirement: Yes
Minimum TOEFL score: 550
Fellowships: 2
Teaching assistantships: 120
Research assistantships: 302
Students reporting specialty: 100%
Students specializing in: agriculture: 6%; architectural: 9%; biomedical: 2%; chemical: 3%; civil: 16%; computer: 6%; computer science: 16%; electrical: 15%; management: 3%; science and physics: 1%; environmental: 1%; materials: 4%; mechanical: 13%; other: 4%

NEVADA

University of Nevada-Las Vegas (Hughes)

4505 Maryland Parkway
Box 544005
Las Vegas, NV 89154-4005
go.unlv.edu/
Public
Admissions: (702) 895-3320
Email: gradcollege@unlv.edu
Financial aid: (702) 895-3697
Application deadline: 08/01
In-state tuition: full time: $9,455; part time: $264/credit hour
Out-of-state tuition: full time: $23,363
Room/board/expenses: $15,142
Full-time enrollment: 189
men: 72%; women: 28%; minorities: 19%; international: 55%
Part-time enrollment: 48
men: 73%; women: 27%; minorities: 31%; international: 17%
Acceptance rate: 68%
GRE requirement: Yes
Avg. GRE: quantitative: 155
TOEFL requirement: Yes
Minimum TOEFL score: 550
Fellowships: 15
Teaching assistantships: 61
Research assistantships: 39
Students reporting specialty: 99%
Students specializing in: biomedical: 1%; civil: 28%; computer science: 24%; electrical: 23%; mechanical: 23%; nuclear: 1%

University of Nevada-Reno

Mail Stop 0256
Reno, NV 89557-0256
www.unr.edu/grad/admissions
Public
Admissions: (775) 784-6869
Email: gradadmissions@unr.edu
Financial aid: (775) 784-4666
Application deadline: rolling
In-state tuition: full time: $371/credit hour; part time: $371/credit hour

Out-of-state tuition: full time: $1,289/credit hour
Room/board/expenses: $20,100
Full-time enrollment: 228
men: 75%; women: 25%; minorities: 14%; international: 65%
Part-time enrollment: 152
men: 76%; women: 24%; minorities: 17%; international: 36%
Acceptance rate: 52%
GRE requirement: Yes
Avg. GRE: quantitative: 159
TOEFL requirement: Yes
Minimum TOEFL score: 550
Fellowships: 5
Teaching assistantships: 81
Research assistantships: 127
Students reporting specialty: 99%
Students specializing in: biomedical: 3%; chemical: 3%; civil: 31%; computer: 34%; computer science: 35%; electrical: 10%; environmental: 31%; materials: 7%; mechanical: 12%

NEW HAMPSHIRE

Dartmouth College (Thayer)
14 Engineering Drive
Hanover, NH 03755
engineering.dartmouth.edu
Private
Admissions: (603) 646-2606
Email: engineering.admissions@dartmouth.edu
Financial aid: (603) 646-3844
Application deadline: 01/01
Tuition: full time: $48,508; part time: N/A
Room/board/expenses: $25,722
Full-time enrollment: 304
men: 71%; women: 29%; minorities: 9%; international: 68%
Part-time enrollment: N/A
men: N/A; women: N/A; minorities: N/A; international: N/A
Acceptance rate: 26%
GRE requirement: Yes
Avg. GRE: quantitative: 165
TOEFL requirement: Yes
Minimum TOEFL score: 600
Fellowships: 49
Teaching assistantships: 32
Research assistantships: 88
Students reporting specialty: 100%
Students specializing in: computer science: 37%; science and physics: 63%

University of New Hampshire
Kingsbury Hall
33 College Road
Durham, NH 03824
www.gradschool.unh.edu/
Public
Admissions: (603) 862-3000
Email: grad.school@unh.edu
Financial aid: (603) 862-3600
Application deadline: 02/15
In-state tuition: full time: $15,315; part time: $750/credit hour
Out-of-state tuition: full time: $28,275
Room/board/expenses: $16,500
Full-time enrollment: 156
men: 73%; women: 27%; minorities: 4%; international: 50%
Part-time enrollment: 115
men: 84%; women: 16%; minorities: 7%; international: 24%
Acceptance rate: 64%
GRE requirement: Yes
Avg. GRE: quantitative: 160
TOEFL requirement: Yes
Minimum TOEFL score: N/A
Fellowships: 9
Teaching assistantships: 70
Research assistantships: 55
Students reporting specialty: 100%

Students specializing in: chemical: 7%; civil: 29%; computer science: 24%; electrical: 14%; materials: 2%; mechanical: 18%; other: 6%

NEW JERSEY

New Jersey Institute of Technology
University Heights
Newark, NJ 07102-1982
www.njit.edu/
Public
Admissions: (973) 596-3300
Email: admissions@njit.edu
Financial aid: (973) 596-3479
Application deadline: 05/01
In-state tuition: full time: $21,152; part time: $1,006/credit hour
Out-of-state tuition: full time: $29,992
Room/board/expenses: $18,300
Full-time enrollment: 1,671
men: 73%; women: 27%; minorities: 8%; international: 87%
Part-time enrollment: 600
men: 78%; women: 22%; minorities: 51%; international: 9%
Acceptance rate: 86%
GRE requirement: Yes
Avg. GRE: quantitative: 157
TOEFL requirement: Yes
Minimum TOEFL score: 550
Fellowships: 4
Teaching assistantships: 80
Research assistantships: 108
Students reporting specialty: 100%
Students specializing in: biomedical: 6%; chemical: 6%; civil: 7%; computer: 3%; computer science: 26%; electrical: 17%; management: 7%; science and physics: 0%; environmental: 1%; industrial: 5%; mechanical: 7%; other: 15%

Princeton University
C230 Engineering Quadrangle
Princeton, NJ 08544-5263
engineering.princeton.edu
Private
Admissions: (609) 258-3034
Email: gsadmit@princeton.edu
Financial aid: (609) 258-3037
Application deadline: N/A
Tuition: full time: $45,350; part time: N/A
Room/board/expenses: $28,425
Full-time enrollment: 568
men: 74%; women: 26%; minorities: 12%; international: 58%
Part-time enrollment: N/A
men: N/A; women: N/A; minorities: N/A; international: N/A
Acceptance rate: 12%
GRE requirement: Yes
Avg. GRE: quantitative: 167
TOEFL requirement: Yes
Minimum TOEFL score: N/A
Fellowships: 159
Teaching assistantships: 144
Research assistantships: 257
Students reporting specialty: 100%
Students specializing in: aerospace: 17%; biomedical: 14%; chemical: 14%; civil: 10%; computer: 22%; computer science: 22%; electrical: 30%; environmental: 10%; mechanical: 17%; other: 8%

Rutgers, The State University of New Jersey-New Brunswick
98 Brett Road
Piscataway, NJ 08854-8058
gradstudy.rutgers.edu
Public
Admissions: (732) 932-7711
Email: gradadm@rci.rutgers.edu
Financial aid: (732) 932-7057
Application deadline: rolling

In-state tuition: full time: $18,346; part time: $678/credit hour
Out-of-state tuition: full time: $29,722
Room/board/expenses: $18,507
Full-time enrollment: 925
men: 78%; women: 22%; minorities: 8%; international: 80%
Part-time enrollment: 430
men: 74%; women: 26%; minorities: 20%; international: 53%
Acceptance rate: 20%
GRE requirement: Yes
Avg. GRE: quantitative: 164
TOEFL requirement: Yes
Minimum TOEFL score: 550
Fellowships: 108
Teaching assistantships: 171
Research assistantships: 149
Students reporting specialty: 100%
Students specializing in: biomedical: 8%; chemical: 13%; civil: 9%; computer science: 22%; electrical: 26%; industrial: 6%; materials: 4%; mechanical: 12%; other: 1%

Stevens Institute of Technology (Schaefer)
Castle Point on Hudson
Hoboken, NJ 07030
www.stevens.edu/ses/index.php
Private
Admissions: (201) 216-5197
Email: gradadmissions@stevens.edu
Financial aid: (201) 216-8143
Application deadline: rolling
Tuition: full time: $33,350; part time: $1,450/credit hour
Room/board/expenses: $15,750
Full-time enrollment: 1,520
men: 73%; women: 27%; minorities: 4%; international: 87%
Part-time enrollment: 553
men: 80%; women: 20%; minorities: 17%; international: 0%
Acceptance rate: 59%
GRE requirement: Yes
Avg. GRE: quantitative: 161
TOEFL requirement: Yes
Minimum TOEFL score: N/A
Fellowships: 42
Teaching assistantships: 134
Research assistantships: 83
Students reporting specialty: 100%
Students specializing in: biomedical: 2%; chemical: 2%; civil: 4%; computer: 5%; computer science: 21%; electrical: 14%; management: 4%; environmental: 2%; materials: 1%; mechanical: 9%; other: 36%

NEW MEXICO

New Mexico Institute of Mining and Technology
801 Leroy Place
Socorro, NM 87801
www.nmt.edu
Public
Admissions: (505) 835-5513
Email: graduate@nmt.edu
Financial aid: (505) 835-5333
Application deadline: rolling
In-state tuition: full time: $6,841; part time: $323/credit hour
Out-of-state tuition: full time: $20,250
Room/board/expenses: $13,488
Full-time enrollment: 143
men: 77%; women: 23%; minorities: 18%; international: 48%
Part-time enrollment: 63
men: 76%; women: 24%; minorities: 30%; international: 11%
Acceptance rate: 45%
GRE requirement: Yes
Avg. GRE: quantitative: 156
TOEFL requirement: Yes

Minimum TOEFL score: N/A
Fellowships: 2
Teaching assistantships: 31
Research assistantships: 35
Students reporting specialty: 100%
Students specializing in: computer science: 12%; electrical: 5%; management: 4%; environmental: 4%; materials: 15%; mechanical: 26%; mining: 11%; petroleum: 23%

New Mexico State University
PO Box 30001
Department 3449
Las Cruces, NM 88003
www.nmsu.edu
Public
Admissions: (575) 646-3121
Email: admissions@nmsu.edu
Financial aid: (505) 646-4105
Application deadline: rolling
In-state tuition: full time: $4,941; part time: $227/credit hour
Out-of-state tuition: full time: $15,107
Room/board/expenses: $13,050
Full-time enrollment: 314
men: 76%; women: 24%; minorities: 18%; international: 68%
Part-time enrollment: 204
men: 75%; women: 25%; minorities: 30%; international: 26%
Acceptance rate: 50%
GRE requirement: Yes
Avg. GRE: quantitative: 157
TOEFL requirement: No
Minimum TOEFL score: N/A
Fellowships: 18
Teaching assistantships: 87
Research assistantships: 128
Students reporting specialty: 99%
Students specializing in: aerospace: 3%; chemical: 8%; civil: 11%; computer science: 18%; electrical: 25%; environmental: 2%; industrial: 26%; mechanical: 7%

University of New Mexico
MSC 01 1140
1 University of New Mexico
Albuquerque, NM 87131
admissions.unm.edu/graduate
Public
Admissions: (505) 277-8900
Email: chat@studentinfo.unm.edu
Financial aid: (505) 277-8900
Application deadline: 07/15
In-state tuition: full time: $5,613; part time: $254/credit hour
Out-of-state tuition: full time: $858/credit hour
Room/board/expenses: $15,684
Full-time enrollment: 853
men: 80%; women: 20%; minorities: 18%; international: 42%
Part-time enrollment: N/A
men: N/A; women: N/A; minorities: N/A; international: N/A
Acceptance rate: 46%
GRE requirement: Yes
Avg. GRE: quantitative: 157
TOEFL requirement: Yes
Minimum TOEFL score: 550
Fellowships: 14
Teaching assistantships: 40
Research assistantships: 332
Students reporting specialty: 97%
Students specializing in: biomedical: 2%; chemical: 3%; civil: 12%; computer: 7%; computer science: 25%; electrical: 21%; industrial: 0%; mechanical: 12%; nuclear: 6%; other: 11%

NEW YORK

Alfred University-New York State College of Ceramics (Inamori)
2 Pine Street
Alfred, NY 14802-1296
nyscc.alfred.edu
Public
Admissions: (800) 541-9229
Email: admwww@alfred.edu
Financial aid: (607) 871-2159
Application deadline: rolling
In-state tuition: full time: $24,634; part time: $810/credit hour
Out-of-state tuition: full time: $24,634
Room/board/expenses: $15,260
Full-time enrollment: 40
men: 80%; women: 20%; minorities: 0%; international: 40%
Part-time enrollment: 15
men: 73%; women: 27%; minorities: 0%; international: 0%
Acceptance rate: 37%
GRE requirement: No
Avg. GRE: quantitative: N/A
TOEFL requirement: Yes
Minimum TOEFL score: N/A
Fellowships: 1
Teaching assistantships: 11
Research assistantships: 14
Students reporting specialty: 0%
Students specializing in: N/A

Binghamton University-SUNY (Watson)
PO Box 6000
Binghamton, NY 13902-6000
watson.binghamton.edu
Public
Admissions: (607) 777-2151
Email: gradsch@binghamton.edu
Financial aid: (607) 777-2428
Application deadline: rolling
In-state tuition: full time: $12,915; part time: $453/credit hour
Out-of-state tuition: full time: $24,255
Room/board/expenses: $17,784
Full-time enrollment: 768
men: 75%; women: 25%; minorities: 7%; international: 82%
Part-time enrollment: 341
men: 80%; women: 20%; minorities: 13%; international: 54%
Acceptance rate: 50%
GRE requirement: Yes
Avg. GRE: quantitative: 159
TOEFL requirement: Yes
Minimum TOEFL score: 550
Fellowships: 4
Teaching assistantships: 106
Research assistantships: 142
Students reporting specialty: 100%
Students specializing in: biomedical: 5%; computer science: 35%; electrical: 18%; industrial: 27%; materials: 2%; mechanical: 9%; other: 4%

Clarkson University
8 Clarkson Avenue
Box 5700
Potsdam, NY 13699
www.clarkson.edu/engineering/graduate/index.html
Private
Admissions: (315) 268-3802
Email: enggrad@clarkson.edu
Financial aid: (315) 268-7929
Application deadline: rolling
Tuition: full time: $1,457/credit hour; part time: $1,457/credit hour
Room/board/expenses: $14,734
Full-time enrollment: 156
men: 76%; women: 24%; minorities: 5%; international: 65%
Part-time enrollment: 17
men: 88%; women: 12%; minorities: 6%; international: 6%
Acceptance rate: 66%
GRE requirement: Yes

Avg. GRE: quantitative: 160
TOEFL requirement: Yes
Minimum TOEFL score: 550
Fellowships: 10
Teaching assistantships: 44
Research assistantships: 66
Students reporting specialty: 100%
Students specializing in: chemical: 12%; civil: 18%; electrical: 24%; science and physics: 3%; environmental: 13%; materials: 4%; mechanical: 25%

Columbia University (Fu Foundation)

500 W. 120th Street
Room 510 Mudd
New York, NY 10027
www.engineering.columbia.edu
Private
Admissions: (212) 854-6438
Email: seasgradmit@columbia.edu
Financial aid: (212) 854-6438
Application deadline: 02/15
Tuition: full time: $47,774; part time: $1,782/credit hour
Room/board/expenses: $27,195
Full-time enrollment: 2,025
men: 70%; women: 30%; minorities: 8%; international: 78%
Part-time enrollment: 1,187
men: 67%; women: 33%; minorities: 10%; international: 68%
Acceptance rate: 24%
GRE requirement: Yes
Avg. GRE: quantitative: 166
TOEFL requirement: Yes
Minimum TOEFL score: 590
Fellowships: 106
Teaching assistantships: 141
Research assistantships: 382
Students reporting specialty: 100%
Students specializing in: biomedical: 5%; chemical: 6%; civil: 8%; computer: 2%; computer science: 17%; electrical: 16%; management: 5%; science and physics: 2%; environmental: 4%; industrial: 19%; materials: 3%; mechanical: 8%; other: 5%

Cornell University

242 Carpenter Hall
Ithaca, NY 14853
www.engineering.cornell.edu
Private
Admissions: (607) 255-5820
Email: engr_grad@cornell.edu
Financial aid: (607) 255-5820
Application deadline: N/A
Tuition: full time: $29,581; part time: $2,038/credit hour
Room/board/expenses: $24,658
Full-time enrollment: 1,908
men: 68%; women: 32%; minorities: 16%; international: 55%
Part-time enrollment: 93
men: 82%; women: 18%; minorities: 34%; international: 2%
Acceptance rate: 28%
GRE requirement: Yes
Avg. GRE: quantitative: 166
TOEFL requirement: Yes
Minimum TOEFL score: N/A
Fellowships: 395
Teaching assistantships: 223
Research assistantships: 440
Students reporting specialty: 100%
Students specializing in: aerospace: 1%; agriculture: 3%; biomedical: 10%; chemical: 10%; civil: 5%; computer: 17%; computer science: 17%; management: 2%; science and physics: 4%; industrial: 9%; materials: 5%; mechanical: 8%; other: 9%

CUNY-City College (Grove)

Convent Avenue at 138th Street
New York, NY 10031
www.ccny.cuny.edu/admissions
Public
Admissions: (212) 650-6853
Email: graduateadmissions@ccny.cuny.edu
Financial aid: (212) 650-6656
Application deadline: 05/01
In-state tuition: full time: $12,147; part time: $505/credit hour
Out-of-state tuition: full time: $870/credit hour
Room/board/expenses: $28,715
Full-time enrollment: 332
men: 68%; women: 32%; minorities: 34%; international: 46%
Part-time enrollment: 210
men: 78%; women: 22%; minorities: 58%; international: 14%
Acceptance rate: 50%
GRE requirement: Yes
Avg. GRE: quantitative: 159
TOEFL requirement: Yes
Minimum TOEFL score: 550
Fellowships: 115
Teaching assistantships: 39
Research assistantships: 125
Students reporting specialty: 97%
Students specializing in: biomedical: 11%; chemical: 10%; civil: 23%; computer science: 18%; electrical: 23%; environmental: 2%; mechanical: 13%

New York University

6 MetroTech Center
Brooklyn, NY 11201
engineering.nyu.edu/
Private
Admissions: (646) 997-3200
Email: engineering.gradinfo@nyu.edu
Financial aid: (646) 997-3182
Application deadline: 02/15
Tuition: full time: $1,546/credit hour; part time: $1,546/credit hour
Room/board/expenses: $30,896
Full-time enrollment: 1,999
men: 75%; women: 25%; minorities: 5%; international: 90%
Part-time enrollment: 497
men: 72%; women: 28%; minorities: 34%; international: 31%
Acceptance rate: 34%
GRE requirement: Yes
Avg. GRE: quantitative: 163
TOEFL requirement: Yes
Minimum TOEFL score: 550
Fellowships: 20
Teaching assistantships: 13
Research assistantships: 237
Students reporting specialty: 100%
Students specializing in: biomedical: 4%; chemical: 2%; civil: 11%; computer: 7%; computer science: 28%; electrical: 22%; management: 16%; environmental: 1%; industrial: 5%; mechanical: 4%

Rensselaer Polytechnic Institute

Jonsson Engineering Center 3004
Troy, NY 12180-3590
www.rpi.edu
Private
Admissions: (518) 276-6216
Email: admissions@rpi.edu
Financial aid: (518) 276-6813
Application deadline: 01/01
Tuition: full time: $50,439; part time: $2,000/credit hour
Room/board/expenses: $16,161
Full-time enrollment: 537
men: 76%; women: 24%; minorities: 10%; international: 55%
Part-time enrollment: 144
men: 77%; women: 23%; minorities: 11%; international: 10%
Acceptance rate: 27%
GRE requirement: Yes
Avg. GRE: quantitative: 163
TOEFL requirement: Yes
Minimum TOEFL score: N/A
Fellowships: 35
Teaching assistantships: 178
Research assistantships: 298
Students reporting specialty: 100%
Students specializing in: aerospace: 5%; biomedical: 7%; chemical: 10%; civil: 4%; computer: 2%; computer science: 15%; electrical: 14%; management: 2%; science and physics: 1%; environmental: 1%; industrial: 2%; materials: 8%; mechanical: 24%; nuclear: 4%

Rochester Institute of Technology (Gleason)

77 Lomb Memorial Drive
Rochester, NY 14623
www.rit.edu
Private
Admissions: (585) 475-2229
Email: gradinfo@rit.edu
Financial aid: (585) 475-5520
Application deadline: rolling
Tuition: full time: $40,426; part time: $1,673/credit hour
Room/board/expenses: $13,944
Full-time enrollment: 999
men: 79%; women: 21%; minorities: 3%; international: 82%
Part-time enrollment: 161
men: 90%; women: 10%; minorities: 8%; international: 35%
Acceptance rate: 39%
GRE requirement: No
Avg. GRE: quantitative: 159
TOEFL requirement: Yes
Minimum TOEFL score: 550
Fellowships: 6
Teaching assistantships: 73
Research assistantships: 170
Students reporting specialty: 100%
Students specializing in: computer: 6%; computer science: 42%; electrical: 18%; management: 2%; science and physics: 2%; industrial: 4%; mechanical: 12%; other: 15%

Stony Brook University-SUNY

Engineering Room 100
Stony Brook, NY 11794-2200
www.grad.stonybrook.edu
Public
Admissions: (631) 632-7035
Email: gradadmissions@stonybrook.edu
Financial aid: (631) 632-6840
Application deadline: N/A
In-state tuition: full time: $12,421; part time: $453/credit hour
Out-of-state tuition: full time: $23,761
Room/board/expenses: $18,514
Full-time enrollment: 1,283
men: 72%; women: 28%; minorities: 9%; international: 80%
Part-time enrollment: 251
men: 76%; women: 24%; minorities: 9%; international: 61%
Acceptance rate: 32%
GRE requirement: Yes
Avg. GRE: quantitative: 165
TOEFL requirement: Yes
Minimum TOEFL score: N/A
Fellowships: 15
Teaching assistantships: 197
Research assistantships: 239
Students reporting specialty: 100%
Students specializing in: biomedical: 5%; computer: 4%; computer science: 33%; electrical: 8%; materials: 9%; mechanical: 12%; other: 29%

SUNY College of Environmental Science and Forestry[1]

227 Bray Hall
Syracuse, NY 13210
www.esf.edu/
Public
Admissions: N/A
Email: esfgrad@esf.edu
Financial aid: N/A
Tuition: N/A
Room/board/expenses: N/A
Enrollment: N/A

Syracuse University

223 Link Hall
Syracuse, NY 13244-1240
www.lcs.syr.edu/
Private
Admissions: (315) 443-4492
Financial aid: (315) 443-1513
Application deadline: rolling
Tuition: full time: $26,632; part time: $1,388/credit hour
Room/board/expenses: $16,490
Full-time enrollment: 973
men: 75%; women: 25%; minorities: 3%; international: 88%
Part-time enrollment: 174
men: 83%; women: 17%; minorities: 14%; international: 43%
Acceptance rate: 34%
GRE requirement: Yes
Avg. GRE: quantitative: 163
TOEFL requirement: Yes
Minimum TOEFL score: 550
Fellowships: 27
Teaching assistantships: 109
Research assistantships: 80
Students reporting specialty: 100%
Students specializing in: aerospace: 6%; biomedical: 6%; chemical: 5%; civil: 9%; computer: 19%; computer science: 16%; electrical: 10%; management: 6%; environmental: 2%; mechanical: 11%; other: 11%

University at Buffalo-SUNY

208 Davis Hall
Buffalo, NY 14260-1900
www.eng.buffalo.edu
Public
Admissions: (716) 645-2771
Email: seasgrad@buffalo.edu
Financial aid: (716) 645-2450
Application deadline: rolling
In-state tuition: full time: $13,165; part time: $453/credit hour
Out-of-state tuition: full time: $24,505
Room/board/expenses: $17,333
Full-time enrollment: 1,691
men: 77%; women: 23%; minorities: 3%; international: 86%
Part-time enrollment: 58
men: 83%; women: 17%; minorities: 14%; international: 0%
Acceptance rate: 31%
GRE requirement: Yes
Avg. GRE: quantitative: 162
TOEFL requirement: Yes
Minimum TOEFL score: N/A
Fellowships: 54
Teaching assistantships: 168
Research assistantships: 203
Students reporting specialty: 100%
Students specializing in: aerospace: 2%; biomedical: 4%; chemical: 7%; civil: 9%; computer science: 36%; electrical: 20%; science and physics: 0%; industrial: 12%; mechanical: 9%

University of Rochester

Lattimore Hall
Box 270076
Rochester, NY 14627-0076
www.Hajim.rochester.edu
Private
Admissions: (585) 275-2059
Email: graduate.admissions@rochester.edu
Financial aid: (585) 275-3226
Application deadline: N/A
Tuition: full time: $1,482/credit hour; part time: $1,482/credit hour
Room/board/expenses: $15,530
Full-time enrollment: 569
men: 75%; women: 25%; minorities: 5%; international: 64%
Part-time enrollment: 33
men: 76%; women: 24%; minorities: 6%; international: 21%
Acceptance rate: 38%
GRE requirement: Yes
Avg. GRE: quantitative: 164
TOEFL requirement: Yes
Minimum TOEFL score: 577
Fellowships: 35
Teaching assistantships: 211
Research assistantships: 205
Students reporting specialty: 99%
Students specializing in: biomedical: 12%; chemical: 9%; computer science: 12%; electrical: 24%; materials: 6%; mechanical: 8%; other: 29%

NORTH CAROLINA

Duke University (Pratt)

305 Teer Building
Durham, NC 27708-0271
www.pratt.duke.edu
Private
Admissions: (919) 684-3913
Email: grad-admissions@duke.edu
Financial aid: (919) 681-1552
Application deadline: 12/08
Tuition: full time: $52,213; part time: $2,875/credit hour
Room/board/expenses: $25,384
Full-time enrollment: 991
men: 67%; women: 33%; minorities: 11%; international: 55%
Part-time enrollment: 76
men: 76%; women: 24%; minorities: 18%; international: 7%
Acceptance rate: 24%
GRE requirement: Yes
Avg. GRE: quantitative: 164
TOEFL requirement: Yes
Minimum TOEFL score: 577
Fellowships: 208
Teaching assistantships: 14
Research assistantships: 333
Students reporting specialty: 100%
Students specializing in: biomedical: 20%; civil: 5%; computer science: 9%; electrical: 22%; management: 29%; mechanical: 7%; other: 8%

North Carolina A&T State University

1601 E. Market Street
651 McNair Hall
Greensboro, NC 27411
www.ncat.edu/academics/schools-colleges1/grad/admissions/index.html
Public
Admissions: (336) 285-2366
Email: grad@ncat.edu
Financial aid: (336) 334-7973
Application deadline: 10/16
In-state tuition: full time: $5,972; part time: $140/credit hour
Out-of-state tuition: full time: $18,732
Room/board/expenses: $11,021
Full-time enrollment: 272
men: 63%; women: 37%; minorities: 50%; international: 42%
Part-time enrollment: 147
men: 71%; women: 29%; minorities: 61%; international: 29%
Acceptance rate: 65%
GRE requirement: Yes
Avg. GRE: quantitative: N/A
TOEFL requirement: Yes
Minimum TOEFL score: 550
Fellowships: 15
Teaching assistantships: 100
Research assistantships: 50
Students reporting specialty: 0%
Students specializing in: N/A

North Carolina State University

PO Box 7901
Raleigh, NC 27695
www.engr.ncsu.edu/
Public
Admissions: (919) 515-2872
Email: graduate_application@ncsu.edu
Financial aid: (919) 515-2421
Application deadline: 06/25
In-state tuition: full time: $10,748; part time: $8,785
Out-of-state tuition: full time: $24,847

Room/board/expenses: $19,284
Full-time enrollment: 2,751
men: 77%; women: 23%;
minorities: 6%; international: 69%
Part-time enrollment: 611
men: 82%; women: 18%;
minorities: 16%; international: 19%
Acceptance rate: 16%
GRE requirement: Yes
Avg. GRE: quantitative: 164
TOEFL requirement: Yes
Minimum TOEFL score: 550
Fellowships: 255
Teaching assistantships: 301
Research assistantships: 830
Students reporting specialty: 100%
Students specializing in:
aerospace: 3%; agriculture:
2%; biomedical: 3%; chemical:
5%; civil: 9%; computer:
6%; computer science: 21%;
electrical: 19%; environmental:
1%; industrial: 4%; materials: 4%;
mechanical: 10%; nuclear: 3%;
other: 8%

University of North Carolina–Chapel Hill

CB #7431, 166 Rosenau Hall
Chapel Hill, NC 27599-7431
www.sph.unc.edu/envr
Public
Admissions: (919) 966-3844
Email: jack_whaley@unc.edu
Financial aid: (919) 966-3844
Application deadline: rolling
In-state tuition: full time: $11,935;
part time: $862/credit hour
Out-of-state tuition: full time:
$28,389
Room/board/expenses: $23,770
Full-time enrollment: 110
men: 39%; women: 61%;
minorities: 6%; international: 28%
Part-time enrollment: 2
men: 50%; women: 50%;
minorities: 0%; international: 0%
Acceptance rate: 37%
GRE requirement: Yes
Avg. GRE: quantitative: 159
TOEFL requirement: Yes
Minimum TOEFL score: 550
Fellowships: 19
Teaching assistantships: 9
Research assistantships: 40
Students reporting specialty: 100%
Students specializing in:
environmental: 100%

University of North Carolina–Charlotte (Lee)

Duke Centennial Hall
9201 University City Boulevard
Charlotte, NC 28223-0001
graduateschool.uncc.edu
Public
Admissions: (704) 687-5503
Email: gradadm@uncc.edu
Financial aid: (704) 687-5504
Application deadline: rolling
In-state tuition: full time: $8,832;
part time: $7,800
Out-of-state tuition: full time:
$21,503
Room/board/expenses: $13,599
Full-time enrollment: 453
men: 80%; women: 20%;
minorities: 2%; international: 78%
Part-time enrollment: 220
men: 78%; women: 22%;
minorities: 18%; international: 41%
Acceptance rate: 51%
GRE requirement: Yes
Avg. GRE: quantitative: 161
TOEFL requirement: Yes
Minimum TOEFL score: 557
Fellowships: 7
Teaching assistantships: 120
Research assistantships: 118
Students reporting specialty: 100%
Students specializing in: civil: 6%;
electrical: 41%; management:
13%; environmental: 8%;
mechanical: 20%; other: 12%

NORTH DAKOTA

North Dakota State University

NDSU Dept. 2450
P.O. Box 6050
Fargo, ND 58108-6050
www.ndsu.nodak.edu/ndsu/cea/
Public
Admissions: (701) 231-7033
Email:
ndsu.grad.school@ndsu.edu
Financial aid: (701) 231-7533
Application deadline: rolling
In-state tuition: full time: $331/
credit hour; part time: $331/
credit hour
Out-of-state tuition: full time: $883/
credit hour
Room/board/expenses: $10,482
Full-time enrollment: 69
men: 83%; women: 17%;
minorities: 64%; international:
77%
Part-time enrollment: 156
men: 81%; women: 19%;
minorities: 57%; international:
61%
Acceptance rate: 38%
GRE requirement: Yes
Avg. GRE: quantitative: 161
TOEFL requirement: Yes
Minimum TOEFL score: 525
Fellowships: 4
Teaching assistantships: 76
Research assistantships: 69
Students reporting specialty: 100%
Students specializing in:
agriculture: 10%; civil: 19%;
electrical: 32%; environmental:
3%; industrial: 10%; mechanical:
12%; other: 14%

University of North Dakota

243 Centennial Drive, Stop 8155
Grand Forks, ND 58202-8155
und.edu/
Public
Admissions: (701) 777-2945
Email: questions@
gradschool.und.edu
Financial aid: N/A
Application deadline: rolling
In-state tuition: full time: $353/
credit hour; part time: $353/
credit hour
Out-of-state tuition: full time: $499/
credit hour
Room/board/expenses: N/A
Full-time enrollment: 127
men: 87%; women: 13%;
minorities: 0%; international: 0%
Part-time enrollment: N/A
men: N/A; women: N/A; minorities:
N/A; international: N/A
GRE requirement: Yes
Avg. GRE: quantitative: N/A
TOEFL requirement: N/A
Minimum TOEFL score: 525
Students reporting specialty: 76%
Students specializing in: chemical:
18%; civil: 11%; electrical: 46%;
mechanical: 25%

OHIO

Air Force Institute of Technology[1]

AFIT/RRA
2950 P Street
Wright Patterson AFB, OH 45433-7765
www.afit.edu
Public
Admissions: (800) 211-5097
Email: counselors@afit.edu
Financial aid: N/A
Tuition: N/A
Room/board/expenses: N/A
Enrollment: N/A

Case Western Reserve University

500 Nord Hall
10900 Euclid Avenue
Cleveland, OH 44106-7220
gradstudies.case.edu
Private
Admissions: (216) 368-4390
Email: gradstudies@case.edu
Financial aid: (216) 368-4530
Application deadline: rolling
Tuition: full time: $41,169; part
time: $1,714/credit hour
Room/board/expenses: $17,010
Full-time enrollment: 607
men: 72%; women: 28%;
minorities: 9%; international: 66%
Part-time enrollment: 64
men: 83%; women: 17%;
minorities: 22%; international:
20%
Acceptance rate: 34%
GRE requirement: Yes
Avg. GRE: quantitative: 165
TOEFL requirement: Yes
Minimum TOEFL score: 577
Fellowships: 46
Teaching assistantships: 33
Research assistantships: 276
Students reporting specialty: 100%
Students specializing in:
aerospace: 2%; biomedical:
18%; chemical: 20%; civil: 3%;
computer: 4%; computer science:
8%; electrical: 17%; management:
9%; materials: 4%; mechanical:
14%; other: 1%

Cleveland State University

2121 Euclid Avenue, FH 104
Cleveland, OH 44115-2425
www.csuohio.edu/engineering
Public
Admissions: (216) 687-5599
Email: graduate.admissions@
csuohio.edu
Financial aid: (216) 687-3764
Application deadline: 07/01
In-state tuition: full time: $531/
credit hour; part time: $531/
credit hour
Out-of-state tuition: full time: $999/
credit hour
Room/board/expenses: $16,856
Full-time enrollment: 479
men: 80%; women: 20%;
minorities: 3%; international: 88%
Part-time enrollment: 239
men: 81%; women: 19%;
minorities: 10%; international:
33%
Acceptance rate: 53%
GRE requirement: Yes
Avg. GRE: quantitative: 157
TOEFL requirement: Yes
Minimum TOEFL score: 525
Fellowships: 0
Teaching assistantships: 66
Research assistantships: 44
Students reporting specialty: 100%
Students specializing in:
biomedical: 7%; chemical: 5%;
civil: 9%; computer science: 11%;
electrical: 44%; environmental:
1%; industrial: 0%; mechanical:
16%; other: 7%

Ohio State University

2070 Neil Avenue
Columbus, OH 43210-1278
engineering.osu.edu/graduate/
admissions
Public
Admissions: (614) 292-9444
Email: gpadmissions@osu.edu
Financial aid: (614) 292-0300
Application deadline: rolling
In-state tuition: full time: $12,935;
part time: $746/credit hour
Out-of-state tuition: full time:
$32,407
Room/board/expenses: $15,274
Full-time enrollment: 1,741
men: 77%; women: 23%;
minorities: 6%; international: 67%
Part-time enrollment: 142
men: 78%; women: 22%;
minorities: 14%; international:
25%

Acceptance rate: 17%
GRE requirement: Yes
Avg. GRE: quantitative: 165
TOEFL requirement: Yes
Minimum TOEFL score: 550
Fellowships: 100
Teaching assistantships: 218
Research assistantships: 732
Students reporting specialty: 100%
Students specializing in:
aerospace: 3%; agriculture:
3%; biomedical: 4%; chemical:
5%; civil: 5%; computer: 16%;
electrical: 27%; management: 1%;
environmental: 1%; industrial: 9%;
materials: 10%; mechanical: 13%;
nuclear: 2%

Ohio University (Russ)

150 Stocker Center
Athens, OH 45701
www.ohio.edu/engineering
Public
Admissions: (740) 593-2800
Email: graduate@ohio.edu
Financial aid: (740) 593-4141
Application deadline: rolling
In-state tuition: full time: $9,810;
part time: $505/credit hour
Out-of-state tuition: full time:
$17,802
Room/board/expenses: $11,500
Full-time enrollment: 260
men: 74%; women: 26%;
minorities: 33%; international:
62%
Part-time enrollment: 271
men: 84%; women: 16%;
minorities: 4%; international: 8%
Acceptance rate: 33%
GRE requirement: Yes
Avg. GRE: quantitative: 159
TOEFL requirement: Yes
Minimum TOEFL score: 500
Fellowships: 15
Teaching assistantships: 117
Research assistantships: 170
Students reporting specialty: 100%
Students specializing in:
biomedical: 2%; chemical: 9%;
civil: 21%; computer science: 7%;
electrical: 24%; management:
22%; industrial: 7%; mechanical:
8%

University of Akron

201 ASEC
Akron, OH 44325-3901
www.uakron.edu/gradsch/
Public
Admissions: (330) 972-7663
Email: gradschool@uakron.edu
Financial aid: (330) 972-7663
Application deadline: rolling
In-state tuition: full time: $10,008;
part time: $442/credit hour
Out-of-state tuition: full time:
$15,514
Room/board/expenses: $14,958
Full-time enrollment: 355
men: 77%; women: 23%;
minorities: 3%; international: 81%
Part-time enrollment: 83
men: 86%; women: 14%;
minorities: 11%; international: 25%
Acceptance rate: 56%
GRE requirement: Yes
Avg. GRE: quantitative: 157
TOEFL requirement: Yes
Minimum TOEFL score: N/A
Fellowships: 1
Teaching assistantships: 134
Research assistantships: 163
Students reporting specialty: 100%
Students specializing in:
biomedical: 7%; chemical:
19%; civil: 23%; computer: 1%;
electrical: 18%; management: 3%;
mechanical: 30%; other: 1%

University of Cincinnati

PO Box 210077
Cincinnati, OH 45221-0077
www.eng.uc.edu
Public
Admissions: (513) 556-6347
Email: engrgrad@uc.edu

Financial aid: (513) 556-3647
Application deadline: 03/15
In-state tuition: full time: $17,604;
part time: $640/credit hour
Out-of-state tuition: full time:
$29,346
Room/board/expenses: $12,819
Full-time enrollment: 775
men: 75%; women: 25%;
minorities: 3%; international: 70%
Part-time enrollment: 33
men: 100%; women: 0%;
minorities: 15%; international: 0%
Acceptance rate: 16%
GRE requirement: Yes
Avg. GRE: quantitative: 161
TOEFL requirement: Yes
Minimum TOEFL score: 580
Fellowships: 43
Teaching assistantships: 129
Research assistantships: 367
Students reporting specialty: 100%
Students specializing in:
aerospace: 15%; biomedical: 2%;
chemical: 5%; civil: 6%; computer:
7%; computer science: 13%;
electrical: 10%; environmental:
8%; materials: 10%; mechanical:
24%

University of Dayton

300 College Park
Dayton, OH 45469-0254
www.udayton.edu/apply
Private
Admissions: (937) 229-4411
Email:
gradadmission@udayton.edu
Financial aid: (937) 229-4311
Application deadline: rolling
Tuition: full time: $951/credit hour;
part time: $951/credit hour
Room/board/expenses: $15,230
Full-time enrollment: 555
men: 80%; women: 20%;
minorities: 5%; international: 64%
Part-time enrollment: 174
men: 77%; women: 23%;
minorities: 4%; international: 44%
Acceptance rate: 15%
GRE requirement: Yes
Avg. GRE: quantitative: 156
TOEFL requirement: Yes
Minimum TOEFL score: 550
Fellowships: 0
Teaching assistantships: 31
Research assistantships: 64
Students reporting specialty: 100%
Students specializing in:
aerospace: 5%; biomedical: 0%;
chemical: 4%; civil: 6%; computer:
0%; electrical: 28%; management:
13%; materials: 9%; mechanical:
15%; other: 19%

University of Toledo

2801 W. Bancroft
Toledo, OH 43606
www.eng.utoledo.edu/coe/
grad_studies/
Public
Admissions: (419) 530-4723
Email: gradoff@eng.utoledo.edu
Financial aid: (419) 530-5812
Application deadline: rolling
In-state tuition: full time: $9,874;
part time: $549/credit hour
Out-of-state tuition: full time:
$17,627
Room/board/expenses: $15,300
Full-time enrollment: 231
men: 81%; women: 19%;
minorities: 2%; international: 86%
Part-time enrollment: 144
men: 79%; women: 21%;
minorities: 2%; international: 63%
Acceptance rate: 64%
GRE requirement: Yes
Avg. GRE: quantitative: 159
TOEFL requirement: Yes
Minimum TOEFL score: 550
Fellowships: 1
Teaching assistantships: 108
Research assistantships: 64
Students reporting specialty: 100%
Students specializing in:
biomedical: 9%; chemical: 10%;
civil: 12%; computer science: 11%;
electrical: 24%; industrial: 3%;
mechanical: 23%; other: 9%

Wright State University

3640 Colonel Glenn Highway
Dayton, OH 45435
www.wright.edu/graduate-school
Public
Admissions: (937) 775-2976
Email: wsugrad@wright.edu
Financial aid: (937) 775-5721
Application deadline: rolling
In-state tuition: full time: $13,082; part time: $604/credit hour
Out-of-state tuition: full time: $22,224
Room/board/expenses: $14,204
Full-time enrollment: 976
men: 74%; women: 26%; minorities: 5%; international: 79%
Part-time enrollment: 234
men: 80%; women: 20%; minorities: 11%; international: 48%
Acceptance rate: 49%
GRE requirement: Yes
Avg. GRE: quantitative: 156
TOEFL requirement: Yes
Minimum TOEFL score: N/A
Fellowships: 0
Teaching assistantships: 55
Research assistantships: 142
Students reporting specialty: 100%
Students specializing in: aerospace: 0%; biomedical: 5%; computer: 5%; computer science: 26%; electrical: 32%; industrial: 7%; materials: 1%; mechanical: 10%; other: 14%

OKLAHOMA

Oklahoma State University

201 ATRC
Stillwater, OK 74078-0535
gradcollege.okstate.edu
Public
Admissions: (405) 744-6368
Email: grad-i@okstate.edu
Financial aid: (405) 744-6604
Application deadline: 02/01
In-state tuition: full time: $196/credit hour; part time: $196/credit hour
Out-of-state tuition: full time: $786/credit hour
Room/board/expenses: $14,530
Full-time enrollment: 303
men: 75%; women: 25%; minorities: 5%; international: 81%
Part-time enrollment: 435
men: 80%; women: 20%; minorities: 15%; international: 46%
Acceptance rate: 27%
GRE requirement: Yes
Avg. GRE: quantitative: 160
TOEFL requirement: Yes
Minimum TOEFL score: 500
Fellowships: 28
Teaching assistantships: 157
Research assistantships: 201
Students reporting specialty: 100%
Students specializing in: aerospace: 17%; agriculture: 5%; chemical: 6%; civil: 10%; computer: 20%; computer science: 11%; electrical: 20%; management: 14%; environmental: 0%; industrial: 14%; materials: 2%; mechanical: 17%

University of Oklahoma

202 W. Boyd, CEC 107
Norman, OK 73019
www.ou.edu/admissions
Public
Admissions: (405) 325-6765
Email: gradadm@ou.edu
Financial aid: (405) 325-4521
Application deadline: rolling
In-state tuition: full time: $191/credit hour; part time: $191/credit hour
Out-of-state tuition: full time: $740/credit hour
Room/board/expenses: $17,315
Full-time enrollment: 425
men: 78%; women: 22%; minorities: 9%; international: 71%
Part-time enrollment: 238
men: 76%; women: 24%; minorities: 13%; international: 54%
Acceptance rate: 26%
GRE requirement: Yes
Avg. GRE: quantitative: 159
TOEFL requirement: Yes
Minimum TOEFL score: N/A
Fellowships: 12
Teaching assistantships: 105
Research assistantships: 253
Students reporting specialty: 100%
Students specializing in: aerospace: 2%; biomedical: 2%; chemical: 6%; civil: 7%; computer science: 14%; electrical: 25%; science and physics: 1%; environmental: 4%; industrial: 11%; mechanical: 5%; petroleum: 17%; other: 9%

University of Tulsa

800 S. Tucker Drive
Tulsa, OK 74104-3189
utulsa.edu
Private
Admissions: (918) 631-2336
Email: grad@utulsa.edu
Financial aid: (918) 631-2526
Application deadline: rolling
Tuition: full time: $1,176/credit hour; part time: $1,176/credit hour
Room/board/expenses: $15,442
Full-time enrollment: 230
men: 82%; women: 18%; minorities: 2%; international: 71%
Part-time enrollment: 16
men: 75%; women: 25%; minorities: 0%; international: 0%
Acceptance rate: 25%
GRE requirement: Yes
Avg. GRE: quantitative: 164
TOEFL requirement: Yes
Minimum TOEFL score: 550
Fellowships: 9
Teaching assistantships: 41
Research assistantships: 99
Students reporting specialty: 100%
Students specializing in: chemical: 11%; computer: 4%; computer science: 20%; electrical: 5%; mechanical: 18%; petroleum: 41%

OREGON

Oregon Health and Science University[1]

3181 S.W. Sam Jackson Park Road, MC: L102GS
Portland, OR 97239
www.ohsu.edu/som/graduate
Public
Admissions: (503) 494-6222
Email: somgrad@ohsu.edu
Financial aid: N/A
Tuition: N/A
Room/board/expenses: N/A
Enrollment: N/A

Oregon State University

101 Covell Hall
Corvallis, OR 97331-2409
engr.oregonstate.edu/
Public
Admissions: (541) 737-4411
Email: osuadmit@orst.edu
Financial aid: (541) 737-2241
Application deadline: 01/15
In-state tuition: full time: $15,702; part time: $505/credit hour
Out-of-state tuition: full time: $24,504
Room/board/expenses: $16,125
Full-time enrollment: 999
men: 80%; women: 20%; minorities: 6%; international: 61%
Part-time enrollment: 151
men: 70%; women: 30%; minorities: 15%; international: 28%
Acceptance rate: 25%
GRE requirement: Yes
Avg. GRE: quantitative: 161
TOEFL requirement: Yes
Minimum TOEFL score: 550
Fellowships: 27
Teaching assistantships: 224
Research assistantships: 359
Students reporting specialty: 100%
Students specializing in: agriculture: 1%; chemical: 7%; civil: 15%; computer science: 18%; electrical: 20%; environmental: 3%; industrial: 7%; materials: 4%; mechanical: 13%; nuclear: 4%; other: 9%

Portland State University (Maseeh)

PO Box 751
Portland, OR 97207
www.pdx.edu/cecs
Public
Admissions: (503) 725-5525
Email: askadm@pdx.edu
Financial aid: (503) 725-3461
Application deadline: rolling
In-state tuition: full time: $12,246; part time: $406/credit hour
Out-of-state tuition: full time: $17,646
Room/board/expenses: $15,681
Full-time enrollment: 438
men: 74%; women: 26%; minorities: 5%; international: 74%
Part-time enrollment: 311
men: 73%; women: 27%; minorities: 21%; international: 27%
Acceptance rate: 48%
GRE requirement: Yes
Avg. GRE: quantitative: N/A
TOEFL requirement: Yes
Minimum TOEFL score: 550
Fellowships: 0
Teaching assistantships: 69
Research assistantships: 67
Students reporting specialty: 100%
Students specializing in: civil: 13%; computer: 44%; computer science: 19%; management: 16%; mechanical: 9%

PENNSYLVANIA

Carnegie Mellon University

5000 Forbes Avenue
Pittsburgh, PA 15213
www.cit.cmu.edu/
Private
Admissions: (412) 268-2478
Financial aid: (412) 268-2482
Application deadline: 01/31
Tuition: full time: $42,746; part time: $2,496
Room/board/expenses: $27,795
Full-time enrollment: 3,288
men: 73%; women: 27%; minorities: 9%; international: 73%
Part-time enrollment: 360
men: 74%; women: 26%; minorities: 13%; international: 71%
Acceptance rate: 22%
GRE requirement: Yes
Avg. GRE: quantitative: 165
TOEFL requirement: Yes
Minimum TOEFL score: N/A
Fellowships: 442
Teaching assistantships: 94
Research assistantships: 943
Students reporting specialty: 97%
Students specializing in: biomedical: 3%; chemical: 5%; civil: 7%; computer science: 39%; electrical: 20%; materials: 4%; mechanical: 9%; other: 14%

Drexel University

3141 Chestnut Street
Philadelphia, PA 19104
www.drexel.edu/engineering
Private
Admissions: (215) 895-6700
Email: enroll@drexel.edu
Financial aid: (215) 895-1600
Application deadline: rolling
Tuition: full time: $32,919; part time: $1,157/credit hour
Room/board/expenses: $22,417
Full-time enrollment: 773
men: 69%; women: 31%; minorities: 57%; international: 51%
Part-time enrollment: 452
men: 78%; women: 22%; minorities: 24%; international: 2%
Acceptance rate: 33%
GRE requirement: Yes
Avg. GRE: quantitative: 160
TOEFL requirement: Yes
Minimum TOEFL score: N/A
Fellowships: 326
Teaching assistantships: 15
Research assistantships: 10
Students reporting specialty: 86%
Students specializing in: architectural: 1%; biomedical: 18%; chemical: 5%; civil: 6%; computer: 4%; computer science: 8%; electrical: 21%; management: 7%; environmental: 4%; materials: 8%; mechanical: 14%; other: 15%

Lehigh University (Rossin)

19 Memorial Drive W
Bethlehem, PA 18015
www.lehigh.edu/engineering
Private
Admissions: (610) 758-6310
Email: ineas@lehigh.edu
Financial aid: (610) 758-3181
Application deadline: 01/15
Tuition: full time: $1,380/credit hour; part time: $1,380/credit hour
Room/board/expenses: $12,800
Full-time enrollment: 740
men: 73%; women: 27%; minorities: 6%; international: 67%
Part-time enrollment: 88
men: 72%; women: 28%; minorities: 19%; international: 7%
Acceptance rate: 26%
GRE requirement: Yes
Avg. GRE: quantitative: 165
TOEFL requirement: Yes
Minimum TOEFL score: N/A
Fellowships: 29
Teaching assistantships: 62
Research assistantships: 183
Students reporting specialty: 100%
Students specializing in: biomedical: 2%; chemical: 9%; civil: 10%; computer: 2%; computer science: 4%; electrical: 9%; management: 1%; environmental: 2%; industrial: 29%; materials: 6%; mechanical: 21%; other: 5%

Pennsylvania State University-University Park

101 Hammond Building
University Park, PA 16802
www.gradsch.psu.edu
Public
Admissions: (814) 865-1795
Email: gswww@psu.edu
Financial aid: (814) 865-6301
Application deadline: rolling
In-state tuition: full time: $21,364; part time: $851/credit hour
Out-of-state tuition: full time: $35,326
Room/board/expenses: $15,316
Full-time enrollment: 1,622
men: 77%; women: 23%; minorities: 6%; international: 68%
Part-time enrollment: 218
men: 85%; women: 15%; minorities: 9%; international: 20%
Acceptance rate: 24%
GRE requirement: Yes
Avg. GRE: quantitative: 164
TOEFL requirement: Yes
Minimum TOEFL score: 550
Fellowships: 67
Teaching assistantships: 394
Research assistantships: 684
Students reporting specialty: 100%
Students specializing in: aerospace: 6%; agriculture: 1%; architectural: 3%; biomedical: 3%; chemical: 6%; civil: 7%; computer: 9%; electrical: 12%; science and physics: 5%; industrial: 11%; materials: 9%; mechanical: 13%; nuclear: 5%; other: 11%

Philadelphia University[1]

4201 Henry Avenue
Philadelphia, PA 19144
www.philau.edu
Private
Admissions: (215) 951-2943
Email: gradadm@philau.edu
Financial aid: N/A
Tuition: N/A
Room/board/expenses: N/A
Enrollment: N/A

Temple University

1947 N. 12th Street
Philadelphia, PA 19122
engineering.temple.edu/
Public
Admissions: (215) 204-7800
Email: gradengr@temple.edu
Financial aid: (215) 204-2244
Application deadline: 03/01
In-state tuition: full time: $968/credit hour; part time: $968/credit hour
Out-of-state tuition: full time: $1,283/credit hour
Room/board/expenses: $19,250
Full-time enrollment: 213
men: 71%; women: 29%; minorities: 6%; international: 71%
Part-time enrollment: 86
men: 77%; women: 23%; minorities: 24%; international: 15%
Acceptance rate: 60%
GRE requirement: Yes
Avg. GRE: quantitative: 158
TOEFL requirement: Yes
Minimum TOEFL score: 550
Fellowships: 11
Teaching assistantships: 58
Research assistantships: 58
Students reporting specialty: 93%
Students specializing in: biomedical: 8%; civil: 6%; computer science: 35%; electrical: 16%; management: 4%; environmental: 6%; mechanical: 7%; other: 17%

University of Pennsylvania

107 Towne Building
Philadelphia, PA 19104
www.seas.upenn.edu/grad
Private
Admissions: (215) 898-4542
Email: gradstudies@seas.upenn.edu
Financial aid: (215) 898-1988
Application deadline: 12/15
Tuition: full time: $31,068; part time: $5,816/credit hour
Room/board/expenses: $20,162
Full-time enrollment: 1,295
men: 70%; women: 30%; minorities: 16%; international: 58%
Part-time enrollment: 282
men: 63%; women: 37%; minorities: 14%; international: 54%
Acceptance rate: 21%
GRE requirement: Yes
Avg. GRE: quantitative: 166
TOEFL requirement: Yes
Minimum TOEFL score: N/A
Fellowships: 146
Teaching assistantships: 0
Research assistantships: 366
Students reporting specialty: 97%
Students specializing in: biomedical: 17%; chemical: 6%; computer science: 26%; electrical: 12%; industrial: 2%; materials: 8%; mechanical: 13%; other: 18%

University of Pittsburgh (Swanson)

109 Benedum Hall
Pittsburgh, PA 15261
www.engineering.pitt.edu
Public
Admissions: (412) 624-9800
Email: ssoeadm@pitt.edu
Financial aid: (412) 624-7488
Application deadline: 03/01
In-state tuition: full time: $25,202;
part time: $1,158/credit hour
Out-of-state tuition: full time:
$40,920
Room/board/expenses: $20,425
Full-time enrollment: 803
men: 74%; women: 26%;
minorities: 9%; international: 68%
Part-time enrollment: 261
men: 84%; women: 16%;
minorities: 15%; international: 10%
Acceptance rate: 33%
GRE requirement: Yes
Avg. GRE: quantitative: 163
TOEFL requirement: Yes
Minimum TOEFL score: 550
Fellowships: 100
Teaching assistantships: 131
Research assistantships: 264
Students reporting specialty: 100%
Students specializing in:
biomedical: 19%; chemical:
8%; civil: 12%; computer: 0%;
computer science: 9%; electrical:
16%; industrial: 7%; materials:
6%; mechanical: 19%; nuclear:
1%; petroleum: 3%; other: 0%

Villanova University[1]

800 E. Lancaster Avenue
Villanova, PA 19085
www.villanova.edu
Private
Admissions: N/A
Email: engineering.grad@
villanova.edu
Financial aid: N/A
Tuition: N/A
Room/board/expenses: N/A
Enrollment: N/A

RHODE ISLAND

Brown University

Box D
Providence, RI 02912
www.brown.edu/academics/
gradschool
Private
Admissions: (401) 863-2600
Email: Admission_Graduate@
brown.edu
Financial aid: (401) 863-2721
Application deadline: rolling
Tuition: full time: $49,346; part
time: $13,142
Room/board/expenses: $16,934
Full-time enrollment: 410
men: 71%; women: 29%;
minorities: 5%; international: 60%
Part-time enrollment: 19
men: 68%; women: 32%;
minorities: 0%; international: 11%
Acceptance rate: 27%
GRE requirement: Yes
Avg. GRE: quantitative: 144
TOEFL requirement: Yes
Minimum TOEFL score: N/A
Fellowships: 94
Teaching assistantships: 39
Research assistantships: 136
Students reporting specialty: 100%
Students specializing in:
biomedical: 16%; chemical: 3%;
computer: 9%; computer science:
37%; electrical: 8%; management:
7%; materials: 6%; mechanical:
14%

University of Rhode Island

102 Bliss Hall
Kingston, RI 02881
www.uri.edu/gsadmis/
Public
Admissions: (401) 874-2872

Email: gradadm@etal.uri.edu
Financial aid: (401) 874-2314
Application deadline: N/A
In-state tuition: full time: $13,342;
part time: $655/credit hour
Out-of-state tuition: full time:
$25,752
Room/board/expenses: $22,650
Full-time enrollment: 115
men: 74%; women: 26%;
minorities: 3%; international: 58%
Part-time enrollment: 105
men: 88%; women: 12%;
minorities: 15%; international: 10%
Acceptance rate: 63%
GRE requirement: Yes
Avg. GRE: quantitative: 154
TOEFL requirement: Yes
Minimum TOEFL score: 550
Fellowships: 0
Teaching assistantships: 28
Research assistantships: 55
Students reporting specialty: 100%
Students specializing in: chemical:
11%; civil: 14%; electrical: 24%;
industrial: 9%; mechanical: 21%;
other: 21%

SOUTH CAROLINA

Clemson University

Room 109, Riggs Hall
Clemson, SC 29634-0901
www.grad.clemson.edu/
Public
Admissions: (864) 656-4172
Email: grdapp@clemson.edu
Financial aid: (864) 656-2280
Application deadline: rolling
In-state tuition: full time: $11,098;
part time: $663/credit hour
Out-of-state tuition: full time:
$21,766
Room/board/expenses: $16,209
Full-time enrollment: 1,190
men: 75%; women: 25%;
minorities: 5%; international: 67%
Part-time enrollment: 267
men: 76%; women: 24%;
minorities: 10%; international:
34%
Acceptance rate: 32%
GRE requirement: Yes
Avg. GRE: quantitative: 162
TOEFL requirement: Yes
Minimum TOEFL score: N/A
Fellowships: 66
Teaching assistantships: 314
Research assistantships: 492
Students reporting specialty: 100%
Students specializing in:
biomedical: 8%; chemical:
3%; civil: 10%; computer: 4%;
computer science: 15%; electrical:
11%; environmental: 6%;
industrial: 14%; materials: 4%;
mechanical: 13%; other: 12%

University of South Carolina

Swearingen Engineering Center
Columbia, SC 29208
www.cec.sc.edu
Public
Admissions: (803) 777-4243
Email: gradapp@mailbox.sc.edu
Financial aid: (803) 777-8134
Application deadline: 07/01
In-state tuition: full time: $15,222;
part time: $516/credit hour
Out-of-state tuition: full time:
$29,370
Room/board/expenses: $10,690
Full-time enrollment: 331
men: 77%; women: 23%;
minorities: 9%; international: 61%
Part-time enrollment: 162
men: 83%; women: 17%;
minorities: 16%; international:
50%
Acceptance rate: 45%
GRE requirement: Yes
Avg. GRE: quantitative: 160
TOEFL requirement: Yes
Minimum TOEFL score: 570
Fellowships: 51
Teaching assistantships: 99
Research assistantships: 168
Students reporting specialty: 98%

Students specializing in:
aerospace: 3%; biomedical:
4%; chemical: 13%; civil: 15%;
computer: 22%; computer
science: 22%; electrical: 18%;
management: 2%; environmental:
15%; mechanical: 17%; nuclear:
6%

SOUTH DAKOTA

South Dakota School of Mines and Technology

501 E. St. Joseph Street
Rapid City, SD 57701-3995
www.sdsmt.edu/
Public
Admissions: (605) 394-2341
Email: graduate.admissions@
sdsmt.edu
Financial aid: (605) 394-2400
Application deadline: rolling
In-state tuition: full time: $225/
credit hour; part time: $225/
credit hour
Out-of-state tuition: full time: $500/
credit hour
Room/board/expenses: $12,300
Full-time enrollment: 148
men: 68%; women: 32%;
minorities: 47%; international: 41%
Part-time enrollment: 140
men: 80%; women: 20%;
minorities: 29%; international:
14%
Acceptance rate: 54%
GRE requirement: Yes
Avg. GRE: quantitative: 155
TOEFL requirement: Yes
Minimum TOEFL score: 520
Fellowships: 26
Teaching assistantships: 49
Research assistantships: 119
Students reporting specialty: 100%
Students specializing in:
biomedical: 5%; chemical: 12%;
civil: 7%; computer science: 3%;
electrical: 3%; management: 19%;
materials: 13%; mechanical: 7%;
mining: 12%; other: 23%

South Dakota State University

CEH 201, Box 2219
Brookings, SD 57007-0096
www3.sdstate.edu/
Public
Admissions: (605) 688-4181
Email: gradschl@adm.sdstate.edu
Financial aid: (605) 688-4695
Application deadline: 04/15
In-state tuition: full time: $219/
credit hour; part time: $219/
credit hour
Out-of-state tuition: full time: $464/
credit hour
Room/board/expenses: $8,220
Full-time enrollment: 291
men: 76%; women: 24%;
minorities: 2%; international: 71%
Part-time enrollment: N/A
men: N/A; women: N/A; minorities:
N/A; international: N/A
Acceptance rate: 51%
GRE requirement: No
Avg. GRE: quantitative: N/A
TOEFL requirement: Yes
Minimum TOEFL score: 527
Fellowships: 6
Teaching assistantships: 67
Research assistantships: 71
Students reporting specialty: 100%
Students specializing in:
agriculture: 8%; civil: 15%;
computer science: 18%;
electrical: 17%; management: 5%;
mechanical: 15%; other: 21%

University of South Dakota

414 E Clark Street
Vermillion, SD 57069
www.usd.edu/
Public
Admissions: N/A

Email: grad@usd.edu
Financial aid: N/A
Application deadline: rolling
In-state tuition: full time: $219/
credit hour; part time: $219/
credit hour
Out-of-state tuition: full time: $464/
credit hour
Room/board/expenses: $9,000
Full-time enrollment: 17
men: 76%; women: 24%;
minorities: 6%; international: 35%
Part-time enrollment: N/A
men: N/A; women: N/A; minorities:
N/A; international: N/A
Acceptance rate: 53%
Avg. GRE: quantitative: N/A
TOEFL requirement: Yes
Minimum TOEFL score: N/A
Students reporting specialty: 0%
Students specializing in: N/A

TENNESSEE

Tennessee State University

3500 John Merritt Boulevard
Nashville, TN 37209-1651
www.tnstate.edu/
Public
Admissions: (615) 963-5107
Email: gradschool@tnstate.edu
Financial aid: N/A
Application deadline: 06/01
In-state tuition: full time: $474/
credit hour; part time: $474/
credit hour
Out-of-state tuition: full time:
$1,056/credit hour
Room/board/expenses: $11,195
Full-time enrollment: 74
men: 69%; women: 31%;
minorities: 97%; international:
76%
Part-time enrollment: 36
men: 69%; women: 31%;
minorities: 58%; international:
31%
Acceptance rate: 74%
Avg. GRE: quantitative: N/A
TOEFL requirement: Yes
Minimum TOEFL score: 525
Students reporting specialty: 100%
Students specializing in: computer:
46%; computer science: 31%;
management: 23%

Tennessee Technological University

N Dixie Avenue
Cookeville, TN 38505
www.tntech.edu/engineering
Public
Admissions: (931) 372-3233
Email: gradstudies@tntech.edu
Financial aid: (931) 372-3073
Application deadline: 07/01
In-state tuition: full time: $10,371;
part time: $511/credit hour
Out-of-state tuition: full time:
$23,771
Room/board/expenses: $16,000
Full-time enrollment: 94
men: 78%; women: 22%;
minorities: 5%; international: 53%
Part-time enrollment: 124
men: 85%; women: 15%;
minorities: 4%; international: 48%
Acceptance rate: 27%
GRE requirement: Yes
Avg. GRE: quantitative: 158
TOEFL requirement: Yes
Minimum TOEFL score: 550
Fellowships: 4
Teaching assistantships: 51
Research assistantships: 75
Students reporting specialty: 100%
Students specializing in: chemical:
15%; civil: 11%; computer science:
13%; electrical: 33%; mechanical:
28%

University of Memphis (Herff)

201 Engineering Administration
Building
Memphis, TN 38152
www.
memphis.edu/herff/index.php
Public
Admissions: (901) 678-2111
Email: recruitment@memphis.edu
Financial aid: (901) 678-4825
Application deadline: 07/01
In-state tuition: full time: $10,197;
part time: $479/credit hour
Out-of-state tuition: full time:
$18,981
Room/board/expenses: $15,656
Full-time enrollment: 89
men: 72%; women: 28%;
minorities: 6%; international: 73%
Part-time enrollment: 84
men: 77%; women: 23%;
minorities: 24%; international:
42%
Acceptance rate: 75%
GRE requirement: Yes
Avg. GRE: quantitative: 158
TOEFL requirement: Yes
Minimum TOEFL score: 550
Fellowships: 32
Teaching assistantships: 0
Research assistantships: 77
Students reporting specialty: 100%
Students specializing in:
biomedical: 21%; civil: 13%;
computer science: 19%; electrical:
19%; science and physics: 40%;
mechanical: 6%

University of Tennessee-Chattanooga

615 McCallie Avenue
Chattanooga, TN 37403
www.utc.edu/college-
engineering-computer-science/
Public
Admissions: N/A
Financial aid: N/A
Application deadline: rolling
In-state tuition: full time: $9,670;
part time: $441/credit hour
Out-of-state tuition: full time:
$25,788
Room/board/expenses: $17,400
Full-time enrollment: 72
men: 65%; women: 35%;
minorities: 58%; international:
64%
Part-time enrollment: 120
men: 81%; women: 19%;
minorities: 41%; international:
23%
Acceptance rate: 40%
GRE requirement: Yes
Avg. GRE: quantitative: N/A
TOEFL requirement: Yes
Minimum TOEFL score: 550
Research assistantships: 52
Students reporting specialty: 96%
Students specializing in: chemical:
4%; civil: 2%; computer
science: 22%; electrical: 14%;
management: 39%; industrial: 1%;
mechanical: 4%; other: 14%

University of Tennessee-Knoxville

124 Perkins Hall
Knoxville, TN 37996-2000
graduateadmissions.utk.edu/
Public
Admissions: (865) 974-3251
Email: graduateadmissions@
utk.edu
Financial aid: (865) 974-3131
Application deadline: 02/01
In-state tuition: full time: $11,906;
part time: $591/credit hour
Out-of-state tuition: full time:
$30,354
Room/board/expenses: $20,914
Full-time enrollment: 764
men: 78%; women: 22%;
minorities: 8%; international: 48%

Part-time enrollment: 244
men: 83%; women: 17%;
minorities: 12%; international: 10%
Acceptance rate: 31%
GRE requirement: Yes
Avg. GRE: quantitative: 160
TOEFL requirement: Yes
Minimum TOEFL score: 550
Fellowships: 95
Teaching assistantships: 205
Research assistantships: 559
Students reporting specialty: 97%
Students specializing in:
aerospace: 3%; agriculture:
2%; biomedical: 2%; chemical:
6%; civil: 13%; computer: 4%;
computer science: 7%; electrical:
14%; management: 0%; science
and physics: 0%; environmental:
1%; industrial: 12%; materials: 8%;
mechanical: 10%; nuclear: 12%;
other: 5%

Vanderbilt University

VU Station B, 351826
2301 Vanderbilt Place
Nashville, TN 37235
engineering.vanderbilt.edu
Private
Admissions: (615) 322-0236
Email: apply@vanderbilt.edu
Financial aid: (615) 322-3591
Application deadline: 12/15
Tuition: full time: $1,818/credit
hour; part time: $1,818/credit hour
Room/board/expenses: $24,004
Full-time enrollment: 482
men: 70%; women: 30%;
minorities: 10%; international:
43%
Part-time enrollment: 21
men: 76%; women: 24%;
minorities: 0%; international: 33%
Acceptance rate: 17%
GRE requirement: Yes
Avg. GRE: quantitative: 163
TOEFL requirement: Yes
Minimum TOEFL score: 570
Fellowships: 48
Teaching assistantships: 124
Research assistantships: 211
Students reporting specialty: 100%
Students specializing in:
biomedical: 15%; chemical: 9%;
civil: 11%; computer science: 17%;
electrical: 20%; environmental:
10%; materials: 6%; mechanical:
13%

TEXAS

Baylor University

One Bear Place, #97356
Waco, TX 76798
www.ecs.baylor.edu/
Private
Admissions: (254) 710-4060
Email: Graduate_Admissions@
baylor.edu
Financial aid: N/A
Application deadline: 02/15
Tuition: full time: $30,150; part
time: $1,515/credit hour
Room/board/expenses: $9,910
Full-time enrollment: 88
men: 84%; women: 16%;
minorities: 11%; international: 35%
Part-time enrollment: N/A
men: N/A; women: N/A; minorities:
N/A; international: N/A
Acceptance rate: 32%
GRE requirement: Yes
Avg. GRE: quantitative: 162
TOEFL requirement: Yes
Minimum TOEFL score: 550
Teaching assistantships: 16
Research assistantships: 28
Students reporting specialty: 100%
Students specializing in:
biomedical: 7%; computer
science: 17%; electrical: 45%;
mechanical: 27%; other: 3%

Lamar University

4400 Martin Luther King
Boulevard
Beaumont, TX 77710
dept.lamar.edu/engineering/coe/
Public
Admissions: (409) 880-8888
Email: admissions@hal.lamar.edu
Financial aid: (409) 880-8450
Application deadline: rolling
In-state tuition: full time: $6,733;
part time: $330/credit hour
Out-of-state tuition: full time:
$11,803
Room/board/expenses: $14,070
Full-time enrollment: 697
men: 87%; women: 13%;
minorities: 4%; international: 95%
Part-time enrollment: 286
men: 84%; women: 16%;
minorities: 5%; international: 93%
Acceptance rate: 60%
GRE requirement: Yes
Avg. GRE: quantitative: 156
TOEFL requirement: Yes
Minimum TOEFL score: 550
Fellowships: 37
Teaching assistantships: 7
Research assistantships: 1
Students reporting specialty: 87%
Students specializing in: chemical:
2%; civil: 7%; computer
science: 29%; electrical: 18%;
management: 7%; environmental:
3%; industrial: 18%; mechanical:
16%

Prairie View
A&M University

PO Box 519, MS 2500
Prairie View, TX 77446
www.pvamu.edu
Public
Admissions: (936) 261-2131
Email: graduateadmissions@
pvamu.edu
Financial aid: (936) 261-1000
Application deadline: 05/01
In-state tuition: full time: $261/
credit hour; part time: $261/
credit hour
Out-of-state tuition: full time: $680/
credit hour
Room/board/expenses: $13,801
Full-time enrollment: 126
men: 63%; women: 37%;
minorities: 32%; international:
57%
Part-time enrollment: 47
men: 74%; women: 26%;
minorities: 64%; international:
21%
Acceptance rate: 99%
GRE requirement: Yes
Avg. GRE: quantitative: 150
TOEFL requirement: Yes
Minimum TOEFL score: 500
Research assistantships: 19
Students reporting specialty: 100%
Students specializing in: computer
science: 33%; electrical: 25%;
mechanical: 42%

Rice University
(Brown)

PO Box 1892, MS 364
Houston, TX 77251-1892
engr.rice.edu
Private
Admissions: (713) 348-4002
Email: graduate@rice.edu
Financial aid: (713) 348-4958
Application deadline: N/A
Tuition: full time: $42,101; part
time: $2,309/credit hour
Room/board/expenses: $16,250
Full-time enrollment: 854
men: 71%; women: 29%;
minorities: 13%; international:
63%
Part-time enrollment: 49
men: 71%; women: 29%;
minorities: 18%; international:
65%
Acceptance rate: 23%
GRE requirement: Yes

Avg. GRE: quantitative: 165
TOEFL requirement: Yes
Minimum TOEFL score: 600
Fellowships: 262
Teaching assistantships: 31
Research assistantships: 355
Students reporting specialty: 100%
Students specializing in:
biomedical: 17%; chemical: 13%;
civil: 3%; computer science: 14%;
electrical: 22%; environmental:
3%; materials: 8%; mechanical:
7%; other: 14%

Southern Methodist
University (Lyle)

3145 Dyer Street
Dallas, TX 75275-0335
www.smu.edu/lyle
Private
Admissions: (214) 768-3913
Email: msaloma@lyle.smu.edu
Financial aid: (214) 768-1501
Application deadline: 07/01
Tuition: full time: $1,165/credit
hour; part time: $1,165/credit hour
Room/board/expenses: $25,710
Full-time enrollment: 488
men: 75%; women: 25%;
minorities: 10%; international:
79%
Part-time enrollment: 625
men: 75%; women: 25%;
minorities: 33%; international:
17%
Acceptance rate: 55%
GRE requirement: Yes
Avg. GRE: quantitative: 159
TOEFL requirement: Yes
Minimum TOEFL score: 550
Fellowships: 0
Teaching assistantships: 51
Research assistantships: 74
Students reporting specialty: 96%
Students specializing in: civil:
4%; computer: 2%; computer
science: 16%; electrical: 30%;
management: 18%; environmental:
4%; industrial: 8%; mechanical:
6%; other: 15%

Texas A&M
University-
College Station
(Look)

Jack K. Williams Administration
Building, Suite 312
College Station, TX 77843-3126
engineering.tamu.edu/graduate
Public
Admissions: (979) 845-7200
Email: gradengineer@tamu.edu
Financial aid: (979) 845-3236
Application deadline: rolling
In-state tuition: full time: $241/
credit hour; part time: $241/
credit hour
Out-of-state tuition: full time: $638/
credit hour
Room/board/expenses: $15,358
Full-time enrollment: 2,867
men: 79%; women: 21%;
minorities: 10%; international: 71%
Part-time enrollment: 613
men: 77%; women: 23%;
minorities: 18%; international:
44%
Acceptance rate: 21%
GRE requirement: Yes
Avg. GRE: quantitative: 163
TOEFL requirement: Yes
Minimum TOEFL score: 550
Fellowships: 416
Teaching assistantships: 397
Research assistantships: 1,070
Students reporting specialty: 100%
Students specializing in:
aerospace: 3%; agriculture: 2%;
biomedical: 3%; chemical: 6%;
civil: 11%; computer science: 9%;
electrical: 21%; industrial: 8%;
materials: 4%; mechanical: 13%;
nuclear: 4%; petroleum: 13%;
other: 3%

Texas A&M
University-Kingsville
(Dotterweich)

MSC 188
Kingsville, TX 78363
www.tamuk.edu/grad
Public
Admissions: (361) 593-2808
Email: gradschool@tamuk.edu
Financial aid: (361) 593-2174
Application deadline: 07/15
In-state tuition: full time: $5,248;
part time: $684/credit hour
Out-of-state tuition: full time:
$12,269
Room/board/expenses: $13,968
Full-time enrollment: 1,320
men: 82%; women: 18%;
minorities: 2%; international: 97%
Part-time enrollment: 373
men: 79%; women: 21%;
minorities: 9%; international: 87%
Acceptance rate: 66%
GRE requirement: Yes
Avg. GRE: quantitative: 152
TOEFL requirement: Yes
Minimum TOEFL score: 550
Fellowships: 0
Teaching assistantships: 90
Research assistantships: 64
Students reporting specialty: 100%
Students specializing in: chemical:
2%; civil: 5%; computer
science: 35%; electrical: 30%;
environmental: 4%; industrial: 6%;
mechanical: 12%; petroleum: 2%;
other: 4%

Texas State
University[1]

601 University Dr.
San Marcos, TX 78666
Public
Admissions: N/A
Financial aid: N/A
Tuition: N/A
Room/board/expenses: N/A
Enrollment: N/A

Texas Tech
University (Whitacre)

Box 43103
Lubbock, TX 79409-3103
www.depts.ttu.edu/coe/
Public
Admissions: (806) 742-2787
Email: gradschool@ttu.edu
Financial aid: (806) 742-3681
Application deadline: rolling
In-state tuition: full time: $270/
credit hour; part time: $270/
credit hour
Out-of-state tuition: full time: $660/
credit hour
Room/board/expenses: $14,705
Full-time enrollment: 712
men: 76%; women: 24%;
minorities: 7%; international: 78%
Part-time enrollment: 180
men: 83%; women: 17%;
minorities: 19%; international:
29%
Acceptance rate: 26%
GRE requirement: Yes
Avg. GRE: quantitative: 159
TOEFL requirement: Yes
Minimum TOEFL score: 550
Fellowships: 0
Teaching assistantships: 117
Research assistantships: 160
Students reporting specialty: 100%
Students specializing in:
biomedical: 1%; chemical: 10%;
civil: 9%; computer science: 12%;
electrical: 23%; environmental:
2%; industrial: 10%; mechanical:
14%; petroleum: 8%; other: 12%

University of
Houston (Cullen)

E421 Engineering Building 2
Houston, TX 77204-4007
www.egr.uh.edu
Public
Admissions: (713) 743-4200

Email: grad-admit@egr.uh.edu
Financial aid: (713) 743-9090
Application deadline: 02/01
In-state tuition: full time: $451/
credit hour; part time: $451/
credit hour
Out-of-state tuition: full time: $941/
credit hour
Room/board/expenses: $15,802
Full-time enrollment: 1,199
men: 75%; women: 25%;
minorities: 6%; international: 85%
Part-time enrollment: 300
men: 76%; women: 24%;
minorities: 23%; international:
48%
Acceptance rate: 31%
GRE requirement: Yes
Avg. GRE: quantitative: 162
TOEFL requirement: Yes
Minimum TOEFL score: 550
Fellowships: 591
Teaching assistantships: 118
Research assistantships: 356
Students reporting specialty: 100%
Students specializing in:
aerospace: 0%; biomedical: 4%;
chemical: 9%; civil: 9%; computer:
4%; computer science: 12%;
electrical: 17%; environmental:
2%; industrial: 14%; materials:
4%; mechanical: 12%; petroleum:
8%; other: 5%

University of
North Texas

1155 Union Circle, #310440
Denton, TX 76203-5017
tsgs.unt.edu/overview
Public
Admissions: (940) 565-2383
Email: gradsch@unt.edu
Financial aid: (940) 565-2302
Application deadline: 06/15
In-state tuition: full time: $228/
credit hour; part time: $228/
credit hour
Out-of-state tuition: full time: $618/
credit hour
Room/board/expenses: $12,846
Full-time enrollment: 475
men: 73%; women: 27%;
minorities: 5%; international: 85%
Part-time enrollment: 146
men: 75%; women: 25%;
minorities: 21%; international:
58%
Acceptance rate: 49%
GRE requirement: Yes
Avg. GRE: quantitative: 158
TOEFL requirement: Yes
Minimum TOEFL score: 550
Fellowships: 4
Teaching assistantships: 48
Research assistantships: 93
Students reporting specialty: 84%
Students specializing in: computer:
10%; computer science: 36%;
electrical: 24%; materials: 15%;
mechanical: 14%

University of
Texas-Arlington

UTA Box 19019
Arlington, TX 76019
www.uta.edu/engineering/
Public
Admissions: (817) 272-2380
Email: graduate.school@uta.edu
Financial aid: (817) 272-3561
Application deadline: rolling
In-state tuition: full time: $8,557;
part time: $6,342
Out-of-state tuition: full time:
$16,311
Room/board/expenses: $14,688
Full-time enrollment: 2,559
men: 77%; women: 23%;
minorities: 4%; international: 93%
Part-time enrollment: 761
men: 79%; women: 21%;
minorities: 16%; international:
59%
Acceptance rate: 48%
GRE requirement: Yes
Avg. GRE: quantitative: 156
TOEFL requirement: Yes
Minimum TOEFL score: 550

Fellowships: 478
Teaching assistantships: 417
Research assistantships: 146
Students reporting specialty: 100%
Students specializing in:
aerospace: 4%; biomedical: 5%; civil: 5%; computer: 1%; computer science: 25%; electrical: 16%; management: 3%; industrial: 13%; materials: 2%; mechanical: 15%

University of Texas-Austin (Cockrell)

301 E. Dean Keeton Street
Stop C2100
Austin, TX 78712-2100
www.engr.utexas.edu/
Public
Admissions: (512) 475-7391
Email:
adgrd@utxdp.its.utexas.edu
Financial aid: (512) 475-6282
Application deadline: rolling
In-state tuition: full time: $9,564; part time: N/A
Out-of-state tuition: full time: $17,506
Room/board/expenses: $18,810
Full-time enrollment: 1,996
men: 79%; women: 21%; minorities: 11%; international: 59%
Part-time enrollment: 377
men: 80%; women: 20%; minorities: 31%; international: 28%
Acceptance rate: 17%
GRE requirement: Yes
Avg. GRE: quantitative: 165
TOEFL requirement: Yes
Minimum TOEFL score: 550
Fellowships: 755
Teaching assistantships: 501
Research assistantships: 981
Students reporting specialty: 100%
Students specializing in:
aerospace: 6%; architectural: 1%; biomedical: 4%; chemical: 8%; civil: 14%; computer: 15%; computer science: 10%; electrical: 13%; management: 3%; environmental: 2%; industrial: 3%; materials: 2%; mechanical: 11%; petroleum: 9%

University of Texas-Dallas (Jonsson)

800 W. Campbell Road
Mail Station EC32
Richardson, TX 75080-3021
www.utdallas.edu
Public
Admissions: (972) 883-2270
Email: interest@utdallas.edu
Financial aid: (972) 883-2941
Application deadline: 07/01
In-state tuition: full time: $11,940; part time: N/A
Out-of-state tuition: full time: $22,282
Room/board/expenses: $14,866
Full-time enrollment: 1,910
men: 72%; women: 28%; minorities: 5%; international: 89%
Part-time enrollment: 642
men: 73%; women: 27%; minorities: 11%; international: 73%
Acceptance rate: 33%
GRE requirement: Yes
Avg. GRE: quantitative: 161
TOEFL requirement: Yes
Minimum TOEFL score: N/A
Fellowships: 66
Teaching assistantships: 215
Research assistantships: 313
Students reporting specialty: 100%
Students specializing in:
biomedical: 3%; computer: 4%; computer science: 46%; electrical: 31%; management: 3%; materials: 2%; mechanical: 7%; other: 4%

University of Texas-El Paso[1]

500 W. University Avenue
El Paso, TX 79968
www.utep.edu/graduate
Public
Admissions: (915) 747-5491
Email: gradschool@utep.edu
Financial aid: (915) 747-5204
Tuition: N/A
Room/board/expenses: N/A
Enrollment: N/A

University of Texas Health Science Center-San Antonio

One UTSA Circle
San Antonio, TX 78249
engineering2.utsa.edu/
Public
Admissions: N/A
Financial aid: N/A
Application deadline: 07/01
In-state tuition: full time: $260/credit hour; part time: $260/credit hour
Out-of-state tuition: full time: $1,001/credit hour
Room/board/expenses: $15,054
Full-time enrollment: 105
men: 58%; women: 42%; minorities: 18%; international: 47%
Part-time enrollment: 1
men: 100%; women: 0%; minorities: 0%; international: 0%
Acceptance rate: 51%
GRE requirement: Yes
Avg. GRE: quantitative: 156
TOEFL requirement: Yes
Minimum TOEFL score: 550
Fellowships: 36
Teaching assistantships: 4
Research assistantships: 6
Students reporting specialty: 100%
Students specializing in:
biomedical: 100%

University of Texas-San Antonio

1 UTSA Circle
San Antonio, TX 78249-0665
www.graduateschool.utsa.edu
Public
Admissions: (210) 458-4330
Email: gradstudies@utsa.edu
Financial aid: (210) 458-8000
Application deadline: 02/01
In-state tuition: full time: $260/credit hour; part time: $260/credit hour
Out-of-state tuition: full time: $1,057/credit hour
Room/board/expenses: $15,054
Full-time enrollment: 446
men: 74%; women: 26%; minorities: 13%; international: 77%
Part-time enrollment: 256
men: 79%; women: 21%; minorities: 35%; international: 30%
Acceptance rate: 59%
GRE requirement: Yes
Avg. GRE: quantitative: 157
TOEFL requirement: Yes
Minimum TOEFL score: 550
Fellowships: 121
Teaching assistantships: 115
Research assistantships: 91
Students reporting specialty: 100%
Students specializing in:
biomedical: 10%; civil: 6%; computer: 6%; computer science: 21%; electrical: 34%; environmental: 4%; industrial: 4%; materials: 2%; mechanical: 13%

University of Texas Southwestern Medical Center-Dallas[1]

5323 Harry Hines Boulevard
Dallas, TX 75390
www.utsouthwestern.edu/education/index.html
Public
Admissions: (214) 648-5617
Email: admissions@utsouthwestern.edu
Financial aid: N/A
Tuition: N/A
Room/board/expenses: N/A
Enrollment: N/A

UTAH

Brigham Young University (Fulton)

270 CB
Provo, UT 84602
www.byu.edu/gradstudies
Private
Admissions: (801) 422-4091
Email: gradstudies@byu.edu
Financial aid: (801) 422-4104
Application deadline: 01/15
Tuition: full time: $6,500; part time: $382/credit hour
Room/board/expenses: $19,308
Full-time enrollment: 385
men: 89%; women: 11%; minorities: 6%; international: 17%
Part-time enrollment: N/A
men: N/A; women: N/A; minorities: N/A; international: N/A
Acceptance rate: 76%
GRE requirement: Yes
Avg. GRE: quantitative: 160
TOEFL requirement: Yes
Minimum TOEFL score: 580
Fellowships: 25
Teaching assistantships: 249
Research assistantships: 713
Students reporting specialty: 100%
Students specializing in: chemical: 12%; civil: 18%; computer science: 19%; electrical: 25%; mechanical: 26%

University of Utah

72 S. Central Campus Drive
1650 WEB
Salt Lake City, UT 84112-9200
www.utah.edu
Public
Admissions: (801) 581-7281
Email: admissions@sa.utah.edu
Financial aid: (801) 581-6211
Application deadline: 04/01
In-state tuition: full time: $8,016; part time: $5,557
Out-of-state tuition: full time: $22,590
Room/board/expenses: $15,362
Full-time enrollment: 940
men: 78%; women: 22%; minorities: 6%; international: 54%
Part-time enrollment: 279
men: 83%; women: 17%; minorities: 13%; international: 26%
Acceptance rate: 36%
GRE requirement: Yes
Avg. GRE: quantitative: 163
TOEFL requirement: Yes
Minimum TOEFL score: 550
Fellowships: 65
Teaching assistantships: 162
Research assistantships: 398
Students reporting specialty: 100%
Students specializing in:
biomedical: 11%; chemical: 7%; civil: 9%; computer science: 30%; electrical: 18%; materials: 3%; mechanical: 15%; mining: 1%; nuclear: 2%; other: 4%

Utah State University

4100 Old Main Hill
Logan, UT 84322-4100
www.engineering.usu.edu/
Public
Admissions: (435) 797-1189
Email: grad.admissions@aggiemail.usu.edu
Financial aid: (435) 797-0173
Application deadline: rolling
In-state tuition: full time: $6,662; part time: $5,825
Out-of-state tuition: full time: $19,133
Room/board/expenses: $11,720
Full-time enrollment: 172
men: 91%; women: 9%; minorities: 15%; international: 34%
Part-time enrollment: 229
men: 84%; women: 16%; minorities: 15%; international: 44%
GRE requirement: Yes
Avg. GRE: quantitative: 166
TOEFL requirement: Yes
Minimum TOEFL score: 550
Students reporting specialty: 100%
Students specializing in:
aerospace: 4%; agriculture: 7%; civil: 27%; computer: 5%; computer science: 19%; electrical: 19%; mechanical: 16%; other: 2%

VERMONT

University of Vermont[1]

109 Votey Hall
Burlington, VT 05405
www.cems.uvm.edu
Public
Admissions: (802) 656-2699
Email: graduate.admissions@uvm.edu
Financial aid: N/A
Tuition: N/A
Room/board/expenses: N/A
Enrollment: N/A

VIRGINIA

George Mason University (Volgenau)

4400 University Drive, MS4A3
Fairfax, VA 22030-4444
admissions.gmu.edu/grad
Public
Admissions: (703) 993-9700
Email: masongrad@gmu.edu
Financial aid: (703) 993-2353
Application deadline: 03/18
In-state tuition: full time: $15,704; part time: $646/credit hour
Out-of-state tuition: full time: $31,424
Room/board/expenses: $23,648
Full-time enrollment: 721
men: 69%; women: 31%; minorities: 10%; international: 73%
Part-time enrollment: 844
men: 79%; women: 21%; minorities: 35%; international: 10%
Acceptance rate: 58%
GRE requirement: Yes
Avg. GRE: quantitative: 158
TOEFL requirement: Yes
Minimum TOEFL score: 570
Fellowships: 0
Teaching assistantships: 177
Research assistantships: 98
Students reporting specialty: 100%
Students specializing in:
biomedical: 1%; civil: 6%; computer: 4%; computer science: 31%; electrical: 32%; industrial: 8%; other: 18%

Old Dominion University[1]

102 Kaufman Hall
Norfolk, VA 23529
www.admissions.odu.edu
Public
Admissions: (757) 683-3685
Email: gradadmit@odu.edu

Financial aid: N/A
Tuition: N/A
Room/board/expenses: N/A
Enrollment: N/A

University of Virginia

Thornton Hall
Charlottesville, VA 22904-4246
www.seas.virginia.edu/
Public
Admissions: (434) 924-3897
Email: seas-grad-admission@virginia.edu
Financial aid: (434) 924-3897
Application deadline: 01/15
In-state tuition: full time: $18,444; part time: $792/credit hour
Out-of-state tuition: full time: $28,006
Room/board/expenses: $20,933
Full-time enrollment: 630
men: 72%; women: 28%; minorities: 11%; international: 49%
Part-time enrollment: 51
men: 86%; women: 14%; minorities: 14%; international: 2%
Acceptance rate: 25%
GRE requirement: Yes
Avg. GRE: quantitative: 164
TOEFL requirement: Yes
Minimum TOEFL score: 600
Fellowships: 274
Teaching assistantships: 113
Research assistantships: 374
Students reporting specialty: 100%
Students specializing in:
biomedical: 11%; chemical: 6%; civil: 9%; computer: 5%; computer science: 12%; electrical: 17%; science and physics: 2%; materials: 9%; mechanical: 14%; other: 14%

Virginia Commonwealth University

PO Box 843068
Richmond, VA 23284-3068
www.egr.vcu.edu/
Public
Admissions: (804) 828-1087
Email: josephl@vcu.edu
Financial aid: (804) 828-3925
Application deadline: 0G/01
In-state tuition: full time: $13,337; part time: $487/credit hour
Out-of-state tuition: full time: $24,913
Room/board/expenses: $22,359
Full-time enrollment: 212
men: 75%; women: 25%; minorities: 15%; international: 55%
Part-time enrollment: 59
men: 71%; women: 29%; minorities: 12%; international: 22%
Acceptance rate: 54%
GRE requirement: Yes
Avg. GRE: quantitative: 159
TOEFL requirement: Yes
Minimum TOEFL score: 550
Fellowships: 4
Teaching assistantships: 66
Research assistantships: 82
Students reporting specialty: 100%
Students specializing in:
biomedical: 19%; chemical: 11%; computer: 23%; computer science: 19%; electrical: 23%; mechanical: 28%; nuclear: 28%

Virginia Tech

3046 Torgersen Hall
Blacksburg, VA 24061-0217
www.grads.vt.edu
Public
Admissions: (540) 231-8636
Email: gradappl@vt.edu
Financial aid: (540) 231-5179
Application deadline: rolling
In-state tuition: full time: $17,307; part time: $673/credit hour
Out-of-state tuition: full time: $30,387
Room/board/expenses: $15,500

Full-time enrollment: 1,869
men: 76%; women: 24%;
minorities: 10%; international:
62%
Part-time enrollment: 388
men: 82%; women: 18%;
minorities: 27%; international:
27%
Acceptance rate: 31%
GRE requirement: Yes
Avg. GRE: quantitative: 163
TOEFL requirement: Yes
Minimum TOEFL score: 550
Fellowships: 126
Teaching assistantships: 386
Research assistantships: 844
Students reporting specialty: 100%
Students specializing in:
aerospace: 8%; agriculture:
3%; biomedical: 3%; chemical:
2%; civil: 14%; computer: 8%;
computer science: 11%; electrical:
18%; science and physics: 3%;
environmental: 2%; industrial:
8%; materials: 3%; mechanical:
15%; mining: 2%; nuclear: 0%;
other: 2%

WASHINGTON

University of Washington

371 Loew Hall
Box 352180
Seattle, WA 98195-2180
www.engr.washington.edu
Public
Admissions: (206) 685-2630
Email: uwgrad@uw.edu
Financial aid: (206) 543-6101
Application deadline: N/A
In-state tuition: full time: $17,496;
part time: $782/credit hour
Out-of-state tuition: full time:
$30,345
Room/board/expenses: $19,425
Full-time enrollment: 1,532
men: 70%; women: 30%;
minorities: 16%; international:
43%
Part-time enrollment: 801
men: 75%; women: 25%;
minorities: 32%; international:
13%
Acceptance rate: 19%
GRE requirement: Yes
Avg. GRE: quantitative: 164
TOEFL requirement: Yes
Minimum TOEFL score: 580
Fellowships: 170
Teaching assistantships: 213
Research assistantships: 672
Students reporting specialty: 100%
Students specializing in:
aerospace: 10%; biomedical:
6%; chemical: 4%; civil: 17%;
computer: 16%; electrical: 16%;

industrial: 5%; materials: 5%;
mechanical: 12%; other: 9%

Washington State University

PO Box 642714
Pullman, WA 99164-2714
www.vcea.wsu.edu
Public
Admissions: (509) 335-1446
Email: gradsch@wsu.edu
Financial aid: (509) 335-9711
Application deadline: 01/10
In-state tuition: full time: $12,745;
part time: $589/credit hour
Out-of-state tuition: full time:
$26,177
Room/board/expenses: $8,016
Full-time enrollment: 542
men: 73%; women: 27%;
minorities: 7%; international: 70%
Part-time enrollment: 190
men: 74%; women: 26%;
minorities: 22%; international:
19%
Acceptance rate: 24%
GRE requirement: Yes
Avg. GRE: quantitative: 161
TOEFL requirement: Yes
Minimum TOEFL score: 550
Fellowships: 11
Teaching assistantships: 118
Research assistantships: 206
Students reporting specialty: 100%
Students specializing in:
agriculture: 11%; chemical:
10%; civil: 10%; computer: 1%;
computer science: 13%; electrical:
15%; management: 11%; science
and physics: 0%; environmental:
2%; materials: 11%; mechanical:
18%

WEST VIRGINIA

West Virginia University

PO Box 6070
Morgantown, WV 26506-6070
www.statler.wvu.edu
Public
Admissions: (304) 293-2121
Email: graduateadmissions@mail.
wvu.edu
Financial aid: (304) 293-5242
Application deadline: 05/01
In-state tuition: full time: $9,720;
part time: $540/credit hour
Out-of-state tuition: full time:
$23,832
Room/board/expenses: $12,600
Full-time enrollment: 528
men: 74%; women: 26%;
minorities: 4%; international: 62%

Part-time enrollment: 175
men: 81%; women: 19%;
minorities: 12%; international:
32%
Acceptance rate: 48%
GRE requirement: Yes
Avg. GRE: quantitative: 160
TOEFL requirement: Yes
Minimum TOEFL score: 550
Fellowships: 16
Teaching assistantships: 86
Research assistantships: 240
Students reporting specialty: 100%
Students specializing in:
aerospace: 4%; chemical:
6%; civil: 10%; computer: 2%;
computer science: 11%; electrical:
16%; industrial: 7%; materials:
1%; mechanical: 15%; mining: 3%;
petroleum: 6%; other: 18%

WISCONSIN

Marquette University

PO Box 1881
Milwaukee, WI 53201-1881
www.grad.marquette.edu
Private
Admissions: (414) 288-7137
Email: mugs@mu.edu
Financial aid: (414) 288-5325
Application deadline: rolling
Tuition: full time: $1,050/credit
hour; part time: $1,050/credit
hour
Room/board/expenses: $17,206
Full-time enrollment: 118
men: 70%; women: 30%;
minorities: 9%; international: 42%
Part-time enrollment: 77
men: 78%; women: 22%;
minorities: 14%; international: 17%
Acceptance rate: 62%
GRE requirement: Yes
Avg. GRE: quantitative: 160
TOEFL requirement: Yes
Minimum TOEFL score: N/A
Fellowships: 8
Teaching assistantships: 29
Research assistantships: 55
Students reporting specialty: 61%
Students specializing in:
biomedical: 27%; civil: 26%;
electrical: 25%; mechanical: 19%;
other: 3%

University of Wisconsin-Madison

2610 Engineering Hall
Madison, WI 53706
www.engr.wisc.edu/
Public
Admissions: (608) 262-2433
Email: gradadmiss@bascom.
wisc.edu
Financial aid: (608) 262-3060

Application deadline: N/A
In-state tuition: full time: $13,012;
part time: $786/credit hour
Out-of-state tuition: full time:
$26,339
Room/board/expenses: $17,814
Full-time enrollment: 1,525
men: 78%; women: 22%;
minorities: 6%; international: 58%
Part-time enrollment: 414
men: 84%; women: 16%;
minorities: 7%; international: 32%
Acceptance rate: 9%
GRE requirement: Yes
Avg. GRE: quantitative: 163
TOEFL requirement: Yes
Minimum TOEFL score: 580
Fellowships: 54
Teaching assistantships: 247
Research assistantships: 868
Students reporting specialty: 100%
Students specializing in:
agriculture: 2%; biomedical: 5%;
chemical: 6%; civil: 7%; computer
science: 19%; electrical: 19%;
science and physics: 7%;
environmental: 1%; industrial: 7%;
materials: 6%; mechanical: 19%;
nuclear: 0%; other: 2%

University of Wisconsin-Milwaukee

PO Box 784
Milwaukee, WI 53201-0784
www.uwm.edu/CEAS
Public
Admissions: (414) 229-6169
Email: bwarras@uwm.edu
Financial aid: (414) 229-4541
Application deadline: rolling
In-state tuition: full time: $11,724;
part time: $1,196/credit hour
Out-of-state tuition: full time:
$24,761
Room/board/expenses: $12,830
Full-time enrollment: 336
men: 71%; women: 29%;
minorities: 5%; international: 81%
Part-time enrollment: 97
men: 85%; women: 15%;
minorities: 23%; international: 0%
Acceptance rate: 52%
GRE requirement: Yes
Avg. GRE: quantitative: 159
TOEFL requirement: Yes
Minimum TOEFL score: 520
Fellowships: 31
Teaching assistantships: 117
Research assistantships: 49
Students reporting specialty: 100%
Students specializing in:
biomedical: 7%; civil: 12%;
computer science: 22%;
electrical: 24%; industrial: 10%;
materials: 8%; mechanical: 17%

WYOMING

University of Wyoming

Department 3295
1000 E. University Avenue
Laramie, WY 82071
www.uwyo.edu/ceas/
Public
Admissions: (307) 766-5160
Email: why-wyo@uwyo.edu
Financial aid: (307) 766-2116
Application deadline: rolling
In-state tuition: full time: $232/
credit hour; part time: $232/
credit hour
Out-of-state tuition: full time: $693/
credit hour
Room/board/expenses: $16,782
Full-time enrollment: 209
men: 74%; women: 26%;
minorities: 2%; international: 64%
Part-time enrollment: 54
men: 76%; women: 24%;
minorities: 6%; international: 48%
Acceptance rate: 23%
GRE requirement: Yes
Avg. GRE: quantitative: 161
TOEFL requirement: Yes
Minimum TOEFL score: 550
Fellowships: 62
Teaching assistantships: 39
Research assistantships: 144
Students reporting specialty: 100%
Students specializing in:
architectural: 1%; chemical: 13%;
civil: 17%; computer science: 10%;
electrical: 16%; mechanical: 17%;
petroleum: 15%; other: 11%

LAW

The law directory lists the 204 schools in the country offering the J.D. degree that were fully or provisionally accredited by the American Bar Association in August 2015. One hundred ninety schools responded to the U.S. News survey conducted in the fall of 2015 and early 2016, and their data are reported here. Nonresponders have abbreviated entries. Minnesota's William Mitchell College of Law and Hamline University School of Law have merged to become Mitchell Hamline School of Law but are listed separately.

KEY TO THE TERMINOLOGY

1. A school whose name is footnoted with the numeral 1 did not return the U.S. News statistical survey; limited data appear in its entry.

N/A. Not available from the school or not applicable.

Admissions. The admissions office phone number.

Email. The address of the admissions office. If instead of an email address a website is listed, the website will automatically present an email screen programmed to reach the admissions office.

Financial aid. The financial aid office phone number.

Application deadline. For fall 2017 enrollment. "Rolling" means there is no deadline; the school acts on applications as they are received. "Varies" means deadlines vary according to department or whether applicants are U.S. citizens or foreign nationals.

Tuition. For the 2015-16 academic year. Includes fees.

Credit hour. The cost per credit hour for the 2015-16 academic year.

Room/board/expenses. For the 2015-16 academic year.

Median grant. The median value of grants to full-time students enrolled in 2015-16. This is calculated for all full-time students (not just those in the first year) who received grants and scholarships from internal sources.

Average law school indebtedness. For 2015 graduates, the average law school debt for those taking out at least one educational loan while in school.

Enrollment. Full and part time, fall 2015. Gender figure is for full and part time.

Minorities. For fall 2015, the percentage of full-time and part-time U.S. students who are black or African-American, Asian, American Indian or Alaska Native, Native Hawaiian or other Pacific Islander, Hispanic/Latino, or two or more races.

Acceptance rate. Percentage of applicants who were accepted for the fall 2015 full-time J.D. program.

Midrange Law School Admission Test (LSAT) score. For full-time students who entered in fall 2015. The first number is the 25th percentile test score for the class; the second, the 75th percentile.

Midrange undergraduate grade point average. For full-time students who entered in fall 2015. The first number is the 25th percentile GPA for the class; the second is the 75th percentile.

Midrange of full-time private sector starting salaries. For the 2014 graduating class, the starting salary is for those employed full time in the private sector in law firms, business, industry or other jobs. The first number is the starting salary at the 25th percentile of the graduating class; the second number is the starting salary at the 75th percentile. When a school has the same salary at the 25th and 75th percentiles, it means that the starting salaries for private sector jobs were the same for a large proportion of the class.

Job classifications. For 2014 graduates, this represents the breakdown for the following types of employment: in law firms, business and industry (legal and nonlegal), government, public interest, judicial clerkship, academia and unknown. Numbers may not add up to 100 percent because of rounding.

Employment locations. For the 2014 graduating class. Abbreviations: **Intl.**, international; **N.E.**, New England (Conn., Maine, Mass., N.H., R.I., Vt.); **M.A.**, Middle Atlantic (N.J., N.Y., Pa.); **S.A.**, South Atlantic (Del., D.C., Fla., Ga., Md., N.C., S.C., Va., W.Va.); **E.N.C.**, East North Central (Ill., Ind., Mich., Ohio, Wis.); **W.N.C.**, West North Central (Iowa, Kan., Minn., Mo., Neb., N.D., S.D.); **E.S.C.**, East South Central (Ala., Ky., Miss., Tenn.); **W.S.C.**, West South Central (Ark., La., Okla., Texas); **Mt.**, Mountain (Ariz., Colo., Idaho, Mont., Nev., N.M., Utah, Wyo.); **Pac.**, Pacific (Alaska, Calif., Hawaii, Ore., Wash.).

ALABAMA

Faulkner University (Jones)[1]
5345 Atlanta Highway
Montgomery, AL 36109
www.faulkner.edu/law
Private
Admissions: (334) 386-7210
Email: law@faulkner.edu
Financial aid: N/A
Tuition: N/A
Room/board/expenses: N/A
Enrollment: N/A

Samford University (Cumberland)
800 Lakeshore Drive
Birmingham, AL 35229
www.samford.edu/cumberlandlaw/
Private
Admissions: (205) 726-2702
Email: lawadm@samford.edu
Financial aid: (205) 726-2905
Application deadline: 04/15
Tuition: full time: $37,096; part time: $21,889
Room/board/expenses: $16,274
Median grant: $15,000
Average student indebtedness at graduation: $124,106
Enrollment: full time: 424; part time: 25
men: 53%; women: 47%; minorities: 13%
Acceptance rate (full time): 65%
Midrange LSAT (full time): 148-153
Midrange undergraduate GPA (full time): 2.98-3.53
Midrange of full-time private-sector salaries of 2014 grads: $49,000-$70,000
2014 grads employed in: law firms: 55%; business and industry: 24%; government: 13%; public interest: 1%; judicial clerk: 7%; academia: 0%; unknown: 0%
Employment location for 2014 class: Intl. 0%; N.E. 1%; M.A. 1%; E.N.C. 0%; W.N.C. 0%; S.A. 26%; E.S.C. 68%; W.S.C. 0%; Mt. 3%; Pac. 2%; unknown 0%

University of Alabama
Box 870382
Tuscaloosa, AL 35487
www.law.ua.edu
Public
Admissions: (205) 348-5440
Email: admissions@law.ua.edu
Financial aid: (205) 348-6756
Application deadline: rolling
In-state tuition: full time: $22,324; part time: N/A
Out-of-state tuition: full time: $37,664
Room/board/expenses: $19,016
Median grant: $15,000
Average student indebtedness at graduation: $74,921
Enrollment: full time: 431; part time: N/A
men: 57%; women: 43%; minorities: 19%
Acceptance rate (full time): 37%

Midrange LSAT (full time): 156-164
Midrange undergraduate GPA (full time): 3.29-3.93
Midrange of full-time private-sector salaries of 2014 grads: $50,000-$110,000
2014 grads employed in: law firms: 52%; business and industry: 16%; government: 11%; public interest: 8%; judicial clerk: 11%; academia: 2%; unknown: 0%
Employment location for 2014 class: Intl. 1%; N.E. 1%; M.A. 3%; E.N.C. 1%; W.N.C. 1%; S.A. 20%; E.S.C. 66%; W.S.C. 4%; Mt. 3%; Pac. 1%; unknown 0%

ARIZONA

Arizona State University (O'Connor)
1100 S. McAllister Avenue
Tempe, AZ 85287-7906
www.law.asu.edu
Public
Admissions: (480) 965-1474
Email: law.admissions@asu.edu
Financial aid: (480) 965-1474
Application deadline: 03/01
In-state tuition: full time: $27,074; part time: N/A
Out-of-state tuition: full time: $42,794
Room/board/expenses: $21,388
Median grant: $20,000
Average student indebtedness at graduation: $106,426
Enrollment: full time: 623; part time: N/A
men: 63%; women: 37%; minorities: 23%
Acceptance rate (full time): 43%
Midrange LSAT (full time): 158-163
Midrange undergraduate GPA (full time): 3.39-3.80
Midrange of full-time private-sector salaries of 2014 grads: $60,000-$105,000
2014 grads employed in: law firms: 46%; business and industry: 18%; government: 19%; public interest: 6%; judicial clerk: 9%; academia: 2%; unknown: 0%
Employment location for 2014 class: Intl. 0%; N.E. 0%; M.A. 1%; E.N.C. 1%; W.N.C. 3%; S.A. 3%; E.S.C. 0%; W.S.C. 4%; Mt. 84%; Pac. 5%; unknown 0%

Arizona Summit Law School[1]
One North Central Avenue
Phoenix, AZ 85004
www.azsummitlaw.edu/
Private
Admissions: (602) 682-6800
Email: admissions@AZSummitLaw.edu
Financial aid: () -
Tuition: N/A
Room/board/expenses: N/A
Enrollment: N/A

University of Arizona (Rogers)

PO Box 210176
Tucson, AZ 85721-0176
www.law.arizona.edu
Public
Admissions: (520) 621-7666
Email:
admissions@law.arizona.edu
Financial aid: (520) 626-1832
Application deadline: 05/15
In-state tuition: full time: $24,500;
part time: N/A
Out-of-state tuition: full time:
$29,000
Room/board/expenses: $21,050
Median grant: $14,362
**Average student indebtedness at
graduation:** $100,902
Enrollment: full time: 359; part
time: 2
men: 60%; women: 40%;
minorities: 24%
Acceptance rate (full time): 33%
Midrange LSAT (full time): 155-162
**Midrange undergraduate GPA (full
time):** 3.22-3.68
**Midrange of full-time private-sector
salaries of 2014 grads:** $70,000-
$110,000
2014 grads employed in: law firms:
38%; business and industry:
10%; government: 18%; public
interest: 2%; judicial clerk: 23%;
academia: 7%; unknown: 2%
**Employment location for 2014
class:** Intl. 3%; N.E. 0%; M.A. 1%;
E.N.C. 2%; W.N.C. 1%; S.A. 2%;
E.S.C. 0%; W.S.C. 1%; Mt. 80%;
Pac. 9%; unknown 1%

ARKANSAS

University of Arkansas-Fayetteville

Robert A. Leflar Law Center
Fayetteville, AR 72701
law.uark.edu/
Public
Admissions: (479) 575-3102
Email: jkmiller@uark.edu
Financial aid: (479) 575-3806
Application deadline: 04/15
In-state tuition: full time: $15,224;
part time: N/A
Out-of-state tuition: full time:
$31,443
Room/board/expenses: $15,726
Median grant: $8,000
**Average student indebtedness at
graduation:** $64,901
Enrollment: full time: 350; part
time: N/A
men: 61%; women: 39%;
minorities: 18%
Acceptance rate (full time): 67%
Midrange LSAT (full time): 151-158
**Midrange undergraduate GPA (full
time):** 3.06-3.65
**Midrange of full-time private-sector
salaries of 2014 grads:** $47,000-
$80,000
2014 grads employed in: law firms:
46%; business and industry:
26%; government: 17%; public
interest: 4%; judicial clerk: 4%;
academia: 3%; unknown: 0%
Employment location for 2014 class:
Intl. 1%; N.E. 0%; M.A. 1%; E.N.C.
3%; W.N.C. 6%; S.A. 4%; E.S.C.
4%; W.S.C. 76%; Mt. 4%; Pac.
2%; unknown 0%

University of Arkansas-Little Rock (Bowen)

1201 McMath Avenue
Little Rock, AR 72202-5142
ualr.edu/law/
Public
Admissions: (501) 324-9903
Email: lawadmissions@ualr.edu
Financial aid: (501) 569-3127
Application deadline: 03/15
In-state tuition: full time: $14,447;
part time: $9,674
Out-of-state tuition: full time:
$29,223
Room/board/expenses: $15,292
Median grant: $7,000
**Average student indebtedness at
graduation:** $68,960
Enrollment: full time: 287; part
time: 112
men: 54%; women: 46%;
minorities: 17%
Acceptance rate (full time): 62%
Midrange LSAT (full time): 146-156
**Midrange undergraduate GPA (full
time):** 2.99-3.55
**Midrange of full-time private-sector
salaries of 2014 grads:** $45,000-
$66,250
2014 grads employed in: law firms:
50%; business and industry:
14%; government: 24%; public
interest: 6%; judicial clerk: 4%;
academia: 1%; unknown: 2%
**Employment location for 2014
class:** Intl. 0%; N.E. 2%; M.A. 2%;
E.N.C. 1%; W.N.C. 0%; S.A. 6%;
E.S.C. 2%; W.S.C. 82%; Mt. 1%;
Pac. 2%; unknown 3%

CALIFORNIA

California Western School of Law

225 Cedar Street
San Diego, CA 92101-3090
www.cwsl.edu
Private
Admissions: (619) 525-1401
Email: admissions@cwsl.edu
Financial aid: (619) 525-7060
Application deadline: 04/01
Tuition: full time: $47,260; part
time: $33,060
Room/board/expenses: $23,792
Median grant: $22,900
**Average student indebtedness at
graduation:** $162,260
Enrollment: full time: 514; part
time: 114
men: 42%; women: 58%;
minorities: 36%
Acceptance rate (full time): 71%
Midrange LSAT (full time): 147-153
**Midrange undergraduate GPA (full
time):** 2.86-3.44
**Midrange of full-time private-sector
salaries of 2014 grads:** $52,000-
$72,000
2014 grads employed in: law firms:
60%; business and industry:
17%; government: 14%; public
interest: 5%; judicial clerk: 1%;
academia: 1%; unknown: 0%
**Employment location for 2014
class:** Intl. 0%; N.E. 0%; M.A. 1%;
E.N.C. 1%; W.N.C. 1%; S.A. 2%;
E.S.C. 0%; W.S.C. 0%; Mt. 3%;
Pac. 92%; unknown 0%

Chapman University (Fowler)

1 University Drive
Orange, CA 92866
www.chapman.edu/law
Private
Admissions: (714) 628-2500
Email: lawadm@chapman.edu
Financial aid: (714) 628-2510
Application deadline: rolling
Tuition: full time: $48,602; part
time: $38,677
Room/board/expenses: $28,315
Median grant: $37,040
**Average student indebtedness at
graduation:** $103,956
Enrollment: full time: 436; part
time: 31
men: 49%; women: 51%;
minorities: 36%
Acceptance rate (full time): 49%
Midrange LSAT (full time): 152-158
**Midrange undergraduate GPA (full
time):** 3.07-3.47
**Midrange of full-time private-sector
salaries of 2014 grads:** $54,500-
$75,000
2014 grads employed in: law firms:
62%; business and industry:
28%; government: 5%; public
interest: 3%; judicial clerk: 1%;
academia: 2%; unknown: 0%
**Employment location for 2014
class:** Intl. 0%; N.E. 0%; M.A. 1%;
E.N.C. 2%; W.N.C. 0%; S.A. 1%;
E.S.C. 0%; W.S.C. 0%; Mt. 2%;
Pac. 94%; unknown 0%

Golden Gate University

536 Mission Street
San Francisco, CA 94105
www.law.ggu.edu
Private
Admissions: (415) 442-6630
Email: lawadmit@ggu.edu
Financial aid: (415) 442-6635
Application deadline: 04/01
Tuition: full time: $46,850; part
time: $34,450
Room/board/expenses: $25,433
Median grant: $20,000
**Average student indebtedness at
graduation:** $143,740
Enrollment: full time: 253; part
time: 94
men: 39%; women: 61%;
minorities: 49%
Acceptance rate (full time): 68%
Midrange LSAT (full time): 146-151
**Midrange undergraduate GPA (full
time):** 2.73-3.22
**Midrange of full-time private-sector
salaries of 2014 grads:** $50,000-
$77,250
2014 grads employed in: law firms:
46%; business and industry:
19%; government: 14%; public
interest: 13%; judicial clerk: 1%;
academia: 8%; unknown: 0%
**Employment location for 2014
class:** Intl. 1%; N.E. 0%; M.A. 0%;
E.N.C. 0%; W.N.C. 0%; S.A. 1%;
E.S.C. 2%; W.S.C. 0%; Mt. 1%;
Pac. 96%; unknown 0%

Loyola Marymount University

919 Albany Street
Los Angeles, CA 90015-1211
www.lls.edu
Private
Admissions: (213) 736-1074
Email: Admissions@lls.edu
Financial aid: (213) 736-1140
Application deadline: 02/01
Tuition: full time: $50,050; part
time: $33,502
Room/board/expenses: $30,276
Median grant: $32,000
**Average student indebtedness at
graduation:** $148,035
Enrollment: full time: 800; part
time: 182
men: 46%; women: 54%;
minorities: 45%
Acceptance rate (full time): 46%
Midrange LSAT (full time): 156-161
**Midrange undergraduate GPA (full
time):** 3.33-3.65
**Midrange of full-time private-sector
salaries of 2014 grads:** $58,200-
$100,000
2014 grads employed in: law firms:
67%; business and industry:
17%; government: 4%; public
interest: 8%; judicial clerk: 4%;
academia: 0%; unknown: 0%
Employment location for 2014 class:
Intl. 1%; N.E. 0%; M.A. 1%; E.N.C.
0%; W.N.C. 0%; S.A. 2%; E.S.C.
0%; W.S.C. 0%; Mt. 1%; Pac.
94%; unknown 0%

Pepperdine University

24255 Pacific Coast Highway
Malibu, CA 90263
law.pepperdine.edu
Private
Admissions: (310) 506-4631
Email: soladmis@pepperdine.edu
Financial aid: (310) 506-4633
Application deadline: 04/01
Tuition: full time: $51,180; part
time: N/A
Room/board/expenses: $28,620
Median grant: $24,485
**Average student indebtedness at
graduation:** $148,959
Enrollment: full time: 598; part
time: 12
men: 49%; women: 51%;
minorities: 31%
Acceptance rate (full time): 49%
Midrange LSAT (full time): 154-161
**Midrange undergraduate GPA (full
time):** 3.24-3.71
**Midrange of full-time private-sector
salaries of 2014 grads:** $60,000-
$80,700
2014 grads employed in: law firms:
49%; business and industry:
18%; government: 11%; public
interest: 3%; judicial clerk: 10%;
academia: 10%; unknown: 0%
Employment location for 2014 class:
Intl. 1%; N.E. 0%; M.A. 1%; E.N.C.
5%; W.N.C. 1%; S.A. 6%; E.S.C.
3%; W.S.C. 4%; Mt. 6%; Pac.
73%; unknown 0%

Santa Clara University

500 El Camino Real
Santa Clara, CA 95053-0421
www.scu.edu/law
Private
Admissions: (408) 554-4800
Email: lawadmissions@scu.edu
Financial aid: (408) 554-4447

Application deadline: 02/15
Tuition: full time: $1,623/credit
hour; part time: $1,623/credit
hour
Room/board/expenses: $23,974
Median grant: $12,000
**Average student indebtedness at
graduation:** $144,130
Enrollment: full time: 506; part
time: 147
men: 50%; women: 50%;
minorities: 42%
Acceptance rate (full time): 61%
Midrange LSAT (full time): 153-157
**Midrange undergraduate GPA (full
time):** 3.07-3.40
**Midrange of full-time private-sector
salaries of 2014 grads:** $67,500-
$160,000
2014 grads employed in: law firms:
47%; business and industry:
36%; government: 8%; public
interest: 6%; judicial clerk: 1%;
academia: 1%; unknown: 1%
**Employment location for 2014
class:** Intl. 1%; N.E. 0%; M.A. 2%;
E.N.C. 0%; W.N.C. 1%; S.A. 1%;
E.S.C. 0%; W.S.C. 1%; Mt. 2%;
Pac. 92%; unknown 1%

Southwestern Law School

3050 Wilshire Boulevard
Los Angeles, CA 90010-1106
www.swlaw.edu
Private
Admissions: (213) 738-6717
Email: admissions@swlaw.edu
Financial aid: (213) 738-6719
Application deadline: 04/03
Tuition: full time: $48,280; part
time: $32,260
Room/board/expenses: $30,123
Median grant: $16,882
Enrollment: full time: 659; part
time: 318
men: 42%; women: 58%;
minorities: 46%
Acceptance rate (full time): 61%
Midrange LSAT (full time): 149-154
**Midrange undergraduate GPA (full
time):** 2.95-3.39
**Midrange of full-time private-sector
salaries of 2014 grads:** $55,500-
$80,000
2014 grads employed in: law firms:
62%; business and industry:
28%; government: 3%; public
interest: 3%; judicial clerk: 1%;
academia: 3%; unknown: 0%
Employment location for 2014 class:
Intl. 0%; N.E. 0%; M.A. 0%;
E.N.C. 0%; W.N.C. 0%; S.A. 0%;
E.S.C. 0%; W.S.C. 1%; Mt. 0%;
Pac. 97%; unknown 37%

Stanford University

Crown Quadrangle
559 Nathan Abbott Way
Stanford, CA 94305-8610
www.law.stanford.edu/
Private
Admissions: (650) 723-4985
Email:
admissions@law.stanford.edu
Financial aid: (650) 723-9247
Application deadline: 02/01
Tuition: full time: $56,274; part
time: N/A
Room/board/expenses: $29,694
Median grant: $22,399
**Average student indebtedness at
graduation:** $132,970

Enrollment: full time: 572; part time: N/A
men: 54%; women: 46%; minorities: 35%
Acceptance rate (full time): 11%
Midrange LSAT (full time): 169-173
Midrange undergraduate GPA (full time): 3.78-3.97
Midrange of full-time private-sector salaries of 2014 grads: $160,000-$160,000
2014 grads employed in: law firms: 49%; business and industry: 6%; government: 2%; public interest: 9%; judicial clerk: 33%; academia: 1%; unknown: 0%
Employment location for 2014 class: Intl. 1%; N.E. 2%; M.A. 20%; E.N.C. 5%; W.N.C. 1%; S.A. 14%; E.S.C. 3%; W.S.C. 3%; Mt. 4%; Pac. 47%; unknown 0%

Thomas Jefferson School of Law
1155 Island Avenue
San Diego, CA 92101
www.tjsl.edu
Private
Admissions: (619) 297-9700
Email: info@tjsl.edu
Financial aid: (619) 297-9700
Application deadline: 08/01
Tuition: full time: $46,200; part time: $34,700
Room/board/expenses: $26,690
Median grant: $12,500
Average student indebtedness at graduation: $172,726
Enrollment: full time: 485; part time: 178
men: 45%; women: 55%; minorities: 51%
Acceptance rate (full time): 84%
Midrange LSAT (full time): 141-148
Midrange undergraduate GPA (full time): 2.46-3.09
Midrange of full-time private-sector salaries of 2014 grads: $48,000-$75,000
2014 grads employed in: law firms: 50%; business and industry: 29%; government: 9%; public interest: 7%; judicial clerk: 3%; academia: 2%; unknown: 0%
Employment location for 2014 class: Intl. 1%; N.E. 1%; M.A. 3%; E.N.C. 2%; W.N.C. 1%; S.A. 7%; E.S.C. 0%; W.S.C. 2%; Mt. 8%; Pac. 70%; unknown 3%

University of California-Berkeley
Boalt Hall
Berkeley, CA 94720-7200
www.law.berkeley.edu
Public
Admissions: (510) 642-2274
Email: admissions@law.berkeley.edu
Financial aid: (510) 642-1563
Application deadline: rolling
In-state tuition: full time: $48,679; part time: N/A
Out-of-state tuition: full time: $52,630
Room/board/expenses: $29,574
Median grant: $19,089
Average student indebtedness at graduation: $144,981
Enrollment: full time: 935; part time: 2
men: 44%; women: 56%; minorities: 39%

Acceptance rate (full time): 21%
Midrange LSAT (full time): 162-168
Midrange undergraduate GPA (full time): 3.66-3.90
Midrange of full-time private-sector salaries of 2014 grads: $160,000-$160,000
2014 grads employed in: law firms: 56%; business and industry: 3%; government: 8%; public interest: 14%; judicial clerk: 17%; academia: 1%; unknown: 0%
Employment location for 2014 class: Intl. 1%; N.E. 1%; M.A. 11%; E.N.C. 2%; W.N.C. 1%; S.A. 9%; E.S.C. 1%; W.S.C. 3%; Mt. 5%; Pac. 67%; unknown 0%

University of California-Davis
400 Mrak Hall Drive
Davis, CA 95616-5201
www.law.ucdavis.edu/jd
Public
Admissions: (530) 752-6477
Email: admissions@law.ucdavis.edu
Financial aid: (530) 752-6573
Application deadline: 03/15
In-state tuition: full time: $47,339; part time: N/A
Out-of-state tuition: full time: $56,590
Room/board/expenses: $21,772
Median grant: $25,000
Average student indebtedness at graduation: $113,765
Enrollment: full time: 494; part time: N/A
men: 47%; women: 53%; minorities: 38%
Acceptance rate (full time): 31%
Midrange LSAT (full time): 159-165
Midrange undergraduate GPA (full time): 3.27-3.68
Midrange of full-time private-sector salaries of 2014 grads: $72,500-$160,000
2014 grads employed in: law firms: 47%; business and industry: 9%; government: 22%; public interest: 12%; judicial clerk: 5%; academia: 3%; unknown: 1%
Employment location for 2014 class: Intl. 1%; N.E. 0%; M.A. 0%; E.N.C. 0%; W.N.C. 1%; S.A. 3%; E.S.C. 0%; W.S.C. 1%; Mt. 3%; Pac. 91%; unknown 0%

University of California (Hastings)
200 McAllister Street
San Francisco, CA 94102
www.uchastings.edu
Public
Admissions: (415) 565-4623
Email: admissions@uchastings.edu
Financial aid: (415) 565-4624
Application deadline: 03/01
In-state tuition: full time: $48,638; part time: N/A
Out-of-state tuition: full time: $54,638
Room/board/expenses: $26,508
Median grant: $13,000
Average student indebtedness at graduation: $135,886
Enrollment: full time: 903; part time: 2
men: 47%; women: 53%; minorities: 44%

Acceptance rate (full time): 42%
Midrange LSAT (full time): 155-161
Midrange undergraduate GPA (full time): 3.28-3.64
Midrange of full-time private-sector salaries of 2014 grads: $72,500-$160,000
2014 grads employed in: law firms: 52%; business and industry: 17%; government: 19%; public interest: 7%; judicial clerk: 3%; academia: 2%; unknown: 0%
Employment location for 2014 class: Intl. 1%; N.E. 0%; M.A. 1%; E.N.C. 1%; W.N.C. 0%; S.A. 3%; E.S.C. 0%; W.S.C. 0%; Mt. 1%; Pac. 92%; unknown 0%

University of California-Irvine
401 East Peltason Drive
Suite 1000
Irvine, CA 92697-8000
www.law.uci.edu/
Public
Admissions: (949) 824-4545
Email: lawadmit@law.uci.edu
Financial aid: (949) 824-8080
Application deadline: 03/01
In-state tuition: full time: $44,765; part time: N/A
Out-of-state tuition: full time: $51,259
Room/board/expenses: $26,366
Median grant: $20,000
Average student indebtedness at graduation: $125,473
Enrollment: full time: 334; part time: N/A
men: 50%; women: 50%; minorities: 43%
Acceptance rate (full time): 27%
Midrange LSAT (full time): 161-165
Midrange undergraduate GPA (full time): 3.38-3.70
Midrange of full-time private-sector salaries of 2014 grads: $65,000-$150,000
2014 grads employed in: law firms: 45%; business and industry: 13%; government: 11%; public interest: 16%; judicial clerk: 13%; academia: 3%; unknown: 0%
Employment location for 2014 class: Intl. 0%; N.E. 0%; M.A. 1%; E.N.C. 1%; W.N.C. 0%; S.A. 6%; E.S.C. 0%; W.S.C. 1%; Mt. 3%; Pac. 88%; unknown 0%

University of California-Los Angeles
71 Dodd Hall
PO Box 951445
Los Angeles, CA 90095-1445
www.law.ucla.edu
Public
Admissions: (310) 825-2260
Email: admissions@law.ucla.edu
Financial aid: (310) 825-2459
Application deadline: 02/01
In-state tuition: full time: $45,284; part time: N/A
Out-of-state tuition: full time: $51,778
Room/board/expenses: $26,368
Median grant: $21,000
Average student indebtedness at graduation: $118,874
Enrollment: full time: 974; part time: N/A
men: 49%; women: 51%; minorities: 34%

Acceptance rate (full time): 30%
Midrange LSAT (full time): 162-169
Midrange undergraduate GPA (full time): 3.51-3.86
Midrange of full-time private-sector salaries of 2014 grads: $85,000-$160,000
2014 grads employed in: law firms: 64%; business and industry: 8%; government: 6%; public interest: 14%; judicial clerk: 7%; academia: 1%; unknown: 0%
Employment location for 2014 class: Intl. N/A; N.E. 1%; M.A. 3%; E.N.C. 1%; W.N.C. 0%; S.A. 5%; E.S.C. 1%; W.S.C. 1%; Mt. 1%; Pac. 87%; unknown N/A

University of La Verne[1]
320 E. D Street
Ontario, CA 91764
law.laverne.edu
Private
Admissions: (909) 460-2006
Email: lawadm@laverne.edu
Financial aid: N/A
Tuition: N/A
Room/board/expenses: N/A
Enrollment: N/A

University of San Diego
5998 Alcala Park
San Diego, CA 92110-2492
www.law.sandiego.edu
Private
Admissions: (619) 260-4528
Email: jdinfo@SanDiego.edu
Financial aid: (619) 260-4570
Application deadline: rolling
Tuition: full time: $48,830; part time: $36,180
Room/board/expenses: $21,170
Median grant: $22,000
Average student indebtedness at graduation: $135,433
Enrollment: full time: 634; part time: 103
men: 51%; women: 49%; minorities: 31%
Acceptance rate (full time): 41%
Midrange LSAT (full time): 156-161
Midrange undergraduate GPA (full time): 3.20-3.64
Midrange of full-time private-sector salaries of 2014 grads: $65,000-$150,000
2014 grads employed in: law firms: 55%; business and industry: 22%; government: 12%; public interest: 6%; judicial clerk: 2%; academia: 1%; unknown: 1%
Employment location for 2014 class: Intl. 0%; N.E. 0%; M.A. 0%; E.N.C. 0%; W.N.C. 0%; S.A. 1%; E.S.C. 0%; W.S.C. 1%; Mt. 5%; Pac. 90%; unknown 0%

University of San Francisco
2130 Fulton Street
San Francisco, CA 94117-1080
www.usfca.edu/law
Private
Admissions: (415) 422-6586
Email: lawadmissions@usfca.edu
Financial aid: (415) 422-6210
Application deadline: 02/01
Tuition: full time: $46,860; part time: $1,670/credit hour
Room/board/expenses: $30,328
Median grant: $23,000

Average student indebtedness at graduation: $162,434
Enrollment: full time: 431; part time: 97
men: 45%; women: 55%; minorities: 52%
Acceptance rate (full time): 63%
Midrange LSAT (full time): 149-154
Midrange undergraduate GPA (full time): 2.87-3.37
Midrange of full-time private-sector salaries of 2014 grads: $52,000-$100,000
2014 grads employed in: law firms: 56%; business and industry: 23%; government: 10%; public interest: 7%; judicial clerk: 2%; academia: 2%; unknown: 0%
Employment location for 2014 class: Intl. 2%; N.E. 1%; M.A. 2%; E.N.C. 1%; W.N.C. 0%; S.A. 2%; E.S.C. 0%; W.S.C. 1%; Mt. 1%; Pac. 90%; unknown 2%

University of Southern California (Gould)
699 Exposition Boulevard
Los Angeles, CA 90089-0071
gould.usc.edu
Private
Admissions: (213) 740-2523
Email: admissions@law.usc.edu
Financial aid: (213) 740-6314
Application deadline: 02/01
Tuition: full time: $58,022; part time: N/A
Room/board/expenses: $22,710
Median grant: $25,000
Average student indebtedness at graduation: $134,673
Enrollment: full time: 598; part time: 4
men: 52%; women: 48%; minorities: 36%
Acceptance rate (full time): 30%
Midrange LSAT (full time): 161-167
Midrange undergraduate GPA (full time): 3.49-3.86
Midrange of full-time private-sector salaries of 2014 grads: $105,000-$160,000
2014 grads employed in: law firms: 59%; business and industry: 11%; government: 11%; public interest: 11%; judicial clerk: 3%; academia: 4%; unknown: 0%
Employment location for 2014 class: Intl. 1%; N.E. 0%; M.A. 3%; E.N.C. 1%; W.N.C. 0%; S.A. 3%; E.S.C. 0%; W.S.C. 1%; Mt. 1%; Pac. 87%; unknown 0%

University of the Pacific (McGeorge)
3200 Fifth Avenue
Sacramento, CA 95817
www.mcgeorge.edu
Private
Admissions: (916) 739-7105
Email: admissionsmcgeorge@pacific.edu
Financial aid: (916) 739-7158
Application deadline: 04/01
Tuition: full time: $48,274; part time: $32,060
Room/board/expenses: $25,495
Median grant: $11,827
Average student indebtedness at graduation: $149,470

Enrollment: full time: 356; part time: 121
men: 45%; women: 55%; minorities: 31%
Acceptance rate (full time): 74%
Midrange LSAT (full time): 149-155
Midrange undergraduate GPA (full time): 2.85-3.43
Midrange of full-time private-sector salaries of 2014 grads: $50,000-$76,000
2014 grads employed in: law firms: 48%; business and industry: 16%; government: 20%; public interest: 9%; judicial clerk: 3%; academia: 4%; unknown: 1%
Employment location for 2014 class: Intl. 1%; N.E. 1%; M.A. 1%; E.N.C. 1%; W.N.C. 1%; S.A. 2%; E.S.C. 0%; W.S.C. 0%; Mt. 4%; Pac. 89%; unknown 0%

Western State College of Law at Argosy University

1 Banting
Irvine, CA 92618
www.wsulaw.edu
Private
Admissions: (714) 459-1101
Email: adm@wsulaw.edu
Financial aid: (714) 459-1120
Application deadline: 07/01
Tuition: full time: $43,350; part time: $29,150
Room/board/expenses: $23,467
Median grant: $21,000
Average student indebtedness at graduation: $122,315
Enrollment: full time: 223; part time: 115
men: 45%; women: 55%; minorities: 58%
Acceptance rate (full time): 65%
Midrange LSAT (full time): 145-151
Midrange undergraduate GPA (full time): 2.83-3.30
Midrange of full-time private-sector salaries of 2014 grads: $49,000-$67,500
2014 grads employed in: law firms: 62%; business and industry: 23%; government: 6%; public interest: 3%; judicial clerk: 1%; academia: 3%; unknown: 1%
Employment location for 2014 class: Intl. 0%; N.E. 1%; M.A. 1%; E.N.C. 1%; W.N.C. 1%; S.A. 2%; E.S.C. 0%; W.S.C. 1%; Mt. 5%; Pac. 88%; unknown 0%

Whittier College

3333 Harbor Boulevard
Costa Mesa, CA 92626-1501
www.law.whittier.edu
Private
Admissions: (800) 808-8188
Email: info@law.whittier.edu
Financial aid: (714) 444-4141
Application deadline: 07/31
Tuition: full time: $44,370; part time: $29,714
Room/board/expenses: $32,136
Median grant: $17,964
Average student indebtedness at graduation: $148,316
Enrollment: full time: 326; part time: 130
men: 41%; women: 59%; minorities: 50%
Acceptance rate (full time): 65%
Midrange LSAT (full time): 146-151
Midrange undergraduate GPA (full time): 2.59-3.28

Midrange of full-time private-sector salaries of 2014 grads: $42,750-$70,233
2014 grads employed in: law firms: 56%; business and industry: 26%; government: 2%; public interest: 4%; judicial clerk: 0%; academia: 11%; unknown: 0%
Employment location for 2014 class: Intl. 0%; N.E. 0%; M.A. 1%; E.N.C. 0%; W.N.C. 1%; S.A. 4%; E.S.C. 0%; W.S.C. 1%; Mt. 1%; Pac. 92%; unknown 1%

COLORADO

University of Colorado-Boulder

Box 401
Boulder, CO 80309-0401
www.colorado.edu/law/
Public
Admissions: (303) 492-7203
Email: law.admissions@colorado.edu
Financial aid: (303) 492-0647
Application deadline: 03/15
In-state tuition: full time: $31,864; part time: N/A
Out-of-state tuition: full time: $38,650
Room/board/expenses: $19,024
Median grant: $11,000
Average student indebtedness at graduation: $107,080
Enrollment: full time: 555; part time: N/A
men: 53%; women: 47%; minorities: 19%
Acceptance rate (full time): 46%
Midrange LSAT (full time): 157-163
Midrange undergraduate GPA (full time): 3.28-3.77
Midrange of full-time private-sector salaries of 2014 grads: $60,000-$115,000
2014 grads employed in: law firms: 40%; business and industry: 12%; government: 18%; public interest: 11%; judicial clerk: 16%; academia: 3%; unknown: 0%
Employment location for 2014 class: Intl. 0%; N.E. 1%; M.A. 4%; E.N.C. 1%; W.N.C. 1%; S.A. 3%; E.S.C. 0%; W.S.C. 3%; Mt. 84%; Pac. 3%; unknown 0%

University of Denver (Sturm)

2255 E. Evans Avenue
Denver, CO 80208
www.law.du.edu
Private
Admissions: (303) 871-6135
Email: admissions@law.du.edu
Financial aid: (303) 871-6362
Application deadline: rolling
Tuition: full time: $44,530; part time: $32,686
Room/board/expenses: $16,643
Median grant: $21,000
Average student indebtedness at graduation: $132,158
Enrollment: full time: 701; part time: 116
men: 50%; women: 50%; minorities: 19%
Acceptance rate (full time): 45%
Midrange LSAT (full time): 154-158
Midrange undergraduate GPA (full time): 3.14-3.63
Midrange of full-time private-sector salaries of 2014 grads: $55,000-$106,250

2014 grads employed in: law firms: 38%; business and industry: 17%; government: 21%; public interest: 3%; judicial clerk: 14%; academia: 7%; unknown: 0%
Employment location for 2014 class: Intl. 0%; N.E. 0%; M.A. 1%; E.N.C. 0%; W.N.C. 0%; S.A. 2%; E.S.C. 0%; W.S.C. 0%; Mt. 94%; Pac. 2%; unknown 1%

CONNECTICUT

Quinnipiac University

275 Mount Carmel Avenue
Hamden, CT 06518
law.quinnipiac.edu
Private
Admissions: (203) 582-3400
Email: law@quinnipiac.edu
Financial aid: (203) 582-3405
Application deadline: 07/01
Tuition: full time: $48,049; part time: $33,859
Room/board/expenses: $19,480
Median grant: $25,000
Average student indebtedness at graduation: $97,335
Enrollment: full time: 208; part time: 59
men: 47%; women: 53%; minorities: 15%
Acceptance rate (full time): 64%
Midrange LSAT (full time): 149-155
Midrange undergraduate GPA (full time): 3.21-3.55
Midrange of full-time private-sector salaries of 2014 grads: $50,000-$73,000
2014 grads employed in: law firms: 48%; business and industry: 25%; government: 15%; public interest: 3%; judicial clerk: 4%; academia: 4%; unknown: 0%
Employment location for 2014 class: Intl. 0%; N.E. 85%; M.A. 9%; E.N.C. 1%; W.N.C. 0%; S.A. 3%; E.S.C. 0%; W.S.C. 0%; Mt. 0%; Pac. 2%; unknown 0%

University of Connecticut

55 Elizabeth Street
Hartford, CT 06105-2296
www.law.uconn.edu
Public
Admissions: (860) 570-5100
Email: law.admissions@uconn.edu
Financial aid: (860) 570-5147
Application deadline: 04/01
In-state tuition: full time: $27,934; part time: $19,502
Out-of-state tuition: full time: $57,852
Room/board/expenses: $17,510
Median grant: $16,625
Average student indebtedness at graduation: $69,195
Enrollment: full time: 328; part time: 105
men: 52%; women: 48%; minorities: 24%
Acceptance rate (full time): 53%
Midrange LSAT (full time): 154-158
Midrange undergraduate GPA (full time): 3.18-3.63
Midrange of full-time private-sector salaries of 2014 grads: $71,000-$120,000
2014 grads employed in: law firms: 39%; business and industry: 26%; government: 13%; public interest: 4%; judicial clerk: 16%; academia: 3%; unknown: 0%

Employment location for 2014 class: Intl. 0%; N.E. 83%; M.A. 6%; E.N.C. 2%; W.N.C. 0%; S.A. 8%; E.S.C. 0%; W.S.C. 0%; Mt. 1%; Pac. 1%; unknown 0%

Yale University

PO Box 208215
New Haven, CT 06520-8215
www.law.yale.edu
Private
Admissions: (203) 432-4995
Email: admissions.law@yale.edu
Financial aid: (203) 432-1688
Application deadline: 02/28
Tuition: full time: $58,050; part time: N/A
Room/board/expenses: $20,276
Median grant: $22,997
Average student indebtedness at graduation: $122,796
Enrollment: full time: 614; part time: N/A
men: 54%; women: 46%; minorities: 33%
Acceptance rate (full time): 10%
Midrange LSAT (full time): 171-176
Midrange undergraduate GPA (full time): 3.86-3.98
Midrange of full-time private-sector salaries of 2014 grads: $160,000-$160,000
2014 grads employed in: law firms: 40%; business and industry: 7%; government: 6%; public interest: 12%; judicial clerk: 31%; academia: 4%; unknown: 0%
Employment location for 2014 class: Intl. 5%; N.E. 10%; M.A. 39%; E.N.C. 8%; W.N.C. 0%; S.A. 17%; E.S.C. 3%; W.S.C. 3%; Mt. 3%; Pac. 13%; unknown 0%

DELAWARE

Widener University

Wilmington, DE 19803-0406
delawarelaw.widener.edu
Private
Admissions: (302) 477-2703
Email: delawarelaw@widener.edu
Financial aid: (302) 477-2272
Application deadline: 05/15
Tuition: full time: $1,396/credit hour; part time: $1,396/credit hour
Room/board/expenses: $20,840
Median grant: $15,000
Average student indebtedness at graduation: $136,992
Enrollment: full time: 317; part time: 139
men: 51%; women: 49%; minorities: 24%
Acceptance rate (full time): 69%
Midrange LSAT (full time): 147-152
Midrange undergraduate GPA (full time): 2.75-3.47
Midrange of full-time private-sector salaries of 2014 grads: $45,000-$75,000
2014 grads employed in: law firms: 39%; business and industry: 24%; government: 13%; public interest: 1%; judicial clerk: 23%; academia: 1%; unknown: 0%
Employment location for 2014 class: Intl. 0%; N.E. 1%; M.A. 70%; E.N.C. 0%; W.N.C. 0%; S.A. 29%; E.S.C. 0%; W.S.C. 0%; Mt. 1%; Pac. 0%; unknown 0%

American University (Washington)

4801 Massachusetts Avenue NW
Washington, DC 20016-8192
www.wcl.american.edu
Private
Admissions: (202) 274-4101
Email: wcladmit@wcl.american.edu
Financial aid: (202) 274-4040
Application deadline: rolling
Tuition: full time: $51,002; part time: $35,776
Room/board/expenses: $23,862
Median grant: $13,000
Average student indebtedness at graduation: $160,274
Enrollment: full time: 1,052; part time: 236
men: 41%; women: 59%; minorities: 39%
Acceptance rate (full time): 60%
Midrange LSAT (full time): 152-158
Midrange undergraduate GPA (full time): 3.02-3.49
Midrange of full-time private-sector salaries of 2014 grads: $68,000-$160,000
2014 grads employed in: law firms: 26%; business and industry: 13%; government: 27%; public interest: 16%; judicial clerk: 12%; academia: 4%; unknown: 1%
Employment location for 2014 class: Intl. 3%; N.E. 1%; M.A. 11%; E.N.C. 1%; W.N.C. 0%; S.A. 73%; E.S.C. 2%; W.S.C. 2%; Mt. 2%; Pac. 5%; unknown 1%

The Catholic University of America

3600 John McCormack Road NE
Washington, DC 20064
www.law.edu
Private
Admissions: (202) 319-5151
Email: admissions@law.edu
Financial aid: (202) 319-5143
Application deadline: 03/15
Tuition: full time: $46,390; part time: $35,230
Room/board/expenses: $23,814
Median grant: $15,000
Average student indebtedness at graduation: $139,803
Enrollment: full time: 283; part time: 137
men: 53%; women: 47%; minorities: 20%
Acceptance rate (full time): 56%
Midrange LSAT (full time): 149-156
Midrange undergraduate GPA (full time): 3.12-3.48
Midrange of full-time private-sector salaries of 2014 grads: $67,500-$125,000
2014 grads employed in: law firms: 19%; business and industry: 25%; government: 35%; public interest: 9%; judicial clerk: 11%; academia: 1%; unknown: 0%
Employment location for 2014 class: Intl. 1%; N.E. 3%; M.A. 8%; E.N.C. 0%; W.N.C. 1%; S.A. 84%; E.S.C. 1%; W.S.C. 0%; Mt. 1%; Pac. 3%; unknown 0%

Georgetown University

600 New Jersey Avenue NW
Washington, DC 20001-2075
www.law.georgetown.edu
Private
Admissions: (202) 662-9015
Email:
admis@law.georgetown.odu
Financial aid: (202) 662-9210
Application deadline: 03/01
Tuition: full time: $55,255; part
time: $37,525
Room/board/expenses: $27,445
Median grant: $20,000
**Average student indebtedness at
graduation:** $160,606
Enrollment: full time: 1,725; part
time: 241
men: 52%; women: 48%;
minorities: 20%
Acceptance rate (full time): 28%
Midrange LSAT (full time): 162-168
**Midrange undergraduate GPA (full
time):** 3.47-3.86
**Midrange of full-time private-sector
salaries of 2014 grads:** $160,000-
$160,000
2014 grads employed in: law firms:
55%; business and industry:
5%; government: 13%; public
interest: 15%; judicial clerk: 9%;
academia: 3%; unknown: 0%
Employment location for 2014 class:
Intl. 2%; N.E. 3%; M.A. 24%;
E.N.C. 4%; W.N.C. 1%; S.A. 51%;
E.S.C. 1%; W.S.C. 2%; Mt. 2%;
Pac. 10%; unknown 0%

George Washington University

2000 H Street NW
Washington, DC 20052
www.law.gwu.edu
Private
Admissions: (202) 994-7230
Email: jdadmit@law.gwu.edu
Financial aid: (202) 994-6592
Application deadline: 03/01
Tuition: full time: $54,114; part
time: $1,905
Room/board/expenses: $26,286
Median grant: $16,000
**Average student indebtedness at
graduation:** $136,662
Enrollment: full time: 1,469; part
time: 237
men: 48%; women: 52%;
minorities: 25%
Acceptance rate (full time): 41%
Midrange LSAT (full time): 158-166
**Midrange undergraduate GPA (full
time):** 3.36-3.79
**Midrange of full-time private-sector
salaries of 2014 grads:** $115,000-
$160,000
2014 grads employed in: law firms:
48%; business and industry:
12%; government: 21%; public
interest: 8%; judicial clerk: 8%;
academia: 1%; unknown: 0%
Employment location for 2014 class:
Intl. 1%; N.E. 2%; M.A. 16%;
E.N.C. 3%; W.N.C. 1%; S.A. 67%;
E.S.C. 1%; W.S.C. 3%; Mt. 2%;
Pac. 5%; unknown 0%

Howard University

2900 Van Ness Street NW
Washington, DC 20008
www.law.howard.edu
Private
Admissions: (202) 806-8009
Email:
admissions@law.howard.edu
Financial aid: (202) 806-8005
Application deadline: 03/15
Tuition: full time: $33,832; part
time: N/A
Room/board/expenses: $27,525
Median grant: $14,000
**Average student indebtedness at
graduation:** $23,197
Enrollment: full time: 413; part
time: N/A
men: 35%; women: 65%;
minorities: 91%
Acceptance rate (full time): 43%
Midrange LSAT (full time): 148-153
**Midrange undergraduate GPA (full
time):** 3.00-3.55
**Midrange of full-time private-sector
salaries of 2014 grads:** $110,000-
$160,000
2014 grads employed in: law firms:
29%; business and industry:
20%; government: 23%; public
interest: 10%; judicial clerk: 17%;
academia: 1%; unknown: 0%
**Employment location for 2014
class:** Intl. 0%; N.E. 4%; M.A.
21%; E.N.C. 2%; W.N.C. 5%; S.A.
55%; E.S.C. 1%; W.S.C. 3%; Mt.
1%; Pac. 4%; unknown 0%

University of the District of Columbia (Clarke)

4200 Connecticut Avenue NW
Building 38 & 52
Washington, DC 20008
www.law.udc.edu
Public
Admissions: (202) 274-7341
Email: vcanty@udc.edu
Financial aid: (202) 274-7337
Application deadline: 04/01
In-state tuition: full time: $11,516;
part time: $369/credit hour
Out-of-state tuition: full time:
$22,402
Room/board/expenses: $26,700
Median grant: $5,500
**Average student indebtedness at
graduation:** $108,095
Enrollment: full time: 156; part
time: 147
men: 39%; women: 61%;
minorities: 57%
Acceptance rate (full time): 31%
Midrange LSAT (full time): 146-151
**Midrange undergraduate GPA (full
time):** 2.65-3.32
**Midrange of full-time private-sector
salaries of 2014 grads:** $47,500-
$94,112
2014 grads employed in: law firms:
27%; business and industry:
29%; government: 16%; public
interest: 11%; judicial clerk: 9%;
academia: 7%; unknown: 1%
**Employment location for 2014
class:** Intl. 0%; N.E. 1%; M.A.
3%; E.N.C. 0%; W.N.C. 0%; S.A.
86%; E.S.C. 0%; W.S.C. 3%; Mt.
1%; Pac. 6%; unknown 0%

FLORIDA

Ave Maria School of Law

1025 Commons Circle
Naples, FL 34119
www.avemarialaw.edu
Private
Admissions: (239) 687-5420
Email: info@avemarialaw.edu
Financial aid: (239) 687-5335
Application deadline: 07/15
Tuition: full time: $41,706; part
time: N/A
Room/board/expenses: $21,800
Median grant: $15,000
**Average student indebtedness at
graduation:** $134,071
Enrollment: full time: 268; part
time: N/A
men: 50%; women: 50%;
minorities: 35%
Acceptance rate (full time): 57%
Midrange LSAT (full time): 142-153
**Midrange undergraduate GPA (full
time):** 2.71-3.39
**Midrange of full-time private-sector
salaries of 2014 grads:** $36,400-
$50,000
2014 grads employed in: law firms:
43%; business and industry:
19%; government: 29%; public
interest: 0%; judicial clerk: 3%;
academia: 2%; unknown: 5%
Employment location for 2014 class:
Intl. 0%; N.E. 3%; M.A. 16%;
E.N.C. 5%; W.N.C. 2%; S.A. 71%;
E.S.C. 0%; W.S.C. 2%; Mt. 2%;
Pac. 0%; unknown 0%

Barry University

6441 E. Colonial Drive
Orlando, FL 32807
www.barry.edu/law/
Private
Admissions: (866) 532-2779
Email: lawadmissions@barry.edu
Financial aid: (321) 206-5621
Application deadline: 05/01
Tuition: full time: $35,844; part
time: $27,070
Room/board/expenses: $26,050
Median grant: $10,000
**Average student indebtedness at
graduation:** $138,410
Enrollment: full time: 476; part
time: 281
men: 44%; women: 56%;
minorities: 49%
Acceptance rate (full time): 62%
Midrange LSAT (full time): 144-150
**Midrange undergraduate GPA (full
time):** 2.62-3.27
**Midrange of full-time private-sector
salaries of 2014 grads:** N/A-N/A
2014 grads employed in: law firms:
56%; business and industry:
14%; government: 22%; public
interest: 3%; judicial clerk: 1%;
academia: 3%; unknown: 1%
Employment location for 2014 class:
Intl. 0%; N.E. 0%; M.A. 6%;
E.N.C. 0%; W.N.C. 1%; S.A. 88%;
E.S.C. 1%; W.S.C. 1%; Mt. 1%;
Pac. 2%; unknown 1%

Florida A&M University[1]

201 Beggs Avenue
Orlando, FL 32801
law.famu.edu/
Public
Admissions: (407) 254-3263
Email: famulaw.admissions@
famu.edu
Financial aid: N/A
Tuition: N/A
Room/board/expenses: N/A
Enrollment: N/A

Florida Coastal School of Law

8787 Baypine Road
Jacksonville, FL 32256
www.fcsl.edu
Private
Admissions: (904) 680-7710
Email: admissions@fcsl.edu
Financial aid: (904) 680-7717
Application deadline: rolling
Tuition: full time: $44,620; part
time: $33,166
Room/board/expenses: $18,446
Median grant: $11,000
**Average student indebtedness at
graduation:** $160,942
Enrollment: full time: 666; part
time: 188
men: 43%; women: 57%;
minorities: 45%
Acceptance rate (full time): 73%
Midrange LSAT (full time): 141-148
**Midrange undergraduate GPA (full
time):** 2.55-3.29
**Midrange of full-time private-sector
salaries of 2014 grads:** $36,200-
$60,000
2014 grads employed in: law firms:
53%; business and industry:
23%; government: 13%; public
interest: 5%; judicial clerk: 3%;
academia: 3%; unknown: 0%
**Employment location for 2014
class:** Intl. 0%; N.E. 1%; M.A. 9%;
E.N.C. 4%; W.N.C. 1%; S.A. 78%;
E.S.C. 1%; W.S.C. 3%; Mt. 3%;
Pac. 2%; unknown 0%

Florida International University

Modesto A. Maidique Campus
RDB 2015
Miami, FL 33199
law.fiu.edu
Public
Admissions: (305) 348-8006
Email: lawadmit@fiu.edu
Financial aid: (305) 348-8006
Application deadline: 05/01
In-state tuition: full time: $21,406;
part time: $14,501
Out-of-state tuition: full time:
$35,650
Room/board/expenses: $27,764
Median grant: $5,000
**Average student indebtedness at
graduation:** $95,331
Enrollment: full time: 374; part
time: 107
men: 48%; women: 52%;
minorities: 64%
Acceptance rate (full time): 30%
Midrange LSAT (full time): 152-158
**Midrange undergraduate GPA (full
time):** 3.15-3.77
**Midrange of full-time private-sector
salaries of 2014 grads:** N/A-N/A

2014 grads employed in: law firms:
60%; business and industry:
19%; government: 17%; public
interest: 2%; judicial clerk: 0%;
academia: 2%; unknown: 0%
**Employment location for 2014
class:** Intl. 0%; N.E. 1%; M.A.
2%; E.N.C. 1%; W.N.C. N/A; S.A.
95%; E.S.C. 1%; W.S.C. N/A; Mt.
N/A; Pac. N/A; unknown 0%

Florida State University

425 W. Jefferson Street
Tallahassee, FL 32306-1601
www.law.fsu.edu
Public
Admissions: (850) 644-3787
Email: admissions@law.fsu.edu
Financial aid: (850) 644-5716
Application deadline: 12/31
In-state tuition: full time: $20,683;
part time: N/A
Out-of-state tuition: full time:
$40,695
Room/board/expenses: $17,000
Median grant: $8,500
**Average student indebtedness at
graduation:** $82,102
Enrollment: full time: 565; part
time: 33
men: 56%; women: 44%;
minorities: 29%
Acceptance rate (full time): 44%
Midrange LSAT (full time): 156-161
**Midrange undergraduate GPA (full
time):** 3.26-3.68
**Midrange of full-time private-sector
salaries of 2014 grads:** $50,000-
$70,000
2014 grads employed in: law firms:
44%; business and industry:
15%; government: 32%; public
interest: 3%; judicial clerk: 5%;
academia: 1%; unknown: 0%
**Employment location for 2014
class:** Intl. 0%; N.E. 1%; M.A. 3%;
E.N.C. 0%; W.N.C. 0%; S.A. 91%;
E.S.C. 1%; W.S.C. 2%; Mt. 1%;
Pac. 1%; unknown 0%

Nova Southeastern University (Broad)

3305 College Avenue
Fort Lauderdale, FL 33314-7721
www.law.nova.edu
Private
Admissions: (954) 262-6117
Email: admission@nsu.law.
nova.edu
Financial aid: (954) 262-7412
Application deadline: 05/01
Tuition: full time: $37,985; part
time: $28,721
Room/board/expenses: $26,735
Median grant: $10,000
**Average student indebtedness at
graduation:** $123,798
Enrollment: full time: 563; part
time: 187
men: 47%; women: 53%;
minorities: 46%
Acceptance rate (full time): 57%
Midrange LSAT (full time): 146-151
**Midrange undergraduate GPA (full
time):** 2.84-3.33
**Midrange of full-time private-sector
salaries of 2014 grads:** $50,000-
$66,000

2014 grads employed in: law firms: 60%; business and industry: 22%; government: 12%; public interest: 4%; judicial clerk: 2%; academia: 1%; unknown: 0% Employment location for 2014 class: Intl. 0%; N.E. 0%; M.A. 3%; E.N.C. 2%; W.N.C. 0%; S.A. 95%; E.S.C. 0%; W.S.C. 0%; Mt. 0%; Pac. 0%; unknown 0%

Stetson University

1401 61st Street S
Gulfport, FL 33707
www.law.stetson.edu
Private
Admissions: (727) 562-7802
Email: lawadmit@law.stetson.edu
Financial aid: (727) 562-7813
Application deadline: 05/15
Tuition: full time: $40,256; part time: $27,892
Room/board/expenses: $15,580
Median grant: $12,000
Average student indebtedness at graduation: $130,079
Enrollment: full time: 672; part time: 164
men: 49%; women: 51%; minorities: 25%
Acceptance rate (full time): 52%
Midrange LSAT (full time): 152-156
Midrange undergraduate GPA (full time): 3.00-3.59
Midrange of full-time private-sector salaries of 2014 grads: $50,000-$83,200
2014 grads employed in: law firms: 49%; business and industry: 16%; government: 20%; public interest: 10%; judicial clerk: 2%; academia: 2%; unknown: 1% Employment location for 2014 class: Intl. 0%; N.E. 0%; M.A. 1%; E.N.C. 1%; W.N.C. 1%; S.A. 93%; E.S.C. 1%; W.S.C. 1%; Mt. 1%; Pac. 0%; unknown 0%

St. Thomas University[1]

16401 N.W. 37th Avenue
Miami Gardens, FL 33054
www.stu.edu
Private
Admissions: (305) 623-2310
Email: admitme@stu.edu
Financial aid: (305) 474-2409
Tuition: N/A
Room/board/expenses: N/A
Enrollment: N/A

University of Florida (Levin)

PO Box 117620
Gainesville, FL 32611-7620
www.law.ufl.edu
Public
Admissions: (352) 273-0890
Email: admissions@law.ufl.edu
Financial aid: (352) 273-0628
Application deadline: 07/15
In-state tuition: full time: $22,299; part time: N/A
Out-of-state tuition: full time: $38,904
Room/board/expenses: $17,330
Median grant: $7,500
Average student indebtedness at graduation: $84,580
Enrollment: full time: 961; part time: N/A
men: 57%; women: 43%; minorities: 30%

Acceptance rate (full time): 62%
Midrange LSAT (full time): 155-160
Midrange undergraduate GPA (full time): 3.28-3.68
Midrange of full-time private-sector salaries of 2014 grads: $55,000-$95,000
2014 grads employed in: law firms: 60%; business and industry: 12%; government: 18%; public interest: 2%; judicial clerk: 5%; academia: 1%; unknown: 2% Employment location for 2014 class: Intl. 0%; N.E. 0%; M.A. 1%; E.N.C. 1%; W.N.C. 0%; S.A. 86%; E.S.C. 0%; W.S.C. 2%; Mt. 1%; Pac. 0%; unknown 9%

University of Miami

PO Box 248087
Coral Gables, FL 33124-8087
www.law.miami.edu
Private
Admissions: (305) 284-2795
Email: admissions@law.miami.edu
Financial aid: (305) 284-3115
Application deadline: 07/31
Tuition: full time: $47,774; part time: $1,670/credit hour
Room/board/expenses: $27,041
Median grant: $25,000
Average student indebtedness at graduation: $155,796
Enrollment: full time: 909; part time: 26
men: 51%; women: 49%; minorities: 39%
Acceptance rate (full time): 54%
Midrange LSAT (full time): 154-160
Midrange undergraduate GPA (full time): 3.15-3.60
Midrange of full-time private-sector salaries of 2014 grads: $50,000-$100,000
2014 grads employed in: law firms: 62%; business and industry: 17%; government: 10%; public interest: 6%; judicial clerk: 3%; academia: 2%; unknown: 0% Employment location for 2014 class: Intl. 1%; N.E. 1%; M.A. 7%; E.N.C. 2%; W.N.C. 0%; S.A. 83%; E.S.C. 1%; W.S.C. 2%; Mt. 1%; Pac. 2%; unknown 0%

GEORGIA

Atlanta's John Marshall Law School[1]

1422 W. Peachtree Street NW
Atlanta, GA 30309
www.johnmarshall.edu
Private
Admissions: (404) 872-3593
Email: admissions@johnmarshall.edu
Financial aid: N/A
Tuition: N/A
Room/board/expenses: N/A
Enrollment: N/A

Emory University

1301 Clifton Road
Atlanta, GA 30322-2770
www.law.emory.edu
Private
Admissions: (404) 727-6802
Email: lawinfo@law.emory.edu
Financial aid: (404) 727-6039
Application deadline: 03/01

Tuition: full time: $51,510; part time: N/A
Room/board/expenses: $23,493
Median grant: $22,000
Average student indebtedness at graduation: $121,278
Enrollment: full time: 836; part time: N/A
men: 50%; women: 50%; minorities: 28%
Acceptance rate (full time): 32%
Midrange LSAT (full time): 156-166
Midrange undergraduate GPA (full time): 3.45-3.88
Midrange of full-time private-sector salaries of 2014 grads: $75,000-$160,000
2014 grads employed in: law firms: 58%; business and industry: 9%; government: 17%; public interest: 7%; judicial clerk: 4%; academia: 5%; unknown: 0% Employment location for 2014 class: Intl. 0%; N.E. 0%; M.A. 13%; E.N.C. 3%; W.N.C. 1%; S.A. 67%; E.S.C. 5%; W.S.C. 4%; Mt. 2%; Pac. 6%; unknown 0%

Georgia State University

PO Box 4049
Atlanta, GA 30302-4049
law.gsu.edu
Public
Admissions: (404) 651-2048
Email: law.gsu.edu/admissions/
Financial aid: (404) 651-2227
Application deadline: 06/01
In-state tuition: full time: $16,858; part time: $13,204
Out-of-state tuition: full time: $36,466
Room/board/expenses: $15,438
Median grant: $4,000
Average student indebtedness at graduation: $66,637
Enrollment: full time: 455; part time: 178
men: 53%; women: 47%; minorities: 27%
Acceptance rate (full time): 29%
Midrange LSAT (full time): 156-160
Midrange undergraduate GPA (full time): 3.16-3.56
Midrange of full-time private-sector salaries of 2014 grads: $55,000-$90,000
2014 grads employed in: law firms: 56%; business and industry: 21%; government: 11%; public interest: 4%; judicial clerk: 8%; academia: 1%; unknown: 0% Employment location for 2014 class: Intl. 0%; N.E. 1%; M.A. 1%; E.N.C. 1%; W.N.C. 0%; S.A. 96%; E.S.C. 0%; W.S.C. 1%; Mt. 0%; Pac. 0%; unknown 0%

Mercer University (George)

1021 Georgia Avenue
Macon, GA 31207-0001
www.law.mercer.edu
Private
Admissions: (478) 301-2605
Email: admissions@law.mercer.edu
Financial aid: (478) 301-5902
Application deadline: 03/15
Tuition: full time: $37,260; part time: N/A
Room/board/expenses: $20,540
Median grant: $12,000

Average student indebtedness at graduation: $138,575
Enrollment: full time: 415; part time: N/A
men: 48%; women: 52%; minorities: 24%
Acceptance rate (full time): 50%
Midrange LSAT (full time): 150-154
Midrange undergraduate GPA (full time): 3.06-3.48
Midrange of full-time private-sector salaries of 2014 grads: $50,000-$65,000
2014 grads employed in: law firms: 58%; business and industry: 4%; government: 15%; public interest: 6%; judicial clerk: 16%; academia: 1%; unknown: 0% Employment location for 2014 class: Intl. 0%; N.E. 0%; M.A. 0%; E.N.C. 1%; W.N.C. 0%; S.A. 96%; E.S.C. 1%; W.S.C. 1%; Mt. 1%; Pac. 1%; unknown 0%

University of Georgia

Herty Drive
Athens, GA 30602
www.law.uga.edu
Public
Admissions: (706) 542-7060
Email: ugajd@uga.edu
Financial aid: (706) 542-6147
Application deadline: 06/01
In-state tuition: full time: $19,476; part time: N/A
Out-of-state tuition: full time: $37,524
Room/board/expenses: $16,962
Median grant: $5,000
Average student indebtedness at graduation: $86,515
Enrollment: full time: 576; part time: N/A
men: 53%; women: 47%; minorities: 17%
Acceptance rate (full time): 33%
Midrange LSAT (full time): 156-164
Midrange undergraduate GPA (full time): 3.36-3.83
Midrange of full-time private-sector salaries of 2014 grads: $50,000-$110,000
2014 grads employed in: law firms: 49%; business and industry: 14%; government: 14%; public interest: 8%; judicial clerk: 13%; academia: 2%; unknown: 0% Employment location for 2014 class: Intl. 1%; N.E. 2%; M.A. 4%; E.N.C. 2%; W.N.C. 1%; S.A. 83%; E.S.C. 3%; W.S.C. 3%; Mt. 2%; Pac. 2%; unknown 0%

HAWAII

University of Hawaii-Manoa (Richardson)

2515 Dole Street
Honolulu, HI 96822-2328
www.law.hawaii.edu/
Public
Admissions: (808) 956-5557
Email: lawadm@hawaii.edu
Financial aid: (808) 956-7966
Application deadline: 02/01
In-state tuition: full time: $20,880; part time: $870/credit hour
Out-of-state tuition: full time: $42,384
Room/board/expenses: $17,560
Median grant: $5,000
Average student indebtedness at graduation: $54,988

Enrollment: full time: 232; part time: 73
men: 50%; women: 50%; minorities: 67%
Acceptance rate (full time): 36%
Midrange LSAT (full time): 151-158
Midrange undergraduate GPA (full time): 2.98-3.63
Midrange of full-time private-sector salaries of 2014 grads: $62,250-$85,500
2014 grads employed in: law firms: 21%; business and industry: 9%; government: 26%; public interest: 8%; judicial clerk: 32%; academia: 0%; unknown: 0% Employment location for 2014 class: Intl. 2%; N.E. 0%; M.A. 0%; E.N.C. 1%; W.N.C. 1%; S.A. 3%; E.S.C. 0%; W.S.C. 1%; Mt. 1%; Pac. 90%; unknown 0%

IDAHO

Concordia University[1]

501 West Front Street
Boise, ID 83702
Private
Admissions: N/A
Financial aid: N/A
Tuition: N/A
Room/board/expenses: N/A
Enrollment: N/A

University of Idaho

875 Perimeter Drive MS2321
Moscow, ID 83844-2321
www.uidaho.edu/law/admissions
Public
Admissions: (208) 885-2300
Email: lawadmit@uidaho.edu
Financial aid: (208) 885-6312
Application deadline: 03/15
In-state tuition: full time: $17,230; part time: N/A
Out-of-state tuition: full time: $31,234
Room/board/expenses: $16,340
Median grant: $6,000
Average student indebtedness at graduation: $32,114
Enrollment: full time: 334; part time: 9
men: 61%; women: 39%; minorities: 20%
Acceptance rate (full time): 66%
Midrange LSAT (full time): 147-155
Midrange undergraduate GPA (full time): 2.94-3.44
Midrange of full-time private-sector salaries of 2014 grads: $43,000-$65,000
2014 grads employed in: law firms: 41%; business and industry: 13%; government: 15%; public interest: 6%; judicial clerk: 19%; academia: 4%; unknown: 2% Employment location for 2014 class: Intl. 1%; N.E. 2%; M.A. 0%; E.N.C. 0%; W.N.C. 2%; S.A. 0%; E.S.C. 0%; W.S.C. 1%; Mt. 69%; Pac. 25%; unknown 0%

ILLINOIS

DePaul University

25 E. Jackson Boulevard
Chicago, IL 60604
www.law.depaul.edu
Private
Admissions: (312) 362-6831
Email: lawinfo@depaul.edu
Financial aid: (312) 362-8091
Application deadline: 03/01

Tuition: full time: $45,450; part time: $29,710
Room/board/expenses: $22,606
Median grant: $15,000
Average student indebtedness at graduation: $131,148
Enrollment: full time: 602; part time: 125
men: 41%; women: 59%; minorities: 27%
Acceptance rate (full time): 69%
Midrange LSAT (full time): 149-154
Midrange undergraduate GPA (full time): 3.15-3.51
Midrange of full-time private-sector salaries of 2014 grads: $45,000-$80,000
2014 grads employed in: law firms: 59%; business and industry: 26%; government: 9%; public interest: 4%; judicial clerk: 2%; academia: 0%; unknown: 0%
Employment location for 2014 class: Intl. 1%; N.E. 1%; M.A. 1%; E.N.C. 90%; W.N.C. 2%; S.A. 2%; E.S.C. 1%; W.S.C. 1%; Mt. 1%; Pac. 2%; unknown 0%

Illinois Institute of Technology (Chicago-Kent)

565 W. Adams Street
Chicago, IL 60661-3691
www.kentlaw.iit.edu/
Private
Admissions: (312) 906-5020
Email: admissions@kentlaw.iit.edu
Financial aid: (312) 906-5180
Application deadline: 03/15
Tuition: full time: $46,822; part time: $34,210
Room/board/expenses: $19,069
Median grant: $20,000
Average student indebtedness at graduation: $115,040
Enrollment: full time: 635; part time: 112
men: 53%; women: 47%; minorities: 30%
Acceptance rate (full time): 64%
Midrange LSAT (full time): 152-158
Midrange undergraduate GPA (full time): 3.13-3.56
Midrange of full-time private-sector salaries of 2014 grads: $55,000-$95,000
2014 grads employed in: law firms: 61%; business and industry: 21%; government: 9%; public interest: 5%; judicial clerk: 2%; academia: 2%; unknown: 0%
Employment location for 2014 class: Intl. 0%; N.E. 0%; M.A. 3%; E.N.C. 86%; W.N.C. 1%; S.A. 4%; E.S.C. 0%; W.S.C. 2%; Mt. 1%; Pac. 2%; unknown 0%

The John Marshall Law School

315 S. Plymouth Court
Chicago, IL 60604
www.jmls.edu
Private
Admissions: (800) 537-4280
Email: admission@jmls.edu
Financial aid: (800) 537-4280
Application deadline: rolling
Tuition: full time: $45,780; part time: $32,127
Room/board/expenses: $28,316
Median grant: $12,000
Average student indebtedness at graduation: $162,264

Enrollment: full time: 744; part time: 277
men: 51%; women: 49%; minorities: 34%
Acceptance rate (full time): 76%
Midrange LSAT (full time): 145-150
Midrange undergraduate GPA (full time): 2.82-3.38
Midrange of full-time private-sector salaries of 2014 grads: N/A-N/A
2014 grads employed in: law firms: 59%; business and industry: 21%; government: 14%; public interest: 3%; judicial clerk: 2%; academia: 1%; unknown: 0%
Employment location for 2014 class: Intl. 1%; N.E. 1%; M.A. 1%; E.N.C. 90%; W.N.C. 0%; S.A. 3%; E.S.C. 0%; W.S.C. 1%; Mt. 1%; Pac. 1%; unknown 0%

Loyola University Chicago

25 E. Pearson Street
Chicago, IL 60611
www.luc.edu/law/
Private
Admissions: (312) 915-7170
Email: law-admissions@luc.edu
Financial aid: (312) 915-7170
Application deadline: 03/01
Tuition: full time: $45,288; part time: $34,198
Room/board/expenses: $21,518
Median grant: $12,000
Average student indebtedness at graduation: $133,052
Enrollment: full time: 582; part time: 72
men: 47%; women: 53%; minorities: 24%
Acceptance rate (full time): 55%
Midrange LSAT (full time): 155-160
Midrange undergraduate GPA (full time): 3.07-3.56
Midrange of full-time private-sector salaries of 2014 grads: $51,000-$100,000
2014 grads employed in: law firms: 49%; business and industry: 24%; government: 12%; public interest: 8%; judicial clerk: 6%; academia: 2%; unknown: 0%
Employment location for 2014 class: Intl. 0%; N.E. 0%; M.A. 2%; E.N.C. 85%; W.N.C. 3%; S.A. 4%; E.S.C. 0%; W.S.C. 0%; Mt. 3%; Pac. 3%; unknown 0%

Northern Illinois University

Swen Parson Hall, Room 276
De Kalb, IL 60115
niu.edu/law
Public
Admissions: (815) 753-8595
Email: lawadm@niu.edu
Financial aid: (815) 753-8595
Application deadline: 04/01
In-state tuition: full time: $22,118; part time: $1,013/credit hour
Out-of-state tuition: full time: $38,374
Room/board/expenses: $19,296
Median grant: $5,000
Average student indebtedness at graduation: $77,975
Enrollment: full time: 241; part time: 11
men: 52%; women: 48%; minorities: 27%
Acceptance rate (full time): 67%
Midrange LSAT (full time): 145-150

Midrange undergraduate GPA (full time): 2.77-3.34
Midrange of full-time private-sector salaries of 2014 grads: $45,000-$62,000
2014 grads employed in: law firms: 56%; business and industry: 15%; government: 23%; public interest: 2%; judicial clerk: 2%; academia: 3%; unknown: 0%
Employment location for 2014 class: Intl. 0%; N.E. 0%; M.A. 0%; E.N.C. 89%; W.N.C. 3%; S.A. 5%; E.S.C. 0%; W.S.C. 0%; Mt. 0%; Pac. 2%; unknown 1%

Northwestern University (Pritzker)

375 E. Chicago Avenue
Chicago, IL 60611
www.law.northwestern.edu
Private
Admissions: (312) 503-8465
Email: admissions@law.northwestern.edu
Financial aid: (312) 503-8465
Application deadline: 02/15
Tuition: full time: $58,398; part time: N/A
Room/board/expenses: $21,506
Median grant: $25,000
Average student indebtedness at graduation: $155,796
Enrollment: full time: 658; part time: 8
men: 52%; women: 48%; minorities: 31%
Acceptance rate (full time): 23%
Midrange LSAT (full time): 163-169
Midrange undergraduate GPA (full time): 3.56-3.85
Midrange of full-time private-sector salaries of 2014 grads: $150,000-$160,000
2014 grads employed in: law firms: 68%; business and industry: 9%; government: 3%; public interest: 6%; judicial clerk: 13%; academia: 1%; unknown: 0%
Employment location for 2014 class: Intl. 3%; N.E. 3%; M.A. 17%; E.N.C. 42%; W.N.C. 4%; S.A. 8%; E.S.C. 2%; W.S.C. 5%; Mt. 2%; Pac. 14%; unknown 0%

Southern Illinois University-Carbondale

Lesar Law Building
Carbondale, IL 62901
www.law.siu.edu
Public
Admissions: (800) 739-9187
Email: lawadmit@siu.edu
Financial aid: (618) 453-4334
Application deadline: 01/08
In-state tuition: full time: $19,474; part time: N/A
Out-of-state tuition: full time: $41,120
Room/board/expenses: $17,471
Median grant: $5,500
Average student indebtedness at graduation: $90,727
Enrollment: full time: 354; part time: 2
men: 57%; women: 43%; minorities: 24%
Acceptance rate (full time): 79%
Midrange LSAT (full time): 145-152
Midrange undergraduate GPA (full time): 2.66-3.32
Midrange of full-time private-sector salaries of 2014 grads: $40,000-$55,000

2014 grads employed in: law firms: 58%; business and industry: 15%; government: 22%; public interest: 0%; judicial clerk: 2%; academia: 2%; unknown: 0%
Employment location for 2014 class: Intl. 0%; N.E. 0%; M.A. 0%; E.N.C. 79%; W.N.C. 15%; S.A. 4%; E.S.C. 2%; W.S.C. 0%; Mt. 0%; Pac. 0%; unknown 0%

University of Chicago

1111 E. 60th Street
Chicago, IL 60637
www.law.uchicago.edu
Private
Admissions: (773) 702-9484
Email: admissions@law.uchicago.edu
Financial aid: (773) 702-9484
Application deadline: 03/01
Tuition: full time: $56,916; part time: N/A
Room/board/expenses: $24,564
Median grant: $15,000
Average student indebtedness at graduation: $129,636
Enrollment: full time: 617; part time: N/A
men: 56%; women: 44%; minorities: 30%
Acceptance rate (full time): 22%
Midrange LSAT (full time): 166-172
Midrange undergraduate GPA (full time): 3.69-3.97
Midrange of full-time private-sector salaries of 2014 grads: $160,000-$160,000
2014 grads employed in: law firms: 65%; business and industry: 6%; government: 4%; public interest: 7%; judicial clerk: 17%; academia: 0%; unknown: 0%
Employment location for 2014 class: Intl. 1%; N.E. 2%; M.A. 20%; E.N.C. 32%; W.N.C. 3%; S.A. 17%; E.S.C. 0%; W.S.C. 4%; Mt. 2%; Pac. 17%; unknown 0%

University of Illinois-Urbana-Champaign

504 E. Pennsylvania Avenue
Champaign, IL 61820
www.law.illinois.edu
Public
Admissions: (217) 244-6415
Email: law-admissions@illinois.edu
Financial aid: (217) 244-6415
Application deadline: 03/15
In-state tuition: full time: $41,328; part time: N/A
Out-of-state tuition: full time: $49,078
Room/board/expenses: $17,900
Median grant: $20,000
Average student indebtedness at graduation: $118,731
Enrollment: full time: 477; part time: N/A
men: 60%; women: 40%; minorities: 28%
Acceptance rate (full time): 46%
Midrange LSAT (full time): 158-163
Midrange undergraduate GPA (full time): 3.26-3.68
Midrange of full-time private-sector salaries of 2014 grads: $60,000-$140,000

2014 grads employed in: law firms: 55%; business and industry: 13%; government: 17%; public interest: 2%; judicial clerk: 8%; academia: 5%; unknown: 0%
Employment location for 2014 class: Intl. 2%; N.E. 0%; M.A. 5%; E.N.C. 68%; W.N.C. 4%; S.A. 11%; E.S.C. 0%; W.S.C. 1%; Mt. 4%; Pac. 5%; unknown 0%

INDIANA

Indiana University-Bloomington (Maurer)

211 S. Indiana Avenue
Bloomington, IN 47405-1001
www.law.indiana.edu
Public
Admissions: (812) 855-4765
Email: lawadmis@indiana.edu
Financial aid: (812) 855-7746
Application deadline: 07/15
In-state tuition: full time: $31,800; part time: N/A
Out-of-state tuition: full time: $51,800
Room/board/expenses: $19,199
Median grant: $22,000
Average student indebtedness at graduation: $91,020
Enrollment: full time: 538; part time: N/A
men: 57%; women: 43%; minorities: 20%
Acceptance rate (full time): 53%
Midrange LSAT (full time): 155-162
Midrange undergraduate GPA (full time): 3.31-3.88
Midrange of full-time private-sector salaries of 2014 grads: $62,500-$110,000
2014 grads employed in: law firms: 46%; business and industry: 16%; government: 17%; public interest: 7%; judicial clerk: 7%; academia: 5%; unknown: 0%
Employment location for 2014 class: Intl. 1%; N.E. 0%; M.A. 5%; E.N.C. 55%; W.N.C. 2%; S.A. 13%; E.S.C. 2%; W.S.C. 5%; Mt. 3%; Pac. 8%; unknown 3%

Indiana University-Indianapolis (McKinney)

530 W. New York Street
Indianapolis, IN 46202-3225
mckinneylaw.iu.edu
Public
Admissions: (317) 274-2459
Email: pkkinney@iupui.edu
Financial aid: (317) 278-2880
Application deadline: 07/31
In-state tuition: full time: $25,625; part time: $19,481
Out-of-state tuition: full time: $45,210
Room/board/expenses: $15,456
Median grant: $13,000
Average student indebtedness at graduation: $106,114
Enrollment: full time: 519; part time: 297
men: 53%; women: 47%; minorities: 18%
Acceptance rate (full time): 68%
Midrange LSAT (full time): 149-156
Midrange undergraduate GPA (full time): 3.10-3.59
Midrange of full-time private-sector salaries of 2014 grads: $50,000-$85,000

2014 grads employed in: law firms: 49%; business and industry: 22%; government: 22%; public interest: 3%; judicial clerk: 3%; academia: 2%; unknown: 0%
Employment location for 2014 class: Intl. 1%; N.E. 0%; M.A. 2%; E.N.C. 89%; W.N.C. 1%; S.A. 4%; E.S.C. 0%; W.S.C. 0%; Mt. 0%; Pac. 2%; unknown 0%

University of Notre Dame

PO Box 780
Notre Dame, IN 46556-0780
law.nd.edu
Private
Admissions: (574) 631-6626
Email: lawadmit@nd.edu
Financial aid: (574) 631-6626
Application deadline: 03/15
Tuition: full time: $52,372; part time: N/A
Room/board/expenses: $19,950
Median grant: $20,000
Average student indebtedness at graduation: $122,822
Enrollment: full time: 581; part time: N/A
men: 59%; women: 41%; minorities: 25%
Acceptance rate (full time): 35%
Midrange LSAT (full time): 161-165
Midrange undergraduate GPA (full time): 3.46-3.79
Midrange of full-time private-sector salaries of 2014 grads: $89,250-$160,000
2014 grads employed in: law firms: 52%; business and industry: 9%; government: 18%; public interest: 7%; judicial clerk: 13%; academia: 1%; unknown: 0%
Employment location for 2014 class: Intl. 1%; N.E. 0%; M.A. 20%; E.N.C. 38%; W.N.C. 2%; S.A. 16%; E.S.C. 2%; W.S.C. 5%; Mt. 6%; Pac. 10%; unknown 0%

Valparaiso University

656 S. Greenwich Street
Wesemann Hall
Valparaiso, IN 46383
www.valpo.edu/law
Private
Admissions: (219) 465-7821
Email: law.admissions@valpo.edu
Financial aid: (219) 465-7818
Application deadline: 07/15
Tuition: full time: $40,372; part time: $24,672
Room/board/expenses: $13,950
Median grant: $19,806
Average student indebtedness at graduation: $131,024
Enrollment: full time: 121; part time: 9
men: 51%; women: 49%; minorities: 32%
Acceptance rate (full time): 68%
Midrange LSAT (full time): 142-148
Midrange undergraduate GPA (full time): 2.63-3.26
Midrange of full-time private-sector salaries of 2014 grads: $51,695-$67,826
2014 grads employed in: law firms: 56%; business and industry: 14%; government: 22%; public interest: 5%; judicial clerk: 2%; academia: 1%; unknown: 0%

Employment location for 2014 class: Intl. 0%; N.E. 0%; M.A. 1%; E.N.C. 81%; W.N.C. 3%; S.A. 7%; E.S.C. 1%; W.S.C. 2%; Mt. 2%; Pac. 3%; unknown 0%

IOWA

Drake University

2507 University Avenue
Des Moines, IA 50311
www.law.drake.edu/
Private
Admissions: (515) 271-2782
Email: lawadmit@drake.edu
Financial aid: (515) 271-2782
Application deadline: 04/01
Tuition: full time: $38,866; part time: $1,336/credit hour
Room/board/expenses: $20,216
Median grant: $20,000
Average student indebtedness at graduation: $107,649
Enrollment: full time: 305; part time: 11
men: 51%; women: 49%; minorities: 16%
Acceptance rate (full time): 75%
Midrange LSAT (full time): 148-154
Midrange undergraduate GPA (full time): 3.00-3.55
Midrange of full-time private-sector salaries of 2014 grads: $45,000-$71,000
2014 grads employed in: law firms: 56%; business and industry: 22%; government: 10%; public interest: 5%; judicial clerk: 4%; academia: 2%; unknown: 1%
Employment location for 2014 class: Intl. 1%; N.E. 1%; M.A. 0%; E.N.C. 7%; W.N.C. 81%; S.A. 2%; E.S.C. 0%; W.S.C. 3%; Mt. 4%; Pac. 1%; unknown 1%

University of Iowa

320 Melrose Avenue
Iowa City, IA 52242
law.uiowa.edu
Public
Admissions: (319) 335-9095
Email: law-admissions@uiowa.edu
Financial aid: (319) 335-9142
Application deadline: 05/01
In-state tuition: full time: $24,177; part time: N/A
Out-of-state tuition: full time: $42,021
Room/board/expenses: $17,310
Median grant: $22,764
Average student indebtedness at graduation: $86,373
Enrollment: full time: 387; part time: 4
men: 59%; women: 41%; minorities: 19%
Acceptance rate (full time): 43%
Midrange LSAT (full time): 156-162
Midrange undergraduate GPA (full time): 3.44-3.79
Midrange of full-time private-sector salaries of 2014 grads: $54,000-$110,000
2014 grads employed in: law firms: 51%; business and industry: 18%; government: 8%; public interest: 6%; judicial clerk: 12%; academia: 4%; unknown: 1%
Employment location for 2014 class: Intl. 2%; N.E. 2%; M.A. 4%; E.N.C. 14%; W.N.C. 56%; S.A. 5%; E.S.C. 0%; W.S.C. 4%; Mt. 7%; Pac. 7%; unknown 0%

KANSAS

University of Kansas

Green Hall
1535 W. 15th Street
Lawrence, KS 66045-7608
www.law.ku.edu
Public
Admissions: (866) 220-3654
Email: admitlaw@ku.edu
Financial aid: (785) 864-4700
Application deadline: 04/01
In-state tuition: full time: $20,718; part time: N/A
Out-of-state tuition: full time: $35,328
Room/board/expenses: $14,570
Median grant: $10,000
Average student indebtedness at graduation: $80,884
Enrollment: full time: 362; part time: N/A
men: 56%; women: 44%; minorities: 14%
Acceptance rate (full time): 66%
Midrange LSAT (full time): 152-159
Midrange undergraduate GPA (full time): 3.16-3.66
Midrange of full-time private-sector salaries of 2014 grads: $60,000-$115,000
2014 grads employed in: law firms: 43%; business and industry: 19%; government: 22%; public interest: 4%; judicial clerk: 7%; academia: 5%; unknown: 0%
Employment location for 2014 class: Intl. 0%; N.E. 0%; M.A. 0%; E.N.C. 2%; W.N.C. 81%; S.A. 6%; E.S.C. 0%; W.S.C. 5%; Mt. 6%; Pac. 2%; unknown 0%

Washburn University

1700 S.W. College Avenue
Topeka, KS 66621
washburnlaw.edu
Public
Admissions: (785) 670-1185
Email: admissions@washburnlaw.edu
Financial aid: (785) 670-1151
Application deadline: 04/01
In-state tuition: full time: $19,964; part time: N/A
Out-of-state tuition: full time: $31,129
Room/board/expenses: $15,299
Median grant: $14,278
Average student indebtedness at graduation: $86,621
Enrollment: full time: 297; part time: N/A
men: 62%; women: 38%; minorities: 14%
Acceptance rate (full time): 59%
Midrange LSAT (full time): 149-155
Midrange undergraduate GPA (full time): 2.86-3.52
Midrange of full-time private-sector salaries of 2014 grads: $50,000-$72,500
2014 grads employed in: law firms: 58%; business and industry: 13%; government: 21%; public interest: 2%; judicial clerk: 3%; academia: 2%; unknown: 0%
Employment location for 2014 class: Intl. 0%; N.E. 0%; M.A. 1%; E.N.C. 1%; W.N.C. 81%; S.A. 2%; E.S.C. 0%; W.S.C. 3%; Mt. 7%; Pac. 3%; unknown 2%

KENTUCKY

Northern Kentucky University (Chase)

Nunn Hall
Highland Heights, KY 41099
chaselaw.nku.edu
Public
Admissions: (859) 572-5841
Email: chaseadmissions@nku.edu
Financial aid: (859) 572-6437
Application deadline: rolling
In-state tuition: full time: $17,576; part time: $14,872
Out-of-state tuition: full time: $28,418
Room/board/expenses: $15,442
Median grant: $12,000
Average student indebtedness at graduation: $84,714
Enrollment: full time: 297; part time: 135
men: 56%; women: 44%; minorities: 15%
Acceptance rate (full time): 83%
Midrange LSAT (full time): 144-153
Midrange undergraduate GPA (full time): 2.91-3.44
Midrange of full-time private-sector salaries of 2014 grads: $45,500-$75,000
2014 grads employed in: law firms: 39%; business and industry: 30%; government: 17%; public interest: 4%; judicial clerk: 7%; academia: 2%; unknown: 0%
Employment location for 2014 class: Intl. 1%; N.E. N/A; M.A. N/A; E.N.C. 43%; W.N.C. N/A; S.A. 4%; E.S.C. 51%; W.S.C. N/A; Mt. N/A; Pac. 1%; unknown 0%

University of Kentucky

209 Law Building
Lexington, KY 40506-0048
www.law.uky.edu
Public
Admissions: (859) 218-1699
Email: uklawadmissions@uky.edu
Financial aid: (859) 257-3172
Application deadline: 03/15
In-state tuition: full time: $21,618; part time: N/A
Out-of-state tuition: full time: $40,836
Room/board/expenses: $15,832
Median grant: $6,000
Average student indebtedness at graduation: $77,793
Enrollment: full time: 374; part time: N/A
men: 57%; women: 43%; minorities: 9%
Acceptance rate (full time): 60%
Midrange LSAT (full time): 152-158
Midrange undergraduate GPA (full time): 3.17-3.69
Midrange of full-time private-sector salaries of 2014 grads: $42,500-$98,000
2014 grads employed in: law firms: 54%; business and industry: 11%; government: 10%; public interest: 4%; judicial clerk: 21%; academia: 1%; unknown: 0%
Employment location for 2014 class: Intl. 0%; N.E. 0%; M.A. 1%; E.N.C. 5%; W.N.C. 1%; S.A. 10%; E.S.C. 81%; W.S.C. 0%; Mt. 2%; Pac. 1%; unknown 0%

University of Louisville (Brandeis)

2301 S. Third Street
Louisville, KY 40292
www.louisville.edu/law
Public
Admissions: (502) 852-6365
Email: lawadmissions@louisville.edu
Financial aid: (502) 852-5511
Application deadline: 04/15
In-state tuition: full time: $20,288; part time: $15,499
Out-of-state tuition: full time: $37,628
Room/board/expenses: $18,806
Median grant: $9,000
Average student indebtedness at graduation: $86,880
Enrollment: full time: 302; part time: 12
men: 56%; women: 44%; minorities: 9%
Acceptance rate (full time): 69%
Midrange LSAT (full time): 151-157
Midrange undergraduate GPA (full time): 3.12-3.69
Midrange of full-time private-sector salaries of 2014 grads: $41,000-$75,000
2014 grads employed in: law firms: 48%; business and industry: 22%; government: 13%; public interest: 9%; judicial clerk: 7%; academia: 2%; unknown: 0%
Employment location for 2014 class: Intl. 0%; N.E. 0%; M.A. 1%; E.N.C. 8%; W.N.C. 0%; S.A. 7%; E.S.C. 81%; W.S.C. 2%; Mt. 1%; Pac. 1%; unknown 0%

LOUISIANA

Louisiana State University-Baton Rouge (Hebert)

400 Paul M. Hebert Law Center
Baton Rouge, LA 70803
www.law.lsu.edu
Public
Admissions: (225) 578-8646
Email: admissions@law.lsu.edu
Financial aid: (225) 578-3103
Application deadline: 06/01
In-state tuition: full time: $21,947; part time: N/A
Out-of-state tuition: full time: $41,297
Room/board/expenses: $22,128
Median grant: $9,675
Average student indebtedness at graduation: $90,609
Enrollment: full time: 525; part time: 9
men: 54%; women: 46%; minorities: 17%
Acceptance rate (full time): 59%
Midrange LSAT (full time): 153-158
Midrange undergraduate GPA (full time): 3.12-3.70
Midrange of full-time private-sector salaries of 2014 grads: $64,375-$141,250
2014 grads employed in: law firms: 50%; business and industry: 15%; government: 11%; public interest: 5%; judicial clerk: 15%; academia: 3%; unknown: 0%
Employment location for 2014 class: Intl. 0%; N.E. 0%; M.A. 0%; E.N.C. 0%; W.N.C. 1%; S.A. 8%; E.S.C. 4%; W.S.C. 84%; Mt. 1%; Pac. 1%; unknown 0%

Loyola University New Orleans

7214 St. Charles Avenue
PO Box 901
New Orleans, LA 70118
law.loyno.edu/
Private
Admissions: (504) 861-5575
Email: ladmit@loyno.odu
Financial aid: (504) 865-3231
Application deadline: rolling
Tuition: full time: $43,410; part time: $32,910
Room/board/expenses: $21,644
Median grant: $20,000
Average student indebtedness at graduation: $124,143
Enrollment: full time: 425; part time: 102
men: 48%; women: 52%; minorities: 25%
Acceptance rate (full time): 78%
Midrange LSAT (full time): 148-154
Midrange undergraduate GPA (full time): 2.93-3.47
Midrange of full-time private-sector salaries of 2014 grads: $60,000-$95,000
2014 grads employed in: law firms: 56%; business and industry: 20%; government: 12%; public interest: 4%; judicial clerk: 8%; academia: 1%; unknown: 0%
Employment location for 2014 class: Intl. 1%; N.E. 0%; M.A. 3%; E.N.C. 1%; W.N.C. 0%; S.A. 10%; E.S.C. 2%; W.S.C. 80%; Mt. 2%; Pac. 2%; unknown 0%

Southern University Law Center

PO Box 9294
Baton Rouge, LA 70813
www.sulc.edu/index_v3.htm
Public
Admissions: (225) 771-5340
Email: Admission@sulc.edu
Financial aid: (225) 771-2141
Application deadline: 02/28
In-state tuition: full time: $13,560; part time: $11,908
Out-of-state tuition: full time: $24,160
Room/board/expenses: $18,703
Median grant: $3,000
Average student indebtedness at graduation: $86,708
Enrollment: full time: 455; part time: 159
men: 46%; women: 54%; minorities: 61%
Acceptance rate (full time): 71%
Midrange LSAT (full time): 141-147
Midrange undergraduate GPA (full time): 2.59-3.25
Midrange of full-time private-sector salaries of 2014 grads: $45,000-$87,500
2014 grads employed in: law firms: 37%; business and industry: 17%; government: 29%; public interest: 4%; judicial clerk: 9%; academia: 3%; unknown: 2%
Employment location for 2014 class: Intl. 0%; N.E. 1%; M.A. 1%; E.N.C. 1%; W.N.C. 0%; S.A. 6%; E.S.C. 3%; W.S.C. 87%; Mt. 0%; Pac. 1%; unknown 0%

Tulane University

6329 Freret Street
John Giffen Weinmann Hall
New Orleans, LA 70118-6231
www.law.tulane.edu
Private
Admissions: (504) 865-5930
Email: admissions@law.tulane.edu
Financial aid: (504) 865-5931
Application deadline: rolling
Tuition: full time: $51,130; part time: N/A
Room/board/expenses: $22,304
Median grant: $25,000
Average student indebtedness at graduation: $153,606
Enrollment: full time: 570; part time: 2
men: 53%; women: 47%; minorities: 18%
Acceptance rate (full time): 60%
Midrange LSAT (full time): 155-161
Midrange undergraduate GPA (full time): 3.15-3.59
Midrange of full-time private-sector salaries of 2014 grads: $67,500-$160,000
2014 grads employed in: law firms: 50%; business and industry: 18%; government: 9%; public interest: 11%; judicial clerk: 9%; academia: 2%; unknown: 0%
Employment location for 2014 class: Intl. 0%; N.E. 2%; M.A. 14%; E.N.C. 5%; W.N.C. 1%; S.A. 12%; E.S.C. 7%; W.S.C. 44%; Mt. 4%; Pac. 8%; unknown 1%

MAINE

University of Maine

246 Deering Avenue
Portland, ME 04102
mainelaw.maine.edu
Public
Admissions: (207) 780-4341
Email: lawadmissions@maine.edu
Financial aid: (207) 780-5250
Application deadline: 04/15
In-state tuition: full time: $23,610; part time: N/A
Out-of-state tuition: full time: $34,680
Room/board/expenses: $15,708
Median grant: $8,000
Average student indebtedness at graduation: $99,617
Enrollment: full time: 241; part time: 9
men: 50%; women: 50%; minorities: 10%
Acceptance rate (full time): 69%
Midrange LSAT (full time): 149-157
Midrange undergraduate GPA (full time): 3.07-3.65
Midrange of full-time private-sector salaries of 2014 grads: $45,000-$70,000
2014 grads employed in: law firms: 46%; business and industry: 17%; government: 14%; public interest: 8%; judicial clerk: 14%; academia: 0%; unknown: 0%
Employment location for 2014 class: Intl. 1%; N.E. 80%; M.A. 5%; E.N.C. 1%; W.N.C. N/A; S.A. 7%; E.S.C. N/A; W.S.C. 1%; Mt. 3%; Pac. 1%; unknown 0%

MARYLAND

University of Baltimore

1420 N. Charles Street
Baltimore, MD 21201-5779
law.ubalt.edu
Public
Admissions: (410) 837-4459
Email: lawadmissions@ubalt.edu
Financial aid: (410) 837-4763
Application deadline: 08/01
In-state tuition: full time: $29,184; part time: $21,782
Out-of-state tuition: full time: $43,002
Room/board/expenses: $19,950
Median grant: $10,000
Average student indebtedness at graduation: $112,008
Enrollment: full time: 496; part time: 283
men: 49%; women: 51%; minorities: 28%
Acceptance rate (full time): 60%
Midrange LSAT (full time): 149-155
Midrange undergraduate GPA (full time): 2.98-3.56
Midrange of full-time private-sector salaries of 2014 grads: $50,000-$75,000
2014 grads employed in: law firms: 39%; business and industry: 21%; government: 13%; public interest: 5%; judicial clerk: 21%; academia: 1%; unknown: 0%
Employment location for 2014 class: Intl. 0%; N.E. 0%; M.A. 3%; E.N.C. 0%; W.N.C. 0%; S.A. 93%; E.S.C. 0%; W.S.C. 1%; Mt. 1%; Pac. 1%; unknown 1%

University of Maryland (Carey)

500 W. Baltimore Street
Baltimore, MD 21201-1786
www.law.umaryland.edu
Public
Admissions: (410) 706-3492
Email: admissions@law.umaryland.edu
Financial aid: (410) 706-0873
Application deadline: 04/01
In-state tuition: full time: $30,177; part time: $23,175
Out-of-state tuition: full time: $43,657
Room/board/expenses: $23,075
Median grant: $9,000
Average student indebtedness at graduation: $114,493
Enrollment: full time: 514; part time: 130
men: 50%; women: 50%; minorities: 34%
Acceptance rate (full time): 57%
Midrange LSAT (full time): 154-160
Midrange undergraduate GPA (full time): 3.25-3.65
Midrange of full-time private-sector salaries of 2014 grads: $51,000-$85,000
2014 grads employed in: law firms: 30%; business and industry: 18%; government: 21%; public interest: 5%; judicial clerk: 22%; academia: 3%; unknown: 0%
Employment location for 2014 class: Intl. 1%; N.E. 1%; M.A. 5%; E.N.C. 1%; W.N.C. 0%; S.A. 86%; E.S.C. 0%; W.S.C. 1%; Mt. 1%; Pac. 3%; unknown 0%

MASSACHUSETTS

Boston College

885 Centre Street
Newton, MA 02459-1154
www.bc.edu/lawschool
Private
Admissions: (617) 552-4351
Email: bclawadm@bc.edu
Financial aid: (617) 552-4243
Application deadline: 03/31
Tuition: full time: $48,670; part time: N/A
Room/board/expenses: $19,360
Median grant: $20,000
Average student indebtedness at graduation: $112,439
Enrollment: full time: 694; part time: N/A
men: 54%; women: 46%; minorities: 24%
Acceptance rate (full time): 45%
Midrange LSAT (full time): 158-163
Midrange undergraduate GPA (full time): 3.39-3.65
Midrange of full-time private-sector salaries of 2014 grads: $76,000-$160,000
2014 grads employed in: law firms: 53%; business and industry: 13%; government: 13%; public interest: 8%; judicial clerk: 12%; academia: 1%; unknown: 0%
Employment location for 2014 class: Intl. 3%; N.E. 54%; M.A. 19%; E.N.C. 3%; W.N.C. 1%; S.A. 13%; E.S.C. 0%; W.S.C. 2%; Mt. 1%; Pac. 3%; unknown 0%

Boston University

765 Commonwealth Avenue
Boston, MA 02215
www.bu.edu/law/
Private
Admissions: (617) 353-3100
Email: bulawadm@bu.edu
Financial aid: (617) 353-3160
Application deadline: 04/01
Tuition: full time: $49,330; part time: N/A
Room/board/expenses: $18,472
Median grant: $20,000
Average student indebtedness at graduation: $102,329
Enrollment: full time: 672; part time: N/A
men: 45%; women: 55%; minorities: 29%
Acceptance rate (full time): 38%
Midrange LSAT (full time): 160-164
Midrange undergraduate GPA (full time): 3.41-3.75
Midrange of full-time private-sector salaries of 2014 grads: $84,550-$160,000
2014 grads employed in: law firms: 55%; business and industry: 16%; government: 14%; public interest: 10%; judicial clerk: 5%; academia: 0%; unknown: 0%
Employment location for 2014 class: Intl. 4%; N.E. 48%; M.A. 19%; E.N.C. 3%; W.N.C. 1%; S.A. 14%; E.S.C. 0%; W.S.C. 4%; Mt. 0%; Pac. 6%; unknown 0%

Harvard University

1563 Massachusetts Avenue
Cambridge, MA 02138
www.law.harvard.edu
Private
Admissions: (617) 495-3109
Email: jdadmiss@law.harvard.edu
Financial aid: (617) 495-4606

Application deadline: 02/01
Tuition: full time: $58,242; part time: N/A
Room/board/expenses: $26,758
Median grant: $21,080
Average student indebtedness at graduation: $149,754
Enrollment: full time: 1,767; part time: N/A
men: 51%; women: 49%; minorities: 33%
Acceptance rate (full time): 18%
Midrange LSAT (full time): 170-175
Midrange undergraduate GPA (full time): 3.75-3.96
Midrange of full-time private-sector salaries of 2014 grads: $160,000-$160,000
2014 grads employed in: law firms: 61%; business and industry: 5%; government: 4%; public interest: 11%; judicial clerk: 19%; academia: 1%; unknown: 0%
Employment location for 2014 class: Intl. 4%; N.E. 10%; M.A. 38%; E.N.C. 5%; W.N.C. 2%; S.A. 18%; E.S.C. 1%; W.S.C. 4%; Mt. 2%; Pac. 14%; unknown 0%

New England Law Boston

154 Stuart Street
Boston, MA 02116
www.nesl.edu
Private
Admissions: (617) 422-7210
Email: admit@nesl.edu
Financial aid: (617) 422-7298
Application deadline: rolling
Tuition: full time: $45,686; part time: $34,284
Room/board/expenses: $19,980
Median grant: $21,994
Enrollment: full time: 466; part time: 222
men: 45%; women: 55%; minorities: 28%
Acceptance rate (full time): 82%
Midrange LSAT (full time): 144-150
Midrange undergraduate GPA (full time): 2.72-3.41
Midrange of full-time private-sector salaries of 2014 grads: $52,000-$75,000
2014 grads employed in: law firms: 41%; business and industry: 29%; government: 13%; public interest: 8%; judicial clerk: 5%; academia: 4%; unknown: 0%
Employment location for 2014 class: Intl. 2%; N.E. 71%; M.A. 14%; E.N.C. 2%; W.N.C. 0%; S.A. 4%; E.S.C. 0%; W.S.C. 1%; Mt. 0%; Pac. 5%; unknown 1%

Northeastern University

416 Huntington Avenue
Boston, MA 02115
northeastern.edu/law
Private
Admissions: (617) 373-2395
Email: lawadmissions@neu.edu
Financial aid: (617) 373-4620
Application deadline: rolling
Tuition: full time: $46,400; part time: N/A
Room/board/expenses: $19,599
Median grant: $15,000
Average student indebtedness at graduation: $127,406

Enrollment: full time: 453; part time: 2
men: 37%; women: 63%; minorities: 29%
Acceptance rate (full time): 35%
Midrange LSAT (full time): 152-162
Midrange undergraduate GPA (full time): 3.30-3.75
Midrange of full-time private-sector salaries of 2014 grads: $70,000-$110,000
2014 grads employed in: law firms: 38%; business and industry: 17%; government: 14%; public interest: 20%; judicial clerk: 5%; academia: 5%; unknown: 1%
Employment location for 2014 class: Intl. 1%; N.E. 54%; M.A. 15%; E.N.C. 1%; W.N.C. 1%; S.A. 8%; E.S.C. 0%; W.S.C. 2%; Mt. 1%; Pac. 5%; unknown 12%

Suffolk University

120 Tremont Street
Boston, MA 02108
www.suffolk.edu/law
Private
Admissions: (617) 573-8144
Email: lawadm@suffolk.edu
Financial aid: (617) 573-8147
Application deadline: 04/01
Tuition: full time: $46,042; part time: $34,530
Room/board/expenses: $15,385
Median grant: $19,480
Average student indebtedness at graduation: $138,724
Enrollment: full time: 788; part time: 393
men: 45%; women: 55%; minorities: 23%
Acceptance rate (full time): 71%
Midrange LSAT (full time): 144-154
Midrange undergraduate GPA (full time): 3.04-3.47
Midrange of full-time private-sector salaries of 2014 grads: $50,000-$90,000
2014 grads employed in: law firms: 43%; business and industry: 33%; government: 15%; public interest: 2%; judicial clerk: 4%; academia: 2%; unknown: 0%
Employment location for 2014 class: Intl. 1%; N.E. 83%; M.A. 7%; E.N.C. 1%; W.N.C. 1%; S.A. 3%; E.S.C. 0%; W.S.C. 0%; Mt. 1%; Pac. 2%; unknown 0%

University of Massachusetts-Dartmouth

333 Faunce Corner Road
North Dartmouth, MA 02747
www.umassd.edu/law/admissions
Public
Admissions: (508) 985-1110
Email: lawadmissions@umassd.edu
Financial aid: (508) 985-1112
Application deadline: 06/30
In-state tuition: full time: $25,016; part time: $18,881
Out-of-state tuition: full time: $32,768
Room/board/expenses: $18,576
Median grant: $11,500
Average student indebtedness at graduation: $102,603
Enrollment: full time: 123; part time: 82
men: 47%; women: 53%; minorities: 26%

Western New England University[1]

1215 Wilbraham Road
Springfield, MA 01119-2684
www.law.wne.edu
Private
Admissions: (413) 782-1406
Email: admissions@law.wne.edu
Financial aid: (413) 796-2080
Tuition: N/A
Room/board/expenses: N/A
Enrollment: N/A

MICHIGAN

Michigan State University

648 N. Shaw Lane, Room 368
East Lansing, MI 48824-1300
www.law.msu.edu
Private
Admissions: (517) 432-0222
Email: law@law.msu.edu
Financial aid: (517) 432-6810
Application deadline: 04/30
Tuition: full time: $39,353; part time: $29,854
Room/board/expenses: $14,442
Median grant: $24,134
Average student indebtedness at graduation: $93,245
Enrollment: full time: 709; part time: 92
men: 51%; women: 49%; minorities: 22%
Acceptance rate (full time): 46%
Midrange LSAT (full time): 151-157
Midrange undergraduate GPA (full time): 3.19-3.72
Midrange of full-time private-sector salaries of 2014 grads: $50,000-$87,500
2014 grads employed in: law firms: 35%; business and industry: 25%; government: 14%; public interest: 13%; judicial clerk: 6%; academia: 7%; unknown: 0%
Employment location for 2014 class: Intl. 3%; N.E. 1%; M.A. 8%; E.N.C. 58%; W.N.C. 2%; S.A. 9%; E.S.C. 2%; W.S.C. 4%; Mt. 4%; Pac. 4%; unknown 4%

University of Detroit Mercy

651 E. Jefferson Avenue
Detroit, MI 48226
www.law.udmercy.edu
Private
Admissions: (313) 596-0264
Email: udmlawao@udmercy.edu
Financial aid: (313) 596-0214
Application deadline: 04/15

Tuition: full time: $40,532; part time: $32,438
Room/board/expenses: $22,853
Median grant: $9,731
Average student indebtedness at graduation: $137,047
Enrollment: full time: 438; part time: 93
men: 45%; women: 55%; minorities: 15%
Acceptance rate (full time): 60%
Midrange LSAT (full time): 148-156
Midrange undergraduate GPA (full time): 2.87-3.38
Midrange of full-time private-sector salaries of 2014 grads: $45,000-$100,000
2014 grads employed in: law firms: 57%; business and industry: 26%; government: 10%; public interest: 2%; judicial clerk: 5%; academia: 1%; unknown: 0%
Employment location for 2014 class: Intl. 30%; N.E. 1%; M.A. 1%; E.N.C. 62%; W.N.C. 0%; S.A. 2%; E.S.C. 0%; W.S.C. 0%; Mt. 3%; Pac. 1%; unknown 0%

University of Michigan-Ann Arbor

625 S. State Street
Ann Arbor, MI 48109-1215
www.law.umich.edu/
Public
Admissions: (734) 764-0537
Email: law.jd.admissions@umich.edu
Financial aid: (734) 764-5289
Application deadline: 02/15
In-state tuition: full time: $53,112; part time: N/A
Out-of-state tuition: full time: $56,112
Room/board/expenses: $18,550
Median grant: $15,000
Average student indebtedness at graduation: $142,572
Enrollment: full time: 932; part time: 3
men: 52%; women: 48%; minorities: 21%
Acceptance rate (full time): 28%
Midrange LSAT (full time): 164-169
Midrange undergraduate GPA (full time): 3.54-3.87
Midrange of full-time private-sector salaries of 2014 grads: $130,000-$160,000
2014 grads employed in: law firms: 53%; business and industry: 5%; government: 12%; public interest: 11%; judicial clerk: 19%; academia: 1%; unknown: 0%
Employment location for 2014 class: Intl. 2%; N.E. 2%; M.A. 22%; E.N.C. 31%; W.N.C. 3%; S.A. 17%; E.S.C. 1%; W.S.C. 4%; Mt. 3%; Pac. 12%; unknown 1%

Wayne State University

471 W. Palmer Street
Detroit, MI 48202
www.law.wayne.edu
Public
Admissions: (313) 577-3937
Email: lawinquire@wayne.edu
Financial aid: (313) 577-3049
Application deadline: 07/01
In-state tuition: full time: $30,111; part time: $16,316
Out-of-state tuition: full time: $32,894

Room/board/expenses: $21,990
Median grant: $17,367
Average student indebtedness at graduation: $82,397
Enrollment: full time: 365; part time: 51
men: 58%; women: 42%; minorities: 14%
Acceptance rate (full time): 55%
Midrange LSAT (full time): 153-159
Midrange undergraduate GPA (full time): 3.22-3.63
Midrange of full-time private-sector salaries of 2014 grads: $55,000-$100,000
2014 grads employed in: law firms: 62%; business and industry: 21%; government: 9%; public interest: 5%; judicial clerk: 1%; academia: 1%; unknown: 0%
Employment location for 2014 class: Intl. 0%; N.E. 0%; M.A. 1%; E.N.C. 90%; W.N.C. 2%; S.A. 1%; E.S.C. 1%; W.S.C. 1%; Mt. 0%; Pac. 3%; unknown 2%

Western Michigan University Thomas M. Cooley Law School

300 S. Capitol Avenue
Lansing, MI 48933
www.cooley.edu
Private
Admissions: (517) 371-5140
Email: admissions@cooley.edu
Financial aid: (517) 371-5140
Application deadline: 09/01
Tuition: full time: $47,890; part time: $28,090
Room/board/expenses: $17,584
Median grant: $15,488
Enrollment: full time: 174; part time: 1,168
men: 45%; women: 55%; minorities: 38%
Midrange LSAT (full time): 145-155
Midrange undergraduate GPA (full time): 2.57-3.23
Midrange of full-time private-sector salaries of 2014 grads: $36,000-$62,400
2014 grads employed in: law firms: 45%; business and industry: 29%; government: 15%; public interest: 5%; judicial clerk: 3%; academia: 3%; unknown: %
Employment location for 2014 class: Intl. 2%; N.E. 1%; M.A. 10%; E.N.C. 63%; W.N.C. 2%; S.A. 9%; E.S.C. 2%; W.S.C. 4%; Mt. 4%; Pac. 3%; unknown 0%

MINNESOTA

Hamline University

1536 Hewitt Avenue
St. Paul, MN 55104-1284
www.hamline.edu/law
Private
Admissions: (651) 523-2461
Email: lawadm@hamline.edu
Financial aid: (651) 523-3000
Application deadline: rolling
Tuition: full time: $40,128; part time: $28,882
Room/board/expenses: $20,007
Median grant: $22,436
Average student indebtedness at graduation: $107,359

Enrollment: full time: 171; part time: 88
men: 51%; women: 49%; minorities: 23%
Acceptance rate (full time): 64%
Midrange LSAT (full time): 149-156
Midrange undergraduate GPA (full time): 3.01-3.52
Midrange of full-time private-sector salaries of 2014 grads: $52,000-$75,000
2014 grads employed in: law firms: 36%; business and industry: 33%; government: 15%; public interest: 4%; judicial clerk: 11%; academia: 2%; unknown: 0%
Employment location for 2014 class: Intl. 0%; N.E. 1%; M.A. 0%; E.N.C. 10%; W.N.C. 77%; S.A. 3%; E.S.C. 0%; W.S.C. 0%; Mt. 2%; Pac. 3%; unknown 4%

University of Minnesota

229 19th Avenue S
Minneapolis, MN 55455
www.law.umn.edu
Public
Admissions: (612) 625-3487
Email: umnlsadm@umn.edu
Financial aid: (612) 625-3487
Application deadline: rolling
In-state tuition: full time: $42,231; part time: N/A
Out-of-state tuition: full time: $50,373
Room/board/expenses: $16,166
Median grant: $22,250
Average student indebtedness at graduation: $92,179
Enrollment: full time: 632; part time: 9
men: 57%; women: 43%; minorities: 19%
Acceptance rate (full time): 44%
Midrange LSAT (full time): 158-166
Midrange undergraduate GPA (full time): 3.48-3.90
Midrange of full-time private-sector salaries of 2014 grads: $65,000-$120,000
2014 grads employed in: law firms: 44%; business and industry: 10%; government: 9%; public interest: 12%; judicial clerk: 23%; academia: 1%; unknown: 0%
Employment location for 2014 class: Intl. 2%; N.E. 0%; M.A. 5%; E.N.C. 7%; W.N.C. 63%; S.A. 7%; E.S.C. 1%; W.S.C. 3%; Mt. 4%; Pac. 8%; unknown N/A

University of St. Thomas

MSL 411
1000 LaSalle Avenue
Minneapolis, MN 55403-2015
www.stthomas.edu/law
Private
Admissions: (651) 962-4895
Email: lawschool@stthomas.edu
Financial aid: (651) 962-6550
Application deadline: 08/01
Tuition: full time: $37,941; part time: N/A
Room/board/expenses: $20,340
Median grant: $20,272
Average student indebtedness at graduation: $101,950

Enrollment: full time: 340; part time: 7
men: 49%; women: 51%; minorities: 15%
Acceptance rate (full time): 64%
Midrange LSAT (full time): 149-157
Midrange undergraduate GPA (full time): 3.21-3.65
Midrange of full-time private-sector salaries of 2014 grads: $44,500-$68,500
2014 grads employed in: law firms: 29%; business and industry: 29%; government: 13%; public interest: 5%; judicial clerk: 21%; academia: 3%; unknown: 0%
Employment location for 2014 class: Intl. 0%; N.E. 1%; M.A. 1%; E.N.C. 5%; W.N.C. 88%; S.A. 1%; E.S.C. 0%; W.S.C. 2%; Mt. 1%; Pac. 2%; unknown 0%

William Mitchell College of Law

875 Summit Avenue
St. Paul, MN 55105-3076
www.wmitchell.edu
Private
Admissions: (651) 290-6476
Email: admissions@wmitchell.edu
Financial aid: (651) 290-6403
Application deadline: 08/01
Tuition: full time: $39,560; part time: $28,690
Room/board/expenses: $19,450
Median grant: $23,040
Average student indebtedness at graduation: $108,678
Enrollment: full time: 375; part time: 363
men: 47%; women: 53%; minorities: 15%
Acceptance rate (full time): 72%
Midrange LSAT (full time): 147-157
Midrange undergraduate GPA (full time): 2.99-3.51
Midrange of full-time private-sector salaries of 2014 grads: $50,000-$85,000
2014 grads employed in: law firms: 39%; business and industry: 27%; government: 11%; public interest: 5%; judicial clerk: 15%; academia: 2%; unknown: 0%
Employment location for 2014 class: Intl. 0%; N.E. 0%; M.A. 1%; E.N.C. 3%; W.N.C. 84%; S.A. 3%; E.S.C. 0%; W.S.C. 2%; Mt. 2%; Pac. 1%; unknown 4%

MISSISSIPPI

Mississippi College

151 E. Griffith Street
Jackson, MS 39201
www.law.mc.edu
Private
Admissions: (601) 925-7152
Email: tpaige@mc.edu
Financial aid: (601) 925-7110
Application deadline: 07/15
Tuition: full time: $33,630; part time: $1,068/credit hour
Room/board/expenses: $21,525
Median grant: $20,000
Average student indebtedness at graduation: $38,213
Enrollment: full time: 380; part time: 11
men: 56%; women: 44%; minorities: 21%
Acceptance rate (full time): 87%
Midrange LSAT (full time): 142-150

Midrange undergraduate GPA (full time): 2.73-3.33
Midrange of full-time private-sector salaries of 2014 grads: $48,000-$80,000
2014 grads employed in: law firms: 60%; business and industry: 16%; government: 10%; public interest: 2%; judicial clerk: 13%; academia: 0%; unknown: 0%
Employment location for 2014 class: Intl. 0%; N.E. 0%; M.A. 2%; E.N.C. 0%; W.N.C. 4%; S.A. 13%; E.S.C. 54%; W.S.C. 25%; Mt. 2%; Pac. 1%; unknown 0%

University of Mississippi

PO Box 1848
University, MS 38677
law.olemiss.edu
Public
Admissions: (662) 915-6910
Email: lawmiss@olemiss.edu
Financial aid: (800) 891-4569
Application deadline: 04/15
In-state tuition: full time: $15,036; part time: N/A
Out-of-state tuition: full time: $32,374
Room/board/expenses: $17,698
Median grant: $10,922
Average student indebtedness at graduation: $71,330
Enrollment: full time: 379; part time: N/A
men: 58%; women: 42%; minorities: 23%
Acceptance rate (full time): 48%
Midrange LSAT (full time): 151-157
Midrange undergraduate GPA (full time): 3.04-3.65
Midrange of full-time private-sector salaries of 2014 grads: $50,000-$80,000
2014 grads employed in: law firms: 57%; business and industry: 15%; government: 13%; public interest: 5%; judicial clerk: 8%; academia: 2%; unknown: 0%
Employment location for 2014 class: Intl. 0%; N.E. 0%; M.A. 3%; E.N.C. 3%; W.N.C. 1%; S.A. 13%; E.S.C. 71%; W.S.C. 6%; Mt. 1%; Pac. 1%; unknown 0%

MISSOURI

St. Louis University

100 N. Tucker
St. Louis, MO 63101
law.slu.edu
Private
Admissions: (314) 977-2800
Email: admissions@law.slu.edu
Financial aid: (314) 977-3369
Application deadline: rolling
Tuition: full time: $39,195; part time: $28,525
Room/board/expenses: $18,940
Median grant: $19,000
Average student indebtedness at graduation: $113,070
Enrollment: full time: 418; part time: 77
men: 50%; women: 50%; minorities: 20%
Acceptance rate (full time): 66%
Midrange LSAT (full time): 152-159
Midrange undergraduate GPA (full time): 3.21-3.68
Midrange of full-time private-sector salaries of 2014 grads: $52,500-$102,500

2014 grads employed in: law firms: 56%; business and industry: 22%; government: 14%; public interest: 4%; judicial clerk: 3%; academia: 1%; unknown: 0%
Employment location for 2014 class: Intl. 0%; N.E. 0%; M.A. 0%; E.N.C. 18%; W.N.C. 70%; S.A. 3%; E.S.C. 0%; W.S.C. 2%; Mt. 3%; Pac. 2%; unknown 0%

University of Missouri

203 Hulston Hall
Columbia, MO 65211-4300
www.law.missouri.edu
Public
Admissions: (573) 882-6042
Email: mulawadmissions@missouri.edu
Financial aid: (573) 882-1383
Application deadline: rolling
In-state tuition: full time: $20,771; part time: N/A
Out-of-state tuition: full time: $38,400
Room/board/expenses: $12,366
Median grant: $10,000
Average student indebtedness at graduation: $81,149
Enrollment: full time: 324; part time: 12
men: 61%; women: 39%; minorities: 17%
Acceptance rate (full time): 59%
Midrange LSAT (full time): 154-159
Midrange undergraduate GPA (full time): 3.08-3.72
Midrange of full-time private-sector salaries of 2014 grads: $50,000-$83,000
2014 grads employed in: law firms: 45%; business and industry: 21%; government: 19%; public interest: 3%; judicial clerk: 9%; academia: 3%; unknown: 0%
Employment location for 2014 class: Intl. 0%; N.E. 0%; M.A. 1%; E.N.C. 6%; W.N.C. 81%; S.A. 2%; E.S.C. 1%; W.S.C. 5%; Mt. 2%; Pac. 2%; unknown 1%

University of Missouri-Kansas City

500 East 52nd Street
Kansas City, MO 64110
www.law.umkc.edu
Public
Admissions: (816) 235-1644
Email: law@umkc.edu
Financial aid: (816) 235-1154
Application deadline: 03/01
In-state tuition: full time: $18,466; part time: $11,251
Out-of-state tuition: full time: $35,110
Room/board/expenses: $16,075
Median grant: $9,806
Average student indebtedness at graduation: $96,639
Enrollment: full time: 387; part time: 75
men: 55%; women: 45%; minorities: 17%
Acceptance rate (full time): 58%
Midrange LSAT (full time): 150-155
Midrange undergraduate GPA (full time): 3.03-3.57
Midrange of full-time private-sector salaries of 2014 grads: $50,000-$70,000
2014 grads employed in: law firms: 45%; business and industry: 27%; government: 13%; public interest: 2%; judicial clerk: 11%; academia: 2%; unknown: 0%

Employment location for 2014 class: Intl. 0%; N.E. 0%; M.A. 0%; E.N.C. 2%; W.N.C. 95%; S.A. 0%; E.S.C. 0%; W.S.C. 0%; Mt. 2%; Pac. 1%; unknown 0%

Washington University in St. Louis

1 Brookings Drive
Box 1120
St. Louis, MO 63130
www.law.wustl.edu
Private
Admissions: (314) 935-4525
Email: admiss@wulaw.wustl.edu
Financial aid: (314) 935-4605
Application deadline: 08/01
Tuition: full time: $51,626; part time: N/A
Room/board/expenses: $22,700
Median grant: $30,000
Average student indebtedness at graduation: $109,232
Enrollment: full time: 684; part time: 5
men: 57%; women: 43%; minorities: 25%
Acceptance rate (full time): 28%
Midrange LSAT (full time): 161-168
Midrange undergraduate GPA (full time): 3.18-3.80
Midrange of full-time private-sector salaries of 2014 grads: $65,000-$150,000
2014 grads employed in: law firms: 50%; business and industry: 20%; government: 16%; public interest: 2%; judicial clerk: 9%; academia: 3%; unknown: 0%
Employment location for 2014 class: Intl. 4%; N.E. 3%; M.A. 13%; E.N.C. 13%; W.N.C. 34%; S.A. 17%; E.S.C. 2%; W.S.C. 7%; Mt. 2%; Pac. 5%; unknown 0%

MONTANA

University of Montana

32 Campus Drive
Missoula, MT 59812
www.umt.edu/law
Public
Admissions: (406) 243-2698
Email: lori.freeman@umontana.edu
Financial aid: (406) 243-5524
Application deadline: 03/15
In-state tuition: full time: $11,393; part time: N/A
Out-of-state tuition: full time: $30,078
Room/board/expenses: $15,346
Median grant: $3,000
Average student indebtedness at graduation: $79,304
Enrollment: full time: 236; part time: N/A
men: 52%; women: 48%; minorities: 14%
Acceptance rate (full time): 65%
Midrange LSAT (full time): 149-156
Midrange undergraduate GPA (full time): 3.06-3.63
Midrange of full-time private-sector salaries of 2014 grads: $48,000-$59,000
2014 grads employed in: law firms: 49%; business and industry: 9%; government: 10%; public interest: 7%; judicial clerk: 22%; academia: 3%; unknown: 0%
Employment location for 2014 class: Intl. 1%; N.E. 0%; M.A. 2%; E.N.C. 0%; W.N.C. 80%; S.A. 4%; E.S.C. 0%; W.S.C. 2%; Mt. 9%; Pac. 2%; unknown 0%

Employment location for 2014 class: Intl. 0%; N.E. 0%; M.A. 1%; E.N.C. 1%; W.N.C. 1%; S.A. 3%; E.S.C. 1%; W.S.C. 1%; Mt. 87%; Pac. 4%; unknown 0%

NEBRASKA

Creighton University

2500 California Plaza
Omaha, NE 68178
www.creighton.edu/law
Private
Admissions: (800) 282-5835
Email: lawadmit@creighton.edu
Financial aid: (402) 280-2352
Application deadline: 08/15
Tuition: full time: $36,258; part time: $1,155/credit hour
Room/board/expenses: $16,925
Median grant: $16,968
Average student indebtedness at graduation: $117,980
Enrollment: full time: 338; part time: 7
men: 56%; women: 44%; minorities: 20%
Acceptance rate (full time): 80%
Midrange LSAT (full time): 149-154
Midrange undergraduate GPA (full time): 2.93-3.56
Midrange of full-time private-sector salaries of 2014 grads: $56,250-$85,000
2014 grads employed in: law firms: 44%; business and industry: 27%; government: 15%; public interest: 4%; judicial clerk: 9%; academia: 1%; unknown: 0%
Employment location for 2014 class: Intl. 3%; N.E. 0%; M.A. 0%; E.N.C. 2%; W.N.C. 70%; S.A. 3%; E.S.C. 0%; W.S.C. 2%; Mt. 18%; Pac. 3%; unknown 0%

University of Nebraska-Lincoln

PO Box 830902
Lincoln, NE 68583-0902
law.unl.edu
Public
Admissions: (402) 472-8333
Email: lawadm@unl.edu
Financial aid: (402) 472-8333
Application deadline: 03/01
In-state tuition: full time: $14,721; part time: N/A
Out-of-state tuition: full time: $33,415
Room/board/expenses: $15,538
Median grant: $14,441
Average student indebtedness at graduation: $58,744
Enrollment: full time: 330; part time: 2
men: 51%; women: 49%; minorities: 8%
Acceptance rate (full time): 62%
Midrange LSAT (full time): 152-158
Midrange undergraduate GPA (full time): 3.40-3.85
Midrange of full-time private-sector salaries of 2014 grads: $48,000-$65,000
2014 grads employed in: law firms: 58%; business and industry: 14%; government: 13%; public interest: 6%; judicial clerk: 7%; academia: 2%; unknown: 0%
Employment location for 2014 class: Intl. 1%; N.E. 0%; M.A. 2%; E.N.C. 0%; W.N.C. 80%; S.A. 4%; E.S.C. 0%; W.S.C. 2%; Mt. 9%; Pac. 2%; unknown 0%

NEVADA

University of Nevada-Las Vegas

4505 S. Maryland Parkway
Box 451003
Las Vegas, NV 89154-1003
www.law.unlv.edu/
Public
Admissions: (702) 895-2440
Email: eric.eden@law.unlv.edu
Financial aid: (702) 895-4107
Application deadline: 03/15
In-state tuition: full time: $25,749; part time: $19,469
Out-of-state tuition: full time: $37,149
Room/board/expenses: $22,516
Median grant: $13,450
Average student indebtedness at graduation: $81,579
Enrollment: full time: 275; part time: 103
men: 54%; women: 46%;
minorities: 31%
Acceptance rate (full time): 34%
Midrange LSAT (full time): 155-161
Midrange undergraduate GPA (full time): 2.92-3.59
Midrange of full-time private-sector salaries of 2014 grads: $62,500-$87,000
2014 grads employed in: law firms: 59%; business and industry: 8%; government: 4%; public interest: 8%; judicial clerk: 19%; academia: 2%; unknown: 0%
Employment location for 2014 class: Intl. 0%; N.E. 0%; M.A. 0%; E.N.C. 2%; W.N.C. 0%; S.A. 2%; E.S.C. 0%; W.S.C. 0%; Mt. 92%; Pac. 4%; unknown 0%

NEW HAMPSHIRE

University of New Hampshire School of Law

2 White Street
Concord, NH 03301
www.law.unh.edu
Public
Admissions: (603) 513-5300
Email: admissions@law.unh.edu
Financial aid: (603) 228-1541
Application deadline: 07/15
In-state tuition: full time: $37,383; part time: $0
Out-of-state tuition: full time: $41,383
Room/board/expenses: $20,877
Median grant: $18,500
Average student indebtedness at graduation: $108,896
Enrollment: full time: 215; part time: 2
men: 56%; women: 44%;
minorities: 13%
Acceptance rate (full time): 53%
Midrange LSAT (full time): 153-159
Midrange undergraduate GPA (full time): 3.18-3.65
Midrange of full-time private-sector salaries of 2014 grads: $52,000-$95,000
2014 grads employed in: law firms: 53%; business and industry: 26%; government: 10%; public interest: 5%; judicial clerk: 4%; academia: 2%; unknown: 0%

Employment location for 2014 class: Intl. 0%; N.E. 65%; M.A. 10%; E.N.C. 4%; W.N.C. 1%; S.A. 10%; E.S.C. 0%; W.S.C. 6%; Mt. 3%; Pac. 3%; unknown 0%

NEW JERSEY

Rutgers, The State University of New Jersey

Camden and Newark, NJ
Public
Admissions: N/A
Financial aid: N/A
Application deadline: 03/15
In-state tuition: full time: $26,842; part time: $22,548
Out-of-state tuition: full time: $39,048
Room/board/expenses: $18,096
Median grant: $11,500
Average student indebtedness at graduation: $85,054
Enrollment: full time: 893; part time: 250
men: 58%; women: 42%;
minorities: 32%
Acceptance rate (full time): 52%
Midrange LSAT (full time): 153-159
Midrange undergraduate GPA (full time): 2.96-3.56
Midrange of full-time private-sector salaries of 2014 grads: $48,500-$125,000
2014 grads employed in: law firms: 35%; business and industry: 16%; government: 7%; public interest: 2%; judicial clerk: 40%; academia: 0%; unknown: 0%
Employment location for 2014 class: Intl. 0%; N.E. 1%; M.A. 90%; E.N.C. 1%; W.N.C. 0%; S.A. 5%; E.S.C. 0%; W.S.C. 0%; Mt. 1%; Pac. 0%; unknown 0%

Seton Hall University

1 Newark Center
Newark, NJ 07102-5210
law.shu.edu
Private
Admissions: (888) 415-7271
Email: admitme@shu.edu
Financial aid: (973) 642-8850
Application deadline: 04/01
Tuition: full time: $51,018; part time: $38,474
Room/board/expenses: $22,344
Median grant: $25,000
Average student indebtedness at graduation: $133,000
Enrollment: full time: 353; part time: 172
men: 52%; women: 48%;
minorities: 26%
Acceptance rate (full time): 51%
Midrange LSAT (full time): 155-160
Midrange undergraduate GPA (full time): 3.24-3.77
Midrange of full-time private-sector salaries of 2014 grads: $50,000-$93,000
2014 grads employed in: law firms: 29%; business and industry: 18%; government: 5%; public interest: 3%; judicial clerk: 46%; academia: 0%; unknown: 0%
Employment location for 2014 class: Intl. 0%; N.E. 1%; M.A. 90%; E.N.C. 0%; W.N.C. 0%; S.A. 3%; E.S.C. 0%; W.S.C. 1%; Mt. 0%; Pac. 2%; unknown 2%

NEW MEXICO

University of New Mexico

1117 Stanford Drive NE
MSC11 6070
Albuquerque, NM 87131-0001
lawschool.unm.edu
Public
Admissions: (505) 277-0958
Email: admissions@law.unm.edu
Financial aid: (505) 277-9035
Application deadline: 03/01
In-state tuition: full time: $16,490; part time: N/A
Out-of-state tuition: full time: $35,183
Room/board/expenses: $15,732
Median grant: $4,745
Average student indebtedness at graduation: $69,366
Enrollment: full time: 344; part time: 2
men: 49%; women: 51%;
minorities: 50%
Acceptance rate (full time): 42%
Midrange LSAT (full time): 150-157
Midrange undergraduate GPA (full time): 3.21-3.73
Midrange of full-time private-sector salaries of 2014 grads: $50,000-$62,000
2014 grads employed in: law firms: 41%; business and industry: 8%; government: 36%; public interest: 6%; judicial clerk: 7%; academia: 2%; unknown: 0%
Employment location for 2014 class: Intl. 1%; N.E. 1%; M.A. 0%; E.N.C. 1%; W.N.C. 0%; S.A. 5%; E.S.C. 1%; W.S.C. 1%; Mt. 91%; Pac. 0%; unknown 0%

NEW YORK

Albany Law School

80 New Scotland Avenue
Albany, NY 12208-3494
www.albanylaw.edu
Private
Admissions: (518) 445-2326
Email: admissions@albanylaw.edu
Financial aid: (518) 445-2357
Application deadline: 06/01
Tuition: full time: $43,398; part time: $32,586
Room/board/expenses: $15,932
Median grant: $19,000
Average student indebtedness at graduation: $125,157
Enrollment: full time: 364; part time: 39
men: 49%; women: 51%;
minorities: 16%
Acceptance rate (full time): 62%
Midrange LSAT (full time): 149-154
Midrange undergraduate GPA (full time): 2.98-3.54
Midrange of full-time private-sector salaries of 2014 grads: $52,000-$75,000
2014 grads employed in: law firms: 42%; business and industry: 21%; government: 24%; public interest: 7%; judicial clerk: 5%; academia: 0%; unknown: 1%
Employment location for 2014 class: Intl. 1%; N.E. 4%; M.A. 89%; E.N.C. 0%; W.N.C. 0%; S.A. 2%; E.S.C. 1%; W.S.C. 1%; Mt. 2%; Pac. 1%; unknown 1%

Brooklyn Law School

250 Joralemon Street
Brooklyn, NY 11201
www.brooklaw.edu
Private
Admissions: (718) 780-7906
Email: admitq@brooklaw.edu
Financial aid: (718) 780-7915
Application deadline: rolling
Tuition: full time: $1,526/credit hour; part time: $1,526/credit hour
Room/board/expenses: $24,396
Median grant: $30,000
Average student indebtedness at graduation: $108,942
Enrollment: full time: 907; part time: 247
men: 52%; women: 48%;
minorities: 27%
Acceptance rate (full time): 54%
Midrange LSAT (full time): 152-158
Midrange undergraduate GPA (full time): 3.12-3.59
Midrange of full-time private-sector salaries of 2014 grads: $63,000-$145,000
2014 grads employed in: law firms: 41%; business and industry: 24%; government: 14%; public interest: 13%; judicial clerk: 7%; academia: 0%; unknown: 1%
Employment location for 2014 class: Intl. 1%; N.E. 3%; M.A. 88%; E.N.C. 1%; W.N.C. 1%; S.A. 2%; E.S.C. 0%; W.S.C. 1%; Mt. 1%; Pac. 3%; unknown 1%

Columbia University

435 W. 116th Street
New York, NY 10027
www.law.columbia.edu
Private
Admissions: (212) 854-2670
Email: admissions@ law.columbia.edu
Financial aid: (212) 854-7730
Application deadline: 02/15
Tuition: full time: $62,700; part time: N/A
Room/board/expenses: $22,942
Median grant: $18,000
Average student indebtedness at graduation: $168,627
Enrollment: full time: 1,165; part time: 2
men: 53%; women: 47%;
minorities: 33%
Acceptance rate (full time): 21%
Midrange LSAT (full time): 168-173
Midrange undergraduate GPA (full time): 3.59-3.81
Midrange of full-time private-sector salaries of 2014 grads: $160,000-$160,000
2014 grads employed in: law firms: 79%; business and industry: 4%; government: 5%; public interest: 7%; judicial clerk: 5%; academia: 0%; unknown: 0%
Employment location for 2014 class: Intl. 4%; N.E. 2%; M.A. 69%; E.N.C. 2%; W.N.C. 1%; S.A. 10%; E.S.C. 0%; W.S.C. 2%; Mt. 1%; Pac. 8%; unknown 0%

Cornell University

Myron Taylor Hall
Ithaca, NY 14853-4901
www.lawschool.cornell.edu
Private
Admissions: (607) 255-5141
Email: jdadmissions@cornell.edu
Financial aid: (607) 255-5141

Application deadline: 02/01

Tuition: full time: $59,900; part time: N/A
Room/board/expenses: $20,232
Median grant: $17,000
Average student indebtedness at graduation: $53,860
Enrollment: full time: 588; part time: N/A
men: 56%; women: 44%;
minorities: 34%
Acceptance rate (full time): 31%
Midrange LSAT (full time): 164-168
Midrange undergraduate GPA (full time): 3.62-3.82
Midrange of full-time private-sector salaries of 2014 grads: $160,000-$160,000
2014 grads employed in: law firms: 71%; business and industry: 3%; government: 6%; public interest: 5%; judicial clerk: 15%; academia: 0%; unknown: 0%
Employment location for 2014 class: Intl. 2%; N.E. 5%; M.A. 64%; E.N.C. 2%; W.N.C. 1%; S.A. 9%; E.S.C. 1%; W.S.C. 4%; Mt. 1%; Pac. 11%; unknown 0%

CUNY

2 Court Square
Long Island City, NY 11101-4356
www.law.cuny.edu/
Public
Admissions: (718) 340-4210
Email: admissions@law.cuny.edu
Financial aid: (718) 340-4284
Application deadline: 05/15
In-state tuition: full time: $14,663; part time: $10,028
Out-of-state tuition: full time: $23,983
Room/board/expenses: $20,261
Median grant: $5,000
Average student indebtedness at graduation: $77,751
Enrollment: full time: 310; part time: 49
men: 36%; women: 64%;
minorities: 45%
Acceptance rate (full time): 49%
Midrange LSAT (full time): 150-157
Midrange undergraduate GPA (full time): 3.13-3.59
Midrange of full-time private-sector salaries of 2014 grads: N/A-N/A
2014 grads employed in: law firms: 19%; business and industry: 13%; government: 16%; public interest: 42%; judicial clerk: 7%; academia: 3%; unknown: 0%
Employment location for 2014 class: Intl. 0%; N.E. 2%; M.A. 90%; E.N.C. 0%; W.N.C. 1%; S.A. 2%; E.S.C. 0%; W.S.C. 0%; Mt. 2%; Pac. 4%; unknown 0%

Fordham University

150 W. 62nd Street
New York, NY 10023-7485
law.fordham.edu
Private
Admissions: (212) 636-6810
Email: lawadmissions@ law.fordham.edu
Financial aid: (212) 636-6815
Application deadline: 03/15
Tuition: full time: $54,116; part time: $40,666
Room/board/expenses: $25,578
Median grant: $15,000
Average student indebtedness at graduation: $149,058

Enrollment: full time: 956; part time: 195
men: 52%; women: 48%; minorities: 28%
Acceptance rate (full time): 36%
Midrange LSAT (full time): 161-165
Midrange undergraduate GPA (full time): 3.35-3.68
Midrange of full-time private-sector salaries of 2014 grads: $80,000-$160,000
2014 grads employed in: law firms: 61%; business and industry: 14%; government: 12%; public interest: 5%; judicial clerk: 6%; academia: 2%; unknown: 0%
Employment location for 2014 class: Intl. 2%; N.E. 1%; M.A. 90%; E.N.C. 1%; W.N.C. 0%; S.A. 2%; E.S.C. 0%; W.S.C. 1%; Mt. 0%; Pac. 2%; unknown 0%

Hofstra University (Deane)

121 Hofstra University
Hempstead, NY 11549
law.hofstra.edu
Private
Admissions: (516) 463-5916
Email: lawadmissions@hofstra.edu
Financial aid: (516) 463-5929
Application deadline: 04/15
Tuition: full time: $54,250; part time: $40,670
Room/board/expenses: $24,547
Median grant: $26,095
Average student indebtedness at graduation: $125,300
Enrollment: full time: 679; part time: 19
men: 48%; women: 52%; minorities: 28%
Acceptance rate (full time): 62%
Midrange LSAT (full time): 147-155
Midrange undergraduate GPA (full time): 2.99-3.60
Midrange of full-time private-sector salaries of 2014 grads: $50,000-$86,250
2014 grads employed in: law firms: 55%; business and industry: 20%; government: 11%; public interest: 8%; judicial clerk: 3%; academia: 3%; unknown: 2%
Employment location for 2014 class: Intl. 0%; N.E. 2%; M.A. 88%; E.N.C. 0%; W.N.C. 0%; S.A. 3%; E.S.C. 0%; W.S.C. 1%; Mt. 1%; Pac. 3%; unknown 1%

New York Law School

185 W. Broadway
New York, NY 10013-2960
www.nyls.edu
Private
Admissions: (212) 431-2888
Email: admissions@nyls.edu
Financial aid: (212) 431-2828
Application deadline: 07/01
Tuition: full time: $49,240; part time: $37,880
Room/board/expenses: $23,663
Median grant: $17,500
Average student indebtedness at graduation: $161,910
Enrollment: full time: 578; part time: 315
men: 46%; women: 54%; minorities: 35%
Acceptance rate (full time): 57%
Midrange LSAT (full time): 150-154
Midrange undergraduate GPA (full time): 2.92-3.49

Midrange of full-time private-sector salaries of 2014 grads: $62,400-$120,000
2014 grads employed in: law firms: 39%; business and industry: 40%; government: 10%; public interest: 5%; judicial clerk: 4%; academia: 1%; unknown: 0%
Employment location for 2014 class: Intl. 1%; N.E. 2%; M.A. 92%; E.N.C. 1%; W.N.C. 0%; S.A. 2%; E.S.C. 0%; W.S.C. 0%; Mt. 0%; Pac. 1%; unknown 1%

New York University

40 Washington Square S
New York, NY 10012
www.law.nyu.edu
Private
Admissions: (212) 998-6060
Email: law.moreinfo@nyu.edu
Financial aid: (212) 998-6050
Application deadline: 02/15
Tuition: full time: $59,330; part time: N/A
Room/board/expenses: $26,634
Median grant: $20,000
Average student indebtedness at graduation: $166,022
Enrollment: full time: 1,395; part time: N/A
men: 50%; women: 50%; minorities: 31%
Acceptance rate (full time): 33%
Midrange LSAT (full time): 166-171
Midrange undergraduate GPA (full time): 3.61-3.87
Midrange of full-time private-sector salaries of 2014 grads: $160,000-$160,000
2014 grads employed in: law firms: 69%; business and industry: 4%; government: 5%; public interest: 12%; judicial clerk: 9%; academia: 1%; unknown: 0%
Employment location for 2014 class: Intl. 2%; N.E. 2%; M.A. 74%; E.N.C. 2%; W.N.C. 0%; S.A. 7%; E.S.C. 0%; W.S.C. 1%; Mt. 1%; Pac. 9%; unknown 0%

Pace University

78 N. Broadway
White Plains, NY 10603
www.law.pace.edu
Private
Admissions: (914) 422-4210
Email: admissions@law.pace.edu
Financial aid: (914) 422-4050
Application deadline: 06/01
Tuition: full time: $45,376; part time: $34,034
Room/board/expenses: $19,362
Median grant: $21,000
Average student indebtedness at graduation: $124,823
Enrollment: full time: 466; part time: 62
men: 44%; women: 56%; minorities: 25%
Acceptance rate (full time): 66%
Midrange LSAT (full time): 147-153
Midrange undergraduate GPA (full time): 2.90-3.49
Midrange of full-time private-sector salaries of 2014 grads: $50,000-$75,000
2014 grads employed in: law firms: 47%; business and industry: 23%; government: 11%; public interest: 10%; judicial clerk: 6%; academia: 0%; unknown: 2%
Employment location for 2014 class: Intl. 0%; N.E. 7%; M.A. 84%; E.N.C. 1%; W.N.C. 0%; S.A. 2%; E.S.C. 1%; W.S.C. 2%; Mt. 1%; Pac. 2%; unknown 1%

St. John's University

8000 Utopia Parkway
Jamaica, NY 11439
www.law.stjohns.edu/
Private
Admissions: (718) 990-6474
Email: lawinfo@stjohns.edu
Financial aid: (718) 990-1485
Application deadline: 04/01
Tuition: full time: $53,290; part time: $39,970
Room/board/expenses: $25,075
Median grant: $38,617
Average student indebtedness at graduation: $115,666
Enrollment: full time: 604; part time: 116
men: 52%; women: 48%; minorities: 30%
Acceptance rate (full time): 42%
Midrange LSAT (full time): 154-159
Midrange undergraduate GPA (full time): 3.26-3.73
Midrange of full-time private-sector salaries of 2014 grads: $60,000-$120,000
2014 grads employed in: law firms: 58%; business and industry: 20%; government: 14%; public interest: 3%; judicial clerk: 2%; academia: 2%; unknown: 0%
Employment location for 2014 class: Intl. 0%; N.E. 1%; M.A. 95%; E.N.C. 0%; W.N.C. 0%; S.A. 2%; E.S.C. 0%; W.S.C. 0%; Mt. 0%; Pac. 1%; unknown 0%

SUNY Buffalo Law School

John Lord O'Brian Hall
Buffalo, NY 14260
www.law.buffalo.edu
Public
Admissions: (716) 645-2907
Email: law-admissions@buffalo.edu
Financial aid: (716) 645-7324
Application deadline: 03/01
In-state tuition: full time: $26,997; part time: N/A
Out-of-state tuition: full time: $45,007
Room/board/expenses: $22,512
Median grant: $6,000
Average student indebtedness at graduation: $86,970
Enrollment: full time: 494; part time: 5
men: 50%; women: 50%; minorities: 17%
Acceptance rate (full time): 52%
Midrange LSAT (full time): 150-157
Midrange undergraduate GPA (full time): 3.21-3.66
Midrange of full-time private-sector salaries of 2014 grads: $50,000-$85,000
2014 grads employed in: law firms: 54%; business and industry: 20%; government: 14%; public interest: 5%; judicial clerk: 4%; academia: 3%; unknown: 0%
Employment location for 2014 class: Intl. 0%; N.E. 1%; M.A. 95%; E.N.C. 1%; W.N.C. 1%; S.A. 3%; E.S.C. 0%; W.S.C. 0%; Mt. 0%; Pac. 0%; unknown 0%

Syracuse University

950 Irving Avenue, Suite 408
Syracuse, NY 13244-6070
www.law.syr.edu
Private
Admissions: (315) 443-1962
Email: admissions@law.syr.edu
Financial aid: (315) 443-1963
Application deadline: 04/01
Tuition: full time: $47,178; part time: $40,682
Room/board/expenses: $18,322
Median grant: $22,000
Average student indebtedness at graduation: $139,753
Enrollment: full time: 505; part time: 3
men: 56%; women: 44%; minorities: 21%
Acceptance rate (full time): 55%
Midrange LSAT (full time): 151-156
Midrange undergraduate GPA (full time): 3.07-3.51
Midrange of full-time private-sector salaries of 2014 grads: $50,000-$90,000
2014 grads employed in: law firms: 47%; business and industry: 22%; government: 11%; public interest: 8%; judicial clerk: 10%; academia: 1%; unknown: 0%
Employment location for 2014 class: Intl. 2%; N.E. 3%; M.A. 65%; E.N.C. 5%; W.N.C. 1%; S.A. 13%; E.S.C. 1%; W.S.C. 1%; Mt. 0%; Pac. 10%; unknown 0%

Touro College (Fuchsberg)

225 Eastview Drive
Central Islip, NY 11722
www.tourolaw.edu
Private
Admissions: (631) 761-7010
Email: admissions@tourolaw.edu
Financial aid: (631) 761-7020
Application deadline: 08/01
Tuition: full time: $45,950; part time: $34,320
Room/board/expenses: $28,974
Median grant: $10,500
Enrollment: full time: 347; part time: 189
men: 44%; women: 56%; minorities: 38%
Acceptance rate (full time): 64%
Midrange LSAT (full time): 145-149
Midrange undergraduate GPA (full time): 2.76-3.28
Midrange of full-time private-sector salaries of 2014 grads: $42,000-$60,000
2014 grads employed in: law firms: 62%; business and industry: 16%; government: 16%; public interest: 6%; judicial clerk: 1%; academia: 1%; unknown: 0%
Employment location for 2014 class: Intl. 0%; N.E. 0%; M.A. 99%; E.N.C. 0%; W.N.C. 0%; S.A. 0%; E.S.C. 0%; W.S.C. 0%; Mt. 0%; Pac. 1%; unknown N/A

Yeshiva University (Cardozo)

55 Fifth Avenue, 10th Floor
New York, NY 10003
www.cardozo.yu.edu
Private
Admissions: (212) 790-0274
Email: lawinfo@yu.edu
Financial aid: (212) 790-0392
Application deadline: 04/01

Tuition: full time: $54,895; part time: $54,895
Room/board/expenses: $26,725
Median grant: $30,000
Average student indebtedness at graduation: $119,294
Enrollment: full time: 852; part time: 75
men: 49%; women: 51%; minorities: 25%
Acceptance rate (full time): 52%
Midrange LSAT (full time): 158-162
Midrange undergraduate GPA (full time): 3.17-3.62
Midrange of full-time private-sector salaries of 2014 grads: $54,000-$120,000
2014 grads employed in: law firms: 49%; business and industry: 25%; government: 10%; public interest: 10%; judicial clerk: 5%; academia: 2%; unknown: 0%
Employment location for 2014 class: Intl. 1%; N.E. 1%; M.A. 90%; E.N.C. 1%; W.N.C. 0%; S.A. 5%; E.S.C. 1%; W.S.C. 1%; Mt. 0%; Pac. 0%; unknown 0%

NORTH CAROLINA

Campbell University

225 Hillsborough Street
Suite 401
Raleigh, NC 27603
www.law.campbell.edu
Private
Admissions: (919) 865-5989
Email: admissions@campbell.edu
Financial aid: (919) 865-5990
Application deadline: 05/01
Tuition: full time: $39,475; part time: $20,175
Room/board/expenses: $26,895
Median grant: $12,500
Average student indebtedness at graduation: $115,128
Enrollment: full time: 399; part time: 33
men: 53%; women: 47%; minorities: 14%
Acceptance rate (full time): 63%
Midrange LSAT (full time): 150-156
Midrange undergraduate GPA (full time): 2.98-3.49
Midrange of full-time private-sector salaries of 2014 grads: $48,000-$67,000
2014 grads employed in: law firms: 54%; business and industry: 15%; government: 20%; public interest: 2%; judicial clerk: 5%; academia: 3%; unknown: 0%
Employment location for 2014 class: Intl. 0%; N.E. 0%; M.A. 1%; E.N.C. 1%; W.N.C. 0%; S.A. 98%; E.S.C. 0%; W.S.C. 1%; Mt. 0%; Pac. 0%; unknown 0%

Charlotte School of Law[1]

201 South College Street
Suite 400
Charlotte, NC 28244
www.charlottelaw.edu/
Private
Admissions: (704) 971-8500
Email: admissions@charlottelaw.edu
Financial aid: (704) 971-8386
Tuition: N/A
Room/board/expenses: N/A
Enrollment: N/A

Duke University

210 Science Drive
Box 90362
Durham, NC 27708-0362
www.law.duke.edu
Private
Admissions: (919) 613-7020
Email: admissions@law.duke.edu
Financial aid: (919) 613-7026
Application deadline: 02/15
Tuition: full time: $57,717; part time: N/A
Room/board/expenses: $19,434
Median grant: $20,000
Average student indebtedness at graduation: $131,073
Enrollment: full time: 668; part time: 18
men: 58%; women: 42%; minorities: 24%
Acceptance rate (full time): 23%
Midrange LSAT (full time): 166-170
Midrange undergraduate GPA (full time): 3.56-3.84
Midrange of full-time private-sector salaries of 2014 grads: $140,000-$160,000
2014 grads employed in: law firms: 65%; business and industry: 5%; government: 7%; public interest: 4%; judicial clerk: 17%; academia: 1%; unknown: 0%
Employment location for 2014 class: Intl. 3%; N.E. 7%; M.A. 30%; E.N.C. 3%; W.N.C. 1%; S.A. 33%; E.S.C. 3%; W.S.C. 7%; Mt. 0%; Pac. 12%; unknown 0%

Elon University

201 N. Greene Street
Greensboro, NC 27401
law.elon.edu
Private
Admissions: (336) 279-9200
Email: law@elon.edu
Financial aid: (336) 278-2000
Application deadline: 07/15
Tuition: full time: $33,334; part time: N/A
Room/board/expenses: $29,060
Median grant: $13,500
Average student indebtedness at graduation: $128,407
Enrollment: full time: 315; part time: N/A
men: 42%; women: 58%; minorities: 27%
Acceptance rate (full time): 47%
Midrange LSAT (full time): 145-150
Midrange undergraduate GPA (full time): 2.80-3.42
Midrange of full-time private-sector salaries of 2014 grads: $42,500-$62,500
2014 grads employed in: law firms: 59%; business and industry: 24%; government: 9%; public interest: 0%; judicial clerk: 4%; academia: 4%; unknown: 0%
Employment location for 2014 class: Intl. 0%; N.E. 1%; M.A. 1%; E.N.C. 1%; W.N.C. 1%; S.A. 91%; E.S.C. 3%; W.S.C. 0%; Mt. 1%; Pac. 0%; unknown 0%

North Carolina Central University

640 Nelson Street
Durham, NC 27707
law.nccu.edu
Public
Admissions: (919) 530-5243
Email: recruiter@nccu.edu
Financial aid: (919) 530-6365

Application deadline: 03/31
In-state tuition: full time: $12,655; part time: $12,655
Out-of-state tuition: full time: $27,696
Room/board/expenses: $22,908
Median grant: $7,139
Average student indebtedness at graduation: $27,972
Enrollment: full time: 470; part time: 112
men: 40%; women: 60%; minorities: 67%
Acceptance rate (full time): 51%
Midrange LSAT (full time): 142-149
Midrange undergraduate GPA (full time): 2.96-3.38
Midrange of full-time private-sector salaries of 2014 grads: N/A-N/A
2014 grads employed in: law firms: 44%; business and industry: 25%; government: 17%; public interest: 5%; judicial clerk: 1%; academia: 3%; unknown: 6%
Employment location for 2014 class: Intl. 0%; N.E. 0%; M.A. 0%; E.N.C. 2%; W.N.C. 3%; S.A. 75%; E.S.C. 0%; W.S.C. 1%; Mt. 0%; Pac. 0%; unknown 19%

University of North Carolina-Chapel Hill

Van Hecke-Wettach Hall
CB No. 3380
Chapel Hill, NC 27599-3380
www.law.unc.edu
Public
Admissions: (919) 962-5109
Email: law_admissions@unc.edu
Financial aid: (919) 962-8396
Application deadline: 08/01
In-state tuition: full time: $23,041; part time: N/A
Out-of-state tuition: full time: $39,672
Room/board/expenses: $23,520
Median grant: $10,000
Average student indebtedness at graduation: $102,828
Enrollment: full time: 657; part time: N/A
men: 49%; women: 51%; minorities: 24%
Acceptance rate (full time): 45%
Midrange LSAT (full time): 160-164
Midrange undergraduate GPA (full time): 3.31-3.68
Midrange of full-time private-sector salaries of 2014 grads: $60,500-$135,000
2014 grads employed in: law firms: 48%; business and industry: 16%; government: 12%; public interest: 7%; judicial clerk: 13%; academia: 4%; unknown: 0%
Employment location for 2014 class: Intl. 0%; N.E. 3%; M.A. 8%; E.N.C. 0%; W.N.C. 0%; S.A. 83%; E.S.C. 1%; W.S.C. 1%; Mt. 2%; Pac. 1%; unknown 0%

Wake Forest University

Reynolda Station
PO Box 7206
Winston-Salem, NC 27109
www.law.wfu.edu
Private
Admissions: (336) 758-5437
Email: lawadmissions@wfu.edu
Financial aid: (336) 758-5437
Application deadline: 03/15

Tuition: full time: $42,738; part time: N/A
Room/board/expenses: $21,818
Median grant: $22,000
Average student indebtedness at graduation: $97,550
Enrollment: full time: 492; part time: 14
men: 50%; women: 50%; minorities: 22%
Acceptance rate (full time): 56%
Midrange LSAT (full time): 157-162
Midrange undergraduate GPA (full time): 3.37-3.73
Midrange of full-time private-sector salaries of 2014 grads: $55,000-$110,000
2014 grads employed in: law firms: 47%; business and industry: 20%; government: 13%; public interest: 6%; judicial clerk: 10%; academia: 4%; unknown: 0%
Employment location for 2014 class: Intl. 0%; N.E. 5%; M.A. 9%; E.N.C. 4%; W.N.C. 0%; S.A. 71%; E.S.C. 3%; W.S.C. 5%; Mt. 2%; Pac. 3%; unknown 0%

NORTH DAKOTA

University of North Dakota

215 Centennial Drive
Stop 9003
Grand Forks, ND 58202
www.law.und.edu
Public
Admissions: (701) 777-2260
Email: benjamin.hoffman@law.und.edu
Financial aid: (701) 777-3121
Application deadline: 07/15
In-state tuition: full time: $11,161; part time: N/A
Out-of-state tuition: full time: $24,836
Room/board/expenses: $16,553
Median grant: $2,500
Average student indebtedness at graduation: $69,058
Enrollment: full time: 224; part time: N/A
men: 53%; women: 47%; minorities: 13%
Acceptance rate (full time): 68%
Midrange LSAT (full time): 145-152
Midrange undergraduate GPA (full time): 2.90-3.45
Midrange of full-time private-sector salaries of 2014 grads: $44,000-$65,000
2014 grads employed in: law firms: 43%; business and industry: 21%; government: 8%; public interest: 0%; judicial clerk: 25%; academia: 2%; unknown: 2%
Employment location for 2014 class: Intl. 2%; N.E. 2%; M.A. 3%; E.N.C. 2%; W.N.C. 89%; S.A. 0%; E.S.C. 0%; W.S.C. 0%; Mt. 3%; Pac. 0%; unknown 0%

OHIO

Capital University

303 E. Broad Street
Columbus, OH 43215-3200
www.law.capital.edu
Private
Admissions: (614) 236-6310
Email: admissions@law.capital.edu
Financial aid: (614) 236-6350
Application deadline: 08/01

Tuition: full time: $1,202/credit hour; part time: $1,202/credit hour
Room/board/expenses: $18,466
Median grant: $15,000
Average student indebtedness at graduation: $116,283
Enrollment: full time: 255; part time: 155
men: 55%; women: 45%; minorities: 21%
Acceptance rate (full time): 76%
Midrange LSAT (full time): 145-152
Midrange undergraduate GPA (full time): 2.93-3.44
Midrange of full-time private-sector salaries of 2014 grads: $40,000-$67,500
2014 grads employed in: law firms: 48%; business and industry: 26%; government: 22%; public interest: 1%; judicial clerk: 1%; academia: 1%; unknown: 0%
Employment location for 2014 class: Intl. 0%; N.E. 0%; M.A. 2%; E.N.C. 89%; W.N.C. 0%; S.A. 4%; E.S.C. 1%; W.S.C. 0%; Mt. 0%; Pac. 1%; unknown 3%

Case Western Reserve University

11075 E. Boulevard
Cleveland, OH 44106-7148
www.law.case.edu
Private
Admissions: (800) 756-0036
Email: lawadmissions@case.edu
Financial aid: (877) 889-4279
Application deadline: 04/01
Tuition: full time: $48,760; part time: N/A
Room/board/expenses: $23,130
Median grant: $32,667
Average student indebtedness at graduation: $105,854
Enrollment: full time: 380; part time: 1
men: 50%; women: 50%; minorities: 19%
Acceptance rate (full time): 42%
Midrange LSAT (full time): 156-162
Midrange undergraduate GPA (full time): 3.12-3.66
Midrange of full-time private-sector salaries of 2014 grads: $50,000-$105,000
2014 grads employed in: law firms: 46%; business and industry: 21%; government: 21%; public interest: 9%; judicial clerk: 2%; academia: 2%; unknown: 0%
Employment location for 2014 class: Intl. 1%; N.E. 1%; M.A. 14%; E.N.C. 59%; W.N.C. 1%; S.A. 16%; E.S.C. 2%; W.S.C. 2%; Mt. 0%; Pac. 4%; unknown 0%

Cleveland State University (Cleveland-Marshall)

2121 Euclid Avenue, LB 138
Cleveland, OH 44115-2214
www.law.csuohio.edu
Public
Admissions: (216) 687-2304
Email: law.admissions@csuohio.edu
Financial aid: (216) 687-2304
Application deadline: 05/01
In-state tuition: full time: $24,887; part time: $20,101
Out-of-state tuition: full time: $34,174

Room/board/expenses: $18,344
Median grant: $9,101
Average student indebtedness at graduation: $93,865
Enrollment: full time: 278; part time: 97
men: 52%; women: 48%; minorities: 16%
Acceptance rate (full time): 47%
Midrange LSAT (full time): 150-156
Midrange undergraduate GPA (full time): 3.10-3.67
Midrange of full-time private-sector salaries of 2014 grads: $47,750-$83,750
2014 grads employed in: law firms: 55%; business and industry: 27%; government: 11%; public interest: 3%; judicial clerk: 3%; academia: 1%; unknown: 0%
Employment location for 2014 class: Intl. 0%; N.E. 0%; M.A. 6%; E.N.C. 85%; W.N.C. 0%; S.A. 5%; E.S.C. 0%; W.S.C. 0%; Mt. 2%; Pac. 2%; unknown 1%

Ohio Northern University (Pettit)

525 S. Main Street
Ada, OH 45810-1599
www.law.onu.edu
Private
Admissions: (877) 452-9668
Email: lawadmissions@onu.edu
Financial aid: (419) 772-2272
Application deadline: 08/15
Tuition: full time: $26,030; part time: N/A
Room/board/expenses: $19,065
Median grant: $19,305
Average student indebtedness at graduation: $102,414
Enrollment: full time: 197; part time: N/A
men: 48%; women: 52%; minorities: 19%
Acceptance rate (full time): 50%
Midrange LSAT (full time): 144-152
Midrange undergraduate GPA (full time): 3.00-3.50
Midrange of full-time private-sector salaries of 2014 grads: $40,000-$55,000
2014 grads employed in: law firms: 41%; business and industry: 32%; government: 16%; public interest: 0%; judicial clerk: 9%; academia: 0%; unknown: 1%
Employment location for 2014 class: Intl. 0%; N.E. 0%; M.A. 14%; E.N.C. 57%; W.N.C. 0%; S.A. 11%; E.S.C. 3%; W.S.C. 3%; Mt. 3%; Pac. 3%; unknown 8%

Ohio State University (Moritz)

55 W. 12th Avenue
Columbus, OH 43210
www.moritzlaw.osu.edu
Public
Admissions: (614) 292-8810
Email: lawadmit@osu.edu
Financial aid: (614) 292-8807
Application deadline: 03/31
In-state tuition: full time: $29,131; part time: N/A
Out-of-state tuition: full time: $44,081
Room/board/expenses: $20,172
Median grant: $11,960
Average student indebtedness at graduation: $96,253

Enrollment: full time: 523; part time: N/A
men: 52%; women: 48%; minorities: 19%
Acceptance rate (full time): 50%
Midrange LSAT (full time): 156-161
Midrange undergraduate GPA (full time): 3.44-3.81
Midrange of full-time private-sector salaries of 2014 grads: $50,000-$100,000
2014 grads employed in: law firms: 46%; business and industry: 26%; government: 17%; public interest: 3%; judicial clerk: 5%; academia: 3%; unknown: 0%
Employment location for 2014 class: Intl. 0%; N.E. 2%; M.A. 4%; E.N.C. 77%; W.N.C. 0%; S.A. 7%; E.S.C. 1%; W.S.C. 1%; Mt. 2%; Pac. 3%; unknown 0%

University of Akron
C. Blake McDowell Law Center
Akron, OH 44325-2901
www.uakron.edu/law
Public
Admissions: (800) 425-7668
Email: lawadmissions@uakron.edu
Financial aid: (800) 621-3847
Application deadline: 03/31
In-state tuition: full time: $24,452; part time: $14,968
Out-of-state tuition: full time: $24,552
Room/board/expenses: $16,524
Median grant: $17,000
Average student indebtedness at graduation: $78,575
Enrollment: full time: 285; part time: 145
men: 58%; women: 42%; minorities: 14%
Acceptance rate (full time): 67%
Midrange LSAT (full time): 148-155
Midrange undergraduate GPA (full time): 2.90-3.57
Midrange of full-time private-sector salaries of 2014 grads: $45,000-$72,000
2014 grads employed in: law firms: 43%; business and industry: 28%; government: 23%; public interest: 3%; judicial clerk: 1%; academia: 2%; unknown: 1%
Employment location for 2014 class: Intl. 0%; N.E. 0%; M.A. 3%; E.N.C. 81%; W.N.C. 0%; S.A. 5%; E.S.C. 0%; W.S.C. 3%; Mt. 2%; Pac. 3%; unknown 4%

University of Cincinnati
PO Box 210040
Cincinnati, OH 45221-0040
www.law.uc.edu
Public
Admissions: (513) 556-6805
Email: admissions@law.uc.edu
Financial aid: (513) 556-0078
Application deadline: 03/15
In-state tuition: full time: $24,010; part time: N/A
Out-of-state tuition: full time: $29,010
Room/board/expenses: $19,268
Median grant: $6,800
Average student indebtedness at graduation: $82,988
Enrollment: full time: 277; part time: 1
men: 56%; women: 44%; minorities: 16%

Acceptance rate (full time): 58%
Midrange LSAT (full time): 152-157
Midrange undergraduate GPA (full time): 3.23-3.78
Midrange of full-time private-sector salaries of 2014 grads: $57,500-$113,000
2014 grads employed in: law firms: 45%; business and industry: 22%; government: 19%; public interest: 7%; judicial clerk: 5%; academia: 1%; unknown: 0%
Employment location for 2014 class: Intl. 0%; N.E. 0%; M.A. 1%; E.N.C. 82%; W.N.C. 2%; S.A. 4%; E.S.C. 7%; W.S.C. 1%; Mt. 4%; Pac. 0%; unknown 0%

University of Dayton
300 College Park
Dayton, OH 45469-2772
www.udayton.edu/law
Private
Admissions: (937) 229-3555
Email: lawinfo@udayton.edu
Financial aid: (937) 229-3555
Application deadline: 05/01
Tuition: full time: $35,665; part time: N/A
Room/board/expenses: $17,500
Median grant: $12,000
Average student indebtedness at graduation: $115,740
Enrollment: full time: 256; part time: N/A
men: 54%; women: 46%; minorities: 20%
Acceptance rate (full time): 58%
Midrange LSAT (full time): 144-151
Midrange undergraduate GPA (full time): 2.84-3.43
Midrange of full-time private-sector salaries of 2014 grads: $50,000-$57,000
2014 grads employed in: law firms: 54%; business and industry: 20%; government: 11%; public interest: 5%; judicial clerk: 6%; academia: 3%; unknown: 0%
Employment location for 2014 class: Intl. 1%; N.E. 0%; M.A. 10%; E.N.C. 63%; W.N.C. 2%; S.A. 10%; E.S.C. 7%; W.S.C. 3%; Mt. 1%; Pac. 4%; unknown 0%

University of Toledo
2801 W. Bancroft
Toledo, OH 43606
www.utoledo.edu/law/admissions
Public
Admissions: (419) 530-4131
Email: law.admissions@utoledo.edu
Financial aid: (419) 530-7929
Application deadline: 08/01
In-state tuition: full time: $19,612; part time: $817/credit hour
Out-of-state tuition: full time: $31,161
Room/board/expenses: $19,140
Median grant: $14,435
Average student indebtedness at graduation: $94,295
Enrollment: full time: 196; part time: 56
men: 54%; women: 46%; minorities: 15%
Acceptance rate (full time): 70%
Midrange LSAT (full time): 148-154
Midrange undergraduate GPA (full time): 3.00-3.53
Midrange of full-time private-sector salaries of 2014 grads: $45,000-$70,000

2014 grads employed in: law firms: 44%; business and industry: 18%; government: 19%; public interest: 7%; judicial clerk: 8%; academia: 3%; unknown: 0%
Employment location for 2014 class: Intl. 2%; N.E. 0%; M.A. 0%; E.N.C. 83%; W.N.C. 0%; S.A. 8%; E.S.C. 0%; W.S.C. 3%; Mt. 2%; Pac. 1%; unknown 0%

OKLAHOMA

Oklahoma City University
2501 N. Blackwelder Avenue
Oklahoma City , OK 73106-1493
www.law.okcu.edu
Private
Admissions: (866) 529-6281
Email: lawquestions@okcu.edu
Financial aid: (800) 633-7242
Application deadline: 08/01
Tuition: full time: $1,065/credit hour; part time: $1,065/credit hour
Room/board/expenses: $23,541
Median grant: $15,000
Average student indebtedness at graduation: $121,607
Enrollment: full time: 385; part time: 64
men: 52%; women: 48%; minorities: 32%
Acceptance rate (full time): 72%
Midrange LSAT (full time): 146-151
Midrange undergraduate GPA (full time): 2.79-3.51
Midrange of full-time private-sector salaries of 2014 grads: $50,000-$90,000
2014 grads employed in: law firms: 56%; business and industry: 26%; government: 18%; public interest: 1%; judicial clerk: 0%; academia: 0%; unknown: 0%
Employment location for 2014 class: Intl. 0%; N.E. 0%; M.A. 0%; E.N.C. 1%; W.N.C. 1%; S.A. 1%; E.S.C. 1%; W.S.C. 92%; Mt. 1%; Pac. 3%; unknown 0%

University of Oklahoma
Andrew M. Coats Hall
300 Timberdell Road
Norman, OK 73019-5081
www.law.ou.edu
Public
Admissions: (405) 325-4728
Email: admissions@law.ou.edu
Financial aid: (405) 325-4521
Application deadline: 03/15
In-state tuition: full time: $19,973; part time: N/A
Out-of-state tuition: full time: $30,398
Room/board/expenses: $18,105
Median grant: $6,000
Average student indebtedness at graduation: $82,818
Enrollment: full time: 467; part time: N/A
men: 56%; women: 44%; minorities: 24%
Acceptance rate (full time): 49%
Midrange LSAT (full time): 154-159
Midrange undergraduate GPA (full time): 3.33-3.80
Midrange of full-time private-sector salaries of 2014 grads: $50,000-$78,211

2014 grads employed in: law firms: 62%; business and industry: 15%; government: 12%; public interest: 5%; judicial clerk: 3%; academia: 2%; unknown: 0%
Employment location for 2014 class: Intl. 0%; N.E. 0%; M.A. 0%; E.N.C. 0%; W.N.C. 4%; S.A. 3%; E.S.C. 1%; W.S.C. 87%; Mt. 2%; Pac. 3%; unknown 0%

University of Tulsa
3120 E. Fourth Place
Tulsa, OK 74104
www.utulsa.edu/law
Private
Admissions: (918) 631-2709
Email: lawadmissions@utulsa.edu
Financial aid: (918) 631-2526
Application deadline: 07/31
Tuition: full time: $35,529; part time: N/A
Room/board/expenses: $19,560
Median grant: $20,000
Average student indebtedness at graduation: $82,954
Enrollment: full time: 238; part time: 24
men: 50%; women: 50%; minorities: 25%
Acceptance rate (full time): 37%
Midrange LSAT (full time): 151-156
Midrange undergraduate GPA (full time): 3.00-3.60
Midrange of full-time private-sector salaries of 2014 grads: $55,000-$92,500
2014 grads employed in: law firms: 59%; business and industry: 22%; government: 9%; public interest: 9%; judicial clerk: 1%; academia: 1%; unknown: 0%
Employment location for 2014 class: Intl. 0%; N.E. 0%; M.A. 3%; E.N.C. 2%; W.N.C. 2%; S.A. 1%; E.S.C. 1%; W.S.C. 85%; Mt. 3%; Pac. 2%; unknown 0%

OREGON

Lewis & Clark College (Northwestern)
10015 S.W. Terwilliger Boulevard
Portland, OR 97219
law.lclark.edu
Private
Admissions: (503) 768-6613
Email: lawadmss@lclark.edu
Financial aid: (503) 768-7090
Application deadline: 03/15
Tuition: full time: $41,328; part time: $31,006
Room/board/expenses: $22,600
Median grant: $15,000
Average student indebtedness at graduation: $140,025
Enrollment: full time: 414; part time: 174
men: 51%; women: 49%; minorities: 23%
Acceptance rate (full time): 60%
Midrange LSAT (full time): 155-161
Midrange undergraduate GPA (full time): 3.08-3.62
Midrange of full-time private-sector salaries of 2014 grads: $48,000-$75,000
2014 grads employed in: law firms: 38%; business and industry: 18%; government: 17%; public interest: 9%; judicial clerk: 17%; academia: 0%; unknown: 1%

Employment location for 2014 class: Intl. 0%; N.E. 1%; M.A. 1%; E.N.C. 1%; W.N.C. 2%; S.A. 4%; E.S.C. 1%; W.S.C. 1%; Mt. 6%; Pac. 83%; unknown 0%

University of Oregon
1221 University of Oregon
Eugene, OR 97403-1221
www.law.uoregon.edu
Public
Admissions: (541) 346-3846
Email: admissions@law.uoregon.edu
Financial aid: (800) 760-6953
Application deadline: 03/01
In-state tuition: full time: $31,506; part time: N/A
Out-of-state tuition: full time: $39,210
Room/board/expenses: $8,918
Median grant: $15,000
Average student indebtedness at graduation: $106,540
Enrollment: full time: 366; part time: N/A
men: 56%; women: 44%; minorities: 18%
Acceptance rate (full time): 49%
Midrange LSAT (full time): 154-159
Midrange undergraduate GPA (full time): 2.97-3.55
Midrange of full-time private-sector salaries of 2014 grads: $48,000-$72,260
2014 grads employed in: law firms: 32%; business and industry: 13%; government: 14%; public interest: 12%; judicial clerk: 19%; academia: 0%; unknown: 1%
Employment location for 2014 class: Intl. 2%; N.E. 0%; M.A. 0%; E.N.C. 1%; W.N.C. 1%; S.A. 1%; E.S.C. 0%; W.S.C. 3%; Mt. 10%; Pac. 82%; unknown 0%

Willamette University (Collins)
245 Winter Street SE
Salem, OR 97301
www.willamette.edu/wucl
Private
Admissions: (503) 370-6282
Email: law-admission@willamette.edu
Financial aid: (503) 370-6273
Application deadline: 04/01
Tuition: full time: $37,625; part time: $26,064
Room/board/expenses: $19,128
Median grant: $12,000
Average student indebtedness at graduation: $133,318
Enrollment: full time: 301; part time: 13
men: 49%; women: 51%; minorities: 19%
Acceptance rate (full time): 67%
Midrange LSAT (full time): 150-157
Midrange undergraduate GPA (full time): 2.80-3.44
Midrange of full-time private-sector salaries of 2014 grads: $50,000-$60,000
2014 grads employed in: law firms: 66%; business and industry: 8%; government: 11%; public interest: 3%; judicial clerk: 13%; academia: 0%; unknown: 0%
Employment location for 2014 class: Intl. 1%; N.E. 0%; M.A. 0%; E.N.C. 0%; W.N.C. 0%; S.A. 1%; E.S.C. 0%; W.S.C. 0%; Mt. 9%; Pac. 88%; unknown 1%

PENNSYLVANIA

Drexel University (Kline)
3320 Market Street, Suite 400
Philadelphia, PA 19104
www.drexel.edu/law/admissions/overview/
Private
Admissions: (215) 895-1529
Email: lawadmissions@drexel.edu
Financial aid: (215) 895-1044
Application deadline: 08/01
Tuition: full time: $1,381/credit hour; part time: N/A
Room/board/expenses: $23,376
Median grant: $18,696
Average student indebtedness at graduation: $100,362
Enrollment: full time: 386; part time: 5
men: 51%; women: 49%; minorities: 17%
Aooceptance rate (full time): 54%
Midrange LSAT (full time): 153-158
Midrange undergraduate GPA (full time): 3.00-3.57
Midrange of full-time private-sector salaries of 2014 grads: $51,000-$80,000
2014 grads employed in: law firms: 43%; business and industry: 16%; government: 18%; public interest: 6%; judicial clerk: 16%; academia: 1%; unknown: 1%
Employment location for 2014 class: Intl. 1%; N.E. 1%; M.A. 87%; E.N.C. 0%; W.N.C. 0%; S.A. 8%; E.S.C. 1%; W.S.C. 0%; Mt. 2%; Pac. 1%; unknown 0%

Duquesne University
600 Forbes Avenue
Pittsburgh, PA 15282
www.duq.edu/law
Private
Admissions: (412) 396-6296
Email: lawadmissions@duq.edu
Financial aid: (412) 396-6607
Application deadline: 03/01
Tuition: full time: $39,766; part time: $30,746
Room/board/expenses: $15,934
Median grant: $11,000
Average student indebtedness at graduation: $104,623
Enrollment: full time: 305; part time: 96
men: 48%; women: 52%; minorities: 6%
Acceptance rate (full time): 67%
Midrange LSAT (full time): 151-155
Midrange undergraduate GPA (full time): 3.16-3.68
Midrange of full-time private-sector salaries of 2014 grads: $50,000-$82,694
2014 grads employed in: law firms: 50%; business and industry: 31%; government: 6%; public interest: 4%; judicial clerk: 9%; academia: 1%; unknown: 0%
Employment location for 2014 class: Intl. 1%; N.E. 0%; M.A. 91%; E.N.C. 0%; W.N.C. 0%; S.A. 7%; E.S.C. 0%; W.S.C. 0%; Mt. 0%; Pac. 0%; unknown 0%

Pennsylvania State University (Dickinson)
150 S. College Street
Carlisle, PA 17013
dickinsonlaw.psu.edu
Public
Admissions: (717) 240-5207
Email: dickinsonlaw@psu.edu
Financial aid: (717) 240-5207
Application deadline: 06/30
In-state tuition: full time: $45,078; part time: N/A
Out-of-state tuition: full time: $45,078
Room/board/expenses: $18,120
Median grant: $21,200
Average student indebtedness at graduation: $116,717
Enrollment: full time: 157; part time: N/A
men: 52%; women: 48%; minorities: 21%
Acceptance rate (full time): 39%
Midrange LSAT (full time): 158-161
Midrange undergraduate GPA (full time): 3.15-3.72
Midrange of full-time private-sector salaries of 2014 grads: $55,000-$89,000
2014 grads employed in: law firms: 43%; business and industry: 16%; government: 14%; public interest: 4%; judicial clerk: 20%; academia: 2%; unknown: 0%
Employment location for 2014 class: Intl. 1%; N.E. 3%; M.A. 60%; E.N.C. 5%; W.N.C. 1%; S.A. 15%; E.S.C. 1%; W.S.C. 4%; Mt. 4%; Pac. 4%; unknown 2%

Pennsylvania State University-University Park
Lewis Katz Building
University Park, PA 16802
pennstatelaw.psu.edu
Public
Admissions: (814) 867-1251
Email: admissions@pennstatelaw.psu.edu
Financial aid: (814) 863-0469
Application deadline: 03/31
In-state tuition: full time: $45,392; part time: N/A/credit hour
Out-of-state tuition: full time: $45,392
Room/board/expenses: $22,704
Median grant: $20,000
Average student indebtedness at graduation: $129,772
Enrollment: full time: 354; part time: N/A
men: 58%; women: 42%; minorities: 19%
Acceptance rate (full time): 43%
Midrange LSAT (full time): 152-159
Midrange undergraduate GPA (full time): 3.15-3.73
Midrange of full-time private-sector salaries of 2014 grads: $55,000-$89,000
2014 grads employed in: law firms: 43%; business and industry: 16%; government: 14%; public interest: 4%; judicial clerk: 20%; academia: 2%; unknown: 0%
Employment location for 2014 class: Intl. 1%; N.E. 3%; M.A. 60%; E.N.C. 5%; W.N.C. 1%; S.A. 15%; E.S.C. 1%; W.S.C. 4%; Mt. 4%; Pac. 4%; unknown 2%

Temple University (Beasley)
1719 N. Broad Street
Philadelphia, PA 19122
www.law.temple.edu
Public
Admissions: (800) 560-1428
Email: lawadmis@temple.edu
Financial aid: (800) 560-1428
Application deadline: 03/01
In-state tuition: full time: $23,336; part time: $18,837
Out-of-state tuition: full time: $36,336
Room/board/expenses: $22,360
Median grant: $12,500
Average student indebtedness at graduation: $86,999
Enrollment: full time: 534; part time: 150
men: 52%; women: 48%; minorities: 26%
Acceptance rate (full time): 44%
Midrange LSAT (full time): 155-163
Midrange undergraduate GPA (full time): 3.30-3.69
Midrange of full-time private-sector salaries of 2014 grads: $60,000-$125,000
2014 grads employed in: law firms: 46%; business and industry: 17%; government: 10%; public interest: 9%; judicial clerk: 16%; academia: 3%; unknown: 0%
Employment location for 2014 class: Intl. 1%; N.E. 0%; M.A. 81%; E.N.C. 0%; W.N.C. 0%; S.A. 11%; E.S.C. 0%; W.S.C. 1%; Mt. 1%; Pac. 4%; unknown 1%

University of Pennsylvania
3501 Sansom Street
Philadelphia, PA 19104-6204
www.law.upenn.edu
Private
Admissions: (215) 898-7400
Email: contactadmissions@law.upenn.edu
Financial aid: (215) 898-7400
Application deadline: 03/01
Tuition: full time: $58,918; part time: N/A
Room/board/expenses: $23,312
Median grant: $18,750
Average student indebtedness at graduation: $144,153
Enrollment: full time: 753; part time: 1
men: 55%; women: 45%; minorities: 27%
Acceptance rate (full time): 19%
Midrange LSAT (full time): 163-170
Midrange undergraduate GPA (full time): 3.52-3.95
Midrange of full-time private-sector salaries of 2014 grads: $150,000-$160,000
2014 grads employed in: law firms: 77%; business and industry: 4%; government: 3%; public interest: 4%; judicial clerk: 12%; academia: 1%; unknown: 0%
Employment location for 2014 class: Intl. 1%; N.E. 3%; M.A. 60%; E.N.C. 3%; W.N.C. 0%; S.A. 18%; E.S.C. 0%; W.S.C. 4%; Mt. 1%; Pac. 9%; unknown 0%

University of Pittsburgh
3900 Forbes Avenue
Pittsburgh, PA 15260
www.law.pitt.edu
Public
Admissions: (412) 648-1805
Email: admitlaw@pitt.edu
Financial aid: (412) 648-1415
Application deadline: 04/01
In-state tuition: full time: $32,426; part time: N/A
Out-of-state tuition: full time: $40,250
Room/board/expenses: $18,788
Median grant: $14,000
Average student indebtedness at graduation: $104,484
Enrollment: full time: 453; part time: 3
men: 57%; women: 43%; minorities: 17%
Acceptance rate (full time): 37%
Midrange LSAT (full time): 153-159
Midrange undergraduate GPA (full time): 3.03-3.63
Midrange of full-time private-sector salaries of 2014 grads: $50,000-$80,000
2014 grads employed in: law firms: 47%; business and industry: 34%; government: 5%; public interest: 6%; judicial clerk: 7%; academia: 1%; unknown: 1%
Employment location for 2014 class: Intl. 1%; N.E. 1%; M.A. 78%; E.N.C. 3%; W.N.C. 0%; S.A. 10%; E.S.C. 0%; W.S.C. 2%; Mt. 2%; Pac. 2%; unknown 0%

Villanova University
299 N. Spring Mill Road
Villanova, PA 19085
www1.villanova.edu/villanova/law.html
Private
Admissions: (610) 519-7010
Email: admissions@law.villanova.edu
Financial aid: (610) 519-7015
Application deadline: 04/01
Tuition: full time: $42,540; part time: N/A
Room/board/expenses: $22,732
Median grant: $28,368
Average student indebtedness at graduation: $110,792
Enrollment: full time: 491; part time: 1
men: 50%; women: 50%; minorities: 17%
Acceptance rate (full time): 49%
Midrange LSAT (full time): 152-158
Midrange undergraduate GPA (full time): 3.27-3.74
Midrange of full-time private-sector salaries of 2014 grads: $62,000-$125,000
2014 grads employed in: law firms: 56%; business and industry: 20%; government: 7%; public interest: 6%; judicial clerk: 14%; academia: 0%; unknown: 0%
Employment location for 2014 class: Intl. 1%; N.E. 1%; M.A. 84%; E.N.C. 0%; W.N.C. 0%; S.A. 13%; E.S.C. 0%; W.S.C. 0%; Mt. 1%; Pac. 1%; unknown 0%

Widener University (Commonwealth)
3800 Vartan Way
Harrisburg, PA 17110
commonwealthlaw.widener.edu
Private
Admissions: (717) 541-3903
Email: admitcwlaw@widener.edu
Financial aid: (717) 541-1924
Application deadline: 05/15
Tuition: full time: $1,396/credit hour; part time: $1,396/credit hour
Room/board/expenses: $20,666
Median grant: $10,000
Average student indebtedness at graduation: $148,496
Enrollment: full time: 137; part time: 67
men: 53%; women: 47%; minorities: 17%
Acceptance rate (full time): 70%
Midrange LSAT (full time): 145-151
Midrange undergraduate GPA (full time): 2.79-3.34
Midrange of full-time private-sector salaries of 2014 grads: $43,000-$70,000
2014 grads employed in: law firms: 45%; business and industry: 20%; government: 18%; public interest: 7%; judicial clerk: 8%; academia: 1%; unknown: 0%
Employment location for 2014 class: Intl. 0%; N.E. 0%; M.A. 85%; E.N.C. 0%; W.N.C. 0%; S.A. 14%; E.S.C. 0%; W.S.C. 0%; Mt. 1%; Pac. 0%; unknown 0%

PUERTO RICO

Inter-American University[1]
PO Box 70351
San Juan, PR 00936-8351
www.metro.inter.edu
Private
Admissions: (787) 765-1270
Financial aid: N/A
Tuition: N/A
Room/board/expenses: N/A
Enrollment: N/A

Pontifical Catholic University of Puerto Rico[1]
2250 Avenida Las Americas
Suite 584
Ponce, PR 00717-0777
www.pucpr.edu
Private
Admissions: (787) 841-2000
Email: admisiones@pucpr.edu
Financial aid: N/A
Tuition: N/A
Room/board/expenses: N/A
Enrollment: N/A

University of Puerto Rico[1]
PO Box 23303
Estacion Universidad
Rio Piedras, PR 00931-3302
www.upr.edu
Public
Admissions: (787) 764-0000
Email: admisiones@upr.edu
Financial aid: N/A
Tuition: N/A
Room/board/expenses: N/A
Enrollment: N/A

RHODE ISLAND

Roger Williams University

10 Metacom Avenue
Bristol, RI 02809-5171
law.rwu.edu
Private
Admissions: (401) 254-4555
Email: Admissions@rwu.edu
Financial aid: (401) 254-4510
Application deadline: 04/01
Tuition: full time: $34,596; part time: N/A
Room/board/expenses: $17,386
Median grant: $18,313
Average student indebtedness at graduation: $123,332
Enrollment: full time: 370; part time: N/A
men: 49%; women: 51%; minorities: 23%
Acceptance rate (full time): 80%
Midrange LSAT (full time): 145-152
Midrange undergraduate GPA (full time): 2.83-3.48
Midrange of full-time private-sector salaries of 2014 grads: $45,000-$61,200
2014 grads employed in: law firms: 43%; business and industry: 28%; government: 8%; public interest: 7%; judicial clerk: 11%; academia: 2%; unknown: 0%
Employment location for 2014 class: Intl. 0%; N.E. 72%; M.A. 13%; E.N.C. 2%; W.N.C. 1%; S.A. 7%; E.S.C. 0%; W.S.C. 1%; Mt. 2%; Pac. 3%; unknown 0%

SOUTH CAROLINA

Charleston School of Law

PO Box 535
Charleston, SC 29402
www.charlestonlaw.edu
Private
Admissions: (843) 377-2143
Email: info@charlestonlaw.edu
Financial aid: (843) 377-1102
Application deadline: 03/01
Tuition: full time: $40,116; part time: $32,256
Room/board/expenses: $22,607
Median grant: $10,500
Average student indebtedness at graduation: $146,230
Enrollment: full time: 297; part time: 56
men: 54%; women: 46%; minorities: 20%
Acceptance rate (full time): 80%
Midrange LSAT (full time): 143-149
Midrange undergraduate GPA (full time): 2.66-3.22
Midrange of full-time private-sector salaries of 2014 grads: $38,000-$60,000
2014 grads employed in: law firms: 53%; business and industry: 17%; government: 6%; public interest: 1%; judicial clerk: 18%; academia: 3%; unknown: 1%
Employment location for 2014 class: Intl. 0%; N.E. 1%; M.A. 1%; E.N.C. 2%; W.N.C. 0%; S.A. 91%; E.S.C. 1%; W.S.C. 1%; Mt. 2%; Pac. 0%; unknown 2%

University of South Carolina

701 S. Main Street
Columbia, SC 29208
www.law.sc.edu/admissions
Public
Admissions: (803) 777-6605
Email: usclaw@law.sc.edu
Financial aid: (803) 777-6605
Application deadline: 03/01
In-state tuition: full time: $24,208; part time: N/A
Out-of-state tuition: full time: $48,472
Room/board/expenses: $18,174
Median grant: $21,206
Average student indebtedness at graduation: $85,006
Enrollment: full time: 618; part time: 2
men: 57%; women: 43%; minorities: 20%
Acceptance rate (full time): 59%
Midrange LSAT (full time): 152-157
Midrange undergraduate GPA (full time): 3.00-3.56
Midrange of full-time private-sector salaries of 2014 grads: $48,000-$85,000
2014 grads employed in: law firms: 50%; business and industry: 13%; government: 15%; public interest: 2%; judicial clerk: 18%; academia: 1%; unknown: 0%
Employment location for 2014 class: Intl. 0%; N.E. 1%; M.A. 1%; E.N.C. 0%; W.N.C. 0%; S.A. 91%; E.S.C. 2%; W.S.C. 1%; Mt. 2%; Pac. 3%; unknown 0%

SOUTH DAKOTA

University of South Dakota

414 E. Clark Street
Vermillion, SD 57069-2390
www.usd.edu/law/
Public
Admissions: (605) 677-6358
Email: law@usd.edu
Financial aid: (605) 677-5446
Application deadline: 07/01
In-state tuition: full time: $14,688; part time: $333/credit hour
Out-of-state tuition: full time: $31,747
Room/board/expenses: $14,364
Median grant: $1,698
Average student indebtedness at graduation: $57,170
Enrollment: full time: 212; part time: 3
men: 59%; women: 41%; minorities: 13%
Acceptance rate (full time): 67%
Midrange LSAT (full time): 144-151
Midrange undergraduate GPA (full time): 3.01-3.67
Midrange of full-time private-sector salaries of 2014 grads: N/A-N/A
2014 grads employed in: law firms: 46%; business and industry: 13%; government: 17%; public interest: 3%; judicial clerk: 20%; academia: 1%; unknown: 0%
Employment location for 2014 class: Intl. 1%; N.E. 0%; M.A. 1%; E.N.C. 3%; W.N.C. 83%; S.A. 3%; E.S.C. 0%; W.S.C. 1%; Mt. 6%; Pac. 1%; unknown 0%

TENNESSEE

Belmont University

1900 Belmont Boulevard
Nashville, TN 37212
www.belmont.edu/law/
Private
Admissions: (615) 460-8400
Email: law@belmont.edu
Financial aid: (615) 460-6403
Application deadline: 07/31
Tuition: full time: $39,070; part time: N/A
Room/board/expenses: $24,500
Median grant: $27,323
Average student indebtedness at graduation: $56,225
Enrollment: full time: 240; part time: N/A
men: 45%; women: 55%; minorities: 16%
Acceptance rate (full time): 63%
Midrange LSAT (full time): 152-158
Midrange undergraduate GPA (full time): 3.07-3.68
Midrange of full-time private-sector salaries of 2014 grads: $45,000-$79,000
2014 grads employed in: law firms: 46%; business and industry: 25%; government: 18%; public interest: 3%; judicial clerk: 7%; academia: 1%; unknown: 0%
Employment location for 2014 class: Intl. 0%; N.E. 0%; M.A. 1%; E.N.C. 0%; W.N.C. 0%; S.A. 4%; E.S.C. 91%; W.S.C. 4%; Mt. 0%; Pac. 0%; unknown 0%

Lincoln Memorial University

601 West Summit Hill Drive
Knoxville, TN 37902
law.lmunet.edu
Private
Admissions: (865) 545-5304
Email: Law.admissions@LMUnet.edu
Financial aid: (423) 869-6465
Application deadline: 07/15
Tuition: full time: $1,073/credit hour; part time: $1,073/credit hour
Room/board/expenses: $20,860
Median grant: $21,938
Average student indebtedness at graduation: $95,495
Enrollment: full time: 66; part time: 25
men: 47%; women: 53%; minorities: 12%
Acceptance rate (full time): 54%
Midrange of full-time private-sector salaries of 2014 grads: N/A-N/A
2014 grads employed in: law firms: 60%; business and industry: 33%; government: 7%; public interest: 0%; judicial clerk: 0%; academia: 0%; unknown: 0%
Employment location for 2014 class: Intl. 0%; N.E. 0%; M.A. 0%; E.N.C. 0%; W.N.C. 0%; S.A. 2%; E.S.C. 98%; W.S.C. 0%; Mt. 0%; Pac. 0%; unknown 0%

University of Memphis (Humphreys)

1 North Front Street
Memphis, TN 38103-2189
www.memphis.edu/law
Public
Admissions: (901) 678-5403
Email: lawadmissions@memphis.edu
Financial aid: (901) 678-2743

Application deadline: 03/15
In-state tuition: full time: $18,387; part time: $867/credit hour
Out-of-state tuition: full time: $26,247
Room/board/expenses: $17,419
Median grant: $7,860
Average student indebtedness at graduation: $77,752
Enrollment: full time: 307; part time: 23
men: 58%; women: 42%; minorities: 27%
Acceptance rate (full time): 60%
Midrange LSAT (full time): 149-156
Midrange undergraduate GPA (full time): 2.89-3.41
Midrange of full-time private-sector salaries of 2014 grads: $42,000-$68,750
2014 grads employed in: law firms: 54%; business and industry: 18%; government: 10%; public interest: 4%; judicial clerk: 10%; academia: 4%; unknown: 0%
Employment location for 2014 class: Intl. 0%; N.E. 0%; M.A. 0%; E.N.C. 1%; W.N.C. 0%; S.A. 5%; E.S.C. 88%; W.S.C. 6%; Mt. 1%; Pac. 0%; unknown 0%

University of Tennessee-Knoxville

1505 W. Cumberland Avenue
Knoxville, TN 37996-1810
www.law.utk.edu
Public
Admissions: (865) 974-4131
Email: lawadmit@utk.edu
Financial aid: (865) 974-4131
Application deadline: 03/01
In-state tuition: full time: $19,256; part time: N/A
Out-of-state tuition: full time: $37,930
Room/board/expenses: $21,072
Median grant: $5,000
Average student indebtedness at graduation: $66,939
Enrollment: full time: 385; part time: N/A
men: 55%; women: 45%; minorities: 19%
Acceptance rate (full time): 37%
Midrange LSAT (full time): 153-161
Midrange undergraduate GPA (full time): 3.31-3.80
Midrange of full-time private-sector salaries of 2014 grads: $45,000-$100,000
2014 grads employed in: law firms: 54%; business and industry: 12%; government: 14%; public interest: 4%; judicial clerk: 10%; academia: 6%; unknown: 0%
Employment location for 2014 class: Intl. 1%; N.E. 0%; M.A. 0%; E.N.C. 0%; W.N.C. 0%; S.A. 13%; E.S.C. 79%; W.S.C. 5%; Mt. 1%; Pac. 0%; unknown 0%

Vanderbilt University

131 21st Avenue S
Nashville, TN 37203-1181
www.vanderbilt.edu/law/
Private
Admissions: (615) 322-6452
Email: admissions@law.vanderbilt.edu
Financial aid: (615) 322-6452
Application deadline: 04/01
Tuition: full time: $51,360; part time: N/A
Room/board/expenses: $24,506

Median grant: $22,500
Average student indebtedness at graduation: $114,447
Enrollment: full time: 538; part time: N/A
men: 51%; women: 49%; minorities: 21%
Acceptance rate (full time): 38%
Midrange LSAT (full time): 161-168
Midrange undergraduate GPA (full time): 3.50-3.83
Midrange of full-time private-sector salaries of 2014 grads: $110,000-$160,000
2014 grads employed in: law firms: 53%; business and industry: 5%; government: 12%; public interest: 11%; judicial clerk: 16%; academia: 2%; unknown: 1%
Employment location for 2014 class: Intl. 1%; N.E. 3%; M.A. 10%; E.N.C. 9%; W.N.C. 2%; S.A. 28%; E.S.C. 30%; W.S.C. 11%; Mt. 2%; Pac. 4%; unknown 1%

TEXAS

Baylor University

1114 S. University Parks Drive
1 Bear Place, # 97288
Waco, TX 76798-7288
www.baylor.edu/law/
Private
Admissions: (254) 710-3239
Email: nicole_neeley@baylor.edu
Financial aid: (254) 710-2611
Application deadline: 03/15
Tuition: full time: $55,547; part time: $1,337/credit hour
Room/board/expenses: $21,247
Median grant: $21,000
Average student indebtedness at graduation: $135,817
Enrollment: full time: 393; part time: 3
men: 54%; women: 46%; minorities: 24%
Acceptance rate (full time): 29%
Midrange LSAT (full time): 158-162
Midrange undergraduate GPA (full time): 3.28-3.72
Midrange of full-time private-sector salaries of 2014 grads: $61,200-$90,000
2014 grads employed in: law firms: 65%; business and industry: 13%; government: 14%; public interest: 2%; judicial clerk: 3%; academia: 3%; unknown: 0%
Employment location for 2014 class: Intl. 0%; N.E. 0%; M.A. 1%; E.N.C. 0%; W.N.C. 3%; S.A. 3%; E.S.C. 0%; W.S.C. 88%; Mt. 3%; Pac. 2%; unknown 1%

Southern Methodist University (Dedman)

PO Box 750116
Dallas, TX 75275-0116
www.law.smu.edu
Private
Admissions: (214) 768-2540
Email: lawadmit@mail.smu.edu
Financial aid: (214) 768-4119
Application deadline: 02/15
Tuition: full time: $49,962; part time: $37,472
Room/board/expenses: $29,370
Median grant: $23,000
Average student indebtedness at graduation: $124,723
Enrollment: full time: 560; part time: 180
men: 52%; women: 48%; minorities: 21%

Acceptance rate (full time): 48%
Midrange LSAT (full time): 156-163
Midrange undergraduate GPA (full time): 3.25-3.75
Midrange of full-time private-sector salaries of 2014 grads: $72,000-$160,000
2014 grads employed in: law firms: 62%; business and industry: 26%; government: 5%; public interest: 1%; judicial clerk: 4%; academia: 2%; unknown: 0%
Employment location for 2014 class: Intl. 1%; N.E. 0%; M.A. 2%; E.N.C. 1%; W.N.C. 1%; S.A. 0%; E.S.C. 0%; W.S.C. 91%; Mt. 3%; Pac. 0%; unknown 0%

South Texas College of Law

1303 San Jacinto Street
Houston, TX 77002-7006
www.stcl.edu
Private
Admissions: (713) 646-1810
Email: admissions@stcl.edu
Financial aid: (713) 646-1820
Application deadline: 03/15
Tuition: full time: $29,490; part time: $19,860
Room/board/expenses: $19,104
Median grant: $3,000
Average student indebtedness at graduation: $121,767
Enrollment: full time: 794; part time: 257
men: 52%; women: 48%; minorities: 38%
Acceptance rate (full time): 66%
Midrange LSAT (full time): 147-153
Midrange undergraduate GPA (full time): 2.81-3.33
Midrange of full-time private-sector salaries of 2014 grads: $70,000-$150,500
2014 grads employed in: law firms: 63%; business and industry: 24%; government: 10%; public interest: 1%; judicial clerk: 1%; academia: 1%; unknown: 0%
Employment location for 2014 class: Intl. 0%; N.E. 0%; M.A. 0%; E.N.C. 0%; W.N.C. 0%; S.A. 0%; E.S.C. 0%; W.S.C. 97%; Mt. 1%; Pac. 0%; unknown 0%

St. Mary's University

1 Camino Santa Maria
San Antonio, TX 78228-8602
www.stmarytx.edu/law
Private
Admissions: (210) 436-3523
Email: lawadmissions@stmarytx.edu
Financial aid: (210) 431-6743
Application deadline: 03/01
Tuition: full time: $34,640; part time: $20,430
Room/board/expenses: $19,334
Median grant: $4,173
Average student indebtedness at graduation: $122,560
Enrollment: full time: 599; part time: 169
men: 55%; women: 45%; minorities: 53%
Acceptance rate (full time): 62%
Midrange LSAT (full time): 149-154
Midrange undergraduate GPA (full time): 2.59-3.39
Midrange of full-time private-sector salaries of 2014 grads: $52,416-$95,500

2014 grads employed in: law firms: 68%; business and industry: 14%; government: 10%; public interest: 5%; judicial clerk: 2%; academia: 1%; unknown: 0%
Employment location for 2014 class: Intl. 1%; N.E. 1%; M.A. 1%; E.N.C. 0%; W.N.C. 0%; S.A. 1%; E.S.C. 1%; W.S.C. 94%; Mt. 1%; Pac. 1%; unknown 0%

Texas A&M University

1515 Commerce Street
Fort Worth, TX 76102
law.tamu.edu/
Public
Admissions: (817) 212-4040
Email: law-admissions@law.tamu.edu
Financial aid: (817) 212-4090
Application deadline: 07/08
In-state tuition: full time: $33,092; part time: $24,069
Out-of-state tuition: full time: $33,092
Room/board/expenses: $24,716
Median grant: $15,000
Average student indebtedness at graduation: $104,200
Enrollment: full time: 396; part time: 185
men: 51%; women: 49%; minorities: 25%
Acceptance rate (full time): 20%
Midrange LSAT (full time): 154-158
Midrange undergraduate GPA (full time): 3.16-3.55
Midrange of full-time private-sector salaries of 2014 grads: $50,400-$75,000
2014 grads employed in: law firms: 54%; business and industry: 33%; government: 8%; public interest: 1%; judicial clerk: 2%; academia: 3%; unknown: 0%
Employment location for 2014 class: Intl. 0%; N.E. 0%; M.A. 2%; E.N.C. 1%; W.N.C. 0%; S.A. 1%; E.S.C. 1%; W.S.C. 96%; Mt. 1%; Pac. 0%; unknown 0%

Texas Southern University (Marshall)[1]

3100 Cleburne Street
Houston, TX 77004
www.tsulaw.edu
Public
Admissions: (713) 313-7114
Email: lawadmit@tsulaw.edu
Financial aid: N/A
Tuition: N/A
Room/board/expenses: N/A
Enrollment: N/A

Texas Tech University

1802 Hartford Avenue
Lubbock, TX 79409-0004
www.law.ttu.edu
Public
Admissions: (806) 834-5024
Email: admissions.law@ttu.edu
Financial aid: (806) 834-3875
Application deadline: 03/01
In-state tuition: full time: $23,262; part time: N/A
Out-of-state tuition: full time: $33,732
Room/board/expenses: $16,060
Median grant: $7,500
Average student indebtedness at graduation: $74,673

Enrollment: full time: 561; part time: N/A
men: 54%; women: 46%; minorities: 25%
Acceptance rate (full time): 54%
Midrange LSAT (full time): 151-156
Midrange undergraduate GPA (full time): 3.07-3.60
Midrange of full-time private-sector salaries of 2014 grads: $54,618-$84,392
2014 grads employed in: law firms: 57%; business and industry: 23%; government: 14%; public interest: 1%; judicial clerk: 5%; academia: 1%; unknown: 0%
Employment location for 2014 class: Intl. 1%; N.E. 0%; M.A. 1%; E.N.C. 1%; W.N.C. 1%; S.A. 0%; E.S.C. 0%; W.S.C. 90%; Mt. 6%; Pac. 1%; unknown 0%

University of Houston

4604 Calhoun Road
Houston, TX 77204-6060
www.law.uh.edu
Public
Admissions: (713) 743-2280
Email: lawadmissions@uh.edu
Financial aid: (713) 743-2269
Application deadline: 02/15
In-state tuition: full time: $29,784; part time: $20,484
Out-of-state tuition: full time: $44,044
Room/board/expenses: $19,460
Median grant: $10,000
Average student indebtedness at graduation: $87,602
Enrollment: full time: 605; part time: 126
men: 53%; women: 47%; minorities: 37%
Acceptance rate (full time): 42%
Midrange LSAT (full time): 155-161
Midrange undergraduate GPA (full time): 3.28-3.70
Midrange of full-time private-sector salaries of 2014 grads: $70,000-$160,000
2014 grads employed in: law firms: 63%; business and industry: 21%; government: 9%; public interest: 3%; judicial clerk: 3%; academia: 2%; unknown: 0%
Employment location for 2014 class: Intl. 0%; N.E. 0%; M.A. 1%; E.N.C. 1%; W.N.C. 1%; S.A. 2%; E.S.C. 0%; W.S.C. 93%; Mt. 0%; Pac. 1%; unknown 0%

University of Texas-Austin

727 E. Dean Keeton Street
Austin, TX 78705-3299
www.utexas.edu/law
Public
Admissions: (512) 232-1200
Email: admissions@law.utexas.edu
Financial aid: (512) 232-1130
Application deadline: 03/01
In-state tuition: full time: $33,162; part time: N/A
Out-of-state tuition: full time: $49,244
Room/board/expenses: $19,354
Median grant: $11,500
Average student indebtedness at graduation: $102,101
Enrollment: full time: 949; part time: 7
men: 56%; women: 44%; minorities: 32%

Acceptance rate (full time): 22%
Midrange LSAT (full time): 162-169
Midrange undergraduate GPA (full time): 3.48-3.86
Midrange of full-time private-sector salaries of 2014 grads: $110,000-$160,000
2014 grads employed in: law firms: 55%; business and industry: 9%; government: 14%; public interest: 7%; judicial clerk: 14%; academia: 1%; unknown: 0%
Employment location for 2014 class: Intl. N/A; N.E. N/A; M.A. N/A; E.N.C. N/A; W.N.C. N/A; S.A. N/A; E.S.C. N/A; W.S.C. N/A; Mt. N/A; Pac. N/A; unknown N/A

UTAH

Brigham Young University (Clark)

243 JRCB
Provo, UT 84602-8000
www.law.byu.edu
Private
Admissions: (801) 422-4277
Email: kulbethm@law.byu.edu
Financial aid: (801) 422-6386
Application deadline: rolling
Tuition: full time: $11,970; part time: N/A
Room/board/expenses: $20,280
Median grant: $5,000
Average student indebtedness at graduation: $62,423
Enrollment: full time: 392; part time: 12
men: 62%; women: 38%; minorities: 14%
Acceptance rate (full time): 40%
Midrange LSAT (full time): 156-164
Midrange undergraduate GPA (full time): 3.45-3.86
Midrange of full-time private-sector salaries of 2014 grads: $60,000-$112,500
2014 grads employed in: law firms: 45%; business and industry: 13%; government: 20%; public interest: 5%; judicial clerk: 16%; academia: 2%; unknown: 0%
Employment location for 2014 class: Intl. 2%; N.E. 0%; M.A. 0%; E.N.C. 1%; W.N.C. 1%; S.A. 5%; E.S.C. 1%; W.S.C. 4%; Mt. 64%; Pac. 23%; unknown 0%

University of Utah (Quinney)

383 South University Street
Salt Lake City, UT 84112
www.law.utah.edu
Public
Admissions: (801) 581-7479
Email: admissions@law.utah.edu
Financial aid: (801) 581-6211
Application deadline: 02/15
In-state tuition: full time: $25,752; part time: N/A
Out-of-state tuition: full time: $48,908
Room/board/expenses: $18,506
Median grant: $11,355
Average student indebtedness at graduation: $79,124
Enrollment: full time: 322; part time: 14
men: 59%; women: 41%; minorities: 13%
Acceptance rate (full time): 47%
Midrange LSAT (full time): 154-160
Midrange undergraduate GPA (full time): 3.36-3.76

Midrange of full-time private-sector salaries of 2014 grads: $60,000-$100,000
2014 grads employed in: law firms: 44%; business and industry: 17%; government: 15%; public interest: 11%; judicial clerk: 11%; academia: 3%; unknown: 0%
Employment location for 2014 class: Intl. 0%; N.E. 1%; M.A. 0%; E.N.C. 0%; W.N.C. 1%; S.A. 3%; E.S.C. 0%; W.S.C. 1%; Mt. 91%; Pac. 4%; unknown 0%

VERMONT

Vermont Law School

Chelsea Street
South Royalton, VT 05068-0096
www.vermontlaw.edu
Private
Admissions: (888) 277-5985
Email: admiss@vermontlaw.edu
Financial aid: (888) 277-5985
Application deadline: 04/15
Tuition: full time: $47,873; part time: N/A
Room/board/expenses: $24,934
Median grant: $20,000
Average student indebtedness at graduation: $156,710
Enrollment: full time: 375; part time: N/A
men: 43%; women: 57%; minorities: 21%
Acceptance rate (full time): 71%
Midrange LSAT (full time): 146-156
Midrange undergraduate GPA (full time): 2.82-3.52
Midrange of full-time private-sector salaries of 2014 grads: $47,000-$62,500
2014 grads employed in: law firms: 28%; business and industry: 22%; government: 24%; public interest: 9%; judicial clerk: 15%; academia: 3%; unknown: 0%
Employment location for 2014 class: Intl. 1%; N.E. 36%; M.A. 13%; E.N.C. 5%; W.N.C. 2%; S.A. 25%; E.S.C. 3%; W.S.C. 2%; Mt. 7%; Pac. 6%; unknown 0%

VIRGINIA

Appalachian School of Law[1]

1169 Edgewater Drive
Grundy, VA 24614-2825
www.asl.edu
Private
Admissions: (800) 895-7411
Email: aslinfo@asl.edu
Financial aid: N/A
Tuition: N/A
Room/board/expenses: N/A
Enrollment: N/A

College of William and Mary (Marshall-Wythe)

PO Box 8795
Williamsburg, VA 23187-8795
law.wm.edu/
Public
Admissions: (757) 221-3785
Email: lawadm@wm.edu
Financial aid: (757) 221-2420
Application deadline: 03/01
In-state tuition: full time: $30,800; part time: N/A
Out-of-state tuition: full time: $39,800

Room/board/expenses: $17,700
Median grant: $10,000
Average student indebtedness at graduation: $110,140
Enrollment: full time: 645; part time: N/A
men: 47%; women: 53%; minorities: 12%
Acceptance rate (full time): 36%
Midrange LSAT (full time): 158-164
Midrange undergraduate GPA (full time): 3.40-3.86
Midrange of full-time private-sector salaries of 2014 grads: $65,000-$135,000
2014 grads employed in: law firms: 43%; business and industry: 12%; government: 24%; public interest: 6%; judicial clerk: 14%; academia: 1%; unknown: 0%
Employment location for 2014 class: Intl. 0%; N.E. 3%; M.A. 20%; E.N.C. 4%; W.N.C. 1%; S.A. 58%; E.S.C. 1%; W.S.C. 4%; Mt. 3%; Pac. 6%; unknown 0%

George Mason University
3301 Fairfax Drive
Arlington, VA 22201-4426
www.law.gmu.edu
Public
Admissions: (703) 993-8010
Email: lawadmit@gmu.edu
Financial aid: (703) 993-2353
Application deadline: 04/01
In-state tuition: full time: $25,351; part time: $905/credit hour
Out-of-state tuition: full time: $40,737
Room/board/expenses: $23,868
Median grant: $10,000
Average student indebtedness at graduation: $121,910
Enrollment: full time: 329; part time: 155
men: 57%; women: 43%; minorities: 22%
Acceptance rate (full time): 34%
Midrange LSAT (full time): 155-162
Midrange undergraduate GPA (full time): 3.15-3.68
Midrange of full-time private-sector salaries of 2014 grads: $63,000-$135,000
2014 grads employed in: law firms: 38%; business and industry: 21%; government: 19%; public interest: 6%; judicial clerk: 11%; academia: 5%; unknown: 0%
Employment location for 2014 class: Intl. 1%; N.E. 1%; M.A. 2%; E.N.C. 1%; W.N.C. 2%; S.A. 85%; E.S.C. 1%; W.S.C. 1%; Mt. 5%; Pac. 2%; unknown 0%

Liberty University
1971 University Boulevard
Lynchburg, VA 24515
law.liberty.edu
Private
Admissions: (434) 592-5300
Email: lawadmissions@liberty.edu
Financial aid: (434) 592-5300
Application deadline: 06/01
Tuition: full time: $31,562; part time: N/A
Room/board/expenses: $16,800
Median grant: $19,500
Average student indebtedness at graduation: $68,667

Enrollment: full time: 172; part time: 1
men: 59%; women: 41%; minorities: 13%
Acceptance rate (full time): 50%
Midrange LSAT (full time): 150-157
Midrange undergraduate GPA (full time): 2.98-3.76
Midrange of full-time private-sector salaries of 2014 grads: $35,000-$60,000
2014 grads employed in: law firms: 49%; business and industry: 20%; government: 20%; public interest: 4%; judicial clerk: 4%; academia: 4%; unknown: 0%
Employment location for 2014 class: Intl. 2%; N.E. 4%; M.A. 5%; E.N.C. 7%; W.N.C. 4%; S.A. 62%; E.S.C. 5%; W.S.C. 5%; Mt. 2%; Pac. 4%; unknown 0%

Regent University
1000 Regent University Drive
Virginia Beach, VA 23464-9880
www.regent.edu/law/admissions
Private
Admissions: (757) 352-4132
Email: lawschool@regent.edu
Financial aid: (757) 352-5137
Application deadline: 06/01
Tuition: full time: $1,140/credit hour; part time: $1,140/credit hour
Room/board/expenses: $20,760
Median grant: $12,750
Average student indebtedness at graduation: $93,142
Enrollment: full time: 246; part time: 11
men: 45%; women: 55%; minorities: 27%
Acceptance rate (full time): 57%
Midrange LSAT (full time): 149-154
Midrange undergraduate GPA (full time): 3.00-3.61
Midrange of full-time private-sector salaries of 2014 grads: $40,000-$70,000
2014 grads employed in: law firms: 30%; business and industry: 26%; government: 13%; public interest: 9%; judicial clerk: 11%; academia: 6%; unknown: 5%
Employment location for 2014 class: Intl. 0%; N.E. 1%; M.A. 10%; E.N.C. 4%; W.N.C. 5%; S.A. 55%; E.S.C. 2%; W.S.C. 3%; Mt. 2%; Pac. 6%; unknown 11%

University of Richmond
28 Westhampton Way
Richmond, VA 23173
law.richmond.edu
Private
Admissions: (804) 289-8189
Email: mrahman@richmond.edu
Financial aid: (804) 289-8438
Application deadline: 03/01
Tuition: full time: $39,950; part time: $2,220/credit hour
Room/board/expenses: $16,220
Median grant: $20,000
Average student indebtedness at graduation: $110,665
Enrollment: full time: 469; part time: 5
men: 53%; women: 47%; minorities: 12%
Acceptance rate (full time): 42%
Midrange LSAT (full time): 155-161
Midrange undergraduate GPA (full time): 3.23-3.66

Midrange of full-time private-sector salaries of 2014 grads: $52,000-$90,000
2014 grads employed in: law firms: 32%; business and industry: 29%; government: 11%; public interest: 7%; judicial clerk: 20%; academia: 2%; unknown: 0%
Employment location for 2014 class: Intl. 4%; N.E. 0%; M.A. 4%; E.N.C. 1%; W.N.C. 1%; S.A. 86%; E.S.C. 1%; W.S.C. 1%; Mt. 1%; Pac. 1%; unknown 0%

University of Virginia
580 Massie Road
Charlottesville, VA 22903-1738
www.law.virginia.edu
Public
Admissions: (434) 924-7354
Email: lawadmit@virginia.edu
Financial aid: (434) 924-7805
Application deadline: 03/06
In-state tuition: full time: $54,000; part time: N/A
Out-of-state tuition: full time: $57,000
Room/board/expenses: $21,323
Median grant: $25,000
Average student indebtedness at graduation: $146,907
Enrollment: full time: 934; part time: N/A
men: 58%; women: 42%; minorities: 21%
Acceptance rate (full time): 20%
Midrange LSAT (full time): 163-170
Midrange undergraduate GPA (full time): 3.59-3.94
Midrange of full-time private-sector salaries of 2014 grads: $136,250-$160,000
2014 grads employed in: law firms: 61%; business and industry: 4%; government: 11%; public interest: 5%; judicial clerk: 20%; academia: 0%; unknown: 0%
Employment location for 2014 class: Intl. 1%; N.E. 2%; M.A. 25%; E.N.C. 5%; W.N.C. 2%; S.A. 46%; E.S.C. 2%; W.S.C. 7%; Mt. 3%; Pac. 8%; unknown 0%

Washington and Lee University
Sydney Lewis Hall
Lexington, VA 24450-0303
law.wlu.edu
Private
Admissions: (540) 458-8503
Email: lawadm@wlu.edu
Financial aid: (540) 458-8729
Application deadline: 07/15
Tuition: full time: $46,497; part time: N/A
Room/board/expenses: $17,613
Median grant: $22,500
Average student indebtedness at graduation: $110,067
Enrollment: full time: 314; part time: N/A
men: 57%; women: 43%; minorities: 21%
Acceptance rate (full time): 49%
Midrange LSAT (full time): 158-162
Midrange undergraduate GPA (full time): 3.08-3.58
Midrange of full-time private-sector salaries of 2014 grads: $65,250-$138,750
2014 grads employed in: law firms: 45%; business and industry: 16%; government: 14%; public interest: 7%; judicial clerk: 16%; academia: 2%; unknown: 0%

Employment location for 2014 class: Intl. 0%; N.E. 5%; M.A. 13%; E.N.C. 5%; W.N.C. 1%; S.A. 57%; E.S.C. 7%; W.S.C. 4%; Mt. 2%; Pac. 7%; unknown 0%

WASHINGTON

Gonzaga University
PO Box 3528
Spokane, WA 99220-3528
www.law.gonzaga.edu
Private
Admissions: (800) 793-1710
Email: admissions@lawschool.gonzaga.edu
Financial aid: (800) 448-2138
Application deadline: 04/15
Tuition: full time: $36,510; part time: N/A
Room/board/expenses: $18,349
Median grant: $16,500
Average student indebtedness at graduation: $125,347
Enrollment: full time: 336; part time: 1
men: 59%; women: 41%; minorities: 17%
Acceptance rate (full time): 66%
Midrange LSAT (full time): 151-156
Midrange undergraduate GPA (full time): 2.98-3.49
Midrange of full-time private-sector salaries of 2014 grads: $45,000-$61,000
2014 grads employed in: law firms: 55%; business and industry: 18%; government: 14%; public interest: 5%; judicial clerk: 6%; academia: 2%; unknown: 0%
Employment location for 2014 class: Intl. 0%; N.E. 0%; M.A. 0%; E.N.C. 2%; W.N.C. 1%; S.A. 0%; E.S.C. 0%; W.S.C. 2%; Mt. 27%; Pac. 68%; unknown 0%

Seattle University
901 12th Avenue
Seattle, WA 98122-1090
www.law.seattleu.edu
Private
Admissions: (206) 398-4200
Email: lawadmis@seattleu.edu
Financial aid: (206) 398-4250
Application deadline: rolling
Tuition: full time: $41,900; part time: $36,302
Room/board/expenses: $23,936
Median grant: $12,500
Average student indebtedness at graduation: $136,889
Enrollment: full time: 557; part time: 151
men: 47%; women: 53%; minorities: 35%
Acceptance rate (full time): 59%
Midrange LSAT (full time): 151-157
Midrange undergraduate GPA (full time): 3.00-3.48
Midrange of full-time private-sector salaries of 2014 grads: $47,500-$80,000
2014 grads employed in: law firms: 51%; business and industry: 21%; government: 12%; public interest: 7%; judicial clerk: 7%; academia: 2%; unknown: 0%
Employment location for 2014 class: Intl. 0%; N.E. 0%; M.A. 0%; E.N.C. 0%; W.N.C. 0%; S.A. 3%; E.S.C. 0%; W.S.C. 0%; Mt. 2%; Pac. 93%; unknown 0%

University of Washington
Campus Box 353020
Seattle, WA 98195-3020
www.law.washington.edu
Public
Admissions: (206) 543-4078
Email: lawadm@u.washington.edu
Financial aid: (206) 543-4078
Application deadline: 03/15
In-state tuition: full time: $31,962; part time: N/A
Out-of-state tuition: full time: $44,124
Room/board/expenses: $19,392
Median grant: $9,000
Average student indebtedness at graduation: $111,003
Enrollment: full time: 496; part time: N/A
men: 54%; women: 46%; minorities: 26%
Acceptance rate (full time): 27%
Midrange LSAT (full time): 159-166
Midrange undergraduate GPA (full time): 3.41-3.78
Midrange of full-time private-sector salaries of 2014 grads: $73,500-$125,000
2014 grads employed in: law firms: 46%; business and industry: 15%; government: 15%; public interest: 9%; judicial clerk: 13%; academia: 2%; unknown: 1%
Employment location for 2014 class: Intl. 1%; N.E. 0%; M.A. 2%; E.N.C. 0%; W.N.C. 1%; S.A. 3%; E.S.C. 0%; W.S.C. 1%; Mt. 1%; Pac. 91%; unknown 0%

WEST VIRGINIA

West Virginia University
PO Box 6130
Morgantown, WV 26506-6130
law.wvu.edu/
Public
Admissions: (304) 293-5304
Email: wvulaw.admissions@mail.wvu.edu
Financial aid: (304) 293-5302
Application deadline: 03/01
In-state tuition: full time: $19,008; part time: $1,056/credit hour
Out-of-state tuition: full time: $35,568
Room/board/expenses: $16,332
Median grant: $17,020
Average student indebtedness at graduation: $85,063
Enrollment: full time: 323; part time: 3
men: 59%; women: 41%; minorities: 11%
Acceptance rate (full time): 53%
Midrange LSAT (full time): 151-157
Midrange undergraduate GPA (full time): 3.11-3.69
Midrange of full-time private-sector salaries of 2014 grads: $50,000-$70,000
2014 grads employed in: law firms: 52%; business and industry: 13%; government: 9%; public interest: 8%; judicial clerk: 16%; academia: 1%; unknown: 2%
Employment location for 2014 class: Intl. 1%; N.E. 1%; M.A. 5%; E.N.C. 2%; W.N.C. 0%; S.A. 85%; E.S.C. 1%; W.S.C. 1%; Mt. 3%; Pac. 0%; unknown 2%

WISCONSIN

Marquette University

Eckstein Hall
PO Box 1881
Milwaukee, WI 53201-1881
law.marquette.edu
Private
Admissions: (414) 288-6767
Email: law.admission@marquette.edu
Financial aid: (414) 288-7390
Application deadline: 04/01
Tuition: full time: $42,270; part time: $26,880
Room/board/expenses: $20,358
Median grant: $8,000
Average student indebtedness at graduation: $138,549
Enrollment: full time: 521; part time: 76
men: 61%; women: 39%; minorities: 17%
Acceptance rate (full time): 78%
Midrange LSAT (full time): 150-155
Midrange undergraduate GPA (full time): 2.88-3.42
Midrange of full-time private-sector salaries of 2014 grads: $50,000-$100,000
2014 grads employed in: law firms: 56%; business and industry: 23%; government: 12%; public interest: 3%; judicial clerk: 4%; academia: 2%; unknown: 0%
Employment location for 2014 class: Intl. 1%; N.E. 1%; M.A. 1%; E.N.C. 85%; W.N.C. 5%; S.A. 4%; E.S.C. 0%; W.S.C. 1%; Mt. 1%; Pac. 2%; unknown 0%

University of Wisconsin-Madison

975 Bascom Mall
Madison, WI 53706-1399
www.law.wisc.edu
Public
Admissions: (608) 262-5914
Email: admissions@law.wisc.edu
Financial aid: (608) 262-5914
Application deadline: 04/01
In-state tuition: full time: $21,378; part time: $1,875/credit hour
Out-of-state tuition: full time: $40,074
Room/board/expenses: $19,064
Median grant: $12,000
Average student indebtedness at graduation: $84,650
Enrollment: full time: 519; part time: 23
men: 53%; women: 47%; minorities: 21%
Acceptance rate (full time): 49%
Midrange LSAT (full time): 155-162
Midrange undergraduate GPA (full time): 3.27-3.76
Midrange of full-time private-sector salaries of 2014 grads: $65,250-$121,500
2014 grads employed in: law firms: 53%; business and industry: 20%; government: 12%; public interest: 7%; judicial clerk: 6%; academia: 1%; unknown: 0%
Employment location for 2014 class: Intl. 4%; N.E. 0%; M.A. 4%; E.N.C. 73%; W.N.C. 6%; S.A. 5%; E.S.C. 1%; W.S.C. 2%; Mt. 1%; Pac. 3%; unknown 0%

WYOMING

University of Wyoming

Department 3035
1000 E. University Avenue
Laramie, WY 82071
www.uwyo.edu/law
Public
Admissions: (307) 766-6416
Email: lawadmis@uwyo.edu
Financial aid: (307) 766-2116
Application deadline: 03/01
In-state tuition: full time: $14,911; part time: N/A
Out-of-state tuition: full time: $31,241
Room/board/expenses: $16,782
Median grant: $6,000
Average student indebtedness at graduation: $77,421
Enrollment: full time: 237; part time: N/A
men: 57%; women: 43%; minorities: 13%
Acceptance rate (full time): 78%
Midrange LSAT (full time): 149-155
Midrange undergraduate GPA (full time): 3.10-3.55
Midrange of full-time private-sector salaries of 2014 grads: $50,000-$60,000
2014 grads employed in: law firms: 50%; business and industry: 19%; government: 4%; public interest: 2%; judicial clerk: 15%; academia: 4%; unknown: 6%
Employment location for 2014 class: Intl. 0%; N.E. 0%; M.A. 2%; E.N.C. 2%; W.N.C. 2%; S.A. 2%; E.S.C. 0%; W.S.C. 0%; Mt. 90%; Pac. 2%; unknown 0%

MEDICINE

This directory lists the 140 schools offering M.D. degrees that were accredited by the Liaison Committee on Medical Education in 2015, plus the 30 schools that offer D.O. degrees and were accredited by the American Osteopathic Association in 2015. Of those, 99 M.D.-granting schools and 17 D.O.-granting schools responded to the U.S. News survey, conducted in the fall of 2015 and early 2016. Their data are reported below. Schools that did not respond have abbreviated entries.

KEY TO THE TERMINOLOGY

1. A school whose name is footnoted with the numeral 1 did not return the U.S. News statistical survey; limited data appear in its entry.

N/A. Not available from the school or not applicable.

Admissions. The admissions office phone number.

Email. The address of the admissions office. If instead of an email address a website is listed, the website will automatically present an email screen programmed to reach the admissions office.

Financial aid. The financial aid office phone number.

Application deadline. For fall 2017 enrollment.

Tuition. For the 2015-16 academic year. Includes fees.

Room/board/expenses. For the 2015-16 academic year.

Students receiving grants. The percentage of the entire student body during the 2014-15 academic year that received grants or scholarships.

Average indebtedness. For 2014 graduates who incurred medical school-related debt.

Enrollment. Total doctor of medicine (M.D.) or doctor of osteopathy (D.O.) degree program enrollment for fall 2015.

Minorities. For fall 2015, percentage of U.S. students who fall in one of these groups: black or African-American, Asian, American Indian or Alaska Native, Native Hawaiian or other Pacific Islander, Hispanic/Latino, or two or more races. The minority percentage was reported by the school.

Underrepresented minorities. For fall 2015, percentage of U.S. students who are black or African-American, American Indian or Alaska Native, Native Hawaiian or other Pacific Islander, Hispanic/Latino, or two or more races. (This category is used only for medical schools. The underrepresented minority percentage was reported by the school.)

Acceptance rate. Percentage of applicants who were accepted for fall 2015 to an M.D. or D.O. degree program.

Median Medical College Admission Test (MCAT) total score. For M.D. or D.O. students who entered the medical or osteopathic program in the fall of 2015. The median total score of verbal reasoning and physical sciences and biological sciences MCAT scores. (These three separate MCAT scores are reported to test-takers on a scale of 1 to 15.)

Median undergraduate grade point average (GPA). For M.D. or D.O. students who entered in the fall of 2015.

Most popular undergraduate majors. For students who entered in the fall of 2015. The main areas are biological sciences, including microbiology; physical sciences, including chemistry; nonsciences, including the humanities; and other, including double majors, mixed disciplines, and other health professions like nursing and pharmacy.

Graduates entering primary care specialties. This is the three-year average percentage of all medical or osteopathic school graduates entering primary care residencies in the fields of family practice, general pediatrics or general internal medicine during 2013, 2014 and 2015.

ALABAMA

University of Alabama-Birmingham
Medical Student Services, VH
Suite 100
Birmingham, AL 35294-0019
www.uab.edu/medicine/admissions
Public
Admissions: (205) 934-2433
Email: medschool@uab.edu
Financial aid: (205) 934-8223
Application deadline: 11/01
In-state tuition: $29,048
Out-of-state tuition: $64,514
Room/board/expenses: $21,452
Percent receiving grants: 41%
Average student indebtedness at graduation: $118,225
Enrollment: 780
men: 56%; women: 44%; minorities: 23%; underrepresented minorities: 14%; in state: 91%
Acceptance rate: 7%
Median MCAT total score: 30
Median GPA: 3.80
Most popular undergraduate majors: biological sciences: 32%; physical sciences: 18%; nonsciences: 11%; other: 39%
Percent of graduates entering primary-care specialties: 43.7%

University of South Alabama[1]
307 University Boulevard
170 CSAB
Mobile, AL 36688
www.usahealthsystem.com/com
Public
Admissions: (251) 460-7176
Financial aid: N/A
Tuition: N/A
Room/board/expenses: N/A
Enrollment: N/A

ARIZONA

University of Arizona
1501 N. Campbell Avenue
Tucson, AZ 85724
www.medicine.arizona.edu/
Public
Admissions: (520) 626-6214
Email: admissions@medicine.arizona.edu
Financial aid: (520) 626-7145
Application deadline: 11/03
In-state tuition: $31,306
Out-of-state tuition: $51,550
Room/board/expenses: $13,000
Percent receiving grants: 79%
Average student indebtedness at graduation: $163,049
Enrollment: 465
men: 48%; women: 52%; minorities: 47%; underrepresented minorities: 27%; in state: 86%
Acceptance rate: 3%
Median MCAT total score: 29
Median GPA: 3.68
Most popular undergraduate majors: biological sciences: 48%; physical sciences: 14%; nonsciences: 10%; other: 28%

Percent of graduates entering primary-care specialties: 37.5%

ARKANSAS

University of Arkansas for Medical Sciences
4301 W. Markham Street, Slot 551
Little Rock, AR 72205
www.uams.edu
Public
Admissions: (501) 686-5354
Email: southtomg@uams.edu
Financial aid: (501) 686-5451
Application deadline: 11/01
In-state tuition: $29,058
Out-of-state tuition: $55,606
Room/board/expenses: $0
Percent receiving grants: 37%
Average student indebtedness at graduation: $160,224
Enrollment: 684
men: 63%; women: 37%; minorities: 20%; underrepresented minorities: 11%; in state: 89%
Acceptance rate: 21%
Median MCAT total score: 29
Median GPA: 3.67
Most popular undergraduate majors: biological sciences: 50%; physical sciences: 31%; nonsciences: 17%; other: 2%
Percent of graduates entering primary-care specialties: 52.3%

CALIFORNIA

California Northstate University
9700 W Taron Drive
Elk Grove, CA 95757
Private
Admissions: N/A
Financial aid: N/A
Application deadline: 12/15
Tuition: $55,850
Room/board/expenses: N/A
Percent receiving grants: 2%
Enrollment: 60
men: 68%; women: 32%; minorities: 68%; underrepresented minorities: 13%; in state: 78%
Acceptance rate: 11%
Median MCAT total score: 32
Median GPA: 3.50
Most popular undergraduate majors: biological sciences: 42%; physical sciences: 6%; nonsciences: 10%; other: 42%
Percent of graduates entering primary-care specialties: N/A

Loma Linda University[1]
24851 Circle Drive
Loma Linda, CA 92350
www.llu.edu/medicine/index.page
Private
Admissions: (909) 558-4467
Email: admissions.sm@llu.edu
Financial aid: N/A
Tuition: N/A
Room/board/expenses: N/A
Enrollment: N/A

Stanford University

300 Pasteur Drive, Suite M121
Stanford, CA 94305
med.stanford.edu
Private
Admissions: (650) 723-6861
Email:
mdadmissions@stanford.edu
Financial aid: (650) 723-6958
Application deadline: 10/15
Tuition: $53,445
Room/board/expenses: $28,440
Percent receiving grants: 65%
Average student indebtedness at graduation: $105,936
Enrollment: 482
men: 51%; women:
49%; minorities: 63%;
underrepresented minorities:
17%; in state: 40%
Acceptance rate: 3%
Median MCAT total score: 35
Median GPA: 3.85
Most popular undergraduate majors: biological sciences:
48%; physical sciences: 24%;
nonsciences: 9%; other: 19%
Percent of graduates entering primary-care specialties: 33.0%

University of California-Davis

4610 X Street
Sacramento, CA 95817
www.ucdmc.ucdavis.edu/
medschool/
Public
Admissions: (916) 734-4800
Email: medadmsinfo@ucdavis.edu
Financial aid: (916) 734-4120
Application deadline: 10/01
In-state tuition: $41,222
Out-of-state tuition: $53,467
Room/board/expenses: $15,736
Percent receiving grants: 91%
Average student indebtedness at graduation: $143,069
Enrollment: 433
men: 43%; women:
57%; minorities: 65%;
underrepresented minorities:
30%; in state: 100%
Acceptance rate: 3%
Median MCAT total score: 29
Median GPA: 3.58
Most popular undergraduate majors: biological sciences:
64%; physical sciences: 5%;
nonsciences: 14%; other: 17%
Percent of graduates entering primary-care specialties: 44.7%

University of California-Irvine

252 Irvine Hall
Irvine, CA 92697-3950
www.som.uci.edu
Public
Admissions: (949) 824-5388
Email: medadmit@uci.edu
Financial aid: (949) 824-6476
Application deadline: 11/01
In-state tuition: $37,734
Out-of-state tuition: $49,979
Room/board/expenses: $12,450
Percent receiving grants: 50%
Average student indebtedness at graduation: $158,929
Enrollment: 437
men: 50%; women:
50%; minorities: 51%;
underrepresented minorities:
18%; in state: 91%
Acceptance rate: 4%
Median MCAT total score: 33
Median GPA: 3.70

Most popular undergraduate majors: biological sciences:
77%; physical sciences: 4%;
nonsciences: 13%; other: 6%
Percent of graduates entering primary-care specialties: 40.0%

University of California-Los Angeles (Geffen)

12-138 CHS
10833 Le Conte Avenue
Los Angeles, CA 90095-1720
apply.medschool.ucla.edu
Public
Admissions: (310) 825-8447
Email: somadmiss@
mednet.ucla.edu
Financial aid: (310) 825-4181
Application deadline: 11/01
In-state tuition: $36,402
Out-of-state tuition: $48,647
Room/board/expenses: $18,060
Percent receiving grants: 92%
Average student indebtedness at graduation: $117,227
Enrollment: 748
men: 50%; women:
50%; minorities: 69%;
underrepresented minorities:
32%; in state: 86%
Acceptance rate: 3%
Median MCAT total score: 35
Median GPA: 3.82
Most popular undergraduate majors: biological sciences:
61%; physical sciences: 10%;
nonsciences: 10%; other: 19%
Percent of graduates entering primary-care specialties: 47.2%

University of California-Riverside[1]

900 University Ave.
Riverside, CA 92521
Private
Admissions: N/A
Financial aid: N/A
Tuition: N/A
Room/board/expenses: N/A
Enrollment: N/A

University of California-San Diego

9500 Gilman Drive
La Jolla, CA 92093-0602
meded.ucsd.edu/
Public
Admissions: (858) 534-3880
Email: somadmissions@ucsd.edu
Financial aid: (858) 534-4664
Application deadline: 11/01
In-state tuition: $36,987
Out-of-state tuition: $49,232
Room/board/expenses: $12,168
Percent receiving grants: 59%
Average student indebtedness at graduation: $99,087
Enrollment: 521
men: 52%; women:
48%; minorities: 52%;
underrepresented minorities:
19%; in state: 86%
Acceptance rate: 3%
Median MCAT total score: 34
Median GPA: 3.77
Most popular undergraduate majors: biological sciences:
60%; physical sciences: 22%;
nonsciences: 10%; other: 8%
Percent of graduates entering primary-care specialties: 39.9%

University of California-San Francisco

513 Parnassus Avenue
Room S224
San Francisco, CA 94143-0410
medschool.ucsf.edu/
Public
Admissions: (415) 476-4044
Email: admissions@
medsch.ucsf.edu
Financial aid: (415) 476-4181
Application deadline: 10/15
In-state tuition: $37,344
Out-of-state tuition: $49,589
Room/board/expenses: $27,720
Percent receiving grants: 81%
Average student indebtedness at graduation: $115,965
Enrollment: 647
men: 49%; women:
51%; minorities: 54%;
underrepresented minorities:
27%; in state: 91%
Acceptance rate: 4%
Median MCAT total score: 34
Median GPA: 3.75
Most popular undergraduate majors: biological sciences:
44%; physical sciences: 12%;
nonsciences: 23%; other: 21%
Percent of graduates entering primary-care specialties: 42.7%

University of Southern California (Keck)

1975 Zonal Avenue, KAM 500
Los Angeles, CA 90033
www.usc.edu/keck
Private
Admissions: (323) 442-2552
Email: medadmit@usc.edu
Financial aid: (213) 740-5462
Application deadline: 11/01
Tuition: $59,388
Room/board/expenses: $19,922
Percent receiving grants: 27%
Average student indebtedness at graduation: $184,149
Enrollment: 743
men: 53%; women:
47%; minorities: 53%;
underrepresented minorities:
16%; in state: 76%
Acceptance rate: 5%
Median MCAT total score: 35
Median GPA: 3.72
Most popular undergraduate majors: biological sciences:
48%; physical sciences: 14%;
nonsciences: 18%; other: 20%
Percent of graduates entering primary-care specialties: 36.3%

University of Colorado

13001 E. 17th Place, MS C290
Aurora, CO 80045
medschool.ucdenver.edu/
admissions
Public
Admissions: (303) 724-8025
Email: somadmin@ucdenver.edu
Financial aid: (303) 724-8039
Application deadline: 12/15
In-state tuition: $37,314
Out-of-state tuition: $63,270
Room/board/expenses: $19,950
Percent receiving grants: 41%
Average student indebtedness at graduation: $164,971

Enrollment: 664
men: 53%; women:
47%; minorities: 42%;
underrepresented minorities:
31%; in state: 72%
Acceptance rate: 4%
Median MCAT total score: 33
Median GPA: 3.71
Most popular undergraduate majors: biological sciences:
41%; physical sciences: 35%;
nonsciences: 5%; other: 19%
Percent of graduates entering primary-care specialties: 41.4%

Quinnipiac University[1]

275 Mt Carmel Ave.
Hamden, CT 06518
Private
Admissions: N/A
Financial aid: N/A
Tuition: N/A
Room/board/expenses: N/A
Enrollment: N/A

University of Connecticut

263 Farmington Avenue
Farmington, CT 06030-1905
medicine.uchc.edu
Public
Admissions: (860) 679-4713
Email: admissions@uchc.edu
Financial aid: (860) 679-1364
Application deadline: 11/15
In-state tuition: $35,622
Out-of-state tuition: $65,630
Room/board/expenses: $20,325
Percent receiving grants: 51%
Average student indebtedness at graduation: $140,051
Enrollment: 392
men: 49%; women:
51%; minorities: 38%;
underrepresented minorities:
17%; in state: 93%
Acceptance rate: 7%
Median MCAT total score: 32
Median GPA: 3.70
Most popular undergraduate majors: biological sciences:
48%; physical sciences: 15%;
nonsciences: 9%; other: 28%
Percent of graduates entering primary-care specialties: 48.0%

Yale University

333 Cedar Street
PO Box 208055
New Haven, CT 06520-8055
medicine.yale.edu
Private
Admissions: (203) 785-2643
Email: medical.admissions@
yale.edu
Financial aid: (203) 785-2645
Application deadline: 10/15
Tuition: $56,645
Room/board/expenses: $13,100
Percent receiving grants: 60%
Average student indebtedness at graduation: $114,314
Enrollment: 396
men: 53%; women:
47%; minorities: 55%;
underrepresented minorities:
21%; in state: 5%
Acceptance rate: 7%
Median MCAT total score: 36
Median GPA: 3.87
Most popular undergraduate majors: biological sciences:
51%; physical sciences: 29%;
nonsciences: 13%; other: 7%

Percent of graduates entering primary-care specialties: 35.0%

Georgetown University

3900 Reservoir Road NW
Med-Dent Building
Washington, DC 20007
som.georgetown.edu/
Private
Admissions: (202) 687-1154
Email: medicaladmissions@
georgetown.edu
Financial aid: (202) 687-1693
Application deadline: 11/07
Tuition: $56,648
Room/board/expenses: $19,250
Percent receiving grants: 51%
Average student indebtedness at graduation: $214,043
Enrollment: 793
men: 48%; women:
52%; minorities: 30%;
underrepresented minorities:
12%; in state: 4%
Acceptance rate: 3%
Median MCAT total score: 31
Median GPA: 3.60
Most popular undergraduate majors: biological sciences:
41%; physical sciences: 17%;
nonsciences: 11%; other: 31%
Percent of graduates entering primary-care specialties: 33.0%

George Washington University

2300 Eye Street NW, Room 708W
Washington, DC 20037
smhs.gwu.edu
Private
Admissions: (202) 994-3506
Email: medadmit@gwu.edu
Financial aid: (202) 994-2960
Application deadline: N/A
Tuition: N/A
Room/board/expenses: N/A
Average student indebtedness at graduation: $197,292
Enrollment: 734
men: 43%; women:
57%; minorities: 51%;
underrepresented minorities:
15%; in state: 0%
Acceptance rate: 3%
Median MCAT total score: 30
Median GPA: 3.70
Most popular undergraduate majors: biological sciences:
45%; physical sciences: 5%;
nonsciences: 17%; other: 33%
Percent of graduates entering primary-care specialties: 37.0%

Howard University[1]

520 W. Street NW
Washington, DC 20059
healthsciences.howard.edu/
education/schools-and-
academics/medicine
Private
Admissions: (202) 806-6279
Email:
sharmon.jones@howard.edu
Financial aid: N/A
Tuition: N/A
Room/board/expenses: N/A
Enrollment: N/A

FLORIDA

Florida Atlantic University[1]
777 Glades Road
Boca Raton, FL 33431
Private
Admissions: N/A
Financial aid: N/A
Tuition: N/A
Room/board/expenses: N/A
Enrollment: N/A

Florida International University (Wertheim)[1]
11200 SW 8th Street
Miami, FL 33199
medicine.fiu.edu/
Public
Admissions: (305) 348-0644
Email: med.admissions@fiu.edu
Financial aid: N/A
Tuition: N/A
Room/board/expenses: N/A
Enrollment: N/A

Florida State University
1115 W. Call Street
Tallahassee, FL 32306-4300
www.med.fsu.edu/
Public
Admissions: (850) 644-7904
Email: medadmissions@med.fsu.edu
Financial aid: (850) 645-7270
Application deadline: 12/01
In-state tuition: $26,110
Out-of-state tuition: $59,393
Room/board/expenses: $15,104
Percent receiving grants: 70%
Average student indebtedness at graduation: $150,008
Enrollment: 485
men: 51%; women: 49%; minorities: 38%; underrepresented minorities: 34%; in state: 100%
Acceptance rate: 2%
Median MCAT total score: 27
Median GPA: 3.66
Most popular undergraduate majors: biological sciences: 60%; physical sciences: 16%; nonsciences: 4%; other: 20%
Percent of graduates entering primary-care specialties: 47.0%

University of Central Florida
6850 Lake Nona Boulevard
Orlando, FL 32827
med.ucf.edu/
Public
Admissions: (407) 266-1350
Email: mdadmissions@ucf.edu
Financial aid: (407) 266-1000
Application deadline: 11/15
In-state tuition: $29,680
Out-of-state tuition: $31,063
Room/board/expenses: $13,850
Percent receiving grants: 100%
Average student indebtedness at graduation: $139,022
Enrollment: 456
men: 51%; women: 49%; minorities: 45%; underrepresented minorities: 14%; in state: 75%
Median MCAT total score: 32
Median GPA: 3.75
Most popular undergraduate majors: biological sciences: 56%; physical sciences: 21%; nonsciences: 7%; other: 16%

University of Florida
Box 100216 UFHSC
Gainesville, FL 32610-0216
www.med.ufl.edu
Public
Admissions: (352) 273-7990
Email: med-admissions@ufl.edu
Financial aid: (352) 273-7939
Application deadline: 12/01
In-state tuition: $37,129
Out-of-state tuition: $49,385
Room/board/expenses: $13,755
Percent receiving grants: 71%
Average student indebtedness at graduation: $151,500
Enrollment: 551
men: 50%; women: 50%; minorities: 34%; underrepresented minorities: 22%; in state: 94%
Acceptance rate: 5%
Median MCAT total score: 33
Median GPA: 3.87
Most popular undergraduate majors: biological sciences: 62%; physical sciences: 8%; nonsciences: 5%; other: 26%
Percent of graduates entering primary-care specialties: 36.7%

University of Miami (Miller)
1120 N.W. 14 Street
Miami, FL 33136
www.med.miami.edu
Private
Admissions: (305) 243-3234
Email: med.admissions@miami.edu
Financial aid: (305) 243-6211
Application deadline: 06/01
Tuition: $37,163
Room/board/expenses: $17,738
Percent receiving grants: 29%
Average student indebtedness at graduation: $158,753
Enrollment: 809
men: 53%; women: 47%; minorities: 40%; underrepresented minorities: 18%; in state: 49%
Acceptance rate: 4%
Median MCAT total score: 33
Median GPA: 3.77
Most popular undergraduate majors: biological sciences: 58%; physical sciences: 31%; nonsciences: 7%; other: 4%
Percent of graduates entering primary-care specialties: 32.3%

University of South Florida
12901 Bruce B. Downs Boulevard, MDC 2
Tampa, FL 33612
mdadmissions@health.usf.edu
Public
Admissions: (813) 974-2229
Email: md-admissions@health.usf.edu
Financial aid: (813) 974-2068
Application deadline: 11/15
In-state tuition: $33,726
Out-of-state tuition: $54,915
Room/board/expenses: $12,250
Percent receiving grants: 59%
Average student indebtedness at graduation: $150,411
Enrollment: 701
men: 56%; women: 44%; minorities: 42%; underrepresented minorities: 16%; in state: 72%
Acceptance rate: 6%
Median MCAT total score: 33
Median GPA: 3.65
Most popular undergraduate majors: biological sciences: 39%; physical sciences: 14%; nonsciences: 4%; other: 43%
Percent of graduates entering primary-care specialties: 47.7%

GEORGIA

Augusta University
1120 15th Street
Augusta, GA 30912-4750
www.gru.edu/medicine/admit/
Public
Admissions: (706) 721-3186
Email: stdadmin@gru.edu
Financial aid: (706) 737-1524
Application deadline: 11/01
In-state tuition: $31,539
Out-of-state tuition: $59,897
Room/board/expenses: $22,566
Percent receiving grants: 25%
Average student indebtedness at graduation: $155,173
Enrollment: 924
men: 56%; women: 44%; minorities: 39%; underrepresented minorities: 16%; in state: 96%
Acceptance rate: 12%
Median MCAT total score: 31
Median GPA: 3.72
Most popular undergraduate majors: biological sciences: 43%; physical sciences: 13%; nonsciences: 16%; other: 28%
Percent of graduates entering primary-care specialties: 32.0%

Emory University
100 Woodruff Circle NE
Atlanta, GA 30322
www.med.emory.edu
Private
Admissions: (404) 727-5660
Email: medadmiss@emory.edu
Financial aid: (404) 727-6039
Application deadline: 10/15
Tuition: $50,860
Room/board/expenses: $23,906
Percent receiving grants: 50%
Average student indebtedness at graduation: $142,857
Enrollment: 562
men: 47%; women: 53%; minorities: 32%; underrepresented minorities: 13%; in state: 30%
Acceptance rate: 6%
Median MCAT total score: 34
Median GPA: 3.70
Most popular undergraduate majors: biological sciences: 34%; physical sciences: 16%; nonsciences: 22%; other: 28%
Percent of graduates entering primary-care specialties: 40.7%

Mercer University[1]
1550 College Street
Macon, GA 31207
medicine.mercer.edu
Private
Admissions: (478) 301-2542
Email: admissions@med.mercer.edu
Financial aid: N/A
Tuition: N/A
Room/board/expenses: N/A
Enrollment: N/A

Morehouse School of Medicine[1]
720 Westview Drive SW
Atlanta, GA 30310
www.msm.edu
Private
Admissions: (404) 752-1650
Email: mdadmissions@msm.edu
Financial aid: (404) 752-1655
Tuition: N/A
Room/board/expenses: N/A
Enrollment: N/A

HAWAII

University of Hawaii-Manoa (Burns)[1]
651 Ilalo Street
Honolulu, HI 96813
jabsom.hawaii.edu
Public
Admissions: (808) 692-1000
Email: medadmin@hawaii.edu
Financial aid: (808) 956-7251
Tuition: N/A
Room/board/expenses: N/A
Enrollment: N/A

ILLINOIS

Loyola University Chicago (Stritch)[1]
2160 S. First Avenue
Building 120
Maywood, IL 60153
www.meddean.luc.edu/
Private
Admissions: (708) 216-3229
Email: ssom-admissions@lumc.edu
Financial aid: N/A
Tuition: N/A
Room/board/expenses: N/A
Enrollment: N/A

Northwestern University (Feinberg)
420 E. Superior Street
(Rubloff Building), 12th Floor
Chicago, IL 60611
www.feinberg.northwestern.edu
Private
Admissions: (312) 503-8206
Email: med-admissions@northwestern.edu
Financial aid: (312) 503-8722
Application deadline: 10/15
Tuition: $58,210
Room/board/expenses: $18,282
Percent receiving grants: 45%
Average student indebtedness at graduation: $174,555
Enrollment: 639
men: 56%; women: 44%; minorities: 45%; underrepresented minorities: 15%; in state: 19%
Acceptance rate: 8%
Median MCAT total score: 36
Median GPA: 3.88
Most popular undergraduate majors: biological sciences: 42%; physical sciences: 19%; nonsciences: 16%; other: 23%
Percent of graduates entering primary-care specialties: 39.4%

Rosalind Franklin University of Medicine and Science[1]
3333 Green Bay Road
North Chicago, IL 60064
www.rosalindfranklin.edu/cms/
Private
Admissions: (847) 578-3204
Email: cms.admissions@rosalindfranklin.edu
Financial aid: N/A
Tuition: N/A
Room/board/expenses: N/A
Enrollment: N/A

Rush University[1]
600 S. Paulina Street
Chicago, IL 60612
www.rushu.rush.edu/medcol/
Private
Admissions: N/A
Email: RMC_Admissions@rush.edu
Financial aid: (312) 942-6256
Tuition: N/A
Room/board/expenses: N/A
Enrollment: N/A

Southern Illinois University-Springfield[1]
801 N. Rutledge
PO Box 19620
Springfield, IL 62794-9620
www.siumed.edu/
Public
Admissions: (217) 545-6013
Email: admissions@siumed.edu
Financial aid: N/A
Tuition: N/A
Room/board/expenses: N/A
Enrollment: N/A

University of Chicago (Pritzker)
5841 S. Maryland Avenue
MC 1000
Chicago, IL 60637-5416
pritzker.bsd.uchicago.edu
Private
Admissions: (773) 702-1937
Email: pritzkeradmissions@bsd.uchicago.edu
Financial aid: (773) 702-1938
Application deadline: 10/15
Tuition: $54,784
Room/board/expenses: $16,800
Percent receiving grants: 87%
Average student indebtedness at graduation: $117,203
Enrollment: 363
men: 52%; women: 48%; minorities: 39%; underrepresented minorities: 19%; in state: 24%
Acceptance rate: 5%
Median MCAT total score: 37
Median GPA: 3.87
Most popular undergraduate majors: biological sciences: 34%; physical sciences: 22%; nonsciences: 19%; other: 25%
Percent of graduates entering primary-care specialties: 40.7%

University of Illinois
1853 W. Polk Street
M/C 784
Chicago, IL 60612
www.medicine.uic.edu
Public
Admissions: (312) 996-5635
Email: medadmit@uic.edu
Financial aid: (312) 413-0127
Application deadline: 11/01
In-state tuition: $39,716
Out-of-state tuition: $76,716
Room/board/expenses: $14,464
Percent receiving grants: 48%
Average student indebtedness at graduation: $207,083
Enrollment: 1,317
men: 54%; women: 46%; minorities: 54%; underrepresented minorities: 36%; in state: 78%
Acceptance rate: 13%
Median MCAT total score: 32

Median GPA: 3.69
Most popular undergraduate majors: biological sciences: 52%; physical sciences: 9%; nonsciences: 17%; other: 22%
Percent of graduates entering primary-care specialties: 40.0%

INDIANA

Indiana University-Indianapolis
340 W. 10th Street, Suite 6200
Indianapolis, IN 46202
www.medicine.iu.edu
Public
Admissions: (317) 274-3772
Email: inmedadm@iupui.edu
Financial aid: (317) 274-1967
Application deadline: 11/17
In-state tuition: $34,602
Out-of-state tuition: $56,230
Room/board/expenses: $11,860
Percent receiving grants: 32%
Average student indebtedness at graduation: $184,843
Enrollment: 1,404
men: 55%; women: 45%; minorities: 33%; underrepresented minorities: 19%; in state: 80%
Acceptance rate: 9%
Median MCAT total score: 30
Median GPA: 3.80
Most popular undergraduate majors: biological sciences: 45%; physical sciences: 28%; nonsciences: 10%; other: 17%
Percent of graduates entering primary-care specialties: 35.0%

IOWA

University of Iowa (Carver)
200 CMAB
Iowa City, IA 52242-1101
www.medicine.uiowa.edu
Public
Admissions: (319) 335-8052
Email: medical-admissions@uiowa.edu
Financial aid: (319) 335-8059
Application deadline: 11/01
In-state tuition: $35,249
Out-of-state tuition: $52,319
Room/board/expenses: $11,040
Percent receiving grants: 60%
Average student indebtedness at graduation: $150,970
Enrollment: 600
men: 55%; women: 45%; minorities: 25%; underrepresented minorities: 11%; in state: 69%
Acceptance rate: 8%
Median MCAT total score: 32
Median GPA: 3.76
Most popular undergraduate majors: biological sciences: 73%; physical sciences: 10%; nonsciences: 10%; other: 7%
Percent of graduates entering primary-care specialties: 38.0%

KANSAS

University of Kansas Medical Center
3901 Rainbow Boulevard
Kansas City, KS 66160
medicine.kumc.edu
Public
Admissions: (913) 588-5245
Email: premedinfo@kumc.edu
Financial aid: (913) 588-5170
Application deadline: 10/15

In-state tuition: $34,469
Out-of-state tuition: $60,431
Room/board/expenses: $16,286
Percent receiving grants: 91%
Average student indebtedness at graduation: $155,241
Enrollment: 838
men: 55%; women: 45%; minorities: 24%; underrepresented minorities: 13%; in state: 92%
Acceptance rate: 7%
Median MCAT total score: 29
Median GPA: 3.78
Most popular undergraduate majors: biological sciences: 54%; physical sciences: 24%; nonsciences: 6%; other: 16%
Percent of graduates entering primary-care specialties: 46.0%

KENTUCKY

University of Kentucky
138 Leader Avenue
Lexington, KY 40506-9983
www.med.uky.edu
Public
Admissions: (859) 323-6161
Email: kymedap@uky.edu
Financial aid: (859) 257-1652
Application deadline: 11/01
In-state tuition: $36,024
Out-of-state tuition: $65,956
Room/board/expenses: $15,000
Percent receiving grants: 40%
Average student indebtedness at graduation: $203,590
Enrollment: 521
men: 58%; women: 42%; minorities: 22%; underrepresented minorities: 9%; in state: 74%
Acceptance rate: 8%
Median MCAT total score: 32
Median GPA: 3.75
Most popular undergraduate majors: biological sciences: 51%; physical sciences: 19%; nonsciences: 9%; other: 21%
Percent of graduates entering primary-care specialties: 37.0%

University of Louisville
Abell Administration Center
H.S.C.
Louisville, KY 40202
www.louisville.edu
Public
Admissions: (502) 852-5193
Email: medadm@louisville.edu
Financial aid: (502) 852-5187
Application deadline: 10/15
In-state tuition: $37,415
Out-of-state tuition: $56,377
Room/board/expenses: $10,446
Percent receiving grants: 35%
Average student indebtedness at graduation: $163,806
Enrollment: 622
men: 58%; women: 42%; minorities: 13%; underrepresented minorities: 6%; in state: 76%
Acceptance rate: 7%
Median MCAT total score: 29
Median GPA: 3.67
Most popular undergraduate majors: biological sciences: 51%; physical sciences: 20%; nonsciences: 10%; other: 20%
Percent of graduates entering primary-care specialties: 40.6%

LOUISIANA

Louisiana State University Health Sciences Center-New Orleans[1]
Admissions Office
1901 Perdido Street
New Orleans, LA 70112-1393
www.medschool.lsuhsc.edu/
Public
Admissions: (504) 568-6262
Email: ms-admissions@lsuhsc.edu
Financial aid: N/A
Tuition: N/A
Room/board/expenses: N/A
Enrollment: N/A

Louisiana State University Health Sciences Center-Shreveport[1]
PO Box 33932
1501 Kings Highway
Shreveport, LA 71130-3932
www.lsuhscshreveport.edu/Education/SchoolofMedicine.aspx
Public
Admissions: (318) 675-5190
Email: shvadm@lsuhsc.edu
Financial aid: N/A
Tuition: N/A
Room/board/expenses: N/A
Enrollment: N/A

Tulane University[1]
1430 Tulane Avenue, SL67
New Orleans, LA 70112-2699
tulane.edu/som/
Private
Admissions: (504) 988-5187
Email: medsch@tulane.edu
Financial aid: N/A
Tuition: N/A
Room/board/expenses: N/A
Enrollment: N/A

MARYLAND

Johns Hopkins University
733 N. Broadway
Baltimore, MD 21205
www.hopkinsmedicine.org
Private
Admissions: (410) 955-3182
Email: somadmiss@jhmi.edu
Financial aid: (410) 955-1324
Application deadline: 10/15
Tuition: $53,804
Room/board/expenses: $22,940
Percent receiving grants: 54%
Average student indebtedness at graduation: $109,471
Enrollment: 472
men: 49%; women: 51%; minorities: 52%; underrepresented minorities: 19%; in state: 21%
Acceptance rate: 6%
Median MCAT total score: 36
Median GPA: 3.90
Most popular undergraduate majors: biological sciences: 51%; physical sciences: 30%; nonsciences: 15%; other: 4%
Percent of graduates entering primary-care specialties: 36.0%

Uniformed Services University of the Health Sciences (Hebert)[1]
4301 Jones Bridge Road
Bethesda, MD 20814
www.usuhs.edu
Public
Admissions: (800) 772-1743
Email: admissions@usuhs.edu
Financial aid: N/A
Tuition: N/A
Room/board/expenses: N/A
Enrollment: N/A

University of Maryland
655 W. Baltimore Street
Room 14-029
Baltimore, MD 21201-1559
medschool.umaryland.edu
Public
Admissions: (410) 706-7478
Email: admissions@som.umaryland.edu
Financial aid: (410) 706-7347
Application deadline: 11/01
In-state tuition: $35,009
Out-of-state tuition: $61,253
Room/board/expenses: $21,500
Percent receiving grants: 65%
Average student indebtedness at graduation: $153,562
Enrollment: 651
men: 42%; women: 58%; minorities: 38%; underrepresented minorities: 11%; in state: 85%
Acceptance rate: 7%
Median MCAT total score: 32
Median GPA: 3.76
Most popular undergraduate majors: biological sciences: 50%; physical sciences: 15%; nonsciences: 16%; other: 19%
Percent of graduates entering primary-care specialties: 38.3%

MASSACHUSETTS

Boston University
72 E. Concord Street, L-103
Boston, MA 02118
www.bumc.bu.edu
Private
Admissions: (617) 638-4630
Email: medadms@bu.edu
Financial aid: (617) 638-5130
Application deadline: 11/01
Tuition: $56,304
Room/board/expenses: $10,688
Percent receiving grants: 65%
Average student indebtedness at graduation: $180,231
Enrollment: 702
men: 52%; women: 48%; minorities: 47%; underrepresented minorities: 19%; in state: 21%
Acceptance rate: 4%
Median MCAT total score: 35
Median GPA: 3.74
Most popular undergraduate majors: biological sciences: 39%; physical sciences: 17%; nonsciences: 13%; other: 31%
Percent of graduates entering primary-care specialties: 42.6%

Harvard University
25 Shattuck Street
Boston, MA 02115-6092
hms.harvard.edu
Private
Admissions: (617) 432-1550
Email: admissions_office@hms.harvard.edu
Financial aid: (617) 432-0449
Application deadline: 10/22

Tuition: $57,485
Room/board/expenses: $17,485
Percent receiving grants: 66%
Average student indebtedness at graduation: $105,671
Enrollment: 710
men: 49%; women: 51%; minorities: 51%; underrepresented minorities: 22%; in state: N/A
Acceptance rate: 4%
Median MCAT total score: 36
Median GPA: 3.92
Most popular undergraduate majors: biological sciences: 36%; physical sciences: 35%; nonsciences: 20%; other: 9%
Percent of graduates entering primary-care specialties: 38.0%

Tufts University
136 Harrison Avenue
Boston, MA 02111
md.tufts.edu/med
Private
Admissions: (617) 636-6571
Email: med-admissions@tufts.edu
Financial aid: (617) 636-6574
Application deadline: 11/01
Tuition: $59,080
Room/board/expenses: $14,620
Percent receiving grants: 37%
Average student indebtedness at graduation: $195,290
Enrollment: 819
men: 47%; women: 53%; minorities: 33%; underrepresented minorities: 14%; in state: 30%
Acceptance rate: 6%
Median MCAT total score: 33
Median GPA: 3.67
Most popular undergraduate majors: biological sciences: 44%; physical sciences: 8%; nonsciences: 24%; other: 24%
Percent of graduates entering primary-care specialties: 45.6%

University of Massachusetts-Worcester
55 Lake Avenue N
Worcester, MA 01655
www.umassmed.edu
Public
Admissions: (508) 856-2323
Email: admissions@umassmed.edu
Financial aid: (508) 856-2265
Application deadline: 10/15
In-state tuition: $34,017
Out-of-state tuition: N/A
Room/board/expenses: $13,909
Percent receiving grants: 44%
Average student indebtedness at graduation: $140,190
Enrollment: 515
men: 47%; women: 53%; minorities: 29%; underrepresented minorities: 9%; in state: 97%
Acceptance rate: 17%
Median MCAT total score: 32
Median GPA: 3.70
Most popular undergraduate majors: biological sciences: 34%; physical sciences: 32%; nonsciences: 2%; other: 32%
Percent of graduates entering primary-care specialties: 51.5%

MICHIGAN

Central Michigan University[1]
1200 S Franklin St.
Mt Pleasant, MI 48859
Private
Admissions: N/A
Financial aid: N/A
Tuition: N/A
Room/board/expenses: N/A
Enrollment: N/A

Michigan State University (College of Human Medicine)
15 Michigan St. NE
Grand Rapids, MI 49503
mdaadmissions.msu.edu
Public
Admissions: (517) 353-9620
Email: MDadmissions@msu.edu
Financial aid: (517) 353-5940
Application deadline: 11/01
In-state tuition: $32,539
Out-of-state tuition: $64,041
Room/board/expenses: $14,616
Percent receiving grants: 32%
Average student indebtedness at graduation: $235,340
Enrollment: 855
men: 48%; women: 52%; minorities: 35%; underrepresented minorities: 18%; in state: 82%
Acceptance rate: 4%
Median MCAT total score: 28
Median GPA: 3.57
Most popular undergraduate majors: biological sciences: 54%; physical sciences: 13%; nonsciences: 15%; other: 18%
Percent of graduates entering primary-care specialties: 44.8%

Oakland University[1]
2200 N. Squirrel
Rochester, MI 48309
Private
Admissions: N/A
Financial aid: N/A
Tuition: N/A
Room/board/expenses: N/A
Enrollment: N/A

University of Michigan-Ann Arbor
1301 Catherine Road
Ann Arbor, MI 48109-0624
www.medicine.umich.edu/medschool/
Public
Admissions: (734) 936-7253
Email: umichmedadmiss@umich.edu
Financial aid: (734) 763-4147
Application deadline: 09/30
In-state tuition: $32,756
Out-of-state tuition: $51,182
Room/board/expenses: $22,775
Percent receiving grants: 55%
Average student indebtedness at graduation: $131,148
Enrollment: 710
men: 47%; women: 53%; minorities: 35%; underrepresented minorities: 13%; in state: 52%
Acceptance rate: 7%
Median MCAT total score: 35
Median GPA: 3.78
Most popular undergraduate majors: biological sciences: 33%; physical sciences: 40%; nonsciences: 12%; other: 15%
Percent of graduates entering primary-care specialties: 44.5%

Wayne State University
540 E. Canfield
Detroit, MI 48201
admissions.med.wayne.edu/
Public
Admissions: (313) 577-1466
Email: admissions@med.wayne.edu
Financial aid: (313) 577-7731
Application deadline: 12/15
In-state tuition: $33,086
Out-of-state tuition: $66,663
Room/board/expenses: $12,350
Percent receiving grants: 68%
Average student indebtedness at graduation: $161,476
Enrollment: 1,219
men: 53%; women: 47%; minorities: 29%; underrepresented minorities: 9%; in state: 81%
Acceptance rate: 11%
Median MCAT total score: 32
Median GPA: 3.70
Most popular undergraduate majors: biological sciences: 56%; physical sciences: 21%; nonsciences: 12%; other: 11%
Percent of graduates entering primary-care specialties: 35.7%

Western Michigan University[1]
1000 Oakland Drive
Kalamazoo, MI 49008
Private
Admissions: N/A
Financial aid: N/A
Tuition: N/A
Room/board/expenses: N/A
Enrollment: N/A

MINNESOTA

Mayo Medical School
200 First Street SW
Rochester, MN 55905
www.mayo.edu/mms/
Private
Admissions: (507) 284-3671
Email: medschooladmissions@mayo.edu
Financial aid: (507) 284-4839
Application deadline: 10/01
Tuition: $49,900
Room/board/expenses: $18,048
Percent receiving grants: 94%
Average student indebtedness at graduation: $57,328
Enrollment: 208
men: 50%; women: 50%; minorities: 35%; underrepresented minorities: 12%; in state: 11%
Acceptance rate: 2%
Median MCAT total score: 34
Median GPA: 3.80
Most popular undergraduate majors: biological sciences: 35%; physical sciences: 29%; nonsciences: 8%; other: 28%
Percent of graduates entering primary-care specialties: 38.0%

University of Minnesota
420 Delaware Street SE
MMC 293
Minneapolis, MN 55455
www.med.umn.edu
Public
Admissions: (612) 625-7977
Email: meded@umn.edu
Financial aid: (612) 625-4998
Application deadline: 11/15
In-state tuition: $39,759
Out-of-state tuition: $53,397
Room/board/expenses: $14,333

Percent receiving grants: 61%
Average student indebtedness at graduation: $174,412
Enrollment: 975
men: 50%; women: 50%; minorities: 20%; underrepresented minorities: 10%; in state: 93%
Acceptance rate: 6%
Median MCAT total score: 32
Median GPA: 3.79
Most popular undergraduate majors: biological sciences: 55%; physical sciences: 18%; nonsciences: 12%; other: 15%
Percent of graduates entering primary-care specialties: 49.4%

MISSISSIPPI

University of Mississippi[1]
2500 N. State Street
Jackson, MS 39216-4505
www.umc.edu/som/
Public
Admissions: (601) 984-5010
Email: AdmitMD@umc.edu
Financial aid: N/A
Tuition: N/A
Room/board/expenses: N/A
Enrollment: N/A

MISSOURI

St. Louis University
1402 S. Grand Boulevard
St. Louis, MO 63104
medschool.slu.edu
Private
Admissions: (314) 977-9870
Email: slumd@slu.edu
Financial aid: (314) 977-9840
Application deadline: 12/15
Tuition: $51,130
Room/board/expenses: $12,600
Percent receiving grants: 53%
Average student indebtedness at graduation: $187,975
Enrollment: 731
men: 53%; women: 47%; minorities: 40%; underrepresented minorities: 10%; in state: 37%
Acceptance rate: 6%
Median MCAT total score: 33
Median GPA: 3.87
Most popular undergraduate majors: biological sciences: 50%; physical sciences: 22%; nonsciences: 8%; other: 20%
Percent of graduates entering primary-care specialties: 47.6%

University of Missouri
One Hospital Drive
Columbia, MO 65212
medicine.missouri.edu
Public
Admissions: (573) 882-9219
Email: MizzouMed@missouri.edu
Financial aid: (573) 882-2923
Application deadline: 10/15
In-state tuition: $30,303
Out-of-state tuition: $57,613
Room/board/expenses: $11,008
Percent receiving grants: 65%
Average student indebtedness at graduation: $142,183
Enrollment: 397
men: 56%; women: 44%; minorities: 16%; underrepresented minorities: 7%; in state: 81%
Acceptance rate: 9%
Median MCAT total score: 30
Median GPA: 3.79
Most popular undergraduate majors: biological sciences: 47%; physical sciences: 19%; nonsciences: 10%; other: 24%

Percent of graduates entering primary-care specialties: 42.7%

University of Missouri-Kansas City[1]
2411 Holmes
Kansas City, MO 64108
www.med.umkc.edu
Public
Admissions: (816) 235-1870
Email: medicine@umkc.edu
Financial aid: N/A
Tuition: N/A
Room/board/expenses: N/A
Enrollment: N/A

Washington University in St. Louis
660 S. Euclid Avenue
St. Louis, MO 63110
mdadmissions.wustl.edu
Private
Admissions: (314) 362-6858
Email: wumscoa@wustl.edu
Financial aid: (314) 362-6671
Application deadline: 12/01
Tuition: $58,460
Room/board/expenses: $12,520
Percent receiving grants: 70%
Average student indebtedness at graduation: $89,812
Enrollment: 484
men: 49%; women: 51%; minorities: 44%; underrepresented minorities: 11%; in state: 11%
Acceptance rate: 9%
Median MCAT total score: 38
Median GPA: 3.88
Most popular undergraduate majors: biological sciences: 34%; physical sciences: 28%; nonsciences: 11%; other: 27%
Percent of graduates entering primary-care specialties: 35.0%

NEBRASKA

Creighton University
2500 California Plaza
Omaha, NE 68178
medicine.creighton.edu
Private
Admissions: (402) 280-2799
Email: medadmissions@creighton.edu
Financial aid: (402) 280-2731
Application deadline: 11/01
Tuition: $54,692
Room/board/expenses: $14,400
Average student indebtedness at graduation: $211,699
Enrollment: 618
men: 50%; women: 50%; minorities: 20%; underrepresented minorities: 7%; in state: 10%
Acceptance rate: 5%
Median MCAT total score: 30
Median GPA: 3.74
Most popular undergraduate majors: biological sciences: 47%; physical sciences: 13%; nonsciences: 20%; other: 20%
Percent of graduates entering primary-care specialties: 38.4%

University of Nebraska Medical Center
985527 Nebraska Medical Center
Omaha, NE 68198-5527
www.unmc.edu/com/admissions.htm
Public
Admissions: (402) 559-2259
Email: grrogers@unmc.edu
Financial aid: (402) 559-4199

Percent of graduates entering primary-care specialties: 64.0%

NEVADA

University of Nevada
Pennington Building
Mailstop 357
Reno, NV 89557-0357
www.medicine.nevada.edu
Public
Admissions: (775) 784-6063
Email: asa@medicine.nevada.edu
Financial aid: (775) 682-8358
Application deadline: 10/15
In-state tuition: $30,120
Out-of-state tuition: $60,474
Room/board/expenses: $15,340
Percent receiving grants: 84%
Average student indebtedness at graduation: $143,485
Enrollment: 277
men: 58%; women: 42%; minorities: 38%; underrepresented minorities: 16%; in state: 96%
Acceptance rate: 6%
Median MCAT total score: 31
Median GPA: 3.76
Most popular undergraduate majors: biological sciences: 48%; physical sciences: 20%; nonsciences: 8%; other: 24%
Percent of graduates entering primary-care specialties: 40.5%

NEW HAMPSHIRE

Dartmouth College (Geisel)
1 Rope Ferry Road
Hanover, NH 03755-1404
geiselmed.dartmouth.edu
Private
Admissions: (603) 650-1505
Email: geisel.admissions@dartmouth.edu
Financial aid: (603) 650-1111
Application deadline: 11/01
Tuition: $60,012
Room/board/expenses: $10,750
Percent receiving grants: 59%
Average student indebtedness at graduation: $140,189
Enrollment: 369
men: 42%; women: 58%; minorities: 45%; underrepresented minorities: 25%; in state: 4%
Acceptance rate: 5%
Median MCAT total score: 32
Median GPA: 3.64
Most popular undergraduate majors: biological sciences: 45%; physical sciences: 16%; nonsciences: 10%; other: 29%
Percent of graduates entering primary-care specialties: 41.6%

NEW JERSEY

Rutgers New Jersey Medical School-Newark

185 S. Orange Avenue
Newark, NJ 07101-1709
www.njms.rutgers.edu
Public
Admissions: (973) 972-4631
Email:
njmsadmiss@njms.rutgers.edu
Financial aid: (973) 972-4376
Application deadline: 12/01
In-state tuition: $41,113
Out-of-state tuition: $62,028
Room/board/expenses: $17,870
Percent receiving grants: 36%
Average student indebtedness at graduation: $163,248
Enrollment: 732
men: 60%; women: 40%; minorities: 60%; underrepresented minorities: 19%; in state: 99%
Acceptance rate: 9%
Median MCAT total score: 32
Median GPA: 3.61
Most popular undergraduate majors: biological sciences: 60%; physical sciences: 16%; nonsciences: 18%; other: 6%
Percent of graduates entering primary-care specialties: 34.7%

Rutgers Robert Wood Johnson Medical School-New Brunswick[1]

125 Paterson Street
New Brunswick, NJ 08903-0019
rwjms.umdnj.edu
Public
Admissions: (732) 235-4576
Email: rwjapadm@umdnj.edu
Financial aid: (732) 235-4689
Tuition: N/A
Room/board/expenses: N/A
Enrollment: N/A

NEW MEXICO

University of New Mexico

Reginald Heber Fitz Hall
Room 107
Albuquerque, NM 87131
som.unm.edu
Public
Admissions: (505) 272-4766
Email: somadmissions@salud.unm.edu
Financial aid: (505) 272-8008
Application deadline: 11/01
In-state tuition: $19,233
Out-of-state tuition: $49,109
Room/board/expenses: $15,848
Percent receiving grants: 68%
Average student indebtedness at graduation: $146,137
Enrollment: 422
men: 48%; women: 52%; minorities: 57%; underrepresented minorities: 49%; in state: 92%
Acceptance rate: 8%
Median MCAT total score: 28
Median GPA: 3.68
Most popular undergraduate majors: biological sciences: 52%; physical sciences: 15%; nonsciences: 13%; other: 21%
Percent of graduates entering primary-care specialties: 45.6%

NEW YORK

Albany Medical College[1]

47 New Scotland Avenue
Albany, NY 12208
www.amc.edu/Academic/
Private
Admissions: (518) 262-5521
Email: admissions@mail.amc.edu
Financial aid: N/A
Tuition: N/A
Room/board/expenses: N/A
Enrollment: N/A

Columbia University

630 W. 168th Street
New York, NY 10032
ps.columbia.edu
Private
Admissions: (212) 305-3595
Email: psadmissions@columbia.edu
Financial aid: (212) 305-4100
Application deadline: 10/15
Tuition: $61,485
Room/board/expenses: $17,079
Percent receiving grants: 68%
Average student indebtedness at graduation: $132,220
Enrollment: 670
men: 50%; women: 50%; minorities: 40%; underrepresented minorities: 25%; in state: 31%
Acceptance rate: 4%
Median MCAT total score: 36
Median GPA: 3.82
Most popular undergraduate majors: biological sciences: 43%; physical sciences: 17%; nonsciences: 20%; other: 20%
Percent of graduates entering primary-care specialties: 30.4%

Cornell University (Weill)

1300 York Avenue
New York, NY 10065
www.weill.cornell.edu
Private
Admissions: (212) 746-1067
Email: wcmc-admissions@med.cornell.edu
Financial aid: (212) 746-1066
Application deadline: 10/15
Tuition: $54,650
Room/board/expenses: $12,880
Percent receiving grants: 69%
Average student indebtedness at graduation: $151,817
Enrollment: 423
men: 51%; women: 49%; minorities: 41%; underrepresented minorities: 17%; in state: 28%
Acceptance rate: 5%
Median MCAT total score: 36
Median GPA: 3.84
Most popular undergraduate majors: biological sciences: 28%; physical sciences: 30%; nonsciences: 14%; other: 28%
Percent of graduates entering primary-care specialties: 41.0%

Hofstra University

500 Hofstra University
Hempstead, NY 11549
medicine.hofstra.edu
Private
Admissions: (516) 463-7519
Email: medicine.admissions@hofstra.edu
Financial aid: N/A
Application deadline: 11/01
Tuition: $48,500
Room/board/expenses: $20,575
Percent receiving grants: 72%

Enrollment: 331
men: 52%; women: 48%; minorities: 39%; underrepresented minorities: 18%; in state: 52%
Acceptance rate: 4%
Median MCAT total score: 33
Median GPA: 3.64
Most popular undergraduate majors: biological sciences: 49%; physical sciences: 21%; nonsciences: 27%; other: 3%
Percent of graduates entering primary-care specialties: 31.0%

Icahn School of Medicine at Mount Sinai

1 Gustave L. Levy Place
PO Box 1217
New York, NY 10029
www.icahn.mssm.edu
Private
Admissions: (212) 241-6696
Email: admissions@mssm.edu
Financial aid: (212) 241-5245
Application deadline: 10/15
Tuition: $53,608
Room/board/expenses: $12,802
Percent receiving grants: 28%
Average student indebtedness at graduation: $151,647
Enrollment: 556
men: 50%; women: 50%; minorities: 43%; underrepresented minorities: 18%; in state: 31%
Acceptance rate: 9%
Median MCAT total score: 35
Median GPA: 3.82
Most popular undergraduate majors: biological sciences: 27%; physical sciences: 20%; nonsciences: 39%; other: 14%
Percent of graduates entering primary-care specialties: 49.3%

New York Medical College

40 Sunshine Cottage Road
Valhalla, NY 10595
www.nymc.edu
Private
Admissions: (914) 594-4507
Email: mdadmit@nymc.edu
Financial aid: (914) 594-4491
Application deadline: 01/31
Tuition: $54,746
Room/board/expenses: $19,388
Percent receiving grants: 51%
Average student indebtedness at graduation: $226,749
Enrollment: 823
men: 52%; women: 48%; minorities: 43%; underrepresented minorities: 21%; in state: 36%
Acceptance rate: 6%
Median MCAT total score: 32
Median GPA: 3.58
Most popular undergraduate majors: biological sciences: 49%; physical sciences: 11%; nonsciences: 16%; other: 24%
Percent of graduates entering primary-care specialties: 38.0%

New York University

550 First Avenue
New York, NY 10016
school.med.nyu.edu
Private
Admissions: (212) 263-5290
Email: admissions@nyumc.org
Financial aid: (212) 263-5286
Application deadline: 10/15
Tuition: $54,030
Room/board/expenses: $15,400
Percent receiving grants: 38%

Average student indebtedness at graduation: $160,702
Enrollment: 615
men: 53%; women: 47%; minorities: 45%; underrepresented minorities: 18%; in state: 34%
Acceptance rate: 5%
Median MCAT total score: 36
Median GPA: 3.87
Most popular undergraduate majors: biological sciences: 36%; physical sciences: 32%; nonsciences: 9%; other: 23%
Percent of graduates entering primary-care specialties: 41.0%

Stony Brook University-SUNY

Office of Admissions
Health Science Center, L4
Stony Brook, NY 11794-8434
medicine.stonybrookmedicine.edu/
Public
Admissions: (631) 444-2113
Email: somadmissions@stonybrookmedicine.edu
Financial aid: (631) 444-2341
Application deadline: 12/01
In-state tuition: $41,401
Out-of-state tuition: $66,411
Room/board/expenses: $11,413
Percent receiving grants: 25%
Average student indebtedness at graduation: $164,148
Enrollment: 516
men: 54%; women: 46%; minorities: 45%; underrepresented minorities: 12%; in state: 90%
Acceptance rate: 7%
Median MCAT total score: 32
Median GPA: 3.70
Most popular undergraduate majors: biological sciences: 55%; physical sciences: 20%; nonsciences: 17%; other: 8%
Percent of graduates entering primary-care specialties: 33.7%

SUNY Downstate Medical Center[1]

450 Clarkson Avenue
Box 60
Brooklyn, NY 11203
www.downstate.edu/college_of_medicine/
Public
Admissions: (718) 270-2446
Email: medadmissions@downstate.edu
Financial aid: N/A
Tuition: N/A
Room/board/expenses: N/A
Enrollment: N/A

SUNY-Syracuse[1]

766 Irving Avenue
Syracuse, NY 13210
www.upstate.edu/com/
Public
Admissions: (315) 464-4570
Email: admiss@upstate.edu
Financial aid: N/A
Tuition: N/A
Room/board/expenses: N/A
Enrollment: N/A

University at Buffalo-SUNY (Jacobs)

155 Biomedical Education Building
Buffalo, NY 14214
medicine.buffalo.edu
Public
Admissions: (716) 829-3466
Email: jjrosso@buffalo.edu

Financial aid: (716) 829-2491
Application deadline: 11/15
In-state tuition: $39,012
Out-of-state tuition: $64,022
Room/board/expenses: $15,113
Percent receiving grants: 22%
Average student indebtedness at graduation: $141,431
Enrollment: 569
men: 56%; women: 44%; minorities: 31%; underrepresented minorities: 16%; in state: 97%
Acceptance rate: 7%
Median MCAT total score: 10
Median GPA: 3.72
Most popular undergraduate majors: biological sciences: 37%; physical sciences: 18%; nonsciences: 29%; other: 16%
Percent of graduates entering primary-care specialties: 37.0%

University of Rochester

601 Elmwood Avenue
Box 706
Rochester, NY 14642
www.urmc.rochester.edu/education/md/admissions
Private
Admissions: (585) 275-4542
Email: mdadmish@urmc.rochester.edu
Financial aid: (585) 275-4523
Application deadline: 10/15
Tuition: $52,799
Room/board/expenses: $17,000
Percent receiving grants: 56%
Average student indebtedness at graduation: $130,512
Enrollment: 435
men: 49%; women: 51%; minorities: 39%; underrepresented minorities: 15%; in state: 50%
Acceptance rate: 5%
Median MCAT total score: 34
Median GPA: 3.79
Most popular undergraduate majors: biological sciences: 38%; physical sciences: 12%; nonsciences: 24%; other: 26%
Percent of graduates entering primary-care specialties: 35.6%

Yeshiva University (Einstein)

1300 Morris Park Avenue
Bronx, NY 10461
www.einstein.yu.edu
Private
Admissions: (718) 430-2106
Email: admissions@einstein.yu.edu
Financial aid: (718) 862-1813
Application deadline: 10/15
Tuition: $54,512
Room/board/expenses: $17,350
Percent receiving grants: 51%
Average student indebtedness at graduation: $155,016
Enrollment: 773
men: 52%; women: 48%; minorities: 30%; underrepresented minorities: 14%; in state: 45%
Acceptance rate: 4%
Median MCAT total score: 33
Median GPA: 3.83
Most popular undergraduate majors: biological sciences: 42%; physical sciences: 14%; nonsciences: 17%; other: 27%
Percent of graduates entering primary-care specialties: 46.0%

NORTH CAROLINA

Duke University

DUMC 3710
Durham, NC 27710
dukemed.duke.edu
Private
Admissions: (919) 684-2985
Email: medadm@mc.duke.edu
Financial aid: (919) 684-6649
Application deadline: 10/15
Tuition: $57,329
Room/board/expenses: $17,304
Percent receiving grants: 68%
Average student indebtedness at graduation: $115,156
Enrollment: 453
men: 53%; women: 47%; minorities: 51%; underrepresented minorities: 17%; in state: 11%
Acceptance rate: 4%
Median MCAT total score: 36
Median GPA: 3.80
Most popular undergraduate majors: biological sciences: 46%; physical sciences: 28%; nonsciences: 10%; other: 16%
Percent of graduates entering primary-care specialties: 44.6%

East Carolina University (Brody)

600 Moye Boulevard
Greenville, NC 27834
www.ecu.edu/bsomadmissions
Public
Admissions: (252) 744-2202
Email: somadmissions@ecu.edu
Financial aid: (252) 744-2278
Application deadline: 11/01
In-state tuition: $22,281
Out-of-state tuition: N/A
Room/board/expenses: $15,536
Percent receiving grants: 85%
Average student indebtedness at graduation: $105,659
Enrollment: 311
men: 51%; women: 49%; minorities: 32%; underrepresented minorities: 16%; in state: 100%
Acceptance rate: 13%
Median MCAT total score: 29
Median GPA: 3.69
Most popular undergraduate majors: biological sciences: 39%; physical sciences: 11%; nonsciences: 11%; other: 39%
Percent of graduates entering primary-care specialties: 56.0%

University of North Carolina–Chapel Hill

CB #7000
4030 Bondurant Hall
Chapel Hill, NC 27599-7000
www.med.unc.edu/admit/
Public
Admissions: (919) 962-8331
Email: admissions@med.unc.edu
Financial aid: (919) 962-6117
Application deadline: 10/15
In-state tuition: $23,772
Out-of-state tuition: $50,651
Room/board/expenses: $33,192
Percent receiving grants: 81%
Average student indebtedness at graduation: $94,354
Enrollment: 829
men: 51%; women: 49%; minorities: 34%; underrepresented minorities: 21%; in state: 93%
Acceptance rate: 4%
Median MCAT total score: 32
Median GPA: 3.73
Most popular undergraduate majors: biological sciences: 41%; physical sciences: 15%; nonsciences: 18%; other: 26%
Percent of graduates entering primary-care specialties: 65.0%

Wake Forest University

Medical Center Boulevard
Winston-Salem, NC 27157
www.wakehealth.edu/school/md-program
Private
Admissions: (336) 716-4264
Email: medadmit@wakehealth.edu
Financial aid: (336) 716-2889
Application deadline: 11/01
Tuition: $51,800
Room/board/expenses: $24,604
Percent receiving grants: 50%
Average student indebtedness at graduation: $173,736
Enrollment: 467
men: 52%; women: 48%; minorities: 27%; underrepresented minorities: 12%; in state: 35%
Acceptance rate: 3%
Median MCAT total score: 31
Median GPA: 3.58
Most popular undergraduate majors: biological sciences: 45%; physical sciences: 19%; nonsciences: 23%; other: 13%
Percent of graduates entering primary-care specialties: 36.0%

NORTH DAKOTA

University of North Dakota[1]

501 N. Columbia Road
Stop 9037
Grand Forks, ND 58202-9037
www.med.und.nodak.edu
Public
Admissions: (701) 777-4221
Financial aid: N/A
Tuition: N/A
Room/board/expenses: N/A
Enrollment: N/A

OHIO

Case Western Reserve University

10900 Euclid Avenue
Cleveland, OH 44106
case.edu/medicine
Private
Admissions: (216) 368-3450
Email: casemed-admissions@case.edu
Financial aid: (216) 368-3666
Application deadline: 11/01
Tuition: $59,303
Room/board/expenses: $20,689
Percent receiving grants: 57%
Average student indebtedness at graduation: $164,062
Enrollment: 883
men: 52%; women: 48%; minorities: 45%; underrepresented minorities: 12%; in state: 21%
Acceptance rate: 10%
Median MCAT total score: 35
Median GPA: 3.73
Most popular undergraduate majors: biological sciences: 30%; physical sciences: 28%; nonsciences: 7%; other: 35%
Percent of graduates entering primary-care specialties: 34.9%

Northeast Ohio Medical University[1]

4209 State Route 44
PO Box 95
Rootstown, OH 44272-0095
www.neomed.edu/
Public
Admissions: (330) 325-6270
Email: admission@neomed.edu
Financial aid: N/A
Tuition: N/A
Room/board/expenses: N/A
Enrollment: N/A

Ohio State University

200 Meiling Hall
370 W. Ninth Avenue
Columbus, OH 43210-1238
medicine.osu.edu
Public
Admissions: (614) 292-7137
Email: medicine@osu.edu
Financial aid: (614) 688-4955
Application deadline: 11/01
In-state tuition: $31,687
Out-of-state tuition: $36,361
Room/board/expenses: $10,810
Percent receiving grants: 79%
Average student indebtedness at graduation: $161,412
Enrollment: 756
men: 52%; women: 48%; minorities: 49%; underrepresented minorities: 23%; in state: 86%
Acceptance rate: 7%
Median MCAT total score: 34
Median GPA: 3.77
Most popular undergraduate majors: biological sciences: 38%; physical sciences: 23%; nonsciences: 11%; other: 28%
Percent of graduates entering primary-care specialties: 43.7%

University of Cincinnati

231 Albert Sabin Way
Cincinnati, OH 45267-0552
www.med.uc.edu
Public
Admissions: (513) 558-7314
Email: MDAdmissions@uc.edu
Financial aid: (513) 558-5991
Application deadline: 11/15
In-state tuition: $32,174
Out-of-state tuition: $50,438
Room/board/expenses: $19,096
Percent receiving grants: 40%
Average student indebtedness at graduation: $173,699
Enrollment: 692
men: 51%; women: 49%; minorities: 32%; underrepresented minorities: 14%; in state: 90%
Acceptance rate: 8%
Median MCAT total score: 33
Median GPA: 3.73
Most popular undergraduate majors: biological sciences: 48%; physical sciences: 24%; nonsciences: 8%; other: 20%
Percent of graduates entering primary-care specialties: 35.4%

University of Toledo

3000 Arlington Avenue
Toledo, OH 43614
hsc.utoledo.edu
Public
Admissions: (419) 383-4229
Email: medadmissions@utoledo.edu
Financial aid: (419) 530-5812
Application deadline: 11/01
In-state tuition: $34,380
Out-of-state tuition: $64,886
Room/board/expenses: $11,634
Percent receiving grants: 17%
Average student indebtedness at graduation: $186,388
Enrollment: 701
men: 56%; women: 44%; minorities: 23%; underrepresented minorities: 5%; in state: 92%
Acceptance rate: 7%
Median MCAT total score: 31
Median GPA: 3.70
Most popular undergraduate majors: biological sciences: 59%; physical sciences: 18%; nonsciences: 12%; other: 11%
Percent of graduates entering primary-care specialties: 37.7%

Wright State University (Boonshoft)

3640 Col. Glenn Highway
Dayton, OH 45435-0001
medicine.wright.edu/
Public
Admissions: (937) 775-2934
Email: som_saa@wright.edu
Financial aid: (937) 775-2934
Application deadline: 12/01
In-state tuition: $37,054
Out-of-state tuition: $54,006
Room/board/expenses: $12,616
Percent receiving grants: 40%
Average student indebtedness at graduation: $176,857
Enrollment: 439
men: 49%; women: 51%; minorities: 28%; underrepresented minorities: 16%; in state: 92%
Acceptance rate: 7%
Median MCAT total score: 28
Median GPA: 3.77
Most popular undergraduate majors: biological sciences: N/A; physical sciences: N/A; nonsciences: N/A; other: N/A
Percent of graduates entering primary-care specialties: 44.1%

OKLAHOMA

University of Oklahoma

PO Box 26901
BMSB 357
Oklahoma City, OK 73126
www.medicine.ouhsc.edu
Public
Admissions: (405) 271-2331
Email: adminmed@ouhsc.edu
Financial aid: (405) 271-2118
Application deadline: 10/15
In-state tuition: $26,176
Out-of-state tuition: $55,522
Room/board/expenses: $20,926
Percent receiving grants: 48%
Average student indebtedness at graduation: $144,155
Enrollment: 648
men: 61%; women: 39%; minorities: 24%; underrepresented minorities: 11%; in state: 91%
Acceptance rate: 10%
Median MCAT total score: 30
Median GPA: 3.78
Most popular undergraduate majors: biological sciences: 40%; physical sciences: 28%; nonsciences: 16%; other: 16%
Percent of graduates entering primary-care specialties: 40.6%

OREGON

Oregon Health and Science University

2730 S.W. Moody Avenue
CL5MD
Portland, OR 97201-3098
www.ohsu.edu/xd
Public
Admissions: (503) 494-2998
Financial aid: (503) 494-7800
Application deadline: 10/14
In-state tuition: $41,312
Out-of-state tuition: $57,856
Room/board/expenses: $19,500
Percent receiving grants: 73%
Average student indebtedness at graduation: $195,632
Enrollment: 556
men: 49%; women: 51%; minorities: 24%; underrepresented minorities: 12%; in state: 72%
Acceptance rate: 4%
Median MCAT total score: 31
Median GPA: 3.68
Most popular undergraduate majors: biological sciences: 43%; physical sciences: 14%; nonsciences: 16%; other: 27%
Percent of graduates entering primary-care specialties: 45.6%

PENNSYLVANIA

The Commonwealth Medical College[1]

525 Pine Street
Scranton, PA 18509
www.tcmc.edu/
Private
Admissions: N/A
Email: admissions@tcmc.edu
Financial aid: N/A
Tuition: N/A
Room/board/expenses: N/A
Enrollment: N/A

Drexel University

2900 Queen Lane
Philadelphia, PA 19129
www.drexelmed.edu
Private
Admissions: (215) 991-8202
Email: Medadmis@drexel.edu
Financial aid: (215) 991-8210
Application deadline: 12/01
Tuition: $54,849
Room/board/expenses: $17,720
Percent receiving grants: 30%
Average student indebtedness at graduation: $219,139
Enrollment: 1,067
men: 50%; women: 50%; minorities: 47%; underrepresented minorities: 14%; in state: 33%
Acceptance rate: 4%
Median MCAT total score: 31
Median GPA: 3.62
Most popular undergraduate majors: biological sciences: N/A; physical sciences: N/A; nonsciences: N/A; other: N/A
Percent of graduates entering primary-care specialties: 38.8%

Pennsylvania State University College of Medicine[1]

500 University Drive
Hershey, PA 17033
med.psu.edu/web/college/home
Public
Admissions: (717) 531-8755
Email: StudentAdmissions@hmc.psu.edu

Financial aid: N/A
Tuition: N/A
Room/board/expenses: N/A
Enrollment: N/A

Temple University (Katz)

3500 N. Broad Street
MERB 1140
Philadelphia, PA 19140
medicine.temple.edu
Private
Admissions: (215) 707-3656
Email: medadmissions@temple.edu
Financial aid: (215) 707-0749
Application deadline: 12/15
Tuition: $48,533
Room/board/expenses: $13,883
Percent receiving grants: 60%
Average student indebtedness at graduation: $217,059
Enrollment: 867
men: 54%; women: 46%; minorities: 36%; underrepresented minorities: 17%; in state: 59%
Acceptance rate: 4%
Median MCAT total score: 31
Median GPA: 3.69
Most popular undergraduate majors: biological sciences: 46%; physical sciences: 17%; nonsciences: 24%; other: 13%
Percent of graduates entering primary-care specialties: 43.0%

Thomas Jefferson University (Kimmel)

1025 Walnut Street
Room 100
Philadelphia, PA 19107-5083
www.tju.edu
Private
Admissions: (215) 955-6983
Email: jmc.admissions@jefferson.edu
Financial aid: (215) 955-2867
Application deadline: 11/15
Tuition: $54,161
Room/board/expenses: $17,391
Percent receiving grants: 48%
Average student indebtedness at graduation: $173,150
Enrollment: 1,056
men: 50%; women: 50%; minorities: 34%; underrepresented minorities: 11%; in state: 47%
Acceptance rate: 4%
Median MCAT total score: 32
Median GPA: 3.70
Most popular undergraduate majors: biological sciences: 36%; physical sciences: 18%; nonsciences: 14%; other: 32%
Percent of graduates entering primary-care specialties: 44.4%

University of Pennsylvania (Perelman)

3400 Civic Center Boulevard
Philadelphia, PA 19104-5162
www.med.upenn.edu
Private
Admissions: (215) 898-8001
Email: admiss@mail.med.upenn.edu
Financial aid: (215) 573-3423
Application deadline: 10/15
Tuition: $56,784
Room/board/expenses: $22,220
Percent receiving grants: 75%
Average student indebtedness at graduation: $118,390

Enrollment: 616
men: 55%; women: 45%; minorities: 46%; underrepresented minorities: 24%; in state: 24%
Acceptance rate: 5%
Median MCAT total score: 38
Median GPA: 3.87
Most popular undergraduate majors: biological sciences: 51%; physical sciences: 20%; nonsciences: 19%; other: 10%
Percent of graduates entering primary-care specialties: 37.0%

University of Pittsburgh

401 Scaife Hall
Pittsburgh, PA 15261
www.medschool.pitt.edu
Public
Admissions: (412) 648-9891
Email: admissions@medschool.pitt.edu
Financial aid: (412) 648-9891
Application deadline: 10/15
In-state tuition: $50,852
Out-of-state tuition: $52,306
Room/board/expenses: $17,190
Percent receiving grants: 56%
Average student indebtedness at graduation: $136,135
Enrollment: 583
men: 53%; women: 47%; minorities: 46%; underrepresented minorities: 15%; in state: 26%
Acceptance rate: 7%
Median MCAT total score: 36
Median GPA: 3.81
Most popular undergraduate majors: biological sciences: 52%; physical sciences: 15%; nonsciences: 15%; other: 18%
Percent of graduates entering primary-care specialties: 39.0%

PUERTO RICO

Ponce School of Medicine[1]

PO Box 7004
Ponce, PR 00732
www.psm.edu
Private
Admissions: (787) 840-2575
Email: admissions@psm.edu
Financial aid: N/A
Tuition: N/A
Room/board/expenses: N/A
Enrollment: N/A

San Juan Bautista School of Medicine[1]

PO Box 4968
Caguas, PR 00726-4968
www.sanjuanbautista.edu
Private
Admissions: (787) 743-3038
Email: admissions@sanjuanbautista.edu
Financial aid: N/A
Tuition: N/A
Room/board/expenses: N/A
Enrollment: N/A

Universidad Central del Caribe[1]

PO Box 60-327
Bayamon, PR 00960-6032
www.uccaribe.edu/medicine/
Private
Admissions: (787) 798-3001
Email: admissions@uccaribe.edu
Financial aid: N/A
Tuition: N/A
Room/board/expenses: N/A
Enrollment: N/A

University of Puerto Rico School of Medicine[1]

PO Box 365067
San Juan, PR 00936-5067
www.md.rcm.upr.edu/
Public
Admissions: (787) 758-2525
Financial aid: N/A
Tuition: N/A
Room/board/expenses: N/A
Enrollment: N/A

RHODE ISLAND

Brown University (Alpert)

222 Richmond Street
Box G-M
Providence, RI 02912-9706
med.brown.edu
Private
Admissions: (401) 863-2149
Email: medschool_admissions@brown.edu
Financial aid: (401) 863-1142
Application deadline: 12/01
Tuition: $57,783
Room/board/expenses: $18,571
Percent receiving grants: 49%
Average student indebtedness at graduation: $126,631
Enrollment: 526
men: 48%; women: 52%; minorities: 54%; underrepresented minorities: 22%; in state: 9%
Acceptance rate: 3%
Median MCAT total score: 33
Median GPA: 3.69
Most popular undergraduate majors: biological sciences: 24%; physical sciences: 14%; nonsciences: 32%; other: 30%
Percent of graduates entering primary-care specialties: 42.0%

SOUTH CAROLINA

Medical University of South Carolina

96 Jonathan Lucas Street
Suite 601
Charleston, SC 29425
www.musc.edu/com1
Public
Admissions: (843) 792-2055
Email: taylorwl@musc.edu
Financial aid: (843) 792-2536
Application deadline: 11/01
In-state tuition: $35,662
Out-of-state tuition: $62,126
Room/board/expenses: $13,340
Percent receiving grants: 53%
Average student indebtedness at graduation: $196,668
Enrollment: 735
men: 57%; women: 43%; minorities: 26%; underrepresented minorities: 17%; in state: 86%
Acceptance rate: 11%
Median MCAT total score: 30
Median GPA: 3.72
Most popular undergraduate majors: biological sciences: 48%; physical sciences: 20%; nonsciences: 6%; other: 26%
Percent of graduates entering primary-care specialties: 29.8%

University of South Carolina[1]

6311 Garners Ferry Road
Columbia, SC 29208
www.med.sc.edu
Public
Admissions: (803) 216-3625
Email: admissions@uscmed.sc.edu
Financial aid: N/A
Tuition: N/A
Room/board/expenses: N/A
Enrollment: N/A

University of South Carolina-Greenville[1]

607 Grove Road
Greenville, SC 29605
Private
Admissions: N/A
Financial aid: N/A
Tuition: N/A
Room/board/expenses: N/A
Enrollment: N/A

SOUTH DAKOTA

University of South Dakota (Sanford)

1400 W. 22nd Street
Sioux Falls, SD 57105
www.usd.edu/medstudentaffairs
Public
Admissions: (605) 658-6302
Email: md@usd.edu
Financial aid: (605) 658-6303
Application deadline: 11/01
In-state tuition: $31,562
Out-of-state tuition: $69,454
Room/board/expenses: $17,981
Percent receiving grants: 84%
Average student indebtedness at graduation: $138,034
Enrollment: 244
men: 55%; women: 45%; minorities: 11%; underrepresented minorities: 7%; in state: 95%
Acceptance rate: 14%
Median MCAT total score: 30
Median GPA: 3.84
Most popular undergraduate majors: biological sciences: 36%; physical sciences: 20%; nonsciences: 11%; other: 33%
Percent of graduates entering primary-care specialties: 39.6%

TENNESSEE

East Tennessee State University (Quillen)

PO Box 70694
Johnson City, TN 37614
www.etsu.edu/com
Public
Admissions: (423) 439-2033
Email: sacom@etsu.edu
Financial aid: (423) 439-2035
Application deadline: 11/15
In-state tuition: $34,271
Out-of-state tuition: $65,457
Room/board/expenses: $11,407
Average student indebtedness at graduation: $184,284
Enrollment: 278
men: 58%; women: 42%; minorities: 12%; underrepresented minorities: 4%; in state: 97%
Acceptance rate: 6%
Median MCAT total score: 28
Median GPA: 3.65

Most popular undergraduate majors: biological sciences: 33%; physical sciences: 21%; nonsciences: 10%; other: 36%
Percent of graduates entering primary-care specialties: 43.9%

Meharry Medical College[1]

1005 D. B. Todd Jr. Boulevard
Nashville, TN 37208
www.mmc.edu/education/som/
Private
Admissions: (615) 327-6223
Email: admissions@mmc.edu
Financial aid: N/A
Tuition: N/A
Room/board/expenses: N/A
Enrollment: N/A

University of Tennessee Health Science Center

910 Madison Avenue
Suite 1002
Memphis, TN 38163
www.uthsc.edu/Medicine/
Public
Admissions: (901) 448-5559
Email: diharris@uthsc.edu
Financial aid: (901) 448-5568
Application deadline: 11/15
In-state tuition: $36,461
Out-of-state tuition: $68,891
Room/board/expenses: $19,380
Percent receiving grants: 49%
Average student indebtedness at graduation: $166,792
Enrollment: 671
men: 59%; women: 41%; minorities: 27%; underrepresented minorities: 14%; in state: 97%
Acceptance rate: 13%
Median MCAT total score: 31
Median GPA: 3.69
Most popular undergraduate majors: biological sciences: 40%; physical sciences: 21%; nonsciences: 13%; other: 26%
Percent of graduates entering primary-care specialties: 52.0%

Vanderbilt University

1211 22nd Avenue South and 201 Light Hall
Nashville, TN 37232-2104
medschool.vanderbilt.edu/md-admissions
Private
Admissions: (615) 322-2145
Email: mdadmissions@vanderbilt.edu
Financial aid: (615) 322-2145
Application deadline: 11/01
Tuition: $50,932
Room/board/expenses: $19,168
Percent receiving grants: 74%
Average student indebtedness at graduation: $140,226
Enrollment: 402
men: 57%; women: 43%; minorities: 40%; underrepresented minorities: 23%; in state: 17%
Acceptance rate: 4%
Median MCAT total score: 37
Median GPA: 3.88
Most popular undergraduate majors: biological sciences: 40%; physical sciences: 17%; nonsciences: 4%; other: 39%
Percent of graduates entering primary-care specialties: 34.9%

TEXAS

Baylor College of Medicine

1 Baylor Plaza
Houston, TX 77030
www.bcm.edu
Private
Admissions: (713) 798-4842
Email: admissions@bcm.tmc.edu
Financial aid: (713) 798-4612
Application deadline: 11/01
Tuition: $18,563
Room/board/expenses: $28,287
Percent receiving grants: 42%
Average student indebtedness at graduation: $105,151
Enrollment: 742
men: 51%; women: 49%; minorities: 56%; underrepresented minorities: 16%; in state: 89%
Acceptance rate: 4%
Median MCAT total score: 35
Median GPA: 3.86
Most popular undergraduate majors: biological sciences: 24%; physical sciences: 25%; nonsciences: 3%; other: 48%
Percent of graduates entering primary-care specialties: 48.3%

Texas A&M Health Science Center

8447 State Highway 47
Bryan, TX 77807-3260
medicine.tamhsc.edu
Public
Admissions: (979) 436-0237
Email: admissions@medicine.tamhsc.edu
Financial aid: (979) 436-0199
Application deadline: 10/01
In-state tuition: $16,432
Out-of-state tuition: $29,532
Room/board/expenses: $15,416
Percent receiving grants: 67%
Average student indebtedness at graduation: $118,501
Enrollment: 801
men: 52%; women: 48%; minorities: 49%; underrepresented minorities: 17%; in state: 96%
Acceptance rate: 16%
Median MCAT total score: 30
Median GPA: 3.72
Most popular undergraduate majors: biological sciences: 50%; physical sciences: 14%; nonsciences: 3%; other: 33%
Percent of graduates entering primary-care specialties: 42.0%

Texas Tech University-El Paso[1]

5001 El Paso Drive
El Paso, TX 79905
Private
Admissions: N/A
Financial aid: N/A
Tuition: N/A
Room/board/expenses: N/A
Enrollment: N/A

Texas Tech University Health Sciences Center

3601 Fourth Street
Lubbock, TX 79430
www.ttuhsc.edu/som/
Public
Admissions: (806) 743-2297
Email: somadm@ttuhsc.edu
Financial aid: (806) 743-3025
Application deadline: 10/01
In-state tuition: $17,737
Out-of-state tuition: $30,837
Room/board/expenses: $15,290
Percent receiving grants: 74%
Average student indebtedness at graduation: $130,917
Enrollment: 665
men: 57%; women: 43%; minorities: 14%; underrepresented minorities: 14%; in state: 90%
Acceptance rate: 8%
Median MCAT total score: 32
Median GPA: 3.62
Most popular undergraduate majors: biological sciences: 51%; physical sciences: 11%; nonsciences: 16%; other: 22%
Percent of graduates entering primary-care specialties: 43.7%

University of Texas Health Science Center-Houston

6431 Fannin Street
MSB G.400
Houston, TX 77030
med.uth.edu
Public
Admissions: (713) 500-5116
Email: ms.admissions@uth.tmc.edu
Financial aid: (713) 500-3860
Application deadline: 10/01
In-state tuition: $20,092
Out-of-state tuition: $31,192
Room/board/expenses: $16,230
Percent receiving grants: 28%
Average student indebtedness at graduation: $108,683
Enrollment: 982
men: 57%; women: 43%; minorities: 44%; underrepresented minorities: 23%; in state: 93%
Acceptance rate: 14%
Median MCAT total score: 32
Median GPA: 3.79
Most popular undergraduate majors: biological sciences: 50%; physical sciences: 22%; nonsciences: 10%; other: 18%
Percent of graduates entering primary-care specialties: 30.4%

University of Texas Health Science Center-San Antonio

7703 Floyd Curl Drive
San Antonio, TX 78229-3900
som.uthscsa.edu
Public
Admissions: (210) 567-6080
Email: medadmissions@uthscsa.edu
Financial aid: (210) 567-2635
Application deadline: 10/01
In-state tuition: $17,661
Out-of-state tuition: $32,068
Room/board/expenses: $15,470

Percent receiving grants: 58%
Average student indebtedness at graduation: $116,909
Enrollment: 859
men: 55%; women: 45%; minorities: 44%; underrepresented minorities: 27%; in state: 90%
Acceptance rate: 10%
Median MCAT total score: 31
Median GPA: 3.68
Most popular undergraduate majors: biological sciences: 54%; physical sciences: 19%; nonsciences: 14%; other: 14%
Percent of graduates entering primary-care specialties: 37.6%

University of Texas Medical Branch-Galveston[1]

301 University Boulevard
Galveston, TX 77555-0133
www.som.utmb.edu/
Public
Admissions: (409) 772-6958
Email: somadmis@utmb.edu
Financial aid: N/A
Tuition: N/A
Room/board/expenses: N/A
Enrollment: N/A

University of Texas Southwestern Medical Center

5323 Harry Hines Boulevard
Dallas, TX 75390
www.utsouthwestern.edu/
Public
Admissions: (214) 648-5617
Email: admissions@utsouthwestern.edu
Financial aid: (214) 648-3606
Application deadline: 10/01
In-state tuition: $19,343
Out-of-state tuition: $32,443
Room/board/expenses: $23,244
Percent receiving grants: 59%
Average student indebtedness at graduation: $104,000
Enrollment: 955
men: 54%; women: 46%; minorities: 49%; underrepresented minorities: 14%; in state: 86%
Acceptance rate: 8%
Median MCAT total score: 34
Median GPA: 3.83
Most popular undergraduate majors: biological sciences: 53%; physical sciences: 27%; nonsciences: 13%; other: 7%
Percent of graduates entering primary-care specialties: 43.5%

UTAH

University of Utah

30 N. 1900 E.
Salt Lake City, UT 84132-2101
medicine.utah.edu
Public
Admissions: (801) 581-7498
Email: deans.admissions@hsc.utah.edu
Financial aid: (801) 581-6499
Application deadline: 11/01
In-state tuition: $36,094
Out-of-state tuition: $67,374

Room/board/expenses: $10,782
Percent receiving grants: 74%
Average student indebtedness at graduation: $166,109
Enrollment: 406
men: 56%; women: 44%; minorities: 21%; underrepresented minorities: 5%; in state: 82%
Acceptance rate: 6%
Median MCAT total score: 30
Median GPA: 3.71
Most popular undergraduate majors: biological sciences: 35%; physical sciences: 33%; nonsciences: 9%; other: 23%
Percent of graduates entering primary-care specialties: 37.3%

VERMONT

University of Vermont

E-126 Given Building
89 Beaumont Avenue
Burlington, VT 05405
www.uvm.edu/medicine/admissions/
Public
Admissions: (802) 656-2154
Email: medadmissions@uvm.edu
Financial aid: (802) 656-5700
Application deadline: 11/15
In-state tuition: $36,216
Out-of-state tuition: $60,776
Room/board/expenses: $10,626
Percent receiving grants: 65%
Average student indebtedness at graduation: $178,064
Enrollment: 464
men: 50%; women: 50%; minorities: 31%; underrepresented minorities: 13%; in state: 30%
Acceptance rate: 4%
Median MCAT total score: 31
Median GPA: 3.65
Most popular undergraduate majors: biological sciences: 46%; physical sciences: 13%; nonsciences: 21%; other: 20%
Percent of graduates entering primary-care specialties: 42.0%

VIRGINIA

Eastern Virginia Medical School

721 Fairfax Avenue
PO Box 1980
Norfolk, VA 23501-1980
www.evms.edu
Public
Admissions: (757) 446-5812
Email: mclendm@evms.edu
Financial aid: (757) 446-5804
Application deadline: 11/15
In-state tuition: $32,616
Out-of-state tuition: $57,802
Room/board/expenses: $14,270
Percent receiving grants: 24%
Average student indebtedness at graduation: $191,619
Enrollment: 580
men: 57%; women: 43%; minorities: 37%; underrepresented minorities: 13%; in state: 51%
Acceptance rate: 5%
Median MCAT total score: 32
Median GPA: 3.56
Most popular undergraduate majors: biological sciences: 50%; physical sciences: 24%; nonsciences: 13%; other: 13%

Percent of graduates entering primary-care specialties: 53.3%

University of Virginia

PO Box 800793
McKim Hall
Charlottesville, VA 22908-0793
www.medicine.virginia.edu/education/medical-students/admissions
Public
Admissions: (434) 924-5571
Email: SOMADM@virginia.edu
Financial aid: (434) 924-0033
Application deadline: 11/01
In-state tuition: $48,036
Out-of-state tuition: $58,160
Room/board/expenses: $21,466
Percent receiving grants: 63%
Average student indebtedness at graduation: $120,301
Enrollment: 629
men: 54%; women: 46%; minorities: 46%; underrepresented minorities: 20%; in state: 51%
Acceptance rate: 10%
Median MCAT total score: 34
Median GPA: 3.86
Most popular undergraduate majors: biological sciences: 42%; physical sciences: 16%; nonsciences: 12%; other: 30%
Percent of graduates entering primary-care specialties: 38.4%

Virginia Commonwealth University

PO Box 980565
Richmond, VA 23298-0565
www.medschool.vcu.edu
Public
Admissions: (804) 828-9629
Email: somume@hsc.vcu.edu
Financial aid: (804) 828-4006
Application deadline: 10/15
In-state tuition: $32,113
Out-of-state tuition: $49,193
Room/board/expenses: $14,834
Percent receiving grants: 48%
Average student indebtedness at graduation: $151,048
Enrollment: 833
men: 54%; women: 46%; minorities: 44%; underrepresented minorities: 13%; in state: 54%
Acceptance rate: 4%
Median MCAT total score: 31
Median GPA: 3.60
Most popular undergraduate majors: biological sciences: 47%; physical sciences: 6%; nonsciences: 5%; other: 43%
Percent of graduates entering primary-care specialties: 50.1%

Virginia Tech Carilion School of Medicine[1]

2 Riverside Circle
Roanoke, VA 24016
www.vtc.vt.edu/
Public
Admissions: (540) 526-2560
Email: VTCAdmissions2015@carilionclinic.org
Financial aid: N/A
Tuition: N/A
Room/board/expenses: N/A
Enrollment: N/A

WASHINGTON

University of Washington

PO Box 356350
Seattle, WA 98195
www.uwmedicine.org/admissions
Public
Admissions: (206) 543-7212
Email: askuwsom@uw.edu
Financial aid: (206) 685-9229
Application deadline: 10/15
In-state tuition: $33,964
Out-of-state tuition: $64,399
Room/board/expenses: $16,890
Percent receiving grants: 77%
Average student indebtedness at graduation: $150,633
Enrollment: 959
men: 46%; women: 54%; minorities: 22%; underrepresented minorities: 9%; in state: 92%
Acceptance rate: 4%
Median MCAT total score: 31
Median GPA: 3.73
Most popular undergraduate majors: biological sciences: 53%; physical sciences: 16%; nonsciences: 12%; other: 19%
Percent of graduates entering primary-care specialties: 56.3%

WEST VIRGINIA

Marshall University (Edwards)

1600 Medical Center Drive
Huntington, WV 25701-3655
musom.marshall.edu
Public
Admissions: (800) 544-8514
Email: warren@marshall.edu
Financial aid: (304) 691-8739
Application deadline: 11/01
In-state tuition: $20,100
Out-of-state tuition: $47,750
Room/board/expenses: $14,560
Percent receiving grants: 60%
Average student indebtedness at graduation: $158,408
Enrollment: 295
men: 63%; women: 37%; minorities: 18%; underrepresented minorities: 9%; in state: 64%
Acceptance rate: 7%
Median MCAT total score: 28
Median GPA: 3.58
Most popular undergraduate majors: biological sciences: 56%; physical sciences: 20%; nonsciences: 10%; other: 14%
Percent of graduates entering primary-care specialties: 42.6%

West Virginia University

1 Medical Center Drive
Morgantown, WV 26506-9111
medicine.hsc.wvu.edu/students
Public
Admissions: (304) 293-2408
Email: medadmissions@ hsc.wvu.edu
Financial aid: (304) 293-3706
Application deadline: 11/01
In-state tuition: $29,295
Out-of-state tuition: $56,673
Room/board/expenses: $15,200
Percent receiving grants: 52%
Average student indebtedness at graduation: $141,807
Enrollment: 429
men: 51%; women: 49%; minorities: 21%; underrepresented minorities: 8%; in state: 60%
Acceptance rate: 4%
Median MCAT total score: 29
Median GPA: 3.73
Most popular undergraduate majors: biological sciences: 43%; physical sciences: 8%; nonsciences: 8%; other: 32%
Percent of graduates entering primary-care specialties: 46.0%

WISCONSIN

Medical College of Wisconsin

8701 Watertown Plank Road
Milwaukee, WI 53226
www.mcw.edu/medical-school/
Private
Admissions: (414) 955-8246
Email: medschool@mcw.edu
Financial aid: (414) 955-8208
Application deadline: 11/01
Tuition: $46,450
Room/board/expenses: $9,500
Percent receiving grants: 66%
Average student indebtedness at graduation: $173,664
Enrollment: 845
men: 55%; women: 45%; minorities: 27%; underrepresented minorities: 13%; in state: 51%
Acceptance rate: 8%
Median MCAT total score: 30
Median GPA: 3.75
Most popular undergraduate majors: biological sciences: 53%; physical sciences: 15%; nonsciences: 5%; other: 28%
Percent of graduates entering primary-care specialties: 40.3%

University of Wisconsin-Madison

750 Highland Avenue
Madison, WI 53705-2221
www.med.wisc.edu/education
Public
Admissions: (608) 263-4925
Email: medadmissions@ med.wisc.edu
Financial aid: (608) 262-3060
Application deadline: 11/01
In-state tuition: $27,259
Out-of-state tuition: $37,155
Room/board/expenses: $22,875
Percent receiving grants: 38%
Average student indebtedness at graduation: $138,339
Enrollment: 727
men: 51%; women: 49%; minorities: 26%; underrepresented minorities: 11%; in state: 76%
Acceptance rate: 6%
Median MCAT total score: 32
Median GPA: 3.80
Most popular undergraduate majors: biological sciences: 49%; physical sciences: 25%; nonsciences: 9%; other: 17%
Percent of graduates entering primary-care specialties: 41.5%

INSTITUTIONS THAT GRANT THE DOCTOR OF OSTEOPATHIC MEDICINE (D.O.) DEGREE

ALABAMA

Alabama College of Osteopathic Medicine[1]
445 Health Sciences Boulevard
Dothan, AL 36303
Private
Admissions: N/A
Financial aid: N/A
Tuition: N/A
Room/board/expenses: N/A
Enrollment: N/A

ARIZONA

A.T. Still University of Health Sciences-Mesa[1]
5850 E. Still Circle
Mesa, AZ 85206
www.atsu.edu/soma/index.htm
Private
Admissions: (866) 626-2878
Email: admissions@atsu.edu
Financial aid: N/A
Tuition: N/A
Room/board/expenses: N/A
Enrollment: N/A

Midwestern University[1]
19555 N. 59th Avenue
Glendale, AZ 85308
www.midwestern.edu
Private
Admissions: (623) 572-3215
Email: admissaz@midwestern.edu
Financial aid: N/A
Tuition: N/A
Room/board/expenses: N/A
Enrollment: N/A

CALIFORNIA

Touro University-California
1310 Club Drive
Vallejo, CA 94592
www.tu.edu
Private
Admissions: (707) 638-5270
Email: steven.davis@tu.edu
Financial aid: (707) 638-5280
Application deadline: 03/15
Tuition: $50,225
Room/board/expenses: $19,686
Percent receiving grants: 8%
Enrollment: 540
men: 57%; women: 43%; minorities: 47%; underrepresented minorities: 5%; in state: 77%
Acceptance rate: 5%
Median MCAT total score: 31
Median GPA: 3.50
Most popular undergraduate majors: biological sciences: 54%; physical sciences: 16%; nonsciences: 5%; other: 25%
Percent of graduates entering primary-care specialties: 57.0%

Western University of Health Sciences
309 E. Second Street
Pomona, CA 91766-1854
prospective.westernu.edu/index.html
Private
Admissions: (909) 469-5335
Email: admissions@westernu.edu
Financial aid: (909) 469-5350
Application deadline: 02/01
Tuition: $53,610

Room/board/expenses: $18,790
Percent receiving grants: 12%
Average student indebtedness at graduation: $258,919
Enrollment: 1,333
men: 54%; women: 46%; minorities: 49%; underrepresented minorities: 7%; in state: 66%
Acceptance rate: 7%
Median MCAT total score: 28
Median GPA: 3.64
Most popular undergraduate majors: biological sciences: 57%; physical sciences: 16%; nonsciences: 22%; other: 5%
Percent of graduates entering primary-care specialties: 53.0%

COLORADO

Rocky Vista University
8401 S. Chambers Road
Parker, CO 80134
www.rvu.edu/aboutCOM.asp
Private
Admissions: (720) 875-2800
Email: admissions@rvu.edu
Financial aid: (720) 875-2800
Application deadline: 03/17
Tuition: $50,030
Room/board/expenses: $16,500
Percent receiving grants: 23%
Average student indebtedness at graduation: $223,543
Enrollment: 632
men: 56%; women: 44%; minorities: 17%; underrepresented minorities: 7%; in state: 40%
Acceptance rate: 6%
Median MCAT total score: 29
Median GPA: 3.61
Most popular undergraduate majors: biological sciences: 60%; physical sciences: 10%; nonsciences: 5%; other: 25%
Percent of graduates entering primary-care specialties: 44.2%

FLORIDA

Nova Southeastern University
3200 S. University Drive
Fort Lauderdale, FL 33328
medicine.nova.edu
Private
Admissions: (954) 262-1101
Email: hpdops@nova.edu
Financial aid: (954) 262-7439
Application deadline: 03/01
Tuition: $49,388
Room/board/expenses: $22,548
Percent receiving grants: 10%
Average student indebtedness at graduation: $240,107
Enrollment: 983
men: 56%; women: 44%; minorities: 48%; underrepresented minorities: 24%; in state: 67%
Acceptance rate: 9%
Median MCAT total score: 27
Median GPA: 3.53
Most popular undergraduate majors: biological sciences: 59%; physical sciences: 8%; nonsciences: 8%; other: 25%
Percent of graduates entering primary-care specialties: 55.0%

ILLINOIS

Midwestern University[1]
555 31st Street
Downers Grove, IL 60515
www.midwestern.edu
Private
Admissions: (630) 515-6171
Email: admissil@midwestern.edu
Financial aid: N/A
Tuition: N/A
Room/board/expenses: N/A
Enrollment: N/A

INDIANA

Marian University College of Osteopathic Medicine[1]
3200 Cold Spring Road
Indianapolis, IN 46222
Private
Admissions: N/A
Financial aid: N/A
Tuition: N/A
Room/board/expenses: N/A
Enrollment: N/A

IOWA

Des Moines University[1]
3200 Grand Avenue
Des Moines, IA 50312
www.dmu.edu/do/
Private
Admissions: (515) 271-1499
Email: doadmit@dmu.edu
Financial aid: N/A
Tuition: N/A
Room/board/expenses: N/A
Enrollment: N/A

KENTUCKY

University of Pikeville
147 Sycamore Street
Pikeville, KY 41501
www.upike.edu
Private
Admissions: (606) 218-5409
Email: kycomadmissions@upike.edu
Financial aid: (606) 218-5407
Application deadline: 02/01
Tuition: $41,320
Room/board/expenses: $22,548
Percent receiving grants: 18%
Average student indebtedness at graduation: $162,306
Enrollment: 532
men: 57%; women: 43%; minorities: 11%; underrepresented minorities: 7%; in state: 44%
Acceptance rate: 7%
Median MCAT total score: 24
Median GPA: 3.50
Most popular undergraduate majors: biological sciences: 64%; physical sciences: 17%; nonsciences: 5%; other: 14%
Percent of graduates entering primary-care specialties: 72.9%

MAINE

University of New England
11 Hills Beach Road
Biddeford, ME 04005
www.une.edu/com/
Private
Admissions: (800) 477-4863
Email: gradadmissions2@une.edu
Financial aid: (207) 602-2404
Application deadline: 02/01
Tuition: $53,485
Room/board/expenses: $12,500
Percent receiving grants: 22%
Average student indebtedness at graduation: $237,275
Enrollment: 649
men: 50%; women: 50%; minorities: 16%; underrepresented minorities: 6%; in state: 13%
Acceptance rate: 9%
Median MCAT total score: 28
Median GPA: 3.57
Most popular undergraduate majors: biological sciences: 52%; physical sciences: 17%; nonsciences: 12%; other: 19%
Percent of graduates entering primary-care specialties: 60.0%

MICHIGAN

Michigan State University (College of Osteopathic Medicine)
A308 E. Fee Hall
East Lansing, MI 48824
www.com.msu.edu
Public
Admissions: (517) 353-7740
Email: com.admissions@hc.msu.edu
Financial aid: (517) 353-5188
Application deadline: 12/15
In-state tuition: $43,478
Out-of-state tuition: $88,788
Room/board/expenses: $17,661
Percent receiving grants: 33%
Average student indebtedness at graduation: $224,321
Enrollment: 1,242
men: 57%; women: 43%; minorities: 24%; underrepresented minorities: 7%; in state: 86%
Acceptance rate: 8%
Median MCAT total score: 29
Median GPA: 3.65
Most popular undergraduate majors: biological sciences: 75%; physical sciences: 7%; nonsciences: 5%; other: 13%
Percent of graduates entering primary-care specialties: 80.0%

MISSISSIPPI

William Carey University College of Osteopathic Medicine[1]
498 Tuscan Avenue
Hattiesburg, MS 39401
www.wmcarey.edu/departments/college-osteopathic-medicine
Private
Admissions: (601) 318-6235
Email: wcucom@wmcarey.edu
Financial aid: N/A
Tuition: N/A
Room/board/expenses: N/A
Enrollment: N/A

MISSOURI

A.T. Still University of Health Sciences-Kirksville[1]
800 W. Jefferson Street
Kirksville, MO 63501
www.atsu.edu/kcom/index.htm
Private
Admissions: (866) 626-2878
Email: admissions@atsu.edu
Financial aid: N/A
Tuition: N/A
Room/board/expenses: N/A
Enrollment: N/A

Kansas City University of Medicine and Biosciences
1750 Independence Avenue
Kansas City, MO 64106-1453
www.kcumb.edu/
Private
Admissions: (800) 234-4847
Email: admissions@kcumb.edu
Financial aid: N/A
Application deadline: 03/01
Tuition: $43,513
Room/board/expenses: $22,250
Percent receiving grants: 26%
Average student indebtedness at graduation: $59,643
Enrollment: 1,032
men: 58%; women: 42%; minorities: 30%; underrepresented minorities: 30%; in state: 22%
Acceptance rate: 9%
Median MCAT total score: 28
Median GPA: 3.62
Most popular undergraduate majors: biological sciences: 59%; physical sciences: 14%; nonsciences: 13%; other: 14%
Percent of graduates entering primary-care specialties: 73.0%

NEW JERSEY

Rowan University
1 Medical Center Drive
Stratford, NJ 08084-1501
www.rowan.edu/som
Public
Admissions: (856) 566-7050
Email: somadm@rowan.edu
Financial aid: (856) 566-6008
Application deadline: 02/01
In-state tuition: $41,883
Out-of-state tuition: $64,412
Room/board/expenses: $15,500
Average student indebtedness at graduation: $170,720
Enrollment: 647
men: 53%; women: 47%; minorities: 53%; underrepresented minorities: 13%; in state: 93%
Acceptance rate: 5%
Median MCAT total score: 29
Median GPA: 3.54
Most popular undergraduate majors: biological sciences: 59%; physical sciences: 12%; nonsciences: 9%; other: 20%
Percent of graduates entering primary-care specialties: 55.3%

NEW YORK

New York Institute of Technology[1]

Old Westbury, Northern
Boulevard
Long Island, NY 11568
www.nyit.edu
Private
Admissions: (516) 686-3747
Email: comadm@nyit.edu
Financial aid: N/A
Tuition: N/A
Room/board/expenses: N/A
Enrollment: N/A

Touro College of Osteopathic Medicine

230 W. 125th Street
New York, NY 10027
www.tourocom.touro.edu
Private
Admissions: (212) 851-1199
Email: admissions.tourocom@touro.edu
Financial aid: (212) 851-1199
Application deadline: 04/01
Tuition: $48,340
Room/board/expenses: $27,942
Percent receiving grants: 3%
Average student indebtedness at graduation: $197,097
Enrollment: 809
men: 54%; women: 46%; minorities: 54%; underrepresented minorities: 13%; in state: 38%
Acceptance rate: 4%
Median MCAT total score: 29
Median GPA: 3.43
Most popular undergraduate majors: biological sciences: 57%; physical sciences: 13%; nonsciences: 19%; other: 12%
Percent of graduates entering primary-care specialties: 52.0%

NORTH CAROLINA

Campbell University (Wallace)[1]

4350 U.S. 421 South
Lillington, NC 27546
Private
Admissions: N/A
Financial aid: N/A
Tuition: N/A
Room/board/expenses: N/A
Enrollment: N/A

OHIO

Ohio University

Grosvenor Hall
Athens, OH 45701
www.ohio.edu/medicine
Public
Admissions: (740) 593-4313
Email: ou-hcom@ohio.edu
Financial aid: (740) 593-2158
Application deadline: 02/01
In-state tuition: $34,380
Out-of-state tuition: $48,040
Room/board/expenses: $15,296
Percent receiving grants: 36%
Average student indebtedness at graduation: $200,876
Enrollment: 711
men: 53%; women: 47%; minorities: 23%; underrepresented minorities: 14%; in state: 98%
Acceptance rate: 7%
Median MCAT total score: 27
Median GPA: 3.65
Most popular undergraduate majors: biological sciences: 66%; physical sciences: 15%; nonsciences: 10%; other: 9%
Percent of graduates entering primary-care specialties: 57.6%

OKLAHOMA

Oklahoma State University

1111 W. 17th Street
Tulsa, OK 74107-1898
healthsciences.okstate.edu
Public
Admissions: (918) 561-8421
Email: sarah.quinten@okstate.edu
Financial aid: (918) 561-8278
Application deadline: 02/01
In-state tuition: $24,094
Out-of-state tuition: $46,225
Room/board/expenses: $18,000
Percent receiving grants: 23%
Average student indebtedness at graduation: $185,484
Enrollment: 440
men: 56%; women: 44%; minorities: 31%; underrepresented minorities: 21%; in state: 92%
Acceptance rate: 13%
Median MCAT total score: 25
Median GPA: 3.61
Most popular undergraduate majors: biological sciences: 66%; physical sciences: 15%; nonsciences: 8%; other: 11%
Percent of graduates entering primary-care specialties: 59.5%

PENNSYLVANIA

Lake Erie College of Osteopathic Medicine

1858 W. Grandview Boulevard
Erie, PA 16509
www.lecom.edu
Private
Admissions: (814) 866-6641
Email: admissions@lecom.edu
Financial aid: (814) 866-6641
Application deadline: 04/01
Tuition: $30,825
Room/board/expenses: $14,500
Percent receiving grants: 30%
Average student indebtedness at graduation: $182,997

Enrollment: 2,263
men: 60%; women: 40%; minorities: 28%; underrepresented minorities: 7%; in state: 37%
Acceptance rate: 9%
Median MCAT total score: 27
Median GPA: 3.50
Most popular undergraduate majors: biological sciences: 73%; physical sciences: 12%; nonsciences: 11%; other: 4%
Percent of graduates entering primary-care specialties: 67.5%

Philadelphia College of Osteopathic Medicine[1]

4170 City Avenue
Philadelphia, PA 19131
www.pcom.edu
Private
Admissions: (800) 999-6998
Email: admissions@pcom.edu
Financial aid: N/A
Tuition: N/A
Room/board/expenses: N/A
Enrollment: N/A

TENNESSEE

Lincoln Memorial University (DeBusk)

6965 Cumberland Gap Parkway
Harrogate, TN 37752
www.lmunet.edu/dcom/admissions
Private
Admissions: (800) 325-0900
Email: dcomadmissions@lmunet.edu
Financial aid: (423) 869-7107
Application deadline: 04/01
Tuition: $46,528
Room/board/expenses: $14,532
Percent receiving grants: 4%
Enrollment: 908
men: 59%; women: 41%; minorities: 25%; underrepresented minorities: 9%; in state: 25%
Acceptance rate: 8%
Median MCAT total score: 26
Median GPA: 3.47
Most popular undergraduate majors: biological sciences: 64%; physical sciences: 6%; nonsciences: 12%; other: 18%
Percent of graduates entering primary-care specialties: 77.5%

TEXAS

University of North Texas Health Science Center

3500 Camp Bowie Boulevard
Fort Worth, TX 76107-2699
www.hsc.unt.edu
Public
Admissions: (800) 535-8266

Email: TCOMAdmissions@unthsc.edu
Financial aid: (800) 346-8266
Application deadline: 10/01
In-state tuition: $19,022
Out-of-state tuition: $34,710
Room/board/expenses: $16,588
Percent receiving grants: 76%
Average student indebtedness at graduation: $137,117
Enrollment: 919
men: 54%; women: 46%; minorities: 47%; underrepresented minorities: 15%; in state: 95%
Acceptance rate: 14%
Median MCAT total score: 28
Median GPA: 3.70
Most popular undergraduate majors: biological sciences: 69%; physical sciences: 6%; nonsciences: 13%; other: 12%
Percent of graduates entering primary-care specialties: 65.7%

VIRGINIA

Edward Via College of Osteopathic Medicine-Virginia, Carolinas, and Auburn

2265 Kraft Drive
Blacksburg, VA 24060
www.vcom.vt.edu
Private
Admissions: (540) 231-6138
Email: admissions@vcom.vt.edu
Financial aid: (540) 231-6021
Application deadline: 03/01
Tuition: $43,250
Room/board/expenses: $0
Percent receiving grants: 29%
Enrollment: 1,546
men: 48%; women: 52%; minorities: 29%; underrepresented minorities: 15%; in state: 11%
Acceptance rate: 11%
Median MCAT total score: 25
Median GPA: 3.63
Most popular undergraduate majors: biological sciences: 72%; physical sciences: 10%; nonsciences: 10%; other: 8%
Percent of graduates entering primary-care specialties: 66.0%

Liberty University College of Osteopathic Medicine[1]

306 Liberty View Lane
Lynchburg, VA 24502
Private
Admissions: N/A
Financial aid: N/A
Tuition: N/A
Room/board/expenses: N/A
Enrollment: N/A

WASHINGTON

Pacific Northwest University of Health Sciences[1]

200 University Parkway
Yakima, WA 98901
www.pnwu.edu/college-of-osteopathic-medicine-com/
Private
Admissions: (509) 452-5100
Email: admission@pnwu.edu
Financial aid: N/A
Tuition: N/A
Room/board/expenses: N/A
Enrollment: N/A

WEST VIRGINIA

West Virginia School of Osteopathic Medicine

400 N. Lee Street
Lewisburg, WV 24901
www.wvsom.edu
Public
Admissions: (800) 356-7836
Email: admissions@osteo.wvsom.edu
Financial aid: (800) 356-7836
Application deadline: 02/15
In-state tuition: $21,650
Out-of-state tuition: $51,400
Room/board/expenses: $14,980
Percent receiving grants: 13%
Average student indebtedness at graduation: $259,177
Enrollment: 833
men: 52%; women: 48%; minorities: 25%; underrepresented minorities: 7%; in state: 30%
Acceptance rate: 7%
Median MCAT total score: 24
Median GPA: 3.52
Most popular undergraduate majors: biological sciences: 55%; physical sciences: 8%; nonsciences: 12%; other: 25%
Percent of graduates entering primary-care specialties: 70.1%

NURSING

Here you'll find information on the 519 nursing schools with master's or doctoral programs accredited by either the Commission on Collegiate Nursing Education or the Accreditation Commission for Education in Nursing. Two hundred sixty-eight schools responded to the U.S. News survey, which was conducted in the fall of 2015 and early 2016. Nursing schools or programs that did not respond have abbreviated entries.

KEY TO THE TERMINOLOGY

1. A school whose name has been footnoted with the numeral 1 did not return the U.S. News statistical survey; limited data appear in its entry.
N/A. Not available from the school or not applicable.
Admissions. The admissions office phone number.
Email. The address of the admissions office. If instead of an email address a website is listed, the website will automatically present an email screen programmed to reach the admissions office.
Financial aid. The financial aid office phone number.
Application deadline. For fall 2016 enrollment. "Rolling" means there is no deadline; the school acts on applications as they are received. "Varies" means deadlines vary according to department or whether applicants are U.S. citizens or foreign nationals.
Degrees offered. Master's, Ph.D. and Doctor of Nursing Practice (DNP)
Tuition. For the 2015-16 academic year for master's, Ph.D. and Doctor of Nursing Practice programs. Doesn't include fees.
Credit hour. The cost per credit hour for the 2015-16 academic year.
Room/board/expenses. For the 2015-16 academic year.
Enrollment. Full-time and part-time, including master's, Ph.D. and DNP candidates, for fall 2015.
Minorities. Full-time and part-time master's, Ph.D., and DNP minority enrollment percentage for fall 2015. Reflects the share of students who are black or African-American, Asian, American Indian or Alaska Native, Native Hawaiian or other Pacific Islander, Hispanic/Latino, or two or more races. The minority percentage was reported by each school.
Acceptance rates. Percentage of applicants who were accepted among those who applied for fall 2015 admission to master's, Ph.D. or DNP nursing programs.
Nursing programs offered in 2015-16. Areas of specialization include administration, case management, clinical nurse leader, clinical nurse specialist, community health/public health, education, forensic nursing, generalist, health management & policy, health care systems, informatics, nurse anesthesia, nurse-midwifery, nurse practitioner, adult-gerontology acute care nurse practitioner, adult-gerontology primary care nurse practitioner, adult nurse practitioner, family nurse practitioner, pediatric primary care nurse practitioner, psychiatric-mental health nurse practitioner–across the lifespan, research, school nursing, other majors, combined nurse practitioner/clinical nurse specialist, dual majors.

ALABAMA

Auburn University
102 Miller Hall
Auburn University, AL 36849
www.auburn.edu/academic/nursing/
Public
Admissions: (334) 844-4700
Email: gradadm@auburn.edu
Financial aid: (334) 844-4634
Application deadline: N/A
Degrees offered: master's
In-state tuition: full time: $8,802, part time: $489/credit hour
Out-of-state tuition: full time: $26,406
Room/board/expenses: $12,584
Full-time enrollment: 13
men: 0%; women: 100%; minorities: 38%; international: 0%
Part-time enrollment: 107
men: 6%; women: 94%; minorities: 15%; international: 1%
Acceptance rate (master's): 57%
Specialties offered: education; nurse practitioner; nurse practitioner: family; dual majors

Auburn University-Montgomery[1]
PO Box 244023
Montgomery, AL 36124
Public
Admissions: N/A
Financial aid: N/A
Tuition: N/A
Room/board/expenses: N/A
Enrollment: N/A

Jacksonville State University
700 Pelham Road N
Jacksonville, AL 36265-1602
www.jsu.edu/nursing/index.html
Public
Admissions: (256) 782-5268
Email: info@jsu.edu
Financial aid: (256) 782-8399
Application deadline: N/A
Degrees offered: master's
In-state tuition: full time: $371/credit hour, part time: $371/credit hour
Out-of-state tuition: full time: $742/credit hour
Room/board/expenses: $7,128
Full-time enrollment: 10
men: 0%; women: 100%; minorities: 40%; international: 0%
Part-time enrollment: 38
men: 3%; women: 97%; minorities: 47%; international: 3%
Acceptance rate (master's): 60%
Specialties offered: community health/public health; education; other majors

Samford University
800 Lakeshore Drive
Birmingham, AL 35229
www.samford.edu/nursing/
Private
Admissions: (205) 726-2047
Email: amaddox@samford.edu
Financial aid: (205) 726-2905
Application deadline: 06/01
Degrees offered: master's, DNP
Tuition: full time: $785/credit hour, part time: $785/credit hour (master's); full time: $785/credit hour, part time: $785/credit hour (DNP)
Room/board/expenses: N/A
Full-time enrollment: 276 (master's); 14 (DNP)
men: 25%; women: 75%; minorities: 19%; international: 0%
Part-time enrollment: N/A (master's); 53 (DNP)
men: 8%; women: 92%; minorities: 23%; international: 0%
Acceptance rate (master's): 72%
Acceptance rate (DNP): 84%
Specialties offered: administration; education; health management & policy health care systems; nurse anesthesia; nurse practitioner; nurse practitioner: family

Spring Hill College[1]
4000 Dauphin Street
Mobile, AL 36608
Private
Admissions: N/A
Financial aid: N/A
Tuition: N/A
Room/board/expenses: N/A
Enrollment: N/A

Troy University-Montgomery[1]
College View Building
Troy, AL 36082
www.troy.edu/healthandhumanservices
Public
Admissions: (800) 551-9716
Email: admit@troy.edu
Financial aid: (800) 414-5756
Tuition: N/A
Room/board/expenses: N/A
Enrollment: N/A

University of Alabama
Box 870358
Tuscaloosa, AL 35487
nursing.ua.edu/index.html
Public
Admissions: (205) 348-5921
Email: gradschool@ua.edu
Financial aid: (205) 348-6756
Application deadline: 04/01
Degrees offered: master's, DNP
In-state tuition: full time: $360/credit hour, part time: $360/credit hour (master's); full time: $360/credit hour, part time: $360/credit hour (DNP)
Out-of-state tuition: full time: $360/credit hour (master's); full time: $360/credit hour (DNP)
Room/board/expenses: N/A

Full-time enrollment: 56 (master's); 58 (DNP)
men: 17%; women: 83%; minorities: 33%; international: 0%
Part-time enrollment: 72 (master's); 118 (DNP)
men: 14%; women: 86%; minorities: 34%; international: 0%
Acceptance rate (master's): 49%
Acceptance rate (DNP): 43%
Specialties offered: case management; clinical nurse leader; nurse practitioner; nurse practitioner: family; nurse practitioner: psychiatric-mental health, across the lifespan; dual majors

University of Alabama-Birmingham

1530 Third Avenue S
Birmingham, AL 35294
www.uab.edu/nursing/home/
Public
Admissions: (205) 975-7529
Email: sonstudaffairs@uab.edu
Financial aid: (205) 934-8223
Application deadline: 09/01
Degrees offered: master's, Ph.D., DNP
In-state tuition: full time: $493/credit hour, part time: $493/credit hour (master's); full time: $493/credit hour, part time: $493/credit hour (Ph.D.); full time: $493/credit hour, part time: $493/credit hour (DNP)
Out-of-state tuition: full time: $493/credit hour (master's); full time: $1,157/credit hour (Ph.D.); full time: $493/credit hour (DNP)
Room/board/expenses: $5,400 (master's); $5,400 (Ph.D.) $5,400 (DNP)
Full-time enrollment: 255 (master's); 13 (Ph.D.); 5 (DNP)
men: 26%; women: 74%; minorities: 32%; international: 0%
Part-time enrollment: 1,101 (master's); 28 (Ph.D.); 145 (DNP)
men: 12%; women: 88%; minorities: 26%; international: 0%
Acceptance rate (master's): 57%
Acceptance rate (Ph.D.): 65%
Acceptance rate (DNP): 83%
Specialties offered: administration; clinical nurse leader; education; informatics; nurse anesthesia; nurse practitioner; nurse practitioner: adult-gerontology acute care; nurse practitioner: adult-gerontology primary care; nurse practitioner: family; nurse practitioner: pediatric primary care; nurse practitioner: psychiatric-mental health, across the lifespan; research; dual majors

University of Alabama-Huntsville

301 Sparkman Drive
Huntsville, AL 35899
uah.edu/nursing
Public
Admissions: (256) 824-6198
Email: deangrad@uah.edu
Financial aid: (256) 824-6650
Application deadline: 04/01
Degrees offered: master's, DNP

In-state tuition: full time: $675/credit hour, part time: $675/credit hour (master's); full time: $366/credit hour, part time: $366/credit hour (DNP)
Out-of-state tuition: full time: $1,500/credit hour (master's); full time: $366/credit hour (DNP)
Room/board/expenses: N/A
Full-time enrollment: 73 (master's); 14 (DNP)
men: 21%; women: 79%; minorities: 25%; international: 0%
Part-time enrollment: 174 (master's); 77 (DNP)
men: 17%; women: 83%; minorities: 16%; international: 0%
Acceptance rate (master's): 90%
Acceptance rate (DNP): 88%
Specialties offered: administration; clinical nurse specialist; nurse practitioner; nurse practitioner: adult-gerontology acute care; nurse practitioner: family

University of Mobile

5735 College Parkway
Mobile, AL 36613-2842
www.umobile.edu/Academics/AcademicAreas/SchoolofNursing.aspx#.VFKIM01ATIU
Private
Admissions: (251) 442-2270
Email: driley@umobile.edu
Financial aid: (251) 442-2239
Application deadline: N/A
Degrees offered: master's
Tuition: full time: $502/credit hour, part time: $502/credit hour
Room/board/expenses: N/A
Full-time enrollment: 8
men: 0%; women: 100%; minorities: 63%; international: 0%
Part-time enrollment: 7
men: 14%; women: 86%; minorities: 57%; international: 0%
Acceptance rate (master's): 83%
Specialties offered: administration; education

University of North Alabama[1]

223 Stevens Hall
Florence, AL 35632
Public
Admissions: N/A
Financial aid: N/A
Tuition: N/A
Room/board/expenses: N/A
Enrollment: N/A

University of South Alabama[1]

5721 USA Drive N, Room 3068
Mobile, AL 36688-0002
Public
Admissions: N/A
Financial aid: N/A
Tuition: N/A
Room/board/expenses: N/A
Enrollment: N/A

ALASKA

University of Alaska-Anchorage[1]

3211 Providence Drive
Anchorage, AK 99508-8030
Public
Admissions: N/A
Financial aid: N/A
Tuition: N/A
Room/board/expenses: N/A
Enrollment: N/A

ARIZONA

Arizona State University

500 N. Third Street
Phoenix, AZ 85004
nursingandhealth.asu.edu/
Public
Admissions: (480) 727-0262
Email: Michael.Mobley@asu.edu
Financial aid: (855) 278-5080
Application deadline: 03/01
Degrees offered: master's, Ph.D., DNP
In-state tuition: full time: $10,610, part time: $758/credit hour (master's); full time: $10,610, part time: $758/credit hour (Ph.D.); full time: $10,610, part time: $758/credit hour (DNP)
Out-of-state tuition: full time: $20,322 (master's); full time: $20,322 (Ph.D.); full time: $20,322 (DNP)
Room/board/expenses: $11,831 (master's); $11,831 (Ph.D.); $11,831 (DNP)
Full-time enrollment: 16 (master's); 20 (Ph.D.); 163 (DNP)
men: 12%; women: 88%; minorities: 29%; international: 4%
Part-time enrollment: 12 (master's); 20 (Ph.D.); 58 (DNP)
men: 11%; women: 89%; minorities: 24%; international: 0%
Acceptance rate (master's): 90%
Acceptance rate (Ph.D.): 38%
Acceptance rate (DNP): 67%
Specialties offered: education; nurse practitioner; nurse practitioner: adult-gerontology primary care; nurse practitioner: family; nurse practitioner: pediatric primary care; nurse practitioner: psychiatric-mental health, across the lifespan; research; other majors

Brookline College[1]

Phoenix, AZ 85021
Private
Admissions: N/A
Financial aid: N/A
Tuition: N/A
Room/board/expenses: N/A
Enrollment: N/A

Grand Canyon University[1]

3300 West Camelback Road
Phoenix , AZ 85061
Private
Admissions: N/A
Financial aid: N/A
Tuition: N/A
Room/board/expenses: N/A
Enrollment: N/A

Northern Arizona University

NAU Box 15035
Flagstaff, AZ 86011
Public
Admissions: N/A
Financial aid: (855) 628-6333
Application deadline: N/A
Degrees offered: master's, DNP
In-state tuition: full time: $458/credit hour, part time: $458/credit hour (master's); full time: $458/credit hour, part time: $458/credit hour (DNP)
Out-of-state tuition: full time: $1,157/credit hour (master's); full time: $1,157/credit hour (DNP)
Room/board/expenses: N/A
Full-time enrollment: 28 (master's); N/A (DNP)
men: 7%; women: 93%; minorities: 18%; international: 0%
Part-time enrollment: 144 (master's); 14 (DNP)
men: 18%; women: 82%; minorities: 25%; international: 0%
Acceptance rate (master's): 86%
Acceptance rate (DNP): 75%
Specialties offered: generalist; nurse practitioner; nurse practitioner: family

University of Arizona

1305 N. Martin Avenue
Tucson, AZ 85721-0203
www.nursing.arizona.edu/
Public
Admissions: (520) 626-3808
Email: studentaffairs@nursing.arizona.edu
Financial aid: (520) 621-1858
Application deadline: 12/15
Degrees offered: master's, Ph.D., DNP
In-state tuition: full time: $800/credit hour, part time: $800/credit hour (master's); full time: $789/credit hour, part time: $789/credit hour (Ph.D.); full time: $789/credit hour, part time: $789/credit hour (DNP)
Out-of-state tuition: full time: $800/credit hour (master's); full time: $1,631/credit hour (Ph.D.); full time: $1,631/credit hour (DNP)
Room/board/expenses: N/A
Full-time enrollment: 158 (master's); 60 (Ph.D.); 235 (DNP)
men: 15%; women: 85%; minorities: 32%; international: 0%
Part-time enrollment: 302 (master's); 20 (Ph.D.); 82 (DNP)
men: 12%; women: 88%; minorities: 32%; international: 0%
Acceptance rate (master's): 31%
Acceptance rate (Ph.D.): 84%
Acceptance rate (DNP): 80%
Specialties offered: generalist; nurse anesthesia; nurse practitioner; nurse practitioner: adult-gerontology acute care; nurse practitioner: family; nurse practitioner: pediatric primary care; nurse practitioner: psychiatric-mental health, across the lifespan; research; other majors

University of Phoenix[1]

4615 E. Elwood Street
Phoenix, AZ 85040
Private
Admissions: N/A
Financial aid: N/A
Tuition: N/A
Room/board/expenses: N/A
Enrollment: N/A

ARKANSAS

Arkansas State University-Jonesboro

State University, AR 72467
www.astate.edu/college/conhp/
Public
Admissions: (870) 972-2031
Email: www.astate.edu/college/graduate-school/
Financial aid: (870) 972-2310
Application deadline: 02/01
Degrees offered: master's, DNP
In-state tuition: full time: $254/credit hour, part time: $254/credit hour (master's); full time: $254/credit hour, part time: $254/credit hour (DNP)
Out-of-state tuition: full time: $506/credit hour (master's); full time: $506/credit hour (DNP)
Room/board/expenses: N/A
Full-time enrollment: N/A (master's); N/A (DNP)
men: N/A; women: N/A; minorities: N/A; international: N/A
Part-time enrollment: 89 (master's); 15 (DNP)
men: 2%; women: 13%; minorities: 11%; international: 0%
Acceptance rate (master's): 77%
Acceptance rate (DNP): 73%
Specialties offered: administration; clinical nurse specialist; education; nurse anesthesia; nurse practitioner: family; school nursing

Arkansas Tech University

Dean Hall 224
402 West O Street
Russellville, AR 72801
www.atu.edu/nursing/
Public
Admissions: (479) 968-0398
Email: gradcollege@atu.edu
Financial aid: (479) 968-0399
Application deadline: 05/01
Degrees offered: master's
In-state tuition: full time: $269/credit hour, part time: $269/credit hour
Out-of-state tuition: full time: $538/credit hour
Room/board/expenses: $1,324
Full-time enrollment: 2
men: 0%; women: 100%; minorities: 50%; international: 50%
Part-time enrollment: 17
men: 18%; women: 82%; minorities: 29%; international: 0%
Acceptance rate (master's): 100%
Specialties offered: administration

University of Arkansas[1]

Room 324
Graduate Education Building
Fayetteville, AR 72701
nurs.uark.edu/
Public
Admissions: (479) 575-4883
Email: admissions.uark.edu
Financial aid: (479) 575-3806
Tuition: N/A
Room/board/expenses: N/A
Enrollment: N/A

University of Arkansas for Medical Sciences[1]

4301 W. Markham Street
Slot 529
Little Rock, AR 72205-7199
Public
Admissions: N/A
Financial aid: N/A
Tuition: N/A
Room/board/expenses: N/A
Enrollment: N/A

University of Central Arkansas

201 Donaghey Avenue
Conway, AR 72035
Public
Admissions: (501) 450-3120
Email: rschlosser@uca.edu
Financial aid: (501) 450-3410
Application deadline: 01/15
Degrees offered: master's, DNP
In-state tuition: full time: $243/
credit hour, part time: $243/
credit hour (master's); full time:
$243/credit hour, part time:
$243/credit hour (DNP)
Out-of-state tuition: full time:
$486/credit hour (master's); full
time: $486/credit hour (DNP)
Room/board/expenses: $5,982
(master's); $5,982 (DNP)
Full-time enrollment: 2 (master's);
N/A (DNP)
men: 50%; women: 50%;
minorities: 0%; international:
50%
Part-time enrollment: 150
(master's); 20 (DNP)
men: 8%; women: 92%;
minorities: 16%; international:
0%
Acceptance rate (master's): 100%
Acceptance rate (DNP): 56%
Specialties offered: clinical
nurse leader; education; nurse
practitioner; nurse practitioner:
adult-gerontology primary care;
nurse practitioner: adult; nurse
practitioner: family

CALIFORNIA

Azusa Pacific University[1]

Graduate Center
Azusa, CA 91702-7000
Private
Admissions: N/A
Financial aid: N/A
Tuition: N/A
Room/board/expenses: N/A
Enrollment: N/A

Brandman University[1]

16355 Laguna Canyon Road
Irvine, CA 92618
Private
Admissions: N/A
Financial aid: N/A
Tuition: N/A
Room/board/expenses: N/A
Enrollment: N/A

California Baptist University

8432 Magnolia Ave
Riverside, CA 92506
www.calbaptist.edu/academics/
schools-colleges/school-nursing/
Private
Admissions: (951) 343-4336
Email: asonke@calbaptist.edu
Financial aid: (951) 343-4236
Application deadline: 08/01
Degrees offered: master's, DNP
Tuition: full time: $742/credit
hour, part time: $742/credit hour
(master's); full time: $1,200/
credit hour, part time: $1,200/
credit hour (DNP)
Room/board/expenses: $10,670
(master's); $10,670 (DNP)
Full-time enrollment: 84 (master's);
N/A (DNP)
men: 18%; women: 82%;
minorities: 45%; international:
5%
Part-time enrollment: 156
(master's); 2 (DNP)
men: 18%; women: 82%;
minorities: 54%; international:
1%
Acceptance rate (master's): 67%
Acceptance rate (DNP): 33%
Specialties offered: clinical
nurse specialist; education;
health management & policy
health care systems; nurse
practitioner: family

California State University-Chico

400 W. First Street
Chico, CA 95929-0200
www.csuchico.edu/nurs
Public
Admissions: (530) 898-6880
Email: graduatestudies@
csuchico.edu
Financial aid: (530) 898-6451
Application deadline: 03/01
Degrees offered: master's
In-state tuition: full time: $8,292,
part time: $5,460
Out-of-state tuition: full time:
$17,220
Room/board/expenses: $11,200
Full-time enrollment:
men: N/A; women: N/A;
minorities: N/A; international: N/A
Part-time enrollment: 20
men: 15%; women: 85%;
minorities: 10%; international:
0%
Specialties offered:
administration; education

California State University-Dominguez Hills

1000 East Victoria Street
Carson, CA 90747
www4.csudh.edu/son/
Public
Admissions: (310) 243-3645
Email: admit@csudh.edu

Financial aid: (310) 243-3691
Application deadline: 06/01
Degrees offered: master's
In-state tuition: full time: $6,738,
part time: $3,906
Out-of-state tuition: full time:
$9,714
Room/board/expenses: $25,580
Full-time enrollment: 11
men: 9%; women: 91%;
minorities: 64%; international:
0%
Part-time enrollment: 265
men: 9%; women: 91%;
minorities: 61%; international: 1%
Acceptance rate (master's): 86%
Specialties offered:
administration; clinical nurse
specialist; education; nurse
practitioner; nurse practitioner:
family

California State University-Fresno[1]

2345 E. San Ramon Avenue
Fresno, CA 93740-8031
Public
Admissions: N/A
Financial aid: N/A
Tuition: N/A
Room/board/expenses: N/A
Enrollment: N/A

California State University-Fullerton[1]

800 N. State College Boulevard
Fullerton, CA 92834
Public
Admissions: N/A
Financial aid: N/A
Tuition: N/A
Room/board/expenses: N/A
Enrollment: N/A

California State University-Long Beach[1]

1250 Bellflower Boulevard
Long Beach, CA 90840
Public
Admissions: N/A
Financial aid: N/A
Tuition: N/A
Room/board/expenses: N/A
Enrollment: N/A

California State University-Los Angeles

5151 State University Drive
Los Angeles, CA 90032-8171
www.calstatela.edu/academic/
hhs/nursing
Public
Admissions: (323) 343-3901
Email: admission@calstatela.edu
Financial aid: (323) 343-6260
Application deadline: 11/30
Degrees offered: master's, DNP
In-state tuition: full time: $7,610,
part time: $4,780 (master's);
full time: $15,182, part time: N/A
(DNP)
Out-of-state tuition: full time:
$16,538 (master's); full time:
$21,878 (DNP)
Room/board/expenses: $12,750
(master's); N/A (DNP)
Full-time enrollment: 188
(master's); N/A (DNP)
men: N/A; women: N/A;
minorities: 71%; international: 0%

Part-time enrollment: 5 (master's);
N/A (DNP)
men: 0%; women: 0%;
minorities: 0%; international: 0%
Acceptance rate (master's): 43%
Specialties offered: education;
nurse practitioner: adult-
gerontology acute care; nurse
practitioner: adult-gerontology
primary care; nurse practitioner:
family; nurse practitioner:
psychiatric-mental health,
across the lifespan

California State University-Sacramento[1]

6000 J Street
Sacramento, CA 95819-6096
Public
Admissions: N/A
Financial aid: N/A
Tuition: N/A
Room/board/expenses: N/A
Enrollment: N/A

California State University-San Bernardino[1]

5500 University Parkway
San Bernadino, CA 92407
Public
Admissions: N/A
Financial aid: N/A
Tuition: N/A
Room/board/expenses: N/A
Enrollment: N/A

California State University-San Marcos[1]

333 S. Twin Oaks Valley Road
San Marcos, CA 92096
Public
Admissions: N/A
Financial aid: N/A
Tuition: N/A
Room/board/expenses: N/A
Enrollment: N/A

California State University-Stanislaus[1]

One University Circle
Turlock, CA 95382
Public
Admissions: N/A
Financial aid: N/A
Tuition: N/A
Room/board/expenses: N/A
Enrollment: N/A

Charles R. Drew University of Medicine and Science[1]

1731 E. 120th Street
Los Angeles, CA 90059
Private
Admissions: N/A
Financial aid: N/A
Tuition: N/A
Room/board/expenses: N/A
Enrollment: N/A

Fresno Pacific University[1]

Fresno, CA 93702
Private
Admissions: N/A
Financial aid: N/A
Tuition: N/A
Room/board/expenses: N/A
Enrollment: N/A

Holy Names University

3500 Mountain Boulevard
Oakland, CA 94619
www.hnu.edu/academics
Private
Admissions: (510) 436-1317
Email: GraduateAdmissions@
hnu.edu
Financial aid: (510) 436-1327
Application deadline: N/A
Degrees offered: master's
Tuition: full time: $984/credit
hour, part time: $984/credit hour
Room/board/expenses: $11,615
Full-time enrollment: 37
men: 14%; women: 86%;
minorities: 78%; international:
0%
Part-time enrollment: 69
men: 14%; women: 86%;
minorities: 71%; international: 0%
Acceptance rate (master's): 69%
Specialties offered:
administration; case
management; education;
informatics; nurse practitioner;
nurse practitioner: family

Loma Linda University[1]

School of Nursing Admissions
Office
Loma Linda, CA 92350
Private
Admissions: N/A
Financial aid: N/A
Tuition: N/A
Room/board/expenses: N/A
Enrollment: N/A

Mount Saint Mary's University[1]

10 Chester Place
Los Angeles, CA 90007
Private
Admissions: N/A
Financial aid: N/A
Tuition: N/A
Room/board/expenses: N/A
Enrollment: N/A

Point Loma Nazarene University

3900 Lomaland Drive
San Diego, CA 92106
www.pointloma.edu/experience/
academics/schools-departments/
school-nursing
Private
Admissions: (619) 563-2846
Email: gradinfo@pointloma.edu
Financial aid: (619) 849-2495
Application deadline: N/A
Degrees offered: master's
Tuition: full time: $735/credit
hour, part time: $735/credit hour
Room/board/expenses: N/A
Full-time enrollment: 1
men: N/A; women: 100%;
minorities: 100%; international:
N/A

Part-time enrollment: 74
men: N/A; women: N/A;
minorities: 46%; international:
3%
Acceptance rate (master's): 88%
Specialties offered: clinical nurse
specialist; generalist

Samuel Merritt University[1]
3100 Summit Street, 3rd Floor
Oakland, CA 94609
www.samuelmerritt.edu/nursing
Private
Admissions: (510) 869-6511
Email:
admission@samuelmerritt.edu
Financial aid: (510) 869-6511
Tuition: N/A
Room/board/expenses: N/A
Enrollment: N/A

San Diego State University[1]
Hardy Tower, Room 58
San Diego, CA 92182-4158
Public
Admissions: N/A
Financial aid: N/A
Tuition: N/A
Room/board/expenses: N/A
Enrollment: N/A

San Francisco State University[1]
Burk Hall, Room 371
San Francisco, CA 94132
Public
Admissions: N/A
Financial aid: N/A
Tuition: N/A
Room/board/expenses: N/A
Enrollment: N/A

San Jose State University
Health Building 420
San Jose, CA 95192-0057
www.sjsu.edu/nursing/
Public
Admissions: (408) 283-7500
Email: graduate@sjsu.edu
Financial aid: (408) 283-7500
Application deadline: 04/01
Degrees offered: master's, DNP
In-state tuition: full time: N/A, part
time: N/A (master's); full time:
N/A, part time: N/A (DNP)
Out-of-state tuition: full time: N/A
(master's); full time: N/A (DNP)
Room/board/expenses: N/A
Full-time enrollment: N/A
(master's); N/A (DNP)
men: N/A; women: N/A;
minorities: N/A; international: N/A
Part-time enrollment: 43
(master's); N/A (DNP)
men: 14%; women: 86%;
minorities: 79%; international:
0%
Acceptance rate (master's): 73%
Specialties offered:
administration; education

Sonoma State University[1]
1801 E.Cotati Avenue
Rohnert Park, CA 94928
Public
Admissions: N/A
Financial aid: N/A
Tuition: N/A

Room/board/expenses: N/A
Enrollment: N/A

United States University[1]
Chula Vista, CA 91911
Private
Admissions: N/A
Financial aid: N/A
Tuition: N/A
Room/board/expenses: N/A
Enrollment: N/A

University of California-Davis
4610 X Street, Suite 4202
Sacramento, CA 95817
www.ucdmc.ucdavis.edu/
nursing/
Public
Admissions: (916) 734-2145
Email: hs-bettyirenemooreson@
ucdavis.edu
Financial aid: (916) 734-4120
Application deadline: 01/15
Degrees offered: master's, Ph.D.
In-state tuition: full time: $21,249,
part time: N/A (master's);
full time: $11,220, part time:
$5,610 (Ph.D)
Out-of-state tuition: full time:
$33,494 (master's); full time:
$26,322 (Ph.D.)
Room/board/expenses: $14,163
(master's); $14,163 (Ph.D.)
Full-time enrollment: 65 (master's);
32 (Ph.D.)
men: 19%; women: 81%;
minorities: 49%; international:
1%
Part-time enrollment: N/A
(master's); N/A (Ph.D.)
men: N/A; women: N/A;
minorities: N/A; international: N/A
Acceptance rate (master's): 57%
Acceptance rate (Ph.D.): 27%
Specialties offered: nurse
practitioner; nurse practitioner:
family; other majors

University of California-Irvine[1]
252 Berk Hall
Irvine, CA 92697
Public
Admissions: N/A
Financial aid: N/A
Tuition: N/A
Room/board/expenses: N/A
Enrollment: N/A

University of California-Los Angeles
700 Tiverton Avenue
Factor Building 2-256
Los Angeles, CA 90097
nursing.ucla.edu
Public
Admissions: (310) 825-9193
Email: rflenoy@sonnet.ucla.edu
Financial aid: (310) 825-2583
Application deadline: 12/01
Degrees offered: master's, Ph.D.
In-state tuition: full time: $21,249,
part time: N/A (master's); full
time: $11,220, part time: N/A
(Ph.D.)
Out-of-state tuition: full time:
$33,494 (master's); full time:
$26,322 (Ph.D.)
Room/board/expenses: $13,932
(master's); $13,932 (Ph.D.)

Full-time enrollment: 316
(master's); 66 (Ph.D.)
men: 14%; women: 86%;
minorities: 57%; international:
2%
Part-time enrollment: N/A
(master's); N/A (Ph.D.)
men: N/A; women: N/A;
minorities: N/A; international: N/A
Acceptance rate (master's): 65%
Acceptance rate (Ph.D.): 72%
Specialties offered: clinical nurse
leader; clinical nurse specialist;
generalist; nurse practitioner;
nurse practitioner: adult-
gerontology acute care; nurse
practitioner: adult-gerontology
primary care; nurse practitioner:
family; nurse practitioner:
pediatric primary care; research;
combined nurse practitioner/
clinical nurse specialist

University of California-San Francisco
2 Koret Way
San Francisco, CA 94143
nursing.ucsf.edu/
Public
Admissions: (415) 476-4801
Email: judy.martin-holland@
ucsf.edu
Financial aid: (415) 476-4181
Application deadline: 02/01
Degrees offered: master's, Ph.D.
In-state tuition: full time: $26,803,
part time: N/A (master's);
full time: $16,810, part time:
$11,200 (Ph.D.)
Out-of-state tuition: full time:
$39,048 (master's); full time:
$31,912 (Ph.D.)
Room/board/expenses: N/A
Full-time enrollment: 400
(master's); 107 (Ph.D.)
men: 14%; women: 86%;
minorities: 41%; international:
5%
Part-time enrollment: N/A
(master's); N/A (Ph.D.)
men: N/A; women: N/A;
minorities: N/A; international: N/A
Acceptance rate (master's): 33%
Acceptance rate (Ph.D.): 30%
Specialties offered: clinical nurse
specialist; community health/
public health; nurse-midwifery;
nurse practitioner; nurse
practitioner: adult-gerontology
acute care; nurse practitioner:
adult-gerontology primary
care; nurse practitioner: family;
nurse practitioner: pediatric
primary care; nurse practitioner:
psychiatric-mental health,
across the lifespan

University of San Diego
5998 Alcala Park
San Diego, CA 92110
www.sandiego.edu/nursing
Private
Admissions: (619) 260-5906
Email: grads@sandiego.edu
Financial aid: (619) 260-2234
Application deadline: 11/01
Degrees offered: master's, Ph.D.,
DNP
Tuition: full time: $1,390/credit
hour, part time: $1,390/credit
hour (master's); full time: $1,420/
credit hour, part time: $1,420/
credit hour (Ph.D.); full time:

$1,420/credit hour, part time:
$1,420/credit hour (DNP)
Room/board/expenses: $12,000
(master's); $12,000 (Ph.D.);
$12,000 (DNP)
Full-time enrollment: 144
(master's); 45 (Ph.D.); 66 (DNP)
men: 16%; women: 84%;
minorities: 47%; international: 1%
Part-time enrollment: 49
(master's); 28 (Ph.D.); 3 (DNP)
men: 16%; women: 84%;
minorities: 41%; international:
0%
Acceptance rate (master's): 26%
Acceptance rate (Ph.D.): 32%
Acceptance rate (DNP): 51%
Specialties offered:
administration; clinical nurse
leader; clinical nurse specialist;
informatics; nurse practitioner;
nurse practitioner: adult-
gerontology primary care;
nurse practitioner: family;
nurse practitioner: pediatric
primary care; nurse practitioner:
psychiatric-mental health,
across the lifespan; research

University of San Francisco
2130 Fulton Street
San Francisco, CA 94117-1080
www.usfca.edu/nursing/
Private
Admissions: (415) 422-6681
Email: nursing@usfca.edu
Financial aid: (415) 422-2020
Application deadline: N/A
Degrees offered: master's, DNP
Tuition: full time: $1,245/credit
hour, part time: $1,245/credit
hour (master's); full time: $1,245/
credit hour, part time: $1,245/
credit hour (DNP)
Room/board/expenses: N/A
Full-time enrollment: 289
(master's); 114 (DNP)
men: 17%; women: 83%;
minorities: 63%; international:
1%
Part-time enrollment: 109
(master's); 51 (DNP)
men: N/A; women: N/A;
minorities: 68%; international:
1%
Acceptance rate (master's): 75%
Acceptance rate (DNP): 93%
Specialties offered:
administration; clinical nurse
leader; nurse practitioner;
nurse practitioner: family; nurse
practitioner: psychiatric-mental
health, across the lifespan;
combined nurse practitioner/
clinical nurse specialist

Vanguard University of Southern California[1]
Costa Mesa, CA 92626
Private
Admissions: N/A
Financial aid: N/A
Tuition: N/A
Room/board/expenses: N/A
Enrollment: N/A

West Coast University[1]
1477 S. Manchester Avenue
Anaheim, CA 92802
Private
Admissions: N/A
Financial aid: N/A
Tuition: N/A
Room/board/expenses: N/A
Enrollment: N/A

Western University of Health Sciences
309 E. Second Street
Pomona, CA 91766-1854
Private
Admissions: N/A
Financial aid: (909) 469-5350
Application deadline: N/A
Degrees offered: master's, DNP
Tuition: full time: $831/credit
hour, part time: $831/credit hour
(master's); full time: $1,087/credit
hour, part time: $1,087/credit
hour (DNP)
Room/board/expenses: $20,498
(master's); $20,498 (DNP)
Full-time enrollment: 272
(master's); 31 (DNP)
men: 16%; women: 84%;
minorities: 85%; international:
1%
Part-time enrollment: N/A
(master's); N/A (DNP)
men: N/A; women: N/A;
minorities: N/A; international: N/A
Acceptance rate (master's): 21%
Acceptance rate (DNP): 95%
Specialties offered:
administration; clinical nurse
leader; nurse practitioner; nurse
practitioner: family; other majors

COLORADO

American Sentinel University[1]
2260 South Xanadu Way
Suite 310
Aurora, CO 80014
www.americansentinel.edu/
nursing
Private
Admissions: (866) 922-5690
Email: admissions@
AmericanSentinel.edu
Financial aid: (800) 729-2427
Tuition: N/A
Room/board/expenses: N/A
Enrollment: N/A

Aspen University[1]
720 South Colorado Boulevard
Denver, CO 80246
Private
Admissions: N/A
Financial aid: N/A
Tuition: N/A
Room/board/expenses: N/A
Enrollment: N/A

Colorado Mesa University[1]
Grand Junction, CO 81501
Public
Admissions: N/A
Financial aid: N/A
Tuition: N/A
Room/board/expenses: N/A
Enrollment: N/A

Colorado State University-Pueblo[1]

2200 Bonforte Boulevard
Pueblo, CO 81001
ceeps.colostate-pueblo.edu/
nursing/
Public
Admissions: (719) 549-2462
Financial aid: (719) 549-2753
Tuition: N/A
Room/board/expenses: N/A
Enrollment: N/A

Regis University

3333 Regis Boulevard, G-8
Denver, CO 80221
regis.edu/RHCHP/Schools/
Loretto-Heights-School-of-
Nursing.aspx
Private
Admissions: (303) 458-4344
Email: healthcare@regis.edu
Financial aid: (303) 458-4126
Application deadline: 01/05
Degrees offered: master's, DNP
Tuition: full time: $620/credit
hour, part time: $620/credit hour
(master's); full time: $825/credit
hour, part time: $825/credit
hour (DNP)
Room/board/expenses: N/A
Full-time enrollment: 348
(master's), 55 (DNP)
men: N/A; women: N/A;
minorities: 14%; international:
0%
Part-time enrollment: N/A
(master's); N/A (DNP)
men: N/A; women: N/A;
minorities: N/A; international: N/A
Acceptance rate (master's): 100%
Specialties offered:
administration; education;
generalist; nurse practitioner;
nurse practitioner: family

University of Colorado

13120 E. 19th Avenue
Aurora, CO 80045
www.ucdenver.edu/academics/
colleges/nursing/Pages/default.
aspx
Public
Admissions: (303) 724-1450
Email:
shane.hoon@ucdenver.edu
Financial aid: (303) 724-8048
Application deadline: 02/15
Degrees offered: master's, Ph.D.,
DNP
In-state tuition: full time: $585/
credit hour, part time: $585/
credit hour (master's); full time:
$550/credit hour, part time:
$550/credit hour (Ph.D.); full
time: $585/credit hour, part time:
$585/credit hour (DNP)
Out-of-state tuition: full time:
$1,020/credit hour (master's);
full time: $1,020/credit hour
(Ph.D.); full time: $1,020/credit
hour (DNP)
Room/board/expenses: N/A
Full-time enrollment: 314
(master's), 39 (Ph.D.), 21 (DNP)
men: 13%; women: 87%;
minorities: 18%; international: 2%
Part-time enrollment: 95
(master's); N/A (Ph.D.), 38 (DNP)
men: 8%; women: 92%;
minorities: 10%; international:
0%
Acceptance rate (master's): 48%
Acceptance rate (Ph.D.): 79%
Acceptance rate (DNP): 100%

Specialties offered:
administration; clinical
nurse specialist; community
health/public health; health
management & policy health
care systems; informatics;
nurse-midwifery; nurse
practitioner; nurse practitioner:
adult-gerontology acute care;
nurse practitioner: adult-
gerontology primary care;
nurse practitioner: adult; nurse
practitioner: family; nurse
practitioner: pediatric primary
care; nurse practitioner:
psychiatric-mental health,
across the lifespan; other
majors; dual majors

University of Colorado-Colorado Springs

1420 Austin Bluffs Parkway
Colorado Springs, CO 80933-7150
www.uccs.edu/~bethel/
Public
Admissions: (719) 255-4490
Email: asilvasm@uccs.edu
Financial aid: (719) 255-3460
Application deadline: 03/15
Degrees offered: master's, DNP
In-state tuition: full time: $11,734,
part time: $4,407 (master's); full
time: $11,734, part time: $4,407
(DNP)
Out-of-state tuition: full time:
$20,068 (master's); full time:
$20,068 (DNP)
Room/board/expenses: $11,020
(master's); $11,020 (DNP)
Full-time enrollment: 11 (master's),
9 (DNP)
men: 15%; women: 85%;
minorities: 10%; international:
0%
Part-time enrollment: 151
(master's), 12 (DNP)
men: 5%; women: 95%;
minorities: 20%; international:
1%
Acceptance rate (master's): 56%
Acceptance rate (DNP): 52%
Specialties offered: education;
nurse practitioner; nurse
practitioner: adult-gerontology
primary care; nurse practitioner:
family

University of Northern Colorado[1]

Gunter 3080
PO Box 125
Greeley, CO 80639
Public
Admissions: N/A
Email: gradsch@unco.edu
Financial aid: N/A
Tuition: N/A
Room/board/expenses: N/A
Enrollment: N/A

CONNECTICUT

Fairfield University

1073 North Benson Road
Fairfield, CT 06824
www.fairfield.edu/nursing
Private
Admissions: (203) 254-4184
Email: gradadmis@fairfield.edu
Financial aid: (203) 254-4125
Application deadline: 08/01
Degrees offered: master's, DNP

Tuition: full time: $850/credit
hour, part time: $850/credit hour
(master's); full time: $950/credit
hour, part time: $950/credit
hour (DNP)
Room/board/expenses: N/A
Full-time enrollment: N/A
(master's); 43 (DNP)
men: 19%; women: 81%;
minorities: 35%; international:
2%
Part-time enrollment: 101
(master's), 80 (DNP)
men: 10%; women: 90%;
minorities: 20%; international:
0%
Acceptance rate (master's): 57%
Acceptance rate (DNP): 61%
Specialties offered: clinical nurse
leader; nurse anesthesia; nurse
practitioner; nurse practitioner:
family; nurse practitioner:
psychiatric-mental health,
across the lifespan; other majors

Quinnipiac University[1]

275 Mount Carmel Avenue
Hamden , CT 06518
www.quinnipiac.edu/nursing
Private
Admissions: (203) 582-8672
Email: graduate@quinnipiac.edu
Financial aid: (203) 582-8588
Tuition: N/A
Room/board/expenses: N/A
Enrollment: N/A

Sacred Heart University

5151 Park Avenue
Fairfield, CT 06825-1000
www.
sacredheart.edu/academics/
collegeofhealthprofessions/
academicprograms/nursing/
Private
Admissions: (203) 365-4827
Email:
gradstudies@sacredheart.edu
Financial aid: (203) 371-7980
Application deadline: N/A
Degrees offered: master's, DNP
Tuition: full time: N/A, part time:
$765/credit hour (master's); full
time: N/A, part time: $920/credit
hour (DNP)
Room/board/expenses: N/A
Full-time enrollment: 6 (master's),
13 (DNP)
men: 5%; women: 95%;
minorities: 21%; international:
0%
Part-time enrollment: 744
(master's), 33 (DNP)
men: 8%; women: 92%;
minorities: 18%; international:
0%
Acceptance rate (master's): 41%
Acceptance rate (DNP): 91%
Specialties offered:
administration; clinical nurse
leader; education; nurse
practitioner; nurse practitioner:
family

Southern Connecticut State University[1]

501 Crescent Street
New Haven, CT 06515
Public
Admissions: N/A
Financial aid: N/A
Tuition: N/A
Room/board/expenses: N/A
Enrollment: N/A

University of Connecticut

231 Glen Brook Road
Storrs, CT 06269-2026
nursing.uconn.edu/
Public
Admissions: (860) 486-1937
Email: nursingadmissions@
uconn.edu
Financial aid: (860) 486-2819
Application deadline: 02/01
Degrees offered: master's, Ph.D.,
DNP
In-state tuition: full time: $13,026,
part time: $724/credit hour
(master's); full time: $13,026,
part time: $724/credit hour
(Ph.D.); full time: $13,026, part
time: $724/credit hour (DNP)
Out-of-state tuition: full time:
$33,812 (master's); full time:
$33,812 (Ph.D.); full time:
$33,812 (DNP)
Room/board/expenses: N/A
Full-time enrollment: 34 (master's),
22 (Ph.D.), 19 (DNP)
men: 11%; women: 89%;
minorities: 25%; international:
3%
Part-time enrollment: 77
(master's), 10 (Ph.D.), 27 (DNP)
men: 16%; women: 84%;
minorities: 18%; international:
0%
Acceptance rate (master's): 54%
Acceptance rate (Ph.D.): 79%
Acceptance rate (DNP): 100%
Specialties offered: clinical nurse
leader; clinical nurse specialist;
nurse practitioner; nurse
practitioner: adult-gerontology
acute care; nurse practitioner:
adult-gerontology primary
care; nurse practitioner: family;
other majors; combined nurse
practitioner/clinical nurse
specialist

University of Hartford

200 Bloomfield Avenue
West Hartford, CT 06117
www.hartford.edu/enhp/
academics/health/default.aspx
Private
Admissions: (860) 768-4371
Email: gradstudy@hartford.edu
Financial aid: (860) 768-4296
Application deadline: N/A
Degrees offered: master's
Tuition: full time: $540/credit
hour, part time: $540/credit hour
Full-time enrollment: N/A
men: N/A; women: N/A;
minorities: N/A; international: N/A
Part-time enrollment: 108
men: 11%; women: 89%;
minorities: 21%; international: 3%
Acceptance rate (master's): 76%
Specialties offered:
administration; community
health/public health; education

University of St. Joseph[1]

1678 Asylum Avenue
West Hartford, CT 06117-2791
Private
Admissions: N/A
Financial aid: N/A
Tuition: N/A
Room/board/expenses: N/A
Enrollment: N/A

Western Connecticut State University[1]

181 White Street
Danbury, CT 06810
www.wcsu.edu/nursing/graduate/
Public
Admissions: N/A
Financial aid: N/A
Tuition: N/A
Room/board/expenses: N/A
Enrollment: N/A

Yale University

100 Church Street S
PO Box 9740
New Haven, CT 06536-0740
nursing.yale.edu
Private
Admissions: (203) 737-1793
Email: melissa.pucci@yale.edu
Financial aid: (203) 737-1790
Application deadline: 11/01
Degrees offered: master's, Ph.D.,
DNP
Tuition: full time: $36,828, part
time: $24,482 (master's); full
time: N/A, part time: N/A (Ph.D.);
full time: N/A, part time: $24,482
(DNP)
Room/board/expenses: N/A
Full-time enrollment: 253
(master's), 13 (Ph.D.), N/A (DNP)
men: 12%; women: 88%;
minorities: 24%; international:
4%
Part-time enrollment: 12
(master's); N/A (Ph.D.), 47 (DNP)
men: 24%; women: 76%;
minorities: 36%; international:
3%
Acceptance rate (master's): 29%
Acceptance rate (Ph.D.): 43%
Acceptance rate (DNP): 47%
Specialties offered: community
health/public health; health
management & policy health
care systems; nurse-midwifery;
nurse practitioner; nurse
practitioner: adult-gerontology
acute care; nurse practitioner:
adult-gerontology primary
care; nurse practitioner: family;
nurse practitioner: pediatric
primary care; nurse practitioner:
psychiatric-mental health,
across the lifespan; research;
dual majors

DELAWARE

University of Delaware[1]

25 N. College Avenue
Newark, DE
www.udel.edu/nursing/index.html
Public
Admissions: (302) 831-2129
Email: gradadmissions@udel.edu
Financial aid: (302) 831-2126
Tuition: N/A
Room/board/expenses: N/A
Enrollment: N/A

Wesley College

120 N. State Street
Dover, DE 19901
www.wesley.edu
Private
Admissions: (302) 736-2400
Email: admissions@wesley.edu
Financial aid: (302) 736-2483
Application deadline: N/A
Degrees offered: master's

Tuition: full time: $502/credit hour, part time: $502/credit hour
Room/board/expenses: N/A
Full-time enrollment: 17
men: 6%; women: 94%;
minorities: 41%; international: 0%
Part-time enrollment:
men: N/A; women: N/A;
minorities: N/A; international: N/A
Acceptance rate (master's): 26%
Specialties offered: clinical nurse specialist

Wilmington University[1]
320 N. DuPont Highway
New Castle, DE 19720-6491
Private
Admissions: N/A
Financial aid: N/A
Tuition: N/A
Room/board/expenses: N/A
Enrollment: N/A

DISTRICT OF COLUMBIA

The Catholic University of America
620 Michigan Ave NE
Washington, DC 20064
nursing.cua.edu/
Private
Admissions: (800) 673-2772
Email: cua-admissions@cua.edu
Financial aid: (202) 319-5307
Application deadline: 07/15
Degrees offered: master's, Ph.D., DNP
Tuition: full time: $41,400, part time: $1,650/credit hour (master's); full time: $41,400, part time: $1,650 (Ph.D.); full time: $41,400, part time: $1,650/credit hour (DNP)
Room/board/expenses: $15,822 (master's); $15,822 (Ph.D.); $15,822 (DNP)
Full-time enrollment: 27 (master's); 7 (Ph.D.); 1 (DNP)
men: 6%; women: 94%;
minorities: 23%; international: 20%
Part-time enrollment: 94 (master's); 80 (Ph.D.); 36 (DNP)
men: 7%; women: 93%;
minorities: 35%; international: 1%
Acceptance rate (master's): 66%
Acceptance rate (Ph.D.): 73%
Acceptance rate (DNP): 57%
Specialties offered: nurse practitioner; nurse practitioner: adult-gerontology primary care; nurse practitioner: family; nurse practitioner: pediatric primary care

Georgetown University
St. Mary's Hall
Washington, DC 20057
nhs.georgetown.edu/nursing
Private
Admissions: (202) 687-1309
Email: bwz2@georgetown.edu
Financial aid: (202) 687-4547
Application deadline: 01/15
Degrees offered: master's, DNP
Tuition: full time: $1,863/credit hour, part time: $1,863/credit hour (master's); full time: N/A, part time: $1,863/credit hour (DNP)
Room/board/expenses: $20,576 (master's); $20,576 (DNP)

Full-time enrollment: 273 (master's); N/A (DNP)
men: 13%; women: 85%;
minorities: 17%; international: 1%
Part-time enrollment: 613 (master's); 22 (DNP)
men: 7%; women: 90%;
minorities: 17%; international: 3%
Acceptance rate (master's): 42%
Acceptance rate (DNP): 52%
Specialties offered: clinical nurse leader; education; nurse anesthesia; nurse-midwifery; nurse practitioner; nurse practitioner: adult-gerontology acute care; nurse practitioner: family; combined nurse practitioner/clinical nurse specialist

George Washington University
900 23rd Street NW
Washington, DC 20037
nursing.gwu.edu
Private
Admissions: (571) 553-0101
Email: sonadmit@gwu.edu
Financial aid: (202) 994-6822
Application deadline: 02/15
Degrees offered: master's, DNP
Tuition: full time: $1,030/credit hour, part time: $1,030/credit hour (master's); full time: $1,030/credit hour, part time: $1,030/credit hour (DNP)
Room/board/expenses: N/A
Full-time enrollment: 39 (master's); 9 (DNP)
men: 8%; women: 92%;
minorities: 44%; international: 0%
Part-time enrollment: 364 (master's); 116 (DNP)
men: 11%; women: 89%;
minorities: 26%; international: 0%
Acceptance rate (master's): 59%
Acceptance rate (DNP): 79%
Specialties offered: administration; education; nurse-midwifery; nurse practitioner; nurse practitioner: adult-gerontology primary care; nurse practitioner: family; other majors

Howard University
516 Bryan Street NW
Washington, DC 20059
healthsciences.howard.edu/education/schools-and-academics/nursing-allied-health
Private
Admissions: (202) 806-5021
Email: tammi.damas@howard.edu
Financial aid: (202) 806-2820
Application deadline: 07/01
Degrees offered: master's
Tuition: full time: $29,090, part time: $1,700/credit hour
Room/board/expenses: $18,213
Full-time enrollment: 7
men: 14%; women: 86%;
minorities: 86%; international: 14%
Part-time enrollment: 24
men: 8%; women: 92%;
minorities: 100%; international: 0%
Acceptance rate (master's): 31%
Specialties offered: education; nurse practitioner; nurse practitioner: family

FLORIDA

Barry University[1]
11300 N.E. Second Avenue
Miami Shores, FL 33161-6695
Private
Admissions: N/A
Financial aid: N/A
Tuition: N/A
Room/board/expenses: N/A
Enrollment: N/A

Florida A&M University[1]
103 Ware-Rhaney Building
Tallahassee, FL 32307
Public
Admissions: N/A
Financial aid: N/A
Tuition: N/A
Room/board/expenses: N/A
Enrollment: N/A

Florida Atlantic University (Lynn)
777 Glades Road
Boca Raton, FL 33431
nursing.fau.edu/
Public
Admissions: (561) 297-2428
Email: nbarragan@fau.edu
Financial aid: (561) 297-3530
Application deadline: 06/01
Degrees offered: master's, Ph.D., DNP
In-state tuition: full time: $304/credit hour, part time: $304/credit hour (master's); full time: $304/credit hour, part time: $304/credit hour (Ph.D.); full time: $304/credit hour, part time: $304/credit hour (DNP)
Out-of-state tuition: full time: $928/credit hour (master's); full time: $928/credit hour (Ph.D.); full time: $928/credit hour (DNP)
Room/board/expenses: $10,518 (master's); $10,518 (Ph.D.); $10,518 (DNP)
Full-time enrollment: 8 (master's); 11 (Ph.D.); 46 (DNP)
men: 5%; women: 95%;
minorities: 60%; international: 3%
Part-time enrollment: 381 (master's); 38 (Ph.D.); 31 (DNP)
men: 7%; women: 93%;
minorities: 28%; international: 0%
Acceptance rate (master's): 52%
Acceptance rate (Ph.D.): 100%
Acceptance rate (DNP): 37%
Specialties offered: administration; clinical nurse leader; education; nurse practitioner; nurse practitioner: adult-gerontology primary care; nurse practitioner: family; research; other majors

Florida Gulf Coast University
10501 FGCU Boulevard S
Fort Myers, FL 33965
www.fgcu.edu/CHPSW/Nursing/index.html
Public
Admissions: (239) 590-1095
Email: admissions@fgcu.edu
Financial aid: (239) 590-7920
Application deadline: 12/15
Degrees offered: master's
In-state tuition: full time: $6,974, part time: N/A

Out-of-state tuition: full time: $28,170
Room/board/expenses: $8,320
Full-time enrollment: 35
men: 43%; women: 57%;
minorities: 29%; international: 0%
Part-time enrollment: 14
men: 21%; women: 79%;
minorities: 0%; international: 0%
Acceptance rate (master's): 69%
Specialties offered: education; nurse anesthesia; nurse practitioner; nurse practitioner: adult-gerontology primary care; nurse practitioner: family

Florida International University
11200 S.W. 8th Street, AHC3
Miami, FL 33199
cnhs.fiu.edu/nursing/graduate/index.html
Public
Admissions: (305) 348-7733
Email: gordony@fiu.edu
Financial aid: (305) 348-2333
Application deadline: 02/15
Degrees offered: master's, Ph.D., DNP
In-state tuition: full time: $628/credit hour, part time: N/A (master's); full time: $456/credit hour, part time: N/A (Ph.D.); full time: $564/credit hour, part time: N/A (DNP)
Out-of-state tuition: full time: $1,133/credit hour (master's); full time: $1,002/credit hour (Ph.D.); full time: $1,068/credit hour (DNP)
Room/board/expenses: N/A
Full-time enrollment: 200 (master's); 8 (Ph.D.); 57 (DNP)
men: 29%; women: 70%;
minorities: 77%; international: 2%
Part-time enrollment: 61 (master's); 14 (Ph.D.); 25 (DNP)
men: 16%; women: 84%;
minorities: 82%; international: 0%
Acceptance rate (master's): 34%
Acceptance rate (Ph.D.): 44%
Acceptance rate (DNP): 35%
Specialties offered: nurse anesthesia; nurse practitioner; nurse practitioner: adult-gerontology primary care; nurse practitioner: family; nurse practitioner: pediatric primary care; nurse practitioner: psychiatric-mental health, across the lifespan; research

Florida Southern College[1]
111 Lake Hollingsworth Drive
Lakeland, FL 33801-5698
Private
Admissions: N/A
Financial aid: N/A
Tuition: N/A
Room/board/expenses: N/A
Enrollment: N/A

Florida State University
102 Vivian M. Duxbury Hall
Tallahassee, FL 32306-4310
nursing.fsu.edu/
Public
Admissions: (850) 644-1328
Email: jfinney@admin.fsu.edu
Financial aid: (850) 644-0539

Application deadline: 04/15
Degrees offered: master's, DNP
In-state tuition: full time: $479/credit hour, part time: $479/credit hour (master's); full time: $479/credit hour, part time: $479/credit hour (DNP)
Out-of-state tuition: full time: $1,111/credit hour (master's); full time: $1,111/credit hour (DNP)
Room/board/expenses: N/A
Full-time enrollment: N/A (master's); 68 (DNP)
men: 12%; women: 88%;
minorities: 25%; international: 0%
Part-time enrollment: 22 (master's); 6 (DNP)
men: 4%; women: 96%;
minorities: 25%; international: 0%
Acceptance rate (master's): 50%
Acceptance rate (DNP): 76%
Specialties offered: education; nurse practitioner; nurse practitioner: family; other majors

Jacksonville University[1]
2800 University Boulevard N
Jacksonville, FL 32211
www.ju.edu/chs/Nursing/Pages/default.aspx
Private
Admissions: N/A
Financial aid: N/A
Tuition: N/A
Room/board/expenses: N/A
Enrollment: N/A

Keiser University
1900 W. Commercial Boulevard
Suite 100
Ft. Lauderdale, FL 33309
www.keiseruniversity.edu/
Private
Admissions: (954) 351-4040
Email: ryounkins@keiseruniversity.edu
Financial aid: N/A
Application deadline: 12/01
Degrees offered: master's, Ph.D., DNP
Tuition: full time: $20,904, part time: N/A (master's); full time: $20,904, part time: N/A (Ph.D.); full time: $20,904, part time: N/A (DNP)
Room/board/expenses: N/A
Full-time enrollment: 4 (master's); N/A (Ph.D.); N/A (DNP)
men: 25%; women: 75%;
minorities: 50%; international: N/A
Part-time enrollment: 73 (master's); 14 (Ph.D.); N/A (DNP)
men: 11%; women: 89%;
minorities: 54%; international: N/A
Acceptance rate (Ph.D.): 61%
Acceptance rate (DNP): 72%
Specialties offered: nurse practitioner

Nova Southeastern University
3200 S. University Drive
Fort Lauderdale, FL 33328
www.nova.edu/nursing
Private
Admissions: (954) 262-1975
Email: www.nova.edu/nursing
Financial aid: (954) 262-3380
Application deadline: N/A

Degrees offered: master's, Ph.D., DNP
Tuition: full time: $660/credit hour, part time: $660/credit hour (master's); full time: $850/credit hour, part time: $850 (Ph.D.); full time: $865/credit hour, part time: $865/credit hour (DNP)
Room/board/expenses: N/A
Full-time enrollment: 2 (master's); N/A (Ph.D.); 2 (DNP) men: N/A; women: N/A; minorities: 0%; international: 0%
Part-time enrollment: 429 (master's); 49 (Ph.D.); 28 (DNP) men: 9%; women: 91%; minorities: 65%; international: 1%
Acceptance rate (master's): 69%
Acceptance rate (Ph.D.): 43%
Acceptance rate (DNP): 50%
Specialties offered: education; health management & policy health care systems; informatics; nurse practitioner; nurse practitioner: family; research

University of Central Florida
12201 Research Parkway
Suite 300
Orlando, FL 32826-3298
www.nursing.ucf.edu/
Public
Admissions: (407) 823-2766
Email: gradnurse@ucf.edu
Financial aid: (407) 823-2827
Application deadline: 02/16
Degrees offered: master's, Ph.D., DNP
In-state tuition: full time: $370/credit hour, part time: $359/credit hour (master's); full time: $370/credit hour, part time: $370/credit hour (Ph.D.); full time: $370/credit hour, part time: $370/credit hour (DNP)
Out-of-state tuition: full time: $1,194/credit hour (master's); full time: $1,194/credit hour (Ph.D.); full time: $1,194/credit hour (DNP)
Room/board/expenses: $9,764 (master's); $9,764 (Ph.D.); $9,764 (DNP)
Full-time enrollment: 31 (master's); 13 (Ph.D.); 13 (DNP) men: 9%; women: 91%; minorities: 26%; international: 2%
Part-time enrollment: 180 (master's); 9 (Ph.D.); 52 (DNP) men: 11%; women: 89%; minorities: 28%; international: 0%
Acceptance rate (master's): 61%
Acceptance rate (Ph.D.): 90%
Acceptance rate (DNP): 52%
Specialties offered: administration; clinical nurse specialist; education; nurse practitioner; nurse practitioner: adult-gerontology primary care; nurse practitioner: family; research

University of Florida
PO Box 100197
Gainesville, FL 32610-0197
nursing.ufl.edu/
Public
Admissions: (352) 273-6409
Email: kimcurry@ufl.edu
Financial aid: (352) 273-6115
Application deadline: 12/31

Degrees offered: Ph.D., DNP
In-state tuition: full time: $531/credit hour, part time: $531/credit hour (Ph.D.); full time: $531/credit hour, part time: $531/credit hour (DNP)
Out-of-state tuition: full time: $1,255/credit hour (Ph.D.); full time: $1,255/credit hour (DNP)
Room/board/expenses: $16,630 (Ph.D.); $16,630 (DNP)
Full-time enrollment: 19 (Ph.D.); 111 (DNP) men: N/A; women: N/A; minorities: 25%; international: 2%
Part-time enrollment: 18 (Ph.D.); 122 (DNP) men: N/A; women: N/A; minorities: 26%; international: 2%
Acceptance rate (Ph.D.): 50%
Acceptance rate (DNP): 41%
Specialties offered: nurse-midwifery; nurse practitioner; nurse practitioner: adult-gerontology acute care; nurse practitioner: adult-gerontology primary care; nurse practitioner: family; nurse practitioner: pediatric primary care; nurse practitioner: psychiatric-mental health, across the lifespan; research; other majors

University of Miami
PO Box 248153
Coral Gables, FL 33124-3850
www.miami.edu/sonhs/index.php/sonhs/
Private
Admissions: (305) 284-4325
Email: nursinggrad@miami.edu
Financial aid: (305) 284-2270
Application deadline: 04/01
Degrees offered: master's, Ph.D., DNP
Tuition: full time: $40,700, part time: $24,420 (master's); full time: $1,850/credit hour, part time: $1,850/credit hour (Ph.D.); full time: $39,900, part time: $19,950 (DNP)
Room/board/expenses: $19,704 (master's); $19,704 (Ph.D.); $19,704 (DNP)
Full-time enrollment: 34 (master's); 23 (Ph.D.); 27 (DNP) men: 13%; women: 87%; minorities: 63%; international: 8%
Part-time enrollment: 135 (master's); N/A (Ph.D.); 30 (DNP) men: 19%; women: 81%; minorities: 70%; international: 0%
Acceptance rate (master's): 53%
Acceptance rate (Ph.D.): 54%
Acceptance rate (DNP): 56%
Specialties offered: informatics; nurse anesthesia; nurse practitioner; nurse practitioner: adult-gerontology acute care; nurse practitioner: adult-gerontology primary care; nurse practitioner: family; nurse practitioner: psychiatric-mental health, across the lifespan; research

University of North Florida
1 UNF Drive
Jacksonville, FL 32224
www.unf.edu/brooks/nursing/
Public
Admissions: (904) 620-1360
Email: graduateschool@unf.edu
Financial aid: (904) 620-5555
Application deadline: N/A
Degrees offered: DNP
In-state tuition: full time: $436/credit hour, part time: $436/credit hour
Out-of-state tuition: full time: $1,017/credit hour
Room/board/expenses: $9,487
Full-time enrollment: 63 men: N/A; women: N/A; minorities: N/A; international: N/A
Part-time enrollment: 83 men: N/A; women: N/A; minorities: N/A; international: N/A
Acceptance rate (DNP): 82%
Specialties offered: nurse anesthesia; nurse practitioner; nurse practitioner: family

University of South Florida
12901 Bruce B. Downs Boulevard
Tampa, FL 33612-4766
health.usf.edu/nursing/index.htm
Public
Admissions: (813) 974-3282
Email: jford2@health.usf.edu
Financial aid: (813) 974-4700
Application deadline: 02/03
Degrees offered: master's, Ph.D., DNP
In-state tuition: full time: $348/credit hour, part time: $348/credit hour (master's); full time: $348/credit hour, part time: $348/credit hour (Ph.D.); full time: $348/credit hour, part time: $348/credit hour (DNP)
Out-of-state tuition: full time: $772/credit hour, part time: $772/credit hour (master's); full time: $772/credit hour, part time: $772/credit hour (DNP)
Room/board/expenses: $9,400 (master's); $9,400 (Ph.D.); $9,400 (DNP)
Full-time enrollment: 83 (master's); 21 (Ph.D.); 55 (DNP) men: 15%; women: 85%; minorities: 6%; international: 41%
Part-time enrollment: 636 (master's); 12 (Ph.D.); 73 (DNP) men: 13%; women: 87%; minorities: 33%; international: 4%
Acceptance rate (master's): 42%
Acceptance rate (Ph.D.): 37%
Acceptance rate (DNP): 58%
Specialties offered: clinical nurse leader; community health/public health; education; nurse anesthesia; nurse practitioner; nurse practitioner: adult-gerontology acute care; nurse practitioner: adult-gerontology primary care; nurse practitioner: family; nurse practitioner: pediatric primary care; dual majors

University of Tampa
401 W. Kennedy Boulevard
Tampa, FL 33606-1490
www.ut.edu/nursing
Private
Admissions: (813) 253-6211
Email: admissions@ut.edu
Financial aid: (813) 253-6219
Application deadline: N/A
Degrees offered: master's
Tuition: full time: $573/credit hour, part time: $573/credit hour
Room/board/expenses: $8,900
Full-time enrollment: 1 men: N/A; women: 100%; minorities: N/A; international: N/A
Part-time enrollment: 153 men: 14%; women: 85%; minorities: 18%; international: 0%
Acceptance rate (master's): 54%
Specialties offered: administration; education; generalist; informatics; nurse practitioner: adult-gerontology primary care; nurse practitioner: family; nurse practitioner: pediatric primary care; other majors

University of West Florida[1]
Pensacola, FL 32514
Public
Admissions: N/A
Financial aid: N/A
Tuition: N/A
Room/board/expenses: N/A
Enrollment: N/A

GEORGIA

Albany State University[1]
504 College Drive
Albany, GA 31705
Public
Admissions: N/A
Financial aid: N/A
Tuition: N/A
Room/board/expenses: N/A
Enrollment: N/A

Armstrong State University[1]
11935 Abercorn Street
Savannah, GA 31419
Public
Admissions: N/A
Financial aid: N/A
Tuition: N/A
Room/board/expenses: N/A
Enrollment: N/A

Augusta University
997 St. Sebastian Way, EG 1030
Augusta, GA 30912
www.gru.edu/nursing
Public
Admissions: (706) 737-1524
Email: admissions@gru.edu
Financial aid: (706) 737-1524
Application deadline: 02/01
Degrees offered: master's, Ph.D., DNP
In-state tuition: full time: $574/credit hour, part time: $514/credit hour (master's); full time: $391/credit hour, part time: $391/credit hour (Ph.D.); full time: $453/credit hour, part time: $453/credit hour (DNP)

Out-of-state tuition: full time: $1,198/credit hour (master's); full time: $1,092/credit hour (Ph.D.); full time: $453/credit hour (DNP)
Room/board/expenses: $5,550 (master's); $5,550 (Ph.D.); $5,550 (DNP)
Full-time enrollment: 311 (master's); 9 (Ph.D.); 65 (DNP) men: 20%; women: 80%; minorities: 26%; international: 0%
Part-time enrollment: 16 (master's); 7 (Ph.D.); 77 (DNP) men: 13%; women: 87%; minorities: 17%; international: 0%
Acceptance rate (master's): 37%
Acceptance rate (Ph.D.): 57%
Acceptance rate (DNP): 67%
Specialties offered: clinical nurse leader; nurse anesthesia; nurse practitioner; nurse practitioner: adult-gerontology acute care; nurse practitioner: family; nurse practitioner: pediatric primary care; nurse practitioner: psychiatric-mental health, across the lifespan; research

Brenau University[1]
500 Washington Street SE
Gainesville, GA 30501
www.brenau.edu/healthsciences/department-of-nursing/
Private
Admissions: (770) 534-6100
Email: admissions@brenau.edu
Financial aid: (770) 534-6152
Tuition: N/A
Room/board/expenses: N/A
Enrollment: N/A

Clayton State University
2000 Clayton State Boulevard
Morrow, GA 30260
www.clayton.edu/health/nursing
Public
Admissions: (678) 466-4108
Email: www.clayton.edu/graduate
Financial aid: (678) 466-4185
Application deadline: 11/15
Degrees offered: master's
In-state tuition: full time: $385/credit hour, part time: $385/credit hour
Out-of-state tuition: full time: $385/credit hour
Full-time enrollment: 16 men: 19%; women: 81%; minorities: 81%; international: 13%
Part-time enrollment: 42 men: 7%; women: 93%; minorities: 88%; international: 0%
Acceptance rate (master's): 48%
Specialties offered: administration; education; nurse practitioner; nurse practitioner: family

Columbus State University[1]
Columbus, GA 31907
Public
Admissions: N/A
Financial aid: N/A
Tuition: N/A
Room/board/expenses: N/A
Enrollment: N/A

Emory University

1520 Clifton Road, NE
Atlanta, GA 30322-4207
www.nursing.emory.edu/
Private
Admissions: (404) 727-7980
Email:
nursingquestions@emory.edu
Financial aid: (404) 712-8456
Application deadline: 03/30
Degrees offered: master's, Ph.D., DNP
Tuition: full time: $1,750/credit hour, part time: $1,750/credit hour (master's); full time: $38,800, part time: $2,156/credit hour (Ph.D.); full time: $1,750/credit hour, part time: $1,750/credit hour (DNP)
Room/board/expenses: N/A
Full-time enrollment: 201 (master's); 29 (Ph.D.); 6 (DNP) men: 8%; women: 92%; minorities: 22%; international: 2%
Part-time enrollment: 27 (master's); N/A (Ph.D.); 11 (DNP) men: 13%; women: 87%; minorities: 45%; international: 0%
Acceptance rate (master's): 81%
Acceptance rate (Ph.D.): 43%
Acceptance rate (DNP): 79%
Specialties offered: health management & policy health care systems; nurse-midwifery; nurse practitioner; nurse practitioner: adult-gerontology acute care; nurse practitioner: adult-gerontology primary care; nurse practitioner: family; nurse practitioner: pediatric primary care; other majors; dual majors

Georgia College & State University

Campus Box 63
Milledgeville, GA 31061
www.gcsu.edu/health/nursing
Public
Admissions: (478) 445-6289
Email: grad-admit@gcsu.edu
Financial aid: (478) 445-5149
Application deadline: 01/12
Degrees offered: master's, DNP
In-state tuition: full time: $373/credit hour, part time: $373/credit hour (master's); full time: $373/credit hour, part time: $373/credit hour (DNP)
Out-of-state tuition: full time: $373/credit hour (master's); full time: $373/credit hour (DNP)
Room/board/expenses: N/A
Full-time enrollment: 62 (master's); 16 (DNP) men: 9%; women: 91%; minorities: 24%; international: 0%
Part-time enrollment: 34 (master's); 6 (DNP) men: 8%; women: 93%; minorities: 25%; international: 0%
Acceptance rate (master's): 94%
Acceptance rate (DNP): 95%
Specialties offered: education; nurse practitioner; nurse practitioner: family; nurse practitioner: psychiatric-mental health, across the lifespan

Georgia Southern University

P. O. Box 8158
Statesboro, GA 30460
chhs.georgiasouthern.edu/nursing/
Public
Admissions: (912) 478-5384
Email: gradadmissions@georgiasouthern.edu
Financial aid: (912) 478-5413
Application deadline: 03/01
Degrees offered: master's, DNP
In-state tuition: full time: $277/credit hour, part time: N/A (master's); full time: $462/credit hour, part time: N/A (DNP)
Out-of-state tuition: full time: $1,105/credit hour (master's); full time: $462/credit hour (DNP)
Room/board/expenses: $9,800 (master's); N/A (DNP)
Full-time enrollment: 18 (master's); 55 (DNP) men: 12%; women: 88%; minorities: 29%; international: 0%
Part-time enrollment: N/A (master's); N/A (DNP) men: N/A; women: N/A; minorities: N/A; international: N/A
Acceptance rate (master's): 0%
Acceptance rate (DNP): 71%
Specialties offered: nurse practitioner; nurse practitioner: family; nurse practitioner: psychiatric-mental health, across the lifespan; other majors

Georgia State University

P. O. Box 3995
Atlanta, GA 30302-3995
snhp.gsu.edu
Public
Admissions: (404) 413-2500
Email: admissions@gsu.edu
Financial aid: (404) 413-2600
Application deadline: 02/01
Degrees offered: master's, Ph.D., DNP
In-state tuition: full time: $388/credit hour, part time: $388/credit hour (master's); full time: $388/credit hour, part time: $388/credit hour (Ph.D.); full time: $382/credit hour, part time: $382/credit hour (DNP)
Out-of-state tuition: full time: $1,249/credit hour (master's); full time: $1,249/credit hour (Ph.D.); full time: $1,243/credit hour (DNP)
Room/board/expenses: $14,160 (master's); $14,160 (Ph.D.); $14,160 (DNP)
Full-time enrollment: 82 (master's); 4 (Ph.D.); 3 (DNP) men: 6%; women: 94%; minorities: 100%; international: 4%
Part-time enrollment: 166 (master's); 17 (Ph.D.); 10 (DNP) men: 10%; women: 90%; minorities: 100%; international: 0%
Acceptance rate (master's): 73%
Acceptance rate (Ph.D.): 71%
Acceptance rate (DNP): 90%
Specialties offered: administration; clinical nurse specialist; informatics; nurse practitioner; nurse practitioner: adult-gerontology acute care; nurse practitioner: adult-gerontology primary care;

nurse practitioner: adult; nurse practitioner: family; nurse practitioner: pediatric primary care; nurse practitioner: psychiatric-mental health, across the lifespan

Kennesaw State University[1]

1000 Chastain Road
Kennesaw, GA 30144-5591
Public
Admissions: N/A
Financial aid: N/A
Tuition: N/A
Room/board/expenses: N/A
Enrollment: N/A

Mercer University

3001 Mercer University Drive
Atlanta, GA 30341
nursing.mercer.edu/
Private
Admissions: (678) 547-6700
Email: nursingadmissions@mercer.edu
Financial aid: (678) 547-6444
Application deadline: 03/01
Degrees offered: master's, Ph.D., DNP
Tuition: full time: $29,784, part time: $1,103/credit hour (master's); full time: $31,443, part time: $1,165/credit hour (Ph.D.); full time: $15,780, part time: $1,165/credit hour (DNP)
Room/board/expenses: N/A
Full-time enrollment: 62 (master's); 8 (Ph.D.); 4 (DNP) men: 8%; women: 92%; minorities: 45%; international: 4%
Part-time enrollment: 26 (master's); 18 (Ph.D.); N/A (DNP) men: 9%; women: 91%; minorities: 27%; international: 0%
Acceptance rate (master's): 70%
Acceptance rate (Ph.D.): 86%
Acceptance rate (DNP): 42%
Specialties offered: nurse practitioner: family

South University[1]

709 Mall Boulevard
Savannah, GA 31406
Private
Admissions: N/A
Financial aid: N/A
Tuition: N/A
Room/board/expenses: N/A
Enrollment: N/A

Thomas University[1]

1501 Millpond Road
Thomasville, GA 31792
Private
Admissions: N/A
Financial aid: N/A
Tuition: N/A
Room/board/expenses: N/A
Enrollment: N/A

University of North Georgia[1]

82 College Circle
Dahlonega, GA 30597
Public
Admissions: N/A
Financial aid: N/A
Tuition: N/A
Room/board/expenses: N/A
Enrollment: N/A

University of West Georgia[1]

1601 Maple Street
Carrollton, GA 30118
nursing.westga.edu/index.php
Public
Admissions: (678) 839-1390
Email: tziglar@westga.edu
Financial aid: (678) 839-6421
Tuition: N/A
Room/board/expenses: N/A
Enrollment: N/A

Valdosta State University[1]

S. Walter Martin Hall
Valdosta, GA 31698-0130
Public
Admissions: N/A
Financial aid: N/A
Tuition: N/A
Room/board/expenses: N/A
Enrollment: N/A

HAWAII

Hawaii Pacific University

45-045 Kamehameha Highway
Kaneohe, HI 96744
www.hpu.edu
Private
Admissions: (808) 236-5847
Email: DKNIGHT@HPU.EDU
Financial aid: (808) 544-1126
Application deadline: 04/15
Degrees offered: master's
Tuition: full time: $1,275/credit hour, part time: $1,275/credit hour
Room/board/expenses: $13,500
Full-time enrollment: 36 men: 19%; women: 81%; minorities: 56%; international: 6%
Part-time enrollment: 20 men: 10%; women: 90%; minorities: 40%; international: 25%
Acceptance rate (master's): 74%
Specialties offered: nurse practitioner; nurse practitioner: adult-gerontology acute care; nurse practitioner: family; dual majors

University of Hawaii-Hilo[1]

Hilo, HI 96720
Public
Admissions: N/A
Financial aid: N/A
Tuition: N/A
Room/board/expenses: N/A
Enrollment: N/A

University of Hawaii-Manoa

2528 McCarthy Mall
Webster Hall
Honolulu, HI 96822
www.nursing.hawaii.edu/home
Public
Admissions: (808) 956-8544
Email: graduate.education@hawaii.edu
Financial aid: (808) 956-7251
Application deadline: 01/04
Degrees offered: master's, Ph.D., DNP

In-state tuition: full time: $933/credit hour, part time: $933/credit hour (master's); full time: $933/credit hour (Ph.D.); full time: $933/credit hour, part time: $933/credit hour (DNP)
Out-of-state tuition: full time: $1,770/credit hour (master's); full time: $1,770/credit hour (Ph.D.); full time: $1,770/credit hour (DNP)
Room/board/expenses: $13,898 (master's); $13,898 (Ph.D.); $13,898 (DNP)
Full-time enrollment: 105 (master's); 8 (Ph.D.); 44 (DNP) men: N/A; women: N/A; minorities: 68%; international: 0%
Part-time enrollment: 57 (master's); 32 (Ph.D.); 16 (DNP) men: 14%; women: 86%; minorities: 58%; international: 2%
Acceptance rate (master's): 77%
Acceptance rate (Ph.D.): 0%
Acceptance rate (DNP): 38%
Specialties offered: administration; clinical nurse specialist; community health/public health; nurse practitioner; nurse practitioner: adult-gerontology primary care; nurse practitioner: family

IDAHO

Boise State University[1]

1910 University Drive
Boise, ID 82537-1840
hs.boisestate.edu/nursing/news/
Public
Admissions: (208) 426-3903
Email: gradcoll@boisestate.edu
Financial aid: (800) 824-7017
Tuition: N/A
Room/board/expenses: N/A
Enrollment: N/A

Idaho State University[1]

921 S. 8th Avenue
Stop 8101
Pocatello, ID 83209-8101
www.isu.edu/nursing
Public
Admissions: (208) 282-2325
Email: profnurs@isu.edu
Financial aid: (208) 282-2756
Tuition: N/A
Room/board/expenses: N/A
Enrollment: N/A

Northwest Nazarene University[1]

623 S. University Boulevard
Nampa, ID 83686
Private
Admissions: N/A
Financial aid: N/A
Tuition: N/A
Room/board/expenses: N/A
Enrollment: N/A

ILLINOIS

Aurora University[1]

347 S. Gladstone Ave.
Aurora, IL 60506
Private
Admissions: N/A
Financial aid: N/A
Tuition: N/A
Room/board/expenses: N/A
Enrollment: N/A

Benedictine University[1]

5700 College Road
Lisle, IL 60532
www.ben.edu/
college-of-education-and-
health-services/nursing-health/
faculty-staff.cfm
Private
Admissions: (630) 366-2981
Email: online.ben.edu/msn/
masters-in-nursing
Financial aid: (630) 829-6415
Tuition: N/A
Room/board/expenses: N/A
Enrollment: N/A

Blessing-Rieman College of Nursing[1]

P. O. Box 7005
Quincy, IL 62305-7005
Private
Admissions: (217) 228-5520
Email: admissions@brcn.edu
Financial aid: (217) 228-5520
Tuition: N/A
Room/board/expenses: N/A
Enrollment: N/A

Bradley University[1]

1501 W. Bradley Avenue
Peoria, IL 61625-0001
Private
Admissions: N/A
Financial aid: N/A
Tuition: N/A
Room/board/expenses: N/A
Enrollment: N/A

Chamberlain College of Nursing

3005 Highland Parkway
Downers Grove, IL 60515
www.chamberlain.edu
Private
Admissions: (888) 556-8226
Financial aid: (888) 556-8226
Application deadline: N/A
Degrees offered: master's, DNP
Tuition: full time: $15,600,
part time: $650/credit hour
(master's); full time: $13,500,
part time: $750/credit hour (DNP)
Room/board/expenses: N/A
Full-time enrollment: 5,367
(master's); 478 (DNP)
men: 10%; women: 90%;
minorities: 32%; international:
0%
Part-time enrollment: 2,078
(master's); 288 (DNP)
men: 9%; women: 91%;
minorities: 31%; international:
0%
Acceptance rate (master's): 96%
Acceptance rate (DNP): 99%
Specialties offered:
administration; education; health
management & policy health
care systems; informatics; nurse
practitioner; nurse practitioner:
family

DePaul University

990 W. Fullerton Avenue
Chicago, IL 60613
csh.depaul.edu/departments/
nursing/
Private
Admissions: (773) 325-7315
Email: graddepaul@depaul.edu
Financial aid: (312) 362-8610
Application deadline: N/A
Degrees offered: master's, DNP
Tuition: full time: $680/credit
hour, part time: $680/credit hour
(master's); full time: $680/credit
hour, part time: $680/credit
hour (DNP)
Room/board/expenses: N/A
Full-time enrollment: 291
(master's); 63 (DNP)
men: 14%; women: 86%;
minorities: 18%; international: 1%
Part-time enrollment: 28
(master's); 25 (DNP)
men: 17%; women: 83%;
minorities: 32%; international:
0%
Acceptance rate (master's): 45%
Acceptance rate (DNP): 97%
Specialties offered: generalist;
nurse anesthesia; nurse
practitioner; nurse practitioner:
adult-gerontology primary care;
nurse practitioner: family

Elmhurst College[1]

190 Prospect Avenue
Elmhurst, IL 60126
Private
Admissions: N/A
Financial aid: N/A
Tuition: N/A
Room/board/expenses: N/A
Enrollment: N/A

Governors State University

1 University Parkway
University Park, IL 60484
www.govst.edu/
Public
Admissions: (708) 534-4490
Email: gsunow@govst.edu
Financial aid: (708) 534-4480
Application deadline: N/A
Degrees offered: master's, DNP
In-state tuition: full time: $7,368,
part time: $307/credit hour
(master's); full time: $16,632,
part time: $693/credit hour
(DNP)
Out-of-state tuition: full time:
$14,736 (master's); full time:
$23,760 (DNP)
Room/board/expenses: $9,638
(master's); $9,638 (DNP)
Full-time enrollment: 3 (master's);
6 (DNP)
men: 0%; women: 100%;
minorities: 33%; international:
0%
Part-time enrollment: 155
(master's); 20 (DNP)
men: 13%; women: 87%;
minorities: 70%; international:
0%
Acceptance rate (master's): 97%
Acceptance rate (DNP): 100%
Specialties offered:
administration; clinical nurse
specialist; nurse practitioner;
nurse practitioner: family

Illinois State University

Campus Box 5810
Normal, IL 61790-5810
nursing.illinoisstate.edu/
Public
Admissions: (309) 438-2181
Email: admissions@ilstu.edu
Financial aid: (309) 438-2231
Application deadline: 03/01
Degrees offered: master's, Ph.D.,
DNP
In-state tuition: full time: $374/
credit hour, part time: $374/
credit hour (master's); full time:
$374/credit hour, part time:
$374/credit hour (Ph.D.); full
time: $374/credit hour, part time:
$374/credit hour (DNP)
Out-of-state tuition: full time: $777/
credit hour (master's); full time:
$777/credit hour (Ph.D.); full time:
$777/credit hour (DNP)
Room/board/expenses: $8,460
(master's); $8,460 (Ph.D.);
$8,460 (DNP)
Full-time enrollment: 10 (master's);
N/A (Ph.D.); N/A (DNP)
men: 20%; women: 80%;
minorities: 0%; international:
10%
Part-time enrollment: 76
(master's); 22 (Ph.D.); 17 (DNP)
men: 9%; women: 91%;
minorities: 6%; international: 0%
Acceptance rate (master's): 54%
Acceptance rate (Ph.D.): 50%
Acceptance rate (DNP): 78%
Specialties offered:
administration; nurse
practitioner; nurse practitioner:
family; research

Lewis University

One University Parkway
Romeoville, IL 60446
www.lewisu.edu/academics/
nursing/
Private
Admissions: (815) 836-5610
Email: grad@lewisu.edu
Financial aid: (815) 836-5263
Application deadline: 04/02
Degrees offered: master's, DNP
Tuition: full time: $770/credit
hour, part time: $770/credit hour
(master's); full time: $760/credit
hour, part time: $760/credit
hour (DNP)
Room/board/expenses: $9,930
(master's); $9,930 (DNP)
Full-time enrollment: 7 (master's);
N/A (DNP)
men: 14%; women: 86%;
minorities: 29%; international:
0%
Part-time enrollment: 351
(master's); 16 (DNP)
men: 6%; women: 94%;
minorities: 28%; international:
0%
Specialties offered:
administration; clinical nurse
specialist; education; nurse
practitioner; nurse practitioner:
adult-gerontology acute care;
nurse practitioner: adult-
gerontology primary care; nurse
practitioner: family; school
nursing; other majors; dual
majors

Loyola University Chicago

6525 North Sheridan Road
Chicago, IL 60626-5385
www.luc.edu/nursing
Private
Admissions: (312) 915-8902
Email: gradapp@luc.edu
Financial aid: (773) 508-7704
Application deadline: 06/01
Degrees offered: master's, Ph.D.,
DNP

McKendree University

701 College Road
Lebanon, IL 62254
www.mckendree.edu/
academics/info/nursing-health/
nursing/index.php
Private
Admissions: (618) 537-6576
Email: graduate@mckendree.edu
Financial aid: (618) 537-6828
Application deadline: N/A
Degrees offered: master's
Tuition: full time: $430/credit
hour, part time: $430/credit hour
Room/board/expenses: N/A
Full-time enrollment: 3
men: 33%; women: 67%;
minorities: 0%; international: 0%
Part-time enrollment: 70
men: 3%; women: 97%;
minorities: 16%; international:
0%
Acceptance rate (master's): 53%
Specialties offered:
administration; education; other
majors; dual majors

Millikin University

1184 W. Main Street
Decatur, IL 62522-2084
www.millikin.edu/
graduate-nursing
Private
Admissions: (217) 424-6210
Email: admis@millikin.edu
Financial aid: (217) 424-6317
Application deadline: N/A
Degrees offered: master's, DNP
Tuition: full time: $750/credit
hour, part time: $750/credit hour
(master's); full time: $857/credit
hour, part time: $857/credit hour
(DNP)
Room/board/expenses: N/A
Full-time enrollment: 21 (master's);
23 (DNP)
men: 39%; women: 61%;
minorities: 14%; international: 2%
Part-time enrollment: 15
(master's); 3 (DNP)
men: 6%; women: 94%;
minorities: 17%; international: 0%
Acceptance rate (master's): 28%

Tuition: full time: $1,060/credit
hour, part time: $1,060/credit
hour (master's); full time: $1,060/
credit hour, part time: $1,060/
credit hour (Ph.D.); full time:
$1,060/credit hour, part time:
$1,060/credit hour (DNP)
Room/board/expenses: $11,500
(master's); $11,500 (Ph.D.);
$11,500 (DNP)
Full-time enrollment: 138
(master's); 25 (Ph.D.); 11 (DNP)
men: 7%; women: 93%;
minorities: 19%; international: 2%
Part-time enrollment: 206
(master's); 7 (Ph.D.); 19 (DNP)
men: 5%; women: 95%;
minorities: 27%; international:
0%
Acceptance rate (master's): 74%
Acceptance rate (Ph.D.): 100%
Acceptance rate (DNP): 88%
Specialties offered: clinical nurse
specialist; health management
& policy health care systems;
informatics; nurse practitioner;
nurse practitioner: adult-
gerontology acute care; nurse
practitioner: adult-gerontology
primary care; nurse practitioner:
family; research; other majors;
dual majors

Northern Illinois University[1]

1240 Normal Road
DeKalb, IL 60115
Public
Admissions: N/A
Financial aid: N/A
Tuition: N/A
Room/board/expenses: N/A
Enrollment: N/A

North Park University[1]

3225 W. Foster Avenue
Chicago, IL 60625-4895
Private
Admissions: N/A
Financial aid: N/A
Tuition: N/A
Room/board/expenses: N/A
Enrollment: N/A

Olivet Nazarene University[1]

3601 Algonquin Road
Rolling Meadows, IL 60008
Private
Admissions: N/A
Financial aid: N/A
Tuition: N/A
Room/board/expenses: N/A
Enrollment: N/A

Resurrection University[1]

1431 N. Claremont Avenue
Chicago, IL 60622
Private
Admissions: N/A
Financial aid: N/A
Tuition: N/A
Room/board/expenses: N/A
Enrollment: N/A

Rush University

600 S. Paulina, Suite 1080
Chicago, IL 60612-3873
www.rushu.rush.edu/servlet/
Satellite?c=RushUnivLevel1Page&
cid=1204497838852&pagename=
Private
Admissions: (312) 942-7110
Email: con_admissions@rush.edu
Financial aid: (312) 942-6523
Application deadline: 01/04
Degrees offered: master's, Ph.D.,
DNP
Tuition: full time: $947/credit
hour, part time: $999/credit hour
(master's); full time: $999/credit
hour, part time: $999/credit hour
(Ph.D.); full time: $999/credit
hour, part time: $999/credit
hour (DNP)
Room/board/expenses: N/A
Full-time enrollment: 276
(master's); N/A (Ph.D.); 79 (DNP)
men: 15%; women: 85%;
minorities: 26%; international:
0%
Part-time enrollment: 61
(master's); 30 (Ph.D.); 644 (DNP)
men: 8%; women: 92%;
minorities: 22%; international:
0%
Acceptance rate (master's): 41%
Acceptance rate (Ph.D.): 86%
Acceptance rate (DNP): 60%

Acceptance rate (DNP): 30%
Specialties offered: education;
nurse anesthesia

Specialties offered: clinical nurse leader; clinical nurse specialist; community health/public health; generalist; health management & policy health care systems; nurse anesthesia; nurse practitioner; nurse practitioner: adult-gerontology acute care; nurse practitioner: adult-gerontology primary care; nurse practitioner: family; nurse practitioner: pediatric primary care; nurse practitioner: psychiatric-mental health, across the lifespan; research; other majors

Southern Illinois University-Edwardsville

Campus Box 1066
Edwardsville, IL 62026-1066
www.siue.edu/nursing/
Public
Admissions: (618) 650-3705
Email: tburrel@siue.edu
Financial aid: (618) 650-3880
Application deadline: 07/18
Degrees offered: master's, DNP
In-state tuition: full time: $293/credit hour, part time: $350/credit hour (master's); full time: $650/credit hour, part time: $650/credit hour (DNP)
Out-of-state tuition: full time: $810/credit hour (master's); full time: $650/credit hour (DNP)
Room/board/expenses: N/A
Full-time enrollment: 117 (master's); 45 (DNP)
men: 19%; women: 81%; minorities: 12%; international: N/A
Part-time enrollment: 69 (master's); 35 (DNP)
men: 10%; women: 90%; minorities: 12%; international: N/A
Acceptance rate (master's): 68%
Acceptance rate (DNP): 43%
Specialties offered: administration; education; nurse anesthesia; nurse practitioner; nurse practitioner: family

St. Anthony College of Nursing[1]

5658 E. State Street
Rockford, IL 61108-2468
sacn.edu
Private
Admissions: (815) 395-5476
Email: angelataillet@sacn.edu
Financial aid: (815) 395-5089
Tuition: N/A
Room/board/expenses: N/A
Enrollment: N/A

St. Francis Medical Center

511 NE Greenleaf
Peoria, IL 61603
www.sfmccon.edu/
Private
Admissions: (309) 655-6362
Email: janice.farquharson@osfhealthcare.org
Financial aid: (309) 655-4119
Application deadline: 04/01
Degrees offered: master's, DNP

Tuition: full time: $10,890, part time: $605/credit hour (master's); full time: $10,890, part time: $605/credit hour (DNP)
Room/board/expenses: $3,400 (master's); $3,400 (DNP)
Full-time enrollment: 13 (master's); N/A (DNP)
men: 8%; women: 92%; minorities: 0%; international: 0%
Part-time enrollment: 224 (master's); 23 (DNP)
men: 11%; women: 89%; minorities: 9%; international: 0%
Acceptance rate (master's): 96%
Acceptance rate (DNP): 86%
Specialties offered: administration; clinical nurse leader; clinical nurse specialist; education; nurse practitioner; nurse practitioner: adult-gerontology primary care; nurse practitioner: family; nurse practitioner: psychiatric-mental health, across the lifespan

St. Xavier University

3700 W. 103rd Street
Chicago, IL 60655
www.sxu.edu/academics/colleges_schools/son/index.asp
Private
Admissions: (773) 298-3096
Email: graduateadmission@sxu.edu
Financial aid: (773) 298-3070
Application deadline: 06/01
Degrees offered: master's
Tuition: full time: $905/credit hour, part time: $905/credit hour
Room/board/expenses: $12,050
Full-time enrollment: 145
men: 9%; women: 92%; minorities: 33%; international: 0%
Part-time enrollment: 134
men: 9%; women: 90%; minorities: 30%; international: 0%
Acceptance rate (master's): 53%
Specialties offered: administration; clinical nurse leader; education; nurse practitioner; nurse practitioner: family; dual majors

University of Illinois-Chicago

845 South Damen Avenue
MC 802
Chicago, IL 60612
nursing.uic.edu
Public
Admissions: (312) 996-7800
Email: conapply@uic.edu
Financial aid: (312) 996-3126
Application deadline: 01/15
Degrees offered: master's, Ph.D., DNP
In-state tuition: full time: $20,120, part time: $13,414 (master's); full time: $20,120, part time: $13,414 (Ph.D.); full time: $22,250, part time: $14,834 (DNP)
Out-of-state tuition: full time: $32,360 (master's); full time: $32,360 (Ph.D.); full time: $34,720 (DNP)
Room/board/expenses: $11,371 (master's); $11,371 (Ph.D.); $11,371 (DNP)

Full-time enrollment: 298 (master's); 39 (Ph.D.); 38 (DNP)
men: 9%; women: 91%; minorities: 30%; international: 9%
Part-time enrollment: 190 (master's); 29 (Ph.D.); 267 (DNP)
men: 10%; women: 89%; minorities: 30%; international: 1%
Acceptance rate (master's): 64%
Acceptance rate (Ph.D.): 49%
Acceptance rate (DNP): 91%
Specialties offered: administration; clinical nurse leader; community health/public health; education; generalist; informatics; nurse-midwifery; nurse practitioner; nurse practitioner: adult-gerontology acute care; nurse practitioner: adult-gerontology primary care; nurse practitioner: family; nurse practitioner: pediatric primary care; nurse practitioner: psychiatric-mental health, across the lifespan; research; school nursing; other majors; dual majors

University of St. Francis

500 Wilcox Street
Joliet , IL 60435
www.stfrancis.edu/academics/college-of-nursing
Private
Admissions: (800) 735-7500
Email: admissions@stfrancis.edu
Financial aid: (866) 890-8331
Application deadline: 03/01
Degrees offered: master's, DNP
Tuition: full time: N/A, part time: $760/credit hour (master's); full time: N/A, part time: $770/credit hour (DNP)
Room/board/expenses: N/A
Full-time enrollment: 70 (master's); 12 (DNP)
men: 12%; women: 88%; minorities: 32%; international: 0%
Part-time enrollment: 303 (master's); 18 (DNP)
men: 8%; women: 92%; minorities: 34%; international: 0%
Acceptance rate (master's): 42%
Acceptance rate (DNP): 44%
Specialties offered: administration; education; nurse practitioner: family; nurse practitioner: psychiatric-mental health, across the lifespan

INDIANA

Anderson University

1100 E. Fifth Street
Anderson, IN 46012
anderson.edu/nursing
Private
Admissions: (765) 641-4388
Email: lmschmidt@anderson.edu
Financial aid: (765) 641-4368
Application deadline: N/A
Degrees offered: master's
Tuition: full time: $460/credit hour, part time: $460/credit hour
Full-time enrollment: 27
men: 15%; women: 85%; minorities: 15%; international: 0%
Part-time enrollment:
men: N/A; women: N/A; minorities: N/A; international: N/A

Acceptance rate (master's): 100%
Specialties offered: administration; education; informatics; dual majors

Ball State University

2000 W. University Avenue
Muncie, IN 47306
www.bsu.edu/nursing
Public
Admissions: (765) 285-9130
Email: nursing@bsu.edu
Financial aid: (765) 285-5600
Application deadline: 02/09
Degrees offered: master's, DNP
In-state tuition: full time: $386/credit hour, part time: $386/credit hour (master's); full time: $386/credit hour, part time: $386/credit hour (DNP)
Out-of-state tuition: full time: $579/credit hour (master's); full time: $579/credit hour (DNP)
Room/board/expenses: $11,116 (master's); $11,116 (DNP)
Full-time enrollment: 9 (master's); N/A (DNP)
men: 11%; women: 89%; minorities: 0%; international: 0%
Part-time enrollment: 321 (master's); 13 (DNP)
men: 7%; women: 93%; minorities: 7%; international: 0%
Acceptance rate (master's): 68%
Specialties offered: administration; education; nurse practitioner; nurse practitioner: family

Bethel College[1]

1001 Bethel Circle
Mishawaka, IN 46545
Private
Admissions: N/A
Financial aid: N/A
Tuition: N/A
Room/board/expenses: N/A
Enrollment: N/A

Goshen College[1]

1700 South Main Street
Goshen, IN 46526
Private
Admissions: N/A
Financial aid: N/A
Tuition: N/A
Room/board/expenses: N/A
Enrollment: N/A

Indiana State University

749 Chestnut Street
Terre Haute, IN 47809-1937
www.indstate.edu/health/department/son
Public
Admissions: (812) 237-3005
Email: Gina.Jordan@indstate.edu
Financial aid: (812) 237-2215
Application deadline: 12/31
Degrees offered: master's, DNP
In-state tuition: full time: $388/credit hour, part time: $388/credit hour (master's); full time: $388/credit hour, part time: $388/credit hour (DNP)
Out-of-state tuition: full time: $485/credit hour (master's); full time: $485/credit hour (DNP)
Room/board/expenses: N/A
Full-time enrollment: N/A (master's); N/A (DNP)
men: N/A; women: N/A; minorities: N/A; international: N/A

Part-time enrollment: 241 (master's); 23 (DNP)
men: 10%; women: 90%; minorities: 8%; international: 0%
Acceptance rate (master's): 75%
Acceptance rate (DNP): 64%
Specialties offered: education; nurse practitioner; nurse practitioner: family

Indiana University East[1]

2325 Chester Boulevard
Richmond, IN 47374
www.iue.edu/nursing/msn
Public
Admissions: N/A
Financial aid: N/A
Tuition: N/A
Room/board/expenses: N/A
Enrollment: N/A

Indiana University-Kokomo[1]

2300 S. Washington Street
Kokomo, IN 46904
Public
Admissions: N/A
Financial aid: N/A
Tuition: N/A
Room/board/expenses: N/A
Enrollment: N/A

Indiana University-Purdue University-Fort Wayne[1]

2101 E Coliseum Boulevard
Fort Wayne, IN 46805
Public
Admissions: N/A
Financial aid: N/A
Tuition: N/A
Room/board/expenses: N/A
Enrollment: N/A

Indiana University-Purdue University-Indianapolis

1111 Middle Drive
Indianapolis, IN 46202-5107
nursing.iu.edu
Public
Admissions: (317) 274-0003
Email: tlabney@iu.edu
Financial aid: (317) 274-5920
Application deadline: 02/15
Degrees offered: master's, Ph.D., DNP
In-state tuition: full time: $503/credit hour, part time: $503/credit hour (master's); full time: $503/credit hour, part time: $503/credit hour (Ph.D.); full time: $1,000/credit hour, part time: $1,000/credit hour (DNP)
Out-of-state tuition: full time: $1,435/credit hour (master's); full time: $1,435/credit hour (Ph.D.); full time: $1,000/credit hour (DNP)
Room/board/expenses: $9,286 (master's); $9,286 (Ph.D.); $9,286 (DNP)
Full-time enrollment: 19 (master's); 10 (Ph.D.); 8 (DNP)
men: 16%; women: 84%; minorities: 22%; international: 0%
Part-time enrollment: 277 (master's); 36 (Ph.D.); 29 (DNP)
men: 10%; women: 90%; minorities: 13%; international: 1%

Acceptance rate (master's): 80%
Acceptance rate (Ph.D.): 73%
Acceptance rate (DNP): 80%
Specialties offered: administration; clinical nurse specialist; education; nurse practitioner; nurse practitioner: adult-gerontology acute care; nurse practitioner: adult-gerontology primary care; nurse practitioner: family; nurse practitioner: pediatric primary care; nurse practitioner: psychiatric-mental health, across the lifespan

Indiana University-South Bend[1]

1700 Mishawaka Avenue
South Bend, IN 46634
www.iusb.edu/nursing/index.php
Public
Admissions: (557) 520-4839
Email: admissions@iusb.edu
Financial aid: (574) 520-4357
Tuition: N/A
Room/board/expenses: N/A
Enrollment: N/A

Indiana Wesleyan University[1]

4201 S. Washington Street
Marion, IN 46953
Private
Admissions: N/A
Financial aid: N/A
Tuition: N/A
Room/board/expenses: N/A
Enrollment: N/A

Purdue University-Calumet[1]

2200 169th Street
Hammond, IN 46323
Public
Admissions: N/A
Financial aid: N/A
Tuition: N/A
Room/board/expenses: N/A
Enrollment: N/A

Purdue University-West Lafayette

502 N. University Street
West Lafayette, IN 47907-2069
www.nursing.purdue.edu/
Public
Admissions: (765) 494-9116
Email: admissions@purdue.edu
Financial aid: (765) 494-5050
Application deadline: 06/01
Degrees offered: master's, DNP
In-state tuition: full time: $10,002, part time: $348/credit hour (master's); full time: $10,002, part time: $348/credit hour (DNP)
Out-of-state tuition: full time: $28,804 (master's); full time: $28,804 (DNP)
Room/board/expenses: N/A
Full-time enrollment: 49 (master's); 3 (DNP)
men: N/A; women: N/A; minorities: 15%; international: 6%
Part-time enrollment: 4 (master's); 24 (DNP)
men: N/A; women: N/A; minorities: 7%; international: 0%
Acceptance rate (master's): 97%
Acceptance rate (DNP): 100%

Specialties offered: nurse practitioner; nurse practitioner: adult-gerontology primary care; nurse practitioner: family; nurse practitioner: pediatric primary care

University of Indianapolis

1400 E. Hanna Avenue
Indianapolis, IN 46227
uindy.edu/nursing
Private
Admissions: (317) 788-3216
Financial aid: (317) 788-3217
Application deadline: 04/15
Degrees offered: master's, DNP
Tuition: full time: N/A, part time: N/A (master's); full time: N/A, part time: N/A (DNP)
Room/board/expenses: N/A
Full-time enrollment: N/A (master's); N/A (DNP)
men: N/A; women: N/A; minorities: N/A; international: N/A
Part-time enrollment: 277 (master's); 13 (DNP)
men: 7%; women: 93%; minorities: 13%; international: 0%
Acceptance rate (master's): 87%
Acceptance rate (DNP): 93%
Specialties offered: administration; education; nurse practitioner; nurse practitioner: adult-gerontology primary care; nurse practitioner: family

University of Saint Francis

2701 Spring Street
Fort Wayne, IN 46808
nursing.sf.edu/
Private
Admissions: (260) 399-8000
Email: gradschool@sf.edu
Financial aid: (260) 399-8000
Application deadline: 05/01
Degrees offered: master's
Tuition: full time: $870/credit hour, part time: $870/credit hour
Room/board/expenses: N/A
Full-time enrollment: 45
men: N/A; women: N/A; minorities: 24%; international: 0%
Part-time enrollment: 58
men: N/A; women: N/A; minorities: 0%; international: 0%
Acceptance rate (master's): 90%
Specialties offered: nurse practitioner; nurse practitioner: family

University of Southern Indiana

8600 University Boulevard
Evansville, IN 47712-3596
www.usi.edu/health/nursing
Public
Admissions: (812) 465-7140
Email: graduate.studies@usi.edu
Financial aid: (812) 464-1767
Application deadline: 02/01
Degrees offered: master's, DNP
In-state tuition: full time: $438/credit hour, part time: $438/credit hour (master's); full time: $488/credit hour, part time: $488/credit hour (DNP)
Out-of-state tuition: full time: $438/credit hour (master's); full time: $488/credit hour (DNP)

Room/board/expenses: $4,140 (master's); $4,140 (DNP)
Full-time enrollment: 104 (master's); 5 (DNP)
men: 10%; women: 90%; minorities: 5%; international: 0%
Part-time enrollment: 323 (master's); 42 (DNP)
men: 12%; women: 88%; minorities: 8%; international: 0%
Acceptance rate (master's): 76%
Acceptance rate (DNP): 82%
Specialties offered: administration; clinical nurse specialist; education; nurse practitioner; nurse practitioner: adult-gerontology acute care; nurse practitioner: adult-gerontology primary care; nurse practitioner: family; nurse practitioner: psychiatric-mental health, across the lifespan

Valparaiso University

LeBien Hall 103
Valparaiso, IN 46383
valpo.edu/nursing
Private
Admissions: (219) 464-5313
Email: graduate.school@valpo.edu
Financial aid: (219) 464-5015
Application deadline: 04/15
Degrees offered: master's, DNP
Tuition: full time: $14,700, part time: $8,400 (master's); full time: $16,800, part time: $8,400 (DNP)
Room/board/expenses: N/A
Full-time enrollment: 23 (master's); 38 (DNP)
men: N/A; women: N/A; minorities: 8%; international: 34%
Part-time enrollment: 12 (master's); 11 (DNP)
men: N/A; women: N/A; minorities: 0%; international: 0%
Acceptance rate (master's): 91%
Acceptance rate (DNP): 89%
Specialties offered: education; nurse practitioner; nurse practitioner: family

IOWA

Allen College

1825 Logan Avenue
Waterloo, IA 50703
www.allencollege.edu/academic-programs.aspx
Private
Admissions: (319) 226-2001
Email: admissions@allencollege.edu
Financial aid: (319) 226-2003
Application deadline: N/A
Degrees offered: master's, DNP
Tuition: full time: N/A, part time: N/A (master's); full time: N/A, part time: N/A (DNP)
Room/board/expenses: N/A
Full-time enrollment: 39 (master's); 4 (DNP)
men: 9%; women: 91%; minorities: 0%; international: 5%
Part-time enrollment: 174 (master's); 3 (DNP)
men: 11%; women: 89%; minorities: 5%; international: 0%
Acceptance rate (master's): 68%
Acceptance rate (DNP): 62%

Specialties offered: administration; community health/public health; education; nurse practitioner: adult-gerontology acute care; nurse practitioner: adult-gerontology primary care; nurse practitioner: family; nurse practitioner: psychiatric-mental health, across the lifespan; dual majors

Briar Cliff University[1]

3303 Rebecca Street
Sioux City, IA 51104
Private
Admissions: N/A
Financial aid: N/A
Tuition: N/A
Room/board/expenses: N/A
Enrollment: N/A

Clarke University

1550 Clarke Drive
Dubuque, IA 52001
www.clarke.edu/page.aspx?id=22047
Private
Admissions: (563) 588-6432
Email: admissions@clarke.edu
Financial aid: (563) 588-6327
Application deadline: 02/01
Degrees offered: DNP
Tuition: full time: $800/credit hour, part time: $800/credit hour
Room/board/expenses: $9,000
Full-time enrollment: 57
men: 4%; women: 96%; minorities: 2%; international: 0%
Part-time enrollment: 8
men: 0%; women: 100%; minorities: 0%; international: 0%
Acceptance rate (DNP): 74%
Specialties offered: administration; education; nurse practitioner; nurse practitioner: family

Grand View University[1]

1200 Grandview Avenue
Des Moines, IA 50316
Private
Admissions: N/A
Financial aid: N/A
Tuition: N/A
Room/board/expenses: N/A
Enrollment: N/A

Kaplan University[1]

1801 East Kimberly Road, Suite 1
Davenport, IA 52807
Private
Admissions: N/A
Financial aid: N/A
Tuition: N/A
Room/board/expenses: N/A
Enrollment: N/A

Mount Mercy University[1]

1330 Elmhurst Drive NE
Cedar Rapids, IA 52402
www.mtmercy.edu/master-science-nursing
Private
Admissions: (319) 363-1323
Email: tom@mtermcy.edu
Financial aid: (318) 363-8213
Tuition: N/A
Room/board/expenses: N/A
Enrollment: N/A

University of Iowa

50 Newton Road
101 College of Nursing Building
Iowa City, IA 52242-1121
www.nursing.uiowa.edu/
Public
Admissions: (319) 335-1525
Email: gradmail@uiowa.edu
Financial aid: (319) 335-1450
Application deadline: 02/01
Degrees offered: master's, Ph.D., DNP
In-state tuition: full time: $14,978, part time: $9,996 (master's); full time: $8,396, part time: $5,604 (Ph.D.); full time: $17,388, part time: $11,592 (DNP)
Out-of-state tuition: full time: $31,608 (master's); full time: $25,574 (Ph.D.); full time: $35,442 (DNP)
Room/board/expenses: $15,010 (master's); $15,010 (Ph.D.); $15,010 (DNP)
Full-time enrollment: N/A (master's); 15 (Ph.D.); 128 (DNP)
men: 19%; women: 80%; minorities: 19%; international: 4%
Part-time enrollment: 14 (master's); 15 (Ph.D.); 55 (DNP)
men: 15%; women: 87%; minorities: 8%; international: 0%
Acceptance rate (master's): 80%
Acceptance rate (Ph.D.): 92%
Acceptance rate (DNP): 77%
Specialties offered: administration; clinical nurse leader; health management & policy health care systems; nurse anesthesia; nurse practitioner; nurse practitioner: adult-gerontology acute care; nurse practitioner: adult-gerontology primary care; nurse practitioner: family; nurse practitioner: pediatric primary care; nurse practitioner: psychiatric-mental health, across the lifespan; research

KANSAS

Fort Hays State University[1]

600 Park Street
Hays, KS 67601-4099
Public
Admissions: N/A
Financial aid: N/A
Tuition: N/A
Room/board/expenses: N/A
Enrollment: N/A

MidAmerica Nazarene University[1]

2030 E. College Way
Olathe, KS 66062
Private
Admissions: N/A
Financial aid: N/A
Tuition: N/A
Room/board/expenses: N/A
Enrollment: N/A

Pittsburg State University[1]

McPherson Building
Pittsburg, KS 66762-7500
Public
Admissions: N/A
Financial aid: N/A
Tuition: N/A

Room/board/expenses: N/A
Enrollment: N/A

University of Kansas

Mail Stop 2029
3901 Rainbow Boulevard
Kansas City, KS 66160
nursing.kumc.edu
Public
Admissions: (913) 588-1619
Email: soninfo@kumc.edu
Financial aid: (913) 588-5170
Application deadline: 12/01
Degrees offered: master's, Ph.D.,
DNP
In-state tuition: full time: $615/
credit hour, part time: $615/
credit hour (master's); full time:
$585/credit hour, part time:
$585/credit hour (Ph.D.); full
time: $600/credit hour, part time:
$600/credit hour (DNP)
Out-of-state tuition: full time: $615/
credit hour (master's); full time:
$655/credit hour (Ph.D.); full
time: $685/credit hour (DNP)
Room/board/expenses: N/A
Full-time enrollment: 5 (master's);
14 (Ph.D.); 25 (DNP)
men: 5%; women: 95%;
minorities: 16%; international:
2%
Part-time enrollment: 90
(master's); 18 (Ph.D.); 150 (DNP)
men: 9%; women: 91%;
minorities: 17%; international: 0%
Acceptance rate (master's): 98%
Acceptance rate (Ph.D.): 100%
Acceptance rate (DNP): 90%
Specialties offered:
administration; clinical nurse
specialist; community health/
public health; informatics;
nurse-midwifery; nurse
practitioner; nurse practitioner:
adult-gerontology primary care;
nurse practitioner: family; nurse
practitioner: psychiatric-mental
health, across the lifespan;
research

Washburn University-Topeka[1]

1700 SW College Avenue
Topeka, KS 66621-1117
www.washburn.edu/sonuk
Public
Admissions: (785) 670-1525
Email:
shirley.dinkel@washburn.edu
Financial aid: (785) 670-2773
Tuition: N/A
Room/board/expenses: N/A
Enrollment: N/A

Wichita State University[1]

1845 Fairmount
Wichita, KS 67260-0041
Public
Admissions: N/A
Financial aid: N/A
Tuition: N/A
Room/board/expenses: N/A
Enrollment: N/A

KENTUCKY

Bellarmine University

2001 Newburg Road
Louisville, KY 40205
www.bellarmine.edu/lansing/
nursing/
Private
Admissions: (502) 272-7200
Email: admissionsoffice@
bellarmine.edu
Financial aid: (502) 272-7300
Application deadline: N/A
Degrees offered: master's, DNP
Tuition: full time: $805/credit
hour, part time: $805/credit hour
(master's); full time: $805/credit
hour, part time: $805/credit
hour (DNP)
Room/board/expenses: N/A
Full-time enrollment: 4 (master's);
N/A (DNP)
men: N/A; women: N/A;
minorities: N/A; international: N/A
Part-time enrollment: 77
(master's); 19 (DNP)
men: N/A; women: N/A;
minorities: 8%; international: 1%
Acceptance rate (master's): 89%
Acceptance rate (DNP): 100%
Specialties offered:
administration; education; nurse
practitioner; nurse practitioner:
family; dual majors

Eastern Kentucky University

521 Lancaster Avenue
Rowlett Building 223
Richmond, KY 40475
bsn-gn.eku.edu
Public
Admissions: (859) 622-1742
Email:
jerry.pogatshnick@eku.edu
Financial aid: (859) 622-2361
Application deadline: 11/01
Degrees offered: master's, DNP
In-state tuition: full time: N/A,
part time: $625/credit hour
(master's); full time: N/A, part
time: $630/credit hour (DNP)
Out-of-state tuition: full time: N/A
(master's); full time: N/A (DNP)
Room/board/expenses: N/A
Full-time enrollment: N/A
(master's); N/A (DNP)
men: N/A; women: N/A;
minorities: N/A; international: N/A
Part-time enrollment: 341
(master's); 59 (DNP)
men: 14%; women: 87%;
minorities: 11%; international: 0%
Acceptance rate (master's): 83%
Acceptance rate (DNP): 63%
Specialties offered:
administration; nurse
practitioner; nurse practitioner:
family; nurse practitioner:
psychiatric-mental health,
across the lifespan

Frontier Nursing University

PO Box 528
Hyden, KY 41749
www.frontier.edu/
Private
Admissions: (606) 672-2312
Email: admissions@frontier.edu
Financial aid: (859) 899-2516
Application deadline: N/A
Degrees offered: master's, DNP

Tuition: full time: $535/credit
hour, part time: $535/credit hour
(master's); full time: $565/credit
hour, part time: N/A (DNP)
Room/board/expenses: N/A
Full-time enrollment: 915
(master's); 99 (DNP)
men: 5%; women: 95%;
minorities: 16%; international:
0%
Part-time enrollment: 499
(master's); N/A (DNP)
men: 4%; women: 96%;
minorities: 21%; international:
0%
Acceptance rate (master's): 49%
Acceptance rate (DNP): 53%
Specialties offered: nurse-
midwifery; nurse practitioner;
nurse practitioner: family

Murray State University[1]

121 Mason Hall
Murray, KY 42071
www.murraystate.edu/
nursing.aspx
Public
Admissions: (270) 809-3779
Email: msu.graduateadmissions@
murraystate.edu
Financial aid: (270) 809-2546
Tuition: N/A
Room/board/expenses: N/A
Enrollment: N/A

Northern Kentucky University[1]

Nunn Drive
Highland Heights, KY 41099
healthprofessions.nku.edu/
Public
Admissions: N/A
Financial aid: N/A
Tuition: N/A
Room/board/expenses: N/A
Enrollment: N/A

Spalding University[1]

851 S. Fourth Street
Louisville, KY 40203-2188
Private
Admissions: N/A
Financial aid: N/A
Tuition: N/A
Room/board/expenses: N/A
Enrollment: N/A

University of Kentucky

315 College of Nursing Building
Lexington, KY 40536-0232
www.uky.edu/nursing/
Public
Admissions: (859) 323-5108
Email: conss@uky.edu
Financial aid: (859) 257-3172
Application deadline: 02/15
Degrees offered: Ph.D., DNP
In-state tuition: full time: $11,652,
part time: $617/credit hour
(Ph.D.); full time: $15,192, part
time: $814/credit hour (DNP)
Out-of-state tuition: full time:
$26,154 (Ph.D.); full time:
$36,136 (DNP)
Room/board/expenses: N/A
Full-time enrollment: 41 (Ph.D.);
106 (DNP)
men: 12%; women: 88%;
minorities: 10%; international:
4%

Part-time enrollment: 4 (Ph.D.);
89 (DNP)
men: 12%; women: 88%;
minorities: 2%; international: 0%
Acceptance rate (Ph.D.): 62%
Acceptance rate (DNP): 94%
Specialties offered: clinical nurse
specialist; health management
& policy health care systems;
nurse practitioner; nurse
practitioner: adult-gerontology
acute care; nurse practitioner:
adult-gerontology primary
care; nurse practitioner: adult;
nurse practitioner: family;
nurse practitioner: pediatric
primary care; nurse practitioner:
psychiatric-mental health,
across the lifespan; research

University of Louisville

555 S. Floyd Street
Louisville, KY 40292
louisville.edu/nursing/
Public
Admissions: (502) 852-3101
Email: gradadm@louisville.edu
Financial aid: (502) 852-5511
Application deadline: 10/01
Degrees offered: master's, Ph.D.
In-state tuition: full time: $11,664,
part time: $649/credit hour
(master's); full time: $11,664, part
time: $649/credit hour (Ph.D.)
Out-of-state tuition: full time:
$24,274 (master's); full time:
$24,274 (Ph.D.)
Room/board/expenses: $7,942
(master's); $7,942 (Ph.D.)
Full-time enrollment: 90 (master's);
20 (Ph.D)
men: 10%; women: 90%;
minorities: 9%; international: 4%
Part-time enrollment: 22
(master's); 1 (Ph.D.)
men: 13%; women: 87%;
minorities: 9%; international: 0%
Acceptance rate (master's): 70%
Acceptance rate (Ph.D.): 56%
Specialties offered: nurse
practitioner; nurse practitioner:
adult-gerontology acute care;
nurse practitioner: adult-
gerontology primary care;
nurse practitioner: family; nurse
practitioner: psychiatric-mental
health, across the lifespan

Western Kentucky University

1906 College Heights Boulevard
#11036
Bowling Green, KY 42101-1036
www.wku.edu/nursing/index.php
Public
Admissions: (270) 745-2446
Email: graduate.admissions@
wku.edu
Financial aid: (270) 745-2755
Application deadline: 04/01
Degrees offered: master's, DNP
In-state tuition: full time: $652/
credit hour, part time: $652/
credit hour (master's); full time:
$643/credit hour, part time:
$643/credit hour (DNP)
Out-of-state tuition: full time:
$652/credit hour (master's); full
time: $833/credit hour (DNP)
Room/board/expenses: N/A
Full-time enrollment: 20 (master's);
23 (DNP)
men: 9%; women: 91%;
minorities: 9%; international: 0%

Part-time enrollment: 99
(master's); 42 (DNP)
men: 10%; women: 90%;
minorities: 8%; international: 0%
Acceptance rate (master's): 50%
Acceptance rate (DNP): 63%
Specialties offered:
administration; education; nurse
practitioner; nurse practitioner:
family; nurse practitioner:
psychiatric-mental health,
across the lifespan

LOUISIANA

Grambling State University[1]

1 Cole Street
Grambling, LA 71245
Public
Admissions: N/A
Financial aid: N/A
Tuition: N/A
Room/board/expenses: N/A
Enrollment: N/A

Louisiana State University Health Sciences Center[1]

1900 Gravier Street
New Orleans, LA 70112
nursing.lsuhsc.edu/default.aspx
Public
Admissions: N/A
Financial aid: N/A
Tuition: N/A
Room/board/expenses: N/A
Enrollment: N/A

Loyola University New Orleans

6363 St. Charles Avenue
New Orleans, LA 70118
css.loyno.edu/nursing
Private
Admissions: (866) 789-9809
Email: nursing@loyno.edu
Financial aid: (504) 865-3231
Application deadline: 12/31
Degrees offered: master's, DNP
Tuition: full time: $818/credit
hour, part time: $818/credit hour
(master's); full time: $818/credit
hour, part time: $818/credit hour
(DNP)
Room/board/expenses: N/A
Full-time enrollment: 271
(master's); 81 (DNP)
men: 8%; women: 92%;
minorities: 23%; international:
0%
Part-time enrollment: 79
(master's); 16 (DNP)
men: 11%; women: 89%;
minorities: 51%; international:
0%
Acceptance rate (master's): 89%
Acceptance rate (DNP): 53%
Specialties offered:
administration; nurse
practitioner; nurse practitioner:
family

McNeese State University

Hardtner Hall, Room 102
Lake Charles, LA 70609
www.mcneese.edu/nursing/
graduate
Public
Admissions: (337) 475-5504
Email: admissions@mcneese.edu
Financial aid: (337) 475-5068

Application deadline: N/A
Degrees offered: master's
In-state tuition: full time: N/A, part time: N/A
Out-of-state tuition: full time: N/A
Room/board/expenses: N/A
Full-time enrollment: 28
men: 18%; women: 82%; minorities: 25%; international: 0%
Part-time enrollment: 128
men: 22%; women: 78%; minorities: 27%; international: 0%
Specialties offered: administration; education; nurse practitioner; nurse practitioner: psychiatric-mental health, across the lifespan

Northwestern State University of Louisiana
1800 Line Avenue
Shreveport, LA 71101-4653
nsula.edu/academics/nursing-allied-health/
Public
Admissions: (318) 357-6171
Email: belle@nsula.edu
Financial aid: (318) 357-5961
Application deadline: 07/06
Degrees offered: master's, DNP
In-state tuition: full time: $10,767, part time: $5,685 (master's); full time: N/A, part time: $425/credit hour (DNP)
Out-of-state tuition: full time: $16,182 (master's); full time: N/A (DNP)
Room/board/expenses: N/A
Full-time enrollment: 15 (master's); N/A (DNP)
men: 13%; women: 87%; minorities: 0%; international: 0%
Part-time enrollment: 202 (master's); 21 (DNP)
men: 14%; women: 86%; minorities: 19%; international: 0%
Acceptance rate (master's): 100%
Acceptance rate (DNP): 100%
Specialties offered: administration; education; nurse practitioner; nurse practitioner: adult-gerontology acute care; nurse practitioner: adult-gerontology primary care; nurse practitioner: family; nurse practitioner: pediatric primary care

Our Lady of the Lake College[1]
7434 Perkins Road
Baton Rouge, LA 70808
Private
Admissions: N/A
Financial aid: N/A
Tuition: N/A
Room/board/expenses: N/A
Enrollment: N/A

Southeastern Louisiana University
SLU Box 10835
Hammond, LA 70402
www.southeastern.edu/acad_research/depts/nurs/index.html
Public
Admissions: (800) 222-7358
Email: admissions@southeastern.edu
Financial aid: (985) 549-2244

Application deadline: 07/15
Degrees offered: master's, DNP
In-state tuition: full time: $6,107, part time: $436/credit hour (master's); full time: $6,107, part time: $436 (DNP)
Out-of-state tuition: full time: $18,584 (master's); full time: $18,584 (DNP)
Room/board/expenses: $7,370 (master's); $7,370 (DNP)
Full-time enrollment: 35 (master's); 6 (DNP)
men: 17%; women: 83%; minorities: 7%; international: 0%
Part-time enrollment: 107 (master's); 27 (DNP)
men: 8%; women: 92%; minorities: 22%; international: 0%
Acceptance rate (master's): 100%
Acceptance rate (DNP): 100%
Specialties offered: education; nurse practitioner

Southern University and A&M College[1]
P.O. Box 11784
Baton Rouge, LA 70813
Public
Admissions: N/A
Financial aid: N/A
Tuition: N/A
Room/board/expenses: N/A
Enrollment: N/A

University of Louisiana-Lafayette
411 E Saint Mary Boulevard
Lafayette, LA 70503
www.louisiana.edu/
Public
Admissions: (337) 482-6965
Email: gradschool@louisiana.edu
Financial aid: (337) 482-6506
Application deadline: 06/30
Degrees offered: master's, DNP
In-state tuition: full time: $5,511, part time: $445/credit hour (master's); full time: $5,511, part time: $445/credit hour (DNP)
Out-of-state tuition: full time: $19,238 (master's); full time: $19,238 (DNP)
Room/board/expenses: $9,073 (master's); $9,073 (DNP)
Full-time enrollment: 44 (master's); 9 (DNP)
men: 11%; women: 89%; minorities: 4%; international: 0%
Part-time enrollment: 100 (master's); 16 (DNP)
men: 12%; women: 88%; minorities: 15%; international: 0%
Acceptance rate (master's): 41%
Acceptance rate (DNP): 45%
Specialties offered: education; nurse practitioner; nurse practitioner: family; nurse practitioner: psychiatric-mental health, across the lifespan

Husson University
1 College Circle
Bangor, ME 04401
www.husson.edu/school-of-nursing
Private
Admissions: (207) 992-4994
Email: graduateschool@husson.edu
Financial aid: (207) 973-1090

Application deadline: 03/30
Degrees offered: master's
Tuition: full time: $547/credit hour, part time: $547/credit hour
Room/board/expenses: $9,676
Full-time enrollment: 27
men: 4%; women: 96%; minorities: 7%; international: 4%
Part-time enrollment: 8
men: 13%; women: 88%; minorities: 13%; international: 0%
Acceptance rate (master's): 27%
Specialties offered: education; nurse practitioner; nurse practitioner: family; nurse practitioner: psychiatric-mental health, across the lifespan

St. Joseph's College[1]
278 Whites Bridge Road
Standish, ME 04084-5263
Private
Admissions: N/A
Financial aid: N/A
Tuition: N/A
Room/board/expenses: N/A
Enrollment: N/A

University of Maine[1]
5724 Dunn Hall
Orono, ME 04469-5724
www.umaine.edu/nursing/
Public
Admissions: (207) 581-3291
Email: graduate@maine.edu
Financial aid: (207) 581-1324
Tuition: N/A
Room/board/expenses: N/A
Enrollment: N/A

University of Southern Maine[1]
96 Falmouth Street
Portland, ME 04104-9300
usm.maine.edu/nursing
Public
Admissions: N/A
Financial aid: (207) 780-5250
Tuition: N/A
Room/board/expenses: N/A
Enrollment: N/A

Bowie State University
14000 Jericho Park Road
Bowie, MD 20715-9465
Public
Admissions: (301) 860-3415
Email: aisaac@bowiestate.edu
Financial aid: (301) 860-4363
Application deadline: N/A
Degrees offered: master's
In-state tuition: full time: $9,384, part time: $7,038
Out-of-state tuition: full time: $16,344
Room/board/expenses: $12,760
Full-time enrollment: 71
men: N/A; women: N/A; minorities: 24%; international: 13%
Part-time enrollment: 96
men: N/A; women: N/A; minorities: 21%; international: 13%
Specialties offered: N/A

Coppin State University (Fuld)[1]
2500 W. North Avenue
Baltimore, MD 21216-3698
Public
Admissions: N/A
Financial aid: N/A
Tuition: N/A
Room/board/expenses: N/A
Enrollment: N/A

Johns Hopkins University
525 N. Wolfe Street
Baltimore, MD 21205-2100
nursing.jhu.edu
Private
Admissions: (410) 955-7548
Email: jhuson@jhu.edu
Financial aid: (410) 955-9840
Application deadline: 01/01
Degrees offered: master's, Ph.D., DNP
Tuition: full time: $36,216, part time: $1,509/credit hour (master's); full time: $41,154, part time: $2,286/credit hour (Ph.D.); full time: $36,530, part time: $1,588/credit hour (DNP)
Room/board/expenses: $12,774 (master's); $12,774 (Ph.D.); $9,000 (DNP)
Full-time enrollment: 188 (master's); 42 (Ph.D.); 17 (DNP)
men: 12%; women: 88%; minorities: 35%; international: 5%
Part-time enrollment: 222 (master's); N/A (Ph.D.); 35 (DNP)
men: 7%; women: 93%; minorities: 23%; international: 5%
Acceptance rate (master's): 57%
Acceptance rate (Ph.D.): 32%
Acceptance rate (DNP): 70%
Specialties offered: clinical nurse specialist; community health/public health; generalist; health management & policy health care systems; nurse practitioner; nurse practitioner: adult-gerontology acute care; nurse practitioner: adult-gerontology primary care; nurse practitioner: family; nurse practitioner: pediatric primary care; nurse practitioner: psychiatric-mental health, across the lifespan; dual majors

Morgan State University[1]
Baltimore, MD 21251
Public
Admissions: N/A
Financial aid: N/A
Tuition: N/A
Room/board/expenses: N/A
Enrollment: N/A

Notre Dame of Maryland University
4701 North Charles Street
Baltimore, MD 21210
www.ndm.edu/academics/school-of-nursing/
Private
Admissions: (410) 532-5108
Email: gradadm@ndm.edu
Financial aid: (410) 532-5735
Application deadline: N/A
Degrees offered: master's

Tuition: full time: $626/credit hour, part time: $626/credit hour
Room/board/expenses: N/A
Full-time enrollment: 19
men: 0%; women: 100%; minorities: 37%; international: 0%
Part-time enrollment: 90
men: 3%; women: 97%; minorities: 52%; international: 0%
Acceptance rate (master's): 96%
Specialties offered: administration; education

Salisbury University
1101 Camden Avenue
Salisbury, MD 21801
www.salisbury.edu/nursing/
Public
Admissions: (410) 677-0047
Email: graduateadmissions@salisbury.edu
Financial aid: (410) 543-6165
Application deadline: 04/15
Degrees offered: master's, DNP
In-state tuition: full time: N/A, part time: $620/credit hour (master's); full time: N/A, part time: $620/credit hour (DNP)
Out-of-state tuition: full time: N/A (master's); full time: N/A (DNP)
Room/board/expenses: N/A
Full-time enrollment: N/A (master's); 22 (DNP)
men: 9%; women: 91%; minorities: 36%; international: 0%
Part-time enrollment: 6 (master's); 1 (DNP)
men: 14%; women: 86%; minorities: 29%; international: 0%
Acceptance rate (master's): 28%
Acceptance rate (DNP): 44%
Specialties offered: education; health management & policy health care systems; nurse practitioner; nurse practitioner: family

Stevenson University
100 Campus Circle
Owings Mills, MD 21117
www.stevenson.edu/graduate-professional-studies/graduate-programs/nursing/
Private
Admissions: (443) 352-4030
Email: www.stevenson.edu/admissions-aid/
Financial aid: (443) 334-3200
Application deadline: N/A
Degrees offered: master's
Tuition: full time: $625/credit hour, part time: $625/credit hour
Full-time enrollment:
men: N/A; women: N/A; minorities: N/A; international: N/A
Part-time enrollment: 183
men: 5%; women: 95%; minorities: 36%; international: 0%
Acceptance rate (master's): 70%
Specialties offered: administration; education; other majors

Towson University[1]
8000 York Road
Towson, MD 21252
Public
Admissions: N/A
Financial aid: N/A
Tuition: N/A

Room/board/expenses: N/A
Enrollment: N/A

Uniformed Services University of the Health Sciences

4301 Jones Bridge Road
Bethesda, MD 20814
www.usuhs.edu/gsn
Public
Admissions: (301) 295-1055
Email:
terry.malavakis@usuhs.edu
Financial aid: N/A
Application deadline: 08/01
Degrees offered: master's, Ph.D., DNP
In-state tuition: full time: N/A, part time: N/A (master's); full time: N/A, part time: N/A (Ph.D.); full time: N/A, part time: N/A (DNP)
Out-of-state tuition: full time: N/A (master's); full time: N/A (Ph.D.); full time: N/A (DNP)
Room/board/expenses: N/A
Full-time enrollment: 1 (master's); 14 (Ph.D.); 172 (DNP)
men: 47%; women: 53%; minorities: 23%; international: 0%
Part-time enrollment: N/A (master's); 3 (Ph.D.); N/A (DNP)
men: 67%; women: 33%; minorities: 67%; international: 0%
Acceptance rate (Ph.D.): 0%
Acceptance rate (DNP): 78%
Specialties offered: clinical nurse specialist; nurse anesthesia; nurse practitioner; nurse practitioner: family; nurse practitioner: psychiatric-mental health, across the lifespan; research

University of Maryland-Baltimore

Suite 516
Baltimore, MD 21201-1579
www.nursing.umaryland.edu
Public
Admissions: (410) 706-0501
Email: admissions@son.umaryland.edu
Financial aid: (410) 706-7347
Application deadline: N/A
Degrees offered: master's, Ph.D., DNP
In-state tuition: full time: $682/credit hour, part time: $682/credit hour (master's); full time: $692/credit hour, part time: $692/credit hour (Ph.D.); full time: $692/credit hour, part time: $692/credit hour (DNP)
Out-of-state tuition: full time: $1,251/credit hour (master's); full time: $1,251/credit hour (Ph.D.); full time: $1,251/credit hour (DNP)
Room/board/expenses: N/A
Full-time enrollment: 235 (master's); 17 (Ph.D.); 118 (DNP)
men: 11%; women: 88%; minorities: 43%; international: 4%
Part-time enrollment: 326 (master's); 37 (Ph.D.); 159 (DNP)
men: 9%; women: 90%; minorities: 37%; international: 0%
Acceptance rate (master's): 56%
Acceptance rate (Ph.D.): 89%
Acceptance rate (DNP): 37%

Specialties offered: administration; clinical nurse leader; clinical nurse specialist; community health/public health; informatics; nurse anesthesia; nurse practitioner: adult-gerontology acute care; nurse practitioner: adult-gerontology primary care; nurse practitioner: adult; nurse practitioner: family; nurse practitioner: pediatric primary care; nurse practitioner: psychiatric-mental health, across the lifespan; research; school nursing; combined nurse practitioner/clinical nurse specialist

MASSACHUSETTS

American International College[1]

1000 State Street
Springfield, MA 01109
Private
Admissions: N/A
Financial aid: N/A
Tuition: N/A
Room/board/expenses: N/A
Enrollment: N/A

Boston College

Cushing Hall
Chestnut Hill, MA 02467
www.bc.edu/nursing
Private
Admissions: (617) 552-4928
Email: csongrad@bc.edu
Financial aid: (617) 552-4928
Application deadline: N/A
Degrees offered: master's, Ph.D.
Tuition: full time: $1,248/credit hour, part time: $1,248/credit hour (master's); full time: $1,248/credit hour, part time: $1,248/credit hour (Ph.D.)
Room/board/expenses: N/A
Full-time enrollment: 171 (master's); 23 (Ph.D.)
men: 12%; women: 88%; minorities: 12%; international: 1%
Part-time enrollment: 63 (master's); 1 (Ph.D.)
men: 9%; women: 91%; minorities: 19%; international: 0%
Acceptance rate (master's): 72%
Acceptance rate (Ph.D.): 82%
Specialties offered: nurse anesthesia; nurse practitioner; nurse practitioner: adult-gerontology primary care; nurse practitioner: family; nurse practitioner: pediatric primary care; nurse practitioner: psychiatric-mental health, across the lifespan

Curry College[1]

1071 Blue Hill Avenue
Milton, MA 02186
Private
Admissions: N/A
Financial aid: N/A
Tuition: N/A
Room/board/expenses: N/A
Enrollment: N/A

Elms College[1]

291 Springfield Street
Chicopee, MA 01013
Private
Admissions: N/A
Financial aid: N/A
Tuition: N/A
Room/board/expenses: N/A
Enrollment: N/A

Emmanuel College[1]

400 The Fenway
Boston, MA 02115
Private
Admissions: N/A
Financial aid: N/A
Tuition: N/A
Room/board/expenses: N/A
Enrollment: N/A

Endicott College[1]

376 Hale Street
Beverly, MA 01915
Private
Admissions: N/A
Financial aid: N/A
Tuition: N/A
Room/board/expenses: N/A
Enrollment: N/A

Fitchburg State University

160 Pearl Street
Fitchburg, MA 01420-2697
www.fitchburgstate.edu/academics/academic-departments/department-homepage-nursing/
Public
Admissions: (800) 705-9692
Email: admissions@fitchburgsatte.edu
Financial aid: (978) 665-3156
Application deadline: N/A
Degrees offered: master's
In-state tuition: full time: $167/credit hour, part time: $167/credit hour
Out-of-state tuition: full time: $167/credit hour
Room/board/expenses: N/A
Full-time enrollment:
men: N/A; women: N/A; minorities: N/A; international: N/A
Part-time enrollment: 32
men: 3%; women: 97%; minorities: 16%; international: 9%
Acceptance rate (master's): 100%
Specialties offered: forensic nursing

Framingham State University[1]

100 State Street
Framingham, MA 01701
www.framingham.edu/academics/graduate-studies/graduate-degree-programs/msn-education
Public
Admissions: (508) 626-4501
Email: ddonovan@framingham.edu
Financial aid: (508) 626-4534
Tuition: N/A
Room/board/expenses: N/A
Enrollment: N/A

MCPHS University[1]

179 Longwood Avenue
Boston, MA 02115
www.mcphs.edu/academics/schools/school%20of%20nursing
Private
Admissions: N/A
Financial aid: N/A
Tuition: N/A
Room/board/expenses: N/A
Enrollment: N/A

MGH Institute of Health Professions[1]

36 First Avenue
Boston, MA 02129-4557
www.mghihp.edu/nursing
Private
Admissions: (617) 726-3177
Email: admissions@mghihp.edu
Financial aid: (617) 726-9549
Tuition: N/A
Room/board/expenses: N/A
Enrollment: N/A

Northeastern University

123 Behrakis Health Sciences Center
Boston, MA 02115
www.northeastern.edu/bouve/nursing/
Private
Admissions: (617) 373-2708
Email: bouvegrad@neu.edu
Financial aid: (617) 373-5899
Application deadline: N/A
Degrees offered: master's, Ph.D., DNP
Tuition: full time: $1,335/credit hour, part time: $1,335/credit hour (master's); full time: $1,335/credit hour, part time: $1,335/credit hour (Ph.D.); full time: $1,335/credit hour, part time: $1,335/credit hour (DNP)
Room/board/expenses: $21,600 (master's); $21,600 (Ph.D.); $21,600 (DNP)
Full-time enrollment: 225 (master's); 15 (Ph.D.); 99 (DNP)
men: 32%; women: 68%; minorities: 20%; international: 1%
Part-time enrollment: 106 (master's); 4 (Ph.D.); 43 (DNP)
men: 12%; women: 88%; minorities: 18%; international: 0%
Acceptance rate (master's): 42%
Acceptance rate (Ph.D.): 70%
Acceptance rate (DNP): 100%
Specialties offered: administration; informatics; nurse anesthesia; nurse practitioner; nurse practitioner: adult-gerontology acute care; nurse practitioner: adult-gerontology primary care; nurse practitioner: family; nurse practitioner: pediatric primary care; nurse practitioner: psychiatric-mental health, across the lifespan; research; school nursing; dual majors

Regis College[1]

235 Wellesley Street
Weston, MA 02493
Private
Admissions: N/A
Financial aid: N/A
Tuition: N/A

Room/board/expenses: N/A
Enrollment: N/A

Salem State University-South Campus[1]

352 Lafayette Street
Salem, MA 01970
Public
Admissions: N/A
Financial aid: N/A
Tuition: N/A
Room/board/expenses: N/A
Enrollment: N/A

Simmons College

300 The Fenway
Boston, MA 02115
www.simmons.edu/snhs
Private
Admissions: N/A
Email: snhs@simmons.edu
Financial aid: (617) 521-2001
Application deadline: 12/01
Degrees offered: master's, Ph.D., DNP
Tuition: full time: $1,271/credit hour, part time: $1,274/credit hour (master's); full time: N/A, part time: N/A (Ph.D.); full time: $1,260/credit hour, part time: $1,260/credit hour (DNP)
Room/board/expenses: N/A
Full-time enrollment: 274 (master's); 59 (Ph.D.); N/A (DNP)
men: 8%; women: 92%; minorities: 20%; international: 2%
Part-time enrollment: 823 (master's); 57 (Ph.D.); 10 (DNP)
men: 9%; women: 91%; minorities: 18%; international: 0%
Acceptance rate (master's): 64%
Specialties offered: nurse practitioner; nurse practitioner: family

University of Massachusetts-Amherst

Arnold House
Amherst, MA 01003-9304
www.umass.edu/nursing
Public
Admissions: (413) 545-0722
Email: gradadm@grad.umass.edu
Financial aid: (413) 545-0356
Application deadline: 12/15
Degrees offered: master's, Ph.D., DNP
In-state tuition: full time: $750/credit hour, part time: $750/credit hour (master's); full time: $12,782, part time: $110/credit hour (Ph.D.); full time: $750/credit hour, part time: $750/credit hour (DNP)
Out-of-state tuition: full time: $750/credit hour (master's); full time: $28,000 (Ph.D.); full time: $750/credit hour (DNP)
Room/board/expenses: N/A (master's); $3,400 (Ph.D.); N/A (DNP)
Full-time enrollment: 1 (master's); 22 (Ph.D.); 44 (DNP)
men: N/A; women: N/A; minorities: 22%; international: 10%

Part-time enrollment: 34
(master's); 30 (Ph.D.); 163 (DNP)
men: N/A; women: N/A;
minorities: 25%; international:
0%
Acceptance rate (master's): 83%
Acceptance rate (Ph.D.): 44%
Acceptance rate (DNP): 71%
Specialties offered: clinical nurse
leader; community health/public
health; nurse practitioner; nurse
practitioner: adult-gerontology
primary care; nurse practitioner:
family; nurse practitioner:
psychiatric-mental health,
across the lifespan; research

University of Massachusetts-Boston

100 Morrissey Boulevard
Boston, MA 02125-3393
www.umb.edu/academics/cnhs
Public
Admissions: (617) 287-6400
Email: bos.gadm.umb.edu
Financial aid: (617) 287-6300
Application deadline: 03/01
Degrees offered: master's, Ph.D.,
DNP
In-state tuition: full time: $16,115,
part time: $671/credit hour
(master's); full time: $16,115, part
time: $671/credit hour (Ph.D.);
full time: $16,115, part time: $671/
credit hour (DNP)
Out-of-state tuition: full time:
$31,115 (master's); full time:
$31,115 (Ph.D.); full time: $31,115
(DNP)
Room/board/expenses: N/A
Full-time enrollment: 49 (master's);
14 (Ph.D.); N/A (DNP)
men: 19%; women: 81%;
minorities: 17%; international:
14%
Part-time enrollment: 93
(master's); 19 (Ph.D.); 38 (DNP)
men: 7%; women: 93%;
minorities: 17%; international: 0%
Acceptance rate (master's): 75%
Acceptance rate (Ph.D.): 53%
Acceptance rate (DNP): 80%
Specialties offered: clinical nurse
specialist; nurse practitioner;
nurse practitioner: adult-
gerontology primary care; nurse
practitioner: family

University of Massachusetts-Dartmouth

285 Old Westport Road
Dartmouth, MA 02747-2300
www.umassd.edu/nursing
Public
Admissions: (508) 999-8604
Email: graduate@umassd.edu
Financial aid: (508) 999-8643
Application deadline: 03/15
Degrees offered: master's, Ph.D.,
DNP
In-state tuition: full time: $2,071,
part time: $86/credit hour
(master's); full time: $2,071, part
time: $86/credit hour (Ph.D.);
full time: $2,071, part time: $86/
credit hour (DNP)
Out-of-state tuition: full time:
$8,099 (master's); full time:
$8,099 (Ph.D.); full time: $8,099
(DNP)
Room/board/expenses: $11,622
(master's); $11,622 (Ph.D.);
$11,622 (DNP)

Full-time enrollment: N/A
(master's); 31 (Ph.D.); N/A (DNP)
men: 3%; women: 97%;
minorities: 10%; international:
0%
Part-time enrollment: 27
(master's); N/A (Ph.D.); 64 (DNP)
men: 9%; women: 91%;
minorities: 13%; international:
0%
Acceptance rate (master's): 100%
Acceptance rate (Ph.D.): 100%
Acceptance rate (DNP): 87%
Specialties offered:
administration; community
health/public health; education;
generalist; nurse practitioner;
nurse practitioner: adult-
gerontology primary care

University of Massachusetts-Lowell

3 Solomont Way
Lowell, MA 01854-5126
www.uml.edu/health-sciences/
Nursing/
Public
Admissions: (978) 934-2373
Email: Graduate_Admissions@
uml.edu
Financial aid: (978) 934-2000
Application deadline: 04/01
Degrees offered: master's, Ph.D.,
DNP
In-state tuition: full time: $1,637,
part time: $91/credit hour
(master's); full time: $1,637, part
time: $91/credit hour (Ph.D.);
full time: $1,637, part time: $91/
credit hour (DNP)
Out-of-state tuition: full time:
$6,425 (master's); full time:
$6,425 (Ph.D.); full time: $6,425
(DNP)
Room/board/expenses: $11,670
(master's); $11,670 (Ph.D.);
$11,670 (DNP)
Full-time enrollment: 22 (master's);
1 (Ph.D.); N/A (DNP)
men: 0%; women: 100%;
minorities: 26%; international:
4%
Part-time enrollment: 48
(master's); 24 (Ph.D.); 18 (DNP)
men: 12%; women: 88%;
minorities: 23%; international: 1%
Acceptance rate (master's): 56%
Acceptance rate (Ph.D.): 100%
Acceptance rate (DNP): 100%
Specialties offered: nurse
practitioner; nurse practitioner:
adult-gerontology primary care;
nurse practitioner: family

University of Massachusetts-Worcester

55 Lake Avenue N
Worcester, MA 01655
www.umassmed.edu
Public
Admissions: (508) 856-3488
Email: gsnadmissions@
umassmed.edu
Financial aid: (508) 856-2265
Application deadline: 12/01
Degrees offered: master's, Ph.D.,
DNP
In-state tuition: full time: $500/
credit hour, part time: $500/
credit hour (master's); full time:
$500/credit hour, part time:
$500/credit hour (Ph.D.); full
time: $500/credit hour, part time:
$500/credit hour (DNP)

Out-of-state tuition: full time:
$750/credit hour (master's); full
time: $750/credit hour (Ph.D.);
full time: $750/credit hour (DNP)
Room/board/expenses: N/A
Full-time enrollment: 90 (master's);
17 (Ph.D.); 34 (DNP)
men: 17%; women: 83%;
minorities: 15%; international: 1%
Part-time enrollment: 12
(master's); 10 (Ph.D.); 5 (DNP)
men: 12%; women: 88%;
minorities: 21%; international:
0%
Acceptance rate (master's): 67%
Acceptance rate (Ph.D.): 75%
Acceptance rate (DNP): 46%
Specialties offered: education;
nurse practitioner; nurse
practitioner: adult-gerontology
acute care; nurse practitioner:
adult-gerontology primary
care; nurse practitioner: family;
research

Worcester State University

486 Chandler Street
Worcester, MA 01602
www.worcester.edu/
Graduate-Programs
Public
Admissions: (508) 929-8127
Email: gradadmissions@
worcester.edu
Financial aid: (508) 929-8056
Application deadline: 06/15
Degrees offered: master's
In-state tuition: full time: $150/
credit hour, part time: $150/
credit hour
Out-of-state tuition: full time: $150/
credit hour
Room/board/expenses: N/A
Full-time enrollment: 1
men: 100%; women: 0%;
minorities: 100%; international:
100%
Part-time enrollment: 114
men: 8%; women: 92%;
minorities: 20%; international:
0%
Acceptance rate (master's): 62%
Specialties offered: community
health/public health; education

MICHIGAN

Davenport University[1]

Grand Rapids, MI 49512
Private
Admissions: N/A
Financial aid: N/A
Tuition: N/A
Room/board/expenses: N/A
Enrollment: N/A

Eastern Michigan University[1]

3111 Marshall Building
Ypsilanti, MI 48197
Public
Admissions: N/A
Financial aid: N/A
Tuition: N/A
Room/board/expenses: N/A
Enrollment: N/A

Ferris State University

200 Ferris Drive
Big Rapids, MI 49307
www.ferris.edu/HTMLS/colleges/
alliedhe/Nursing/homepage.htm
Public
Admissions: (800) 433-7747
Financial aid: (231) 591-2110
Application deadline: N/A
Degrees offered: master's
In-state tuition: full time: $527/
credit hour, part time: $527/
credit hour
Out-of-state tuition: full time:
$790/credit hour
Room/board/expenses: N/A
Full-time enrollment:
men: N/A; women: N/A;
minorities: N/A; international: N/A
Part-time enrollment: 95
men: 12%; women: 88%;
minorities: 13%; international:
0%
Acceptance rate (master's): 43%
Specialties offered:
administration; education;
informatics

Grand Valley State University[1]

301 Michigan Street NE
Grand Rapids, MI 49503-3314
www.gvsu/kcon
Public
Admissions: (616) 331-2025
Email: admissions@gvsu.edu
Financial aid: (616) 331-3234
Tuition: N/A
Room/board/expenses: N/A
Enrollment: N/A

Madonna University

36200 Schoolcraft Road
Livonia, MI 48150-1253
www.madonna.edu/academics/
departments/nursing-graduate/
Private
Admissions: (734) 432-5667
Email: grad@madonna.edu
Financial aid: (734) 432-5663
Application deadline: 01/02
Degrees offered: master's, DNP
Tuition: full time: $760/credit
hour, part time: $760/credit hour
(master's); full time: $760/credit
hour, part time: $760/credit
hour (DNP)
Room/board/expenses: $9,230
(master's); $9,230 (DNP)
Full-time enrollment: 3 (master's);
1 (DNP)
men: 25%; women: 75%;
minorities: 25%; international:
25%
Part-time enrollment: 243
(master's); 36 (DNP)
men: 13%; women: 87%;
minorities: 16%; international: 1%
Acceptance rate (master's): 41%
Acceptance rate (DNP): 32%
Specialties offered:
administration; nurse
practitioner; nurse practitioner:
adult-gerontology acute care;
nurse practitioner: adult-
gerontology primary care; other
majors; dual majors

Michigan State University

A117 Life Sciences Building
East Lansing, MI 48824-1317
nursing.msu.edu
Public
Admissions: (517) 432-9515
Email: nurse@hc.msu.edu
Financial aid: (517) 353-5940
Application deadline: N/A
Degrees offered: master's, Ph.D.,
DNP
In-state tuition: full time: $672/
credit hour, part time: $672/
credit hour (master's); full time:
$672/credit hour, part time:
$672/credit hour (Ph.D.); full
time: $672/credit hour, part time:
$672/credit hour (DNP)
Out-of-state tuition: full time:
$1,320/credit hour (master's);
full time: $1,320/credit hour
(Ph.D.); full time: $1,320/credit
hour (DNP)
Room/board/expenses: $10,412
(master's); $10,412 (Ph.D.);
$10,412 (DNP)
Full-time enrollment: 71 (master's);
14 (Ph.D.); 15 (DNP)
men: 18%; women: 82%;
minorities: 9%; international: 5%
Part-time enrollment: 105
(master's); 2 (Ph.D.); 2 (DNP)
men: 10%; women: 90%;
minorities: 11%; international: 0%
Acceptance rate (master's): 40%
Acceptance rate (Ph.D.): 83%
Acceptance rate (DNP): 100%
Specialties offered: clinical nurse
specialist; nurse anesthesia;
nurse practitioner; nurse
practitioner: adult-gerontology
primary care; nurse practitioner:
family

Oakland University

428 O'Dowd Hall
Rochester, MI 48309-4401
www.oakland.edu/nursing
Public
Admissions: (248) 370-3167
Email: gradmail@oakland.edu
Financial aid: (248) 370-2550
Application deadline: N/A
Degrees offered: master's, DNP
In-state tuition: full time: $15,720,
part time: $655/credit hour
(master's); full time: $15,720,
part time: $655/credit hour
(DNP)
Out-of-state tuition: full time:
$24,648 (master's); full time:
$24,648 (DNP)
Room/board/expenses: $9,250
(master's); $9,250 (DNP)
Full-time enrollment: 144
(master's); 5 (DNP)
men: N/A; women: N/A;
minorities: 6%; international: 1%
Part-time enrollment: 45
(master's); 25 (DNP)
men: N/A; women: N/A;
minorities: 23%; international:
3%
Acceptance rate (master's): 21%
Acceptance rate (DNP): 57%
Specialties offered: nurse
anesthesia; nurse practitioner;
nurse practitioner: adult-
gerontology acute care; nurse
practitioner: adult-gerontology
primary care; nurse practitioner:
adult; nurse practitioner: family;
nurse practitioner: pediatric
primary care

Saginaw Valley State University

7400 Bay Road
University Center, MI 48710
www.svsu.edu/nursing/
Public
Admissions: (989) 964-6096
Email: gradadm@svsu.edu
Financial aid: (989) 964-4103
Application deadline: N/A
Degrees offered: master's, DNP
In-state tuition: full time: $514/credit hour, part time: $514/credit hour (master's); full time: $565, part time: $565 (DNP)
Out-of-state tuition: full time: $980/credit hour (master's); full time: $1,037 (DNP)
Room/board/expenses: N/A
Full-time enrollment: 7 (master's); 2 (DNP)
men: 22%; women: 78%; minorities: 0%; international: 0%
Part-time enrollment: 41 (master's); 39 (DNP)
men: 14%; women: 86%; minorities: 8%; international: 3%
Acceptance rate (master's): 72%
Acceptance rate (DNP): 85%
Specialties offered: administration; clinical nurse leader; education; nurse practitioner: family

Spring Arbor University[1]

106 E. Main Street
Spring Arbor, MI 49283
Private
Admissions: N/A
Financial aid: N/A
Tuition: N/A
Room/board/expenses: N/A
Enrollment: N/A

University of Detroit Mercy

4001 W. McNichols Road
Detroit, MI 48221-3038
healthprofessions.udmercy.edu/programs/nursing/index.htm
Private
Admissions: (313) 993-1245
Email: admissions@udmercy.edu
Financial aid: (313) 993-3350
Application deadline: 02/15
Degrees offered: master's, DNP
Tuition: full time: $925/credit hour, part time: $925/credit hour (master's); full time: $925/credit hour, part time: $925/credit hour (DNP)
Room/board/expenses: N/A
Full-time enrollment: 72 (master's); N/A (DNP)
men: 39%; women: 61%; minorities: 21%; international: 3%
Part-time enrollment: 132 (master's); 12 (DNP)
men: 13%; women: 88%; minorities: 36%; international: 3%
Acceptance rate (master's): 25%
Acceptance rate (DNP): 63%
Specialties offered: clinical nurse leader; clinical nurse specialist; education; health management & policy health care systems; nurse anesthesia; nurse practitioner: family

University of Michigan-Ann Arbor

400 N. Ingalls
Ann Arbor, MI 48109-0482
nursing.umich.edu/
Public
Admissions: (734) 763-5237
Email: umsn-mastersadmissions@med.umich.edu
Financial aid: (734) 763-6730
Application deadline: 03/01
Degrees offered: master's, Ph.D., DNP
In-state tuition: full time: $20,550, part time: $1,142/credit hour (master's); full time: $20,550, part time: $1,142/credit hour (Ph.D.); full time: $20,550, part time: $1,142/credit hour (DNP)
Out-of-state tuition: full time: $42,282 (master's); full time: $42,282 (Ph.D.); full time: $42,282 (DNP)
Room/board/expenses: $14,248 (master's); $14,248 (Ph.D.); $14,248 (DNP)
Full-time enrollment: 151 (master's); 34 (Ph.D.); 5 (DNP)
men: 9%; women: 91%; minorities: 16%; international: 8%
Part-time enrollment: 176 (master's); 5 (Ph.D.); 22 (DNP)
men: 12%; women: 88%; minorities: 11%; international: 1%
Acceptance rate (master's): 67%
Acceptance rate (Ph.D.): 64%
Acceptance rate (DNP): 100%
Specialties offered: administration; clinical nurse specialist; health management & policy health care systems; informatics; nurse-midwifery; nurse practitioner; nurse practitioner: adult-gerontology acute care; nurse practitioner: adult-gerontology primary care; nurse practitioner: adult; nurse practitioner: family; nurse practitioner: pediatric primary care; research; combined nurse practitioner/clinical nurse specialist; dual majors

University of Michigan-Flint

303 E. Kearsley Street
Flint, MI 48502-1950
www.umflint.edu/nursing
Public
Admissions: (810) 762-3171
Email: graduate@umflint.edu
Financial aid: (810) 762-3444
Application deadline: 08/01
Degrees offered: master's, DNP
In-state tuition: full time: $9,554, part time: $531/credit hour (master's); full time: $9,554, part time: $531/credit hour (DNP)
Out-of-state tuition: full time: $14,319 (master's); full time: $14,319 (DNP)
Room/board/expenses: $8,706 (master's); $8,706 (DNP)
Full-time enrollment: 12 (master's); 119 (DNP)
men: 13%; women: 87%; minorities: 26%; international: 1%
Part-time enrollment: 1 (master's); 74 (DNP)
men: 12%; women: 88%; minorities: 31%; international: 1%
Acceptance rate (DNP): 77%

Specialties offered: nurse anesthesia; nurse practitioner; nurse practitioner: adult-gerontology acute care; nurse practitioner: adult-gerontology primary care; nurse practitioner: family; nurse practitioner: psychiatric-mental health, across the lifespan

Wayne State University

5557 Cass Avenue
Detroit, MI 48202
nursing.wayne.edu/
Public
Admissions: (313) 577-8141
Email: gradadmissions@wayne.edu
Financial aid: (313) 577-2100
Application deadline: 01/31
Degrees offered: master's, Ph.D., DNP
In-state tuition: full time: $805/credit hour, part time: $805/credit hour (master's); full time: $805/credit hour, part time: $805/credit hour (Ph.D.); full time: $805/credit hour, part time: $805/credit hour (DNP)
Out-of-state tuition: full time: $1,463/credit hour (master's); full time: $1,463/credit hour (Ph.D.); full time: $1,463/credit hour (DNP)
Room/board/expenses: $9,133 (master's); $9,133 (Ph.D.); $9,133 (DNP)
Full-time enrollment: 50 (master's); 21 (Ph.D.); 56 (DNP)
men: 6%; women: 94%; minorities: 27%; international: 9%
Part-time enrollment: 91 (master's); 4 (Ph.D.); 37 (DNP)
men: 9%; women: 91%; minorities: 29%; international: 4%
Acceptance rate (master's): 18%
Acceptance rate (Ph.D.): 33%
Acceptance rate (DNP): 67%
Specialties offered: community health/public health; education; nurse-midwifery; nurse practitioner; nurse practitioner: adult-gerontology acute care; nurse practitioner: adult-gerontology primary care; nurse practitioner: family; nurse practitioner: pediatric primary care; nurse practitioner: psychiatric-mental health, across the lifespan; research; other majors

Western Michigan University

1903 West Michigan Avenue
Kalamazoo, MI 49008-5200
www.wmich.edu/nursing/
Public
Admissions: (269) 387-2000
Email: ask-wmu@wmich.edu
Financial aid: (269) 387-6000
Application deadline: 05/30
Degrees offered: master's
In-state tuition: full time: $530/credit hour, part time: $530/credit hour
Out-of-state tuition: full time: $1,123/credit hour
Room/board/expenses: $9,238
Full-time enrollment: 14
men: 14%; women: 86%; minorities: 7%; international: 0%

Part-time enrollment: 3
men: 0%; women: 100%; minorities: 0%; international: 0%
Acceptance rate (master's): 64%
Specialties offered: clinical nurse leader; education

MINNESOTA

Augsburg College[1]

2211 Riverside Avenue S
Minneapolis, MN 55454
Private
Admissions: N/A
Financial aid: N/A
Tuition: N/A
Room/board/expenses: N/A
Enrollment: N/A

Bethel University[1]

3900 Bethel Drive
St. Paul, MN 55112
Private
Admissions: N/A
Financial aid: N/A
Tuition: N/A
Room/board/expenses: N/A
Enrollment: N/A

Capella University[1]

225 South 6th Street
9th Floor
Minneapolis, MN 55402
Private
Admissions: N/A
Financial aid: N/A
Tuition: N/A
Room/board/expenses: N/A
Enrollment: N/A

College of St. Scholastica

1200 Kenwood Avenue
Duluth, MN 55811
www.css.edu/academics/school-of-nursing.html
Private
Admissions: (218) 733-2240
Email: geoadmin@css.edu
Financial aid: (218) 723-6000
Application deadline: 12/15
Degrees offered: DNP
Tuition: full time: $800/credit hour, part time: N/A
Room/board/expenses: $16,713
Full-time enrollment: 93
men: 12%; women: 88%; minorities: 9%; international: N/A
Part-time enrollment: 16
men: 13%; women: 88%; minorities: 25%; international: N/A
Acceptance rate (DNP): 62%
Specialties offered: informatics; nurse practitioner; nurse practitioner: adult-gerontology primary care; nurse practitioner: family; nurse practitioner: psychiatric-mental health, across the lifespan

Metropolitan State University[1]

730 Hennepin Avenue
Minneapolis, MN 55403-1897
Public
Admissions: N/A
Financial aid: N/A
Tuition: N/A
Room/board/expenses: N/A
Enrollment: N/A

Minnesota State University-Mankato[1]

College of Graduate Studies and Research
Mankato, MN 56001
ahn.mnsu.edu/nursing/
Public
Admissions: N/A
Financial aid: N/A
Tuition: N/A
Room/board/expenses: N/A
Enrollment: N/A

Minnesota State University-Moorhead

1104 Seventh Avenue South
Moorhead, MN 56563
www.mnstate.edu/graduate-nursing/
Public
Admissions: (218) 477-2134
Email: graduate@mnstate.edu
Financial aid: (218) 477-2251
Application deadline: N/A
Degrees offered: master's
In-state tuition: full time: $430/credit hour, part time: $430/credit hour
Out-of-state tuition: full time: $860/credit hour
Room/board/expenses: N/A
Full-time enrollment:
men: N/A; women: N/A; minorities: N/A; international: N/A
Part-time enrollment: 83
men: 20%; women: 80%; minorities: 13%; international: 0%
Specialties offered: administration; education

St. Catherine University

2004 Randolph Avenue
Mail #F-22
St. Paul, MN 55105-1794
www2.stkate.edu/nursing/home
Private
Admissions: (651) 690-6933
Email: graduate_study@stkate.edu
Financial aid: (651) 690-6607
Application deadline: N/A
Degrees offered: master's, DNP
Tuition: full time: $751/credit hour, part time: $751/credit hour (master's); full time: $940/credit hour, part time: $940/credit hour (DNP)
Room/board/expenses: N/A
Full-time enrollment: 175 (master's); 11 (DNP)
men: 8%; women: 92%; minorities: 15%; international: 1%
Part-time enrollment: 11 (master's); 9 (DNP)
men: 10%; women: 90%; minorities: 5%; international: 5%
Acceptance rate (master's): 95%
Acceptance rate (DNP): 83%
Specialties offered: education; generalist; nurse practitioner; nurse practitioner: adult-gerontology primary care; nurse practitioner: pediatric primary care

University of Minnesota-Twin Cities

308 Harvard Street SE
Minneapolis, MN 55455
www.nursing.umn.edu/
Public
Admissions: (612) 625-7980

Email: sonstudentinfo@umn.edu
Financial aid: (612) 624-4138
Application deadline: 03/01
Degrees offered: Ph.D., DNP
In-state tuition: full time: $15,844, part time: $1,320/credit hour (Ph.D.); full time: $950/credit hour, part time: $950/credit hour (DNP)
Out-of-state tuition: full time: $24,508 (Ph.D.); full time: $950/credit hour (DNP)
Room/board/expenses: N/A
Full-time enrollment: 32 (Ph.D.); 308 (DNP)
men: 12%; women: 87%; minorities: 15%; international: 1%
Part-time enrollment: 9 (Ph.D.); 40 (DNP)
men: 14%; women: 84%; minorities: 20%; international: 0%
Acceptance rate (Ph.D.): 85%
Acceptance rate (DNP): 54%
Specialties offered: administration; clinical nurse specialist; community health/public health; informatics; nurse anesthesia; nurse-midwifery; nurse practitioner; nurse practitioner: adult-gerontology primary care; nurse practitioner: family; nurse practitioner: pediatric primary care; nurse practitioner: psychiatric-mental health, across the lifespan; research; other majors

Walden University[1]
100 Washington Avenue S
Suite 900
Minneapolis, MN 55401
Private
Admissions: N/A
Financial aid: N/A
Tuition: N/A
Room/board/expenses: N/A
Enrollment: N/A

Winona State University-Rochester[1]
859 30th Avenue SE
Rochester, MN 55904
Public
Admissions: N/A
Financial aid: N/A
Tuition: N/A
Room/board/expenses: N/A
Enrollment: N/A

MISSISSIPPI

Alcorn State University[1]
15 Campus Drive
Natchez, MS 39122-8399
Public
Admissions: N/A
Financial aid: N/A
Tuition: N/A
Room/board/expenses: N/A
Enrollment: N/A

Delta State University
P.O. Box 3343
1003 West Sunflower Road
Cleveland, MS 38733
www.deltastate.edu/school-of-nursing/
Public
Admissions: (662) 846-4700
Email: grad-info@deltastate.edu
Financial aid: (662) 846-4670
Application deadline: 02/01

Degrees offered: master's, DNP
In-state tuition: full time: $6,012, part time: $334/credit hour (master's); full time: $6,012, part time: $334/credit hour (DNP)
Out-of-state tuition: full time: $6,012 (master's); full time: $6,012 (DNP)
Room/board/expenses: N/A
Full-time enrollment: 27 (master's); 11 (DNP)
men: 18%; women: 82%; minorities: 26%; international: 0%
Part-time enrollment: 6 (master's); 6 (DNP)
men: 8%; women: 92%; minorities: 50%; international: 0%
Acceptance rate (master's): 77%
Acceptance rate (DNP): 43%
Specialties offered: nurse practitioner; nurse practitioner: family

Mississippi University for Women
1100 College Street
MUW-910
Columbus, MS 39701-5800
www.muw.edu/nslp
Public
Admissions: (662) 329-7142
Email: www.muw.edu/graduates/admission
Financial aid: (662) 329-7145
Application deadline: 02/01
Degrees offered: master's, DNP
In-state tuition: full time: $5,681, part time: $321/credit hour (master's); full time: $5,681, part time: $321/credit hour (DNP)
Out-of-state tuition: full time: $15,747 (master's); full time: $15,747 (DNP)
Room/board/expenses: $6,591 (master's); $6,591 (DNP)
Full-time enrollment: 33 (master's); 8 (DNP)
men: 10%; women: 90%; minorities: 12%; international: 0%
Part-time enrollment: 2 (master's); 3 (DNP)
men: 40%; women: 60%; minorities: 40%; international: 0%
Acceptance rate (master's): 39%
Acceptance rate (DNP): 100%
Specialties offered: nurse practitioner; nurse practitioner: family

University of Mississippi Medical Center[1]
2500 N. State Street
Jackson, MS 39216-4505
Public
Admissions: N/A
Financial aid: N/A
Tuition: N/A
Room/board/expenses: N/A
Enrollment: N/A

University of Southern Mississippi
118 College Drive
PO Box 5095
Hattiesburg, MS 39406-5095
www.usm.edu/nursing
Public
Admissions: (601) 266-4369

Email: Karen.Coats@usm.edu
Financial aid: (601) 266-4813
Application deadline: 03/01
Degrees offered: master's, Ph.D., DNP
In-state tuition: full time: $10,836, part time: $7,566 (master's); full time: $10,836, part time: $7,566 (Ph.D.); full time: $10,836, part time: $7,566 (DNP)
Out-of-state tuition: full time: $24,141 (master's); full time: $24,141 (Ph.D.); full time: $24,141 (DNP)
Room/board/expenses: $8,719 (master's); $8,719 (Ph.D.); $8,719 (DNP)
Full-time enrollment: 80 (master's); 13 (Ph.D.); 64 (DNP)
men: 32%; women: 68%; minorities: 11%; international: 0%
Part-time enrollment: 31 (master's); 13 (Ph.D.); 1 (DNP)
men: 7%; women: 93%; minorities: 18%; international: 0%
Acceptance rate (master's): 88%
Acceptance rate (Ph.D.): 100%
Acceptance rate (DNP): 100%
Specialties offered: nurse anesthesia; nurse practitioner; nurse practitioner: family; nurse practitioner: psychiatric-mental health, across the lifespan; research; other majors

William Carey University
498 Tuscan Avenue
Hattiesburg, MS 39401
www.wmcarey.edu/schools/school-nursing
Private
Admissions: (800) 962-5991
Email: admissions@wmcarey.edu
Financial aid: (601) 318-6486
Application deadline: N/A
Degrees offered: master's, Ph.D.
Tuition: full time: $350/credit hour, part time: $350/credit hour (master's); full time: $450/credit hour, part time: $450/credit hour (Ph.D.)
Room/board/expenses: $1,470 (master's); $1,470 (Ph.D.)
Full-time enrollment: 39 (master's); 39 (Ph.D.)
men: 13%; women: 87%; minorities: 51%; international: 0%
Part-time enrollment: 40 (master's); 35 (Ph.D.)
men: 9%; women: 91%; minorities: 36%; international: 0%
Acceptance rate (master's): 97%
Acceptance rate (Ph.D.): 80%
Specialties offered: administration; case management; education; generalist; dual majors

MISSOURI

Central Methodist University[1]
411 Central Methodist Square
Fayette, MO 65248
Private
Admissions: N/A
Financial aid: N/A
Tuition: N/A
Room/board/expenses: N/A
Enrollment: N/A

Cox College[1]
1423 N. Jefferson Avenue
Springfield, MO 65802
Private
Admissions: N/A
Financial aid: N/A
Tuition: N/A
Room/board/expenses: N/A
Enrollment: N/A

Goldfarb School of Nursing at Barnes-Jewish College[1]
4483 Duncan Avenue
St. Louis, MO 63110
Private
Admissions: N/A
Financial aid: N/A
Tuition: N/A
Room/board/expenses: N/A
Enrollment: N/A

Graceland University[1]
1401 W. Truman Road
Independence, MO 64050
Private
Admissions: N/A
Financial aid: N/A
Tuition: N/A
Room/board/expenses: N/A
Enrollment: N/A

Maryville University of St. Louis
650 Maryville University Drive
St. Louis, MO 63141
www.maryville.edu/hp/nursing/
Private
Admissions: (314) 529-9350
Email: admissions@maryville.edu
Financial aid: (314) 529-9360
Application deadline: N/A
Degrees offered: master's
Tuition: full time: $781/credit hour, part time: N/A
Room/board/expenses: N/A
Full-time enrollment: 17
men: 6%; women: 94%; minorities: 12%; international: 12%
Part-time enrollment: 145
men: 8%; women: 92%; minorities: 8%; international: 1%
Specialties offered: nurse practitioner; nurse practitioner: adult-gerontology acute care; nurse practitioner: adult-gerontology primary care; nurse practitioner: adult; nurse practitioner: family; nurse practitioner: pediatric primary care

Missouri Southern State University[1]
Health Sciences Building 243
Joplin, MO 64801
Public
Admissions: N/A
Financial aid: N/A
Tuition: N/A
Room/board/expenses: N/A
Enrollment: N/A

Missouri State University[1]
Professional Building, Suite 300
Springfield, MO 65897
Public
Admissions: N/A
Financial aid: N/A
Tuition: N/A
Room/board/expenses: N/A
Enrollment: N/A

Missouri Western State University[1]
4525 Downs Drive
Murphy Hall, Room 309
St. Joseph, MO 64507
Public
Admissions: N/A
Financial aid: N/A
Tuition: N/A
Room/board/expenses: N/A
Enrollment: N/A

Research College of Nursing[1]
2525 E. Meyer Boulevard
Kansas City, MO 64132
Private
Admissions: N/A
Financial aid: N/A
Tuition: N/A
Room/board/expenses: N/A
Enrollment: N/A

Southeast Missouri State University
1 University Plaza
Cape Girardeau, MO 63701
semo.edu/nursing
Public
Admissions: (573) 651-2590
Email: admissions@semo.edu
Financial aid: (573) 651-2253
Application deadline: 04/01
Degrees offered: master's
In-state tuition: full time: $261/credit hour, part time: $261/credit hour
Out-of-state tuition: full time: $487/credit hour
Room/board/expenses: $8,285
Full-time enrollment: 12
men: 17%; women: 83%; minorities: 8%; international: 0%
Part-time enrollment: 15
men: 0%; women: 100%; minorities: 13%; international: 7%
Acceptance rate (master's): 50%
Specialties offered: education; nurse practitioner; nurse practitioner: family

Southwest Baptist University[1]
Bolivar, MO 65613
Private
Admissions: N/A
Financial aid: N/A
Tuition: N/A
Room/board/expenses: N/A
Enrollment: N/A

St. Louis University
3525 Caroline Mall
St. Louis, MO 63104-1099
nursing.slu.edu
Private
Admissions: (314) 977-2500
Email: www.slu.edu
Financial aid: (314) 977-2350
Application deadline: N/A

Degrees offered: master's, Ph.D., DNP
Tuition: full time: $1,050/credit hour, part time: $1,050/credit hour (master's); full time: $1,050/credit hour, part time: $1,050/credit hour (Ph.D.); full time: $1,050/credit hour, part time: $1,050/credit hour (DNP)
Room/board/expenses: N/A
Full-time enrollment: 210 (master's); 30 (Ph.D.); 27 (DNP)
men: 15%; women: 85%; minorities: 14%; international: 7%
Part-time enrollment: 127 (master's); 3 (Ph.D.); 10 (DNP)
men: 15%; women: 85%; minorities: 15%; international: 1%
Acceptance rate (master's): 69%
Acceptance rate (Ph.D.): 71%
Acceptance rate (DNP): 74%
Specialties offered: clinical nurse leader; nurse practitioner; nurse practitioner: adult-gerontology acute care; nurse practitioner: adult-gerontology primary care; nurse practitioner: family; nurse practitioner: pediatric primary care; nurse practitioner: psychiatric-mental health, across the lifespan

University of Central Missouri

UHC 106A
Warrensburg, MO 64093
www.ucmo.edu/nursing
Public
Admissions: (660) 543-4621
Financial aid: (660) 543-8266
Application deadline: N/A
Degrees offered: master's
In-state tuition: full time: $278/credit hour, part time: $278/credit hour
Out-of-state tuition: full time: $557/credit hour
Room/board/expenses: $8,102
Full-time enrollment: 4
men: 0%; women: 100%; minorities: 25%; international: 0%
Part-time enrollment: 79
men: 4%; women: 96%; minorities: 3%; international: 0%
Specialties offered: education; nurse practitioner: nurse practitioner: family

University of Missouri

Columbia, MO 65211
nursing.missouri.edu
Public
Admissions: (573) 882-0277
Email: nursing@missouri.edu
Financial aid: (573) 882-7506
Application deadline: 03/01
Degrees offered: master's, Ph.D., DNP
In-state tuition: full time: $422/credit hour, part time: $422/credit hour (master's); full time: $422/credit hour, part time: $422/credit hour (Ph.D.); full time: $422/credit hour, part time: $422/credit hour (DNP)
Out-of-state tuition: full time: $422/credit hour (master's); full time: $422/credit hour (Ph.D.); full time: $422/credit hour (DNP)
Room/board/expenses: N/A
Full-time enrollment: 1 (master's); 27 (Ph.D.); 42 (DNP)
men: 3%; women: 97%; minorities: 14%; international: 4%

Part-time enrollment: 39 (master's); 18 (Ph.D.); 160 (DNP)
men: 8%; women: 92%; minorities: 12%; international: 2%
Acceptance rate (master's): 81%
Acceptance rate (Ph.D.): 82%
Acceptance rate (DNP): 80%
Specialties offered: administration; clinical nurse specialist; education; generalist; nurse practitioner; nurse practitioner: family; nurse practitioner: pediatric primary care; nurse practitioner: psychiatric-mental health, across the lifespan; research; other majors; combined nurse practitioner/clinical nurse specialist; dual majors

University of Missouri-Kansas City

2464 Charlotte
Kansas City, MO 64108
www.umkc.edu/nursing
Public
Admissions: (816) 235-1111
Email: admit@umkc.edu
Financial aid: (816) 235-1154
Application deadline: 12/15
Degrees offered: master's, Ph.D., DNP
In-state tuition: full time: $400/credit hour, part time: $400/credit hour (master's); full time: $400/credit hour, part time: $400/credit hour (Ph.D.); full time: $400/credit hour, part time: $400/credit hour (DNP)
Out-of-state tuition: full time: $400/credit hour (master's); full time: $400/credit hour (Ph.D.); full time: $400/credit hour (DNP)
Room/board/expenses: N/A
Full-time enrollment: 9 (master's); 2 (Ph.D.); 51 (DNP)
men: 31%; women: 69%; minorities: 18%; international: 0%
Part-time enrollment: 105 (master's); 41 (Ph.D.); 114 (DNP)
men: 8%; women: 92%; minorities: 26%; international: 0%
Acceptance rate (master's): 82%
Acceptance rate (Ph.D.): 83%
Acceptance rate (DNP): 74%
Specialties offered: education; nurse anesthesia; nurse practitioner: adult-gerontology primary care; nurse practitioner: family; nurse practitioner: pediatric primary care; nurse practitioner: psychiatric-mental health, across the lifespan; research

University of Missouri-St. Louis

One University Boulevard
St. Louis, MO 63121
www.umsl.edu/divisions/nursing/
Public
Admissions: (314) 516-5458
Email: gradadm@umsl.edu
Financial aid: (314) 516-5526
Application deadline: 02/15
Degrees offered: master's, Ph.D., DNP
In-state tuition: full time: $436/credit hour, part time: $436/credit hour (master's); full time: $436/credit hour, part time: $436/credit hour (Ph.D.);

full time: $436/credit hour, part time: $436/credit hour (DNP)
Out-of-state tuition: full time: $1,049/credit hour (master's); full time: $1,049/credit hour (Ph.D.); full time: $1,049/credit hour (DNP)
Room/board/expenses: $11,971 (master's); $11,971 (Ph.D.); $11,971 (DNP)
Full-time enrollment: 2 (master's); 2 (Ph.D.); 20 (DNP)
men: 4%; women: 96%; minorities: 0%; international: 4%
Part-time enrollment: 200 (master's); 21 (Ph.D.); 18 (DNP)
men: 5%; women: 95%; minorities: 13%; international: 0%
Acceptance rate (master's): 55%
Acceptance rate (Ph.D.): 100%
Acceptance rate (DNP): 94%
Specialties offered: education; nurse practitioner; nurse practitioner: adult-gerontology primary care; nurse practitioner: family; nurse practitioner: pediatric primary care; nurse practitioner: psychiatric-mental health, across the lifespan; research

Webster University

470 E. Lockwood Avenue
St. Louis, MO 63119
www.webster.edu/arts-and-sciences/academics/nursing/
Private
Admissions: (800) 753-6765
Email: admit@webster.edu
Financial aid: (800) 983-4623
Application deadline: N/A
Degrees offered: master's
Tuition: full time: $685/credit hour, part time: $685/credit hour
Room/board/expenses: $10,860
Full-time enrollment: 1
men: 0%; women: 100%; minorities: 0%; international: 0%
Part-time enrollment: 122
men: 2%; women: 98%; minorities: 18%; international: 1%
Acceptance rate (master's): 93%
Specialties offered: education; other majors

MONTANA

Montana State University

PO Box 173560
Bozeman, MT 59717-3560
www.montana.edu/nursing/
Public
Admissions: (406) 994-2452
Email: admissions@montana.edu
Financial aid: (406) 994-2845
Application deadline: 02/15
Degrees offered: master's, DNP
In-state tuition: full time: $267/credit hour, part time: $267/credit hour (master's); full time: $267/credit hour, part time: $267/credit hour (DNP)
Out-of-state tuition: full time: $892/credit hour (master's); full time: $892/credit hour (DNP)
Room/board/expenses: N/A
Full-time enrollment: N/A (master's); 43 (DNP)
men: 19%; women: 81%; minorities: 9%; international: 0%

Part-time enrollment: 17 (master's); 32 (DNP)
men: 4%; women: 96%; minorities: 6%; international: 0%
Acceptance rate (master's): 100%
Acceptance rate (DNP): 70%
Specialties offered: clinical nurse leader; education; nurse practitioner; nurse practitioner: family; nurse practitioner: psychiatric-mental health, across the lifespan

NEBRASKA

Bryan College of Health Sciences[1]

5035 Everett Street
Lincoln, NE 68506
Private
Admissions: N/A
Financial aid: N/A
Tuition: N/A
Room/board/expenses: N/A
Enrollment: N/A

Clarkson College

101 S. 42nd Street
Omaha, NE 68131-2715
www.clarksoncollege.edu/about/
Private
Admissions: (402) 552-2796
Email: Admissions@clarksoncollege.edu
Financial aid: (402) 552-2470
Application deadline: 11/01
Degrees offered: master's, DNP
Tuition: full time: $535/credit hour, part time: $535/credit hour (master's); full time: $803/credit hour, part time: $803/credit hour (DNP)
Room/board/expenses: N/A
Full-time enrollment: 264 (master's); 2 (DNP)
men: 10%; women: 89%; minorities: 9%; international: 0%
Part-time enrollment: 244 (master's); 3 (DNP)
men: 10%; women: 90%; minorities: 9%; international: 0%
Acceptance rate (master's): 49%
Acceptance rate (DNP): 60%
Specialties offered: administration; education; nurse anesthesia; nurse practitioner; nurse practitioner: adult-gerontology primary care; nurse practitioner: family; other majors

College of St. Mary[1]

7000 Mercy Road
Omaha, NE 68106
Private
Admissions: N/A
Financial aid: N/A
Tuition: N/A
Room/board/expenses: N/A
Enrollment: N/A

Creighton University

2500 California Plaza
Omaha, NE 68178
nursing.creighton.edu/
Private
Admissions: (402) 280-2703
Email: nursing@creighton.edu
Financial aid: (402) 280-2351
Application deadline: N/A
Degrees offered: master's, DNP
Tuition: full time: $800/credit hour, part time: $800/credit hour (master's); full time: $800/credit

hour, part time: $800/credit hour (DNP)
Room/board/expenses: N/A
Full-time enrollment: 42 (master's); 89 (DNP)
men: 9%; women: 91%; minorities: 10%; international: 1%
Part-time enrollment: 63 (master's); 153 (DNP)
men: 7%; women: 93%; minorities: 11%; international: 0%
Acceptance rate (master's): 100%
Acceptance rate (DNP): 86%
Specialties offered: administration; clinical nurse leader; nurse practitioner; nurse practitioner: adult-gerontology acute care; nurse practitioner: adult-gerontology primary care; nurse practitioner: family; nurse practitioner: pediatric primary care; other majors

Nebraska Methodist College

720 N. 87th Street
Omaha, NE 68114
Private
Admissions: (402) 354-7202
Email: admissions@methodistcollege.edu
Financial aid: (402) 354-7225
Application deadline: N/A
Degrees offered: master's, DNP
Tuition: full time: $698/credit hour, part time: $698/credit hour (master's); full time: $770/credit hour, part time: $770/credit hour (DNP)
Room/board/expenses: $7,320 (master's); $7,320 (DNP)
Full-time enrollment: 89 (master's); 25 (DNP)
men: 3%; women: 97%; minorities: 11%; international: 0%
Part-time enrollment: 23 (master's); 2 (DNP)
men: 0%; women: 100%; minorities: 4%; international: 0%
Acceptance rate (master's): 50%
Acceptance rate (DNP): 47%
Specialties offered: administration; education; informatics; nurse practitioner; nurse practitioner: family

Nebraska Wesleyan University

5000 Saint Paul Avenue
Lincoln, NE 68504
Private
Admissions: N/A
Financial aid: (402) 465-2167
Application deadline: N/A
Degrees offered: master's
Tuition: full time: $395/credit hour, part time: $395/credit hour
Room/board/expenses: $9,000
Full-time enrollment: 70
men: 7%; women: 93%; minorities: 6%; international: 4%
Part-time enrollment: 15
men: 13%; women: 87%; minorities: 13%; international: 7%
Acceptance rate (master's): 100%
Specialties offered: administration; education; other majors; dual majors

University of Nebraska Medical Center

985330 Nebraska Medical Center
Omaha, NE 68198-5330
www.unmc.edu/nursing/
Public
Admissions: (402) 559-6639
Email: rolee.kelly@unmc.edu
Financial aid: (402) 559-4199
Application deadline: 02/01
Degrees offered: master's, Ph.D., DNP
In-state tuition: full time: $447/credit hour, part time: $447/credit hour (master's); full time: $447/credit hour, part time: $447/credit hour (Ph.D.); full time: $447/credit hour, part time: $447/credit hour (DNP)
Out-of-state tuition: full time: $933/credit hour (master's); full time: $933/credit hour (Ph.D.); full time: $933/credit hour (DNP)
Room/board/expenses: N/A
Full-time enrollment: 117 (master's); 12 (Ph.D.); 36 (DNP)
men: 7%; women: 93%; minorities: 14%; international: 2%
Part-time enrollment: 155 (master's); 13 (Ph.D.); 16 (DNP)
men: 8%; women: 92%; minorities: 11%; international: 0%
Acceptance rate (Ph.D.): 66%
Acceptance rate (Ph.D.): 86%
Acceptance rate (DNP): 65%
Specialties offered: administration; clinical nurse specialist; education; nurse practitioner; nurse practitioner: adult-gerontology acute care; nurse practitioner: adult-gerontology primary care; nurse practitioner: family; nurse practitioner: pediatric primary care; nurse practitioner: psychiatric-mental health, across the lifespan; research

NEVADA

University of Nevada-Las Vegas[1]

4505 Maryland Parkway
Las Vegas, NV 89154-3018
Public
Admissions: N/A
Financial aid: N/A
Tuition: N/A
Room/board/expenses: N/A
Enrollment: N/A

University of Nevada-Reno

1664 North Virginia Street
Reno, NV 89557-0042
Public
Admissions: N/A
Financial aid: N/A
Application deadline: N/A
Degrees offered: master's, DNP
In-state tuition: full time: N/A, part time: N/A (master's); full time: N/A, part time: N/A (DNP)
Out-of-state tuition: full time: N/A (master's); full time: N/A (DNP)
Room/board/expenses: N/A
Full-time enrollment: 31 (master's); 12 (DNP)
men: N/A; women: N/A; minorities: N/A; international: N/A

Part-time enrollment: 80 (master's); 6 (DNP)
men: N/A; women: N/A; minorities: N/A; international: N/A
Specialties offered: clinical nurse leader; education; nurse practitioner; nurse practitioner: adult-gerontology acute care; nurse practitioner: family; nurse practitioner: psychiatric-mental health, across the lifespan; dual majors

NEW HAMPSHIRE

Franklin Pierce University[1]

40 University Drive
Rindge, NH 03461
Private
Admissions: N/A
Financial aid: N/A
Tuition: N/A
Room/board/expenses: N/A
Enrollment: N/A

Rivier University

420 S. Main Street
Nashua, NH 03060
www.rivier.edu/academics.aspx?menu=76&id=521
Private
Admissions: (603) 897-8507
Email: admissions@rivier.edu
Financial aid: (603) 897-8510
Application deadline: N/A
Degrees offered: master's
Tuition: full time: N/A, part time: N/A
Room/board/expenses: N/A
Full-time enrollment: 6
men: N/A; women: 100%; minorities: N/A; international: N/A
Part-time enrollment: 166
men: 7%; women: 93%; minorities: 8%; international: N/A
Acceptance rate (master's): 59%
Specialties offered: community health/public health; education; nurse practitioner; nurse practitioner: adult-gerontology primary care; nurse practitioner: family; nurse practitioner: psychiatric-mental health, across the lifespan; other majors

Southern New Hampshire University[1]

Hooksett, NH 03106
Private
Admissions: N/A
Financial aid: N/A
Tuition: N/A
Room/board/expenses: N/A
Enrollment: N/A

University of New Hampshire[1]

Hewitt Hall
4 Library Way
Durham, NH 03824-3563
Public
Admissions: N/A
Financial aid: N/A
Tuition: N/A
Room/board/expenses: N/A
Enrollment: N/A

NEW JERSEY

College of New Jersey[1]

PO Box 7718
Ewing, NJ 08628-0718
Public
Admissions: N/A
Financial aid: N/A
Tuition: N/A
Room/board/expenses: N/A
Enrollment: N/A

College of St. Elizabeth[1]

2 Convent Road
Morristown, NJ 07960
Private
Admissions: N/A
Financial aid: N/A
Tuition: N/A
Room/board/expenses: N/A
Enrollment: N/A

Fairleigh Dickinson University[1]

1000 River Road
H-DH4-02
Teaneck, NJ 07666
Private
Admissions: N/A
Financial aid: N/A
Tuition: N/A
Room/board/expenses: N/A
Enrollment: N/A

Felician University

262 S. Main Street
Lodi, NJ 07644
felician.edu/
Private
Admissions: (201) 355-1465
Email: admissions@felician.edu
Financial aid: (201) 559-6036
Application deadline: 08/25
Degrees offered: master's, DNP
Tuition: full time: $965/credit hour, part time: $965/credit hour (master's); full time: $965/credit hour, part time: $965/credit hour (DNP)
Room/board/expenses: N/A
Full-time enrollment: 38 (master's); 6 (DNP)
men: 9%; women: 91%; minorities: 55%; international: 2%
Part-time enrollment: 85 (master's); 10 (DNP)
men: 7%; women: 93%; minorities: 47%; international: 0%
Acceptance rate (master's): 83%
Acceptance rate (DNP): 75%
Specialties offered: administration; education; nurse practitioner; nurse practitioner: adult-gerontology primary care; nurse practitioner: family

Kean University[1]

1000 Morris Avenue
Union, NJ 07083
www.kean.edu/academics/college-natural-applied-health-sciences/school-nursing
Public
Admissions: N/A
Financial aid: N/A
Tuition: N/A
Room/board/expenses: N/A
Enrollment: N/A

Monmouth University

400 Cedar Avenue
West Long Branch, NJ 07764
www.monmouth.edu/school-of-nursing-health/department-of-nursing.aspx
Private
Admissions: (732) 571-3452
Email: gradadm@monmouth.edu
Financial aid: (732) 571-3463
Application deadline: 07/15
Degrees offered: master's, DNP
Tuition: full time: $1,047/credit hour, part time: $1,047/credit hour (master's); full time: $1,047/credit hour, part time: $1,047/credit hour (DNP)
Room/board/expenses: N/A
Full-time enrollment: 14 (master's); N/A (DNP)
men: 14%; women: 86%; minorities: 36%; international: 0%
Part-time enrollment: 240 (master's); 4 (DNP)
men: 7%; women: 93%; minorities: 32%; international: 0%
Acceptance rate (master's): 99%
Specialties offered: administration; education; forensic nursing; nurse practitioner; nurse practitioner: adult-gerontology primary care; nurse practitioner: family; nurse practitioner: psychiatric-mental health, across the lifespan; school nursing

Ramapo College of New Jersey[1]

505 Ramapo Valley Road
Mahwah, NJ 07430
Public
Admissions: N/A
Financial aid: N/A
Tuition: N/A
Room/board/expenses: N/A
Enrollment: N/A

Rutgers University-Newark

180 University Avenue
Newark, NJ 07102
nursing.rutgers.edu
Public
Admissions: (973) 353-5293
Email: snRecruiter@sn.rutgers.edu
Financial aid: (973) 972-7030
Application deadline: 04/01
Degrees offered: master's, Ph.D., DNP
In-state tuition: full time: $775/credit hour, part time: $775/credit hour (master's); full time: $775/credit hour, part time: $775/credit hour (Ph.D.); full time: $775/credit hour, part time: $775/credit hour (DNP)
Out-of-state tuition: full time: $1,124/credit hour (master's); full time: $1,124/credit hour (Ph.D.); full time: $1,124/credit hour (DNP)
Room/board/expenses: $11,730 (master's); $11,730 (Ph.D.); $11,730 (DNP)
Full-time enrollment: 30 (master's); 11 (Ph.D.); 99 (DNP)
men: 9%; women: 91%; minorities: 46%; international: 2%

Part-time enrollment: 286 (master's); 22 (Ph.D.); 298 (DNP)
men: 13%; women: 87%; minorities: 52%; international: 1%
Acceptance rate (master's): 62%
Acceptance rate (Ph.D.): 38%
Acceptance rate (DNP): 53%
Specialties offered: clinical nurse leader; education; health management & policy health care systems; informatics; nurse anesthesia; nurse-midwifery; nurse practitioner; nurse practitioner: adult-gerontology acute care; nurse practitioner: adult-gerontology primary care; nurse practitioner: adult; nurse practitioner: family; nurse practitioner: pediatric primary care; nurse practitioner: psychiatric-mental health, across the lifespan; research; school nursing; other majors

Seton Hall University

400 S. Orange Avenue
South Orange, NJ 07079
www.shu.edu/search.cfm?q=College%20of%20Nursing
Private
Admissions: (973) 761-9107
Email: thehall@shu.edu
Financial aid: (800) 222-7183
Application deadline: 04/01
Degrees offered: master's, Ph.D., DNP
Tuition: full time: $1,135/credit hour, part time: $1,135/credit hour (master's); full time: $1,135/credit hour, part time: $1,135/credit hour (Ph.D.); full time: $1,135/credit hour, part time: $1,135/credit hour (DNP)
Room/board/expenses: N/A
Full-time enrollment: 41 (master's); N/A (Ph.D.); N/A (DNP)
men: N/A; women: N/A; minorities: 20%; international: 0%
Part-time enrollment: 223 (master's); 26 (Ph.D.); 31 (DNP)
men: N/A; women: N/A; minorities: 20%; international: 0%
Acceptance rate (master's): 50%
Acceptance rate (Ph.D.): 63%
Acceptance rate (DNP): 52%
Specialties offered: administration; case management; clinical nurse leader; nurse practitioner; nurse practitioner: adult-gerontology acute care; nurse practitioner: adult-gerontology primary care; nurse practitioner: pediatric primary care; research; school nursing; dual majors

Stockton University[1]

PO Box 195
Pomona, NJ 08240
Public
Admissions: N/A
Financial aid: N/A
Tuition: N/A
Room/board/expenses: N/A
Enrollment: N/A

St. Peter's University[1]

Hudson Terrace
Englewood Cliffs, NJ 7632
Private
Admissions: N/A
Financial aid: N/A
Tuition: N/A

Room/board/expenses: N/A
Enrollment: N/A

Thomas Edison State College[1]

101 West State Street
Trenton, NJ 08608
Public
Admissions: N/A
Financial aid: N/A
Tuition: N/A
Room/board/expenses: N/A
Enrollment: N/A

William Paterson University of New Jersey[1]

300 Pompton Road
Wayne, NJ 7470
Public
Admissions: N/A
Financial aid: N/A
Tuition: N/A
Room/board/expenses: N/A
Enrollment: N/A

NEW MEXICO

New Mexico State University

1335 International Mall, HSS110
Las Cruces, NM 88003-8001
schoolofnursing.nmsu.edu
Public
Admissions: (575) 646-3121
Email: admissions@nmsu.edu
Financial aid: (575) 646-4105
Application deadline: 02/01
Degrees offered: master's, Ph.D., DNP
In-state tuition: full time: $4,088, part time: $227/credit hour (master's); full time: $4,088, part time: $227/credit hour (Ph.D.); full time: $4,088, part time: $227/credit hour (DNP)
Out-of-state tuition: full time: $14,254 (master's); full time: $14,254 (Ph.D.); full time: $14,254 (DNP)
Room/board/expenses: $8,064 (master's); $8,064 (Ph.D.); $8,064 (DNP)
Full-time enrollment: 3 (master's); 2 (Ph.D.); 19 (DNP) men: 25%; women: 75%; minorities: 58%; international: 4%
Part-time enrollment: 18 (master's); 28 (Ph.D.); 44 (DNP) men: 11%; women: 89%; minorities: 39%; international: 0%
Acceptance rate (master's): 80%
Acceptance rate (Ph.D.): 100%
Acceptance rate (DNP): 48%
Specialties offered: administration; community health/public health; nurse practitioner; nurse practitioner: adult-gerontology primary care; nurse practitioner: family; nurse practitioner: psychiatric-mental health, across the lifespan

University of New Mexico[1]

MSC09 5350
Albuquerque, NM 87131-0001
Public
Admissions: N/A
Financial aid: N/A
Tuition: N/A

Room/board/expenses: N/A
Enrollment: N/A

NEW YORK

Adelphi University[1]

1 South Avenue
Garden City, NY 11530-0701
Private
Admissions: N/A
Financial aid: N/A
Tuition: N/A
Room/board/expenses: N/A
Enrollment: N/A

American University of Beirut

3 Dag Hammarskjold Plaza
New York, NY 10017
aub.edu.lb/~webson
Private
Admissions: (961) 137-4374
Email: admissions@aub.edu.lb
Financial aid: (961) 137-4374
Application deadline: 04/01
Degrees offered: master's
Tuition: full time: $763/credit hour, part time: $763/credit hour
Room/board/expenses: $12,978
Full-time enrollment: 5 men: 0%; women: 100%; minorities: 0%; international: 20%
Part-time enrollment: 51 men: 16%; women: 84%; minorities: 0%; international: 8%
Acceptance rate (master's): 90%
Specialties offered: administration; community health/public health; other majors

Binghamton University-SUNY

PO Box 6000
Binghamton, NY 13902-6000
www.binghamton.edu/dson
Public
Admissions: (607) 777-2151
Email: gradadmission@binghamton.edu
Financial aid: (607) 777-2428
Application deadline: 04/15
Degrees offered: master's, Ph.D., DNP
In-state tuition: full time: $10,870, part time: $453/credit hour (master's); full time: $10,870, part time: $453/credit hour (Ph.D.); full time: $23,230, part time: $968/credit hour (DNP)
Out-of-state tuition: full time: $22,210 (master's); full time: $22,210 (Ph.D.); full time: $42,880 (DNP)
Room/board/expenses: N/A
Full-time enrollment: 61 (master's); 10 (Ph.D.); 5 (DNP) men: 14%; women: 86%; minorities: 13%; international: 13%
Part-time enrollment: 64 (master's); 19 (Ph.D.); 10 (DNP) men: 18%; women: 82%; minorities: 17%; international: 0%
Acceptance rate (master's): 85%
Acceptance rate (Ph.D.): 100%
Acceptance rate (DNP): 100%
Specialties offered: administration; clinical nurse specialist; community health/public health; education; forensic nursing; nurse practitioner;

nurse practitioner: adult-gerontology primary care; nurse practitioner: family; nurse practitioner: psychiatric-mental health, across the lifespan; other majors

College of Mount St. Vincent[1]

6301 Riverdale Avenue
Riverdale, NY 10471
Private
Admissions: N/A
Financial aid: N/A
Tuition: N/A
Room/board/expenses: N/A
Enrollment: N/A

College of New Rochelle

29 Castle Place
New Rochelle, NY 10805-2308
www.cnr.edu/web/school-of-nuring
Private
Admissions: (914) 654-5085
Email: kcavanagh@cnr.edu
Financial aid: (914) 654-5225
Application deadline: N/A
Degrees offered: master's
Tuition: full time: $894/credit hour, part time: N/A
Full-time enrollment: men: N/A; women: N/A; minorities: N/A; international: N/A
Part-time enrollment: 117 men: 10%; women: 90%; minorities: 68%; international: 0%
Specialties offered: N/A

Columbia University

630 West 168th Street
Mailbox 6
New York, NY 10032
nursing.columbia.edu/
Private
Admissions: (212) 305-5756
Email: nursing@columbia.edu
Financial aid: (212) 305-8147
Application deadline: 01/04
Degrees offered: master's, Ph.D., DNP
Tuition: full time: $1,408/credit hour, part time: $1,408/credit hour (master's); full time: $1,820/credit hour, part time: $1,820/credit hour (Ph.D.); full time: $1,820/credit hour, part time: $1,820/credit hour (DNP)
Room/board/expenses: $24,000 (master's); $24,000 (Ph.D.); $24,000 (DNP)
Full-time enrollment: 317 (master's); 24 (Ph.D.); 19 (DNP) men: 13%; women: 87%; minorities: 38%; international: 3%
Part-time enrollment: 161 (master's); 1 (Ph.D.); 20 (DNP) men: 7%; women: 93%; minorities: 38%; international: 3%
Acceptance rate (master's): 37%
Acceptance rate (Ph.D.): 56%
Acceptance rate (DNP): 76%
Specialties offered: nurse anesthesia; nurse-midwifery; nurse practitioner; nurse practitioner: adult-gerontology acute care; nurse practitioner: adult-gerontology primary care; nurse practitioner: adult;

nurse practitioner: family; nurse practitioner: pediatric primary care; nurse practitioner: psychiatric-mental health, across the lifespan; research

CUNY-Hunter College

695 Park Ave
New York, NY 10065
www.hunter.cuny.edu/nursing
Public
Admissions: (212) 396-6049
Email: gradadmissions@hunter.cuny.edu
Financial aid: (212) 772-4820
Application deadline: 04/01
Degrees offered: master's, DNP
In-state tuition: full time: $10,437, part time: $425/credit hour (master's); full time: $13,677, part time: $560/credit hour (DNP)
Out-of-state tuition: full time: $19,026 (master's); full time: $22,147 (DNP)
Room/board/expenses: N/A
Full-time enrollment: 3 (master's); 18 (DNP) men: 19%; women: 81%; minorities: 38%; international: 0%
Part-time enrollment: 492 (master's); 11 (DNP) men: 14%; women: 86%; minorities: 56%; international: 2%
Acceptance rate (master's): 47%
Acceptance rate (DNP): 60%
Specialties offered: administration; clinical nurse specialist; community health/public health; nurse practitioner; nurse practitioner: adult-gerontology primary care; nurse practitioner: psychiatric-mental health, across the lifespan; dual majors

CUNY-Lehman College[1]

250 Bedford Park Boulevard
West Bronx, NY 10468-1589
Public
Admissions: N/A
Financial aid: N/A
Tuition: N/A
Room/board/expenses: N/A
Enrollment: N/A

CUNY-Staten Island[1]

2800 Victory Boulevard
Building 55, Room 213
Staten Island, NY 10314
Public
Admissions: N/A
Financial aid: N/A
Tuition: N/A
Room/board/expenses: N/A
Enrollment: N/A

Daemen College[1]

4380 Main Street
Amherst, NY 14226
www.daemen.edu/
Private
Admissions: N/A
Financial aid: N/A
Tuition: N/A
Room/board/expenses: N/A
Enrollment: N/A

Dominican College

470 Western Highway
Orangeburg, NY 10962
www.dc.edu/gradnursing
Private
Admissions: (845) 848-7800
Email: admissions@dc.edu
Financial aid: (845) 848-7818
Application deadline: N/A
Degrees offered: master's, DNP
Tuition: full time: N/A, part time: $839/credit hour (master's); full time: N/A, part time: $908/credit hour (DNP)
Room/board/expenses: N/A
Full-time enrollment: 17 (master's); N/A (DNP) men: 6%; women: 94%; minorities: 53%; international: N/A
Part-time enrollment: 54 (master's); 7 (DNP) men: 13%; women: 87%; minorities: 38%; international: 2%
Specialties offered: nurse practitioner; nurse practitioner: family

D'Youville College[1]

320 Porter Avenue
Buffalo, NY 14201-9985
www.dyc.edu/academics/nursing/
Private
Admissions: (800) 777-3921
Email: graduateadmissions@dyc.edu
Financial aid: (716) 829-7500
Tuition: N/A
Room/board/expenses: N/A
Enrollment: N/A

Excelsior College[1]

7 Columbia Circle
Albany, NY 12203-5159
Private
Admissions: N/A
Financial aid: N/A
Tuition: N/A
Room/board/expenses: N/A
Enrollment: N/A

Keuka College[1]

141 Central Avenue
Keuka Park, NY 14478
asap.keuka.edu/programs/ms-nursing/
Private
Admissions: N/A
Financial aid: N/A
Tuition: N/A
Room/board/expenses: N/A
Enrollment: N/A

Le Moyne College

1419 Salt Springs Road
Syracuse, NY 13214-1301
www.lemoyne.edu/nursing
Private
Admissions: (315) 445-5444
Email: nursing@lemoyne.edu
Financial aid: (315) 445-4400
Application deadline: 05/01
Degrees offered: master's
Tuition: full time: $683/credit hour, part time: $683/credit hour
Room/board/expenses: N/A
Full-time enrollment: men: N/A; women: N/A; minorities: N/A; international: N/A
Part-time enrollment: 46 men: 15%; women: 85%; minorities: 7%; international: 2%
Acceptance rate (master's): 96%

Specialties offered: administration; education; informatics; nurse practitioner; nurse practitioner: family

LIU Brooklyn[1]
1 University Plaza
Brooklyn, NY 11201-8423
Private
Admissions: N/A
Financial aid: N/A
Tuition: N/A
Room/board/expenses: N/A
Enrollment: N/A

LIU Post[1]
720 Northern Boulevard
Brookville, NY 11548
Private
Admissions: N/A
Financial aid: N/A
Tuition: N/A
Room/board/expenses: N/A
Enrollment: N/A

Mercy College
555 Broadway
Dobbs Ferry, NY 10522
www.mercy.edu/
health-and-natural-sciences/
Private
Admissions: (877) 637-2946
Email: admissions@mercy.edu
Financial aid: (877) 637-2946
Application deadline: N/A
Degrees offered: master's
Tuition: full time: $828/credit hour, part time: $828/credit hour
Room/board/expenses: $13,700
Full-time enrollment: 6
men: 17%; women: 83%; minorities: 67%; international: 0%
Part-time enrollment: 160
men: 5%; women: 95%; minorities: 65%; international: 0%
Acceptance rate (master's): 77%
Specialties offered: administration; education

Molloy College
1000 Hempstead Avenue
Rockville, NY 11571-5002
www.molloy.edu/academics/
graduate-programs/
graduate-nursing
Private
Admissions: (516) 323-4014
Email: admissions@molloy.edu
Financial aid: (516) 323-4200
Application deadline: 04/15
Degrees offered: master's, Ph.D., DNP
Tuition: full time: $1,025/credit hour, part time: $1,025/credit hour (master's); full time: $1,150/credit hour, part time: $1,150/credit hour (Ph.D.); full time: $1,150/credit hour, part time: $1,150/credit hour (DNP)
Room/board/expenses: N/A
Full-time enrollment: 13 (master's); N/A (Ph.D.); N/A (DNP)
men: 0%; women: 100%; minorities: 77%; international: 0%
Part-time enrollment: 501 (master's); 37 (Ph.D.); 12 (DNP)
men: 6%; women: 94%; minorities: 56%; international: 0%
Acceptance rate (master's): 70%
Acceptance rate (Ph.D.): 75%

Acceptance rate (DNP): 53%
Specialties offered: clinical nurse specialist; education; informatics; nurse practitioner; nurse practitioner: adult-gerontology primary care; nurse practitioner: family; nurse practitioner: pediatric primary care; nurse practitioner: psychiatric-mental health, across the lifespan; other majors; dual majors

Mount St. Mary College
330 Powell Avenue
Newburgh, NY 12550
www.msmc.edu/Academics/
Graduate_Programs/
Master_of_Science_in_Nursing
Private
Admissions: (845) 569-3225
Email: graduateadmissions@msmc.edu
Financial aid: (845) 569-3700
Application deadline: N/A
Degrees offered: master's
Tuition: full time: $750/credit hour, part time: $750/credit hour
Room/board/expenses: $13,588
Full-time enrollment: 5
men: 20%; women: 80%; minorities: 60%; international: 0%
Part-time enrollment: 114
men: 10%; women: 90%; minorities: 34%; international: 0%
Acceptance rate (master's): 83%
Specialties offered: nurse practitioner; nurse practitioner: adult-gerontology acute care; nurse practitioner: adult-gerontology primary care; nurse practitioner: family

New York University
726 Broadway, 10th Floor
New York, NY 10003
www.nursing.nyu.edu
Private
Admissions: (212) 998-5317
Email: admissions.nursing@nyu.edu
Financial aid: (212) 998-4444
Degrees offered: master's, Ph.D., DNP
Tuition: full time: $40,024, part time: $20,416 (master's); full time: $40,024, part time: $20,416 (Ph.D.); full time: $40,024, part time: $20,416 (DNP)
Room/board/expenses: $25,170 (master's); $25,170 (Ph.D.); $25,170 (DNP)
Full-time enrollment: 48 (master's); 18 (Ph.D.); N/A (DNP)
men: 11%; women: 89%; minorities: 53%; international: 12%
Part-time enrollment: 552 (master's); 19 (Ph.D.); 26 (DNP)
men: 11%; women: 89%; minorities: 55%; international: 3%
Acceptance rate (master's): 69%
Acceptance rate (Ph.D.): 50%
Acceptance rate (DNP): 59%
Specialties offered: administration; education; informatics; nurse-midwifery; nurse practitioner; nurse practitioner: adult-gerontology acute care; nurse practitioner:

adult-gerontology primary care; nurse practitioner: family; nurse practitioner: pediatric primary care; nurse practitioner: psychiatric-mental health, across the lifespan; research; dual majors

Pace University
861 Bedford Road
Pleasantville, NY 10570
www.pace.edu/lienhard/
Private
Admissions: (212) 346-1531
Email: graduateadmission@pace.edu
Financial aid: (212) 346-1309
Application deadline: 03/01
Degrees offered: master's, DNP
Tuition: full time: $1,150/credit hour, part time: $1,150/credit hour (master's); full time: N/A, part time: $18,370 (DNP)
Room/board/expenses: N/A
Full-time enrollment: 2 (master's); N/A (DNP)
men: 0%; women: 100%; minorities: 100%; international: 0%
Part-time enrollment: 366 (master's); 35 (DNP)
men: 7%; women: 93%; minorities: 46%; international: 0%
Acceptance rate (master's): 66%
Acceptance rate (DNP): 71%
Specialties offered: clinical nurse leader; education; nurse practitioner; nurse practitioner: adult-gerontology acute care; nurse practitioner: family

Roberts Wesleyan College
2301 Westside Drive
Rochester, NY 14624
www.roberts.edu/
graduate-nursing-programs.aspx
Private
Admissions: (585) 594-6686
Email: gradnursing@roberts.edu
Financial aid: (585) 594-6391
Application deadline: N/A
Degrees offered: master's
Tuition: full time: $772/credit hour, part time: N/A
Full-time enrollment: 70
men: 3%; women: 97%; minorities: 21%; international: 10%
Part-time enrollment:
men: N/A; women: N/A; minorities: N/A; international: N/A
Acceptance rate (master's): 57%
Specialties offered: administration; education

The Sage Colleges[1]
65 1st Street
Troy, NY 12180
Private
Admissions: N/A
Financial aid: N/A
Tuition: N/A
Room/board/expenses: N/A
Enrollment: N/A

St. John Fisher College
3690 East Avenue
Rochester, NY 14618
www.sjfc.edu/academics/nursing/about/index.dot
Private
Admissions: (585) 385-8161
Email: www.sjfc.edu/admissions/graduate/
Financial aid: (585) 385-8042
Application deadline: N/A
Degrees offered: master's, DNP
Tuition: full time: $860/credit hour, part time: $860/credit hour (master's); full time: $1,200/credit hour, part time: $1,200/credit hour (DNP)
Room/board/expenses: N/A
Full-time enrollment: 7 (master's); 15 (DNP)
men: 5%; women: 95%; minorities: 23%; international: 5%
Part-time enrollment: 129 (master's); 12 (DNP)
men: 6%; women: 94%; minorities: 40%; international: 1%
Acceptance rate (master's): 50%
Acceptance rate (DNP): 89%
Specialties offered: clinical nurse specialist; nurse practitioner; nurse practitioner: adult-gerontology acute care; nurse practitioner: adult-gerontology primary care; nurse practitioner: family; nurse practitioner: psychiatric-mental health, across the lifespan

St. Joseph's College[1]
206 Prospect Avenue
Syracuse, NY 13203
Private
Admissions: N/A
Financial aid: N/A
Tuition: N/A
Room/board/expenses: N/A
Enrollment: N/A

Stony Brook University-SUNY
Health Science Center
Stony Brook, NY 11794-8240
nursing.stonybrookmedicine.edu/
Public
Admissions: (631) 444-3554
Email: Karen.Allard@stonybrook.edu
Financial aid: (631) 444-2111
Application deadline: 01/15
Degrees offered: master's, DNP
In-state tuition: full time: $10,870, part time: $453/credit hour (master's); full time: $968/credit hour, part time: $968/credit hour (DNP)
Out-of-state tuition: full time: $22,210 (master's); full time: $1,787/credit hour (DNP)
Room/board/expenses: $8,460 (master's); $8,170 (DNP)
Full-time enrollment: 10 (master's); 34 (DNP)
men: 9%; women: 91%; minorities: 55%; international: 11%
Part-time enrollment: 788 (master's); 30 (DNP)
men: 12%; women: 88%; minorities: 34%; international: 5%
Acceptance rate (master's): 58%
Acceptance rate (DNP): 81%

Specialties offered: education; nurse-midwifery; nurse practitioner; nurse practitioner: adult-gerontology primary care; nurse practitioner: family; nurse practitioner: pediatric primary care; nurse practitioner: psychiatric-mental health, across the lifespan; other majors

SUNY Downstate Medical Center
450 Clarkson Avenue
Box 22
Brooklyn, NY 11203-2098
www.downstate.edu
Public
Admissions: (718) 270-4744
Email: admissions@downstate.edu
Financial aid: (718) 270-2488
Application deadline: 11/30
Degrees offered: master's
In-state tuition: full time: $10,870, part time: $453/credit hour
Out-of-state tuition: full time: $22,210
Room/board/expenses: N/A
Full-time enrollment: 126
men: 25%; women: 75%; minorities: 63%; international: 0%
Part-time enrollment: 84
men: 6%; women: 94%; minorities: 76%; international: 0%
Acceptance rate (master's): 23%
Specialties offered: clinical nurse specialist; nurse anesthesia; nurse-midwifery; nurse practitioner; nurse practitioner: family

SUNY Polytechnic Institute
PO Box 3050
Utica, NY 13504
sunypoly.edu/graduate/
Public
Admissions: (315) 792-7347
Email: graduate@sunyit.edu
Financial aid: (315) 792-7210
Application deadline: 07/15
Degrees offered: master's
In-state tuition: full time: $453/credit hour, part time: $453/credit hour
Out-of-state tuition: full time: $925/credit hour
Room/board/expenses: $12,778
Full-time enrollment: 53
men: 11%; women: 89%; minorities: 21%; international: 2%
Part-time enrollment: 152
men: 9%; women: 91%; minorities: 13%; international: 0%
Acceptance rate (master's): 41%
Specialties offered: education; nurse practitioner: family

SUNY Upstate Medical Center[1]
750 East Adams Street
Syracuse, NY 13210-2375
Public
Admissions: N/A
Financial aid: N/A
Tuition: N/A
Room/board/expenses: N/A
Enrollment: N/A

University at Buffalo-SUNY

103 Wende Hall
3435 Main Street
Buffalo, NY 14214
nursing.buffalo.edu
Public
Admissions: (716) 829-2537
Email: nursing@buffalo.edu
Financial aid: (716) 645-8232
Application deadline: 01/01
Degrees offered: master's, Ph.D., DNP
In-state tuition: full time: $10,870, part time: $453/credit hour (master's); full time: $10,870, part time: $453/credit hour (Ph.D.); full time: $34,224, part time: $968/credit hour (DNP)
Out-of-state tuition: full time: $22,210 (master's); full time: $22,210 (Ph.D.); full time: $58,973 (DNP)
Room/board/expenses: $15,260 (master's); $15,260 (Ph.D.); $15,260 (DNP)
Full-time enrollment: N/A (master's); 3 (Ph.D.); 58 (DNP) men: 39%; women: 61%; minorities: 18%; international: 0%
Part-time enrollment: 8 (master's); 21 (Ph.D.); 104 (DNP) men: N/A; women: N/A; minorities: 20%; international: 5%
Acceptance rate (master's): 63%
Acceptance rate (Ph.D.): 50%
Acceptance rate (DNP): 55%
Specialties offered: administration; nurse anesthesia; nurse practitioner; nurse practitioner: adult-gerontology primary care; nurse practitioner: family; nurse practitioner: psychiatric-mental health, across the lifespan; research

University of Rochester

601 Elmwood Avenue
Rochester, NY 14642
son.rochester.edu/
Private
Admissions: (585) 275-2375
Email: son_admissions@urmc.rochester.edu
Financial aid: (585) 275-3226
Application deadline: 01/04
Degrees offered: master's, Ph.D., DNP
Tuition: full time: $24,192, part time: $1,344/credit hour (master's); full time: $24,192, part time: $1,344/credit hour (Ph.D.); full time: $24,192, part time: $1,344/credit hour (DNP)
Room/board/expenses: $14,580 (master's); $14,580 (Ph.D.); $14,580 (DNP)
Full-time enrollment: 2 (master's); 19 (Ph.D.); N/A (DNP) men: 5%; women: 95%; minorities: 29%; international: 14%
Part-time enrollment: 200 (master's); 1 (Ph.D.); 14 (DNP) men: 18%; women: 82%; minorities: 13%; international: 0%
Acceptance rate (master's): 71%
Acceptance rate (Ph.D.): 20%
Acceptance rate (DNP): 100%

Specialties offered: clinical nurse leader; education; health management & policy health care systems; nurse practitioner; nurse practitioner: adult-gerontology acute care; nurse practitioner: adult-gerontology primary care; nurse practitioner: family; nurse practitioner: pediatric primary care; nurse practitioner: psychiatric-mental health, across the lifespan; research

Wagner College[1]

1 Campus Road
Staten Island, NY 10301
Private
Admissions: N/A
Financial aid: N/A
Tuition: N/A
Room/board/expenses: N/A
Enrollment: N/A

NORTH CAROLINA

Duke University

Box 3322, Medical Center
Durham, NC 27710-3322
nursing.duke.edu
Private
Admissions: (877) 415-3853
Email: SONAdmissions@dm.duke.edu
Financial aid: (877) 344-4680
Application deadline: 12/01
Degrees offered: master's, Ph.D., DNP
Tuition: full time: $1,568/credit hour, part time: $1,568/credit hour (master's); full time: $50,880, part time: $2,875/credit hour (Ph.D.); full time: $1,568/credit hour, part time: $1,568/credit hour (DNP)
Room/board/expenses: $17,304 (master's); $17,304 (Ph.D.); $17,304 (DNP)
Full-time enrollment: 94 (master's); 33 (Ph.D.); 79 (DNP) men: 15%; women: 85%; minorities: 23%; international: 7%
Part-time enrollment: 380 (master's); N/A (Ph.D.); 115 (DNP) men: 12%; women: 88%; minorities: 20%; international: 1%
Acceptance rate (master's): 49%
Acceptance rate (Ph.D.): 27%
Acceptance rate (DNP): 42%
Specialties offered: administration; case management; education; health management & policy health care systems; informatics; nurse anesthesia; nurse practitioner; nurse practitioner: adult-gerontology acute care; nurse practitioner: adult-gerontology primary care; nurse practitioner: family; nurse practitioner: pediatric primary care; research; other majors

East Carolina University

Library, Allied Health and Nursing Building
Greenville, NC 27858
www.ecu.edu/nursing/
Public
Admissions: (252) 744-6477
Email: gradnurs@ecu.edu
Financial aid: (252) 328-6610

Application deadline: 03/15
Degrees offered: master's, Ph.D., DNP
In-state tuition: full time: $342/credit hour, part time: $342/credit hour (master's); full time: $6,684, part time: $333/credit hour (Ph.D.); full time: $342/credit hour, part time: $342/credit hour (DNP)
Out-of-state tuition: full time: $960/credit hour (master's); full time: $19,286 (Ph.D.); full time: $960/credit hour (DNP)
Room/board/expenses: $12,640 (master's); $12,640 (Ph.D.); $12,640 (DNP)
Full-time enrollment: 59 (master's); 1 (Ph.D.); 78 (DNP) men: 13%; women: 87%; minorities: 21%; international: 0%
Part-time enrollment: 308 (master's); 27 (Ph.D.); 44 (DNP) men: 7%; women: 93%; minorities: 21%; international: 0%
Acceptance rate (master's): 68%
Acceptance rate (Ph.D.): 50%
Acceptance rate (DNP): 75%
Specialties offered: administration; clinical nurse specialist; education; nurse anesthesia; nurse-midwifery; nurse practitioner: adult-gerontology primary care; nurse practitioner: family

Gardner-Webb University

PO Box 7286
Boiling Springs, NC 28017
www.gardner-webb.edu/academics/areas-of-study/nursing/index
Private
Admissions: (704) 406-4723
Email: gradschool@gardner-webb.edu
Financial aid: (704) 406-4247
Application deadline: 01/15
Degrees offered: master's, DNP
Tuition: full time: $433/credit hour, part time: $433/credit hour (master's); full time: $716/credit hour, part time: $716/credit hour (DNP)
Room/board/expenses: N/A
Full-time enrollment: 212 (master's); 29 (DNP) men: 7%; women: 93%; minorities: 18%; international: 0%
Part-time enrollment: 1 (master's); 7 (DNP) men: 0%; women: 100%; minorities: 13%; international: 13%
Acceptance rate (master's): 68%
Specialties offered: administration; education; nurse practitioner; nurse practitioner: family; dual majors

Lenoir-Rhyne University[1]

Hickory, NC 28601
Private
Admissions: N/A
Financial aid: N/A
Tuition: N/A
Room/board/expenses: N/A
Enrollment: N/A

Queens University of Charlotte

1900 Selwyn Avenue
Charlotte, NC 28274
www.queens.edu/
Private
Admissions: (704) 337-2314
Email: PSONAdmissions@queens.edu
Financial aid: (704) 688-2713
Application deadline: N/A
Degrees offered: master's
Tuition: full time: $490/credit hour, part time: $490/credit hour
Room/board/expenses: N/A
Full-time enrollment: 70 men: 6%; women: 94%; minorities: 29%; international: 1%
Part-time enrollment: 19 men: 5%; women: 95%; minorities: 37%; international: 11%
Acceptance rate (master's): 81%
Specialties offered: administration; clinical nurse leader; education

University of North Carolina-Chapel Hill

Carrington Hall, CB #7460
Chapel Hill, NC 27599-7460
nursing.unc.edu/
Public
Admissions: (919) 966-4260
Email: nursing@unc.edu
Financial aid: (919) 962-8396
Application deadline: 01/12
Degrees offered: master's, Ph.D., DNP
In-state tuition: full time: $14,143, part time: $10,607 (master's); full time: $9,143, part time: $6,857 (Ph.D.); full time: $14,143, part time: $10,607 (DNP)
Out-of-state tuition: full time: $31,354 (master's); full time: $26,354 (Ph.D.); full time: $31,354 (DNP)
Room/board/expenses: $17,008 (master's); $17,008 (Ph.D.); $17,008 (DNP)
Full-time enrollment: 138 (master's); 48 (Ph.D.); 51 (DNP) men: 11%; women: 89%; minorities: 29%; international: 7%
Part-time enrollment: 80 (master's); N/A (Ph.D.); 11 (DNP) men: 9%; women: 91%; minorities: 24%; international: 0%
Acceptance rate (master's): 29%
Acceptance rate (Ph.D.): 55%
Acceptance rate (DNP): 29%
Specialties offered: administration; clinical nurse leader; education; informatics; nurse practitioner; nurse practitioner: adult-gerontology primary care; nurse practitioner: family; nurse practitioner: pediatric primary care; nurse practitioner: psychiatric-mental health, across the lifespan; research; other majors; dual majors

University of North Carolina-Chapel Hill (School of Public Health)[1]

135 Dauer Drive
Chapel Hill, NC 27599
Public
Admissions: N/A
Financial aid: N/A
Tuition: N/A
Room/board/expenses: N/A
Enrollment: N/A

University of North Carolina-Charlotte

9201 University City Boulevard
Charlotte, NC 28223-0001
nursing.uncc.edu
Public
Admissions: (704) 687-5503
Email: graduateschool.uncc.edu
Financial aid: (704) 687-7010
Application deadline: 02/02
Degrees offered: master's, DNP
In-state tuition: full time: $4,128, part time: $3,096 (master's); full time: $8,928, part time: $6,696 (DNP)
Out-of-state tuition: full time: $16,799 (master's); full time: $21,599 (DNP)
Room/board/expenses: N/A
Full-time enrollment: 133 (master's); 14 (DNP) men: 16%; women: 84%; minorities: 16%; international: 0%
Part-time enrollment: 77 (master's); N/A (DNP) men: 1%; women: 99%; minorities: 30%; international: 0%
Acceptance rate (master's): 21%
Acceptance rate (DNP): 67%
Specialties offered: administration; community health/public health; education; nurse anesthesia; nurse practitioner; nurse practitioner: adult-gerontology acute care; nurse practitioner: family

University of North Carolina-Greensboro

PO Box 26170
Greensboro, NC 27402-6170
nursing.uncg.edu
Public
Admissions: (336) 334-5596
Financial aid: (336) 334-5702
Application deadline: 05/15
Degrees offered: master's, Ph.D., DNP
In-state tuition: full time: $4,872; part time: $609/credit hour (master's); full time: $4,872, part time: $609/credit hour (Ph.D.); full time: $7,991, part time: N/A (DNP)
Out-of-state tuition: full time: $13,448 (master's); full time: $13,448 (Ph.D.); full time: $19,852 (DNP)
Room/board/expenses: $8,000 (master's); $8,000 (Ph.D.); $8,000 (DNP)

Full-time enrollment: 89 (master's); 40 (Ph.D.); 87 (DNP)
men: 19%; women: 81%; minorities: 32%; international: 3%
Part-time enrollment: 50 (master's); 3 (Ph.D.); N/A (DNP)
men: 19%; women: 81%; minorities: 26%; international: 0%
Acceptance rate (master's): 84%
Acceptance rate (Ph.D.): 43%
Acceptance rate (DNP): 49%
Specialties offered: administration; education; nurse anesthesia; nurse practitioner; nurse practitioner: adult-gerontology primary care; research

University of North Carolina-Pembroke

Pembroke, NC 28372
www.uncp.edu/nursing
Public
Admissions: (910) 521-6271
Email: grad@uncp.edu
Financial aid: (910) 521-6255
Application deadline: 05/15
Degrees offered: master's
In-state tuition: full time: $3,474, part time: $1,737
Out-of-state tuition: full time: $13,266
Room/board/expenses: $8,292
Full-time enrollment: 3
men: 0%; women: 100%; minorities: 0%; international: 0%
Part-time enrollment: 31
men: 6%; women: 94%; minorities: 55%; international: 0%
Acceptance rate (master's): 100%
Specialties offered: case management; clinical nurse leader; education

University of North Carolina-Wilmington[1]

601 S. College Road
Wilmington, NC 28403-5995
Public
Admissions: N/A
Financial aid: N/A
Tuition: N/A
Room/board/expenses: N/A
Enrollment: N/A

Western Carolina University-Cullowhee

1459 Sand Hill Road
Candler, NC 28715
nursing.wcu.edu
Public
Admissions: N/A
Financial aid: N/A
Application deadline: N/A
Degrees offered: master's, DNP
In-state tuition: full time: $7,000, part time: $3,500 (master's); full time: N/A, part time: N/A (DNP)
Out-of-state tuition: full time: $18,000 (master's); N/A (DNP)
Room/board/expenses: N/A
Full-time enrollment: 78 (master's); 10 (DNP)
men: 18%; women: 82%; minorities: 15%; international: N/A

Part-time enrollment: 85 (master's); N/A (DNP)
men: 7%; women: 93%; minorities: 4%; international: N/A
Specialties offered: N/A

Winston-Salem State University

601 S. Martin Luther King Jr. Drive
Winston-Salem, NC 27110
www.wssu.edu/school-health-sciences/departments/nursing/default.aspx
Public
Admissions: (336) 750-2078
Email: www.wssu.edu/admissions/default.aspx
Financial aid: (336) 750-3296
Application deadline: 02/15
Degrees offered: master's, DNP
In-state tuition: full time: $3,758, part time: $2,818 (master's); full time: $3,758, part time: $2,818 (DNP)
Out-of-state tuition: full time: $13,314 (master's); full time: $13,314 (DNP)
Room/board/expenses: $6,700 (master's); $6,700 (DNP)
Full-time enrollment: 100 (master's); 15 (DNP)
men: N/A; women: N/A; minorities: 70%; international: 0%
Part-time enrollment: 30 (master's); 2 (DNP)
men: N/A; women: N/A; minorities: 47%; international: 0%
Acceptance rate (master's): 59%
Acceptance rate (DNP): 86%
Specialties offered: education; nurse practitioner; nurse practitioner: family

NORTH DAKOTA

North Dakota State University[1]

NDSU Department 2820
Fargo, ND 58108
www.ndsu.edu/nursing/
Public
Admissions: N/A
Financial aid: N/A
Tuition: N/A
Room/board/expenses: N/A
Enrollment: N/A

University of Mary[1]

7500 University Drive
Bismarck, ND 58504-9652
Private
Admissions: (701) 355-8030
Email: marauder@umary.edu
Financial aid: (701) 355-8142
Tuition: N/A
Room/board/expenses: N/A
Enrollment: N/A

University of North Dakota[1]

Box 9025
Grand Forks, ND 58202
nursing.und.edu/
Public
Admissions: (701) 777-4535
Email: questions@gradschool.und.edu
Financial aid: (701) 777-3092
Tuition: N/A
Room/board/expenses: N/A
Enrollment: N/A

OHIO

Capital University[1]

1 College and Main
Columbus, OH 43209-2394
Private
Admissions: N/A
Financial aid: N/A
Tuition: N/A
Room/board/expenses: N/A
Enrollment: N/A

Case Western Reserve University

10900 Euclid Avenue
Cleveland, OH 44106-4904
fpb.case.edu/
Private
Admissions: (216) 368-2529
Email: admissionsfpb@case.edu
Financial aid: (216) 368-0517
Application deadline: 03/01
Degrees offered: master's, Ph.D., DNP
Tuition: full time: $1,891/credit hour, part time: $1,891/credit (master's); full time: $1,714/credit hour, part time: $1,714/credit hour (Ph.D.); full time: $1,891/credit hour, part time: $1,891/credit hour (DNP)
Room/board/expenses: $26,270 (master's); $26,270 (Ph.D.); $6,150 (DNP)
Full-time enrollment: 147 (master's); 43 (Ph.D.); 64 (DNP)
men: 15%; women: 85%; minorities: 44%; international: 10%
Part-time enrollment: 140 (master's); 6 (Ph.D.); 79 (DNP)
men: 18%; women: 82%; minorities: 24%; international: 2%
Acceptance rate (master's): 71%
Acceptance rate (Ph.D.): 58%
Acceptance rate (DNP): 89%
Specialties offered: administration; education; nurse anesthesia; nurse-midwifery; nurse practitioner; nurse practitioner: adult-gerontology acute care; nurse practitioner: adult-gerontology primary care; nurse practitioner: family; nurse practitioner: pediatric primary care; nurse practitioner: psychiatric-mental health, across the lifespan; research; other majors; combined nurse practitioner/clinical nurse specialist; dual majors

Cedarville University

251 N. Main Street
Cedarville, OH 45314
www.cedarville.edu/Academics/Nursing.aspx
Private
Admissions: (800) 233-2784
Email: admissions@cedarville.edu
Financial aid: (877) 233-2784
Application deadline: N/A
Degrees offered: master's
Tuition: full time: $536/credit hour, part time: $536/credit hour
Room/board/expenses: $6,542
Full-time enrollment: 18
men: 6%; women: 94%; minorities: 50%; international: 0%
Part-time enrollment: 35
men: 9%; women: 91%; minorities: 23%; international: 0%

Acceptance rate (master's): 81%
Specialties offered: community health/public health; nurse practitioner: family

Cleveland State University

2121 Euclid Avenue, RT 1416
Cleveland, OH 44115-2214
www.csuohio.edu/nursing
Public
Admissions: (216) 687-5411
Email: graduate.admissions@csuohio.edu
Financial aid: (216) 687-5411
Application deadline: 03/01
Degrees offered: master's
In-state tuition: full time: $531/credit hour, part time: $531/credit hour
Out-of-state tuition: full time: $541/credit hour
Room/board/expenses: N/A
Full-time enrollment:
men: N/A; women: N/A; minorities: N/A; international: N/A
Part-time enrollment: 47
men: 2%; women: 98%; minorities: 26%; international: 0%
Acceptance rate (master's): 46%
Specialties offered: clinical nurse leader; education; forensic nursing; other majors

Franciscan University of Steubenville[1]

1235 University Boulevard
Steubenville, OH 43952
Private
Admissions: N/A
Financial aid: N/A
Tuition: N/A
Room/board/expenses: N/A
Enrollment: N/A

Kent State University

PO Box 5190
Henderson Hall
Kent, OH 44242
www.kent.edu/nursing
Public
Admissions: (330) 672-7911
Email: bsn@kent.edu; msn@kent.edu
Financial aid: (330) 672-2972
Application deadline: 02/01
Degrees offered: master's, Ph.D., DNP
In-state tuition: full time: $495/credit hour, part time: $495/credit hour (master's); full time: $495/credit hour, part time: $495/credit hour (Ph.D.); full time: $495/credit hour, part time: $495/credit hour (DNP)
Out-of-state tuition: full time: $837/credit hour (master's); full time: $837/credit hour (Ph.D.); full time: $837/credit hour (DNP)
Room/board/expenses: $10,000 (master's); $10,000 (Ph.D.); $10,000 (DNP)
Full-time enrollment: 46 (master's); 26 (Ph.D.); 7 (DNP)
men: 28%; women: 72%; minorities: 18%; international: 16%
Part-time enrollment: 389 (master's); 10 (Ph.D.); 21 (DNP)
men: 12%; women: 88%; minorities: 12%; international: 1%
Acceptance rate (master's): 69%
Acceptance rate (Ph.D.): 100%

Acceptance rate (DNP): 100%
Specialties offered: clinical nurse specialist; education; health management & policy health care systems; nurse practitioner; nurse practitioner: adult-gerontology acute care; nurse practitioner: adult-gerontology primary care; nurse practitioner: family; nurse practitioner: pediatric primary care; nurse practitioner: psychiatric-mental health, across the lifespan; dual majors

Lourdes University[1]

6832 Convent Boulevard
Sylvania, OH 43560
Private
Admissions: (800) 878-3210
Email: gradschool@lourdes.edu
Financial aid: (419) 824-3732
Tuition: N/A
Room/board/expenses: N/A
Enrollment: N/A

Malone University

515 25th Street NW
Canton, OH 44709
www.malone.edu/academics/snhs/
Private
Admissions: (330) 471-8145
Email: admissions@malone.edu
Financial aid: (330) 471-8159
Application deadline: N/A
Degrees offered: master's
Tuition: full time: $668/credit hour, part time: $668/credit hour
Room/board/expenses: N/A
Full-time enrollment:
men: N/A; women: N/A; minorities: N/A; international: N/A
Part-time enrollment: 49
men: 12%; women: 88%; minorities: 4%; international: 0%
Acceptance rate (master's): 81%
Specialties offered: nurse practitioner; nurse practitioner: adult-gerontology acute care; nurse practitioner: family

Mount Carmel College of Nursing[1]

127 S. Davis Avenue
Columbus, OH 43222
Private
Admissions: N/A
Financial aid: N/A
Tuition: N/A
Room/board/expenses: N/A
Enrollment: N/A

Mount St. Joseph University

5701 Delhi Road
Cincinnati, OH 45233
www.msj.edu/academics/divisions-departments/division-of-health-sciences/department-of
Private
Admissions: (513) 244-4531
Email: admission@msj.edu
Financial aid: (513) 244-4418
Application deadline: N/A
Degrees offered: master's, DNP
Tuition: full time: $595/credit hour, part time: $595/credit hour (master's); full time: $620/credit hour, part time: $620/credit hour (DNP)
Room/board/expenses: $8,810 (master's); $8,810 (DNP)

Full-time enrollment: 96 (master's); N/A (DNP)
men: 19%; women: 81%; minorities: 20%; international: 1%
Part-time enrollment: 60 (master's); 24 (DNP)
men: 0%; women: 100%; minorities: 4%; international: 0%
Acceptance rate (master's): 34%
Acceptance rate (DNP): 95%
Specialties offered:
administration; clinical nurse leader; education; generalist; nurse practitioner

Ohio State University

1585 Neil Avenue
Columbus, OH 43210
nursing.osu.edu/
Public
Admissions: (614) 292-4041
Email: nursing@osu.edu
Financial aid: (614) 292-8595
Application deadline: 01/15
Degrees offered: master's, Ph.D., DNP
In-state tuition: full time: $723/credit hour, part time: $723/credit hour (master's); full time: $723/credit hour, part time: $723/credit hour (Ph.D.); full time: $723/credit hour, part time: $723/credit hour (DNP)
Out-of-state tuition: full time: $1,940/credit hour (master's); full time: $1,940/credit hour (Ph.D.); full time: $723/credit hour (DNP)
Room/board/expenses: $814 (master's); $814 (Ph.D.); $814 (DNP)
Full-time enrollment: 445 (master's); 20 (Ph.D.); 29 (DNP)
men: 17%; women: 83%; minorities: 14%; international: 1%
Part-time enrollment: 182 (master's); 6 (Ph.D.); 28 (DNP)
men: 9%; women: 91%; minorities: 17%; international: 0%
Acceptance rate (master's): 58%
Acceptance rate (Ph.D.): 70%
Acceptance rate (DNP): 83%
Specialties offered:
administration; clinical nurse leader; clinical nurse specialist; community health/public health; health management & policy health care systems; nurse-midwifery; nurse practitioner; nurse practitioner: adult-gerontology acute care; nurse practitioner: adult-gerontology primary care; nurse practitioner: adult; nurse practitioner: family; nurse practitioner: pediatric primary care; nurse practitioner: psychiatric-mental health, across the lifespan; research; other majors; dual majors

Ohio University[1]

Grover Center, E365
Athens, OH 45701-2979
Public
Admissions: N/A
Financial aid: N/A
Tuition: N/A
Room/board/expenses: N/A
Enrollment: N/A

Otterbein University[1]

1 Otterbein College
Westerville, OH 43081
Private
Admissions: N/A
Financial aid: N/A
Tuition: N/A
Room/board/expenses: N/A
Enrollment: N/A

University of Akron[1]

209 Carroll Street
Akron, OH 44325-3701
Public
Admissions: N/A
Financial aid: N/A
Tuition: N/A
Room/board/expenses: N/A
Enrollment: N/A

University of Cincinnati

3110 Vine Street, ML 0038
Cincinnati, OH 45221-0038
nursing.uc.edu/
Public
Admissions: (513) 558-3600
Email: nursing1@uc.edu
Financial aid: (513) 556-9171
Application deadline: 02/15
Degrees offered: master's, Ph.D., DNP
In-state tuition: full time: $14,468, part time: $724/credit hour (master's); full time: $14,468, part time: $724/credit hour (Ph.D.); full time: $14,468, part time: $724/credit hour (DNP)
Out-of-state tuition: full time: $26,210 (master's); full time: $26,210 (Ph.D.); full time: $26,210 (DNP)
Room/board/expenses: N/A
Full-time enrollment: 225 (master's); 19 (Ph.D.); 6 (DNP)
men: 18%; women: 82%; minorities: 17%; international: 2%
Part-time enrollment: 1,252 (master's); 8 (Ph.D.); 33 (DNP)
men: 12%; women: 88%; minorities: 20%; international: 0%
Acceptance rate (master's): 56%
Acceptance rate (Ph.D.): 67%
Acceptance rate (DNP): 76%
Specialties offered:
administration; nurse anesthesia; nurse-midwifery; nurse practitioner; nurse practitioner: adult-gerontology acute care; nurse practitioner: adult-gerontology primary care; nurse practitioner: family; nurse practitioner: pediatric primary care; nurse practitioner: psychiatric-mental health, across the lifespan; research; other majors

University of Toledo

3000 Arlington Avenue, MS1026
Toledo, OH 43614
www.utoledo.edu/nursing/index.html
Public
Admissions: (419) 383-5841
Email: admitnurse@utoledo.edu
Financial aid: (419) 530-8700
Application deadline: 12/15
Degrees offered: master's, DNP
In-state tuition: full time: $13,166, part time: $549/credit hour (master's); full time: $16,560, part time: $690 (DNP)

Out-of-state tuition: full time: $23,502 (master's); full time: $23,785 (DNP)
Room/board/expenses: $11,046 (master's); $11,046 (DNP)
Full-time enrollment: 74 (master's); 10 (DNP)
men: 18%; women: 82%; minorities: 46%; international: 4%
Part-time enrollment: 132 (master's); 23 (DNP)
men: 10%; women: 90%; minorities: 13%; international: 0%
Acceptance rate (master's): 91%
Acceptance rate (DNP): 88%
Specialties offered: clinical nurse leader; education; nurse practitioner; nurse practitioner: adult; nurse practitioner: family; nurse practitioner: pediatric primary care

Urbana University[1]

101 Miller Hall
Springfield, OH 45505
www.urbana.edu/academics/college-of-professional-applied-studies.html
Private
Admissions: (937) 772-9200
Email: admissions@urbana.edu
Financial aid: N/A
Tuition: N/A
Room/board/expenses: N/A
Enrollment: N/A

Ursuline College

2550 Lander Road
Pepper Pike, OH 44124
www.ursuline.edu
Private
Admissions: (440) 449-4200
Email: graduateadmissions@ursuline.edu
Financial aid: (440) 449-4200
Application deadline: 12/31
Degrees offered: master's, DNP
Tuition: full time: N/A, part time: N/A (master's); full time: N/A, part time: N/A (DNP)
Room/board/expenses: N/A
Full-time enrollment: 219 (master's); 16 (DNP)
men: 10%; women: 90%; minorities: 18%; international: 5%
Part-time enrollment: 118 (master's); 6 (DNP)
men: 3%; women: 97%; minorities: 19%; international: 0%
Acceptance rate (master's): 90%
Acceptance rate (DNP): 75%
Specialties offered: clinical nurse specialist; nurse practitioner; nurse practitioner: adult-gerontology primary care; nurse practitioner: family

Walsh University[1]

North Canton, OH 44720
Private
Admissions: N/A
Financial aid: N/A
Tuition: N/A
Room/board/expenses: N/A
Enrollment: N/A

Wright State University

3640 Colonel Glenn Highway
Dayton, OH 45435-0001
nursing.wright.edu
Public
Admissions: (937) 775-5700
Email: admissions@wright.edu
Financial aid: (937) 775-5405
Application deadline: 08/24
Degrees offered: master's, DNP
In-state tuition: full time: $13,082, part time: $604/credit hour (master's); full time: $15,360, part time: $711/credit hour (DNP)
Out-of-state tuition: full time: $22,224 (master's); full time: $24,544 (DNP)
Room/board/expenses: $9,304 (master's); $9,304 (DNP)
Full-time enrollment: 121 (master's); 13 (DNP)
men: N/A; women: N/A; minorities: 10%; international: 1%
Part-time enrollment: 107 (master's); 12 (DNP)
men: N/A; women: N/A; minorities: 19%; international: 2%
Specialties offered:
administration; clinical nurse specialist; education; nurse practitioner; nurse practitioner: adult-gerontology acute care; nurse practitioner: family; nurse practitioner: pediatric primary care; nurse practitioner: psychiatric-mental health, across the lifespan; school nursing; other majors

Xavier University

119 Cohen Center
Cincinnati, OH 45207
www.xavier.edu/nursing
Private
Admissions: (513) 745-3301
Email: xuadmit@xavier.edu
Financial aid: (513) 745-3142
Application deadline: 01/15
Degrees offered: master's, DNP
Tuition: full time: N/A, part time: N/A (master's); full time: N/A, part time: N/A (DNP)
Room/board/expenses: N/A
Full-time enrollment: 61 (master's); N/A (DNP)
men: 26%; women: 74%; minorities: 18%; international: 0%
Part-time enrollment: 166 (master's); 22 (DNP)
men: 6%; women: 94%; minorities: 10%; international: 0%
Acceptance rate (master's): 86%
Acceptance rate (DNP): 96%
Specialties offered:
administration; clinical nurse leader; education; forensic nursing; generalist; informatics; nurse practitioner: family; school nursing; other majors

Youngstown State University[1]

1 University Plaza
Youngstown, OH 44555
Public
Admissions: N/A
Financial aid: N/A
Tuition: N/A
Room/board/expenses: N/A
Enrollment: N/A

Northeastern State University

600 N. Grand Avenue
Tahlequah, OK 74464
academics.nsuok.edu/healthprofessions/DegreePrograms/Graduate/NursingEducationMSN.aspx
Public
Admissions: (918) 444-2093
Email: graduatecollege@nsuok.edu
Financial aid: (918) 444-3456
Application deadline: 11/01
Degrees offered: master's
In-state tuition: full time: $227/credit hour, part time: $227/credit hour
Out-of-state tuition: full time: $500/credit hour
Room/board/expenses: N/A
Full-time enrollment: men: N/A; women: N/A; minorities: N/A; international: N/A
Part-time enrollment: 27
men: 7%; women: 93%; minorities: 30%; international: 0%
Acceptance rate (master's): 100%
Specialties offered: education

Oklahoma Baptist University[1]

111 Harrison Avenue
Oklahoma City, OK 73104
Private
Admissions: N/A
Financial aid: N/A
Tuition: N/A
Room/board/expenses: N/A
Enrollment: N/A

Oklahoma City University

2501 N. Blackwelder
Oklahoma City, OK 73106
Private
Admissions: (405) 208-5094
Email: gadmissions@okcu.edu
Financial aid: (405) 208-5848
Application deadline: N/A
Degrees offered: master's, Ph.D., DNP
Tuition: full time: $10,620, part time: $7,080 (master's); full time: $11,940, part time: $5,970 (Ph.D.); full time: $11,940, part time: $5,970 (DNP)
Room/board/expenses: $9,682 (master's); $9,682 (Ph.D.); $9,682 (DNP)
Full-time enrollment: 5 (master's); 16 (Ph.D.); 16 (DNP)
men: 30%; women: 70%; minorities: 30%; international: 41%
Part-time enrollment: 17 (master's); 22 (Ph.D.); 79 (DNP)
men: 7%; women: 93%; minorities: 31%; international: 3%
Specialties offered:
administration; education; nurse practitioner; nurse practitioner: family

Southern Nazarene University[1]

6729 N.W. 39th Expressway
Bethany, OK 73008-2605
Private
Admissions: N/A
Financial aid: N/A
Tuition: N/A
Room/board/expenses: N/A
Enrollment: N/A

University of Oklahoma Health Sciences Center

PO Box 26901
Oklahoma City, OK 73190
nursing.ouhsc.edu
Public
Admissions: (405) 271-2428
Email: Nursing@OUHSC.edu
Financial aid: (405) 271-2118
Application deadline: 12/31
Degrees offered: master's, Ph.D., DNP
In-state tuition: full time: $259/credit hour, part time: $259/credit hour (master's); full time: $191/credit hour, part time: $191/credit hour (Ph.D.); full time: $446/credit hour, part time: $446/credit hour (DNP)
Out-of-state tuition: full time: $835/credit hour (master's); full time: $740/credit hour (Ph.D.); full time: $1,072/credit hour (DNP)
Room/board/expenses: N/A
Full-time enrollment: 52 (master's); 8 (Ph.D.); 4 (DNP)
men: 8%; women: 92%;
minorities: 20%; international: 3%
Part-time enrollment: 149 (master's); 3 (Ph.D.); 14 (DNP)
men: 11%; women: 89%;
minorities: 25%; international: 0%
Acceptance rate (master's): 46%
Acceptance rate (Ph.D.): 55%
Acceptance rate (DNP): 100%
Specialties offered: administration; clinical nurse specialist; education; nurse practitioner: family

OREGON

Oregon Health and Science University

3455 S.W. U.S. Veterans Hospital Road
Portland, OR 97239-2941
www.ohsu.edu/xd/education/schools/school-of-nursing/
Public
Admissions: (503) 494-7725
Email: proginfo@ohsu.edu
Financial aid: (503) 494-7800
Application deadline: N/A
Degrees offered: master's, Ph.D., DNP
In-state tuition: full time: $572/credit hour, part time: $572/credit hour (master's); full time: $564/credit hour, part time: $564/credit hour (Ph.D.); full time: $564/credit hour, part time: $564/credit hour (DNP)
Out-of-state tuition: full time: $740/credit hour (master's); full time: $729/credit hour (Ph.D.); full time: $729/credit hour (DNP)
Room/board/expenses: N/A

Full-time enrollment: 153 (master's); 18 (Ph.D.); 11 (DNP)
men: 21%; women: 79%;
minorities: 23%; international: 2%
Part-time enrollment: 37 (master's); 13 (Ph.D.); 25 (DNP)
men: 5%; women: 84%;
minorities: 7%; international: 1%
Acceptance rate (master's): 34%
Acceptance rate (Ph.D.): 55%
Acceptance rate (DNP): 57%
Specialties offered: education; health management & policy health care systems; nurse anesthesia; nurse-midwifery; nurse practitioner; nurse practitioner: adult-gerontology acute care; nurse practitioner: family; nurse practitioner: pediatric primary care; nurse practitioner: psychiatric-mental health, across the lifespan; research

University of Portland

5000 N. Willamette Boulevard
MSC 153
Portland, OR 97203
nursing.up.edu/
Private
Admissions: (503) 943-7107
Email: gradschl@up.edu
Financial aid: (503) 943-7311
Application deadline: 01/15
Degrees offered: master's, DNP
Tuition: full time: $685/credit hour, part time: $685/credit hour (master's); full time: $1,120/credit hour, part time: $1,120/credit hour (DNP)
Room/board/expenses: N/A
Full-time enrollment: 8 (master's); 34 (DNP)
men: 7%; women: 93%;
minorities: 14%; international: 2%
Part-time enrollment: N/A (master's); N/A (DNP)
men: N/A; women: N/A;
minorities: N/A; international: N/A
Acceptance rate (master's): 100%
Acceptance rate (DNP): 32%
Specialties offered: clinical nurse leader; education; nurse practitioner; nurse practitioner: family

PENNSYLVANIA

Alvernia University[1]

400 St. Bernardine Street
Reading, PA 19607
Private
Admissions: N/A
Financial aid: N/A
Tuition: N/A
Room/board/expenses: N/A
Enrollment: N/A

Bloomsburg University of Pennsylvania[1]

3109 McCormick Center for Human Services
Bloomsburg, PA 17815-1301
Public
Admissions: N/A
Financial aid: N/A
Tuition: N/A
Room/board/expenses: N/A
Enrollment: N/A

California University of Pennsylvania

250 University Avenue
California, PA 15419
www.calu.edu/academics/online-programs/nursing-administration/index.htm
Public
Admissions: (866) 595-6348
Email: msonline@calu.edu
Financial aid: (724) 938-4415
Application deadline: N/A
Degrees offered: master's
In-state tuition: full time: $470/credit hour, part time: $470/credit hour
Out-of-state tuition: full time: $479/credit hour
Room/board/expenses: N/A
Full-time enrollment: 83
men: 23%; women: 77%;
minorities: 1%; international: 1%
Part-time enrollment:
men: N/A; women: N/A;
minorities: N/A; international: N/A
Acceptance rate (master's): 80%
Specialties offered: administration

Carlow University[1]

3333 Fifth Avenue
Pittsburgh, PA 15213
Private
Admissions: N/A
Financial aid: N/A
Tuition: N/A
Room/board/expenses: N/A
Enrollment: N/A

Cedar Crest College

100 College Drive
Allentown, PA 18104
www.cedarcrest.edu/ca/academics/nursing/index.shtm
Private
Admissions: (610) 606-4666
Email: sage.cedarcrest.edu/graduate/nursing-scienc
Financial aid: (610) 606-4602
Application deadline: N/A
Degrees offered: master's
Tuition: full time: $772/credit hour, part time: $772/credit hour
Room/board/expenses: N/A
Full-time enrollment:
men: N/A; women: N/A;
minorities: N/A; international: N/A
Part-time enrollment: 12
men: 0%; women: 100%;
minorities: 8%; international: 0%
Acceptance rate (master's): 75%
Specialties offered: administration; education

Chatham University[1]

Woodland Road
Pittsburgh, PA 15232
Private
Admissions: N/A
Financial aid: N/A
Tuition: N/A
Room/board/expenses: N/A
Enrollment: N/A

Clarion University-Edinboro University[1]

1 Morrow Way
Slippery Rock, PA 16057
www.clarion.edu/academics/colleges-and-schools/venango-college/school-of-health-scien
Public
Email: gradstudies@clarion.edu

Financial aid: (814) 393-2315
Room/board/expenses: N/A
Enrollment: N/A

DeSales University[1]

2755 Station Avenue
Center Valley, PA 18034-0568
www.desales.edu/home/academics/divisions-departments/department-of-nursing-and-health
Private
Admissions: (610) 282-1100
Email: gradadmissions@desales.edu
Financial aid: (610) 282-1100
Tuition: N/A
Room/board/expenses: N/A
Enrollment: N/A

Drexel University

Bellet Building
Philadelphia, PA 19102-1192
www.drexel.edu/cnhp/academics/graduate/gradNursing/
Private
Admissions: (215) 895-6172
Email: randall.c.deike@drexel.edu
Financial aid: (215) 571-4531
Application deadline: 05/01
Degrees offered: master's, Ph.D., DNP
Tuition: full time: $890/credit hour, part time: $890/credit hour (master's); full time: $1,157/credit hour, part time: $1,157/credit hour (Ph.D.); full time: $890/credit hour, part time: $890/credit hour (DNP)
Room/board/expenses: N/A
Full-time enrollment: 38 (master's); 3 (Ph.D.); N/A (DNP)
men: 24%; women: 76%;
minorities: 17%; international: 5%
Part-time enrollment: 1,225 (master's); N/A (Ph.D.); 95 (DNP)
men: 11%; women: 89%;
minorities: 20%; international: 2%
Specialties offered: administration; clinical nurse leader; education; nurse anesthesia; nurse practitioner; nurse practitioner: adult-gerontology acute care; nurse practitioner: adult-gerontology primary care; nurse practitioner: adult; nurse practitioner: family; nurse practitioner: pediatric primary care; nurse practitioner: psychiatric-mental health, across the lifespan; other majors

Duquesne University

600 Forbes Avenue
Pittsburgh, PA 15282-1760
www.duq.edu/academics/schools/nursing
Private
Admissions: (412) 396-6550
Email: nursing@duq.edu
Financial aid: (412) 396-6607
Application deadline: 03/01
Degrees offered: master's, Ph.D., DNP
Tuition: full time: $1,218/credit hour, part time: $1,218/credit hour (master's); full time: $1,218/credit hour, part time: $1,218/credit hour (Ph.D.); full time: $1,218/credit hour, part time: $1,218/credit hour (DNP)
Room/board/expenses: N/A

Full-time enrollment: 91 (master's); 38 (Ph.D.); 17 (DNP)
men: 9%; women: 91%;
minorities: 19%; international: 2%
Part-time enrollment: 87 (master's); 17 (Ph.D.); N/A (DNP)
men: 12%; women: 88%;
minorities: 16%; international: 1%
Acceptance rate (master's): 82%
Acceptance rate (Ph.D.): 54%
Acceptance rate (DNP): 80%
Specialties offered: education; forensic nursing; nurse practitioner; nurse practitioner: family

Gannon University[1]

109 University Square
Erie, PA 16541
www.gannon.edu/
Private
Admissions: N/A
Financial aid: N/A
Tuition: N/A
Room/board/expenses: N/A
Enrollment: N/A

Gwynedd Mercy University[1]

1325 Sumneytown Pike
Gwynedd Valley, PA 19437
www.gmercyu.edu/academics/graduate-programs/nursing
Private
Admissions: N/A
Financial aid: N/A
Tuition: N/A
Room/board/expenses: N/A
Enrollment: N/A

Holy Family University[1]

9801 Frankford Avenue
Philadelphia, PA 19114
www.holyfamily.edu/choosing-holy-family-u/academics/schools-of-study/philadelphia-sch
Private
Admissions: (267) 341-3327
Email: gradstudy@holyfamily.edu
Financial aid: (267) 341-3233
Tuition: N/A
Room/board/expenses: N/A
Enrollment: N/A

Immaculata University[1]

1145 King Road
Immaculata, PA 19345-0500
Private
Admissions: N/A
Financial aid: N/A
Tuition: N/A
Room/board/expenses: N/A
Enrollment: N/A

Indiana University of Pennsylvania

Johnson Hall
1010 Oakland Avenue, Room 210
Indiana, PA 15705
www.iup.edu/rn-alliedhealth/
Public
Admissions: (724) 357-4413
Email: graduate-admissions@iup.edu
Financial aid: (724) 357-2218
Application deadline: N/A
Degrees offered: master's, Ph.D.
In-state tuition: full time: $495/credit hour, part time: $495/credit hour (master's); full time: $520/credit hour, part time: $520/credit hour (Ph.D.)

Out-of-state tuition: full time: $742/credit hour (master's); full time: $779/credit hour (Ph.D.)
Room/board/expenses: $11,730 (master's); $11,730 (Ph.D.)
Full-time enrollment: 26 (master's); men: 15%; women: 85%; minorities: 0%; international: 92%
Part-time enrollment: 32 (master's); 39 (Ph.D.) men: 4%; women: 96%; minorities: 4%; international: 1%
Acceptance rate (master's): 74%
Acceptance rate (Ph.D.): 55%
Specialties offered: administration; education

La Roche College[1]

9000 Babcock Boulevard
Pittsburgh, PA 15237-5898
www.laroche.edu/Academics/Academic_Divisions/Education_and_Nursing_Division/NURSING/D
Private
Admissions: (412) 536-1266
Financial aid: (412) 536-1125
Tuition: N/A
Room/board/expenses: N/A
Enrollment: N/A

La Salle University

1900 W. Olney Avenue
Philadelphia, PA 19141-1199
www.lasalle.edu/snhs/
Private
Admissions: (215) 951-1322
Email: dillonp@lasalle.edu
Financial aid: (215) 951-1070
Application deadline: N/A
Degrees offered: master's, DNP
Tuition: full time: $870/credit hour, part time: $870/credit hour (master's); full time: $930/credit hour, part time: $930/credit hour (DNP)
Room/board/expenses: N/A
Full-time enrollment: N/A (master's); N/A (DNP)
men: N/A; women: N/A; minorities: N/A; international: N/A
Part-time enrollment: 315 (master's); 28 (DNP)
men: 16%; women: 84%; minorities: 28%; international: 1%
Acceptance rate (master's): 61%
Acceptance rate (DNP): 92%
Specialties offered: administration; clinical nurse leader; clinical nurse specialist; community health/public health; nurse anesthesia; nurse practitioner; nurse practitioner: adult-gerontology primary care; nurse practitioner: family; school nursing

Mansfield University of Pennsylvania[1]

G24 South Hall
Mansfield, PA 16933
Public
Admissions: N/A
Financial aid: N/A
Tuition: N/A
Room/board/expenses: N/A
Enrollment: N/A

Millersville University of Pennsylvania[1]

127 Caputo Hall
Millersville, PA 17551
Public
Admissions: N/A

Financial aid: N/A
Tuition: N/A
Room/board/expenses: N/A
Enrollment: N/A

Misericordia University[1]

301 Lake Street
Dallas, PA 18612
Private
Admissions: N/A
Financial aid: N/A
Tuition: N/A
Room/board/expenses: N/A
Enrollment: N/A

Moravian College[1]

1200 Main Street
Bethlehem, PA 18018
moravian.edu/nursing
Private
Admissions: (800) 441-3191
Email: admissions@moravian.edu
Financial aid: (610) 861-1330
Tuition: N/A
Room/board/expenses: N/A
Enrollment: N/A

Neumann University[1]

1 Neumann Drive
Aston, PA 19014-1298
Private
Admissions: N/A
Financial aid: N/A
Tuition: N/A
Room/board/expenses: N/A
Enrollment: N/A

Pennsylvania State University-University Park

201 Health and Human Development E
University Park, PA 16802-1589
www.nursing.psu.edu/
Public
Admissions: (814) 863-1795
Email: nursinggrad@.psu.edu
Financial aid: (814) 865-6301
Application deadline: 02/15
Degrees offered: master's, Ph.D., DNP
In-state tuition: full time: $16,905, part time: $805/credit hour (master's); full time: $19,328, part time: $805/credit hour (Ph.D.); full time: $16,100, part time: $805/credit hour (DNP)
Out-of-state tuition: full time: $29,001 (master's); full time: $33,142 (Ph.D.); full time: $16,100 (DNP)
Room/board/expenses: $12,852 (master's); $12,852 (Ph.D.); N/A (DNP)
Full-time enrollment: 64 (master's); 7 (Ph.D.); 2 (DNP)
men: 16%; women: 84%; minorities: 14%; international: 5%
Part-time enrollment: 88 (master's); 9 (Ph.D.); 18 (DNP)
men: 10%; women: 90%; minorities: 10%; international: 0%
Acceptance rate (master's): 46%
Acceptance rate (Ph.D.): 35%
Acceptance rate (DNP): 74%
Specialties offered: administration; clinical nurse specialist; education; nurse practitioner; nurse practitioner:

adult-gerontology acute care; nurse practitioner: adult-gerontology primary care; nurse practitioner: family; dual majors

Robert Morris University

6001 University Boulevard
Moon Township, PA 15108
www.rmu.edu/Undergraduate/AcademicOfferings/Nursing
Private
Admissions: (800) 762-0097
Email: graduateadmissionsoffice@rmu.edu
Financial aid: (412) 397-6250
Application deadline: 05/01
Degrees offered: master's, DNP
Tuition: full time: N/A, part time: $495/credit hour (master's); full time: N/A, part time: $900/credit hour (DNP)
Room/board/expenses: N/A
Full-time enrollment: N/A (master's); N/A (DNP)
men: N/A; women: N/A; minorities: N/A; international: N/A
Part-time enrollment: 69 (master's); 128 (DNP)
men: 13%; women: 87%; minorities: 12%; international: 1%
Acceptance rate (master's): 71%
Acceptance rate (DNP): 17%
Specialties offered: education; generalist; nurse practitioner: adult-gerontology primary care; nurse practitioner: adult; nurse practitioner: family; nurse practitioner: psychiatric-mental health, across the lifespan

Temple University

1801 N. Broad Street
Philadelphia, PA 19122
cph.temple.edu/nursing/home
Public
Admissions: (215) 707-4618
Email: tunurse@temple.edu
Financial aid: (215) 204-2244
Application deadline: 02/14
Degrees offered: DNP
In-state tuition: full time: $881/credit hour, part time: $881/credit hour
Out-of-state tuition: full time: $1,212/credit hour
Room/board/expenses: $13,620
Full-time enrollment: 7
men: 0%; women: 100%; minorities: 57%; international: 0%
Part-time enrollment: 55
men: 15%; women: 85%; minorities: 56%; international: 0%
Acceptance rate (DNP): 49%
Specialties offered: nurse practitioner: adult-gerontology primary care; nurse practitioner: family

Thomas Jefferson University

901 Walnut Street
8th Floor
Philadelphia, PA 19107
www.jefferson.edu/nursing
Private
Admissions: (215) 503-1040
Email: erin.finn@jefferson.edu
Financial aid: (215) 955-2867
Application deadline: 02/15
Degrees offered: master's, DNP

Tuition: full time: $1,075/credit hour, part time: $1,075/credit hour (master's); full time: $1,075/credit hour, part time: $1,075/credit hour (DNP)
Room/board/expenses: N/A
Full-time enrollment: 46 (master's); N/A (DNP)
men: 30%; women: 70%; minorities: 11%; international: 0%
Part-time enrollment: 384 (master's); 36 (DNP)
men: N/A; women: N/A; minorities: 18%; international: 0%
Acceptance rate (master's): 55%
Acceptance rate (DNP): 64%
Specialties offered: clinical nurse specialist; community health/public health; informatics; nurse anesthesia; nurse practitioner; nurse practitioner: adult-gerontology acute care; nurse practitioner: adult-gerontology primary care; nurse practitioner: family; nurse practitioner: pediatric primary care; combined nurse practitioner/clinical nurse specialist; dual majors

University of Pennsylvania

420 Guardian Drive
Philadelphia, PA 19104-6096
www.nursing.upenn.edu
Private
Admissions: (215) 898-4271
Email: admissions@nursing.upenn.edu
Financial aid: (215) 898-8191
Application deadline: 07/01
Degrees offered: master's, Ph.D.
Tuition: full time: $38,060, part time: $1,196/credit hour (master's); full time: $31,068, part time: $971/credit hour (Ph.D.)
Room/board/expenses: $27,310 (master's); $27,310 (Ph.D.)
Full-time enrollment: 208 (master's); 54 (Ph.D.)
men: 14%; women: 86%; minorities: 28%; international: 5%
Part-time enrollment: 353 (master's); 4 (Ph.D.)
men: 8%; women: 92%; minorities: 25%; international: 0%
Acceptance rate (master's): 48%
Acceptance rate (Ph.D.): 50%
Specialties offered: administration; clinical nurse specialist; nurse anesthesia; nurse-midwifery; nurse practitioner; nurse practitioner: adult-gerontology acute care; nurse practitioner: adult-gerontology primary care; nurse practitioner: family; nurse practitioner: pediatric primary care; nurse practitioner: psychiatric-mental health, across the lifespan; other majors; dual majors

University of Pittsburgh

Victoria Building
Pittsburgh, PA 15261
www.nursing.pitt.edu/
Public
Admissions: (412) 624-6910
Email: sao50@pitt.edu
Financial aid: (412) 624-7488

Application deadline: 05/01
Degrees offered: master's, Ph.D., DNP
In-state tuition: full time: $37,392, part time: $1,016/credit hour (master's); full time: $37,392, part time: $1,016/credit hour (Ph.D.); full time: $37,392, part time: $1,016/credit hour (DNP)
Out-of-state tuition: full time: $43,290 (master's); full time: $43,290 (Ph.D.); full time: $43,290 (DNP)
Room/board/expenses: N/A
Full-time enrollment: 120 (master's); 31 (Ph.D.); 68 (DNP)
men: 19%; women: 81%; minorities: 9%; international: 6%
Part-time enrollment: 58 (master's); 4 (Ph.D.); 97 (DNP)
men: 20%; women: 80%; minorities: 10%; international: 1%
Acceptance rate (master's): 34%
Acceptance rate (Ph.D.): 52%
Acceptance rate (DNP): 60%
Specialties offered: administration; clinical nurse leader; clinical nurse specialist; informatics; nurse anesthesia; nurse practitioner; nurse practitioner: adult-gerontology acute care; nurse practitioner: adult-gerontology primary care; nurse practitioner: adult; nurse practitioner: family; nurse practitioner: pediatric primary care; nurse practitioner: psychiatric-mental health, across the lifespan; research; other majors

University of Scranton[1]

800 Linden Street
Scranton, PA 18510
www.scranton.edu/nursing
Private
Admissions: (570) 941-4416
Email: cgce@scranton.edu
Financial aid: (570) 941-7700
Tuition: N/A
Room/board/expenses: N/A
Enrollment: N/A

Villanova University

800 Lancaster Avenue
Villanova, PA 19085
www1.villanova.edu/villanova/nursing.html
Private
Admissions: (610) 519-4000
Email: gotovu@villanova.edu
Financial aid: (610) 519-4010
Application deadline: N/A
Degrees offered: master's, Ph.D., DNP
Tuition: full time: $837/credit hour, part time: $837/credit hour (master's); full time: $1,049/credit hour, part time: $1,049/credit hour (Ph.D.); full time: $1,375/credit hour, part time: $1,375/credit hour (DNP)
Room/board/expenses: $17,410 (master's); $17,410 (Ph.D.); $17,410 (DNP)
Full-time enrollment: 142 (master's); 61 (Ph.D.); 16 (DNP)
men: 10%; women: 90%; minorities: 11%; international: 7%
Part-time enrollment: 108 (master's); N/A (Ph.D.); N/A (DNP)
men: 11%; women: 89%; minorities: 11%; international: 0%
Acceptance rate (master's): 86%
Acceptance rate (Ph.D.): 48%

Acceptance rate (DNP): 100%
Specialties offered: administration; education; nurse anesthesia; nurse practitioner; nurse practitioner: adult-gerontology primary care; nurse practitioner: family; nurse practitioner: pediatric primary care; research

Waynesburg University[1]

51 West College Street
Waynesburg, PA 15370
www.waynesburg.edu/graduate/graduate-majors/nursing
Private
Admissions: (724) 743-7612
Email: sstoneci@waynesburg.edu
Financial aid: (724) 852-3208
Tuition: N/A
Room/board/expenses: N/A
Enrollment: N/A

West Chester University of Pennsylvania[1]

222 Sturzebecker Health Sciences Center
West Chester, PA 19383
Public
Admissions: N/A
Financial aid: N/A
Tuition: N/A
Room/board/expenses: N/A
Enrollment: N/A

Widener University[1]

One University Place
Chester, PA 19013-5892
Private
Admissions: N/A
Financial aid: N/A
Tuition: N/A
Room/board/expenses: N/A
Enrollment: N/A

Wilkes University

109 S. Franklin Street
Wilkes-Barre, PA 18766
wilkes.edu/academics/colleges/school-of-nursing/index.aspx
Private
Admissions: (800) 945-5378
Email: GraduateStudies@wilkes.edu
Financial aid: (570) 408-2000
Application deadline: N/A
Degrees offered: master's, DNP
Tuition: full time: $625/credit hour, part time: $625/credit hour (master's); full time: N/A, part time: $840/credit hour (DNP)
Room/board/expenses: N/A
Full-time enrollment: 10 (master's); N/A (DNP)
men: 20%; women: 80%; minorities: 20%; international: 0%
Part-time enrollment: 410 (master's); 112 (DNP)
men: 9%; women: 91%; minorities: 24%; international: 0%
Acceptance rate (master's): 90%
Acceptance rate (DNP): 93%
Specialties offered: administration; education; informatics; nurse practitioner; nurse practitioner: adult-gerontology primary care; nurse practitioner: psychiatric-mental health, across the lifespan

York College of Pennsylvania[1]

York College of Pennsylvania
York, PA 17405
Private
Admissions: N/A
Financial aid: N/A
Tuition: N/A
Room/board/expenses: N/A
Enrollment: N/A

PUERTO RICO

Universidad del Turabo[1]

PO Box 3030
Gurabo, PR 00778-3030
Private
Admissions: N/A
Financial aid: N/A
Tuition: N/A
Room/board/expenses: N/A
Enrollment: N/A

University of Puerto Rico[1]

Box 365067
San Juan, PR 00936-5067
Public
Admissions: N/A
Financial aid: N/A
Tuition: N/A
Room/board/expenses: N/A
Enrollment: N/A

RHODE ISLAND

Rhode Island College[1]

600 Mount Pleasant Avenue
Providence, RI 02908-1991
www.ric.edu/nursing/
Public
Admissions: N/A
Financial aid: (401) 456-8033
Tuition: N/A
Room/board/expenses: N/A
Enrollment: N/A

University of Rhode Island

White Hall
Kingston, RI 02881-2021
web.uri.edu/nursing/
Public
Admissions: (401) 874-2872
Email: gradadm@etal.uri.edu
Financial aid: (401) 874-9500
Application deadline: 04/15
Degrees offered: master's, Ph.D., DNP
In-state tuition: full time: $11,796, part time: $655/credit hour (master's); full time: $11,796, part time: $655/credit hour (Ph.D.); full time: $11,796, part time: $655/credit hour (DNP)
Out-of-state tuition: full time: $24,206 (master's); full time: $24,206 (Ph.D.); full time: $24,206 (DNP)
Room/board/expenses: N/A
Full-time enrollment: 25 (master's); 10 (Ph.D.); 4 (DNP)
men: 21%; women: 79%; minorities: 23%; international: 8%

Part-time enrollment: 42 (master's); 28 (Ph.D.); 14 (DNP)
men: 8%; women: 92%; minorities: 10%; international: 0%
Specialties offered: administration; education; nurse practitioner: adult-gerontology acute care; nurse practitioner: adult-gerontology primary care; nurse practitioner: family; research; combined nurse practitioner/clinical nurse specialist

SOUTH CAROLINA

Charleston Southern University[1]

9200 University Boulevard
North Charleston, SC 29406
Private
Admissions: N/A
Financial aid: N/A
Tuition: N/A
Room/board/expenses: N/A
Enrollment: N/A

Clemson University

524 Edwards Hall
Clemson, SC 29634
www.clemson.edu/hehd/departments/nursing
Public
Admissions: (864) 656-3195
Email: grdapp@clemson.edu
Financial aid: (864) 656-2280
Application deadline: 03/01
Degrees offered: master's
In-state tuition: full time: $9,882, part time: $663/credit hour
Out-of-state tuition: full time: $20,550
Room/board/expenses: N/A
Full-time enrollment: 68
men: N/A; women: N/A; minorities: 12%; international: 0%
Part-time enrollment: 18
men: N/A; women: N/A; minorities: 11%; international: 0%
Acceptance rate (master's): 100%
Specialties offered: administration; clinical nurse specialist; education; nurse practitioner; nurse practitioner: adult-gerontology primary care; nurse practitioner: family

Francis Marion University[1]

Florence, SC 29506
Public
Admissions: N/A
Financial aid: N/A
Tuition: N/A
Room/board/expenses: N/A
Enrollment: N/A

Medical University of South Carolina

99 Jonathan Lucas Street
Charleston, SC 29425
musc.edu/nursing
Public
Admissions: (843) 792-7408
Email: hudsonly@musc.edu
Financial aid: (843) 792-2536
Application deadline: 03/15
Degrees offered: master's, Ph.D., DNP

In-state tuition: full time: $24,348, part time: $835/credit hour (master's); full time: $24,348, part time: $835/credit hour (Ph.D.); full time: $24,348, part time: $835/credit hour (DNP)
Out-of-state tuition: full time: $28,659 (master's); full time: $28,659 (Ph.D.); full time: $28,569 (DNP)
Room/board/expenses: N/A
Full-time enrollment: 15 (master's); 11 (Ph.D.); 142 (DNP)
men: 7%; women: 93%; minorities: 13%; international: 0%
Part-time enrollment: 11 (master's); 49 (Ph.D.); 61 (DNP)
men: 5%; women: 95%; minorities: 31%; international: 0%
Acceptance rate (master's): 18%
Acceptance rate (Ph.D.): 57%
Acceptance rate (DNP): 41%
Specialties offered: administration; generalist; nurse practitioner; nurse practitioner: adult-gerontology primary care; nurse practitioner: family; nurse practitioner: pediatric primary care; research

University of South Carolina

1601 Greene Street
Columbia, SC 29208-0001
www.sc.edu/nursing
Public
Admissions: (803) 777-7412
Email: sburgess@mailbox.sc.edu
Financial aid: (803) 777-8134
Application deadline: 04/01
Degrees offered: master's, Ph.D., DNP
In-state tuition: full time: $714/credit hour, part time: $714/credit hour (master's); full time: $516/credit hour, part time: $516/credit hour (Ph.D.); full time: $714/credit hour, part time: $714/credit hour (DNP)
Out-of-state tuition: full time: $1,304/credit hour (master's); full time: $1,106 (Ph.D.); full time: $1,304/credit hour (DNP)
Room/board/expenses: N/A
Full-time enrollment: 101 (master's); 7 (Ph.D.); 10 (DNP)
men: 10%; women: 90%; minorities: 15%; international: 1%
Part-time enrollment: 119 (master's); 5 (Ph.D.); 69 (DNP)
men: 10%; women: 90%; minorities: 23%; international: 0%
Acceptance rate (master's): 82%
Acceptance rate (Ph.D.): 38%
Acceptance rate (DNP): 71%
Specialties offered: administration; nurse practitioner; nurse practitioner: adult-gerontology acute care; nurse practitioner: family; nurse practitioner: psychiatric-mental health, across the lifespan; research

SOUTH DAKOTA

National American University[1]

925 29th Street SE
Watertown, SD 57201
www.national.edu/programs/school-nursing
Private
Admissions: (877) 398-0118
Email: graduateadmissions@national.edu
Financial aid: (855) 459-3629
Tuition: N/A
Room/board/expenses: N/A
Enrollment: N/A

South Dakota State University

SNF 217
Brookings, SD 57007
www.sdstate.edu/nurs/index.cfm
Public
Admissions: (605) 688-4181
Email: sdsu_gradschool@sdstate.edu
Financial aid: (800) 952-3541
Application deadline: 04/15
Degrees offered: master's, Ph.D., DNP
In-state tuition: full time: $313/credit hour, part time: $313/credit hour (master's); full time: $313/credit hour, part time: $313/credit hour (Ph.D.); full time: $313/credit hour, part time: $313/credit hour (DNP)
Out-of-state tuition: full time: $582/credit hour (master's); full time: $582/credit hour (Ph.D.); full time: $582/credit hour (DNP)
Room/board/expenses: $9,450 (master's); $9,450 (Ph.D.); $9,450 (DNP)
Full-time enrollment: 8 (master's); 1 (Ph.D.); 25 (DNP)
men: 6%; women: 94%; minorities: 3%; international: 0%
Part-time enrollment: 62 (master's); 21 (Ph.D.); 74 (DNP)
men: 10%; women: 90%; minorities: 6%; international: 0%
Acceptance rate (master's): 41%
Acceptance rate (Ph.D.): 100%
Acceptance rate (DNP): 92%
Specialties offered: administration; clinical nurse leader; clinical nurse specialist; education; nurse practitioner; nurse practitioner: family; nurse practitioner: pediatric primary care; nurse practitioner: psychiatric-mental health, across the lifespan; research

TENNESSEE

Aquinas College[1]

Nashville, TN 37205
Private
Admissions: N/A
Financial aid: N/A
Tuition: N/A
Room/board/expenses: N/A
Enrollment: N/A

Belmont University

1900 Belmont Boulevard
Nashville, TN 37212
www.belmont.edu/gradnursing/
Private
Admissions: (615) 460-6107
Email: bill.nichols@belmont.edu
Financial aid: (615) 460-6403
Application deadline: 05/01

Degrees offered: master's, DNP
Tuition: full time: $1,140/credit hour, part time: N/A (master's); full time: $21,860, part time: N/A (DNP)
Room/board/expenses: N/A
Full-time enrollment: 27 (master's); 40 (DNP)
men: 10%; women: 90%; minorities: 10%; international: 0%
Part-time enrollment: 22 (master's); N/A (DNP)
men: 5%; women: 95%; minorities: 5%; international: 0%
Acceptance rate (master's): 54%
Acceptance rate (DNP): 72%
Specialties offered: nurse practitioner; nurse practitioner: family

Carson-Newman University[1]

1646 Russell Avenue
Jefferson City, TN 71883
Private
Admissions: N/A
Financial aid: N/A
Tuition: N/A
Room/board/expenses: N/A
Enrollment: N/A

East Tennessee State University

Campus Box 70617
Johnson City, TN 37614-0617
www.etsu.edu/nursing
Public
Admissions: (423) 439-4221
Email: gradsch@etsu.edu
Financial aid: (423) 439-4300
Application deadline: 02/01
Degrees offered: master's, Ph.D., DNP
In-state tuition: full time: $519/credit hour, part time: $519/credit hour (master's); full time: $519/credit hour, part time: $519/credit hour (Ph.D.); full time: $519/credit hour, part time: $519/credit hour (DNP)
Out-of-state tuition: full time: $1,292/credit hour (master's); full time: $1,292/credit hour (Ph.D.); full time: $1,292/credit hour (DNP)
Room/board/expenses: $4,800 (master's); $4,800 (Ph.D.); $4,800 (DNP)
Full-time enrollment: 58 (master's); 2 (Ph.D.); 47 (DNP)
men: 14%; women: 86%; minorities: 8%; international: 0%
Part-time enrollment: 270 (master's); 27 (Ph.D.); 28 (DNP)
men: 11%; women: 89%; minorities: 7%; international: 0%
Acceptance rate (master's): 77%
Acceptance rate (Ph.D.): 13%
Acceptance rate (DNP): 76%
Specialties offered: administration; clinical nurse leader; education; nurse practitioner; nurse practitioner: adult-gerontology primary care; nurse practitioner: family; nurse practitioner: psychiatric-mental health, across the lifespan; research

King University[1]

1350 King College Road
Bristol, TN 37620
Private
Admissions: N/A
Financial aid: N/A
Tuition: N/A
Room/board/expenses: N/A
Enrollment: N/A

Lincoln Memorial University[1]

6965 Cumberland Gap Parkway
Harrogate, TN 37752
Private
Admissions: N/A
Financial aid: N/A
Tuition: N/A
Room/board/expenses: N/A
Enrollment: N/A

Southern Adventist University[1]

PO Box 370
Collegedale, TN 37315
Private
Admissions: N/A
Financial aid: N/A
Tuition: N/A
Room/board/expenses: N/A
Enrollment: N/A

Tennessee Board of Regents[1]

1415 Murfreesboro Road
Suite 350
Nashville, TN 37217-2833
Public
Admissions: N/A
Financial aid: N/A
Tuition: N/A
Room/board/expenses: N/A
Enrollment: N/A

Tennessee State University[1]

3500 John A. Merritt Boulevard
Box 9590
Nashville, TN 37209-1561
Public
Admissions: N/A
Financial aid: N/A
Tuition: N/A
Room/board/expenses: N/A
Enrollment: N/A

Union University

1050 Union University Drive
Jackson, TN 38305
www.uu.edu/academics/son/
Private
Admissions: (731) 661-6545
Email: nursingadmissions@uu.edu
Financial aid: (731) 661-5015
Application deadline: 01/15
Degrees offered: master's, DNP
Tuition: full time: $560/credit hour, part time: $560/credit hour (master's); full time: $840/credit hour, part time: $840/credit hour (DNP)
Room/board/expenses: $10,356 (master's); $14,358 (DNP)
Full-time enrollment: 79 (master's); 113 (DNP)
men: 24%; women: 76%; minorities: 21%; international: 0%

Part-time enrollment: 15 (master's); 17 (DNP)
men: 6%; women: 94%; minorities: 22%; international: 0%
Acceptance rate (master's): 57%
Acceptance rate (DNP): 43%
Specialties offered: administration; education; nurse anesthesia; nurse practitioner; nurse practitioner: adult-gerontology primary care; nurse practitioner: family; nurse practitioner: pediatric primary care; nurse practitioner: psychiatric-mental health, across the lifespan

University of Memphis (Loewenberg)[1]

610 Goodman
Memphis, TN 38152
Public
Admissions: N/A
Financial aid: N/A
Tuition: N/A
Room/board/expenses: N/A
Enrollment: N/A

University of Tennessee-Chattanooga

615 McCallie Avenue
Chattanooga, TN 37403
www.utc.edu/nursing/
Public
Admissions: (423) 425-4666
Email: gsadmin@utc.edu
Financial aid: (423) 425-4677
Application deadline: 10/01
Degrees offered: master's, DNP
In-state tuition: full time: $694/credit hour, part time: $694/credit hour (master's); full time: $534/credit hour, part time: $534/credit hour (DNP)
Out-of-state tuition: full time: $1,589/credit hour (master's); full time: $581/credit hour (DNP)
Room/board/expenses: $3,000 (master's); $3,000 (DNP)
Full-time enrollment: 65 (master's); 27 (DNP)
men: 34%; women: 66%; minorities: 13%; international: 0%
Part-time enrollment: N/A (master's); N/A (DNP)
men: N/A; women: N/A; minorities: N/A; international: N/A
Acceptance rate (master's): 24%
Acceptance rate (DNP): 85%
Specialties offered: administration; nurse anesthesia; nurse practitioner; nurse practitioner: family

University of Tennessee Health Science Center[1]

877 Madison Avenue
Memphis, TN 38163
Public
Admissions: N/A
Financial aid: N/A
Tuition: N/A
Room/board/expenses: N/A
Enrollment: N/A

University of Tennessee-Knoxville

1200 Volunteer Boulevard
Knoxville, TN 37996-4180
nursing.utk.edu
Public
Admissions: (865) 974-3251
Email: gradschool@utk.edu
Financial aid: (865) 974-1111
Application deadline: 02/01
Degrees offered: master's, Ph.D., DNP
In-state tuition: full time: $634/credit hour, part time: $634/credit hour (master's); full time: $634/credit hour, part time: $634/credit hour (Ph.D.); full time: N/A, part time: $634/credit hour (DNP)
Out-of-state tuition: full time: $1,660/credit hour (master's); full time: $1,660/credit hour (Ph.D.); full time: N/A (DNP)
Room/board/expenses: N/A
Full-time enrollment: 98 (master's); 9 (Ph.D.); N/A (DNP)
men: 22%; women: 78%; minorities: 5%; international: 0%
Part-time enrollment: 26 (master's); 23 (Ph.D.); 20 (DNP)
men: 12%; women: 88%; minorities: 3%; international: 0%
Acceptance rate (master's): 54%
Acceptance rate (Ph.D.): 67%
Acceptance rate (DNP): 70%
Specialties offered: administration; clinical nurse specialist; health management & policy health care systems; nurse anesthesia; nurse practitioner; nurse practitioner: family; nurse practitioner: pediatric primary care; nurse practitioner: psychiatric-mental health, across the lifespan; research

Vanderbilt University

464 21st Avenue S
Nashville, TN 37240
www.nursing.vanderbilt.edu/
Private
Admissions: (615) 322-3800
Email: vusn-admissions@vanderbilt.edu
Financial aid: (615) 322-8986
Application deadline: 09/15
Degrees offered: master's, Ph.D., DNP
Tuition: full time: $1,219/credit hour, part time: $1,219/credit hour (master's); full time: $1,818/credit hour, part time: $1,818/credit hour (Ph.D.); full time: $1,219/credit hour, part time: $1,219/credit hour (DNP)
Room/board/expenses: N/A
Full-time enrollment: 408 (master's); 26 (Ph.D.); 34 (DNP)
men: N/A; women: N/A; minorities: 19%; international: 2%
Part-time enrollment: 203 (master's); 5 (Ph.D.); 134 (DNP)
men: N/A; women: N/A; minorities: 14%; international: 0%
Acceptance rate (master's): 53%
Acceptance rate (Ph.D.): 29%
Acceptance rate (DNP): 66%
Specialties offered: administration; informatics; nurse-midwifery; nurse practitioner; nurse practitioner: adult-gerontology acute care; nurse practitioner: adult-

gerontology primary care; nurse practitioner: family; nurse practitioner: pediatric primary care; nurse practitioner: psychiatric-mental health, across the lifespan; other majors; dual majors

TEXAS

Angelo State University

ASU Station 10902
San Angelo, TX 76909-0902
www.angelo.edu/dept/nursing/
Public
Admissions: (325) 942-2169
Email: graduate.school@angelo.edu
Financial aid: (325) 942-2246
Application deadline: 04/01
Degrees offered: master's
In-state tuition: full time: $477/credit hour, part time: $477/credit hour
Out-of-state tuition: full time: $778/credit hour
Full-time enrollment: 56
men: 13%; women: 88%; minorities: 16%; international: 0%
Part-time enrollment: 27
men: 26%; women: 74%; minorities: 30%; international: 0%
Acceptance rate (master's): 60%
Specialties offered: education; nurse practitioner; nurse practitioner: family

Baylor University

3700 Worth Street
Dallas, TX 75246
www.baylor.edu/nursing_grad/
Private
Admissions: (214) 820-3361
Email: bu_nursing@baylor.edu
Financial aid: (214) 820-4143
Application deadline: N/A
Degrees offered: master's, DNP
Tuition: full time: $1,515/credit hour, part time: $1,515/credit hour (master's); full time: $1,515/credit hour, part time: $1,515/credit hour (DNP)
Room/board/expenses: N/A
Full-time enrollment: 15 (master's); 21 (DNP)
men: 11%; women: 89%; minorities: 31%; international: 0%
Part-time enrollment: 5 (master's); 3 (DNP)
men: 13%; women: 88%; minorities: 75%; international: 0%
Acceptance rate (master's): 70%
Acceptance rate (DNP): 63%
Specialties offered: administration; nurse-midwifery; nurse practitioner; nurse practitioner: family

Hardin-Simmons University[1]

2149 Hickory Street
Abilene, TX 79601
Private
Admissions: N/A
Financial aid: N/A
Tuition: N/A
Room/board/expenses: N/A
Enrollment: N/A

Lamar University

4400 Martin Luther King
Boulevard
Beaumont, TX 77710
artssciences.lamar.edu/nursing/
Public
Admissions: (409) 880-8890
Email: gradmissions@lamar.edu
Financial aid: (409) 880-7011
Application deadline: N/A
Degrees offered: master's
In-state tuition: full time: N/A, part
time: $318/credit hour
Out-of-state tuition: full time: N/A
Full-time enrollment: 2
men: 0%; women: 100%;
minorities: 50%; international:
0%
Part-time enrollment: 73
men: 12%; women: 88%;
minorities: 44%; international:
0%
Acceptance rate (master's): 43%
Specialties offered:
administration; education; dual
majors

Lubbock Christian University

5601 19th Street
Lubbock, TX 79407
www.lcu.edu/admissions/
graduate/nursing
Private
Admissions: (806) 720-7599
Email: patricia.moulton@lcu.edu
Financial aid: (806) 720-7178
Application deadline: N/A
Degrees offered: master's
Tuition: full time: $410/credit
hour, part time: $410/credit hour
Full-time enrollment: 16
men: 6%; women: 94%;
minorities: 38%; international:
6%
Part-time enrollment: 91
men: 13%; women: 87%;
minorities: 32%; international:
9%
Acceptance rate (master's): 69%
Specialties offered: education;
nurse practitioner: nurse
practitioner: family

McMurry University (Shelton)[1]

2149 Hickory Street
Abilene, TX 79601
Private
Admissions: N/A
Financial aid: N/A
Tuition: N/A
Room/board/expenses: N/A
Enrollment: N/A

Midwestern State University[1]

3410 Taft Boulevard
Wichita Falls, TX 76308
Public
Admissions: N/A
Financial aid: N/A
Tuition: N/A
Room/board/expenses: N/A
Enrollment: N/A

Patty Hanks Shelton School of Nursing[1]

Abilene, TX 79601
Private
Admissions: N/A
Financial aid: N/A
Tuition: N/A
Room/board/expenses: N/A
Enrollment: N/A

Prairie View A&M University

6436 Fannin Street
Houston, TX 77030
www.pvamu.edu/nursing/
Public
Admissions: (713) 797-7000
Email:
graduatenursing@pvamu.edu
Financial aid: (936) 261-1000
Application deadline: 06/01
Degrees offered: master's, DNP
In-state tuition: full time: $261/
credit hour, part time: $261/
credit hour (master's); full time:
$261/credit hour, part time: $261/
credit hour (DNP)
Out-of-state tuition: full time:
$680/credit hour (master's); full
time: $680/credit hour (DNP)
Room/board/expenses: $8,418
(master's); $8,418 (DNP)
Full-time enrollment: 55 (master's);
10 (DNP)
men: 11%; women: 89%;
minorities: 88%; international:
3%
Part-time enrollment: 77
(master's); 1 (DNP)
men: 9%; women: 91%;
minorities: 91%; international:
4%
Acceptance rate (master's): 100%
Acceptance rate (DNP): 83%
Specialties offered:
administration; education;
generalist; nurse practitioner

Tarleton State University

Stephenville, TX 76401
www.tarleton.edu/nursing/
Public
Admissions: N/A
Financial aid: (254) 968-9070
Application deadline: 06/01
Degrees offered: master's
In-state tuition: full time: $204/
credit hour, part time: $204/
credit hour
Out-of-state tuition: full time:
$594/credit hour
Room/board/expenses: N/A
Full-time enrollment:
men: N/A; women: N/A;
minorities: N/A; international: N/A
Part-time enrollment: 19
men: 89%; women: 11%;
minorities: 32%; international:
0%
Acceptance rate (master's): 100%
Specialties offered:
administration; education;
generalist

Texas A&M University-Texarkana[1]

7101 University Avenue
Texarkana, TX 75503
Public
Admissions: N/A
Financial aid: N/A
Tuition: N/A
Room/board/expenses: N/A
Enrollment: N/A

Texas A&M International University[1]

5201 University Boulevard
Laredo, TX 78041
Public
Admissions: N/A
Financial aid: N/A
Tuition: N/A
Room/board/expenses: N/A
Enrollment: N/A

Texas A&M University-Corpus Christi[1]

6300 Ocean Drive, Unit 5805
Corpus Christi, TX 78412
nursing.tamucc.edu/index.html
Public
Admissions: (361) 825-2177
Email: gradweb@tamucc.edu
Financial aid: (361) 825-2338
Tuition: N/A
Room/board/expenses: N/A
Enrollment: N/A

Texas Christian University

2800 W. Bowie Street
Fort Worth, TX 76019
www.harriscollege.tcu.edu
Private
Admissions: (817) 257-6726
Email: m.allred@tcu.edu
Financial aid: (817) 257-7858
Application deadline: N/A
Degrees offered: master's, DNP
Tuition: full time: $1,415/credit
hour, part time: $1,415/credit
hour (master's); full time: $1,415/
credit hour, part time: $1,415/
credit hour (DNP)
Room/board/expenses: N/A
Full-time enrollment: 55 (master's);
202 (DNP)
men: 29%; women: 71%;
minorities: 22%; international:
0%
Part-time enrollment: 14
(master's); 11 (DNP)
men: 8%; women: 92%;
minorities: 16%; international:
4%
Acceptance rate (master's): 80%
Acceptance rate (DNP): 36%
Specialties offered: clinical nurse
leader; clinical nurse specialist;
education; nurse anesthesia

Texas State University

San Marcos, TX 78666
www.nursing.txstate.edu/
Public
Admissions: (512) 245-2581
Email: gradcollege@txstate.edu
Financial aid: (512) 245-2315
Application deadline: 04/01
Degrees offered: master's
In-state tuition: full time: $6,024,
part time: $301/credit hour
Out-of-state tuition: full time:
$13,824
Room/board/expenses: $7,840
Full-time enrollment: 68
men: 12%; women: 88%;
minorities: 28%; international: 1%
Part-time enrollment: 1
men: N/A; women: 100%;
minorities: 100%; international:
N/A
Acceptance rate (master's): 37%

Texas Tech University Health Sciences Center

3601 4th Street, MS 6264
Lubbock, TX 79430
www.ttuhsc.edu/son
Public
Admissions: (800) 851-8240
Email: songrad@ttuhsc.edu
Financial aid: (806) 743-3025
Application deadline: 02/15
Degrees offered: master's, DNP
In-state tuition: full time: $2,133,
part time: $237/credit hour
(master's); full time: $2,133, part
time: $237/credit hour (DNP)
Out-of-state tuition: full time:
$5,643 (master's); full time:
$5,643 (DNP)
Room/board/expenses: N/A
Full-time enrollment: 7 (master's);
55 (DNP)
men: 19%; women: 81%;
minorities: 19%; international:
0%
Part-time enrollment: 498
(master's); 6 (DNP)
men: 19%; women: 81%;
minorities: 40%; international:
0%
Acceptance rate (master's): 34%
Acceptance rate (DNP): 38%
Specialties offered:
administration; education;
informatics; nurse-midwifery;
nurse practitioner: nurse
practitioner: adult-gerontology
acute care; nurse practitioner:
family; nurse practitioner:
pediatric primary care

Texas Woman's University

PO Box 425498
Denton, TX 76204-5498
www.twu.edu
Public
Admissions: (940) 898-3188
Email: admissions@twu.edu
Financial aid: (940) 898-3064
Application deadline: N/A
Degrees offered: master's, Ph.D.,
DNP
In-state tuition: full time: $298/
credit hour, part time: $298/
credit hour (master's); full time:
$303/credit hour, part time:
$303/credit hour (Ph.D.); full
time: $303/credit hour, part time:
$303/credit hour (DNP)
Out-of-state tuition: full time:
$688/credit hour (master's); full
time: $693/credit hour (Ph.D.);
full time: $693/credit hour (DNP)
Room/board/expenses: $7,443
(master's); $7,443 (Ph.D.);
$7,443 (DNP)
Full-time enrollment: 31 (master's);
4 (Ph.D.); 4 (DNP)
men: 5%; women: 95%;
minorities: 41%; international:
36%
Part-time enrollment: 819
(master's); 96 (Ph.D.); 44 (DNP)
men: 7%; women: 93%;
minorities: 57%; international:
2%
Acceptance rate (master's): 69%
Acceptance rate (Ph.D.): 39%
Acceptance rate (DNP): 62%

Specialties offered: nurse
practitioner; nurse practitioner:
family

administration; clinical
nurse leader; education;
health management & policy
health care systems; nurse
practitioner; nurse practitioner:
adult-gerontology acute care;
nurse practitioner: adult-
gerontology primary care;
nurse practitioner: adult; nurse
practitioner: family; nurse
practitioner: pediatric primary
care; other majors

University of Houston-Victoria[1]

3007 N. Ben Wilson
Victoria, TX 77901
Public
Admissions: N/A
Financial aid: N/A
Tuition: N/A
Room/board/expenses: N/A
Enrollment: N/A

University of Mary Hardin-Baylor[1]

900 College Street
Belton, TX 76513
umhb.edu/nursing
Private
Admissions: N/A
Financial aid: (254) 295-4515
Tuition: N/A
Room/board/expenses: N/A
Enrollment: N/A

University of Texas-Arlington

411 S. Nedderman Drive
PO Box 19407
Arlington, TX 76019
www.uta.edu/nursing
Public
Admissions: (817) 272-3275
Financial aid: (817) 272-3561
Application deadline: 06/01
Degrees offered: master's, Ph.D.,
DNP
In-state tuition: full time: $8,553,
part time: $6,586 (master's); full
time: $8,169, part time: $5,492
(Ph.D.); full time: $8,169, part
time: $5,492 (DNP)
Out-of-state tuition: full time:
$16,307 (master's); full time:
$15,922 (Ph.D.); full time:
$15,922 (DNP)
Room/board/expenses: $8,970
(master's); $8,970 (Ph.D.);
$8,970 (DNP)
Full-time enrollment: 72 (master's);
9 (Ph.D.); N/A (DNP)
men: 12%; women: 88%;
minorities: 30%; international:
19%
Part-time enrollment: 1,842
(master's); 26 (Ph.D.); 42 (DNP)
men: 12%; women: 88%;
minorities: 46%; international:
1%
Acceptance rate (master's): 57%
Acceptance rate (Ph.D.): 17%
Acceptance rate (DNP): 38%
Specialties offered:
administration; education;
nurse practitioner; nurse
practitioner: adult-gerontology
acute care; nurse practitioner:
adult-gerontology primary
care; nurse practitioner: family;
nurse practitioner: pediatric

primary care; nurse practitioner: psychiatric-mental health, across the lifespan; research; other majors

University of Texas-Austin

1710 Red River
Austin, TX 78701
www.nursing.utexas.edu
Public
Admissions: (512) 471-7927
Email: tdemchuk@
mail.nur.utexas.edu
Financial aid: (512) 475-6282
Application deadline: 10/01
Degrees offered: master's, Ph.D., DNP
In-state tuition: full time: $11,572, part time: $4,180 (master's); full time: $11,572, part time: $4,180 (Ph.D.); full time: $18,000, part time: $9,000 (DNP)
Out-of-state tuition: full time: $21,155 (master's); full time: $21,155 (Ph.D.); full time: $18,000 (DNP)
Room/board/expenses: $9,600 (master's); $9,600 (Ph.D.); $9,600 (DNP)
Full-time enrollment: 205 (master's); 29 (Ph.D.); N/A (DNP)
men: 15%; women: 85%; minorities: 31%; international: 2%
Part-time enrollment: 41 (master's); 11 (Ph.D.); N/A (DNP)
men: 13%; women: 87%; minorities: 19%; international: 4%
Acceptance rate (master's): 57%
Acceptance rate (Ph.D.): 78%
Specialties offered: administration; clinical nurse specialist; community health/public health; nurse practitioner: family; nurse practitioner: pediatric primary care; nurse practitioner: psychiatric-mental health, across the lifespan; research; other majors

University of Texas-El Paso

500 W. University Avenue
El Paso, TX 79902
nursing.utep.edu/
Public
Admissions: (915) 747-5491
Email: gradschool@utep.edu
Financial aid: (915) 747-5204
Application deadline: N/A
Degrees offered: master's, DNP
In-state tuition: full time: $419/credit hour, part time: $419/credit hour (master's); full time: $419/credit hour, part time: $419/credit hour (DNP)
Out-of-state tuition: full time: $843/credit hour (master's); full time: $843/credit hour (DNP)
Room/board/expenses: N/A
Full-time enrollment: 273 (master's); 16 (DNP)
men: 18%; women: 82%; minorities: 65%; international: 1%
Part-time enrollment: 23 (master's); N/A (DNP)
men: 17%; women: 83%; minorities: 61%; international: 4%
Acceptance rate (master's): 96%
Acceptance rate (DNP): 82%

Specialties offered: administration; education; nurse practitioner; nurse practitioner: adult-gerontology acute care; nurse practitioner: family; nurse practitioner: pediatric primary care

University of Texas Health Science Center-Houston

6901 Bertner Avenue
Houston, TX 77030
nursing.uth.edu/
Public
Admissions: (713) 500-2101
Email: soninfo@uth.tmc.edu
Financial aid: (713) 500-3860
Application deadline: 04/01
Degrees offered: master's, Ph.D., DNP
In-state tuition: full time: $244/credit hour, part time: $244/credit hour (master's); full time: $244/credit hour, part time: $244/credit hour (Ph.D.); full time: $244/credit hour, part time: $244/credit hour (DNP)
Out-of-state tuition: full time: $946/credit hour (master's); full time: $946/credit hour (Ph.D.); full time: $946/credit hour (DNP)
Room/board/expenses: N/A
Full-time enrollment: 179 (master's); 13 (Ph.D.); 44 (DNP)
men: 16%; women: 84%; minorities: 47%; international: 5%
Part-time enrollment: 244 (master's); 36 (Ph.D.); 60 (DNP)
men: 17%; women: 83%; minorities: 56%; international: 1%
Acceptance rate (master's): 57%
Acceptance rate (Ph.D.): 88%
Acceptance rate (DNP): 44%
Specialties offered: administration; education; nurse anesthesia; nurse practitioner; nurse practitioner: adult-gerontology acute care; nurse practitioner: adult-gerontology primary care; nurse practitioner: family; nurse practitioner: psychiatric-mental health, across the lifespan; research; dual majors

University of Texas Health Science Center-San Antonio

7703 Floyd Curl Drive
San Antonio, TX 78229-3900
nursing.uthscsa.edu
Public
Admissions: (210) 567-5805
Email: nursing.uthscsa.edu/students/index.asp
Financial aid: (210) 567-2635
Application deadline: 02/01
Degrees offered: master's, Ph.D., DNP
In-state tuition: full time: $6,379, part time: $3,987 (master's); full time: $6,379, part time: $3,987 (Ph.D.); full time: $6,379, part time: $3,987 (DNP)
Out-of-state tuition: full time: $17,659 (master's); full time: $17,659 (Ph.D.); full time: $17,659 (DNP)
Room/board/expenses: $18,560 (master's); $18,560 (Ph.D.); $18,560 (DNP)

Full-time enrollment: 109 (master's); 4 (Ph.D.); 24 (DNP)
men: 15%; women: 85%; minorities: 55%; international: 4%
Part-time enrollment: 87 (master's); 17 (Ph.D.); 5 (DNP)
men: 19%; women: 81%; minorities: 57%; international: 0%
Acceptance rate (master's): 37%
Acceptance rate (Ph.D.): 80%
Acceptance rate (DNP): 75%
Specialties offered: administration; clinical nurse leader; nurse practitioner; nurse practitioner: adult-gerontology acute care; nurse practitioner: family; nurse practitioner: pediatric primary care; nurse practitioner: psychiatric-mental health, across the lifespan

University of Texas Medical Branch-Galveston

301 University Boulevard
Galveston, TX 77555-1132
nursing.utmb.edu/
Public
Admissions: (409) 772-8205
Email: dpearro@utmb.edu
Financial aid: (409) 772-1215
Application deadline: 12/01
Degrees offered: master's, Ph.D., DNP
In-state tuition: full time: $285/credit hour, part time: $285/credit hour (master's); full time: $285/credit hour, part time: $285/credit hour (Ph.D.); full time: $285/credit hour, part time: $285/credit hour (DNP)
Out-of-state tuition: full time: $675/credit hour (master's); full time: $675/credit hour (Ph.D.); full time: $675/credit hour (DNP)
Room/board/expenses: $14,424 (master's); $14,424 (DNP)
Full-time enrollment: 110 (master's); 23 (Ph.D.); N/A (DNP)
men: 11%; women: 89%; minorities: 52%; international: 1%
Part-time enrollment: 381 (master's); 22 (Ph.D.); 25 (DNP)
men: 11%; women: 89%; minorities: 52%; international: 1%
Acceptance rate (master's): 27%
Acceptance rate (Ph.D.): 60%
Acceptance rate (DNP): 53%
Specialties offered: administration; clinical nurse leader; education; nurse practitioner: adult-gerontology primary care; nurse practitioner: family; research

University of Texas-Rio Grande Valley

Brownsville, TX 78520
www.utrgv.edu/en-us/academics/colleges/health-affairs
Public
Admissions: (956) 665-3661
Email: gradcollege@utrgv.edu
Financial aid: (956) 665-2170
Application deadline: 04/01
Degrees offered: master's
In-state tuition: full time: $5,329, part time: $303/credit hour
Out-of-state tuition: full time: $12,349

Full-time enrollment: 72
men: N/A; women: N/A; minorities: 88%; international: 0%
Part-time enrollment: 103
men: N/A; women: N/A; minorities: 93%; international: 0%
Acceptance rate (master's): 84%
Specialties offered: administration; education; nurse practitioner; nurse practitioner: family

University of Texas-Tyler

3900 University Boulevard
Tyler, TX 75799
www.uttyler.edu/nursing/college/
Public
Admissions: (903) 566-7457
Email: ogs@uttyler.edu
Financial aid: (903) 566-7180
Application deadline: 02/15
Degrees offered: master's, Ph.D.
In-state tuition: full time: $731/credit hour, part time: $731/credit hour (master's); full time: $342/credit hour, part time: $342/credit hour
Out-of-state tuition: full time: $1,123/credit hour (master's); full time: $732/credit hour
Room/board/expenses: N/A
Full-time enrollment: 84 (master's); 42
men: 13%; women: 87%; minorities: 25%; international: 0%
Part-time enrollment: 268 (master's); 28
men: 12%; women: 88%; minorities: 32%; international: 0%
Acceptance rate (master's): 48%
Acceptance rate (Ph.D.): 53%
Specialties offered: administration; education; nurse practitioner; nurse practitioner: family; research

University of the Incarnate Word

4301 Broadway
San Antonio, TX 78209
uiw.edu/nursing/
Private
Admissions: (210) 829-6005
Email: admis@uiwtx.edu
Financial aid: (210) 829-6008
Application deadline: N/A
Degrees offered: master's, DNP
Tuition: full time: $850/credit hour, part time: $850/credit hour (master's); full time: $850/credit hour, part time: $850/credit hour (DNP)
Room/board/expenses: N/A
Full-time enrollment: 3 (master's); N/A (DNP)
men: 0%; women: 100%; minorities: 33%; international: 33%
Part-time enrollment: 29 (master's); 37 (DNP)
men: 17%; women: 83%; minorities: 62%; international: 3%
Acceptance rate (master's): 53%
Acceptance rate (DNP): 40%
Specialties offered: clinical nurse leader; clinical nurse specialist; nurse practitioner: family; nurse practitioner: psychiatric-mental health, across the lifespan

Wayland Baptist University[1]

Plainview, TX 79072
Private
Admissions: N/A
Financial aid: N/A
Tuition: N/A
Room/board/expenses: N/A
Enrollment: N/A

West Texas A&M University[1]

Killgore Research Center
Room 102
Canyon, TX 79016
Public
Admissions: N/A
Financial aid: N/A
Tuition: N/A
Room/board/expenses: N/A
Enrollment: N/A

UTAH

Brigham Young University

400 SWKT
Provo, UT 84602
nursing.byu.edu
Private
Admissions: (801) 422-4091
Email: graduatestudies@byu.edu
Financial aid: (801) 422-4104
Application deadline: 12/01
Degrees offered: master's
Tuition: full time: $382/credit hour, part time: $382/credit hour
Room/board/expenses: $11,412
Full-time enrollment: 30
men: 27%; women: 73%; minorities: 0%; international: 0%
Part-time enrollment:
men: N/A; women: N/A; minorities: N/A; international: N/A
Acceptance rate (master's): 32%
Specialties offered: nurse practitioner; nurse practitioner: family

University of Utah

10 S. 2000 E
Salt Lake City, UT 84112
nursing.utah.edu
Public
Admissions: (801) 581-3414
Email: info@nurs.utah.edu
Financial aid: (801) 585-1671
Application deadline: 01/15
Degrees offered: master's, Ph.D., DNP
In-state tuition: full time: $13,805, part time: N/A (master's); full time: $11,658, part time: N/A (Ph.D.); full time: $16,259, part time: N/A (DNP)
Out-of-state tuition: full time: $34,479 (master's); full time: $28,181 (Ph.D.); full time: $41,680 (DNP)
Room/board/expenses: $10,782 (master's); $10,782 (Ph.D.); $10,782 (DNP)
Full-time enrollment: 27 (master's); 21 (Ph.D.); 231 (DNP)
men: 22%; women: 78%; minorities: 14%; international: 3%
Part-time enrollment: 18 (master's); 21 (Ph.D.); 18 (DNP)
men: 23%; women: 77%; minorities: 7%; international: 0%
Acceptance rate (master's): 86%
Acceptance rate (Ph.D.): 54%
Acceptance rate (DNP): 56%

Specialties offered: case management; education; informatics; nurse-midwifery; nurse practitioner; nurse practitioner: adult-gerontology acute care; nurse practitioner: adult-gerontology primary care; nurse practitioner: family; nurse practitioner: pediatric primary care; nurse practitioner: psychiatric-mental health, across the lifespan; research; other majors; dual majors

Utah Valley University[1]
800 W. University Parkway
Orem, UT 84058
Public
Admissions: N/A
Financial aid: N/A
Tuition: N/A
Room/board/expenses: N/A
Enrollment: N/A

Weber State University[1]
3875 Stadium Way
Department 3903
Ogden, UT 84408
weber.edu/nursing
Public
Admissions: (801) 626-6753
Email: rholt@weber.edu
Financial aid: N/A
Tuition: N/A
Room/board/expenses: N/A
Enrollment: N/A

Western Governors University[1]
4001 S. 700 E
Salt Lake City, UT 84107
Private
Admissions: N/A
Financial aid: N/A
Tuition: N/A
Room/board/expenses: N/A
Enrollment: N/A

Westminster College[1]
1840 S. 1300 E
Salt Lake City, UT 84105
Private
Admissions: N/A
Financial aid: N/A
Tuition: N/A
Room/board/expenses: N/A
Enrollment: N/A

VERMONT

Norwich University[1]
158 Harmon Drive
Northfield, VT 05663
online.norwich.edu/
degree-programs/masters/
master-science-nursing/overview
Private
Admissions: (800) 460-5597
Email: msn@online.norwich.edu
Financial aid: (802) 485-2969
Tuition: N/A
Room/board/expenses: N/A
Enrollment: N/A

University of Vermont
216 Rowell Building
Burlington, VT 05405
www.uvm.edu/~cnhs/nursing/
Public
Admissions: (802) 656-3858
Email: cnhsgrad@uvm.edu

Financial aid: (802) 656-5700
Application deadline: N/A
Degrees offered: master's, DNP
In-state tuition: full time: $611/credit hour, part time: $611/credit hour (master's); full time: $611/credit hour, part time: $611/credit hour (DNP)
Out-of-state tuition: full time: $1,544/credit hour (master's); full time: $1,544/credit hour (DNP)
Room/board/expenses: $9,904 (master's); $9,904 (DNP)
Full-time enrollment: 40 (master's); 30 (DNP)
men: 16%; women: 84%; minorities: 7%; international: 0%
Part-time enrollment: 8 (master's); 13 (DNP)
men: 24%; women: 76%; minorities: 10%; international: 0%
Acceptance rate (master's): 100%
Acceptance rate (DNP): 45%
Specialties offered: clinical nurse leader; nurse practitioner; nurse practitioner: adult-gerontology primary care; nurse practitioner: family

VIRGINIA

Eastern Mennonite University[1]
1200 Park Road
Harrisonburg, VA 22802
Private
Admissions: N/A
Financial aid: N/A
Tuition: N/A
Room/board/expenses: N/A
Enrollment: N/A

George Mason University
4400 University Drive
Fairfax, VA 22030-4444
chhs.gmu.edu/nursing/index.cfm
Public
Admissions: (703) 993-2400
Email: admissions@gmu.edu
Financial aid: (703) 993-2353
Application deadline: 02/01
Degrees offered: master's, Ph.D., DNP
In-state tuition: full time: $505/credit hour, part time: $505/credit hour (master's); full time: $505/credit hour, part time: $505/credit hour (Ph.D.); full time: $505/credit hour, part time: $505/credit hour (DNP)
Out-of-state tuition: full time: $1,260/credit hour (master's); full time: $1,260/credit hour (Ph.D.); full time: $1,260/credit hour (DNP)
Room/board/expenses: $16,928 (master's); $16,928 (Ph.D.); $16,928 (DNP)
Full-time enrollment: 18 (master's); 7 (Ph.D.); 29 (DNP)
men: 17%; women: 83%; minorities: 44%; international: 11%
Part-time enrollment: 98 (master's); 22 (Ph.D.); 64 (DNP)
men: 9%; women: 91%; minorities: 39%; international: 2%
Acceptance rate (master's): 48%
Acceptance rate (Ph.D.): 42%
Acceptance rate (DNP): 59%

Specialties offered: administration; education; nurse practitioner; nurse practitioner: adult-gerontology primary care; nurse practitioner: family; nurse practitioner: psychiatric-mental health, across the lifespan; research

Hampton University[1]
100 E. Queen Street
Hampton, VA 23668
Private
Admissions: N/A
Financial aid: N/A
Tuition: N/A
Room/board/expenses: N/A
Enrollment: N/A

James Madison University
MSC 4305
Harrisonburg, VA 22807
jmu.edu/nursing
Public
Admissions: N/A
Email: walshmd@jmu.edu
Financial aid: (540) 568-7820
Application deadline: N/A
Degrees offered: master's, DNP
In-state tuition: full time: $524/credit hour, part time: $524/credit hour (master's); full time: $524/credit hour, part time: $524/credit hour (DNP)
Out-of-state tuition: full time: $1,225/credit hour (master's); full time: $1,225/credit hour (DNP)
Room/board/expenses: N/A
Full-time enrollment: 14 (master's); N/A (DNP)
men: 7%; women: 93%; minorities: 14%; international: 0%
Part-time enrollment: 57 (master's); 17 (DNP)
men: 18%; women: 82%; minorities: 3%; international: 0%
Acceptance rate (master's): 64%
Acceptance rate (DNP): 100%
Specialties offered: administration; clinical nurse leader; nurse-midwifery; nurse practitioner: family

Jefferson College of Health Sciences[1]
101 Elm Avenue, SE
Roanoke, VA 24013
Private
Admissions: N/A
Financial aid: N/A
Tuition: N/A
Room/board/expenses: N/A
Enrollment: N/A

Liberty University
1971 University Boulevard
Lynchburg, VA 24502
www.liberty.edu/academics/arts-sciences/nursing/index.cfm?PID=188
Private
Admissions: (800) 424-9596
Email: gradadmissions@liberty.edu
Financial aid: (434) 582-2270
Application deadline: N/A
Degrees offered: master's, DNP
Tuition: full time: $540/credit hour, part time: $590/credit hour (master's); full time: $570/credit hour, part time: $570/credit hour (DNP)

Room/board/expenses: N/A
Full-time enrollment: 68 (master's); 40 (DNP)
men: 7%; women: 93%; minorities: 18%; international: 0%
Part-time enrollment: 507 (master's); 1 (DNP)
men: 11%; women: 89%; minorities: 19%; international: 0%
Acceptance rate (master's): 34%
Acceptance rate (DNP): 19%
Specialties offered: administration; education; nurse practitioner; nurse practitioner: family

Lynchburg College
1501 Lakeside Drive
Lynchburg, VA 24501
www.lynchburg.edu/graduate/online-master-of-science-in-nursing/
Private
Admissions: (800) 426-8101
Email: admissions@lynchburg.edu
Financial aid: (434) 544-8228
Application deadline: N/A
Degrees offered: master's
Tuition: full time: $475/credit hour, part time: $475/credit hour
Full-time enrollment: 2
men: 0%; women: 100%; minorities: 0%; international: 50%
Part-time enrollment: 32
men: 6%; women: 94%; minorities: 13%; international: 3%
Acceptance rate (master's): 33%
Specialties offered: clinical nurse leader

Marymount University
2807 N. Glebe Road
Arlington, VA 22207-4299
www.marymount.edu/Academics/Malek-School-of-Health-Professions
Private
Admissions: (703) 284-5901
Email: grad.admissions@marymount.edu
Financial aid: (703) 284-1530
Application deadline: 05/01
Degrees offered: master's, DNP
Tuition: full time: N/A, part time: $910/credit hour (master's); full time: N/A, part time: $910/credit hour (DNP)
Room/board/expenses: N/A
Full-time enrollment: 12 (master's); N/A (DNP)
men: 8%; women: 92%; minorities: 33%; international: 0%
Part-time enrollment: 39 (master's); 13 (DNP)
men: 10%; women: 90%; minorities: 33%; international: 2%
Acceptance rate (master's): 47%
Acceptance rate (DNP): 89%
Specialties offered: nurse practitioner; nurse practitioner: family

Old Dominion University[1]
Office of Admissions
Norfolk, VA 23529-0500
Public
Admissions: N/A
Financial aid: N/A
Tuition: N/A
Room/board/expenses: N/A
Enrollment: N/A

Radford University[1]
PO Box 6964
Radford Station
Radford, VA 24142
Public
Admissions: N/A
Financial aid: N/A
Tuition: N/A
Room/board/expenses: N/A
Enrollment: N/A

Shenandoah University
1460 University Drive
Winchester, VA 22601
www.nursing.su.edu/
Private
Admissions: (540) 665-4581
Email: admit@su.edu
Financial aid: (540) 665-4538
Application deadline: 04/15
Degrees offered: master's, DNP
Tuition: full time: $830, part time: $830 (master's); full time: $830, part time: $830 (DNP)
Room/board/expenses: $9,920 (master's); $9,920 (DNP)
Full-time enrollment: 24 (master's); 4 (DNP)
men: 7%; women: 93%; minorities: 21%; international: 0%
Part-time enrollment: 35 (master's); 3 (DNP)
men: 11%; women: 89%; minorities: 26%; international: 3%
Acceptance rate (master's): 79%
Acceptance rate (DNP): 100%
Specialties offered: health management & policy health care systems; informatics; nurse-midwifery; nurse practitioner; nurse practitioner: family; nurse practitioner: psychiatric-mental health, across the lifespan

University of Virginia
PO Box 800826
Charlottesville, VA 22908-0926
www.nursing.virginia.edu/
Public
Admissions: (434) 924-0067
Email: ChristopherDLC@virginia.edu
Financial aid: (434) 924-0067
Application deadline: 11/01
Degrees offered: master's, Ph.D., DNP
In-state tuition: full time: $14,856, part time: $802/credit hour (master's); full time: $14,518, part time: N/A (Ph.D.); full time: $14,856, part time: $802/credit hour (DNP)
Out-of-state tuition: full time: $24,288 (master's); full time: $24,316 (Ph.D.); full time: $24,288 (DNP)
Room/board/expenses: N/A

Full-time enrollment: 108
(master's); 30 (Ph.D.); 35 (DNP)
men: 16%; women: 84%;
minorities: 23%; international:
3%
Part-time enrollment: 157
(master's); 10 (Ph.D.); 31 (DNP)
men: 12%; women: 88%;
minorities: 18%; international: 1%
Acceptance rate (master's): 43%
Acceptance rate (Ph.D.): 62%
Acceptance rate (DNP): 60%
Specialties offered: clinical nurse
leader; clinical nurse specialist;
community health/public health;
health management & policy
health care systems; nurse
practitioner; nurse practitioner:
adult-gerontology acute care;
nurse practitioner: family;
nurse practitioner: pediatric
primary care; nurse practitioner:
psychiatric-mental health,
across the lifespan; research;
combined nurse practitioner/
clinical nurse specialist

Virginia Commonwealth University

730 E. Broad Street
Richmond, VA 23298
www.nursing.vcu.edu
Public
Admissions: (804) 828-5171
Email: VCU_Nurse@vcu.edu
Financial aid: (804) 828-6669
Application deadline: 02/01
Degrees offered: master's, Ph.D.,
DNP
In-state tuition: full time: $12,397,
part time: $590/credit hour
(master's); full time: $10,230,
part time: $487/credit hour
(Ph.D.); full time: $12,600, part
time: $700/credit hour (DNP)
Out-of-state tuition: full time:
$25,492 (master's); full time:
$21,806 (Ph.D.); full time:
$12,600 (DNP)
Room/board/expenses: $9,586
(master's); $9,586 (Ph.D.);
$9,586 (DNP)
Full-time enrollment: 75 (master's);
11 (Ph.D.); N/A (DNP)
men: 7%; women: 93%;
minorities: 14%; international: 2%
Part-time enrollment: 147
(master's); 11 (Ph.D.); 14 (DNP)
men: 6%; women: 94%;
minorities: 19%; international: 1%
Acceptance rate (master's): 54%
Acceptance rate (Ph.D.): 54%
Acceptance rate (DNP): 71%
Specialties offered:
administration; nurse
practitioner; nurse practitioner:
adult-gerontology acute care;
nurse practitioner: adult-
gerontology primary care;
nurse practitioner: family; nurse
practitioner: psychiatric-mental
health, across the lifespan

WASHINGTON

Gonzaga University[1]

502 E. Boone Avenue
Spokane, WA 99258-0038
www.gonzaga.edu/SNHP
Private
Admissions: (509) 313-6239
Email: burdette@gonzaga.edu
Financial aid: (800) 793-1716
Tuition: N/A

Room/board/expenses: N/A
Enrollment: N/A

Pacific Lutheran University

121st and Park Avenue
Tacoma, WA 98447-0029
www.plu.edu/nursing
Private
Admissions: (253) 535-8570
Email: gradadmission@plu.edu
Financial aid: (253) 535-8725
Application deadline: 01/15
Degrees offered: master's, DNP
Tuition: full time: $960/credit
hour, part time: $960/credit hour
(master's); full time: $1,100/credit
hour, part time: $1,100/credit
hour (DNP)
Room/board/expenses: $8,500
(master's); $8,500 (DNP)
Full-time enrollment: 89 (master's);
12 (DNP)
men: N/A; women: N/A;
minorities: 10%; international: 1%
Part-time enrollment: N/A
(master's); 3 (DNP)
men: 0%; women: 100%;
minorities: 0%; international: 0%
Acceptance rate (master's): 33%
Acceptance rate (DNP): 81%
Specialties offered:
administration; clinical nurse
leader; education; generalist;
nurse practitioner; nurse
practitioner: family; dual majors

Seattle Pacific University[1]

3307 Third Avenue W
Seattle, WA 98119-1922
Private
Admissions: N/A
Financial aid: N/A
Tuition: N/A
Room/board/expenses: N/A
Enrollment: N/A

Seattle University

901 12th Avenue
Seattle, WA 98122-4340
www.seattleu.edu/nursing
Private
Admissions: (206) 220-8010
Email: grad-admissions@
seattleu.edu
Financial aid: (206) 220-8020
Application deadline: 01/11
Degrees offered: master's, DNP
Tuition: full time: $690/credit
hour, part time: $690/credit hour
(master's); full time: $712/credit
hour, part time: $712/credit hour
(DNP)
Room/board/expenses: N/A
Full-time enrollment: 190
(master's); 14 (DNP)
men: N/A; women: N/A;
minorities: 18%; international:
N/A
Part-time enrollment: N/A
(master's); N/A (DNP)
men: N/A; women: N/A;
minorities: N/A; international: N/A
Acceptance rate (master's): 21%
Acceptance rate (DNP): 86%
Specialties offered: community
health/public health; nurse-
midwifery; nurse practitioner;
nurse practitioner: adult-
gerontology acute care; nurse
practitioner: adult-gerontology
primary care; nurse practitioner:
family; nurse practitioner:

psychiatric-mental health,
across the lifespan

University of Washington

PO Box 357260
Seattle, WA 98195
nursing.uw.edu/
Public
Admissions: (206) 543-8736
Email: sonsas@uw.edu
Financial aid: (206) 543-6107
Application deadline: 01/15
Degrees offered: master's, Ph.D.,
DNP
In-state tuition: full time: $21,370,
part time: $16,095 (master's); full
time: $16,425, part time: $14,078
(Ph.D.); full time: $24,010, part
time: $17,679 (DNP)
Out-of-state tuition: full time:
$31,542 (master's); full time:
$29,274 (Ph.D.); full time:
$34,182 (DNP)
Room/board/expenses: $14,625
(master's); $14,625 (Ph.D.);
$14,625 (DNP)
Full-time enrollment: 12 (master's);
46 (Ph.D.); 206 (DNP)
men: 12%; women: 88%;
minorities: 23%; international:
12%
Part-time enrollment: 49
(master's); 14 (Ph.D.); 69 (DNP)
men: 14%; women: 86%;
minorities: 36%; international:
2%
Acceptance rate (master's): 84%
Acceptance rate (Ph.D.): 56%
Acceptance rate (DNP): 51%
Specialties offered: clinical nurse
specialist; community health/
public health; informatics; nurse-
midwifery; nurse practitioner;
nurse practitioner: adult-
gerontology acute care; nurse
practitioner: adult-gerontology
primary care; nurse practitioner:
family; nurse practitioner:
pediatric primary care; nurse
practitioner: psychiatric-mental
health, across the lifespan;
research

Washington State University

PO Box 1495
Spokane, WA 99210-1495
nursing.wsu.edu
Public
Admissions: (509) 324-7279
Email: cefitzgerald@wsu.edu
Financial aid: (509) 335-9711
Application deadline: 01/10
Degrees offered: master's, Ph.D.,
DNP
In-state tuition: full time: $17,756,
part time: $888/credit hour
(master's); full time: $17,756, part
time: $888/credit hour (Ph.D.);
full time: $17,756, part time:
$888/credit hour (DNP)
Out-of-state tuition: full time:
$32,814 (master's); full time:
$32,778 (Ph.D.); full time:
$32,778 (DNP)
Room/board/expenses: $11,356
(master's); $11,356 (Ph.D.);
$11,356 (DNP)
Full-time enrollment: 5 (master's);
11 (Ph.D.); 63 (DNP)
men: 17%; women: 83%;
minorities: 24%; international:
4%

Part-time enrollment: 34
(master's); 24 (Ph.D.); 69 (DNP)
men: 14%; women: 86%;
minorities: 14%; international: 2%
Acceptance rate (master's): 69%
Acceptance rate (Ph.D.): 73%
Acceptance rate (DNP): 51%
Specialties offered:
administration; community
health/public health; education;
health management & policy
health care systems; nurse
practitioner; nurse practitioner:
family; nurse practitioner:
psychiatric-mental health,
across the lifespan; research

WEST VIRGINIA

Marshall University[1]

100 Angus E. Peyton Drive
South Charleston, WV 25303
Public
Admissions: N/A
Financial aid: N/A
Tuition: N/A
Room/board/expenses: N/A
Enrollment: N/A

West Virginia University

One Medical Drive
PO Box 9600
Morgantown, WV 26506-9600
nursing.hsc.wvu.edu/
Public
Admissions: (304) 293-5908
Email: mmmichael@hsc.wvu.edu
Financial aid: (304) 293-3706
Application deadline: 02/01
Degrees offered: master's, Ph.D.,
DNP
In-state tuition: full time: $9,054,
part time: $503/credit hour
(master's); full time: $9,054, part
time: $503/credit hour (Ph.D.);
full time: $9,054, part time:
$503/credit hour (DNP)
Out-of-state tuition: full time:
$21,996 (master's); full time:
$21,996 (Ph.D.); full time:
$21,996 (DNP)
Room/board/expenses: N/A
Full-time enrollment: 53 (master's);
N/A (Ph.D.); N/A (DNP)
men: 11%; women: 89%;
minorities: 8%; international: 0%
Part-time enrollment: 67
(master's); 13 (Ph.D.); 14 (DNP)
men: 9%; women: 91%;
minorities: 4%; international: 0%
Acceptance rate (master's): 83%
Acceptance rate (Ph.D.): 90%
Acceptance rate (DNP): 67%
Specialties offered: nurse
practitioner; nurse practitioner:
family; nurse practitioner:
pediatric primary care

West Virginia Wesleyan College[1]

59 College Avenue
Buckhannon, WV 26201
Private
Admissions: N/A
Financial aid: N/A
Tuition: N/A
Room/board/expenses: N/A
Enrollment: N/A

Wheeling Jesuit University[1]

316 Washington Avenue
Wheeling, WV 26003
Private
Admissions: (304) 243-2359
Email: adulted@wju.edu
Financial aid: (304) 243-2304
Tuition: N/A
Room/board/expenses: N/A
Enrollment: N/A

WISCONSIN

Alverno College

300 S. 43 Street
Milwaukee, WI 53234-3922
www.alverno.edu/academics/
academicdepartments/
joannmcgrathschoolofnursing
Private
Admissions: (800) 933-3401
Email: admissions@alverno.edu
Financial aid: (414) 382-6046
Application deadline: N/A
Degrees offered: master's
Tuition: full time: $921, part
time: N/A
Room/board/expenses: N/A
Full-time enrollment: 102
men: 7%; women: 93%;
minorities: 26%; international:
1%
Part-time enrollment: 100
men: 5%; women: 95%;
minorities: 23%; international:
0%
Acceptance rate (master's): 95%
Specialties offered: clinical nurse
specialist; nurse practitioner;
nurse practitioner: family; nurse
practitioner: psychiatric-mental
health, across the lifespan

Bellin College[1]

3201 Eaton Road
Green Bay, WI 54311
Private
Admissions: N/A
Financial aid: N/A
Tuition: N/A
Room/board/expenses: N/A
Enrollment: N/A

Cardinal Stritch University[1]

6801 N. Yates Road
Milwaukee, WI 53217-3985
Private
Admissions: N/A
Financial aid: N/A
Tuition: N/A
Room/board/expenses: N/A
Enrollment: N/A

Concordia University

12800 N. Lake Shore Drive
Mequon, WI 53097
www.cuw.edu/Programs/nursing/
index.html
Private
Admissions: (262) 243-4590
Email:
michelle.hoffman@cuw.edu
Financial aid: (262) 243-2025
Application deadline: 05/01
Degrees offered: master's, DNP
Tuition: full time: $662/credit
hour, part time: $662/credit hour
(master's); full time: $730, part
time: $730 (DNP)
Room/board/expenses: N/A

Full-time enrollment: 201 (master's); N/A (DNP) men: 8%; women: 92%; minorities: 19%; international: 0%
Part-time enrollment: 490 (master's); 54 (DNP) men: 8%; women: 92%; minorities: 16%; international: 0%
Acceptance rate (master's): 84%
Acceptance rate (DNP): 94%
Specialties offered: education; nurse practitioner; nurse practitioner: adult-gerontology primary care; nurse practitioner: family

Edgewood College[1]
1000 Edgewood College Drive
Madison, WI 53711
Private
Admissions: (608) 663-2294
Email: admissions@edgewood.edu
Financial aid: (608) 663-4300
Tuition: N/A
Room/board/expenses: N/A
Enrollment: N/A

Herzing University-Milwaukee[1]
525 N. 6th Street
Milwaukee, WI 53203
Private
Admissions: N/A
Financial aid: N/A
Tuition: N/A
Room/board/expenses: N/A
Enrollment: N/A

Marian University
45 S. National Avenue
Fond du Lac, WI 54935-4699
www.marianuniversity.edu/nursing/
Private
Admissions: (800) 262-7426
Email: admission@marianuniversity.edu
Financial aid: (920) 923-7614
Application deadline: N/A
Degrees offered: master's

Tuition: full time: $710/credit hour, part time: $710/credit hour
Room/board/expenses: N/A
Full-time enrollment: 14 men: 0%; women: 100%; minorities: 7%; international: 0%
Part-time enrollment: 59 men: 12%; women: 88%; minorities: 5%; international: 0%
Acceptance rate (master's): 57%
Specialties offered: education; nurse practitioner; nurse practitioner: adult-gerontology primary care; nurse practitioner: family

Marquette University
PO Box 1881
Milwaukee, WI 53201-1881
www.marquette.edu/nursing/index.shtml
Private
Admissions: (414) 288-7137
Email: gradadmit@mu.edu
Financial aid: (414) 288-5325
Application deadline: 02/15
Degrees offered: master's, Ph.D., DNP
Tuition: full time: $1,050/credit hour, part time: $1,050/credit hour (master's); full time: $1,050/credit hour, part time: $1,050/credit hour (Ph.D.); full time: $1,050/credit hour, part time: $1,050/credit hour (DNP)
Room/board/expenses: $13,770 (master's); $13,770 (Ph.D.); $13,770 (DNP)
Full-time enrollment: 119 (master's); 5 (Ph.D.); 10 (DNP) men: 16%; women: 84%; minorities: 10%; international: 1%
Part-time enrollment: 182 (master's); 24 (Ph.D.); 30 (DNP) men: 9%; women: 91%; minorities: 8%; international: 1%
Acceptance rate (master's): 57%
Acceptance rate (Ph.D.): 100%
Acceptance rate (DNP): 95%
Specialties offered: administration; clinical nurse leader; clinical nurse specialist; generalist; nurse-midwifery; nurse practitioner; nurse practitioner: adult-gerontology acute care; nurse practitioner:

adult-gerontology primary care; nurse practitioner: pediatric primary care; other majors

University of Wisconsin-Eau Claire
Nursing 127
Eau Claire, WI 54702-4004
www.uwec.edu/CONHS/index.htm
Public
Admissions: (715) 836-5415
Email: admissions@uwec.edu
Financial aid: (705) 836-3373
Application deadline: 01/04
Degrees offered: master's, DNP
In-state tuition: full time: $7,641, part time: $425 (master's); full time: $13,200, part time: N/A (DNP)
Out-of-state tuition: full time: $16,771 (master's); full time: $23,100 (DNP)
Room/board/expenses: $7,322 (master's); $7,322 (DNP)
Full-time enrollment: 1 (master's); 25 (DNP) men: 8%; women: 92%; minorities: 8%; international: 0%
Part-time enrollment: 3 (master's); 57 (DNP) men: 8%; women: 92%; minorities: 3%; international: 0%
Acceptance rate (master's): 100%
Acceptance rate (DNP): 76%
Specialties offered: administration; clinical nurse specialist; education; nurse practitioner; nurse practitioner: adult-gerontology primary care; nurse practitioner: family

University of Wisconsin-Madison[1]
600 Highland Avenue
Madison, WI 53792-2455
Public
Admissions: N/A
Financial aid: N/A
Tuition: N/A
Room/board/expenses: N/A
Enrollment: N/A

University of Wisconsin-Milwaukee
1921 E. Hartford Avenue
Milwaukee, WI 53201
www.uwm.edu/nursing
Public
Admissions: (414) 229-2494
Email: rjens@uwm.edu
Financial aid: (414) 229-4541
Application deadline: N/A
Degrees offered: master's, Ph.D., DNP
In-state tuition: full time: $11,724, part time: $1,196/credit hour (master's); full time: $11,724, part time: $1,196/credit hour (Ph.D.); full time: $11,724, part time: $1,196/credit hour (DNP)
Out-of-state tuition: full time: $24,761 (master's); full time: $24,761 (Ph.D.); full time: $24,761 (DNP)
Room/board/expenses: $9,315 (master's); $9,315 (Ph.D.); $9,315 (DNP)
Full-time enrollment: 103 (master's); 43 (Ph.D.); 42 (DNP) men: 15%; women: 85%; minorities: 14%; international: 7%
Part-time enrollment: 4 (master's); 45 (Ph.D.); 63 (DNP) men: 7%; women: 93%; minorities: 19%; international: 0%
Acceptance rate (master's): 84%
Acceptance rate (Ph.D.): 88%
Acceptance rate (DNP): 97%
Specialties offered: administration; clinical nurse leader; clinical nurse specialist; community health/public health; generalist; health management & policy health care systems; informatics; nurse practitioner; nurse practitioner: family; research; dual majors

University of Wisconsin-Oshkosh
800 Algoma Boulevard
Oshkosh, WI 54901
con.uwosh.edu/
Public
Admissions: (920) 424-1223
Email: gradschool@uwosh.edu

Financial aid: (920) 424-3377
Application deadline: 04/01
Degrees offered: master's, DNP
In-state tuition: full time: $484/credit hour, part time: $484/credit hour (master's); full time: $731/credit hour, part time: $731/credit hour (DNP)
Out-of-state tuition: full time: $991/credit hour (master's); full time: $1,238/credit hour (DNP)
Room/board/expenses: N/A
Full-time enrollment: 11 (master's); 43 (DNP) men: 11%; women: 89%; minorities: 17%; international: 4%
Part-time enrollment: 31 (master's); 39 (DNP) men: 3%; women: 97%; minorities: 4%; international: 0%
Acceptance rate (master's): 89%
Acceptance rate (DNP): 89%
Specialties offered: clinical nurse leader; education; nurse practitioner; nurse practitioner: family

Viterbo University[1]
900 Viterbo Drive
La Crosse, WI 54601
Private
Admissions: N/A
Financial aid: N/A
Tuition: N/A
Room/board/expenses: N/A
Enrollment: N/A

WYOMING

University of Wyoming[1]
Department 3065
Laramie, WY 82071
Public
Admissions: N/A
Financial aid: N/A
Tuition: N/A
Room/board/expenses: N/A
Enrollment: N/A

BUSINESS

EDUCATION

ENGINEERING

MEDICINE

INDEX